digest of papers

February 29 – March 4, 1988

spring COMPCON 88

San Francisco

THIRTY-THIRD IEEE COMPUTER SOCIETY INTERNATIONAL CONFERENCE
CATHEDRAL HILL HOTEL, SAN FRANCISCO, CALIFORNIA

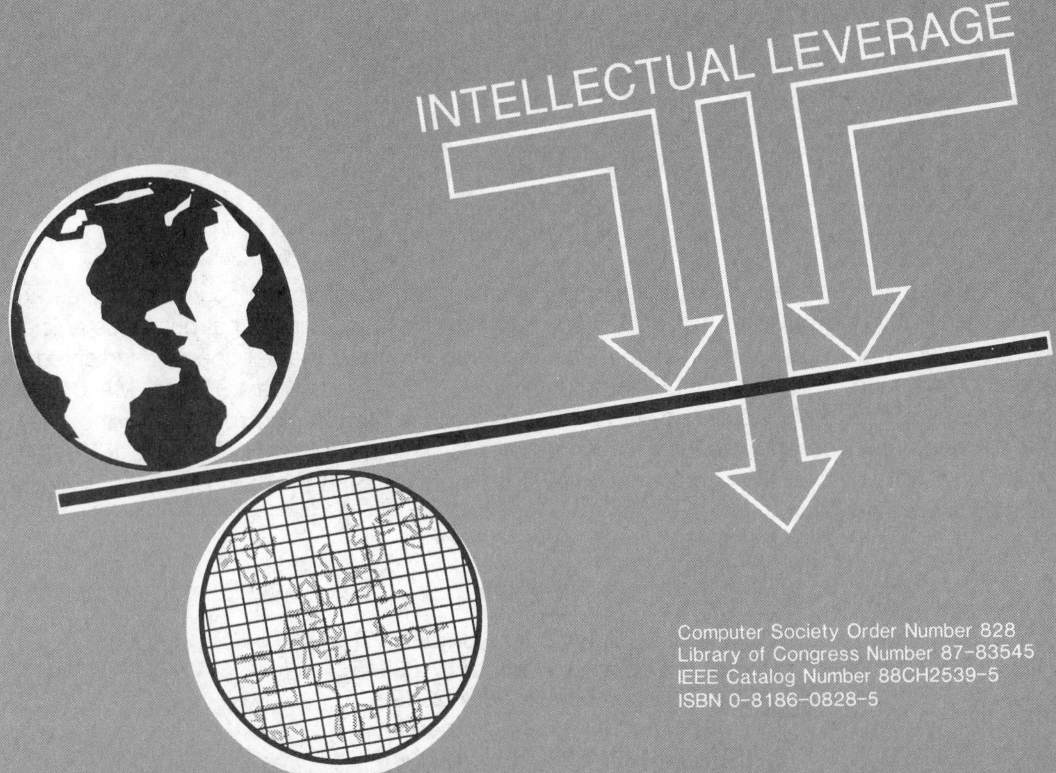

Computer Society Order Number 828
Library of Congress Number 87-83545
IEEE Catalog Number 88CH2539-5
ISBN 0-8186-0828-5

THE COMPUTER SOCIETY OF THE IEEE
THE INSTITUTE OF ELECTRICAL AND ELECTRONICS ENGINEERS, INC
IEEE
COMPUTER SOCIETY PRESS

Published by Computer Society Press of the IEEE
1730 Massachusetts Avenue, N.W.
Washington, D.C. 20036-1903

Cover designed by Jack I. Ballestero

Computer Society Order Number 828
Library of Congress Number 87-83545
IEEE Catalog Number 88CH2539-5
ISBN 0-8186-0828-5 (paper)
ISBN 0-8186-4828-7 (microfiche)
ISBN 0-8186-8828-9 (case)

Order from: Computer Society of the IEEE
Terminal Annex
Post Office Box 4699
Los Angeles, CA 90080

IEEE Service Center
445 Hoes Lane
P.O. Box 1331
Piscataway, NJ 08855-1331

Computer Society of the IEEE
Avenue de la Tanche, 2
B-1160 Brussels
BELGIUM

IEEE
THE INSTITUTE OF ELECTRICAL AND ELECTRONICS ENGINEERS, INC.

General Chairman's Message

Welcome to Compcon Spring 88 which continues the intellectual leverage theme of previous years. Compcon Spring continues to be a broad perspective computing conference designed to keep the practitioner up to date in the constantly expanding computer-related field. Unlike previous years, Compcon Spring 88 will have five featured sessions which are designed to bring the audience up to date on recent advances in key computing fields. The Program Committee, ably chaired by Hasan Al-Khatib, has chosen Computer Market Update by Gorden Bell, Developments in Integrated Device Technologies by Mike Callahan, Update on RISC Architectures by John Hennessy, Developments in Neural Networks by Federico Faggin, and Emerging Workstation Platforms by Andrew Heller for these featured sessions. In addition to the featured sessions, the Program Committee has done an outstanding job of putting together program tracks on Processor Architecture, Parallel Processing Systems, Artificial Intelligence, Storage Technologies, Software Engineering, Workstations, CAD, Neural Networks, and Databases, as well as an assortment of critical "potpourri."

Preceding and following the main conference again this year are full days of tutorials. This year the choice of tutorials includes Software Reuse Update, VHDL Tutorial, Computer Architecture Choices, Software Quality Control, an Introduction to Artificial Neural Networks, Microchannel Interfacing, and Fault-Tolerant Software. Special thanks go to Joseph Fernandez for arranging the tutorials and to the tutorial instructors who have prepared a day's program to give background and perspective in these important fields.

This conference has been deeply dependent upon the Standing Committee, headed by Sid Fernbach, the hardworking and dedicated Program Committee, and the many persons and committees involved in Compcon Spring 88. These people have given generously to ensure that program, tutorials, arrangements, publicity, accounting, registration, publishing, and other matters go well. I would also like to thank the session chairpersons for volunteering to organize and run the sessions, and the speakers who provide the real content of the conference.

K.G. Stevens, Jr.
General Chairman
Compcon Spring 88

Program Chairman's Message

On behalf of myself and the Program Committee I would like to welcome you to the 33rd International Computer Conference, Compcon Spring 88. It is the annual tradition of Compcon to provide a high quality forum for computer professionals to gather and listen to the latest research and development in computer science and engineering. Compcon has been and continues to be a general computer conference spanning a diverse range of topics. The technical program of the conference is a reflection of what the Program Committee perceives as the current hot issues in the computer field. The Program Committee has worked diligiently to put together a well-balanced program that emphasises breadth of scope and quality. Some of the leaders in academia and industry have been invited and have kindly accepted to present at the conference their latest contributions in the field.

This year's program provides full-day focus tracks in several key areas. It is our goal to strike a balance between subject emphasis and breadth of scope. The Featured Sessions at the beginning of each day of the conference are to provide broad update presentations on some key issues relating to computers today. The tutorials, on the other hand, provide extended updates, and represent an integral part of the technical program. Some of the key issues covered include the emergence of new powerful workstations, including personal supercomputers, which has been fueled by the rapid develpment in processor speeds. The comeback of Neural Networks has been given full attention this year. Databases, Software Engineering, Computer Aided Design, Artificial Intelligence, Distributed Processing, and Storage Technologies are other main features in the program. A track on Legal Issues has been introduced to provide you with the latest information about the copyright laws in software and hardware.

Compcon has managed over the years to preserve its excellent technical quality through the hard work of its volunteers in both the Program and the Steering Committees. I wish to thank the members of the Program Committee: Dennis Allison, Richard Belgard, Alan Bell, Fred Buelow, Fred Clegg, Michael Fehling, Jim Gray, Ted Laliotis, Glen Langdon, Bahram Mahbod, Creve Maples, Jai Menon, Stan Mazor, Ken Muira, Yale Patt, Alan Smith, Ken Stevens, Will Tracz, Jim Warren, John Wharton, and Sally Wood. I would also like to express my gratitude to the members of the Steering Committee for their trust and support, especially Dr. Sid Fernbach. Ms. Jacky Olila deserves special thanks for helping collect the authors' contributions in time to include them in the Digest.

Hasan S. AlKhatib
Program Chairman
Compcon Spring 88

Compcon Spring 88 Standing Committee

Sidney Fernbach, Standing Committee Chairman, Consultant
Ken Stevens, General Chairman, NASA-Ames Research Center
Hasan AlKhatib, Program Chairman, Santa Clara University
Fred Buelow, Standing Committee Chairman-Elect, AIDA Corp.
Joseph Fernandez, Tutorials, IBM
Bob Fink, Local Arrangements Chairman, Lawrence Berkeley Lab.
David Hunt, Treasurer, Lawrence Livermore National Lab.
Glen Langdon, Publicity, University of Calif., Santa Cruz
Roy Lee, Registration, Sandia National Lab.
Kenneth Majithia, Local Liaison, IBM
Jacquelyn S. Olila, Digest, SRI International
Lori Goerz, Registration, Lawrence Livermore National Lab.
Ross Gaunt, Computer Manager, Lawrence Livermore National Lab.

Compcon Spring 88 Program Committee

Hasan AlKhatib, Program Chair, Santa Clara University
Dennis Allison, Stanford University
Richard Belgard, Consultant
Alan Bell, Xerox PARC
Fred Buelow, AIDA Corp.
Michael Fehling, Rockwell International
Jim Gray, Tandem
Ted Laliotis, Hewlett-Packard
Glen Langdon, UC Santa Cruz
Bahram Mahbod, Hewlett-Packard Lab.
Creve Maples, Sandia National Lab.
Jai Menon, IBM Almaden Research
Stan Mazor, Consultant
Ken Muira, Fujitsu America, Inc.
Yale Patt, UC Berkeley
Alan Smith, UC Berkeley
Ken Stevens, NASA-Ames Research
Will Tracz, Stanford University
Jim Warren, Silicon Gulch Gazette
John Wharton, Applications Research
Sally Wood, Santa Clara University

Table of Contents

WORKSTATIONS Track

SONY NEWS Workstation

Sun Microsystems SPARC Architecture

The New Apollo Workstations

CAD Track

Update on New Standards for Hardware Design: VHDL and EDIF

Advances in the VHDL Design Environment

FEATURED SESSION

TRENDS IN SCIENTIFIC AND ENGINEERING COMPUTING

Gordon Bell

Dana Computer, Inc.
Sunnyvale, California

Many, new high performance computers for scientific, engineering, and real time applications are emerging from DARPA's Strategic Computing Initiative based on parallelism and gains in VLSI. These have stimulated both traditional companies and initiated venture capital backed start-ups to build the new computers.

Power available from a single computer due to parallelism is doubling almost every year while circuit technology power gains at the maximum clock speed continue to double every 5 years or roughly 14% per year. This maximum power will not be available to a single job unless parallelism is conquered. Neither the user nor computer science community is moving rapidly enough to understand and exploit the potential performance gains coming from an increasing number of parallel processors which are scaleable and compatible to a very high degree.

The "main line" of scientific computing for the next generation (1988-1994) will be a vector multiprocessor with 4-6 and evolving to 64 processors. A range of supers (>$10M), minisupers (<$1M), and personal or solo supers (<$100K) continues to evolve. No economy of scale, measured by processing operations/sec./$, will be observable over the range... in fact, the new class of solo supers may provide a dis-economy of scale for general purpose computing. The lack of a high performance National Research Network to couple users to regional computers and increasing needs for visualizing results, favor a highly distributed environment for most applications.

Multiprocessors, sans vector processing, with a very large number of processors have not yet been adopted for a wide range of applications. Poor microprocessor floating point performance and lack of parallelizing compilers limit them in technical applications. However, such computers are clearly superior to existing large systems for transaction processing, batch data, and program development. Furthermore, a wide range of computers from two to several hundred processors can be constructed using the same basic components to achieve economy through scaleability.

Plain Old one chip micro-Processors (POPs) are becoming very fast, and approach the speed for scalar/integer work of the largest mainframes and supers. Attached vector units will make such uniprocessors very useful and cost-effective in workstations and small computers. A factor of 5-10 is feasible by the early 1990s by switching from CMOS to ECL technology.

Multicomputers, a collection of 32-1024 interconnected computers communicating with one another via passing messages are the most cost-effective for single scientific jobs, provided the problem is compatible with the computer. Multicomputers require reprogramming, are used on one problem at a time, achieve supercomputer power, and cost $25K-$1M depending on the number of computers and their power.

A single instruction, massively large data (SIMD) computer, the Connection Machine, has become the supercomputer for several applications. The current Connection Machine, CM2, is scaleable and comes in a variety of sizes from 8K to 64K processing elements. Like other programmed applications-specific computers the Connection Machine runs only one (or a few) programs at a given time, with a resulting performance/price advantage of a factor of 10 over a general purpose computer.

A variety of other computer structures based on parallelism have proven themselves and are either emerging or show great promise. These are truly applications-specific for vision, speech, text, database, etc. By binding the application in hardware and software at design time, a factor of 10**4 in performance, cost reduction, or performance/price is possible.

A path to a computer capable of executing 10**12 floating point operations per second (flops) by 1994 looks possible utilizing either the multicomputer or SIMD (e.g. Connection Machine) approach. IBM Research has a project to build such a machine, the TF1.

Training and involvement by the computer science and engineering community to achieve high performance on real scientific and engineering applications is a serious barrier to progress. The only training program is around the NSF supercomputer centers, which is limited to simple vectorization of existing FORTRAN programs. Computer science has yet to embrace vectors as a machine primitive to be incorporated in texts and courses.

A program to install, use, and understand the new parallel, vector processors is needed. Only then can faculty rewrite the obsolete texts and train students. Embracing vector processing is a trivial, but necessary first step. Finally, government must support a balanced program in universities to facilitate the change from selective, inaccessible, regional supercomputing to a wide-scale distributed, cost-effective environment for all research.

PROCESSORS Track

Implementations of the SPARC Architecture

Chair: F. Buelow

Design Considerations For A Bipolar Implementation Of SPARC

Anant Agrawal, Emil W. Brown, Joseph Petolino, James R. Peterson

Sun Microsystems, Inc.
2550 Garcia Avenue
Mountain View, CA 94043

Bipolar Integrated Technology
1050 NW Compton Drive
Beaverton, OR 97006

ABSTRACT

Sun Microsystems' Scalable Processor Architecture (SPARC™) defines an architecture that provides a migration path to higher performance levels as new technologies become available. Bipolar ECL processes such as the BIT1™ process from Bipolar Integrated Technology, make it feasible to implement the SPARC architecture in ECL cost effectively.

The cycle times of ECL machines are much shorter than those of CMOS machines and thus I/O and wiring delays become more significant. The well defined division between system and silicon considerations seen in CMOS microprocessor systems is not as obvious in ECL; many system concerns must be accounted for in the design of the silicon.

This paper describes the BIT1 ECL process, and design considerations which must be made for an ECL implementation of SPARC. Bus structures, cache concerns, interface considerations, and power density are all discussed.

1. VLSI ECL

In the past ECL had a well deserved reputation for low density and extremely high power levels. This has changed with the advent of BIT1. BIT1 maintains the high performance of ECL, but offers VLSI density and significantly reduced power when compared to other ECL processes. It provides minimum geometry transistors of 14 μm^2. Gates exhibit typical propagation delays of 300 ps and power dissipation of 300 μW. Using fully self-aligned transistors with polysilicon contacts and resistors, the BIT1 minimum feature size is 2 μm. The BIT1 process has demonstrated its high density potential with devices such as the B3110/20 floating point ALU and multiplier chip set, each of which contain more than 65,000 transistors. The B3110/20 offer the option of either TTL or ECL interfaces.

BIT1 allows three level series gating, which enables separate logic functions to share the same current tree. This feature saves devices and power, and enables complex functions to be implemented in a single gate delay. For example, a single gate delay two input multiplexer/latch requires less than 4000 μm^2, and a 32-bit add can be accomplished in four gate delays.

Bipolar transistors provide advantages both on and off the chip. A bipolar device is much better than a MOS device at driving large capacitive loads, due to better transconductance. This allows signals to be driven between chips at high speeds. Also, by using small voltage swings, gate delays and capacitive charging times are minimized. For example, at a 1 V/ns slew rate, a CMOS rail-to-rail transition would take about 2.5 ns to the 50% point while an ECL transition would take about 300 ps.

CMOS and TTL outputs are generally not designed to drive transmission lines, even though that is what they must do in a circuit board environment. Their uncontrolled output impedance, and the typical lack of termination make it difficult to maintain good signal quality. As TTL and CMOS chips strive for higher performance, the faster edge rates make system design even more difficult. Chip output overshoot and $\partial i/\partial t$ caused by gate transitions inside CMOS chips are a significant source of noise. With multiple outputs changing in the same direction, output overshoot can be significantly worse than for a single output transition, and the delay through the part may be longer than the specified delay. This is because CMOS and TTL delays are typically specified for a single output transition.

In the core of an IC, ECL has the advantage of using constant current, so signal transitions do not generate noise in the power supply and ground. The outputs of ECL chips are designed to drive transmission lines and have a slew rate that is matched to their propagation delay. With proper attention to return currents, the ECL system environment will be noise free.

2. System Considerations

SPARC implementations achieve high performance by reducing the number of cycles required to execute an instruction. The SPARC instruction set is optimized so that most instructions execute in one cycle. To execute instructions at this rate the memory system must provide one instruction every cycle, and in truly high performance designs it must also provide 20% to 30% additional bandwidth for loads and stores. To achieve this, all of SUN's SPARC based systems to date have used a tightly coupled Virtual Address Cache (VAC). By using virtual addresses, the penalty of address translation is avoided between the CPU and the cache. The VAC is designed as an integral part of the CPU rather than an adjunct part of the memory system.

The following few sections of this paper discuss some of the issues we have encountered implementing and incorporating SPARC in a high speed ECL system.

2.1. Transmission Lines

Unlike an NMOS or CMOS microprocessor with a cycle time in the 40 to 100 ns range, an ECL processor must be designed from conception to fit into a high speed transmission line environment. This includes considerations for characteristic impedance matching and trace delays.

The experience of designing machines based on SPARC processors has shown that the cache access path is likely to be one of the longest paths in the system. In an ECL system the cache access is even more critical because the address and data busses must be considered as transmission lines with trace delays that are a significant percentage of the cycle time. To minimize the trace delay of a transmission line it should have exactly one driver and one terminator. Consequently, we accepted as axioms that the cache address bus should only be driven by the CPU, and the cache data bus should only be driven by the cache RAMs. Furthermore, we believe that additional components such as discrete address latches or buffers would ultimately slow the cache access. Therefore, the CPU chip should drive the RAM array directly.

The implications of this are significant. All addresses from sources other than the CPU must pass *through* the CPU to address the cache, including cache fill addresses. The data bus from the cache cannot be bidirectional, so separate load and store busses are mandated. ECL RAMS typically provide separate data-in and data-out ports for this purpose. The axiom of allowing only the cache RAMs to drive the data bus implies that *all* data must pass through the cache RAMs, including non-cached data. This may require invalidating a cache line, or using a buffer to save the previous contents of the line.

2.2. Cache Organizations

Cache design is a major discipline in itself, but the number of options is quickly reduced by looking at the available technology and gaining an early understanding of the critical paths. Set-associative caches increase performance in multi-tasking environments by allowing some cache sharing. Two-way set associativity provides most of the gain. Unfortunately data selection between two associativities is always in the critical path and it depends on the result of the cache tag access and comparison. The result is a longer cycle time. The benefit of set-associativity did not justify the cycle time penalty in our studies of large application programs.

With ECL cycle times, the number of cycles required to process a cache miss will be greater than in slower CMOS/TTL systems, so low miss rates are even more important. We studied the effect of cache size by simulating large programs and found that the miss rate increases rapidly as the cache size decreases below 64-kilobyte. On the other hand, extremely large caches are not cost effective because miss rates may not drop below a certain threshold for real programs running on multi-tasking machines. Furthermore, a large cache requires physically long address and data busses, potentially increasing the cycle time. Based on the current RAM technology and future trends we believe that in ECL systems the cache size would be on the order of 128-kilobyte.

The CPU requires data and instructions at a rate that exceeds the capability of all but the fastest ECL static RAMs. RAMs with access times at or below 15ns are readily available today from several vendors. These RAMs range in size up to 64K bits. Access times are shrinking to the sub 10ns range.

Using an array of eight 16K×4 RAMs, it is possible to build a 32-bit wide, 64-kilobyte cache. Two of these arrays could be used to build a 128-kilobyte combined instruction/data cache or two separate caches for data and instructions. The combined cache can be organized in a 32-bit or a 64-bit width. Depending on the organization, a number of RAMs must be distributed evenly along the address transmission lines. These lines are heavily loaded, resulting in very low characteristic impedances due to capacitive effects. Propagation delay along these transmission lines, added to the processor's input and output buffer delays, is comparable to the read access time of the RAMs.

In earlier implementations of SPARC, memory reference instructions required multiple cycles. This was primarily due to the single 32-bit instruction/data bus between the cache and the processor. One of the goals of this design was to improve the load and store instruction performance. We looked at a number of alternatives which centered around various cache organizations.

One way to achieve our goal would be to provide independent access paths for data and instructions. Using two independent RAM arrays of 64-kilobyte each, a split instruction and data cache could be built. Each cache requires its own 32-bit address bus (the full 32-bits is required to do tag checking), and its own 32-bit data bus. Each address wire would be loaded with 8 data RAMs plus a few tag RAMs. The chip would require 64 output drivers for addresses, 32 inputs for instructions, 32 inputs for load data and 32 output drivers for store data. Thus 160 pins are required just for the busses to support this configuration.

A second way to achieve our goal would be to provide a single 64-bit interface to a combined instruction/data cache. This approach provides twice the required instruction-fetch bandwidth. By saving some of the excess instructions on the CPU chip, some cycles can be used to access data without reducing the instruction execution rate. The configuration easily supports the required additional bandwidth of 20% to 30% data accesses. The pin requirement for busses is 64 input pins, plus 32 address outputs and 32 store-data outputs for a total of 128. An added advantage of this scheme could be improved performance for floating-point double precision computation.

We also considered a number of techniques to decrease the system cycle time, while still meeting the bandwidth requirement of greater than one word per cycle. In particular, we explored using a two-cycle cache access path. There are several possibilities which include (1) an interleaved cache in which odd and even words are accessed in parallel from two banks, (2) a pipelined access in which the latency of access is two cycles, but the data rate is one access per cycle, and (3) a duplicated cache in which the same data can be accessed from two different banks.

If we can depend on the processor to access words sequentially most of the time, it is productive to assign consecutive words to different cache banks. A pipeline that supports a stage between address generation and data return is used. The processor would require separate address busses for each bank, and would alternate their usage. Separate data-in busses would also be required. Stalls would occur whenever consecutive accesses are made to the same bank.

Another kind of pipeline can be designed if RAMs are available with internal address registers. This allows the first cycle of a two cycle access to be used in driving the address transmission line, and the second cycle in accessing the RAMs and sending the data back to the processor. This design relies on RAM vendors to produce special RAM parts.

The best choice among these possibilities is governed by the performance goals and the expected usage of the machine. We rejected the two-cycle access methods on the basis of pin requirements, complexity, and reduced performance.

2.3. Stores

The ECL RAM write cycle presents special problems because the write-pulse width specification is usually as long as or longer than the address access time, and there is address and data setup time to the pulse's leading edge and hold time from the pulse's trailing edge. There are two approaches. Allow the write cycle to increase the cycle time, or use multiple cycles to perform stores. Our data has shown that large SPARC programs execute about 5% store instructions and 15% load instructions. The remaining bandwidth is used to fetch instructions. Because the store percentage is quite low (mainly due to the large on-chip register file) we believe that it is better to have an additional cycle for stores than to allow a longer cycle time.

2.4. Chip Crossings

Once the timing of the primary cache access path is analyzed, attention must be given to the control signals. At high speeds, the cost of crossing any chip boundary can be as high as 60% to 80% of the system cycle time. This was considered from the very beginning of design when interfaces were being defined. We avoid interfaces that require more than one or two levels of logic in a chip crossing path and double chip crossings. These restrictions resulted in some interfaces being logically complex in order to accomplish simple functions, and forced some operations to use additional cycles. Tradeoffs were made between lengthening the cycle time and increasing the number of cycles required for frequent operations.

Since the cache interface in this design requires a large number of pins, care had to be taken when adding functionality at the cost of more pins. Most processor status information has been encoded into a single bus that provides more information to the external system than the earlier SPARC implementations.

3. Floating-point Performance

Floating-point performance has historically been low in microprocessor based machines because the operations take longer than simple integer operations. Simple systems could not afford the multiple functional units that give supercomputers their floating-point speed. In the domain of ECL microprocessors however, the issue of floating-point performance cannot be ignored.

ECL densities are not yet sufficient to support floating-point hardware on the CPU chip, especially not multiple arithmetic units. BIT has developed the first ECL floating-point chip set that supports very high performance computation. The B3110/20 chip set can perform double precision multiply in 50 ns, and double precision add in 25 ns, without internal pipelining. This level of performance can lead to low latency as well as high throughput floating-point performance.

The B3110/20 in combination with the B3210 high-speed register file can be used as a floating-point co-processor with a SPARC microprocessor to provide performance unprecedented in a microprocessor based system. SPARC defines a floating-point instruction set which is compatible with the B3110/20, and supports concurrent operation between the two floating point chips as well as with the integer CPU.

Floating-point performance comes down to two cases: load/store limited problems and computational limited problems. Calculations such as a matrix times a vector are likely to be computation limited when the matrix is constant because the number of FLOPS is of order N^2, while the load and store operations are of order N. The Linpack benchmark, which solves a system of linear equations, is load/store limited. The number of floating point operations per data word accessed is less than one. Thus the requirement for consistently good floating-point performance can be met by using the B3110/20, *and* by providing sufficient data bandwidth.

4. Cooling and Package Considerations

System designers using ECL must pay close attention to thermal management. Even though BIT1 gates provide lower power dissipation than other ECL technologies, an implementation which contains more than 20,000 BIT1 gates may dissipate 10 watts or more. This level of power requires special packaging techniques. BIT products are housed in ceramic pin grid array (PGA) packages designed to give users maximum flexibility in thermal management. These PGA packages use a cavity down configuration and incorporate a copper/tungsten slug brazed into the cavity. The silicon die is mounted directly to the slug using a silver glass paste. A path of low thermal resistance is thus provided from the silicon chip to the external area of the slug, and is estimated to be approximately 0.2° C/W.

To simplify thermal management at the system level BIT standard products have heat sinks attached to the slug. These thermal dissipators were designed to provide a low thermal resistance from junction to ambient, which ensures that the junction temperature does not exceed 125° C when the ambient temperature is 70° C or less, with 500 linear feet per minute (LFM) airflow across the heat-sink. Designers can also obtain BIT parts without a heat sink and attach their own, for added flexibility.

Using the standard heat sink, thermal concerns are reduced to airflow considerations and ambient temperature specifications. Although these standard devices are specified for 500 LFM and 70° C ambient temperature, a system may need to meet more stringent requirements. Since these specifications must be met at the device, any obstructions to the airflow upstream from the device must be accounted for. For example, if a B3120 is 0.5 inches downstream from a B3110, the upstream device will cause the downstream device to be subjected to a slightly higher temperature and lower airflow. If a part is dissipating 10 watts and causes 0.25° C/W rise in ambient temperature downstream, the downstream part will actually see 2.5° C higher temperature. Additionally, studies indicate that 0.5 inches downstream from a B3110, the airflow may drop by more than 100 LFM due to turbulence effects on the air-stream caused mainly by the heat sink. This decrease in airflow could be countered in a number of ways, such as increasing the upstream airflow, placing the devices orthogonal to the air-stream, or spacing the parts further apart.

The decisions that maximize performance also force a high pin count. With a large number of signal outputs, power supply allocation becomes very important. The potential for output ringing and cross-talk must be simulated and minimized. For example, the cache address lines must not be affected, after they have settled, by the transitions of outputs that have a different timing. A large percentage of all pads on a die may have to be allocated to power supplies. This helps reduce supply inductance to the output drivers which minimizes output ringing and cross-talk.

5. Conclusion

The implementation of a microprocessor in high speed technologies, such as the BIT1 ECL process, requires that system level design considerations be made a part of the chip design. Careful analysis of critical timing paths and accounting for wiring and I/O delays are some of the issues which must be solved when designing an ECL microprocessor.

The scalable nature of the SPARC architecture makes migration to ECL a natural progression, and the integration capabilities of BIT1 makes such a migration possible.

Acknowledgements

The ECL implementation of the SPARC architecture is being carried out as a joint development program between Sun Microsystems and Bipolar Integrated Technology. In addition to the authors Trevor Creary, Tom Guthrie, Mike Klein, Arthur Leung, Dave Murata, Susan Rohani, Tom Tate, Jim Testa, Chris Yau, David Yen from Sun Microsystems and Bob Elkind, Duane Jacobson, Paul Kingzett, Jim Russell, and Mark Slamowitz from Bipolar Integrated Technology are contributing to the implementation and verification of the design. Thanks to Robert Garner for reviewing and suggesting improvements to this paper.

SPARC is a trade mark of Sun Microsystems. BIT and BIT1 are trade marks of Bipolar Integrated Technology.

References

"The SPARC Architecture Manual", Sun Microsystems, Inc., Mountain View, CA. Also published by Fujitsu Microelectronics, Inc., 3320 Scott Blvd., Santa Clara, CA 95054.

Robert Garner, Anant Agrawal, Fayé Briggs, Emil W. Brown, David Hough, Bill Joy, Steve Kleiman, Steven Muchnick, Masood Namjoo, Dave Patterson, Joan Pendleton, & Richard Tuck, "The Scalable Processor Architecture (SPARC)," This proceedings.

M. Namjoo, A. Agrawal, D. Jackson, Le Quach, "CMOS Gate Array Implementation of the SPARC Architecture," this proceedings.

M. Namjoo, et. al., "CMOS Custom Implementation of the SPARC Architecture," this proceedings.

Bob Leibowitz, Greg Taylor, "ECL gains ground in battle against CMOS," Computer Design, April 1, 1987.

Jim Peterson, Bob Leibowitz, "Processor chip set shrinks latency, boosts throughput'" Electronic Design, February 5, 1987.

George Wilson, "Creating Low-Power Bipolar ECL at VLSI Densities'" VLSI Systems Design, May, 1986.

CMOS GATE ARRAY IMPLEMENTATION OF THE SPARC ARCHITECTURE

*Masood Namjoo, Anant Agrawal, Donald Clark Jackson, Le Quach**

Sun Microsystems, Inc. Mountain View, CA.

INTRODUCTION

This article describes MB86900 processor, the first implementation of the SPARC architecture. MB86900, refered to here as the Integer Unit (IU), is a high-performance microprocessor designed with Fujitsu's high-speed CMOS gate-array technology. In a typical system the MB86900 IU works with a companion floating-point controller chip, MB86910, two commercial floating-point arithmetic processors, and a cache which is an essential component of the system.

The MB86900 has a reduced-instruction-set-computer (RISC) architecture. The architecture defines a simple, yet efficient set of instructions. Most of these instructions execute in a single cycle, resulting in a very low average number of cycles per instruction (CPI). Instructions that cannot finish in a single cycle, such as loads and stores, use a minimum number of additional cycles.

The simplified format of instructions allows the source operands to be read immediately from the register file without any delay caused by the decoding of instructions. This significantly decreases the cycle time, contributing to the processor's speed. The processor has a large on-chip register file that reduces the overhead of load and store operations considerably, allowing a peak execution rate of approximately 1 cycle per instruction when all operands are kept inside the processor's register file. More information on the architecture can be found in the companion paper.

PROCESSOR MICROARCHITECTURE

The entire IU is implemented in a single 20,000-gate CMOS gate-array chip fabricated by Fujitsu. This gate-array is based on a 1.5 micron technology (with 10% gate shrink), yielding a worst case cycle time of 60ns (16.6 MHz) for the processor. One quarter of this gate-array is occupied by a 4K-bits register file and the other three quarters are used by the data path and control circuitry. The circuitry inside the IU has been partitioned, hierarchically, into blocks, sub-blocks and sub-sub-blocks allowing easy place and route and predictable post-layout wire delays for the entire chip. The processor chip has a total of 156 I/O signals and uses a 256 pin PGA (Pin Grid Array) package.

As shown in Figure 1, the chip consists of four major units.

1) REGISTER FILE UNIT (R_UNIT) -- The R_UNIT contains a total of 120 32-bit general purpose registers, from which eight registers are global and the rest are divided into seven overlapped frames (windows) of 24 registers each. Although the MB86900 processor implements only seven windows, the actual number of windows is implementation dependent and future implementations can have more. A pointer in the Processor Status Register, called Current Window Pointer (CWP), is used to point to the current window in the register file. The register file has two read ports and a single write port. The uniform format of instructions allows reading both source operands of any instruction and writing the result of a previously fetched instruction into the register file, through the write port. The entire process occurs in a single cycle.

2) EXECUTION UNIT (E_UNIT) -- This unit consists of a fast 32-bit carry-look-ahead ALU (which performs all arithmetic and logic operations), a 32-bit barrel shifter, condition code generation logic, load and store alignment logic, and related pipeline registers required to save the operands and intermediate results. All arithmetic and logic instructions use the E_UNIT for a single cycle to complete their execution. The data path incorporates two bypass paths for handling dependencies between the operands and results of consecutive instructions. The first bypass path feeds the output of the ALU directly to the input of the operand registers. This bypass is activated when a source operand of an instruction depends on the results of its previous instruction. The second bypass path feeds the output of the result register to the input of the operand registers. It is activated when a source operand of an instruction depends on the result of the instruction prior to the previous instruction in the pipeline.

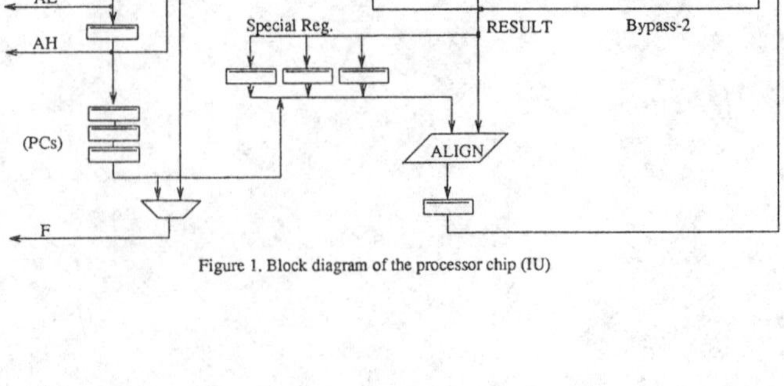

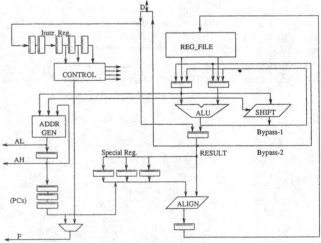

Figure 1. Block diagram of the processor chip (IU)

3) INSTRUCTION FETCH UNIT (I_UNIT) -- This unit consists of the processor's program counters and instruction/data address generation circuitry. There are four program counters corresponding to the four stages of the instruction pipeline (see section on processor pipeline). These program counters are necessary and are used in the case of exceptions that may occur as late as the last stage in the processor pipeline. This unit also includes the circuitry for the Trap Base register (TBR), Trap Type register (TT), Y register (used by multiply step instruction), and Window Invalid Mask register (WIM).

4) CONTROL UNIT (C_UNIT) -- This unit implements the main state machine, instruction pipeline, instruction decoder, Processor Status Register (PSR), circuitry for exception/trap handling, and the interface to the cache and floating-point unit. The C_UNIT maintains a copy of the instructions that execute in different stages of the pipeline. The majority of the control signals for other units are generated in this unit.

PROCESSOR PIPELINE

The processor has a four-stage deep pipeline. Each stage of the processor pipeline performs a subset of operations that are needed to complete the execution of an instruction. All operations performed in a given pipeline stage occur in one full clock cycle. A brief description of each pipeline stage follows:

1) Fetch Stage -- In this stage of the pipeline, a new instruction is fetched. The fetched instruction enters the processor's pipeline at the completion of this stage.

2) Decode Stage -- In this stage, the instruction is decoded and source operands are read from the register file. The source operands read during this stage are passed to both the E_UNIT and the I_UNIT for execution of the instruction in later stages. The decode stage of the pipeline is also used to generate the next instruction address (and in the case of branches, the branch target address). More precisely, while instruction I(n) is being decoded in the decode stage, the address for instruction I(n+2) is being calculated by the I_UNIT.

3) Execute Stage -- In this stage, the E_UNIT performs arithmetic and logic operations on the operands read during the decode stage. The results of these operations are saved in a temporary result register before they are actually written into the destination register.

4) Write Stage -- The write stage marks the end of of an instruction execution in the pipeline. In this stage a decision is made whether to write the results into the register file, which means the instruction has completed successfully, or to prohibit any changes in the state of the processor. The write stage will abort if an exception is raised during the execution of that instruction.

As shown in Figure 2, four instructions can execute simultaneously in the processor pipeline. While instruction I(n) is being fetched, instruction I(n-1) is being decoded in the decode stage, instruction I(n-2) is being executed in the execute stage, and instruction I(n-3) is writing its results into the destination register.

In this processor since branch instructions are delayed by one instruction, all taken PC-relative branches execute in a single cycle. This is done by fetching the target instruction before the condition codes are ready. If after evaluation of the condition codes it is determined that the branch should have not been taken, the processor ignores the target instruction and continues to fetch the next instruction in the sequence.

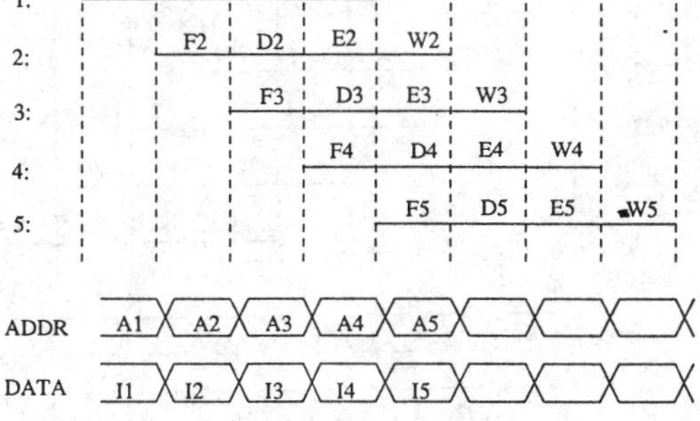

Figure 2. Four stage instruction pipeline

INSTRUCTION BUFFER -- The IU uses a dual-instruction buffer in order to keep the pipeline full at all times. These buffers are used to prefetch instructions during the execution of multiple-cycle instructions and to speed up the execution by utilizing the data bus more efficiently. The buffer is empty when the processor is executing a sequence of single-cycle instructions in a row. When a multiple-cycle instruction enters into the pipeline, its following instructions are prefetched into the buffer until the multiple-cycle instruction is complete.

INTERNAL INSTRUCTIONS -- All control circuitry in the IU has been implemented using random logic (no PLA's). The state machine and controls are designed so that each multiple-cycle instruction behaves like several consecutive single-cycle instructions. This is accomplished using *internal instructions* which are generated automatically by the IU and are injected into the processor's pipeline as they are needed. Load and store instructions are examples of instructions that need more than one cycle to complete. Figure 3 shows a single-word load instruction which takes one extra cycle and Figure 4 shows a single-word store instruction which takes two extra cycles in the pipeline to complete.

TRAPS AND EXCEPTIONS -- A given instruction may raise several exceptions (traps) during the course of its execution. When multiple traps are raised simultaneously, the trap handling logic guarantees that the highest priority trap is taken by the IU. Traps are vectored and an on-chip trap base address register (TBR) is used to point to the trap table. Traps may be synchronous such as privileged instruction trap or asynchronous such as external interrupts. The IU provides 15 External Interrupt Levels that are maskable (with the exception of Level-15) by a 4-bit Processor Interrupt Level. All external interrupts are ignored when traps are disabled. If a synchronous trap is detected while traps are disabled, the IU enters into an Error Mode and remains in that mode until it is reset externally. At reset the IU enters into an initial state and starts execution from memory address 'zero'.

CACHE/MEMORY INTERFACE

The IU uses two separate 32-bit busses, *A_BUS* and *D_BUS*, for address and data to access the storage. As shown in Figure 5, the address bus is divided into two parts: AL (low address, bits 17..0) and AH (high address, bits 31..16). AL and AH bits are overlapped in bits 16 and 17, allowing direct addressing of a cache with a size up to 256K bytes.

Every cycle in this processor is either an instruction fetch cycle, a load cycle, or a store cycle. For every instruction fetch, the IU sends the AL in the cycle before the fetch cycle. The AL is latched externally and used to fetch the instruction in the fetch cycle.

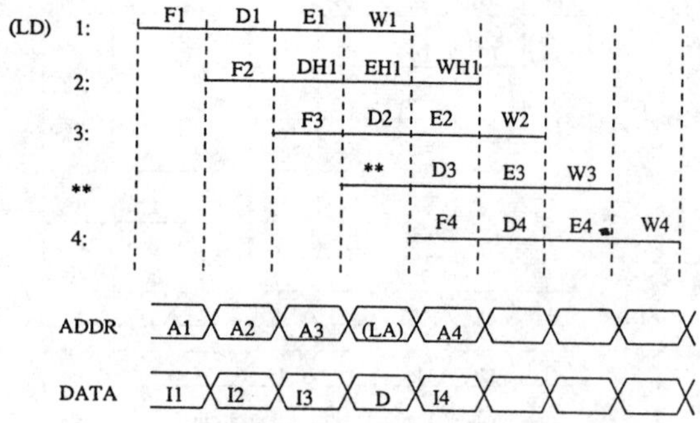

** Load data cycle

Figure 3. Execution of a single-word load instruction

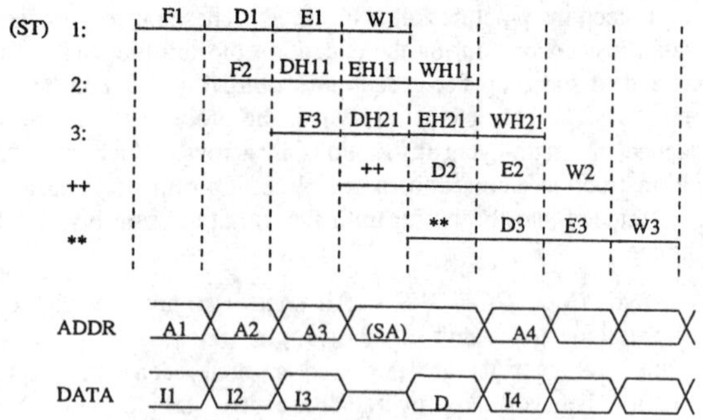

++ Tag comparison for store

** Store data cycle

Figure 4. Execution of a single-word store instruction

Within the same cycle, the cache tags are read and checked against AH. In the case of a cache-hit, the IU treats the fetched instruction as a correct instruction and continues to fetch the next instruction in the following cycle. However, if the cache is missed, the external cache controller logic must hold the IU in the cycle following the fetch cycle. This can be done by asserting one of the MHOLD input signals that forces the processor pipeline into a WAIT state for the duration of the time that the signal is asserted. During this period, the cache controller fills the missed cache line and strobes (using MDS signal) the missed instruction into the IU's instruction register. The IU, in this case, ignores the previous instruction and uses the new instruction as the correct one to be executed. The cache-miss for load and store instructions is handled in a similar way.

Since a new instruction address is sent every cycle before the tag comparison result for the previous address is ready, the cache address must be saved by the external circuitry for one extra cycle. This delayed address will be needed by the cache only in the case of a cache-miss; otherwise it is ignored.

Bus request/grant operations are implemented in very simple manner. Basically, the processor may be forced into a WAIT state in any cycle for any duration of time using BHOLD signal. A LOCK signal is provided and is asserted when the processor is in the middle of a multi-cycle bus transaction that should not be aborted. Normally, a device that needs the bus simply asserts the BHOLD signal in the first cycle that it sees the LOCK signal is inactive. Once the processor is in the WAIT state, AOE and DOE control signals may be used to turn off the output drivers of the chip. The LOCK signal is guaranteed to be deasserted for at least one cycle during any

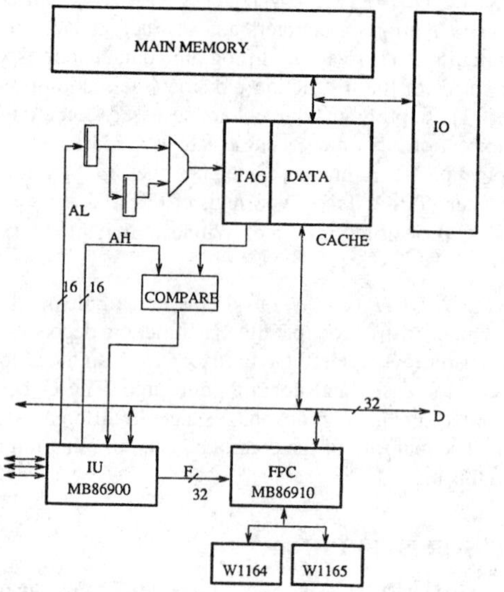

Figure 5. A typical cache-based system configuration

instruction, preventing the I/O from being locked out.

All I/O devices are memory mapped and load/store instructions are used to read from or write into the I/O devices. For every memory access, the IU sends out an 8-bit Address Space Identifier (ASI) field. Normally, ASI bits carry information such as processor mode (user/superuser) and the type of memory access (instruction/data). During the execution of alternate load/store instructions, these bits carry the ASI field specified by the instruction. (See the MB86900 data sheet for more information on pin descriptions)

FLOATING-POINT UNIT INTERFACE

In MB86900 processor, floating-point instructions are executed by the MB86910 floating-point controller chip, refered to here as FPC. The FPC, also designed using Fujitsu's 20,000 gate CMOS gate-array, consists of thirty-two 32-bit floating-point registers, a Floating-Point Status Register (FSR) and a Floating-Point Queue (FQ). The floating-point controller chip handles the execution of floating-point instructions as well as floating-point loads/stores concurrent with the execution of integer instructions.

Floating-point instructions and their addresses are sent to the FPC through a dedicated 32-bit *F_BUS* in two consecutive cycles. This information is maintained in the floating-point queue of the FPC and is used for later execution of the instruction by the arithmetic units (WTL1164 multiplier and WTL1165 alu). Each entry of the queue consists of two pieces of information: the floating-point instruction and its address. The contents of the queue can be read out and used by the trap handler when floating-point exceptions occur.

Both single and double precision load/stores are supported. For these instructions, the IU computes the memory address for the operands and the FPC either receives the data from the data bus (for loads) or puts the data on the data bus (for stores). The floating-point controller holds the processor when there is a dependency between the operands of loads/stores and the operands of previous instructions in the floating-point queue.

Branch on floating-point condition instructions behave very similar to the branch on integer condition instructions. The only difference is that the condition code bits for these instructions are generated by the floating-point controller. The IU enters into a wait state whenever it needs the floating-point conditions and these condition bits are not ready.

MB86910 does not implement square root (SQRT) and extended precision instructions. These instructions will generate floating-point exception if they are executed. Floating-point exceptions are signaled to the IU using FEXC signal. In general, these exceptions are asynchronous with respect to the processor's pipeline. The reasons are (1) integer instructions are executed concurrently with the floating-point instructions and (2) different floating-point instructions take a different number of cycles to complete their execution or generate an exception. In the MB86900 processor, floating-point exceptions are taken in a synchronous manner. This is done by taking the exception immediately, if the current instruction is a floating-point, or delaying the exceptions until the next floating-point instruction, if the current instruction is not a floating-point. All integer instructions with the exception of SWAP instruction are implemented by the IU.

MB86900 PERFORMANCE

In addition to the cycle time, there are two other important factors that affect the performance. These are (1) the average number of cycles per instruction (CPI) and (2) the average number of instructions needed to complete a given task, which is a function of compilers and the efficiency of the instruction set. As was mentioned earlier, some instructions take more than one cycle to complete. Table 1 gives a summary of the number of cycles used to execute each instruction.

Table 1: Instruction Execution Times

Instruction Type	# of cycles	# of Internal Instr.
Load (word/halfword/byte)	2	1
Load (double)	3	2
Store (word/halfword/byte)	3	2
Store (double)	4	3
Atomic Load and Store	4	3
Floating-point ops	2+Cf	1
Jump and Rett	2	1
Branch (untaken)	2	0
Branch (taken)	1	0
All Other instructions	1	0

(Note: Cf is the number of cycles needed by the floating-point arithmetic unit to complete a floating-point instruction. This number varies depending on the type of floating-point operation. The WTL1164/1165 arithmetic units perform single precision add/multiply in 10 cycles, double precision add in 13 cycles, and double precision multiply in 15 cycles.)

For large C programs an instruction mix ratio of about 15% loads, 5% stores, 15% taken branches and 5% untaken branches is observed. Based on the above table, the contribution of loads, stores, branches, annulled instructions, load interlocks (assuming 50% of loads cause interlock with the next instruction), and jumps to the CPI, excluding cache-misses would be approximately 1.47. The contribution of cache-misses for a 128K-byte cache (with approximately 1% miss-ratio and 10 cycles miss penalty) would be:

$$CACHE\_MISS\_COST = 0.01 * (1 + 0.15 + 0.05) * 10 = 0.12$$

Therefore, the average CPI for the processor would be:

$$CPI = 1.47 + 0.12 = 1.59$$

CONCLUSIONS

In this paper we described the first implementation of SPARC architecture on a single gate-array. With a worst case cycle time of 60ns and an average CPI of approximately 1.59, this processor delivers a performance that exceeds most existing 32-bit microprocessors. In this implementation, some instructions, such as loads and stores, take more than one cycle to complete, resulting in a slight increase in the average CPI. The reason for this is mainly due to limitations of the single 32-bit data bus, which is used in this design. The CPI can be improved in future implementations with a different bus structure.

The gate-array approach, chosen for this implementation, proved to be a low-risk, low-cost solution and resulted in early availability of functional parts which were used in debugging of prototype systems. The entire design of IU uses an equivalent of approximately 12000 2-input nand gates and a custom designed 3-port register file. This gate count includes the overhead for additional circuitry needed for a fully scannable design in order to facilitate testing of the chips. Both IU and FPC designs were simulated and verified using a large set of diagnostics. The extensive amount of simulations paid off eventually once the first silicon of these chips ran the multiuser Unix in a prototype system of SUN 4/200 work station.

ACKNOWLEDGMENTS

The authors would like to thank all members of the MB86900 design team. K.G. Tan and Wayne Rosing managed this project. J.K. Lu, Rick Iwamoto and Larry Yang helped in logic simulation and design verification. Phil Mak, Susan Rohani and Quyen Vu helped in timing verification tools and other cad support. Will Brown wrote an architectural and machine cycle simulator. Ed Kelly and Robert Garner designed the Sun-4/200 processor board and helped design the IU/cache interface. Many others including Bill Joy, David Patterson, Steven Muchnick, Steve Kleiman, Dock Williams, David Weaver, David Hough, Richard Tuck, and Alex Wu helped in developing the architecture.

REFERENCES

[1] D. A. Patterson, "RISC," *Eighth Annual Symposium on Computer Architecture,* May 1981.

[2] J. Hennesey, "VLSI Processor Architecture," *IEEE Transactions on Computers,* December 1984.

[3] R. Garner et al., "The Scalable Processor Architecture (SPARC)," *this proceedings.*

[4] S. Kleiman, D. Williams, "UNIX on SPARC," *this proceedings.*

[5] S. Muchnick, C. Aoki, V. Ghodssi, M. Helft, M. Lee, R. Tuck, D. Weaver, A. Wu, "Optimizing Compilers for the SPARC Architecture: An Overview," *this proceedings.*

[6] M. Namjoo and A. Agrawal, "Implementing SPARC: A High Performance 32-bit RISC Microprocessor," *Sun Microsystems Technical Publications,* Sun Microsystems, Inc., 1987.

[7] MB86900 Processor Data Sheet, *Fujitsu Microelectronics Technical Publication,* Fujitsu Microelectronics, Santa Clara, CA, 1987.

CMOS GATE ARRAY IMPLEMENTATION OF SPARC

Le Quach and Richard Chueh

Fujitsu Microelectronics Inc.

Abstract

This paper describes the implementation of the 32-bit RISC based SPARC microprocessor chip set MB86900 and MB86910 using Fujitsu's CMOS 20K UH Gate Array to meet tight development schedule while achieving high performance with high degree of testability.MB86900 is the CPU and MB86910 is the floating point controller(FPC). Although they were implemented in a gate array,the performance exceeds that of most of the existing commercial full custom microprocessors.

(I) Introduction

The joint development project of the SPARC chip set MB86900 and MB86910 between SUN and Fujitsu started in 1985 when Fujitsu's CMOS 20K UH gate array was just introduced at the ISSCC conference[1].MB86900 is the SPARC CPU and MB86910 is the floating point controller(FPC). MB86910 is designed to work with 2 commercial floating point arithmetic processors(Weitek W1164 multiplier and W1165 ALU) to form the SPARC floating point coprocessor.The goal was to develop a new 32-bit high performance microprocessor chip set based on RISC architecture.In order to meet the tight schedule, it had to be a high speed high density gate array chip set instead of a full custom one. Furthermore,both MB86900 and MB86910 require on-chip RAM to implement the large register files, thus made the newly announced Fujitsu CMOS 20K gate array the best candidate available at that time. As a result we built the fastest 32-bit testable gate array microprocessor with a performance exceeding that of most of the existing commercial full custom microprocessors.

(II) Key implementation features

* 3 layer metalization

One of the key features of using Fujitsu's C20K UH gate array is the availability of three layer metalization technology.It helps to shorten the wire length and at the same time improve routability.

* Fixed clock network

Fixed clock network is implemented using fixed location clock buffers (IAB and/or IBB) and block clock buffers (KAB and/or KBB) as shown in Figure 1. With the use of fixed clock network,the clock skew is automatically minimized. The on-chip clock skew of MB86900 and MB86910 are both at 1.3 ns worst case.

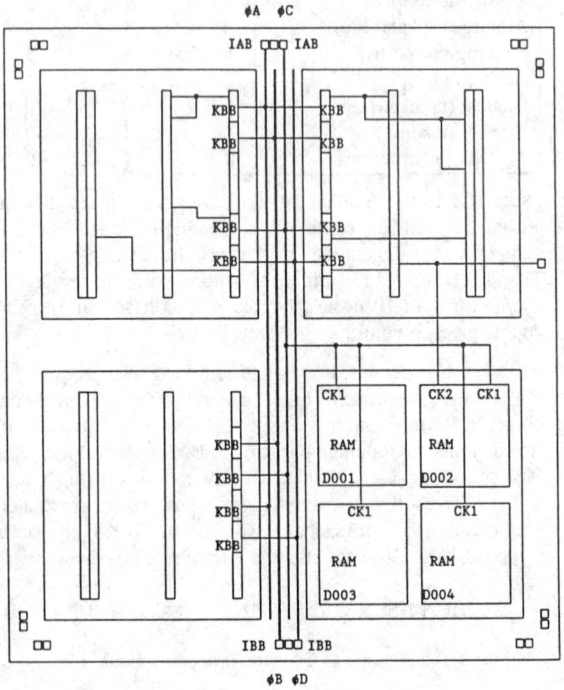

Figure 1 Fixed Clock Network

CH2539-5/88/0000/0014$01.00

* SCAN design

In order to use the Fujitsu Automatic Test pattern Generator (ATG),all the flip-flops used in the chip set are scannable and have their SCAN in/out pins connected together to form a shift register when the chip is in SCAN mode. With the support of ATG, the fault coverage of both MB86900 and MB86910 is higher than 97%.

* 3 port RAM used in SPARC chip set

The large integer register file of 128*32-bit is implemented with 2 identical 3 port RAM cells, and the floating point register file of 32*32-bit is implemented using 2 dual port RAM cells. All of them are fully tested after fabrication.

* New unit cells for SPARC

In order to save gate count and improve performance,8 new unit cells have been developed. Because these are gate array cells,the cell development time is much shorter than that of a standard-cell approach.

(III) Design tools and techniques used in the SPARC implementation

* Use of a static timing verifier

The SPARC logic design is supported by a timing verification package developed for the SPARC project which includes a static timing verifier, a pre-layout wire loading estimator, a post layout actual wire back annotation program and some cross reference list generators . Because this is a synchronized design, the static timing verifier, which does not require test vector to exercise long/short paths, becomes very useful and powerful. Before layout it works with a cross reference list generator to report all the potential long /short paths in the workstation database . After layout it works with another cross reference list generator to report all the long wires in the long paths in the mainframe physical layout pattern database. With the help of the timing verification package, we managed to pass pre-layout and post-layout simulation of the CPU and FPC on the mainframe at the first run, and to improve 12% of the performance of CPU in terms of cycle time by manually shortening 15 wires reported by the timing verifier in only 2 days. Manual layout improvement of the FPC took less than a day.

* Logic partitioning

Because of the special silicon structure of the C20K G/A,the partition of logic blocks was done carefully so that the whole design is placeable and routable and that the post-layout wire loading would be consistent with the pre-layout estimation. For example, we could always design a 500 basic cell block in level 3 which has a recommended size of only 200 basic cells. The wire loading would be estimated using values for level 3 which would look very impressive but would cause timing problem after layout.

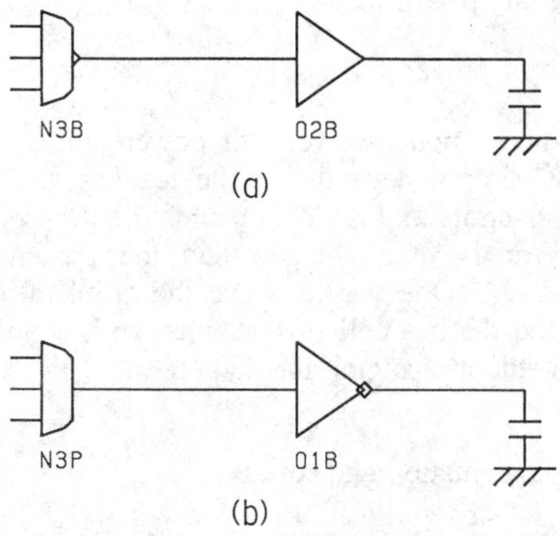

Figure 2 Proper use of cells improves performance

* Proper use of cells

In a CMOS gate array design, it is very important that the right cell is used in the right place. Due to the specific silicon structure of CMOS gate array,the rising and falling delays of a cell could be very different. Without paying attention to the difference of rising and falling delays of a path, a long path usually has timing problem at the rising edge while having a wide timing margin at the falling edge or vise versa. This kind of problem can be solved by changing the combination of the logic cells along the path. Figure 2 shows a simple example where in (a) a power NAND cell N3B is driving an output buffer and in (b) a power AND cell N3P is driving an output inverter. Note that in Fujitsu C20K G/A cell library, both N3B and N3P use 3 basic cells. Assuming a typical wire capacitive loading of 20 lu (lu is the normalized loading unit),(a) will be rising 1 ns slower and falling 1.5 ns faster than (b). Depending on the rising and falling arrival times at the inputs of the NAND or the AND, there will either be a saving of 1 ns or 1.5 ns.

* Use of bigger cells

The use of bigger cells reduces the number of interconnections of the chip which improves the routability and in most cases improves the post layout timing performance.

* Use of power cells

Whether a nonpower cell or power cell should be used simply depends on the loading and the decision is simple. Problem occurs when the post-layout wire is much longer than the pre-layout estimated one. One way to solve the problem is to replace the driving cell of that wire with a power version without changing the layout.

(IV) Implementation and results

In order to push for performance,the design was done in an iterative way with the help of the static timing verifier until all the internal and external paths met the targeted timing specifications. The pre-layout timing verification was done with estimated wire loading. All the pre-layout long paths were eliminated by either the redesigning of sub-block or minor modification of pipeline.The post-layout timing verification was done with actual wire loading. All the post-layout long paths were improved by shortening all the long wires in the paths reported by the timing verifier,especially those driven by cells which have poor drive, and/or replacing the driving cell with a power version. The preliminary designs of both the CPU and FPC were not optimized for timing and had no maunal modification of the layout. They were performed automatically by the layout program and each took only 2~3 hours of CPU time. The corresponding working CPU and FPC chips came out in April 1986 and July 1986 respectively. Both of them run with a cycle time of 90 ns. After the redesigning of sub-blocks and some manual modification of layout,the final versions of CPU and FPC, which are both in gate-shrinked version, are both running at a cycle time of 60ns worst case . The chip layout photographs of the CPU and FPC are shown in Figure 3 and 4, respectively.

(VI) Future plan

Fujitsu is in the process of porting the design to a more advanced CMOS technology known as AUH and it will be a standard cell instead of gate

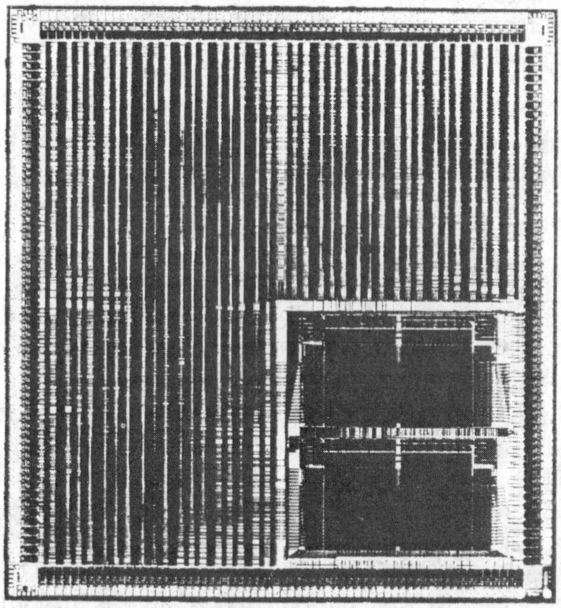

Figure 3 Layout photo of MB86900

array. There are 2 performance improvement factors in doing this: better cell specifications(AUH vs UH)and better design approach(standard cell vs gate array). Shrinking to a faster technology is always under considerations. To obtain an even better performance in addition to technology shrinking, the following items are also under considerations :

(1) customizing critical function blocks in the data path such as ALU, SHIFTER etc.
(2) restructuring the pipeline scheme to support new instructions and better interface between CPU and FPC.
(3) designing faster floating point arithmetic chip set.
(4) using different type of technology, namely, ECL, GaAs, and HEMT.

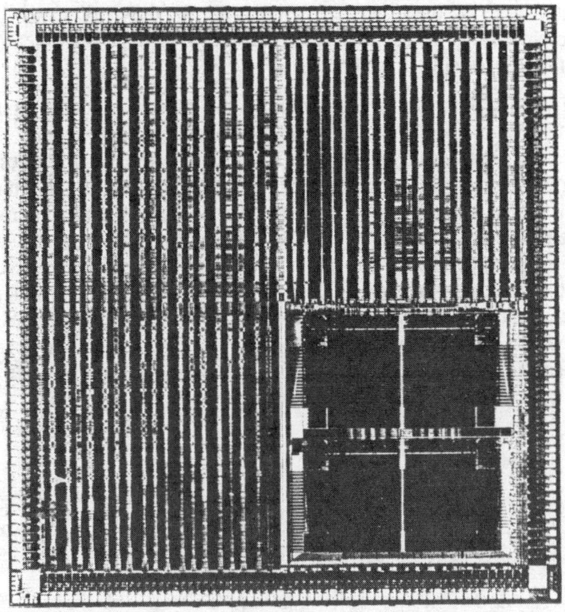

Figure 4 Layout Photo of MB86910

Acknowledgment

The authors would like to thank R. Hoshikawa's group especially Y. Takayama for their contributions to this project.

References

[1] Y. Takayama , S. Fujii , T. Tanabe,K. Kawauchi , T. Yoshida , K. Yamashita , "A 1ns 20K CMOS Gate Array Series with configurable 15ns 12K Memory",ISSCC 85, pp 916~917,Feb.

[2] T. Aikyo , Y. Hatano , J. Ishii , N. Karasawa , S. Fujii , "An Automatic Test Generation System for Large Scale Gate Arrays", Compcon, pp 445~449, May 1986.

CMOS CUSTOM IMPLEMENTATION OF THE SPARC ARCHITECTURE

M. Namjoo[1], F. Abu-Nofal[1], D. Carmean[2], R. Chandramouli[1], Y. Chang[2], J. Goforth[2], W. Hsu[2], R. Iwamoto[1], C. Murphy[2], U. Naot[1], M. Parkin[1], J. Pendleton[1], C. Porter[2], J. Reaves[1], R. Reddy[1], G. Swan[1], D. Tinker[2], P. Tong[1], L. Yang[1]

1. INTRODUCTION

Using custom circuitry, a higher level of performance is achieved for a new implementation of the SPARC™ architecture. CYC601 processor (integer unit), running at a clock rate of 25-33 MHz, implements the complete set of SPARC instructions in a 0.8 micron CMOS technology. This paper gives an overview of the processor chip and its interface to the external cache, floating-point unit, and a generic coprocessor. Companion papers provide more information on the SPARC architecture and software tools.

2. PROCESSOR MICROARCHITECTURE

Figure 1 shows a block diagram of the processor chip. The major components are: (1) a 4-stage instruction pipeline with a dual instruction buffer which is used to maximize its throughput, (2) a three port register file with 136 32-bit general purpose registers, configured as eight overlapped windows (each with twenty-four registers) and eight global registers, (3) a fast precharged arithmetic and logic unit, (4) a separate 32-bit adder for branch target calculation, and (5) the circuitry for load/store alignment and special registers (PSR, TBR, WIM, and Y).

In the basic pipeline operation, the processor fetches an instruction during the fetch-stage (F). The fetched instruction is decoded in the decode-stage (D) and source operands are read from the register file. In the execute-stage (E), the instruction is executed and in the write-stage (W) the results are written into the destination register. The write-stage is aborted if a trap or exception is raised while the instruction is being executed.

All instructions with the exception of loads/stores and jump/return execute in a single cycle. Execution of load and store instructions take more than one cycle because they use the same bus for accessing instructions as well as operands from the memory. Jump/return instructions take one extra cycle because they use register-indirect operands and the processor must read the operands from the register file before calculating the target address. All Conditional branch instructions, however, are performed in a single cycle. The single-cycle branch execution, which applies to both taken and untaken branches, results from the early availability of the condition codes generated by a highly optimized ALU and condition code evaluation logic.

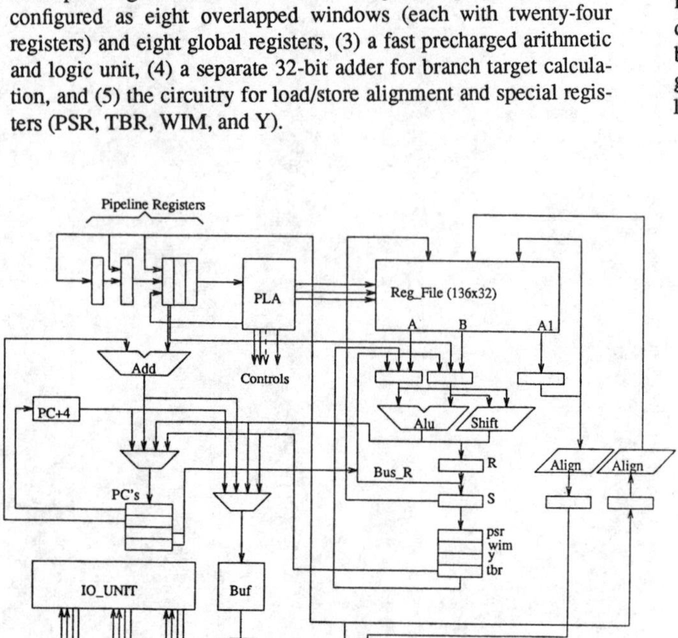

Figure 1. Chip block diagram

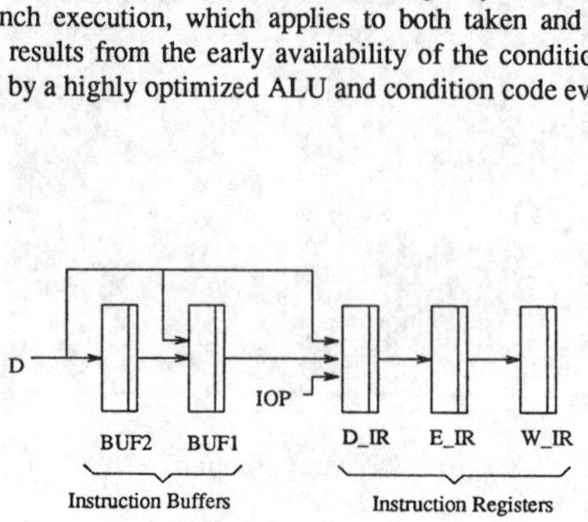

Figure 2. Instruction buffer

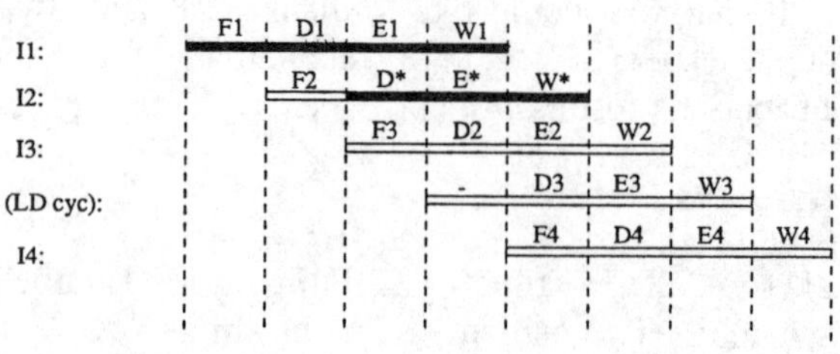

Note: I1 is the Load instruction.

Figure 3. Execution of a single-word load instruction

[1] The author is with Sun Microsystems, Inc., Mountain View, CA.
[2] The author is with Cypress Semiconductor, Inc., San Jose, CA.

The instruction pipeline consists of various fields of instructions corresponding to the decode, execute and write stages of the pipeline and a two-stage instruction buffer. The instruction buffer, shown in Figure 2, continues to prefetch new instructions once the processor encounters an instruction that needs more than one cycle to complete. This buffer is empty during a sequence of single-cycle instructions and is used only when a multi-cycle instruction is decoded. Multi-cycle instructions use one or more internally generated opcodes to complete execution. These internal opcodes are generated using a small on-chip PLA and are jammed into the pipeline as needed. Figure 3 shows the execution of a single-word load instruction that uses an extra cycle in the pipeline to complete.

3. EXTERNAL INTERFACE

The processor provides a simple interface to the cache, the floating-point unit, and a generic coprocessor. Almost all output signals of the processor are sent unlatched and are available a cycle before the cycle in which they are needed. In a typical system these signals should be latched externally before they are used.

3.1. CACHE/MEMORY INTERFACE

The chip uses two major buses for accessing the cache: a 32-bit address-bus (*A<31:0>*) and a 32-bit bi-directional data-bus (*D<31:0>*). In addition, the chip generates an 8-bit address-space-identifier (*ASI<7:0>*) which carry information such as processor mode (user/super-user) and memory access type (instruction/data). Figure 4 shows the processor bus cycles during load and store operations.

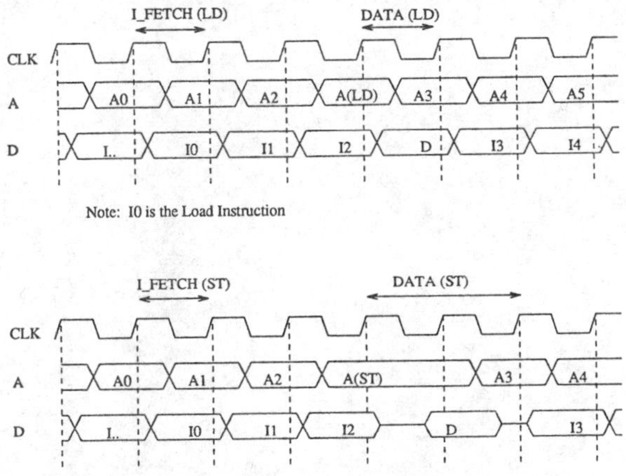

Figure 4. Load/Store bus cycles

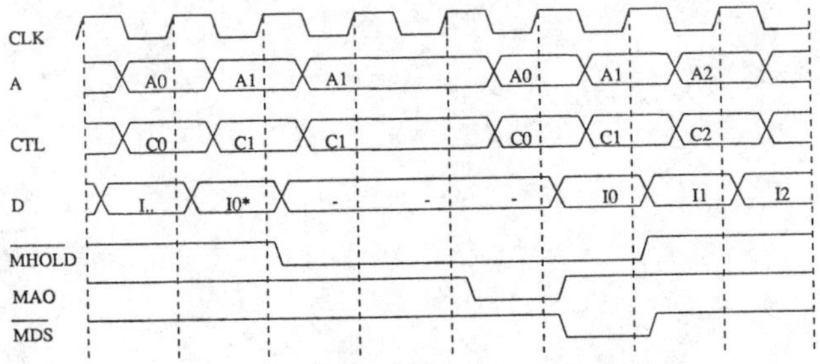

Figure 5. Cache miss on instruction fetch

In a typical cache-based system, the latched value of the address is used to access the cache data as well as cache tags. During the same cycle the cache tags are checked and depending on the result (miss or hit) the cache controller either stops the processor chip to handle the cache-miss or continues as normal in the case of a cache-hit. Figure 5 shows a timing diagram in which instruction I0 causes a cache-miss. In this case the cache controller stops the processor chip (using MHOLD signal) in the cycle following the fetch cycle and starts the cache-fill sequence. Once the cache is ready, it asserts the MAO (missed-address-output select) signal that forces the processor to put the address and controls for the missed instruction on the bus. The missed instruction is then strobed into the processor's instruction register using the MDS (memory-data-strobe) signal.

3.2. FLOATING-POINT/COPROCESSOR INTERFACE

The processor chip supports two identical coprocessor ports. One of these ports is used for interface to the floating-point unit (FP) and the other port may be used for interface to a generic user-defined coprocessor (CP). In this interface, as shown in Figure 6, the coprocessors are connected directly to the address and data bus. For every instruction fetch, both FP and CP capture the instruction and its address from the data-bus and address-bus respectively. These instructions are entered into the pipeline registers of both floating-point and coprocessor units. The integer chip provides all necessary control signals for synchronizing its pipeline with the pipeline in FP and CP. When a floating-point/coprocessor instruction is decoded by the integer chip, it signals the FP/CP to start executing it immediately. Note that this decision has to be made by the integer chip because instructions may be flushed from the pipeline due to traps and nullification which are known only by the integer chip. All floating-point and coprocessor instructions take only one cycle in the integer chip. Therefore, a new floating-point or coprocessor instruction can be started in every cycle.

The coprocessors have their own set of registers (thirty-two 32-bit registers each), a status register, a queue for holding the instructions that need to be executed, and the logic for decoding instructions, checking dependencies between instructions, dispatching instructions to the arithmetic units, and performing load/store operations from or to the cache.

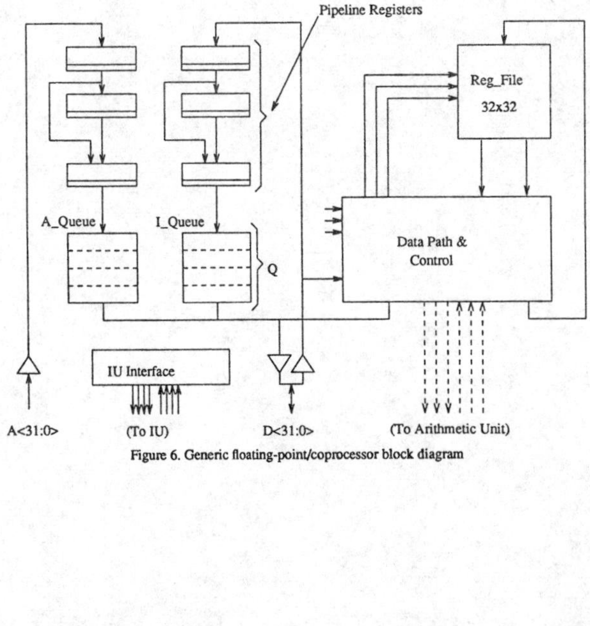

Figure 6. Generic floating-point/coprocessor block diagram

3.3. I/O AND INTERRUPTS

I/O devices are memory mapped and accessed using basic load and store operations. The architecture defines a set of alternate load and store instructions that allow the user to select different I/O devices using different ASI values.

Internal traps (synchronous) and external traps (asynchronous) are handled in the same manner. Basically, once the processor detects a trap condition, it enters into a trap sequence, saves the necessary state, flushes the instructions in the pipeline and then resumes execution from the address defined by the trap base address (TBR) and the trap-type value.

External interrupts are given to the processor chip using four input signals. Any level other than "0" on these pins is detected as a valid interrupt level. An on-chip synchronizer is used to synchronize the interrupts and prevent spurious interrupts.

4. SUMMARY AND CONCLUDING REMARKS

CYC601 with a cycle time in the range of 30 to 40 ns can perform integer instructions at a peak rate of 25 to 33 MIPS. The average number of cycles per instruction (CPI) for this processor is approximately 1.54. This assumes an instruction mix with 15% loads (which take one extra cycle), 5% stores (which take two extra cycles), 20% branches (which execute in a single cycle -- no penalty), and additional cycles lost due to load interlocks, jump/returns, nullification of delay-slot instruction in branches, and penalty for a 128 Kbyte cache-miss on instructions as well as data.

ACKNOWLEDGMENTS

This project was jointly developed by Sun Microsystems, Inc., under the supervision of Jim Slager and Cypress Semiconductor, Inc., under the supervision of Uday Kapoor and Chris Porter. Many others contributed to this project including Al Marston in the area of circuit design, Ken Okin, Chien Nguyen, Larry Goss in the area of external pin specification, Chuck Tucker, Gary Formica, Matt Clayson, Bob Davidson, and Debbie Weed in layout design, Joe Sirott, Mike Klein, Rajiv Kane, David Cooke in CAD development, and Chris Christensen, Mike Russo, and Joseph Yang in CAD support.

REFERENCES

[1] R. Garner et al., "The Scalable Processor Architecture (SPARC)," *this proceedings.*

[2] S. Kleiman, D. Williams, "UNIX on SPARC," *this proceedings.*

[3] S. Muchnick, C. Aoki, V. Ghodssi, M. Helft, M. Lee, R. Tuck, D. Weaver, A. Wu, "Optimizing Compilers for the SPARC Architecture: An Overview," *this proceedings.*

[4] M. Namjoo, A. Agrawal, D.C. Jackson, L. Quach "CMOS Gate Array Implementation of the SPARC Architecture," *this proceedings.*

TRON Project Overview

Chair: K. Sakamura

AN IMPLEMENTATION BASED ON THE BTRON SPECIFICATION

Yoshihiko Imai,Makoto Ando*,Masaaki Kobayashi*,Yoshiaki Kushiki*,Ken Sakamura***

* Central Research Laboratories, Matushita Electric Industrial Co., LTD.

**Department of Information Science,Faculty of Science, The University of Tokyo

ABSTRACT

BTRON stands for the Business-oriented operating system (OS) specification of the TRON(The Realtime Operating system Nucleus) project and is a computer architecture for office workstations. The major objective is to offer an unified man-machine interface (MMI) and handling multi-media data. Special features of the BTRON specification are (1) unified MMI method, (2) data transportability, (3) handling multi-media data. In order to achieve these objectives, the BTRON specification proposes a data model called the real object/virtual object model. To evaluate the BTRON specification ,the nucleus and extended nucleus were developed on the experimental 80286 based system.

KEY WORDS
BTRON, 80286, Nucleus, Extended Nucleus, the real object/ virtual object model

1. INTRODUCTION [1],[2],[3],[4]

The most important objective of the BTRON design is to offer an unified and easy-to-use man-machine interface and to assure data compatibility among systems built according to the BTRON specification. The second is to establish a method to pass control and data among application programs so that computers can simulate the division of labor found in society. The third is to realize a documentation management system which has the expressive power of ordinary paper, such as the capability to mix text and figures, and which can reflect the logical structure of documents. The fourth is to treat many different character sets including Japanese in a uniform manner.

We have proposed a new data model called the real object/virtual object model in order to achieve the third objective, namely the implementation of a documentation management system with rich expressive power and structure.

In this paper, the implementation of the real object/ virtual object model on our experimental system based upon the BTRON specification is described.

2. IMPLEMENTATION OF THE REAL OBJECT/VIRTUAL OBJECT MODEL

In the BTRON specification-based OS , the accumulation of data is referred to as a real object , and this is referenced by a tag called a virtual object. On a bitmapped display , virtual objects are shown as a collection of rectangles. By pointing to the rectangles with a pointing device, the viewport displayed on the bitmapped display becomes an "opened" virtual object. Opened virtual objects display the contents of the real objects. Specific applications can handle the displayed contents of opened virtual objects.

In the real object/virtual object model, a file corresponds to the real object and a link corresponds to the virtual object one to one. The virtual object is directly managed by the BTRON file management system. The contents of the virtual object are kept by the same function of the BTRON file management system. The features of the BTRON real object/virtual object model can be summarized as follows:

1) Relationships between real objects are expressed as linked network configurations;

2) Links in real objects are expressed by virtual object and/ or "opened" virtual objects;

3) Data in real objects can be arrayed in one and/or two dimensions;

4) Links can co-exist with data and can be handled in the same way as data;

5) "Opened" virtual objects operate as viewports which describe the contents of a real object.

The real object/virtual object model is realized by the functions of the file management system in the BTRON nucleus, and the real object/virtual object manager, in the extended nucleus, which expresses the data structure visually and manages the execution of application programs.

Application programs become executable in the BTRON system by means of registering to the real object/virtual object manager. On the other hand, application programs request the file management system to take out the link pointer(See 3.1) and access to the files. Further, application programs request the MMI manager and the display primitive to operate viewports and display menus, characters and figures(See 3.2).

The relationship of the above-mentioned software are shown in Figure 1.

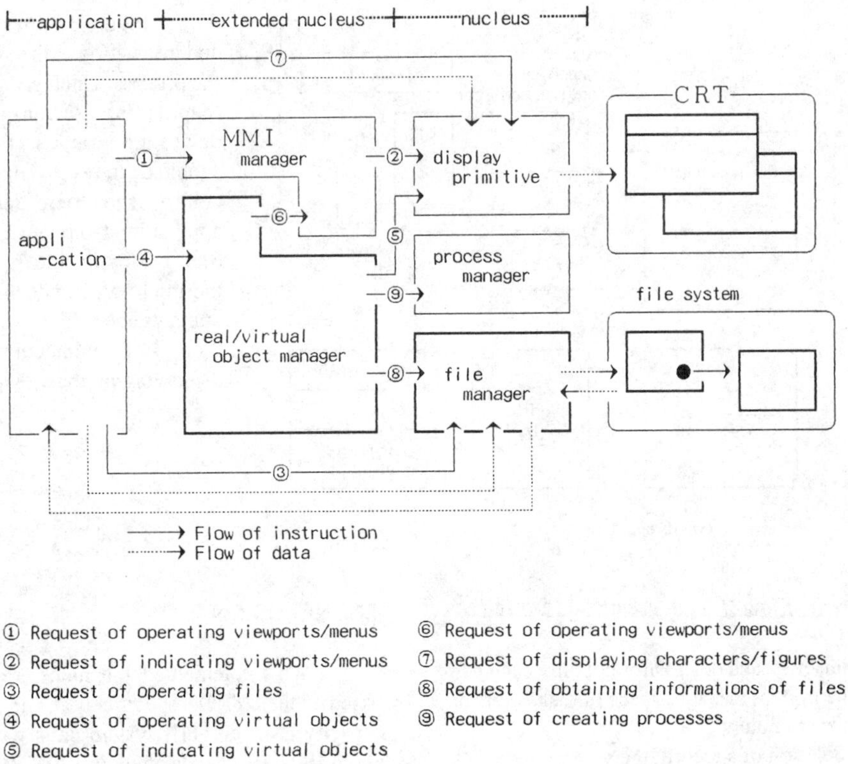

Figure 1. Relationship of software in order to implement the real object/virtual object model

The real object/virtual object manager is one of the external nucleus and offers several functions of supporting the real object/virtual object model. Application programs can visually operate the real objects and virtual objects by means of calling extended system calls. The real object/virtual object manager offers the functions of registering/deleting programs, so usually all application programs are controlled by that manager.

The followings are picked up as the functions of the real object/virtual object manager.

1) Indicating/operating virtual objects,

2) Management of application programs(for example registration and deletion of an application),

3) Setting up menus,

4) Management of attaching file systems.

3. IMPLEMENTATION OF NUCLEUS AND EXTENDED NUCLEUS

(For realizing the real object/virtual object model)

3.1 NUCLEUS

In order to realize the data management model of the real object/virtual object, variable-length record stream, network-like directory and file access control capabilities are supported on the file management system in the nucleus. In the real object/virtual object model, the accumulation of data is referred to as a "file", and this is referenced by a pointer called a "link"(Figure 2). So the file corresponds to Real object and the link corresponds to Virtual objects. The file consists of an ordered sequence of variable-length records (record stream) and the link is a sort of records. Therefore the file(Real object) may include plural links(Virtual object). Then the file may be pointed to by plural links. Consequently the real object/virtual object model implements network-like relations.

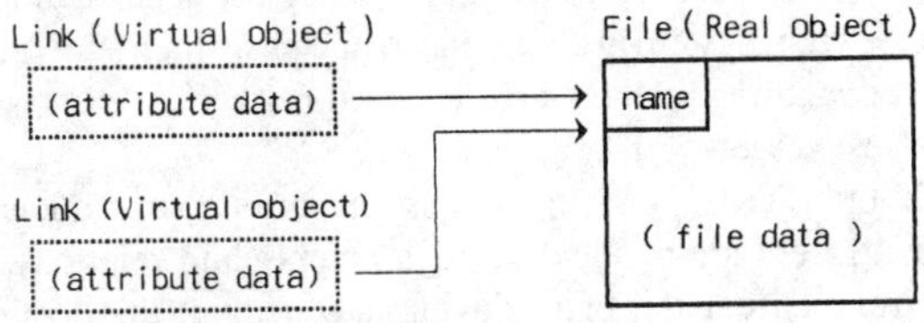

Figure 2. File and Link

For supporting this data structure, it is necessary to control multiple relationship between one file and multiple links, to treat networks without depending on devices and manage files which consist of a stream of variable-length records, efficiently.

Then file management controls the reference relationship by plural links, using a reference counter. A reference relationship independent on devices is implemented, using an indirect link.

The file doesn't consist of a stream of bytes but a stream of records and it is possible to read, write, insert, delete and truncate each record. To implement these operations efficiently, the file management system provide the following features.

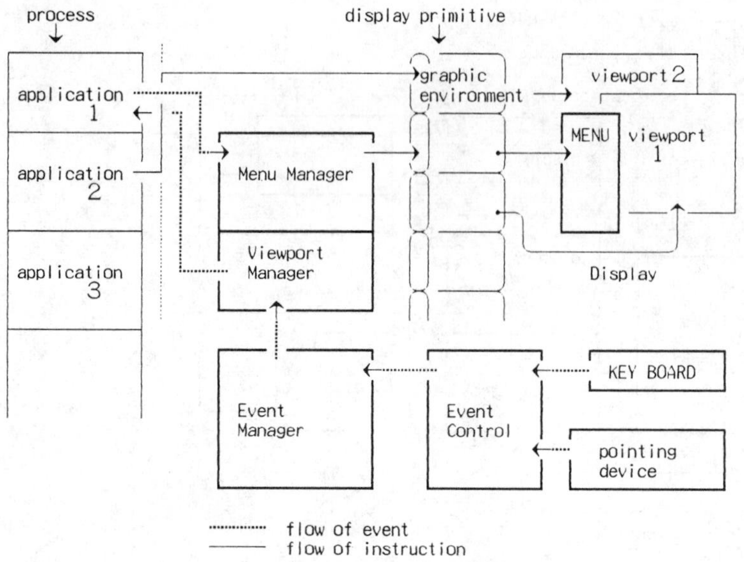

Figure 3. Flow of Input event and Instruction

Figure 3 shows the flow of input event and instruction in the system. Application 1 is the process which possess the dialog-status.
Step 1: Inputs from keyboard or pointing device are grouped as events, and events are supplied to event manager through event control subsystem, and then supplied to application from viewport manager.
Step 2: Application 1, which is woken up by the input event, checks the input event, and operates according to the input event content.
Step 3: Simultaneously, Application 2 is displaying on the viewport2.

1) As data can be inserted and deleted for not only each file but each record, the system manages space of disks, not for each block, but more minutely.
2) In insertion or deletion of a record, the system updates a record index efficiently.
3) Even though records are deleted or inserted while a file to which these records belong is being accessed, the system function is to continue to access a present record in this file.
4) The system has a function to access massive data such as image and voice, speedly.

3.2 EXTENDED NUCLEUS

In the BTRON concept, the object handling method is based on the real object/virtual object model. Special features of the viewport system in the extended nucleus,which supports the object handling method, are discussed below:

(1) Nested viewport.

In the BTRON concept, document structure and document management are handled through parent-child relations. The environment capable of displaying and operating this document structure and document management uses a multi-viewport system that fulfills the requirements of such parent-child relationships. Thus viewports may be nested.

(2) All viewports can be displayed simultaneously.

All viewports which a running process possess can be displayed simultaneously under the multi-tasking operating system.

In order to handle the real object/virtual object, the following methods are adopted :

1) Event-driven system. Input events from the keyboard and a pointing device wake up the responsible application in real-time.

2) Well-balanced coordination of MMI system and application programs.

4.CONCLUSION

We implemented the nucleus and extended nucleus based on the BTRON specification, and evaluated function and capacity (Nucleus:116 system calls with a program code of about 180 KB and data of about 140 KB. Extended nucleus:150 functions with a program code of about 215 KB and data of about 126 KB). Performance evaluation is yet to be required along with performance measurements such as speed , response time and ease of use. The tune up of the nucleus and extended nucleus and the addition to system call are under investigation. Moreover we plan to investigate to support extended functions like network environment , and to transport to other CPU's.

Finally , we would like to acknowledge the support and cooperation from the member of TRON project of the Japan Electronic Industry Development Association and the project members of our company.

REFERENCES

[1] K. Sakamura, "BTRON: The Business-oriented Operating System," IEEE MICRO, Vol.7, No.2, April 1987, pp.53-65.

[2] K. Sakamura, New Concepts from the TRON project, Iwanami-Shoten, Tokyo, 1987 (In Japanese).

[3] M. Kobayashi, S. Takenouchi, Y. Kushiki, K. Sakamura, "THE SOFTWARE STRUCTURE OF EXTENDED NUCLEUS BASED ON BTRON SPECIFICATION," T2B(TRON and Logic Programming Architecture) Session, Proceedings of the FJCC, October 1987.

[4] Y. Kushiki, M.Ando, M. Kobayashi,Y. Imai, K. Sakamura, "An Implementation based upon the BTRON specification," The 3rd technical meeting on TRON real-time architecture, Institute of Electronics ,Information and Communication Engineers of Japan, November 1987.

DESIGN CONSIDERATIONS FOR 32BIT MICROPROCESSOR TX3

Kosei Okamoto, Misao Miyata, Hidechika Kishigami, Takashi Miyamori and Tai Sato

Semiconductor Device Engineering Laboratory
Toshiba Corporation

Abstract

TX3 is Toshiba's implementation of the TRON-CHIP32 specification and supports the full instruction set, including the decimal, floating point and other complex instructions. Average performance above 10MIPS is expected. This performance level is obtained by the use of an 8KByte instruction cache, 8KByte data cache, decoded instruction loop buffer, three instruction execution units, and the ability to issue up to two instructions per cycle. In this paper, we discuss the design architecture for the TX3.

1 INTRODUCTION

1.1 TRONCHIP Architecture

TRONCHIP [1,2] is one of the subprojects of TRON project [3,4]. The TRON project is an integrated computer system design including a CPU architecture, bus, man-machine interface and operating system for high performance workstations (BTRON), and real time operating system (ITRON). The TRON architecture is defined to be expandable from 32 bits to 64 bits. TRONCHIP32 has 32 address bits and 32 data bits, TRONCHIP48 has 48 address bits and 64 data bits, and TRONCHIP64 has 64 address bits and 64 data bits. The TRON functional architecture includes the following:

- Register set: Sixteen 32-bit general-purpose registers, including the Stack pointer and Frame pointer. There are also a Program Counter, Processor Status Word, several Control Registers, and sixteen 80-bit floating point registers.
- Addressing modes: Twelve basic addressing modes and three multiple-indirect addressing(chained addressing); the chained addressing modes permit multilevel indirection with scaling and offsets.
- Instruction format: A basic set of 2-byte instructions (mostly register to register), and a larger set of variable length instructions, with orthogonal choice of operand types and addressing modes. All instructions are a multiple of 2 bytes in length.
- Instruction set: The instruction set is defined on three levels: <L0>, <L1>, and <L2>. <L0> instructions are fundamental instructions. <L1> instructions include BCD (decimal) and RING operations. <L2> instructions include other more complicated operations and additional decimal operations. These instructions include high-level instructions supporting the ITRON and BTRON operating system.
- Memory Management: Address translation uses two level page tables. A four level ring structured protection system (similar to that implemented in Multics [5]) is provided, and protection is specified on a page basis.

1.2 TX3 Outline

TX3[6] implements the 32bit TRONCHIP specification and provides all instructions defined at levels <L0>, <L1>, and <L2>. TX3 also provides floating-point instructions and TRONCHIP32 standard memory management. TX3 is intended to be used in high performance office and engineering workstations, and is being designed with a performance goal of over 10 MIPS average. To obtain this level of performance, TX3 has two large caches, a TLB, a decoded instruction loop buffer, and three parallel execution units. Table 1 shows TX3 features.

Table 1. TX3 Features

Operating Freq.	33MHz
Process Technology	CMOS 0.8μm
TLB	32 entries
Caches	8KB Instruction 8KB Data
Decimal Instructions	15 instructions
Floating Point Instructions	18 instructions
Target Performance	10 MIPS(average)

2. IMPLEMENTATION

2.1 Basic features for high performance

To achieve high performance, TX3 adopts three advanced features that do not appear in conventional microprocessors.

CH2539-5/88/0000/0025$01.00 © 1988 IEEE

a) Large On Chip Caches

TX3 has separate instruction and data caches of 8Kbytes each on chip; they can be accessed in one cycle. This design permits one instruction fetch, and one data read or write every cycle, which is four times as much bandwidth as would be obtained from a single, off chip, unified (instructions and data) cache.

b) Decoded Instruction Loop Buffer

TX3 has a Decoded Instruction Loop Buffer (DILB), similar to that used in the CRISP [7] microprocessor. Each entry in the DILB consists of two fields. The first field holds an arbitrary (decoded) TX3 instruction; the second field can hold (only) a simple instruction with no memory operand. One DILB entry can be issued every cycle; i.e. two instructions can be issued to the execution unit in one cycle; an estimate of the performance benefit from this feature is given later. The DILB also has two additional benefits: first, it is later in the pipeline than the instruction fetch stage, and thus a branch which hits in the DILB causes less of a pipeline hole than would otherwise occur. Second, the DILB permits many branches to be avoided completely, through branch folding.

c) Parallel Instruction Execution

TX3 has three instruction execution units, and these units can operate simultaneously. The first unit is a simple R-R (register to register) instruction processor, the second unit is a general integer instruction processor and the last unit is floating point processor.

2.2 Block Diagram of TX3

Figure 1 shows the Block Diagram of TX3. It consists of an Instruction Fetch Unit (IFU), Decode Unit (DCU), Instruction Issue Unit (IIU), Execution Unit (EXU), Memory Management Unit (MMU) and Cache Control Unit (CCU). The IFU includes an 8KB Instruction Cache and a Prefetcher. The DCU includes the Decoder and the Decoded Instruction Loop Buffer. The IIU includes Branch Prediction Logic[8], Instruction Issue Logic, two General Register Files and the Reorder Buffer [9], which is explained later. The EXU includes the three Execution Processors. The MMU includes the Address Generator and the TLB. The CCU includes the large Data Cache and the Store Buffer.

The three processors in the EXU are the Integer Execution Processor (IEP), the Floating point Execution Processor (FEP) and the Simple integer Execution Processor (SEP). The IEP executes not only simple arithmetic and logic instructions but also complex instructions such as bit field instructions, string instructions, system call/return instructions, and context switch instructions; the IEP is microprogrammed. The FEP executes floating point instructions and it is also controlled by a microprogram. The SEP executes only simple one cycle instructions that have no memory operand, and is hardwired.

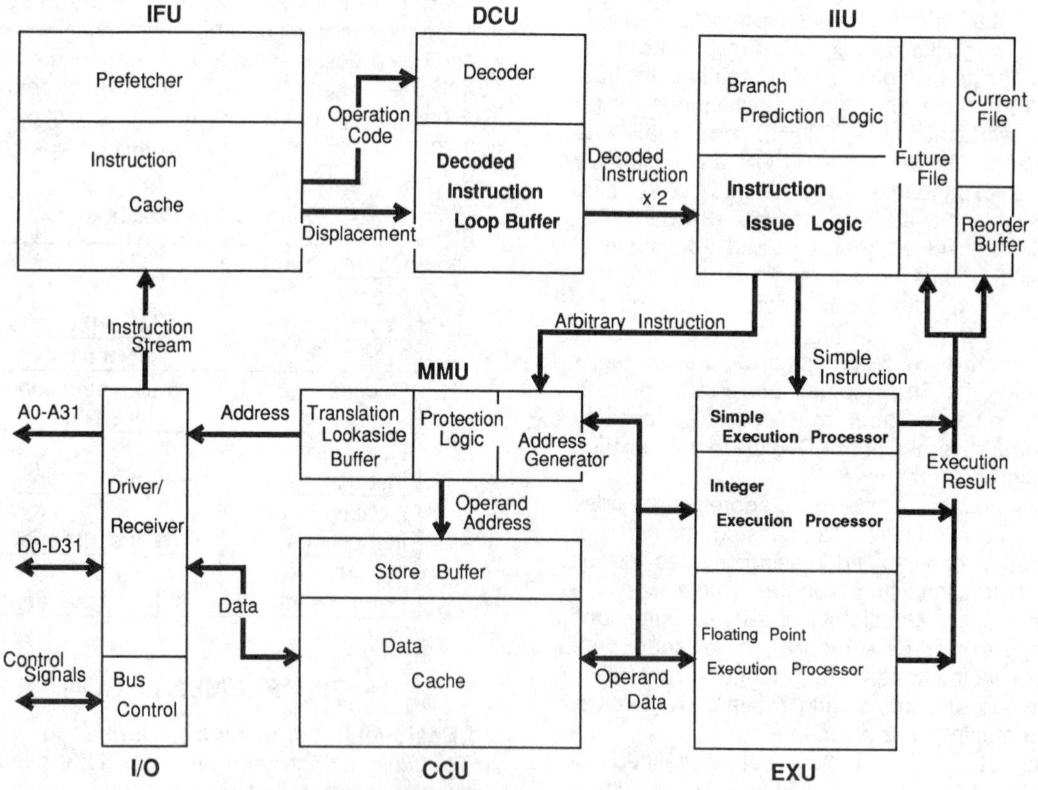

Figure 1. Block Diagram of TX3

The pipeline structure of TX3 is divided into two parts, which are "Instruction Fetch to Decode" and "Issue of Decoded Instruction to Execution". Between these two parts, there is a Decoded Instruction Loop Buffer, which permits the two halves of the pipeline to operate largely independently.

Figure 2 shows part of the TX3 pipeline design, excluding instruction fetch and decode. This latter part of TX3's pipeline scheme for complex instructions (CI) and simple instruction with memory operand (SIm) type instructions consists of six stages, which are: issue of decoded instruction by Instruction Issue Logic (IIL), operand address calculation by Address Generator (OAG), address translation by TLB (MMU), operand read from data cache (DCR), execution by IEP (IEP), and data cache write(DCW). The corresponding pipeline section for simple instruction with register operand (SIr) consists of two stages, which are issue of decoded instruction by Instruction Issue Logic (IIL) and execution by SEP (SEP). Each stage except IEP finishes it's processing in one cycle.

(SIm)
IIL --> OAG --> MMU --> DCR --> IEP --> DCW
(SIr)
IIL --> SEP

Figure 2. Latter Part of TX3's Pipeline Scheme

Each decoded instruction is issued in order of program sequence, but instructions may complete out of order because of differences in execution time or number of pipeline stages. In order to ensure precise interrupts and traps, TX3 has a Reorder Buffer and two general register files which are the Current GR file and the Future GR file. (Precise interrupts and traps require that all instructions prior to the interrupted instruction have completed and all instructions following the interrupted instruction have not begun.) The Future GR file maintains the copies of the registers used for normal program execution, and the Current GR file holds the state of the registers to be used in case of an interrupt or trap. The Reorder Buffer keeps track of which instructions have been issued, and in what order. Register writes are sent immediately to the Future GR file, but are queued by the Reorder buffer to be written to the Current GR file as the immediately previous instruction completes. (Additional logic ensures that results are computed before they are read.)

Figure 3(a) shows the timing of the pipeline stream of a program sequence 'CI1-SIr1-SIr2-SIr3'. (CI1 means complex instruction and SIri means simple instruction with register operand.)

In Figure 3(a), both CI1 and SIr1 are issued in cycle 1. As noted earlier, this is because each entry of the Decoded Instruction Loop Buffer may consist of two instruction fields, one of which must be a simple instruction with no memory operand. If the program sequence is 'CI-SIr', both CI and SIr can be issued in the same cycle.

Figure 3(b) also shows the timing of the pipeline stream of a program sequence of 'CI1-SIr1-CI2-SIr2-CI3-SIr3----CIn-SIrn'. In this case, all the simple instructions with register operand (SIri) can be issued simultaneously with a complex instruction (CIi) and can be executed in the SEP. So if no register hazard occurs, this program sequence will be finished in close to n+4 cycles and the execution time for the simple instructions (SIri) is effectively zero.

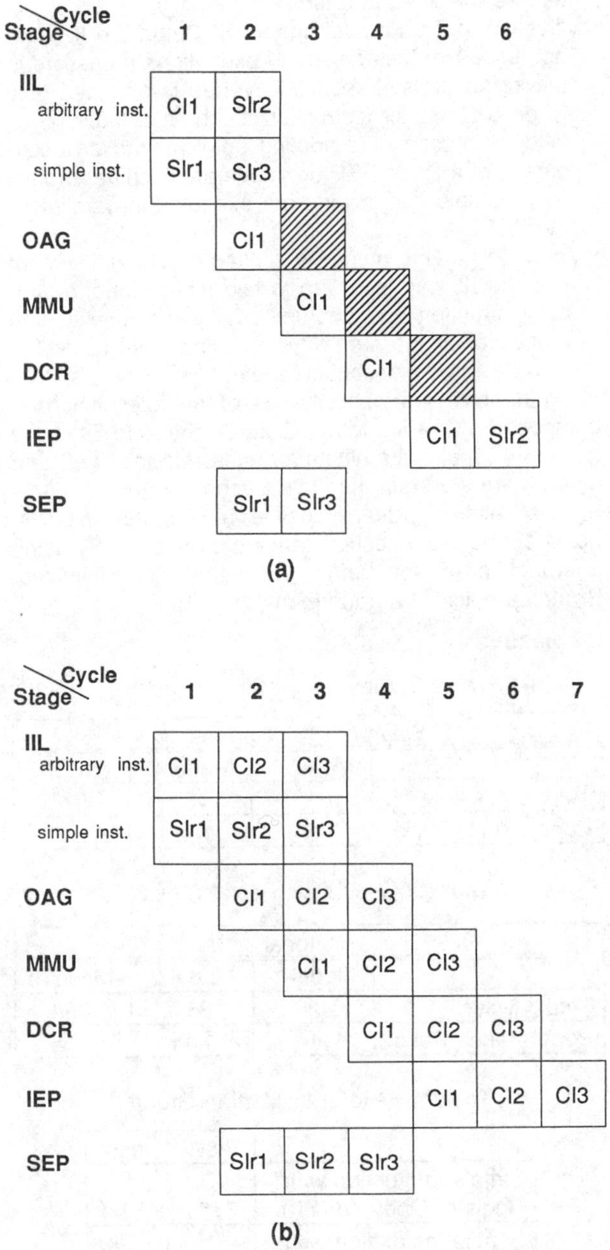

Figure 3. Example of TX3's Pipeline Stream

3 SIMULATION

3.1 Simulation Model

One of the more important aspects of the TX3 design is the incorporation of three execution processors, SEP, IEP, and FEP. These processors can execute independent instructions simultaneously. To evaluate the effect on performance of these multiple processors, three simulation models are evaluated.

<Model-1> This model is similar to an ordinary sequential pipeline scheme and does not have an SEP for simple instructions. Only one instruction can be executed at a time.

<Model-2> This model has an SEP, but the IIL cannot issue two instructions to execution processors in the same cycle. Execution overlap is obtained only when a Complex Instruction, such as a multiply, bit field instruction or a floating point instruction occupies the IEP or FEP for several machine cycles, while simple instructions are executed in parallel by the SEP.

<Model-3> This model is similar to Model-2 except that the IIL can issue up to two instructions, a simple instruction and another one, to each execution processor in the same cycle; this model is for the TX3 design, as described above.

To analyze the performance of an execution part composed of the IIL, MMU, Data Cache, and EXU, we assume that all instructions are stored in the DILB and all data are stored in the Data Cache.

This relatively deep pipeline means that pipeline hoies due to branches are many cycles long. By using a branch prediction buffer, this penalty is minimized. Branch prediction is done in the IIU.

3.2 Results

Table 2. Simulation Result (Test1)

Sieve of Eratosthenes			
	Model-1	Model-2	Model-3
Total Cycles	513	485	322
Performance Ratio	1	1.06	1.59

Table 3. Simulation Result (Test2)

Factorial			
	Model-1	Model-2	Model-3
Total Cycles	426	384	309
Performance Ratio	1	1.11	1.38

Table 4.Ratio of Instruction Group

	test1	test2
Simple Instruction with Register Operand (SIr)	37%	29%
Simple Instruction with Memory Operand(SIm)	63%	65%
Complex Instruction(CI)	0%	6%

Two simple benchmark programs have been used for preliminary evaluation of these three models. One was the 'Sieve of Eratosthenes' [10](Test1) and the other was 'Factorial' (Test2). Since no compiler is yet available, we have been limited to small programs which can be reasonably written in assembly language. Table 2 and Table 3 show the results. In the case of Test1, 6% performance improvement is observed for Model-2 and 59% for Model-3. The corresponding figures for Test2 are 11% and 38%. The different degrees of improvement for the two programs is due to the difference in the frequency of simple instructions. Table 4 shows the percentage of simple instruction with register operand (SIr), simple instruction with memory operand (SIm) and complex instruction (CI) in Test1 and Test2. Another reason for the smaller performance improvement in Test2 is that register hazards occur more often in Test2. (A register hazard is when an instruction wishes to read a register which has not yet been written. This condition is detected and the appropriate interlock imposed.) As can be seen, the performance improvement for Model-2 is about 10%, and for Model-3, 30% or more.

In order to estimate the performance advantage actually obtained from the Decoded Instruction Loop Buffer, we have to estimate it's hit ratio. Our DILB has 128 entries, and is estimated to have about a 50% hit ratio. (We consider the DILB to be analogous to an instruction cache of 128 4-byte lines, since the average TRON instruction is expected to be about 4-bytes, and the DILB is loaded one instruction at a time. From [11], we see that such a cache will have in the neighborhood of a 50% miss ratio.) That implies that the actual performance improvement is about half of the performance gain estimated above. Thus the over all improvement is about 30% in case of 'Sieve of Erathosthenes' and about 20% in case of 'Factorial'.

Other more complicated programs may have a higher frequency of complex instructions including floating point instructions. For such programs, more overlap between complex and simple instructions can be obtained (i.e. a greater improvement from Model-1 to Model-2), but since pairs of complex instructions cannot be issued together or overlapped in execution, less improvement is likely in going from Model-2 to Model-3.

We also note another advantage of the decoded instruction buffer: branch folding [7] allows the elimination of all unconditional branches and many conditional branches. This will be especially effective for a CISC architecture such as TRON, where successful branches are likely to be 20% to 25% of all instruction executions.

4 CONCLUSION

The TX3 32-bit microprocessor incorporates several features for high performance. The decoded instruction loop buffer permits two instructions to be issued in one cycle, and also permits branch folding. There are three execution units, all of which can be active at the same time; these are the simple instruction execution unit, the integer execution unit and the floating point execution unit. Performance improvements in the range of 38% to 59% are expected from the ability to issue and execute multiple instructions simultaneously.

TX3 also contains 8KB each of instruction and data cache on chip. The effectiveness of this cache along with branch target buffer and branch folding will be discussed at the conference.

Acknowledgement

The authors would like to thank Prof. Ken Sakamura of University of Tokyo, who provided many helpful suggestions. They are also grateful to Prof. Alan Jay Smith of UC Berkely for valuable comments and critical reading of the manuscript.

References

[1] K. Sakamura, "Architecture of the TRON VLSI CPU", IEEE, Vol.7,No.2, April, 1987, pp.17-31

[2] K. Sakamura, "TRON VLSI CPU: Concepts and Architecture", TRON Project 1987, Springer-Verlag, pp.199-238

[3] K. Sakamura, "The TRON Project", IEEE Micro, Vol.7, No.2, April, 1987, pp.8-14

[4] K. Sakamura, "The Objectives of the TRON Project", TRON Project 1987, Springer-Verlag, pp.3-16

[5] Michael Schroeder and Jerome H. Saltzera, "A Hardware Architecture for Implementing Protection Rings", CACM, 15, 3, March, 1972, pp. 157-170.

[6] K. Namimoto, T. Sato and A. Kanuma, "TX series based on TRONCHIP Architecture", TRON Project 1987, Springer-Verlag, pp.291-308

[7] D. R. Ditzel and H. R. Melellan, "Branch Folding in the CRISP Microprocessor: Reducing Branch Delay to Zero", Proc. of 14th Annual International Symposium on Computer Architecture, 1987, pp.2-9

[8] Johnny K. F. Lee and Alan Jay Smith, "Prediction Strategies and Branch Target Buffer Design", COMPUTER, January, 1984, pp. 6-22

[9] J. E. Smith and A. R. Pleszkun, "Implementation of Precise Interrupts in Pipelined Processors", Proc. of 12th Annual International Symposium on Computer Architecture, 1985, pp.36-44

[10] BYTE Editorial Staff, "High-Tech Horsepower", BYTE, July, 1987, pp.101-108

[11] Alan Jay Smith, "Line (Block) Size Choice for CPU Cache Memories", IEEE Transactions on Computers, September, 1987, pp.1063-1075

A 32-bit Microprocessor Based on the TRON Architecture: Design of the GMICRO/100

Toru Shimizu, Toyohiko Yoshida, Yuichi Saito,
Masahito Matsuo and Tatsuya Enomoto

LSI Research and Development Laboratory
Mitsubishi Electric Corporation
4-1 Mizuhara, Itami 664 Japan

Abstract

This paper covers the special features of the GMICRO/100 including the branching and pipelining methodologies, as well as system modeling and verification.

1. Introduction

The GMICRO/100 is a 32-bit microprocessor in the GMICRO microprocessor series. The GMICRO family includes the GMICRO/100 for application system's core processors, the GMICRO/200 for engineering workstations and the GMICRO/300 for office workstations. They implement the TRON CPU architecture and are software compatible with each other. (The TRON CPU architecture was proposed by Professor Ken Sakamura.[1]) This paper provides an overview of the GMICRO/100 design.[2]

2. GMICRO/100 Design Strategies

The GMICRO/100 is being designed as a core processor for applications in a variety of systems with the following strategies in mind:

Compact design for system integration

As a core processor, a compact design is required to enable the integration of the GMICRO/100 processor and the application specific circuits on a single chip. The processor size requirement was determined to be smaller than 10 mm $\times$ 10 mm. In order to achieve this, peripheral units, such as cache memory, memory management unit and floating point unit, have been moved off chip.

Optimized design for the basic instructions

As the chip area resources are limited for the GMICRO/100, optimum performance is impossible for all instructions. Therefore the basic instructions are implemented directly in hardware; other instructions are mainly supported with microprograms. The basic, pipelined instructions are data transfer, comparison, arithmetic, logical, shift and branch instructions. The microprogrammed instructions are bit manipulation, bit-field manipulation, variable-length bit-field manipulation, string manipulation, queue manipulation, etc.

Enhanced support for the system control

Since the GMICRO/100 is a system controller, system control functions have been given special design consideration. It provides interrupt handling mechanisms and queue manipulation instructions for the

Table 1. GMICRO/100 Specification

	GMICRO/100
Instructions	Data transfer Arithmetic Logical Bit manipulation Bit-field manipulation Variable-length bit-field manipulation String manipulation Queue manipulation Control transfer Others
Registers	Sixteen 32-bit registers (Frame pointer = R14, stack pointer = R15.)
Address space	4.3 billion bytes (Virtual memory is not supported.)
Interrupt level	7 levels
Address bus	32 bits
Data bus	32 bits
Instruction cycle (minimum)	2 machine cycles
Bus cycle (minimum)	2 machine cycles
Pipeline scheme	5 stages with branch prediction mechanism

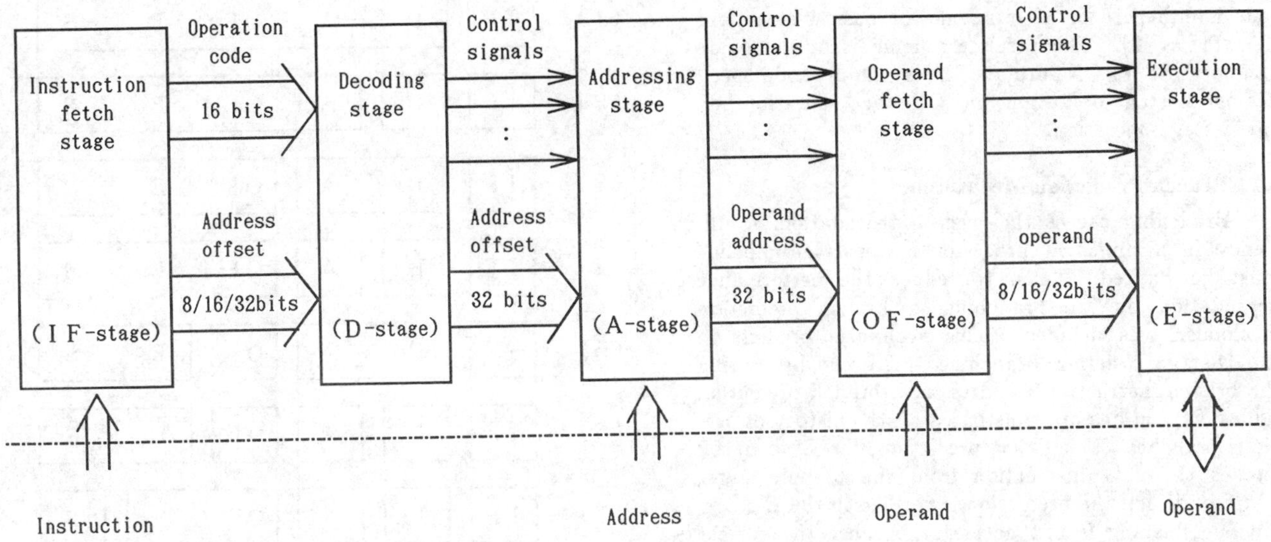

Figure 1. GMICRO/100 Pipeline Scheme

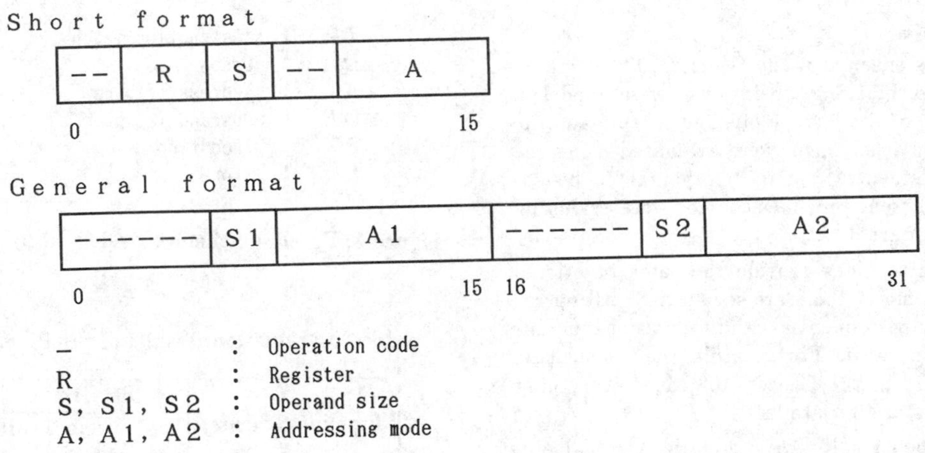

Figure 2. TRON Instruction Formats

operating-system implementation, as well as variable-length bit-field manipulation instructions for the bit-map display control.

3. GMICRO/100 Specifications

The GMICRO/100 has 32-bit address and data busses. It has 16 registers which are also 32-bit wide. As its optimum rate, it can perform 32-bit data operations and/or access memory, every two machine cycles. The specifications are detailed below in Table 1.

4. GMICRO/100 Pipeline Scheme

The GMICRO/100 employs a 5-stage pipeline scheme with a branch prediction mechanism to reduce the number of pipeline flushings due to branching. The pipeline is designed to handle the TRON instruction formats efficiently.

4.1. 5-stage Pipeline

The GMICRO/100 pipeline consists of: 1) an instruction fetch (IF) stage, 2) a decoding (D) stage, 3) an addressing (A) stage, 4) an operand fetch (OF) stage and 5) an execution (E) stage. These stages are operated simultaneously by their corresponding functional units. The pipeline scheme is illustrated in Figure 1.

The IF-stage fetches instructions from memory and sends them to the D-stage as an operation code and an address offset. In the D-stage, the operation code is decoded into control signals. The address offset is passed, unchanged, to the A-stage. In the A-stage, the address offset is translated into an operand address. This is then passed to the OF-stage. Here, the operand data is fetched based on the operand address. Finally, in the E-stage, the operand is used to execute the instruction and store the result.

In the TRON instruction format, the instruction code is either 16 or 32-bits wide for basic instructions (See Figure 2). The pipeline scheme is optimized to handle these TRON formats. Every 16-bit code specifies one A-stage operation, one OF-stage operation and one E-stage operation.

4.2. Branch Prediction Mechanism

Branching causes the biggest degradation of efficiency in a pipelined processor because the pipeline must be flushed. Thus, to reduce the performance degradation due to branching, a branch prediction mechanism was included.[3] This mechanism predicts, in the D-stage, whether branching will occur by storing the branch instruction's address in a branch prediction table. Predictions are thus based on the history of previous branches. Using that prediction, the GMICRO/100 fetches the next instruction from the branch target address. When the prediction is verified in the E-stage, pipeline flushing is not necessary because the correct branch target instructions are preprocessed in the pipeline. Table 2. outlines the branch prediction strategies for the GMICRO/100.

4.3. Evaluations

The pipeline scheme of the GMICRO/100, including the flushing and blocking operations, were modeled. The performance of the 5-stage pipeline scheme and the branch prediction mechanism were evaluated using the "Sieve of Eratosthenes"[4] and "Dhrystone"[5] benchmarks. Eight different pipeline schemes were evaluated as described in Figure 3.

Each of the schemes provide the same functional operations but some of them are sequential. All operations in a box are sequential, and operations in different boxes are parallel. For example, the 6th scheme, which is employed in the GMICRO/100, does everything but execute and store in parallel.

The evaluation results are summarized in Table 3. The scheme chosen for the GMICRO/100 was the second-best of the 8 schemes; it had a 10% performance improvement with branch prediction. The best one, the 8th scheme, was rejected because it provides little performance improvement with complicated controls.

Table 2. GMICRO/100 Branch Prediction Strategies.

Branch Instruction	Predictions
Branch Always	The branch will occur (JUMP).
Conditional Branch (for the first occurrence)	The branch will not occur (NOT JUMP).
Conditional Branch (for successive occurrences)	The same as the last execution of the branch (CONDITIONAL).
Loop Branch	The branch will occur (JUMP).

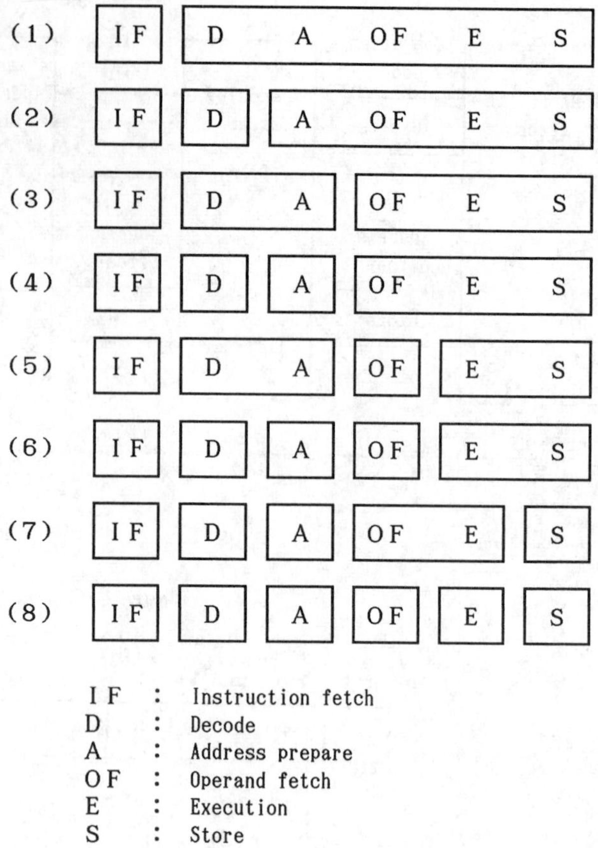

Figure 3. Pipeline Schemes Evaluated by the Simulation

Table 3. Evaluation Results of the Pipeline Schemes

Pipeline Scheme	Performance Ratio	
	no branch prediction	with branch prediction
Scheme (1)	1.00	1.02
Scheme (2)	1.18	1.29
Scheme (3)	1.61	1.68
Scheme (4)	1.76	1.97
Scheme (5)	1.71	1.80
Scheme (6) (for GMICRO/100)	2.22	2.45
Scheme (7)	1.81	2.01
Scheme (8)	2.37	2.56

5. Conclusions

The GMICRO/100 microprocessor was designed to take advantage of the special features of the TRON CPU architecture, such as the instruction format. It uses a 5-stage pipeline scheme and branch prediction mechanism, which have been validated by simulation.

The GMICRO/100 chip is now under development, along with software development tools such as compilers and operating systems. The chip will be implemented using a 1.0 micron double-metal CMOS process.

Acknowledgements

We would like to express our appreciation to Professor Ken Sakamura for helpful discussions. We also wish to thank Dr. K. Shibayama, Dr. H. Nakata and all the engineers involved in this project.

References

[1] K.Sakamura, "Architecture of the TRON VLSI CPU", IEEE MICRO, vol.7, no.2, pp.17-31 (Apr.1987).

[2] O.Tomisawa, T.Yoshida, M.Matsuo, T.Shimizu and T.Enomoto, "Design Considerations of the GMICRO/100", TRON Project 1987, Springer-Verlag, pp.249-258 (Nov.1987).

[3] J.K.F. Lee and A.J. Smith, "Branch Prediction Strategies and Branch Target Buffer Design", IEEE Computer, vol.17, no.1, pp.6-22 (Jan.1984).

[4] J. Gilbreath and G. Gilbreath, "Eratosthenes Revisited: Once More through the Sieve", BYTE, pp.283-326 (Jan.1983).

[5] R.P. Weicker, "Dhrystone: A Synthetic Systems Programming Benchmark", Communications of the ACM, vol.27, no.10, pp.1013-1030 (Oct.1984).

Emerging Processors

Chair: Y. Patt

V60/V70 Microprocessor and its Systems Support Functions

Yoichi Yano, Yasuhiko Koumoto, and Yoshikuni Sato

Microcomputer Division
NEC Corporation
1753 Shimo-numabe, Nakahara, Kawasaki, 211 Japan

Abstract *This paper will describe advanced 32-bit microprocessors, V60 and V70 (μPD70616 and μPD70632, respectively), and their support functions for operating systems and high-reliable systems. Various operating systems functions are provided by the V60/V70 architecture, but three of them, namely the virtual memory support functions, context-switch functions, and asynchronous trap functions will be described in this paper. As a basic mechanism for highly-reliable systems implementation, FRM (Functional Redundancy Monitoring) is also provided. The FRM allows to design a system in which multiple V60s (or V70s) form a redundant processor configuration. One processor in the system acts as a master, while the others act as monitors. As an example of FRM implementation, an FRM board which uses three V60s in its redundant core is introduced.*

Introduction

Rapid progresses in semiconductor manufacturing technology now allow us to design a VLSI system of some hundred-thousand transistors on a single chip. A good example of such VLSI systems includes 32-bit microprocessors with 32-bit internal configuration and pipelined CPU structure. In designing such microprocessors, main architectural support for software system should be operating system support functions as well as highly-reliable system support functions. The former requirement is a direct outcome of current microprocessor software trends, namely a complex system needs operating system as run-time environment for software. The latter requirement is also from current system design trend in large systems, such as the Electrical Switching System (ESS) and the Private Branch Exchange (PABX).

The V60/V70 microprocessors were designed to support these requirements [1][2]. Advanced 1.5μm CMOS technology allowed us to realize 32-bit microprocessors with 375,000 transistor on a single chip (V60) and 385,000 transistor version (V70). Six-stage pipelined structure also provides 3.5MIPS (V60) and 6.6 MIPS (V70) performance at 16MHz and 20MHz operation, respectively.

Their architectural supports for the above requirements include

- Virtual memory management
- Context-switch function
- Asynchronous traps

and

- FRM (Functional Redundancy Monitoring).

In Section 1, we briefly describe the architecture of V60/V70, and their hardware structure. In Section 2, Operating systems support functions are introduced. In Section 3, the FRM function is explained. In Section 4, a testbed of the FRM function evaluation, the V60 FRM board, is explained. Section 5 closes this paper.

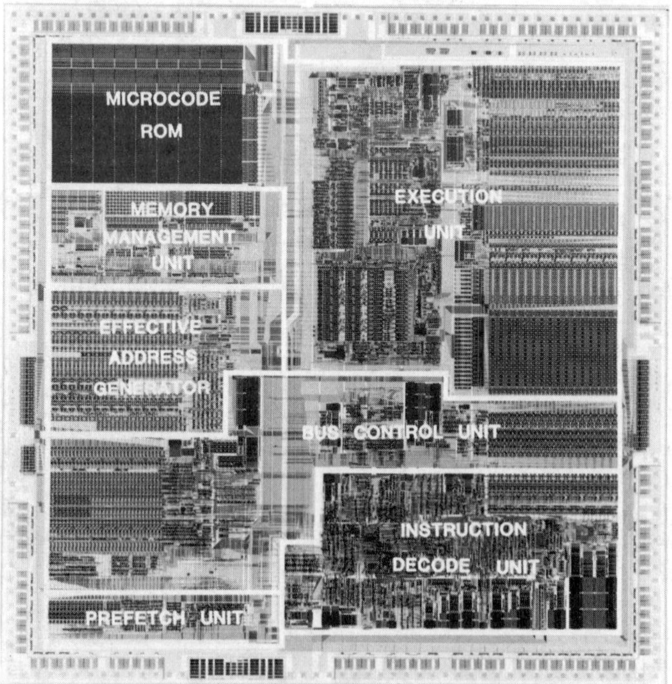

CH2539-5/88/0000/0036$01.00

1. Architecture of the V60/V70

This section introduces architecture of V60/V70 microprocessor.

(1) V60 and V70: V60 and V70 are 32-bit microprocessors with on-chip memory management unit (MMU) and floating-point arithmetic unit (FPU) in addition to six-unit pipelined CPU structure. Both microprocessors have the same instruction set architecture. Differences in these two are shown in the table 1. As is shown in the table, V60 is a 16-bit data bus version, while V70 is full 32-bit bus version of the same architecture. Number of transistors vary because the bus data/control part have been extended in V70. Fig.1 is a chip microphotograph of the V70. Inside the chips, both microprocessor have almost the same internal structure. The following shows these blocks:

- PFU: prefetch unit
- IDU: instruction decode unit
- EAG: effective address generator
- MMU: memory management unit
- BCU: bus control unit
- EXU: execution unit

These six units form a pipelined instruction execution structure. Up to four instructions can be processed at one time in various instruction processing stages, e.g., instruction code fetch, instruction decode, address translation, and instruction execution [1][2].

Item	V60	V70
Product Name	μPD70616	μPD70632
Technology	1.5μm 2-Al CMOS	
Transistors	375,000	385,000
Internal Struct.	32-bit Data/32-bit Address	
Ext. Data Bus	16-bit	32-bit
Ext. Address Bus	24-bit	32-bit
Min. Bus Cycle	3-clock	2-clock
Package	68-pin PGA	312-pin PGA
Performance	3.5MIPS (16MHz)	6.6 MIPS (20MHz)
Introduction	1986/2	1987/4

Table.1 V60/V70 Comparison

(2) Register Set: V60/V70 employs general-purpose register based architecture. Thirty-two 32-bit general purpose registers, 32-bit program counter (PC) and a program status word (PSW) which is a set of conditional/control flags form program register set. Operating system routines can access privileged register set which includes various control registers, such as stack pointer caches, task control registers, system control registers, virtual memory management registers and trap registers. Fig.2 shows the V60/V70 register set.

(3) Register Usage: The general purpose registers provide an opportunity for better object code by optimizing compilers, because the large number of registers are suited for global optimization, such as the

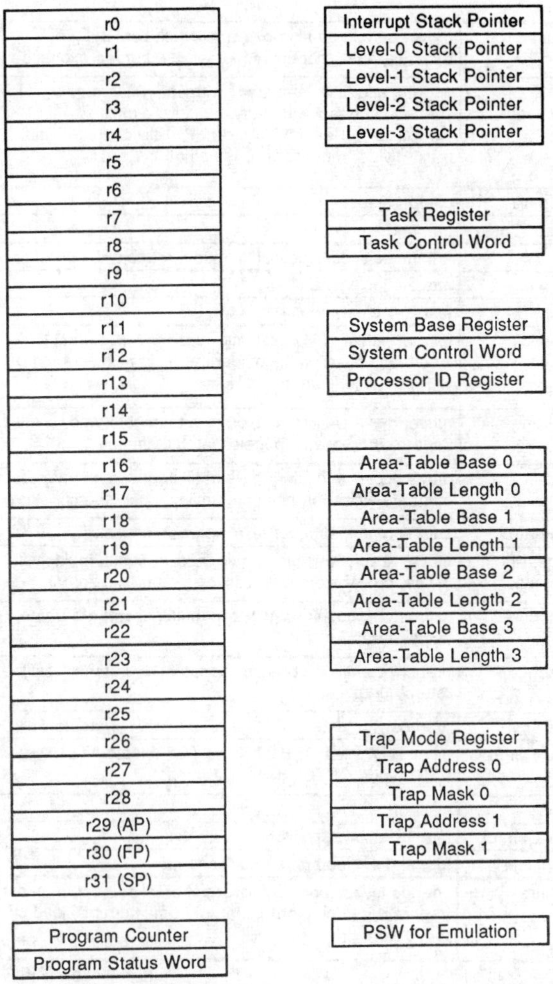

Fig.2 V60/V70 Register Set

global register allocation. Allocation reduces the number of memory traffics, hence reduces the cost of accessing (relatively) slow main memory. Three out of 32-registers are reserved for special usages in procedure call/return sequence.

- R29 : Argument Pointer
- R30 : Frame Pointer
- R31 : Stack Pointer

Register 29 is assigned as an argument pointer (AP) which holds the base address of arguments (parameters). Register 30 is for frame pointer that designates base address of local variables in current procedure execution context. Register 31 is a stack pointer. Its points the top of stack (TOS) address.

(4) Instruction Set: V60/V70 instruction set consists of 119 instructions. Table 2 lists V60/V70 instructions. Basic instruction format allows to designate two addressing modes (operands) as source and destination operands. Because an addressing mode can be specified as register, immediate, or memory, the instruction format permits memory-to-memory operation as an instruction.

Transfer	move, move with sign-ext., move with zero-ext., truncate, push, pop, byte reorder, bit reorder, exchange
Integer Arithmetic	negate, add, increment, add with carry, decrement, subtract, subtract with carry, multiply, u-multiply, ext-multiply, u-ext-multiply, divide, u-divide, ext-divide, u-ext-divide, remainder, u-remainder
Compare	compare, test
Logical Ops	not, and, or, exclusive or
Shift	arithmetic shift, logical shift, rotate, rotate with carry
Address	move effective address
Single-Bit	test, set, clear, negate
Bit-Field	extract with sign-ext., extract with zero-ext., extract to right, insert left, insert right, compare with sign-ext., compare with zero-ext., compare to right
Bit-String	move, move with negate, or, or with negate, and, and with negate, xor, xor with negate, serch 0, search 1
Character String	move, move with filler, move until stopper, compare, compare with filler, compare until stopper, search, skip
Decimal	add, subtract, subtract reverse, pack, unpack
Floating-Point Arithmetic	move, absolute value, negate, add, subtract, multiply, divide, power, compare, conversion, integerize, trap
Procedure	call, return, push multiple, pop multiple, prepare frame, dispose frame
Branch	branch, conditiona branch, loop, test and branch, call, return, jump
PSW Ops	read psw, update psw, set byte by flag, update psw all*
MMU Controls	clear TLB*, clear TLB all*, get ATE*, update ATE*, get PTE*, update PTE*, get real address*
In/Out	in*, out*
Task Control	load task context*, store task context*
Indivisible	test and set, compare and exchange
Et Cetra	change level, check access, nop, breakpoint, trap on ovf, trap, retrun from interrupt, return from interrupt*, load priv reg.*, store priv reg.*, halt*

* : Priviledged Instruction

Table.2 V60/V70 Instruction Set Summary

(5) Virtual Memory System: V60/V70 has 4G-byte of addressing space that is defined by 32-bit pointer in the instruction set architecture. The address space can be realized in either in real address mode or virtual address mode. In virtual mode, the address space is implemented by paging-based virtual memory system. To bring efficient virtual space structure, the address space is divided into three levels of hierarchy, namely

- section (1GB section x 4 = address space),
- area (1MB area x 1024 = section), and
- page (4KB page x 256 = area).

According to this partition, a virtual address is translated to real address by referring a register set (Area Table Base/Length Register), and two types of address translation tables (Area Table and Page Table). The address translation is supported by on-chip memory management unit (MMU) which has 16-entry full associative translation look-aside buffer (TLB) for high-speed translation by eliminating table memory accesses. Fig.3 shows address translation process.

(6) Protection: V60/V70 architecture emphasizes run-time systems safety by a unique protection mechanism. Programs are defined as running in certain execution level (EL) which is specified by the EL bits in PSW. If the level is 0, programs are running in priviledged mode in which priviledged instruction execution and priviledged register accesses are permitted. Larger the number is, the lower the priority. A data in memory is protected by using two types of protection mechanisms.

- execution level and area-level protection
- page-level protection

Suppose a data item is shared by two processes. One process is a producer (writer) and the other is consumer (reader). The data item acts as a pipe between two processes. Further suppose that the data item should be read and written only by privileged routines (e.g., OS kernel). In this case, the data can be set to "readable by level-0 routines" for the reader process and "writable by level-0 routines" for the writer process. Area-level protection mechanism enables this specification. Two Area Table Entries are defined. One defines "readability" which is attached to the reader process' address space, and the other defines "writability" which is attached to the writer. Two processes share the data by referring it through different Area Table Entries. Accesses through these entries are possible if and only if the process runs at certain execution level and the area-level protection allows the access. In page-level protection, the page is defined as certain combination of readability, writability, and executability which is defined by data items in the page. In the above example, the data is readable and writable, but non-executable. The page is set to non-executable by resetting "executable" bit in corresponding Page Table Entry. The data is accessible if both two protection mechanisms allow access.

Fig.3 Address Translation Process

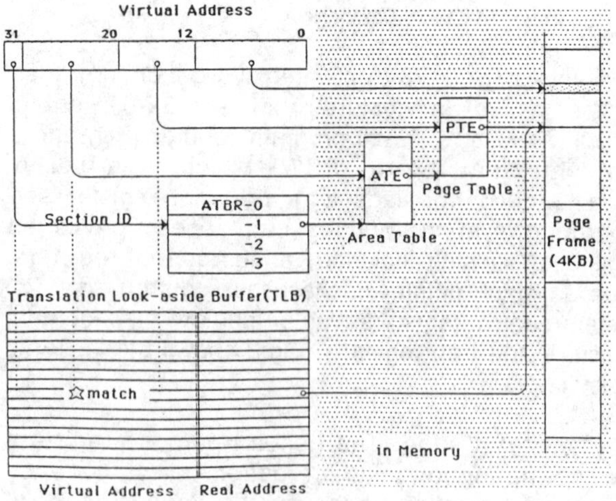

2. OS Support Functions

This section describes operating system support functions in V60/V70.

(1) Virtual Memory Support: Basic support mechanisms for virtual memory system was introduced in Section 1. An example of usage of the virtual memory support function is an MVSC (Multiple Virtual Space Configuration). The standard virtual address space configuration can be defined to all processes, namely a process can have its own addressing space as its execution environment. Up to 4G-byte of address space is provided to each task. This concept is named "Multiple Virtual Space Configuration." Fig.4 shows this configuration example. Application codes and data are located in different address spaces to have basic protected environment (in a sense that an application is independent from crash of other applications). Operating system codes, in turn, should be accessible from all the processes to enjoy OS services through system calls. Shared address segment can be realized by sharing a section. Also the protection mechanism is used to separate execution levels among OS codes and application codes.

(2) Context Switch Support: The instruction set includes context-switch related instructions. They are

- STTASK : store current task context
- LDTASK : load task context

A task is defined by a Task Control Block (TCB) in memory. Execution environment is saved and restored from a TCB which corresponds a task. Swapping task context usually takes long time, but only a subset of TCB can be swapped at the point of context switch, because not all the TCB resources are used by a task. STTASK/LDTASK instructions have operands that support variable-size TCB. The following registers are candidates for subsetting:

- Memory Management Registers
  - Area Table Base Register
  - Area Table Length Register
- Stack Pointers
- General-Purpose Registers

If a system uses only a limited virtual address sections for each task, only a subset of Area Table Base/Length Registers are swapped at the context switch. If a system uses only a limited execution levels, we can save stack pointers' swappings. If operating system's entry library and interrupt handler save certain general purpose registers inside them, not all the general purpose registers are saved at the switch.

(3) Asynchronous Traps: Asynchronous trap means a way of noticing event occurrence to software by postponing the notice to certain entry point. Quick response to an event is necessary, but it usually introduces complicated software structure (spaghetti structure) in operating systems. Two types of asynchronous trap are provided. One is a trap to system routine, the AST (Asynchronous System Trap). Another one is a trap to task routine, the ATT (Asynchronous Task Trap). Trap occurs just after the "Return From Interrupt/Exception" instruction.

(4) Asynchronous System Trap: AST is used inside operating system routines. An example is dispatcher. If a task is set to ready by an event, such as expiration of waiting time, the task should be rescheduled by dispatcher. Direct control transfer to the dispatcher from timer interrupt handler in this example, cannot isolate the handler from dispatcher in a sense of module design. In addition, time in interrupt-disabled status is lengthened because each routine is indivisible and two routines are executed without permitting further interrupt. AST saves such situation. The timer handler sets a request for AST if task(s) should be rescheduled. Then, the routine finishes execution by executing the "Return From Interrupt" instruction at the end of handler. AST occurs at this point, and the control is transferred to dispatcher, if entry point to the dispatcher is registered as AST handler address. This simplifies the design, because two routines are isolated, and interrupt can be sensed at the execution of "Return From Interrupt" instruction. AST occurs if a request is registered and the execution level changes to defined level. In this case, the event handling is postponed to the time of end of handler execution.

(5) Asynchronous Task Trap: If a trap handler is attached to task execution environment, ATT is useful. In the above example, AST is used because the dispatcher is inside operating system. But a routine is for a task, such as exception handler, ATT traps to the handler if a request is registered and the execution level changes to task's level. In this case, event handling is postponed to the time of task dispatching.

Fig.4 Multiple Virtual Space Configuration Example

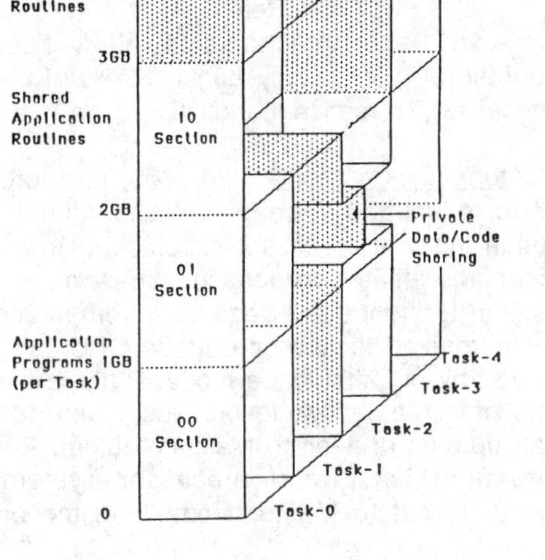

3. Functional Redundancy Monitoring

This section introduces the FRM (Functional Redundancy Monitoring) in V60/V70 microprocessors.

(1) Introduction: One can define a highly reliable system by "a digital system which can correctly continue its all or partial operation without total system-down, even if faults may degrade the performance of the system". Some hardware components may be lost due to the fault, but redundant hardware units replace their functions so that continuous operation can be achieved. The VLSI components have changed the concept in high-reliability. Components, such as functional units inside a VLSI chip, have much higher reliability than ones by vacuum tubes. Highly reliable system can be achieved by considering only system-level configuration. Generally speaking, a high reliability system provides the following procedural steps for fault recovering:

1. Identify a fault
2. Isolation of the faulty component
3. Diagnose the fault
4. Repair/replace the component
5. Recover the process
6. Reconfigure the system

Step-1 identify a component that does not operate as expected, and notice it to external interface. Step-2 tries to eliminate the faulty component from the system to prevent fault propagation, as well as activation of redundant module for reconfiguration. Step-3 and step-4 try to inspect the faulty unit and repair it. Step-5 recovers the process that was interrupted, and step-6 reconfigures the system by hardware and software.

(2) FRM Function: The FRM function consists of following mechanisms:

- Master/Checker Mode
  - Monitoring
  - Match/Mismatch Status
- Bus-Cycle Control
  - Bus-Freeze Operation
  - Bus-Cycle Retry

These two basic mechanisms allow redundant configuration. In V60, only about 0.24% of chip area was necessary to realize the function.

(3) Master/Checker Mode: V60 (V70) microprocessor has two execution modes. One is Master Mode execution that the processor executes instructions. In Checker Mode, the processor does not execute instruction. It fetches and read data from memory that are synchronized to a Master Mode CPU, but it does not drive any outputs in the mode. Rather, it "listens" outputs of a Master Mode processor and compares (virtual) outputs of itself to Master's output. A minimal configuration is a dual processor system. One processor is set to Master Mode, and the other as Checker Mode. They share a same processor clock.

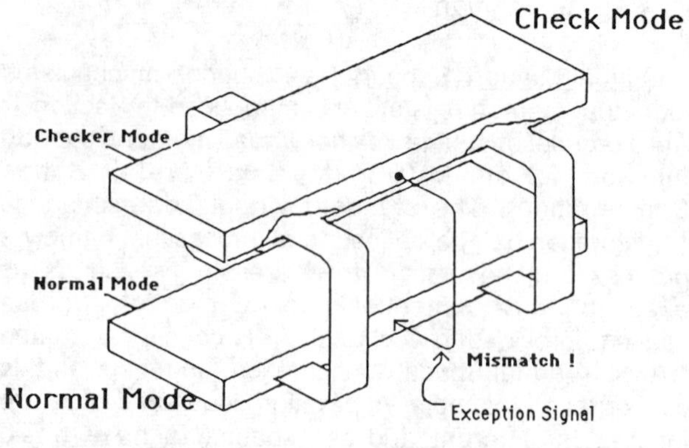

Fig.5 FRM Configuration Concept

The Checker compares the output of Master's in every bus-cyle If mismatch occurs, it drives "Mismatch" signal to indicate to external hardware. Fig.5 shows the FRM configuration.

(4) Bus-Cycle Control: Comparison takes place in bus-cycles. As a basic mechanism of bus-cycle operation, V60 (V70) provides bus-cycle freeze and bus-cycle retry operations. One can "freeze" current bus-cycle by setting Bus-Cycle Freeze signal. Bus-cycle operation is terminated and suspended, and later it can be resumed by resetting the signal. Bus-Cycle Retry operation is also provided. Setting retry request, processor retries current bus-cycle. If mismatch occurs, first freeze the bus-cycle. The bus-cycle terminates as if it were normally terminated. But further bus-cycles are not activated by the processor(s). Detect faulty processor, and eliminate it from the configuration. Reconfigure the system, and retry the bus-cycle. The suspended bus-cycle is again executed. In this process, one can change processors' mode from Checker to Master or Master to Checker. Mode can be dynamically changed.

(5) System Configuration: The FRM function provides basic mechanism for designing redundant system. It provides functions that correspond to the basic concept:

1. Identify a fault	: Monitoring
	: Match/Mismatch
2. Isolation	: Bus-Freeze
3. Diagnose the fault	: --
4. Repair/replace it	: --
5. Recover the process	: --
6. Reconfiguration	: Master/Checker
	: Reconfiguration
	: Bus-Cycle Retry

Basic mechanisms are provided, and a real system implementation example is explained in the following section.

4. V60 FRM Board

This section describes the V60 FRM board.

(1) Basic Structure: The V60 FRM board is a single board computer for Multibus-I bus. The board consists of following sub-units:

- CPU core : V60 x 3 (in TMR)
- MINC : Majority Decision and Reconfiguration
- 2MB of Dual-ported main memory with Write-backup for for multi-board system
- FRM configuration test circuit
- Peripheral controllers : Timers, Serial/Parallel Interface, etc.

Fig.6 shows board photograph.

(2) The TRM CPU core: The board has three V60 microprocessors in Triple Redundancy Module (TRM) configuration. One out of three acts as a Master Mode processor, while the other two act as monitors in Checker Mode at the start-up time. In this *Three CPU Mode*, let us denote them by CPU0, CPU1, and CPU2.

- CPU0 --- Master Mode
- CPU1 --- Checker Mode
- CPU2 --- Checker Mode

Fig.7 shows TRM configuration.

(3) Three CPU Mode: Suppose there occurs a mismatch after executing some instructions. Then, we can say that one CPU is faulty. The system automatically configures itself into *two CPU mode*. Majority decision takes place in this reconfiguration process.The following shows the faulty processor and related reconfiguration operation:

CPU1	CPU2	Fault	Operation
match	match	none	Continue execution
match	mismatch	CPU2	Cut off CPU2, then continue
mismatch	match	CPU1	Cut off CPU1, then continue
mismatch	mismatch	CPU0	Cut off CPU0, then set CPU1 as master mode and continue

Here, "match"/"mismatch" shows that the CPUn provides "match"/"mismatch" status by comparison. Reconfiguration occurs automatically under hardware control. The MINC (Mismatch Control) circuit controls this majority decision and reconfiguration process. Fig.8 shows this operation. Software routines can not know this in time, but the reconfiguration is displayed in an I/O port. Polling this port allows software routine, such as timer interrupt handler, to know the reconfiguration.

(4) Two CPU Mode: After reconfiguration to *Two CPU Mode*, the board can continue execution. But further mismatch occurrence does not allow the CPU core to continue execution, because, if mismatch occurs, we cannot tell which CPU is faulty. Further mismatch occurrence stops the board operation, and signals to the other board(s) for interruption.

Fig.7 Triple Mode Redundancy Configuration

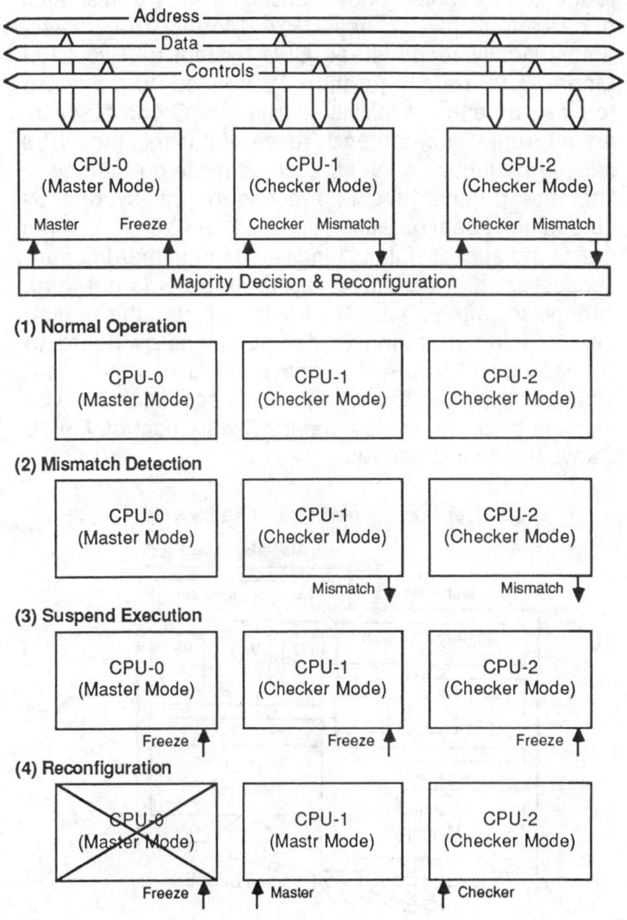

(5) Dual Board Configuration: The board can be configured as dual system by master/stand-by setting, as shown in Fig.9. Although the boards are identical, a jumper switch is provided to distinguish whether a board should start as master board or stand-by board. Initializing software (boot program) has to read this switch, then it continues its execution if it were set to master board, otherwise it waits for wake-up interrupt in halt mode.

(6) Write-Backup: To ensure the identity of two boards in dual board configuration, autonomous memory update function is provided. If the memory contents in master board is updated, the same data is transferred to the stand-by board through Multibus-I bus. This concept is close to the store-through cache implementation strategy.

(7) Evaluation Circuit: For evaluation of board circuitry and software routines, a circuit which forces mismatch occurrence is provided. The circuit, which consists of timers and controls, outputs signals that forces mismatch occurrence. It is under software control. Memory error which enables write back-up control is also provided.

(8) Software Considerations: Software routines are requested to control above functions. After a mismatch occurrence in Three CPU Mode, the MINC automatically reconfigures CPU system to Two CPU Mode. The reconfiguration is noticed to software routines by either explicitly polling an I/O port bit or by an interrupt. Since an occurrence of mismatch may be caused by tentative event, such as noise on the power line, the routine tries to reconfigure the system by outputting reconfiguration request to an I/O port. If the trial is not successful, it is indicated in another I/O port. successful, it is assumed that the error was not fatal. Otherwise, after a couple of times of trial, the routine can transfer operation to another stand-by board to continue execution. All the above operations are under software control. Memory systems reconfiguration, by memory back-up, is also under software control. Fig.10 shows the flow of control.

Fig.9 Board Configuration and Write Back-Up

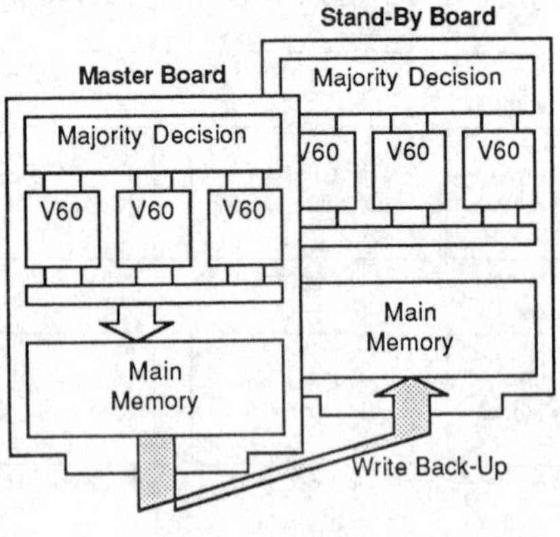

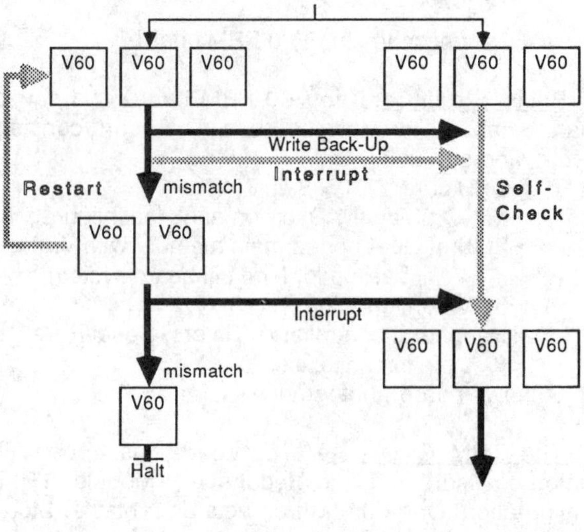

Fig.10 Flow of Control

5. Conclusion

The basic systems support functions by V60/V70 microprocessor were introduced. Operating system support functions, such as virtual memory management for basic system structuring, context switch support functions for shorter context switch time, and asynchronous trap mechanism for module oriented software design, are the key for short OS development. Also, FRM function supports highly-reliable systems design, and an example of such configuration, the FRM board, shows easiness of implementation.

The V60/V70 microprocessors have other system related functions, such as the address trap mechanism for debugging and V20/V30 emulation mode for multiple-OS structure, but they will be reported in other papers.

Acknowledgement : The authors would like to thank members in V60/V70 project. The limited space does not allow the authors to acknowledge all of them, but they would like to give special thanks to Dr.K.Kani, M.Kimura, and I.Fujitaka for their helpful suggestions and supports.

References

[1] Y.Yano et al [1986] : A 32-bit Microprocessor with On-Chip Virtual Memory Management, ISSCC Digest of Technical Papers, Feb., 1986.

[2] H.Kaneko et al [1986] : A 32-bit CMOS Micro-processor with Six-stage Pipeline Structure, Fall Joint Computer Conference, 1986.

ARCHITECTURE OF THE WE®32200 CHIP SET

Matthew S. Nelson, Jorge Cruz-Rios, Benjamin Ng, and William S. Wu

AT&T Information Systems
Crawfords Corner Rd.
Holmdel, NJ 07733

Abstract

In this paper we will describe four members of the WE32200 chip set, the WE32200 Central Processing Unit (CPU), the WE32201 Memory Management Unit (MMU), the WE32204 Direct Memory Access Controller (DMAC), and the WE32206 Math Acceleration Unit (MAU).

These chips provide substantial performance improvements over the present generation AT&T microsystem chip set and constitute the core of the next generation of VLSI chips.

The CPU, MMU, DMAC, and MAU are implemented using 1.0 micron CMOS technology and are designed to initially run at 24 MHz.

1. INTRODUCTION

Extensive studies of the many applications currently using the WE32100 chip set have pointed the way to many enhancements that provide increased system performance. These enhancements have been implemented while at the same time providing an upward hardware and software migration path from the current chip set.

2. The WE32200 CPU

The WE32200 microprocessor[1], a third generation CPU, is the follow-on to the single-chip, 32-bit WE32100 microprocessor[2]. The performance goal for the microprocessor at 24 MHz is two times the performance of the WE32100 microprocessor at 14 MHz. To make use of the existing software base and board designs, the microprocessor is protocol and object code upward compatible.

The microprocessor has separate 32-bit address and data buses, a flexible protocol that adjusts dynamically to the size of the data bus, a high performance, general coprocessor interface and a rich set of interrupt support features.

The WE32200 microprocessor has an extensive and orthogonal instruction set to support efficient execution of high-level languages. In addition, it has operating system instructions that establish an environment that permits process switching and interrupt handling with a minimum of operating system support.

In what follows, an overview of the internal architecture of the microprocessor will first be presented. The new features of the WE32200 CPU will then be presented.

The WE32200 microprocessor consists of the four major sections shown in Figure 1. These are the main controller, the fetch unit, the execution unit, and the bus interface control. The main controller is responsible for acquiring and decoding instruction opcodes and directing the action of the fetch and execute controllers. It is also responsible for responding to and directing the handling of interrupts and exception conditions.

The fetch unit handles the instruction stream and performs memory-based operand accesses. It consists of a fetch controller, an instruction cache, an instruction queue, an immediate and displacement extractor and an addressing arithmetic unit.

The execute unit performs all arithmetic and logic operations, performs all shift and rotate operations, and computes condition flags. It consists of an execute controller, 32 32-bit registers, working registers, an ALU and a 32 bit barrel shifter.

The bus interface control provides all the strobes and control signals necessary to interface with peripherals.

The WE32200 CPU has a total of 32 32-bit user visible registers. The upper 16 registers are additions to the WE32100 CPU architecture. Of these 16 registers, 8 of them are user registers. They are user readable and writable. The other 8 registers are kernel registers, which are kernel readable and writable. The user can read the kernel registers, but cannot modify them. The same "register related addressing modes" for the lower 16 registers are supported for these 16 new registers. In addition, they can be used for base register addressing, which is a new addressing mode supported by the WE32200 CPU.

The larger register set allows more data to be stored in the CPU, and thus reduces CPU to Memory traffic and execution time. However, there is a tradeoff of process switching time and the number of registers to be saved

CH2539-5/88/0000/0043$01.00 © 1988 IEEE

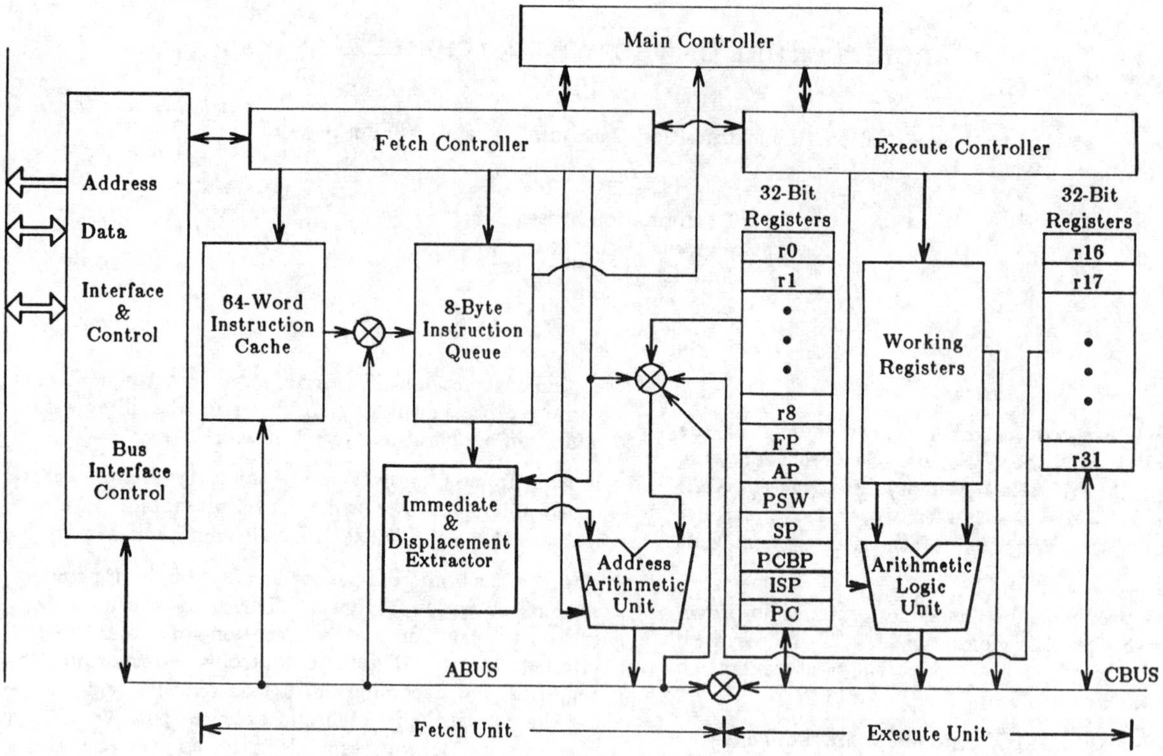

Figure 1. WE32200 Microprocessor Block Diagram

on process switch. The WE32200 CPU provides the choice of two process models. Support is provided in the process-handling instructions to optionally save the 14 registers (in WE32100 CPU compatible mode) or the 14 registers plus the 8 new user registers.

The WE32100 CPU supports a rich set of addressing modes. They are absolute and absolute deferred, displacement and displacement deferred, immediates, register and register deferred, and expanded-operand type that performs data type conversion. In addition to the above, the WE32200 CPU supports auto post/pre inc/dec, index and scaled index modes. The new addressing modes are added to further enhance the string manipulations and table/array accessing of the WE32100 CPU instruction set architecture. With these new addressing modes operations like change encodings, move strings, remove multiple blanks, remove extraneous characters, etc., which are used heavily in COBOL and in compilers, will speed up significantly.

To provide stronger support for COBOL, the WE32200 CPU supports packed BCD addition and subtraction and pack and unpack data conversion instructions. In addition, loop control instructions, which test the condition flags and then decrement a counter and test it against 0 are added. The loop control instructions, again, enhance the string manipulations and table/array accessing of the WE32100 CPU instruction set architecture.

The WE32200 CPU supports dynamic bus sizing. This feature allows the CPU to connect directly to 32-bit and 16-bit data busses. For example, while the main memory system may be 32 bits wide, 16 bit wide bootup ROMs can be used.

The WE32200 microprocessor supports arbitrary byte alignment for data. This feature enhances the capability of the microprocessor in accessing databases consisting of non-aligned data. Furthermore, the feature is important for message passing by communicating processes in a multiprocessor environment.

3. The WE32201 MMU

The WE32201 Memory Management Unit (MMU) is a third generation MMU and is a successor to the WE32101 MMU.[3] [4] Although the MMU provides upward migration from the 32101, its internal architecture has been redesigned to provide several performance enhancing features. The MMU consists of 2 distinct functions, memory management and data caching.

3.1 Memory Management

The MMU supports a 4 Gbyte virtual address space as well as a 4 Gbyte physical address space. Access rights checking for all 4 execution levels of the WE32100 CPU are provided. The MMU supports both contiguous as well as paged segments, and both types of segments may be supported at the same time. Shared segments are supported, facilitating interprocess communication. Miss processing and history bit updating are provided in hardware. Fast context switching performance is supported by managing and caching descriptors for multiple contexts on chip.

The MMU assumes a three level table structure which provides mapping from virtual to physical address spaces. The first level is a four entry table called the Section Table. Each Section Table entry provides a physical address pointer to the second level which contains the Segment Descriptor Tables. Each Segment Descriptor Table entry describes either a contiguous segment or a paged segment. For contiguous segments, the Segment Descriptor points to the base of the contiguous segment. For paged segments, the Segment Descriptor points to the Page Descriptor Table. The Page Descriptors point to the location in physical memory of each of the pages of the segment.

The Segment Descriptor also contains information on whether the segment is cacheable. This information provides a data cache (virtual or physical) with information on whether the data can be cached. Memory buffers being filled from disk and UART address space are typical memory areas that are not cached.

In order to increase the performance of memory translation, a fully associative 64 entry Page Descriptor Cache has been implemented on chip. A pseudo-LRU algorithm is used as the replacement policy for the PDC. An 8 entry directly mapped Segment Descriptor Cache serves to reduce the miss processing time.

The MMU can be configured for various page sizes. Page sizes of 2K, 4K, and 8K bytes are supported. This allows the system designer the flexibility to use the optimal page size for their application.

The MMU also supports multiple contexts with the management of the identification of each of the contexts provided by on chip hardware. This hardware consists of a fully associative 16 entry ID Cache and a 4 entry Current ID RAM. A hardware LRU stack has been implemented to support the LRU replacement policy for the ID Cache. The support for multiple contexts tends to improve the PDC hit ratio, especially in applications where context switches occur frequently. This feature may be optionally turned off in order to maintain compatibility with the 32101 MMU.

Simulations show that for typical environments, hit rates of over 99 percent can be expected for the PDC.

A probe feature has also been implemented in the MMU. This feature provides a facility by which the system may check permissions at a given execution level for a virtual address. In addition, the address of the Segment Descriptor, Page Descriptor, or the corresponding physical address may be returned.

3.2 Physical Data Cache

In addition to the memory management functions, the MMU supports a physical data cache on chip. This implementation, provides the data as well as the tag portions of the cache. The 4K byte cache is organized in a 2 way set associative configuration with 2 32 bit words per block and 1 word per sector. There are therefore 256 tags per set. The data cache performs a lookup in parallel with the address translation. This allows the MMU to provide the CPU with data without incurring wait states on a data cache hit. On data cache misses, the CPU access incurs only latency due to address translation. A write through policy is implemented with the data cache updating the cache data only if there was a cache hit.

The data cache provides the capability of automatically maintaining cache coherency. This capability is provided by implementing on chip hardware which monitors the bus when the MMU is idle. Cache coherency is necessary if other processors can modify data cached in the MMU. It is also necessary in systems where multiple MMUs are used. In this case, different MMUs may contain data from the same physical address because different virtual addresses may be mapped to the same physical address.

System simulations show that the hit rate for the data cache may vary from 80 to 90 percent.

3.3 Multiple MMUs

In those systems where an additional increase in performance is desired, additional MMUs may be used. The use of multiple MMUs can provide additional sections, reduce miss processing by virtue of a larger Page Descriptor Cache, or increase hit rate in the data cache by providing a larger data cache. The virtual address is used to select among 2 or 4 MMUs.

4. The WE32206 MAU

The WE32206 Math Acceleration Unit (MAU) provides single chip floating point capability for the WE32200 Microprocessor and is fully compatible with the IEEE standard 754 for binary floating point arithmetic.[5] It provides single (32-bit), double (64-bit), double-extended (80-bit) precision, 18 digit binary coded decimal, and 32-bit integer data formats.

It supports add, subtract, multiply, divide, remainder, square root, compare, sine, cosine and arctan operations. The operand, result, and status and command information transfers take place over a 32-bit bidirectional data bus that provides the interface to the host microprocessor. The 32206 MAU is footprint, software, and protocol upward compatible with the 32106 MAU.[6] [7] Upward compatibility is desired in order to provide a smooth migration path from the 32106 to the 32206. The rest of this section will focus on the new features of the 32206 MAU.

The 32206 has four new instructions: SIN, COS, ATAN, and PI, to provide high performance support for trigonometric calculations. The first three functions use the CORDIC[8] algorithm to generate their results. Over the range of $-\pi/2 < x < +\pi/2$ for sine and cosine and the range of $-1 \leq x \leq +1$ for arctan, the functions are guaranteed to be accurate to at least one bit in the last place for single and double precision. The instruction PI returns the value of π in the desired precision and rounding mode.

The number of 80 bit user registers has been increased from four to eight, thereby allowing more data to be stored internally in the 33206. The selection fields for the original four registers did not change, thereby insuring upward compatibility.

In the 32106, selection of the rounding mode is determined in the Auxiliary Status Register (ASR). Changing the rounding mode requires writing the ASR. There are cases, however, such as a Fortran float to integer conversion, which require a specific rounding mode, Round to Nearest, independent of the rounding mode in effect at the time. The 32206 provides for additional rounding control in the Control Register (CR), which is already automatically written during every instruction, thereby saving the extra instruction.

The performance objective of the 32206 at 20 MHz is to be twice the floating point performance of the 32106 at 14 MHz. Taking the 32106 at its base frequency of 14 MHz, increasing the frequency to 20 MHz provides a straight 43% improvement in all benchmarks. To achieve the goal of 2X improvement, another 40% gain had to be found.

The inclusion of the three trigonometric functions in the 32206 provides a significant performance improvement over software implementations. Additionally, examinations of the algorithms used allowed the iteration count for the single precision implementation to be halved, therefore making it almost twice as fast as the double precision implementation. This performance gain is determined automatically from the precision of the destination operand. In a single precision Whetstone benchmark, the use of the hardware trigonometric functions provides a 25% performance improvement.

The algorithm for square root was changed from a restoring to a non-restoring procedure which doubled the performance. Halving the iteration count for single precision caused a total improvement of approximately 4X. The iteration count for single precision calculations was also halved for multiply and divide.

The total performance improvement from the features examined above is 36% for the single precision Whetstone benchmark. Combined with the frequency gain, the total improvement is 95%. This number does not include any gains from the 32200 CPU. This additional improvement puts the 32206 over its 2X improvement goal.

5. *WE 32204 DMAC*

The WE 32204 Direct Memory Access Controller (DMAC) was designed to solve one of the most critical computer system bottle necks: the I/O subsystem. The I/O subsystem becomes a bottle neck because there are disparities between the bandwidth and protocols of the system and peripheral buses. The WE 32204 DMAC dual-bus architecture, buffering scheme and packing/unpacking of data fully decouples the peripheral bus from the system bus. The decoupling of the buses and buffering of data allows for higher parallelism between the two buses which prevent slow peripherals from degrading the system performance.

The WE 32204 DMAC has four fully independent channels which can perform four types of data transfers: peripheral to memory (PTM), memory to peripheral (MTP), memory to memory (MTM) and memory fills (MF). Each channel has eight registers to manage data transfers. Three of the registers (status and control, mode, and device control registers) specify parameters for data transfers, peripheral device configuration, and the system and peripheral bus protocols. The remaining five registers hold the number of bytes to be transferred, a pointer to a link list, and the source and destination addresses for the data transfer. Each channel also has a 32 byte data buffer and a packing/unpacking data block. The data buffer is used by the DMAC to temporarily store data. The packing/unpacking data block is used to assemble bytes from the peripheral into 32 bit words (PTM transfers) or disassemble 32 bit words into four bytes (MTP transfers).

5.1 System Bus

System performance is largely affected by the availability of the system bus to the CPU. The WE 32204 DMAC optimizes the system bus bandwidth utilization four ways. First, it supports a block mode access that can transfer in a single access 8 or 16 bytes (the DMAC also supports byte, half word (16 bits) and word accesses). Second, the buffering scheme used by the DMAC insures that the system bus is utilized efficiently. The WE 32204 DMAC will request the bus and transfer data to the system memory only when the internal buffer of a particular channel has at least 16 bytes (this will provide enough data for the DMAC to perform a block mode access). The same strategy is used when reading data from the system memory: the DMAC transfers data to the channel's buffer only when there is at least room for 16 bytes. Third, the DMAC supports chain transfers which virtually eliminates the need for the CPU to load new parameters into the DMAC for each individual transfer. The CPU intervention is only needed to load three registers of the DMAC and to set up a request block in memory. The request block is a singlely linked list of structures, each containing the source and destination addresses for a transfer, the byte count, and the pointer to the next structure in the list. The linked list allows for modifications to the request block without halting DMA activities.

When the DMAC becomes the bus master, it is capable of transferring data in burst or cycle steal mode (the burst mode transfers can be interrupted to prevent blocking of high priority interrupts or external accesses to local memory). The DMAC is also capable of handling bus exceptions like faulted and retried accesses. Polling and interrupt generation are supported by the DMAC. Each channel has its own interrupt vector which is driven on the system bus during an interrupt acknowledge cycle. The DMAC requests an interrupt when a channel terminates (normally or abnormally) and the channel is allowed to interrupt the CPU. The status of the channel's termination is embedded in the interrupt vectors to speed up response to abnormally terminated transfers.

5.2 Peripheral bus

The peripheral bus is eight bits wide and supports up to four devices. All four devices share a data strobe which signals the presence of valid data on the bus, a data acknowledgement signal used to end asynchronous accesses and a peripheral done signal which can be used to terminate peripheral to memory transfers. Beside the shared signals, each device has its own bus request and chip select signals.

The DMAC supports synchronous and asynchronous protocols for each device on the peripheral bus. The synchronous protocol is the simplest because the peripheral device is not required to assert a data acknowledgement. Beside the two protocols, the DMAC supports two types of data transfers. The first is the single byte transfer in which the peripheral transfers one byte and then relinquishes the bus. The second is a burst transfer, in which up 65536 bytes can be transferred without relinquishing the bus (intended for fast peripherals).

5.3 DMAC Performance

The performance of DMAC transfers at 24 MHz clock rate can be divided into three categories. First, memory fills which are performed at a rate of 34.9 Mbytes/sec. Second, memory to memory transactions which achieve a transfer rate of 19.2 Mbytes/sec. Third, memory to peripheral and peripheral to memory transfers are performed at a rate of 12 Mbytes/sec.

6. Summary

The WE32200 chip set provides substantially increased performance over the WE32100 chip set. Various features increasing performance and functionality have been added to the CPU and the MAU. The MMU provides a physical data cache as well as new memory management features. The DMAC solves the most critical computer system bottleneck: the I/O subsystem. These chips constitute the VLSI core of a general purpose computing environment supporting virtual memory and IEEE standard floating point.

7. Acknowledgements

The authors wish to acknowledge the contributions made by the following persons to the architecture of the WE32200 chip set: S. Altabet, D. Blevins, S. Boyles, U. V. Gumaste, N. M. Hayes, P. Kumar, F. D. LaRocca, Z. J. Mao, M. E. Reynolds, W. Pekrul, R. Piepho, J. W. Seery, and M. E. Thierbach.

REFERENCES

1. "The WE32200, AT&T's High Performance 32 Bit CMOS Microprocessor", W.S. Wu *et al.*, Conference Proceedings, ICCD, Rye, N.Y., 1987.
2. UNIX Microsystem-WE32100 Microprocessor Information Manual, AT&T Technologies, Inc., Morristown, N.J., Jan. 1985.
3. "Architecture of a VLSI MAP for Bellmac-32 Microprocessor," P. M. Lu *et al.*, Digest of Papers-Compcon Spring 83, San Francisco, CA., Feb.-Mar. 1983, pp.213-217.
4. "A VLSI Memory Management Chip: Design Considerations and Experience," A. K. Goksel *et al.*, IEEE J. Solid-State Circuits, Vol. SC-19, No. 3, June 1984, pp. 325-328.
5. "IEEE Standard for Binary Floating-Point Arithmetic", ANSI/IEEE Std 754-1985.
6. "The Design of an IEEE Standard Math Accelerator Unit", P.W. Diodato *et al.*, IEEE Journal of Solid-State Circuits, Vol. SC-20, No. 5, October 1985, pp. 993-997.
7. "An IEEE standard floating point chip", A.K. Goksel *et al.*, ISSCC, February, 1985.
8. "A Unified Algorithm for Elementary Functions", J.S. Walther, AFIPS Conf. Proc., Vol. 38, 1971, SJCC, pp. 379-385.

Regulus: A High Performance VLSI Architecture

S. Sims, J. Benkual
Computer Consoles Incorporated
Computer Products Division
Irvine, California

Abstract

The Regulus Processor is a high performance microprocessor specifically designed to take full advantage of custom VLSI. Regulus is designed to minimize control area and maximize the amount of on-chip memory. It is a general-purpose 32-bit architecture. The instruction set is very simple, with memory addressed only through load and store instructions. The first design is implemented with a 1.2-micron double metal CMOS technology. The architecture is implemented with two full custom CMOS VLSI devices, the Instruction Processor (IP) and the Arithmetic Processor (AP). This paper deals primarily with the Instruction Processor (IP) chip. Some of the innovative features of the architecture and design are described.

Architectural Overview

The Regulus architecture[1] is based on Reduced Instruction Set Computer[2] (RISC) principles. It is a load/store architecture with simple addressing modes. It supports a small number of basic instruction types. It has thirty-two 32-bit general-purpose registers. The architecture supports a paged memory management scheme that provides four gigabytes of virtual address space as well as memory protection for each page. Implicit in the architecture is an on-chip cache memory that is used to hold frequently accessed instructions and data.

The instruction set is optimized for the C programming language. It contains a complete set of integer and floating point operations. Instructions are all in a single 64-bit format. The fields of the instruction are very simple to decode. This is to minimize the time required for instruction decoding. The current design uses a simple two-stage pipeline. The instruction set design allows for separate and concurrent control of instruction sequencing and data loop operations. This feature also provides for a delayed branch mechanism.

Special support for fast and efficient call/return and parameter passing is designed into the architecture. A high bandwidth data path between the register file and the cache provide the ability to load and store the registers very quickly.

The AP is a slave co-processor to the IP. It supports the IEEE floating point standard for single and double precision formats. It performs all floating point arithmetic operations. It also performs the integer multiply and divide instructions. The AP contains accumulators, both floating and integer, which hold the results for all AP operations. To perform an AP operation, the IP sends commands and data to the AP. The AP then performs the operation and saves the result in the appropriate accumulator. The programmer may then retrieve the result from the accumulator or use it in subsequent AP operations.

The IP is a large device of about 450 mils per side. It contains over 560,000 devices. A 10- kilobyte internal cache is used for instructions, data, page table entries and special data and instructions for virtual to physical address translation. The cache is implemented with a three-transistor dynamic memory cell. In addition, there are static memory blocks that are used for register file and instruction buffering. About 65 percent of the IP chip area is used for memory (about 470,000 transistors). The AP is about 360 mils by 360 mils. It contains about 200,000 devices.

Instruction Processor

Figure 1 shows a simplified block diagram of the IP chip. There are seven distinct areas of the chip: the Unified Cache, the Instruction Buffer, the Data Loop, the Instruction Address Block, the Shifter, the Window Pointer Block and the External Reference Block.

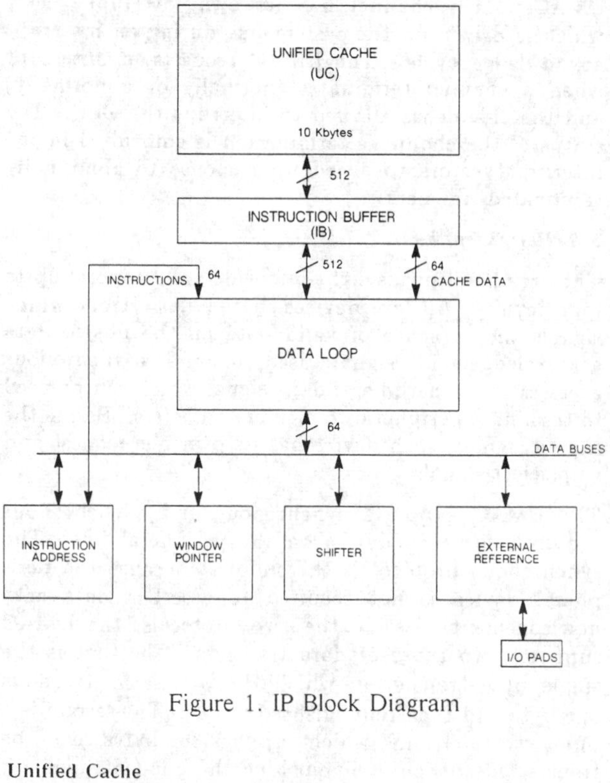

Figure 1. IP Block Diagram

Unified Cache

The Unified Cache (UC) is broken into three sections. Eight kilobytes are used for combined instructions and data. One kilobyte is for page table entries and one kilobyte for special data and instructions used for address translation. This design was chosen to minimize the impact of circuit overhead associated with the cache, e.g., sense amps, write amps, etc. The cache is organized as a two-way associative structure with a line size of eight quadwords. The two-way associativity is accomplished with a single tag comparator by using a single bit per cache block that toggles on a miss and references a second line of the cache. With this approach, the behavior of a two-set cache is obtained without the normally associated costs. On stores, the data is written only to the cache and a "write back" cache replacement strategy is employed.

Instruction Buffer

The Instruction Buffer (IB) is used to hold the most recently used instructions. It is designed to supply instructions at a rate that is comparable to the execution rate of the data loop. It also serves to greatly reduce the contention for the Unified Cache between instruction accesses and data accesses. The buffer is organized into four fully associative lines of instructions. The line size is eight quadwords. The data path between the cache and the buffer is 512 bits wide. On a buffer miss and a cache hit, an entire line in the buffer is replaced in one cache cycle.

Data Loop

The Data Loop block contains the logic necessary for execution of most of the instructions. The register file, the ALU, a special equal comparator, data steering logic and the main control PLA are all contained in this block. Most instructions can be executed within this block; only instructions requiring other units, e.g., the shifter, need to leave this block. Operations are performed in this block in two cycles. In the first cycle, a typical arithmetic instruction would fetch operands from the register file and get through the first level of logic in the ALU. In the following cycle the ALU operation would be completed and the result written back to the register file. These two cycles are overlapped so that the effective rate is one operation per cycle. Since the results of the previous operation might be required in the current operation, there is logic to detect this case and the data is forwarded back into the ALU while the result is being written to the register file.

Instruction Address Block

This block is used to control the sequencing of instructions. It is mostly independent of the data loop. It contains the Program Counter (PC), the Branch Address (BA) register, and the Instruction Address (IA) register. The IA contains the address of the instruction that is being fetched. The BA contains the address of the instruction that is to be fetched on the successful branch operation. On Regulus the BA is different from other architectures, since it is part of the process state. This means that it is apparent to the programmer and can be loaded independently. This block also contains the control logic for the Instruction Buffer block, including the LRU logic for the buffer as well as logic to issue a prefetch of instructions as execution nears a line boundary in the buffer.

Shifter

The Shifter block has two separate functions. The first is to provide a full 32-bit barrel shifter. Because the barrel shifter is relatively large and shift instructions are quite infrequent, this unit was not placed in the main data loop where it would have slowed down the execution of all instructions. Consequently, shift instructions take two cycles to execute. The second function of this block is to perform the byte and word extraction that is required by load and store instructions that are not of the type longword. Again, since the most common data type is longword, a small time penalty is charged to the byte and word data types. On loads of bytes or words, the data is moved toward the least significant bit of a register with the upper bits either cleared or sign extended. On stores, the control performs a read of the addressed longword and the shifter block inserts the byte or word to be stored into the appropriate location. The modified longword is then written to the cache.

Window Pointer

The Window Pointer block contains logic that is necessary to map the Register File into the virtual memory space. Local variables are intended to be allocated in the Register File. In many programming languages, the address of a variable can be obtained and referenced through pointers. Therefore, it becomes necessary for the contents of a register to be accessed as if they were memory. In the Regulus architecture this mapping takes place on the first 16 registers. The Window Pointer block contains a register called the Window Pointer (WP) and a comparator that compares the address of memory references on load and store instructions with the WP. If the address is within 16 longwords of the WP, the data is accessed in the Register File rather than memory. WP points to R0, WP+4 points to R1, etc. There is also a Return Window Pointer (RWP), which contains a predecremented copy of WP to accelerate the return instruction. An incrementer/decrementer in this block maintains these pointers.

External Reference Block

This block contains all of the logic necessary to transfer data to and from the internal buses of the chip and the I/O pins. It also contains all of the signals that perform the handshaking and control the flow of the data.

Call/Return Processing

The performance of the procedure call/return and the associated overhead is a dominant part of the overall performance of any architecture. For this reason, a very substantial part of the Regulus machine revolves around this function. Recently, many approaches to speed up this function have been proposed.[3 4 5 6 7] Most involve the use of large register files. A large register file allows many variables to be stored in the relatively fast register structure. The register file may also serve as a means for passing parameters to and from a called procedure.

The main disadvantage of a large register file is that as the size of the file increases, the access time to the registers also increases. To overcome this problem and still have the advantages that the large file has to offer, the Regulus architecture uses a technique made possible by VLSI technology. First, a very high bandwidth path between the register file and the on-chip cache is provided. This is accomplished with a 512-bit data path. This means that sixteen 32-bit registers can be stored or loaded in one cache cycle. Second, the register file itself contains 32 registers. This allows for very fast access times to the registers, which makes the cycle time for the more frequent data manipulation instructions short. Lastly, a parameter passing mechanism similar to other RISC machines is implemented. The register file is partitioned into four sections. Registers R0 to R7 are used for incoming parameters and local variables. Registers R8 to R14 are for local variables. Register R15 always contains zero and is a place holder for the PC on call instructions. R16 to R23 are for outgoing parameters. R24 to R31 are for temporaries and other software defined uses. There is hardware in the register file addressing logic that switches the logical to physical addressing of registers R0 to R7 and R16 to R23.

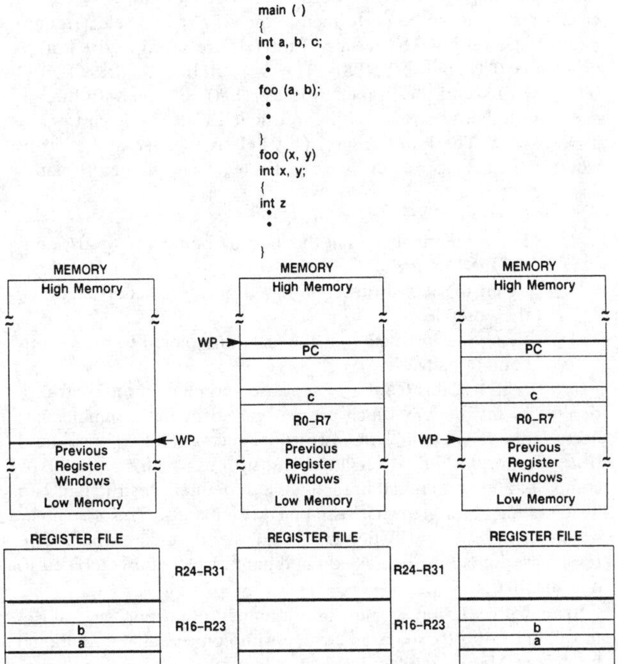

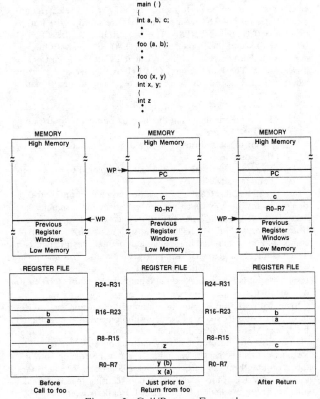

Figure 2. Call/Return Example

Refer to Figure 2 for the following description of a procedure call and return. As the main program is preparing to call process foo, it moves the parameters a and b into r16 and r17. It then executes a call instruction. The call instruction saves R0 through R14 and the PC at the location pointed to by the Window Pointer. The Window Pointer is then incremented by 64 and the addressing of the register file is swapped as described above. The result is that the parameters being passed to process foo appear in R0 and R1. Since the calling procedures registers are saved, process foo can now use the register file as required. Similarly, this mechanism is carried out for calls to other processes within foo. This can continue until the amount of virtual space allocated for the saving of windows is exhausted. This means that the Regulus register file does not require any special handling, as is the case with other architectures.

The return is just the inverse of the call operation. The addressing of the register file is swapped and the saved registers are restored from a predecremented copy of the Window Pointer. The PC is restored and execution is continued. The entire call/return sequence, including parameter passing, is completed in seven cycles. For aggregate data types such as arrays and structures, or when more than eight parameters are to be passed, a more traditional frame stack is defined by software and the parameters are passed there.[8]

63		60	59						32	31 ... 0
JC	BA	AC	ALU	TY	CTL	G	OP3	OPA	OPB	LITERAL

Figure 3. Regulus Instruction Format

Instruction Sequencing

The design of the Regulus instruction set allows for separate and concurrent control of the data loop portion and the instruction sequencing. The single format instruction is shown in Figure 3. The literal is in bits 0 to 31. Bits 32 to 59 are used to control the data loop. Included in these bits are operand specifiers, the ALU operation to be performed, and a six-bit field that contains the encoding of the 17 basic instructions. Bits 60 through 63 are used to control the sequencing of the instructions. The Assert Condition (AC) bit causes a subtract to be performed in the ALU and a selected condition to be tested. The results of the test are saved in the Condition Code (CC) bit of the PSL. The Load Branch Address (LBA) bit is used to load the Branch Address (BA) Register with the address in the literal portion of the instruction. The BA is part of the process state. The Jump Control (JC) field is encoded and controls where the next instruction is to be fetched. The four possibilities are:

1. Continue to the next instruction
2. Fetch the instruction at the location pointed to by BA conditioned by the CC bit
3. Fetch the next instruction based on a prediction made by the compiler
4. Fetch the instruction at the location pointed to by BA unconditionally.

In order to use this feature of separate and concurrent control, a rich set of instructions which are recognized by the assembler has been defined. These include instructions such as add registers, load from memory, shift, etc.. Other instructions, such as load BA, compare, and conditional branch are also defined. Instructions can be combined using special assembler commands. The assembler knows the rules of instruction combination and validates them. The results are functions such as add and jump, which are combined in one instruction.

Branch Prediction Regulus uses a branch prediction mechanism to minimize the penalties associated with conventional conditional branches. Many architectures statically choose a direction, either always false or true, and fetch the instruction appropriately. The Regulus compiler issues a conditional branch instruction with the direction based on the particular looping construct. The hardware then fetches according to the prediction, causing pipeline breaks only when the prediction is incorrect. Careful analyses of UNIX* system utilities and benchmarks were used to determine the best prediction for each looping construct.[8] The prediction is also maintained through each level of optimization.

```
WITH DELAYED BRANCH              WITHOUT DELAYED BRANCH
  .micro
    movl    r0, r21              movl r0, r21
    ldba    branch address       addl $1, R0
  .mend                          mvl $FE, R1
    cmpeq   $FE, r21             cjeqt R1, R21, $branch address
  .micro
    addl    $1, R0
    cbr
  .memd
```

Figure 4. Delayed Branch Example

Conditional Branching The conditional branch mechanism is implemented using a single Condition Code (CC) bit in the PSL. If the AC bit of the instruction is set, the ALU is forced to perform a subtract and a condition to be tested is specified in the ALU field of the instruction. The result of the conditional test, true or false, is stored in the CC bit. When a conditional branch type instruction is executed, the next instruction fetch is done according to the state of the CC bit. This allows for a delayed branch type function to be performed. Figure 4 shows a code sequence that illustrates how the delayed branching and instruction combination works. The first instruction is formed by combining the **movl** with a load of the BA register. This is possible because the literal field is not used. Second, a compare instruction is used to set the CC bit. Lastly, a conditional branch is combined with an **addl**. The result in this example is a savings of one clock cycle if the prediction is correct or two clock cycles if the prediction was incorrect.

Conclusion

The Regulus architecture was designed to provide very high performance by taking advantage of custom VLSI technology. The target cycle time for the first chips is 18 nanoseconds. Most design tradeoffs were made in favor of the cycle time. An efficient call/return and parameter passing mechanism was achieved while still maintaining a very fast register file. Also, a large on-chip cache was made possible with the small register file. Very flexible and powerful instruction sequencing was achieved.

Acknowledgment

Special thanks go to Mark Halvorsen, Dave Unterseher, Elad Loker, Dave Hill, Paul Sweere, Bruce Troutman, Larry Johnson, Bob Krebs, Kim Chang, Duc Nguyen, Laura Haug, Lydia Korownyk, Hilda Turner, Jeff Arnold, Jack Slingwine, Duane Grigsby, John McCurry, Elvyn Donawerth and Doug Forehand for their participation in the IP and AP design efforts.

References

1. S. Sims, et al. "The Regulus Architecture," Proceedings of ICCD '87, pp. 534–538.
2. D. A. Petterson and C. H. Sequin, "A VLSI RISC", *Computer*, Vol. 15 No. 9, pp. 8–22, Sept. 1982.
3. D. Ditzel and R. McLellan, "Register Allocation for Free: The C Machine Stack Cache," Proc. Symp. Architectural Support for Programming Languages and Operating Systems, ACM, pp. 48–56, Mar. 1982.
4. A. D. Berenbaum, et al, "Introduction to the CRISP Instruction Set Architecture," Proceedings of the IEEE Spring COMPCON '87, pp. 86–90.
5. A. D. Berenbaum, et al, "Architectural Innovations in the CRISP Microprocessor," Proceedings of the IEEE Spring COMPCON '87, pp. 91–95.
6. M. Namjoo and A. Agrawal, "Preserve High Speed in CPU-to-cache Transfers," *Electronic Design*, Aug. 20, 1987, pp. 91–96.
7. B. Case, "32-bit Microprocessor Opens System Bottlenecks," *Computer Design*, Apr. 1, 1987, pp. 79–86.
8. J. Letz and J. Slingwine, "Living With RISC: Software Issues in the Regulus Architecture," Proc. Int. Conf. Computer Design, IEEE, Oct. 1987.

ARTIFICIAL INTELLIGENCE Track

Recent Developments in Intelligent Machine Technology

Chair: R. Harrigan

INTELLIGENT CONTROL OF ROBOT MANIPULATORS IN HAZARDOUS ENVIRONMENTS

Raymond W. Harrigan
Sandia National Laboratories
Albuquerque, New Mexico 87185

ABSTRACT

The characteristics of hazardous environments and the impact these have on robot manipulator system control are reviewed. In particular, computer based reasoning must be integrated into the control of robot manipulators to allow successful application to such environments. Computing architectures and the concomitant software structures necessary to support both the high level reasoning and low level servo control requirements are discussed in the context of prototype robot systems.

INTRODUCTION

This review paper focuses upon the impact that hazardous environments have on the control and computing requirements of robot manipulator systems. The technical challenges associated with operating robot manipulators in hazardous environments are first reviewed. Then robots are defined as mechanical systems capable of reasoning and dealing with uncertainties in the environment. The requirement for reasoning and dealing with uncertainties leads to a discussion of appropriate distributed computing architectures which incorporate both supervisory and real-time control and support environmental sensing. Finally, the necessity for manual operation is recognized and the impact this requirement has on the system control architecture is also discussed. A computing architecture employed in protoype robot systems at Sandia National Laboratories is employed to focus the discussion.

Hazardous environments tend to be tightly contained and characterized by limited personnel access. Examples of such environments include hot cells for handling radioactive materials and chemical processing cells for the manufacture of toxic and explosive materials. These environments are frequently used for batch processing of materials and, while carefully controlled, the location of objects within the cells may not be well defined due to the difficulty of locating and placing objects with remote handling equipment. Such environments are characterized as *semistructured.* Most industrial environments employing robots, on the other hand, tend to be highly structured where the location of objects are carefully controlled and the robots operate without adapting to the environment.

Perhaps the most traditional means of handling materials remotely in hazardous environments is the use of master/slave mechanisms in which a remote mechanical manipulator (the slave) is directly coupled to a mechanism (the master) controlled by an operator. The slave manipulator typically repeats the master's movements exactly. Due to the restricted dexterity (the manipulators rarely have the degrees of freedom of a human arm) of such devices and limited environmental sensing, remote manipulation using master/slave devices tends to be difficult even for experienced operators [1]. As a result, there has been increased interest in the development of robotic manipulators for application to such environments.

Robots, in the context of this paper, are robot manipulators. The terms robot and robot manipulator are used interchangeably. Robot manipulators vary considerably in design and capabilities. They range from fixed location, articulated arms with a very localized workspace such as a bench top to large gantry, crane-like, mechanisms having large workspaces such as hot cells. In all cases, robot manipulators have well defined work envelopes.

TECHNICAL CHALLENGES

Hazardous environments present unique technical challenges to robot manipulator systems not typically found in more common industrial environments. Due to the limited personnel access of most hazardous environments, robot manipulators must typically be programmed off-line within the context of a model of the environment rather than *taught. Teaching,* which is the most common mode of robot manipulator programming, involves manually moving the manipulator's endpoint to a location in the environment and storing that position

Work supported by the U.S. Department of Energy at Sandia National Laboratories under Contract DE-AC04-76DP00789 (usually based upon encoder readings) in the robot's computer memory. During operation, the robot manipulator is instructed to return to some predetermined sequence of these previously visited locations. Thus, the human operator serves as the reasoning agent by, for example, selecting robot movements which avoid collisions with obstacles. With the highly restricted personnel access associated with most hazardous environments, this manual approach to robot programming is difficult. Thus, much of the reasoning task must be transferred from the human to the robotic system.

In addition to the requirement for the robot manipulator system to reason about its environment for the purpose of off-line programming, environmental sensing must also be provided. Sensing allows the robot to adapt to the environment to compensate for uncertainties in the world model used during off-line programming. In addition, sensing helps insure that the reliability of the robot system is high and that the robot causes no damage. Under no circumstances may the robot be allowed to increase the hazard associated with the already hazardous environment. If this occurred, the robot manipulator could not be used because, typically, safety is an overriding issue when dealing with hazardous environments. Sensing must be integrated with the robot control to provide updates to the model of the environment so that the system's reasoning process is based upon a valid model.

DEFINITION OF ROBOTICS

Since the most common commercial application of robot manipulators is for repetitive *pick-and-place* operations requiring no sensing or decision making on the part of the robot, robot manipulators are frequently envisioned as devices capable of only this type of behavior. Based upon the discussion above, hazardous environments clearly require robot systems with more advanced operational characteristics. Thus, for clarity, it is worthwhile to define what the term robotics means in the context of this review paper.

For the purposes of the following discussion, the term robotics will be defined starting with a definition proposed by John Hopcroft [2] that robotics may be viewed as the study of representing and reasoning about physical objects in a computer. Incorporating the more traditional mechanistic view of robotics into this computer science viewpoint provides the definition used here.

> *Robotics is the integration of the sciences of sensing, representing and reasoning about physical objects in a computer coupled with electromechanical systems to carry out purposeful actions.*

A reasonable goal for a robotic system operating in a hazardous environment is to serve as a supervised electromechanical system possessing sufficient intellect to serve in the place of a similarly supervised human. In the event a robot manipulator cannot accomplish its task due to errors, it either replans or requests help from the supervisor (typically in the form of manual operation) much as the replaced human would do. While intelligent robotic systems possessing the full range of capabilities implied by this goal are beyond the current state of the technology, significant strides are being made.

Critical to achieving this goal is the formulation of a control architecture which incorporates high level reasoning based upon static and dynamic knowledge of the environment derived from a priori and sensory information. A basic computer science issue is the integration of many levels of control into a hierarchical computing architecture which allows the construction of intelligent, responsive systems that can safely operate in environments about which there is incomplete information.

CONTROL ARCHITECTURE

In order to satisfy the performance characteristics described above, a structured computing system must be developed which allows the incorporation of the wide range of capabilities required for the successful operation of robot manipulator systems in hazardous environments. These capabilities range from fast, servo level response based on sensor inputs (*e.g.*, follow a surface contour based upon interaction forces) to slower responses in which evaluation of various alternatives is involved (*e.g.*, planning a trajectory for the manipulator endpoint). The computing environment must integrate all levels of control into an efficiently executed control strategy which smoothly transitions from one control mode to the next. An example of a control architecture used for a robot manipulator system operating in a hazardous environment [3] is shown in Figure 1. The hierarchical control environment has two main systems: the reasoning system in which high level control processes are performed and the real-time control system in which fast response control processes are carried out.

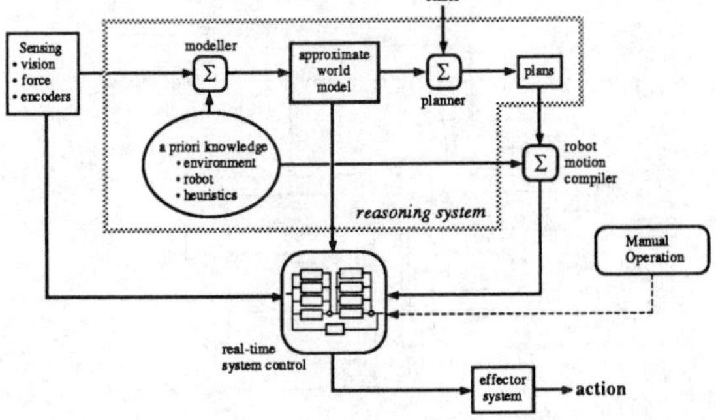

Figure 1: Hierarchical System Control.

Within the reasoning system, the computer constructs an approximate world model based upon knowledge about the environment (*e.g.*, a map), robot manipulator characteristics (*e.g.*, kinematics) and heuristics about objects in the environment and their behavior (*e.g.*, physical limitations of the robot). This world model is modified by sensory information and provides the foundation for generating plans (*e.g.*, a collision free robot trajectory) which are translated into robot manipulator motion primitives. The control processes taking place within the reasoning system can be quite complex and may require considerable computing time.

Within the real-time control system, servo control of the robot manipulator is accomplished. Responsiveness of the control system is extremely important as it is responsible for executing the robot motions developed by the reasoning system or supplied by direct intervention by the operator. A slow real-time control system would introduce delays between the commanding of movement and the execution of that movement by the robot leading to instabilities in the system. Sensors and a model of the environment are employed to monitor the execution of these motions and to perturb the robot motions if necessary to provide safe operation while accomplishing the desired task. Manual operation in the form of direct operator commands (see below) is distinct from the reasoning system and interfaces directly to the real-time control system.

The real-time control system must possess several characteristics. It must provide for both model driven control and real-time servo control and it must achieve the intent of the commanded robot manipulator motions in a safe, reliable fashion. A layered control structure for the real-time control system [4] has been investigated which successfully integrates these attributes. Figure 2 shows the basic elements of this layered control structure and their interactions. While Figure 2 shows only force and torque constraints explicitly, other sensory constraints such as ultrasonic proximity sensors could also be employed if desired. This would simply provide additional layers to the real-time control system as

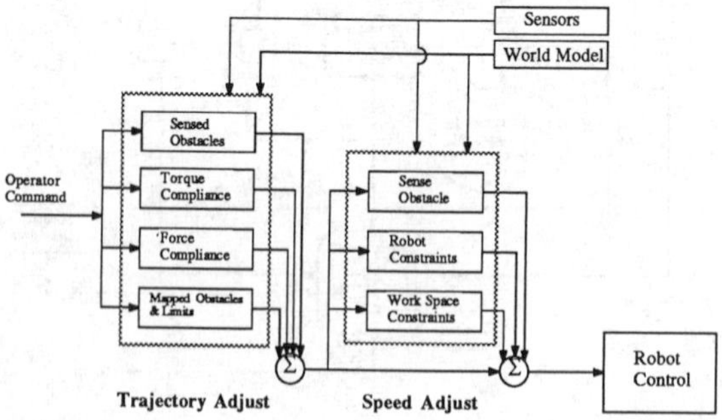

Figure 2: Real-Time Control Architecture.

indicated by the *Sense Obstacle* module. Basically, the real-time control system perturbs the two commands (direction and speed) to which a conventional robot manipulator can respond.

As the robot approaches the vicinity of either a sensed or known obstacle, the speed of the robot is gradually reduced. The intent is to reduce the robot's speed either to allow time for the robot's control system to respond in the event the robot inadvertently strikes an object or to allow time for the reasoning system to replan the robot's trajectory based upon new sensor information.

Perhaps the most important feature of the layered real-time control system shown in Figure 2 is the fact that both the world model developed in the reasoning system and the sensory information pervade the real-time control system at all levels. Following the lead of Brooks [5], adopting a layered structure for the control system reduces computational bottlenecks that slow the control system response. Each layer of control within the real-time control system runs continuously with each control layer contributing perturbations to the original commanded robot motion if appropriate. In addition, the reasoning system also operates continuously but asynchronously from the real-time control system. Thus, the real-time control system is provided with updated world model information without impeding the robot manipulator's ability to respond quickly.

The nature and magnitude of the output from each level of the controller is determined through analysis of the commanded robot manipulator motions with respect to the world model and sensory inputs. The outputs from each layer of the real-time control system are then combined (as represented by the summing nodes) to produce a perturbed trajectory and speed command. The timing requirements and coordination of the different layers within the real-time control system are discussed in reference 4.

Due to the nature of the computations involved, different layers of the control environment represented by Figure 1 should be implemented in different computing environments. For example, the reasoning system might best be implemented in a computer designed to efficiently execute a high level language such as LISP. The real-time control system, in contrast, might best be implemented in a computing environment specifically designed to execute languages such as C and that supports efficient interrupt structures to quickly respond to new sensory information. In fact, some applications may benefit (particularly if very fast response is required) from a highly parallel computing environment in which each layer within the real-time control system resides on a separate processor specially designed to execute the control algorithms associated with that level.

The Role of Sensing in Control

Sensing provides dynamic updates to a priori knowledge of the environment and allows the robot system to function when the world model is incomplete. In addition, sensing provides the real-time feedback required for servo control. Thus, sensory information must enter into all levels of the system control architecture. A complete ensemble of sensors provides a set of complementary sensing modalities each selected to support the various system control layers. Selection of sensors parallels development of the system control architecture and individual sensors are chosen that support the requirements of the individual control layers.

Rather than attempt to present a comprehensive discussion of the sensors available for application to robotic systems operating in hazardous environments, it is perhaps more appropriate to discuss general sensor characteristics and the desired complementarity of these characteristics to provide effective sensor ensembles. Experience at Sandia National Laboratories in developing intelligent robot manipulator systems for application to hazardous environments has shown that, at a minimum, three basic classes of sensors are desirable: spatial, proximity and contact.

Global, low to medium resolution spatial sensors, such as cameras, allow the system controller to verify and update maps of the robot's environment. These sensors interface to those layers of the control system which involve tasks ranging from path planning to object recognition. They usually provide good two dimensional spatial information but low resolution depth information. Typically, processing of the data from such sensors is slow and is not, except for special purpose hardware, designed for real-time control.

Medium to high resolution proximity sensors, such as laser range finders, provide high quality three dimensional information. However, such systems are frequently expensive and require significant signal processing times. More typically, fast acting, nonimaging proximity sensors, such as ultrasonic sensors, are used. These sensors allow the approach to and avoidance of objects in the environment. Thus, proximity sensors, while providing some updates to the world model, most strongly influence the real-time control system by providing fast servo-controlled approaches to physical objects in the environment.

Contact (force) sensors serve mainly in the real-time control system to allow controlled interactions with objects in the environment. Typically, force sensors are employed to manipulate objects. No world model is accurate enough to allow damage free interactions with the environment without monitoring and responding to interaction forces.

The basic reason for classifying desirable sensors into these three categories is that their characteristics complement each other. An ensemble of such sensors would allow a robot to not only safely move about in an environment without collisions, but would also allow approach to and controlled contact with objects in the environment.

Integration of Manual Control

A final issue which must be addressed in any robot manipulator system is that of manual control. At some point during the operation of any robotic system manual control will be desirable. Situations requiring manual operation vary from the teaching of robot locations to the recovery from errors with which the robot control system is unable to cope. As discussed above, experience with master/slave manipulators [1] suggests that even highly trained operators experience considerable difficulty when executing remote manipulations using these devices. The problem is compounded with robot manipulator systems. If the robotic system performs as desired, manual operation will be an infrequent event, thus depriving the operator of significant experience with manual operation of the system. Therefore, the better the robot manipulator system performs, the more difficulty the operator should experience during any manual operation.

An approach to this dilemma is to provide computer assisted manual control. This approach, termed telerobotics, has been investigated by various researchers particularly in the remote control of space based robots by operators on earth [1,6,7]. Much of this work has been directed at providing sufficient feedback so that the operators feel as if they were in the environment performing the operations. Computers synthesize the feedback to provide the artificial environment which the operator senses and responds to.

An alternative approach is to moderate the operator commands such that the remote robot manipulator system executes complex operations without requiring the operator to provide every detailed robot command [4]. Thus, within the context of Figure 1, the operator takes on the role of the planner and develops the commands for the robot manipulator to execute. However, the computing and sensory systems maintain their role as developers of approximate world models and real-time controller. Much in the manner that the real-time control system perturbs the robot commands of the supervisor, the real-time control system now perturbs the commands of the operator within the context of a world model and sensory system. The real-time control system assists the operator in automatically avoiding obstacles and executing controlled interactions with the environment while the operator performs the high level task and path planning. Such computer assisted approaches to manual operation have proven effective in providing responsive robot manipulator systems capable of safe flexible operation when manually operated [4].

CONCLUSION

Hazardous environments provide strong incentives for the development of sensor based computer reasoning systems. In addition, computing architectures which support both real-time control and high level reasoning tasks such as planning are required for the safe operation of robot manipulator systems in these environments. Typically, no single computing system will serve effectively for such diverse special purpose requirements. Distributed, multiprocessor systems with special purpose architectures matched to the requirements of the individual control layers are required for effective control of these robot systems.

Research is needed in all aspects of this control problem. Conflict resolution strategies for distributed control in multiprocessor systems needs development. Reuseable, device independent software must also evolve to reduce software development time and improve software reliability. In addition, the networking aspects of distributed intelligent control must be investigated. On line analysis of network status, prediction of failure and development of techniques to insure network integrity in the event of node failures is required.

REFERENCES

[1] Stark, *etal,* "Telerobotics: display, control and communication problems", IEEE Journal of Robotics and Automation, Vol 3, No 1, pp 67-75, Feb. 1987.

[2] Hopcroft, John E., "The Impact of Robotics on Computer Science", Communications of the ACM, Vol 29, No 6, pp 486-498, June 1986.

[3] Thunborg, Siegfried, "A Robotic Radiation Survey and Analysis System", American Nuclear Society Winter Meeting, Los Angeles, November 1987.

[4] Boissiere, P. T. and Harrigan, Raymond W. "Telerobotic Operation of Conventional Robot Manipulators", submitted for presentation at the 1988 IEEE International Conference on Robotics and Automation, April 25-29, Philadelphia.

[5] Brooks, R. A., "A Robust Layered Control System for a Mobile Robot", IEEE Journal of Robotics and Automation, Vol RA-2, No 1, pp 14-23, 1986.

[6] Mohr, G. C., "Robotic Telepresence", 1987 IEEE Proceedings: Annual Reliability and Maintainability Symposium, pp 25-30, January 1987, Philadelphia.

[7] Sheridan, T. B., "Human Supervisory Control of Robot Systems", Proceedings of the 1986 IEEE International Conference on Robotics and Automation, Vol 2, pp 808-812, 1986.

Artificial Intelligence and Robotics

Leslie Pack Kaelbling
Artificial Intelligence Center
SRI International

Abstract

The AI and robotics communities, although addressing similar problems, typically focus on very different aspects of those problems. The two fields interact profitably in the area of building intelligent agents; this interaction has resulted in important developments in the areas of vision and planned action. To enable further progess on building intelligent agents, the AI community must make more advances, particularly in the areas of belief revision and learning.

Introduction

The ultimate goal of designing and building intelligent agents that perceive, reason about, and act upon our everyday world is shared by artificial intelligence (AI) and robotics. Despite their common goal, however, the two fields of research have become very specialized and employ quite different methods for solving their problems. In this paper, we shall examine the disparate orientations of the two fields, then focus on the problem of building intelligent agents. Because this task requires significant contributions from both disciplines, it can serve as a focal point for integration of the methodologies of AI and robotics. We shall discuss progress made by the artificial intelligence community in solving some of the problems of intelligent agents, then go on to discuss further advances that are essential for eventual success this area.

The robotics community has traditionally focused on problems of sensing, manipulation, and locomotion. Work on sensing includes visual recognition of known objects in a carefully controlled environment, force sensing to aid in manipulation, and proximity sensing for collision avoidance and simple navigation. Manipulation research has addressed such problems as planning the motion of arms through space and computing appropriate angles from which a manipulator should grasp an object. As regards locomotion, control systems are developed for widely divergent styles of movement, including robots on wheels or with one or more legs, as well robots that swim and fly.

The AI community, on the other hand, typically considers the more abstract problems of a system reasoning about its environment. Problems in this domain include planning complex sequences of actions to achieve a goal, efficiently determining the consequences of a set of beliefs (if an agent believes that there is a rock in front of it and, furthermore, believes that it cannot drive over rocks, what process must it then undergo in ascertaining that it cannot drive forward?), and understanding utterances in natural language. Computer vision is an important subdiscipline of AI, as well as of robotics. The AI vision community often studies a more general aspect of the vision problem, one in which the objects to be recognized and their environment are much less carefully controlled. This includes problems of outdoor vision and the analysis of aerial photographs.

Intelligent Agents

Artificial intelligence and robotics come into close contact in the study of intelligent agents. These are machines that have physical interactions with the world, but, unlike factory robots, do so in a flexible and intelligent manner. There are many important practical applications for intelligent agents—for example, work in hazardous environments, military reconnaissance missions, and delivery of materials in factories. The recent resurgence of interest in the problems of intelligent agents offers an ideal opportunity for productive interaction by the AI and robotics communities.

The AI community, with its typical focus on simple test problems, can benefit tremendously from work on intelligent agents because it will stretch the limits of current techniques and encourage the integration of many types of subsystems, from abstract reasoning modules to numerical control programs. It will be the task of the AI community to create systems that can integrate the disparate and contradictory information gathered by the agent's sensors (some of which will be the output of robotic software systems) and determine a robust plan of action for controlling the agent's effectors.

One of the first intelligent robotic agents was Shakey, developed by SRI International [11]. Built in the late 1960's, Shakey served as a focal point of integration for many advanced software and hardware technologies. Shakey operated in a artificial blocks world, perceiving its environment with a computer vision system and laser rangefinder, and acting by pushing blocks from room to room. The work done on Shakey inspired the development of many important AI systems and techniques, including the STRIPS planning system. When provided with a logical description of (1) the robot's situation, (2) the goal situation, and (3) the effects of all of the actions it could perform, the STRIPS system would determine a sequence of actions that, if performed by the robot, would result in the goal being achieved. The plan was passed to an execution system that caused the robot to carry out the prescribed actions, retrying them if they failed, and taking advantage of serendipitous conditions (such as the unexpected presence of a block in the same room as the robot). Another important result of the

CH2539-5/88/0000/0059$01.00

work on STRIPS was a system that learned *macro-operators.* Macro-operators are sequences of the atomic actions available to the robot. The planning system was able to work much more efficiently when it remembered generalized versions of previous plans it had made.

Although the Shakey project was a success and gave impetus to a great deal of important work in AI, it operated at speeds that made it impractical for real applications. It would take the robot many minutes to analyze a scene visually and then develop a plan to execute. Shakey depended crucially on the fact that it was the only agent in its world, presuming that nothing could change unless it was a result of the robot's actions. In the real world, systems must be able to notice changes in the world quickly and react to them effectively. As a result of the Shakey project, many researchers in the AI community have been pursuing methods of perception and planning that work more efficiently and allow agents to respond promptly to changing environments. In the sections that follow, we shall explore briefly the progress that has been achieved in real-time perception and planning.

Vision for Intelligent Agents

Many traditional approaches in the development of computer vision concentrate on the analysis of a single image without any a priori knowledge of what that image represents. Some of the techniques devised for dealing with this difficult and underconstrained problem have met with success, but have required an inordinate amount of computation time (many hours). While these techniques are of great theoretical interest and have useful application in the analysis of still pictures, they are nevertheless unsuitable for use in intelligent agents.

Vision may be done much more efficiently and successfully when the system knows what it is looking for. This is the essence of a computer vision subfield called *model-based* vision. Model-based vision has been applied most successfully in industrial contexts, where the task is to find the location and orientation of a part (or one of a small number of possible parts) on a conveyor belt. These techniques can also be used in an intelligent agent: because the agent has a continuing interaction with the world, it can utilize prior knowledge to predict what it will see. Thus, an agent that knows it is in an office can prime its vision system to look for a few things that are typically found in offices, such as telephones and computer terminals.

Another method of acquiring visual information efficiently is to build low-level visual procedures into the agent, almost as virtual sensors. A robot that navigates along hallways in an office environment can derive a great deal of useful information simply from knowing the locations of the rows of overhead lights. Vision can also be used to determine depth information, allowing the robot to where material surfaces are, even if it cannot recognize them as particular objects. This information can be obtained with stereo cameras or through the depth-from-motion method (essentially the use of triangulation to determine the distance to a particular feature, two views of which are available). The general versions of algorithms for stereo vision and depth-from-motion are computationally expensive, but they can be made efficient by using low resolution images [5] or by focusing on prominent individual features [8].

Planning and Action

The model of planning used in Shakey, namely, choosing a sequence of actions that achieves a goal, has been extended and generalized, and has been studied extensively by the AI community. Although the model is of some theoretical interest, it has not only been shown to be computationally intractable [6], but is considered by many to be psychologically implausible as well [1]. Humans and other living creatures spend the majority of their time performing routine tasks without devoting time to thinking about how to do them. Occasionally we have to stop and plan the most efficient sequence in which to perform a set of errands, or a plan a route on a map, but that sort of activity is very much out of the ordinary. Some AI and cognitive-science researchers study planning for exactly this reason—it is a uniquely human activity that requires sophisticated intelligence. Many of those whose goal it is to construct intelligent agents have chosen to concentrate instead on building mechanisms for routine behavior rather than planning.

There are two practical reasons that make it difficult to use planning as the model of action for an agent in a dynamic world: during the time it takes the agent to plan what to do, the current state of the world may change in such a way as to invalidate its plan; if the agent is not carefully constructed, it may ignore its sensory inputs while it is planning, and, without being aware of it, become endangered.

One way to avoid these difficulties is through *reactive planning* [7], in which the agent embarks on preformed plans but continuously monitors the world to assure itself that the plan it is executing is indeed appropriate to the circumstances. The plans in such a system still make reference to the state of the world through a central symbolic data base.

Another approach is to design the agent to act as much as possible on the basis of sensory inputs, avoiding the computational and semantic difficulties of large databases of facts. In the simplest of these systems, the agent executes a continuous mapping from the values of its sensors to those of its effectors. Although this method affords maximum reactivity, it is susceptible to the many criticisms of stimulus-response systems. State can be added gradually to such a system, allowing it to remember more about the context of its actions while retaining much of its computational efficiency. A very appealing approach to creating systems of this kind is developed by Brooks [4], in which the agent is built up hierarchically from component behaviors of increasing degrees of sophistication. Systems of this kind have been applied to the problems of manipulator control [3] and mobile robots [4, 9], have been propounded as constituting a psychologically plausible model of everyday activity [2], and have been given a formal logical foundation [10].

Important Areas in AI

The problems associated with building intelligent agents have motivated the significant advances in perception and planning discussed above, but there are a number of areas in AI that are still not up to the challenge of intelligent agents. Two of the more important ones are belief revision and learning.

Belief revision is the process of arriving at a new state of belief on the basis of new information. If an agent is to behave rationally, it must have a consistent belief state. When new information received through its sensors contradicts some conclusion previously arrived at, the agent must cease to believe the latter, as well as any beliefs that depended upon it. The difficulty of this task is compounded by the need for *default reasoning*, that is, drawing conclusions that do not necessarily follow from the current belief state, but that are nonetheless usually true. Upon hearing about a particular bird, a reasoning system should make the default inference that it can fly, because most birds can fly. It must also possess the means of retracting this conclusion in the case that it later discovers that the bird is a penguin (we assume it knows penguins cannot fly). Another dimension is added to the problem if we wish to consider degrees of belief. Then the system must perform *evidential reasoning*, weighing evidence for and against a particular fact to determine the degree to which it is believed. This variety of belief-updating and inference methods is essential to the proper functioning of an intelligent agent. Techniques exist for performing all of these types of belief revision, but they are generally quite inefficient.

The ability to learn is another aspect of AI that plays an important role in the design and construction of intelligent agents. It is very complicated and tedious to program robots to act effectively in the real world. A large part of the problem is that humans find it extremely difficult to articulate the knowledge they use in recognizing the walls of a corridor or in differentiating the faces of two people. If we could discover effective methods for automatic learning, much of the difficulty of programming could be alleviated. Both supervised learning (in which a teacher presents an agent with a series of examples of a concept) and unsupervised learning (in which the robot acts in the world to try to achieve its goal and is told whether or not it has succeeded) are important to the success of building intelligent agents. There is an active community of researchers in the area of machine learning, but the emphasis tends to be on learning to solve circumscribed symbolic problems, such as puzzles, in worlds devoid of noise. Robots in the world receive noisy inputs, many of which are irrelevant to any specific problem, making it very difficult to learn. One promising methods for learning in such environments is *connectionist learning* [12], in which networks of simple processors (modeled loosely on neurons) can be taught to recognize statistically salient properties of the environment and to compute functional mappings from their inputs to their outputs. While these methods are computationally tractable, the learning of simple concepts may require a substantial amount of experience.

Conclusions

The problem of building intelligent agents is a crucial meeting point for the AI and robotics communities. The necessity of providing solutions that work efficiently in the real world has propelled AI research along significant new paths of investigation in perception and planning. For the endeavor to succeed, further advances will be needed from AI in the areas of belief revision and learning.

References

[1] Philip E. Agre. *Routines.* Technical Report AIM-828, MIT Artificial Intelligence Laboratory, Cambridge, Massachusetts, 1985.

[2] Philip E. Agre and David Chapman. Pengi: an implementation of a theory of activity. In *Proceedings of the Sixth National Conference on Artificial Intelligence*, pages 268–272, Morgan Kauffman, Seattle, Washington, 1987.

[3] James S. Albus. *Brains, Behavior, and Robotics.* BYTE Books, Subsidiary of McGraw-Hill, Peterborough, New Hampshire, 1981.

[4] Rodney A. Brooks. *A Robust Layered Control System for a Mobile Robot.* Technical Report AIM-864, MIT Artificial Intelligence Laboratory, Cambridge, Massachusetts, 1985.

[5] Rodney A. Brooks, Anita M. Flynn, and Thomas Marill. *Self Calibration of Motion and Stereo Vision for Mobile Robot Navigation.* Technical Report AIM-984, MIT Artificial Intelligence Laboratory, Cambridge, Massachusetts, 1987.

[6] David Chapman. Planning for conjunctive goals. *Artificial Intelligence*, 32(3):333–378, 1987.

[7] Michael P. Georgeff and Amy L. Lansky. Reactive reasoning and planning. In *Proceedings of the Sixth National Conference on Artificial Intelligence*, pages 677–682, Morgan Kauffman, Seattle, Washington, 1987.

[8] William M. Wells III. Visual estimation of 3-d line segments from motion—a mobile robot vision system. In *Proceedings of the Sixth National Conference on Artificial Intelligence*, pages 772–776, Morgan Kauffman, Seattle, Washington, 1987.

[9] Leslie Pack Kaelbling. An architecture for intelligent reactive systems. In Michael P. Georgeff and Amy L. Lansky, editors, *Reasoning About Actions and Plans*, pages 395–410, Morgan Kauffman, 1987.

[10] Stanley J. Rosenschein Leslie Pack Kaelbling. The synthesis of digital machines with provable epistemic properties. In Joseph Halpern, editor, *Proceedings of the Conference on Theoretical Aspects of Reasoning About Knowledge*, pages 83–98, Morgan Kauffman, 1988. An updated version appears as Technical Note 412, Artificial Intelligence Center, SRI International, Menlo Park, California.

[11] Nils J. Nilsson. *Shakey the Robot.* Technical Report 323, Artificial Intelligence Center, SRI International, Menlo Park, California, 1984.

[12] David E. Rumelhart and James L. McClelland, editors. *Parallel Distributed Processing.* Volume 1, MIT Press, Cambridge, Massachusetts, 1986.

Prolog Update

Chair: Y. Patt

PROLOG AT BERKELEY

Alvin M. Despain

Computer Science Division
Univ. of Calif.; Berkeley, CA 94720

1. INTRODUCTION

The Aquarius project at Berkeley is centered on the high performance execution of logic programs in general and Prolog in particular. Even more generally its goal is to determine how a very large improvement in performance can be achieved in a machine specialized to solve some difficult problems characterized by both symbolic and numerical calculations both within a search space. The particular problem domain of this type that we are currently concerned with is design automation of single VLSI chip microprocessors. The processors support Prolog execution and the design tools are written in Prolog, as are the high level specifications of the processors. Interestingly, we are thus developing high performance processors in VLSI to help execute the design automation tools that are being used to help design these same processors.

The Aquarius project has been going on for several years now, and and there is no possible way to do justice to the wide range of activities in this short digest paper. So an overview is provided and the reader is referred to the papers and reports listed in the references for in depth discussions.

2. ASP

The Advanced Silicon-compiler in Prolog (ASP) accepts a high level specification of an instruction set architecture (ISA) as input, and produces a CIF (Caltech Intermediate Form) file as output. CIF files can be submitted to the MOSIS fabrication service and fabricated VLSI chips will be returned. Since the specification is written in Prolog, it is executable by a Prolog system. This provides a simulator at no extra cost. An example specification (partial) of a very simple, classic Von-Neumann machine is:

```
%Specification of a very simple machine.

p(AC,PC):- fetch(PC,OP,X), P1 is PC + 1,
        exec(OP,X,AC,A,P1,P), p(A,P).
p(_,_).

fetch(PC,OP,X) :- m(PC,OP,X).

exec(add,X,AC,A,PC,PC):- m(X,T),A is T+ AC.

exec(jump,X, AC, AC,PC, X ).
 ... etc ...

% Example program:
m(0,add,8).  .. etc ..  m(8,2).  .. etc ..

% Command to simulate ISA
p(0,0),m(10,Ans)?
```

So far ASP can synthesize an ISA of about eight instructions producing a complete CIF level design, except for the pad frame. Work is continuing, and we plan to produce much more complex designs as our work progresses.

ASP is currently about 10,000 lines of Prolog code. It has provided valuable insights into those features of Prolog that support design automation programming well, and those that don't. This has led us to consider extensions to the Prolog language to provide support for those constructs needed by ASP but missing from 'standard' Prolog. This topic is discussed next.

3. BXP

Berkeley Extended Prolog (BXP) is basically an extension of 'standard' Prolog to include efficient built-in predicates. Because we are designing and building processors to support Prolog, we can provide hardware support to make these predicates fast and efficient, where strictly software solutions might not be satisfactory.

An example of such predicates is the 'replarg' predicate. It is used to effectively replace the argument of a Prolog structure, but in such a way as to not modify the semantics of 'quasi-pure' Prolog by just bashing the argument. The argument value is restored on backtracking. This feature allows efficient execution of algorithms that require array and other complex data structure operations.

BXP is not finished, and experimentation is still in progress.

4. SDDA

The Berkeley Static Data Dependency Analyzer (SDDA) is a Prolog Program that analyzes Prolog programs for their data dependencies. It yields a collection of data dependency graphs (one for each clause). These are used for three main purposes:

(1) To discover and mark those parts of the input program that are independent so that they can be executed in parallel.

(2) To locate and mark 'intelligent' choice points in the input Prolog program so that during execution, backtracking can directly return to that part of the program that is causing (through a dependency) the current failure.

(3) To indicate (for later possible use) those unifications that can be executed in parallel.

The output of the SDDA is fed to a compiler where it is used to compile machine language programs with parallel execution instructions and intelligent backtracking instructions.

5. COMPILER

Our Prolog compiler is also written in Prolog. It produces 'W-code', which is the assembly language for our PLM (see below) processor. W-code is a concrete machine-level language that was directly derived from the Warren abstract machine (WAM) specification. We have extensively used the compiler (compiling part of itself) as a benchmark program, and it has been very influential in determining what Prolog features need hardware support.

6. Parallel Execution

We have been studying parallel models of execution of compiled Prolog programs. We started with modifications of the W-code, mentioned above, and more extensive modifications are under consideration. These are intended to support only that subset of parallelism that can be discovered at compile time by our SDDA (see above), and matches the type of applications that we are interested in. Thus far we have been investigating only the following types of parallelism:

(1) Independent AND

(2) Single Solution OR

(3) Intelligent Backtracking

(4) Unification

We may study other types that are more difficult to support (such as stream parallelism, or other run time types of parallelism) in the future.

7. BAM

Our studies of the WAM, our evaluations of our own machines and our work on parallel execution models have led us to consider a new abstract model, the Berkeley Abstract Machine (BAM). BAM is intended to support both BXP and the our parallel model of execution. BAM is still under study but it appears that we will employ it to derive our future processor instruction set architectures. Perhaps its biggest change from the WAM is the added support for built-in predicates.

8. PLM

The Programmed Logic Machine (PLM) was the first experimental processor of the Aquarius project. It was composed of about TTL 300 chips, ranging from simple gates to LSI circuits (e.g. PLA's). This processor and its caches, interfaces and host was our Aquarius-I experimental system. A commercial version of this processor is now available from Xenologic Inc, of Newark CA.

We designed a VLSI version of the PLM, to be used in an experimental multiprocessor system, Aquarius-II. This system will employ the parallel model of execution mentioned above. At the time of this writing, the VLSI chip had been fabricated but not yet tested.

9. HPS

We have investigated two major microarchitectures to support the execution of W-code. The first is a classic parallel and pipelined data path statically controlled by a microprogram. The second is a new, innovative, but untried approach called 'High Performance Substrate' (HPS). HPS is a restricted data flow microarchitecture. It is an expansion and generalization of ideas originally put forward in the floating point unit of the IBM 360/91. Our approach is to implement the architecture in tiers, Software control at the top, classical Von Neumann machine control flow in the middle, and fine granularity dynamic data flow at the bottom. The bottom layer is HPS. The HPS studies are not yet finished, but it appears that HPS will be quite effective in extracting parallelism dynamically, in contrast to the static extraction of the SDDA approach.

10. CONCLUSIONS

The Aquarius Project is an on-going activity. We have some interesting accomplishments in our Aquarius-I system. We have made a fair amount of progress in our studies of the parallel execution of Prolog programs. We have been able to incorporate some of what we have learned into our ASP design system, and we plan to expand the capabilities of the ASP system.

We have found Prolog to be very helpful in writing compilers, program analyzers and design automation systems. Prolog seems to be a good specification language as well. We believe modest extensions to Prolog, and the availability of powerful execution environments will make it attractive for even a wider range of programming tasks.

11. ACKNOWLEDGMENTS

The Aquarius team is led by myself and my close colleagues Yale Patt and Vason Srini. We have had the good fortune to work with a fine group of students, all who have made important contributions. These are: Philip Bitar, William Bush, Michael Carlton, Gino Cheng, Chien Chen, Jung-Herng Chang, Wayne Citrin, Tep Dobry, Barry Fagin, Jeff Gee, Bruce Holmer, Wen-mei Hwu, Shen Lin, Steve Melvin, Tam Nguyen, Carl Ponder, Steve Schoettler, Michael Shebanow, Ashok Singhal, Jerric Tam, Herve Touati, Peter Van Roy , and Robert Yung. We also acknowledge the stimulating interactions with our colleagues R. Fateman, W. Kahan, Richard M. Karp, Paul Hilfinger, Eugene Lawler, and Alan Smith. Finally, we acknowledge the financial support of several institutions. In particular, this work was partially sponsored by the Defense Advanced Research Projects Agency (DOD) under contract no. N00039-84-C-0089 and and by the California MICRO program. We also thank the Digital Equipment Corporation, the NCR Corporation, ESL, Xenologic Inc., Apollo, Mentor, Valid, Bellcore, and CSELT for their generous contributions of equipment, and for funding part of the work done on the project.

References

1. Alvin Despain and Yale Patt, "The Aquarius Project," *Proceedings, COMPCON 1984, IEEE Press*, pp. 364-367.

2. Alvin Despain and Yale Patt, "Aquarius – A High Performance Computing System for Symbolic Numeric Applications." *Proceedings, COMPCON Spring 85,* San Francisco, California, February 25-28, 1985.

3. T.P. Dobry, A.M. Despain and Y.N. Patt "Performance Studies of a Prolog Machine Architecture" *Proceedings for 12th International Symposium on Computer Architecture* Boston, Massachusetts, June 17-19, 1985.

4. Peter Van Roy "A Prolog Compiler for the PLM" *Technical Report No. UCB/CSD 84/203,* Computer Science Division, University of California, Berkeley, November 1984.

5. Jung-Herng Chang, Alvin Despain and Doug de Groot, "Semi-Intelligent Backtracking of Prolog Based on a Static Data Dependency Analysis" *Proceedings, The Symposium on Logic Programming 1985* Boston, July 1985.

6. Wayne Citrin, Peter VanRoy and Alvin Despain, "A Prolog Compiler" *Proceedings, Hawaii International Conference on System and Science,* Honolulu, Hawaii, January 7-10, 1986.

7. Wayne Citrin, Peter VanRoy and Alvin M. Despain "Compiling Prolog for the Berkeley PLM" *Proceedings, Hawaii International Conference on System and Science,* Honolulu, Hawaii, January 7-10 1986.

8. T.P.Dobry, Y.N. Patt and A.M. Despain, "Design Decisions Influencing the Microarchitecture for a Prolog Machine" *Proceedings, the 17th Annual Microprogramming Workshop* New Orleans, Louisiana, October 30 - November 2, 1984.

9. Carl C. Ponder, and Yale Patt, "Alternative Proposals for Implementing Prolog Concurrently and Implications Regarding their Respective Microarchitectures" *Proceedings for the 17th Annual Microprogramming Workshop,* New Orleans, Louisiana, October 30 - November 2, 1984.

10. T. P Dobry, J.H. Chang, A.M Despain and Y.N. Patt "Extending a Prolog Machine for Parallel Execution" *Proceedings, Hawaii International Conference on System and Science,* Honolulu, Hawaii, January 7-10, 1986.

11. Barry Fagin, and Alvin Despain, "Goal Caching in Prolog" *Proceedings, Hawaii International Conference on System and Science* Honolulu, Hawaii, January 7-10, 1986.

12. Yale Patt, Wen-Mei Hwu and Michael Shebanow, "HPS, A New Microarchitecture: Rationale and Introduction" *Proceedings, the 18th Microprogramming Workshop* Asilomar/Pacific Grove, California, December 3-6, 1985.

13. Yale Patt, Stephen Melvin, Wen-Mei Hwu and Michael Shebanow, "Critical Issues Regarding HPS, A High Performance Microarchitecture" *Proceedings, the 18th Microprogramming Workshop* Asilomar/Pacific Grove, California. December 3-6.

14. Barry Fagin, Yale Patt, Vason Srini and Alvin Despain, "Compiling Prolog into Microcode: A Case Study Using the NCR/32-000" *Proceedings, the 18th Microprogramming Workshop,* Asilomar/Pacific Grove, California, December 3-6, 1985.

15. Philip Bitar and Alvin Despain, "Multiprocessor Caches: Cache Synchronization and Busy-Wait Locking, Waiting and Unlocking" *Presented at Thirteenth Annual IEEE International Symposium on Computer Architecture, Tokyo, June 3-5, 1986.*

16. Jonathan Pincus and Alvin Despain, "Delay Reduction Using Simulated Annealing" *Presented at 23rd ACM/IEEE Design Automation Conference,* Las Vegas, Nevada, June 29 - July 2, 1986.

17. Patrick McGeer, William Bush, Jonathan Pincus and Alvin Despain, "Design Considerations for a Prolog Silicon Compiler" *Presented at 23rd ACM/IEEE Design Automation Conference,* Las Vegas, Nevada, June 29 - July 2, 1986.

18. Jung-Herng Chang, "High Performance Execution of Prolog Programs Based on a Static Data Dependency Analysis" *Technical Report No. UCB/CSD 86/263, Computer Science Division, University of California, Berkeley, October 1986.*

19. Nasser Lone, "A Replacement Algorithm for Prolog Goal Caches" *Master's Thesis, Department of Electrical Engineering and Computer Sciences* University of California, Berkeley, December 1985.

20. Ashar Butt, and Alvin Despain, "Cell Design in Prolog," *Technical Report No. UCB/CSD 85/286, Computer Science Division,* University of California, Berkeley, August 1985.

21. A.M. Despain, Y.N. Patt, T.P. Dobry, J.H. Chang and W. Citrin, "High Performance Prolog, The Multiplicative Effect of Several Levels of Implementation" *Proceedings COMPCON Spring 86,* San Francisco, California, March 3-6, 1986.

22. Michael Shebanow, Yale Patt, Wen-Mei Hwu and Steve Melvin, "A C Compiler for HPS I, A Highly Parallel Execution Engine" *Proceedings, Hawaii International Conference on System and Science* Honolulu, Hawaii, January 7-10, 1986.

23. Yale Patt, Wen-Mei Hwu, Stephen Melvin, Michael Shebanow, Chien Chen and Jiajuin Wei, "Experiments with HPS, A Restricted Data Flow Microarchitecture for High Performance Computers" *Proceedings, COMPCON Spring 86,* San Francisco, California, March 3-6, 1986.

24. Wen-mei Hwu, Steve Melvin, Mike Shebanow, Chien Chen, Jiajuin Wei and Yale Patt, "An HPS Implementation of VAX, Initial Design and Analysis" *Proceedings, Hawaii International Conference on System and Science* Honolulu, January 7-10, 1986.

25. Wen-mei Hwu and Yale Patt, "HPSm, A High Performance Restricted Data Flow Architecture Having Minimal Functionality" *Proceedings, 13th International Symposium on Computer Architecture,* Tokyo, June 3-5, 1986.

26. Alvin M. Despain, Vason Srini, Yale Patt, Barry Fagin "Architecture Research for Prolog Based on NCR/32" University of California, Berkeley 1986

27. Alvin M. Despain "High Performance Hardware Architecture for Design Automation" *Aerospace Applications of Artificial Intelligence Conference, Oct, 1986* University of California & Xenologic Inc. Sept. 1986

28. Yale N. Patt, "Several Implementations of Prolog, the Microarchitecture Perspective" *Proceedings 1986 IEEE International Conference,* October, 1986

29. Yale N. Patt, Stephen Melvin, "A Microcode-Based Environment for Non-Invasive Performance Analysis" *Proceedings, 19th Microprogramming Workshop,* October, 1986

30. Yale N. Patt, Stephen W. Melvin, Wen-mei Hwu, Michael Shebanow, Chien Chen, Jiajuin Wei, "Run-Time Generation of HPS Microinstructions from a VAX Instruction Stream" *Proceedings 19th Microprogramming Workshop,* Oct. 1986

31. Jeff Gee, Stephen W. Melvin, Yale N. Patt, "The Implementation of Prolog via VAX 8600 Microcode" *Proceedings, MICRO 19, New York* October 1986

32. Wen-mei Hwu and Yale N. Patt "Design Choices for the HPSm Microprocessor Chip" *Proceedings- 20th Annual Hawaii International Conference on System Sciences,* Kona, Hawaii, January 1987

33. Stephen W. Melvin, Yale Patt, "A Clarification of the Dynamic/Static Interface" *Proceedings, 20th Annual Hawaii International Conference on Systems Sciences* Kona Hawaii, January 1987

34. Wen-mei Hwu, Yale N. Patt, "CheckPoint Repair for Out-of-Order Execution Machines" *Proceedings, 14th Annual International Symposium on Computer Architecture* Pittsburgh, Pa., June 1987

35. John Swensen and Yale Patt "Fast Temporary Storage for Serial and Parallel Execution" *Proceedings, 14th Annual International Symposium on Computer Architecture* Pittsburgh, Pa., June 1987

36. Peter Van Roy, Bart Demoen, Yves Williams, "Improving the Execution Speed of Compiled Prolog with modes, clause selection, and determinism" *Proceedings, International Joint Conference on Theory and Practice of Software Development (TAPSOFT), Pisa, Italy, March, 1987*

37. Patrick McGeer, Robert K. Brayton, "Efficient Algebraic Prime Factorization of Logic Expressions and Applications" *International Workshop on Logic Synthesis* MC - North Carolina May 12-15,1987 (No Proceedings)

38. Jeff Gee, Stephen W. Melvin, Yale N. Patt, "Advantages of Implementing Prolog by Microprogramming a Host General Purpose Computer" *Proceedings 4th International Conference on Logic Programming* Melbourne, Australia May, 1987

39. Vason Srini, Jerric Tam, Tam Nguyen, Chien Chen, Allen Wei, Jim Testa, Yale N. Patt, Alvin Despain, "VLSI Implementation of a Prolog Processor" *Stanford VLSI Conference, March 1987*

40. Barry Fagin, Alvin M. Despain, "Performance Studies of a Parallel Prolog Architecture" *14th ICSA, June 1987*

41. William R.Bush, Gino Cheng, Patrick C. McGeer, Alvin M. Despain, "Experience with Prolog as A Hardware Specification Language" *Symposium of Logic Programming, 1987.*

42. Patrick C. McGeer Robert K. Brayton "Efficient, Stable Algebraic Operations on Logic Expressions *VLSI, 1987*

43. William R. Bush, Gino Cheng, Patrick McGeer, Alvin M.Despain "An Advanced Silicon Compiler in Prolog" *Proceedings, ICCAD, 1987*

44. A. Despain, Y. Patt, V. Srini, P. Bitar, W. Bush, C. Chien, W. Citrin, B. Fagin, W. Hwu, S. Melvin, R. McGeer, A. Singhal, M. Shebanow, P. Van Roy, "Aquarius" *Computer Architecture News* March, 1987.

45. Tep Dobry "A High Performance Architecture for Prolog" *UCB, Technical Report #87/352* May, 1987

46. Erling Wold "Nonlinear Parameter Estimation of Acoustic Models" *U.C.B, Technical Report # 87/354* May , 1987.

47. Vason P. Srini,,Jerric Tam, Tam Nguyen, Yale N. Patt, Alvin M. Despain "A CMOS Chip for Prolog" *Proceedings, ICCD* New York, 1987,

48. Patrick McGeer, Alvin Despain, "Data Structures and Destructive Assignment in Prolog" *UCB, Technical Report # 87/356* July, 1987

49. Patrick McGeer, William R. Bush, Gino Cheng, Alvin M. Despain, "Prolog for VLSI Layout: Experiences in the Design and Implementation of Topolog, A Prolog Based Module Generation and layout System" *UCB,Technical Report # 87/363* July 1987

50. Herve Touati, and Alvin M. Despain "An Empirical Study of the Warren Abstract Machine" *Proceedings Symposium on Logic Programming* September 1987

51. Barry Fagin, "A Parallel Execution Model for Prolog" *U.C.B. Technical Report #87/380* November, 1987.

PROLOG AT THE UNIVERSITY OF ILLINOIS*

M. M. Gooley L. V. Kalé D. A. Padua B. Ramkumar U. S. Reddy D. C. Sehr W. W. Shu B. W. Wah

University of Illinois at Urbana–Champaign

Abstract. **This paper presents a brief description of four logic programming research projects under way at the University of Illinois at Urbana–Champaign. Three of these projects deal with the design of Prolog interpreters and compilers. The other project deals with the design of languages that combine then functional programming and the logic programming paradigms and with the transformation of programs written in these languages.**

Introduction

The logic programming language Prolog was developed about fourteen years ago by A. Colmerauer and P. Roussel [Rous75]. Prolog in particular, and logic programming languages in general are today the subject of increasing interest on the part of many research groups. This paper presents a brief description of four of the logic programming research projects under way at the University of Illinois at Urbana–Champaign. The first three section of the paper describe projects dealing with the design of Prolog interpreters and compilers emphasizing efficiency and parallelism. The first project deals with the use of heuristics to reduce the search space. The second project concentrates on efficient OR–parallel execution of standard sequential Prolog programs. The third project studies the use of both AND and OR parallelism. The last project presented here deals with the design of languages that combine the functional programming and the logic programming paradigms and with the transformation of programs written in these languages.

Heuristic guiding and pruning

We have performed an extensive survey of computers, from both the hardware and software perspectives, to support artificial intelligence processing [WaLi86a, WaLi86b, Wah87, WaLi88]. We have found that the execution of Prolog programs is inefficient due to redundant searches. Our research on efficient execution of Prolog programs is centered around two themes: reducing the search space through heuristic guiding and pruning, and efficient execution of Prolog programs by parallel processing [LiWa86e].

In heuristic guiding, we have studied two related problems: the identification of attributes that can be used to guide the evaluation of Prolog programs, and the static reordering of programs at compile time to reduce redundant searches.

In identifying attributes to guide the search, we model the evaluation of a Prolog program as the search of an AND–OR tree. An attribute that has been found to be useful to characterize the merit of evaluating a subtree is the ratio of success probability of the subtree to the corresponding overhead (cost) of evaluation [LiWa85]. If a depth–first search is used and all nodes in the search tree are independent, then an optimal search strategy to minimize the expected total cost is to reorder the descendents of AND nodes by increasing the ratios of success probability to cost and to reorder OR nodes by decreasing the ratios of success probability to cost [LiWa86d]. In a best–first search, the AND–OR tree has to be transformed so that all OR nodes are in the top part of the search tree and all AND nodes are in the lower part. An optimal strategy to search the transformed tree is to search all OR nodes by decreasing ratios of success probability to cost and all AND nodes by increasing ratios of success probability to cost [LiWa85]. It should be noted that when the search tree is transformed as described above, its size is increased by an exponential order.

In practice, nodes in the AND–OR search tree are dependent and may be traversed more than once due to backtracking. We study the effects of backtracking by modeling the evaluation of subgoals in a clause and clauses with the same head as an absorbing Markov Chain [LiWa85]. Such an approach is heuristic in nature because nodes in the search tree may be dependent, while nodes in the Markov Chain are independent and satisfy the memoryless property. The evaluation of success probabilities and costs is recursive. That is, the success probabilities and costs in the lower part of the search tree are evaluated first. This will provide success probabilities and costs to clauses that call these subgoals, and their success probabilities and costs can then be evaluated.

* The work of L. V. Kalé, B. Ramkumar, and W. W. Shu was supported in part by the the National Science Foundation under Grant NSF–CCR–8700988. The Work of D. A. Padua and D. C. Sehr was supported in part by the National Science Foundation under Grant NSF–MIP–8410110, the Department of Energy under Grant DOE DE–FG02–85ER25001, and a donation from IBM Corporation to the Center for Supercomputing Research and Development. D. C. Sehr holds a fellowship from the Office of Naval Research. The work of U. S. Reddy was supported in part by the National Aeronautics and Space Administration under Grant NAG 1–613. The work of B. W. Wah and M. M. Gooley was supported in part by the National Aeronautics and Space Administration under Grant NCC 2–481.

Based on the technique described above, to approximate the merit of evaluating a clause or subgoal, we have studied the static reordering of Prolog subgoals and clauses to minimize the expected total cost [GoWa88]. Two major problems have been addressed. First, it is necessary to define the equivalence of results when the execution order is changed. Equivalence can be thought of as what is acceptable to the users as an equivalent solution set. We have defined four classes of equivalence: reflexive, set, tree, and inequivalent executions. In reflexive equivalence, the results in the solution set are obtained in the same order; this can only be achieved through minimal or no reordering. In set equivalence, the same set of results are obtained but possibly in a different order. In tree equivalence, a superset of subset of solutions may be generated, while in inequivalence, any result can be generated. Reordering may result in set, tree, or inequivalent executions. Our objective is to maintain set equivalence in the presence of side effects and control predicates. The second problem addressed in this research is the characterization of restrictions on reordering and the development of methods to detect these restrictions. Restrictions on reordering are governed by fixity, semi-fixity, and control predicates. We have designed a new system of calling modes for Prolog, geared to reordering, and a system for inferring them automatically. We have developed an approach that used multiple versions of the same clause in different modes, each with different order of execution. We improved the Markov-Chain method for determining a good goal order for Prolog clauses, and used it as the basis for a reordering system, showing how it could be guided by information about modes and restrictions to generate reordered Prolog programs that behaved correctly.

In heuristic guiding, we have studied the detection of redundant evaluations in a Prolog program, the abstraction of previous evaluations by explanation-based learning, and the storage of previous solution sets by caching [WaLi88].

In parallel processing of logic programs, we are currently simulating a parallel processing system that evaluates Prolog programs based on the Markov-Chain method described above, the maintenance of equivalence of solution sets, and the automatic detection of precedence order of execution. The architectural model assumed is a multiprocessing system with a hybrid of tightly coupled multiprocessors and loosely coupled distributed computers [Li85,LiWa85]. The objective here is to develop methods to coordinate the search in a distributed fashion, without violating precedence while maintaining equivalence of results, and investigate strategies to avoid detrimental anomalies in parallelism [LiWa86c].

OR–parallelism in the presence of side–effects

The goal of this project is the design and implementation of a Prolog compiler that accepts standard sequential Prolog as input language and produces efficient code for a parallel processor. The translation of sequential programs into equivalent parallel versions has several advantages. The programmer's task is simplified since there is no longer the need to deal with parallelism explicitly, and sequential programs can be easily ported between different classes of machines. Research on this same compiling strategy for FORTRAN and other languages was pioneered at the University of Illinois many years ago. Techniques developed at Illinois are used today in the FORTRAN compilers of many supercomputers and minisupercomputers.

In the early stages of this project we decided to take advantage of OR–parallelism only, and leave to the project described in the next section the study of the interaction between AND and OR–parallelism. OR–parallelism was chosen because it seemed more likely to achieve good speedups on conventional multiprocessors. The reason for this is that, under OR–parallelism, the target parallel program can be organized in such a way that there is little interaction between the different processes cooperating in the search for solutions. Also, restricting the work to only one form of parallelism will allow us to concentrate more on the quality of the analysis and code generation phases. We hope that the outcome of this work will be a compiler capable of generating very efficient parallel code in a reasonable time.

The project is organized into three phases. During the first phase, an interpreter was written. During the second phase we will explore different strategies and assess their performance potential, and during the third phase we will write the compiler based on the techniques and measurements obtained during the first two phases.

The central structure in the interpreter or target parallel program is a representation of an *evolving OR–tree* whose root corresponds to the input query. In this tree, each node represents a set of bindings and a conjunction of goals. Each descendant of a node corresponds to a successful unification of its leftmost goal with a different clause. The clause used for generating a node will be called its *originating clause*. The bindings produced by the unification become the bindings of the new node. Also, the query of a node is the query of its parent with the leftmost goal replaced by the right–hand side of the originating clause. A node containing an empty query is called a *success*, and a node whose leftmost goal cannot be unified with any clause is called a *failure*.

The target parallel program consists of several cooperating processes. Assume first that there are no goals with side–effects in the Prolog program. Under this assumption, execution proceeds as follows. When execution starts, the OR–tree is just the root node containing the user input query. One of the cooperating processes grabs this node while the others remain idle. The process then tries to unify the leftmost goal with every clause in its procedure. A child node is created for every successful unification. The binding set and the query of each child node are also computed as described above, and both items are stored in the child node. Execution terminates if all the children of the root node are successes, or if no unification is possible, i.e. the root is a failure. Otherwise there will be some children that are *ready nodes*, i.e. nodes that are neither successes nor failures and whose children have not been generated.

After processing the root, the search of the OR–tree proceeds in a similar way. At any given time, there may be several ready nodes in the evolving OR–tree which gives the opportunity for parallelism by having each of several processes work on a different ready node. The work on each of these nodes is the same as the one described for the root node. Execution terminates when no ready nodes remain.

When predicates with side–effects such as `assert`, `retract`, and `write` are present, the processes have to perform the action corresponding to these predicates before generating the child node. In our system, predicates with side–effects other than cut are evaluated one at a time and in the order specified by the Prolog program. This is achieved by linking the nodes of the evolving OR–tree in post–order to form the *scheduling queue*. Processes look for work in this queue, and predicates with side–effects other than cut are evaluated only when they are the leftmost goal of the leftmost ready node in the scheduling queue.

The three most important issues with respect to this work are scheduling, how to handle different simultaneous bindings to the same variable, and how to correctly process the side–effect predicates. We decided to concentrate, at least at the beginning on the scheduling and side–effect issues which have not been studied as extensively as the multiple bindings issue. In the current version of the interpreter, we have implemented some of the models described in the literature [HaCH87,Warr87] with the purpose of studying their behavior before selecting one or trying to design a new scheme.

Next we discuss briefly the algorithms we use to handle the predicates with side–effects. The main idea of these algorithms is easy to describe. The details, however, are lengthy, and cannot be presented here due to space limitations. They can be found in [KaPS88].

Executing a cut is done by deleting from the scheduling queue the nodes between the cut node and the parent of its frame. This is a constant time operation in our system. When the children of a ready node, say *N*, are generated, the identification of *N* is inserted in a list associated with the procedure of the leftmost goal of *N*. When a clause is asserted into a procedure, this list is used to insert an additional child for all the appropriate nodes in the list. Similarly, when a new node is added to the tree, its identification is inserted into a list associated to its originating clause. This list is used to handle `retract`.

An important issue is the interaction between scheduling, garbage collection and the processing of `assert`, `retract`, and cut. The major difficulty is that care has to be given to the scheduling and the garbage collection algorithms to avoid redundant and useless work. For example, when a subtree is cut from the OR–tree, a process working in that subtree should be redirected towards another part of the tree to avoid wasting computation. Also, it may not be beneficial to garbage collect subtrees removed by cut, since the cut itself could later be removed by another cut.

The REDUCE–OR process model

The main motivation behind this research is a premise that massively parallel machines will be available in near future. We then need to extract maximal parallelism from given logic programs. This is particularly important for many combinatorially explosive AI computations. As a consequence, we cannot rely solely on AND or OR parallelism, but must pursue both sources of parallelism *in concert*.

We found that the AND–OR trees, which are a usual representation of logic computations, are not adequate for representing parallel computations. Firstly, as the binding information is spread through the tree, the nodes don't represent independent subproblems. Secondly, the tree hides an important form of parallelism, as there is only one OR child–node for every literal of an AND node [KaWa84]. The REDUCE–OR process model [Kale87a] is based on the REDUCE–OR trees which we developed as a representation of logic computations suitable for parallel interpretation.

We will use a simple example to illustrate the basic operation of the model. Figure 1 depicts a data join graph (DJG: a form of data dependence graph), for a clause. I is the input value given to this clause. Assume that p,q and r are non–deterministic, and return multiple solutions. As the graph indicates, p computes values for X that q and r can use in parallel. The ROPM starts a new instance of q and r as soon as a X value is returned from p. Every Y value returned from q is paired with each Z value that has been returned by r and that shares the same X value as an ancestor. (Similar, symmetric, pairing happens when a Z value arrives from r) For every new pair so formed, a new instance of s process is started to compute a T value. Thus, if p returns two X values, and q and r each give 3 values for every X value, the ROPM will form 9 Y–Z pairs for each X value, and may have 18 s processes running in parallel at a time. In contrast, the AND–OR process model (AOPM) [Cone83] can have only one instance of s running at a time. A pure OR process model will of course miss the parallelism between q and r. The AOPM does execute alternate clauses for p in parallel. Similarly, for each X value, it will have 3 processes each for q and r running in parallel. But as it deals with one binding for each variable at a time, it misses the parallelism between multiple instances of a consumer literals. We call this *consumer instance parallelism*. We find that it is an important source of parallelism in AI computations where the generate–and–test paradigm prevails. In an 8–queens program, admittedly a toy example, the ROPM obtains about 26,400 parallel actions in contrast to 4,544 obtained by a pure OR model, and just 7 obtained by AOPM. (The AOPM can get the same degree

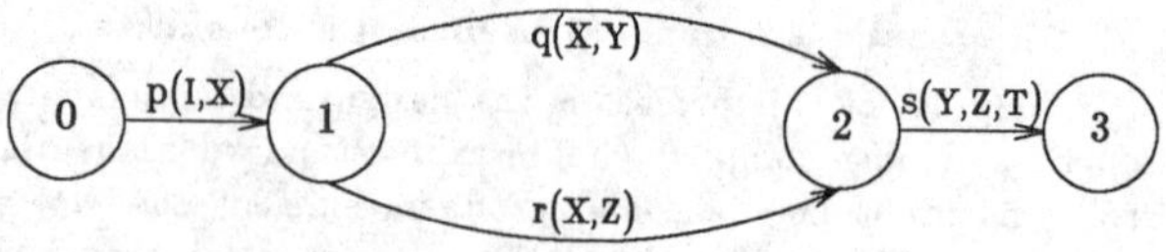

Figure 1: The Operation of ROPM

of parallelism by rewriting the Logic program).

We have shown in [Kale87b] that ROPM is *complete* and that it produces more parallelism than most proposed models. This 'maximal parallelism' comes at a price. The ROPM has to do much more book-keeping than the AOPM, say. As a simple example of the complexities involved, notice that the Y values and Z values coming from q and r (in Figure 1) have to appropriately distinguished to ensure that a solution for q(x1,Y) is not paired with a solution for r(x2,Z). For a model such as the AOPM, this is no problem because it allows only one X value to be alive at a time. The challenge is then to develop techniques and algorithms that control the overhead in ROPM. In fact, we aim at reducing the overhead to the extent that even on computations where ROPM generates the same parallelism as AOPM, it should be as efficient as AOPM (and within a small factor of sequential compiled execution). We intend to achieve that by following the venerable dictum: pay the overhead for a feature only when you use it (which is, of course, easier said than done).

Consequently, we are focusing on optimizations to our basic algorithm. One optimization deals with the consistency problem mentioned above. Instead of requiring a full relational join of the XYZ values kept in relations at the p and q arcs, it allows us to access only the consistent values, by maintaining a few additional pointers. Many such optimizations are under investigation. The other techniques involve dynamically trading a part of our asset, the parallelism, for a reduction in overhead. These may lead to a tunable process model, which generates more or less parallelism depending on the runtime conditions in the parallel system. Throttling techniques which take over when the system memory starts to overflow are also being developed.

A major source of improvement will come from static analysis of given programs. Logic Programming is a very high level language, and our process model is also a more general one in that it attempts to handle different kinds of parallelism at once. In any particular clause the full generality of the basic algorithms is not usually needed. Compilation gives us an opportunity to handle each clause and each call differently, and static analysis should provide information useful to simplifying code for individual clauses. The kind of information we have found useful includes: a bound on the number of 'embedded' variables returned by a call, the variables that a given variable 'depends on' at a given point in the program, etc.

An interpreter for the ROPM has been implemented. It runs on an ALLIANT FX/8 (a shared memory machine), and on an Intel hypercube with 32 nodes. (The ROPM is implemented as a message passing system. A shared memory system provides additional opportunities for optimizations, and simplifies load distribution). It also runs on ORACLE, a multiprocessor simulation system that can simulate a variety of architectures. Related ongoing research includes
(1) Message-selection strategies, which significantly affect many performance metrics including the memory usage;
(2) load-balancing strategies for message-passing systems
(3) An 'operating system' (called the *chare kernel*) that can support many types of parallel symbolic computations including Logic programming.

Functional logic programming

The functional logic programming project at University of Illinois is involved in the investigation of languages that combine functional programming and logic programming paradigms into a unified framework. Our position, explained in [Redd85], is that *logic programming* means performing computations based on the notion of *solving* for variables. The notion of solving is not limited to predicates, it can be applied to functional expressions as well. The operational mechanism used for solving for variables in functional expressions is called *narrowing* [Fay79, Hull80, Redd85]. Narrowing essentially involves performing function application using unification for parameter passing, rather than pattern matching.

For example, consider a function for appending lists, defined by the equations

append(nil, Y) –> Y
append(A.X, Y) –> A.append(X,Y)

In a conventional implementation of functional programming, such a definition can only be used for evaluating applications of append to *ground* (variable-free) terms. But, in an implementation using the narrowing mechanism, append can also be applied to *nonground* terms. The variables in the argument terms are instantiated by unifying the arguments with the formal parameter terms on the left hand sides of the definition equations. For example, the evaluation of the function application append(L, M) can be unified with the left hand sides of both the equations. Each such evaluation yields a pair of results <s, e> where s is a substitution on the initial expression, and e the result of evaluation using the substitution. For the expression append(L, M), the first step of evaluation produces two such pairs:

1. substitution: L → nil, result: M
2. substitution: L → A.X, result: A.append(X, M)

Further evaluation of the second result term again yields two pairs:

2.1. substitution: L → A.nil, result: A.M
2.2. substitution: L → A.A'.X, result: A.A'.M

This then makes up the narrowing search space, and traversing it in a complete manner produces all possible solutions. Using backtracking to traverse the search space, though incomplete, provides an operationally viable method to enumerate the solutions, one by one. Each "solution" answers the question "for what instantiation of the variables does the initial expression reduce to a value, and what is its value under that instantiation?"

A functional logic language based on these ideas, called Scope, is being used as the *specification language* in the FOCUS program derivation system discussed later. In addition to the usual functional programming constructs, it contains 4 constructs which facilitate the introduction of logical variables in expressions and solving for them. These are

1. if p then e
2. e ; e'
3. forsome(X) e
4. unionover(X) s

where p is boolean valued expression, e, e' are any expressions, and s is a set-valued expression. (The terminology "set" is historical [Turn81], but these are in reality multisets, i.e., with possible duplicates). The first expression denotes the value of e if the expression p is true, and is undefined otherwise. The second construct denotes the choice of e and e'. If any one of them is defined, then it denotes the value of the defined expression. If both of them are defined, but have different values, then the expression is erroneous. The third construct, similar to existential quantification in predicate logic, means the value of e for some instantiation of X that makes e defined. Again, if e has different values for different instantiations of X, then the expression is erroneous. The fourth construct yields a set of values rather than a single value. It yields the union of all set values of s for all instantiations of X. The formal semantics of this language together with a set of examples illustrating its use may be found in [Redd87a].

The second aspect of our research is in using the narrowing mechanism for *transforming specifications into efficient programs.* We are constructing an interactive program transformation system called FOCUS [Redd87b] for this purpose. Most programs that can be expressed abstractly and concisely using the logical features of Scope have poor performance. (For example, maximum of a list can be expressed as its largest element, and sort of a list can be expressed as an ordered permutation of it). The FOCUS system allows the user to use such programs as specifications and transform them step by step into efficient programs.

The FOCUS system structures program derivations as trees, and uses a tree editor called XTED for its user interface. The program specification is entered in the root node of the derivation tree. Then nodes are created for each function that the user wishes to transform. Selecting a function to transform (together with its specification) is called *focusing.* A tree structure follows from the fact that in transforming a function, subsidiary foci may be needed for transforming its subexpressions. Focusing is also performed on *properties* of functions which need to be proved and then used in transformations. A number of transformation and deduction operations are provided to manipulate expressions and to prove theorems. The most often used transformation operations are *simplification* (evaluation without instantiation of any variables), *expansion* (evaluation with instantiation), and *recursing* or *application-introduction* (replacing instances of function specifications by function applications, or invoking inductive hypotheses). The deduction operations closely correspond to natural deduction inference rules.

The use of the FOCUS system operations ensures that the derived programs are equivalent to the original specifications. Moreover, the system also documents all the derivation activity performed in each focus node. Such a documentation is called a *derivation script.* When a specification is altered, the scripts off all the nodes are *replayed* to redo the derivation automatically. In this use, the FOCUS system acts much like a compiler, except that the optimizations performed are not preprogrammed by the compiler-writer, but programmed by the user himself in earlier derivation effort. The user is alerted to the situations where the replay *breaks* (i.e., where the old script is not applicable to the new specification or where it produces significantly different results from the earlier derivation). These situations are then handled by rederivation. Replaying is also used to modify a derivation. The system keeps track of the dependencies between focus nodes. When the derivation of a node is changed, the scripts of the other dependent nodes are replayed. Using the replay facility, changes can be propagated through entire programs semi-automatically. Thus, the FOCUS system supports the *automation-based software development* paradigm widely recognized to be the future software technology [Balz83].

References

[Balz83] R. Balzer, E. Cheatham, and C. Green. " Software technology in the 1990's: Using a new paradigm," *Computer*, Vol. 16, No. 11, Nov. 1983, pp. 39–45.

[Cone83] J. S. Conery. "The And/OR Process Model for Parallel Interpretation of Logic Problems", Ph.D. Thesis, University of California, June 1983.

[Fay79] M. Fay. "First order unification in an equational theory," *Fourth Workshop on Automated Deduction*, pp. 161–167, 1979.

[GoWa88] M. M. Gooley and B. W. Wah. "Efficient Reordering of Prolog Programs", to appear in *Proc. of 4th International Conference on Data Engineering*, Los Angeles, California, Feb. 1988.

[HaCH87] B. Hausman, A. Ciepielewski, and S. Haridi. "OR-parallel Prolog made efficient on shared memory multiprocessors," *Proc. of the 1987 International Symposium on Logic Programming*, San Francisco, California, 1987

[Hull80] J.-M. Hullot. "Canonical forms and unification," *Conference on Automated Deduction*,1980, pp. 318–334.

[Kale87a] L. V. Kalé. "Parallel execution of Logic Programs: the REDUCE-OR process model", *Proc. of Fourth International Conference on Logic Programming*, May 1987.

[Kale87b] L. V. Kalé. "'Completeness' and 'Full Parallelism' of Parallel Logic Programming Schemes", *Proc. of the 1987 Symposium on Logic Programming*, San Francisco, California.

[KaPS88] L. V. Kalé, D. A. Padua, and D. C. Sehr. "OR–parallelism in standard sequential Prolog," forthcoming.

[KaWa84] L. V. Kalé and D. S. Warren. "A Class of Architectures for Prolog Machine", *Proc. of the Conference on Logic Programming*, Uppsala, Sweden, July 1984, pp. 171-182.

[Li85] G. J. Li. "Parallel Processing of Combinatorial Search Problems", Ph.D. Thesis, School of Electrical Engineering, Purdue University, Dec. 1985.

[LiWa85] G.–J. Li and B. W. Wah. "MANIP–2: A Multicomputer Architecture for Evaluating Logic Programs", *Proc. of International Conference on Parallel Processing*, Aug. 1985, pp. 123–130.

[LiWa86a] G.–J. Li and B. W. Wah. "Coping with Anomalies in Parallel Branch–and–Bound Algorithms", *IEEE Transactions on Computers*, Vol. C–34, No. 6, June 1986, pp. 568–573.

[LiWa86b] G.–J. Li and B. W. Wah. "How Good are Parallel and Ordered Depth–First Searches?", *Proc. of International Conference on Parallel Processing*, Aug. 1986, pp. 992–999.

[LiWa86c] G.–J. Li and B. W. Wah. "Multiprocessing of Logic Programs", *Proc. of International Conference on Systems, Man and Cybernetics*, Oct. 1986, pp. 563–567.

[Redd85] U. S. Reddy. "Narrowing as the operational semantics of functional programs," *Symposium on Logic Programming*, Boston, Mass., 1985.

[Redd87a] U. S. Reddy. "Functional logic languages, Part I," in *Graph Reduction*, J. H. Fasel and R. M. Keller (eds.), Springer–Verlag Lecture Notes in Computer Science, Vol. 279, pp. 401–425, 1987.

[Redd87b] U. S. Reddy. *The FOCUS program derivation system: project report*, University of Illinois, 1987.

[Rous75] P. Roussel. *Prolog, manuel de reférence et d'Utilisation,* Univ. of Marseilles, France, 1975.

[Turn81] D. A. Turner, *KRC Language Manual*, University of Kent, UK, 1981.

[Wah87] B. W. Wah. "Guest Editor's Introduction: New Computers for Artificial Intelligence Processing", *Computer*, Vol. 20, No. 1, Jan. 1987, pp. 10–15.

[WaLi86a] B. W. Wah and G.–J. Li. "A Survey of Special Purpose Computer Architectures for AI", *SIGART Newsletter*, April 1986, pp. 28–46.

[WaLi86b] B. W. Wah and G.–J. Li. "Tutorial in Computers for Artificial Intelligence Applications", *IEEE Computer Society Press*, May 1986.

[WaLi88] B. W. Wah and G.–J. Li. "Design of Multiprocessing Systems for Artificial Intelligence Applications", to appear in *Transactions on System, Man, and Cybernetics*, 1988.

[Warr87] D. H. D. Warren. "OR–parallel execution models of Prolog," *Proc. of the 1987 International Joint Conference on Theory and Practice of Software Development*, Pisa, Italy, Springer–Verlag, 1987, pp. 243–259.

Logic Programming Research in Oregon

John S. Conery
University of Oregon, Eugene, Oregon, USA

This paper is a high level overview of various research projects at the University of Oregon and elsewhere in the state of Oregon. Instead of trying to describe each project in detail, I will give a qualitative overview, with references to key papers that are more authoritative sources of information.

Research at the University of Oregon

The current logic programming research projects at the University of Oregon have grown from efforts to implement the AND/OR Process Model for parallel execution of logic programs [2]. In the last few years, we have built several interpreters that execute pure logic programs, in order to study implementation techniques. Our current projects, based on experience with these interpreters, are (1) development of binding environments for OR-parallel programs in the AND/OR model, and, (2) implementation of a virtual machine for the model. Another project, which was initially inspired by concerns for writing an operating system for the virtual machine, is to develop a new logic programming language that incorporates notions of object-oriented programming.

Closed Environments

The binding environments used by most other implementations of OR-parallel logic programs can be characterized as generalizations of the standard 3-stack method used in sequential Prolog systems. In this method, variables are allocated in local stack frames, and instances of complex structures are built on a heap. The unification of unbound logical variables results in pointers from cells in the stack to either other cells lower in the stack or cells on the heap. When a variable is passed as a parameter to a procedure that has multiple OR-parallel solutions, the new processes will share references to the variable. The central problem in adapting the three-stack scheme for parallel execution is how to share existing binding information, so copies of the stacks do not have to be made for each new process, while at the same time giving each parallel process its unique copy of shared variables, to avoid conflicting bindings. There are a number of proposals for solving this problem (a survey and analysis of three of them can be found in an excellent paper by Crammond [6]).

A common attribute of these methods is that they require a shared memory multiprocessor, since all rely on sharing the main stack and heap structures while mapping unbound variables into data local to each process. The goal of the closed environment model is to enable systems to run on non-shared memory architecture. Attributes of this method are:

- Pointers representing the unification of two variables are arranged in such a way that the environment of an active process never contains a reference to a variable in the environment of another process (this is the meaning of *closed environment*).

- Since environments are closed, they can be relocated anywhere in the system, and a process that executes a program fragment will not make nonlocal references to environments residing in other memories.

- Complex terms are represented in such a way that sibling processes can share the same instance of a term when both are in the same memory; *i.e.* instance terms contain no variables, but relative pointers to variables that can be dereferenced to actual variables in each process.

- When a process is relocated to a different memory space by the task allocator in the system, any complex terms it references will have to be copied to the memory space of the new node.

CH2539-5/88/0000/0074$01.00 © 1988 IEEE

The overhead of the closed environment model is that local environments of a process will have to expand to contain variables that would reside in the heap in a three-stack representation, and some instance terms have to be copied when they are passed as parameters to lower level processes. In addition, an environment closing algorithm that is comparable in complexity to unification has to be executed after each procedure call. Details can be found in [3].

OM

Closed environments were first used in an interpreter for the AND/OR Process Model written by More [9]. This interpreter, known as OPAL (for *O*regon *P*arallel *L*ogic), ran either as a single Unix process or as multiple Unix processes communicating with sockets. Our original plans were to port the interpreter directly to a small multiprocessor. However, OPAL creates a large number of processes, and does an inordinate amount of copying of process states and binding environments. Instead, we designed a virtual machine for OPAL programs, as a means of cutting down on memory use, and at the same time making OPAL programs run faster. The machine is named OM (*O*PAL *M*achine). It also runs as a single Unix process, and we are currently porting it to the multiprocessor.

OM is similar to the Warren Abstract Machine [10], in that it does "open coded unification" by having a compiler generate code that is specific for each call or clause head. Where it differs from the WAM is that binding environments are closed environments, and control instructions are for a parallel execution instead of sequential execution. For example, instead of **call**, we have **start_or**, which starts a new OR process for the head of a procedure, and instead of **proceed**, we have **succeed**, which sends a success message to the parent of the currently executing process.

OM makes more efficient use of space than the OPAL interpreter by cutting down on the number of copies of environments, and the fact that environments and complex terms are variable-sized data structures tailored for each process. In OPAL, an OR process has to make a copy of the parent's AND process for each potential unification, and keep the copy for each successful unification. The stored copy is used to create a success message for the parent, if and when the body of the corresponding process succeeds. In the virtual machine, environments are kept in registers. This makes it easier to extend an environment (no need to allocate a larger structure in memory), make copies for each new unification (we just restore the registers from a backup set), and avoid allocating environments until we know a unification succeeds. In addition, we are exploring a technique that should allow us to avoid storing copies of the parent environment for each active descendant.

Another aspect of OM that makes it more efficient than OPAL is open coded environment closing. Just as the WAM is more efficient than a Prolog interpreter as a result of executing **get** and **put** instructions that are specific to each particular clause, OM is more efficient than OPAL because it executes instructions for environment closing that are tailored to each clause. These instructions, known as **cput** and **cget**, are generated by the OM compiler to be executed after the corresponding unification instructions. OM's **put** and **get** instructions are implemented in such a way that they always create closed environments for new processes, and the **cput** and **cget** instructions are used to close a descendant's environment so it can later send a result back to its parent.

An early version of OM is described in [5]. A more recent description has just been submitted for publication, and Craig Thornley's M.S. project, to be completed later this year, will contain more details on the current machine.

Object Oriented Programming with Logic

Our technique for doing object oriented programming within the framework of a logic programming language grew out of discussions of the nature of an operating system for OM. Such a system would do task distribution, message routing, *etc.*, and it will be advantageous to write it in a logic programming language so it is executed by OM along with user programs.

The basic idea is that, unlike Prolog, where each literal on the right hand side of an implication is interpreted as a procedure call, we will interpret some literals as descriptions of object states. To keep things straight, the predicates that name object literals are separate from the predicates that name procedures. To write procedures that modify objects, we use an object literal in the head of a procedure. If there is another object literal with the same predicate in the body of the clause, we can view this clause as describing an object transformation, *e.g.*

```
s(X) :- p(X,Y), s(Y).
```

What this clause means is: if there is an object (negative literal) with state `s(X)` in the current goal statement, and the goal `p(X,Y)` is solvable, then create a new object with state `s(Y)`. Note that the new object is a negative literal in the goal statement derived by the clause and the input goal statement, which is what we expect.

To be useful, we need a means to control when objects should be transformed. As described above, there is no control information that tells an interpreter when to replace an object literal by a new object. For this, we introduce a new type of logical formula, called an *object clause*, that has a conjunction of two positive literals in the head, instead of the single positive literal found in a Horn clause. One of the positive literals will be a regular procedure literal, and the other an object literal:

```
p(X) ∧ s(Y) :- q(X,Y,Z), s(Z).
```

This "clause" (which isn't really a clause, by the strict definition of clausal form) means: if the current goal statement contains a goal (procedure call) that can be unified with `p(X)`, and it also contains an object state that can be unified with `s(Y)`, then the clause can be invoked as a procedure. The call and the input state in the current goal statement are replaced by the goals and output state in the body of the clause. The system-wide control strategy, with this new type of rule, is to ignore object states in a goal statement until there is a call to a procedure defined by an object clause, at which time we have to search the goal statement for an object that matches the object literal in the object clause.

Here is a familiar example, the definition of a stack as an abstract type:

```
class stack.
new(ID) :- stack(ID,[]).
push(X,ID) ∧ stack(ID,S) :-
    stack(ID,[X|S]).
pop(X,ID) ∧ stack(ID,[X|S]) :-
    stack(ID,S).
top(X,ID) ∧ stack(ID,[X|S]) :-
    stack(ID,[X|S]).
end stack.
```

The first line tells the system that `stack` is a predicate that will be used in object states and not procedure calls. The second line is a regular Horn clause which, when called, creates a new stack by putting an object literal into the derived goal statement. The three object clauses are procedures that operate on stacks. Note that by requiring the procedure head and object head of an object clause to unify simultaneously with the call and input object, we make sure a call is paired up with the right object instance. Thus a program can use the above definition of a stack and create many different stacks, each with a unique ID passed to `new_stack`, and later operate on the proper stack by passing an ID in one of the object clause calls.

This new type of logical formula is called a clause because it is easy to show that it can be transformed into two Horn clauses. A paper that defines this transformation, proves that the inference rule described above is sound (and equivalent to two successive resolutions on the corresponding Horn clauses), and describes the semantics of the new language is available as a University of Oregon technical report [4].

The new language has several interesting properties of both object oriented and logic programming languages. As in object oriented languages, we can enforce a rule that says the collection of statements inside a class definition is the only way to operate on the object; for example, we won't allow an object clause with `stack` as the object outside the class shown above. Thus our class has become an abstract type, with the representation of the stack known only inside the class, and the only way to operate on the stack described by the clauses inside the class. It is also possible to define inheritance mechanisms, class methods, and other features of Smalltalk and other object oriented languages within this framework.

The new language is similar to Prolog in the nondeterministic programming style and pattern matched invocation. There are two sources of nondeterminism here: when a procedure inside a class is called, there may be more than one object clause with a matching procedure head. Using terminology from Smalltalk, we could send a message to an object, telling it to transform itself; later, if a procedure fails, the system would backtrack, and have the object handle the message via a different clause, perhaps changing to a different state this time. The second source of nondeterminism is that there may be many different object states that could be chosen for a call to an object clause; for example, `ID` could be unbound in a call to `push`. Again in Smalltalk terms, it corresponds to sending a message that could be handled by a number of different objects. If the wrong one is used, leading to a failure, the system backtracks, restores the object to its old state, and picks a different object. Finally, and perhaps most interesting, object states can contain logical variables, meaning they can represent partial data structures. This can lead to some serious aliasing problems that are not found in current object oriented languages, but at the same time it provides an interesting avenue of exploration in programming styles. The logical variable is one of the distinguishing features of Prolog, and it will be interesting to see how it can be exploited in an object oriented language.

Other Research Centers in Oregon

Many other organizations in Oregon have researchers actively engaged in logic programming research. They are mentioned briefly in this section, and references to their work is included in the bibliography.

Oregon State University

Tom Dietterich's lab at Oregon State University is working on a logic programming language based on DeKleer's assumption-based truth maintenance system. Their language, FORLOG, allows forward chaining inference, as opposed to the strict backward chaining in Prolog, and extends the basic ATMS formalism to allow logical variables in expressions [7].

Oregon Graduate Center

David Maier and Jianhua Zhu at the Oregon Graduate Center, in Beaverton, are working on a data model and language that are based on a combination of logic and object-oriented programming. The formal underpinnings are captured in "O-Logic," which is a first-order system whose terms resemble feature structures of unification grammars, but also includes object identity and a type hierarchy. They, along with Hitomi Ohkawa, are implementing a database language, called TEDM (Tektronix Engineering Data Model), for use in engineering applications, which takes its semantics from O-Logic [8].

Harry Porter's Ph.D. research at OGC resulted in the development of a formalism, known as *Inheritance Grammars*, that allows left recursive rules and semantic inheritance (in the form of is-a relations) that are difficult with the definite clause grammars known to Prolog programmers.

Tektronix

Peter Borgwardt, at Tektronix Labs in Beaverton, is continuing research he started at the University of Minnesota. He and Carolyn Hakansson at OGC just finished an implementation of an AND-parallel model on a Sequent shared-memory machine (see [1] for a description of this model). He is currently working with Doug Pase, also of OGC, on load balancing techniques for OR-parallelism in a message-passing network.

Intel

Joe Brandenburg, at Intel Scientific Computers, is monitoring work done at Weizmann Institute in Israel on implementing Concurrent Prolog on Intel's iPSC hypercube. Intel is planning on implementing CP on their next generation hypercube.

References

[1] Borgwardt, P. and Rea, D. Distributed semi-intelligent backtracking for a stack-based AND-parallel Prolog. In *Proceedings of the 1986 Symposium on Logic Programming*, (Salt Lake City, UT, Sep. 22–25), 1986, pp. 211–222.

[2] Conery, J.S. *Parallel Execution of Logic Programs.* Kluwer Academic Publishers, Boston, MA, 1987.

[3] Conery, J.S. Binding environments for parallel logic programs in non-shared memory multiprocessors. In *Proceedings of the 1987 IEEE Symposium on Logic Programming*, (San Francisco, CA, Aug 31 – Sep 4), 1987, pp. 457–467.

[4] Conery, J.S. *Object Oriented Programming with First Order Logic.* Tech. Rep. 87-09, Univ. of Oregon, Aug. 1987.

[5] Conery, J.S. and Meyer, D.M. *OM: A Virtual Processor for Parallel Logic Programs.* Tech. Rep. 87-01, University of Oregon, 1987.

[6] Crammond, J.A. A comparative study of unification algorithms for OR-parallel execution of logic languages. In *Proceedings of the 1985 International Conference on Parallel Processing*, (August 20–23), 1985, pp. 131–138.

[7] Flann, N.S., Dietterich, T.G., and Corpron, D.R. Forward chaining logic programming with the ATMS. In *AAAI-87*, (Seattle, WA, July 13–17), Am. Assoc. for Artificial Intelligence, 1987, pp. 24–29.

[8] Maier, D. *A Logic for Objects.* Tech. Rep. CS/E-86-012, Oregon Graduate Center, Nov. 1986.

[9] More, N. *Implementing the AND/OR Process Model.* Master's thesis, Univ. of Oregon, 1986.

[10] Warren, D.H.D. *An Abstract Prolog Instruction Set.* Tech. Note 309, SRI International, Oct. 1983.

HIGH PERFORMANCE COMPUTER SYSTEMS Track

Myths vs. Reality 1: Using Parallel Computers

Chair: H.D. Simon

PARALLEL PROGRAMS ON THE CRAY AND ON THE ALLIANT: A COMPARATIVE EVALUATION

Michael Bieterman

Engineering and Scientific Services Division
Boeing Computer Services
Seattle, Washington

Abstract

The microtasking capabilities of two computers are examined. Microtasking is a loop-based form of multitasking on MIMD computers in which much of the synchronization and control of parallel tasks in a user's program is managed by vendor software. The machines used in this study are the CRAY X-MP/4 and Alliant FX/8. We describe differences in their microtasking features, compare the processes of applying them to different types of partial differential equation software, and present performance results from several experiments. A number of problems delayed completion of the experiments past the time of this writing. At the conference these problems are described and written summaries of the experiments are provided.

Introduction

A pressing question in the scientific community is whether any but a small group of its members will ever be able to efficiently write, convert, or optimize software for parallel computers. Microtasking is a form of multitasking on MIMD computers which addresses many of this community's needs. In microtasking, tasks are the work carried out in independent iterations of a DO loop. This loop orientation, with its implicit synchronization of tasks, makes it quite tractable for programmers to identify and exploit much of the parallelism in today's application software. When the extent of tasks does not cross procedure boundaries (i.e. loops don't contain (nested) subprogram calls), and the loops aren't too complicated, this parallelization process can be carried out automatically by a compiler.

We examine and compare the microtasking mechanisms available on two vector multiprocessor computers: the Alliant FX/8 and the CRAY X-MP/4. The Alliant FX/8 is an eight-processor virtual memory system. It's real memory is hierarchical in that data is supplied from main memory to the processors via one or two high speed caches shared by the processors. The CRAY X-MP/4 is a four-processor real memory system in which data is transferred to the processors directly at high speed from the interleaved main memory.

The present study involves comparing the effort required to microtask different types of partial differential equation software on the two machines and the resulting performance achieved. Typically, experiments conducted to measure performance are run in dedicated, single-job environments. The results we present are from experiments in both single-job and multiprogramming environments. There is a great need for examination of parallel processing performance in multiuser mode since a great many of the cycles used on Alliant and Cray computers today are used in such environments. Such an examination was made previously [2] for the CRAY X-MP by the author.

Unfortunately, several problems were encountered during our preliminary work and initial experiments. Since identification of the sources of some of these difficulties is underway at the time of this writing, it seemed prudent to delay presentation of any comparative performance results. Written descriptions of the experiments and their results can be obtained at the conference from the author.

Here, we restrict our attention to a comparison of the microtasking features on the two machines.

Microtasking on the Alliant FX and CRAY X-MP

A common attribute of the microtasking mechanisms of these computers is that each iteration of a microtasked loop is executed sequentially by one processor. The two implementations differ in many respects, however.

On the Alliant FX [1], when a user enables a compiler option, the compiler automatically detects and microtasks many loop constructs. These include some second level outer loops, and single vector loops, whose iterations are partitioned across the available processors in "vector concurrent" mode. Microtasking can be controlled on a loop to loop basis on the Alliant by a programmer with compiler directives. This is required, for example, when loop iterations cross procedure boundaries. Critical regions (e.g., where global variables are updated) are not permitted within microtasked loops. The compiler can recognize and parallelize certain reduction operations (e.g., dot product and sum), however.

Microtasked loops can occur anywhere in a program package on the Alliant FX. The only code processed by more than one processor in a program unit containing such loops is that in the loops. While the Alliant FX can automatically partition program units into microtasked loops and single threaded portions of code, it can be necessary for a programmer to participate in the partitioning by pulling code out of line and creating subroutines. This is the case, for example, when critical regions occur in loops or when one wishes to parallelize third level outer loops.

On the CRAY X-MP, all microtasking is directed by a programmer through insertion of preprocessor directives into his software. The directives mark, among other constructs, microtaskable loops. The iterations in any loop so marked will be concurrently executed by available processors. Critical regions can occur inside a microtasked loop on the CRAY X-MP and are protected with user-supplied directives. Hence, a programmer has considerable freedom in choosing the granularity and type of work to be microtasked. No "vector concurrent" mode is available as on the Alliant FX. A person wishing to partition a vector operation into a set of smaller vector operations for concurrent processing must do so explicitly by creating an outer microtasked loop. Microtasking on the CRAY X-MP can be directed to occur anywhere in a program package where it is deemed appropriate, provided this occurs in a subroutine.

Execution of such a subroutine follows a much different set of rules than on the Alliant FX. A "master" processor, which is that which executes all unitasked program units, signals for other available "slave" processors to join in its execution of microtasked loops. The master continues its execution without waiting for the slaves. The slave processors join by entering the subroutine at the top. They execute all local initialization code in the subroutine not marked with user-supplied directives and procede until they find and enter the microtasked loop in which the master processor is active. This implementation requires a programmer to understand dependencies in, and to impose structures on, an entire subroutine. When a subroutine is very complex, a person always can pull desired loops out of line to create a new subroutine where scoping and protecting data is more easily accomplished.

References

1. Alliant Computer Systems Corporation, FX/FORTRAN Programmer's Handbook, Acton, Massachusetts, March, 1986.

2. Bieterman, M., The Impact of Microtasked Applications in a Multiprogramming Environment, Proceedings of the Fall 1987 Cray User Group Meeting, Bologna, Italy, September 22-26, 1987.

3. Cray Research, Inc., Chapter 12: Microtasking, in Multitasking User Guide, Cray Computer Systems Technical Note, Pub. No. SN-0222, Mendota Heights, Minnesota, October, 1986.

CHALLENGES IN MATCHING PARALLEL ARCHITECTURES AND MATRIX ALGORITHMS[a]

R. E. Benner

Sandia National Laboratories
Albuquerque, NM 87185

Abstract

Most classes of numerical algorithms for solving matrix equations are not 'embarrassingly' parallel and, therefore, are a challenge to implement efficiently on parallel computers. Direct solution methods based on Gauss elimination and its variants are of particular interest because they readily expose memory limitations and communication bottlenecks of parallel architectures, are integral components of other, more highly parallel matrix algorithms, and can solve poorly conditioned problems on which other methods fail. The parallel implementation and performance of a class of direct methods is examined on three architectures: CRAY X-MP/48, ELXSI 6400, and NCUBE/ten. Further algorithmic innovations are mandated by the demands of massive parallelism, *i.e.*, thousands of floating-point processors.

1. Introduction

There are several routes to efficient parallelism in numerical algorithms. Some approaches map well to one class of parallel architectures and poorly to others. For example, *microtasking* and *self-scheduling* provide medium to fine-grain parallelism, e.g., at the DO-loop level in Fortran, but are presently effective and practical only on shared-memory machines. At the other extreme, *macrotasking* provides coarse-grain parallelism, *e.g.*, at the subroutine level in Fortran. Macrotasking often requires more programming effort to implement, such as significant restructuring or even replacement of traditional uniprocessor algorithms. However, the effort can result in new and significantly better parallel algorithms. In addition, macrotasking is the most practical route to parallelism on the current generation of distributed memory machines, on which high-latency communications discourage fine-grain parallelism.

Domain decomposition is a standard technique for creating subroutine-level parallelism in numerical simulations based on a computational grid, *e.g.*, partial differential equations. Figure 1 shows a computational domain and a potentially useful decomposition. Domain dissection introduces

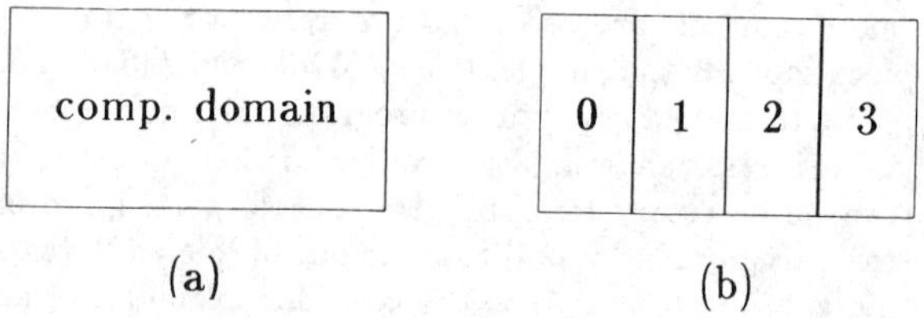

Figure 1: Domain decomposition strategy: (a) a computational domain, and (b) a domain dissection appropriate for a four-processor, shared-memory architecture.

the desired high-level parallelism into the matrix algorithm: the domain is divided or dissected one or more times to produce a set of subdomains, and a subdomain is then assigned to each parallel process. Each subdomain may contain thousands of finite elements or finite difference grid cells.

Figure 2 contrasts two kinds of domain decomposition based on one-way and two-way mesh dissection. Two-way mesh dissection represents the algorithmic approaches needed to use parallel computers with thousands of processors effectively, but poses difficulties for parallel direct methods, as discussed below.

Domain decomposition is currently a research vehicle for creating entirely new parallel algorithms, some of which feature special iterative techniques to handle equations that are shared by neighboring processor subdomains[1–2], while others are ***hybrid*** methods that combine direct and iterative matrix solvers[3–4]. However, domain decomposition is also applicable to traditional direct and iterative solution methods.

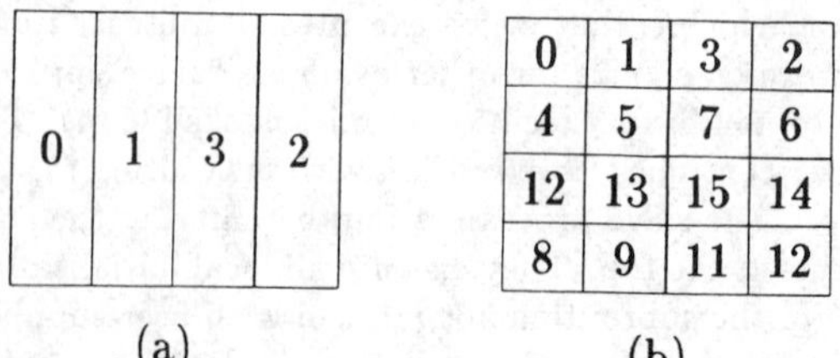

Figure 2: Domain decompositions with processor assignments, given by standard binary-reflected gray code, which map well to local-memory architectures such as hypercubes: (a) one-way domain dissection suitable for a small number of parallel processes, and (b) two-way mesh dissection.

[a]This work was performed at Sandia National Laboratories which is operated for the U. S. Department of Energy under contract number DE-AC04-76DP00789.

The following sections outline a parallel direct method in the context of domain decomposition and discuss performance of the algorithm on three distinct parallel machines. Results on CRAY X-MP and ELXSI computers have been presented in detail elsewhere[5], so only key features are reviewed below. More attention is devoted to the present status of the parallel direct method on the NCUBE and to future changes needed in the algorithm to better utilize massively-parallel computers. In particular, a published algorithm[6] developed on the Intel hypercube is a promising step in this direction.

2. A Parallel Direct Method

Direct methods deservedly suffer from a serious 'image problem' in the parallel processing research community: in addition to being compute-intensive they are notoriously memory intensive, particularly for numerical simulations in three spatial dimensions. However, direct methods remain important in many scientific and engineering applications because they can solve a variety of poorly-conditioned problems on which iterative methods fail (*e.g.*, large structural mechanics simulations with a plain stress constitutive model). Parallel direct solvers are also important as: (1) a component of a stable and highly-parallel hybrid method, (2) a coarse-mesh solver for parallel multigrid, or (3) a close relative of incomplete matrix factorization preconditioners for conjugate gradient iteration.

The frontal method, a popular implementation of Gauss elimination in finite element analysis, was first used[7] as an efficient matrix solver on sequential machines with limited core memory. There are frontal solvers that are highly vectorized and optimized for the current generation of supercomputers. A particular extension known as multifrontal, developed on the Cray 1[8], is a natural framework in which to exploit parallelism by domain dissection[9]. In the multifrontal algorithm, matrix assembly and factorization can proceed simultaneously in many processor subdomains, as shown in Figure 3.

Parallelization of a multifrontal method raises two key issues[5]: (1) a bottleneck in the algorithm, an elimination tree (Figure 3(b)) that idles most processors and grows with the number of concurrent processes, and (2) additional numerical computations required in the parallel algorithm. The first issue is a serious limitation when large numbers of processors are available, while the second can represent a significant portion of the computational effort on as few as four processors.

3. Test Problems

The parallel algorithm described above was originally applied on the CRAY and ELXSI to a nonlinear finite element code that models oscillations of drops confined to a spherical container[10]. The oscillating drop model is both nonlinear and spatially heterogenous, because a portion of the drop surface is free (modeled by a Bernoulli-type equation), while the rest of the drop surface simply meets the solid container. The parallel direct method, as well as several parallel iterative methods, has more recently been applied on the NCUBE and ELXSI to symmetric positive definite matrix equations which arise in well-conditioned Laplace equations and poorly-conditioned bending beam problems in two dimensions.

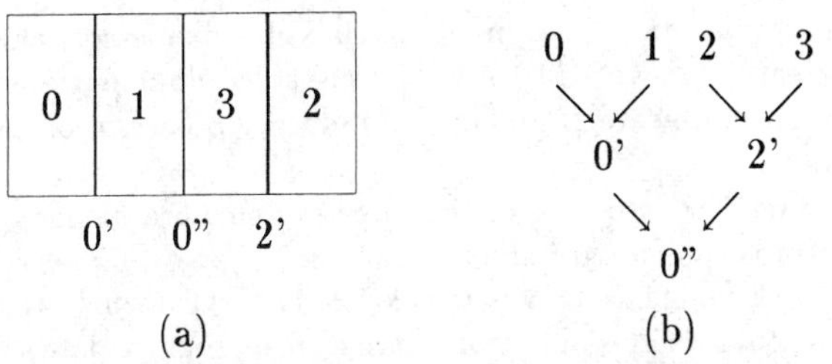

Figure 3: Direct Method: (a) nested dissection of a mesh and (b) elimination tree. Processes 0-3 operate in parallel on the numbered submeshes of (a), followed by processes 0', 2' and 0" which solve equations associated with the numbered dissection boundaries.

4. Performance Analysis

Performance of the parallel algorithm on the shared memory machines (CRAY and ELXSI) is expressed below in terms of parallel speedup. Parallel speedup is generally defined as the elapsed time to solve a problem on one processor with the serial version of the code (no multitasking added) divided by the elapsed time needed to solve the same problem (i.e., the same number of equations) with N processors using a multitasked version of the code. However, speedup is an impractical measure of performance on a distributed memory machine, because a problem that uses a thousand processors efficiently is not likely to fit in the limited local memory available to a single processor.

Performance on a distributed memory machine is best expressed in terms of efficiency. Parallel efficiency is generally defined as the elapsed time to solve a problem on one processor divided by the elapsed time to solve a problem N times as large on N processors. Given parallel efficiency, one can, in turn, calculate a *scaled speedup* as N times efficiency.

Note that the timings, speedups, and efficiencies reported here include the effects of I/O and other sequential and parallel pre- and post-processing tasks involved in finite element analysis, not just a key computational kernel like the matrix solver.

5. Results and Discussion: One-way Decomposition

Results are summarized from research with parallel direct methods on a four processor CRAY X-MP/48, ten processor ELXSI 6400, and 1024 node NCUBE/ten computers. The CRAY features fast vector processors, whereas the ELXSI and NCUBE have slower scalar processors. The first generation of ELXSI processors, model 6410's, has a clock cycle of 50 ns and a sustained double-precision computation rate of about 1.1 Mflop per processor. NCUBE nodes, which are a proprietary VLSI processor chip plus six memory chips, currently run at 8 MHZ with a sustained double-precision computation rate of about 0.1 Mflop per processor on Fortran code.

Memory resources of the three systems are distinct, as are preferred programming strategies. For example, each NCUBE node has 0.5 Mbyte of local memory, of which about 0.48 Mbyte is available to user programs, program data, and message buffers. A 1024-node configuration has 512 Mbyte of total memory. Alternatively, the CRAY X-MP machines have a large central memory (currently 128 Mbytes) with all data in Fortran COMMON available by default for sharing. The ELXSI also has a large central memory (32 Mbytes at Sandia), but each processor has a much faster, small (16 Kbyte) cache.

A programming style has been outlined[11] which streamlines algorithm and code development and improves parallel performance in a multitasking environment such as the ELXSI's. Two key objectives are minimization of shared memory and cacheability of as much of the remaining shared memory as possible. Shared memory use is reduced by restructuring an algorithm to make as much data local to individual processes as possible. Uncached data must be accessed directly from central memory each time it is needed, while cached data can be brought into each high-speed cache and retained there. However, caching increases the complexity of code development efforts on the ELXSI, because cached data is not automatically updated in the central memory. The user is responsible for maintaining cache coherency by flushing portions of each cache as necessary with Fortran subroutine calls.

The effective use of the multiple memory levels on the ELXSI is of particular interest because it results in direct and iterative matrix algorithms suitable for conversion to distributed memory machines: most data is already local to individual processors. Also, manual flushing of cached, shared data corresponds very closely to the communication calls required, for example, on the NCUBE to pass the same data as messages between processes.

5.1. Shared Memory Computers: Drop Problem

Similar speedups are obtained on both the CRAY and ELXSI although two very different programming strategies are required. On the CRAY X-MP all data has been shared. Various sources of performance degradation limit speedup of the oscillating drop code to 2.9 on four X-MP processors[5]. In addition to idle processes, load imbalance is introduced by boundary conditions and floating-point overhead in the multifrontal algorithm.

On an ELXSI 6400 the same algorithm, code and test problem achieves a speedup of only 1.4 when run on four scalar processors. Of course, the ELXSI's additional memory level, local processor cache, has been ignored in the algorithm's design for the CRAY. The cache acts as a buffer between the slower main memory and each processor's registers. The parallel algorithm has been redesigned to take advantage of the cache; *e.g.*, 8 Mbytes of uncached, shared memory become 0.5 Mbytes of cached shared memory and 0.5 Mbytes of local data per process. These modifications double the parallel speedup on the ELXSI to 2.8 on four processors. However, further speedup is difficult to gain on larger numbers of processors, with parallel speedups of 3.1 on eight processors and 4.3 on 16 processors observed and simulated, respectively[5].

5.2. Local Memory Computer: Laplace Equation

The parallel direct solver based on one-way mesh dissection has been implemented on the NCUBE hypercube. The results of Table 1 indicate that for this particular algorithm, reasonable parallel efficiencies and scaled speedups are observed for problems of modest size (73737 equations on 1024 processors) relative to the largest possible size (currently, in excess of 4.5 million equations) which are solved on the hypercube using preconditioned conjugate gradient methods. Table 1 shows an efficiency of 33% on 1024 nodes, which initially might not seem good and indicates that there is more research to be done. However, it is important to notice that the elapsed time of 6.2 sec. on this medium size problem is equal to or better than the elapsed time performance a CRAY X-MP processor would give. Therefore, the algorithm achieves the excellent price/performance effectiveness expected of massively parallel computers. If the size of the problem can be increased, the corresponding increase in efficiency will further increase the effectiveness of the massively parallel approach.

Of course, one-way mesh dissection on a thousand processors is a technique with limited applicability (very long beams and related structural models could qualify). It is also a technique for which iterative methods such as Jacobi preconditioned conjugate gradients (JPCG) will fare poorly in terms of convergence behavior and run time on large problems. JPCG achieves a much better parallel efficiency of 0.7 on the above problem, but has an elapsed time of 467 sec., because of the large number of iterations (7400) required to reach convergence. (It is worth noting that parallel effi-

Table 1. Multifrontal Solver: Parallel Performance

Finite Element Analysis of 2-D Laplace equation (NCUBE/ten, 16 biquadratic elements/processor)

Number of Processors	Number of Equations	Elapsed Time [s]	Parallel Efficiency	Scaled Speedup
1	81	2.019	1.	1.
2	153	2.087	0.967	1.93
4	297	2.572	0.785	3.14
8	585	2.795	0.722	5.78
16	1161	3.018	0.669	10.7
32	2313	3.256	0.620	19.8
64	4617	3.597	0.561	35.9
128	9225	3.897	0.518	66.3
256	18441	4.280	0.472	120.
512	36873	4.921	0.410	210.
1024	73737	6.157	0.328	336.

ciencies $\geq 95\%$ are achieved with JPCG based on two-way mesh dissection on problems with thousands of unknowns per processor.[12] Again, for these problems, massive parallelism is superior to any uniprocessor approach.) Attention is now shifted to the prospects for parallel direct methods based on two-way mesh dissection.

6. Discussion: Two-way Domain Dissection

Current research is focused on development of a massively parallel direct solver. An algorithm based on two-way mesh dissection would seem to be the simplest practical approach to solving a reasonable variety of 2D and 3D problems on hundreds or thousands of processors.

Three research directions are under investigation. The first, which has been tested on the NCUBE, is based on a straightforward extension of its one-way dissection counterpart plus a preprocessor that statically assigns a nesting order to the processes that solve the domain dissection boundary equations (cf. Figure 3(b) in the one-way dissection case). At four processors and about 1000 finite element equations, the new code achieves a parallel speedup of 3.0 and a scaled speedup of 2.5 on the NCUBE. However, this algoirhtm is not extendable to either larger problems or a larger number of processors. One problem is that as dissection boundaries are treated, their equations are held by the relatively few processors that participate. Thus, most of the available memory in the cube stands idle, and the portion that is used is quickly swamped. Another problem is that when a process passes its boundary data to another (*e.g.*, processor 3 to processor 2 in Figure 3(b)) an entire set of matrix entries associated with boundary equations is passed. These *large* messages can easily overflow processor message buffers on a machine such as the NCUBE hypercube. Therefore, this strategy has proven unproductive as an initiative in massively-parallel computing.

A second approach, a partial solution to the dilemma posed by the first strategy, has been developed and tested by an independent research team[6] on an Intel hypercube. The authors statically distribute processor boundary equations among *all* processors and make use of medium-grain parallelism, *i.e.*, as a processor eliminates one of its equations it broadcasts needed information about the factorization step to the other processors. The preprocessing required to assign boundary equations to processors is minimal. The new algorithm is clearly an improvement – speedups and scaled speedups in the range of 10 to 12 are reported for 16 processors. However, the algorithm is not suitable for massive parallelism, due to the large amount of communication that is introduced by sacrificing locality.

A third approach has been formulated and is now under investigation. This initiative recognizes that the ideal situation would be to maintain as much locality in the solution of processor boundary equations as possible. That is, at each stage of the algorithm each of the remaining processor boundaries can be *dynamically* distributed among processors belonging to a common subcube. This scheme can greatly reduce the size of interprocessor messages and better utilize all available memory. However, the preprocessing required to set the dynamic allocation of equations to processors will certainly be nontrivial and may prove quite difficult.

7. Concluding Remarks

The ongoing development of parallel direct matrix methods provides a route to performance, via massive parallelism, beyond that available on current supercomputers. Given the above case history of a parallel direct method, there is no question that parallel processing forces changes in the way one looks at numerical algorithms, programming styles (and languages), performance evaluation, memory usage and many other aspects of hardware/software interaction. Nowhere are the changes more acute than on the new frontier of massive parallelism, where thousands of floating point processors dictate the evolutionary path of both algorithms and software.

References

1. Chan, T. F., and Resasco, D. C. 1987. Adv. Comput. Meth. PDEs. VI. New Brunswick, New Jersey: IMACS, pp. 317:322.

2. Chin, R. C. Y., Hedstrom, G. W., Scroggs, J. S., and Sorenson, D. C. 1987. Adv. Comput. Meth. PDEs. VI. New Brunswick, New Jersey: IMACS, pp. 375:381.

3. Nour-Omid, B., and Park, K. C. 1986. C3P-273A, Pasadena: California Institute of Technology.

4. Benner, R. E., Montry, G. R., and Weigand, G. G. 1987. Adv. Comput. Meth. PDEs. VI. New Brunswick, New Jersey: IMACS, pp. 419:424.

5. Benner, R. E., Montry, G. R., and Weigand, G. G. 1987. Internat. J. Supercomp. Appl. 1(3):26-44.

6. Farhat, C., Wilson, E. L. and Powell, G. 1987. Engng. Comput. 2:157-165.

7. Irons, B. M. 1970. Int. J. Num. Meth. Engr. 2:5-32.

8. Duff, I. S. and Reid, J. K. 1983. ACM Trans. Math. Soft. 9:302-325.

9. Duff, I. S. 1985. ANL/MCS-TM-49. Argonne, IL: Argonne National Laboratory.

10. Bixler, N. E., and Benner, R. E. 1985 July 9-12, Swansea U.K. Proc. 4th Int. Conf. Numer. Meth. Lam. Turb. Flow, Swansea, U.K.:Pineridge Press, pp. 1336-1347.

11. Montry, G. R., and Benner, R. E. 1987. Proc. 2nd Int. Conf. Supercomputing, St. Petersburg, Florida: ISI Inc. 2:64-71.

12. Gustafson, J. L., and Montry, G. R. 1988. Compcon Spring'88 Conference, Washington, D.C.:IEEE Computer Society Press, in press.

Myths vs. Reality 2: Programming and Performance on Advanced Computer Systems

Chair: C. Maples

THE GOOD, THE BAD AND THE UGLY: COMPARING HIGH SPEED COMPUTER SYSTEMS

Kirk E. Jordan

Computing and Telecommunications Systems
Exxon Research and Engineering Company
Annandale, New Jersey 08801

Abstract

In this report, several different classes of high speed computer systems for scientific computing are investigated. These include mainframes, mainframes with vector facilities, mini-supercomputers, vector supercomputers and vector multiprocessor mini-super and supercomputers. In this investigation a particular application code is run on several high speed computer systems. The particular code is a finite-difference elastic wave code. The numerical scheme is based on a dimensional splitting. This dimensional splitting leads in a natural way to efficient parallel and vector implementations on many high speed computer systems. Through executing this code on various high speed computer systems, several hardware and software features of thses systems which can affect overall performance if not considered by the code developer have been exposed. In order to comment on these features performance results are included for some model problems.

1. Introduction

In this paper, I describe my experience on various high speed computers for scientific computing. I describe the good, the bad, and the ugly that I encountered while trying to run various codes on a variety of machines. The intent here is to give a general overview of things to consider beyond just CPU speed when comparing high speed computer systems. The discussion here is not meant to be a benchmark study. Such a study should compare machines in a relatively short time span and simulate as much as possible the environment that will exist on the machine. For details of such a study see[1].

The comparison presented here is given to suggest that computational speed is not the only parameter that should be considered when evalutating high speed computer systems. With the announcement of new hardware for scientific compting a frequent occurance each with differing architecture, system software, and application software, many factors come into play as to the relative merits of the various systems. Some of these factors include sofistication of the compilers for automatic parallelization and vectorization, memory access time, and size of cache as well as clock speed, number of arithmetic units and number of processors.

I compare differing classes of architectures. The classes discribed here include mainframe computers, mainframes with vector facilities, vector supercomputers, mini-supercomputers and parallel-vector mini-supercomputers and supercomputers. Each class has different merits but one question that arises is how do they compare with each other. To try to answer this, I will discuss my observations in running a single application code on these different classes of machines.

The particular application code is a fourth-order accurate in space and second-order accurate in time finite-difference scheme for the computation of waves in an elastic medium. The numerical scheme is a fourth-order accurate variant of the MacCormack scheme[2] which was shown to be effective for accoustic wave propagation[3]. This fourth-order scheme was initially developed for a single processor machine[4]. On vector and shared-memory parallel computers[5], this algorithm has proven to be very efficient this is in part due to efforts to minimize memory references and to enhance chaining in the implementation. This algorithm was among several used for a comparison of vector machines the results of this performance comparison can be found in[1].

The motivation for obtaining a numerical scheme with high performance on high speed computer systems lies in the fact that geophyscists and siesmologists are typically interested in problems whose physical domain covers 10,000 feet in the horizontal direction and 20,000 feet in the vertical direction. The physical domain is further complicated by interior interfaces across which the elastic parameters are discontinuous. The mesh size is governed by the wave speed of the faster shear waves typically requiring mesh spacing of the order of 10 feet or less for the desired accuracy. In order to accurately solve the problems of interest, the equations must be solved at many mesh points. Fast solutions are required as the problems are solved many times for a variety of the elastic parameters and the entire parameter studies must be carried out in some timely fashion.

2. Equations of Elastodynamics

In this section, I give the mathematical formulation of the equations of linear elastodynamics that the fourth-order accurate scheme is based on. A detailed description of this numerical scheme can be found in[4]. The discussion below will therefore be brief and will emphasize the salient points needed for an understanding of the implementation of this numerical scheme.

The equations of linear isotropic elastodynamics for the stresses and velocities in Cartesian coordinates are

$$\begin{aligned}
\rho u_t &= \tau_{11,x} + \tau_{12,y} \\
\rho v_t &= \tau_{12,x} + \tau_{22,y} \\
\tau_{11,t} &= (\lambda + 2\mu) u_x + \mu v_y \\
\tau_{22,t} &= \mu u_x + (\lambda + 2\mu) v_y \\
\tau_{12,t} &= \mu (v_x + u_y).
\end{aligned} \tag{2.1}$$

In equation (2.1), u and v are the horizontal and vertical velocities, respectively, and τ_{ij} are the components of the stress tensor. The elastic parameters are the density ρ and the Lamé constants λ and μ. The compressional and shear wave speeds, C_p and C_s, are given by

$$\begin{aligned}
C_p^2 &= (\lambda + 2\mu)/\rho \\
C_s^2 &= \mu/\rho
\end{aligned} \tag{2.2}$$

and $C_p > C_s$.

For seismic problems, one finds that one can take $C_p/C_s = \sqrt{3}$, see[4] for a detailed discussion of this. As a result of this, it follows that the shear wavelengths are about 60 percent smaller than the compressional wavelengths. The spatial resolution requirements, therefore, must be based on the shorter shear wavelengths. There may also exist interface and surface waves whose wavelengths typically are smaller than the shear wave lengths. Although in some applications these interface and surface waves are not considered important, nevertheless, it is necessary to sufficiently resolve these waves to prevent a spurious transfer of energy into other wave modes. We also do not want numerical dispersion for these waves to interfer with the generation and interpretation of the waves of interest. This puts further constraints on the spatial resolution requirements.

Equation (2.1) can be written in vector form as

$$W_t = AW_x + BW_y \tag{2.3}$$

where $W = (u, v, \tau_{11}, \tau_{22}, \tau_{12})^T$, and the matrices A and B consist of the coefficients of equation (2.1).

The numerical method is based on equation (2.3). Equation (2.3) can be put into divergence-free form, the details are in[4].

3. Model Problems

Next, I describe two model problems used in comparing the various machines. The first problem referred to as the large problem consists of Rayleigh wave scattering from a fluid-elastic interface. The physical domain is shown in Figure 1. This problem was run on all the machines given here. A second problem, the small problem, consists of scattering from three layers of differing materials. This problem was used to compare some performance issues on the Alliant FX/8 and the Cray X-MP. The physical domain for this second problem is shown in Figure 2.

The domain of definition for the large problem is

$$0 \le x \le L_1; \ -L_2 \le y \le 0 . \tag{3.1}$$

For purposes of this example, L_1=2100 feet and L_2=900 feet. In both the elastic and acoustic region, I use equations (2.1). However, in the acoustic region the shear modulus is set to zero, i.e. C_s=0.

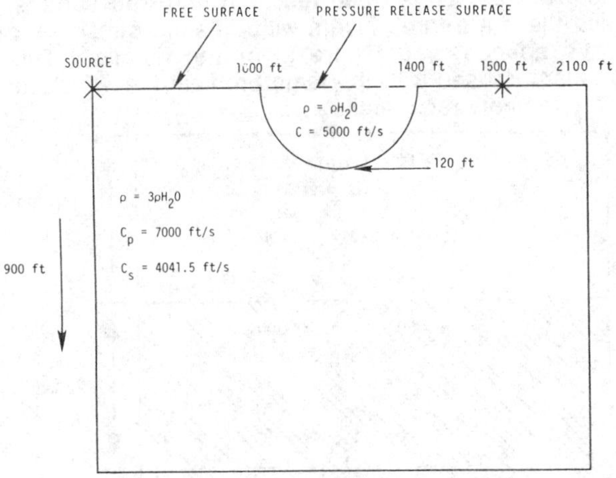

Figure 1. The physical domain for the large problem.

There is one physical boundary (y=0) and three artificial boundaries along which boundary conditions must be prescribed. Along the physical boundary, y=0, we apply a free surface boundary condition ($\tau_{12}=\tau_{22}=0$) over the elastic medium and a pressure release boundary condition ($\tau_{11}=\tau_{22}=0$) over the fluid.

In addition to the physical boundary, on the three artificial boundaries, x=0, x=L_1, and y=-L_2, appropriate absorbing boundary conditions are imposed. Based on a one-dimensional analysis, characterisitic equations can be derived. We impose the boundary condition that the incoming characteristic variable is zero. Using the first-order system (2.1), this condition becomes a Dirichlet condition. This is somewhat of a simplification of the absorbing boundary conditions but suffices for the numerical solution of the problem. For further discussion on the appropriateness of these boundary conditions we refer to[4].

A source function needs to be impose. We take a surface line source, i.e.

$$\tau_{22} = f(t)\delta(x) \tag{3.2}$$

on the free surface. The source function f has the form

$$f(t) = -4/\sigma^2(e^{-2(t-t_s)^2/\sigma^2} - e^{-2(t_s/\sigma)^2})(t - t_s). \tag{3.3}$$

The parameters of the source function are σ=0.0017 sec. and the time shift t_s=0.285 sec. The delta function is approxiamted by a discrete function which is zero except at the location of the source and there it is 1/h (h the mesh size). Equations (2.1), (3.2) together with the boundary conditions form our model initial-boundary value problem.

The small problem is similar to the large problem in terms of its definition. Here $L_1=L_2$=700 feet. The source is similarly defined as in equations (3.2) and (3.3). The main difference is that the source and the receivers are buried 200 feet from the free surface. Also there are three layers with differing density and wave speeds, see Figure 2 for the details. This problem is used with the large problem the effects of large memory requirements.

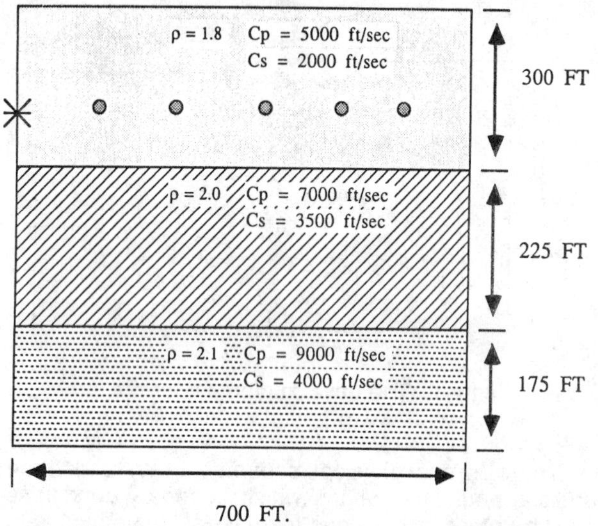

Figure 2. The physical domain for the small problem.

4. Numerical Algorithm

In general terms, I give a brief discussion of the numerical algorithm before turning to the specifics of the vector and parallel implementations of this algorithm. More details are in[4]. This algorithm is based on the method of dimensional splitting. The essence of the numerical method is, the two-dimensional problem (2.3) is updated for one timestep by first solving the equation in the x-direction and then in the y-direction. For the next timestep, the order of the x and y updates is reversed. The solution is advanced from time level n to level n+2 using the formula

$$W^{n+2} = L_xL_yL_yL_xW^n \tag{4.1}$$

where L_x, L_y represent the solutions of the one-dimensional problems

$$W_t = AW_x$$
$$W_t = BW_y, \tag{4.2}$$

respectively. Each of the L_x, and L_y are solved using a MacCormack's predictor-corrector type scheme. I use a scheme that is second-order in time and fourth-order in space (see[2]).

I now describe the parallel and vector implemetations of this numerical algorithm. To advanced the solution of (2.3) one timestep, I solve (2.3) using only the terms involving the x derivatives. I then use these new values for the dependent variables and solve (2.3) using only terms involving y derivatives. This gives the solution at time level n+1. To update to the next time level, I repeat the procedure but reverse the order of the x and y updates. Reversing the order results in a scond-order accurate scheme in time.

Each of the L_x and L_y in (4.1) represents a subroutine in the code. Each of these subroutines consists of a nested set of Fortran Do-Loops two loops deep. The inner loops are the predictor-corrector MacCormick scheme for the problems (4.2). These inner loops vectorize on all the vector machines. The outer loops run over the other spatial dimension not associated with the inner loops. For example, I solve the first equation in (4.2) for each y=constant and all the x updates for each line y=constant can be done independently. As a result of this observation, each subroutine for the L_x and L_y is a candidate for parallelization or multitasking.

Since the parallelization is occurring at the outer loop level, this code is appropriate for parallel execution on the Alliant FX/8 and for microtasking on the Cray X-MP. For a detailed discussion of microtasking this code see[5]. For more information on the differences between macrotasking and microtasking on the Cray X-MP see[6]. For the Alliant FX/8, a brief description of how the compiler parallelizes code is in[7].

5. Some Numerical Results

In this section, I present some numerical results for the elastic wave code of the previous section on the large model problem described in section 3. The acoustic fluid is treated by setting the shear modulus to zero and differencing across the interface.This model problem is designed to demonstrate that the numerical scheme is accurate and stable at a fluid-elastic interface. The dynamics of the model problem consist of the impinging Rayleigh wave generating an interfacial wave which travels along the elastic-fluid interface and a wave that travels throughout the fluid. The slow velocity of the interfacial wave governs the resolution requirements of the problem. At the interface body waves are generated and propogate away from the fluid.

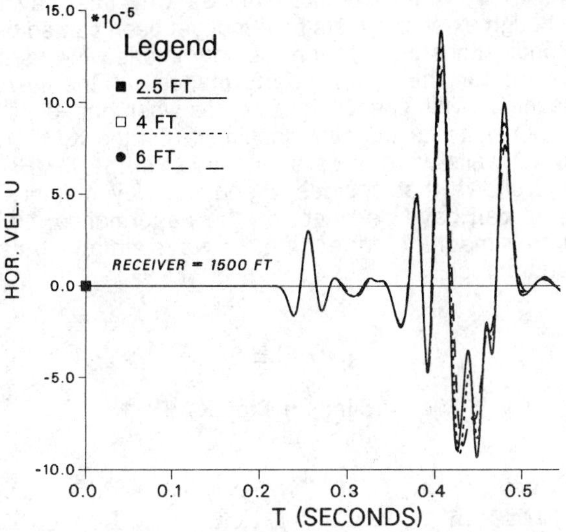

Figure 3.
Comparison of Horizontal Velocity on 3 Different Grids.

Although I do not have an exact solution to compare with, I assess the accuracy of the scheme by examining time traces for different grids. By selecting a receiver location of 1500 ft, I can see the effects of the slow interfacial wave. In Figure 3, I compare the solutions obtained with grid sizes of 6, 4 and 2.5 ft. Further refinement beyond 2.5 ft shows no appreciable difference in the solution and I therefore conclude the solution converges as the grid is refined. A more thorough discussion of the numerical accuracy and stability is contained in[4] and I do not wish to repeat it here.

6. Performance Results

It is interesting to the compare the performance of this code on a variety of supercomputers in order to assess the vector content in our implementation. In Table 1, I compare the CPU time of this code on several different machines, including mainframes with vector facilities, vector processors and parallel/vector processors. I also contrast this with how the exact same problem was solved on the ER&E IBM 3033 AP. It is interesting to note that the large model problem with a grid of 701 x 301 points and a run for 1280 timesteps, required 11 CPU hours on the IBM 3033AP, 12 CPU mintues on a single processor of a (9.5 nsec.) Cray X-MP, 6 CPU minutes on the Amdahl VP 1200 and 3 CPU minutes on 4 processors of a (8.5 nsec) Cray X-MP. Using one of the tools available on the Amdahl machines, the single processor implementation of the code for this model problem was estimated to have 99% vector content.

TABLE 1

Comparison of CPU Time on Various Processors

Machines	CPU Sec.
Alliant FX/8 (1Proc.)	112507.09
IBM 3033AP	39648.00
IBM 3090	12164.00
Convex C1-XP	20906.40
Alliant FX/8 (8Proc.)	16078.62
IBM 3090VF	16025.28
Cray 1-S	1145.65
Amdahl VP 500	778.65
Cray X-MP (1Proc.)	714.90
Amdahl VP 1200	360.00
Cray X-MP (4Proc.)	187.00

Some comments on the IBM 3090VF are in order. Note that this code actually ran longer on the Vector Facility (VF) than on the IBM 3090 without the VF. As mentioned above this code does have high vector content. There is some speculation that either the compiler or the cache were responsible for the problem encountered here. The IBM vectorizing compiler had early on been known to generate less than optimal code through the choice of loops it vectorized in a set of nested loops. Careful inspection of the compiler listing has indicated that the compiler at least vectorized the expected vector loops. The other problem that others have noted has been cache stumbling when the Vector Facility deals with long vectors. The cache stumbling results from the fact that the vectors can not fit in cache and data must be fetched from main memory at the slower access time than the cache. The data structure of this code would for large dimensions lead to cache misses and result in the cache stumbling problem. For a detailed description of both these problems I refer to the book by W. Schonauer[8]. What is interesting here is the code developer must now consider the effects that cache may have on his code and design the data structure appropriately. Since cache misses are hard to monitor, it is difficult to know if infact one has obtained an optimal data structure without extensive testing.

The mini-supercomputers, Alliant FX/8 and Convex C1-XP, and the vector supercomputers, the one processor Crays and the Amdahls, as noted above perform relatively well on this code due to the high vector content in the code. The mini-supercomputers are factor of two or better over the IBM 3033AP. The vector supercomputers range from a factor of fifty to over one hundred times faster than the IBM 3033AP. The Alliant FX/8 one processor run is included for comparison purposes. Its slower clock speed is evident here.

The Convex C1-XP like the IBM 3090 and the Alliant has a cache. However, for vector processing the Convex C1-XP by passes the cache. This gives improved performance for vector codes. However, if the vectors are not unity stride but offset by some constant stride degraded performance occurs. The elasitic wave code has both vectors with unity stride and nonunity constant stride. The subroutines that have unity stride performing essentially the same work as the subroutines with nonunity constant stride ran two to three times faster.

Turning to the parallel and vector processors, some work was involved in order to parallelize this code. For the parallel/vector version of the numerical scheme for the Cray X-MP, the work involved modifying the original implementation to take advantage of microtasking on this machine. The original version of the microtasked code ran on a Cray X-MP/48. This machine has a clock cycle of 9.5 nanoseconds. Also, the original microtasked version of the code used an earlier version of microtasking which used calls rather than directives for the microtasking preprocessor.

One often wonders how much effort must be expended in converting a sequential code to a mutlitasking code. Like vectorizing, conversion to multitasking is code and problem dependent. For my problem, I note that the microtasked version of the code on the Cray X-MP required only 17 lines of Fortran be changed along with the microtasking directives.

In evaluating performance on multiprocessor machines, the speedup or ratio of uniprocessor CPU time to time to execute on N processors should be considered. The efficiency of the processors utilization can then be determined by the ratio of speedup to the number of processors. In Table 2, I give the speedup and efficiency I obtained using the early version of microtasking on the older Cray X-MP. The effficiency gives an indication of the microtasking overhead associated with this implementation of our numerical scheme. As our code also measured MFLOPS (Million Floating Point Operations Per Second), we have included these values in Table 2. I note that the improvement in using four processors with the microtasked code is 3.9 which gives me an efficiency factor of 97.5%. Further note from Table 2 that I obtain a sustained 83 MFLOPS rate on the uniprocessor version and 329 MFLOPS when using four processors.

TABLE 2

Microtasking on Cray X-MP/48
(9.5 nsec Cycle)

Number Processors	CPU Secs	MFLOPS Rate	Speedup Factor	Effcy. Factor
1	756	83	1.0	100.0%
4	191	329	3.9	97.5%

Table 3, contains the results of microtasking our numerical scheme on the newer Cray X-MP/416. I also used a later version of the microtasking library. This newer version uses directives instead of subroutine calls. In addition, the Cray X-MP/416 differs from the Cray X-MP/48 used above in the memory interleaving. The X-MP/48 had 64 way interleaving while the X-MP/416 had only 32 way interleaving. Although extensive tests have not yet been carried out, all indications point to the memory interleaving as the reason for the poorer performance on the newer machine. This speculations comes when one looks at the IO waits for the two machines. On the X-MP/416 the IO waits were twice as many as on the X-MP/48. This shows that besides speed the way memory is setup can have an effect on the performance, i.e. a faster machine does not always imply better performance.

TABLE 3

Microtasking on Cray X-MP/416
(8.5 nsec Cycle)

Number Processors	CPU Secs	MFLOPS Rate	Speedup Factor	Effcy. Factor
1	676	100	1.0	100%
2	336	199	2.0	100%
3	238	298	2.8	95%
4	187	385	3.6	90%

The Alliant FX/8, like the Cray X-MP, is a multiprocessor shared memory machine. The Alliant FX/8 can have up to 8 processors. Table 4 contains the CPU time, speedup factors and the machine efficiency for the large model problem running on various numbers of processors on the Alliant FX/8. Note that when using 4 processors on this problem I have quite good machine efficiency even better than the X-MP. Even with all eight processors the machine efficiency remains high at 87.5%. This correponds closely with that of the Cray X-MP.

The effort involved in multitasking the elastic wave code on the Alliant FX/8 was more than on the Cray X-MP. This is surprising when one considers that the compiler generates the multitasked code. However, the compiler can only make the outer loop of a set of nested loops concurrent if the set of nested loops is relatively simple. In this case, the more complicated nested loops had to be split into two sets of simpler loops. In addition, several one dimensional arrays which were used to store some intermediate values had to be promoted to two dimesnional arrays. The addition of these two dimensional arrays resulted in 30% more storage requirements.

TABLE 4

Multitasking on Alliant FX/8
(8 Processors in Cluster)

Number Processors	CPU Secs	Speedup Factor	Effcy. Factor
1	112507	1.00	100.0%
2	56994	1.97	98.7%
3	38652	2.91	97.0%
4	29820	3.80	94.7%
5	24251	4.64	92.8%
6	20480	5.50	91.6%
7	18073	6.23	88.9%
8	16078	7.00	87.5%

Even though the speedup factors and machine efficiency was high for the large model problem, comparing with the single processor Cray X-MP, the CPU time seemed to be larger than expected. See Table 5 for this comparison. Since the Alliant FX/8 has a cache and given that for the large model problem, the memory requirements were increased, I conjectured that the comparison to the X-MP might be more favorable for a problem requiring less memory. This lead to the formulatiuon of the small model problem described in section 3. In Table 5, one sees the improved ratio between the FX/8 and X-MP for the small problem. This implies that as the problem sizes increase performance falls off. For more information on this phenomena on the Alliant FX/8 see[9].

TABLE 5

Comparison of
Alliant FX/8 and Cray X-MP

Problem Size	FX/8-CPU sec (8-Processors)	X-MP-CPU sec (1-Processor)	Ratio
Small	513.5	81.8	6.3
Large	16078.6	714.9	22.5

Finally, I should note one other phenomena observed while running this small model problem on the Alliant FX/8. This was that when the 8 processor run was compared with the 1 processor run the speedup factor dropped to 5. Although I have not carried out any experiments to investigate this, Hanson[10] has conducted parameter studies where he varies the mesh sizes for a specific problem and observed with smaller meshes his speedups were less than with larger meshes on the FX/8. Further work to understand this phenomena should be carried out.

7. Conclusions

Through an example code, the elastic wave code, I have related several observations that can have implications for performance if ignored by code developers on many high speed computer systems. The dimensional splitting used in this code leads naturally to vector and parallel implementations of the code for high speed computer systems. However, certain hardware and software features can have an adverse effect perfromance as illustrated.

The work presented is not intended to imply that one computer system is better than another. How a particular computer system handles one code is not conclusive of its overall merits. Certainly cost/performance is a factor that needs to be taken into account when judging value of a high speed computer system. No cost/performance is given nor is any implied. The objective here has been to suggest certain hardware and software features that warrant closer scrutiny on the various high speed computer systems presented.

More importantly, the code developer or numerical analysis can nolonger have just a superficial acquaintance with the architecture of the high speed computer system. He must now understand the many different components such as memory access pattern and how they work together. High performance can not be achieved through mere use of compiler options but may require rewriting portions of code in order to fully utilize the machine. One may argue that this is not new. What is important is that with the variety of architectures now available, different components of the architecture, hardware and software, can dramatically effect performance of a particular code. This is particular true as one starts using vector multiprocessors.

8. Acknowledgements

The author wishes to thank M. Booth, C. Grassl and R. Selva of Cray Research Inc. for their assistance in microtasking this code and for showing the author how to efficiently use the Cray X-MP. Further, the author would like to thank the Benchmark Services Group of Cray Research Inc. for providing access to the Cray X-MP's at Mendota Heights.

The author also wishes to acknowledge A. Bayliss for his many helpful discussions and support during the efforts to multitask the elastic wave program.

The author would also like to thank his colleagues in the Mathematics and Computer Science Division at Argonne National Laboratory for their help while the author was visiting Argonne on a Department of Energy Laboratory Technology Exchange Program and also for access to the Advanced Computer Research Facility at Argonne where all the Alliant FX/8 tests were run.

9. References

1. K.E. Jordan, "Perfromance comparison of large-scale scientific computers: scalar mainframes, mainframes with vector facilities, and

supercomputers," Computer, pp. 10-23, March 1987.

2. D. Gottlieb and E. Turkel, "Dissipative two-four method for time dependent problems," Math. Comp. vol. 30, pp. 703-723, 1976.

3. L. A. Maestrello, A. Bayliss, and E. Turkel, "On interaction of a sound impluse with the shear layer of an axisymmetric jet," J. Sound Vib. vol. 74, pp. 281-301, 1981.

4. A. Bayliss, K. E. Jordan, B. J. LeMesurier, and E. Turkel, "A fourth-order accurate finite-difference scheme for the computation of elastic waves," Bul. Seism. Soc. of Am., vol. 76, pp. 1115-1132, August 1986.

5. K. E. Jordan, "On Multitasking of an Elastic Wave Code," in Advances in Computer Methods for Partial Differential Equations VI, R. Vichnevetsky and R. S. Stepleman (eds.), IMACS, New Brunswick, N.J., pp. 220-224, June 1987.

6. Multitasking user guide, Cray Computer Systems Technical Note, Publication No. SN-0222, Cray Research Inc., March 1986.

7. Alliant FX/Series Product Summary, Alliant Computer Systems Corporation, Acton MA, June 1985.

8. W. Schonauer, **Scientific Computing on Vector Computers**, private communication.

9. W. Abu-Sufah and A. D. Maloney, "Vector Processing on the Allinat FX/8 Multiprocessor," in Proccedings of 1986 Int. Conf. Par. Processing, K. Hwang et al., eds., IEEE Computer Society Press, Piscataway, N.J., pp. 559-566, 1986.

10. F. B. Hanson, "Computational Dynamic Programming for Stochatic Optimal Control on a Vector Multiprocessor," private communication.

Programming and Performance on a Cube-Connected Architecture

John L. Gustafson and Gary R. Montry

Sandia National Laboratories
Albuquerque, NM 87185

ABSTRACT

The first generation of commercial hypercube[6] multiprocessors is now over two years old. We have discovered the weaknesses of these machines and learned to program around them; also, we have discovered their strengths and utilized them to our advantage. This discussion will focus on the strengths and weaknesses of this first generation of machines and their effects on meaningful software development and implementation. In particular, we will address these issues with respect to hypercubes of *a thousand or more* processing elements.

INTRODUCTION

The issues discussed here pertain to the authors' experiences with a limited class of application programs: fluid dynamics, factoring large numbers, structural analysis, sieving prime numbers, and electrostatics. Hence, these discussions only represent a subset of the vast range of applications which might be put on a large computer. However, improvements in architecture suggested by some classes of applications will generally improve performance of the computer over a much wider range of programs. The observations in this paper are for problems that are

- Fairly regular in space decomposition
- Explicit in stepping through time or iterations
- Decomposable with static methods
- Parallel enough for a 1024-processor ensemble

The large number of processors forces one to consider *every sequential aspect* of a run, including loading the program and viewing results. Unlike systems with, say, ten or fewer processors, the 1024-processor environment is very unforgiving of old-fashioned serial programming habits. Some of the issues presented here stem from the hypercube interconnect; others are the result of massive ensemble parallelism generally.

HYPERCUBES AT SANDIA

Sandia obtained a completely functioning 10-dimensional (1024 processors) hypercube on November 20, 1987. There are also a number of *development systems*, low-order hypercubes based on personal computers, that are compatible with the large system. The Sandia hypercube environment is shown in Figure 1.

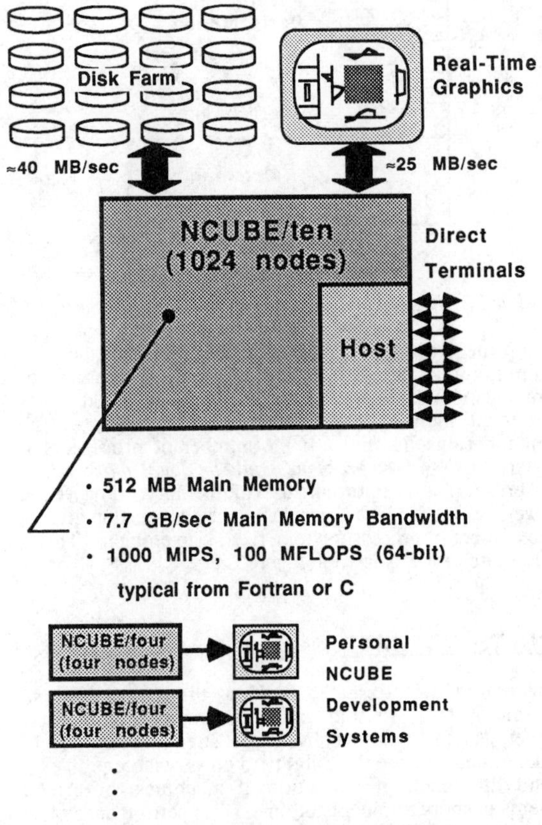

Figure 1. Sandia Hypercube Environment

The NCUBE hypercubes[4] currently use an Intel 80286 host, the same microprocessor used in the IBM® PC-AT; however, the processor does not run in 8088-compatibility mode or under MS-DOS®. Both the large system and the development systems run under a UNIX-style operating system that controls the multitasking and system device resources. The hypercube is accessed from the host operating system just like any other device, via the /dev directory.

The NCUBE processors are proprietary, highly-integrated chips that are compatible with the 80286 host only in that they have the same storage format for floating-point and integer data. The NCUBE node resembles a VAX-11/780® with Floating Point Accelerator, in both architecture and performance. Each node has 512 KBytes of memory, of which 480 KBytes is available for program and data (depending on the size of communication buffers).

THE ENSEMBLE PARADIGM

Large ensembles should be used on large problems. This simple principle is widely ignored in the research community, which tends to seek parallel solutions and evaluate parallel performance for fixed-size problems. The issue is illustrated in Figure 2.

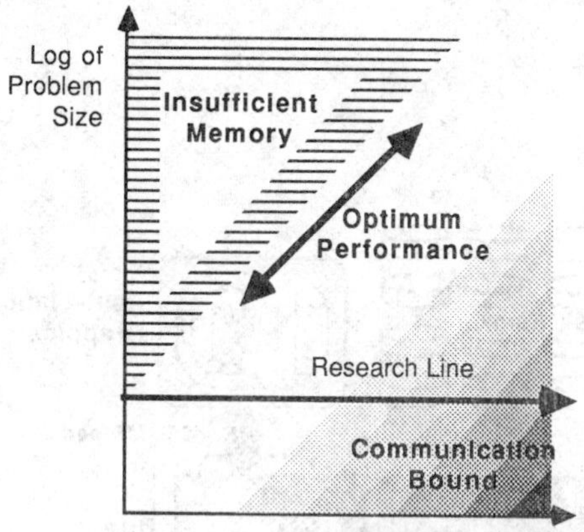

Figure 2. Ensemble Computing Performance Pattern

To keep the arithmetic hardware as busy as possible, one seeks to minimize the percent of time spent in interprocessor communication. This implies that the problem should use as much local memory as possible, to keep most of the communications internal. If the number of processors is doubled, *the size of the problem should be doubled as well,* so as to preserve this optimum use of memory. For years, however, "efficiency" has been defined as the speedup divided by the number of processors, for a fixed-size problem. This is the "Research Line" shown in Figure 2.

RESULTS TO DATE

We recognize the "Research Line" as the region of some academic interest to the computer science community; however, as a practical matter, the real strength in massively parallel systems lies in their ability to do very large problems beyond the reach of conventional machines, not fixed problems in shorter amounts of time. This performance view is illustrated by the "Optimum Performance" line in Figure 2.

Along the "Research Line," we have recently achieved the following speedups over the serial algorithms on four applications of importance to Sandia, using all 1024 processors:

Beam Bending (Finite Elements) using Conjugate Gradients	**>350x**
Nonlinear Second-Order CFD using the Flux-Corrected Transport method	**>450x**
Acoustic Wave Propagation using Explicit Finite Differences	**>600x**
Finding All Primes in [1, 2×10^6] using the Sieve of Eratosthenes	**>600x**

Our initial results along the "Optimum Performance" line have been even more encouraging. The conjugate gradient solver, when the number of degrees of freedom is scaled to the number of processors, essentially runs a thousand times faster on a thousand nodes compared to a hypothetical single processor with memory large enough to run such a problem. We refer to this as "scaled speedup."

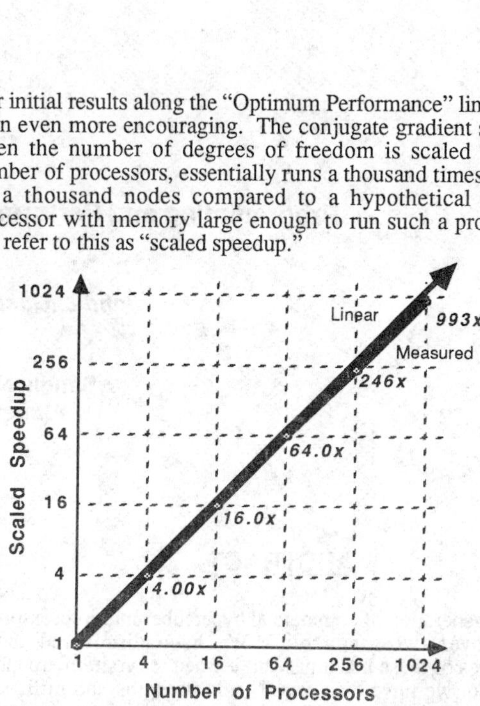

Figure 3. Scaled Performance — Structural Analysis

Similar performance curves have been obtained for the Wave Equation and Computational Fluid Dynamics.

PROGRAM LOADING

One must attend to *program loading* on distributed memory machines with a little more diligence than on their shared memory counterparts. A hypercube with only a single data path between the mass storage device and the ensemble of processors must ensure that the program load uses much of the available bandwidth between the host and the hypercube. For example, a modest-sized executable file of 100 KBytes loaded into the full 1024 processors requires the (redundant) loading of more than 100 MBytes of data. In order to accomplish this feat gracefully, one *must* take advantage of the fact that a binary spanning tree (requiring time of order $\log_2 N$, where N is the number of processors) is a subset of the hypercube interconnect[5]. The difference between an order N and an order $\log_2 N$ algorithm is a factor of 100 on our hypercube! Loading from the host, one processor at a time, takes several minutes on our system. This worst-case situation need only occur when a different program is loaded onto every node, a rare situation indeed. Most of our applications use exactly the same program on every node, permitting a logarithmic fan-out as shown in Figure 4 for a set of 16 processors labeled 0000 to 1111.

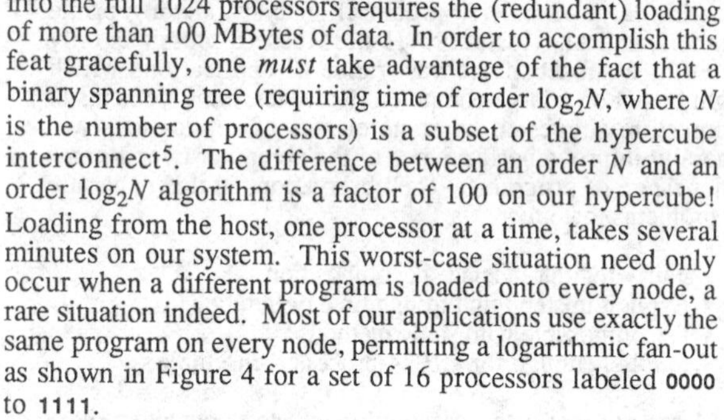

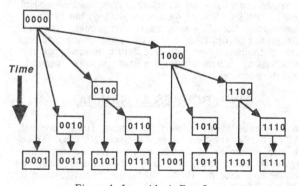

Figure 4. Logarithmic Fan-Out

This approach makes it possible to load programs into the entire hypercube in a few seconds.

The program load time for parallel processors might not seem like an important factor. But it is not unusual to want to run a job that involves only 10 billion floating-point operations, which would take about a minute and a half on the hypercube for the actual computation. It is clearly a waste of resource if the program load takes twice as long as its execution.

In addition to loading, the logarithmic communication concept is necessary for a variety of functions during program execution. For example, if an inner product must be computed across all processors, or a maximum element found, or a vote must be taken as to whether a technique has converged to a solution, or answers consolidated for output, then there is an order N technique that burdens the host or an order $\log_2 N$ technique that uses the nodes with a hundred times more parallelism. This is an important concept for multi-processors generally; even if the application appears to need only toroidal interconnect, massive parallelism will be degraded unless the ensemble has a fast binary (or higher) tree in its interconnect.

LANGUAGE

The NCUBE has Fortran, C, and assembler, for both the 80286 host and the processing nodes. In this first-generation machine, the compilers are obviously less mature regarding optimization than on a machine such as a VAX, so there is still reason to code critical sections of a program in assembler for improved performance. Many excellent features of the NCUBE processor (automatic constant-stride addressing, repeat-and-decrement instructions, floating-point hardware for argument reduction) remain inaccessible from C and Fortran at the time of writing.

Programming the ensemble involves writing *two* programs: one for the host and (at least) one for the hypercube. [If sophisticated graphics output is desired at high speed, one must also write a program for nodes dedicated to graphics I/O… or load existing graphics routines.] The program for the host, ideally, does little more than fetch the program and initial data from disk, load it onto the nodes, receive results, and display or store those results. Even serial parts of the application are best handled by the nodes rather than the host, since an individual node is about five times faster than the host microprocessor. The host is simply the hub of all the devices in the system. The node program, which need not be in the same language as the host program, resembles the non-I/O part of a conventional application program.

Communication between nodes is handled with simple subroutine calls. It is this point that causes the greatest confusion about what it means to program a hypercube. There is no need to extend the language syntax itself. Hypercube communication uses a half-dozen calls for sending and receiving messages that are quickly learned and in no way revolutionize the language.

DEBUGGING

While developing programs on hypercubes, the most common mode of failure is that the system deadlocks as the result of failed interprocessor communication. There is no automatic reporting of the cause of the lockup. It is therefore absolutely essential that the system possess a debugger capable of interrogating the ensemble either globally or on a node-by-node basis. This is probably the most important piece of support software that a vendor can supply.

COMMUNICATIONS

There are several shortcomings in the communication protocols of the first generation of cubes that need to be addressed in the next generation.

The first of these weaknesses is unnecessary overhead, not just for message startup, but *during the actual transfer*. For a typical domain-decomposition problem, a message is *quadruple-buffered*, which cuts communication speed by several times. If a two-dimensional subdomain is stored in typical lexicographic order, then either the left-right or the top-bottom edges will not be stored contiguously. The current generation of hypercubes requires that a message be in a contiguous block of memory, so the edge must first be copied to a contiguous buffer before it is sent. The operating system call to write the message does *not* move that buffer, but first copies it to a dedicated area in system memory, and then returns control to the program. The reason for this is that one might otherwise alter the data while it is being sent, resulting in hard-to-detect and hard-to-repeat bugs. On the receiving end, the process is duplicated in reverse (See Figure 5).

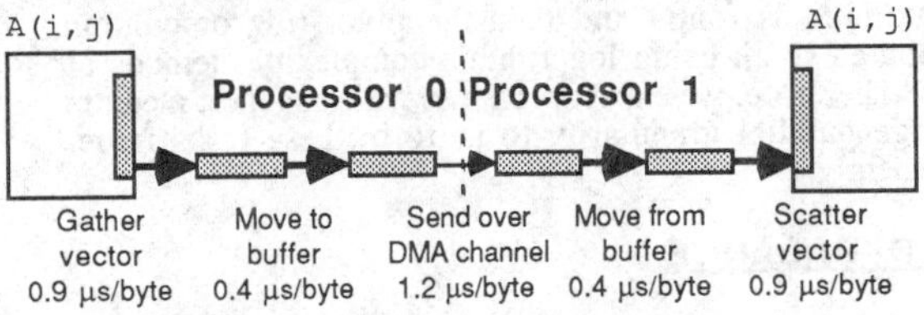

Figure 5. Quadruple Buffering

The gathering and scattering of the vector can be eliminated with hardware/software support for constant-stride DMA. The move to and from system buffers should be an option that can be disabled for higher performance once bugs have been otherwise eliminated.

A related communications efficiency issue is the availability of truly overlapped internode communications. The hooks for non-blocking reads are available in the software for these machines, but have yet to be fully implemented. The buffering shown in Figure 5 also means that at least half the time of the communication is spent using the processor to do memory-to-memory moves, and hence it is very difficult to get more than two DMA writes operating simultaneously. It is possible in principle for hypercubes to *completely overlap* their communication with the computation for most applications, which will further improve efficiency for all sizes of hypercubes. Note that if a separate processing entity (such as a simple finite-state machine) is provided to handle the communication, then no communication cost is incurred by the node processor itself except for the subroutine call. This paradigm appears to us to be highly desirable for cubes with thousands of processing elements.

The current generation of hypercubes is notorious for the relatively large startup times of message transmission. Much of this is caused by handshaking and routing protocol. We look forward to leaner protocol that recognizes nearest-neighbor connections only, and to hardware assistance in reducing message startup time. The high latency forces a programming style, at least in Fortran, that is somewhat opaque… using `EQUIVALENCE` statements to consolidate data wherever possible, changing the order of algorithm steps to batch messages together, and similar tricks.

ALGORITHM ISSUES

Large ensemble parallel processors greatly extend the applicable range of iterative methods and explicit methods for the solution of PDE's. Generally, explicit application programs can be written that require only one global operation per timestep. The remaining interprocessor communications can be reduced to nearest-neighbor data exchanges within the hypercube. The number of data exchanges between adjacent nodes can be greatly reduced by data structure rearrangement (see the preceding section). Explicit methods are local, load-balanced, low in synchronization and communication cost, and clearly the method of choice for the first generation of hypercubes.

The first generation of hypercube multiprocessors does not seem well-suited to *direct solvers* that arise, for example, in discretized representations of partial differential equations[1]. Direct inversion of matrices appears to require a large ratio of off-node communication to computation, regardless of the algorithm used. The direct solvers in use today are rife with sequential bottlenecks and non-local communication patterns. For example, the pivoting step makes all processors wait while a maximum is found and then the pivot row or column distributed (both using logarithmic complexity methods at best). Therefore, we expect machines which support medium to large parallel granularity to perform these tasks rather inefficiently.

LOAD BALANCE

Load balance on *shared memory* multiprocessors can be maintained by static decomposition of the computational domain or via the dynamic method of "self-scheduling," where units of work are parcelled out centrally on a first-come, first-served basis.

There is no reason that dynamic self-scheduling cannot be used on distributed memory machines, except that the global communication implied by a central scheduling entity is not efficient on a machine with high interprocessor message latency (on the order of a millisecond). As a result, research into the decomposition of irregular domains has focused on new techniques for determining optimized *static* decomposition of the problem. These techniqes include simulated annealing[3] and neural networks[7]; they are typically too expensive to use at run time.

The techniques necessary to efficiently load balance problems with data-dependent computational and communication loads, such as adaptive grids and Lagrangian (moving grid) dynamics, are still open for intensive research.

SUMMARY

The first generation of hypercubes has proved to be useful on a selected set of applications when more than 1000 processors are used. However, our work on large hypercubes illustrates deficiencies in the hardware and software that suggest improvements for the next generation. None of these deficiencies are inherent in the hypercube approach or technically difficult to correct; they simply require attention.

REFERENCES

(1) Benner, R.E., Montry, G.R., and Weigand, G.C., "Concurrent Multifrontal Methods: Shared Memory, Cache, and Frontwidth Issues," *Int. Journal of Supercomputer Applications,*, Vol 1, No.3, Fall 1987, pp.26-44

(2) Fox, G.C., *et. al., Solving Problems on Concurrent Processors*, 1987, (in publication), California Institute of Technology, 1987

(3) Laarhoven, J.M., and Aarts, E.H.C., *Simulated Annealing: Theory and Application*, D. Reidel Publishing Co. 1987.

(4) *NCUBE Users Handbook*, NCUBE Corporation, Beaverton, Oregon, 1987.

(5) Saad, Y., and Schultz, M.H., "Topological Properties of Hypercubes," *Research Report YALEU/DCS/RR-389*, June 1985.

(6) Seitz, C., "The Cosmic Cube," *Communications of the ACM*, January 1985, Vol.28, #1, pp.22-33

(7) Williams, R.E., "Optimization by Computational Neural Nets," CALT-68-1409, California Institute of Technology, September, 1986

Experiences with the BBN Butterfly

John M. Mellor-Crummey*

University of Rochester

Abstract

The BBN Butterfly™ Parallel Processor is a shared-memory multiprocessor built around a scalable high-bandwidth switching network. The architecture is flexible and efficiently supports many different models of computation. While the Butterfly provides a high performance testbed for parallel processing research, it lacks a file system and a strong development environment making program development difficult.

1 Introduction

The BBN Butterfly™ Parallel Processor was developed by BBN Laboratories, Inc. in the mid 1970's for the DARPA Voice Funnel project. Since 1984, the Computer Science Department at the University of Rochester has acquired 3, 16, and 120 processor Butterflys. These machines have served as a testbed for parallel processing research. This research ranges over a diverse set of topics including computer vision, operating systems, concurrent data structures, artificial intelligence, parallel programming languages, and development of a parallel programming environment. This paper is a synthesis of our collective experience using the Butterfly at the University of Rochester over the past $3\frac{1}{2}$ years.

2 Hardware/Software Overview

2.1 Butterfly Hardware

The Butterfly Parallel Processor is a MIMD shared-memory multiprocessor which consists of up to 256 processing nodes connected by a scalable radix 4 FFT switching network. All of the memory in the system resides on individual nodes, but any processor can address any memory through the high-bandwidth switching network. In the absence of contention for a particular memory module, all processors can simultaneously invoke an operation on different remote memory modules. In contrast, bus-based machines serialize access to shared memory.

Currently there are three versions of the Butterfly architecture. For clarity, we distinguish these machines as the B/68000, the B/68020 and the B/Plus. Each B/68000 node is built around an 8 MHz MC68000 that uses 24 bit virtual addresses. An AMD2901-based bit-slice co-processor interprets every memory reference issued by the 68000 and is used to communicate with other nodes across the switching network. The B/68020 is identical to the B/68000, except that the 68000 is replaced by a daughter board containing a MC68020 and a 68881 floating point co-processor. Each processing node can acommodate a maximum of 4MB of RAM. A remote memory reference (read) on the B/68000 and B/68020 takes about 4 *us.*, roughly 5 times as long as a local reference.

The Butterfly Plus (B/Plus), a second-generation Butterfly architecture announced in the fall of 1987, is built around a Motorola chipset consisting of a 68020 processor, a 68881 floating point co-processor, and a 68851 memory management chip. Unlike the other two machines, the 2901 co-processor is not on the path between the processor and the local memory; instead, it is used solely as an interface to I/O and the switching network. Each processing node can accomodate 4MB of RAM, expandable to 16MB with the arrival of 1Mb DRAMs. Individual nodes of the B/Plus are faster than those of the original B/68000: local memory accesses are four times as fast; remote memory accesses are twice as fast. Doubling the ratio of time required for remote vs. local memory references increases the penalty for using remote references. This will encourage programmers to carefully limit their use of remote references in order to achieve optimum performance.

Most of the experience at Rochester is with the B/68000, the earliest of the Butterfly machines. Many of the experiences generalize to the new machine, but our experiences must be examined in their proper context.

2.2 Chrysalis Operating System

Chrysalis [2], the Butterfly operating system, consists largely of a protected subroutine library that implements operations on a set of primitive data types including synchronization events, atomic queues, atomic short integers, shared memory segments, and a global name table. Objects of these types

*The research reported here was supported by U.S. Army ETL contract no. DACA76-C-001, NSF CER grant no. DCR-8320136, and NSF grant no. CCR-8704492.

can be shared among all processes executing on the machine. Chrysalis provides low-level operations on these data types; many of these operations rely on microcode support. These primitives provide a general framework for building efficient high-level communication protocols and software systems.

Chrysalis lacks a file system, so the B/68000 and B/68020 are currently usable only as back-end machines. However, the B/Plus is intended to run Mach [1] as well as Chrysalis. Mach will provide a file system enabling the B/Plus to run as a stand-alone machine.

2.3 Uniform System

The Uniform System (US) is a runtime library that supports a user view of the Butterfly architecture consisting of lightweight tasks and shared memory. The US creates a manager process on each node involved in the computation that is responsible for allocating the processor to a series of lightweight tasks which operate on the shared memory. Usually a task is as a small procedure to be applied to a subset of the shared memory. Each task is represented as a pair of indices and a procedure to be called.

3 Experiences

3.1 Memory Architecture

While the Butterfly currently supports a maximum of 1GB of memory for 256 nodes, on both the B/68000 and B/68020, the virtual address space of each process is limited to 16MB by the memory architecture. Using data areas larger than 16MB requires processes to explicitly swap segments in and out of their own address space. The B/Plus provides processes with a 32-bit virtual address space and the potential to address 4GB of memory. This additional capability facilitates construction of applications that manipulate large amounts of data using a shared memory model of computation.

There is no support for virtual memory on the B/68000 or B/68020 machines. All processes and shared data structures on these machines must reside in physical memory. The B/Plus removes this restriction by using 68020 processors with restartable instructions and an MMU enabling the B/Plus to support virtual memory with demand paging.

3.2 Using Chrysalis

Chrysalis's use of the memory architecture on the B/68000 and B/68020 precludes a high degree of multi-programming with a high degree of sharing on a node. In these machines, the hardware provides segment address mapping registers which are used for address translation. These mapping registers are a critical resource under Chrysalis. Each process receives a static allocation of 8–248 mapping registers at process creation. Since only 512 such registers exist on each B/68000 and B/68020 node, Chrysalis's static allocation strategy severely limits the degree of multi-programming. Also, since the range of virtual addresses available to each process is directly proportional to the number of mapping registers allocated to it, the amount of data that may be shared between processes on the same node is inversely proportional to the number of processes on that node that may share it.

The low-level mechanisms provided by Chrysalis enable nearly total control of the hardware and support construction of efficient software systems. Efficient implementations of Lynx (a language for programming distributed applications) [14], Modula-2 [13], and SMP (a run-time library supporting message passing) [9] have been developed for the Butterfly. Protection has been sacrificed for performance in Chrysalis; however, this is appropriate since the primary purpose of parallel machines is to provide better performance. While the flexibility provided by the low-level primitives is clearly an asset, the lack of higher level abstractions makes the Chrysalis environment cumbersome for programmers to use directly.

In our experience, Chrysalis has not proven to be a particularly stable base for program development. Chrysalis has been vulnerable to program errors and resource limitations; bugs sometimes manifest themselves in the form of processor node crashes or other mysterious symptoms.

3.3 Using the US Shared Memory Model

Programmers find building programs using the US much easier than building them from scratch, regardless of how well the application fits the shared memory model. A weakness of the US is that it treats shared memory as having uniform access time and does not encourage the programmer to exploit locality. To write efficient programs using the US, a programmer must recognize the non-uniform nature of the memory (local memory access is substantially faster than remote access) and use block transfers to cache shared data on the local node during computations, copying it back after the computation is complete. Block transfers amortize overhead associated with remote references and can significantly improve performance.

3.4 Using a Message Passing Model

A study of message passing on the Butterfly has shown that the shared memory model of computation is not the only model suitable for the Butterfly [8]. The particular model of computation in use is less important than how well it is matched to the application. Also, the performance of an application depends not only on the efficiency of the underlying communication, but to the extent to which the underlying model encourages or discourages communication. In particular, an implementation based on very efficient communication (*e.g.*, shared memory) may perform worse than one based on a less efficient mechanism (*e.g.*, message passing), if such efficiency encourages too much communication. An example of this principle studied by LeBlanc [8] is a US Gaussian elimination program in which each task copies a row into local memory, eliminates an entry and copies the resulting row back into shared memory. Using a message passing model exploits locality and avoids one of these copies since each row to be modified is local to some process in the computation. The SMP message passing system is an outgrowth of these studies.

3.5 Using the Atomic Primitives

The Butterfly hardware provides several atomic primitives for communication and synchronization. On the B/68000 and B/68020, the read-modify-write primitive *atomic-clear-then-add* can be applied to any 16-bit word with various arguments to provide *fetch-and-add*, *fetch-and-ior*, *fetch-and-and*, and *fetch-and-store*. These primitives are synchronous; this avoids shared memory consistency problems present in systems that use pipelining and delayed writeback to update shared memory.

One of the primary functions of these primitives is to facilitate construction of concurrent data structures for sharing information among cooperating processes. Such data structures are of considerable importance for programs targeted to parallel architectures. Several concurrent data structures have been developed at Rochester with the intent to implement them on the Butterfly [6,10].

The Butterfly's atomic primitives provide only limited support for building concurrent data structures. *Fetch-and-ior* can be used as *test-and-set* to provide critical sections. *Fetch-and-add* can be used to regulate access to bounded length static data structures (*i.e.*, providing indices for entries in a ring buffer). Dynamic data structures require pointer manipulation. Since pointers on the B/68000 and B/68020 use 24-bit addresses, the 16-bit atomic primitives are inadequate for efficient atomic manipulation of pointers. Operations manipulating pointers require critical sections to provide atomicity. The B/Plus provides 32-bit atomic operations that enable efficient pointer manipulation, facilitating construction of concurrent data structures.

3.6 Probing the Internals

The Butterfly is an open architecture about which BBN has made available extensive information. Systems researchers can use this information to experiment with new operating systems and communication strategies. At the University of Rochester five people developed a prototype of Elmwood, an RPC based operating system for the Butterfly, over the course of a single term [11]. Another project is currently under way to develop Psyche [15], a general-purpose operating system for shared-memory multiprocessors. Without the availability of low-level details about the hardware, development of both of these systems would have been impossible.

3.7 Ease of Programming

Programming the Butterfly has proven to be a difficult task. The low-level interface provided by the operating system requires programs to manage a considerable amount of detail even to perform simple tasks such as process creation. The lack of a good development environment makes program development difficult. Chrysalis uses catch/throw style exception handling. Often, obscure faults propogate back to the user from the operating system requiring one to delve into operating system source code to determine the root of the error.

The lack of a good subroutine library for parallel programming and library implementations of abstract data types (*i.e.*, parallel queues, sets) has made development of individual applications more difficult.

Several programming packages now exist for the Butterfly including Lynx, SMP, and the Uniform System. While these packages simplify the task of programming the Butterfly, often they are not used in practice for developing performance critical applications as they don't provide the control necessary to achieve high performance.

One common difficulty is that all stages of a problem solution do not fit well into a single computational model. Currently, all the programming environments available for the Butterfly support a single model of computation, which severely restricts the choice of algorithms for the problem solution. In short, the current programming environments do not reflect the underlying flexibility of the architecture.

3.8 Performance

The Butterfly has proven to be a unique resource for investigating algorithm performance. In our experience, many parallelization issues do not show up when using less than 64 processors.

Although the Butterfly provides a large degree of parallelism, the lack of floating point hardware on the B/68000 has proven crippling for achieving high performance on scientific computations. On a series of benchmark programs developed to study image processing on parallel architectures [3,12], the B/68000 performed relatively poorly against fast sequential machines due to the lack of floating point support and the lack of a hardware integer multiply instruction. Floating point hardware was added to the B/68020 and B/Plus to correct this deficiency.

Applications that do not use floating point perform well after a substantial investment of effort in parallelizing the computations [4,5,7]. The University of Rochester Connectionist Simulator [7], a simulator for neural-like computational units, benefits both from the large memory and from the availability of many processors to run simulations. A sample network with 100,000 units, each unit receiving input from 30 randomly chosen units, was built using memory distributed over 100 nodes.[1] Sequentially building the network took 2.85 hours. Building the same network in parallel using 100 processors took 56 seconds. This better than linear speedup is due to concurrency, and data locality. In tests executing a single computational step of a network, it was found that

[1]It is necessary to distribute the network across the nodes since the network requires more memory than available on a single node.

90 processors could provide the effective performance of between 70 and 81 processors, depending on how much computation was required to compute the new output for each unit. The higher the ratio of computation to communication, the greater the effective speedup.

In carefully coded applications, memory and switch contention does not pose a serious problem. Consider the results using a global name table implemented for the Connectionist Simulator. A table containing 90,000 names was distributed over 90 processors. It took a single processor 401 seconds to look up all 90,000 names with all other processors idle. When 90 processors simultaneously looked up 90,000 names each (the names were generated in a different order for each processor so no two processors were looking up the same name at the same time), the total lookup time was 409 seconds. Surprisingly, the intense switch traffic generated by this test caused less than a 2% increase in the running time.

4 Summary

At the University of Rochester we have become "wizards" with the Butterfly, knowledgeable about many of the internal details of the hardware and the Chrysalis operating system. For us, the choice of the Butterfly architecture was good. The B/68000 and B/68020 have served us well as research machines and their flexibility to handle a wide range of applications has proved a significant asset. However, in order to program the machine, it is necessary to understand many low-level details about it. Most end users will find this unsatisfactory. The B/Plus retains the flexibility of the earlier machines while correcting many aspects of the design that have made the B/68000 and B/68020 so difficult to program. This, along with the introduction of the Mach operating system which provides a substantially improved development environment, a file system and virtual memory support, makes the B/Plus architecture substantially more attractive than the B/68000 and B/68020 as a system for both research and applications development.

Acknowledgements

Many thanks to Liudvikas Bukys, Alan Cox, Lawrence Crowl, Peter Dibble, Tom LeBlanc, Brian Marsh and Michael Scott who provided input for this paper. Many of the experiences presented here have been distilled from the University of Rochester Butterfly Project Report series, and I gratefully acknowledge the contribution of their authors.

References

[1] M. Accetta et al. Mach: a new kernel foundation for unix development. In *Proceedings of the Summer 1986 USENIX Technical Conference and Exhibition*, Pittsburgh, PA, June 1986.

[2] BBN. *Chrysalis Programmer's Manual.* BBN Laboratories, Cambridge, Massachusetts, June 1985.

[3] C. Brown et al. *DARPA Parallel Architecture Benchmark Study.* BPR 13, Department of Computer Science, University of Rochester, Oct. 1986.

[4] L. Bukys. *Connected Component Labeling and Border Following on the BBN Butterfly Parallel Processor.* BPR 11, Department of Computer Science, University of Rochester, Oct. 1986.

[5] J. Costanzo, L. Crowl, L. Sanchis, and M. Srinivas. *Subgraph Isomorphism on the BBN Butterfly Multiprocessor.* BPR 14, Department of Computer Science, University of Rochester, Oct. 1986.

[6] C. Ellis and T. Olson. Parallel first fit memory allocation. In *Proceedings of the 1987 International Conference on Parallel Processing*, pages 502–511, Aug. 1987.

[7] M. Fanty. *A Connectionist Simulator for the Butterfly.* TR 164, Department of Computer Science, University of Rochester, Jan. 1986.

[8] T. LeBlanc. Shared memory versus message-passing in a tightly-coupled multiprocessor: a case study. In *Proceedings of the 1986 International Conference on Parallel Processing*, pages 463–466, Aug. 1986.

[9] T. LeBlanc, N. Gafter, and T. Ohkami. *SMP: A Message-Based Programming Environment for the BBN Butterfly.* BPR 8, Department of Computer Science, University of Rochester, July 1986.

[10] J. Mellor-Crummey. *Concurrent Queues: Practical Fetch-and-Φ Algorithms.* TR 229, Department of Computer Science, University of Rochester, Nov. 1987.

[11] J. Mellor-Crummey, T. LeBlanc, L. Crowl, N. Gafter, and P. Dibble. *Elmwood – An Object-Oriented Multiprocessor Operating System.* BPR 20, Department of Computer Science, University of Rochester, Sept. 1987.

[12] T. Olson. *Finding Lines with the Hough Transform on the BBN Butterfly Parallel Processor.* BPR 10, Department of Computer Science, University of Rochester, Sept. 1986.

[13] T. Olson. *Modula-2 on the BBN Butterfly Parallel Processor.* BPR 4, Department of Computer Science, University of Rochester, Jan. 1986.

[14] M. Scott. *LYNX Reference Manual.* BPR 7, Department of Computer Science, University of Rochester, March 1986.

[15] M. Scott and T. LeBlanc. *Psyche: A General-Purpose Operating System for Shared-Memory Multiprocessors.* BPR 19, Department of Computer Science, University of Rochester, July 1987.

Mini-Supercomputers

Chair: K. Miura

Cydra™ 5 Directed Dataflow Architecture

Dr. B. Ramakrishna Rau

CYDROME Inc.
1589 Centre Pointe Dr.
Milpitas, CA 95035

ABSTRACT

CYDROME™ has merged several innovative technologies into a balanced and functionally complete mini-supercomputer called the CYDRA™ 5 Departmental Supercomputer:

- Directed Dataflow™ (Cydrome proprietary architecture)
- Compiler optimizing technology
- High-speed memory with guaranteed bandwidth
- Tightly integrated multiple optimized processors
- Parallel processing
- Parallelized UNIX® compatible operating system.

The Cydra 5 makes extensive use of industry standards, such as AT&T UNIX System V.3, ANSI FORTRAN 77, and the IEEE 754 floating point standard, to take advantage of customers' investments in applications software. In addition, the open architecture of the Cydra 5, including the use of the VME bus, makes it an attractive platform for systems integrators. Most important, the sophistication of the technology enables Cydrome to present customers with a very simple and familiar user interface.

INTRODUCTION

The building and testing of prototypes is as important to the engineer's job as the conducting of experiments is to the scientist's work. Also common to both activities are the high costs in time and money. Hence, computer simulations, which provide much faster turnaround and dramatically lower cost, have triggered a revolution in science and engineering.

The extremely visible success of computer simulations in such fields as computer-aided design has validated the use of this technique in engineering and science. As confidence in computer simulation has increased, so has dependence on it. Larger problems are being tackled and at a finer level of detail. The net result is a sharp increase in the need for computing power. Users who were formerly content with their departmental minicomputer now find it quite inadequate.

The architecture of the Cydra 5 Numeric Processor and the compiler technology that goes hand-in-hand with it, as well as the Cydra 5 system architecture, provide a complete solution to user needs. The chief virtue of this combination is its ability to excel with a broad spectrum of computations. It enables users to achieve large performance gains over superminis without re-engineering their existing application software and algorithms.

ARCHITECTURAL ALTERNATIVES FOR HIGH PERFORMANCE

The Nature of Parallelism in Applications

Any serious attempt at high performance computing involves the concurrent execution of multiple operations. The methods of achieving concurrent execution can be classified as fine-grained parallelism and coarse-grained parallelism.

Fine-grained parallelism is the simultaneous execution of multiple primitive operations such as additions and multiplications. This type of parallelism is usually exploited at a low level of operations in a piece of straight-line code or across the multiple iterations of an innermost loop. It is the form of parallelism used by uniprocessor architectures, such as vector and sequential processors, which overlap the execution of successive operations.

Coarse-grained parallelism refers to larger computations run in parallel and can be exploited by running multiple outer loop iterations or subroutine invocations in parallel on different processors. The term "parallel processing" generally refers to this type of computation. Each coarse-grained computation has some fine-grained parallelism that can be exploited by the individual processors in the parallel processor system. Thus, fine-grained and coarse-grained parallelism are complementary forms of parallelism that can be exploited individually or jointly.

Because most scientific and engineering programs are written in FORTRAN, a sequential language, it is up to the compiler to detect parallelism in the sequentially expressed program. The compiler must, in effect, prove to itself that two operations are independent of each other before it can exploit the parallelism inherent in a program.

Current compiler technology and the nature of the FORTRAN language allow the compiler to do a reasonably good job at the level of fine-grained parallelism. The task of proving that coarse-grained parallelism exists is considerably more difficult, if not impossible, for the compiler. As a rule, the user must either modify the program and indicate where opportunities for coarse-grained parallelism lie or use a language other than FORTRAN. Either alternative would simplify the compiler's task, but users are generally opposed to both alternatives.

CH2539-5/88/0000/0106$01.00 © 1988 IEEE

The Attraction of Parallel Processing

Despite the difficulties, coarse-grained parallel processing continues to attract a lot of attention as a means of achieving high performance. The reason may be that the uniprocessor's performance does not increase proportionately with its price. Empirically, the achieved performance of the most cost-effective uniprocessor computer in each price band is proportional to the price of the product raised to a power less than 1. This is shown by the dashed curve in Figure 1.

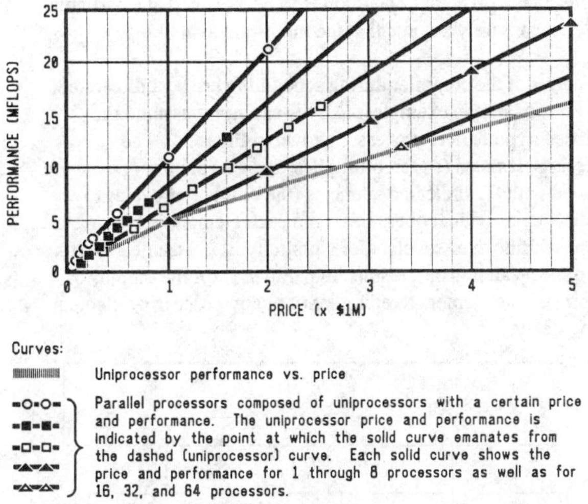

PERFORMANCE (MFLOPS)
0
5
10
15
20
25
PRICE (x $1M)
0
1
2
3
4
5
Curves:
Uniprocessor performance vs. price
Parallel processors composed of uniprocessors with a certain price and performance. The uniprocessor price and performance is indicated by the point at which the solid curve emanates from the dashed (uniprocessor) curve. Each solid curve shows the price and performance for 1 through 8 processors as well as for 16, 32, and 64 processors.

Figure 1. Comparison of Uniprocessor Performance With the Idealized Performance of Parallel Processors

Assuming that on a single parallel job one could get a linear improvement in performance as the number of processors increased, one could achieve an arbitrarily large performance advantage over the best uniprocessor. This is demonstrated by the solid curves in Figure 1. Note that in this figure the generous assumption is made that the price of the parallel processor increases only linearly with the number of uniprocessors that comprise it. Furthermore, it would appear to be more advantageous to use many slower uniprocessors than a few faster processors. Therein lies the seductive appeal of the massively parallel processor.

In reality, the situation is quite different. As the number of processors increases, the time spent in executing the parallel portion of the job decreases but there is no effect on the sequential portion of the job. Eventually this fact determines the minimum execution time and limits the attainable performance, regardless of the number of processors used.

To make matters worse, executing a job in parallel invariably incurs some overhead cost. This overhead results from the time required to start up each parallel process, the time spent in communicating data from one process to another, and the time lost while one process waits on another or contends for some essential resource. The net effect is that the achieved performance eventually decreases as the number of processors increases. Each processor begins to spend more time on overhead activities than it does on useful work.

Figure 2 demonstrates this effect. Given a uniprocessor with a certain price and performance (lying on the dashed curve), the initial effect of increasing the number of processors is to increase the performance of the parallel processor above that of the equivalently priced uniprocessor. Beyond a certain point, however, the parallel processor's performance flattens and drops off, while the uniprocessor's performance rises steadily.

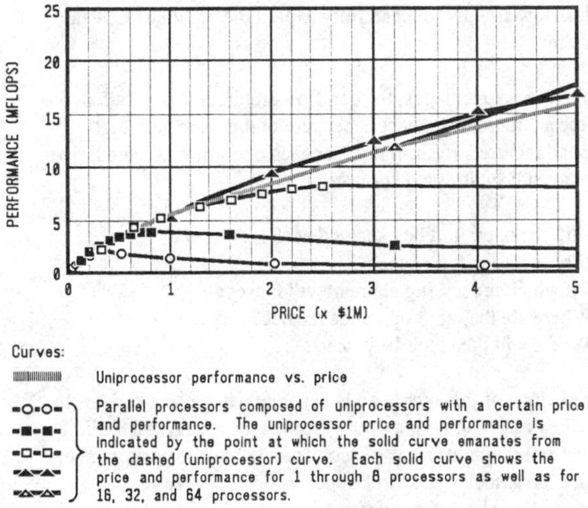

PERFORMANCE (MFLOPS)
0
5
10
15
20
25
PRICE (x $1M)
0
1
2
3
4
5
Curves:
Uniprocessor performance vs. price
Parallel processors composed of uniprocessors with a certain price and performance. The uniprocessor price and performance is indicated by the point at which the solid curve emanates from the dashed (uniprocessor) curve. Each solid curve shows the price and performance for 1 through 8 processors as well as for 16, 32, and 64 processors.

Figure 2. Comparison of Uniprocessor Performance With the Realizable Performance of Parallel Processors

The proponents of parallel processing tend to focus on the speedup that is possible with multiple processors while ignoring the fact that an equivalently priced uniprocessor might give almost the same, if not better, performance. This is not to say that the parallel processor architecture is without merit. A parallel architecture makes sense in applications where the fraction of sequential computation and the overhead are small, or where the level of performance required makes it impossible to use a uniprocessor regardless of cost. Also, a parallel processor can be profitably used to run multiple independent jobs requiring a single processor for a job. This is the most common and beneficial way to use a multiple processor system.

In any event, whether a uniprocessor is intended for use as an individual processor or as the building block for a parallel processor, it is essential that its architecture be most effective at exploiting fine-grained parallelism.

Dataflow Architecture

From a theoretical viewpoint, the most desirable architecture for fine-grained parallelism is dataflow. Dataflow is the only architecture that can exploit all forms of parallelism in a program; hence, it achieves higher performance over a broader class of computations than any other architecture.

In a dataflow processor, computation is viewed as a computation graph that explicitly represents *all* the dependencies between operations. Consider, for instance, the code segment and its corresponding computation graph in Figure 3. It is clear that the operation labeled A1 cannot be executed until operations M1 and M2 have completed, since M1 and M2 provide the inputs to A1.

Operations R1, R2, R3 and R4, however, are all independent of one another and could be executed in parallel.

Of all processor architectures, the dataflow architecture places the minimum constraints on when operations may be executed. A dataflow processor can execute an operation any time after all its inputs are available, i.e., when all inputs have been computed and have arrived at the point of execution. By maximizing the number of operations that are eligible for execution at any point in time, the dataflow architecture can fully exploit the parallelism in an algorithm.

Despite these advantages, the dataflow architecture has failed to become a commercial success because of the extremely high overhead incurred at run-time. For each operation executed, five issues must be addressed at run-time:

- Will the operation be executed at all?
- If so, when will it execute?
- On which processing element will it execute?
- Where are the input operands located?
- Where will the result be placed?

The net effect of this overhead is apparent when one considers that a dataflow machine with a peak performance of, say, 50 million floating-point operations per second would have to perform about 400 million associative searches per second--clearly an enormously expensive proposition.

$$Q = U*Y$$
$$Y = X - Q$$
$$X = Q + V*X$$

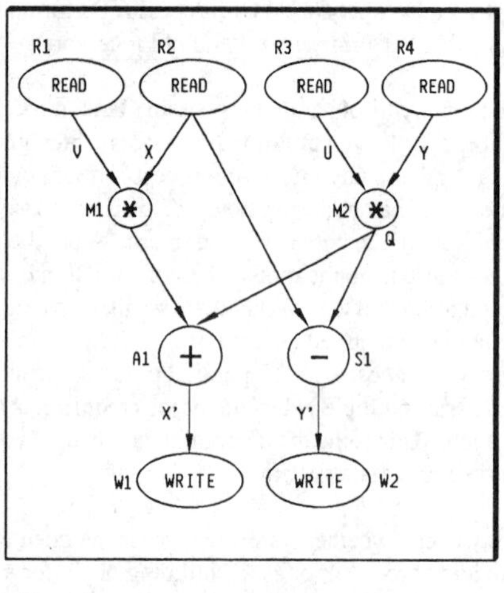

Figure 3. Code Segment and Corresponding Computation Graph

Directed Dataflow Architecture

Directed Dataflow, the Cydra 5 proprietary architecture, retains the important benefits of the dataflow architecture but makes the concept commercially viable by moving as much decision-making as possible from run-time to compile-time. As a consequence, the cost of the hardware is comparable to that of other machines providing the same peak performance, but a significantly larger fraction of peak performance is consistently delivered.

In the dataflow architecture, the five issues listed above must be addressed at run-time for each operation that is executed. With the Directed Dataflow architecture, these issues are settled at compile-time to the extent possible. Where it is not possible, the processor hardware provides the support needed to resolve issues at run-time.

Scheduling of Computation Graphs. Conceptually, the compiler simulates the decision-making processes of the dataflow processor and creates a schedule that details when and where each operation is to be performed. The compiler has a slight advantage in that it can look ahead in the computation and make decisions that are globally more optimal. The dataflow processor cannot do this because its scheduling decisions are made in real-time.

The compiler's schedule is incorporated into the program that is executed by the Directed Dataflow processor. If the program specifies that a particular operation is to be executed at a particular time, one can safely assume that the inputs are available.

The actions of the compiler during scheduling are best illustrated by a series of simple examples. All the examples assume the simplified hypothetical processor shown in Figure 4. The processing elements (adder, multiplier, and two memory ports) are pipelined with the indicated latencies (the number of cycles to complete an individual operation), and each element is able to start a new operation every cycle. For simplicity, it is assumed that the interconnect can transmit results, in parallel, from the outputs of each processing element to either input of any processing element with no delay.

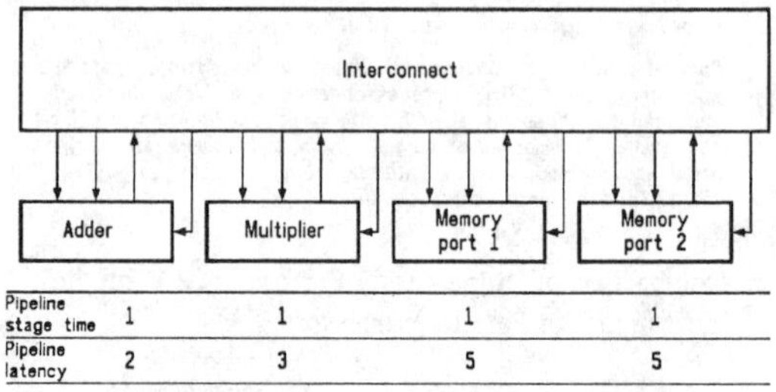

Figure 4. Simplified Directed Dataflow Processor

Scheduling of Straight-Line Code. Table 1 shows the schedule that the compiler would prepare for the code and the corresponding computation graph in Figure 3. The schedule is designed for execution on the processor in Figure 4.

Table 1. Compiler Schedule for the Code Segment in Figure 3

Time	Memory Port 1	Memory Port 2	Multiplier	Adder
0	R1	R2		
1	R3	R4		
2				
3				
4				
5			M1	
6			M2	
7				
8				
9				A1
10				S1
11	W1			
12	W2			

At the outset, the only operations that can be executed are read operations R1 through R4. Operations R1 and R2 are scheduled for execution at time 0 on Memory Ports 1 and 2, respectively. Given the 5-cycle execution latency for read operations, both inputs of M1 will be available at time 5 and may be scheduled for execution at 5 or any time thereafter. Operations R3 and R4 are scheduled for execution at time 1, making M2 eligible for execution at time 6 or any time thereafter.

Operations M1 and M2 are scheduled for execution on the multiplier at times 5 and 6, respectively. Since the multiplier latency is 3 cycles, A1 and S1 are scheduled for execution at times 9 and 10, respectively. Write operations W1 and W2 have been delayed with respect to A1 and S1 by the 2-cycle adder latency and are scheduled at times 11 and 12, respectively.

This rather simple procedure can exploit the fine-grained parallelism within a single segment of straight-line code. The operations corresponding to the third FORTRAN statement, viz., R1, R2, A1, and W1, have been scheduled to execute in parallel with the operations of the first two FORTRAN statements. Assuming the same processing unit structure and pipeline latencies, a simple sequential processor would take at least 32 cycles to execute this code sequence, and even a rather sophisticated overlapped scalar processor would take 26 cycles. In contrast, the 13-cycle schedule for the Directed Dataflow processor represents a significant performance improvement, especially when one considers the simplicity of the hardware that controls the execution of the processing elements.

Nevertheless, the processor is considerably underutilized, owing to the pipeline latencies of the operations, the data dependencies between them, and insufficient amounts of parallelism. Note the number of empty slots in the schedule of Table 1. This processor, which is capable of starting four operations every cycle, ends up starting only 10 operations in 13 cycles, yielding a performance that is less than 25 percent of its peak performance.

Increasing the number of processing elements is not the solution. A processor with a larger number of processing elements would only achieve a lower utilization and very little improvement in performance. In fact, with an unlimited number of processing elements, the schedule length would reduce by only one cycle. As with parallel processing, it is far better to have fewer but faster processing elements. To use this processor more fully, one must exploit the far larger amounts of parallelism that exist between successive iterations of a loop.

Scheduling of Simple Loops. Let us now assume that the code sequence in Figure 3 is the body of an innermost loop, as shown in Figure 5. The computation graph now consists of multiple copies of the graph in Figure 3, with one copy for each iteration of the loop.

When there are no data dependencies between operations in different iterations of the loop, the dataflow architecture allows the processor to execute any number of iterations in parallel, limited only by the number of processing elements. For a compiler doing compile-time scheduling for the Directed Dataflow processor, the challenge is to exploit the inter-iteration parallelism to the point where the most heavily used processing element is fully utilized.

```
   DO 10 I = 1,N
   Q = U(I)*Y(I)
   Y(I) = X(I) - Q
   X(I) = Q + V(I)*X(I)
10 CONTINUE
```

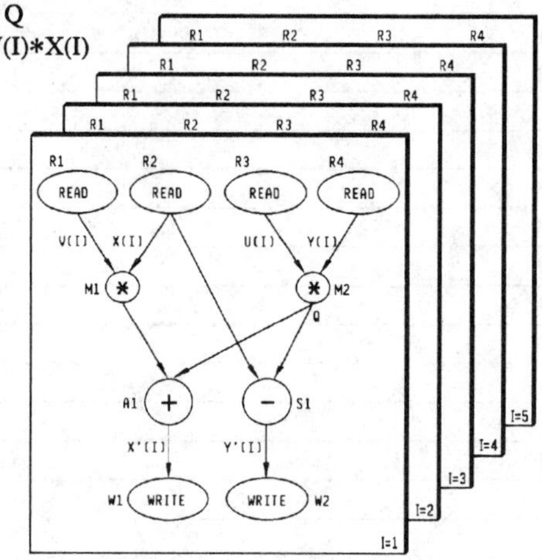

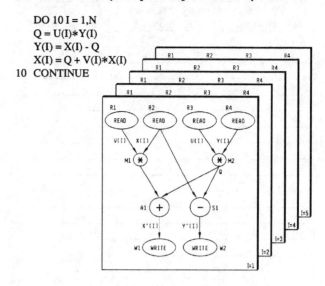

Figure 5. Code for a Simple Vectorizable Loop and Computation Graph for the Loop Body

The first step is to determine which processing element is most heavily used. Each iteration performs two operations on the adder and multiplier, respectively, and six memory operations. Since there are two memory ports, this represents three operations per memory port. Thus, the memory ports are the most heavily used processing elements. The objective of maximizing performance on the loop can be served by scheduling successive iterations to start as frequently as possible. The interval between the initiation of two consecutive iterations is the "initiation interval". Clearly, the initiation interval cannot be less than the number of times the most heavily used processing element is used per iteration. (A shorter initiation interval would require the use of some processing elements more than 100%, which is impossible.) In our example, the minimum initiation interval is 3. This corresponds to optimal performance.

The schedule shown in Table 2 is based on the assumption that a new iteration is started every 3 cycles. Therefore, scheduling the first iteration implicitly schedules all subsequent iterations. For example, when R1 for the first iteration is scheduled on Memory Port 1 at time 0, corresponding R1 operations for subsequent iterations are implicitly scheduled at times 3, 6, 9, 12, et cetera. Thus, every time slot for Memory Port 1 which is at time 0 modulo 3 is crossed off as unavailable. With this additional "modulo" constraint, the scheduling of the rest of the operations proceeds as before.

The first time this constraint makes a difference to the schedule is when W2 is scheduled. From the viewpoint of input availability, W2 may be scheduled at time 12 or later. If it were scheduled at time 12, it would conflict with R2 of the fifth iteration. Thus, W2 is scheduled for execution at time 14, the next available time slot.

Table 2. Schedule for One Iteration of the Loop in Figure 5

Time	Time Modulo 3	Memory Port 1	Memory Port 2	Multiplier	Adder
0	0	R1	R2		
1	1	R3	R4		
2	2				
3	0	---	---		
4	1	---	---		
5	2			M1	
6	0	---	---	M2	
7	1	---	---		
8	2			---	
9	0	---	---	---	A1
10	1	---	---		S1
11	2	W1		---	
12	0	---	---	---	---
13	1	---	---		---
14	2	---	W2	---	

This schedule can be replicated, with successive copies staggered at 3-cycle intervals. The iterations will dovetail perfectly. Table 3 shows the results when the schedule is executed at run-time. From the end of the initial start-up phase to the last few iterations, both memory ports--the most heavily used processing elements--are fully utilized. This result represents optimal performance. The processor now issues 10 operations every 3 cycles, which is 83% of its peak capability of four operations per cycle.

Table 3. Schedule of Multiple Iterations of the Loop in Fig. 6, Overlapped in Time

Time	Time Modulo 3	Memory Port 1	Memory Port 2	Multiplier	Adder
0	0	R1	R2		
1	1	R3	R4		
2	2				
3	0	R1	R2		
4	1	R3	R4		
5	2			M1	
6	0	R1	R2	M2	
7	1	R3	R4		
8	2			M1	
9	0	R1	R2	M2	A1
10	1	R3	R4		S1
11	2	W1		M1	
12	0	R1	R2	M2	A1
13	1	R3	R4		S1
14	2	W1	W2	M1	
15	0	R1	R2	M2	A1
16	1	R3	R4		S1
17	2	W1	W2	M1	

Table 3. Schedule of Multiple Iterations of the Loop in Fig. 6, Overlapped in Time (continued)

Time	Time Modulo 3	Memory Port 1	Memory Port 2	Multiplier	Adder
18	0	R1	R2	M2	A1
19	1	R3	R4		S1
20	2	W1	W2	M1	
21	0	R1	R2	M2	A1
22	1	R3	R4		S1
:	:	:	:	:	:
:	:	:	:	:	:

Scheduling of Recurrence Loop. The loop in the previous example is one of the simpler types of loops; it contains no data dependencies between the operations in one iteration and the same operations in subsequent iterations. This type of loop can be "vectorized", i.e, reduced to a set of vector operations. All instances of M1, in all iterations, can be executed in their entirety as one vector operation; then all instances of M2 can be executed as one vector operation, and so on.

Now consider the example in Figure 6, where the value referenced as Y(I) on one iteration is the value computed for Y(I-1) on the previous iteration. In the computation graph of Figure 6, an arc is drawn from S1 in one iteration to M2 in the next iteration. This indicates that the result computed by S1 is used by M2 in the next iteration. This cyclic dependency is a recurrence; hence, this loop cannot be vectorized. Clearly, the vector operation corresponding to S1 cannot be performed until the vector operation for M2 is complete, because S1 is dependent on M2. Nor can the M2 vector operation be performed first, because the second operation in it is dependent on the first operation in the S1 vector operation. The sequence of M2 and S1 operations must happen in an interleaved order, which a vector processor cannot do. The vector processor would have to execute this loop in a degraded scalar mode.

```
    DO 10 I = 1,N
    Q = U(I)*Y(I-1)
    Y(I) = X(I) -Q
    X(I) = Q + V(I)*X(I)
10  CONTINUE
```

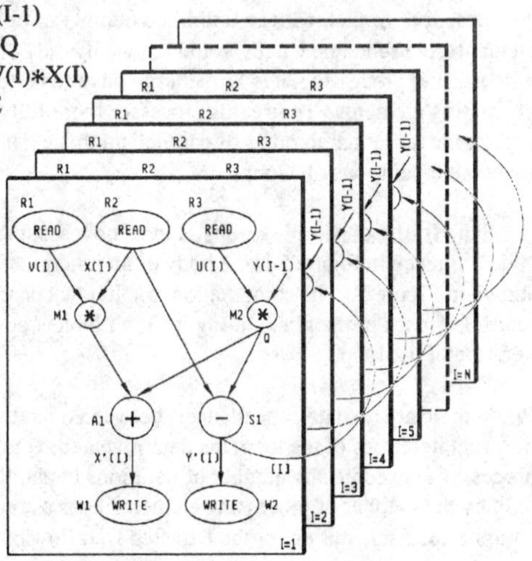

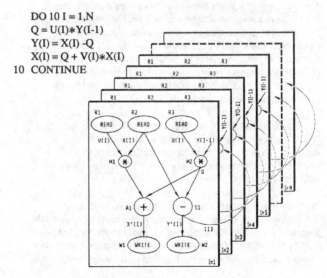

Figure 6. Code for a Recurrence Loop and Computation Graph for the Loop Body

Scheduling of recurrence loops poses no major problems for the Directed Dataflow processor. It only requires a different initiation interval from the one used in the previous loop schedule. The nature of the recurrence data dependency requires that M2 of the second iteration be scheduled at least 2 cycles after S1 of the first iteration. In the first iteration, S1 must be scheduled at least 3 cycles after M2. Therefore, the interval between the M2 operations for two consecutive iterations must be at least 5 cycles. After computing this initiation interval, the compiler constructs the schedule shown in Table 4.

The inter-iteration dependency prevents the compiler from overlapping successive iterations as much as processing element usage alone would have permitted. Although the Directed Dataflow processor's performance on the recurrence loop is 40 percent less than on the vectorized loop, it is considerably better than a vector processor could achieve using scalar execution.

Table 4. Schedule for One Iteration of the Loop

Time	Time Modulo 5	Memory Port 1	Memory Port 2	Multiplier	Adder
0	0	R1	R2		
1	1	R3	R4		
2	2				
3	3				
4	4				
5	0	---	---	M1	
6	1	---	---	M2	
7	2				
8	3				
9	4				A1
10	0	---	---	---	S1
11	1	---	---	---	
12	2	W1	W2		

The advantage of the Directed Dataflow architecture becomes even more evident as the order of the recurrences increases. Suppose we change the first statement in the loop body (Figure 6) to read Y(I-2) instead of Y(I-1). The statement now constitutes a second-order recurrence, because the data dependency is between iterations that are two removed. Now the M2 operations from iterations that are two removed must be at least 5 cycles apart. In other words, twice the initiation interval must be at least 5 cycles; hence, the initiation interval must be at least 2.5, viz., 3. This initiation interval allows the Directed Dataflow processor to achieve the same performance it would achieve if the loop were vectorizable. It is this ability to perform well on linear as well as nonlinear recurrences that sets the Directed Dataflow architecture apart from the vector architecture.

Hardware Support for Loop Scheduling. A result generated by the execution of an operation must reside in some storage location, either memory or register, until is has been used by all the operations to which it is an input. Concurrent instances of a result must reside in different storage locations, and a mechanism must exist to ensure that each instance is matched to the correct operation. In the dataflow architecture, each iteration of a loop or invocation of a procedure constitutes a distinct "context" with a distinct name. Confusion is averted by tagging each result with the name of the context in which the result will be used. Associative searching is used to find matching inputs tagged with the same context name.

In the case of procedure calls, the conventional method of handling this problem is to allocate separate stack frames to hold the results computed on the various invocations of the procedure. While it appears that the results from each invocation are written to the same location, the frame pointer actually guides the results to equivalent locations in separate stack frames.

The Directed Dataflow architecture uses this conventional mechanism to handle multiple invocations of the same procedure. In addition, it employs iteration frames to handle parallel execution of multiple iterations of loops. At compile-time each result is assigned a definite location. At run-time the processor steers different instances of the same result to equivalent locations in separate iteration frames. This mechanism avoids the cost of associative storage.

Scheduling of Conditional Loop Bodies. One decision that cannot be made at compile-time is whether a data-dependent branch will be taken at run-time. Data-dependent branching complicates the task of loop scheduling, since the computations performed vary from one iteration to the next and make it impossible to devise a single schedule that can be replicated and overlapped at periodic intervals.

In the sequential mode of computing, the decision to execute an operation is made by data-dependent branches that direct the flow of control either to or away from the code containing the operation.

In the dataflow architecture, this issue is determined by data switches controlled by data-dependent conditions. The switches either inhibit or permit the input data to flow into the computation graph containing the operation. Consider the example in Figure 7 of a loop with some conditional branching. The switch operations transmit their input data down one of their two outgoing arcs (depending on the value of the boolean input) and control data flow into the subgraph of the computation. If the condition is false, no data flows into the subgraph consisting of operation W1. (This is the equivalent of branching away in the conventional sequential program.)

```
   DO 10 I = 1,N
   IF (X(I) .LT. X(I-1) = X(I-1)
   Y(I) = X(I) - X(I-1)
10 CONTINUE
```

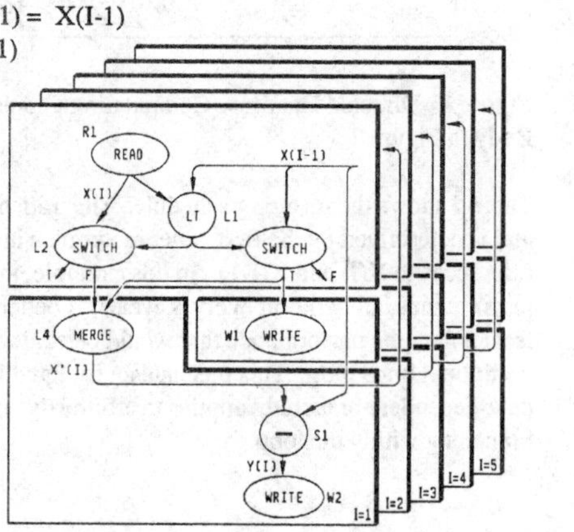

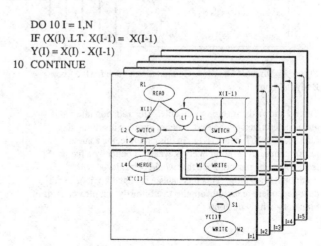

Figure 7. Code for a Loop With Conditional Branching and Dataflow Graph for the Loop Body

Because data-dependent conditions obviously cannot be evaluated at compile-time, the Directed Dataflow architecture uses a different but equivalent approach. Instead of inhibiting the flow of data into a computation graph, it inhibits the *execution of the operations* in the graph. Control over the execution of operations is provided by a third boolean input to the operation. This input is computed at run-time and reflects the data-dependent condition. The boolean input is treated exactly like the other inputs for purposes of determining when an operation can be executed.

Figure 8 displays the Directed Dataflow computation graph for the example in Figure 7. Every operation now has an additional boolean input, shown entering the operation at the side. If the input is TRUE, the operation is executed normally. If it is FALSE, the operation becomes a "null" operation. (Operations shown without the boolean input actually have a boolean input that is constantly TRUE.) The SELECT operation selects either the left or the right input as its result, depending on the value of the boolean input.

The hardware support for the conditional execution of operations makes it unnecessary to branch around the operations that will not be executed. Because no branching is involved in the Directed Dataflow computation, the task of scheduling the computation is no harder than in the earlier examples and proceeds as described in those examples.

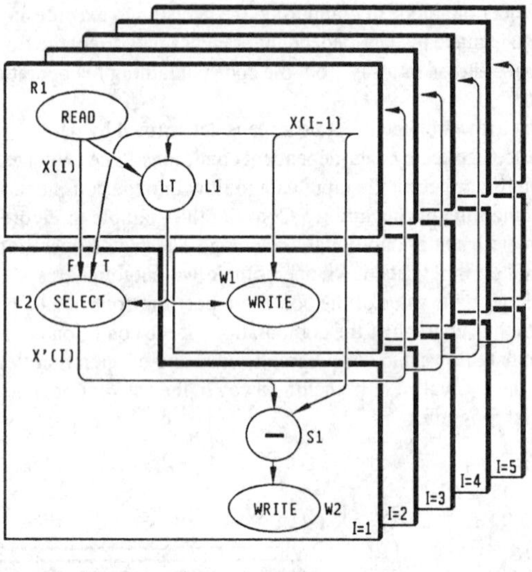

Figure 8. Directed Dataflow Computation Graph for the Loop Body in Figure 7

Table 5 shows the resulting schedule. The initiation interval is 4 and is determined by the first-order recurrence involving the references to X(I) and X(I-1). In this example, the achieved performance, an iteration every 4 cycles, is better by a factor of at least 3 than the performance that would be achieved with traditional branching. This mechanism for handling loops with data-dependent branching applies to arbitrarily complex patterns of branching within the loop.

Table 5. Schedule for One Iteration of the Loop

Time	Time Modulo 4	Memory Port 1	Memory Port 2	Multiplier	Adder
0	0	R1			
1	1				
2	2				
3	3				
4	0	---			
5	1				L1
6	2				
7	3	W1			L2
8	0	---			
9	1				---
10	2				S1
11	3	---			---
12	0	---			
13	1				---
14	2	W2			

Generality of the Directed Dataflow Architecture

Code containing fine-grained parallelism can be classified as:

- Code with vectorizable innermost loops
- Sequential code with little parallelism
- Code with innermost loops containing recurrences, condition branches, or irregular array accesses.

With vectorizable innermost loops, the Directed Dataflow architecture has a modest advantage over the vector architecture for two reasons. First, the Directed Dataflow architecture can chain an unlimited number of vector operations by spacing successive operations of one vector operation sufficiently to allow other vector operations to run concurrently, interleaved in time, on the same pipeline. This amortizes the vector startup penalty over a large number of vector operations. Second, because all the vector operations are chained, the Directed Dataflow architecture only needs to store a small part of each vector temporary; viz., the part that has been generated by one vector operation but has not yet been used as an input for the last time. Strip mining is unnecessary, which further reduces the vector startup penalty. (Strip mining is the partitioning of a long vector operation into short vectors the size of a vector register.)

With sequential code with little parallelism, the Directed Dataflow processor does better than the vector processor operating in its scalar mode. This is because the Directed Dataflow processor can execute operations out of sequence.

With code containing sets of innermost loops with recurrences, conditional branches, or irregular array accesses, the Directed Dataflow architecture has the greatest advantage. Whereas the vector processor drops to a sequential mode of execution, the Directed Dataflow processor continues to exploit any parallelism that exists.

Central to the superiority of the Directed Dataflow architecture are the compiler techniques and the supporting hardware. The hardware provides efficient allocation of register storage for the iteration frames and conditional execution of operations. The compiler and the hardware are inseparable design considerations. Even the most complex compiler techniques would fail to fully exploit fine-grained parallelism if the hardware failed to provide the appropriate architectural features.

THE CYDRA 5 SYSTEM

The Cydra 5 Departmental Supercomputer is a heterogeneous multi-processor system designed to be a functionally complete data processing solution for serious users in the engineering and scientific disciplines. It draws upon the most appropriate technology to meet each need.

As shown in Figure 9, the Cydra 5 is designed around a central bus and supports three types of processor: the Numeric Processor, the Interactive Processors (general processors), and the I/O Processors. Each of these processors is optimized for a particular type of task.

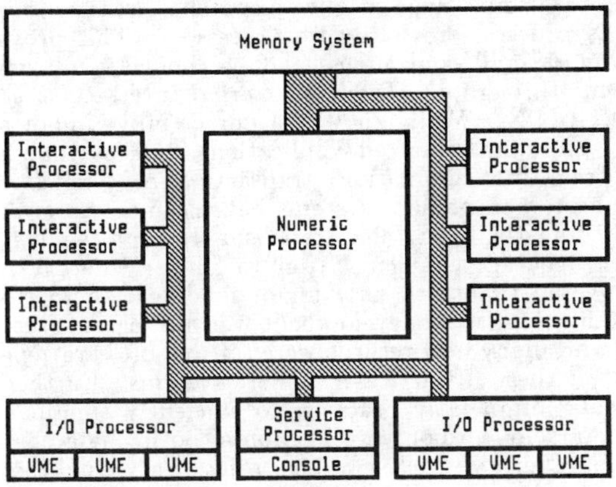

Figure 9. Cydra 5 System Diagram

The Numeric Processor has been optimized for the task of running large floating-point intensive applications. By virtue of its Directed Dataflow architecture, it can sustain high performance over a much broader spectrum of computations than other mini-supercomputer processors. Consequently, it is better equipped to meet the user's need for high performance without re-engineering of the application software.

Maintaining a balance with the high-performance Numeric Processor requires a high bandwidth memory system. Although the Numeric Processor has an instruction cache, it avoids data caching in order to avoid the anomalous performance that results when working with large data sets. The highly interleaved main memory incorporates a unique architecture that guarantees a uniformly high memory bandwidth regardless of how data is placed and referenced in memory. These features have been provided to meet a very important design objective: the user must be able to use the computer without perceiving any anomalous characteristics or performance shortfalls.

While the Numeric Processor is intended to execute numerically intensive applications, Cydrome recognizes that the typical user will run other jobs that are not numerically intensive, such as text editors, compilers, and interactive tasks. Rather than tie up the Numeric Processor with such tasks, Cydrome designed a tightly integrated general-purpose subsystem that shares memory with the Numeric Processor. This subsystem provides most of the operating system services, leaving the Numeric Processor free to run applications continuously. By tightly integrating the Numeric Processor and the general-purpose subsystem, Cydrome avoided the clumsiness of the host/attached-processor combination.

To avoid the bottleneck that occurs when the operating system does not execute the application's I/O requests fast enough, Cydrome has designed a UNIX V.3-compatible operating system with greatly improved I/O handling capability. This CYDRIX™ operating system executes on the general-purpose subsystem, which contains multiple general-purpose processors (the Interactive Processors). Cydrix is designed to execute as a set of parallel processes operating in a symmetric parallel mode on multiple processors.

In running Cydrix, the general-purpose subsystem functions as a parallel processor. UNIX, being a procedure-oriented system, is inherently parallelizable. Its execution consists of the joint activity of all user processes that are currently in kernel mode. This potential parallelism has been successfully exploited in Cydrix by modifying the kernel to make it re-entrant.

With multiple independent non-numeric user tasks, the Interactive Processors function as a multiprocessor, achieving near-linear speedup with the number of processors. In this mode, the Interactive Processors yield considerably better cost-performance than an equivalently priced uniprocessor.

High I/O performance is also achieved by using multiple processors. These microprocessor-based I/O processors can perform gather/scatter operations and handle tens of I/O transfers in both directions simultaneously. The total I/O bandwidth and storage capacity are more than adequate to ensure a balance with the performance capability of the Numeric Processor.

CONCLUSION

The Cydra 5 Departmental Supercomputer combines a radically different internal design with a familiar and comfortable user interface. It achieves significantly higher performance than superminis and higher cost-performance than conventional mini-supercomputers without re-engineering of applications. Cost-effective Directed Dataflow architecture and sophisticated compiler technology work hand-in-hand to provide an innovative solution to the computing needs of the engineering and scientific communities.

SYMMETRY: A SECOND GENERATION "PRACTICAL PARALLEL"

Gary N. Fielland

Sequent Computer Systems, Inc., Beaverton, Oregon

ABSTRACT

In the last three years there has been over a four fold improvement in the raw processor performance of VLSI integrated processors. There is a corresponding increase in the memory bandwidth demand. This article explores the issues of managing this increased bandwidth while retaining compatibility with a first generation shared-memory, bus-based, symmetric, transparent multiprocessor.

March 1, 1988

VLSI integrated processor technology is evolving faster than any other computer implementation technology. This rate of change is due to continued progress in VLSI circuit technology as fueled by the mass market for commercial microprocessors. In the last decade we have seen the integer performance of commercial microprocessors increase over 30 fold. In the same period the architecture of these machines has matured to the point that they are comparable in both performance and features with current high end minicomputer architectures. Further, due to the very large software base for popular microprocessors, these machines enter the market well adorned with a wealth of powerful software. And this ever increasing capability is presented to the systems designer at approximately fixed cost.

It is natural to consider building a parallel computer which can multiply the performance and cost effectiveness of this powerful underlying technology. Special purpose, often massively, parallel computer systems offer perhaps the largest potential gain to sophisticated users. But the tradeoff is fairly extreme complexity imposed on these users, requiring fundamentally new operating and applications software to attain even a fraction of the potential gain. The mainstream computer markets have little tolerance for such change. They insist on the ability to utilize familiar software and hardware standards, with little or no recoding required.

In December 1984, Balance was introduced as the first "Practical Parallel". This symmetric shared-memory multiprocessing system tightly integrates twelve one-MIP processors on a common bus. There is an 8KB, two-way set associative, write-thru cache per processor which improves scalar performance while simultaneously reducing the memory bandwidth demand on the shared bus. Full cache coherency is continuously and automatically maintained by the hardware providing full transparency to both operating and applications software. In 1986 the implementation was mechanically extended to support up to 30 such processors on the shared bus.

These systems feature a reentrant, fully symmetric, transparent multiprocessing UNIX operating system, named Dynix. Dynix dynamically dispatches ready to run UNIX processes to hardware processors. This provides automatic and continuous load balancing to maximize system throughput. Dynix's external interface is standard UNIX. Well known, commercially important, large-grain, multitasked applications such as timesharing, real-time simulation, transaction processing, and database management systems benefit immediately and often linearly from the parallelism without requiring a single coding change. After a little time it was discovered that with only minor modification to UNIX makefiles, software development was also easily parallelized and many new records were set for software generation on these "Practical Parallel" systems. Further, it appears imminently practical to efficiently timeshare a single machine among a collection of both singleton jobs and parallel jobs each running on its own virtual (parallel) machine.

Substantial progress has also been made in environments and tools to help with the parallelization of monolithic, sequential, compute-intensive programs. Early work on Balance systems demonstrated, for instance, that the well known sequential Linpack benchmark could be easily run in parallel merely by adding a single comment-card directive. And the gains are impressive -- 28 fold reduction in run time on a 30 processor system. More recently these tools have been enhanced by the introduction of KAP/Sequent, a restructuring Fortran compiler which can automatically or interactively transform monolithic sequential programs to an efficient parallel form. These tools combined with a multi-windowed parallel debugger have proven that fairly straightforward extensions of the familiar sequential programming paradigm are still very effective for parallel programming.

As mentioned above the underlying VLSI technology is moving very quickly indeed. Today's commodity microprocessors already offer over 4 MIPS of integer performance with respectable floating point. Symmetry is a second generation implementation of the general purpose Balance architecture designed to incorporate these higher performance processors while maintaining a high

CH2539-5/88/0000/0114$01.00 © 1988 IEEE

degree of compatibility. Any such design entails an enormous amount of engineering effort, but perhaps the single biggest design issue was that of maintaining the level of parallelism while tracking the over four fold improvement in raw processor performance.

The approach taken in Symmetry is two-fold. The first architectural enhancement is made to the shared bus. Balance uses a pipelined, packet-oriented, 32-bit data path. In Symmetry this bus is "unfolded" yielding a 64-bit data path which includes as a subset the Balance bus. Some minor protocol enhancements are implemented but the 10Mhz Balance bus clock rate is retained. The resulting Symmetry bus and memory system offer a little over twice the sustained bandwidth of the Balance bus while still fully supporting all first generation 32-bit bus agents (bus couplers, IO processors, etc).

The second architectural enhancement employed yields an even greater benefit. Major enhancements are made in the per-processor cache architecture. The Symmetry cache uses an integrated (both instructions and data), 64KB, two-way set associative, copy-back organization. The eight fold larger cache substantially improves the hit ratio, while a larger line size both improves the cold-start performance and matches more closely the granularity of the memory organization. But the biggest improvement is attributed to the new copy-back write policy. This design still offers fully automatic hardware maintained cache coherency while drastically reducing the bus traffic over that incurred in a write-thru design. Smith, in his landmark "Cache Memories" paper, provides simulation results indicating a fourteen fold reduction in bus traffic resulting from this write policy change alone at the 64KB cache size. His data is derived from simulations of a static load and may not accurately reflect the actual improvement, but it is indicative of a large gain. Further, the copy-back write policy together with a few other changes offered the opportunity for a major reduction (twenty-five fold) in primitive synchronization operation time for parallel programs.

A very high degree of compatibility is achieved. Balance systems can be field upgraded to Symmetry using their existing cabinet and peripheral complement in under an hour. Symmetry offers exactly the same rich Dynix operating environment and in fact there is a single source tree maintained in common for both Balance and Symmetry. User programs need only be recompiled to take advantage of the new level of performance.

Early indications are that Symmetry has also achieved all of its performance goals. The performance characterization indicates that single processor performance is not sacrificed and if anything, Symmetry appears to attain even better linearity at 30 processors than does Balance. The result is a parallel system which offers over 100 MIPS of integer performance and over 100 Megawhetstones of floating point performance to mainstream applications.

THE SUPERTEK S-1 MINI-SUPERCOMPUTER

Dr. Mike Fung

Supertek Computers, Inc.
2975 Bowers Ave., Suite 203, Santa Clara, CA 95051

ABSTRACT

The Supertek S-1 is a Cray X-MP/416™ compatible minisupercomputer which offers 40 MFLOPS peak performance. It is implemented in advanced high-speed TTL/CMOS technologies. The system features compactness, low-power consumption, and high reliability/maintenability. The S-1 design was optimized for the Cray X-MP architecture, with a central control mechanism which schedules hardware resources for maximal concurrent operations. The 4-ported, 16-way interleaved main memory, the 18-ported vector register file, and other multi-ported register files/buffers are the key to high performance for a wide range of applications in the scientific and engineering fields.

Introduction

The S-1 is a high-performance 64-bit computer which executes the Cray X-MP/416™ instruction set, with hardware support for scatter/gather, compressed index, and extended addressing mode. This line of first-generation mini-supercomputers from Supertek Computers, Inc. are single-CPU implementations, providing peak performance of 40 MFLOPS and 20 MIPS for vector and scalar operations respectively.

Such Cray X-MP compatibility allows the S-1 to execute programs currently running on a Cray with little or no modification. The Cray compatibility allows Supertek to capitalize on the wealth of application programs and system software available on the Cray supercomputers ---- which have the largest user base and have become the *de facto* industry standard today. The Cray compatibility feature also provides S-1 users with an upward growth path to high-end Cray machines in the GFLOPS performance range.

The S-1 is based on state-of-the-art IC technologies with outstanding speed/power ratios, such as advanced Schottky TTL and certain high-speed CMOS logic devices; it also uses high-density CMOS static RAMs in the main memory subsystem. Currently, no custom or semi-custom integrated circuits are being employed in the system. By taking advantage of mature, multiple-sourced off-the-shelf components, the S-1 offers performance higher than its competitors at a substantially lower price.

The S-1 is implemented on 15.2"x19" multilayer printed circuit boards. The CPU and main memory are packaged in a single 26"-wide card cage which contains up to 31 boards for a maximum of 64 MBytes of main memory. The entire system (without peripherals) consumes less than 2,000 watts of power and is fan cooled. Such simple packaging requirements will not only cut down manufacturing costs, but will offer higher reliability and maintenability.

Central Processing Unit

The entire S-1 system runs with a single-phased 50 ns. clock. Its architecture is based on five major, tightly-coupled subsystems which operate concurrently: the Instruction Unit, Vector Unit, Scalar Unit, Main Memory Subsystem, and I/O Subsystem. The S-1 CPU contains a total of thirteen functional units, and its control mechanism allow concurrent floating point, integer, and logical operations on vector, scalar, and address operands. The S-1 structure, optimized for the Cray X-MP instruction set, yields relatively high throughput for a wide range of applications with various degrees of vectorizability or inherent parallelism.

The Instruction Unit (IU) is organized in two pipeline stages. For single-parcel (16-bit) instructions (e.g. arithmetic types) , the maximal instruction issue rate is 1 issue/cycle; for two-parcel instructions (e.g. branch and memory types), the maximal rate is 1 issue/2 cycles. In the S-1 design, conditional branch instructions do not incur any penalty whether or not the branch is taken. This design not only reduces branch instruction overheads, but also simplifies the IU pipeline which does not have any "hiccup" in handling branch instructions.

The IU consists of four instruction buffers each storing 128 parcels. The I-Buffer switch time is only one cycle. In the event of an I-miss, all four ports of the Main Memory Subsystem participate in filling up the I-Buffers in order to minimize the time (18 cycles) required to refill them.

The S-1 CPU is under the control of a "scoreboard" responsible for resource scheduling: availability of a resource is determined by its state of reservation. Examples of reservation are: Vector Register as operand or result, Scalar Register as result, Address Register as result, Memory Port busy, and T/B Registers busy. The IU provides the primary level of control in resource scheduling by performing *test and set* operations on reservation state registers. These scoreboard registers will be *reset* by the individual resources as soon as they are releasable. The secondary level of control is distributed over all the relevant resources (e.g. vector control unit handles chaining, and memory control unit resolves memory bank conflicts).

The Vector Unit (VU) contains a multiported vector register file (V) which supports as many as 16 word transfers per clock cycle through ten read ports and eight write ports ---- with a total bandwidth of 2.56 GBytes/s. The VU control supports flexible chaining operations, allowing the result vector register of an instruction to be used as the operand vector register of a subsequent instruction with minimal delay. In the S-1 design, after a vector register becomes an operand in a vector instruction, the same register can be used immediately as a result register in another vector instruction. The VU supports all concurrent vector operations including vector-memory and vector-scalar data transfers. Hence, peak or near-optimal vector performance can be readily sustained in most applications.

The Scalar Unit (SU) contains a 5-ported scalar register file (S) that supports simultaneous scalar operations with low latencies. It also contains a 64-word scalar buffer (T). The SU is complemented by a 5-ported address register file (A), a 64-register address buffer (B), as well as an address multiplier and adder. With 20 MIPS peak performance for 64-bit scalar operations, supported by an IU which can issue instructions at the maximal rate of one per cycle, the S-1 is well suited for many scalar applications.

Main Memory Subsystem

The S-1 Memory Unit (MU) serves the other major subsytems at very high data transfer rates. Its 4-ported memory design has an aggregate bandwidth of 640 MB/s and supports two vector reads, one vector write, and one I/O transfer. The S-1 MU design provides fast access time for vector-memory operations it takes only 13 cycles to fetch the first element of a vector from memory. The MU supports full complement of 128 MBytes of main memory, with single-error-correction, double-error-detection (SECDED) protection.

The memory's 16-way, fully interleaved structure reduces memory bank conflicts to a minimum. Coupled with the multi-ported vector register file and a built-in vector chaining capability, the Memory Unit makes most vector operations run as efficient register-to-register operations.

I/O Subsystem

The S-1 Series I/O Subsystem is comprised of multiple, highly intelligent I/O Processors (IOPs) each attached to a 160 MB/sec Central Memory Channel (CMC). Each IOP is an autonomous processor with its own control store and local memory.

The S-1 supports up to four IOPs and takes full advantage of this architecture by distributing operating system functions across the central processing unit and the multiple IOPs. Each IOP is controlled by a real-time, event-driven operating system (RTIOS™) that processes external interrupts and Central Processor I/O requests and executes peripheral driver routines. The central operating system and the IOP's communicate via messages and queues. By thus shifting the peripheral processing burden to the I/O Subsystem, The central processor is free for high performance computation.

Reliability-Availability-Serviceability

Each S-1 system incorporates sophisticated features to support a well conceived Reliability/Availability/Serviceability program.

The Master IOP supports an independent Service Processor Unit (SVP) which controls the S-1's adavanced diagnostic subsystem, the central operating system "bootstrap", and S-1 CPU initialization. The SVP also maintains a log of the system's detected and corrected errors. A self-contained subsystem, the SVP includes its own processor and local memory, an 800 MByte disk, cartridge tape drive, and communications ports for the operator's console and or remote diagnosis.

The SVP can set and examine the state of internal registers and step the functional units through execution cycles using the independent diagnostic scanbus. This approach provides quick fault detection with a high level of confidence.

Supertek UNIX™ with Supercomputing Extensions

Supertek UNIX™ sets a new standard for ease of use and efficiency among supercomputer operating systems. Designed specifically for the S-1 series of mini-supercomputers, Supertek UNIX provides the optimal computing environment for engineering and scientific users.

Derived from AT&T UNIX System V, Supertek UNIX provides extensive functionality specifically designed to support the broad range of applications in the scientific computing enviroment. By combining the familiar and proven timesharing capabilities of UNIX with Supertek designed extensions to support a large-scale, performance intensive scientific computing enviroment, Supertek UNIX creates an outstanding enviroment for interactive applications development as well as for long running, large production jobs.

Supercomputing features added to UNIX by Supertek include multi-stream batch processing, asynchronous disk I/O, a new user-specified priority scheme, a highly vectorized applications and system runtime enviroment, resource and job accounting facilities, a process restart and recovery capability for long running production applications, and a channel-based I/O interface with multiple, independent, intelligent I/O processors. Following are some highlights of the Supertek software:

UNIX™ Operating System ATT SYSTEM V/IEEE POSIX **Standard**

Supercomputing Extensions.
- - - Distributed I/O Subsystem.
- - - Interactive/Batch Access.
- - - Process & Job Recovery.
- - - High-Performance I/O.
- - - User Specified Process Priority Levels.

Multi-User Environment.
Hierarchical file system.
Interprocess communication.
Windowing capability.

FORTRAN Applications Development Environment

sft (Supetek FORTRAN compiler)
- - - ANSI '77.
- - - Scalar optimization.
- - - Automatic vectorization.
- - - VMS™ FORTRAN extrensions.

ddt (Dynamic Debug Tool)
- - - Interactive, Source-level, Symbolic debugging without requiring code recompilation.
- - - User may specify execution breakpoints/tracepoints, examine and alter values of variables.

upd (Source code control)
- - - Source code management librarian.
- - - Audit trail of code changes.
- - - Reversibility of changes.

Math/Science Libraries.
- - - Optimized for maximum runtime performance.

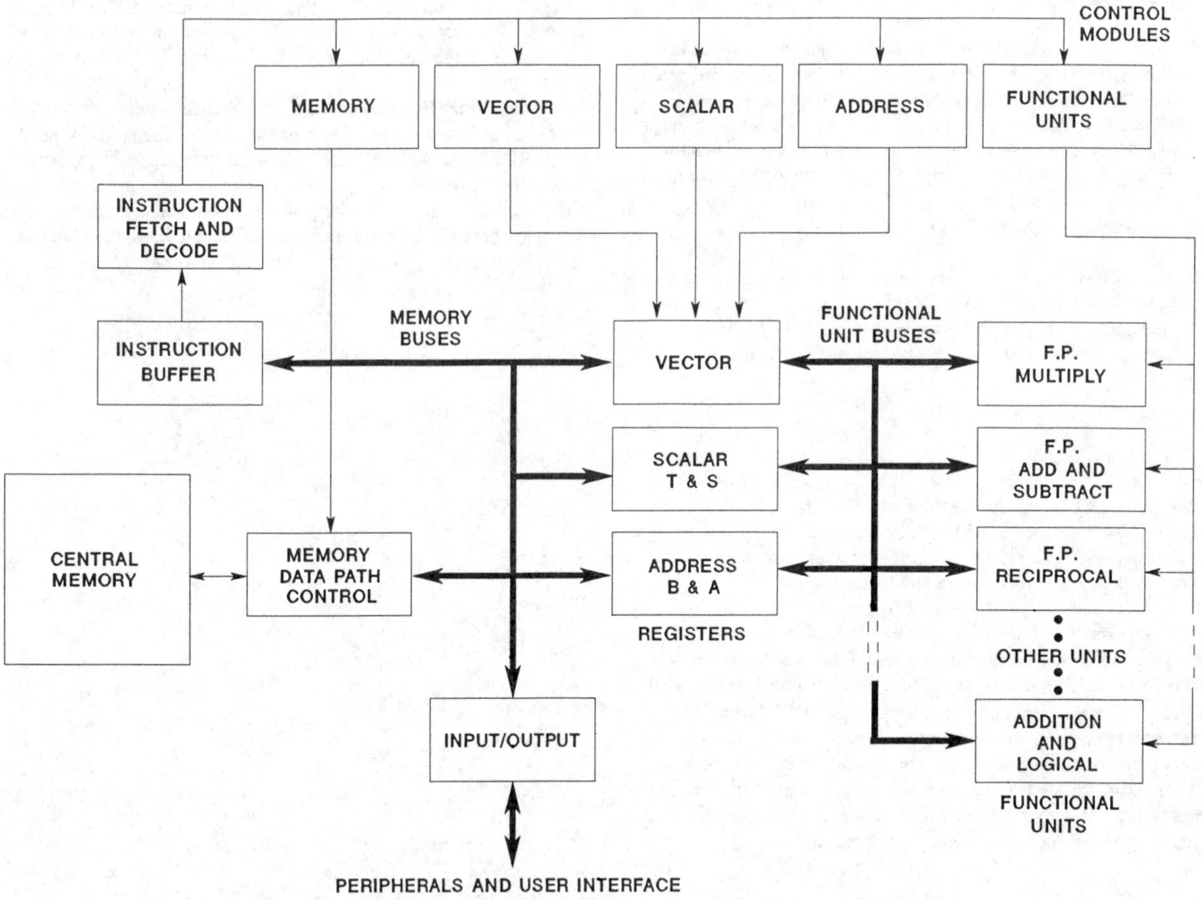

SUPERTEK S-1 FUNCTIONAL BLOCK DIAGRAM

STORAGE TECHNOLOGIES AND SYSTEMS Track

Magnetic Storage Devices

Chair: A. Hoagland

ROTARY HEADS: NEW DIRECTIONS FOR TAPE BACKUP

Juan A. Rodriguez

Exabyte Corporation

Abstract

This paper addresses the application of rotary head recording technology as a solution for the current capacity problems that exist with tape backup devices.

Current and future rotary head (helical scan) tape backup subsystems are based on technology derived from commercially available video recorders. These products take advantage of an established technology that is mass produced. This paper will specifically discuss the adaptation of the technology used in 8mm video recorders for data storage applications. It covers the technology that is used in rotary head devices, the market need for these products, the general applications, and existing and future products based upon the technology.

Introduction

There is an existing need for high capacity, low cost, removable data storage devices, to keep pace with the exploding demand for information. Winchester disk technology has continued to outpace tape technology in terms of linear recording densities and tracks per inch (tpi). As a result, the gap that exists between storage capacities of tape products and state-of-the-art disk products has increased significantly in the last few years. This phenomenon has compounded the level of manual intervention required to perform the time-consuming, labor-intensive system backup.

Major advances in tape recording technology have taken flexible recording media to new levels of reliability and capacity, made it available now on a worldwide basis, and set new standards for quality. The combination of rotary head (helical scan) recording technology and 8mm metal particle tape enable storage of over 2 Gigabytes of data on a tape that is the size of a deck of playing cards, providing a solution to applications that were previously unattainable for industrial and business applications. Now, large volume data backup, archiving, interchange and acquisition can be accomplished on a small form factor device which is available at an economical price.

Technical Description

Helical scan technology enables tape capacity to meet, and possibly exceed that of disk. It has been used to create a storage device that makes unattended backup a reality - dramatically reducing the costs associated with this time-consuming and expensive task for even the smallest of today's computer systems.

Helical scan recording has existed for some time in the form of videotape cassette recorders (VCRs). The technology has been through several generations of VCR products over the last 25 years. In its current state, it provides the high reliability and low cost of a mass produced product that has been through several iterations of improvements. Seldom has the computer industry had the opportunity to take advantage of a technology this mature.

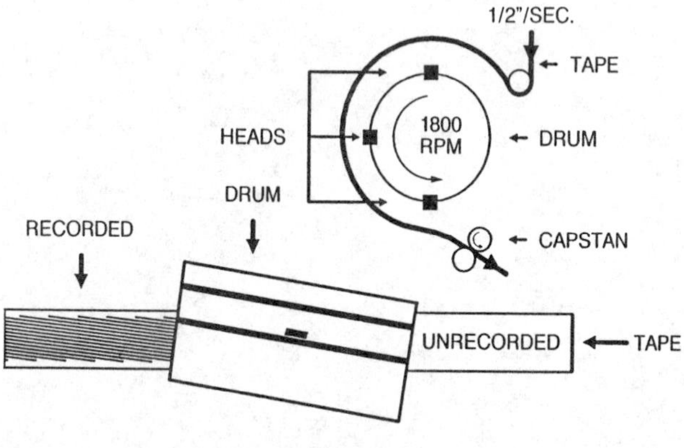

Figure 1. - Helical Scan Recording

Helical scan devices record data using heads that are mounted on a rotating drum (See Figure 1.). The tape is slowly moved around the drum in a C-wrap fashion. Very narrow (25 micron) tracks are written at an acute angle of approximately 5 degrees to the edge of tape in a diagonal pattern. In this way a track length is created which is nearly ten times longer than the

CH2539-5/88/0000/0122$01.00 © 1988 IEEE

width of the tape. Tracks can be accurately positioned by the geometry of the tape path, thus facilitating very high tpi, resulting in very high areal bit density.

Stationary head recording devices have limited tracks per inch mainly because of the tolerances required for the manufacturing of metal laminate multiple track read/write heads. Even though new thin-film, batch-fabricated heads can shrink the geometries and tolerances, the tolerance build-ups necessary to keep the heads aligned with the tape for data interchange is still the major problem which limits the potential areal density of these systems. The amount of data recorded is limited by the number of tracks that fit onto the width of the tape while still assuring data interchange.

In comparison, the tolerance problem for helical scan is greatly reduced because only one head is needed to write data. A track-following servo is used to keep the head aligned with the track, whereby a reading system is able to adapt to the recorded information of the writing system. This means that the tolerance build-up is automatically compensated, therefore more tracks per inch are able to be recorded.

Not only does helical scan recording increase the number of tracks per inch, it easily provides high data throughput as well. By using a head that is rotating on a cylinder at 1800 rpm and with the tape moving at one-half inch per second, an effective head to tape velocity of 150 inches per second can be attained. This results in a data transfer rate of 246 KBytes/sec.

In tape systems, a high relative head to tape velocity is required to produce read signals. Conventional parallel track tape recording systems employ a moving tape and a stationary head. The power that is required to start or stop a tape reel is tremendous and the tape must be relatively thick to withstand stretching from sudden acceleration transients. Helical scan recording mechanisms using low inertia tape cartridges provide gentle tape handling, and therefore can use the thinner, 8mm tape. The slow tape motion permits excellent velocity control, low stress on the tape and minimum power consumption. By reducing the acceleration forces by a factor of 10,000, electro-mechanical and tape path reliability are greatly improved, yielding a Mean Time Between Failure (MTBF) for the tape subsystem of greater than 20,000 hours.

In helical scan, alternate azimuth track recording (See Figure 2.) is frequently used to maximize the number of tracks per inch, thereby greatly improving the off track read channel performance. The rotating cylinder has two heads that are positioned at 180 degree angles. One head has a plus 10 degrees azimuth and the other a minus 10 degree azimuth.

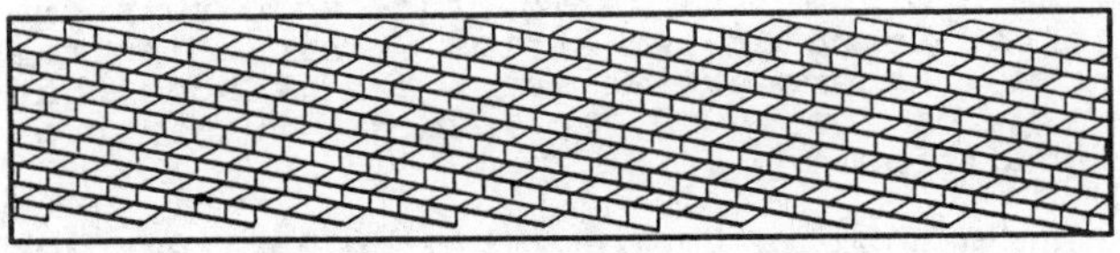

Figure 2. - Alternate Azimuth Track Recording

Therefore, every track is written at an opposite azimuth angle (herringbone pattern) to the adjacent track. In this way, tracks that are physically next to each other cannot be read by a head that is slightly off-track. Tracks can be written extremely close together because the possibility of picking up in-band noise from the adjoining track is eliminated. With stationary heads, tracks are normally separated by an erased guard band to keep the heads from picking up noise from the next track, which is another reason the track density available to conventional linear recording systems is limited.

To achieve the data reliability that is needed in data processing applications, helical scan devices must have at least two heads on the cylinder positioned at the same azimuth angle for concurrent read after write capability. This error avoidance technique enables errors to be detected immediately after they occur, dramatically increasing the reliability of the data.

Data that is determined to be defective or unacceptable during the read check is immediately re-written on a different area of the tape (See Figure 3.). Read margin can be provided by intelligent management of write checking criteria. Erasure of defective blocks is neither necessary nor desirable. This eliminates the need for tape repositioning and thereby maintains the high data transfer rate.

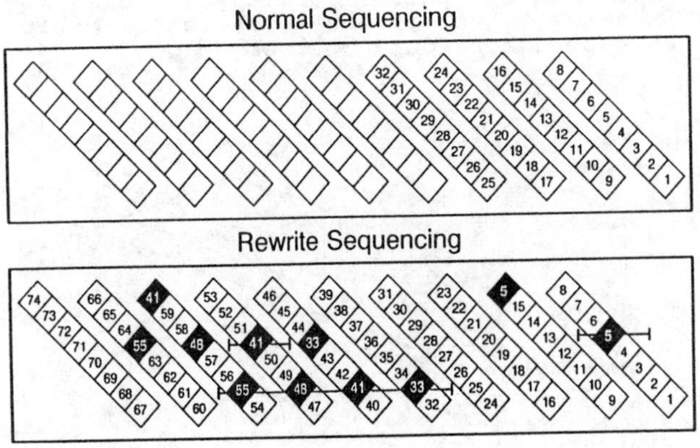

Figure 3. - Read After Write

An error correction code (ECC) can be used to assure that the probability of a permanent data error is less than one in 10E13 bits read. Research has shown that media defects typically occur parallel to the edge of a tape and that statistically, the probability is low for more than one error to occur per stripe. This being the case, there are at least two methods that may be employed to avoid this error condition.

One method is to re-write the entire track after holding the stripe in memory until an error-free space is found. This method of avoidance is cost-effective although data throughput performance may suffer when blank spots in the data stream occur due to rewrites. In this method a track would be an ECC entity.

A second method offers an alternative to re-writing whole tracks by dividing the track into a series of blocks. When an error occurs, only the block where the error occurred will have to be re-written instead of the entire track. Read data throughput performance is minimally degraded because only one-eighth of the data is effected. In this method, a block would be an ECC entity.

The incorporation of an intelligent SCSI interface allows tasks normally conducted by the host, such as error recovery procedures, to be performed by the tape drive, thereby relieving the host and enhancing overall system performance. For example, the EXB-8200 from Exabyte Corporation (Boulder, Colorado) supports SCSI bus transfer rates of up to 1.5 MBytes per second and, assuming the host is capable, can maintain a continuous data transfer rate of 246 KBytes per second. An internal 256 Kbyte speed-matching cache buffer provides the drive with virtual start-stop performance. Additionally, a fast forward file search may be performed at ten times nominal speed while rewind operation is 75 times nominal speed.

8mm Metal Particle Tape

The tape media that is utilized with EXABYTE's EXB-8200 is 8mm metal particle tape. The superior quality of this tape is a key factor in the subsystem's ability to record more data in less space.

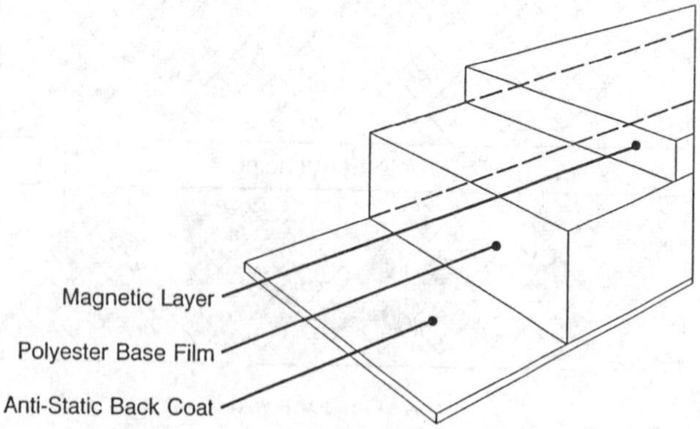

Figure 4. - Composition of Tape

8mm tape is produced starting with the base film (See Figure 4.), a wafer-thin, smooth polyester layer which is coated on the back with an anti-static backing material. The smoothness of this film is an important factor in increasing the recording density of the tape because the stability of the head/tape interface is directly proportional to the film's smoothness. Coverage of the magnetic layer over a rough surface creates dropouts or non-uniform signal when the tape is used. Head and tape wear diminishes as smoothness increases.

The magnetic material used in 8mm tape is the key difference over conventional tape that has been used for data storage. 8mm tape is made up of pure metal particles whereas previous tape used oxide particles. Each needle-shaped particle is about 1/25th the volume of iron-oxide particles and is only 0.15 microns in length. The binder used in this tape is also less likely to break down and shed as the head passes over the tape thereby head abrasion and wear is minimized.

The coercivity of magnetic media is an important factor for high frequency recording. The metal particles give the 8mm tape a superior quality because the metal particles have a higher coercivity, that is, once they are aligned, they tend to stay aligned and are not affected by adjacent domains. The key to its high coercivity comes from the composition of the materials that are used.

The coercivity of magnetic media is measured in units called Oersteds. 8mm tape has a coercivity of 1500 Oersteds. In contrast, other forms of cartridge tapes range between 300 to 550 Oersteds. This tape also provides a remanence of 2400 gauss which results in high read output signal.

The packaging of 8mm tape is designed to withstand the rigorous uses of a video camcorder by the general public, which is more than sufficient to withstand a typical, climate-controlled computer environment. All of these elements add up to a tape that is far more superior to what has been available in the past.

Market

The recent trend in the computer industry towards higher capacity disk drives and the corresponding increase in online databases has placed tremendous demands on current removable media, archival storage devices. This demand stems not only from the traditional requirements for cost-effective backup and data interchange devices, but from the expanded role of magnetic tape into real-time data acquisition and image storage/retrieval applications.

The explosion of these removable data storage requirements found traditional tape devices to be lacking in one or more parameters: capacity, performance, size, or cost. This led to work on new forms of storage devices to meet these growing demands. Rotary head tape technology is one result, using a data storage medium that is well understood by the industry: tape.

To address the market's need for removable storage, a device was needed that could deliver high capacity, performance, small size and low cost. The major use for removable storage is backup. As such, a backup device needs a high capacity unit of media; an average data transfer rate commensurate with the processor; a low-cost, compact, rewriteable, mass-produced removable storage medium; an industry standard interface; a device cost less than any single disk drive in the system; and the capability to perform an unattended backup for a large system. Additional requirements, based upon the implementation, include a small form-factor, light weight and minimal average power consumption.

Applications

In data processing, traditional system backup is still a high priority, and the most frequently performed tape application. Unfortunately, it is also a very time-consuming and labor-intensive application, and therefore, one of the most costly. An 8mm device provides the capacity, performance and storage medium to perform a backup with little or no manual intervention. This enables the backup to be completed in far less time, at significantly reduced costs. Additionally, an 8mm device is also capable of supporting all the tasks associated with traditional data processing applications including journaling, archiving, data interchange, and data acquisition, as well as backup and restore.

In the data acquisition environment, an 8mm device is well suited for recording test instrumentation data such as seismic, satellite or telemetry, and is well matched for document storage and retrieval. In addition, the relatively high data bandwidth of an 8mm device meets the needed requirements for real-time image capture and processing.

An emerging application is in the medical imaging arena, where image capture and retrieval is combined with document storage and retrieval. A commercial turnkey system is available that digitizes X-rays and combines them with medical transcription files. A complete patient history is stored on a single 8mm tape cartridge.

An 8mm rotary head tape device is well suited to meet all of today's traditional tape processing requirements, as well as being poised to handle the application needs due to the potential for additional capacity and higher performance.

Existing Products

Relatively few products based on helical scan recording technology have been marketed for use as computer peripheral devices. Previous helical scan products were developed for special applications, as in the case of the IBM Corporation 3850 MSS, or for niche markets, as in the case of the ALPHA MICRO SYSTEMS adaptor for attaching standard VHS video recorders to personal computers.

Exabyte Corporation introduced the EXB-8200 8mm Cartridge Tape Subsystem which was the first helical scan product intended for general use as a removable, sequential access, data storage device. The EXB-8200 features data storage capacity in excess of 2 Gigabytes in a 5.25 inch form factor at a low cost, and clearly establishes significant competitive advantages relative to linear track products. The concept for helical scan has been rapidly accepted in the marketplace, and in less than a year no fewer than four manufacturers have publicly announced intentions to develop helical scan products.

Small numbers of other helical scan products are built today for special applications that transfer data at 50 MBytes/sec and store 100 GBytes. These products may not be practical for general use because of their high cost, but they are indicative of the very high levels of performance which are achievable with helical scan recording technology.

Future Products

The range of performance of helical scan products developed and introduced over the next few years is likely to be bounded on the low end at 100 KBytes/sec transfer rate and 1 GByte capacity, and on the high end at 1 MByte/sec transfer rate and 10 GBytes capacity. Form factor is important and will evolve from 5.25 inch, full-height and half-height units into 3.5 inch units, as in the case of Digital Audio Tape (DAT)-based products. A very high percentage of the market demand will be for products operating near the low end of the performance range packaged in small form factors. These products will be derivatives of existing consumer recording devices and media; higher performance models will be based on multiple head scanners, improvements in format efficiency, and data compression.

Maximum storage density for the 8mm cartridge as written by the EXB-8200 is approximately 440 MBytes/cubic inch, and media costs are less than 0.005 $/MByte. Very high storage density and low media cost are characteristic of helical scan products; no other existing data storage technology is as dense or as cost-effective. Because of these economies, the 8mm cartridge is particularly well suited for storage of archival data. The small size of the cartridge, its rugged design, and its ease of manipulation are excellent qualities in a media product for application in an automated library device, although no products or development efforts have been publicly announced. However, the feasibility of developing automated library systems based on 8mm media and cartridge tape subsystems is excellent.

The basic technology of the 8mm format has almost unlimited potential for consumer, industrial and professional applications. For this reason, follow-on digital data products based on 8mm Helical Scan technology have a bright future. The operational characteristics of next generation 8mm cartridge tape drives could include greatly improved data transfer rates as well as a series of incremental improvements in capacity that would extend as high as 8 GBytes.

Generally, these sort of advancements would still use standard 8mm metal particle tape, but involve the active development and use of non-conventional video components, and/or more efficient data modulation and error correction codes. More importantly, these modified components and recording techniques would be designed to operate well within established limits for 8mm media.

Summary

Rotary head recording, especially coupled with a standard SCSI interface, affords an attractive solution to the high capacity, removable storage problem that the computer industry is experiencing. It also paves the road for further research into smaller tape sizes with smaller form factors to match the direction that disk has taken. The technology is sound and reliable, and has a high enough storage capacity with a low enough price, to firmly establish 8mm cartridge tape as a viable solution to increasing data storage capacity requirements.

Acknowledgment

Many thanks to Kelly Beavers, Kristin Garrett, Harry Hinz, Marty McCoy and Mark Vallee, all from EXABYTE, for their input and editorial contributions.

Optical Storage

Chair: G. Bate

THE LIMITS TO MAGNETIC RECORDING

Geoffrey Bate

Santa Clara University

Abstract

The data storage requirements of high data capacity and transfer rate and low access time and cost are apparently impossible to satisfy in a single technology and so we accept the need for a storage hierarchy. The fast-access level of the hierarchy has been occupied over the last 30 years by a succession of technologies: Williams tubes, ferrite cores, and semiconductors but during this time only one technology, magnetic recording, has been used at the high-capacity position in the hierarchy. Its success came from three key positive attributes, 1) no processing between writing and reading, 2) infinite reversibility and 3) the storage density could always be increased as needed. But now there are signs that the rate of improvement in the latter is slowing down. This is a warning that we may be approaching the limits to the technology.

Storage Density

The attributes of magnetic recording for data storage that are particularly important are: reliability, durability, cost, compatibility, consistency, performance (data rate and access time), and storage density. Storage density is the product of bits/inch (bpi) measured along the track and tracks/inch (tpi) measured along a radius in the case of disks [or perpendicular to the tracks in a general medium]. Storage density is measured in bits/square inch and is an areal density. It is the property that we shall examine first since it is the one that shows most clearly that magnetic recording is a mature and aging technology.

The development over time of any performance parameter of any technology whether it be the areal density of a rigid disk or the top speed of a jet-powered aircraft, follows the S-shaped curve shown in the first figure. The rate of improvement is slow at first but begins to increase when the factors that govern progress are identified and improved. After a period of rapid growth, in the middle of the curve, we reach the point where the easier problems have all been solved and we are left with the more difficult problems. Not surprisingly the rate of improvement begins to decline, gradually at first but then more rapidly until progress effectively stops and we have reached the limit of that particular technology. Long before the end is reached we need to identify what is happening to the technology and begin the search for alternative technologies that offer the promise of higher levels of performance (on other, higher S-curves).

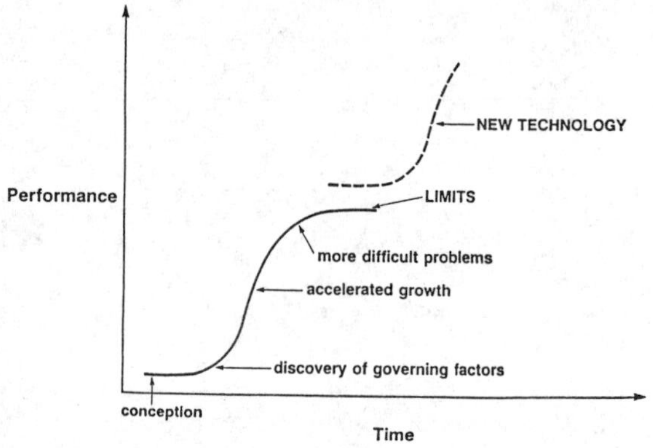

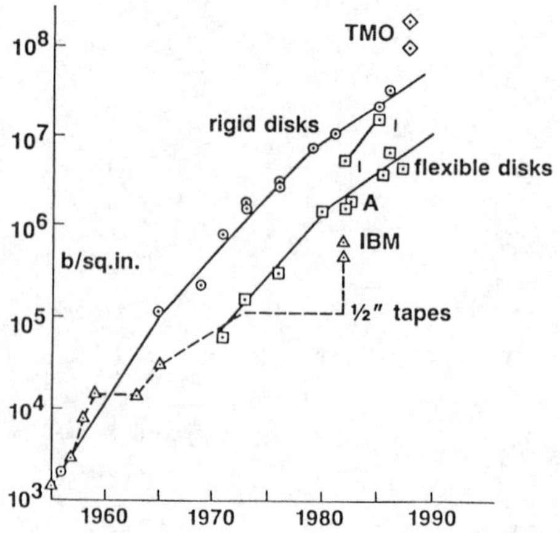

CH2539-5/88/0000/0128$01.00 © 1988 IEEE

Clearly, with any technology, it is important to know where we are on the curve and this means examining graphs of bits/sq. in., for example, against time for signs of a decreasing slope. The second figure shows bits/sq. in. for both rigid disks and flexible disks, plotted on a logarithmic scale versus time and clearly shows that a decrease in the slope occurred around 1980. The problem is that both bpi and tpi are reaching a period of diminishing improvement over time.

Bits Per Inch

The major problem with bpi is that the signal that we write on and read from the disk depends exponentially on the product of bpi and the flying height of the read-write head above the surface of the disk. Thus, every time we try to double the bpi we must half the flying height in order to keep the signal constant. The highest bpi rigid disk drives in use today operate at a flying height of 6 microinches. This is about the average distance that a molecule of oxygen or nitrogen in air travels between collisions with other molecules. This is certainly not a fundamental limit i.e. a limit imposed by the laws of physics but it is clear from the next figure that progress in reducing flying height is harder and harder to achieve. A smaller head-medium separation (in fact, contact) is achieved with tapes and flexible disks because the flexible medium represents a more compliant and forgiving interface, but the head-medium velocity (and so also the data rate and access time) are generally lower in this case. The figures show the relationships between bpi and flying height and also the thickness of the recording medium. from these it is clear that two and not just one critical dimension must be reduced in order to achieve high bpi.

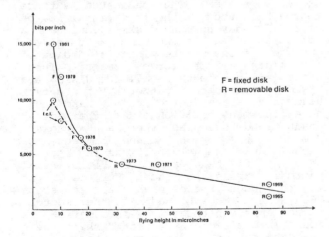

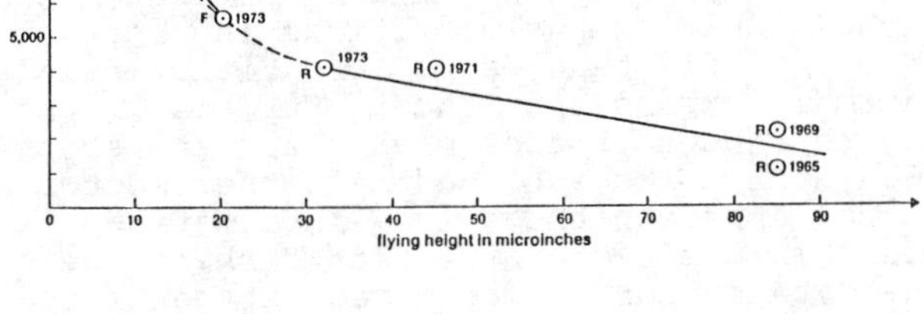

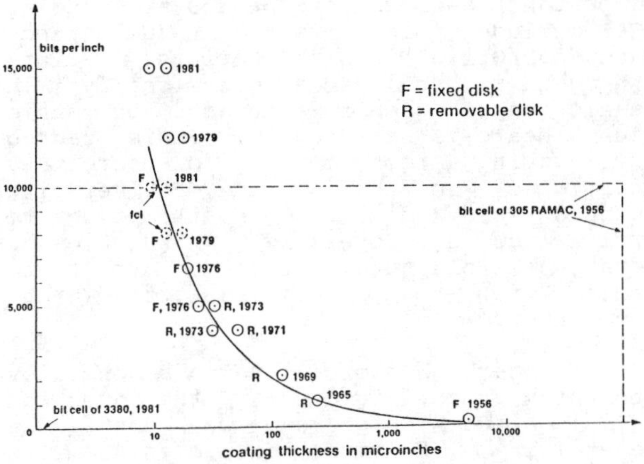

The other parameter controlling bpi is the coercivity H_c of the magnetic material of which the disk or tape is composed. Coercivity is not a dimension but a measure of the magnetic field strength needed to reverse the magnetic materials (particles or thin films) that form the information storage part of the disk or tape coating. Information is stored in terms of the direction of magnetization of discrete areas (bits) in the coating. The non-magnetic part of the disk or tape is the substrate and plays a passive role in the magnetic properties of the medium but is otherwise very active in such properties as reliability, durability, cost, consistency etc., etc. In order to write on or erase the medium it is necessary to apply a magnetic field that is about twice the coercivity.

Coercivity is measured in oersteds (Oe) and a typical rigid disk, flexible disk, or 1/2" tape of early 1980's would be made of particles of gamma iron oxide having a coercivity of about 300 Oe (about 600x the strength of the earth's magnetic field in U.S.A.). Recently cobalt-impregnated particles of iron oxide, having a coercivity of 600-650 Oe have been used to increase the bpi to 15,000 bpi in rigid or 24,000 bpi in flexible media. In the R-DAT (digital audio tape), small particles of almost pure iron, rather than iron oxide, and having a coercivity of 1,500 Oe are used to achieve about 58,000 bpi.

Coercivity is a measure of the average switching field of millions of particles of different shapes and sizes. Like all averages it can be misleading and needs another parameter such as variance or standard deviation to make it more meaningful. The additional parameter here is the Switching Field Distribution (SFD) which should be as small as possible, corresponding to a very narrow distribution of switching fields. The important recording properties affected by SFD include "print-through" in audio tapes and "overwrite" in disk coatings. Print-through is noticeable occasionally in audio tapes when a faint echo of music just heard is heard again. It is caused by having too many low-coercivity particles in the coating. Overwrite occurs when a disk head in attempting to write new data over old, is unable to erase all old data. It is due to there being too many particles of high-coercivity.

Since high coercivity leads generally to high recording density the question arises "How high can we push the coercivity of small particles?" The answer is that we know how to make particles with coercivities of tens of thousands of oersteds but this in not the limiting factor. We accomplish nothing if we are able to make particles of extremely high coercivity but are unable to write on nor erase them. And this is the situation. At present we do not know how to make materials for magnetic heads that can switch particles whose coercivity is higher than about 2,000 Oe. Over the last few years our ability to make magnetic particles has outstripped our ability to make improved head materials and unfortunately there are no encouraging signs that this deficiency will soon be corrected.

It is possible to increase the bits/inch without changing the medium or reducing the flying height. This can be done by changing the modulation code which translates the bits to be recorded into the sequence of reversals of magnetization on the recording medium. In this way the number of bits per inch is 1.5 x the number of flux changes per in. (fci) in both the IBM 3380 disk drives and the IBM 3480 tape system. This increase in density does not come free of cost. When the bpi is greater than fci the precision with which the flux changes must be recorded and detected is correspondingly increased. This in turn increases the sensitivity to the cross-talk from adjacent tracks, the signal remaining from previously written data and in general, all forms of in-band noise.

Tracks Per Inch

The width of a written track is equal to the width of the pieces of magnetic material forming the read-write head and so the most obvious approach to the problem of increasing the track density is to develop methods of making narrower heads. The most common material used to make heads is a magnetic ceramic known as "ferrite" --- a distant relation of gamma iron oxide. Like most ceramics, ferrites are rather brittle and therefore, are not easily formed into very thin structures and those structures tend to be fragile. However it happens that the major problem in achieving high tpi is not how to write and read narrow tracks it is rather how to find and follow them. Predicting where on the disk the desired track should be is clearly only half the problem; we must also know where the head is at present. And getting the head from here to there cannot be done simply by a combination of arithmetic and mechanical engineering --- at least it cannot be done at track densities of more than a few hundred tpi. To reach higher track densities it is necessary to use tracking servo techniques that constantly feed to the head a position-error signal which enables the head not only to find the correct track (out of thousands on the disk) but also to follow it despite non-circularities in the disk, bearings that have wobble, disks that deform differently in different directions as the temperature (or in the case of flexible disks, the humidity) changes, and mechanical parts that vibrate over a range of frequencies.

With the aid of improved mechanical design and track-following servos it has been possible to increase the track densities in rigid disks from less than 200 tpi in the 1960's to almost 2,000 tpi in 1988. But where are the limits?

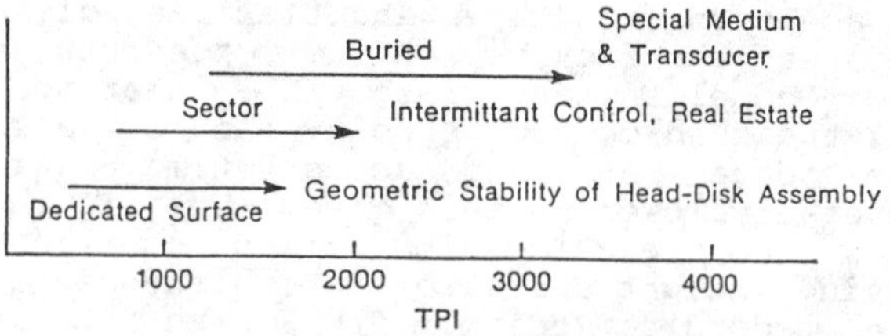

The figure shows the tpi that are being achieved and might be achieved in the future by using three different types of servo system. The dedicated surface approach is used in the traditional large disk drive having many disks spinning on a common spindle. As the name suggests, one surface of one of the disks is dedicated to holding all the servo tracks. Then, since all the heads on all the disks are rigidly connected together, the "servo" head reads the servo tracks and thus determines the position of all the "data" heads (and thus also, the data tracks). Clearly this approach cannot correct for such situations as vibrations in one or more of the head arms or differential thermal expansions etc. But, as the figure shows it does enable up to about 1600 tpi to be achieved. In the sector-servo approach the servo information is found in the sectors of each disk between the data sectors. The disadvantage of the sector approach is that the position error signal is discontinuous; when the head is traversing the data part of the track it is not receiving the error signals. However the servo information is on every disk and on balance, this approach enables higher tpi $\leq$ 2000 to be achieved. The best method would be to find some way of burying the servo information under the data (as is done on optical disks!). Then the error-signal would be continuous and the servo information would be stored as close as possible to the data. Unfortunately, solving the track-following servo problem does not guarantee that high track densities can be reliably achieved. Part of the remaining problem comes from the geometry of a head. A toroid made of magnetic material and having a gap built into it (so that the circle is almost complete but not quite) is wound with a few turns of fine wire. When the magnetization in the disk or tape changes (as when a "1" is stored) a change occurs in the magnetic flux that the magnetic medium causes to flow around the head. During writing the gap in the head serves to define where each bit will be written and during reading the gap allows the head to distinguish the bit being read from the preceding and succeeding bits. The head gap, however, is just as capable of writing and reading sideways with the result that a guard band or dead space must be left between recorded tracks to prevent the data on adjacent tracks from either being changed (during writing) or contributing unwanted signals to the data being read. This is a fundamental problem of magnetic heads which cannot be completely solved by changing the design or the material of the head. It can be minimized in some cases as in the case of video cassette recorders where two rotating heads write adjacent tracks alternately. The gaps of the heads are not parallel to each other and the angle between them is chosen to minimize the cross-talk. This solution cannot easily be applied to disk recording.

BPI Versus TPI

There are sound reasons both magnetic and signal-to-noise, for desiring that tpi should be greater than bpi but looking at the figure we see that bit densities have always been greater than track densities rather than the reverse. The smallest (most desirable) ratio of bpi/tpi (=5) was actually in the very first disk drive, the IBM 305 RAMAC in 1956. Since then the ratio has ranged about an average of 14 to a high of 22.

Track densities have increased by a factor of about 70 since 1956 while the bit densities have grown by x 150. In tapes (all kinds) the factors are: tpi = x 140, bpi = x 500. These ratios clearly reflect the fact that improving bpi has been EASIER (thus far) than increasing tpi.

					In Micro Inches		
Year	Device	Bits/In	Tracks/In	Bits/In^2	Spacing	Gap	Thickness
1956	IBM 350	100	20	2000	1000	800	1200
1961	IBM 1301	500	50	25000	500	500	500
1964	IBM 2311	1100	100	110000	125	200	250
1965	IBM 2314	2200	100	220000	85	105	85
1970	IBM 3330	4040	192	775680	50	100	41
1973	IBM 3340	5600	300	1.68×10^6	17	60	41
1975	IBM 3350	6425	476	3.06×10^6	17	60	41
1978	STC 8650	6425	952	6.12×10^6	17	60	40
1979	IBM 3370	12134	635	7.71×10^6	15	24	35
1980	IBM 3380	15000	801	1.20×10^7	11	24	26
1981	NTT PATTY*	13970	1092	1.53×10^7	8	32	7
1984	NTT PATTY*	25400	1800	4.57×10^7	6	20	7
1985	IBM 3380(E)	15000+	~1400	2.30×10^7	—	—	—

prototypes

Limits

The limits discussed thus far are limits that are imposed by our imperfect command of the technologies involved. But no matter how much we improve our control of those technologies there will always be limits imposed by the laws of physics which will ultimately bring progress to a halt. In the case of magnetic recording the fundamental limit is the size of the smallest stable magnetic particle or region. Fortunately this size is known because the transition from stable single-domains to superparamagnetism as the size is reduced occurs at about 500Å. This translates into a maximum possible bit density of 500,000 bpi and, since the same laws must apply to track density, the limit is 500,000 tpi also. It is important to remember that these are fundamental limits. There is no guarantee that they will ever be reached, they are simply the ultimate goals.

ERROR MANAGEMENT IN OPTICAL DISK RECORDING

Ian Turner

Laserdrive Limited. Santa Clara, California

Abstract

The observed raw bit error rate of typical recordable optical storage media, is in the range of 10^{-4} to 10^{-6} errors per bit. In addition, the error rate increases by two or three times as the media ages and the disk becomes contaminated with dust particles and other airborne debris. To provide a corrected error rate to the user, in excess of 10^{-12}, it is necessary for an optical storage system to utilize a multiple level error management scheme. The challenge to the system designer is to meet the corrected error rate goals with a minimum of overhead in excess of the user data. This paper outlines some of the techniques which are commonly used.

Introduction

Optical storage can readily achieve areal bit densities of in excess of 2.0×10^8 bits per square inch. At the bit dimensions used to achieve these densities, microscopic media defects are numerous, and result in multiple bit dropouts of various lengths.

Apart from the obvious bit errors which these defects cause, the high error rate makes the use of any single recording feature such as a header or data mark so unreliable that they cannot be used to achieve initial synchronization with a data sector. In addition, the nature of the recording channel and the encoding scheme used, may be such that in extreme circumstance, bit synchronization may be lost during a sector read.

The increased error rate over the life of the media poses an additional problem in that simple read verification of written data does not guarantee its integrity at the end of life.

Elements of an error management scheme

An effective error management scheme for optical storage will consist of several or all of the following elements:

1. A strategy for reliably detecting sector headers.

2. A technique for locating the start of a data sector.

3. An error detection and correction method (EDAC), for correcting multiple bit errors of varying burst length within a data field.

4. The use of media certification at either the media manufacturer or the user location.

5. A technique for the detection and correction of a loss or slip of bit synchronization.

6. Detection of a fault during writing such as a focus or tracking error caused by shock.

7. A method for flaw mapping large numbers of defective sectors.

8. A CRC or other checking method beneath the basic EDAC scheme to ensure that undetected data errors are minimized.

9. A method for scanning previously written data to locate areas where the EDAC scheme is nearing its limits of recovery.

Header and data location techniques

A typical sector header will be six to ten bytes long. The probability that an error will occur within a feature of this length is approximately 10^{-3}. It is clear that a system which depends on one header to locate a sector, will be totally unreliable.

A variety of methods are available to the system designer. Firstly, multiple, redundant headers may be used. The number must be chosen so that the probability of every redundant header being damaged is less than the error rate requirement of the system. This requires four or five headers to be used. The key issue is that overhead is increased significantly.

An alternative approach is to use one header per sector, but to establish the context of any required sector by the headers of previous sectors. Two issues must be dealt with in this case. Following a seek, context may be slow to establish, impacting access time, and secondly, the accuracy of the context system must be sufficiently high so that the length which must be reserved for a written sector is not greatly increased by the positional uncertainty of the context system.

Once a reliable method for locating and writing a data sector has been designed, a method for locating the start bit of the data field must be provided so that the read channel hardware can be synchronized. Once again, a single data mark feature cannot be used since its integrity will be too low to meet system error rate requirements.

A technique to overcome this problem is to use multiple data marks per data field, written sufficiently close together so that the loss of any data following a lost data mark is correctable by the EDAC system. Each of these marks may be unique so that the hardware can identify the exact byte count of the following data.

Error detection and correction

Given that a data buffer can be successfully filled from a given sector written on the disk surface, the probability that a data error has occurred within the sector is approximately 10^{-1}. A variety of EDAC schemes are available to the system designer. The choice of any particular technique will depend on the error rate and burst length statistics of the particular media being used. Interleaved Reed-Solomon codes are highly favored.

The ability of any given EDAC system to correct errors, depends to a large extent on the overhead which the method requires. In general, the correction of long burst length errors requires a large number of overhead bytes. The statistics of the number of separate error events within the sector is another factor which must be considered.

Another key issue when selecting the EDAC scheme is the processing time required to correct the data. Some schemes detect the errors using hardware but require processor activity to correct the data in a buffer. This can result in an inability to stream contiguous sectors, with a resulting loss of data thruput.

Media certification

The distribution of defects on optical media is such that the majority are of a size which is of the order of one code bit. However, there are also lesser numbers of defects significantly greater than one bit in size up to a typical maximum of one hundred code bits.

The system designer must decide if the EDAC scheme chosen will be able to correct the maximum size error burst expected. In this case the EDAC overhead will be very large and the capacity of the store reduced.

Media certification offers the possibility of eliminating sectors containing these large defects so that a lower overhead EDAC scheme may be used. The nature of the distribution of defect numbers versus size is such that the effect of retiring sectors containing defects of greater than one byte in length, reduces the number of available sectors by approximately one percent. The remaining sectors then contain defects of less than one byte at the start of life which can be corrected using an EDAC scheme of moderate redundancy.

In the event that the media is stored unwritten or partially unwritten, it is desirable to include the capability for certification, in the optical disk drive, at the users location. This extends the shelf life of the media prior to writing and also offers the user the ability to confirm the integrity of media exposed to an undesirable storage environment.

Synchronization loss and correction

Long burst length errors can create the possibility of the read channel loosing bit synchronization. In the event that this occurs, the data following the sync slip will be completely corrupted unless the bit slip can be detected and corrected.

The obvious solution is to include a repeating re-synchronization pattern in the data field so that the read channel can detect and correct for slip loss continuously. The spacing between synchronization patterns must be such that the EDAC scheme can correct for a worst case loss of synchronization, and in addition the system designer must include the probability that these patterns will be damaged in his design.

Detection of write faults

Optical storage is relatively shock sensitive due to the high accuracies required in the laser beam track-following system. During a read operation, a shock which causes an off track condition is of minor concern since a retry of the read is possible. In the case of writing, the consequences are far more severe. It is critically important to terminate the write operation before the laser has moved off track sufficiently to damage the adjacent track of data.

Read after write verification may be used for confirming the integrity of written data, but this reduces the thruput of the system dramatically.

To avoid the need for a second pass of the track for verification, it is possible to include read during write verification. Such systems avoid the need for reading after writing, but most techniques require a real time response from host level software if the data is to be rewritten in the next available unused sector. Automatic sector remapping by the optical disk controller can be used to avoid the need for real time host level activity.

Flaw mapping of defective sectors

If certification is used, the number of flawed sectors which must be retired, although a small percentage of the total, is still a very large number compared to that found on a typical magnetic disk. Mapping the flaws by tracks is not efficient since up to ten percent of the tracks will contain flawed sectors. It is therefore highly desirable to perform flaw mapping at the sector level.

To illustrate the scope of this problem, consider the example of a one gigabyte optical disk using 512 byte sectors. Such a disk contains almost 2,000,000 sectors. If the disk is certified so that the sector retirement rate is one percent, the flaw map will require 20,000 entries. The responsibility for manipulation of such a flaw map may be in the host or alternatively in the optical disk controller. In either case, significant amounts of RAM will be required for this task.

Undetected error rate issues

EDAC schemes, particularly when exposed to error rate conditions near to the maximum which is correctable, have a small but finite probability of performing a correction incorrectly. In this circumstance the host would be passed corrupted data without the knowledge of the EDAC scheme.

To reduce this probability to an acceptable level, it is common to apply a CRC, or other check to the data before the EDAC overhead bytes are computed. In this way the probability of undetected errors can be reduced to a vanishingly small number.

Data integrity scanning

When an optical disk has been stored for a very long time, new defects will incubate and old defects will grow in size. It is these factors which ultimately govern the storage lifetime of an optical disk, since eventually the EDAC scheme will be unable to recover the data at the specified error rate.

It is possible to provide a read scanning mode in an optical disk system which will evaluate the degree of damage of each sector before the EDAC system reaches the point of failure to correct. Sectors which fail some criteria can be rewritten into new sectors so that the overall life of the disk can be extended. It is difficult to evaluate the exact effect of such a strategy, but it is possible that storage life may be more than doubled.

Conclusions

The inherent error rate of optical storage systems is very poor. Typical error rates are such that no single event or feature recorded on the disk can be used to ensure data integrity. The use of redundancy in both the data and other essential surface format features is therefore an essential part of the working of any optical storage system.

By combining a variety of error management techniques in a mathematically balanced way, the system designer can trade off media quality, capacity, thruput, storage life, data integrity and system cost and complexity.

SYSTEMS, APPLICATIONS, AND IMPLICATIONS OF OPTICAL STORAGE

Richard G. Zech, PhD.

Rothchild Consultants

ABSTRACT *Optical storage technology, has been under active investigation by the leading computer and mass storage peripheral vendors for over 25 years. Only in the past 18 months have the hardware and software been available to permit serious system integration plans to evolve efforts. Plug and play optical disk subsystems, turnkey systems, and automated mass storage libraries are now available for PCs to mainframes. The future of optical storage is bright, but some complex system integration issues must still be resolved.*

1. INTRODUCTION

Few technologies are as diverse as optical storage. There are optical disks, cards, and tapes. Optical media is removable and can be read only, write once, or erasable -- and sometimes all three. Disk libraries, or jukeboxes, have created a new level in the mass storage hierarchy called *near-line storage*. No implementable storage technology even comes close to optical storage's proven areal density. In this brief overview, the marketing/applications and technology basics are presented. Although this survey is brief, it should be adequate to motivate an enthusiastic evaluation of optical storage's potential as an enabling technology.

2. OPTICAL MEMORY TECHNOLOGY

Today's optical storage devices are precision electro-mechanical/electro-optical systems capable of storing information at densities exceeding 500 million bits per square inch. The supporting technology and engineering infrastructure are complex and sophisticated. In this section the basic concepts are reviewed and relevant comparative background provided.

2.1 Advantages of Optical Storage

Various favorable attributes of optical storage have motivated the strong interest of end users, computer OEMs, and system integrators. Very high capacity, removability, and the potential for a high level of operating and storage reliability are considered the foremost. The security implied by a cartridge that can be vaulted is appreciated by business and military users. An examination of the inherent advantages of optical storage via typical specifications and operating parameters reveals the strengths and certain weaknesses of the technology.

The best known advantage of optical storage is its high storage density. This is due almost entirely to its ability (1) to write track densities exceeding 15,000 tracks per inch (tpi) in commercial products (15,875 tpi, corresponding to a track pitch of 1.6 um, is a de facto standard), and now close to 25,000 tpi, and (2) to reliably acquire and follow these tracks during read with an accuracy often better than ± 0.1 u m. When this is combined with recording densities in the 11,500 - 43,000 bits per inch (bpi) range, the result is very high storage densities and surface capacities.

Current 5¼" write-once optical disks store between 120 MB and 500 MB per side (750 - 1000 MB is the next target). The larger 8" and 12" optical disks store up to 0.75 or 2 GB, respectively. It's expected that 12" drives with 2 - 5 GB per side will be available in 1989 to compete with both 14" disks and jukeboxed or arrayed 5¼" drives. **Eastman Kodak** announced in March 1987 a 14" system that has a capacity of 3.4 GB per side and a data transfer rate of 1 megabyte per second (MBps). Kodak's subsidiary, **Verbatim**, is expected to begin delivery of 3½" erasable drives in Q3 1988.

High surface capacity translates into large amounts of storage in a relatively small volume, with reduced weight and power consumption. Today, two 5¼" full-height write-once optical drives with 500 - 1000 MB of total capacity, fit in a single 19" rack mount. Three to five years from now, the same volume will accommodate four 5¼" half-height drives with 2 GB of write-once and 1 GB of erasable optical storage. No other storage technology comes close to matching this level of capacity and functionality.

Another inherent advantage of optical storage is the potential for a high level of operational reliability, particularly in high stress environments. The following reliability aspects merit discussion.

- First, there can never be a head crash or slap with an optical drive. The optical head is positioned several millimeters above the surface of the optical disk, which is about 10,000 times higher than a magnetic head flies to achieve comparable recording densities. Moreover, the optical head doesn't fly over the optical disk, it is suspended over it.

- Second, the data surface of the optical disk is covered or sandwiched. This renders it immune to all

CH2539-5/88/0000/0135$01.00 © 1988 IEEE

but the most severe scratch, abrasion, and dust problems. For a removable medium this is a must, even if a protective case or caddy is employed.

■ Third, there is a read-after-write option (RAW or "direct read during write", DRDW) that permits data to be verified in real time, and for defective sectors or data blocks to be rewritten and mapped.

■ Fourth, because of unavoidable defects on the surface of the optical disk, graceful aging effects, and potentially catastrophic burst errors, powerful error detection and correction codes (EDAC or ECC) have been developed. A depth four interleaved Reed-Solomon code over a 512 byte sector can correct a 10^{-4} raw bit error rate to an industry acceptable 10^{-12}, or better, with less than 10 - 20% overhead. This error protection can be obtained in a small, low cost chip set, implemented in gate array logic.

The removability of optical media is often taken for granted. Neither magnetic disk nor tape cartridge or cassette drives offer the performance obtainable from optical disk drives. The throughput of a magnetic drive may be better today and the capacity of a magnetic tape may be comparable to today's low-end optical disks, but neither by itself provides the high capacity, removability, high throughput, and reliability found in an optical disk drive.

Unlike magnetic drives, both the write and read energy of an optical drive are in the optical head (the laser diode). The energy, moreover, scales linearly with the recording density (spot size). This implies that storage density in optical drives is limited only by laser spot size, and whatever challenges that size may create for the focus and tracking servos. Laboratory systems can handle spot sizes as small as 0.25 um, or the equivalent storage density of over 2 GB/inch^2.

In contrast, magnetic drives have the write energy in the magnetic heads and the read energy in the magnetic media. At very high recording densities, the signal or read margin becomes very small and the error rate increases (any separation loss adds to the problem); evidence of this problem comes from the increasing use of ECC.

Finally, optical drives can be designed for extremely wide bandwidth, multichannel recording. In the past this required acousto-optic page composers and high power argon gas lasers. With the advent of laser diode arrays, compact and reliable optical drives having data transfer rates of 100 Mbps or higher, can be developed. For example, an eight data channel (byte wide) optical head writing at 20,000 bpi on a 5¼" disk spinning at 3,600 revolutions per minute (rpm) would yield a data transfer rate of 75 Mbps; with a 14" optical disk it would be over 200 Mbps. Only very advanced magnetic tape instrumentation recorders with up to 100 channels match or exceed these rates.

2.2 Technology Trends

Most of the optical drives being considered for small computer system applications are based on technology perfected over the past five years. Engineering and packaging have helped to mature this technology, but have not solved some important performance and functional problems. Current technology trends suggest a new generation of optical drives that will be very attractive for all applications. The following overview suggests important trends:

■ **Capacity** -- Higher areal densities (greater surface capacity). Expect 1 Gbit/in^2 densities (40,000 bpi and 25,000 tpi) by early 1990s. Multiple disks per spindle for fixed optical disks (greater volume capacity). Expect IBM 3380 performance in an 8" rack mount product by 1991.

■ **Erasability** -- Magneto-optic (MO), phase change, and dye/polymer media have excellent storage parameters, but only MO currently looks like a commercial product. Most reliability problems that caused concern about MO media have been solved. Sampling of MO drives began in Q3 1987. Late 1988 and 1989 will see the introduction of the first DASD competitive erasable optical drives.

■ **Data Transfer Rate** -- Higher laser diode power, laser diode arrays, and faster rotational speeds will permit rates to move into the 1-2 MBps regime for small form factor drives, and beyond 3 MBps for large form factor drives.

■ **Access Time** -- New small mass optical heads (using holographic optical elements) and better actuators will greatly improve seek times, and result in average access times below 75 msec in 1988 and below 30 msec by late 1989. Less than 45 msec has been demonstrated for 3½" drives; less than 20 is feasible.

■ **Smaller Sizes** -- 3½" and 5¼" erasable drives are under development and are expected to come to market in early 1988. Some 3½" and 5¼" drives will directly replace magnetic DASD in PCs and workstations.

■ **Intelligence** -- Intelligent interfaces with a SCSI host bus adapter, large write and read buffers, and a 680XX or 80X86 microprocessor will simplify integration of large capacity systems through transparency and programmability. Many optical drives are today sold only as subsystems which are plug and play with computers running under MS-DOS, UNIX, VMS, and MVS (TSO and CICS) operating systems.

The net effect of these advances should be a number of new products with the potential for satisfying important computer system data and digital image storage requirements. The following matrix summarizes the possible performance ranges:

Disk Size	Capacity Range (MB)	Rate (Mbps)	Type	Available
3½	100-250	10	E	Q4 88
5¼	500-1,000	5-20	WO,E	Q2 88
8/12	2,000-4,000	10-25	WO,E	Q4 88
14	5,000-15,000	10-100	WO,E	Q4 89

3. MARKETS AND APPLICATIONS

3.1 Definition of Terms

Like its magnetic counterpart, optical storage systems come in many types and forms, including optical disks, cards, and tapes (the latter is being designed almost exclusively for mainframe backup, digital high definition TV, and wideband data collection applications). Moreover, optical media can be:

- **Read-only** (an optical read-only memory, or OROM),

- **Write-once/Read-many** (often called write-once, WO, or "WORM"), or

- **Erasable/Re-writeable** (which is a different concept from "**overwriteable**", or the ability to write directly new information over old, as in the case of magnetic media).

Finally, one class of optical drives is being designed to read or read/write all (or at least most) types of optical media. These drives are called "**multifunction**" drives.

Although there are no formal standards for the large majority of optical storage devices, the physical attributes of optical drives have tended to mimic those of magnetic storage devices whenever possible. Available and announced 3½", 5¼", 8", 12", and 14" drive designs have attempted to satisfy some minimal form factor or packaging constraint. For 3½" and 5¼" drives there is strict adherence to industry-standard form factor volume rules. Most 8", 12", and 14" drives are designed to fit comfortably in standard 19" rack mounts. Complete physical and certain format standards for all disk sizes are being pursued through working documents submitted to the **American National Standards Institute** (ANSI) technology subcommittee, X3B11.

The 120 mm CD-ROM is the only worldwide standardized optical data disk product, being completely defined in great detail both physically and logically by its co-inventors N.V. Philips of the Netherlands and Sony of Japan and recently adopted **International Standards Organization (ISO)** standards for file labeling and structure (mainly the work of the **High Sierra Committee**).

ANSI/ISO standards are now in place for 5¼" write-once as of October 1987. Both **composite continuous, spiral and sampled servo formats** have been promulgated. Only the exact details of the file structure and labeling, essential to disk interchange across product lines, remains to accomplished.

There are no standards for either optical tape or cards, although an ANSI committee is working to develop one for the latter. The large number of announced and planned optical card readers and reader/writers, most of which are based on **Drexler Technology Corporation** licenses, makes a compelling argument for an early adoption of standards.

With the possible exception of optical tape, all types and forms of optical storage will be specified for computer data and image storage applications. The smaller capacity, lower performance optical devices will most often be integrated into single user (personal) and document management systems, whereas the larger capacity, higher performance devices will most likely be shared in multi-user systems or networked.

3.2 Market and Application Analysis

Applications that may require optical storage products have a number of similar characteristics. The most prominent may have one or more of the following:

- Removability and large capacity on a single media unit (100s of megabytes);

- Removability and relatively high throughput (greater than 1 Mbps data transfer rate and less than 1 second average access time at the upper limit). This opens the door to direct replacement of floppy disks, tape cartridges, disk cartridges, and Bernoulli boxes;

- Very large capacity (1000s of megabytes) and on-line (drive arrays) or near-line (automated optical disk libraries) accessibility;

- Exceptional media reliability (in use, on the shelf, and in long term storage). This relates, in particular, to the important notion of "archival" storage, which offers significant economic advantage compared to magnetic tape.

- Replication and distribution of large amounts of data (software systems and/or value-added databases);

- Harsh environment survivability (militarized and ruggedized equipment). This appears to be one of the areas in which optical storage has a real opportunity to replace magnetic disk and tape, especially in avionics and shipboard applications.

3.2.1 Major Market Segments

With this background in place, we can now summarize the basic parameters of what are perceived to be the most promising markets for optical storage products. These include small computer system applications, office and transaction document storage, engineering and manufacturing document and image storage, and mainframe computer applications.

- **Banking, Financial Services, and Insurance Companies**

  - 14", 12", and 5¼" write-once main opportunities; PC to mainframe applications
  - Jukebox near-line storage can have significant positive impact on productivity
  - Very intensive processing and information needs
  - Security (audit trails and data vaulting) important
  - Dynamic transaction oriented environment
  - Complex legal and regulatory considerations
  - 3½" erasable and CD-ROM for data transport

- **Fortune 1000 Industrial/Manufacturing Companies**

  - 14", 12", and 5¼" write-once and 5¼" and 3½" erasable main opportunities; PC to mainframe applications
  - Productivity/marketing/global competition driven
  - Computerized and robotic production lines/systems may

require ruggedized, high capacity storage peripherals
- Office document management applications also very important, as productivity benefits are readily obtainable with relatively small investments and risk
- Jukebox near-line storage important for both administration and production

■ **Federal/State Government**

- 14", 12", 8", 5¼" write-once main opportunities
- Jukebox near-line storage essential for magnetic tape library replacement
- Very significant data generators and collectors
- Most activities mandated by laws and regulations
- Standards are very important
- On-line departmental/agency document files needed
- Longer than average sales cycle
- CD-ROM and 5¼" and 3½" OROM for data distribution

■ **Medium Size Businesses/Large Professional Offices**

- 5¼" and 3½" erasable and write-once main opportunities; some opportunities for 14", 12', and 8" write-once for document management systems.
- Have an estimated installed base of $33 billion in small computer systems
- Looking for better approach to save/restore and backup/archive functions
- Cost sensitive, but a moderately fast reacting segment

■ **Medium and Large Data Processing Centers**

- 14" and 12" write-once and jukebox systems primary opportunities; 5¼" erasable and write-once also represent important opportunities, especially for mid-range computer systems
- Tape drive replacement for save/restore (12", 8" and 5¼" erasable)
- Tape drive replacement for backup/archive (14" and 12" write-once)
- Tape library compression using jukeboxes
- Standards and support very important
- Must be compatible with existing computing environment

■ **Military and Rugged**

- 14", 12", and 5¼" write-once main opportunities, although erasable is also required
- 3½" erasable and read-only variants needed for terminals and small vehicles
- Mission support and data collection are initial applications; general data processing applications for erasable drives to follow
- Reliability and performance are top priorities

3.2.2 Primary (General) Applications

■ **Hard Disk Complement**

Hard disk complement defines the use of write-once or lower performance erasable optical disk drives as a partner of a fixed magnetic disk drive. This concept derived from the observation that most files are inactive and that the ratio of read requests to write requests is often greater than 5 to 1. The optical disk drive provides large, on-line capacity with the advantages of removability, permanence, and security. For this reason, it may also be referred to as an "on-line or active archive." The magnetic disk drive is primarily used for scratch pad I/O (system boot, application program loading, etc. are done from the optical disk) and temporary file storage. Data to be stored indefinitely is written to and read from the optical disk.

There are several advantages to this arrangement. First, the magnetic drive's capacity need not be large (e.g., 10 - 20 MB for a small computer system) for most systems. This, in turn, allows the magnetic drive to be designed for maximum throughput, greater reliability, and lower cost. The capacity burden falls on the optical drive, which can currently provide from 115 MB to 3,400 MB of removable on-line storage. This design allows each device to be separately optimized relative to its strongest features (performance is measured relative to the combined devices).

For most computer systems the data on hard disks is read-only (true in many cases even for mainframe systems, where a large number of relatively inactive records are kept on-line more for convenience than necessity). Typical examples are documents, databases, and software that may be seldom accessed, but still have some intrinsic value. Generally, these data are backed up on floppy disks or tapes, and are stored on shelves or in file drawers. These files can safely, less expensively, and more conveniently be stored on a high capacity write-once or erasable optical disk, and be maintained on-line for rapid access when needed. In simple terms, the concept of hard disk complement permits all data and software to reside on-line and eliminates the need for floppy disk or tape backup.

Implementation of hard disk complement will be relatively straightforward for erasable optical drives. For write-once optical drives, an operating system and user procedure issue that arises is how to most efficiently use the disk capacity. Currently, no computer operating system recognizes as a valid peripheral a write-once optical disk drive. Hence, system software must be written that makes the optical drive transparent to the operating system. In this instance, the write-once optical drive functions as a typical hard disk.

An easier approach, one that matches the characteristics of write-once quite well, is to "spool" (an acronym for simultaneous peripheral operation on-line) to the hard disk, and write on command any files that are to be permanently stored. On the read side, the usual DMA techniques are available, and provide with suitable optimization techniques rather impressive throughput rates. Alternatively, a file or collection of files can be "staged" (copied over) to the hard disk for subsequent processing.

Despite some obvious advantages, the concept of hard disk complement has not sold well. The two main issues are cost and, for small computer systems, front panel priority (i.e., which storage peripherals are to be mounted in the front panel; this is a market driven consideration). Attachable subsystems circumvent the problem, but they take up extra desk or floor space.

The introduction of the hard card solved the root problem for small computer systems by moving the hard disk out of the front panel into the chassis.

Interestingly, no 5¼" or 3½" optical drive vendor has publicly exploited this important development to stake claim to the abandoned front panel volume, which has created a minimum of 250,000 new sales opportunities for 5¼" and 3½" write-once and erasable disk drives, CD-ROM readers, and optical card reader/writers (in the near future some desktop computer manufacturers may design in hard cards and use the abandoned space for more add-in board slots).

Cost is still a major issue at the low end of the small computer system market, where a $1,500 - $2,000 per unit pain threshold exists for storage peripherals. In contrast, the price of optical storage at the higher end of the market is low enough to motivate system integrators to do extensive development work on disk and tape emulation and document storage systems. Value added via system integration hides the cost of the optical drive.

■ Hard Disk Replacement

Hard disk replacement is the substitution of an erasable optical disk drive for a magnetic hard disk drive. This implies a minimum set of characteristics which include a sub-100 msec average access time (less than 50 msec is desired), and a data transfer rate of at least 5 Mbps (10 Mbps is preferred). Optical drives for high end workstations and PCs and large computer systems will need even higher levels of performance, whereas those intended for data collection systems and transportable computers will be acceptable with lower levels of performance (often a trade-off with power consumption). By the early 1990s, there will probably be an optical solution for every requirement.

For an optical disk drive to be a better than or equal replacement for a magnetic disk drive, the optical drive must provide superior price/performance and it must integrate with the same familiarity to design engineers as the magnetic drive. This means commonalty of drivers, controllers, interfaces, etc. Today, this can be handled via a host level interface such as SCSI (small computer system interface) or with a drive level interface such as ESDI (enhanced small device interface). Controllers have been designed that support both a high performance magnetic drive and a write-once optical drive; similar support will be even easier for erasable optical drives. Because of inherent differences in their design, optical drives will probably always be different from magnetic drives. However, from an integrator or end user perspective, the differences will be negligible.

■ Archive/Backup

The hallmark characteristics of optical storage media are large capacity per surface, removability and, stability. This has long suggested that a primary application of optical storage be for archiving or backing up operational or historical data. Archive and backup generally imply off-site or secure storage (as in a vault) of the medium and infrequent accession of the data on the medium. The term backup is often used synonymously, but incorrectly, for save/restore. In fact, a large percent of backed up data may never be used, and is commonly disposed of, or should be, on a regularly scheduled basis. Archived data is often used only to make working copies of the data sets, thus limiting the opportunities for accidental or intentional data losses.

This can be a write-once or read-only application, since there is seldom a need to change the data. The data permanence of write-once and read-only media is a distinct advantage where legal requirements demand a tangible, certifiable audit trail or historical record. The high volumetric storage density of an optical disk is another advantage in terms of cost savings for storage space and minimization of the number of data storage elements that must be handled when a record request is initiated.

■ Save/Restore

In large dynamic data processing environments, the content of records, files, and data volumes is constantly changing. This is especially true in applications involving transaction processing and recording such as in the airline and banking industries. However, even many business and professional users of small computer systems, whether single or multiuser, generate significant daily changes to their databases.

To prevent catastrophic loss of data, many system managers or end users dump the entire content of their hard disks onto tape, magnetic disk or Bernoulli cartridges, floppies, or even disk packs. Depending on the application, this may be done hourly, twice a day, daily, or weekly. The objective is to minimize data loss to the amount captured during the time between save/restore operations. In many instances, save/restore is viewed as an expensive inconvenience, and many individuals and businesses simply do without it, despite the risks.

The save/restore function was developed as a form of insurance to protect vital records in the event of hard disk failure. Until recently, mean time between failures (MTBF) for rotating mass storage devices was around 5,000 hours; today, many vendor spec sheets claim 30,000 hours, or more. However infrequently they occur, failures still remain random events, often with catastrophic results. There is generally no interest in or need for saving the disk image after the most recent dump. However, some users do vault tape cartridges as a means of preserving time slices or snapshots of their database; this then becomes what has been defined as archiving/backup.

Thus, this application requires (1) an erasable medium, although very inexpensive write-once disks, essentially throw away consumables, might also serve a small part of this market and (2) a system with sufficient throughput to permit fast, simple save/restore operations.

The first generation of 5¼" magneto-optic (MO) disk drives (including several multifunction types) will fit the application profile very well for small computer systems. With a typical 300 MB capacity per side and data transfer rates of up to 1 MBps, these devices are strong competition for ¼" tape drives and Bernoulli boxes.

One side of a magneto-optic disk has more capacity than about 90% of the hard disks being used with small computer systems. This allows automated save/restore operations on a pre-scheduled basis without the need in most cases for disk swap or turn or other user intervention.

For larger computer systems, 12" multifunction drives are expected to be available in 1989 with surface capacities exceeding 1,000 MB and data transfer rates approximating current 3 - 4.5 MBps mainframe data transfer rates.

For many single user systems, the 50 - 100 MB per side 3½" magneto optic drive and media under development by **Verbatim (Sunnyvale, California)** and several Japanese companies will be very attractive. Early and deep penetration of this market will be driven by price and features (based on current ¼" tape drive and Bernoulli box pricing, an erasable optical subsystem priced in the $1,200 - $1,600 price range should sell well). Competition from 3½" will also be a factor.

4. CONCLUDING REMARKS

Optical storage is rapidly becoming a viable mass storage peripheral alternative. All major computer and office automation OEMs have either announced products, will be announcing soon, or have a development program in progress. No significant factor in the computer industry can afford to ignore the competitive advantage or threat that optical storage offers.

The current generation of optical storage is an enabling technology, not a displacement one. There are very few applications for which optical is a one for one replacement for magnetic DASD. That opportunity will have its genesis when the next generation of erasable, high performance optical drives come to market.

In the mean time, existing optical drives and media provide an abundance of system configuration options for compressing magnetic tape libraries, automating order fulfillment, creating near-line engineering drawing and document libraries, designing avionic subsystems for flight optimization, and so forth. Whether an entrepreneur, MIS manager, system integrator, or a business executive with a critical operating problem, optical storage offers new and cost effective solutions to those with imagination and vision. The cost/benefit equation of optical storage is now well enough defined and positive to encourage action now.

STATUS OF OPTICAL MEDIA

David H. Davies

3M Company
420 North Bernardo Avenue
Mountain View, California 94043

The criticality of media to laser optical storage is first detailed followed by a discussion of the basic forms of media. The various options in substrates, construction, formatting, encoding and active layer selection are discussed in the light of major trade-offs involved in practical selection.

Prerecorded and recordable media are included with the latter encompassing both write-once and erasable varieties.

Introduction

The emergence of laser optical storage offers significant potential for improving the utility of computer systems particularly in image and data base related applications. It is generally recognized that the disc media plays a critical role in this technology, indeed a larger role than in most conventional storage technologies. The reasons for this lie in the added functionality that media brings to, and requires from, the system. For example, the radial density that is unique to optical results from the specific media based tracking schemes employed. The very high density also results in significant media intrinsic errors. This requires sophisticated error correction (ECC) and detection schemes that then in turn require that the media error distributions and error deterioration patterns are consistent enough to remain within the scope of the ECC. The great advantage of laser optical storage, the noncontacting nature of the interaction which results in media portability and the archival like properties, also places burdens on the media. For example, the reflective nature of the off-contact focus servo places severe restrictions on the media's infrared reflectivity uniformity. Another aspect is the preformatting utilized in most recordable optical storage; this preembossing is a major savings in cost and time for the user but places a difficult validation and certification task on the media maker. Further, the read and tracking schemes must be operational without problem over the very different detector signal responses of the post written and preformatted data. This constrains the mechanisms, places a further media reflectivity limit and requires a high degree of microstructure 'feature' consistency on the embossed surface.

Despite the constraints, viable cost effective media has been realized on a commercial scale for all the forms of optical storage. This paper outlines the status of these medias and discusses problems and issues relating to them.

The Forms of Optical Media

The basic division in optical media results in four categories; prerecorded or user-recordable and digital or analog. Hybrids are also possible and table (1) illustrates the present status in outline and gives an illustrative reference for the most important categories.

Table 1

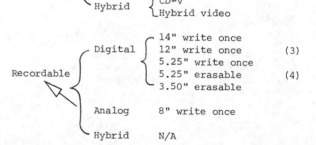

Prerecorded	Digital	O-ROM	
		CD-Audio	
		CD-I	
		CD-ROM	(1)
		DVI	
		Digital video	
	Analog	Laser video	(2)
	Hybrid	CD-V	
		Hybrid video	
Recordable	Digital	14" write once	
		12" write once	(3)
		5.25" write once	
		5.25" erasable	(4)
		3.50" erasable	
	Analog	8" write once	
	Hybrid	N/A	

There are fifteen major variants, with new ones appearing rapidly, please refer to the references for specific descriptions. The degree of category variety is superimposed over a wide range of construction and mechanistic options creating an enormous number of potential variants.

Substrate and Construction

There are four materials presently used for media construction; they are glass, polycarbonate (PC), polymethyl methacrylate (PMMA), and aluminum.

Substrate choice is determined largely by media active layer environmental sensitivities, a high sensitivity to oxidation or hydrolysis forces a glass solution (e.g., tellurium based write once). Nonsensitive media will in general use plastic for cost and weight, also to avoid breakage risk. Generally, the smaller formats use PC rather than PMMA since molding of polycarbonate without birefringence is very difficult above 6" diameter. Aluminum is selected if precise flatness is needed. Typically this arises if access time and data rate needs have forced disk rotation rates above the cost effective servo limits for plastic.

The vast majority of today's optical disks are plastic. Table (2) lists the major plastic performance attributes required and details illustrative data relative to those attributes (see below).

Construction options are illustrated in Table (3). The grading numbers are explained below.

Table 3

A <u>Air sandwich - S.I.</u>

good 2 bad 4

B <u>Air sandwich cover incident</u>

good 3 bad 4

C <u>Laminate - S.I.</u>

good 1,2 bad 3

D <u>Laminate cover A.I.</u>

good 1 bad 4

E <u>Single piece - face up</u>

good 4 bad 2

F <u>Single piece - face down</u>

good 4 bad 2

S.I. - substrate incident, A.I. - air incident; see Fig. (1) which illustrates these options.

The selection variables are as follows:

1) size and related physical run out (TIR) requirements
2) need to protect active layer from environment
3) need to maximize media sensitivity to laser power and hence avoid heat sinking at the active layer
4) cost, including moldability, intrinsic simplicity and raw material cost.

Generally, these trade-offs have resulted in the following primary selections...prerecorded video-C, prerecorded audio/data - F, write once recordable - A,B and erasable - C. Other options are also in use.

Tracking

The four options for a media tracking scheme are as follows: (a) no media tracking, (b) far field tracking, (c) sampled servo tracking, and (d) data tracking. Figure (2) illustrates option (b). See ref. (5) for further details.

The major trade-offs are as follows:

a) no media based tracking

good....lowers media cost
bad.....media interchange difficult

b) far field tracking

good....data density increased
bad.....media complexity

c) sampled servo tracking

good....cross talk limitation
bad.....reliability

d) data tracking

good....simplifies read:write channel
bad.....only applies to prerecorded

In practice all prerecorded media use data tracking and the majority of recordable medias have used far field with a move to sampled servos being

Table 2

Performance of Typical Plastics

Property	Unit	PC	PMMA	Epoxy[(1)]	PO[(2)]
Transmission (780-830nm)	%	90±1	92±1	92±1	93
Refractive Index	-	1.55-1.59	1.49-1.52	1.51-1.54	1.55
Birefringence	nm	<20	<10	<5	<20
Glass Transition Temp.	^0C	143-145	89-100	115-125	155
Deformation Temp.	^0C	125-136	80-88	125-135	129-136
Rockwell Hardness	M-scale	5	82	85-90	75
Water Absorption	%	0.2	0.3	0.25-0.3	0.01
Water Vapor Transmission	g/m^2-24 hrs	3.6	2.8	1.30-2.5	?

[1]Published data by Sumitomo Bakelite.
[2]Amorphous polyolefine, published data by Mitsui Petrochemical.

driven by the better compatibility with the detectors used in magneto-optic erasable media. In the absence of media based preembossed tracking, the user drive is sometimes designed with sufficient precision to meet the interchange tolerances or the media is prewritten at the initial formatter and this provides a tracking functionality.

Media Encoding

The coding method that translates media pit to data bits has a significant impact on total system design and on media operation. For an explanation of encoding methods for optical discs, see ref. (6).

The trade-offs can be summarized as follows.

Table 4

Encoding Trade-offs

	efficiency	media tolerant	system tolerant	typical use
2,7	+	--	--	erasable optical
8,14	-	+	+	CD
NRZ	0	+	+	write once

The error detection and correction coding methods employed are very much media dependent. Ref. (7) provides a good theoretical base for the area of coding theory.

Active Layer Selection

The material system that is used to provide the function of storage is the most important variable in optical storage. Unlike magnetic storage, there are a wide range of options available and this has tended to reduce standardization. Prerecorded media need only to reflect the laser light and generally aluminum is used either alone or doped for stability. The major options for write once media are shown below.

Write-once Active Layer Options

The following options are currently commercial.

.... low melting metals that ablate e.g., tellurium doped with other elements to enhance chemical stability
.... low melting alloys that comingle to form a reflective or absorbing phase e.g., antimony: selenium:tellurium
.... dye systems e.g., cyanine dyes, with or without polymeric hosts
.... high melting refractories that are optically enhanced e.g., chromium oxide in trilayer construction. See Fig. (3).

All the above systems are in use today with varying degrees of success. All achieve >50 db CNR at typical write power levels of 5 mW at the disc surface (500-1800 rpm, 0.5 NA, 820nm). Ref. (8) details an example of refractory optically enhanced media in use today.

Erasable Optical

There are three currently distinct approaches;
.... dye-polymer materials e.g., melt and remelt
.... phase change e.g., reversible cyclic amorphous to crystalline
.... magneto-optic e.g., ternary rare earth transition metal (RE-TM) alloys

Only the latter approach is commercial, Fig. (4) illustrates the principle. The major issue of both phase change and dye-polymer is cyclic stability and of magneto-optic is bit overwrite. Several approaches to solve bit overwrite have been proposed recently. These generally utilize the self orienting internal fields possible with some high coercivity alloys in the RE-TM class. Ref. (4) details specific performance parameters of a typical magneto-optic media.

Conclusion

The complexity of laser optical media for storage purposes has made the commercialization of this technology a significant challenge. It appears that currently the major issues are resolved and media availability is no longer a critical issue.

References

1. CD-ROM - The New Papyrus, ed. S. Lambert, S. Ropiequet, Microsoft Press, Redmond, WA., 1986.
2. The Videodisc Book: A guide and directory, Daynes, R. & Butler, B., J. Wiley & Sons Inc., 1984.
3. "Optical Storage Media", Proc. SPIE, Vol. 420, ed. A.E. Bell, Arlington, VA., 1983.
4. R.P. Freese, International Conf. on Optical Mass Data Storage, Vol. 529, ed. R.A. Sprague, pp. 6-9, 1985.
5. Principles of Optical Disc Systems, ed. G. Bouwhuis, Adam Hilger, Ltd., Bristol, England, 1985.
6. J. Isailovic, Proc. SPIE, Vol. 529, ed. R.A. Sprague, pp. 161.
7. Algebraic Coding Theory, E.R. Berlekamp, McGraw-Hill Co., New York, N.Y., 1968.
8. D.H. Davies, Proc. SPIE on Optical Storage Media, Vol. 420, ed. A.E. Bell, p. 250, 1985.

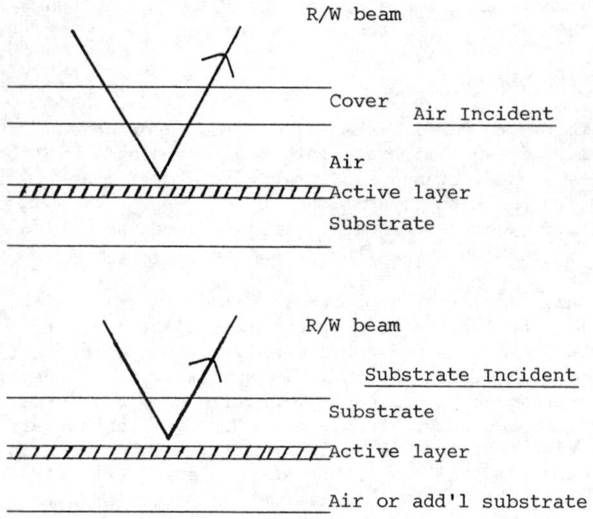

Figure 1

Construction Principles

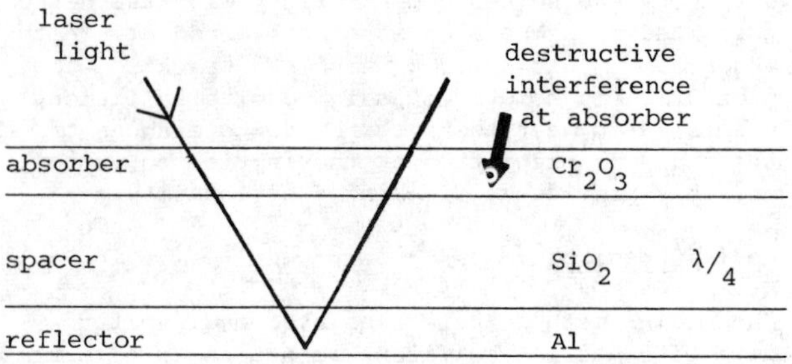

Figure 3

Optically Enhanced Refractory Metal Write Once Media

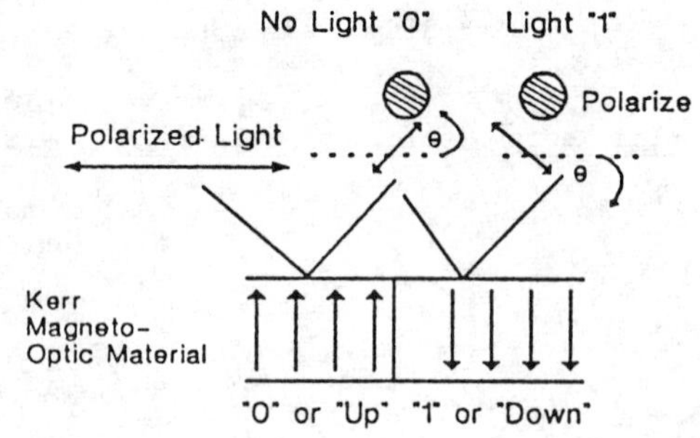

Figure 4

Principle of Magneto-optic Media

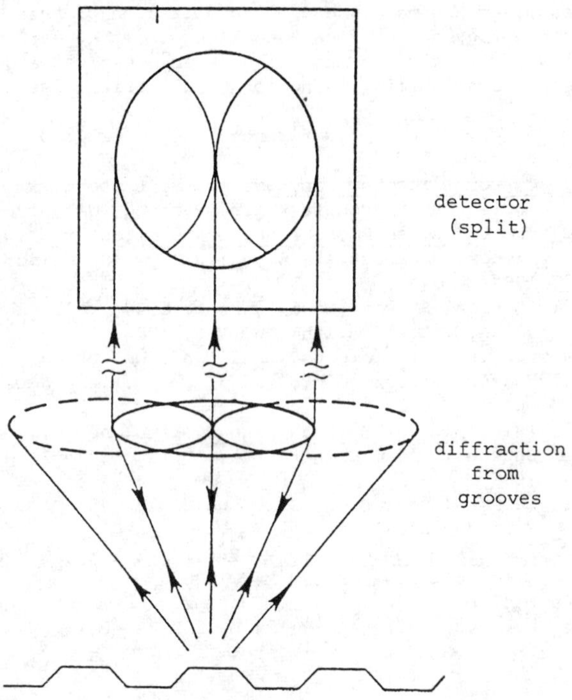

Figure 2

Principle of Far Field Tracking

Disk Caching

Chair: J. Menon

The IBM 3990 Disk Cache

Jai Menon

IBM Almaden Research Center
San Jose, California 95120-6099

Mike Hartung

IBM Tucson Laboratory
Tucson, Arizona 85744

Abstract

This report gives a brief overview of the IBM 3990 Model 3 cache control unit. Some new performance and RAS features are described and some modelling results on performance are presented.

Introduction

Disk caches that are used to extend the performance of high-end computer systems have been implemented by several vendors (see [SMITH85] for a list of some of these vendors). This paper describes the IBM 3990 cached disk control unit, which is the most modern IBM disk cache to date ([IBM3990]).

The 3990 is available in three models ([IBM3990]), and the structure and features of the 3990 family of control units represent a significant improvement over the structure and features of the older 3880 family of control units ([IBM3880, IBM232]). The 3990 Model 1 and the 3990 Model 2 are uncached control units, and we will not describe them any more in this report. The 3990 Model 3 is a cached disk control unit, and the rest of this paper will be devoted to a description of the 3990 Model 3. For simplicity, in the rest of this report, we will often use the term "3990" when we really mean the "3990 Model 3". We will also sometimes refer to a disk as DASD (direct access storage device), which is the IBM terminology for disk.

The 3990 is a separate, stand-alone control unit, which attaches to the host CPU over ***channels*** and to the IBM 3380 disk via an internally defined disk interface. For an overview of a typical I/O in IBM architecture, and a summary of what functions are typically performed in a channel and what functions are typically performed in a control unit, the reader is referred to [BOHL81].

Frequently referenced records from the disk are stored in high-speed electronic storage in the 3990. When the host CPU asks for a record from a disk, the 3990 first checks to see if the requested record is in the electronic storage (cache) in the 3990. If so, the record is returned from the cache and there is no need to access the disk. The more often requested data is found in the cache (a ***cache hit*** occurs), the better the performance of the control unit. If a copy of the record is in the cache when the host initiates a read request, we will refer to that as a ***read hit***. On the other hand, if a copy of the record is in the cache when the host initiates a write request, we will call that a ***write hit***.

The rest of this paper will be organized as follows. We will begin with a diagram and overview of the paths in the 3990. Then, we will describe the performance and cache features of the 3990. Following this, we describe the dual copy feature and other reliability, availability and serviceability features of the 3990. Finally, we will present some results indicating the expected performance that can be obtained by using a 3990 disk cache.

3990 Overview

In Figure 1 on page 2, we show an overview of the 3990 Model 3. As can be seen, it consists of two independent ***storage clusters***. Each cluster provides a separate power and service region and two separate paths to the string of DASDs. Loss of power to one cluster does not disable the 3990, since processing continues through the other storage cluster.

CH2539-5/88/0000/0146$01.00

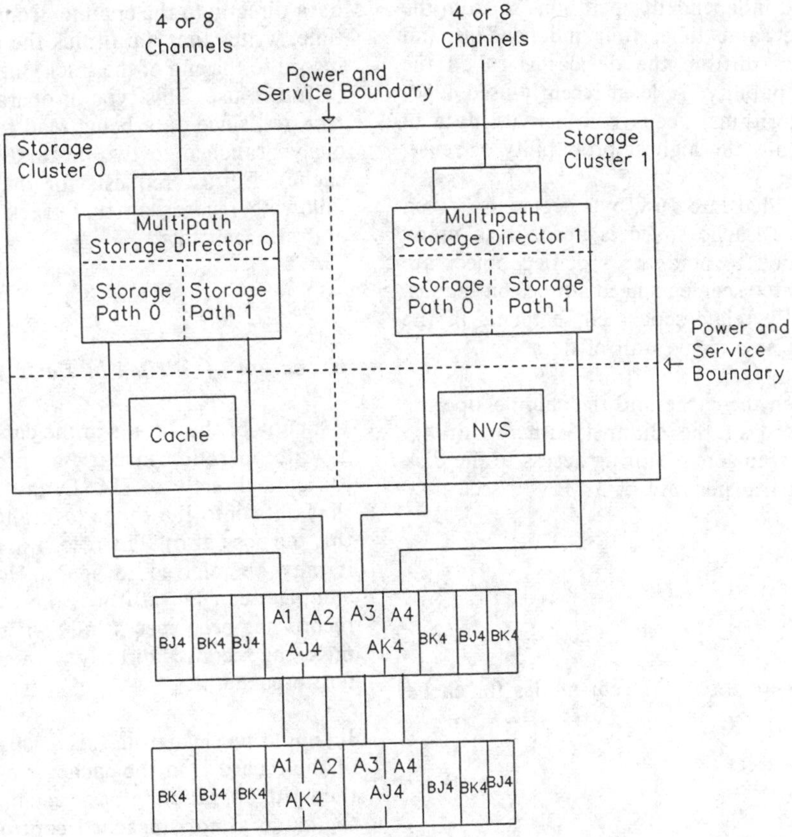

Figure 1: The IBM 3990 Disk Cache

Each storage cluster attaches to host CPUs via four or eight channels. Each of the possible total of 16 channels can operate at either 3 or 4.5 Mbytes/sec.

As a new standard of data availability and overall performance, twice as many storage paths are provided in the 3990 than in the older 3880 Model 23 ([IBM231, IBM232]). When attached to the new 4-path 3380 Models AJ4/AK4 ([IBM3380]), the 3990 can access any device over any one of ***four*** paths using the ***device level selection enhanced*** (DLSE) mode. To repeat, DLSE provides four paths to each actuator and simultaneous data transfer to any four actuators in the attached 4-path strings of devices. In Figure 1, each AJ4, AK4, BJ4 or BK4 actually represents four devices (actuators). Thus, a total of 64 devices are represented in the figure. The J and K in AJ4, AK4, BJ4 and BK4 refer to different capacity 3380 disks, and, as is apparent from Figure 1, any combination of the J and K disks may be intermixed. For further details on these devices, and the difference between the AJ4 (AK4) and the BJ4 (BK4), the reader is referred to [IBM3380].

The 3990 has cache sizes of 32, 64, 128 or 256 Mbytes. Cache is in a separate power region from the storage clusters. If a storage cluster is off-line, cache processing still continues through the other storage cluster.

Finally, the 3990 has nonvolatile storage (NVS) which provides random-access electronic storage. However, as will become apparent later in the paper, the NVS is not used as a cache. The NVS has its own separate power region for data protection and is used to perform functions like DASD fast write and dual copy, which will be described later. If power is lost to the 3990 before certain data in NVS has been copied to disk, a battery-backup system maintains power in the nonvolatile storage for up to 48 hours with a fully-charged battery to prevent data loss. When power is restored, the 3990 destages any data in NVS to disk and completes any operation in process at the time of the failure.

Details of the 3990 Cache

The cache in the 3990 which is shared by all the storage paths uses IBM's one million bit DRAM chip. At any time, there may be as many as four different devices that are sending data to be placed in the cache, and there may be as many as four different channels that are accessing data from the cache. Thus, the cache permits eight simultaneous accesses. This capability of the 3990 cache to allow four simultaneous and independent operations to/from the channels and, at the same time, four independent and simultaneous transfers to/from the devices is called the ***dual data transfer*** capability. A least-recently-used algorithm (and other algorithms) keeps high-activity data in the cache because it has the highest probability of reuse.

The 3990 cache is divided into 16K byte segments. When a specified amount of cache space is needed, as many segments as are needed to hold the specified object are allocated. These allocated segments need not be contiguous. The 3990 can logically relate separated segments in the cache and treat them as a single unit of data.

Data transfers between the cache and the channel operate at the maximum speed of the channel, either 3 or 4.5 Mbytes/sec. All data transfers requiring access to the disk will occur at the disk transfer rate of 3 Mbytes/sec.

Cache Operations

With the 3990, there are three different modes for cache operations:

- Basic caching
- DASD fast write
- Cache fast write

With basic caching, only read operations benefit from cache. This mode of caching was the only one provided in the earlier IBM 3880 control unit. The 3990 provides two new modes of caching operations - ***DASD fast write*** and ***cache fast write***. For simplicity, we will refer to a write operation executed in DASD fast write mode as a DASD fast write and to a write operation executed in cache fast write mode as a cache fast write. With DASD fast write and cache fast write, the performance benefits of caching are extended to write operations.

The I/O command must specify which of the three modes of caching is to be employed. Read operations are executed similarly in all three caching modes and will be described first. Write operations are executed differently depending on the mode, as will become clear from the following discussion.

Execution of Reads in All Three Modes

If a copy of the data is in the cache when the host initiates a read request (read hit), the 3990 transfers the desired data from the cache to the channel. If a copy of the data is not in cache (read miss), the 3990 sends the requested data directly to the channel from the disk and, at the same time, writes that data (plus the rest of the data from that record to the end of the track) into the cache in anticipation of future use. This type of operation is called a ***branching transfer***, since data being read from the disk is simultaneously branched to two destinations (the channel and the cache). Future requests for the referenced record or for following records on that track are read from the cache and are read hits.

Execution of Writes in Basic Caching Mode

If a copy of the data is in the cache when the host initiates a write operation in basic caching mode, the 3990 writes the data directly to DASD and, at the same time, writes that data into the cache (a branching transfer is used for this purpose also). The record in cache is updated because it may be referred to again. However, before operation complete can be returned, the 3990 also ensures that the record has been successfully written to DASD. On a write miss, the record is directly written to DASD and not written to cache.

It should be clear from this discussion that whether a copy of the record is in the cache or not, the total I/O time for the write operation in basic caching mode is approximately the same as for uncached control units, and is governed by the actual disk access and transfer times.

Execution of Writes in the Two Fast Write Modes

Next, let us describe the operation of the 3990 cache in executing write operations in the two fast write modes. Both types of fast write operations - DASD fast write and cache fast write can improve performance for write hits or full track format write operations. Most write operations are hits because typical applications read a record before updating it, or the write operation itself creates a new record. This last operation is called a ***format write***. In a format write, the new record is written, and the rest of the track is formatted for new data. Thus, there is no need to verify the data on the track before allowing the cache write. Hence, format writes can be considered as cache hits.

Unlike write operations in the basic caching mode, fast writes use NVS as will be described shortly.

DASD Fast Write

DASD fast write improves storage subsystem performance because immediate access to DASD is not required for write hits and full track format writes. DASD fast write stores data simultaneously in cache and in nonvolatile storage using a branching transfer. Access to DASD is not required to complete the DASD fast write operation. Because a copy of the data is put into the NVS, the 3990 returns operation complete at the end of data transfer to cache and NVS. This allows the program in the host CPU to continue processing without waiting for the data to be put on DASD. The data remains in cache and in NVS until the data is written to DASD to free space in the cache or NVS. Thus, most write operations operate directly with the cache and NVS without going to DASD, resulting in the same performance as a read hit.

On a write miss in DASD fast write mode, the 3990 writes the data to DASD and cache simultaneously. The remainder of the track is staged into the cache.

Cache Fast Write

Cache fast write is an option of the 3990 designed for use with special kinds of data, such as temporary work files produced during sorting. Such data does not need to be written to disk, and the I/O is considered complete as soon as data is written into the cache. Unlike DASD fast write, a copy of the data is not written into NVS. The data may never get written to disk.

On a write miss in cache fast write mode, the 3990 writes the data to DASD and cache simultaneously. The remainder of the track is staged into the cache. Thus, write misses work similarly in DASD fast write and cache fast write modes.

Cache Algorithms

Caching algorithms include ***normal***, ***sequential***, ***bypass-cache*** and ***inhibit cache loading***. Normal caching algorithms are used unless otherwise directed in the I/O command. This means that data is staged to the cache after being referred to in a read operation and remains in the cache until LRU algorithms permit the data to be overlaid by other data. During sequential caching, the 3990 pre-stages anticipated data so that up to five tracks are in the cache. Bypass-cache does not use the cache and operations go directly to the disk. Inhibit cache loading uses existing copies of tracks if they are in the cache, but does not load any new tracks into the cache.

Dual Copy in the 3990

Dual copy allows the 3990 to maintain a duplicate copy of the data on a device on a different device. This improves the availability of data. The status of the dual copy operation is kept in NVS.

The two physical devices are a ***duplex pair*** - a primary device and a secondary device. The dual copy operation is managed by the 3990. All I/O operations are directed to the primary device. The 3990 automatically updates both copies of the data. Data is accessed from the secondary device if the primary device is not available.

Because the secondary device is off-line, the host knows only of one device - the primary device. The 3990 orients to the primary device and does a branching transfer of the data to the primary device and to the cache. It also updates status information in the NVS to indicate that the primary device has been updated and that the secondary device has not yet been updated. At this point, the 3990 returns operation complete to the host. Later, the 3990 completes the write operation from the cache to the secondary device. This write operation is transparent to the host.

The DASD fast write capability and the dual copy capability can be combined to form a ***fast dual copy***. Using fast dual copy results in an optimum of data availability, performance and reliability. The method of operation for fast dual copy depends on whether a write hit or a write miss occurs. On a write miss, the operation is similar to that for dual copy described above. For fast dual copy with write hit, the 3990 does a branching transfer of the data to cache and NVS. It then updates status information in the NVS regarding the state of the dual copy operation. At this point, the 3990 returns operation complete to the host. Later, the 3990 completes the write operation from the cache to the primary device, and, later still, from the cache to the secondary device.

RAS Features on the 3990

The 3990 provides a number of reliability, availability and serviceability (RAS) features. A major improvement in RAS for the storage subsystem is provided by dual copy, which we have already described. A second RAS feature is the use of a pair of independent storage clusters in the 3990. A clear benefit of each of the clusters is that they are independent components with separate power and service regions. Each storage cluster has its own support facility. A major RAS enhancement, the support facility permits concurrent maintenance and provides a remote maintenance support capability. Among other tasks, the support facility monitors subsystem activity, generates service information messages (SIMs), communicates with the other support facility, runs maintenance analysis programs and diagnostics, and logs error conditions on diskette storage.

As a consequence of concurrent maintenance, one storage cluster can continue to access cache and DASD while maintenance activities are taking place on the other storage cluster. Also, a service action can be performed on the cache while direct access to DASD is provided through the storage clusters, and a service action can be performed on NVS while caching operations and direct access to DASD continues through the storage clusters.

The remote maintenance support capability permits a support representative to establish communication with either storage cluster through an external modem. Once established, the remote service representative can analyze the error data and send maintenance information to the service representative on site.

The 3990 has a writeable diskette which contains 3990 microcode, microcode patches, error log, and maintenance analysis procedures. During either local or remote maintenance, microcode patches can be transmitted to the 3990 support facility and stored on the 3990's diskette. Microcode patches written on the diskette are not lost across IMLs and are not installed until the installation asks a local service representative to do so.

Performance Modelling Results for the 3990

In this section, we present performance results from mathematical models. The different operating environments and processing workloads used with the model were obtained through studies of representative production systems. Some of these models have not yet been validated against 3990s running in a production environment, so the results must be taken with appropriate caution.

For the studies, we modelled a single 3990 with 32 Mbytes of cache, and 32 devices operating in the TSO environment. For this environment, the average block size has been measured to be 5496 bytes, the read hit ratio to be 91% and the write hit ratio to be 98%.

Performance numbers are typically given in terms of I/Os per second at a given response time. At 22 msecs response time, we found that the given configuration could provide 500 I/Os per second. Assuming that fast dual copy was performed on all 32 devices (in other words, there were physically 64 devices), the I/O rate dropped to 380 per second at the same 22 msec response time. Finally, with DASD fast write, the given configuration of 32 devices could provide 590 I/Os per second. These results were obtained assuming 4.5 Mb/sec channels. When these numbers were compared to a similar configuration using the older 3880 Model 23 disk cache, we found that the 3990 provided 20% higher throughput using fast dual copy and 90% higher throughput using DASD fast write.

Next, we compared the response times at a fixed I/O rate of 150 per second. The 3880 Model 23 provided 8.5 msecs response time, the 3990 provided 6.0 msecs response time, which dropped to 4.2 msecs with fast dual copy and 4.0 msecs with DASD fast write.

Conclusions

The IBM 3990 disk cache is designed to meet and exceed the data availability, performance and reliability requirements that businesses demand today. To improve performance, it uses cache sizes as large as 256 Mbytes, uses improved cache slot segmentation resulting in more efficient cache space utilization, provides two new fast write capabilities - DASD fast write and cache fast write, allows for branching and dual data transfers, and provides four paths to DASD. To improve RAS, it provides a dual copy capability, two independent storage clusters, separate power and service regions for cache and nonvolatile storage and concurrent and remote maintenance support. Overall, the 3990 represents a new dimension in disk caching.

Bibliography

[BOHL81] Bohl, M., Introduction to IBM Direct Access Storage Devices, SRA (1981).

[IBM231] IBM 3880 Storage Control Model 23 Description, *IBM Publication* **GA32-0083** (Tucson, 1985).

[IBM232] IBM 3880 Storage Control Model 23 Introduction, *IBM Publication* **GA32-0082** (Tucson, 1985).

[IBM3380] IBM 3380 Direct Access Storage Introduction, *IBM Publication* **GC26-4491-0**.

[IBM3880] IBM 3880 Storage Control Models 1, 2, 3 and 4 Description Manual, *IBM Publication* **GA26-1661**.

[IBM3990] IBM 3990 Storage Control Introduction, *IBM Publication* **GA32-0098-0**.

[SMITH85] Smith, A. J., Disk Cache - Miss Ratio Analysis and Design Considerations, *ACM Transactions on Computer Systems* **3** (Aug. 1985) pp. 161—203.

THE MPE XL DATA MANAGEMENT SYSTEM
EXPLOITING THE HP PRECISION ARCHITECTURE
FOR HP'S NEXT GENERATION COMMERCIAL COMPUTER SYSTEMS

Alan J. Kondoff
Hewlett-Packard

The Hewlett Packard Precision Architecture provides the basis for low overhead, high throughput data management under the commercial MPE XL operating system. Large address spaces and large main memories offer the opportunity for system software to obviate sophisticated disc I/O subsystems in order to achieve efficient, high throughput commercial data management systems.

MPE XL FILE SYSTEM

The HP Precision Architecture (HPPA) presented operating systems designers with an extremely large address space[1,3] (2^64 bytes) and initial implementations providing 128 Mbytes of main memory. The opportunities possible for data management subsystems to exploit these capabilities had been researched, implemented, and refined through experiences incorporating main memory disc caching in Hewlett-Packard's current MPE VE based architecture[2].

Two primary objectives needed to be satisfied through the implementation of a new, high-level data management subsystem for MPE XL. These were:

- o Exploit the price / performance advantages available through MPE XL services on the HP Precision Architecture (HPPA).
- o Provide an extensible base that can track functional and availability evolutionary directions of MPE XL.

PERFORMANCE ADVANTAGES
Single Level Store

The most significant advantage of the HP Precision Architecture, exploited by the data management subsystem, is its extremely large virtual address space and main memories. All access to secondary store (disc) is performed via machine load and store instructions to objects (disc files) mapped into the machine's virtual address space. This eliminates the need for explicit disc file buffer management and location. Buffer management functions are handled by standard MPE XL memory management facilities, while buffer location is performed by HPPA hardware.

By providing a byte-array abstraction of secondary store to the disc access methods, a simple, deliberate code algorithm can be designed to access each type of disc file. To an access method, a disc file appears as a four gigabyte array of bytes onto which it can impose its specific organizational and semantic rules.

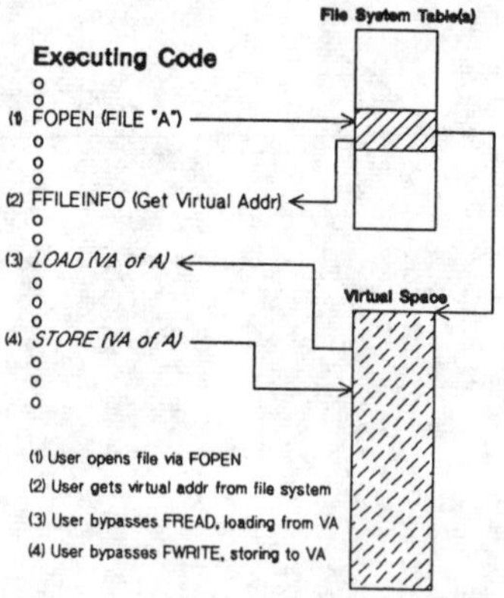

Figure 1: User Mapped File

A fallout of the single level store nature of disc file access on MPE XL is the notion of a user mapped file. Certain access methods allow users to directly modify the contents of a disc file without going through the access methods. A virtual address can be passed back to the application (user) through which accesses to the disc file can be performed via a simple, dereferenced pointer. The application now has access to a disc file at HPPA load/store machine instruction speed without incurring the additional overhead of file system access methods.

Since user mapped files are under control of the MPE XL File System, all security, protection, and rendezvous mechanisms are defined and enforced identically to conventionally accessed

CH2539-5/88/0000/0152$01.00 © 1988 IEEE

files. This allows applications to make use of user mapped files as shared, named common storage between programs, as a basis for their own specific disc access method, or as retained working storage. Mapped files offer applications the opportunity to achieve high levels of performance through conventional programming practices.

Integrated Mechanisms

Key secondary storage management mechanisms have been integrated with disc storage management to effect the most optimal system resource utilization possible under varying load conditions.

The behavior and reference pattern of disc accesses has been extensively measured and modeled for a wide range of application mixes on commercial HP systems. Through these analysis and experiences with internal disc caching on MPE-VE based computer systems, a set of relevant metrics and mechanisms emerged. Disc prefetch, posting, extent allocation, and placement were among the mechanisms selected for integration.

When a page fault against a disc file is detected or projected to occur on MPE XL, a strategy routine is invoked to determine how much data should actually be brought in, or prefetched, from disc. The goal of this strategy routine is to provide enough data to keep the application running without unnecessarily over committing disc or main memory resources. The strategy routine consults and adjusts a set of metrics, against which it makes its decision.

The prefetch strategy routine views the essence of both global and local references against a disc file, and makes a heuristic determination of how much data should be prefetched from disc. The algorithm used is deliberately simple. Disc file metrics consulted reflect file consumption rate, access pattern (sequential or random), fault rate, access method hints, and global main memory availability. Through this localized file view and global feedback metrics from the prefetch mechanism, the file system can adjust to varying application demand, CPU availability, and main memory availability to provide the best global result in a dynamic environment.

The posting (physical write to disc) strategy routine uses the same set of metrics as does the prefetch routine, but to a slightly different set of goals. The posting routines attempt to judiciously manage main memory occupancy, file consistency windows, and disc utilization.

Main memory occupancy of file pages is primarily the responsibility of the memory manager. The file system posting routines assist the memory manager's job in several ways. When sequential access is performed to a file, the posting strategy routine explicitly requests the memory manager to post large, consecutive virtual address ranges. In addition, memory manager is also informed that there is a low probability that these pages will be referenced in the short term, which makes them readily available for replacement if main memory is needed. This input to memory manager eases its ability to claim needed main memory pages on demand while minimizing the number of visits to disc in order to post modified pages (minimizing disc utilization).

The posting strategy routines are also concerned with file consistency. The notion of dependency queues have been implemented in the memory manager to satisfy atomic post and asynchronous post order constraints. File posts (or writes from the user perspective) can be piggybacked on one another without waiting for physical completion to disc. Applications can now post any number of files without wait and be guaranteed that the order of the posts are maintained. By merely waiting for the last post to physically complete on a dependency queue, the entire chain of requests are guaranteed to be durable on disc. This allows the greatest possible disc throughput while minimizing process stops otherwise required for transaction serialization or ordering.

Disc utilization is optimized through the previously mentioned prefetch and post strategies, along with extent management. When a page fault occurs on a portion of a disc file that does not have disc space allocated, a strategy routine is invoked which will determine the size and placement of the file extent to be created. File extent sizes on MPE XL are variable, with no practical limit on the number of extents in a file. The metrics consulted when determining the new extent characteristics are dominant access mode (sequential or random), file capacity, access method hints, and extent fault frequency.

Sequentially accessed files will tend to have large extents consecutively located on a disc drive. This allows the prefetch and post strategy routines to minimize visits to the disc, increasing effective disc utilization. Random access files will tend to have smaller extents spread across disc drives, allowing highly parallel access to data for both prefetching and posting. Extent allocation size may also be modified due to actual remaining disc space on a drive, allowing full (100%) utilization of the media by the file system.

Specialized Mechanisms

The throughput of the data management subsystem has been enhanced through the implementation of specialized mechanisms in MPE XL. These mechanisms address systematic problems in commercial computing systems. The areas can be loosely categorized into increased data concurrency and repeated disc file reference.

MPE XL has integrated a full functioned transaction management facility within its disc storage management subsystem. This facility allows the MPE XL data management services to optionally make use of integrated lock, write-ahead log, and recovery facilities.

All permanent data structures managed by the MPE XL File System have the transaction management property enabled. This allows highly concurrent access to system directories and disc file labels through shared or exclusive locks. Additionally, over 50% of all physical writes to files currently under transaction management are eliminated due to usage of the write ahead log. MPE XL Transaction Management is beyond the scope of this paper, and will be addressed in a future document.

Granular use of shared and exclusive semaphores in data management services has virtually eliminated artificial points of serialization in data management. Concurrent file opens, closes, page faults, disc file map-ins to virtual space, and name space resolution can occur. If contention does arise, automatic process priority elevation mechanisms alleviate convoy effects. In many instances, like exclusive file access, all locks are avoided by access methods to give optimal performance.

Repeated reference to disc files are enhanced due to a closed file LRU (least recently used) list. All files that are closed (no users) on MPE XL are placed on LRU and remain mapped into virtual space with file pages remaining in main memory. When an initial file open operation locates a file on the LRU, it is merely removed from the LRU and reactivated. The file open operation and subsequent accesses can potentially occur with no disc accesses. This is especially significant for operating system functions like directory scans, or job steps in user applications where the output of one program feeds the next.

Temporary or new files are also treated specially in MPE XL. By virtue of their transient nature, the MPE XL file system will avoid posting data to disc unless main memory is required. It is possible for a temporary file in MPE XL to be created, accessed, and deleted without a single disc file access.

Accessing new portions of new disc files, or extending the end-of-file on existing files, also has special optimizations. When a page fault is detected on one of these previously untouched or virgin pages while accessing a file, a disc transfer to read the page is avoided. Memory manager merely claims available page(s) in memory and initializes it to the file's fill character (usually blanks or zeros).

The memory manager, managing a single main memory resource, equitably allocates pages between files, code, and transient data in a uniform manner. Occupancy of main memory is determined by reference and is replaced by an approximation of a LRU algorithm. Since main memory caches access to all discs, memory occupancy tends to reflect workload skews on disc. As references to certain discs become dominant, MPE XL's memory manager will dynamically adjust its allocation to those discs.

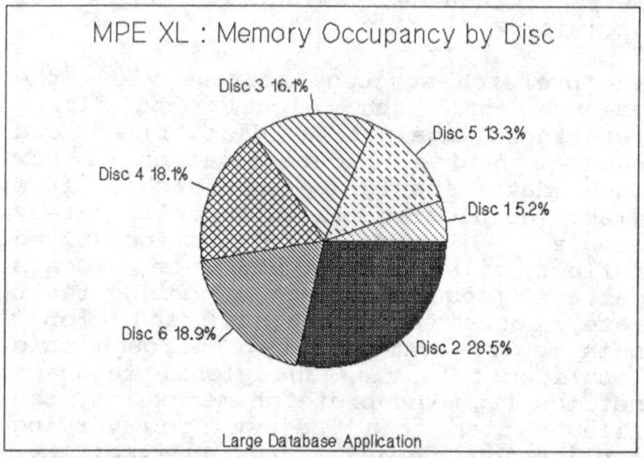

Additionally, this same memory manager algorithm dynamically apportions main memory resources between disc files and active processes on the system. If there is one process, such as a single batch job, main memory will most likely be dominated by file pages. This is especially true of commercial database applications. All available system resources are applied to most effectively increase the throughput of that application. As the system multiprogramming level (MPL) increases, occupancy of main memory by file pages erodes to pages associated with the additional executing tasks.

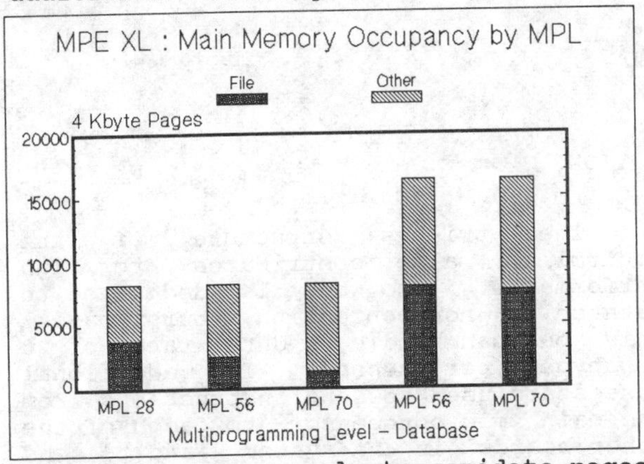

As memory manager selects canidate pages to replace in main memory, it employs a gather write strategy. Since dirty disc file pages tend to be adjacent in virtual space, a single page replacement canidate replacement can many times be combined with adjacent pages in a single physical disc I/O. MPE XL's strategy currently limits gather writes to 64 Kbytes, or 16 pages. This feature tends to amortize fixed costs with performing physical disc I/O to create large holes of recoverable main memory.

FILE SYSTEM ARCHITECTURE
Overview

The organization of the MPE XL File System has been optimized to efficiently support multiple operating system environments via a common set of file system services. Three levels constitute the primary access method path in the file system, and are called the storage management, type management, and intrinsic interface layers.

The highest level of the file system hierarchy is the intrinsic interface. Each intrinsic interface module can efficiently support the procedural interface, semantics, and error conventions of a specific subsystem. For the first release of MPE XL on HPPA, the MPE Intrinsic Interface module will be included in the file system.

Type managers occupy the middle level of the file access hierarchy. They define a consistent set of interfaces and operators which may be applied to a file through the intrinsic interface. All intrinsic environments access a specific file type through the same type manager, insuring integrity of the file. Access to a particular type manager, or type

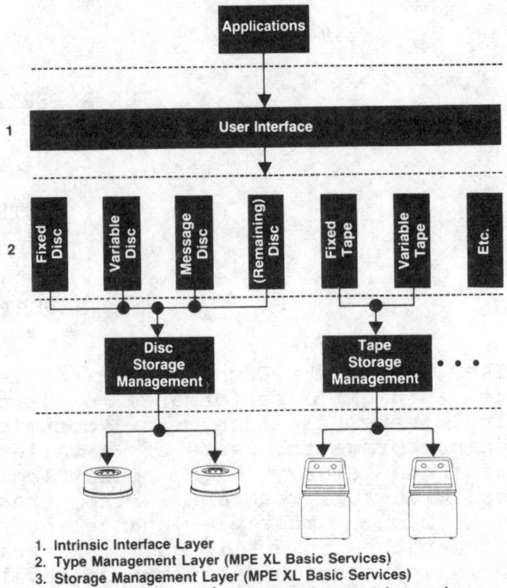

Figure 4 : File System Structure

manager operator, may be restricted by an intrinsic interface, but is not enforced by the type manager. Internally, type managers provide a logical abstraction (fixed, variable, byte stream, keyed, etc) of the specific storage management module being accessed.

Storage management is the lowest layer of the three abstract layers of the MPE XL File System. It defines the set of basic operators that can be performed against a specific class of devices (discs, tapes, terminals, etc). Within the disc storage management module, additional subsystems such as transaction and disc volume management are also included. The architecture also provides for any number of storage managers to exist within a class, such as disc storage management. This is necessary to accomodate differing strategies based on varied topologies or specialized functional requirements.

REFERENCES

1. J.S. Birnbaum and W.S. Worley, Jr., "Beyond RISC: High Precision Architecture," Hewlett-Packard Journal, Vol. 36, no. 8, August 1985, pp. 4-10.
2. J.R. Busch and A.J. Kondoff, "Disc Caching in the System Processing Units of the HP3000 Family of Computers," Hewlett-Packard Journal, Vol. 36, no. 2, February 1985, pp. 21-39.
3. M.J. Mahon, et al, "Hewlett-Packard Precision Architecture: The Processor," Hewlett-Packard Journal, Vol. 37, no. 8, August 1986, pp. 4-21.

THE AMPERIF CACHE DISK SYSTEM

STEPHEN FULD

AMPERIF CORPORATION

The Amperif Cache Disk System provides high performance, large capacity, very flexible, low cost of ownership storage for users of a variety of mainframe CPUs. High speed logic combined with full read and write, track oriented cache, multiple channel ports and data paths as well as disk array design give a high performance level. The modular architecture of the system provides flexibility for a variety of host interfaces, storage configurations and operating modes. The system uses a fraction of the floor space, power and air conditioning of comparable products. Of course, due care was taken to assure data integrity throughout the system.

The Amperif Cache Disk System is a large capacity, high performance, caching disk controller for selected mainframe environemnts. It has been adapted for a variety of interfaces and a variety of configurations. This paper gives an overview of the system and explains how the design elements contribute to high performance, flexability, low cost of ownership and data integrity.

High Performance

Several design features combine to give a high performance system. The system caches full disk tracks. This allows the caching operation to begin anywhere on the track and complete in one disk revolution, effectively eliminating the rotational latency and possible RPS misses of sector oriented caches. The track organization makes the number of cache entries smaller than a sector cache for any given cache size. This allows the implementation of high speed cache search hardware. The hardware performs searches and keeps the pointer stack in LRU order at the rate of 1.25 million entries per second. Thus the typical search time is 20 to 30 microseconds. Future versions will increase the rate to 5 million entries per second.

The tri-bus structure of the controller also contributes to high performance. One bus is dedicated to data on a non-contention, burst basis. This bus can handle a data rate of 20 megabytes per second. Two additional busses are used to send instructions from the main microprocessor to each of the other boards in the system, and to send control parameters and receive status from the other boards. The main microprocessor uses bit slice technology executing one instruction every 200 nanoseconds. Even this isn't fast enough to handle data so all the data paths are under direct hardware control. The basic protocol for a data transfer is for the main microprocessor to tell the sending board to put data on the bus, the receiving board to take it; then initiate both boards and wait for a completion status.

Another factor that contributes to high performance is the use of dual data control paths and up to eight channel interfaces. A request can be sent to any one of the eight and be processed by whichever of the two data control paths isn't busy. This reduces control unit busy time.

Flexibility

Because of the building block structuring of the Amperif Cache Disk System, components can be changed and intermixed in a variety of ways. For example, the system supports up to 32 logical units, each of which can be disk, cache disk, or solid state storage. The disks available span a wide capacity range allowing up to 32 gigabytes of storage on a string. Optionally, two disks can be treated as one by the microcode to allow larger capacities on systems where the number of units is a constraint.

For each cache disk unit, there are three operating modes. Bypass mode allows a cache disk unit to function as a non cache unit; all operations bypass the cache and go directly to/from the disk. Write thru allows caching with utmost assurance of data integrity. Read

CH2539-5/88/0000/0156$01.00 © 1988 IEEE

operations are handled from the cache and write operations are written to both the cache and the disk. The completion status is delayed until successful completion of the disk write. Full or post store cache is the same as write thru except the completion status for writes is given after the data is in cache. This provides the maximum performance mode of the system. Each unit's operating mode can be changed, concurrently with full operations, either by the operator or through system commands.

The system supports a variety of host computer interfaces. The ones presently existing or in development include Unisys (Sperry) word channel, IBM block multiplexor (FBA mode), CDC Cyber channel, Unisys (Burroughs) DLP, and IPI-3. Thus a user can protect his investment by buying a system that operates with his current and possible future computers. In some cases, multiple interfaces can be mixed on the same controller for flexibility in multi-vendor shops.

Low Cost of Ownership

By using a disk array design, the system reduces cost of ownership. For one thing, it uses very little floor space. A system with two controllers, all associated interface hardware, 16 gigabytes of disk, 32 megabytes of cache, and 45 megabytes of solid state storage fits in one 12 square foot cabinet. An additional 16 gigabytes of disk takes only 6 square feet. Another benefit of the disk array concept is the reduction in power and air conditioning required. Typically, the Amperif system uses about one half the power of competing systems.

Data Integrity

The high performance, flexibility, and low cost are worthless if the disk doesn't do the one thing that you expect it to do; store and transfer data without losing or gaining even a single bit. Features are designed into the Amperif Cache Disk System to assure the data integrity that mainframe users require. For cache and solid state systems, there is a UPS that prevents data loss in a power outage. Additionally, to handle the cases where the 15 minutes provided by the UPS isn't sufficient, there is a data save disk. If the power is out for more than 1 minute, the contents of the cache and Solid State Disk are copied to the data save disk. Then, no matter how long the outage is, when the power comes on again, the data can be copied back to the cache and Solid State Disk from the data save disk. Thus no data will be lost.

The controllers are designed to high standards of hardware integrity. There is parity on all internal busses. Data is through checked to prevent a part failure from causing undetected data corruption. Both the disk and the memory use modern ECC algorithms. If the controller sees correctable ECC errors on the memory, it corrects that data, then dynamically downs that block of memory in order to prevent any future uncorrectable errors. The critical block number to cylinder, head and record number division is checked by multiplying the numbers back and testing for the original number. By these means, the rate of undetected data corruption is reduced to one in 50 years.

By combining a modular design with intelligent caching strategies and using disk arrays, the Amperif Cache Disk System provides an alternative to the storage typically provided by mainframe vendors.

SOFTWARE POTPOURRI Track

Object Oriented Programming

Chair: D. Bryan

SELF: The Power of Simplicity*

David Ungar
Stanford University

Randall B. Smith
Xerox PARC

To thine own self be true.
—William Shakespeare

Abstract

SELF is a new object-oriented language for exploratory programming based on a small number of simple and concrete ideas: prototypes, slots, and behavior. Prototypes combine inheritance and instantiation to provide a framework that is simpler and more flexible than most object-oriented languages. Slots unite variables and procedures into a single construct. This permits the inheritance hierarchy to take over the function of lexical scoping in conventional languages. Finally, because SELF does not distinguish state from behavior, it narrows the gap between ordinary objects and procedures. SELF's simplicity and expressiveness offer new insights into object-oriented computation.

Introduction

Object-oriented programming languages are gaining acceptance, partly because they offer a useful perspective for designing computer programs. However, they do not all offer exactly the *same* perspective; there are many different ideas about the nature of object-oriented computation. In this paper we present SELF, a programming language with a new perspective on objects and message passing.

Like the Smalltalk-80** language [GoR83], SELF is designed to support exploratory programming [She83], and therefore includes runtime typing (i.e. no type declarations) and automatic storage reclamation. But unlike Smalltalk, SELF includes neither classes nor variables. Instead, SELF has adopted a prototype metaphor for object creation [Bor81 Bor86, Lie86, LTP86].

Furthermore, while Smalltalk and most other object-oriented languages support variable access as well as message passing, SELF objects access their state information by sending messages to "self," the receiver of the current message. Naturally this results in many messages sent to "self," and the language is named in honor of these messages. One of strengths of object-oriented programming lies in the uniform access to different kinds of stored and computed data, and the ideas in SELF result in even more uniformity, which results in greater expressive power. We believe that these ideas offer a new and useful view of object-oriented computation.

Figure 1. Two SELF point objects

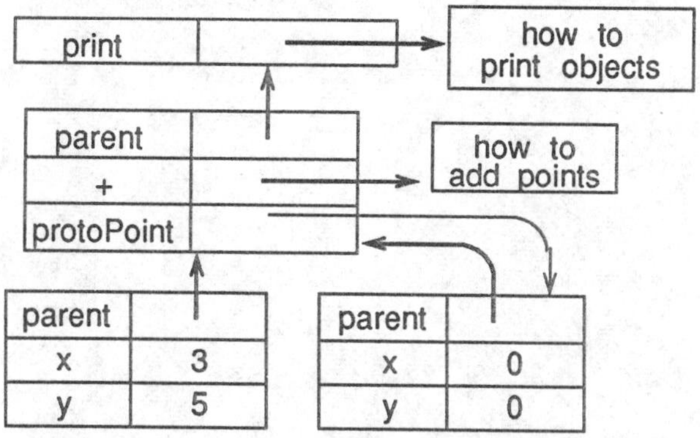

Prototypes Blend Classes and Instances

In Smalltalk, unlike C++, Simula, Loops, or ADA, everything is an object and every object contains a pointer to its class, an object that describes its format and holds its behavior. In SELF too, everything is an object. But, instead of a class pointer, a SELF object contains named slots which may store either state or behavior. If an object receives a message and it has no matching slot, the search continues via its *parent* pointer. This is how SELF implements inheritance. Inheritance in SELF allows objects to share behavior, which in turn allows the programmer to alter the behavior of many objects with a single change. For instance, Figure 1 shows a point† object with slots for its non-shared characteristics: x and y. Its parent holds the behavior shared among all points: +, -, etc.

* This is a digest of the original paper, see [UnS87].

** Smalltalk-80 is a trademark of ParcPlace Systems. In this paper, the term "Smalltalk" will be used to refer to the Smalltalk-80 programming language.

† Throughout this paper we appeal to point objects in examples. A Smalltalk point represents a point in two-dimensional Cartesian coordinates. It contains two instance variables, an x and a y coordinate.

CH2539-5/88/0000/0162$01.00 © 1988 IEEE

To create a new object in SELF, the **clone** message is sent to an existing object. Such existing objects serve as *prototypes* to create similar objects. In Figure 1, the **protoPoint** slot in the root contains the prototypical point. Since the slot is in the root, any object can create a point by first sending itself the **protoPoint** message, then sending **clone** to the result.

SELF's treatment of inheritance, prototypes, and object creation provides some benefits over class-based systems:

Simpler relationships. In a class–based language, one must grasp two relationships: the "is a" relationship, that indicates that an object is an *instance* of some class, and the "kind of" relationship, that indicates that an object's class is a *subclass of* some other object's class. In a system with prototypes instead of classes such as SELF, there is only one relationship, "inherits from," that describes how objects share behavior and state. This structural simplification makes it easier to understand the language and easier to formulate an inheritance hierarchy.

Creation by copying. Creating new objects from prototypes is accomplished by a simple operation, copying, which we refer to as *cloning*. Creating new objects from classes is accomplished by instantiation, which includes the interpretation of format information in a class. Instantiation is similar to building a house from a plan. Copying appeals to us as a simpler metaphor than instantiation.

Examples of preexisting modules. Prototypes are more concrete than classes because they are *examples* of objects rather than *descriptions* of format and initialization. These examples may help users to reuse modules by making them easier to understand. A prototype–based systems allows the user to examine a typical representative rather than requiring him to make sense out of its description.

Support for one–of–a–kind objects. SELF provides a framework that can easily include one–of–a–kind objects with their own behavior. Since each object has named slots, and slots can hold state or behavior, any object can have unique slots or behavior. Class–based systems are designed for situations where there are many objects with the same behavior. There is no linguistic support for an object to possess its own unique behavior, and it is awkward to create a class that is guaranteed to have only one instance. SELF suffers from neither of these disadvantages. Any object can be customized with its own behavior. A unique object can hold the unique behavior, and a separate "instance" is not needed.

Elimination of meta–regress. No object in a class–based system can be self sufficient; another object (its class) is needed to express its structure and behavior. This leads to a conceptually infinite meta–regress: an object is an instance of its class, which is an instance of the class's class, which is an instance of the class's class's class, ad infinitum. On the other hand, in prototype–based systems an object can include its own behavior; no other object is needed to breathe life into it. Prototypes eliminate meta regress.

Blending state and behavior

In SELF, there is no direct way to access a variable; instead objects send messages to access data residing in named slots. So, to access its "x" value, a point sends itself the ''x'' message. The message finds the "x" slot, and evaluates the object found therein. Since the slot contains a number, the result of the evaluation is just the number itself. In order to change contents of the "x" slot to, say 17, instead of performing an assignment like ''x←17,'' the point must send itself the ''x:'' message with 17 as the argument. The point object (or one of its ancestors) must contain a slot named ''x:'' containing the assignment primitive. Of course, all these messages sent to ''self'' would make for verbose programs, so our syntax allows the ''self'' to be elided. The result is that accessing state via messages in SELF becomes as easy to write as accessing variables directly in Smalltalk; ''x'' accesses the slot by the same name, and "x: 17" stores seventeen in the slot.

Accessing state via messages makes inheritance more powerful. Suppose we wish to create a new kind of point, whose x coordinate is a random number instead of a stored value. We copy the standard point, remove the x: slot (so that x cannot be changed) and replace the contents of the x slot with the code to generate a random number. (See Figure 2.) If instead of modifying the x slot, we had replaced the x: slot with a ''halt'' method, we would obtain a breakpoint on write. Thus, SELF can express the idioms associated with *active variables* and *dæmons.* Accessing state via messages also makes it easier to share state. To create two points that share the same x coordinate, the x and x: slots can be put in a separate object that is the parents of each of the two points. (See Figure 3.)

In most object–oriented languages, accessing a variable is a different operation than sending a message. This dilutes the message passing model of computation with assignment and access. As a result,

Figure 2. Customized Behavior

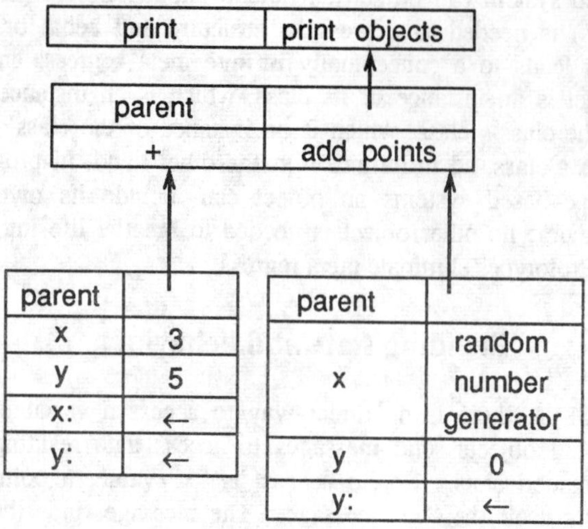

Figure 3. Shared state

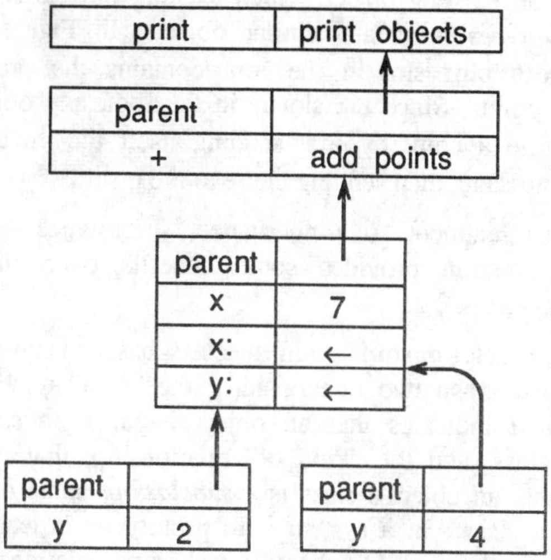

message passing becomes less powerful. For instance, the inclusion of variables makes it harder for a specialization (subclass) to replace a variable with a computed result, because there may be code in a superclass that directly accesses the variable. Also, class–based languages typically store the names and orders of instance variables in an object's class. This further limits the power of inheritance; the specification within a class unnecessarily restricts an instance's format. Finally, variable access requires scoping rules, yet a further complication. For instance Smalltalk has five kinds of variables: local variables (temporaries), instance variables, class variables, pool variables, and global variables, whose scopes roughly correspond to rungs on the ladder of instantiation.

Speculation: Where is SELF headed?

In the designing of SELF, we have been led to some rather strange recurring themes. We present them here for the reader to ponder.

Behaviorism. In most object languages (Actors excepted), objects are passive; an object is what it is. In SELF, an object is what it *does*. Since variable access is the same as message passing, ordinary passive objects can be regarding merely as methods that always return themselves. For example, consider the number 17. In Smalltalk, the number 17 represents a particular (immutable) state. In SELF, the number 17 is just an object that returns itself and behaves a certain way with respect to arithmetic. The only way to know an object is by its actions.

Computation viewed as refinement. In Smalltalk, the number 17 is a number with some particular state, and the state information is used by the arithmetic primitives—addition for example. In SELF, 17 can be viewed as a *refinement of shared behavior* for numbers that responds to addition by returning 17 more than its argument. Since in SELF, an activation record's parent gets set to the receiver of the message, method activation can be viewed as the creation of a short–lived *refinement* of the receiver. Likewise block, or closure activation can be viewed as the creation of a *refinement* of the activation record for the enclosing context scope.

In our examples, we render the shared behavior object for points as an ordinary *passive* object. Another twist would be to build class–like objects out of *methods*. In SELF, the shared behavior object for points could be a method with code that simply returned a clone of the prototypical point. This method could then be installed in the "Point" slot of the root object. One object would then be serving two roles: its code would create new points, and its slots (locals) would hold the shared behavior for points. At this writing, we do not believe that this is the best way to construct a system, but the use of methods to hold shared behavior for a group of objects is an example of the flexibility afforded by SELF.

Parents viewed as shared parts. Finally, one can view the parents of an object as shared parts of the object. From this perspective, a SELF point contains a private part with x and y slots, a part shared with other points containing +, -, etc. slots, and a part shared with all other objects containing behavior common to all objects. Viewing parents as shared parts broadens the applicability of inheritance.

Status

Craig Chambers, Elgin Lee, and Martin Rinard have built a prototype environment for SELF including a browser, inspector, debugger, and interpreter. This system is intended to help us gain a deeper understanding of the language and implementation challenges. We have written and run small SELF programs in this environment.

Chambers, Lee, and Ungar are constructing a complete, efficient programming environment. The new system has run small programs.

Related Work and Acknowledgments

We would like to express our deep appreciation to the past and present members of the System Concepts Laboratory at Xerox PARC for blazing the trail with Smalltalk [GoR83]. In addition, SELF owes much to "O" [Deu86], Trellis/Owl [SCB86], Lieberman's prototypes [Lie86], ARK [Smi86], ThingLab [Bor81, Bor86], DeltaTalk [BoO86], Scheme [ASS84, Ste76], and OakLisp [LaP86]. Readers interested in the ideas of slots and prototypes may also want to research Exemplars [LTP86] and Strobe [Smi83].

This work is partially supported by Xerox, and partially by the National Science Foundation Presidential Young Investigator Award DCK 8657631, Apple Computer, IBM, NCR, and Texas Instruments.

Conclusions

SELF offers a new paradigm for object–oriented languages that combines both simplicity and expressiveness. Its simplicity arises from realizing that classes and variables are not needed. Their elimination banishes the metaclass regress, dispels the illusory distinction between instantiation and subclassing, and allows for the blurring of the differences between objects, procedures, and closures. Reducing the number of basic concepts in a language can make the language easier to explain, understand, and use.

Making SELF simpler made it more powerful. SELF can express idioms from traditional object–oriented languages such as classes and instances, but can go beyond them to express one–of–a–kind objects, active values, inline objects and classes, and the overriding of instance variables. We believe that contemplation of SELF provides insights into the nature of object–oriented computation.

References

[Bor86] A. Borning, "Classes versus Prototypes in Object–Oriented Languages," Proceedings of the ACM / IEEE Fall Joint Computer Conference, Dallas, TX, November, 1986, 36-40.

[Deu86] L. P. Deutsch, "O," private communication, 1986.

[GoR83] A. J. Goldberg and D. Robson, Smalltalk–80™: The Language and Its Implementation, Addison-Wesley Publishing Company, Reading, MA, 1983.

[LTP86] W. R. LaLonde, D. A. Thomas and J. R. Pugh, "An Exemplar Based Smalltalk," OOPSLA'86 Conference Proceedings, Portland, OR, 1986, 322–330. Also published as a special issue of SIGPLAN Notices Vol. 21, No. 11, Nov. 86.

[LaP86] K. J. Lang and B. A. Pearlmutter, "Oaklisp: An Object-Oriented Scheme with First Class Types," OOPSLA'86 Conference Proceedings, Portland, OR, 1986, 30-37. Also published as a special issue of SIGPLAN Notices Notices, Vol. 21, No. 11, Nov. 86.

[Lie86] H. Lieberman, "Using Prototypical Objects to Implement Shared Behavior in Object-Oriented Systems," OOPSLA'86 Conference Proceedings, Portland, OR, 1986, 214–223. Also published as a special issue of SIGPLAN Notices Notices, Vol. 21, No. 11, Nov. 86.

[SCB86] C. Schaffert, T. Cooper, B. Bullis, M. Kilian and C. Wilpolt, "An Introduction to Trellis/Owl," OOPSLA'86 Conference Proceedings, Portland, OR, 1986, 9-16. Also published as a special issue of SIGPLAN Notices, Vol. 21, No. 11, Nov. 86.

[She83] B. Sheil, "Environments for Exploratory Programming," Datamation, February, 1983.

[Smi83] R. G. Smith, "Strobe: Support for Structured Object Knowledge Representation," Proceedings of the 1983 International Joint Conference On Artificial Intelligence, 1983, 855–858.

[Smi86] R. B. Smith, "The Alternate Reality Kit: An Animated Environment for Creating Interactive Simulations," Proceedings of 1986 IEEE Computer Society Workshop on Visual Languages, Dallas, TX, June, 1986, 99–106.

[Ste76] G. L. Steele Jr., "Lambda, the Ultimate Imperative," AI Memo 353, 1976.

[UnS87] D. Ungar and R. B. Smith, "Self: The Power of Simplicity," OOPSLA '87 Conference Proceedings, Orlando, FL, 1987, 227-241. Available as SIGPLAN Notices, Vol. 22, No. 12, December 1987.

The Objective–C Environment *Past, Present, and Future*

Brad J. Cox

Productivity Products International

Abstract

The Objective–C environment is a growing collection of tools and reusable components (Software–ICs®) for large–scale production system–building. Its goal is to make it possible for its users to build software systems in the way that hardware engineers build theirs, by reusing Software–ICs supplied by a marketplace in generic components rather than by building everything from scratch. The environment is based on conventional technology (C and Unix–style operating systems), which it includes and extends. The extensions presently include a compiled and an interpreted implementation of Objective–C (an object–oriented programming language based on C) and several libraries of reusable components (ICpaks®).

Motivation

The Objective–C environment was born of frustration. We wanted to build systems whose primary focus is helping people coordinate their activities as part of a larger organization, rather than traditional solitary tools that only help individuals with their solitary tasks. And we discovered that we couldn't get there from here, at least not without first bringing together a foundation of tools and concepts that were unavailable in any single environment, but are scattered across incompatible environments as diverse as Unix/C, CommonLoops/Lisp, and Smalltalk–80. We'd have to build the missing substrate before we could build tools to address what we see as the major cause of poor software productivity, coordination losses in managing large groups of people toward a common end.

Systems like these demonstrate the problem that faces many software developers today; the desired system is (a) clearly worth building, (b) clearly buildable on today's hardware platforms, but (c) clearly *not* buildable at reasonable cost with today's programming tools and techniques. Production environments as powerful as C and Unix do not provide tools for building such systems reliably, nor do prototyping environments like Smalltalk–80.

The problem is that the products that system–builders would most like to build must provide meaningful support for each of the role–players in the process they're supporting. For example, a full coordination system for software development organizations should support not only the programmers, but also those responsible for requirements–writing, architecting, designing, testing, repairing, evolving, documenting, managing, pricing, selling, and marketing the evolving product. Each role–player needs a user interface that fully supports his or her needs. And the current state of the product, stored as data structures inside the system, would have to be projected to each of the diverse role–players as role–specific views and held reasonably consistent as the software product, and also the system within which it is being developed, evolves over time.

Such systems are well beyond the state of the art today, not because of hardware limitations, but because of limitations in the facilities system–builders have for managing complexity and controlling change in large–scale system–building projects. Accordingly, we set aside our long–range goal until we could first accumulate the missing tools into a hybrid environment for production system–building that we call the *Objective–C Environment*. The Objective–C environment is based on, includes, and extends the facilities of its host operating system, of which Unix, VMS, and MS–DOS are presently–supported examples. For brevity in what follows, I'll use Unix to mean any of these base environments.

Host Environment: Production vs Prototyping

We chose traditional operating systems like Unix as the base because large–scale, technically ambitious systems are built by large numbers of developers, evolved over long periods of time, supported on many hardware platforms, and used hard every day by large numbers of users. We needed the portability, machine-efficiency, and support for programming in the large that production programming environments provide and are often less advanced in prototyping environments like Smalltalk-80. C provides satisfactory and highly efficient tools for the micro-granularity end of system-building (data structures, functions), and Unix provides outstanding support for the macro-granularity end (files, pipes, filters, configuration management tools, networking, remote procedure calls, etc). We concentrated on identifying and then providing the missing pieces as incremental additions to an Objective-C environment that would grow steadily over time.

Objective-C, The Language

One of the most critical shortcomings in C and Unix-like operating systems is the lack of language support for object-oriented programming, particularly of the variety that supports loosely coupled cooperation between suppliers and consumers of code. This is strategically vital for large-scale system-building because it lets large numbers of programmers contribute to a larger undertaking without the restrictively tight coupling that results when suppliers try to use statically bound tools like Ada, C, or even C++, to package code for reuse by large communities of diverse consumers.

The critical insight was that static binding is, as a rule, a *bad* idea. It is the root of the technical obstacle that has until now prevented programmers from overcoming the software crisis by creating a robust marketplace in reusable code analogous to the hardware integrated circuit market. It optimizes a cheap resource, the machine, at the expense of a very expensive one, the programmer, by making it technically impossible for suppliers to package their work for sale and reuse.

Static binding requires that the consumer's environment (the static types of the arguments the consumer will pass to the supplier's code) be known when the supplier's code is compiled. This is possible only when the supplier and the consumer operate in the tightly coupled fashion that is admittedly the rule today, but only because of the absence of tools that avoid premature binding. Without delayed binding, the only way a supplier can provide code that is independent of the consumer's environment is by providing sources that the consumer can recompile its new environment. But this makes the marketplace impractical because the supplier is then unable to protect (e.g. to derive income from) his source code.

A common misconception is that static binding and dynamic binding are two 'equivalent' ways of accomplishing a similar end, and thus to be chosen by the designer of a programming language, not by its users. For example, Smalltalk-80's designers chose in favor of dynamic binding, and Ada's chose static binding. Static and dynamic binding are very different tools for very different purposes. Programming languages should offer both tools to be picked up or laid aside according to the job at hand.

Since C is reasonably adequate for the low-level micro-granularity problems of large-scale system-building, we defined Objective-C as a hybrid between C and Smalltalk-80. It is a strict superset of C that in addition supports the dynamically bound, object-oriented style of programming from Smalltalk-80. Objective-C language is identical to C language, but with a small number of syntactic additions for declaring object identifiers, sending messages to objects, and defining new classes and their methods. The additional syntax is described in [Cox86a]. We're also addressing some of C's long-standing deficiencies by adding many of the statically-bound features pioneered in C++ (in-line procedures, operator overloading, etc).

Notice that Objective-C was not motivated by a desire to define an ambitious programming *language*, but only to provide the features missing from C that we needed to provide an ambitious programming *environment*. This orientation is similar to that of Smalltalk-80, and in opposition to that taken by most other language development efforts including Fortran, Pascal, C, and C++. As the descriptions to follow will make clear, didn't stop after merely building a compiler. We've expended a great deal of energy providing useful libraries, and we supported both ends of the software development process by also providing an interpreter for the same programming language. Additional tools are planned, but not yet released.

Objective-C Compiler

The first and oldest tool in the Objective-C environment is a compiler for transforming Objective-C source files into binary files. It does this by emitting ordinary C statements as a machine-independent representation for the program, thus relying on the native C compiler for machine-dependent transformations. This means that Objective-C programs (and the compiler itself, since it is written in Objective-C) are as portable as any ordinary C program, and are automatically compatible with other tools such as linkers and debuggers.

ICpak101: Foundation Library

We supply with the compiler a comprehensive library of foundation classes that provide such things as the basic classes that define characteristics inherited by all objects (*Object*, various *Arrays*, etc). This library also provides a large and still growing library of Collection classes; *Set, OrderedCollection, Dictionary*, etc. The presence of this library demonstrates our belief that the potential of any programming language is relatively small compared to the potential of well-designed, well-tested, libraries of reusable components. The Objective-C compiler was never an end unto itself; just a necessary step towards acquiring large libraries of useful and reusable components.

Objective-C Interpreter

The second piece missing from C and Unix is adequate support for the rapid prototyping end of the software development lifecycle. Accordingly, our next addition was the *Objective-C Interpreter*, which supports precisely the same language as the compiler, but with instantaneous turnaround between making a change and seeing the effects in the executing code.

The interpreter is often used in conjunction with compiled code from the compiler. Stable code is generally compiled and linked into the interpreter, so that only the code that is actually under development need be interpreted. If a bug is discovered in compiled code, it can be fixed by changing the source and interpreting it, immediately overriding the compiled version with an interpreted one, or even by dynamically linking in previously compiled object code.

ICPak 201: Iconic User Interface Library

The third piece missing from C and Unix was a solution for Unix's user interface inadequacies. We've recently filled this gap with *ICpak201*, a library of Software-ICs that customers use to build multi-window iconic user interfaces so that their applications are immediately portable to any engineering workstation.

The key component in this library is a class called *Layer*, which implements the abstraction of a transparent sheet of acetate. Layers can be attached to other layers, sized, and positioned just like the acetate sheets that animation artists use to build animated movies. Specialized layer subclasses override a specific method, *display*, to in effect define 'paint' that overrides the transparency that they inherit by default. Layers can be dynamically repositioned to obtain dynamic effects like movement of a figure against a background as when scrolling text or moving and opening icons.

Most of the Software-ICs in this library are specialized Layer subclasses that are already cut to size, painted with relevant images, and pre-wired with relevant behaviors for use as scrollbars, close boxes, windows, menus, and so forth. This layer-based approach to iconic user interface construction is described in [Cox86a,b].

Distributed Objects; Persistent Objects; Garbage Collection

Products for removing several other deficiencies in C and Unix are under development. For example, C is basically a program-building language, not a system-building language, because it makes no provision for addressing objects in other programs on the same machine, in programs on different machines on a network, or objects that outlive the program that created them. ICpak products that relieve these restrictions, and others including automatic garbage collection, can be expected as early as 1988.

These libraries extend the traditional process model in three stages. The first, the *Coroutining* stage, removes the assumption that processes of the base operating system (*Domains*) contain only a single thread of control and generalizes how input/output is managed so that I/O by any coroutine will not block the others from execution. The second, the *Distributed Object* stage, introduces *Capability* objects that remove the assumption that all objects live in a single domain by encoded message requests and responses into packets for execution in a remote process. They also impose restrictions on what messages the local domain is allowed to send. The third stage, the *Persistent Object* stage, provides remote domains that know how to manage their objects permanently on a back-end database system.

Objective-C Environment

Once these substrate facilities are in place, we hope to return to our original goal of building a comprehensive coordination system for software development organizations. This is clearly an ambitious goal that can only be achieved incrementally. Its success rests on a single critical, heretofore missing lever that was contributed by object-oriented technology, the ability for one programmer to provide a large piece of functionality, say an integrated text and graphics editor, as Software-ICs that other programmers can customize and reuse in their own applications.

But this lever must still be powered by lots of muscle to crack the full coordination system nut. The object-oriented lever must also be supported and complimented by additional levers that we're drawing from other domains, such as 'expert' systems, and integrating as Software-IC libraries, particularly non-procedural approaches such as constraint solving and rule processing, to name only a couple.

[Cox86a] *Object-oriented Programming, An Evolutionary Approach,* Brad Cox, Addison Wesley Publishing Company, 1986.

[Cox86b] *Objects, Icons, and Software-ICs*, Brad Cox and Bill Hunt, Byte Magazine, August 1986.

Object Oriented Database

Chair: D. Fishman

Abstract Types and Storage Types in an OO-DBMS

Craig Damon and Gordon Landis
Ontologic, Inc.
47 Manning Road
Billerica, Mass. 01821

Abstract

The Vbase object-oriented database management system (OO-DBMS) extends the basic paradigm offered by other object-oriented systems, by allowing the creation of "storage classes", in the same way other systems allow the creation of abstract classes. Storage classes control object storage, including dereferencing, object faulting, clustering, sharing and persistence.

This facility is based upon the notion of a storage manager. Storage managers are types, which are organized into a hierarchy, similar to but orthogonal to the hierarchy of abstract types. The storage manager type hierarchy is user-extensible by subtyping, just as the abstract type hierarchy is. The implementation of the storage manager abstraction relies upon generalizations to operation dispatching and reference resolution.

1. Introduction

Section 1 of this paper provides an introduction to the concepts of object-oriented programming, including a definition of an Object-Oriented DBMS, and a brief outline of the Vbase data model. Section 2 describes what a storage manager is and how it is used in Vbase. Section 3 describes some features of our implementation. Finally, Section 4 offers some conclusions based on our experiences.

1.1. What is an OO-DBMS ?

Even within object-oriented circles, there is not a clear consensus on what an object-oriented database is, but we will start with the guidelines given in [Wegner87]. He defines an object-oriented language as possessing three characteristics: objects, classes, and inheritance. An *object* is a combination of state and a set of operations defined on that state. A *class* (or *type*) is a definition of the state and operations that are valid for all objects that are members of the class. *Inheritance* is the ability to make subtypes by "inheriting" all of the operations defined by a supertype.

To define an object-oriented database, we add three additional criteria: persistence, sharing and transactions. *Persistence* simply means that objects may live longer than the process that created them. *Sharing* means that objects are accessible to multiple processes (which might run concurrently or sequentially). A *transaction* lumps one or more actions into a single atomic action, which is both indivisible, in that either all of it happens or none of it happens, and non-interfering, in that it does not see the effects of another concurrent transaction [Weihl82]. Note that there are other features commonly associated with a database, such as query capabilities, but these are less fundamental to the notion of a database, and we do not take them to be definitional.

1.2. Introduction to Vbase

Vbase incorporates these basic concepts, adding to them the notions of data abstraction and static type checking, both heavily influenced by the CLU programming language [Liskov81]. In a system supporting *data abstraction*, an object's state and implementation are accessible only through operations defined by the type. *Static type checking* requires that all validation of type compatibility can happen at compile time.

In Vbase, an object's abstract behavior is defined by an abstract typing mechanism. This behavior may have been defined by the object's abstract type, or directly inherited from its supertype, or inherited from the supertype with a refinement by the type. In a *refinement*, the subtype adds some additional behavior to the behavior defined by the supertype. A type must provide the implementation for all behavior that it defines and for the additional behavior that it has added through refinements.

When an operation is invoked, Vbase uses a mechanism called *dispatching* to determine which

CH2539-5/88/0000/0172$01.00 © 1988 IEEE

subtype's implementation to execute, based on the abstract type of the supplied argument.

At the top of the abstract type hierarchy is the type Entity. All objects in the Vbase system are instances of Entity. Subtypes of Entity (including user-defined types) define additional state and operations to model application-specific behaviors.

To model state, an abstract type defines properties for its instances. Unlike the notions of state in many traditional data models, Vbase properties do not give the user direct access to the object's internal implementation. Instead, the user accesses the state through a collection of abstract operations. A typical property consists of three operations: Get, Set and Init.

The state of an object is stored in one or more representation pieces defined by the abstract type of the object. Each piece of representation is itself an object. The representation of a primitive Vbase type is Space, which is in turn its own representation.

Typically, each type defines a single representation piece, containing all of the state needed for the behavior defined by the type. The actual storage used to represent the object is allocated and managed by a type called a *storage manager*.

2. Vbase Storage Managers

2.1. Overview

Every Vbase object is an instance of some abstract type, and derives all of its visible behavior from that type (and, via the inheritance mechanism, from the supertypes of that type). The behaviors associated with the object's storage, however, are implemented not by the object's abstract type, but by its storage manager. These behaviors include the object's persistence, location, its clustering with other objects, its paging (or "object-faulting") behavior, etc.

These behaviors are not directly visible at the abstract level, but are used internally by the type to manipulate its instances. Most types, however, will choose to export the higher level features of the storage manager, by allowing the user to specify, when an object is created, which storage manager to use, and how to cluster the object (thus determining the object's persistence, paging behaviors, etc.)

For example, when a user creates an instance of type Document, or CircuitDesign, or, say, Cat, the type might allow specification of whether the cat should be stored in persistent storage, or in temporary storage. Many types, however, will limit the set of allowable storage managers, either for semantic or performance reasons. If the set is limited to only one allowable storage manager, then the type most likely will not allow user specification of the storage manager at all.

Storage managers are much like other types, in that they define a set of behaviors, can have subtypes, etc. They differ, though, in that they do not have instances in the same sense as abstract types do. Instead, their operations apply to pieces of storage, which might be used to store instances of other types.

There is a strong analogy between the way an application makes calls on the operations defined by abstract types, and the way an abstract type makes calls on a storage manager. For example, an application could invoke an operation on a Cat, like GetHairColor (defined, say, on type Mammal), and it would dispatch to the appropriate subtype of Cat, based on the actual abstract type of the argument (Fig. 1)

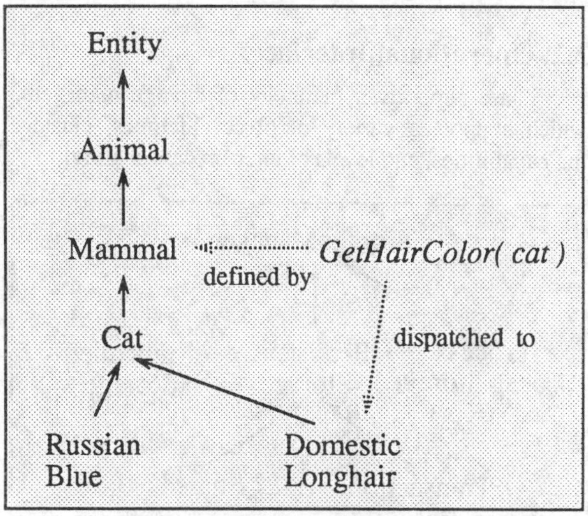

Fig 1. Dispatching an Abstract Operation

Internally, the type Cat processes the GetHairColor operation by accessing the instance's storage, by invoking the StorageManager$Wire operation. This operation will dispatch the appropriate subtype of StorageManager, based on the actual storage manager of the argument (Fig. 2).

Note that if the cat in question is of the type RussianBlue, then the original GetHairColor operation will dispatch to this type. In this case, the question can be answered without looking at any storage at all: the operation can simply return the value

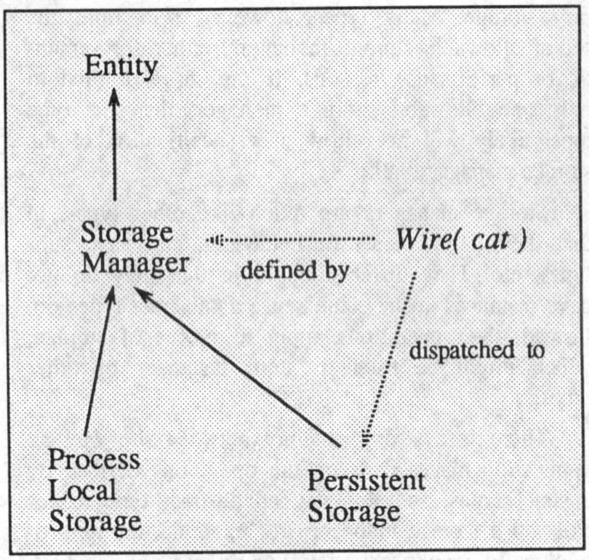

Fig 2. Dispatching a Storage Manager Operation

Blue, because all instances of RussianBlue cats are blue.

2.2. Operational Interface.

Vbase supports a hierarchy of storage managers, which support a variety of object lifetimes, clustering capabilities, and levels of inter-process sharing.

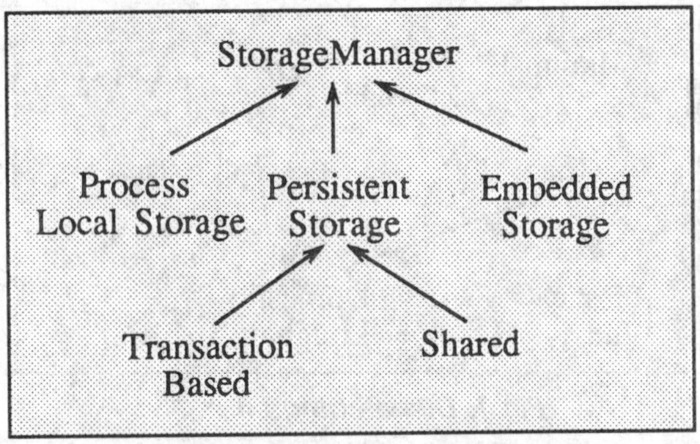

Fig 3. Storage Manager Hierarchy

The type StorageManager defines operations for allocating, deallocating, and accessing storage. There are nine operations altogether for managing storage, which are defined by type StorageManager, and refined by its subtypes.

```
Allocate( storagemanagerindex: integer,
          size: integer,
          where: entity,
          hownear: cluster )
    returns( space );

Deallocate( e: space );

Wire( e: space )
    returns( pointer );

Unwire( e: space,
        modified:boolean );

Resize( e: space,
        delta: integer );

Getsize( e: space )
    returns( integer );

BeginTransaction(
    timestamp: time );

CommitTransaction(
    timestamp: time );

AbortTransaction( );
```

Allocate: The arguments to the Allocate operation are a "StorageManagerIndex", indicating which storage manager to use (described in the section on Implementation); the size of the storage piece to allocate (in bytes); an entity with which to cluster the new storage; and a cluster-specification, indicating how closely to cluster it. (These last two arguments are optional and are described in the section on Clustering.) Allocate returns a reference to a piece of storage, which is used by the abstract type (which made the call) to store an instance. The type of the return from the Allocate operation is Space. Space is the type used as the representation for the primitive system types (out of which, in turn, the non-primitive types build *their* representation).

Deallocate: The Deallocate operation takes only a single argument, the piece of storage to be deleted.

Wire: The Wire operation brings a piece of storage into memory, and returns a Pointer to it. A Pointer is the abstract equivalent of a virtual memory address. Once this Pointer is returned by the storage manager, it is guaranteed that the storage piece will remain fixed ("wired") in virtual memory until a corresponding Unwire operation is called.

Unwire: The Unwire operation releases a wired object from its virtual memory address. This operation takes two arguments: a piece of storage (which must be currently wired) and a boolean, indicating whether the storage was modified. If the storage was modified, the storage manager will take appropriate measures to ensure that the changes are preserved. If the storage manager supports persistent object storage, then this will mean writing the object out to stable storage at the end of the transaction. If the storage manager supports only transient (process-local) object storage, then the Modified flag might well be ignored.

Resize: The Resize operation changes the size of a previously allocated piece of storage. It takes two arguments: a piece of storage, and a delta, indicating the number of bytes to add or remove.

Getsize: The Getsize operation simply returns the current size in bytes of a piece of storage. It takes one argument, a piece of storage, and returns an integer.

BeginTransaction: This storage manager operation is called by the user-visible operation, Transaction$Begin. Not all storage managers support the transaction protocol. In fact, one Vbase storage manager, SharedStorage, is specifically designed for implementing objects that are used for inter-transaction communication. If these objects obeyed the normal transaction protocol of non-interference (that is, the effects of one transaction are not visible to another concurrent transaction), then inter-transaction communication would be impossible.

For those storage managers that do support the transaction protocol, BeginTransaction starts a transaction scope. The timestamp argument controls the resolution of future Wire calls: the storage manager will ensure that this transaction will not see the changes made by other transactions whose commit time is later than this transaction's start time.

CommitTransaction: This operation has the effect of making the current transaction's changes visible to subsequent transactions (probably by writing the changes out to stable storage). If the storage manager does not support a transaction protocol, this operation might be a no-op.

AbortTransaction: This operation throws away all of the current transaction's changes. Again, if the storage manager does not support the transaction protocol, this might be a no-op.

2.3. Clustering

Raising the storage problem to being a semantically visible portion of the system has advantages for clustering. *Clustering* is the ability to store logically related objects close together.

The storage managers all support a series of hierarchical clustering levels. The normal arrangement is to support chunks (contiguous storage), segments (a clustering of chunks) and areas (a clustering of segments). Any storage manager, however, is free to support more levels of clustering or ignore some or all of these standard levels. For the default persistent storage type, a segment is the unit of transfer to and from disk, and an area maps to a disk partition or file. As alternatives, process local objects have only two levels of clustering: chunks and segments, where segments are built along operating system paging boundaries in a virtual memory system; while a distributed storage manager might add another higher level of clustering: a node.

The user can cluster an object's storage explicitly by making use of the clustering arguments to the abstract type's create operation, but types also generally provide a default clustering. The user's preferences, or the type's defaults if no preferences are given, are passed on to the Allocate operation via the *where* and *hownear* arguments. These specify an object to cluster with and how tight (area, segment or chunk) the clustering should be.

Since all storage managers support the same basic model of clustering, it becomes a much simpler problem to export a strong clustering pragma language to the type implementor. In Vbase, objects may be clustered at any clustering level, along semantic relationships. Typically, all of the storage pieces required to implement an object are clustered within the same chunk. This chunk is then clustered within the same segment as the chunk(s) implementing another related object. For example, in a CAD application, all of the subpieces of an assembly might be clustered within the same segment, thus requiring only a single disk transfer when accessing the assembly.

In some cases, it is even desirable to state what you do *not* want clustered together. For example, if an object has a raster image as part of its representation, it is likely that having the image clustered in the same paging unit as the rest of the object would severely degrade the access time to other parts of the object's state, due to the disk-read cost associated with bringing a large image into memory.

3. Implementation

3.1. Reference Resolution

When a piece of storage is allocated, the storage manager returns a reference to the storage. This reference is only interpretable by the storage manager. It may or may not map directly to a physical address. (This allows the storage manager to shuffle the storage under its control to facilitate its management functions.)

This reference serves as the only handle that the type manager has on the underlying piece of storage. The type manager then (typically) passes this reference on to the user, as the user's only handle on the abstract object being created. The reference is a surrogate for the object, and as far as the user is concerned, it *is* the object.

The user accesses or updates the object by passing the reference to an operation of the abstract type. The type in turn calls the storage manager to dereference the storage, map it into memory, and return a pointer to it. Upon completing its access, the abstract type relinquishes the storage piece, thus allowing the storage manager to move the object within memory, or page it out to disk.

3.2. Dispatching

Just as with the abstract operations, storage manager operations must be dispatched to the appropriate implementation. But this dispatching is based on the storage manager of the object, rather than its abstract type.

When dispatching an abstract operation, it is necessary to determine (at runtime, in general) the abstract type of the entity being operated on. This is typically done by examining the object's storage, which contains a reference to the object's type. When dispatching a storage manager operation, however, it is not possible to examine the object's storage to determine what storage manager to dispatch to, as this would result in a recursion problem. This means that the storage manager must be directly inferred from the reference.

To accomplish this, one field of the reference, called the StorageManagerIndex, is reserved for indicating the storage manager of the object. The remainder of the reference is considered the storage address of the object, and its use is defined by the particular storage manager.

The actual dispatch occurs by using the form as an index into a table of dispatch tables. Each operation (together with its refinements) is assigned a unique index into the dispatch table. The corresponding entry in the dispatch table is a list of pointers to the method or methods that implement the given operation. Since this table is brought into memory when the database is opened, storage manager dispatching is very fast.

4. Experiences

In contrast with most object systems, which provide only a single storage type for all instances [Goldberg83], or perhaps a single storage type for all instances of a single abstract type [Stroustrup86], Vbase provides a set of storage managers. These can be employed on an object-by-object basis to store the instances of any type. Vbase has storage managers that implement temporary, process local objects, and both shared and non-shared permanent, database resident objects. Depending upon the lifetime and other features of the object in question, any one of the available storage managers might be the most appropriate.

An important goal of the design of the storage manager facility in Vbase was to make the storage class of an object independent of its abstract class. Just as the use of inheritance in traditional object-oriented systems makes it possible for a user to define a new type, and immediately begin to make use of that type in existing code, a user of Vbase can add new storage managers, and immediately begin to make use of these storage managers in existing abstract types.

When we started this project, we had only a single storage manager (for persistent database-resident objects). We have since added two others (for process-local storage, and shared storage). Because existing types interfaced with the storage subsystem only through the interface defined by type StorageManager, the integration of these new storage managers was straightforward. We could immediately begin creating instances stored in the new storage managers, and the users of the abstract types involved were unaffected by the change.

We are now engaged in work to add a stronger clustering model and a richer transaction interface at the abstract level. We also expect to add versioning and distribution support to our storage managers.

References

[Goldberg83] Goldberg A., Robson D., Smalltalk-80 The Language and Its Implementation, Addison-Wesley 1983.

[Liskov81] Liskov B., Atkinson R., Bloom T., Moss E., Schaffert C., Scheifler R., Snyder A., CLU Reference Manual, Springer-Verlag 1981.

[Stroustrup86] Stroustrup B., The C++ Programming Language, Addison-Wesley 1986.

[Wegner87] Wegner P., Dimensions of Object-Based Language Design, OOPSLA 87.

[Weihl82] Weihl W., Liskov B., Specification and Implementation of Resilient, Atomic Data Types, MIT Technical Memo 1982.

AN OVERVIEW OF THE IRIS OBJECT-ORIENTED DBMS

D. H. Fishman

Hewlett-Packard Laboratories
Palo Alto, CA 94304

Abstract

The Iris database management system is a research prototype of a next-generation DBMS. Iris is intended to meet the needs of new and emerging database applications such as office information and knowledge-based systems, engineering test and measurement, and hardware and software design. These applications require a rich set of capabilities that are not supported by current generation DBMSs. In addition to providing for permanence of data, controlled sharing, backup, and recovery, Iris will also provide a number of needed new capabilities that include: rich data modeling constructs, uniform access to specialized storage subsystems and to foreign DBMSs, novel data types (images, voice, text, vectors, matrices), prolonged transactions, direct database support for inference, and version control. Iris will also provide sharing of objects across applications and programming languages.

Introduction

Below is a depiction of the layered architecture of Iris, including the database interfaces, the object management component, and the storage capability, which includes the native Iris Storage Manager, and hooks to other data sources. This paper briefly describes the capabilities provided at each layer of the architecture. A more complete description of the Iris DBMS may be found elsewhere[6]. Space limitations have prevented me from describing our approach to version control[1].

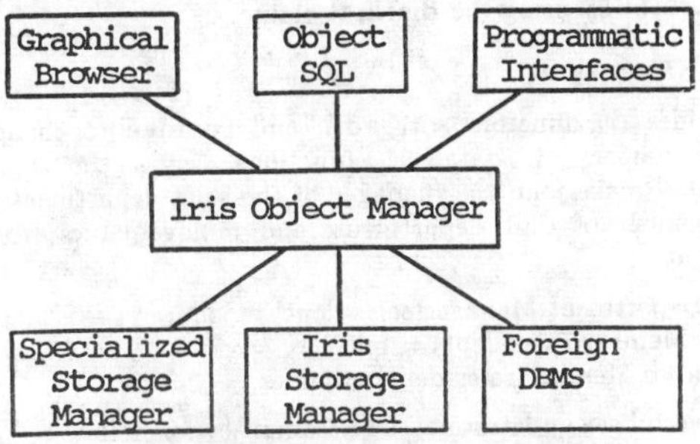

The Iris Object Manager

The Iris Object Manager[11] implements the Iris Data Model[4,5] by providing support for schema definition, data manipulation, and query processing. The Iris data model supports high-level structural abstractions such as classification, generalization/specialization, and aggregation[7,12] as well as behavioral abstractions[2]. The data model is based on the three constructs, *objects, types* and *functions.* The model supports inheritance and generic properties, constraints, complex or non-normalized data, user-defined operations, version control, inference, and extensible data types. The interface to the Object Manager is defined by a library of C language subroutines whose capabilities are illustrated in this section.

The query processor is a rule-based system that translates and optimizes Iris queries and operations into an extended relational algebra format that is interpreted against the stored database. We rely on the relational algebra as our theory of computation[10], rather than inventing a totally new formalism upon which to base the correct behavior of our system. This has proven very convenient in terms of coexisting with and migrating from existing database applications.

Objects

Objects are unique entities in the database that can be referred to, regardless of their attribute values, by a system-assigned, system-wide, unique object identifier (OID). OIDs are used to provide direct support for referential integrity.

Objects can only be accessed and manipulated in terms of functions (operations). As long as the semantics of the operations remain the same, the database can be physically and logically reorganized without affecting application programs. This provides a very high degree of data abstraction and data independence.

Literal objects, such as character-strings and numbers, are distinguished from *non-literal objects* such as persons and departments. Literal objects are directly represented, whereas non-literal objects are represented by OIDs. A non-literal object may be referenced in terms of its property values, e.g., "the person named 'Randy Newman'," or in terms of its relationships with other objects, e.g., "the spouse of the person named 'Sandy Newman'."

Operations are provided for explicitly creating and deleting non-literal objects, and for assigning and updating their property values. Referential integrity is supported by cascaded deletion of objects and relationships. When a given object is deleted, all references to that object are deleted as well.

Types and Type Hierarchies

Objects are classified by type. Types are named collections of objects, all of whose members share common properties. A property is a function of one argument defined on a type, such as a Name or an Age function defined on Persons. Types constrain the permissible operations that can be applied to an object.

Types are organized in a type structure that supports generalization and specialization. A type may be declared to be a subtype of another type. In that case, *all* instances of the subtype are also instances of the supertype. It follows that properties defined on the supertype are also defined on the subtype. We say that the properties are *inherited* by the subtype. The Iris type structure is a directed acyclic graph. A given type may have multiple subtypes and multiple supertypes. Iris properties may be *generic.*

The type Object is the supertype of all other types and therefore contains every object. Types are objects themselves, and their relationships to subtypes, supertypes, and instances are expressed as functions in the system[9].

In order to support graceful database evolution, Iris allows the type graph to be changed dynamically. New types may be created and existing types deleted and objects may gain or lose types throughout their lifetime. Currently, new subtype/supertype relationships among existing types cannot be created.

CH2539-5/88/0000/0177$01.00 © 1988 IEEE

Functions and Rules

Functions are defined on types and are applicable to the instances of the types. User-defined functions are compiled and stored by the system, and executed when invoked.

The specification of an Iris function consists of a *declaration* and an *implementation*. By separating the function declaration from its implementation, users are allowed to change the implementation without affecting application programs. A function declaration specifies the name of the operation and the number and types of its arguments and results, e.g.,

> **New function** Marriage(p/Person)
> = (spouse/Person, date/Charstring);

declares a function called Marriage. Functions can be either single-valued or multi-valued, and they can return compound results. The Marriage function can be invoked as follows ("bob" is a variable):

> **Find** s/Person, d/Charstring
> **where** <s, d> = Marriage(bob);

Iris functions may be implemented either as *stored functions, derived functions,* or *foreign functions,* as described below.

Stored Functions. A stored function is implemented as a table that maps input values to corresponding result values. The **store** operation specifies that a function is to be implemented this way, e.g.,

> **Store** Marriage;

causes a table to be created with, in this case, three columns for the Person, Spouse, and Date. The mappings of several functions may be stored together in a single table, e.g.,

> **Store** Name **on** Person, Age **on** Person;

would create a table containing Persons with their Names and Ages.

Derived Functions. The definition of a function may be specified in terms of other functions, e.g.,

> **Define** Emp-Manager(e/Employee) = **Find** m/Manager
> **where** m = Department-Manager(Emp-Department(e));

This simple definition specifies how the manager of an employee may be derived from other functions. In general, function definitions may contain arbitrary queries and may include calls to any implemented function. (At present, only conjunctive, disjunctive, and non-recursive queries are supported.) The following function calls a derived function, Emp-Manager, a stored function, Salary, and a foreign function (see below), Date-Older.

> **Define** Important-Manager () = **Find** m/Manager
> **where forsome** e/Employee
> Salary(e) > 10000 **and** m = Emp-Manager(e) **and**
> Date-Older(BirthDate(e),BirthDate(m));

In Iris, *rules* are simply functions. This is suggested by the definitions for Grandparent and Older-Cousin, below:

> **Define** Grandparent(Person p) = **Find** gp/Person
> **where** gp = Parent(Parent(p));

> **Define** Older-Cousin(Person p) = **Find** c/Person
> **where** c = Child(Sibling(Parent(p))) **and** Age(c) > Age(p);

Iris functions can return multiple results, and a nested function call returns the concatenation of the sets of results obtained from calling the inner function. E.g.,

> Children(Member(sales-dept));

returns all of the children of all of the members of the sales department.

Foreign Functions. Functions may be implemented in a general-purpose programming language, such as C. We call these *foreign* functions because they are written in a language that Iris does not understand, and hence cannot optimize. Foreign functions allow the user to extend Iris's capabilities in unanticipated ways. Foreign functions allow access to arbitrary sources of data such as the underlying file system, specialized storage managers, foreign DBMSs, high-speed in-memory data structures, and algorithmic generation of data. They also permit specialized operations as may be associated with new, user-defined data types. Foreign functions also provide operator extensibility. Although Iris cannot optimize the *implementation* of foreign functions, it can optimize their *usage*. One can add rules to Iris's rule-based optimizer appropriate to any particular foreign function.

Foreign functions appear to the Iris user as ordinary Iris functions. In their most general form, foreign functions may perform any computation, however, they are currently restricted from invoking Iris recursively.

Sets and Aggregate Functions

The previous sections describe functions defined on individual objects. Function may be defined over sets of objects via nested **find** statements, similar to the use of nested queries in SQL. For example, the following query computes the average salary of all employees.

> **Find** y/Real
> **where** y = Average (
> **Find** z/Real **where forsome** x/Employee z = Salary(x));

The set of values returned by the nested **find** statement are input to the Average function. The nested **find** statement may refer to variables defined outside its scope. Such variables link the results of the nested **find** statement to the outer query. For example, the following query computes the average salary of each department.

> **Find** c/Charstring, y/Real
> **where forsome** d/Department
> c = Dept-Name(d) **and** y = Average (
> **Find** z/Real **where forsome** x/Employee
> z = Salary(x) **and** d = Emp-Department(x));

Note that Iris sets are really multi-sets or *bags* since they may contain duplicates. Duplicates may be eliminated in any nested **find** statement by using the **distinct** clause.

Update Operations

Iris provides the functors **set, add,** and **remove** to change the future behavior of database functions, e.g., the following statements: make john the manager of the sales department; make bill a member of that department; and remove james from the department.

> **Set** Department-Manager(sales-dept) = john;
> **Add** Member(sales-dept) = bill;
> **Remove** Member(sales-dept) = james;

More powerful set updates may be accomplished as follows:

> **Set** Member(sales-dept) = Member(toy-dept);
> **Remove** Member(sales-dept) = e/Employee
> **where** e = Member(sales-dept) **and** Age(e) > 50;

Delete Operations

The **delete** operation deletes any user-defined object, type or function, with the effect cascaded to all related information. For example, the operation

> **Delete** Engineer;

will cause the type Engineer and all its instances to be deleted, together with all functions with type Engineer as an argument or a result.

Iris Interfaces

Iris is accessible both through interactive and programmatic interfaces. Three interactive interfaces are currently supported: (i) Object SQL (OSQL), an object-oriented extension to SQL, will be described in this section; (ii) a graphical browser that is being extended to support direct update both to schema and data, and (iii) a driver for the raw Object Manager interface.

Iris also supports three kinds of programmatic interfaces: (i) a straightforward embedding of OSQL into Lisp and C; (ii) an encapsulation of Iris as a programming language *object*[3,13] whose methods correspond to the C functions in the Object Manager interface; and (iii) a mapping of programming language objects directly and transparently onto Iris objects, thereby providing persistent, sharable objects across applications and languages.

Object SQL

We chose to extend SQL rather than invent a totally new language because of the importance of SQL and because the extensions are fairly natural. OSQL is at a somewhat higher level than the Object Manager interface, primarily because of OSQL's ability to bundle property functions with the definition of an object.

Three main extensions are needed to adapt SQL to the Iris model:

- Types, objects, and functions are manipulated rather than tables.
- Direct references to objects are supported, in addition to keys. Interface variables may be bound to objects on creation or retrieval, and may then be used to refer to the objects in subsequent statements.
- User-defined functions and Iris system functions may appear in **where** and **select** clauses to give concise and powerful retrieval.

Also, a few new keywords have been introduced. It is possible to mechanically reinterpret all existing keywords, but some of the keywords would be very misleading to users when applied to the object model.

The remainder of this section consists of examples intended to illustrate both the general similarity of OSQL to SQL, and the advantages of an object-based query language. Suppose we wish to automate some office procedures for obtaining approvals for documents, some of the actions and corresponding OSQL statements could be as shown below.

Start a new database called Approvals, connect to this database and start a new session, implicitly begining a new transaction:

```
Start Approvals;
Connect Approvals;
```

Create a type called Person, with the property functions name, address, netaddress, and phone. Each Person object must have a value for the name function:

```
Create type Person
    (name Charstring required,
     address Charstring,
     netaddress Charstring,
     phone Charstring);
```

Create a type called Approver as a subtype of Person, with one multi-valued property function called expertise (we assume Topic is a previously defined type); also create a type called Author as a subtype of Person; and create a type called Document:

```
Create type Approver subtype of Person
    (expertise Topic many);

Create type Author subtype of Person;

Create type Document
    (title Charstring required,
     authorOf Author required many,
     prim Topic,
     sec Topic,
     status Charstring required,
     approverOf Approver many);
```

Create a stored function called grade which for a given document and a given approver returns the grade assigned to the document by the approver, and create three instances of type Approver and assign values to the property functions name (*inherited* from type Person) and expertise. Bind the interface variables Smith, Jones, and Robinson to the objects created:

```
Create function grade (Document, Approver) -> Integer;

Create Approver (name, expertise)
  instances
    Smith ("Albert Smith", software),
    Jones ("Isaac Jones", (finance, marketing)),
    Robinson ("Alan Robinson", (marketing, personnel));
```

Add the type Author to the two objects referred to by the interface variables Smith and Robinson, (this shows objects being given multiple types), and enter documents written by Smith and Robinson:

```
Add type Author to Smith, Robinson;

Create Document (title, authorOf, status)
  instances
    d1 ("The Flight from Relational", Smith, "Received"),
    d2 ("DBMS Market Projections", Robinson, "Received");
```

Next, assign approvers to the document d1; assign to the document d1 the grade of 3 given by Jones; make a type for approved documents; approve the document d1; and commit the current transaction and start a new one:

```
Set approverOf(d1) = (Jones, Robinson);
Set grade(d1, Jones) = 3;
Create type ApprovedDocument subtype of Document;
Add type ApprovedDocument to d1;
Commit;
```

Lastly, make the following queries and end the current session, implicitly committing the current transaction: get the title of document d5; get the titles of all the approved documents; find the titles of all the documents Robinson is approving; find the names of all authors with some documents approved.

```
Select title(d5);

Select title
  for each ApprovedDocument;

Select title
  for each Document d
    where Robinson = approverOf(d);

Select distinct authorOf
  for each Document d
    where status(d) = "Approved";

End;
```

It is interesting to consider OSQL as a potential evolutionary growth path for SQL. It would be possible to use a subset of OSQL that is very similar to SQL, or to begin to make sparing use of new features such as the implicit keys, or to move to a style which takes full advantage of derived and nested functions in queries. Some of the new features of OSQL could be supported in a straightforward way on a relational system, while others require a more ambitious object manager. Migration is never easy, but the OSQL approach could smooth the path for migration of both users and programs from SQL to the objects world.

The Iris Storage Manager

The Iris Storage Manager is (currently) a conventional relational storage subsystem, namely that of HP's relational DBMS product, HP-SQL[8]. Relations can be created and dropped at any time. The system supports transactions with savepoints and restores to savepoints, concurrency control, logging and recovery, archiving, indexing and buffer management. It provides tuple-at-a-time processing with commands to retrieve, update, insert and delete tuples. Indexes and threads (links between tuples in the same relation) allow users to access the tuples of a relation in a predefined order. Additionally, a predicate over column values can be defined to qualify tuples during retrieval. We plan to extend and modify this storage subsystem to better support the Iris data model and to provide support for foreign operators and long fields.

Foreign Operators

Currently, the Query Interpreter module of the Object Manager evaluates operations involving multiple tables (joins), complex operations over a single table (aggregation) and foreign functions. However, we plan to extend the Storage Manager so that it can evaluate any operator or foreign function defined on a single table. This implies that columns returned from the Storage Manager may not even be stored in the database (e.g., they could be the result of an arithmetic operation). Note that a long term goal will be to support operators over sets of tuples, such as aggregate operators. Just as the operator '=' can be executed directly by a finite state machine or indirectly by retrieval via a hashing or B-tree access method, foreign operators will be allowed to have several implementations. Depending on their presence and estimated cost, the query optimizer will decide which implementation to choose.

Long Fields

The Storage Manager will also be extended to support field lengths well in excess of the maximum page size of 4K bytes. Each long field will be assigned a unique identifier by the Storage Manager. Tuples may use this identifier to reference the entire long field or some subset identified by a list of offsets and lengths. The basic operations on long fields will be retrieval and update. The retrieval of long fields will be allowed by reference or by value and may include a length. A retrieval request will return the requested bytes as a single byte stream. An update request similarly may be by reference or value and essentially will replace one byte sequence with another. This may cause the long field to expand or contract.

Types, such as "voice", "text", "bitmap", etc. will be associated with long fields. Foreign functions and operators will be allowed on long fields as on any other fields. Space efficient versioning facilities will be available for long fields to avoid almost identical copies of large amounts of data.

Acknowledgements

The author wishes to thank the entire Iris team for making this enterprise as successful and exciting as it has been. All should be listed as coauthors of this paper, as I have freely borrowed from their work.

References

1. Beech, D. and Mahbod, B., "Generalized Version Control in an Object-Oriented Database," *IEEE 4th Intl. Conf. on Data Engineering,* to appear, February 1988.

2. Brodie, M. L. "On Modeling Behavioral Semantics of Data." In *Proceedings of the 7th International Conference on Very Large Data Bases.* Cannes, France, September, 1981.

3. Cox, B. J., *Object Oriented Programming: An Evolutionary Approach,* Addison-Wesley, Reading, Massachussets, 1986.

4. Derrett, N., Kent, W., and Lyngbaek, P., "Some Aspects of Operations in an Object-Oriented Database," *Database Engineering,* (8),4, IEEE Computer Society, December, 1985.

5. Derrett, N., Fishman, D. H., Kent, W., Lyngbaek, P., Ryan, T. A. "An Object-Oriented Approach to Data Management." In *Proceedings of Compcon 31st IEEE Computer Society International Conference.* San Francisco, California, March, 1986.

6. Fishman, D. H., et al. "Iris: An Object-Oriented Database Management System," *ACM Transactions on Office Information Systems,* (5), 1, January 1987, 48-69.

7. Hammer, M. and McLeod, D. Database Description with SDM: A Semantic Database Model. *ACM TODS,* 6(3),351-386, September, 1981.

8. *HPSQL Reference Manual, Part Number 36217-90001,* Hewlett-Packard Company, Palo Alto, CA.

9. Lyngbaek, P. and Kent, W. "A Data Modeling Methodology for the Design and Implementation of Information Systems." In *Proceedings of International Workshop on Object-Oriented Database Systems.* Pacific Grove, California, September, 1986.

10. Lyngbaek, P. and Vianu, V. "Mapping a Semantic Database Model to the Relational Model." *SIGMOD 87,* San Francisco, Ca., May, 1987.

11. Lyngbaek, P., Derrett, N., Fishman, D. H., Kent, W., Ryan, T. A. "Design and Implementation of the Iris Object Manager." In *Proceedings of a Workshop on Persistent Object Systems: Their Design, Implementation and Use,* Scotland, Aug. 1987.

12. Smith, J. M. and Smith D. C. P. "Database Abstractions: Aggregation and Generalization," *ACM TODS,* 2(2),105-133, June, 1977.

13. Snyder, A. "CommonObjects: An Overview," To appear in *Sigplan Notices.*

Distributed Processing Systems

Chair: A. Elmagarmid

Distributed Shared Memory in a Loosely Coupled Distributed System

Brett D. Fleisch
University of California, Los Angeles

EXTENDED ABSTRACT

Introduction

In this work we describe new implementation experiences with a distributed shared memory system implemented in a loosely coupled distributed system. Our goal was to investigate the feasibility of distributed shared memory (dsm) in an operating system kernel. Li[LI86] demonstrated the feasibility of such a system outside of the kernel with a number of numeric applications, but it remained a relatively open question as to how well dsm performs for a variety of non-numeric applications and what the effects of dsm are on other kernel services. The organization of dsm we describe resembles a cross-processor segmented paging system.

Our talk relates implementation experiences and preliminary performance results. We plan to report results from experiments with symbolic computation, which emphasizes rearragement of data, where often the sequence of operations is highly data dependent and less amenable to compile time analysis than numerical computation. One general goal of this work is to describe a set of software primitives and to identify hardware features that can be used to support the conversion of applications from nondistributed shared memory to distributed shared memory. These features may include hints, user advice, control primitives, and architectural modifications that will improve functionality and performance.

Motivations for Distributed Shared Memory

One of the most popular communication schemes in the past has been the message passing approach. However, a significant limitation of message passing has been that to transfer a large amount of data between processes required a significant number of message exchanges[RASH86]. Often, data had to be broken up into discrete packets typically of 1K or 4K and transferred sequentially. This impacted on the efficiency of the message system and on the complexity of interactions. Accent[RASH81] and Mach[ACCE86] addressed the issue of accommodating bulk transfers in message passing systems. It relied, however, on a scarcely available hardware provision: copy-on-write support. With copy-on-write, no copy of the data is made when data is transferred if both communicants only read the data transmitted. Instead, shared memory is used (actually sharing through the maps) rather than paying the overhead of having the data copied.

The use of sharing for high performance message passing suggests exploration of a more direct sharing model in a distributed network environment. Our new model is a separate and distinct shared memory facility. It may be used for sharing and data exchange between sites in a transparent *distributed* manner in the Locus system[POPE81]. It differs from copy-on-write schemes which preserve "copy" semantics since direct sharing is used. In this system the programmer assumes a single site shared memory system (with UNIX System V IPC semantics) and the underlying operating system manages the distribution of shared memory data across sites. Applications written for a single site model of computation will work transparently across sites.

It has been argued that a distributed shared memory model can be a powerful basis for a decentralized computer service. In particular, Cheriton[CHER85] imagines a common name space tied together with a global shared directory system. Such a system would have global directories residing in the shared memory. As another example of the power of such a service, the machines could agree on the time of day by storing the time in this shared memory. At the extreme, Cheriton argues assuming the shared memory was large enough, the system could put everything in this shared memory and operate just like a shared memory multiprocessor. Further, much power is derived because it is easy to program applications in a shared memory model. The management of shared program state is familiar to programmers and transparently managed by the underlying operating system. This simplifies the amount of familiarity the programmer needs of the system's distributed configuration. Even remote procedure call (RPC) does not provide such a high degree of application level transparency because currently there is no good way to pass pointers in RPC paradigms. To avoid this problem, distributed languages are designed so that there are no application visible pointers in the language or so that passing pointers across site boundaries is prohibited.

The implementation we propose uses software support rather than building the shared memory in hardware. By implementing shared memory using the software segments mentioned earlier, a wide range of experimental parameters can be varied. Experimental parameters include number of processors, amount of multi-segment consistency, amount of memory, and variety in applications. We may be able to experiment with fiber optics at some later stage in this work.

The Model of Shared Memory

Figure 1 shows the organization of our distributed shared memory system. Depicted are a number of sites connected by a communication medium. Also shown is one shared memory *image* (or *segment).* The image is seen by all sites which have it "attached". When a site attaches the image all machine instructions are directed to a *local segment* which is a logical copy of the shared memory image. Each site with the shared memory image attached has a local segment which reflects the contents the entire image's data.

Our talk will describe the model in more detail and touch upon issues of segment distribution, locality, granularity, coherence, problem-oriented shared memories, network partitioning, and scaling.

The Status

At the conference the new status of our implementation will be presented and our progress towards acheiving our goals will be described. Further information may be found in [FLEI86,87a,87b].

References

[ACCE86] Accetta, M., Baron R., Bolosky W., Golub, D., Rashid, R. F., Tevanian, A., and Young, M., "Mach: A New Kernel Foundation for UNIX Development," Computer Science Department Technical Report, Carnegie-Mellon University, Pittsburgh, PA, May 1986.

[CHER85] Cheriton, D. R., Preliminary Thoughts on Problem-Oriented Shared Memory: A Decentralized Approach to Distributed Systems, *Operating Systems Review*, v. 19, n. 4, October 1985, pp. 26-33.

[FLEI86] Fleisch, B. D., Distributed System V IPC in Locus: A Design and Implementation Retrospective, Proceedings SIGCOMM 86 Symposium on Communications Architectures and Protocols, Stowe, Vermont, August 1986, pp. 386-396. Also appears in UCLA Computer Science Department Quarterly, 14, 2, Spring 1986, pp. 131-144.

[FLEI87a] Fleisch, B. D., Distributed Shared Memory in a Loosely Coupled Distributed System, Prospectus for the Dissertation, University of California, Los Angeles, CA, November, 1987.

[FLEI87a] Fleisch, B. D., Distributed Shared Memory in a Loosely Coupled Distributed System, Proceedings SIGCOMM 87 Workshop on Frontiers in Computer Communications Technology, Stowe, Vermont, August, 1987.

[LI86] Li, K., Memory Coherence in Shared Virtual Memory Systems, *5th ACM SIGACT-SIGOPS Symposium on Principles of Distributed Computing*, Calgary, Canada, 1986.

[POPE81] Popek, G. J., Walker, B. J., et. al., LOCUS: A Network Transparent, High Reliability Distributed System, *Proceedings of the Eighth Symposium on Operating System Principles*, Pacific Grove, CA, December, 1981, pp. 169-177.

[RASH81] Rashid, R. F., Robertson, G. R., Accent: A Communication Oriented Network Operating System Kernel, *Proceedings of the Eighth Symposium on Operating System Principles*, Pacific Grove, CA, December, 1981, pp. 64-75.

[RASH86] Rashid, R. F, From RIG to Accent to Mach: The Evolution of A Network Operating System, *Proceedings of the 1986 Fall Joint Computer Conference*, Dallas, Texas, November 2-6, 1986, pp. 1128-1137.

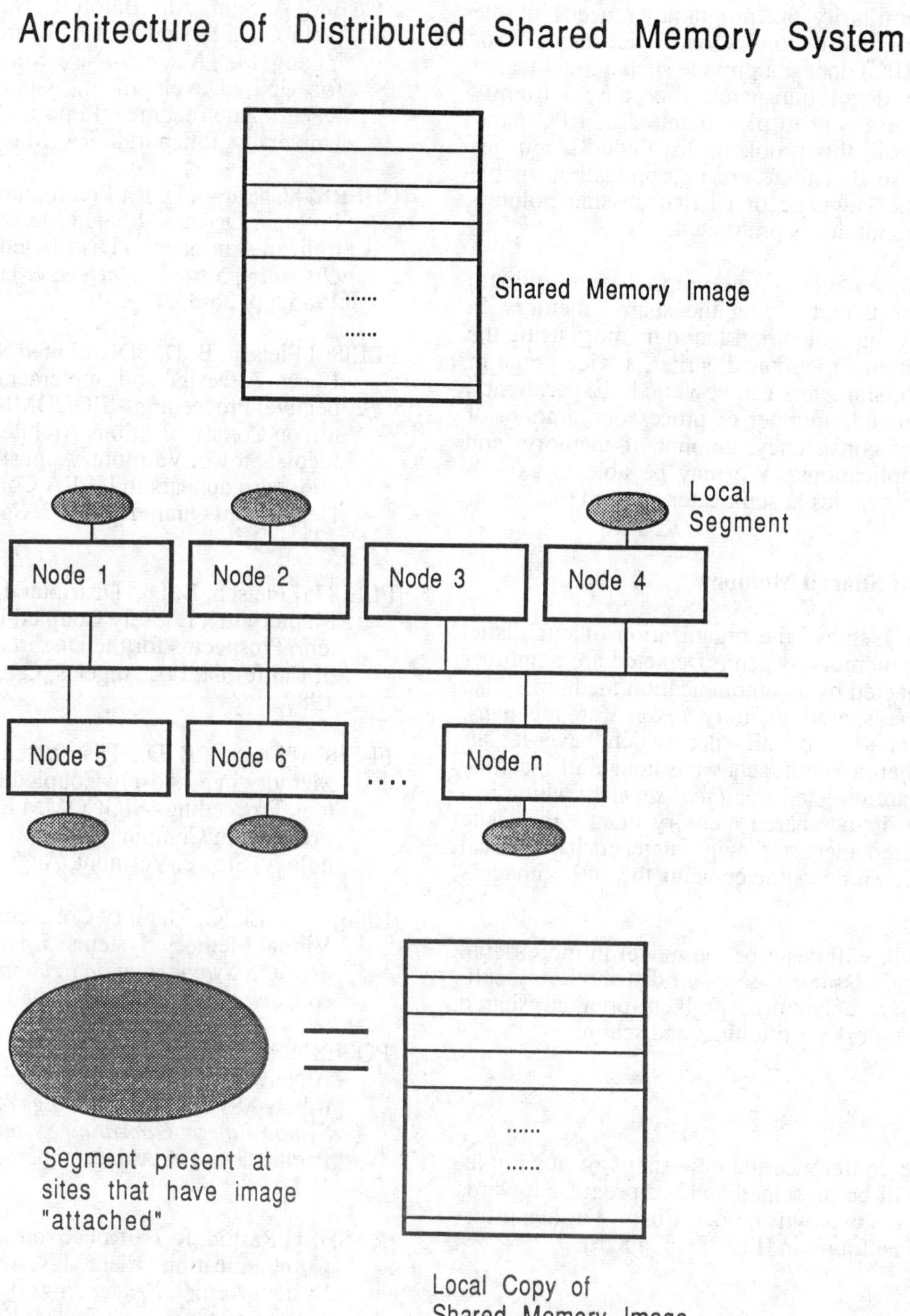
Architecture of Distributed Shared Memory System
Shared Memory Image
Local Segment
Node 1
Node 2
Node 3
Node 4
Node 5
Node 6
Node n
Segment present at sites that have image "attached"
Local Copy of Shared Memory Image

Figure 1

Design and Implementation of a Distributed Transaction Processing System

Dhamir N. Mannai and Ahmed K. Elmagarmid
Computer Engineering Program
Electrical Engineering Department
The Pennsylvania State University
University Park, PA. 16802

Abstract

Higher reliability could be achieved by integrating fault–tolerance in both the hardware and the software components of a system. Transactions have proved to be powerful tools for the implementation of fault–tolerant software. The extension of the transaction concept to the distributed environment has introduced new problems not present in centralized systems. Among them are those due to the communication network. The latter has become the major speed limitation factor. This suggests that minimizing communication in distributed transactions is as crucial as minimizing disk access for centralized systems. This paper presents a system for distributed transaction processing that reflects this concern. It introduces a new construct, called 'execute', that allows the initiation and execution of a group of remote operations with one command.

1 Transactions and Distributed Systems

The transaction concept has simplified the construction of reliable software. Transactions either run to completion or have no effect at all. If they complete successfully, then they preserve system consistency and integrity. A transaction is a transformation of state which has the properties of atomicity, durability, serializability, and isolation. Atomicity prevents partial effects of transactions, serializability assures proper concurrent execution of transactions, isolation provides the confinement of faults in a failed transaction to prevent their propagation to others, and durability assures the permanent effect of committed transactions. Higher reliability can be achieved if transactions are made resilient to as many failure types as possible and then used as the only means of accessing the database and operating on objects.

Several factors have motivated the decentralization of computer systems and have made distributed systems economically as well as architecturally interesting; and it became a necessity to extend transaction–based applications to distributed systems. Transactions that require services at more than one site are called **distributed transactions** and should still preserve the same transaction properties as the centralized ones. But, the decentralization of transactions raises new issues that are not present in a centralized system. Among these are communication failures and distributed transaction commitment.

A distributed system consists of a computer network in which hosts cooperate towards a goal. This computer network consists of autonomous computers that communicate via a communication network. Message exchanges and data transfers in such a loosely coupled system are prone to more failures than in a tightly coupled system. In addition, they are relatively slow. For real–time (interactive) transaction processing such characteristics are undesirable. One way to improve performance and increase reliability is to minimize the communication overhead of distributed transactions. The transaction processing model presented in this paper reflects such an idea by introducing a new construct, called 'execute', that allows the grouping of several transaction operations under one command.

2 System Description

The distributed transaction processing model proposed in this paper is aimed at reducing communication in distributed transactions. This communication involves both data transfers and control messages. the latter. The reason being that the amount of data transfer is dictated more by the application whereas the amount of control messages is dependent mostly on the approach taken to process transactions. The next few sections present a description of the model and a discussion of its 'execute' primitive.

The underlying system consists of several nodes that can communicate via a network. Each node has a global transaction manager (GTM), a local transaction manager (LTM), one data manager (DM), a storage facility for the database files, and a log management system. The log management system consists of an on–line log storage, a log storage manager (LSM), and an off–line log storage. The logical structure of one node of the system is shown in figure 1. Both the GTM and the LTM have some method of direct access to the on–line storage of the log management system. This is provided so that log information can be forced directly to stable storage. The log files that are no longer needed are transferred periodically to the off–line storage. This operation is controlled by the log storage manager (LSM). The log manager may incorporate some log compression schemes that will speed up the recovery process.

2.1 Transaction Processing:

The primitives issued by a distributed transaction are begin_transaction, read, write, execute, and commit or abort. They are processed according to the schemes outlined below. The algorithms can be found in [1]:

Begin_transaction: Upon invocation of this operation, the global transaction manager (GTM) writes a begin_transaction record in the log, interprets the request, and decides which nodes are going to be accessed to complete the transaction. Next, it initializes a run–time global table for the transaction. This table has a column for each participating node. The header of the column is the identifier of the called node. Then, it issues a local_begin_transaction primitive to all participating nodes. The local transaction managers (LTMs) of these nodes respond by writing a local_begin_transaction record in the log and creating and initializing new columns in their run–time local tables. Each of the headers of these columns contains the global transaction number and the identifier of the calling node.

Read(Xvalue): The GTM looks in its run_time global tables to find the table of the involved transaction. Next, It looks for the column of the participating node that contains Xvalue. If it finds a value for Xvalue then it returns it to the calling transaction. If not, it issues a local_read(Xvalue) primitive to the appropriate node. The LTM of the latter, in turn, issues a disk_read(Xvalue) primitive to the data manager of its data storage files. It gets the requested value, adds it as an entry in the cor-

CH2539-5/88/0000/0185$01.00 © 1988 IEEE

responding column of the calling global transaction, and sends it to the GTM. The latter adds the information as an entry in the appropriate column of its table and returns the value to the transaction.

Write(Xitem:Nvalue): The GTM checks the transaction's table for an entry of the item. If it finds it, then it updates it and issues a local_write(Xitem:Nvalue) to the corresponding LTM and writes a log record of the action. The latter, in turn, updates its copy of the item. Note that if the item has a copy in the global table then it must have a copy in the local table as well. However, If the GTM does not find a copy of the item, then it adds it as a new entry in its table and issues a local_write(Xitem:Nvalue) primitive to the corresponding LTM. The LTM, in turn, looks for a copy of the item in its tables. Obviously it does not find it and therefore adds it as a new entry.

Execute(Mod_ID,P1,P2, ... ,PN): Upon receipt of this primitive, the GTM writes the record to the log, records the necessary information in the run-time global table of the transaction, and issues a local_execute primitive to the appropriate LTM. Depending on the identification of the module (Mod_ID) and the parameters supplied (P1, P2, ... , PN) the LTM determines the data items to be accessed and the operations to be performed on them, writes a record to the log, performs the operations and records them in the transaction's column, and sends the results, if any, back to the GTM. Note that the type of operations performed and their corresponding logs vary according to the module executed and, possibly, the values of some data. The commitment of the operations of an executed module is fully taken care of by the LTM. Executing a module might require reading and writing data items. These data items are all recorded in the transaction's column, which resides at the local site, but not in its run-time global table, which resides at the site of the GTM. The only information kept at the global table is that of the operation's Mod_ID and its parameters P1, P2, ... , PN.

Commit: Upon receipt of this primitive, the GTM starts the atomic commitment part of the process using the 2-phase-commit protocol. It writes a Prepare_for_com- mit record in the log, sends the message to all participating LTMs, activates a timeout device, and waits for a response from each one of them. The LTMs in turn reply by writing a ready or not_ready record in the log and sending the message to the GTM. If a LTM sends a ready message then it must ensure that it is capable of committing its part of the transaction even in presence of failures. If all of the LTMs respond positively, then the GTM writes a global_commit record in the log and issues the primitive to all of the LTMs. Every LTM,in turn, commits its part of the transaction, writes a final_commit record in the log, sends the message to the GTM, and removes the transaction's entries from its tables. Upon receipt of the final_commit messages from all the participants, the GTM writes a global_final_commit record to the log, deletes the run-time global table of the transaction, and informs the end user. If any participant responds with a not_ready message, then the GTM must abort the whole transaction.

Abort: To abort a transaction, the GTM writes a global abort record in the log, issues the global_abort primitive to all the participating LTMs, and activates a timeout device. The LTMs, in turn, write local_abort records in the log, abort their parts of the global transaction, remove the corresponding columns from the tables, and send final_abort messages to the GTM. Upon receipt of these messages, the GTM writes a global_final abort record in the log, deletes the run-time global table of the transaction, and warns the end user. However, if the timeout period expires and the GTM does not receive responses from all of the participants, then it writes a timeout record in the log and proceeds as in the previous case.

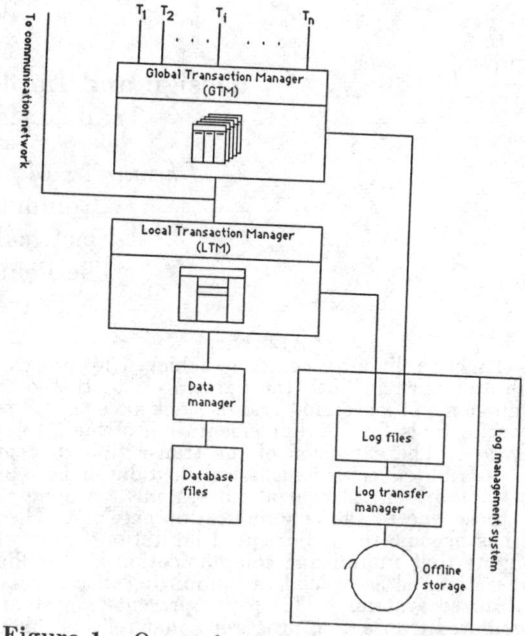

Figure 1. One node of the distributed transaction processing model.

2.2 The 'Execute' Construct

Transactions submitted to a particular site are serviced by the GTM and LTM of that site. However, when a transaction requires accessing items at remote sites, the GTM forwards the requests on behalf of the transaction directly to the LTMs at the corresponding nodes. The LTMs are capable of performing several operations on data stored at their sites on behalf of the GTMs. A requested operation could be simple, as read or write, or compound. The initiation of the latter type of operations is done using an "execute" call.

The **execute** construct is a one-level macro that translates into the basic **read** and **write** primitives at the local transaction manager's level and is issued by the global transaction managers. This construct enables the programmer to use fewer communications to execute many commands that would otherwise cause heavy traffic due to both data transfers and control-message exchanges. Suppose, for example, that a global transaction needs to perform N read and write operations at one particular remote site. To initiate one operation, we need a local_read or local_write message from the GTM to the LTM. In order to initiate the N operations we need N messages across the communication network. If the programmer can group all of these operations under one module name then it can be initiated by only one network message from the GTM to the LTM. This represents a significant gain and the advantage becomes very clear when the communication across the network is expensive, unreliable, or has considerably long delays.

Another advantage of using the execute construct is to be able to perform some processing and subtransaction control locally (at the remote site). This will allow better performance through parallel initiation and execution of many operations by sending only a few messages across the communication network.

The execute construct is basically a compound operation that utilizes the proposed architecture. There are however other constructs, such as nested transactions and remote procedure calls (RPCs), that provide a way to group operations together and it would be of interest to compare them to the execute construct.

Execute vs. Nested Transactions: The concept of a nested transaction [2,3] is an extension of the traditional one. In a system that supports transaction-nesting, there are two types of transactions: Top-level and nested. A top-level transaction may have several other transactions nested within it. These nested transactions must preserve the same transaction properties as the top-level ones and may have other child transaction. This concept introduces a hierarchy (tree) of transactions with the top-level one as the root. Nested transactions must begin after their parents and finish before them, and their commitment is conditional upon the commitment of the parent. The idea of nesting transactions introduces concurrency control and recovery concepts to within the transaction. In order to support nested transactions an additional mechanism that enforces transaction properties for the nested ones is needed. One major advantage of using nested transactions is the control of interaction between multiple processes within a single transaction. Another advantage is that a transaction may partially fail (i.e. at the level of the nested ones) and yet recover and retry other alternatives without aborting. That is because if one operation of a nested transaction fails then the nested transaction may simply be aborted and restarted by the parent. This feature is very useful in real-time systems where aborting a lengthy transaction may result in considerable delays or intolerable expenses, which will reduce the cost of transaction failures. Of course in some cases the whole transaction may have to be aborted because of the continuous failure of a child.

The 'execute' construct differs from nested transactions in several ways. First, it is a one-level macro that does not permit any further nesting whereas nested transactions do. Second, it does not utilize an additional mechanism to enforce transaction properties. It simply gets translated, at the LTM's level, into local read and write operations that are handled by the LTM just as if they were issued as such by the GTM. The software needed to support the 'execute' construct will be a module that is part of the LTM. Third, unlike nested transactions, it does not allow partial failure and recovery of the global transaction (in the sense discussed above).

Execute vs. Remote Procedure Calls: A procedure call is the invocation of a procedure, henceforth called the callee, by a user program, henceforth called the caller, where both the callee and the caller belong to the same address space. A remote procedure call (RPC) is a facility that extends this concept to the distributed environment. In other words, RPCs provide the user with a method to initiate and execute modules residing in different address spaces (namely, at different sites). Unlike local procedure calls, RPCs cannot guarantee a return since they are affected by communication and remote site failures over which they have no control. However, they do employ some schemes to cope with some of the unreliability issues. Nelson [4] describes these schemes by their call semantics.

In distributed systems, the implementation of atomic actions requires the provision of a special protocol for atomic commitment among sites as well as some recovery capability at every participating site. The software that supports atomic actions (or transactions) contains all the reliability tools such as do-redo-undo log management, 2PC protocols, etc. This software for atomic actions uses some mechanism for communication. The implementation of the latter could include a RPC facility, a message passing facility, and the underlying hardware, as shown in figure 2 [5].

The semantics and implementation of the reliability capabilities of the RPC facility used by a transaction processing system have to be well suited for the application. One example of the issues to be considered is the possible repeated executions of the remote call at the server.

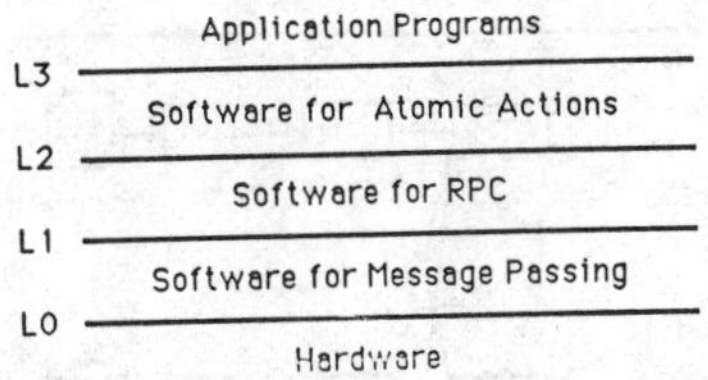

Figure 2 Hierarchy of software interfaces

RPC is a facility built on top of a message passing mechanism and may be used by the atomic action software for communicating with remote sites. The execute construct, on the other hand, is part of the atomic action (or transaction processing) software. In our implementation, the communication between sites is based on a RPC facility that was modified to accomodate restrictions posed by the nature of the application.

2.3 Proposed Model vs. The TM/DM Model

The operations requested by transactions fall into one of two categories; process management or data management requests. The begin_transaction, execute, and commit primitives are process management requests; and the read and write primitives are data management requests. In the light of this classification of requested operations we compare the proposed model to the TM/DM one.

In the TM/DM model, a transaction is represented by one particular process running at one site and controlling the whole transaction. Therefore, the control of the processing of distributed transactions is totally centralized. In the proposed model, however, a distributed transaction is represented by a cooperation of agents. The agents are the LTMs that reside at the different participating sites. The processing of the subtransactions of a global transaction are controlled by the local sites and thus making the control of processing a distributed operation. Figure 3 shows the logical structure of the proposed model.

In the TM/DM model, the transaction manager that initiates the distributed transaction is the only one that handles process management requests. The other participating sites handle, exclusively, data management requests. In the proposed model, on the other hand, the local sites handle process management as well as data management requests. This capability reduces to a great extent the amount of data and control messages transferred back and forth between the initiating site (GTM) and the participating sites (LTMs). Another advantage of the model is that transaction commitment at the local level is handled by the LTMs.

3 The Concurrency Controller

Concurrency control is handled by the data manager (DM) of the site where the requested data resides. For the time being, we are assuming that there is no replication of data. The locking methods of concurrency control resolve conflicts as soon as they arise by blocking the conflicting transactions. The optimistic methods, on the other hand, allow transactions to run to completion before testing for conflicts. Conflicts are then resolved by aborting the conflicting transactions. The choice for the appropriate concurrency control method is very dependent on the application at hand. Several studies however showed that in most applications the concurrency controllers that use locking perform better than those using optimistic methods. Locking induces more rejections while optimistic approaches induce more aborts.

In our system we use locking as the method for concurrency control. Transactions do not need to explicitly request locks. Appropriate locks are automatically granted for all read and write operations and released at commit time.

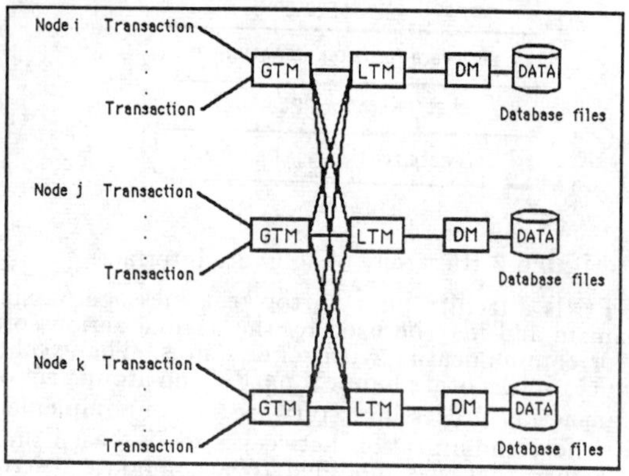

Figure 3 Logical Structure of the Model

4 The Recovery Mechanism

Recovery deals to a large extent with the problem of preserving transaction atomicity in the presence of failures [5–11]. In distributed systems, the implementation of atomic actions requires the provision of a special protocol for atomic commitment among sites (global) as well as some recovery capability at every participating site (local).

In the proposed model, atomic commitment is based on the 2–Phase–Commit protocol. This protocol is resilient to all failures in which no log information is lost. During the commitment stage (see section 2.1), when a LTM answers with a ready message to the global commit call, it takes the responsibility of committing its part of the transaction even in the presence of failures. Therefore, if the global decision is to commit and a local failure occurs, local recovery must be provided to restore the consistency of the local site. In short, recovery must be provided at both local and global levels.

Recovery at The Local Level: Recovery at the local level is provided by the local site. In our implementation, when a local failure occurs, the local recovery procedure uses the log records to restore the consistency of the database. The only recoverable failures considered are system failures (loss of volatile storage) and media failures that do not involve log files.

Recovery at the Global Level: Atomicity of the distributed transaction depends on atomicity at both the local and global levels. At the local level, and at each participating site, the LTMs must guarantee that all or none of the actions are performed. At the global level, the GTM must guarantee that all the LTMs take the same decision with respect to the commitment or abortion of their parts of the transaction. We have already discussed the recovery at the local level and need only consider recovery from failures at the global level.

The main global system component that is vulnerable to failures is the communication network that connects the different sites of the distributed system. In terms of the communication facility, we assume that if site X sends a message to site Y and Y receives it, then it was correct and in the proper sequence with respect to other X–Y messages, and within a reasonable predefined period of time Max_Delay. Furthermore, If two sites X and Y cannot communicate, then the network is partitioned into at least two groups, one containing X and the other containing Y. This is based on the assumption that as long as there is a path the communication network is capable of routing messages and delivering them properly. The communication mechanism just described was inplemented on top of a remote procedure call facility.

The failures to be considered are those resulting from lost messages and site crashes. When communication failures occur during transaction processing but before the commit operation, then the transaction is simply aborted. However if all operations are successfully completed and a failure occurs at commit time, then it is handled by the 2–phase–commit protocol. A more detailed discussion of the behaviour of the 2PC protocol in the presence of the various failures can be found in [1].

5 The Implementation

The proposed system is implemented in a UNIX environment on a collection of computers interconnected by a local area network. We have also implemented a remote procedure call facility on top of which we built the communication mechanism. The system is operational and being tested for performance data. It will also be used as a testbed for some database research at our laboratory.

6 Conclusions

This paper gave an overview of a distributed transaction processing system. The model used is aimed at minimizing data transmissions and message exchanges between remotely located sites. This communication reduction will decrease the probability of failures that are due to communication problems as well as increase parallelism in the execution. This will increase both the reliability and the efficiency of the distributed system. The 'execute' construct, a one–level macro, was compared with both nested transactions and remote procedure calls. The system is implemented in a UNIX environment on a collection of computers connected via a LAN. Investigations of the applicability of this transaction model in heterogeneous environments is under way.

References

[1] A.K. Elmagarmid and D.N. Mannai "A Transaction Processing Model for Fault–Tolerant Distributed Computing," Computer Engineering Technical Report TR – 86 – 010, The Pennsylvania State University, 1986.

[2] J.E.B. Moss, "Nested Transactions: An Approach to Reliable Distributed Computing," Ph.D. Dissertation, MIT, 1981.

[3] C. Pu and J.D. Noe, "Nested Transactions for General Objects: The Eden Implementation," Technical Report, University of Washington, Dec. 1985.

[4] B.J. Nelson, "Remote Procedure Call," Ph.D. Dissertation, Computer Science Department, Carnegie – Mellon University, Pittsburgh, Technical Report CMU – CS – 81– 119, Xerox PARC, Technical Report CSL – 81 – 9, April 1982.

[5] S.K. Shrivastava and F. Panzieri, "The Design of a Reliable Remote Procedure Call Mechanism," IEEE Transactions on Computers, Vol. C–31, No. 7, July 1982, pp. 692–697.

[6] J.N. Gray, "The Transaction Concept: Virtues and Limitations," Proceedings of the Seventh International conference on VLDB., Cannes, 1981.

[7] S. Ceri and G. Pelagatti, "Distributed Databases, Principles and Systems," McGraw Hill, 1984, pp. 173–206.

[8] P.A. Bernstein, V. Hadzilacos, and N. Goodman, "Concurrency Control and Recovery in Database Systems," Addison–Wesley Publishing Company, 1987, p. 20.

[9] A.Z. Spector and P.M. Schwarz, "Transactions: A Construct for Reliable Distributed Computing," ACM Operating System Review, Vol. 17, No. 2, 1983.

[10] J.N. Gray, "Notes on Database Operating Systems," Operating Systems: An Advanced Course, Springer–Verlag, 1979, pp. 393 481.

[11] W.H. Kohler, "A Survey of Techniques for Synchronization and Recovery in Decentralized Computer Systems," ACM Computing Surveys, Vol. 13, No.2, 1981.

A PARADIGM AND SYSTEM FOR DESIGN AND TEST OF DISTRIBUTED APPLICATIONS

Johan Fagerström and Lars Strömberg

Programming Environments Laboratory
Department of Computer and Information Science
Linköping University, Sweden

Abstract

It is well known that programming and testing distributed systems can be extremely difficult. Reasons for this include non-deterministic behavior, non-reproducibility of events, complex timing of events, and complex states. This paper presents a paradigm and system that will support a programmer when designing, programming, and testing a distributed application. Our main point is that the structure introduced by the paradigm must be kept and exploited during design, programming, and testing. One is not helped by a programming method which introduces a structure just to break it down again. We have developed a structural model based on common structures in distributed systems. This structural model is used to describe the logical relationships between components in a system. It is also integrated into a programming environment.

Background

Designers of large programs traditionally start with high-level structural design. People introduced to programs also generally try to understand global structures before looking at sub-components. Structures and understanding of structural relationships is thus of vital importance for design and programming. Enforcing programs to conform to the designed structures not only guarantees up to date documentation but it also simplifies testing. This paper presents a structural model of distributed applications based on a few observations of common structures in such systems. The model is very general but specific enough to allow us to integrate it into a programming environment. The programmer can thus use structural relationships introduced by the designer when debugging. For instance, he can change viewpoints of the system consistent with abstraction levels in the design. This 'meta-level' debugging is a necessary methodology since debugging of distributed systems is complicated by non-deterministic behavior, complex causal relationships between events, complex timing of events, and complex states.

Introduction

The **PEPSy** project (**P**rogramming **E**nvironments for **P**arallel **Sy**stems)[1,2] is an attempt to provide programmers with a suitable paradigm and appropriate tools for design and test of distributed applications. By "paradigm" we understand a conceptual framework for structuring ideas and concepts when solving problems. Our main point is that the structure introduced by the paradigm must be kept and exploited both during design and testing. One is not helped by a programming method that introduces a structure in the design phase just to break it down again later. An example on a small scale; it is common to implement complex knowledge structures in Lisp and still debug the program in terms of low-level primitives such as CARs and CDRs. Several formal models for describing parallel systems exist, for instance CCS[3] and CSP[4]. Both can be used to describe communicating processes, concepts like encapsulation, observation and tracing, and even system design. However, they are primarily models to be used in the specification and formal analysis of systems. They do not support later phases, such as testing, especially well. We have developed a structural model that explain distributed systems in terms of processes, logical channels, interfaces and abstract objects. This structural model is used to describe the logical relationships between components in the system. We use communication for process composition and encapsulation to provide abstraction. At the same time the model is integrated into a programming environment. It supports distributed system construction in several ways:

- Documentation of system components and their relationships can be done in a consistent and intuitive way. It is focused around a graphical representation of the design.

- The paradigm can be used to enforce a limited and structured mechanism for incremental changes in the system. There are two reasons for this. First, the paradigm results in hierarchical designs. Secondly, this hierarchy is enforced. We have made 'change' a design issue.

- Programming environment tools can be improved since more knowledge of the system can be built into them. The main reason for this is the fact that knowledge introduced by the designer and the programmer is kept and exploited by the programming environment.

Our model strongly resembles the HPC - model[5,6]. Both models have the same purpose: to use process structures explicitly in the design of distributed systems.

A paradigm for design and test of distributed applications

Summary

We base our model on processes which are combined into so called software ICs. (We acknowledge Brad J. Cox[7] for this appropriate name, we have previously used various other names). The nature of processes is language dependent. For now, think of them as containing state and code. They have an interface and they communicate via logical channels. These channels are uni-directional. A software IC is a set of communicating processes encapsulated into a black box by means of a so called control unit. The control unit is responsible for linking and un-linking logical channels inside the software IC. It is also used to construct well-defined states locally inside the Software IC, so called clean points[8]. A complete description of the model and its implementation and integration with the programming environment is given in [9].

Processes

The first architectural component in the paradigm is the **process**. Our processes corresponds to the usual concept of logical process. The paradigm is language independent. The only requirement is that processes must be able to "communicate" with the outside world. This can be done either explicitly, using for instance SEND and RECEIVE primitives, or implicitly, dependent on the language used. A processes is created as an instantiation of a class. A class is a template that describes a generic process. On instantiation a few specializations on the process are always done. At least, the process is given a globally unique name. This name is known to its creator and the process itself. Names are used for resource management, testing, and monitoring the system, not for binding communication partners. It is also possible to initialize local state or instantiate types. For instance, a queue template can be used to generate a queue-process with buffer elements of a certain type (SIMULA-syntax[10]):

```
ref (queue) queue#1;
queue#1 :- new queue (#elements,typeOfElements);
```

Processes can be written in almost any language. The only requirement is that it supports some means of communication with the outside world. However, for the purpose of this paper the reader can assume a language with explicit send and receive primitives.

Interfaces & channels

Processes communicate with each other using message passing through well-defined **interfaces**. The message passing is between interfaces, the coupling between the interface and the associated process is where the language independent model meets a language. An interface is always created together with a process (or more generally, together with an object). An interface consists of a fixed number of **ports**. From the outside a port can be seen as an abstraction of a function implemented by the associated object. Logical channels can be set up between ports. Messages are sent on these channels asynchronously. Ports are named. The extra level of indirection introduced by using portnames instead of direct naming simplifies process migration and location transparency. This is not an implementation issue since entries can be simulated by direct naming and calculated GOTOs. Figure 1 shows our view of an interface.

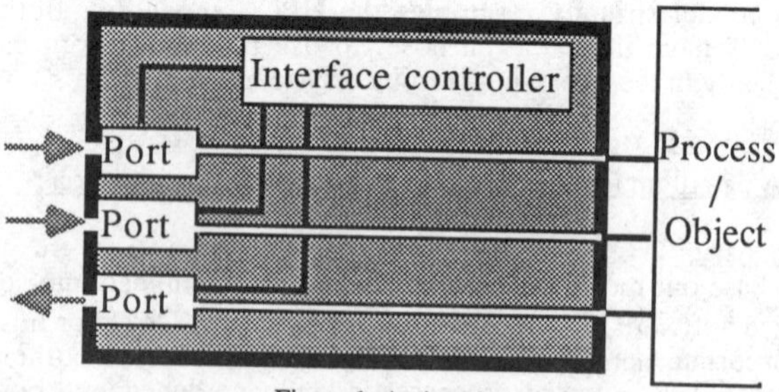

Figure 1: An interface

This particular interface consists of three ports and an interface controller. The interface controller will intercept messages sent to the interface itself, e.g. a request to link a port to some other interface. We have also indicated that two ports are used for input and one for output. Keeping to the queue example, the three ports can be named `controlPort`, `queuePut`, and `queueGet` respectively. From the process point of view, entries (defined inside the process and connected to the interface) are used for sending and receiving messages. Processes have thus no direct control over communication paths, this simplifies testing, process migration and fault-handling. An example of a physical realization of a port is shown in figure 2.

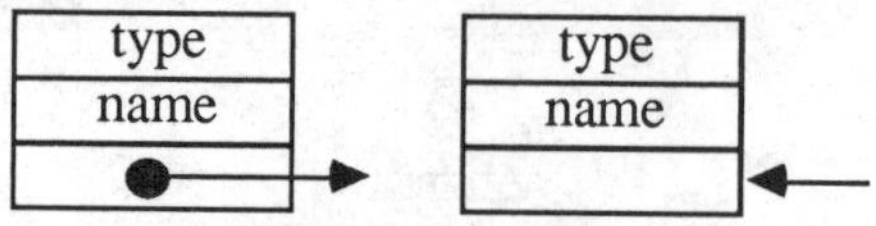

Figure 2: A port implementation

The port consists of three fields: a type, a name, and a register. The name is a constant. The register can either be used as an input register or as a placeholder for an output pointer. The output pointer either points to another port or it is `nil`. Incoming data will temporarily be stored in an input register. If it is not used it will contain `nil`. Values sent or received on `nil`-valued ports are lost. If the output pointer is writeable it will be possible to dynamically change communication partners.

Encapsulations

Abstraction is an important tool often used in design and programming. The model introduces **encapsulations** as an abstraction mechanism. The user can specify a border around an arbitrary set of objects. This border together with a name defines a new object. Figure 3 is an example of an encapsulation with three component object, one of which is itself an encapsulation.

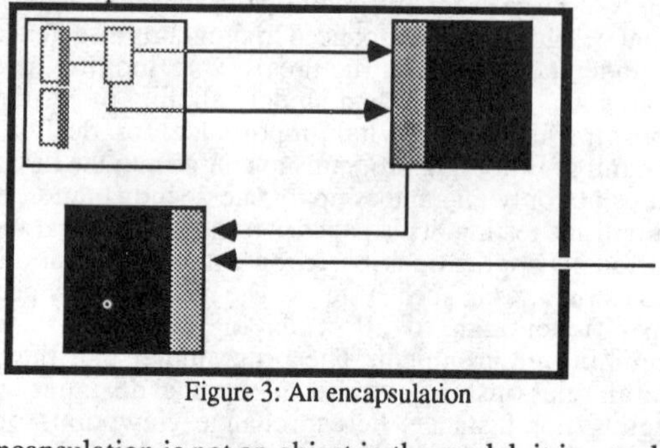

Figure 3: An encapsulation

An encapsulation is not an object in the model, it is a tool used in the programming environment. This mechanism is very influential on the debugging of the system. We describe this idea here since it is reflected in the model by our next type of object. One can trace and examine an encapsulation as a single object. (Within reasonable limits.) This kind of multi-level abstraction is useful in many situations.

Software ICs

An encapsulation is transparent. One can observe and even change sub-components. It is also passive (as an object). In order to make it opaque we must transform it into an active object. Logically, an encapsulation can be turned into a black box by introducing a **control unit**. (In practice one does not start from an encapsulation, since they represent a user-defined categorization of instances, not a class). This new type of object is called a **Software IC**. A control unit is thus a part of a Software IC. It will set up and tear down logical channels between interfaces in the Software IC, so called **internal interfaces**. The control unit also controls the interface to the environment (the **external interface**). A software IC is opaque, its internal structure can not be observed or manipulated from the outside. It can not be distinguished from a single process. (Our implementation guarantees this by enforcing scope rules for process naming consistent with the design). In figure 4 an encapsulation (figure 3) has been turned into a software IC by introducing a control unit. We have also included a new logical channel from the environment, a channel directly to the control unit. It could represent a control channel used for sending interrupts, debug commands, etc.

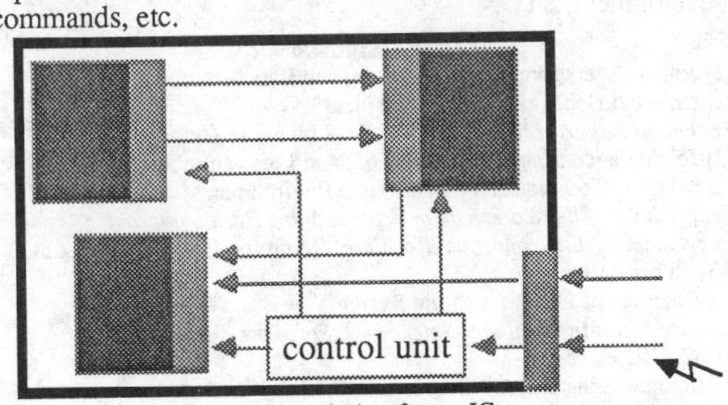

Figure 4: A software IC

The control unit has the following responsibilities:

- creating new instances of objects and their interfaces
- requesting termination or suspension of objects
- setting up and tearing down logical channels between objects
- setting up and tearing down logical channels between objects and the external interface.

The control unit is the only object in the system that can directly manipulate other objects. In this way we allow limited structured changes in the system. Unlimited creation, suspension and termination of objects in a distributed system very quickly leads to chaos.

Programming environment tools

Distributing systems introduce a number of new dimensions to the system design problem. For instance, designers must take time delays and limited bandwidth into account. Distributed systems also introduce a number of new types of possible bugs (in particular bugs introduced by failing nodes), and debugging is further complicated by non-reproducibility of events, non-determinism and complex timing of events. If robust, reliable, and correct programs are to be constructed, we must handle this extra complexity compared to sequential systems. We will examine a number of programming environment tools in light of our model in particular and distributed systems in general.

Editor, compiler, interpreter, linker, and loader

Traditional tools like these play an important role for program development. They must be re-evaluated in the distributed case. For example, the optimizing pass in compilers might try to add code to increase parallelism and thus performance[11]. "Objects" also provide an appropriate component for editing, compiling, and distributing. Incrementality can thus be provided at varying granularities. A related project has presented results on statement level incremental compilation in a host-target situation[12,13]. Incrementality in our case must be on larger objects (processes) of varying sizes. We have two editors, one at a process level (language dependent) and one structure editor which is used to create software ICs (language independent). The structure of the latter is shown in figure 6.

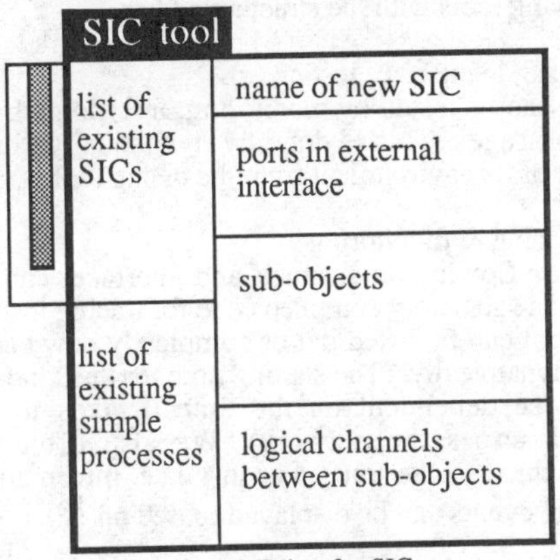

Figure 6: Editor for SIC

When entered the structure editor automatically creates a sub-class of the class **control unit**, an external interface and various control channels to the external world. The programmer can then use the editor to record the appropriate configuration code executed by the control unit when it is started (by pointing and using menus). Commands include creating and deleting sub-objects, and linking and un-linking channels between interfaces. The code for this (the configuration code) is generated and stored in the control unit. For sub-units, the editor will automatically create the appropriate interface and link it to the control unit via control ports (using symbolic names). The programmer can incrementally add, change and delete the configuration code. He/she can also inform the editor to generate a template (or a set of templates) for sending or receiving data on channels and insert data into the configuration code. Code for tracing (conditional or unconditional) and demons can be installed from the editor on ports, interfaces and channels. The appropriate code for this will then be generated. When the editing session is finished, the software IC and the control unit as sub-classes will be stored in the class hierarchy. (One can, of course, also start with an old sub-class of software IC and change it.) The programmer can create numerous instances of the structure editor and the language editor so that various part of the design can be designed and accessed in parallel using the window system. Finally, he/she can load and start the system from the editor. This is implemented as an instantiation of the control unit which executes its configuration code. Space does not allow us to discuss resource allocation. However, the programmer has the freedom to specify (or not specify) resource requirements consistent with the model structure.

Debugging tools

The backbone of any debug system is a traditional debugger for sequential processes. It provides services such as conditional breakpoints, single-stepping and tracing. Sequential debuggers can be allocated on a one per object basis, together with a master debugger residing on the host from where the user interacts with the system. In our case we can provide more structure than this. The debug system will have knowledge about component relationships. The most important aspect of a debugger is that it presents the system in a way consistent with the users conceptual view. The debugger must thus know about encapsulations, control units, and interfaces. To support this we need a kernel which keeps track of logical structures and a name server which maps logical names into addresses. The model itself also simplifies debugging by introducing centralized control at various places: the control unit. For debugging purposes we have integrated the following tools with the structure editor:

- module interface testing

protocols can be tested by monitoring, inserting, changing, or adding messages. This is done by dynamically "lifting" the object out of its environment from the debug tool.

- tracing & monitoring

Information flowing on channels and interfaces can be stored on a file. The statically compiled code for tracing installed with the SIC tool can be lifted out or completely new code can be installed dynamically. (The starting time for this kind of tracing is of course dependent on the time it takes to send the command across the network). We also offer tools for browsing through the trace. For instance, information about ordering of events can be displayed (based on [14]).

- automatic surveillance

Traditionally the term 'demon' has been used for a process that observes a database. The demon consists of a trigger and an action. The action associated with an instance of a demon is performed when the trigger condition is fulfilled. Demons recognize database changes that occur after their activation. Demons, in our case, is part of the debug tools watching and controlling objects. The user specifies the conditions which must be fulfilled for an action to occur, and the action itself. Typically, demons are used for testing relations between structures in the system (i.e., "protocols"). They can be considered as part of the debugger distributed into the system itself.

- control over the system

Single-stepping, tracing, peek and poking on processes can be done via a traditional sequential debugger, allowing the user to introduce his own debugging techniques. This is similar to the probe-mechanism used in[15]

These tools (except the last) can be used on processes, encapsulations and software ICs. For instance, by tracing the external interface of a software IC the programmer avoids generating the (possibly large) trace of all its sub-components. Debugging can thus be done in a bottom-up fashion where single components are tested before integrating them into a software IC. When all sub-components are believed to function correctly one can study their combined behavior. All control units have built-in methods for cooperating with the debug tool. Interfaces are also prepared for tracing and demon handling. We can thus manipulate objects within the system in several ways. It is also possible to manipulate logical channels in similar ways.

Implementation status

A prototype implementation has been constructed in Smalltalk-80[16]. It was used as a tool when studying the model. All objects, e.g. interfaces, are represented as processes making the system very slow.Present work includes refinement of the model and the tools, and porting the prototype onto a distributed system (using CONIC[17] on a set of SUN workstations). This version will use tables operated on by name servers to implement several model objects. This will improve performance considerably.

Conclusions

We have presented a unifying view of distributed computations based on a structural model and briefly discussed the consequences for programming environments. The model is based on communication for process composition, and encapsulation as an abstraction tool. The programming environment benefit since more knowledge is introduced and exploited. This provides a conceptual adequate view of the system to the user. Structures are enforced by the system and protocols can be tested in a hierarchical way. The model supports both structuring (interfaces, logical channels, and processes) and layering (encapsulations and software ICs).

This work is supported by the Swedish Board for Technical Development, STU.

References

[1] Johan Fagerström, Yngve Larsson, and Lars Strömberg
"Distributed Debugging - Collected ideas"
Technical Report, LITH-IDA-R-86-21, Linköping University
[2] Johan Fagerström, Yngve Larsson, and Lars Strömberg
"Debugging Techniques for Distributed Environments"
Proceedings of the Workshop on Programming Paradigms and Programming Environments, Roskilde, Denmark, Oct. 1986, pp. 65-73
[3] Robin Milner
"A Calculus of Communicating Systems"
Lecture Notes in Computer Science 92, Springer - Verlag , 1980
[4] C.A.R. Hoare
"Communicating Sequential Processes"
Prentice Hall International Series in Computer Science, 1985
[5] Thomas J. LeBlanc and Stuart A. Friedberg
"Hierarchical Process Composition in Distributed Operating System"
Computer Science Department, University of Rochester
[6] Thomas J. LeBlanc and Stuart A. Friedberg
"HPC: A Model of Structure and Change in Distributed Systems"
Computer Science Department, University of Rochester
[7] Brad J. Cox
"Object Oriented Programming - An Evolutionary Approach"
Addison - Wesley Publishing Company, 1986
[8] J. Bryan Lyles, Zebo Peng, and Johan Fagerström
"Naming Services in a Distributed Computer Architecture"
Nordic Symp. on VLSI in Comp. & Comm. Tampere, Finland, June 84
[9] Johan Fagerström
"A paradigm and system for design of distributed systems"
Forthcoming thesis, Linköping University
[10] O-J. Dahl, B. Myhraug and K. Nygaard
"Simula Common Base Language" *Norsk Regnecentral*, 1970
[11] P.G. Hibbard and T.L. Rodeheffer
"Optimizing for a Multiprocessor: Balancing Synchronization Cost against Parallelism"
Proce. of the 5th Intern. Symp. on Programming, Torino, Italy, 1982
[12] Peter Fritzson
"Symbolic Debugging through Incremental Compilation in an Integrated Environment"
The Journal of System and Software, 1983 pp.285-294
[13] Peter Fritzson
"Preliminary Experience from the DICE System - a Distributed Incremental Compiling Environment"
Proce.of the ACM SIGSOFT/SIGPLAN Software Engineering Symp. on Practical Software Development Environments, Pittsburgh, Pennsylvania, April 1984, pp. 113-123
[14] Leslie Lamport
"Time, Clocks and the Ordering of Events in Distributed Systems"
CACM, Vol.21, No.7, (1978), pp.558-565
[15] Partha Dasgupta
"A Probe-Based Monitoring Scheme for an Object-Oriented Distributed Operating System" *Proceedings of OOPSLA '86*, pp.57-66
[16] Adele Goldberg and David Robson
"Smalltalk-80: The language and its implementation"
Addison-Wesley Publishing Company, 1983
[17] J. Kramer et al
"The CONIC Programming Language, Version 2.4"
Research Report DOC 84/19
Imperial College of Science and Technology, London

PARALLEL PROCESSING Track

Parallel Processing Systems

Chair: K. Stevens, Jr.

THE AMT DAP 500

by D. Parkinson, D.J. Hunt and K.S. MacQueen,

Active Memory Technology

Abstract
The Active Memory Technology DAP 500 series is the first commercial offering of a range of upwards compatible parallel processors. The DAP 500 is a 32 x 32 array of bit-organised processors based on two previous generations of DAP systems. The DAP 500 is an attached processor available on a wide range of host computers such as the SUN or VAX*.

DAP 500 Hardware

The DAP 500 has four main components (as shown in Figure 1):
- Host connection unit
- Master control unit
- Processor element (PE) and memory array
- Fast data channel

The total system is contained within a single cabinet that fits beneath a desk. It is powered directly from a standard power outlet socket, requires no special environmental control and consumes only 800 watts. Connection to a SUN host is via a SCSI interface with a nominal capacity of 2 MBytes/sec, or to a VAX host via a VME bus interface.

The prime design criteria are to provide outstanding price/ performance plus a programming environment that eases the task of the application programmer.

Host Connection Unit
The host connection unit is responsible for all communication between the host computer and the DAP 500. Provision is made for a VAX host using either ULTRIX* or VMS* as an operating system, or a SUN host using UNIX**. The host connection unit incorporates a Motorola 68020 32-bit microprocessor, SCSI and VME bus interfaces and two RS232 serial ports.

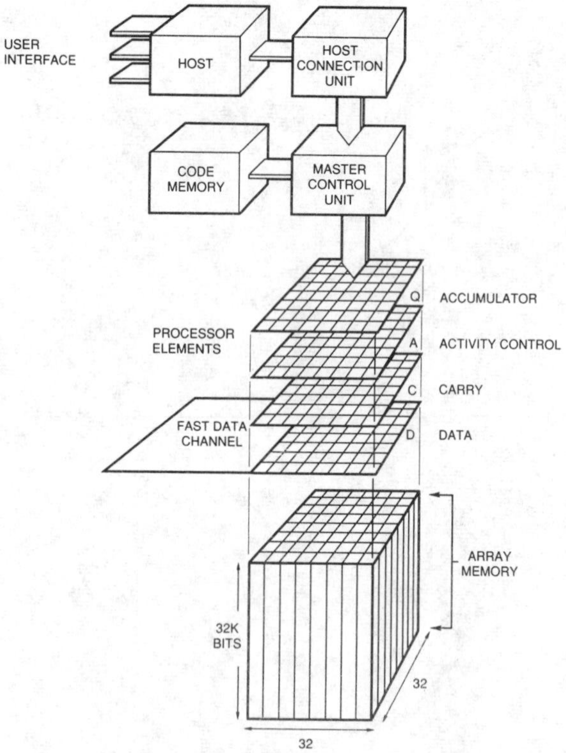

Figure 1: Schematic of the DAP 500.

Master Control Unit
The master control unit is the 'nerve centre' of the DAP 500 - it takes instructions from the code memory, interprets them and then controls the array of processors and data transfers. The master control unit also performs scalar operations. The arithmetic operations are duplicated and checked by master/slave comparison. The code memory has a minimum size of 512 KBytes and can be field upgraded to 2 MBytes.

Array of Processor Elements
The single instruction multiple data (SIMD) architecture of the DAP 500 series has 1024 single-bit processor

---

* VAX, ULTRIX and VMS are trademarks of Digital Equipment Corporation

** UNIX is the trademark of Bell Telephone Laboratories Ltd

CH2539-5/88/0000/0196$01.00 © 1988 IEEE

elements (PEs) arranged as a two-dimensional 32 x 32 array. It is implemented using 16 semi-custom chips, each containing 64 PEs. A duplicate set of 16 array chips is included as a slave to the master set. All PE operations are checked by master/slave comparison.

Each PE is provided with connections to nearest neighbours. In addition, a bus system connects processors by rows and columns (see Figure 2). These row and column data paths provide rapid data broadcasting or fetching facilities. The nearest neighbour connection scheme gives the high level of connectivity required for many applications.

All PEs simultaneously execute the same instruction, but an activity control register in each PE allows individual PEs or groups of PEs to be 'switched off'. The control bits can be generated from a predetermined pattern or from a previous calculation.

Array Memory
Each processor has a direct connection to its own memory. The minimum store size is 32K bits per PE, which provides 4 MBytes in total. The architecture of the DAP 500 series can support up to 1 Mbits/PE, or 128 MBytes total for a 32 x 32 array.

Fast Data Channel
A plane of data (1024 bits) can be transferred between the array memory and the D plane in one machine cycle. The data may be input to or output from the D plane over the fast data channel at a transfer rate of 50 MBytes/sec. Only 5% of the processor cycles are used in this I/O process. Currently a high resolution colour display is available as a fast data channel peripheral (1024 x 1024 x 8-bit pixels) via a framestore. Future options will provide for attachment of other input/output devices.

Performance and Reliability

Performance
The DAP 500 offers high performance through having many processors operating in parallel.

The cycle time of the DAP is determined mainly by the array memory technology. In the first commercially available system, the cycle speed is 10 MHz; this version is thus designated the DAP 510.

Some examples of performance on the DAP 510 are:
- Transfer between memory and processors at 1200 MBytes/sec.
- Logic or Boolean operations at 10,000 million operations /sec.
- Character handling at 1000 million/sec.
- 8-bit integer multiply (2 address) at 400 million operations/sec.

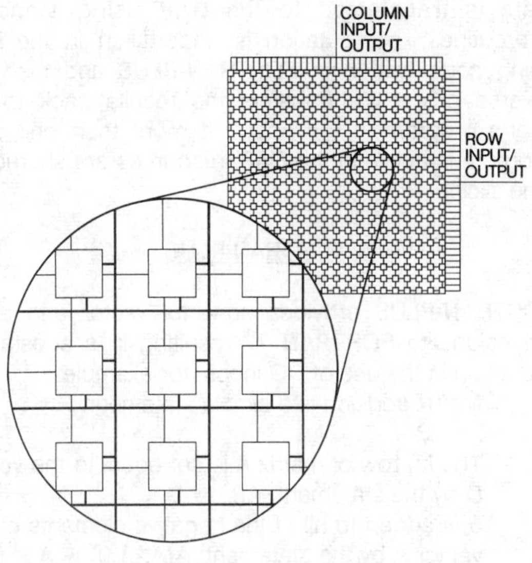

Figure 2: Connectivity of the array of processors.

Reliability
The DAP 500 series is designed to be resilient, reliable, maintainable and offer a high level of integrity. All data paths and memory in the system are parity checked. The complete array of processors is duplicated and all operations are checked by master/slave comparison. The master control unit also uses master/slave comparison to validate its scalar operations.

Programming the DAP

High level programming support is provided for the DAP 500 series systems using a version of the FORTRAN language which includes extensions for dealing with vectors and arrays. This is called FORTRAN-PLUS, a forerunner of the ISO standard FORTRAN 8X which will be offered once the standard is ratified.

A complete suite of software is available to the user which includes a FORTRAN-PLUS compiler, the APAL assembly level language, run-time aids, an extensive library of subroutines and simulators for the DAP hardware. The software is provided for SUN hosts using UNIX as an operating system and for VAX hosts using ULTRIX or VMS.

A key to high productivity is the continuity which is offered to DAP users by allowing them to create and run programs using their host system. DAP program development is undertaken through the host which also provides the user's run-time interface. Access to standard input/output facilities, including filestore, is available via the host. That part of the computation that is appropriate for the DAP is selected by the programmer.

Data is transferred to the DAP using standard subroutines; computation is undertaken in the DAP using code written in FORTRAN-PLUS and then the reverse procedure transfers the results back to the user's program in the host. If more than one user program is active in the DAP, resources are shared by time slicing.

FORTRAN-PLUS

FORTRAN-PLUS provides powerful vector and array extensions to FORTRAN 77 resulting in a substantial reduction in the use of DO loops, for example:

- Matrix addition is a simple statement: A = B + C.
- The Ith row of matrix A is set equal to the vector D by the statement: A(I,) = D.
- 5 is added to all of the negative elements of the vector A by the statement: A(A.LT.0) = A + 5.

These examples are listed in Table 1.

FORTRAN-PLUS code is typically a factor of three to five times shorter than standard FORTRAN 77. A second advantage is that programs are more easily understood because FORTRAN-PLUS statements bear a strong resemblance to the equivalent mathematical expressions. A third advantage is that the user will be exploiting some of the ISO/ANSI standard FORTRAN 8X concepts in advance of the final definition of the standard.

FORTRAN-PLUS allows a wide range of data types, from 1-bit variables to 8-byte precision. It has many other useful extensions that result in coding flexibility.

Table 1: Comparison of coding

FORTRAN-PLUS	FORTRAN
A = B + C	DO 4 M = 1,32 DO 4 N = 1,32 4 A(M,N) = B(M,N) + C(M,N)
A(I,) = D	DO 5 M = 1,32 A(1,M) = D(M) 5 CONTINUE
A(A.LT.0) = A + 5	DO 9 M = 1,32 DO 9 N = 1,32 IF (A(M,N).GE.0) GOTO 9 A(M,N) = A(M,N) + 5 9 CONTINUE

The compiler generates efficient code and the average user will have no need of the assembler language APAL - although many of the library routines utilised will make extensive use of this efficient language.

Application Support Library

Active Memory Technology's application support software includes an extensive library of subroutines which simplifies the task of developing code, enhances programming efficiency, makes code more readable and generates code with high efficiency at execution. There are about 150 routines currently available and the library is being extended rapidly. In many cases the 'routines' are very close to application packages.

The library contains routines for:

- Matrix manipulation (eg multiplying, inverting, calculating eigenvalues)
- Signal processing (eg calculating Fourier transforms)
- Image processing (eg windowing, histogramming, calculating convolutions)
- Data manipulation (eg sorting, permutations)
- Auxiliary functions (eg generating random numbers, evaluating transcendental functions)
- Graphics

Low Level Assembler - APAL

A low level assembler - APAL - is provided for the user who requires facilities or performance not available in FORTRAN-PLUS. This is for users who wish to manipulate data in ways not supported by FORTRAN-PLUS. Two contrasting examples are short word length for image processing and 128,000 bit arithmetic to search for large prime numbers. Even in these cases, APAL will normally only be required for small sections of the code. FORTRAN-PLUS and APAL routines can be combined during compilation.

Run Time Software

The run-time support environment resides partly in the host and partly in the DAP. The host component provides interfaces whereby a standard host program can control the running of an associated DAP program.

A DAP-based component monitors the progress of DAP programs. Run-time computational errors (eg dividing by zero) are trapped by this system which then informs the user on the host, and automatically enters an interactive analysis mode. In this mode the user can request the value of variables by name. APAL users may obtain the values of data items by specifying their address. As an alternative to analysing the program state at runtime, a dump can be taken at this point for later interactive study. When in analysis mode, the user may choose at any time to resume the program from where it was interrupted, or to abandon it.

Parallel Data Transforms

Effective exploitation of parallel processing requires a solution to the problem of communicating data between processors. This solution must satisfy demands in performance, ease of use and generality.

Table 2: Some DAP applications in various sectors

Area	Applications
ACADEMIC SECTOR	
Artificial intelligence	neural networks
Astronomy	image analysis
Earth resources	image analysis
Fluid flow	Navier-Stokes equations
Genetics	DNA sequencing
Geophysics	climatic modelling
High energy physics	lattice gauge theory
Hydraulics research	wave-equation in shallow water
Mechanical engineering	finite element analysis
Solid state theory	Ising model
Vision research	image analysis
INDUSTRIAL SECTOR	
Aerospace	fluid flow, Navier-Stokes equations
Biotechnology	DNA sequencing
Electronics	routing on a chip and logic simulation
Legal and Patents	syntactical retrieval from GByte files
Oil exploration	signal processing of seismographic data
Ordnance Survey	digital cartography
Pharmaceutical	molecular modelling
Robotics	image analysis
DEFENCE SECTOR	
Command systems	speech recognition
Electronic support measures	signal processing
Radar systems	signal processing
Terrain modelling	image processing and graphics
Vision support	image processing

The array abstractions implicit in the definition of the language FORTRAN-PLUS satisfy these demands for general use. Their implementation relies on hardware, software and a general algebra of data routing known as Parallel Data Transforms (PDTs). As well as helping to provide the underlying support for FORTRAN-PLUS, PDTs may be employed to produce higher level library routines and applications code. In these roles, PDTs provide a unique and powerful tool for the development of high performance parallel software.

Simulation Software

DAP simulation software is available that runs on the host computers. This suite of software allows users to develop and test programs without access to DAP hardware. The simulator suite executes normal DAP object code and hence is a real development tool - while it runs orders of magnitude slower than on DAP hardware, it provides estimates of execution speed to be expected on the real hardware.

DAP Applications

The DAP 500 is a development of earlier DAPs built by International Computers Ltd (ICL). Six systems of 4096 processors were delivered and twelve systems of 1024 processors (Mini-DAPs) were also built. Some applications of these machines are shown in Table 2.

It is usual to refer to the DAP 500 series as special purpose machines, but the wide range of applications casts some doubt upon such a viewpoint. The DAP 500 has a number of outstanding attributes that are instrumental in making its architecture ideally suited to a broad range of applications involving large data structures. Examples of the performance of the DAP 510 are:

- Transfer rate between memory and processors of 1200 MBytes/sec.
- Ability to undertake Boolean operations at 10,000 million operations/sec (MOPS).
- Character handling ability of a 1000 million/sec.
- Integer arithmetic at 60-400 MOPS in 8-bit precision or 30-200 MOPS in 16-bit precision.
- 32-bit floating point operation in the range 6-60 MFLOPS.
- A fast input-output capability of 50 MBytes/sec.
- A flexibility of functionality that is determined by software at the bit level, making variable word length in fixed or floating point computations possible.
- A high level language, software tools and aids that help program development and greatly improve the efficiency of software production.

M31 : A LARGE-SCALE MULTIPROCESSOR VAX FOR PARALLEL PROCESSING RESEARCH

Matthew H. Reilly John R. Sopka
Digital Equipment Corporation

Abstract

M31 is a custom-designed, large-scale multiprocessor VAX for support of research and experimentation within Digital Equipment Corporation in the area of parallel processing. It is a shared-memory design with all processors having equal access to all physically available memory over a common bus. A large amount of 'snoopy' cache is provided to reduce memory access traffic on the bus while providing software- transparent coherency among the multiple caches in use by multiple processors. High-speed, programmable probe processors are provided which are capable of selectively capturing trace information on the software execution on the individual VAX processors non-intrusively. This report describes the general characteristics of the hardware and software design for this system and plans for its exploitation.

Overview

The design of the M31 system was motivated by the desire to achieve high performance through architectural features rather than technological innovation. With this in mind, the development team set about designing a modular multiprocessor built from "off the shelf" microprocessors, and readily available memory and I/O subsystems. Modules were constructed almost entirely with semi-custom CMOS and TTL components. Only the clock distribution system was implemented in a high speed (ECL) technology.

Within the bounds enumerated here – the machine had to be implemented in a conservative technology and achieve high performance by exploiting innovative architectural features – there were more specific goals and requirements that drove architectural decisions.

Architectural Goals

Early in the development effort five goals were enumerated for the project team [Egg84].

- The compute power of the system should be "interesting". That is, the compute power of a multimicroprocessor must be significantly greater than that which is achievable by conventional means.

  In order to achieve such performance without undertaking the development of a new instruction set processor, the system would need to allow at least thirty-two processors to cooperate on the same problem. M31 was designed to allow modular configurations of from four to sixty-four processors.

- The system should provide an hospitable software development environment.

  This was part of the motivation for ensuring that M31 would be a suitable platform for Digital's VMS operating system. Ease of programming was also a strong argument for the presence of a completely transparent means of data sharing and cache consistency enforcement.

- The chosen processor building block must have a future.

  The overall aim of the project was, after all, to allow Digital to explore multiprocessor concepts with an eye toward possible future product development. The choice of the MicroVAX-II chip processor was a natural one.

- Performance monitoring and tuning assists must be built into the system from the beginning.

  M31 supports an integral performance monitor system that allows programmers and hardware designers difficult to obtain insights into program and system behavior.

- There must be a solution to the problem of program decomposition.

  It was clear from the start that this last goal could not be achieved without actually building and gaining experience with a multiprocessor that fulfills the first four goals.

A Brief Description of the Hardware

An M31 system is a VAX multiprocessor that may be configured with up to 64 processors in 4 processor increments. The processors are connected to a large shared memory via a single interleaved bus, as are the I/O devices. Caches are interposed between the processors and the system bus to reduce bus traffic and the effects of memory latency.

Each cache is shared by a group of four processors. A single group of four processors and one cache is contained within a *Processor-Cache* (PC) module. I/O is via a connection to a VAXcluster using Digital's *Computer Interconnect* (CI). Two CI adaptors reside on the M31 bus. Memory is connected to the system through two *Memory Master* (MM) modules. The actual memory arrays are in two cabinets separate from the main processor system. Memory configurations can range from 4 to 256 MegaBytes. The system also includes a central bus arbiter and an interrupt controller in the *Interrupt-Arbiter* (IA) module. Finally, a *Console Control* (CC) module and a *Bus Recorder* (BR) module are provided for diagnosis and bootstrapping. (See Figure 1.)

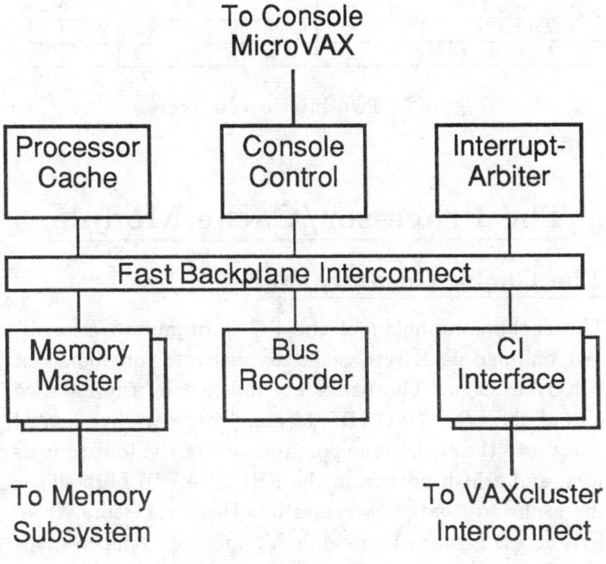

Figure 1: M31 System Diagram

In addition, each PC is connected to a *Processor Monitor* (PM) module. The PM contains three microprogrammable sensors that are connected to three of the four processors on a PC module. A microprocessor on the PM collects data from the sensors and transmits the data over an Ethernet connection to a VAX host for post-processing. The intent was to provide a sensor for each of the four processors on a PC module, but physical space constraints on the PM module forced the designer to eliminate the fourth sensor. (See Figure 2.)

The Interconnect

One of the major innovations in the M31 design is the *Fast Backplane Interconnect* (FBI) that connects the various system components. The FBI is an eight way interleaved bus that is designed to support the cache consistency scheme with a minimum of overhead.

Cache Consistency

The M31 architecture allows shared data to be stored in a processor's cache. In order to guarantee that every processor "sees" data change in a consistent manner, the system supports a cache consistency protocol. The actual cache behavior will be discussed below, but it is sufficient for the discussion of the bus protocol to say that for any processor access that *may* be to a shared location, the access will cause a bus transaction to occur. The originating processor will be informed if such a transaction actually results in an access to a shared location.

The FBI Protocol

A single bus transaction is divided into three phases: arbitration, command, and response. Excluding the arbitration time, a transactions takes 800 ns to complete. This is referred to as a "major cycle". Each part of a transaction takes place within a particular 100 ns window of a major cycle, this window is called a "minor cycle". Minor cycles are numbered 0 through 7.

For purposes of illustration, let us assume that a processor module (or I/O device) **X** is to perform a READ of

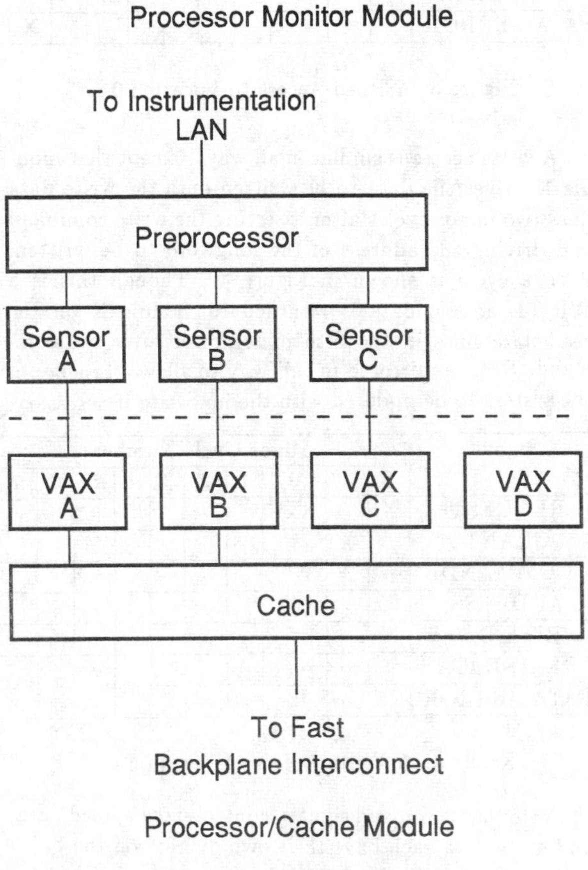

Figure 2: The Processor Monitor and Processor Cache Modules

location 0 in the M31 physical address space. Two minor cycles before the command is to occur, the module makes a request to the arbiter. The arbiter examines all of the current requests and, using a modified "round-robin" algorithm, grants the bus in the next minor cycle. In the minor cycle following the grant, module **X** issues a read command by asserting the read signal and driving the address of interest (0) on the bus. (The minor cycle in which this command is asserted is refered to as minor cycle zero and, for reference, begins at time zero.) Five minor cycles later, the data at location 0 is driven onto the bus by the MM module. If the access resulted in an error, **X** will be granted access to the FBI again in the seventh minor cycle, so that the access may be re-attempted. In the seventh minor cycle after the command in a retried access, a fatal error signal is asserted if the re-attempted access resulted in an error. Figure 3 describes a typical (error-free) access schematically.

Signal	Minor Cycle Number									
	6	7	0	1	2	3	4	5	6	7
REQUEST	X									
GRANT		X								
COMMAND			RD							
ADDRESS			000							
READ-DATA								X		
FATAL-ERROR										X

Figure 3: A Read Access to Location 0

A write access is similar in all ways, except that module **X** drives the data to be written onto the write data lines two minor cycles after asserting the write command and driving the address of the longword to be written. Such a cycle is shown in Figure 4. Though this is a WRITE access, data is returned to module **X** on the read data lines in the fifth minor cycle after the command. Data is mirrored in this way to allow all caches in the system to be updated with the new data if necessary.

Signal	Minor Cycle Number									
	6	7	0	1	2	3	4	5	6	7
REQUEST	X									
GRANT		X								
COMMAND			WT							
ADDRESS			000							
WRITE-DATA					X					
READ-DATA								X		
FATAL-ERROR										X

Figure 4: A Write Access to Location 0

Note that command signals, control signals, read data, and write data each have their own "wires" on the backplane. The access described above used each signal for just 1 minor cycle out of the eight that it took to complete the access. The other seven cycles are in fact put to use by interleaving bus accesses. If a second module **Y** (**Y** and **X** could in fact even be the same module) were to access a longword at address a the command and address would be driven during minor cycle (a / 4) MOD 8. The arbitration request would occur two minor cycles previous to this, and the response signals would be similarly shifted in time. Figure 5 shows a read of location 200_{16} interleaved with a write to location $3EC_{16}$.

Signal	Minor Cycle Number												
	6	7	0	1	2	3	4	5	6	7	0	1	2
REQUEST	X			Y									
GRANT		X			Y								
COMMAND			RD			WT							
ADDRESS			200			3EC							
WRITE-DATA								Y					
READ-DATA								X			Y		
FATAL-ERROR										X			Y

Figure 5: Two Interleaved Accesses

The Processor/Cache Module

The Cache Organization

The cache component of the PC is organized as a direct mapped 64 KByte cache divided into four banks of 16KBytes each. The banks are indexed by the low two bits of the LONGWORD address. There are five logical ports into the cache: one port for each of the four processors, and a fifth port from the FBI. The FBI port allows the cache to "watch" accesses by other processors. If an FBI access is made by module **Y**, and the cache on module **X** contains the most recent copy of the data being addressed, the cache on module **X** will supply this most recent copy to **Y** and to the memory controller. At the same time, the entry in both **X**'s and **Y**'s cache will be marked as shared so that all future modifications of the entry will cause the new data to be written through the cache to the FBI and main memory.

Using this mechanism, the M31 architecture ensures that traffic between processors and main memory is minimized but is still sufficient to provide transparent cache consistency. Data that is not shared is cached as if it were stored in a "write-back" cache, while shared data is cached as if it were stored in a "write-through" cache. This idea was proposed in [Goo83] and improved upon by Stephen Shaffer at Digital.

The Cache State Machine

In the implementation of the M31 cache each entry has associated with it an entry STATE (essentially an elaboration of the "full" and "empty" states in a uniprocessor cache). The state of an entry determines whether an access to that entry by a processor will cause a write to the FBI. Further, the state determines what action will be taken if an FBI access matches the address tag for the entry.

Accesses from any of the four processors may affect the state of an entry. So too may accesses from modules on the FBI. The two tables below describe the state transitions and the actions necessary to maintain consistency of cached data throughout an M31 system.

As an example, imagine two processors on different modules – processor **A** and processor **B**. They are sharing a location **T**. One of the two processors must be the first to read **T**, as only one memory transaction can occur at a time. If **A** reads **T** first, then a copy of **T** will be cached on **A**'s module in the *single* state. At some point later, **B** reads **T**. **A**'s cache notices this request on the FBI and asserts the TRANSACTION_MULTIPLE signal. This causes **B**'s cache to set the state of location **T** to *multiple*. The state of **T** in **A**'s cache is also set to multiple. From that point forward all writes to **T** by either **A** or **B** will be written through to the FBI for as long as the cached locations for **T** are in the *multiple* state.

If at some point **B** flushes its copy of **T** from its cache, then the next write to **T** that **A** performs will not result in TRANSACTION_MULTIPLE being asserted. This will cause the state of **T**'s entry in **A**'s cache to transition

CURRENT STATE	ACCESS TYPE	ACTION	TRANS_MULTIPLE?	NEXT STATE
Invalid	Read	RFA	No	Single
	Read	RFA	Yes	Multiple
	Write	WFA	No	Single
	Write	WFA	Yes	Multiple
Single	Read Hit	RC	NA	Single
	Read Miss	RFA	No	Single
	Read Miss	RFA	Yes	Multiple
	Write Hit	WC	NA	Single
	Write Miss	WFA	No	Single
	Write Miss	WFA	Yes	Multiple
Dirty	Read Hit	RC	NA	Dirty
	Read Miss	FRFA	No	Single
	Read Miss	FRFA	Yes	Multiple
	Write Hit	WC	NA	Dirty
	Write Miss	FWFA	No	Single
	Write Miss	FWFA	Yes	Multiple
Multiple	Read Hit	RC	NA	Multiple
	Read Miss	FRFA	No	Single
	Read Miss	FRFA	Yes	Multiple
	Write Hit	WT	NA	Multiple
	Write Miss	FWFA	No	Single
	Write Miss	FWFA	Yes	Multiple

KEY TO ACTION CODES	
RC	Read from cache.
WC	Write to cache.
RFA	Read from FBI and allocate cache entry.
WFA	Write to FBI and allocate cache entry.
FRFA	Flush entry to FBI, read from FBI, and allocate cache entry.
FWFA	Flush entry to FBI, write to FBI, and allocate cache entry.
WT	Write to FBI and cache.

Figure 6: M31 Cache State Transitions for Processor Accesses

to *single*. A second write by **A** to **T** will cause its state to change to *dirty*. Note that this write action did not propagate to the FBI, since the cache controller for **A**'s cache knows that it owns the only copy of **T**. (**T** could not be in the *single* state otherwise.) As long as there are no other copies of **T** in the system, the entry for **T** will remain in the *dirty* state and writes to **T** will be to the cache entry only.

CURRENT STATE	ACCESS TYPE	ACTION	NEXT STATE
Single	Read Hit	T	Multiple
Single	Write Hit	T	Multiple
Dirty	Read Hit	ST	Multiple
Dirty	Write Hit	UT	Multiple
Multiple	Read Hit	T	Multiple
Multiple	Write Hit	UT	Multiple

KEY TO ACTION CODES	
T	Assert TRANS_MULTIPLE.
ST	Substitute data from cache to FBI and assert TRANS_MULTIPLE.
UT	Update cache with data from FBI and assert TRANS_MULTIPLE.

Figure 7: M31 Cache State Transitions for Bus Accesses

The Memory Subsystem

The Memory Organization

An M31 system may be configured with up to 256 MBytes of memory that is shared between all of the devices on the FBI. The memory is interleaved eight ways in the same manner as the FBI, so that at any time all eight banks may be servicing a request. The memory arrays are housed in two standard VAX 11/780 style memory expansion cabinets. Each cabinet contains four banks of memory and is connected to a single *Memory Master* module. (See Figure 8.)

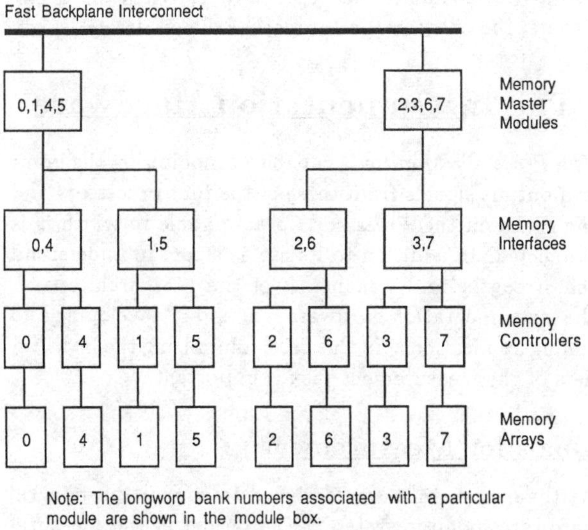

Figure 8: M31 Memory Subsystem

The Interlock Table

The VAX architecture includes a large group of instructions designed to allow multiple actors to share a single data item. These include instructions to insert and remove an entry from the head or tail of a queue (INSQHI, REMQHI, INSQTI, and REMQTI), test and set or clear a bit (BBSSI and BBCCI), and atomically increment a word in memory (ADAWI). Atomicity for each of the resulting accesses to shared data is ensured by an exclusive read and exclusive write bus operation. Between an exclusive read of a location and its companion exclusive write no other exclusive reads are allowed to that location.

VAX processors have implemented this exclusion by a variety of means. The choices span the range from implementing mutual exclusion at the bus level (following an exclusive read to location T all other exclusive reads to any location are "locked out" until the companion exclusive write to T occurs) to – in the case of the M31 system – locking out exclusive reads to a block of locations containing the currently locked location.

Specifically, when a processor (or I/O device) performs an exclusive read to a location T, a bit is set in the Interlock Table corresponding to the address T. The table is however much smaller than the size of the full memory subsystem. The index into the interlock table is a function of T that maps T (a 30 bit address) into the range <0..65535>. This index function extracts T<17:2> from the address. If a second processor attempts to perform an exclusive read to a second location S where S<17:2> = T<17:2> then the exclusive read access is refused. The processor recieving such a refusal will continue to attemt the read lock access until it is successfully completed. Successful completion will occur only after the processor that performed the exclusive read to location T has also performed an exclusive write to T. When this access occurs, the entry in the Interlock Table is cleared.

The Instrumentation Hardware

The *Processor Monitor* is capable of monitoring the input and output signals from three of the four processors and the cache on the *Processor Cache* module to which it is connected. In addition to its use as a tool to understand the strengths and weaknesses of the M31 architecture, the instrumentation hardware is an aid in developing and tuning applications. In this case, minimizing the invasiveness of the measurement task is important.

Goals for Measurement

At the outset, M31 was designed to support an integral hardware monitor system. The design of the measurement hardware was driven by the need to support both hardware and software experiments. In describing these needs two major goals were identified

- Cache and processor control signals must be visible to the PM, and the PM must be capable of reacting to changes in these signals.

  (Many of the questions that were seen as important required the PM to monitor events that lasted only a very short time and that were not visible to software executing on the M31 processors.)

- The PM must be able to detect the occurence of high level software events such as process activation, fault activity and subroutine entry and exit.

In general, the task of the PM is to track all processor events (primarily memory references) with minimal interference, and it must reduce the stream of those events to a data set that is relevant to the experiment being conducted.

Hardware Capabilities

The diagrams in Figures 9 and 10 describe the PM design that was implemented for the M31 system.

Figure 9 shows three processor/cache sensors connected to an Ethernet port via a PDP-11 microprocessor. The microprocessor executes a real time executive that was written especially to support measurement activities. This microprocessor is refered to as the "preprocessor" because it *preprocesses* the data from each of the sensors before sending the data over the Ethernet connection to the experimentation host.

Figure 10 describes the *sensor* submodule. The sensor is divided into five parts; the counters and control registers, the trace memory, the micro-sequencer, the pattern matcher, and the lookup table. The micro-sequencer determines the flow of control of the sensor program based on the results of pattern matching against the signals

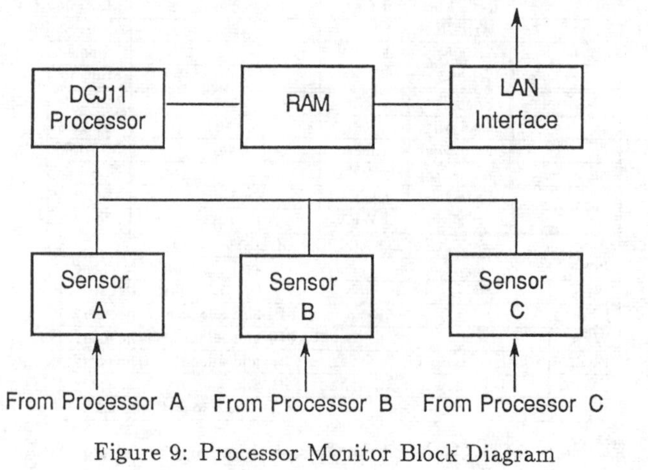

Figure 9: Processor Monitor Block Diagram

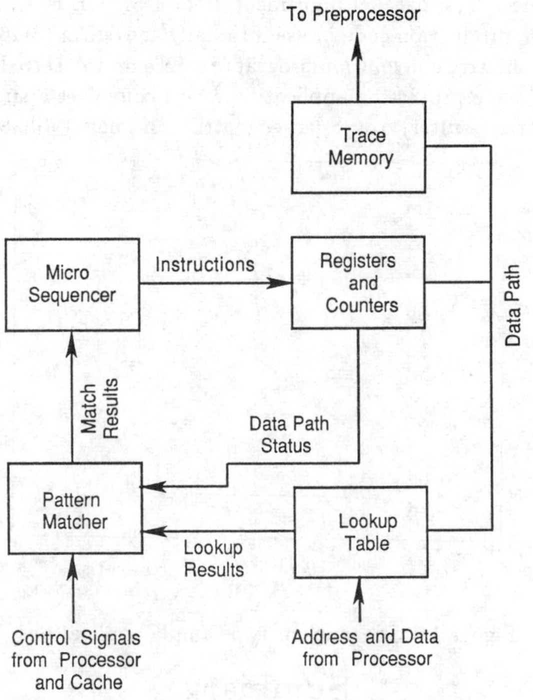

Figure 10: Processor Monitor Sensor Block Diagram

from the attached *Processor Cache* module and against the results from the lookup table. Microinstructions executed by the microsequencer may cause data to be stored into the trace memory, transfer information from one register to another, and increment any of the counters within the data path.

The Processor Monitor has been used so far to measure such things as cache hit ratio, memory access times, subroutine execution times, process activation and deactivation behavior and scheduler performance.

Software Development

Software Objectives

The software work on the M31 systems is focused on three specific objectives:

- explore the limits and obstacles to parallel execution performance
- use realistic production-scale applications pertinent to Digital Equipment Corporation and its customers
- work within a standard program development and execution environment

This exploration is intended to expose the current state-of-the-art in parallel processing software technology and to suggest potential directions for future developments in this area. The work is intended to range over the many levels of problem and program formulation which must be dealt with for effective utilization of parallel processing. The applications of greatest interest are primarily computationally intensive scientific and engineering simulation and design tools. The area of symbolic processing for artificial intelligence applications such as expert systems is not being ignored however.

The standard environment within which this work is being done is that of the VAX/VMS operating system with its rich set of languages and programming support tools. The VAX architecture provides interlocked instructions for atomic setting and clearing of individual bits, atomic queue insertion and removal operations, and an atomic addition operation. VMS provides support for shared, common address space among a set of independent threads of execution. Separate execution streams can invoke the interlocked instructions when manipulating data locations within such shared address space to construct higher-level synchronization and communication abstractions. The M31 is a powerful platform for developing understanding of what parallel processing extensions and enhancements can most effectively be made in the VAX language compilers, their run-time support, and their debug and execution analysis tools.

Foundational Software Work

In order to provide access to groups throughout Digital Equipment Corporation M31 has been connected to Digital's corporate-wide internal computer network running VAX/VMS as a VAXcluster member. This means that:

- a familiar programming and execution environment is provided for a majority of internal users;
- programs may be developed and executed on any VAX/VMS system within the network;
- once a program executes correctly on a uni- or dual-processor VAX it can be transferred electronically over the network to the M31 system for much larger-scale parallel execution; and
- remote login for execution and monitoring of such applications can be made available from any DEC location world-wide.

In order to achieve this status the VAX/VMS operating system had to be ported to execute on the M31 hardware and the existing support for dual- processor VAXes had to be generalized to tens of processors. Further enhancements and extensions to the basic operating system are now being explored as we gain experience in its use in this new environment. The robust design of VMS provides considerable flexibility in user authorizations and system control parameters which has made much of this work more a matter of tuning and balancing than of reworking the internals of the kernel.

The following operating system adaptations specific to the M31 hardware components were made:

- a privileged software image running on the console sub-system for interrogation and setting of the physical characteristics of the M31 modules connected to its FBI backplane. The console sub-system the M31 is an independent MicroVAX-II system with a custom-built interface between its Q-bus backplane and the M31 Console Control Module.
- an extensive suite of hardware diagnostic exercisers specific to to the M31 modules and components.
- a set of privileged images for system configuration and boot procedures which run cooperatively on the console MicroVAX and on individual M31 processors permit boot-time selection of physical components and the simultaneous booting of multiple copies of VMS on separate sets of processors.
- a driver for the signaling and handling of interprocessor interrupts between M31 processors.
- a driver which runs on the M31 and a gateway driver which runs on another member of the VAXcluster to provide interactive terminal access to the M31 over the CI interconnect based on Digital's established LAT terminal server protocol.

Applications Decomposition and Debug

The applications targeted for experimentation and analysis on the M31 are full production-scale programs which exhibit parallelism with at least a medium grain size of one to several hundred machine instructions. Programs which contain sizable DO-loops with independent iterations or independent tasks of this approximate size are our initial target applications. Initially the dependency analysis on these programs is being done by the applications programmer until we can develop adequate analysis tools and eventually lauguage compiler support for performing this function.

The programs are written or modified to run in the context of separate VMS processes running the same image and all sharing major portions of their address spaces. Both the program code segments and the global shared data segments of the processes are mapped to single copies within the system and only local stack and process control data space are maintained separately for the separate processes. The shareable image and mapped global section services of VMS are available to implement this model of cooperating processes.

The separate processes are implemented to make use of the VAX architecture's interlocked instructions or of VMS operating system services for coordinating their accesses and modifications to data structures within the shared data segments. Figure 11 shows the speedup achieved by two separate applications using these techniques. The parallel implementation of SPICE is a full-scale production code in use internally at Digital [BG86]. The matrix convolution program represents the kernel of an image processing application which convolves a small matrix (a filter) over a larger matrix (an image) [Sha87].

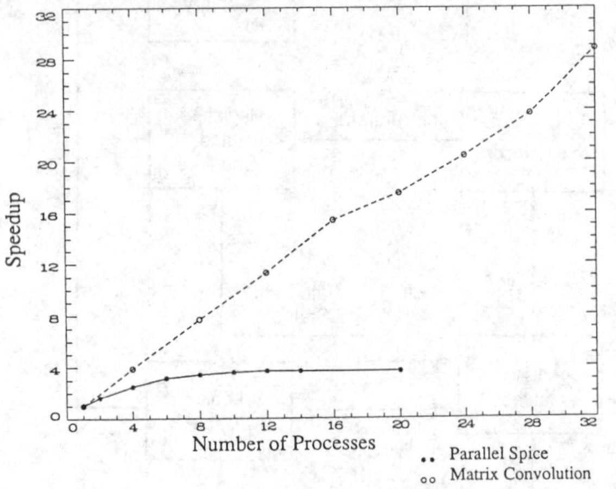

Figure 11: Speedup for two sample applications

Summary

The M31 system is a larger-scale implementation of a bus-based multiprocessor than is commercially available today. This larger scale is feasible as a result of an appropriate balance between the processor, cache, bus and memory components of the system. We have described many of the innovative design features which have been contributed to the implementation of this critical balance. While some applications will exceed the aggregate capacity of one or more of these components an important objective of developing this system is to provide the opportunity to explore as wide a range of parallel processing as possible within such a symmetric architectural design.

Software experience to date has been limited by hardware availability but it clearly demonstrates that the capacities of this system exceed what most production-scale applications can be adapted to utilize. The effective exploitation of a parallel processor of this scale is clearly dependent on the development of powerful analysis and monitoring software tools which are now the major focus of this project.

References

[Bis86] Gabriel Bischoff and Steven Greenberg. "Cayenne: A Parallel Implementation of the Circuit Simulator SPICE." In *Proceedings of the International Conference on Computer Aided Design*, 1986.

[Egg84] Thomas W. Eggers. Unpublished internal memorandum, 1984.

[Goo83] J. R. Goodman. *Using Cache Memory to Reduce Processor-Memory Traffic.* Technical Report, University of Wisconsin, Department of Computer Science, 1983.

[Sha87] John Shakshober. Unpublished internal memorandum, 1987.

A VLSI Family for Multiprocessing Systems

Chair: J.L. Payne

Architecture of The NS32532 - A Single Chip VLSI High Performance CPU

David J. Schanin
Chief Scientist - 32000 Architecture
National Semiconductor
2900 Semiconductor Drive
M.S. D-3768 - P.O. Box 58090
Santa Clara, CA 95052

Abstract

The 32-bit NS32532 is a VLSI component fabricated in 1.25 micron, double metal CMOS, which achieves a scalar performance of 15 MIPS peak, 8-10 MIPS average, and can execute 15 million floating point operations per second. This paper presents the VLSI CPU's four stage instruction execution pipeline, its unique floating point arithmetic support, the architecture of its internal instruction and data caches, and its branch prediction mechanism. The special instructions and cache coherency mechanisms for multiprocessing support will also be described.

Introduction

Designing a high performance, 32-bit Central Processing Unit (CPU) is no longer simply a device design problem. With performance capabilities of 15 Million Instructions Per Second (MIPS) peak, 8-10 MIPS average, a comprehensive system architecture is required so that the overall performance will remain balanced when designing a complete computer system with the NS32532. A CPU's scalar and floating point execution rate, and its memory bandwidth must all be equalized so that no one attribute negatively impacts performance. In addition, perturbations to the instruction and data stream, the worst being pipeline breakage due to branches, must be minimized. Finally, the growing body of knowledge and expertise in the field of multiprocessing cannot be ignored, and the proper system support for multiprocessing must be incorporated into the architecture.

Architecture Overview

The NS32532 is a highly integrated VLSI device containing 370,000 transistors, running at a 30Mhz clock rate. It is the third evolution of the Series 32000 microprocessors, maintaining binary compatibility with its predecessors. The NS32532 integrates several functional units into one component. These include the scalar execution and floating point instruction pipelines, separate instruction and data caches, a Memory Management Unit (MMU), a branch prediction unit, and a highly efficient Bus Interface Unit (BIU). Figure 1 details the internal structure of the NS32532.

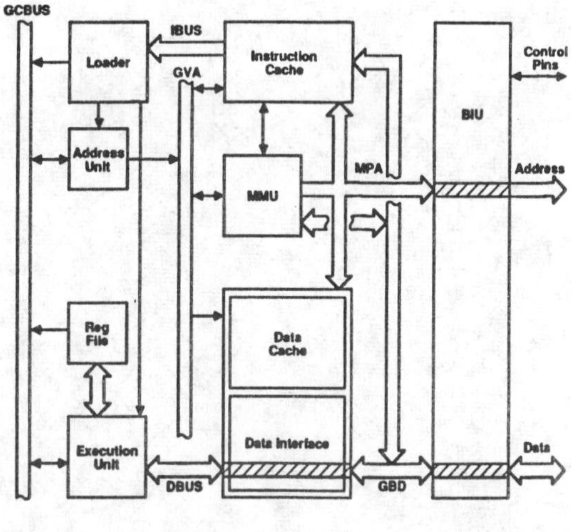

Figure 1 - NS32532 Block Diagram

CH2539-5/88/0000/0208$01.00 © 1988 IEEE

Scalar Pipeline

The heart of the NS32532's performance lies in its instruction execution pipeline. This pipeline is built in four stages, as illustrated in figure 2.

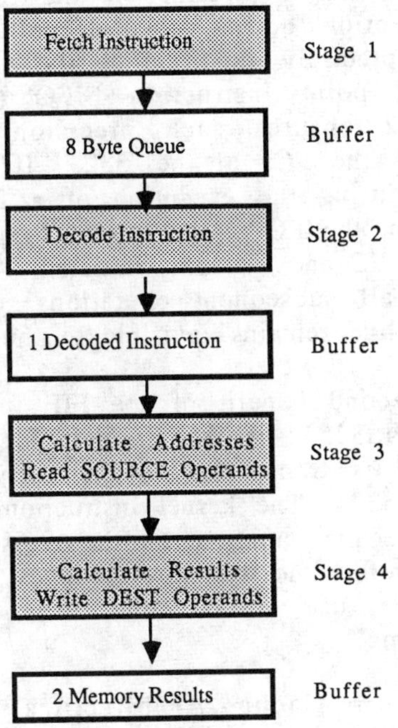

Figure 2 - NS32532 Pipeline

Most of the pipeline's stages are separated by buffers which help smooth the flow of instructions through the pipeline. The first buffer stores bytes of the instruction stream (prefetched by the loader) to ensure continued pipeline operation while instruction cache misses are resolved. The buffer following stage two holds one fully decoded instruction ready for execution. The last buffer in the pipeline holds the data for up to two write operations. These writes to memory are completed when the system bus has available bandwidth.

Several special function units are provided in both the address and data paths to avoid most pipeline bottlenecks, and to enhance the execution of important complex instructions. A shifter in the Address Calculate stage is dedicated to the scaled index addressing mode. In the Execute stage, a barrel shifter and mask generator are used for bit and field operations. The ALU in the pipe implements a modified Booth's algorithm for multiplication operations.

The pipeline in the '532 is interlocked, so that all data dependencies are detected and resolved in hardware. An example of such a dependency occurs when the destination of an instruction is used by a subsequent instruction in an address calculation or as the source operand. Special circuitry detects the most common of these data dependencies, that being when a destination register of one instruction is used as a source register for the next instruction. This circuitry fowards the register information to the Execution stage directly to avoid the delay of performing the register write and then the read. Another example of hardware resolved dependencies involves the buffered memory writes previously described. The address of all data reads is checked against those of the buffered writes, which are still not written through to the caches. If an address match is detected, the execution pipeline stalls until the write has been completed to insure data consistency.

In order to keep the pipeline fully operational, the loader attempts to prefetch instructions into the instruction cache prior to their actually being required by the pipeline. The primary obstacle to achieving this is unexpected changes in the instruction stream due to conditional branch instructions. These instructions can force the pipeline to be flushed and a new instruction stream to be fetched, if the conditional branch is taken. A branch prediction mechanism is supplied in the NS32532 to minimize this pipeline breakage. This prediction mechanism is built into the Instruction Decode stage of the pipeline, and has a dedicated adder to calculate the target address. A prediction is made regarding whether the conditional branch will take based on the direction (forward or backward) and the type of condition being tested, and the loader is told to continue prefetching along the predicted path. The physical address of the branch not predicted is stored in a small local cache. Of course, the condition cannot be resolved until the branch operation reaches the Execute stage of the pipeline. At this time, if the branch was incorrectly predicted, the pipeline is flushed and fetching of the alternate instruction stream begins immediately since the address of the new instruction stream had already been calculated and cached. Measurements show that 71% of the total branches are predicted correctly, significantly reducing pipeline stalls that could be caused by conditional branches.

The pipeline's peak throughput is 2.0 clock cycles per instruction, or 15 MIPS. This performance is achieved for all register to register operations, and for register to memory or memory to register operations where there are data cache hits and the write buffer is not full. In a real system, with cache misses, memory access delays, and a mix of simple and complex instructions, the NS32532 yields an average throughput of 8-10 MIPS with an average instruction execution rate of 3.5 clock cycles per instruction.

Floating Point Instruction Pipeline

In order to balance the floating point performance and the scalar performance of the '532, a pipelined approach to floating point instruction execution was required. The NS32532 supports two external Floating Point Units (FPU):

1. The NS32381, which is a single CMOS chip supporting the Series 32000 architecture registers and basic floating point instruction set.

2. The NS32580, which is a single CMOS device which acts as an interface between the NS32532 and a single CMOS chip from Weitek, Inc., the WTL3164 multiplier and adder. The NS32580 also supports the Series 32000 architecture registers and basic floating point instruction set. In addition, the NS32580 supports Multiply And Accumulate (MAC) and SQuare Root (SQRT) instructions.

The '381's performance is comparable to that of other 32-bit microprocessor vendor's FPU offerings. It's microcoded execution engine is compute bound rather than bus bound, so it would derive little benefit from a pipelined interface. It is provided with a traditional, interlocked interface.

However, the '580 and the WTL 3164 form a very powerful complex capable of performing a floating point operation every two CPU clock cycles in pipelined mode. It is therefore not compute bound, and could benefit from a fully pipelined interface to the '532. However, the problem of supporting both a pipelined and a non-pipelined interface to an FPU goes beyond the simple design problems of a bus interface. When dealing with pipelined floating point operations, in keeping with the IEEE specification on floating point exceptions, one must ensure the precision of exception handling. This requires that the PC be stored for each floating point operation that is pipelined to the '580 so that if an exception occurs, the offending instruction can be precisely identified by the software. The Floating point Instruction FIFO (FIF) in the NS32532 ensures such precision. The FIF pipelines the PCs of the '532. If an exception occurs during the execution of a floating point operation, the PC at the top of the FIF becomes the new PC and a trap is initiated. The NS32580 flushes all subsequent operations, ensuring that the pipeline remains invisible to the software.

A second benefit of the FIF implementation in the NS32532 is that support for the '381 or the '580 is transparent to the software running on the '532. The kernel instructions in the two FPUs are the same, as is the register structure, and therefore no software changes are required for their use unless one uses the special extensions.

Cache Architecture

The scalar and floating point pipelines require a constant stream of instructions and data to operate at maximum performance. The best method to insure adequate bandwidth is to provide large caches on the CPU chip itself. The '532 provides a .5K byte direct mapped instruction cache, and a 1.0K byte two way set associative data cache. These two caches each yield cache hits rates of over 80%, significantly reducing the load on the memory system and improving the performance of the '532. As can be seen in figure 1, both of these caches have separate internal buses which provides for an effective bandwidth of 240 MB/Sec. Figure 3 shows the architecture of the data cache.

Both on-chip caches use physical addresses as their index. This was required for multiprocessing support, which will be described later. However, in order to eliminate any performance penalty that might occur by requiring the virtual address to be translated to a physical address before accessing the cache, this translation is done by the MMU in parallel with the cache access. Both the cache access and the translation are done simultaneously, and then the tag address and the physical address are compared to determine if a hit in the cache has occurred.

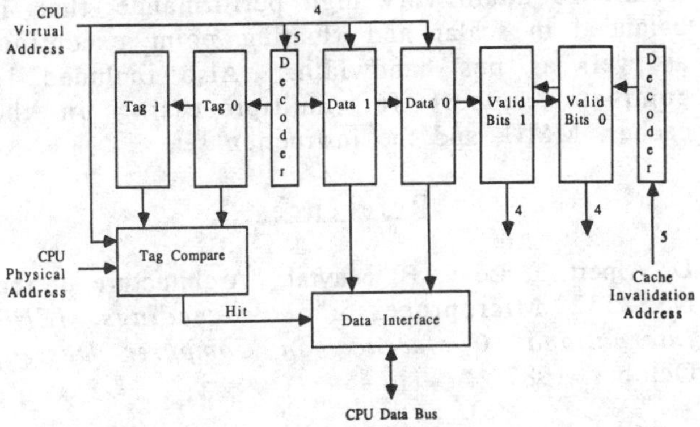

Figure 3 - Data Cache Architecture

MMU Architecture

The NS32532 contains a completely functional on-chip MMU. The MMU supports a 4G byte physical and virtual address space with 4K byte pages, and is fully demand paged. Two level page tables are supported for efficient physical memory usage, as illustrated in figure 4. The MMU has a 64 entry, fully associative TransLation Buffer (TLB), which yields a hit ratio of over 99%. MMU misses are handled by hardware which is independent of the execution unit, and therefore TLB operations do not perturb the pipeline. As previously described, MMU translations are overlapped with cache accesses, so no performance penalty is incurred for MMU translations when the entry is in the TLB. Multiprocessing support is integrated into the MMU, and this will be discussed below.

Multiprocessing Support - Interlocks

Supporting a multiprocessing environment requires careful design on a systems level, as well as support from the CPU. One such support mechanism is a means for interlocking operations to memory for semaphore support. This is accomplished in the NS32532 using the bit set, interlocked and bit clear, interlocked instructions. When these instructions are executed in the NS32532, an external signal, InterLOcked (ILO), is asserted during the data read and write operations. This signal allows the memory and bus system to be interlocked during these operations to avoid semaphore corruption.

Multiprocessing Support - Caches

A second multiprocessing support mechanism built into the '532 is the internal caches. These caches use only physical addresses as their index. This feature is required to prevent aliasing, where more than one virtual address can be mapped into one physical address, requiring multiple cache invalidations on a single system write to the physical location. Detecting address aliasing would require a fully associate cache tag store, which is prohibitive in cost.

Cache coherency is a feature that is highly desirable in any system supporting DMA, and is a requirement in a multiprocessor system. Cache coherency ensures that stale data will not be left behind in a cache when the main memory copy of that location is modified by another system member. Cache coherency could be maintained using software invalidations in a low performance, single CPU system. However, performance will suffer because of the software overhead involved in such invalidations. In a multiprocessing system, the software overhead becomes overwhelming, as interprocessor message communication would be required for each such invalidation. Finally, software based on providing such support will be tied directly to one particular hardware implementation. Such a binding is in conflict with today's thrust towards open systems. Therefore, hardware cache coherency is required, where the address of any location that is modified in the system is passed to the CPU chip for matching and possible invalidation.

Hardware cache coherency allows cache invalidations to occur as needed, without software knowledge or support. However, the problem in supporting hardware based cache coherency is to do so without degrading the performance of the system by contending for either the CPU's tag store or the CPU's bus. The NS32532 solves the former problem by using alternate phases of the internal clock to perform CPU tag store lookups and bus tag invalidations. The latter problem is solved by using a separate bus to supply the CPU with invalidation addresses.

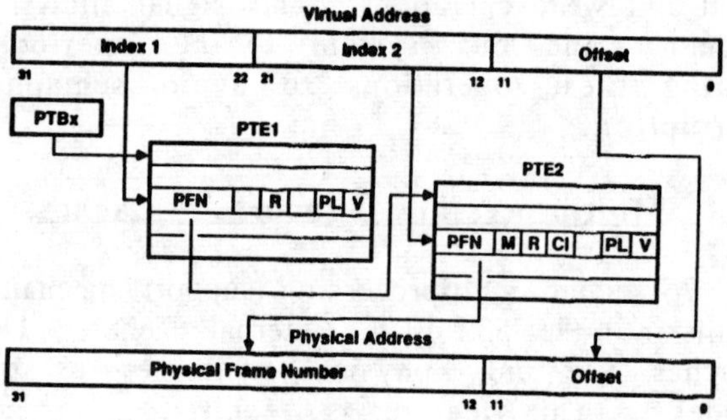

Figure 4 - Page Table Structure

Finally, the most efficient invalidation methodology supports invalidating only those locations in the CPU's cache that are at the exact physical address as the location being modified in the system. This support is typically integrated into an external cache's bus snooper. To do so, the user must duplicate the CPU's tag store external to the CPU chip so that the system bus can be snooped. To support such an external tag store, the NS32532 must provide the user with real time information regarding line placement within its associative cache. This is done through dedicated signals on the '532 so that the external tag store can exactly mirror the internal tag store.

Multiprocessing Support - MMU

The NS32532's MMU has several mechanisms to provide support for multiprocessing. When performing page table modifications, such as to mark pages as dirty or accessed, all such operations are done under interlock so that multiple CPUs sharing a common page table entry will not corrupt the bits being set and/or cleared. In addition, the MMU supports the marking of pages as non-cacheable, to support, for example, dual port memory architectures. This information is passed to the external interface of the '532 to provide for maintaining external caches coherent with the internal CPU cache.

Conclusions

The NS32532 32-bit microprocessor exploits VLSI technology and superminicomputer architecture to attain very high performance that is balanced in scalar and floating point execution, as well as bus bandwidth. Also included is complete support for multiprocessing in the caches, MMU, and the instruction set.

References

D. Alpert, J. Levy, B. Maytal, "Architecture of the NS32532 Microprocessor", *Proceedings IEEE International Conference on Computer Design,* October 1987

M. Baron and S. Iacobovici, "Supermini on a chip Juggles Several Jobs", *Electronic Products,* June 1, 1987, p. 57-60

M. Baron and S. Iacobovici, "32-bit CMOS CPU Chip Acts Like a Mainframe", *Electronic Design,* April 16, 1987, p. 95-100

C. Hunter, *Series 32000 Programmer's Reference Manual,* Prentice Hall Inc., 1987

D. Schanin, "Microprocessor Cache Coherency", *VLSI Systems Design,* August 1987, p. 40-42

D. Schanin, "Cache Coherency in Microprocessor Based Systems", *Electronics Engineering,* October 1987, p. 57-63.

U. Weiser, et. al., "Design of the NS32532 32-Bit Microprocessor", in *Proceedings IEEE International Conference on Computer Design,* October 1987

Architecture of the NS32580 Floating-Point Controller

S. Ben-Chorin
National Semiconductor Corporation
2900 Semiconductor Drive Santa Clara CA 95051

ABSTRACT

The NS32580 Floating-Point Controller and it's companion device, Weitek's WTL 3164 Floating-Point Data Path, are a high-performance floating-point solution for high end NS32532 based systems. The NS32580-WTL3164 with the NS32532 CPU executes single- and double- precision ADD, SUB, MUL, MACf with a peak throughput of 15 MFlops keeping precise exception handling. Using an improved slave protocol, the NS32580 interfaces between the NS32532 microprocessor and the WTL 3164 floating-point data path to form a software upwardly compatible floating-point unit in National Semiconductor Corporation's Series 32000 family.

INTRODUCTION

The NS32580 is a VLSI floating-point controller (FPC) that interfaces between the NS32532 CPU and WTL 3164 floating-point data path (FPDP). The FPC adapts the pipelining technique to achieve sustained peak performance of 15 MFlops. The FPC-FPDP supports IEEE standard 754-1985 for Binary Floating-Point Arithmetic. The FPC is fabricated in 1.25 micron double-metal CMOS technology and operates at a frequency of 30 Mhz. The FPC translates the instructions received from the CPU, to FPDP operations (or sequences of operations in some of the instructions). FPC supports on chip all the Series 32000 floating-point instructions that are not supported by the FPDP and keeps the upward software compatibility with existing Series 32000 family floating-point units.

Fig 1 shows the internal architecture of the NS32580. The FPC has a three stage pipeline. The first instruction is latched in the Instruction FIFO and the operand for that instruction is latched in the Data FIFO. The second instruction is waiting for execution at the output of the instruction decoder (and the inputs of the interlock detection mechanism). The third instruction is being executed at the state machine, register mapping and FPDP control word generation block. as can be seen from the block diagram the interface with the CPU and the interface with the FPDP are totally isolated. The following section demonstrates the execution of one isolated instruction in the FPC.

An instruction from the CPU is detected by the CPU Interface State machine, that controls the Instruction and Data FIFOs, to latch the instruction and operands from the CPU data bus. The operands (if any) are then transferred to the data FIFO in the FPDP by the Operand Transfer Controller. Simultaneously the instruction is decoded by the

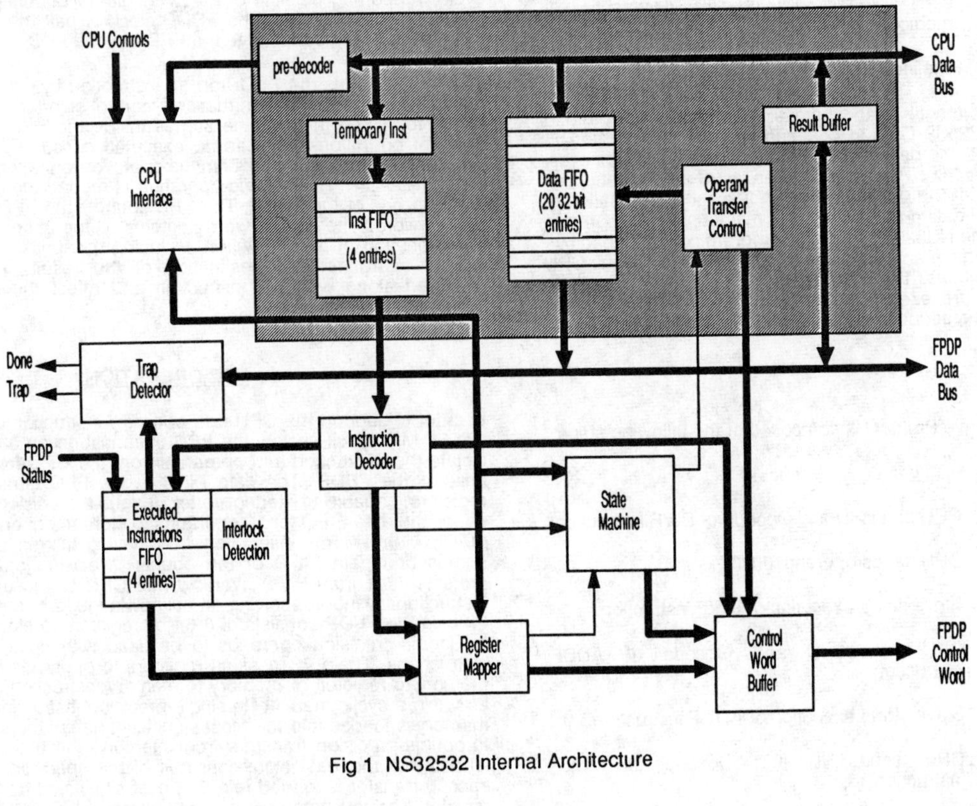

Fig 1 NS32532 Internal Architecture

CH2539-5/88/0000/0213$01.00 © 1988 IEEE

Instruction Decoder. When the operands are ready in the FPDP and no interlocks are detected by the Interlock Detector the State Machine will start the execution of the instruction. Simultaneously the Register Mapper issues the source and destination registers addresses, using information from the Instruction Decoder. The control Word Buffer collects information from the other blocks and generates a control word for the execution of the instruction in the FPDP. FPDP status is read into the Executed Instruction FIFO at the end of each instruction (the Instruction Decoder issues a count number for each instruction). There is a counter for each executed instruction to sample the status at the right time. The status is then transferred to the Trap Detector that generates the acknowledgment signals to the CPU.

NS32532 INTERFACE

The NS32580 uses the Series 32000 32-bit slave protocol supported by the NS32532 microprocessor. This 32-bit protocol supports the delivery of an instruction or operands every two clock cycles at 30 Mhz. The slave protocol is a well defined protocol for instruction and operand transfers between the CPU and the slave coprocessors (FPC, and Custom Slave). Only the CPU can initiate a slave cycle or access the memory to fetch operands. The communication between the CPU and the FPC occurs at the beginning of the floating-point instruction, when the CPU transfers the Opcode and possible operands. At the end of the instruction, the FPC signals successful or unsuccessful conclusion of the floating-point instruction and the CPU transfers operands from the FPC, if applicable. The CPU broadcasts the ID and Opcode to all slave processors, one of which will recognize it and from this point the CPU is communicating only with one slave processor.

SLAVE PROTOCOL

The 32-bit Slave Protocol is composed of the following steps:

STEP	STATUS	ACTION
1	ID (h'1F)	CPU sends ID and Operation Word.
2	OP (h'1D)	CPU sends required operands (if any).
3	--	Slave starts execution (CPU prefetches).
4	--	Slave pulses DONE or TRAP.
5	ST (h'1E)	CPU Reads Status Word (If TRAP was signaled).
6	OP (h'1D)	CPU Reads Result (if destination is memory).

Pipelined Slave Protocol

The pipelined slave protocol is an improved communication protocol supported by the NS32532 CPU to communicate with the FPC. This 32-bit protocol supports the delivery of an instruction or operands every two clock cycles at 30 Mhz . The NS32532 can issue a new instruction before the completion of the previous instructions, if the destination of the instruction is a floating-point register, maintaining the precise exception handling. The NS32532 holds the program count of up to five floating-point instructions in an instruction FIFO (FIF), allowing the CPU to back up five instructions. The FPC receives up to five instructions with operands, which are executed simultaneously. For example the CPU sends the following sequence of instructions to the FPC:

```
DIVF  0(R0), F1
ADDF  F2, F3
MULF  F4, F5
```

The Pipelined 32-bit Slave Protocol is composed of the following steps:

STEP	STATUS	ACTION
1	ID (h'1F)	CPU sends ID and Opcode of DIVF instruction.
2	OP (h'1D)	CPU sends operand 0(R0).
3	--	Slave starts execution of DIVF instruction.
4	ID (h'1F)	CPU sends ID and Opcode of ADDF instruction.
5	--	Slave starts execution of ADDF instruction.
6	ID (h'1F)	CPU sends ID and Opcode of MULF instruction.
7	--	Slave starts execution of MULF instruction.
8	--	Slave pulses DONE or TRAP for the DIVF instruction.

If TRAP occurred, the rest of the instructions will be aborted.

9	ST (h'1E)	CPU Reads Status Word (If TRAP was signaled).
10	--	Slave pulses DONE or TRAP for the ADDF instruction.

If TRAP occurred, the rest of the instructions will be aborted.

11	ST (h'1E)	CPU Reads Status Word (If TRAP was signaled).
12	--	Slave pulses DONE or TRAP for the MULF instruction.
13	ST (h'1E)	CPU Reads Status Word (If TRAP was signaled).

The three instructions and operands in the example are sent to the FPC before completing the execution of the first instruction (DIVF). The ADDs and MULs are executed concurrently with the DIVF instruction. If result exception occurred in the DIVF instruction, the CPU gets an indication from the FPC for the unsuccessful completion of the DIVF instruction. The CPU will back up it's program counter to the DIVF PC and exit the program to the exception handling routine. As a result of the exception, the FPC flushes it's instruction queue and changes the registers to the original data stored before the execution of the instruction. Although highly pipelined, the FPC does not destroy valid data in registers, if an instruction ended with exception. The FPC receives a new single- or double-precision instruction every two clock cycles at 30 Mhz and delivers the result to the floating-point registers at the same rate.

WTL 3164 INTERFACE

The FPC uses Weitek's WTL 3164 Floating-Point Data Path (FPDP) as the computational unit. The FPDP is capable of supporting 32-bit and 64-bit IEEE floating-point operations. The FPDP consists of a Multiplier, ALU, Divide/Sqrt unit, 32 X 64-bit, Six-Port Register file, I/O port, and control unit. There are six major internal 64-bit wide data buses, used for data transfers between the different blocks inside the FPDP. Using six data buses allows an input of two double-precision operands to a selected unit and to output one double-precision result in one 15 Mhz cycle, supporting pipeline of a new single- or double-precision instruction every clock cycle. (The FPDP clock is half the frequency of the system clock and supplied to the FPDP by the FPC.)

The FPC controls the FPDP on an instruction by instruction basis and not clock by clock. The instruction's control signals are delayed in the FPDP to match the pipeline stages inside the FPDP. There are two types of operations that can be executed concurrently on the FPDP. The first is floating-point arithmetic operation done with operands from the register file. The second operation is a Load/Store operation using the data bus of the FPDP. The FPC controls the FPDP, using a 33-bit control word. The control word contains all the information needed for the execution of an instruction, including the function to be executed, source operands and destination of the result. The controls are pipelined along with the instruction and affect the operation at the appropriate times.

FPC OPERATION

In order to support the CPU rate of a new instruction or operand every two 30 Mhz clock cycles, the FPC uses instruction and data FIFOs to isolate the instruction and operands from the CPU from the execution units in the FPDP. The data FIFO in the FPC consists of 20 32-bit registers, capable of storing up to 10 double-precision operands. FPC needs the data FIFO for 10 operands to store the operands of up to five MACL Mem, Mem instructions. By having Instructions FIFO of five entries and data FIFO of ten double- precision operands the FPC protects itself from FIFO overflow (the CPU can issue up to five new instructions without receiving an acknowledge from the FPC). The data FIFO in the FPDP consists of 8 64-bit registers to store up to 8 single- or double-precision operands to be used with up to four concurrent instructions. The FPC assigns registers to operands from memory (in memory to register, or memory to memory instructions) by the order of arrival in a cyclic manner. In single-precision instructions the data from memory is loaded into the most significant half of the specified register. In double-precision transfers from memory, the first 32-bit transfer is loaded into the least significant half of the specified register and the second transfer is loaded into the most significant half of the specified register. The registers used as the operand FIFO can not be accessed by the user program and the assignment of registers is transparent to the program. An independent operand transfer machine is responsible to transfer operands from the FPC data FIFO to the FPDP data FIFO. By using this mechanism, all the instructions (including instructions with operands in memory) can be treated as register to register instructions inside the FPDP. Another independent machine is responsible for issuing a new instruction to the FPDP, when all the operands are in the FPDP register file. This machine considers all the possible interlock situations.

INTERLOCK DETECTION

There are three groups of interlocks: Operand interlocks, execution unit interlocks (div/sqrt unit interlock) and Instruction interlocks. The operand interlock can be source interlock, when the result of instruction is being used by the next instruction (or by the second next instruction). For example:

```
ADDL  l1, l2
MULL  l2, l3
```

Operand interlock can also occur when the destination of the first instruction is the same as the destination of the second instruction. The second instruction will destroy (overwrite) the original data of the first instruction. If an exception occurred in the first instruction the data can not be recovered. The second instruction will only be sent when the first instruction ends without exception (for more details refer to Register File Control). For example:

```
MULF  f0, f1
NEGF  f2, f1
```

Execution unit interlock occurs when two or more DIVf/SQRTf instructions are sent to the FPC. The FPDP div/sqrt unit can execute one instruction at the time and the execution takes multiple clock cycles. For example:

```
DIVL   l0, l1
SQRTL  l2, l3
```

Instruction interlock occurs when executing SFSR instruction (store status register) LFSR (load status register) and instructions that change rounding mode inside the FPDP (ROUND, FLOOR, TRUNC). Those instructions are interlocked because they are affected or can affect another instructions executed concurrently in the pipe.

New instructions are not sent to the FPDP when it can not start execution in the next clock cycle, allowing the load/store machine to prepare operands for the next instruction. If interlock condition is detected by the FPDP all the operations including load/store are halted for the duration of the interlock. By preventing the interlocks in the FPDP, the FPC can utilize the FPDP more efficiently. Four different instructions can be executed simultaneously in the FPDP, each can take a different number of clock cycles. Status from FPDP is sent to the FPC after completion of an instruction. If the FPDP status is out of order, relative to the sequence of the instructions in the executed program, the FPC still keeps the order of the acknowledgements to the CPU for successful execution or exception of the instructions. To synchronize between the status from FPDP and the acknowledgement to the CPU, the FPC has a four entry FIFO for status latching. This FIFO is also used by the interlock prevention unit. Each entry in the FIFO contains information about the instruction, and a counter to signal when an instruction is finished (to latch FPDP status and to issue the new instruction). The latched status is transferred to the Trap detection unit in the right order for evaluation. The Trap detection unit compares the FPDP status with the enabled exceptions and generates "Done" or "Trap" signals and updates the corresponding flags in the FPC status register (the FSR register).

REGISTER FILE CONTROL

Two problems were found when using the WTL 3164. The first problem was the incompatibility of the FPDP register file and Series 32000 architecture. The FPDP has 32 registers in the register file, each register is 64 bits wide. The same register is used for single- or double operands. When using the register as a single-precision register, only the upper 32 bits of the register are used.

```
63 62        52 51                                        0
+-+-----------+-------------------------------------------+
|S|   EXP     |                 FRACTION                  |
+-+-----------+-------------------------------------------+
```

Figure 2 Double-Precision Register in FPDP

```
63 62    55 54                32 31                        0
+-+--------+-------------------+---------------------------+
|S|  EXP   |     FRACTION      |0 0 0 .................0 0 0|
+-+--------+-------------------+---------------------------+
```

Figure 3 Single-Precision Register in FPDP

In the Series 32000 architecture, double-precision operands are stored in two consecutive registers. The even register holds the least significant half of the floating-point operand and the odd register contains the most significant half. The user can use the MOVL instruction to move two single-precision operands in one floating-point instruction and then use the two halves of the double-precision operand as two single-precision operands.

```
 31                       0  31                         0
+-------------------------+ +--------------------------+
|        F1/L0 MS         | |        F0/L0 LS          |
+-------------------------+ +--------------------------+
```

Figure 4 Data Registers in Series 32000

```
63                       32 31                        0
+-+------+----------------+-+------+------------------+
|S| EXP  |   FRACTION     |S| EXP  |    FRACTION      |
+-+------+----------------+-+------+------------------+
```

Figure 5 Two Single-Precision Operands as one Double-Precision Operand

In this case, there was incompatibility between the register file of the FPDP and the registers in the Series 32000 architecture. Compatibility was achieved by assigning separate registers in the register file to the even single-precision registers F0, F2, F4, F6. These registers can be loaded as a half-double-precision operand and used as a single-precision operand. An automatic register copy is only done for MOVL from memory into L0, L2 L4 or L6 registers. The LS half of the double-precision operand is copied into F0, F2, F4 or F6 accordingly. Special mechanism is responsible for detecting any mismatch in the register file and to update the proper register with the correct data.

The second incompatibility related to the exception handling. The FPDP updated a register and detected a result exception at the same time. Therefore, if a result exception occurred, the destination register destroyed by the FPDP. In the Series 32000 architecture, an instruction that ended with exception (and trap is enabled) does not update the destination address. The FPDP can not avoid destruction of the destination register and special handling is needed. The solution to the problem is a set of shadow registers similar to the main register set. The use of shadow registers is transparent to the user and to the algorithms of the different instructions. The control of the shadow registers is done by hardware mechanism. As can be seen by the following example, when result exception is being detected, an abort signal is asserted. The abort cancels the current and the previous instructions (the current instruction is N3 and the previous instruction is N2) therefore N0 that caused the exception and N1 the next instruction after N0 will finish execution and update the destination register.

```
FPDP    +----+    +----+    +----+    +---+   +----+
Clock   | 0  |    | 1  |    | 2  |    | 3 |   | 4  |
     ---+    +----+    +----+    +----+   +---+    +-+

Inst. +---+    +---+    +---+    +---+
Code  |N0 |    |N1 |    |N2 |    |N3 |
      +---+    +---+    +---+    +---+

Execution
Pipe        +---+    +---+    +---+    +---+
Stage 1/2   |N0 |    |N1 |    |N2 |    |N3 |
            +---+    +---+    +---+    +---+
                +---------++---------++---------++------
Stage 1         |   N0    ||   N1    ||   N2    ||   N3
                +---------++---------++---------++--------
                          +---+    +---+    +---+    +---+
Stage 1/2                 |N0 |    |N1 |    |N2 |    |N3 |
                          +---+    +---+    +---+    +---+
                               +---+    +---+
Write to Register              |N0 |    |N1 |
                               +---+    +---+
                                 +---+
Abort                            |   |
                                 +---+
```

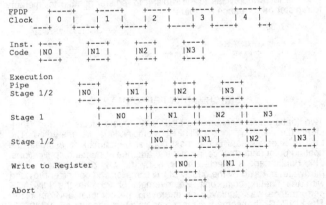

Figure 6 Result Exception in FPDP

The FPDP has a three address architecture, therefore, for each instruction as many as two source addresses and one destination address can be specified. When executing floating-point instruction, the destination of the result will be the shadow register instead of the source register. The only difference between a register and it's shadow is the most significant bit of the address. For example, if R2 (00010) is the source register, the shadow register is R18 (10010) and if R16 (10000) is the source register, R0 (00000) will be the shadow. Instruction ADDL L0, L2 for example, will be translated to ADDL Reg 0, Reg 2 --> Reg 18. The FPDP executes the instruction and at the end of the execution Reg 18 holds the new result. (Reg 0 and Reg 2 holds the source operands). If no exception occurred, the next time that instruction will try to use L2 instead of using Reg 2, the FPC will assign Reg 18, which becomes the source register. If exception occurred in the instruction ADDL L0, L2, the register Reg 2 will still hold the source operand. The shadow bit of Reg 18 will be toggled again and Reg 2 will become L2, as if the instruction were not executed.

```
        63          32 31          0              63          32 31          0
        +-----------+-----------+                 +-----------+-----------+
Reg  0  | F1/L0 MS  | L0 LS (F0)|        Reg 16   | F1/L0 MS  | L0 LS (F0)|
        +-----------+-----------+                 +-----------+-----------+
Reg  1  |  L1 MS    |   L1 LS   |        Reg 17   |  L1 MS    |   L1 LS   |
        +-----------+-----------+                 +-----------+-----------+
Reg  2  | F3/L2 MS  | L2 LS (F2)|        Reg 18   | F3/L2 MS  | L2 LS (F2)|
        +-----------+-----------+                 +-----------+-----------+
Reg  3  |  L3 MS    |   L3 LS   |        Reg 19   |  L3 MS    |   L3 LS   |
        +-----------+-----------+                 +-----------+-----------+
Reg  4  | F5/L4 MS  | L4 LS (F4)|        Reg 20   | F5/L4 MS  | L4 LS (F4)|
        +-----------+-----------+                 +-----------+-----------+
Reg  5  |  L5 MS    |   L5 LS   |        Reg 21   |  L5 MS    |   L5 LS   |
        +-----------+-----------+                 +-----------+-----------+
Reg  6  | F7/L6 MS  | L6 LS (F6)|        Reg 22   | F7/L6 MS  | L6 LS (F6)|
        +-----------+-----------+                 +-----------+-----------+
Reg  7  |  L7 MS    |   L7 LS   |        Reg 23   |  L7 MS    |   L7 LS   |
        +-----------+-----------+                 +-----------+-----------+
Reg  8  |    F0     | X X....X X|        Reg 24   |    F0     | X X....X X|
        +-----------+-----------+                 +-----------+-----------+
Reg  9  |FIFO 0 MS  | FIFO 0 LS |        Reg 25   |FIFO 4 MS  | FIFO 4 LS |
        +-----------+-----------+                 +-----------+-----------+
Reg 10  |    F2     | X X....X X|        Reg 26   |    F2     | X X....X X|
        +-----------+-----------+                 +-----------+-----------+
Reg 11  |FIFO 1 MS  | FIFO 1 LS |        Reg 27   |FIFO 5 MS  | FIFO 5 LS |
        +-----------+-----------+                 +-----------+-----------+
Reg 12  |    F4     | X X....X X|        Reg 28   |    F4     | X X....X X|
        +-----------+-----------+                 +-----------+-----------+
Reg 13  |FIFO 2 MS  | FIFO 2 LS |        Reg 29   |FIFO 6 MS  | FIFO 6 LS |
        +-----------+-----------+                 +-----------+-----------+
Reg 14  |    F6     | X X....X X|        Reg 30   |    F6     | X X....X X|
        +-----------+-----------+                 +-----------+-----------+
Reg 15  |FIFO 3 MS  | FIFO 3 LS |        Reg 31   |FIFO 7 MS  | FIFO 7 LS |
        +-----------+-----------+                 +-----------+-----------+
```

Figure 7 Register Organization in the FPDP

NS32580 RAW PERFORMANCE

The execution time is given for register to register instructions. Time is given in clock cycles and includes the CPU protocol.

Inst.	Latency reg, reg	Throughput reg, reg
ADDf/l	13	2
SUBf/l	13	2
MULf/l	13	2
MOVf/l	13	2
MACf/l	15	6
DIVf	29	Up to 29
DIVl	43	Up to 43
SQRTf	41	Up to 41
SQRTl	69	Up to 69

Add the following cycles to the register to register number for memory to register performance numbers:

Inst.		Latency	Throughput
Monadic/Diadic Single-Precision	mem, reg	0	2
Monadic/Diadic Double-Precision	mem, reg	2	4

BENCHMARKS PERFORMANCE

Two floating-point benchmarks LINPACK (double-precision) and Whetstone (DP) with various CPU-FPU combinations were studied. The LINPACK benchmark is the most popular benchmark to estimate the floating-point performance in scientific and heavy numeric applications. This benchmark is affected not only by the raw performance of the hardware, but also by the quality of the compiler and optimizer provided with the floating-point unit. Improvement of 25% in the LINPACK performance was achieved by improving the compiler and optimizer. The LINPACK benchmark is presented as a test case for the NS32532-NS32580-WTL3164 combination. Through profiling of the LINPACK we found that 90% of the time is spent in one routine (the LINPACK-core) that has the following structure:

```
DO  20  I=1 , N
        A[I] = A[I] + B * C[I]
    20  CONTINUE
```

One iteration of this loop is considered as 2 flops.

Using the CTP-f77 compiler the LINPACK-core was translated to the following code:

```
L:
        movl    0(r3), l0
        mull    l1, l0
        addl    l0, 0(r2)

        addqd   $(1), r1
        addd    $(8), r3
        addd    $(8), r2
        cmpd    r1, 1640(sp)
        ble     L
```

The estimated number of clock cycles:

Floating-point operations:	41 cycles
Loop control (integer overhead)	12 cycles
Data cache misses (50% DC misses)	5 cycles

Total:	58 cycles

Scaling to 30 Mhz: 2 * 30 / 58 = 1.04 Mflops/sec

Using a new compiler that does unrolling of 4 and code reordering the following code was generated:

```
L:
# Fetch all memory operands to registers
        movl    0(r2), l0
        movl    8(r2), l2
        movl    16(r2), l3
        movl    24(r2), l4

        mull    l1, l0
        mull    l1, l2
        mull    l1, l3
        mull    l1, l4

        addl    0(r3), l0
        addl    8(r3), l2
        addl    16(r3), l3
        addl    24(r3), l4

# Delay all stores to memory to the end of the loop.

        movl    l0, 0(r3)
        movl    l2, 8(r3)
        movl    l3, 16(r3)
        movl    l4, 24(r3)

        addqd   $(4), r1
        addd    $(32), r2
        addd    $(32), r3
        cmpd    r1, 1640(sp)
        ble     L
```

The estimated number of clock cycles (4 loops):

Floating-point operations:	144 cycles
Loop control (integer overhead)	12 cycles
Data cache misses (50% DC misses)	20 cycles

Total:	176 cycles
Average cycles/loop:	44 cycles

Scaling to 30 Mhz: 2 * 30 / 44 = 1.35 Mflops/sec (Total improvement of 30%)

SELECTED PERFORMANCE COMPARISON

System	LINPACK DP (Mflops/sec)	Whetstone DP (Mwhet/sec)
Intel 80386+80387 @20Mhz	0.2	1.73
Intel 80386+1167(Weitek) @20Mhz	0.38	2.59
Sun-3/260 68020 @25Mhz + 68881 @20Mhz	0.11	1.23
Sun-3/260 Weitek FPA @16.6Mhz	0.46	2.6
Mips M/500 @8 Mhz	0.58	4.45
Mips M/800 @12.5 Mhz	0.8	6.9
National 32532+32381 @30Mhz	0.4	2.3
National 32532+32580 @30Mhz + 3164 @15Mhz	1.35	8.0

The performance numbers were taken from [Mips 87]

CONCLUSION

The NS32580 floating-point controller provides an efficient interface between the NS32532 CPU and the WTL3164 floating-point data path. With sustained peak performance of 15 Mflops, the FPC-FPDP pair are a powerful solution for scientific and number crunching applications. The FPC-FPDP are heavily pipelined for maximum performance, yet the FPC is upwardly compatible with existing Series 32000 family software and supports precise exception handling.

REFERENCES

[Mips 87] Performance Brief, Mips M/800 and M/500 Systems, Issue 2.2 April 2,1987 P 11,13

D. Alpert, J. Levy, B. Maytal "Architecture of the NS32532 Microprocessor" 1987 IEEE International Conference on Computer Design VLSI in Computers & Processors P 168-172

D. Hough "Floating-Point Programmers Guide for the Sun Workstation", Sun Microsystems, September 1986.

THE NS32605 CACHE CONTROLLER

Lisa K. Quinones
National Semiconductor Corporation
2900 Semiconductor Drive
Santa Clara, California 95052

Abstract

The NS32605 Cache Controller, currently under development, integrates the tag store, control logic, and data buffering into a single VLSI component. Supporting up to 256K bytes of external cache memory, as well as a variety of caching protocols and configurations, the NS32605 continues the thrust towards low cost multiprocessing.

Introduction

Increased densities of VLSI components have made multiprocessing systems with between two and four processors per board possible. These systems typically share main memory by connecting processors to a common system bus. This makes bus throughput critical to increased system performance. In order to minimize bus traffic, cache memory is often placed between the processor and the shared bus. Until recently, cache memories were often designed with discrete logic. In designing a standard cache controller for a multiprocessing environment, performance translates into a high hit ratio on the cache with zero wait states for cache hits and minimal delay for cache misses. In addition, there must be little or no delay on processor writes. Optimization of the processor port includes integration of those functions necessary to keep the internal processor caches enabled as well as those to minimize glue logic between the processor and cache controller. Finally, the processor clock should be decoupled from the system, allowing the maximum CPU clock speed to be used regardless of the system speed. On the system side of the cache controller, the goal is to minimize the frequency and duration of bus accesses. This requires support for the most efficient cache coherence protocols and high speed data block transfers. The system port must be optimized for interfacing to industry-standard buses, while allowing enough flexibility for the cache controller to be integrated into both synchronous and asynchronous environments.

The NS32605 cache controller, currently in development, continues the trend towards higher integration while allowing enough flexibility to tune the

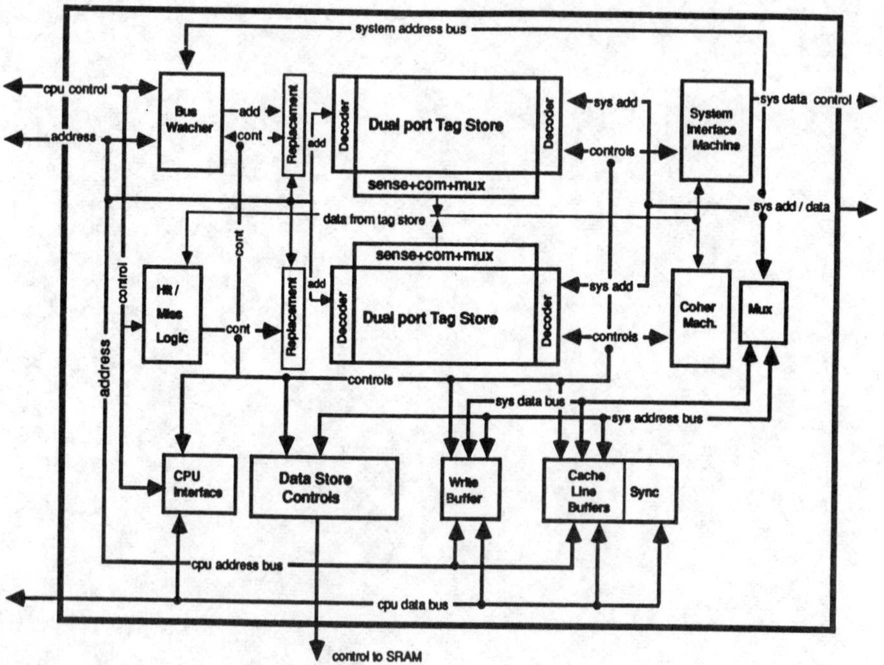

Figure 1. Block Diagram of NS32605

CH2539-5/88/0000/0218$01.00

device for any particular class of applications. This paper will discuss each of the design considerations mentioned above and will describe the structures which were integrated as a result.

General Features

The NS32605 cache controller can be configured to support up to 256K bytes of external cache memory with parity. Its design is optimized for operating with the NS32532 and Futurebus, while allowing users the flexibility to support multiple coherence protocols. Programmable features include the cache size, cache line size, and set associativity. A novel circuit technique enables optimal matching to various static RAM cycle times. Advanced packaging has also allowed the data path to be integrated on-chip. This enables the designers to incorporate coherent data buffers on-board. The major functional blocks of the cache controller are shown in Figure 1.

Maximizing Cache Performance

Maximizing Hit Ratio

Many studies have focused on quantifying cache hit ratios for various applications.[1] While simulations have been limited to small caches under 32K bytes, these studies suggest that the single most important factor for improving the cache hit ratio is the size of the cache memory. By varying the line size between 16 bytes and 64 bytes, the cache memory can be configured from 32K bytes to 256K bytes, allowing a variety of cost/performance goals to be achieved. In addition, the cache may be constructed as either direct-mapped or two-way set associative to allow optimal performance of programs exhibiting differing degrees of locality.

To achieve zero wait state access on cache hits, a 2K tag directory has been included on-chip as well as all control signals for external static RAMs. Implemented as a dual-port RAM, the tag directory provides the minimum address latency for access by both the processor and system ports. This tag directory supports either a sectored or non-sectored cache to allow for maximum cache size. While a non-sectored cache associates a single line with each tag, the sectored cache associates two lines with each tag, maintaining state information for each line independently. The flexibility that these various configurations allows is exhibited in Table 1.

Tag Entries	2K Direct-mapped OR 2-Way Set Associative					
Sectoring	Sectored			Non-Sectored		
Cache Size	64KB	128KB	256KB	32KB	64KB	128KB
Line Size	16B	32B	64B	16B	32B	64B

Table 1. Cache Configurations

Minimizing Miss Penalty

Although cache performance is often equated with hit ratio, the cost of a cache miss (the miss penalty) cannot be ignored, particularly in a copy-back cache. In such a design, the miss penalty varies, and it may be twice that of a write-through cache. When a cache miss occurs, if the line selected for replacement is a line which has been modified, it will have to be flushed to main memory before the new line can enter the cache.

To reduce this miss penalty, the write cache line buffer of the NS32605 is used to store the modified line being evicted from the cache, allowing the read to occur as soon as the bus is acquired. The modified line is transferred from the cache memory to the write cache line buffer concurrently with the arbitration for the system bus. When the cache controller receives mastership of the bus, the bus cycle is used to read the data requested by the processor. The bus cycle following the data read may then be used to perform the flush, or the evicted line may reside in the write cache line buffer if the bus is being requested by another module. This reduction of the miss penalty by allowing the data read to preceed the write of the evicted line is shown in Figure 2.

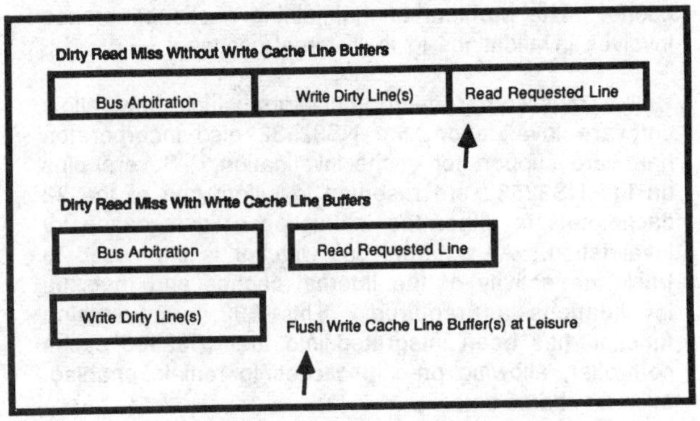

Figure 2. Benefits of the Write Cache Line Buffers

If the cache is configured as a sectored cache, the replacement may require the eviction of up to two lines of modified data. For this reason, there are two separate write cache line buffers within the cache controller. Each cache line buffer is composed of 64 bytes of data to allow for the maximum line size, in addition to the address, parity, and status bits. The data portion acts as a FIFO, accessible from both sides simultaneously. If the write cache line buffers are still occupied from the previous flush, simultaneous access allows the previous data to be flushed from the buffer as the newer evicted data is being transferred from the cache memory. Since a dirty line(s) may reside in the write cache line buffer, the address and status portions must be available for snooping on both the system and processor sides.

Minimizing Write Delay

In a write-through cache without buffering, the processor might have to wait for the write to complete, since the system bus may not be immediately available. To minimize this possibility, a write buffer has been included in the NS32605 cache controller. The write buffer consists of four double-words of data, with address, status, and parity bits associated with each double-word. Byte gathering is also performed within the write buffer, although it is restricted to the double-word most recently written. Inclusion of this write buffer allows a minimum of four processor writes to occur before the system bus is actually acquired. As with the cache line buffers, the address and status portions of the write buffer are available to both the system and processor ports for snooping.

Processor Port Optimizations

Optimization of the processor port for operation with the NS32532 centers around minimizing the external components required between the processor and cache controller and maintaining the coherence of the processor's on-chip caches. With the integration of a 532-compatible bus watcher into the cache controller, the only external components required at the processor interface consist of buffers to provide the high drive required by the RAM array. Since the internal data cache and of the NS32532 implements a write-through protocol, all processor writes are passed to the external cache. The problem of maintaining cache coherence involves invalidations to the internal caches.

Unlike most other microprocessors which only allow software invalidation, the NS32532 also incorporates hardware support for cache invalidation.[2] Several pins on the NS32532 are reserved to select one of the 32 cache sets in either the instruction or data cache for invalidation. An external bus watcher is then used to track the activity of the internal caches and to issue invalidations as required. This 532 bus watching function has been integrated into the NS32605 cache controller, allowing on-chip caches to remain enabled, even for shared data.

The bus watcher block in the NS32605 contains copies of the 96 tag entries - 32 for the internal instruction cache and 64 for the internal data cache of the NS32532. The tag directories have the same structures and replacement algorithms as the processor tag directories. By monitoring the CPU bus, the tag directories of the bus watcher are kept equivalent to those of the processor. The system bus is then monitored simultaneously, comparing addresses to those in the tag directory and issuing invalidations as required.

Since the line size of the cache controller can vary from 16 to 64 bytes, the external cache line size can be from one to four times the length of the internal cache line size. Whenever the external cache line size is a multiple of the internal cache line size, multiple invalidations may be required. The bus watcher is responsible for performing the appropriate number of tag comparisons and for generating the invalidations whenever a match occurs.

Decoupling Clock Speeds

To achieve the highest performance, the processor should be allowed to run at its maximum frequency. The optimal processor speed, however, rarely matches the optimal clock frequency of the rest of the system. One of the most valuable functions of the NS32605 cache controller is to decouple the processor clock from the other clocks in the system, while protecting against metastability.

Allowing the processor/cache module and system bus to run asynchronously requires that there be a point of resynchronization at the interface, where mutually asynchronous events are reconciled. The penalty for this resynchronization is measured as the delay from the time a data word is received until it is absorbed by the cache controller. Although the resynchronization penalty is incurred for each data transfer, this delay can be amortized across a block data transfer if the interface can store each data word. The same number of resynchronization delays will occur; however, they will be resolved in parallel rather than serially.

The read cache line buffer of the NS32605 serves as a buffer for all data entering the cache controller. In addition to allowing for the amortization of the resynchronization penalty, the read cache line buffer also minimzes the duration of the bus cycle by allowing the system bus to run at its maximum frequency. The structure of the read cache line buffer is similar to that of the write cache line buffer, consisting of 64 bytes of data and the associated address, parity, and status bits. The data requested by the processor is delivered as soon as it arrives and is also simultaneously copied into the cache memory. Although the remaining contents of the read cache line buffer are transferred to the cache memory as soon as the processor is satisfied, the address and status bits must be available for snooping the system bus while this transfer occurs.

System Port Optimizations

In order to minimize the frequency and duration of bus accesses, the most efficient cache coherence protocols are supported. In addition to the write-through protocol, the enhanced Futurebus-compatible system port provides all of the status information and support of complex transactions necessary for implementation of copy-back protocols. Although many varieties of copy-back protocols have been implemented, the actual state transitions can be summarized with the MOESI state model.[3] Three attributes of cached data exist: validity, denoting that the data is correct and up-to-date; ownership, denoting that the particular cache must respond to requests in place of shared memory; and, exclusiveness, denoting that no other cache in the system shares the data. In the MOESI state model, these three attributes of cached data are combined to form five meaningful states, as pictured in Figure 3. Each state is represented by a single letter that stands for the most important attribute of the state. As can be seen from the diagram, there are four valid states. In the "M", or "modified" state, data is not shared by any other cache and is incorrect in shared memory. The "E", or "exclusive" state is very similar, the main difference being that it is correct in shared memory. In the "O", or "ownership" state, the data may be shared by other caches in the system; however, it is the responsibility of the owning cache to respond to any requests for the data. The only attribute for the "S" state, or "shared" state, is that the data is valid. Finally, in the "I" state, or "invalid" state, the data in the cache is not accessible by its processor. Within the tag directory, three bits signifying the attributes are used to denote the state of each cache line. As data is read or modified, both by the cache master and by other caches within the system, status information will be communicated over the shared bus, resulting in possible state transitions within each cache.

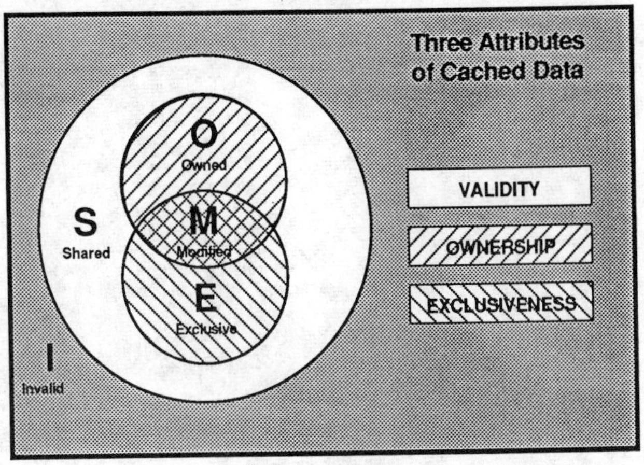

Figure 3. MOESI State Model

To support a copy-back protocol, since the shared memory may be incorrect, there must be a class of transactions to ensure that any processor can reliably read modified data. This is accomplished with the support of three-party transactions known as *reflection* and *intervention*. In these two types of transactions, the owning cache will respond to the request in place of shared memory. When using *intervention*, the shared memory is disabled and the value of the data in shared memory will remain incorrect. When using *reflection*, the shared memory also participates in the transaction, monitoring the data on the bus as it is being sent from the owning cache and storing the updated value. In the NS32605 cache controller, the user may choose to perform either reflection or intervention by programming a bit in the configuration register.

The other requirement in supporting a copy-back protocol is to make sure that any processor can modify data without leaving copies of data accessible that are not updated. This is accomplished with either of two bus transactions: invalidation or broadcast write. Under the write-through protocol, if cached data is externally changed, the cache will invalidate its entry. This same invalidation approach can be applied to the copy-back protocol with the use of address-only transactions. For highly shared data, however, it may be advantageous to avoid invalidation of all copies just because one sharer changes a portion of the cache line. In this case, a broadcast write transaction may be used to simultaneously update all caches holding a copy of the line. Implementation of either of these two methods may cause a program to execute more efficiently; however, the efficiency will be dependent on the nature of the program. Invalidation may cause thrashing as the polling of a semaphore causes the cache line to be refetched. The broadcast write transaction may also lead to inefficiencies as each processor whose cache contains a copy of the updated line is stalled, even if the data is no longer needed by the sharing cache module. Since neither approach is shown to be universally better, the NS32605 cache controller also leaves this implementation choice up to the user. Either the invalidation or broadcast write transaction may be chosen for execution by programming a bit in the configuration register.

Parity Support

Since the cache memory may be configured to support up to 256K bytes of external RAM, parity is also supported in the static RAM array. In fact, parity can be checked and generated at both the system and processor ports independently. If the system bus or cache master supports parity, the parity of all data entering the cache controller will be checked and then stored in the external RAM. If either of the ports does not support parity, parity will be generated upon entry. All data leaving the cache memory will have its associated parity checked. Detection of a parity error at any location will be detected and flagged.

Scalability and Partitioning

Systems which require more than 256K bytes of cache may cascade two cache controllers. The cache controllers can be divided into non-overlapping address spaces by connecting one of the address pins to a cache select pin. Configured in this manner, only one of the cache controllers will be activated for any processor request.

Although the cache controller supports a unified cache, either a single cache controller or two cache controllers can be used to partition the memory into instruction/data portions or user/supervisor portions. Using a single cache controller, this partitioning is achieved by configuring the cache as two-way set associative, one column being used for each portion. Using two cache controllers, the configuration may remain as either direct-mapped or two-way set associative since the partitioning is between caches. For each processor request that results in a hit, the tag comparison and data fetching is performed in the usual manner. Partitioning is only used when a cache line requires replacement. Upon replacing a cache line, the status bits are examined to determine the nature of the request; the appropriate column or cache is then selected for replacement.

Conclusion

The NS32605 cache controller optimally interfaces to the NS32532 microprocessor and to Futurebus, providing support for a variety of caching protocols. While supporting up to 256K bytes of external cache memory with parity contributes to a reduction in the miss ratio, integration of data buffering structures helps minimize the miss penalty. In addition to targeting for the highest performance, the cache controller is also targeted for maximum flexibility. Many features, such as the line size and set associativity, are programmable to allow tuning specific applications.

References

[1] A. J. Smith, "Cache Evaluation and the Impact of Workload Choice," *The 12th Annual International Symposium on Computer Architecture*, pp. 64-75, 1985.

[2] D. Alpert, J. Levy, B. Maytal, "Architecture of the NS32532 Microprocessor," *IEEE International Conference on Computer Design: VLSI in Computers*, pp. 168-172, 1987.

[3] P. Sweazey and A. J. Smith, "A Class of Compatible Cache Consistency Protocols and their Support by the IEEE Futurebus," *The 13th Annual International Symposium on Computer Architecture*, pp. 414-423, 1986.

A New Mid-Range VAX Multiprocessor System

Chair: D. Bhandarkar

SOFTWARE ENGINEERING Track

Engineering Information Systems: Panel

Chair: M. Ketabchi

ENGINEERING INFORMATION SYSTEMS
PROSPECTS AND PROBLEMS OF INTEGRATION

Gio Wiederhold
Stanford University

The spectrum of services that an EIS must provide ranges far. We can recognize two orthogonal dimensions:

1. Design: The reduction of informal specifications to precise mechanical dimensions of the objects being designed, with complete material specification.

2. Flow: A product has to move through the phases of design for functionality, design tests, design for manufacturability, prototype building and test, production planning, manufacture, product test, maintenance, and engineering changes.

Activities pertaining to a design object should proceed in parallel along both dimensions. As the functional specification of a design become firm, tests can be defined, and manufacturability begins to be considered. As the product design nears completion, the flow has reached questions of maintenance, and once it is firmed up, further alterations become engineering changes.

We can, using these dimensions, view the design process as a wavefront, starting small at the origin of our plan, and wideming while proceeding in parallel over all phases. The greatest effort takes place where the wavefront is widest, at the time that the design is nearly complete, but other phases of the product flow are still lagging.

This note is based on experience gained within the US Air Force VHSIC datamanagement task force, supported through a contract with Universal Energy Systems. Research support for this area is supported by DARPA contract N39-84-C211, and NSF grant DTMP 8619595. It was written while the author was a guest investigator with IBM Deutschland, at the LILOG project in Stuttgart.

Given this model, we notice that there are continuously active parallel tasks to be served by an EIS. Strict task serialization would not only extend the product development time excessively, but also inhibit the necessary feedback. Information from later phases in the product must be able to affect the design tasks before the design is completed, otherwise we are forced to use longer iterative cycles. The feedback effectively creates conflicts between the contibuing design task and the product development flow. Methods must be developed which signal possible conflicts without inhibiting cooperative parallel work.

At the stages where multiple phases are active, the data within the EIS will be viewed from very different aspects. An optimal data structure for the design phase is likely to be unwieldy for a testing phase. Distinct activities within a phase will themselves have differing requirements.

Most task specific design tools have today employ data structures that are specifically well-suited to the task at hand, but because of that view, the data structures chosen are rarely well suited to other tasks. Questions to be posed in regard to the data organization are:

1. Adequacy of information content.

2. Adequacy of recognized relationships.

One specific design task is likely to ignore interesting descriptive data about the design object that are not relevant to the task. The data will be organized according to the hierarchical decomposition inherent in the design or evaluation paradigm of that task.

Problems induced by these two aspects are information loss and locality loss.

If the information is needed in phase i-1 and phase i+1, and phase i ignores that information, it must be reobtained, merged, and possibly transformed to be available in phase i+1. Similarly, structures have to be rebuilt from phase to phase.

The use of a central database with an EIS seems to have the potential of dealing with the first problem in information loss. The database provides a central resource, the tasks are limited to views. Mapping functions will have to be programmed until we have query languages that permit object construction and view update.

Locality management remains a problem, since locality and access issues are based on accessing requirements, beyond the knowledge of the database system and schema. They must be solved to provide adequate performance for engineering users.

If a database for an EIS can provide dynamic rebinding capabilities, which permit adjustment to current usage patterns, a third of the problems is solved. The remaining issues are: how does one application advise the database system of its access needs and how does the database integrate the diversity of requirements? As databases for EIS become a reality these questions will have to be addressed.

GOALS OF THE ENGINEERING INFORMATION SYSTEMS PROJECT*

Robert I. Winner

Institute for Defense Analyses
1801 N. Beauregard St., Alexandria, VA 22311

1. Introduction

The complexity of engineered systems is increasing dramatically. Advances in the miniaturization of electronics have increased the complexity of electronic designs by an order of magnitude within the last few years. Further, the advent of VHSIC technology promises to increase the complexity of single-chip designs by another order of magnitude.

The complexity of current systems already is so great that it would be practically impossible to carry out the engineering process without computer assistance. Thus, many different tools and support systems for computer aided design (CAD), computer aided manufacturing (CAM), computer integrated manufacturing (CIM), and (generically) computer aided engineering (CAE) have been evolved and continue to be introduced. Since these tools essentially shoulder a portion of the complexity of an engineered system, the amount of complexity that engineers must bear is substantially reduced.

Yet, the usefulness of these tools and systems is reduced in the current situation since no particular vendor has an integrated tool set that performs all of the steps needed and/or desired for engineering a system from the requirements phase, through specification and design, all the way to manufacturing and maintenance. Thus, the creation of an adequate tool set requires that tools from different vendors be integrated. The problem here is that tools from different vendors utilize different models and formats for representing the same information in a design. Different user interfaces are employed; similarly, different approaches are used in implementing administrative and management capabilities. These differences create additional complexity in the engineering process; the elimination of this complexity would allow the potential productivity gains from CAE tools to be more fully realized.

A second problem brought about by the increased complexity of engineered systems is that it is no longer possible in most cases for a single engineer to design the entire system. Rather, complex designs must be subdivided into smaller units and the designs must be handled by design teams rather than by individual designers.

The decomposition of a design often creates highly interrelated subtasks that must be pursued concurrently, yet the designers must use or revise each other's results. Thus, there is a need for controlled sharing of the design information, tracking of design information, tracking of design dependencies and changes, and monitoring of the design process. In short, there is a need for a system that provides database management functions for engineering information.

In response to these problems, an Engineering Information System (EIS) was conceived that provides a framework for tool integration based on information sharing. In this document, the term **EIS** is used to describe a particular class of systems whose concepts and requirements are defined in this document and not in an universal way. Like an operating system, the EIS offers facilities and defines interfaces to be used by applications. Also like an operating system, the EIS controls and allocates resources (here, data resources), provides concurrency controls, archiving, and an *ad hoc* query capability.

The basic functions of the EIS are:

- Tool Integration--the ability to operate, efficiently and uniformly, a number of tools with different data and hardware requirements.
- Data Exchange--the ability to translate and to communicate data among different hosts and tools not only within the EIS but also between the EIS and external systems (including other EISs).
- Engineering Management and Control--the facilities to monitor the design process and to impose automatic and manual controls on accessing and modifying data.
- Information Management--the facilities to describe and to control globally available EIS data (including the creation and manipulation of data, the imposition of data validity (or constraint) checking, the management of versions and of configurations, the control of concurrent transactions, and the management of backup and archived data).

* Most of the information in this paper is from Joseph L. Linn and Robert I. Winner, editors, *The Department of Defense Requirements for Engineering Information Systems (EIS), Volume I: Operational Concepts,* IDA Paper P-1953, Institute for Defense Analyses, Alexandria, VA, July 1986.

- EIS Administration--the tools and the specifications for managing the data dictionary, tools, workstations, user profiles, and control rules.

The EIS is a set of services and specifications; it is **not** a single implementation of a specific system; rather, it is a framework for providing the necessary functions. It is intended to apply to a number of different engineering tasks and organizations. Therefore, it must offer a means for tailoring to meet the individual requirements of each. It must be able to evolve to meet the challenges of new design processes and tools, and it also must be able to function efficiently in a distributed environment that includes different types of mainframes and workstations. Finally, the system itself must be portable across different systems.

2. EIS Program Goals

The EIS program pursues two primary objectives. The first is to produce a set of reference specifications for use by industry that can form the basis for a standardization effort and that covers various data interchange and tool portability aspects. The second is to produce a prototype system that demonstrates how short-term requirements for an EIS can be satisfied using those reference specifications. This section discusses the goals that underlie the two objectives.

The EIS framework consists of a set of fundamental services, much like an all-purpose operating system, and a series of specifications, forming a baseline for communication and implementation. The goals of the EIS, then, are to provide the services and specifications that are essential to build information systems to support computer-aided engineering design. Furthermore, these services and specifications must be acceptable to a wide body of industrial and government vendors and users.

Integration and Uniformity

The EIS is intended to integrate the tools and processes, engineering and managerial, used in the engineering environment, and to allow different organizations (teams, departments, corporations, or agencies) to exchange pertinent information. These goals can be stated more specifically as:

(1) Provide a framework for integrating design tools in a cost effective manner.

The EIS will not be a complete, self-contained design automation system; instead it must provide mechanisms (e.g., services and specifications) that facilitate the integration of new and existing tools requiring the least possible modification of the tools themselves. This acknowledges the fact that there is no single, small set of tools that covers all design aspects and activities and is acceptable to all design engineers.

(2) Encourage the portability of tools.

The EIS cannot mandate or ensure the portability of tools among different run-time and design management environments, since it is not itself a tool provider. However, the EIS can provide services and specifications that, when utilized, greatly improve tool portability without greatly restricting tool applicability. Use of these services and specifications should result in cost savings to tool builders as an additional incentive.

(3) Encourage a uniform design environment.

The design environment is implied by the operating environment that the tools create for its users, for example, through the methods of interfacing with the end-user. A frequent reason for lack of uniformity is the absence of a suitable reference specification for user and system interface services that are portable among host environments. The EIS should provide specifications and services that can serve as the basis for significant improvements in this area.

(4) Facilitate the exchange of design information.

Design data is exchanged among different physical processing components, among different software tools, among different engineering departments in the same company, and among different corporations and agencies. The EIS should contain facilities that can be used to provide a uniform tool environment, tools that can perform generic application services (for example, design format translators), and specifications that can serve as a reference for data exchange.

(5) Provide a framework for supporting design management and reuse of previous designs.

Large designs typically are performed by engineering teams. This requires, for example, controlled sharing of preliminary design data, protection of released design information, and monitoring of design methods and progress. Also, with the rapid accumulation of design data, the reuse of past designs is becoming increasingly dependent upon support from automated tools. An EIS that does not offer design management support would be incomplete.

Acceptability

There is a wide-spread desire for integrated design environments throughout the industry. If this desire led to the development of many incompatible engineering information systems, many of the primary goals expressed above would not be achieved. Hence, a critical factor for the success of the EIS can be expressed as the following goal:

(6) Achieve wide-spread acceptance of the EIS by the electronics industry.

Extra effort may be needed for achieving acceptance on a large scale. For example, the EIS must appeal to end-users as well as decision makers. In addition to demonstrating its usefulness and cost-effectiveness, the EIS must also exhibit the key properties of being adaptable and extensible.

Adaptability and Extensibility

In order for the EIS to be widely accepted, it must be able to adapt to the changing needs of different organizations over time. Its scope must be broad enough, and its generality great enough, to accommodate and integrate new engineering activities. This observation leads to the following two goals:

(7) Be adaptable to future changes in engineering methods.

The EIS architecture must be technology-independent, where functional components can be easily replaced, without compromising other system features such as ease of use.

(8) Although concentrating initially on electronic design, be extensible to all life-cycle activities and other engineering disciplines.

Because the EIS is a framework, it can be extended to cover more engineering applications by incorporating new or different tools and expanding the scope of data that it manages.

Evolutionary Approach

It will be necessary to insert the EIS into existing design environments. A revolutionary approach is likely to fail for cost reasons. This leads to another key constraint as an EIS goal:

(9) Provide a transition path for existing design environments that is cost-effective.

The EIS needs to offer means for a phased transition, offering services that facilitate and reduce the cost of the transition process--including adaptation of design and management tools, acquisition and installation of needed system services and resources, definition of management procedures, transition of existing data, and training of future system users.

3. Background

Computer aided engineering (CAE) systems have evolved in such a way that there is considerable overlap in the functions of the tools provided in such systems. Because of this overlap, it can be very difficult to get the tools to work together. The objective of this program is to provide a framework for the integration of CAE tools and systems. As the development schedule for the project is very ambitious, success may be achieved only by building upon the extensive existing base of design automation tools and systems. Since EIS environments must build from the existing engineering support environments, it is critically important to determine how current nonintegrated systems may evolve to participate in an integrated EIS environment.

3.1. Project Organization

The EIS effort was initiated through the efforts of the VHSIC (Very High Speed Integrated Circuits) Program Office. There is a great need for this work in industry; however, no successful unified set of standards, de facto or otherwise, has emerged. Interested parties include the IEEE, the ACM, the ASME, numerous industry concerns, and the United States government.

The technical project manager is 1Lt. Jack Ebel, AFWAL/AAL, Wright-Patterson Air Force Base. Questions about the EIS program should be directed to him.

The project is being executed under contract to Honeywell Information Systems, Inc. The overall project manager is Dr. Jay Patel. Subcontractors on the team include Computer Corporation of America, TRW, CLSI, Inc., McDonnell Douglas and Arizona State University.

3.2. Project History

A large amount of work has gone into automating various areas of engineering, especially electrical engineering. This program was initiated to search for a means to integrate existing engineering systems and tools. At first, it was thought that this is essentially a database problem; as it turns out, the scope of the problem is far greater. In defining an EIS environment, the issues to be considered include inter-tool interfaces, network and operating system interfaces, consistent user interfaces, standardization efforts and policies, and the migration of existing tools and systems into an integrated EIS environment. In addition, the concept of extensibility is a pervasive influence on all other system concepts.

A fundamental tenet of the approach adopted in this program is that the environment issues that the EIS is intended to address can be considered separately from the tool set that is to populate the environment. Thus, the solutions obtained should be applicable across wide ranges of tool sets; that is, tool sets from various engineering disciplines should be equally appropriate in an EIS environment. However, the prototype EIS will explore only the digital electronics field. Similarly, there are many facets of the design of digital electronic systems; the prototype EIS will concentrate on the design of such systems.

4. Community Involvement

Previously, workshops were held in November, 1985, and January, 1986. In the first workshop, the participants were divided into two working groups in order to identify technical issues concerning the development of standards and the prototype EIS. The workshop identified eight overlapping areas of concern including: Current Representation Capabilities, Man-Machine Interfaces, Computing Systems, Information Management and Control, Information Models, Functional Architecture, Workstations, and Application Program Information Requirements.

In preparation for the January workshop, the Institute for Defense Analyses (IDA) prepared a document entitled "Operational Concepts and Requirements for an

Engineering Information System" (OCREIS). The OCREIS document served as a starting point for discussions in the working groups of the January workshop. The working groups were chartered to provide input to the next documents. These comments were important in reformulating the original OCREIS document to obtain the next document, OCREIS version 2.

OCREIS version 2 was submitted to a qualified panel of experts and to the attendees of the previous workshops for consideration and comment. Based on these new comments and a parallel requirements analysis effort, IDA produced the next document, OCREIS version 3. Another expert panel (actually a superset of the previous panel) reviewed the third version of the document. Their comments and an ongoing requirements conflict analysis has yielded the current, final version of the document, the one that is operative for the EIS prototype development.

As of this writing, an EIS Technical Working Group (EIS TWG) is being formed to provide advice to the EIS Project Office on the overall technical direction of the project. Also, links are being formed with IEEE DASS working groups. In connection with these, there are several open EIS Special Interest Groups dealing with specific technical aspects of the project. The first meeting of these groups was at a workshop at Arizona State University in January, 1988.

THE ENGINEERING INFORMATION SYSTEM PROGRAM

John L. Ebel, 1Lt, USAF

Air Force Wright Aeronautical Laboratories (AFWAL/AADE)
Wright-Patterson Air Force Base, OH

ABSTRACT

The phenomenal growth in integrated circuit fabrication technology over the last decade has led to the need for a robust, multi-user, integrated design environment for electronic systems. Attempts to develop "integrated" design environments have highlighted the present lack in design tool interoperability. The Very High Speed Integrated Circuits (VHSIC) program has recognized the importance of integrated design environments for the design of future defense electronic systems and for the insertion of new technologies into existing electronic systems, and is attempting to ease the task of integrating disparate electronic system design aids by addressing the design tool interoperability problem. This paper briefly describes the rationale for the Engineering Information System (EIS) program, highlights the goals of the effort, and outlines the general structure of the program.

INTRODUCTION

The Very High Speed Integrated Circuit (VHSIC) Program has developed an integrated circuit capability which can significantly increase the performance of defense electronic systems. In order to economically realize this capability, the Department of Defense must be able to efficiently design and insert VHSIC technology into new and existing electronic defense systems. This goal will require the development of an integrated design environment that supports design, documentation, and life-cycle maintenance of complex electronic systems from the initial system specification through fabrication and test. A design system with this degree of functionality is not available commercially because the development of such a large and complex "turn-key" system would require more resources than any one business can afford. As a result, organizations which use design automation tools are forced to integrate an assorted set of design aids developed either internally or by different vendors. The integration task is complicated by the multi-user, distributed, heterogeneous design environment, and by the unique, proprietary, internal data representation of each vendor's design system. The difficulties associated with the integration of disparate design tools are well known [2,3], but the benefits derived from integration are indispensable [4]. The objective of the Engineering Information System (EIS) Program is to reduce the present difficulties involved with integrating different vendors' design tools by developing a candidate set of interface standards and demonstrating their usefulness. From [1], the basic functions which an EIS must provide are:

1. Tool Integration - The ability to operate, efficiently and uniformly, a number of different tools with different data and hardware requirements.

2. Data Exchange - The ability to translate and to communicate data among different hosts and tools not only within the EIS but also between the EIS and external systems (including other EISs).

3. Engineering Management and Control - The facilities to monitor the design process and to impose automatic and manual controls on accessing and modifying data.

4. Information Management - The facilities to describe and control globally available EIS data (including the creation and manipulation of data, the imposition of validity (or constraint) checking, the management of versions and of configurations, the control of concurrent transactions, and the management of backup and archived data).

5. EIS Administration - The tools and the specifications for managing the data dictionary, tools, workstations, user profiles, and control rules.

EIS PROGRAM GOALS

The EIS program has two primary goals. The first is to develop candidate standard specifications in the five functional areas mentioned above for use by industry. The second goal is to develop prototype software to demonstrate that the needs of the user community can be met through the use of the specifications developed.

The specific goals to be met by an EIS as described in reference [1] are:

1. Provide a framework for integrating design tools in a cost effective manner - The EIS is not a self-contained system, it is a set of services and specifications that facilitate the integration of new and existing tools.

2. Encourage the portability of tools - The EIS will provide services and specifications which, when used by tool builders, will greatly improve tool portability and result in a cost savings to the tool builder.

3. Encourage a uniform design environment - The EIS will provide a user interface toolkit and guidelines which will allow the development of uniform user interfaces in different host environments.

4. Facilitate the exchange of design information - The EIS will provide a uniform interface to tools for data exchange, and a set of specifications that can serve as a reference model for data translation.

5. Provide a framework for supporting design management and reuse of previous designs - Design data is a valuable resource which must be managed and controlled. The EIS will provide facilities to support this function.

6. Achieve wide-spread acceptance of the EIS by the electronics Industry - The goals of tool interoperability and EIS-compatible commercial tool availability will not be met unless there is wide-spread acceptance of the EIS specifications. This goal requires involvement of industry in the formation of the EIS specifications.

7. Be adaptable to future changes in engineering methods - The CAD/CAE environment is rapidly, and constantly changing. The EIS should be technology independent, and allow for easy change technology dependent functional parts of the system.

8. Be extensible to life cycle activities and other engineering disciplines - Other engineering disciplines (mechanical,software) are facing the same difficulties addressed by EIS in the electrical domain. The EIS should be extensible into these areas through the integration of new or different tools.

9. Provide a cost-effective transition path for existing environments - Users have a large investment in the tools and data of their existing systems. The EIS must provide a cost-effective way to move from the existing environment to the EIS environment.

PROGRAM ORGANIZATION

The Engineering Information System Program has been organized into three phases. Phase I is comprised of the specification, documentation and delivery of a preliminary set of EIS specifications based upon user requirements captured in reference [1]. This phase began in July 1987, and will last nineteen months. Phase II and Phase III will last a combined total of 22 months, and will consist of the implementation and testing (Phase II), and demonstration (Phase III) of the information management system and the interface specifications.

These initial specifications from Phase I will be evaluated by industry, academia and the Government in order to determine their adequacy. User community participation in this process is strongly encouraged. The evaluation process will be aided by a workshop just prior to the end of Phase I in which the salient features of the specifications will be reviewed. The results of the review workshop will be incorporated into the final specification.

Following analysis of the results of the review workshop, Phase II will begin. The second phase of the program will involve the detailed design of EIS prototype specifications and software. Phase II will be organized as a sequence of incremental developments. Each incremental development will serve to further refine the definition of the design environment and its implementation. The system will be demonstrated for evaluation by the user community and Government during Phase III. Evaluation feedback will be used to determine the strong and weak areas of the system, and potential areas for standardization.

The EIS standardization process will depend critically on feedback from the EIS user community. The EIS user community includes everyone who might be affected by future EIS standards. As the EIS program proceeds, the development team will be required to keep the user community informed, and will solicit and analyze their inputs. User community feedback will be necessary to determine which parts of the specifications implemented by the prototype might form the basis of a standard, and how those specifications should be tailored or extended before standardization. User community feedback will also be essential in ensuring that any standards developed do not favor any particular (proprietary) methodology which would undermine their acceptance.

At the completion of this effort, the user community will have a set of candidate standard interface specifications which will facilitate the integration of disparate design aids into a tightly coupled electronic system design environment along with prototype demonstration software.

REFERENCES

1. R. Winner, J.Linn, editors, "DOD Requirements for Engineering Information Systems", July 1986.

2. R. Katz, "Managing the Chip Design Database," IEEE Computer Magazine, V 16, N 12, December 1983.

3. Y, Kalay, "A Database Management Approach to CAD/CAM Systems Integration," Proc. 22nd ACM/IEEE Design Automation Conference, June 1985.

4. H. Brown, C. Tong, G. Foyster, "Palladio: An Exploratory Environment for Circuit Design," IEEE Computer Magazine, V 16, N 12, December 1983.

Software Reusability

Chair: W. Tracz

The Economics of Reuse

Tom Love

Productivity Products International, Inc.
Sandy Hook, CT

With current technology we cannot build the software that the market demands. Current approaches result in too little functionality and too many errors. Significant commercial experience now exists using object-oriented programming. The paper does an economic analysis of the use of object-oriented programming and concludes that it provides the technical key to higher productivity and quality.

About 10 years ago while designing an early Computer Aided Software Engineering (CASE) system within General Electric Company, it became obvious that we had neither the time nor the budget to build all the components of that system. I began to tell the development team, "Buy the best, build the rest". It seemed like our only hope.

But problems arose. While it was easy to find people willing to sell software products to GE, it was nearly impossible to find two products that would work together. We needed specification tools, design tools, coding tools, testing tools and documentation tools. All of these tools needed to operate in a seamlessly integrated environment with a consistent graphical user interface and operating with a single database containing all the relevant project information.

Later I heard someone else working on an integrated office environment describe software products as **slabs.** If the slab did what you required or was a pure subset of what you needed, it could be used within your system. But if elements of several slabs were required, you had no recourse but to design and build your system from scratch. Slabs don't integrate.

From an economic perspective, building software from scratch makes about as much sense as building special purpose computers from scratch -- designing fully custom circuits, boards, racks and systems. Or designing individual bricks within a large building.

I began to wonder, "Could there be some technical barrier which prevents systems designers from 'buying the best and building the rest' "? Have we failed to standardize something as fundamental as the voltage level required in our circuits or the sockets which allow our components to fit on uniform circuit boards? After a few years, I found the answer.

The problem with software reusability is that we have pretended we know what we can't and we encrypt what we do know.

We pretend when we build software that we can know what that program will be subjected to during its lifetime. Furthermore, we imbed this "knowledge" uniformly throughout the program -- resulting in a cipher that would make the Inigma machine pale by comparison. This "knowledge" is contained in branching statements (If-then-else, switch, etc.) throughout our programs.

Among other things branching statements test a variable or data structure to determine its type or value and alter the program's flow of control as a result. A test for a value may be a disguised test for the type of the data structure; e.g., if x is GT 25 bytes in size it must be polygon. Our assumptions about the range of data that will be acceptable to a program become built into the branching statements throughout the program --

CH2539-5/88/0000/0238$01.00 © 1988 IEEE

regardless of its size. If a set of assumptions about this program is altered, an indeterminate number of branching statements anywhere in the program might be affected. The "maintenance challenge" is to find and modify all the appropriate branching statements. For systems of any significant size, this task becomes impossible.

Software is not routinely reused; because it takes more effort to reuse someone else's code than build it from scratch. Programmers are not charlatans or ego maniacs who refuse to use previously developed code and insist upon developing systems from scratch. **There are fundamental technical barriers which must be overcome before reusability becomes technically possible.**

As with most scientific advances, the reusability breakthrough has been lying around dormant in academic institutions for more than 25 years! When the demand became so great to construct systems of a size and complexity which was not possible by building from scratch, a breakthrough was found.

The solution to the reusability problem requires only a small change in the way we structure our software systems, so it appears quite evolutionary. Software professionals can learn how to apply this solution in a matter of hours. Yet the change turns out to be more revolutionary than evolutionary. Like the introduction of microprocessors (a natural evolution of semiconductory technology), the ultimate impact was be enormous.

The solution to the reusability problem is objects. Objects change the way our programs are organized and packaged. Objects bind procedures to the particular types of data that those procedures were designed to work with. Pure data and pure functions are recognized for the fantasy they really are -- "there is no such thing as a sort routine, Alice". A sorting function can only be defined for data of a particular type. Sorting 747's on the runway at O'Hare is quite different from sorting employees by payroll number. Our uniquely human ability to cope with concepts such as sorting and correctly apply these concepts to a wide spectrum of situations is not shared by our electronic automatons. Our automatons require considerably more precision and clarification of assumptions.

At this point I could delve into "Objects 101" and give you a little better understanding of this important new technology. You would be totally unsatisfied by such a cursory introduction. Instead read Brad Cox's *Object-Oriented Programming* published by Addison-Wesley in 1986. It is the best available description of the concepts of object-oriented programming.

Instead of "Objects 101", I want to describe some of the experiences commercial developers have had using object-oriented software engineering techniques and conclude with a simply economic analysis of the implications of this technology.

Sources of productivity

Productivity gains using PPI's Workplace and IC-Paks result from three sources:

- the Objective-C language
- improved development tools
- reuse of existing components

Let's consider these effects and attempt to quantify their respective effects on productivity.

The Language

The Objective-C language is an extensible language which raises the level of C language. With a higher level language, the amount of effort required to do a given job is reduced across the board by some quantity depending upon the match between the language and the application or system domain. For example to build a large package of statistical functions, C is not significantly better than Fortran to express the equations within such a package. But for the portion of the system involving parsing or graphics or user interfaces, C is a much more suitable language and would be much more efficient to use.

Controlled scientific studies have not been done comparing Objective-C with C over any reasonable range of application and system types and which control for individual differences between programmers. Actual experiences obtained from industrial users suggests that Objective-C results in as much as a 2 to 1 reduction in the number of non-commented source lines of code to accomplish a given application or system.

This reduction in development effort comes from internal reuse within the application due to inheritance and from the reuse of existing components. Generic behaviors can be inherited by one or more subclasses.

The Workplace

PPI's interpretive environment for building Objective-C programs allows a programmer to modify a program and test that program in 10 to 20 seconds versus 3 to 5 minutes using typical compiled environments. Only 13% of the development process involves code development and testing.[1] Thus the 20 to 1 (10 - 20 sec vs 180 - 300 sec) time savings to do a particularly common task during the code and test phases only may result as little as 20% productivity gain in the project as a whole.

Let's be conservative and only attribute a 10% overall improvment due to today's interpretive environment provided with Objective-C.

Component Reuse

A Software-IC typically involves 10 to 15 methods and 200 to 300 non-commented source lines of code. Experience to date suggest that it takes about 1 person month of effort to build one Software-IC yet only 1 person day of effort to reuse that same component. This twenty to one discrepancy is the predominant productivity effect resulting from object-oriented programming.

The following table shows the effect of this reusability within a system involving 100 Software-ICs under the assumption that the effort to construct new Software-ICs is constant regardless of the number of components within the system.

	Develop (PMs)	Reuse (PDs)	Total (PYrs)	Savings
No reuse	100	0	8.33	0
10% reuse	90	10	7.55	9%
30% reuse	70	30	5.97	28%
50% reuse	50	50	4.39	47%
80% reuse	20	80	2.03	76%

A comparison of the effort to construct a system with 100 Software-ICs with 4 levels of reuse. (PM = person months; PD = person days; PY = person days)

If fact it is well known and often demonstrated that the effort to construct a system grows logarithmically with the size of the system.

Effort = n $\log_{10}$ n

[1] B. Boehm. Software Engineering Economics. Prentice-Hall, 1981, page 341.

If we recast the above table taking into account this established fact, it produces the following results:

	components reused		effort	savings
none	100	0	200	0
10%	90	10	176	12%
30%	70	30	131	34%
50%	50	50	89	56%
80%	20	80	33	84%

We find that this relationship is consistent with PPI's own development experience and with the experience of our commercial customers. Customers building research prototypes which do not require complete documentation and quality assurance can take even less time to build systems with components.

Suppose that 50% of the components required for your next commercial system involving 100 components could be purchased at a price equal to your development cost.[1] As a developer, your technical risk would be reduced considerably; your time to market would be faster; you could develop the product with 111 person months less effort; and your energies could be directed toward the value-added aspects of the system, not a lot of scaffolding or substrate which your customers are not interested in paying for anyway.

By purchasing components, your risk of total project failure is much lower; your profits begin months earlier; the quality of the purchased components could be higher than you could have afforded to make them; and the documentation for these acquired components is first rate. Besides, you are comparing a fixed expenditure versus a historically inaccurate estimate. It's a "no-brainer" -- even if you had to pay what it would cost you to develop those components.

In fact, component suppliers supply components for a fraction of the original development effort depending upon the size of the market for each component package and the degree of innovation involved in the components themselves.

[1] From previous experience, you believe that the supplier produces quality components.

The Overall Productivity

As we combine the effects of using PPI's workplace tools for Objective-C and the available library of components, we can see the following benefits on a 200 component development project where 50 components have been purchased and reused.

components	*reused*	*effort in OC*	*effort w/ C*	*savings*
		(person months)		
200	0	460	1,104	
150	50	330		774

This model demonstrates that by acquiring PPI's Workplace and 50 Software-ICs (actually nearly 80 are available), 774 person months of effort or more than 64 person years of effort could be saved on this one project compared to building the same system in the C language using the usual UNIX development tools. That will amount to a savings of at least $6,000,000 deducting the one time cost of acquiring the Workplace and IC-paks.

The actual savings must also include the benefits to the company of having the product available to the market 4.6 years earlier! In fact 5 year development projects rarely make sense, so we either have to substantially increase the development staff or more likely, significantly reduce the functionality of the system.

Even if the entire job were done in Objective-C, 130 person months could be saved by acquiring 50 components rather than building them from scratch. If we assume that 14 people could develop the required 330 components in 2 calendar years. It would take that same 14 person team another 9 or 10 months to build the additional components instead of purchasing them for the cost of 4 person months of effort.

Summary

The economics are compelling. If quality software components can be purchased which accomplish any significant portion of the functionality required by the system under development and if those components can be acquired for less than their original development costs, they should be acquired.

On economic grounds, my favorite slogan holds up one more time:

Buy the best, build the rest.

The Software Productivity Consortium Reuse Program

Arthur Pyster and Bruce Barnes

Software Productivity Consortium
Reston VA 22091

Systematic software reuse offers the greatest potential for significant gains in software development productivity. Many forms of reuse exist, each offering different potential productivity gains. The Software Productivity Consortium has a broad approach towards reuse in order to maximize the impact on its customers and to improve its internal development productivity.

1. The Problem

The biggest gains in software development productivity will come from increased software reuse [Boehm, et al 84 and Brooks 87]. Even though this proposition is now well accepted, there are still relatively few organizations that have integrated reuse into their development paradigm in any significant way. The failure of software organizations to integrate reuse into their development methods is reflected in the lack of commerically available reusable parts. The hardware world takes reuse for granted and has well-developed terminology, concepts, tools, and infrastructure to support reuse. Nothing that mature exists for software [Kang and Levy 85]; e.g., only a handful of vendors sell reusable components in what can only be called a tough market [Booch 87, EVB 87, PPI 87].

The problem in achieving a high degree of systematic reuse can be characterized by the lack of:

1. Well understood and accepted terminology and concepts to describe reusability.
2. Tools and techniques that support software reuse.
3. An economic model that explains the real benefits and costs of software reuse, and that offers a method to software development organizations for them to analyze their situation [Barnes-et al 87].
4. A corporate infrastructure that encourages and rewards reuse.

The Software Productivity Consortium, founded by 14 U.S. aerospace companies, is tasked with dramatically increasing its owners' software development productivity. The Consortium has an ongoing program that directly addresses the first three reuse problems and that is trying to understand what is required to solve the fourth problem. Most of the work to date has centered around reusable designs and code. Over time this focus will expand to include other lifecycle objects such as requirements, schedules, and test cases.

2. Consortium Reuse Projects

The Consortium reuse methodology assumes a software development process in which new lifecycle parts are created and old ones modified over time. As shown in Figure 1, the material for creation and modification comes from three sources: project library, reuse libraries, and outside vendors. A *project library* is a repository for all technical and managerial information relevant to a single project. At any given time it contains a snapshot of the project's current state of development. When development is finished, the project library contains the final lifecycle parts such as requirements, design, user manuals, code, test plans, test cases, test results, and quality assurance plans. A *reuse library* is a repository for parts that are available across projects.

To systematically support reuse, a software development organization must have:

1. Tools within the project library for managing and accessing reuse libraries.
2. Reuse libraries relevant to the organization's business area.

3. A methodology that states when and how to apply reuse libraries to compose new project library parts and update old ones.

The Consortium's reuse projects address these three needs. There are four reuse-oriented projects currently underway: *Reuse Libraries, Synthesis, Methodology,* and *Measurement*. The Reuse Libraries Project is addressing the first problem by developing a general framework for cataloging, storing, and retrieving reusable software parts. It is also supplying sample reuse libraries. The Synthesis Project is addressing the second problem by developing a method for creating and applying very general design parts described in Section 6, and is building example reusable parts useful to the Consortium's customers and to itself. In addition, the Methodology Project is addressing such concerns as what makes a part reusable and how developers can be encouraged to create and apply reusable parts. The Libraries and Methodology Projects are maturing rapidly and will lead to relatively near-term Consortium products. The Synthesis Project will lead to later products. Finally, the Measurement Project is a research effort that is developing and validating models that relate the proportion of software reused, the cost of establishing reuse libraries, the cost of using library components during application development, and the number of library users [Barnes-et al 87]. Models are also being developed and validated relating the parameters of software reuse to development schedules and software quality.

3. Assumptions

The primary assumptions on which the Consortium's reuse program is based are:

1. Software reuse will grow only if developers are presented with a cost effective way to routinely build and apply reusable parts.
2. Limited but effective reuse is possible even with a relatively small number of parts; i.e., start-up costs are not overwhelming. However, the degree of reuse should rise as the number of parts increases.
3. Any software lifecycle part can potentially be reused; e.g., requirements specification, source code, management plan, and test case.
4. The implementation of a system should be specified by its visible behavior, not its internal structure. An implementation so described is called a *module* [Parnas-et al 83]. (See [Clements 82] for examples of module descriptions.) Currently, design and code are the only parts for which behavioral descriptions have been written. A complete behavioral description specifies both functional and non-functional characteristics; e.g., it is important to know the run-time performance of a module to be reused in real-time systems, and the space characteristics of a module to be reused in memory-limited applications.
5. Modules whose similarities are more revealing than their differences can best be viewed as variants within a single *module family*. Each family is specified in a *module family description*.
6. People will only reuse modules in which they have confidence. Accurate and precise characterization of modules is critical to their reuse. Testing is one common method of determining the accuracy of a module description. If the description of behavior is accurate but imprecise, a developer may choose not to reuse a module.
7. Designers should explicitly anticipate points of flexibility and stability in their modules, and provide insight into how to modify a module around anticipated flexibility points.

The Consortium is developing a methodology around these assumptions and tools to support that methodology. To a large degree this methodology is an adaptation of the work by Parnas and others at the Naval Research Laboratory on the A7 project [Parnas 76, Parnas-Clements 86]. The Consortium's reuse-oriented tools will support this emerging methodology. This methodology is also being applied during the Consortium's own tool development both to validate the methodology and to improve the Consortium's own productivity.

4. Modules, Families, and Reuse Libraries

The primary units of reuse are modules, and reuse libraries are organized around module families. For example, the Stack family contains all modules that satisfy the Stack family description. That description states the basic properties and operations of a stack such as the definition of the familiar push and pop operations. Each implementation, while unique, would still satisfy those basic properties and support those fundamental operations. A library user could read the family and module descriptions to understand the commonalities and variations among stack modules.

There are at least two interesting relationships among module families. First, a family may be subdivided into smaller constituent families to facilitate explanation and organization; e.g., a user interface family might by subdivided into families for character-oriented and bit-mapped displays. The bit-mapped display family might be further subdivided into families for windows, menus, and scrollbars.

Second, a family may be described using other families; e.g., a Booch diagram may be described as a special type of graph useful for displaying design dependencies in Ada programs, and an Assessment diagram as another type of graph useful for showing the dynamic properties of programs. The family description for Booch diagrams can reference information in the description of the Graph Family. Major economies of description are possible by describing one module family in terms of another.

The description of one module family in terms of other family descriptions does not say anything about how the members of the first family are actually designed. A Booch diagram implementation may or may not use the implementation of a Graph even if it is described that way. One way to document a module's design is by describing structural relationships between it and other modules.

A family description states what is common among the members of the family and what differences among members are anticipated; e.g., one section describes fundamental properties expected to hold among all members. Another identifies a range of behavioral differences anticipated among members. For example, one of the basic assumptions of the Graph Family is that zero or more arcs may connect two vertices. All members should satisfy that assumption. On the other hand, a member may vary in whether the system or the user handles garbage collection of storage associated with a graph. This possibility is explicitly noted in the family description because developers usually care about the amount of storage that an implementation consumes. The description of a family member would state which storage policy that member uses.

It is important to note that complete behavioral equivalence among family members is not expected, nor even desirable. Equivalence modulo the family description is all that is normally expected. This allows grouping of implementations that are *slightly* different in their behavior under a common name, reflecting how people would likely want to view them. This grouping policy is analogous to calling robins, ostriches, and penguins by the same term, *bird*, even though they are very different in many behaviorally visible ways. The Stack Family illustrates member variation well. Stacks are normally implemented using either arrays or linked lists. The basic operations of push, pop, top, create, copy, etc. can, for the most part, be described behaviorally without regard to the representational choice. However, there is one important behavioral difference. Array implementations normally have a fixed size at run-time, while list implementations can grow. A developer being presented with two candidate implementations that behaved similarly except for stack growth would still view them both as *stacks*. In a well stocked library, the developer would actually find both kinds of implementations. One of the past inhibitors of software reuse has been the inflexibility of candidate parts presented to potential users. Although offering one implementation choice per family supports some reuse, it is usually too limiting for widespread application.

The Methodology Project is trying to foster a spirit within the Consortium that encourages developers to describe software behaviorally and develop it with reuse in mind. Several Consortium projects are currently using this approach under the tutelage of the Methodology group. All are eventually expected to follow. For example, each of the data access and user interface services developed by the Consortium for its toolbuilding efforts will be described behaviorally, cataloged using a standard template, and placed in a reuse library.

5. Domain Analysis

There are two methods for finding modules with which to stock a reuse library's shelves. The first is essentially ad hoc as targets of opportunity are presented; e.g., a developer realizes he needs a coordinate conversion routine for a navigational system and no appropriate one is in the reuse library. Through proper guidance or luck he produces a version that is flexible enough for others to use. It is certified, cataloged, and inserted into the library. The strength of ad hoc collection is that it takes advantage of activities people are doing anyhow and requires relatively little advance planning. The weakness, of course, is that many opportunities will be missed. The second method is by performing a *domain analysis*; i.e., determining for a particular area such as flight navigation or database management which module families are important and describing both the families and their relationships. Such an analysis then becomes the basis for stating which implementations are needed to support that domain. Implementations can be sought from internal development or outside vendors depending on availability.

One of the most widely known examples of a domain analysis was done in the CAMP project by McDonnell Douglas for cruise missile flight control [McNicholl 86]. Although their terminology and organization were different than the Consortium's, CAMP produced the equivalent of several dozen module families to support certain aspects of flight control and partially populated those families with implementations. The Consortium is mapping the CAMP work into its own framework, and attempting to generalize on it as a basis for conducting domain analysis in other areas.

6. Canonical Design and Synthesis

One form of software design is the description of the modules that comprise the software plus the relationships among those modules. Such a design describes the implementation of *one* system. If a module description is replaced by a module family description, that design describes *many* systems. A different system results from each combination of member selections from the families. A design built from module family descriptions is called *canonical* to reflect the fact that it actually describes a set of related designs. Designs that are not canonical are *specialized*.

Having a canonical design opens up the possibility of either manually or automatically deriving specialized designs that satisfy a stated set of design constraints or higher level system requirements. Associating implementations with each of the module descriptions in a specialized design can potentially lead to automatically generating a runnable system from that design. Such generation, called *synthesis*, is a hard problem. There is a combinatorial explosion if a canonical design contains a large number of module families each of which has several alternative implementations. For complex modules such as Kalman filters or integrators the set of alternative implementations may be very large. Another interesting possibility is modifying the canonical design to meet design and requirements objectives. The choice of one module may make another module inappropriate or simply unnecessary. It may also suggest an extension or restriction on an existing module. In general there will be many constraints which must be simultaneously satisfied in order for a specialized design to meet user design and requirement specifications. Understanding and expressing such constraints and verifying that a specialized design satisfies them is difficult.

7. Relating Reuse to Prototyping

Development risk may arise because of uncertainties about a systems's requirements, feasibility or implementation strategy. One method of understanding risk is to construct a model of the system and analyze it with respect to known risk areas. Such investigation using models is also called *prototyping*. To the extent that prototyping is relatively rapid and inexpensive compared to building and rebuilding the full system, it is valuable.

One of the areas where reuse can offer enormous leverage is in prototyping. Models of complex systems can be constructed rapidly if there is a collection of parts from the domain of interest plus the necessary composition tools. One of the best understood examples of this is in the user interface domain. If a risk area is the correct specification of the user interface, or a user interface is required in order to effectively address other risk issues, a toolkit for rapidly prototyping user interfaces is extremely helpful. For a workstation oriented display, such a toolkit would contain parts that support interfaces involving windows, menus, buttons, etc. A primitive composition tool would be a programming language such as C or Ada in which to invoke toolkit services written as subroutines. A much better composition tool would support interactively constructing the user interface without having to resort to explicit programming.

The developer would never actually see the toolkit parts, but the composition tool would invoke them as needed.

The user interface domain is only one example where reusable parts effectively support model building. In such diverse arenas as signal processing, flight navigation, data base management, and graphics editors, a ready stock of reusable parts plus tools for quickly combining those parts and analyzing the results offers tremendous opportunities which the Consortium is attempting to exploit.

Reuse supports prototyping by providing the materials from which to construct models rapidly; in turn, prototyping supports reuse in two ways. First, if one of the goals of a project is to produce a reusable module, an explicit goal of prototyping might be to assess the suitability of a proposed module for reuse. Sucessful prototyping should lead to a production quality module more likely to be reused. Second, if prototyping really reduces overall development costs, then the cost of building production quality reusable parts that are first prototyped should be less than those built using other methods. Keeping the cost of creating parts low is critical to successfully stocking libraries.

8. Status

Four reuse-oriented projects are currently underway at the Consortium. The first reuse library has been partially constructed for the data structures domain by the Reuse Libraries Project. Several development projects are beginning to reuse that library and are writing module family descriptions and module descriptions for their software. Over the next several months, this form for documenting software should become routine within the Consortium and provide the basis for stocking the library shelves with additional modules. The Consortium's first product release and prototypes of second round products will be built taking advantage of such libraries.

The Synthesis Project is chartered with constructing canonical designs for application areas of interest, developing methods for constructing canonical designs, and where possible with constructing synthesizers around existing canonical designs. Initially this project is basing its work on the CAMP project, which provides many module implementations and descriptions of module families (although it obviously uses notations quite different from those adopted by the Consortium). An early prototype synthesizer can produce a certain class of autopilots for cruise missiles from high level design constraints entered by a developer. The autopilots use CAMP parts, are written in Ada, and can be run on either an Apollo or a VAX computer. The synthesizer uses a knowledge-based system to organize the domain analysis and select the correct members of each family in the one canonical design that has been built. In many cases the alternative implementations in a module family are actually constructed as one parameterized program segment, often as an Ada generic. The synthesizer determines the correct parameter values based on user input. If the prototyping effort is successful, this synthesizer will eventually become a Consortium product and additional synthesizers built.

Validation of parts generated by the Consortium but not used to build Consortium tools will become a problem in the future. The Consortium is not currently organized or staffed to perform meaningful validation on synthesized autopilots or other aerospace domain parts. The lack of adequate validation facilities will be addressed by the Consortium in 1988.

The Methodology Project is developing guidelines explaining how to write a module so that it is more reusable and is attempting to extend the concept of behavioral descriptions to lifecycle objects other than design and code. It is working with the staff to ensure they understand and are applying the methodology.

Finally, the Measurement Project is very early in its development, but has developed several preliminary reuse models that it is now attempting to refine and validate.

If the reuse program is successful, extensive systematic reuse should be possible within the Consortium by the end of 1988, and be supported by the Consortium's first product release to its customers.

9. Acknowledgements

The authors gratefully acknowledge the careful review and contributions by Tom Durek, Rick Lutowski, Bill Riddle, Terry Tyler, and David Weiss.

10. References

[Barnes-et al 87] B. Barnes, T. Durek, J. Gaffney, and A. Pyster, *A Framework and Economic Foundation for Software Reuse*, SPC-TN-87-011, Software Productivity Consortium, Reston, June 1987.

[Boehm, et al 84] B.W. Boehm, M. Penedo, A. Pyster, E.D. Stuckle, R.D. Williams, "An environment for improving software productivity", *Computer*, June 1984.

[Booch 87] G. Booch, *Software Components with Ada*, Benjamin Cummings, Menlo Park, 1987.

[Brooks 87] F.P. Brooks, "No silver bullet", *Computer*, April 1987.

[Clements 82] P. Clements, *Interface Specification for the A-7E Shared Services Module*, NRL Report 4863, September 1982.

[EVB 87] EVB Software Engineering, Inc. *Grace Notes*, 1987.

[Kang and Levy 85] K.C. Kang and L.S. Levy, "Software Reuse: What's Behind the Buzzword," AT&T Bell Laboratories, Warren NJ, pp. 20, 1985.

[McNicholl 86] D.G. McNicholl, *Common Ada Missle Packages (CAMP)*, AFATL-TR-85-93, McDonnell Douglas Astronautics Co., May, 1986.

[Parnas 76] D. Parnas, "On the design and development of program families," *IEEE Trans. on SE*, 2, 1, March 1986.

[Parnas-Clements 86] D. Parnas and P. Clements, "A rational design process: how and why to fake it," *IEEE Trans. on SE*, 12, 2, February 1986.

[Parnas-et al 83] D. Parnas, P. Clements, and D. Weiss, "Enhancing reusability with information hiding," *Workshop on Reusability in Programming*, September 1983.

[PPI 87] Productivity Products International. *Hope with objects*, presentation at the National Conference on Software Productivity, sponsored by the DPMA Education Foundation, 1987.

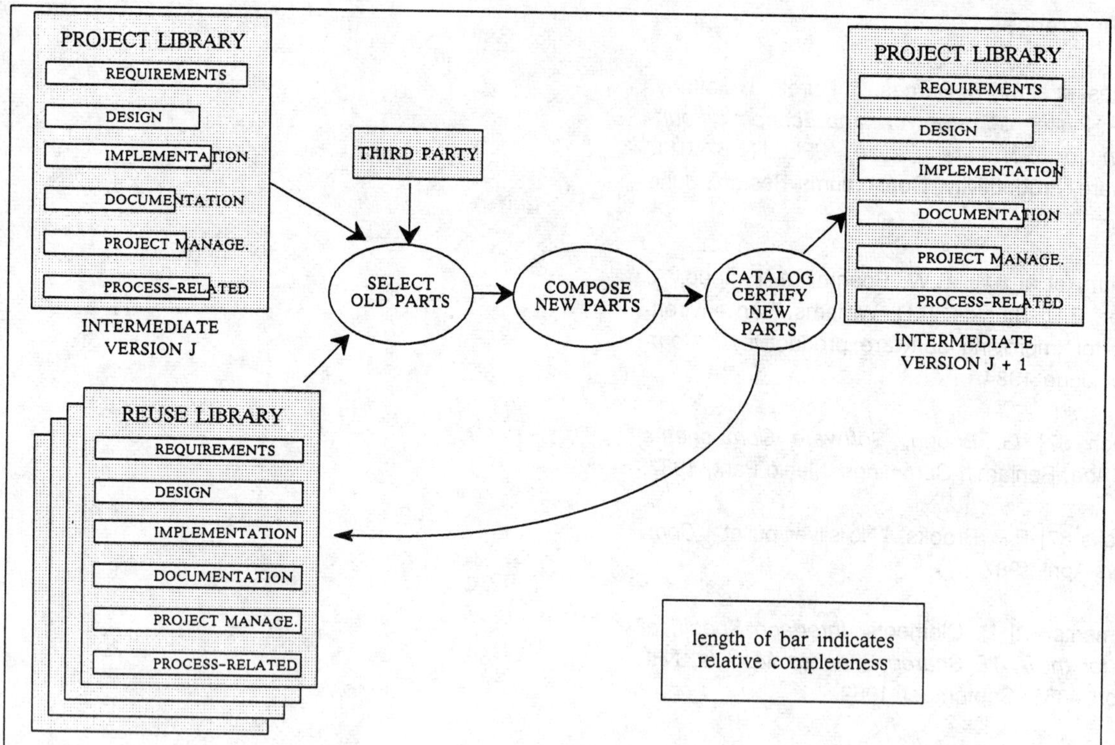

Figure 1. Software System Evolution With Reuse

The Use of Integrated Project Support Environments, IPSE, for Large-Scale Software Development

Chair: R. Banin

Market Impact of Integrated Software Development Environments

Andrew S. Rappaport and Victoria L. Hinder

The Technology Research Group, Inc.

Abstract

Integrated software development environments offer software development tool and process integration, two functions critical to address spiraling software complexity demands. Tool integration offers the ability to integrate leading-edge technology from different sources into sophisticated development systems. Process integration offers overall productivity gains, through automation of project management, documentation, and communication. The potential U.S. market for frameworks for creating integrated environments, excluding specific design tools, is estimated to be $233 million cummulative over the next three years. Software development automation tool suppliers must develop and adhere to a small number of standard environment specifications to ensure success for their own products, as well as the CASE merchant market overall.

Introduction

Integrated project support environments for software development perform two related functions: They provide data connectivity among discrete tools oriented toward individual development tasks and furnish a framework for support of project management and documentation. Both of these functions are increasingly critical to the development process as growing software complexity forces changes in development methodologies and extensions to development systems. By contributing to the structure and manageability of development systems, integrating environments do more than directly benefit program developers. They contribute to the development of advanced CASE tools and a vigorous software-development automation industry by adding to the usefulness of individual tools developed outside of the context of a fully integrated development system.

Tool integration

The integration of an array of disparate tools supplied by multiple vendors is becoming increasingly important to the majority of software developers worldwide. As code complexity increases, development methodologies are changing to allow more emphasis in analysis and design phases and less in coding and debugging. This results in demand for new front-end design tools able to feed such conventional back-end tools as compilers and debuggers. In most cases, developers seek new tools able to link directly to tools already in place.

In a recent survey of 1600 software developers and development managers in the United States, conducted by The Technology Research Group, Inc., and L.F. Rothschild and Co., only 23% of respondents reported general satisfaction with the development tools they currently have in place[1]. More than 60% are actively seeking new tools.

These same respondents indicate that compatibility with the hardware and software tools they now own are the most important criteria when selecting new tools. Roughly 80% of respondents cite hardware compatibility and 60% cite software compatibility as playing a big role in the selection of new tools (figure 1). Investments in hardware, software and training make abandoning present development systems impractical.

Although hardware and software compatibility is vital, the majority of developers are not interested in purchasing tools from a single source. They perceive leading-edge technology to be furnished by a number of specialized tools start-ups, not the few established companies offering complete software, or hardware/software solutions. Over 60% of respondents expect the bulk of tools acquired over the next two years to come from specialized software-development tool suppliers (figure 2). By comparison, only 20% of respondents cite the availability of a complete tool suite from one vendor, and the availability of hardware and software as a complete system to be important criteria for tool selection.

Developers' desire to add new tools from several suppliers to existing systems is itself not a clear-cut case for the importance of integrating environments, but the structure developers hope to achieve in their systems is. More than 45% of respondents to the Technology Research Group/L.F. Rothschild survey cite common user interface and common database as important factors in the selection of tools. The only means for developers to achieve tool connectivity, aside from purchasing all of their tools from a single source, is to purchase only those tools that work within a consistent environment. Such environments, and tools designed to work within them have much greater commercial appeal than tools designed to stand alone.

Software tools are not the only source of disparity in the software development systems--development hardware is another. Respondents indicate that software

CH2539-5/88/0000/0250$01.00 © 1988 IEEE

development systems are distributed across an array of hardware platforms including centralized mainframes and superminis, and desk-top personal computers and supermicros. Not all developers use all types of platforms, but the large majority use more than one type. Developers using multiple platform types benefit from systems capable of distributing tasks across hardware types.

Desktop resources need to offer access to centralized resources in order to offer maximum integration, both in terms of data connectivity, and in terms of accessing all tools from one interface. Integration mandates platform connectivity, increasingly so as developers purchase new single-user platforms while continuing to use their older multi-user developemnt platforms.

Developers demands for integrated tool structures stem from the dual desires to preserve existing investments in hardware and software and to ensure access to the most effective tools for individual development tasks, regardless of evolving methodologies and automation technology. Developers are not only concerned about their ability to purchase and integrate new merchant-market tools as they become available, but also seek to develop and integrate new tools themselves. More than 30% of respondents develop tools internally, a percentage expected to decrease only slightly over the next few years, despite the emergence of greatly improved and more numerous commercial tools. For these developers, compatibility of new tools with internally developed ones is also a key requirement.

Process integration

The second key aspect of integrating environments, the integration of discrete tools into a system capable of supporting a product development process, seems subtler than promoting tool connectivity but is actually much more important. Software development automation, like other forms of design automation, has evolved from a set of discrete tools, each oriented to a single task or narrow range of related tasks. But software development is a large collection of tasks as dissimilar as code generation and project management. Merely connecting tools targeted to different *tasks* does not directly create a system geared toward the automation of an entire *process*. Automating the development process requires the integration of tools in a framework that keeps track of the flow of data and project status as projects progress.

The process-creation aspects of environments are critical at the end-user level as well as at the team level. Few developers spend the majority of their time on a single task. Most divide their time among a range of tasks, each requiring different tools, and almost all spend a considerable amount of time on management and documentation. Structures that make the transition from tool to tool easier and faster and that automate documentation and project management can result in significant productivity improvements at the individual contributor level.

Respondents to the Technology Research Group/L.F. Rothschild survey report that the software professional spends only 30% to 40% of the day on tasks directly related to his or her principal responsibility. For example, programmer/analysts report that they typically spend 20% of their time actually coding; systems analysts spend an average of 38% of their time on analysis (figure 3). The rest of the day is roughly evenly divided between other development tasks and management overhead. According to the study, the typical software work-group member spends about 25% of his or her time on project management and communicating with co-workers and about 8% on project documentation. Assuming that loaded labor costs are distributed evenly across the development process, these figures suggest that roughly one third of a project's development costs is represented by management overhead, making it the single largest cost contributor. As reported elsewhere in the study, coding and maintenance are next largest, at roughly 24% each for an average software development work group.

Assuming that an integrated environment that includes integral project management, communication, and documentation tools cuts each individuals typical management burden by half, a net work-group-wide productivity gain of 15% or more is feasible without the addition of any new tools. This productivity improvement is greater than the improvement afforded by almost any single task-oriented tool as it affects the entire work group.

Large potential market

The penetration of structured development systems will ultimately be evenly distributed among developers of all types of software, but they will be adopted first among developers of military/aerospace code. Not only are these developers under pressure to conform to increasingly rigid and comprehensive documentation standards, but they are also the developers of the most complex software systems. Military/aerospace developers write the longest programs with the fastest rate of increase in program complexity. Programs in this sector now average more than 36,000 lines and are expected to grow to more than 67,000 lines, on average, over then next two years. Developers of other industrial software and scientific/engineering applications are next most likely to adopt integrating environments, as their programs are next longest and growing nearly as rapidly. In contrast, typical MIS applications are now only 8000 lines long and are not expected to grow appreciably over the next two years. The MIS segment, although very large compared to other groups, will be the late adopters of most CASE tools.

Assuming that, over the next three years, third-party integrating frameworks appeal to the most sophisticated 15% of software professionals, the potential U.S. market includes roughly 110,000 professionals. Given an average work-group size of 20 professionals among this group, the potential unit market for these frameworks equals about 5500 systems. If each work group devotes 10% of its tools budget to frameworks over the three-year period, that represents a potential cumulative U.S. market of $233 million, or $42,000 per unit.

Frameworks able to create useful, usable systems from collections of disparate tools are crucial to delivering systems required by the most advanced software developers. But promulgating such frameworks throughout the software-development community requires a concentrated effort towards standardization. It is as infeasible for suppliers of tools to support many competing environmental standards as it is to support none. In many ways, the growth and health of the CASE industry--and the software industry itself--depends on the emergence of a small number of widely adopted environment specifications, supported by viable commercial frameworks. CASE developers that fail to base their tools around the most popular such frameworks risk not only missing the mark with customers seeking to assemble their own systems optimized for their requirements, but also limit their own options for incorporation of new tools from other vendors into their product offerings.

Hardware suppliers must also play their part in developing integrated environments. Adequate compatibility among operating systems, and communications among different platforms are necessary to offer the seamless environment sought by software developers.

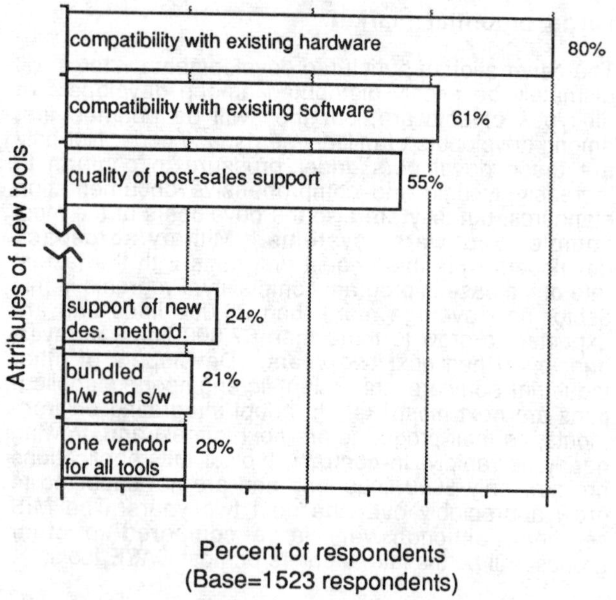

Figure 1: Factors ranked as having a big impact on purchases of new CASE tools

Long-term, the CASE industry will compete not on the basis of the framework environments themselves--a few standards will emerge preempting that competition. Instead, they will compete on the basis of the quality of task-oriented tools developed for those frameworks and project management and documentation tools that take advantage of them. Initially however, the incorporation into tool sets of open, structured integrating frameworks will differentiate vendors with like task-oriented tools. Companies with a process solution embracing the best individual tools--their own and other--will leverage their market position, and maximize their opportunity to become one of the standards.

References

1. *Software Development Automation--1987*, The Technology Research Group, Inc., Boston, MA 1987.

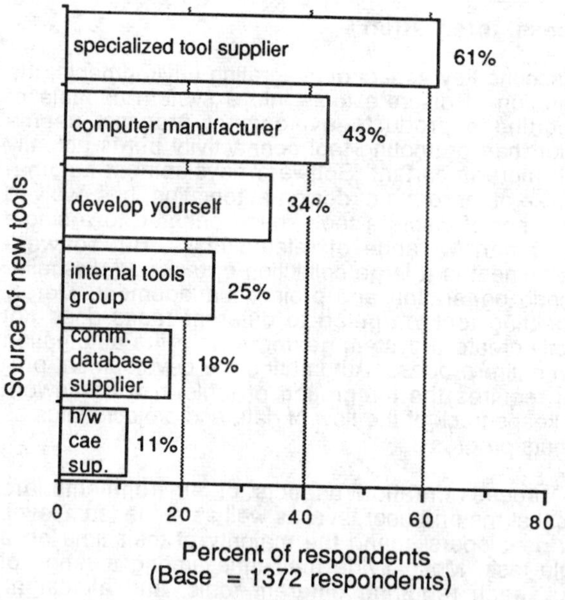

Figure 2: Anticipated sources of new CASE tools, 1987 through 1989

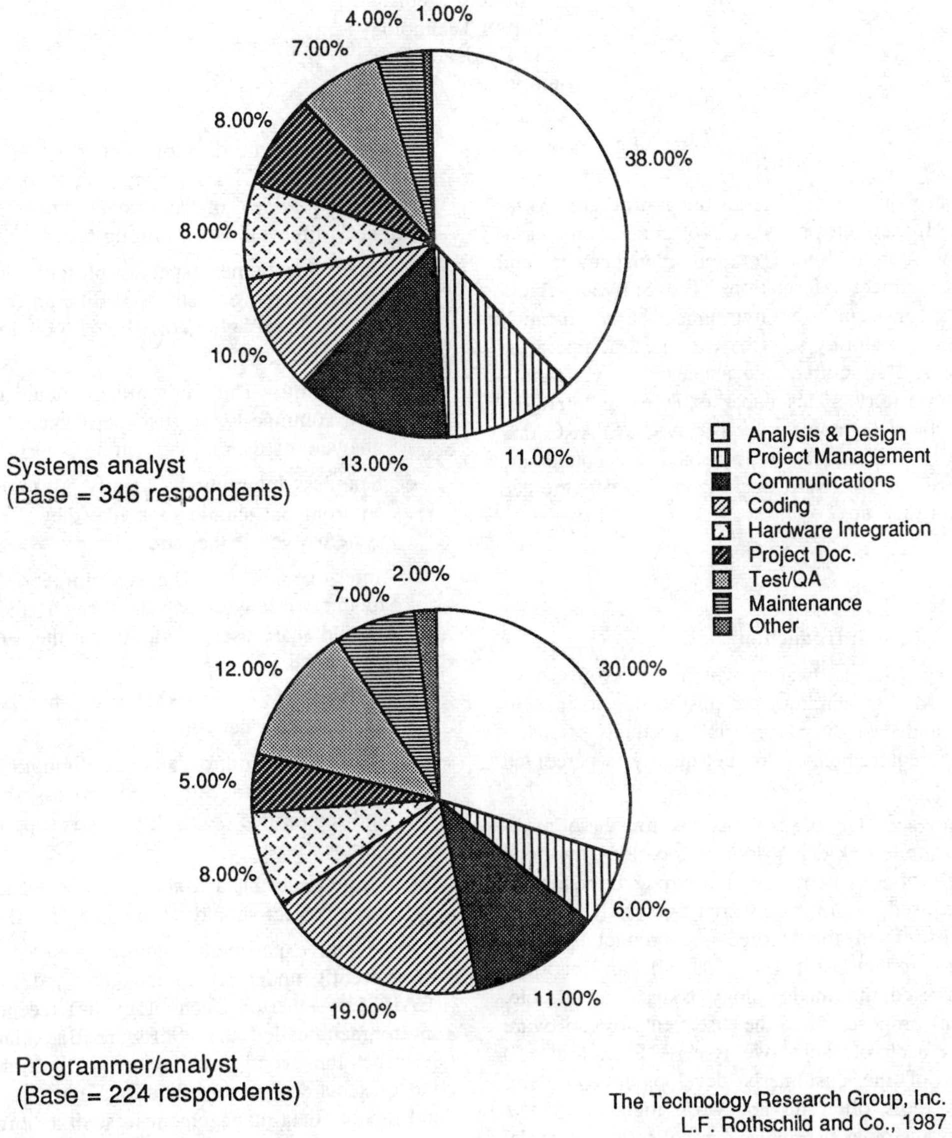

Figure 3: Percent of time spent on software development and maintenance tasks

Architecture of an Integration and Portability Platform

William Paseman
Atherton Technology
1333 Bordeaux Drive
Sunnyvale CA. 94089

Abstract

The Software BackPlane™ is an Integration and Portability Platform. It facilitates software tool integration, portability, workflow control, configuration management and shared access to project information. The Software BackPlane provides a consistent user environment based on the X Window standard, portability services via a generic operating system interface and structured data management via a multilayered data repository. This paper explores architectural alternatives for the data repository. The ANSI/SPARC taxonomy is used to characterize the external, conceptual and internal model of the Software BackPlane's object oriented data management facilities.

Introduction

It is no secret that software development efforts have their problems. Market windows are missed due to inaccurate scheduling and cost overruns. Final products often do not comply with requirements. Product quality is perceived as low.

There is no shortage of explanations for these problems: the edit-compile-link-debug loop is too slow, the code isn't documented, code isn't reused, the wrong implementation language is used, requirements aren't correctly defined, requirements are defined and ignored, the product is tested incorrectly, the product isn't tested at all, an incorrect methodology is used, no methodology is used at all, etc. Current wisdom proposes that the user employ software tools to address each of the above issues. Such tools do relieve portions of the customer's development problem. However, these tools often do not work together. As a result, when the customer assembles his collection of tools, he must integrate the tools together himself. Unfortunately, since each tool uses a different, incompatible data format, the user cannot query the assemblage as a whole. For example, the user cannot ask: "What requirement hasn't the code met yet?", since no single tool is aware of both the requirement tool's data representation and the code development tool's data representation. Worse yet, the user may have to enter the same data twice into two separate tools. For example, he may keep a list of bug fixes for release 4.03.01 both in each module he fixed, and in the final product release note. Worst of all, this duplicated data may become inconsistent, much to the development manager's chagrin and the customer's fury. Clearly, managing a consistent, useful (i.e. "queryable") view of all development data across the customer's lifecycle is a daunting task.

Enter now a new species of tool: the "environment". What does an environment do? Like an operating system, it provides the basic "glue" that holds tools together. Ideally, it should provide:

- Portability - The environment should treat the hardware as a commodity, so that, performance aside, the user is unaware of which platform he is on.
- Seamless Integration - Ideally, all tools operating in the environment should look like they are part of the same system, even if they are third party tools.
- Inter-operability - The environment should allow tools to interwork with one another. At the very least, tools should share user input, so that the user need enter data only once.
- Universality - Tools should be able to transparently use data across a network.
- Workflow Control and Configuration Management - The software development process should be modeled and controlled explicitly, and support organizational policies.
- Large Scale Data Management - All the data used in a large project should be handled effectively.

Several experimental environment development efforts are currently underway in the U.S. and Europe [PCTE86], [CAIS85]. Atherton Technology has recently introduced an environment called the "Software BackPlane". This paper describes the overall architecture of the Software BackPlane and presents design considerations and tradeoffs for efficient and flexible data management in such an environment.

Software BackPlane Overview

Atherton's Software BackPlane (Figure I) is functionally divided into three main sections. The section most visible to the user is the User Interface (UI) section, which provides a consistent user environment. Underlying the entire architecture is the Generic Operating System (GOS), which provides environment and tool portability across industry standard platforms. The final section is the data repository which has three goals: to structure tool data and make it a public resource, to allow concurrent read/write access to the same data by several tools, and to allow transparent access to data distributed across a network.

All these sections share several common characteristics. Each provides functionality that is complete enough to support necessary tools. Whenever possible, each is based on existing, implemented, standards. This promotes wider acceptance. Each complements existing native functionality. Therefore, the user can use the platform's native capability (e.g. the native operating system or window system) without interference. Each possesses an object oriented flavor. In the case of GOS and UI, this is reflected simply in the interface naming syntax, which is structured as an object/action pair (e.g. process_delete). As will be described later, the data repository uses the object oriented paradigm to greater effect. Each section is accessible via a set of public procedure interfaces. Both the UI and the data repository have a built in user extension capability. Each section was evolved internally through several releases before being presented publicly. Finally, the GOS and UI sections provide performance comparable to the native platform's OS services.

The Generic Operating System (GOS) interfaces to an unmodified version of the native OS. The entire Software BackPlane is supported on VAX VMS™ and Sun UNIX™ via this GOS layer.

The User Interface (UI) is based on version 10.4 of X Window. It will migrate to version 11 of X Window when that becomes available. It provides an extensible "toolkit" approach to user interface construction. This approach allows the user to construct user visible objects, such as dialogue boxes, from smaller, more primitive user visible objects, such as buttons and scroll panes. UI works compatibly with both UIS on VAX/VMS and SunTools™ on Sun/UNIX.

The data repository provides general query capability, data integration, data integrity, data and query consistency and schema extensibility.

The data repository will now be described in more detail.

Data Repository Alternatives - File Systems

File Systems are the traditional repositories of software development data. They are useful data stores. They store data persistently (i.e. the data remains after the power is off). They allow data to be accessed by name. They support an explicit structuring mechanism (directories). However, file systems have a number of limitations.

Files are coarse grained or "heavy". This means that there is a large space overhead for each data item stored as a file, and that there is a large time overhead to open, read and close a file. Often, there is no direct user control over where data is stored. This sometimes results in inefficient disk access.

Files have no semantic content. They don't restrict the type of data they can contain, so they can store anything. On the other hand, they can't do type enforcement and can't support type specific queries. This forces the user to do file typing by convention (often using file name suffixes).

File systems have no knowledge of file contents. If you wish to ask "which files #include(stdio.h)", you must use an application that searches the file system. In addition, since you are likely to have several versions of stdio.h floating around, you might like to know which version was included by what files in which system release. Unfortunately, that knowledge is determined by the preprocessor that compiled the file, and the preprocessor information is thrown away at the end of the compile. So you may never know the real answer to the question "which files #include(stdio.h)".

File systems have an inconvenient multiuser sharing model. They range from the UNIX approach, where two users can simultaneously access a file and overwrite portions of each other's work, to an exclusive locking approach, where two users must serialize their file accesses. Neither approach is meant to support "long transactions", transactions which may last for weeks at a time.

Data Repository Alternatives - Databases

Databases provide four basic services [BERN87]: storage management, type management, associative access and transaction management.

The storage management service allocates secondary storage transparently to the user. Instead of viewing data as consisting of two major types, file based and memory based, storage managers provide a model that allows the developer to dismiss the distinction between the two. The manager also provides operations to cheaply retrieve and update small objects (e.g. "get" and "set" as opposed to "open/read/close" or "open/write/close"). In other words, the storage manager is fine grained, or "light". The storage manager also buffers popular objects in main memory.

The type management service allows the user to define new data types, much as he would in C, Pascal or Ada. As the database accesses each object, the type manager interprets objects relative to their types, permitting, for example, concatenation operations on objects of type "string", and forbidding the same operations on objects of type "float". This "type checking" helps ensure that objects are consistent, and meet their type definition.

Associative access services support value based retrieval of objects. This means that the database can search for all "person" objects where the "hair" field is "blond" and the "eyes" field is "blue". Storage systems (as opposed to databases) cannot do this because they have no "data dictionary". Data Dictionaries are where databases record the fine (record) structure of the objects they store. The associative access services often maintain tables (called indices) to speed up retrieval of objects that are frequently accessed. Finally, the associative access services may provide high level associative operators to aid in querying the database. Examples of these operators are select, project and join.

Transaction management services provide serializable concurrency control and fault tolerance [GRAY81]. Fault tolerance is usually implemented using shadowing or logging.

All these advantages led Atherton to implement the data repository using a database approach.

Generic Database Taxonomy

The ANSI/SPARC standard decomposes databases into three layers (Figure II).

The outer layer is called the External Model Layer. This layer defines the user view of the data; the objects he perceives and uses in his day to day work. The "objects" that software developers encounter day to day include: Shells (or Sessions), Files, Directories, Action Requests, Tools, Users, Mail, Software Releases and Executables.

The middle layer is called the Conceptual Model Layer. This layer defines the logical primitives that the user uses to create the external view. In a relational database, the conceptual model is based on tables which have columns and rows. For example, in a relational database, a "user" (again, "user" is an external model concept) may be modeled as a table, which has a primary key (column) called "name", and and other columns called "social security number" and "project". In an object oriented database, the conceptual model is based on a type hierarchy which classifies objects and their associated variables and methods. The conceptual model layer is where the Software BackPlane implements its type manager and associative access service. We will discuss the object oriented conceptual model in more detail later.

The lowest layer is called the Internal Model Layer. This layer concerns itself with the physical storage of the data. In a relational database, this layer is usually optimized for sequential access of fixed width tabular records. In an object-oriented database, the internal model is generally optimized for random access of variable sized data. The internal model layer is where the Software BackPlane implements its storage and transaction manager. We will discuss our internal model in more detail later.

The Software BackPlane External Model

The primary objects that the user encounters day to day are "shells/sessions", "files" and "directories". These user concepts are modeled and extended using Software BackPlane Services. Since we alter the semantics of each of these objects, we've defined analogs for each object in the Software BackPlane environment. The analog of "shell/session" is "context". The analog of "file" is "version". The analog of "directory" is "collection".

Shells/Sessions provide a command interface into the system. Shells are single threaded. Only one user (keyboard) at a time can enter input into it. Shells contain variables, such as the "current directory" the user is working in, and a "history" of user interaction.

Contexts provide these capabilities and more. Contexts are persistent. Contexts track the versions of all tools they invoke via a "toolset". Contexts help provide a non-interfering view of the multiuser database. They support the "long transaction" concept alluded to earlier.

Files provide persistent data storage. In addition, they provide a model of multiuser access.

Versions also provide persistent data storage, but add a checkpointing capability, so that the user can rollback to a prior version state. More importantly, versions provide an extended multiuser access model. This model provides parallel access without interference. Let's briefly illustrate this in terms of a protocol chart (Table I).

UNIX has a very simple sharing protocol; the user can access data at any time. This protocol provides parallel access at the expense of consistency (i.e. the user can always access the data, but the data might get accidentally overwritten).

VMS allows a user to lock a resource, then write it, and finally release it. This protocol ensures consistency at the expense of serializing access (i.e. the data is always guaranteed to be consistent, but the user may not always be able to access it).

The Software BackPlane allows the user to first "check out" the version (which produces a private, writable, *copy* of the data), then write the private copy, and finally "check in" the private copy (which makes the copy both public and read only). Multiple people can access the same data in parallel, but eventually, the "copies" (or "branches") must be merged. This protocol guarantees parallel access and consistency, at the expense of an extra operation. Table II summarizes the characteristics of the approaches.

Directories provide hierarchical structuring (via a "parent-child" relationship) which helps a single user organize his work. Directories also serve to partition work on multi-user projects. They are persistent and have the same sharing model as files.

Collections provide the same organization and persistence characteristics as directories. However, they also have the same sharing model and checkpointing capability as Versions. This checkpointing capability is important, since system structure is typically stored in the Collections.

Figure III shows an example configuration of Contexts, Collections and Versions.

The Software BackPlane Conceptual Model

The conceptual layer allows the user to formally define the "user visible" objects described at the external layer. The Software BackPlane does this by allowing the user to define an "Ada-like" package interface for each "type" of object described above [ADA84]. Each object type is defined in terms of the:

- "messages" it responds to (procedure interfaces that can be called)
- "methods" that process the messages (procedure bodies) and the
- "instance variables" it has (persistent, externally visible variables).

Variable types include binary relations. This type is not usually present in object oriented systems. It enhances the query capability of the database considerably.

Messages and instance variables for the types described in the Software BackPlane external model are listed in Table III.

Notice that Versions and Collections share a number of properties and messages. In fact, Collections are identical to

Versions in behavior except that Collections have "children" plus a way of attaching and detaching them. The Software BackPlane allows objects to share behavior through a "type hierarchy" [SMAL83]. The type hierarchy allows the the user to structure types by factoring out common messages and instance variables. Let's represent the contents of Table III using a type hierarchy.

Root_Object		(Type)
		[subtype_of]
	Context	(History,Current_Directory,Toolset)
		[change,invoke]
	Version	(Owner, Parent)
		[checkout, checkin, status]
	Collection	(Children)
		[attach,detach]

The Root_Object is at the hierarchy's root. It has one instance variable called "Type". "Type" indicates the object type. Root_Object has one message defined on it: "subtype_of". This message lets the caller establish the parent child relationships that exist in the type hierarchy.

Contexts have all the variables and messages defined in the Formal User Model Specification. In addition, Contexts inherit the interface definition of the Root_object. This means that Contexts also have the variable: "Type", and also respond to the "subtype_of" message.

Similarly, Versions inherit all the Root_object's messages and variables. Collections inherit all of Version's messages and variables, as well as the Root_Object's.

Each type must implement a piece of code to respond to the message sent. This piece of code is called the "method". A type has three alternative "method" implementation approaches: it may pass the message directly to its supertype, it may implement the method totally itself, or it may do some local processing and have the supertype do some more. This approach provides good extensibility.

Suppose now that we wish to integrate a Dataflow Diagramming tool. We could do this by defining the following type:

Dataflow_Diagram	*(Process_scan, Flow_scan, Store_scan)*
	[open]

and placing it under Version in the type hierarchy. This allows all Dataflow_Diagrams to inherit Version's capabilities, and to provide other types with a well defined interface to Dataflow_Diagram's internal data. This interface allows another type to search a particular Process_scan for a particular process, for example.

The Software Backplane Internal Model

The internal model concerns itself with the physical storage of the objects. Objects are identified via a unique ID. They are variable sized and can be "clustered" together by the application that creates them. This clustering ensures a cache hit when a group of related objects are brought into memory. Objects have a space overhead of 6 bytes. They can be fetched at speeds in the order of tens of microseconds when a cache hit occurs.

Summary

The dramatic increase in size and complexity of software projects has created a growing gap between the needs of software developers and the capabilities offered by individual software tools and present day operating systems. Major aspects of the software development process which are not adequately supported include:

- Tool integration and portability
- Work flow control and configuration management
- Multithreaded access to shared project information

Our experience with the Software Backplane indicates that the integrated environment approach to the software development problem is the most promising solution to date. Furthermore, object-oriented database technology provides an optimal engineering solution to the data management requirements of such environments.

Bibliography

[ADA84] U.S. D.O.D., "*Reference Manual for the Ada Programming Language*", ANSI/MIL-STD-1815A-1983, Springer-Verlag, (1984).

[BERN87] Bernstein, P., "*Database System Support for Software Engineering, --An Extended Abstract--*", 9th International Conference on Software Engineering, Monterey, Ca., (March 30, 1987), 166-178.

[CAIS85] Ada Joint Program Office, "*Military Standard Common Apse Interface Set (CAIS)*", AD-A157 589, National Technical Information Service, (Jan 85).

[GRAY81] Gray, Jim, "*The Transaction Concept: Virtues and Limitations*", Tandem Computers, Cupertino Ca., (April 1981).

[PCTE86] Esprit, "*PCTE, A Basis for a Portable Common Tool Environment- Functional Specifications*", Fourth Edition, Commission of the European Communities, Brussels, (1986).

[SMAL83] Goldberg, et.al., "*Smalltalk-80, The Language and its Implementation*", Addison-Wesley, (1983).

Table I - Protocol Comparison of Multiuser Sharing Models			
Update Protocol	UNIX Operation	VMS Operation	BackPlane Operation
Reserve	n/a	Get Lock	Check Out
Update	Write	Write	Write
Release	n/a	Release Lock	Check In
Merge	n/a	n/a	Merge

Table II - Characteristics of Multiuser Sharing Models			
	UNIX	VMS	BackPlane
Access Approach	Parallel	Serial	Parallel
Shared Data Consistency	Not Assured	Assured via Serialization	Assured via Merge

Table III - Formal User Model Specification		
Type	(Type Variables)	[Type Messages]
Context	(History,Current_Directory,Toolset)	[change,invoke]
Version	(Owner,Parent)	[checkout,checkin,status]
Collection	(Owner,Parent,Children)	[checkout,checkin,status,attach,detach]

Software Backplane Architecture

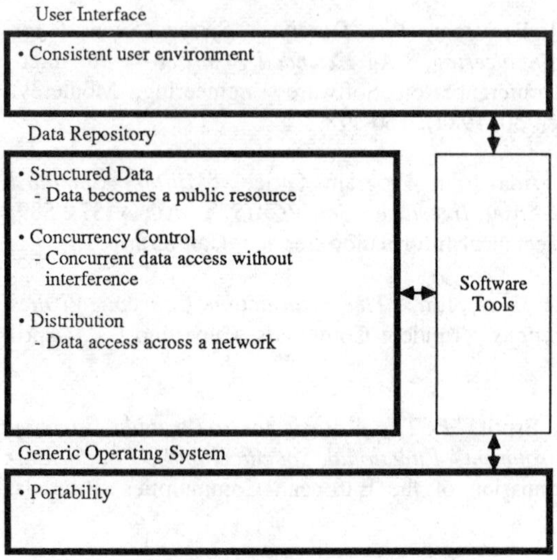

Figure I

Generic Database Taxonomy

ANSI/SPARC Definition	Relational Approach	Object Oriented Approach
External Model - User View	Shell, File, Directory, Action Request, Tool, User, Mail, Release, Executable	
Conceptual Model - Logical Primitives	Table, Row, Column	Type Hierarchy, Object, Instance Variable, Message, Method
Internal Model - Physical Organization	Sequential, Fixed Size Records	Random Accessed, Variable Size Records

Figure II

External Model Example

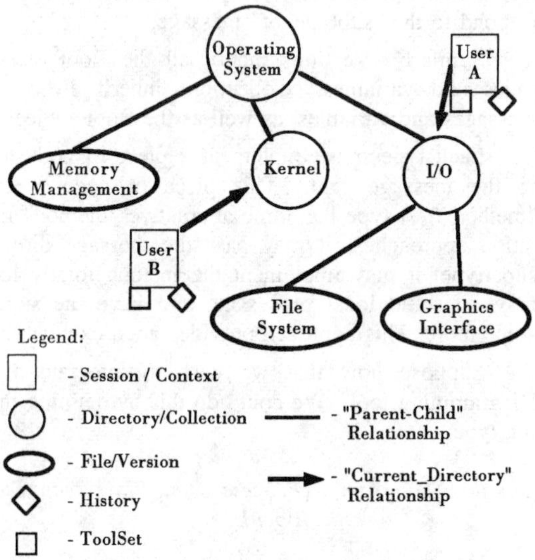

Figure III

TRENDS IN SOFTWARE DEVELOPMENT ENVIRONMENTS FOR LARGE SOFTWARE SYSTEMS

Robert J. Ellison

Software Engineering Institute
Carnegie Mellon University
Pittsburgh, PA 15213-3890

Abstract

Software development environments have evolved considerably over the last twenty years. In particular, there are an increasing number of commercially available environments designed to manage large software development efforts. This paper discusses some trends in such environments with an emphasis on support for management of the development process.

1. Introduction

Over the last three years, the Software Engineering Institute has evaluated a number of software development environments, concentrating on their support for programming [6], and has categorized the trends in environment research and development [2]. In the development of very large systems, project management plays a dominant role, and the earlier SEI work on a method for environment evaluation [5] has been extended to deal with project management issues [4]. This note presents a number of observations derived from the above work as it applies to environments intended for the management of large software projects.

The taxonomy defined in [2] specifies technology trends and defines the following categories:

1. *Language-Centered* environments are built around one language, thereby providing a tool set suited to that language. These environments are highly interactive, with limited support for programming-in-the-large.
2. *Structure-Oriented* environments incorporate techniques that allow the user to manipulate structures directly. The language-independence of the techniques led to the notion of generators for environments.
3. *Toolkit* environments provide a collection of tools which include language-independent support for programming-in-the-large tasks such as configuration management and version control. There is little, if any, environment-defined control and management of tool usage.
4. *Method-Based* environments incorporate support for a broad range of activities in the software development process, including programming-in-the-many issues such as team and project management. These environments also incorporate tools for particular specification and design methods.

The recent activity for large-scale development environments has been in the language-centered and method-based environments. The work in language-centered environments has been concentrated on environments for Ada. The method-based category includes CASE (Computer Assisted Software Engineering) tool sets as well as environments such as GENOS from GEC and ISTAR from Imperial Software Technology that concentrate more on management of the full software process.

2. Management Support

While discussions of environment for large-scale development often concentrate on issues of scale, data management, and full life-cycle coverage, a view of environment work from the perspective of the management of the development activity raises a number of important issues that should be addressed. For this paper, we take a broad view of the role of project management. Management support as provided by the environment can include:

- management of resources - project planning and control
- management of the product - version control, configuration management, and system modeling
- management of the process - task management and change request procedures
- management of the environment - introduction or replacement of tools, change in project policies, and migration to new hardware

CH2539-5/88/0000/0259$01.00 © 1988 IEEE

The above categories give a view of the current state of software support environments. Management of resources is reasonably well supported by a number of tools, although those tools are not necessarily well integrated into the actual development process. Product management is relatively mature, and there is considerable commercial activity with respect to configuration management. Process management has received considerable attention as of late, and there is support from some commercial systems such as ISTAR [3]. Finally, support for the management of the environment is a new requirement that arises from the need to tailor an environment for a specific product or development process.

The general requirements listed in the above categories are not necessarily conflicting. Most large-scale development environments are in the early stages of development, and the implementations have often been optimized for a specific kind of management support. The early state of environment management support tends to magnify the differences in approaches.

One current difference in management support is exemplified by a comparison of a language-centered environment such as the Rational Ada environment and a process-oriented design such as ISTAR. Historically, the language-centered environments have stressed product rather than process management. They started with basic language support and extended that to provide support for larger scale software development. The language-centered environments are typically strong on object management. They primarily deal with language defined objects such as functions, modules, or packages, or extensions to those concepts, such as the subsystems as defined by Rational [1], which are used to manage versions and configurations better. These objects have well defined static semantics. Project management in such environments can often be done in terms of access control to the product components and in terms of version control and configuration management. The more recent process-oriented environments have started with activity management and concentrate on *how* a task should be described or monitored. ISTAR, for example, has defined primitives such as the *contract* to support task management. A contract might consist of a description of the task to be completed, an appropriate schedule or set of milestones, as well as a set of criteria to be met when that task is completed. The contract primitive also provides the means to describe a large project in terms of nested contracts. An ISTAR environment may be organized in terms of workbenches that correspond to a major activity such as design or coding.

3. Implications on Environment Design

The language-centered and method-based environments currently have very different architectures and significant differences in critical areas such as data management. It is not the case that one approach is necessarily better than the other, but that they optimize different aspects of environment support. The language-centered environments have taken what might be considered a *bottom-up* approach. Such environments start with a good set of tools for one specific development activity, coding, and extend it to support project management and detailed design. The underlying data management may be optimized for representing language semantic information as well as versioning or configuration support. The process-driven systems might be described as taking a more *top-down* approach to environment design. In an ISTAR environment, each contract has an associated database. The data organization reflects more how the system was managed rather than the organization of final system.

The support for process and product management also influences some other requirements for environments such as *tailorability* of the environment. For example, from the perspective of product management, we may want to specialize an environment for a particular kind of product such as a process control system. Tailorability in this case could mean the ability to integrate very specialized design tools, test harnesses, or run-time support systems. The environment might assist this effort by supporting common operating system interfaces to achieve tool portability or by following standards for data interchange. Tailorability in a method-based environment addresses the support of a variety of process models, such as incremental development or rapid prototyping, as well as support for organization or project specific policies for quality assurance and configuration management. The issue in this case is to manage how a tool is used. The latter is a particularly hard problem when the tools were designed to be used also in a stand alone state with few constraints. These two approaches to tool integration and management are solving two different problems, but the approaches will have to be compatible.

The issue of environment management has received relatively little attention. It will take on a more important and perhaps critical role. Compared to using a new tool such as a compiler or design aid, an environment can have a major impact on a software project. The first available environment products were similar to *turnkey* systems. Most of the tools were already integrated into the system and in many instances could not be replaced. Such an environment might replace almost every software tool used by that organization, as well as fundamentally change the methodology behind the development effort and its management. Many of the more recent commercial offerings follow a strategy that attempts to use as many of the existing project tools as possible and, over time, replace those tools or integrate them better into the environment. The same practice is applied to the process management so that the environment can support existing practice rather than imposing a new model. Thus, tailorability of the initial environment is a critical requirement, and a project will probably require a specialist to perform that task on a continuing basis. From one perspective, some of the standard practices such as configuration management are being applied to the environment and its underlying tool set, but experience with a number of environments suggests that it a very complex task.

4. Conclusion

We conclude with one prediction. The problem of change control at the level of major system releases will be a excellent testbed for resolving the current tension between product and process management. A new release for a large system can involve changes to more than 20% of the source and in itself represents a large project development effort. Most existing large-scale environments have concentrated on supporting the development of the initial version of the system. One major task in the planning of a new release is to use the internal structure of the system to design a schedule and task plans which permit as much parallel activity as possible and avoid creating deadlocks as multiple groups modify different components of the existing system. This effort requires a mix of good product and project management, in particular a way of describing dependencies between major product components.

Acknowledgments

This work is supported by the Department of Defense.

References

[1] James E. Archer, Jr. and Michael T. Devlin. Rational's Experience Using Ada for Very Large Systems. In *First International Conference on Ada Programming Language Applications for the NASA Space Station*, pages B.2.5.1-B.2.5.11. Houston, TX, June, 1986.

[2] Susan A. Dart, Robert J. Ellison, Peter H. Feiler, A. N. Habermann. Trends in Software Development Environments. *IEEE Computer* , November, 1987.

[3] M. Dowson. ISTAR - An Integrated Project Support Environment. In *2nd ACM SIGSOFT/SIGPLAN Symposium on Practical Software Development Environments*, pages 27-33. ACM, December, 1986.

[4] Peter H. Feiler and Roger Smeaton. Managing Development of Very Large Systems: Implications on Integrated Environments. In *Proceedings of International Workshop on Software Version and Configuration Control.* German Chapter ACM, GI, Siemens AG, Teubner Verlag, Grassau, W-Germany, January, 1988.

[5] N.H. Weiderman; A.N. Habermann; M. Borger; and M. Klein. A Methodology for Evaluating Environments. In *2nd ACM SIGSOFT/SIGPLAN Symposium on Practical Software Development Environments*, pages 199-207. ACM, December, 1986.

[6] N.H. Weiderman, et al. *Evaluation of Ada Environments.* Technical Report CMU/SEI-87-TR-1, Software Engineering Institute, March, 1987.

WORKSTATIONS Track

SONY NEWS Workstation

Chair: Y. Takeyari

System Design of the NEWS Workstation

Masao Hori, Ken Kurihara, Hiroyuki Kobayashi, Hiroshi Tezuka, Koichi Tanaka

Sony Corporation

Abstract

The NWS-1800 is a new series of NEWS workstations being developed at Sony. Using two Motorola MC68030 microprocessors, one for the main processor and the other for the I/O processor, it provides superlative performance in an exceptionally compact package. The MC68030 contains a data/instruction cache and an MMU (Memory Management Unit) and supports 2-cycle synchronous bus transfer and burst data transfer between the processor and the external devices. Taking full advantage of this microprocessor, therefore, the new NWS-1800 Series offers more than 5-MIPS performance. In addition, I/O processing, including displays, SCSI devices, serial I/O and the Ethernet network, are handled by the I/O processor, giving this series of workstations performance required of servers.

1. Introduction

In January 1987, Sony started to market a family of 32-bit engineering workstations called NEWS. The first to appear on the market was the NWS-800 Series, which was also the first in Japan to offer the Japanese version of UNIX 4.2BSD, NFS, and the X-Window System. This series of compact, low-cost and high-performing workstations, with the added benefit of distributed processing, is now accepted as the de facto standard for the industry. The NWS-1800 Series is the upgraded version of this NWS-800 Series built around the MC68020. Combining the remarkable features of the NWS-800 Series with the capabilities of the MC68030, it can yield dramatically improved performance.

2. Design Concept

The NWS-1800 series has been designed to realize a network environment where individuals can each work at their own machine. In line with the concepts listed below our basic policy was to move maximum use of the latest, readily available technologies.

(1) Compact Size and Low Cost

To provide each user with a workstation of his own, the machine must be made as small and inexpensive as possible. Compact size is an essential requirement for any machine to be used in Japanese offices on a one machine per person basis. Therefore, the goal has been a desktop unit with dimensions about the same as those of a home video cassette recorder. The unit price was set at less than one million yen, with consideration given to a standard system which consists of about 6 diskless workstations for individual users, plus server workstations.

(2) High Performance

In addition to compact size and low cost, high performance is an important aspect of any engineering workstation. In designing NEWS, therefore, careful attention has been paid not only to the CPU processing speed but also to the speed of the network, displays and disks, so that excellent overall performance can be achieved.

(3) Short-Term Development

To keep up with the rapid advances in hardware for timely introduction of new models, the time required for development must be made as short as possible. NEWS meets this requirement by using only those components that are most up-to-date but immediately available at the time of development.

(4) Open Architecture

General-purpose workstations must offer standard interfaces so that they can be used in a heterogeneous, easily expandable system. That's why NEWS employs an Ethernet controller, a SCSI bus for interfacing with external storage devices, and a VME bus as an additional I/O interface bus and standard software on NEWS includes Japanese-language versions of UNIX 4.2BSD, NFS and the X-Window System.

The NWS-1800 Series is in the process of development, with consideration given to the principles described above. The main processor and the I/O processor of this series are designed with the MC68030. With respect to performance, the MC68030 is inferior to the RISC chip. However, it has been adopted for the reason that it offers such desirable features as on-chip MMU and cache, burst transfer mode, and software compatibility.

Because of the use of MMU on the MC68030, the external cache can serve perfectly as a physical cache for the CPU, eliminating the need for complex processing required to maintain consistency.

CH2539-5/88/0000/0266$01.00

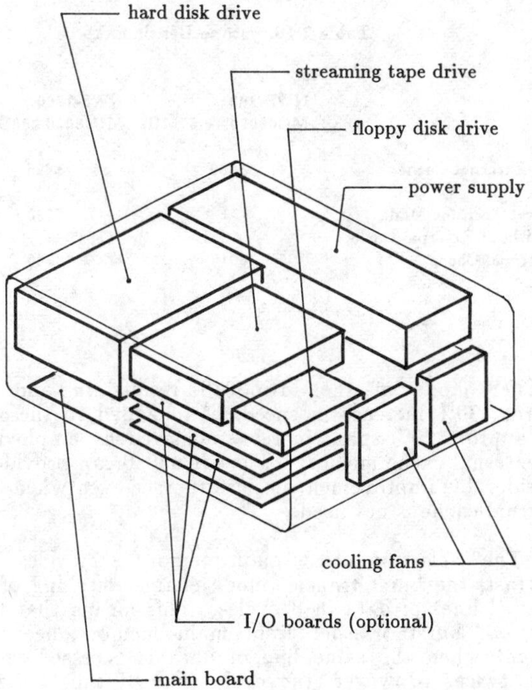

Figure 1 Internal Structure of the NWS-1800

Table 1 Specification of the NWS-1800

Main processor	MC68030 (25MHz)
I/O processor	MC68030 (25MHz)
Floating Point Co-Processor	MC68882 (25MHz)
Cache memory	
Type	direct mapping store through
Capacity	64KByte (16Byte/line x 4096line)
Data bus width	64bit (main memory to cache memory) 32bit (cache memory to processors)
Main memory	
Capacity	16MByte standard (expandable to 32MByte)
Data bus width	64bit (32bit x 2bank)
Cycle time	280ns/16byte (burst transfer) 200ns/32bit (store/bank)
Store buffer	1stage/bank
Error detection	Byte parity
Standard I/O	286MByte hard disk drive 125MByte streaming tape drive 1.44MByte 3.5" floppy disk drive Ethernet controller SCSI bus Serial port (RS232C) 2 channels Parallel port (centronics)
Display options	1280x1024x8 color bitmap display 816x1024 B/W bitmap display
Dimensions	430mm x 370mm x 145mm approx. (17" x 14.5" x 5.7")
Weights	20kg(44lbs.) approx.
Power	90-132V 300W max.

The burst transfer mode of the MC68030 enables high-speed data transfer between the main memory and the cache/CPU. System software of the current NEWS, except that for memory management, needed only a few modifications to be incorporated in the NWS-1800 Series. In addition, user software is perfectly compatible on the object level. These are the main reasons why we can bring about the compact high-performance NWS-1800 Series in such a short period of time.

3. Architecture

The internal structure and the specifications of the high-end model in the NWS-1800 Series are shown in Figure 1 and Table 1 respectively.

Compact Design

The NWS-1800 Series is about the same size as the current NWS-800 Series. It is compact enough to use on a desk. In addition to two MC68030, the main board packs a 16M-byte - 32M-byte main memory, a 64K-byte cache memory, Ethernet and SCSI controllers, Centronics and RS232C interfaces, a timer, and real-time clock. Built-in drives include a 286M-byte (formatted) hard disk drive, a 125M-byte streaming tape drive, and a 1.44M-byte (formatted) floppy disk drive. There are also three I/O slots for optional boards. Figure 2 illustrates the architecture of the NWS-1800 Series.

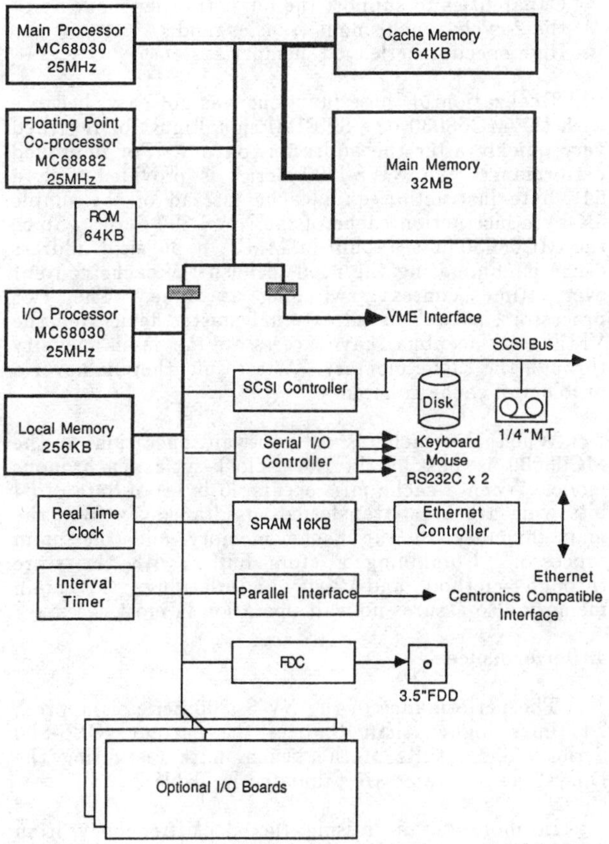

Figure 2 Architecture of the NWS-1800

Dual Processors

The NWS-1800 Series uses the 25MHz MC68030 for the main processor and the I/O processor to ensure compatibility with the I/O boards and peripheral units for the NWS-800 Series. A simple message-based multi-task monitor is running on the I/O processor with a 256K-byte static RAM. Communication between the two processors is enabled by transmitting an interrupt signal. The messages from the main processor is passed to a task on I/O processor and the response from a task on I/O processor is returned to the main processor through a part of the main memory. According to the message from the main processor, the I/O processor performs all I/O processing to take the burden off the main processor, which include complicate control of bitmap/graphic display, and high-speed data transfer between the main memory and I/O devices. Adoption of the MC68030 for the I/O processor means that sophisticated I/O control and DMA (Direct Memory Access) functions can be packed compactly into a single chip and the I/O processing speed is approx. 5 MIPS.

Cache Memory/Burst Transfer

To take advantage of the MC68030, the following had to be designed into the NWS-1800 Series.

- Higher-frequency clock
- Capabilities to support the burst transfer mode and the 2-cycle synchronous transfer mode
- High-speed, interleaved memory system

Realization of these functions was not easy, because with the MC68030, the STERM signal must be returned very quickly after the address is output. For improved performance, the NWS-1800 Series is provided with a 64K-byte instruction/data cache instead of the simple 8K-byte instruction cache of the NWS-800 Series. Since the MC68030 has a built-in MMU, a physical address cache is eliminating the need to flush the cache content every time context switching is done. The two processors, as well as all external master devices on the VME interface bus, have access to the main memory through the cache memory. As a result, there is never a problem of cache coherency.

When the cache is hit, no-wait operation of the MC68030 is possible in the 2-clock-cycle synchronous mode. When a cache miss occurs, 16 bytes of data of 64 bits wide are burst-transferred simultaneously from the main memory to the cache memory and the main processor. Combining a store buffer with the store through method and 2-way interleaving, the main memory also assures no-wait operation in most cases.

4. Performance

The performance of the NWS-1800 Series is approx. 2.1 times higher than that of the current NWS-800 Series. The results of the bench mark test using the Dhrystone programs are tabulated in Table 2.

In more detail, raising the clock frequency from 16.67MHz to 25MHz brings approx. 50% increase in speed. The increased transfer speed between the processor and the memory made possible by the burst transfer mode of the MC68030 results in another approx. 30% increase in speed. And added to these is the approx. 20% speed increase achieved by employing an external cache memory. The MC68030 can provide a considerable improvement in performance even when the external cache is not used.

Table 2 Dhrystone Benchmark

	NWS-800 MC68020 16.67MHz	NWS-1800 MC68030 25MHz
No External Cache	3800	5625
Burst Transfer Mode without External Cache	----	7250
External Cache	4010	8500

The cycle time of the main memory is 7 cycles. In contrast, the burst transfer mode enables fetching of 16 bytes (1 line) of data in 8 cycles. This means that the effect of burst transfer from main memory becomes evident when the same line of data is accessed more than twice. However, the cycle time of the external cache memory is 2 cycles, while that of the burst transfer mode is 5 cycles. Thus the actual improvement obtained by burst transfer from the external cache is 1 to 3 cycles even if the same line is accessed more than 3 times.

All this means that the most efficient way of achieving high performance is to avoid burst transfer between the processor and the external cache memory and to use it between the external cache and the main memory. When the external cache is not hit, the processor directly accesses the main memory for 4 bytes of data it needs. At the same time, the external cache is filled with 1 line of data burst-transferred from the main memory. With the NWS-1800 Series, however, burst transfer is enabled between the processor and the external cache for the reasons that the external cache is shared by both the main processor and the I/O processor and that the use of the external cache by the main processor has to be minimized.

The data transfer speed of the I/O processor is approx. 1.5 times faster than that of the processor used in the NWS-800 Series. It is approx. 3M bytes/sec when measured between the main memory and the buffer for the Ethernet network, and approx. 2M bytes/sec when measured between the main memory and the SCSI controller.

5. Conclusion

The NEWS family of Sony workstations are highly acclaimed for their compact size, low cost and superb performance. They are widely used as the standard engineering workstations in Japan. A new addition to this family of workstations, the NWS-1800 Series is built around two 25MHz MC68030 microprocessors. To get the most out of the high-performance MC68030, it also incorporates a high-speed, interleaved memory system designed with standard components.

Resultantly, the NWS-l800 Series provides approx. 5-MIPS performance, which is twice as high as that of the NWS-800 Series. Designed based on the NEWS concept for compact size and low cost, it is also small in dimensions and offers an exceptional price/performance ratio. Software for the NWS-800 Series are compatible at the object level. Moreover, the 25MHz MC68030 I/O processor can handle heavy I/O loads, making it possible for the NWS-1800 Series to operate as the server for diskless workstations in a high-performance.

Acknowledgement

The authors are grateful to Dr. Toshitada Doi, Mr. Yukio Takeyari and colleagues for their contribution on this work.

Trademarks.

UNIX is a trademark of AT&T Bell Laboratories.
NFS is a trademark of Sun Microsystems, Inc.
The X Window System is a trademark of the Massachusetts Institute of Technology.

Japanese Language Processing on the NEWS Workstation

Katsutoshi Doi, Koji Koshiba, Masaki Takeuchi

Sony Corporation

Abstract

This paper describes Japanese language processing on Sony's NEWS workstation. The NEWS workstation incorporates the Berkeley version of UNIX, Sun Microsystems Inc.'s Network File System (NFS), and the X Window System developed at Massachusetts Institute of Technology, all of which are not only used widely but also being established as the de facto standard. Described below is how Japanese language processing has been achieved with this system software.

1. Introduction

The NEWS workstation is designed to be used with system software developed originally in the USA. In order to provide the NEWS workstation with a Japanese language processing capability, the following had to be achieved:

- Japanization of the Berkeley version of UNIX
- Development of a front-end processor for Japanese language input
- Japanization of the X Window System.

2. Japanization of the Berkeley Version of UNIX

The items which had to be Japanized were:

(1) Kernel
(2) Language Processor
(3) Library
(4) Commands

In determining to what extent each of these items had to be Japanized, we considered it important to maintain the original functions of UNIX. That is, we carefully avoided making alternations that would restrict the capabilities of UNIX.

2-1 Code Set

The Japanese written language consists of two types of characters called Kanji(Chinese characters) and Kana(Indigenous Japanese syllabary) used together.
The Japanese code used on NEWS for internal processing is the Shift-JIS Kanji code. This code is employed in a wide range of personal computers in Japan to provide the following features:

(1) No SI (shift-in) and SO (shift-out) means that a shift code is unnecessary, eliminating the need to be concerned about the current shift condition.

(2) Because the string length is proportional to the display width, it is quite easy to erase keyboard inputs, as well as to operate the cursor through a screen editor.

The Shift-JIS Kanji code includes the following.

(a) Kanji code (The first byte)

0x81 - 0x9f and 0xe0 - 0xfc

(b) Kanji code (The second byte)

0x40 - 0x7e and 0x80 - 0xfc

(c) Kana code

0xal - 0xdf

(d) ASCII code

0x21 - 0x7e

(e) ASCII control code

0x00 - 0x20 and 0x7f

As can be seen from the above list, the Kanji code (the second byte) overlaps with the ASCII code. This overlapped portion contains those characters that are used as special characters in the shell and the editor ([, \,], ^, ‘, {, |, }, ˜). Special care must therefore be taken to distinguish between the Kanji code and the ASCII code when Japanizing the shell and the editor.

2-2 Kernel

Adding new capabilities to the tty driver is the major modification to the kernel. The 4.2 BSD tty driver could not handle 8-bit codes and thus needed modification in this respect.

Modifying the tty driver so that it can handle an 8-bit code suffices if only the Kana code is used. When using the Kanji code, however, the tty driver must be provided with an ability to make it possible to handle two bytes as one character. This is because when erasing, two bytes (the equal of one Kanji character) must be removed from the queue of the tty driver when

CH2539-5/88/0000/0270$01.00 © 1988 IEEE

an erase character of one byte is input. At the same time, the sequence for evoking the delete operation of the respective character on the display must be echoed back. To achieve all this, therefore, functions to enable queue handling in two-bytes units were added to the tty driver.

One more aspect of the kernel which was subjected to Japanization is the way file names are written. With the NEWS design, however, writing the file names in Japanese is not allowed for the following reasons.

(1) Files with Japanese file names cannot be accessed from a terminal which cannot handle Japanese. They cannot be referred to using the "ls" command, thereby putting a limitation on the original UNIX capabilities.

(2) Files with Japanese file names cannot be accessed by machines using different code systems when files are remote-mounted via an NFS.

2-3 Language Processor

The language processor was modified to enable the following.

(1) Use of Japanese comments

(2) Use of the Japanese code for the character string

(3) Input/output processing of the Japanese code

2-4 Library

A function was added to make it possible to decide whether a code is a part of the Kanji code or not. Functions used for handling regular expressions, as well as those used for display operations, were also modified.

2-5 Commands

Most commands on UNIX are designed with no consideration given to 8-bit codes. This means that if we were to use Japanese on UNIX, a number of commands must be modified. The reason why 8-bit codes cannot be used on UNIX resides in the fact that the 8th bit of UNIX commands is used as a flag or for such purposes as shown below.

(1) Shell
With the shell, the 8th bit is used to indicate a character sequence marked by ''', '"' and so on.

(2) ed, ex
With ed and ex, the 8th bit is used for regular expression.

There is also a problem of cursor manipulation when a word or sentence contains both full-size and half-size characters.

3. Front-End Processor for Japanese Language Input

To enable Japanese language input, the SJ2 front-end processor was developed.

3-1 Principles of Japanese Input Processing

All Kanji can be expressed as Kana and for language processing purposes, all sentences are expressed in Kana. Thus, for Japanese language input, the following is required.

(1) A Kana-Kanji dictionary that contains information about Kanji and can be accessed by Kana.

(2) A Kana-to-Kanji translation module that converts input Kana characters to Kanji characters, using the dictionary.

(3) An Alphabet-to-Kana translation module when an alpha-numeric keyboard is used. (Any Kana character is represented using the alphabet.)

3-2 Input Systems for Japanese Language

There are several methods available for implementing the above mentioned software on UNIX.

(1) Library Method
A library necessary for Kana-to-Kanji translation is included in each application software.

(2) Driver Method
The tty driver includes Kana-to-Kanji translation.

(3) Front-End Method
The Kana-to-Kanji conversion function is built into the front-end processor.

The front-end method is employed in NEWS, because it offers the following advantages over other methods.

(a) Input in the form of Japanese can be handled using the same interface for a variety of applications.

(b) Commands can be Japanized easily. In addition, those commands on which Japanese inputs have no effect can be used without modification.

(c) The application program can be made small, since there is no need for each application to include Kana-to-Kanji translation software.

(d) User interfaces can be switched simply by changing the front-end processor.

(e) The kernel does not have to be modified for Kana-to-Kanji translation.

3-3 The SJ2 Front-End Processor

The SJ2 uses the UNIX 4.2BSD's pty driver to implement a front-end processor for Japanese inputs on UNIX. Making use of the functions of this driver, the process necessary for Kana-to-Kanji translation is run between the tty driver and each application. The relationship between the tty and pty drivers and the SJ2 and each application when the SJ2 is initiated is shown in Figure 1.

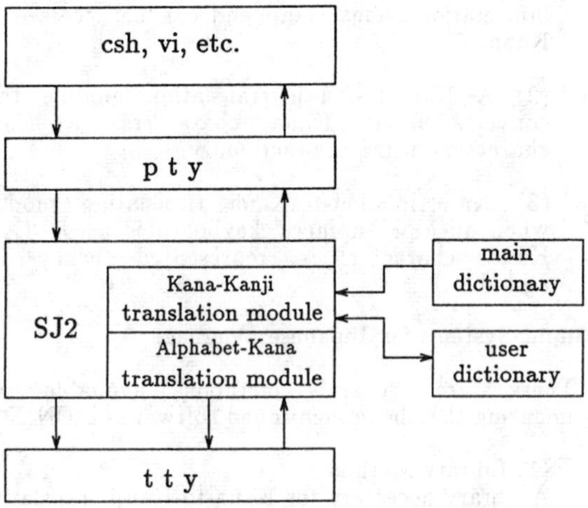

Figure 1 Implementaion of the SJ2 Front-End Processor

3-4 Dictionary

The dictionary used by the SJ2 is divided into a main dictionary and a user dictionary. The main dictionary contains Kanji and its various Kana equivalents, plus the information about special usage. The user dictionary is used to store Kanji and their Kana equivalents registered by the user.

A single Kanji might be represented by any of several possible Kana, depending on its order in a combination of Kanji and its intended meaning. Because of this, a "learning function" is included in the user dictionary so that when a particular Kana is selected, the Kanji previously deemed appropriate by the user is offered as the first possibility.

The main dictionary is shared by all users. Placed under the home directory, the user dictionary can be customized by each user.

3-5 Kana-to-Kanji Translation

The major job of the front-end processor for Japanese inputs is conversion of Kana into Kanji. Among the many methods for achieving this conversion, the SJ2 employs the sentence-by-sentence translation system. At the touch of a key, this system makes it possible to convert the entire sentence written in Kana into the normal way of writing using Kanji and Kana. As a result, this system not only offers improved efficiency but also enables the user to concentrate without being distracted by key operations. The translation routine accesses the dictionary, analyzes the Kana sequence, and converts it into a mixed Kanji and Kana sequence.

3-6 Kana-to-Kanji Translation Library

As part of the Japanese Language Processing environment, the Kana-to-Kanji translation routine of the SJ2 of NEWS is offered in the form of a library so that it can be included in each user's application software.

3-7 User Interface

The Japanese-input front-end processor is controlled with the function keys. These keys provide control over translation of the character sequence, selection of the desired character type, and editing of the character sequence. With the SJ2 front-end processor, the above functions are assigned to the escape sequences mapped on the function keys of the NEWS keyboard. This key assignment, however, can easily be changed using the setup file in each user's home directory, enabling the user to use the escape sequence and control code of his choice.

4. Japanization of the X Window System

The X Window System developed at Massachusetts Institute of Technology is standard on NEWS. Japanese language processing on this window system has been achieved by the adoption of a Japanese terminal emulator and the extension of the X server.

4-1 Kanji and Kana Font Sets

Font sets are available for Kanji (16 x 16 dots) and Kana (8 x 16 dots). The Kanji font set corresponds with the character set of two-bytes code and includes more than 6,000 characters of both first and second levels as specified by JIS (Japanese Industrial Standard) X 0208. Each character is a bitmap of 16 x 16 dots. The Kana font set corresponds with the character set of one-byte code and includes one-byte Kana characters in addition to the ASCII characters. Each character in this font set is a bitmap of 8 x 16 dots.

4-2 Extension of Font Format and the X server

Ordinary font formats and the X server are not suitable for use with the NEWS Kanji font set, which exceeds 200K bytes. The format of the font file is thus extended to enable use of the large number of characters contained in the Kanji font set. The X server is also equipped with the Kanji font loading function.

4-3 Japanese Terminal Emulator (jterm)

NEWS incorporates the jterm terminal emulator, which is a Japanese version of xterm (the terminal emulator software for the X Window System). Together with the Japanese-input front-end processor and the Japanese editor, this terminal emulator makes it possible to input, display and edit Japanese. The jterm terminal emulator can use both Kanji and Kana font sets. Selection of the font set to be used is automatically done by detecting the number of bytes of the character to be displayed. Figure 2 shows Japanese language processing performed on the X window System. Besides jterm, we also offers a Japanese ditroff (device independent troff) previewer.

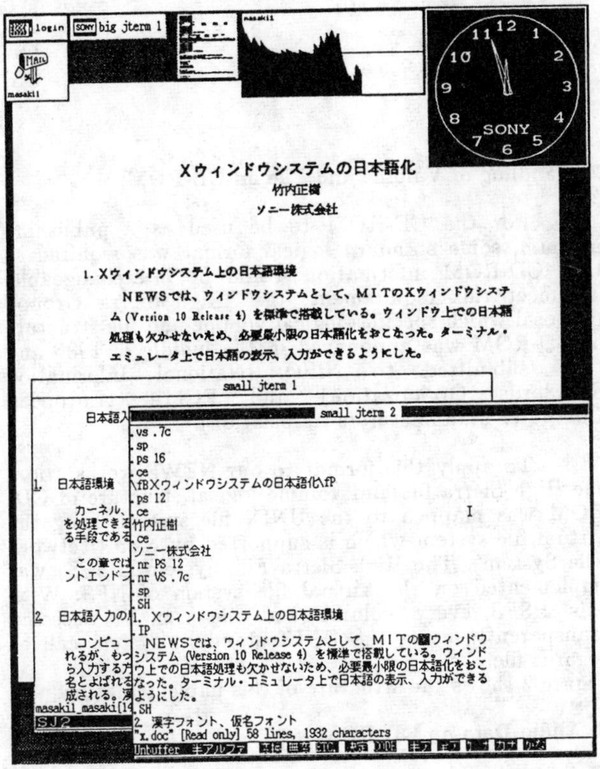

Figure 2 Japanese Language Processing on the X Window System

5. Conclusion

With the Japanese language processing functions described above, NEWS provides a unique language processing environment where Japanese users can use and develop Japanese application software, while benefiting from the original capabilities of UNIX.

References

1. "UNIX Programmer's Manual, 4.2 Berkeley Software Distribution", University of California, Berkeley, August 1983

2. James Gettys, "Problems Implementing Window Systems in UNIX", MIT, 1985

3. Jim Gettys, Ron Newman and Tony Della Fera "Xlib - C Language X Interface, Protocol Version 10", MIT, November 1986

Trademarks.

UNIX is a trademark of AT&T Bell Laboratories.

NFS is a trademark of Sun Microsystems, Inc.

The X Window System is a trademark of the Massachusetts Institute of Technology.

CD-ROM System based on the NEWS Workstation

Keiji Kimura, Akihide Demura, Tatsuya Igarashi, Yukio Takeyari

Sony Corporation

Abstract

To fully utilize the CD-ROM (Compact Disc-Read Only Memory) as an electronic publishing multimedia on the NEWS workstation, a newly developed audio bit-rate reduction system and a function to access the standard logical format of volume and file on a CD-ROM have been implemented to meet the requirements of a wide range of applications.

1. Overview

In 1983, the CD (Compact Disc) was developed by Sony and Philips as an audio medium. Based on this technology, the CD-ROM was developed in order to utilize the Compact Disc as a data storage medium which can provide a massive storage capacity with high reliability. Significant features of this medium are as follows.

- Mass productivity, low production cost
- Storage of 540 million bytes on a disc
- Compactness of 4.75 inches diameter
- Lightness of about 0.7 ounce weight
- A highly durable medium

The enormous capacity of the CD-ROM makes it especially attractive as a medium which can store text, data, sound and images. This flexibility, as well as the ease and rapidity of data retrieval, suggest that the CD-ROM has the capability of becoming a publishing medium with many new applications.

The workstation system which incorporates the CD-ROM was developed for the series of NEWS workstations which can provide high processing speed and a high-resolution display. Our developmental goals were as follows.

i) To enable the CD-ROM system to handle the standard volume and file format of the CD-ROM as a UNIX file system.

ii) To expand features of audio data handling using a new bit-rate reduction system. (To solve a problem of the trade-off between audio sound quality and storage capacity.)

Figure 1 shows the prototype of the NEWS CD-ROM workstation and Table I shows its basic configuration.

2. Handling of Volume and File on CD-ROM

For the CD-ROM to be used as a publishing medium, some standard logical format was required so that CD-ROM information would be interchangeable. To meet this requirement, the "High Sierra Group" proposal which specifies logical volume and file structure of CD-ROM was announced in the middle of 1986 and then submitted to NISO (National Information Standards Organization) and ECMA (European Computer Manufacturers Association).

To apply this format to our NEWS workstation, the High Sierra file and volume logical structure of CD-ROM was mapped to the UNIX file system using the virtual file system which is supported by NFS (Network File System). The High Sierra File System (HSFS) was implemented on the virtual file system of NFS. With this HSFS every volume and file can be accessed transparently using the UNIX standard system call as regards file.
Figure 2 shows the structure of this implementation.

3. Audio Data on CD-ROM

Three Different Sound Quality Levels

The CD-DA, CD audio standard format is based on a sampling frequency of 44.1kHz, and a number of bits used per sample of 16, and can provide about 60 minutes of stereo audio. The sound quality of this format is outstanding. On the other hand, to utilize CD-ROM as a multimedia which can handle data, text, images and graphics, more an efficient audio data format is required. To meet this requirement, we use a newly developed audio bit-rate reduction format. This format provides three levels of sound quality to match specific application requirements. - Level A, Level B and Level C.

Level A: 8-bit ADPCM encoding with a sampling frequency of 37.8kHz. The sound quality is almost the same as that of CD-DA. 2 hours of stereo audio or 4 hours of mono can be stored on a disc.

Level B: 4-bit ADPCM encoding with a sampling frequency of 37.8kHz. The sound quality is slightly lower than that of Level A. 4 hours of stereo audio or 8 hours of mono can be stored on a disc.

Level C: 4-bit ADPCM encoding with a sampling frequency of 18.9kHz. The sound quality is suitable for high quality speech. 8 hours of stereo audio or 16 hours

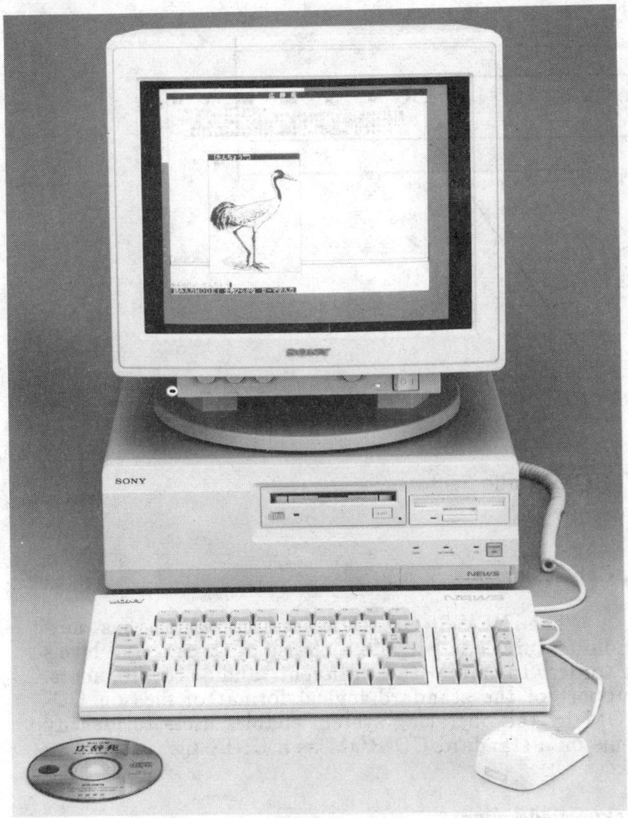

Figure 1 NEWS CD-ROM System

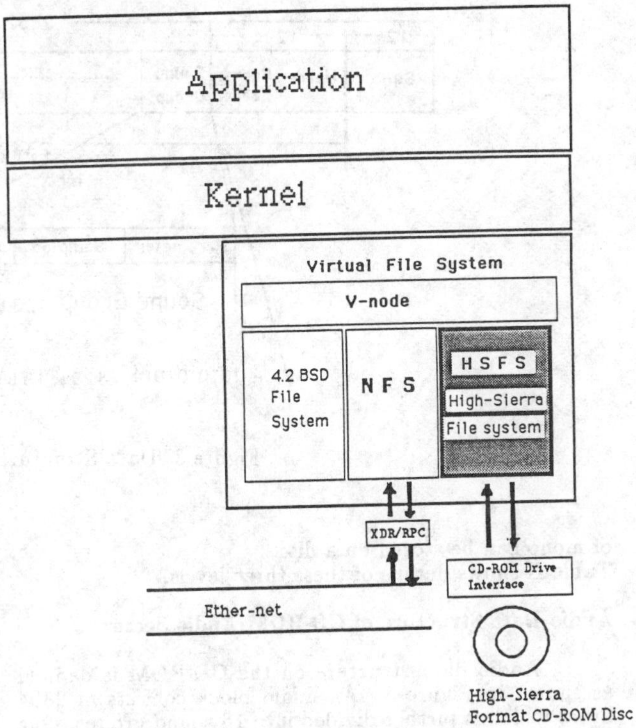

Figure 2 HSFS Implementation

Table I Basic Configuration of NEWS CD-ROM System

CPU	I/O Processor	Co-Processor	Audio Processor	Main Memory	Storage		
					FDD	HD	CD-ROM
68020 16.67 MHz	68020 16.67 MHz	68881 16.67MHz	ADPCM 8/4 bit	4 MB	1.44MB	286MB	540MB

Table II Overview of the Sound Quality Levels

Level	Sampling Frequency (kHz)	Bit per Sample	Channel number	Channel Bit Rate (Kbits/Sec)
A	37.8	8	2 Stereo 4 Mono	309
B	37.8	4	4 Stereo 8 Mono	159
C	18.9	4	8 Stereo 16 Mono	80

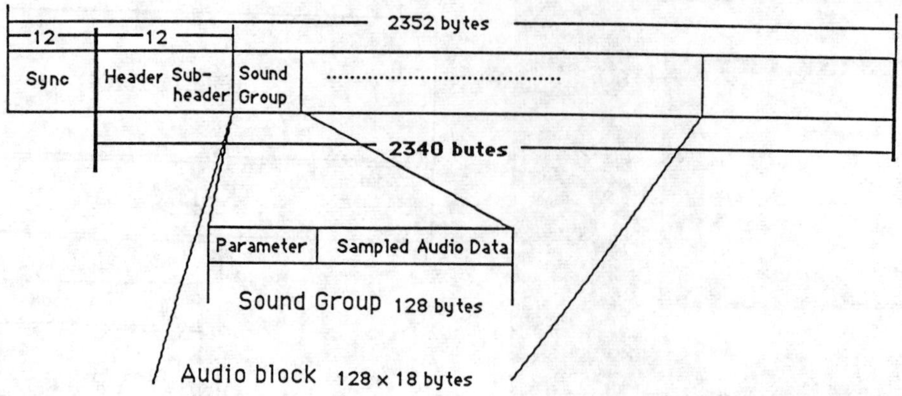

Figure 3 Data Structure of CD-ROM Audio Sector

of mono can be stored on a disc.
Table II shows details of these three levels.

Audio Data Structure of CD-ROM Audio Sector

Audio data structure on the CD-ROM is defined as shown in Figure 3. An audio block consists of 2304 bytes which is further divided into 18 sound groups. One sound group consists of a sound parameter and sampled audio data. In a sampled audio data field 4 or 8 sound blocks are included depending on the level. In level A there are 4 sound blocks in one sound group, and 8 sound blocks in level B and level C. The sound block is the basic unit with which bit compression and decompression are carried out.

Implementation on NEWS

The audio capability which is made possible by the new bit-rate reduction format is implemented on the NEWS workstation as shown in Figure 4. A dedicated decoder LSI has been developed for this new format. This ADPCM processor supports error compensation, block decoding, bit-rate reduction decoding, and can generate linear 16-bit data. The audio data of all levels is decoded to 16-bit data by this processor and directly transferred to a D/A converter. CD-DA audio data is also inputted directly into a D/A converter.

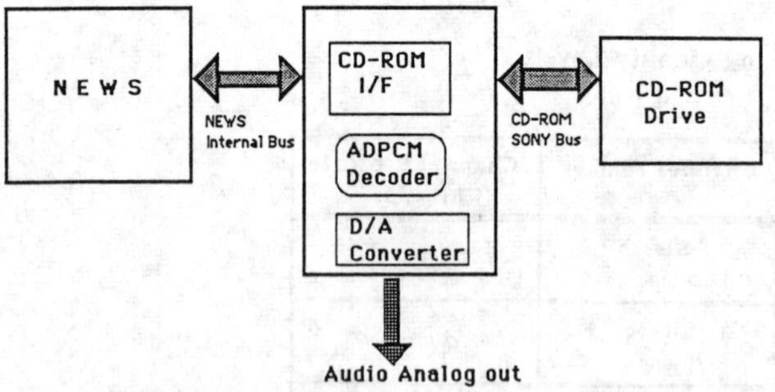

Figure 4 Implementation of Audio Processor on NEWS

4. Conclusion

The NEWS CD-ROM system which has new audio features can provide a choice of three sound levels in order to meet the different audio requirements. Support of the standard logical format of files on CD-ROM by the operating system enables users to identify a file on a standard CD-ROM as a UNIX file.

Acknowledgement

We would like to thank the members in Sony Information Systems Research Center for the development and design of a new audio format.

References

1. M. Nishiguchi, K. Akagiri and T. Suzuki "A New Audio Bit Rate Reduction System For The CD-I Format" Audio Engineering Society, November, 1986

2. M. Nishiguchi and K. Akagiri, "Audio Bit Rate Reduction System", Proc. Spring Meet. Acoust. Soc. Jpn., 313-314, 1984

3. CDROM Ad Hoc Advisory Committee, "Working Paper for Information Processing - Volume and File Structure of Compact Read Only Optical Discs for Information Interchange", May 28, 1987

4. "Information processing - Volume and file structure of CDROM for information interchange", Draft of International Standard, ISO/DIS 9660, 1987

Trademarks.

Sun Microsystems SPARC Architecture

Chair: D. Ditzel

The Scalable Processor Architecture (SPARC)

Robert B. Garner, Anant Agrawal, Fayé Briggs, Emil W. Brown, David Hough,
Bill Joy, Steve Kleiman, Steven Muchnick, Masood Namjoo,
Dave Patterson†, Joan Pendleton, & Richard Tuck

Sun Microsystems, Inc.
2550 Garcia Avenue
Mountain View, CA 94043

ABSTRACT

Sun Microsystems' SPARC architecture, based on the RISCs and SOAR architectures developed at UC Berkeley, was designed for easily pipelined, cost-effective, high-performance, multi-technology implementations. The goal is that the cost/performance ratio of successive implementations should scale with, or track, improvements in circuit technology while remaining ahead of CISC-based systems. The simple instruction set, well-matched to compiler technology, allows for implementations with very high MIPS rates and short development cycles.

The combined integer and floating-point architecture includes multiprocessor, coprocessor, and tagged arithmetic support. System functions, such as an MMU, are not integrated into the architecture.

Sun Microsystems is encouraging other companies to implement SPARC. Its first implementation is a pair of 20K-gate CMOS gate arrays plus two float chips; higher-performance custom CMOS and ECL are under development.

1. Introduction

The Scalable Processor Architecture (SPARC™) defines a general-purpose, 32-bit integer, IEEE-standard floating-point, 32-bit byte-addressed processor architecture. The design goal was that successive SPARC implementations should achieve increasingly higher levels of performance via faster and possibly less dense circuit technologies. The simple nature of the architecture enables easily pipelined, cost-effective, high-performance implementations across a range of device integration levels and technologies.

SPARC was defined at Sun Microsystems over the period 1984 to 1987. The genesis of the architecture was the Berkeley RISC and SOAR designs [PattSeq81, Katevenis83, Ungar84, Pendleton86]. Changes, including extensions for multiprocessors, floating-point and tightly coupled coprocessors, were made with the guidance of an operating system/compiler/hardware team.

We implemented the first SPARC processor with a pair of Fujitsu 20K-gate, 1.5-micron CMOS gate arrays, a pair of floating-point accelerator chips, and a 128-Kbyte cache giving a 60 ns (16.67 MHz) instruction cycle time. The first SPARC-based workstations and servers, the Sun-4/200™ series, were announced concurrently with the architecture and a large set of vendor application software on July 8, 1987.

Unlike other existing commercial CPU architectures, Sun Microsystems is encouraging companies to design and market implementations of the architecture. In addition to the project with Fujitsu Microelectronics, Sun is working with Cypress Semiconductor to develop a custom 0.8-micron CMOS implementation and with Bipolar Integrated Technology on a custom ECL implementation. Sun and AT&T are also defining an Application Binary Interface (ABI) for third-party software vendors to be supported by a future version of UNIX® System V. SPARC conforms to the DARPA and Software Engineering Institute "Core Set of Assembly Language Instructions." [Core87]

This paper introduces the SPARC architecture and its more interesting features. A complete, implementation-independent specification is available elsewhere [SPARC87]. We also describe the differences from the Berkeley RISC/SOAR designs. Companion papers cover compilers [Muchnick88], how Sun's operating system uses the architecture [Kleiman88], and the Fujitsu [Namjoo88, Quach88], Cypress [NamjCypr88], and BIT implementations [Agrawal88]. An introduction to RISCs is in [Patterson85].

2. Registers

A SPARC processor is divided into two parts: an Integer Unit (IU) and a Floating-Point Unit (FPU). An optional coprocessor (CP) can also be present. Each of these units contains its own set of registers, and all registers are 32 bits wide.

2.1. Window Registers

The IU may contain from 40 to 520 registers, depending on the implementation.[1] These are partitioned into 2 to 32 overlapping register windows plus 8 *global* registers. (The *global* register g0 always delivers the value zero.) At any one time, a program can address 32 general-purpose registers: the 8 *ins*, 8 *locals*, and 8 *outs* of the active window and the 8 *globals*. The *outs* of a given window correspond to the *ins* of the next window and each window has its own set of *locals*. The active window is identified by the 5-bit Current Window Pointer (CWP). Decrementing the CWP at procedure entry causes the next window to become active and incrementing the CWP at procedure exit causes the previous window to become active. The accompanying compiler paper explains how windowed registers can be used [Muchnick88].

Register windows have several advantages over a fixed set of registers. Their principal advantage is a reduction in the number of load and store instructions required to execute a program. As a consequence, there is also a decrease in the number of data cache misses. The reduced number of loads and stores is also beneficial in implementations that have multi-cycle load or store instructions and in tightly coupled multiprocessors.

† Current affiliation is Computer Science Division, EECS, University of California, Berkeley, CA, 94720.

[1] A minimal, 40-register, two-window implementation comprises 8 *ins*, 8 *locals*, 8 *outs*, 8 *globals*, and 8 trap handler *locals*. An implementation with 40 registers functions as if there were no windows, although window-based code would execute properly, though less efficiently.

CH2539-5/88/0000/0278$01.00 © 1988 IEEE

For large C programs, dynamic trace data show that about 20% of executed SPARC instructions are loads and stores, including the window overflow/underflow processing overhead. This compares to about 30% to 40% of executed instructions for RISCs without register windows.

Register windows also work well in incremental compilation environments such as LISP and in object-oriented programming environments such as Smalltalk, where interprocedural register allocation is impractical. Even though these exploratory programming languages benefit from register windows, SPARC does **not** preclude interprocedural register allocation optimizations since the subroutine call and return instructions are distinct from the instructions that advance and retract the window pointer.

Register window overflow and underflow conditions are handled in software by a kernel trap handler. An IU state register, the Window Invalid Mask (WIM), can tag any window (or set of windows) so that an overflow or underflow trap is generated whenever the CWP is about to point to a tagged window. To implement the usual LIFO stack of overlapping windows, one of the WIM bits is set to identify the boundary between the oldest and the newest window. Note that on process switches only the active windows are saved, **not** the entire set of windows.[2] See the accompanying system paper for a more detailed description of window overflow/underflow handling.

In specialized systems, the register windows can be managed in a variety of different ways. For example, in device controller applications that require rapid context switching, the windows can be partitioned into non-overlapping pairs, with one pair allocated per process. Each process would have—not including the 8 *globals*—24 private registers plus a set of 8 registers for trap handling. The WIM would protect each process's registers from the other processes.

The register windows also allow for fast trap handling. When a trap or interrupt occurs, the CWP is decremented—as for a procedure call—making available to the trap handler six of the *local* registers of the next window. (Two of the *locals* are written with the IU's two Program Counters.) Thus, the interrupt latency to a simple handler can be as small as a few cycles.

2.2. Floating-Point Registers

The FPU has thirty-two 32-bit-wide registers. Double-precision values occupy an even-odd pair and extended-precision values occupy an aligned group of four registers. The FPU's registers are accessed externally only via load and store instructions; there is no direct path between the IU and the FPU. The instruction set defines doubleword (64-bit) floating-point loads and stores to boost double-precision performance. Also, in order to decrease context switch time, the FPU can be disabled so that its registers need not be saved when switching from a process that does not use floating-point.

SPARC allows floating-point operations, such as multiply and add, to execute concurrently with each other, with floating-point loads and stores, and with integer instructions. This concurrency is hidden from the programmer: a program generates the same results —including traps—as if all instructions were executed sequentially.

Because of this concurrency, the IU's Program Counters can advance beyond floating-point instructions in the instruction stream. There is a special group of registers, the Floating-point Queue (FQ), that records the floating-point instructions (and their addresses) that were pending completion at the time of a floating-point trap. The queue's head contains the unfinished instruction (and its address) that caused the floating-point trap.

[2]The cost of saving or restoring a window is not large: on the Sun-4/200, it approximates the overhead of 7 cache misses.

Format 1 (CALL):

op	displacement
2	*30*

Format 2 (SETHI):

op	rd	op	immediate
2	*5*	*3*	*22*

Format 2 (Bicc, FBfcc, CBcc):

op	a	cc	op	displacement
2	*1*	*4*	*3*	*22*

Format 3 (Remaining instructions, i=0):

op	rd	op	rs1	i	asi *or* fp-op	rs2
2	*5*	*6*	*5*	*1*	*8*	*5*

Format 3 (Remaining instructions, i=1):

op	rd	op	rs1	i	immediate
2	*5*	*6*	*5*	*1*	*13*

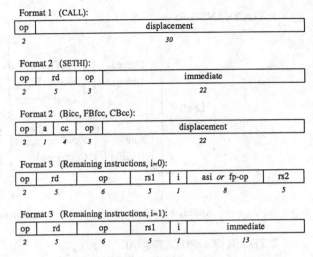

Figure 1. SPARC Instruction Formats

3. Instructions

SPARC defines 55 basic integer and 13 floating-point instructions. Figure 1 illustrates the instruction formats and Figure 2 summarizes the instruction set.

3.1. Instruction Formats

All instructions are 32 bits wide. The first format holds a 30-bit word displacement for the PC-relative CALL instruction. Thus a PC-relative call or an unconditional branch can be made to an arbitrarily distant location in a single instruction. (Note that there is also a register-indirect call encoded via a format 3 instruction.) The return address of the CALL is stored into *out* register 7.

Format 2 defines two instruction types: SETHI and branches. SETHI loads the 22-bit immediate value into the high 22 bits of the destination IU register and clears its low 10 bits. SETHI, in conjunction with a format 3 instruction, is used to create 32-bit constants. (Note that the immediate fields of formats 2 and 3 overlap by three bits.) Format 2's 22-bit word displacement defines the ±8-Mbyte displacement for PC-relative conditional branch instructions.

Format 3, which has specifiers for two source registers and a destination register, encodes the remaining instructions. Like Berkeley's RISC and SOAR, if the *i* bit is set, a sign-extended 13-bit immediate substitutes for the second register specifier. The upper 8 bits of this field are used as an opcode extension field for the floating-point instructions and as an "address space identifier" for the load/store instructions (see Section 3.2).

3.2. Load/Store Instructions

Only the load/store instructions access memory. For the floating-point and coprocessor load/stores, the IU generates the memory address and the FPU or coprocessor sources or sinks the data. The load/store halfword (16-bit), word (32-bit), and doubleword (64-bit) instructions trap if the data are not aligned on halfword, word, and doubleword boundaries, respectively. The aligned doubleword constraint allows for faster load/store double instructions in implementations with 64-bit data buses.

The load/store instructions assume "big-endian," Motorola 68000-compatible byte ordering: byte 0 is the most significant and byte 3 is the least significant byte in a word. We chose one arrangement without an option for the other to preclude incompatibility problems between binaries that access sharable data records.

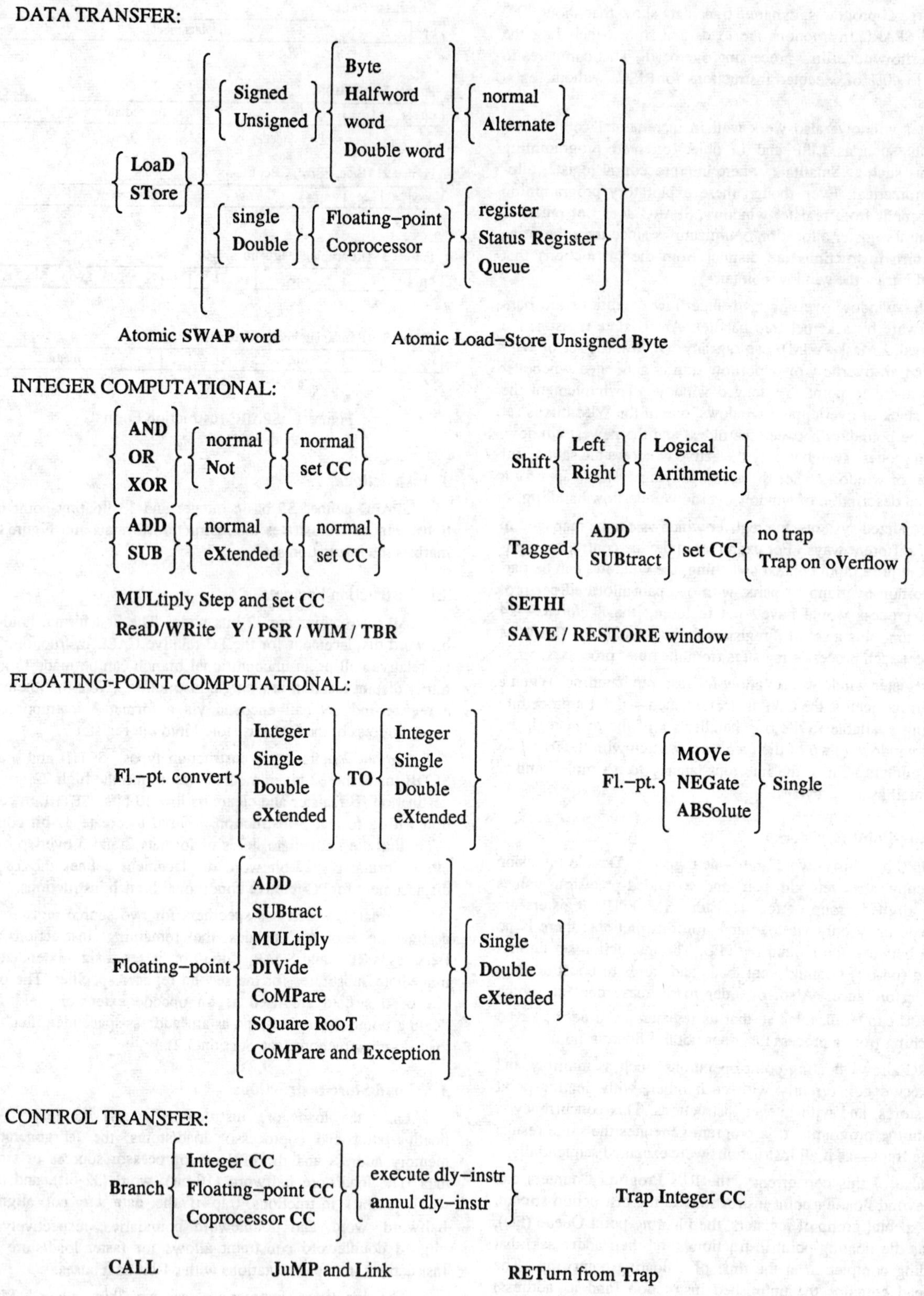

Figure 2. SPARC Instruction Set Summary

(This summary implies several nonexistent instructions: e.g., STore Signed, Shift Left Arithmetic, and Fl.-pt. convert self to self.)

Two memory addressing modes are supported via the 3rd format: "reg_1 + reg_2" or "reg + signed_13-bit_constant". Register indirect and absolute addressing modes are implied when g0 is specified. The two addressing modes are defined for both load and store instructions.[3]

Unlike some other RISCs that implement "delayed" loads, the instruction that immediately follows a load may use the load data. This feature simplifies the scheduling of instructions by compilers. In some SPARC implementations there may be a performance advantage if the instruction placed after a load does not specify the register being loaded.

For all instruction and normal data fetches from the uniform 32-bit memory address space, the IU indicates a user or supervisor reference by sending to the memory system the user/supervisor bit from the Processor Status Register (PSR). This, in conjunction with a data/instruction indicator define an Address Space Identifier (ASI) that can be matched against protection bits in a system's Memory Management Unit (MMU) (See Section 5).

The privileged load/store integer "alternate" instructions define a mechanism that allows the supervisor to access an arbitrary, or alternate, ASI. Either the user instruction or user data spaces or up to 252 other system-dependent, 32-bit address spaces can be specified by an constant from the instruction. The MMU itself, for example, might be mapped into an alternate space.

There are two special instructions for tightly coupled multiprocessor support: SWAP and load-store unsigned byte (LDSTUB). SWAP atomically exchanges the contents of an IU register with a word from memory. It can be used in conjunction with a memory-mapped coprocessor to implement other synchronizing instructions, such as the non-blocking "fetch and add" instruction [GottKrus81]. The second instruction, LDSTUB, atomically reads a byte from memory into an IU register and then rewrites the same byte in memory to all ones. It is the atomic instruction necessary for the blocking synchronization schemes, such as semaphores [Dubois88]. Since word-wide registers are not necessarily aligned in general-purpose I/O buses, LDSTUB reads and writes bytes to preclude the occurrence of processor alignment errors.

3.3. Integer Computational Instructions

Format 3 integer instructions compute a two's complement result that is a function of two source operands, and either write the result into a destination IU register or discard it. Most have two versions: one that modifies the integer condition codes and one that does not. The "subtract and set condition codes" instruction (SUBcc) with a destination of g0 is the generic compare instruction.

The shift instructions shift left or right by a distance specified in a register or an immediate value in the instruction. The "multiply step" instruction (MULScc) is used to generate the 64-bit product of two signed or unsigned words. It shifts by one bit the 64-bit product formed by concatenating a general-purpose IU register with the 32-bit Y register. At each step, the LSB of the Y register determines whether the multiplicand—another IU register—is added to the product. A 32x32 signed multiply requires 36 cycles. As mentioned in the companion compiler paper, higher-level language multiplications execute in an average of 6 cycles.

[3]The "reg_1 + reg_2" mode does not significantly affect the performance of store instructions since most caches require more than one cycle, on the average, to accept both the data and the address.

There are four special instructions for languages that can benefit from operand tags, such as LISP and Smalltalk. The "tagged add/subtract" instructions (TADDcc, TSUBcc) set the overflow condition code bit if either of the operands has a nonzero tag (or a normal arithmetic overflow occurs), where the tag is the least significant two bits of a word. (Thus, these instructions assume left-justified, 30-bit signed integers.) Normally, a tagged add/subtract is followed by a conditional branch instruction (BVS), which, if the overflow bit has been set, transfers control to code that further deciphers the operand types. There are also two variants, TADDccTV and TSUBccTV, that trap if the overflow bit has been set and can be used to detect operand type errors.

There are two special instructions used to adjust the Current Window Pointer: SAVE and RESTORE which respectively decrement and increment the CWP, or trap if the adjustment would cause a window overflow or underflow. They also operate like an ordinary ADD instruction and thus can be used to atomically adjust both the CWP and a program stack pointer.

3.4. Control Transfer Instructions

Most control transfers, such as "branch on integer condition codes" (Bicc) and "jump and link" (JMPL) are delayed by one instruction: they take effect after the instruction that follows the control transfer is executed. This "delay" instruction is usually executed irrespective of the outcome of the branch. However, three kinds of control transfers are not delayed:

(1) The conditional branch instructions, in addition to the condition specifier, have a special "annul" bit. If the annul bit is set, the delay instruction—normally executed—is **not** executed if the conditional branch is **not** taken. This feature can shorten execution time by allowing compilers to move an instruction from within a loop into the delay slot of a loop-terminating branch, or move an instruction from one arm of an IF-THEN-ELSE statement into the other. By use of the annul bit, compiled code contains less than 5% NOPs.

(2) A special interpretation of the annul bit is made by the "branch always" (BA) instruction. If a BA with the annul bit set is executed, its delay instruction is **not** executed. This unique instruction is like the traditional, non-delayed branch. It can be used to efficiently emulate unimplemented instructions if, at run-time, the unimplemented instruction is replaced with an annulling BA whose target is the emulation code.

(3) The "trap on integer condition codes" (Ticc) instruction, without a delay, conditionally transfers control to one of 128 software trap locations. Ticc's are used for kernel calls and compiler run-time checking. The Trap Base Register (TBR) holds the location of the software/hardware trap table. The low bits of this register are set to the trap type when a trap is taken.

3.5. Floating-Point Computational Instructions

The "floating-point operate" instructions (FPop) compute a single, double, or extended-precision result that is a function of two source operands in FPU registers and write the result into FPU registers. The floating-point compare instructions write a 2-bit condition code in the FPU's Floating-point Status Register (FSR) that can be tested by the "branch on floating-point condition codes" (FBfcc) instruction. The operands and results for all FPops are of the same precision so there are instructions that convert between all formats, including integers. The FPop's are encoded via the 9-bit "opf" field of two format 3 instructions.

As mentioned previously, the floating-point computational instructions can execute concurrently with floating-point loads and stores and with integer instructions. In all implementations, they also execute concurrently with cache misses. If a floating-point store attempts to write a result whose computation has not yet finished, the IU stalls until the floating-point operation is complete. A "store FSR" instruction also causes the FPU to wait for outstanding floating-point operations to finish.

In general, a user program sees a complete ANSI/IEEE 754-1985 implementation, even though the hardware may not implement every nuance of the standard, such as gradual underflow. Software emulates missing hardware functionality via FPU-generated traps.

3.6. Coprocessor Instructions

SPARC has instruction support for a single coprocessor (in addition to the floating-point unit). The coprocessor instructions mirror the floating-point instructions: load/store coprocessor, "branch on coprocessor condition codes", and "coprocessor operate" (CPop). Coprocessor operate instructions can execute concurrently with integer instructions.

4. Comparison to Berkeley RISC and SOAR

We adopted Berkeley's register windows for SPARC, although unlike SOAR [Pendleton86], windowed registers do not have main memory addresses. Because it is a condition-code and three-register-address based instruction set, the instruction formats are nearly identical to RISC I/II [PattSeq81, Katevenis83] and SOAR [Ungar84]. Seriously considered as alternatives were different windowing schemes, "compare-and-branch" instructions, and SOAR's word-addressed memory and absolute branch addresses. Gate count limitations of the architecture's first implementation had a positive effect by encouraging simplicity. Opcode space has been reserved for future expansion. Unimplemented instructions trap and reserved fields are zero.

We added these features to the Berkeley instruction sets: a floating-point and coprocessor architecture, atomic load/store for multiprocessors, load/store alternate, multiply step, the branch annul bit (similar to the nullification bit in HP's Precision Architecture [Mahon86]), the Window Invalid Mask, SAVE/RESTORE, and single instructions for all 16 functions of two binary variables (e.g., and_not, nor). Although SOAR supports conditional trapping and tags, these are defined differently in SPARC.

5. System Architecture

SPARC does not specify I/O interfaces, cache/memory architectures, or memory management units (MMUs). Although the instruction set has no intrinsic bias favoring either virtual or real address caches, in order to minimize cycle time, many system implementations are based on virtual caches. Since the architecture of an MMU is best established by the particular requirements of the system hardware/software designers, and is not a performance bottleneck in virtual address caches, SPARC does not define an MMU. System issues are discussed further in the operating system paper [Kleiman88].

6. Performance

SPARC's performance depends on many interrelated parameters. In general, a processor's ability to execute a compute-bound task is proportional to the product of the average number of instructions executed per second (MIPS) and the number of instructions required to execute the program.

The number of instructions depends on the quality of the code generated by compilers and the efficiency of the instruction set. Based on data from C and Fortran programs, SPARC machines execute from 0 to 25% more instructions than CISCs (e.g., VAX®, Motorola 68000). The companion compiler paper includes data on static code expansion.

The native MIPS rate is a function of an implementation's cycle time, average memory access time, and microarchitecture. It is influenced by the available circuit technologies and the system's cost, performance, and time-to-market goals. SPARC's simple instruction set allows for implementations with very high MIPS rates and short product development cycles.

7. Conclusion

The SPARC instruction set allows for high-performance processor and system implementations at a variety of price/performance technology points. The architecture is simple and powerful enough that we could implement its integer portion in a single CMOS gate array that executes instructions from a 128-Kbyte cache at a peak rate of 16 MIPS and yet far exceeds the performance of existing CISC-based systems [Schafir87, Chu87].

Acknowledgements

In addition to the authors, many people at Sun Microsystems contributed to the definition of the architecture, including K.G. Tan, Wayne Rosing, Don Jackson, Dave Weaver, Dave Goldberg, Tom Lyon, Alex Wu, and John Gilmore. The gate-array IU (Fujitsu MB86900) was designed by Anant Agrawal and Masood Namjoo and the FPC (Fujitsu MB86910), which interfaces with the Weitek WTL1164/65 floating-point chips, was designed by Don Jackson with help from Rick Iwamoto and Larry Yang. Will Brown wrote an architectural and machine cycle simulator. Ed Kelly and Robert Garner designed the Sun-4/200 processor board. K.G. Tan and Wayne Rosing managed the gate-array and architecture projects.

Thanks to Dave Ditzel, Dave Weaver, Ed Kelly, and Joe Petolino for their useful suggestions in improving this paper.

References

[Agrawal88] A. Agrawal, E. W. Brown, J. Petolino, D. Russel, J. Peterson, "Design Considerations for a Bipolar Implementation of SPARC," this proceedings.

[Chu87] N. Chu, L. Poltrack, J. Bartlett, J. Friedland, A. MacRae, **Sun Performance**, Sun Microsystems, Inc., Mountain View, CA.

[Core87] **Core Set of Assembly Language Instructions for MIPS-based Microprocessors**, Software Engineering Institute, Pittsburgh, PA.

[Dubois88] M. Dubois, C. Scheurich, & F. Briggs, "Synchronization, Coherence and Ordering of Events in Multiprocessors," to appear in *IEEE Com.*, March 1988.

[GottKrus81] A. Gottlieb & C. Kruskal, "Coordinating parallel processors: A Partial unification," *Comp. Arch. News*, vol. 9, no. 6, Oct. 1981.

[Katevenis83] M. Katevenis, **Reduced Instruction Set Computer Architectures for VLSI**, Ph.D. dissertation, Computer Science Div., Univ. of California, Berkeley, 1983. Also published by M.I.T. Press, Cambridge, MA.

[Kleiman88] S. Kleiman & D. Williams, "SunOS on SPARC," this proceedings.

[Mahon86] M. Mahon, R. B. Lee, T. C. Miller, J.C. Huck, & W. R. Bryg, "Hewlett-Packard Precision Architecture: The Processor," *HP J.*, vol. 37, no. 8, Aug. 1986.

[Muchnick88] S. Muchnick, C. Aoki, V. Ghodssi, M. Helft, M. Lee, R. Tuck, D. Weaver, & A. Wu, "Optimizing Compilers for the SPARC Architecture: An Overview," this proceedings.

[Namjoo88] M. Namjoo, A. Agrawal, D. Jackson, Le Quach, "CMOS Gate Array Implementation of the SPARC Architecture," this proceedings.

[NamjCypr88] M. Namjoo, et. al., "CMOS Custom Implementation of the SPARC Architecture," this proceedings.

[Patterson85] D. Patterson, "Reduced Instruction Set Computers," *CACM*, vol. 28, no. 1, Jan. 1985.

[PattSeq81] D. Patterson & C. Sequin, "RISC I: A Reduced Instruction Set VLSI Computer," *Proc. of 8th Annual Intl. Symp. on Comp. Arch.*, May 1981.

[Pendleton86] J. Pendleton, S. Kong, E. W. Brown, F. Dunlap, C. Marino, D. Ungar, D. Patterson, & D. Hodges, "A 32-bit Microprocessor for Smalltalk," *IEEE J. of Solid-State Circuits*, vol. SC-21, no. 5, Oct. 1986.

[Quach88] L. Quach & R. Chueh, "CMOS Gate Array Implementation of the SPARC Architecture," this proceedings.

[Schafir87] M. Schafir & A. Nguyen, **Sun-4/200 Benchmarks**, Sun Microsystems, Inc., Mountain View, CA.

[SPARC87] **The SPARC™ Architecture Manual**, Sun Microsystems, Inc., Mountain View, CA. Also published by Fujitsu Microelectronics, Inc., 3320 Scott Blvd., Santa Clara, CA 95054.

[Ungar84] D. Ungar, R. Blau, P. Foley, A. Samples, & D. Patterson, "Architecture of SOAR: Smalltalk on a RISC," *Proc. of 11th Annual Intl. Symp. on Comp. Arch.*, June 1984.

Optimizing Compilers for the SPARC Architecture
An Overview

Steven S. Muchnick, Christopher Aoki, Vida Ghodssi, Michel Helft,
Meng Lee, Richard Tuck, David Weaver & Alexand Wu

Sun Microsystems, Inc.
2550 Garcia Avenue
Mountain View, CA 94043

ABSTRACT

Sun Microsystems' SPARC architecture is tuned to provide high performance in a variety of hardware implementation technologies. The user programming model and compiler technology are major components in achieving SPARC's full performance. The user model was designed in tandem with the architecture so as to best exploit advances in processor design and code optimization.

Sun provides compilers for C, FORTRAN 77 with VMS® extensions, Pascal and Modula-2 for SPARC, all based on the same code generation and optimization technology. Other languages, such as Smalltalk, Ada, Common Lisp and Prolog are or will be provided in the future, some by Sun and some from other sources.

1. Introduction

This paper discusses Sun Microsystems' user programming model for the SPARC™ architecture and the optimizing compilers for the SPARC-based Sun-4 workstations. The architecture and its first implementation are discussed in a companion paper [GarA88] and another [Klei88] describes the Sun implementation of UNIX® for SPARC. Here we concern ourselves with two broad areas: how the compilers use the architecture and the design of the compilers themselves.

As seen by a compiler, SPARC is a reduced instruction set (RISC) architecture in the Berkeley RISC II and SOAR tradition [Kate83, UngB84], with register windows, delayed branches and delayed loads with hardware interlocks, a floating-point coprocessor, and a few special instructions to support tagged data. All instructions are 32 bits long and most take only a single machine cycle to execute. Since there are only a few choices (or, in many cases, only one) for the proper instructions and addressing modes to use for a given operation, compilers can generate locally optimal code for expressions with relative ease, leaving more time available for the developers to address questions of the run-time environment and global code optimization.

Sun provides compilers for C, FORTRAN 77 with VMS® extensions, Pascal and Modula-2 for SPARC, all based on the same code generation and optimization technology. In addition, Sun will provide Ada® and Common LISP for SPARC (derived from products of third parties) and others provide Smalltalk [Smal87] and will provide Prolog and other languages. We deal with support for the first set of languages in depth here and mention some of the others peripherally.

2. Registers

The use of registers is typically among the most important resource allocation issues for a compiler. The load/store nature of RISC architectures makes this even more so. An accompanying paper [GarA88] describes SPARC's registers in some detail. Here we provide a synopsis of the features of greatest importance to the compiler writer.

SPARC provides three sets of registers visible to the user program at any time: 1) global integer registers, 2) global floating-point registers and 3) windowed integer registers. Global integer register `g0` reads as zero and discards values written to it. The other global integer registers are managed by software using the caller-saves protocol. These registers could also be used for global variables and pointers, either visible to the programmer or maintained as part of the program's execution environment. For instance one could, by convention, address global variables by offsets from a global register, allowing quick access to 2^{13} bytes of storage per register so dedicated. The global floating-point registers are also managed entirely by software. Our compilers use them as caller-saved register variables.

The windowed registers are further subdivided into three sets: the *ins*, *outs*, and *locals*. The `save` instruction executed as part of a procedure prologue (see Section 4.1) changes the machine's interpretation of register numbers so that the calling procedure's *outs* become the called procedure's *ins*, and a new set of *locals* and *outs* is provided. The `save` also allocates a new stack frame, by setting the new stack pointer from the old one. Similarly, the `restore` instruction executed in the procedure epilogue restores the register number interpretation to its previous state, and simultaneously cuts back the stack. Since an implementation can provide only a bounded set of windows, provision is made for a trap to occur when a procedure is entered if all windows are in use, and when a procedure is exited if the window being returned to does not have the proper values in it. The operating system can then spill or refill register windows as needed.

The overlap of *in* and *out* registers provides a way to pass most parameters in registers. One of the *outs* receives a call's return address, and another is the caller's stack pointer, which becomes the callee's frame pointer. This leaves six registers for user parameters.[1] If more parameters are provided, they are passed on the memory stack. A procedure returns a value by writing it to one or more *in* registers, where it is available to the caller as the corresponding *out*.

[1] Six is more than adequate, since the overwhelming majority of procedures take fewer than six parameters. The average number of parameters, measured statically or dynamically, is no greater than 2.1 [Weic84].

CH2539-5/88/0000/0284$01.00 © 1988 IEEE

Unused *in* registers and all the *locals* are available for a procedure's automatic storage and temporaries.

Register Names		
Register numbers	Alternate numbering	Names
r24 to r31	i0 to i7	*ins* (windowed)
r16 to r23	l0 to l7	*locals* (windowed)
r8 to r15	o0 to o7	*outs* (windowed)
r0 to r7	g0 to g7	*globals*

3. Addressing and Stack Models

SPARC's computational instructions obtain all their data from registers and immediate fields in instructions and put their results in registers. Only load and store instructions access memory. The load and store instructions have two addressing modes, one which adds the contents of two integer registers and one which adds the contents of an integer register and a 13-bit signed immediate. The semantics of `g0` makes an absolute addressing mode available also.

All but one of the integer computational instructions use the same means to specify their operands and results, i.e. one operand comes from a general register and the other either comes from a register or is a sign-extended 13-bit immediate, and the result is stored in a register. The exception is the `sethi` instruction, which is used to construct 32-bit constants and addresses for access to global data. It loads an immediate 22-bit constant into the high end of a register and zeros the other 10 bits. Thus, for example, the sequence

```
sethi%hi(loc),%i1
ld        [%i1+%lo(loc)],%i2
```

can be used to load the word at address `loc` into `i2`. While the need for an extra instruction to construct 32-bit constants and addresses may appear to be a disadvantage, it is fully in line with RISC design principles: it helps make the common cases fast without significantly slowing down the low frequency ones, since constants are usually short and the address construction is frequently optimizable to a single instruction because `%hi(loc)` turns out to be a common subexpression or loop invariant.

Parameters beyond the sixth, if any, are passed on the memory stack. Since registers do not have memory addresses, parameters which must be addressable are stored in the stack at entry to a procedure. Space is reserved on the stack for passing a one-word hidden parameter. This is used when the caller is expecting to be returned a C language *struct* by value, and gives the address of stack space allocated by the caller for that purpose. Also, space is reserved on the stack for the window overflow trap handler to store the procedure's *in* and *local* registers. Automatic variables which must be addressable, including automatic arrays and automatic records, are kept there also, as are some compiler-generated temporaries. Also, space is reserved for saving floating-point registers across calls. Automatic variables on the stack are addressed relative to `fp`, while temporaries and outgoing parameters are addressed relative to `sp`. When a procedure is active, its stack frame appears as in Figure 1.

4. Synthesized Instructions

We use the term synthesized instruction to refer to one which is generally provided in a more complex architecture, such as the DEC VAX® or IBM 370, but which is replaced by a series of instructions or a special-case subroutine call in a RISC system. In SPARC the most important instances are for procedure call, multiply and divide.

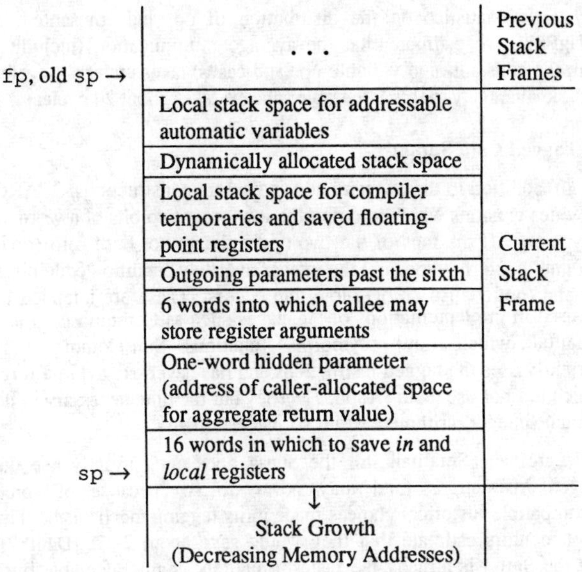

Figure 1. Memory Stack Layout for an Active Routine

4.1. Procedure Call

SPARC provides two instructions which can be used to call a procedure, namely the PC-relative `call` and the register-indirect `jmpl`. Additional instructions are required to pass parameters and to move from one register window to the next. The latter is done by the `save` instruction as part of the entry point sequence of the called routine, and a corresponding `restore` instruction is done on exit. The `save` and `restore` also set the callee's stack pointer and reset it for the caller. Thus the comparatively common case of a leaf routine (one which calls no other routines) which can allocate its local variables in its *in* registers and the global registers (and hence needs no local memory and no local registers) can be entered and exited with the minimum possible overhead by omitting the `save` and `restore`. This also reduces the number of register window overflows and underflows incurred.

4.2. Integer Multiplication and Division

SPARC provides no integer multiply, divide or remainder instructions, so these operations are synthesized from more elementary instructions. There is a multiply step instruction `mulscc`[2], but even that is not used to multiply variables by constants. Instead multiplication by constants known at compile time is done using sequences of shifts and adds (subtracts are used also if overflow detection is not an issue). Multiplication of variables by variables and all divisions and remainders other than by powers of 2 are done by calling special leaf routines. Based on statistics gathered from running an instrumented version of the system, the routines are biased so as to terminate quickly for the common cases, namely either operand being short in a multiply and the operands of a divide or remainder being about the same length. For example, the cycle count for multiplication is about $1.75 * n + 14$ for $n \le 16$ and 60 for $17 \le n \le 32$, where n is the length of the smaller operand.[3]

[2]The "cc" indicates that the instruction sets the integer condition codes.

[3]These are for the case of a positive multiplier. Negative multipliers require one more cycle for up to 16 bits and up to four more cycles for longer operands.

Given the statistics on the distribution of operands presented in [MagP87], we estimate that the average multiplication (including both the constant- and variable-operand cases) takes under six cycles and the average variable × variable subcase takes about 24 cycles.

5. Tagged Data Support

In addition to the ordinary add and subtract instructions, SPARC provides versions which interpret the low-order two bits of a word as a type tag. If the tags of the two operands are not both zero (or if arithmetic overflow occurs) the integer overflow condition code bit is set and (optionally) an overflow trap occurs. These are intended to be used in implementations of languages such as Common Lisp and Smalltalk which allow polymorphic functions. Sun Common Lisp currently uses the tagged instructions and has never existed in a form which did not use them [Kaph87]. They cut the time necessary to do fixnum (integer) arithmetic from six cycles to two.

ParcPlace Smalltalk for the Sun-4 does not currently use the tagged instructions (and may never do so) because of some incompatible historical choices made in its tagging mechanism. The implementors estimate that they would save about 2.4% [Deut87], but the Sun-4 is already the fastest Smalltalk engine available by a large margin anyway [Smal87].

6. SPARC Compilers

As noted above, Sun provides SPARC compilers for C, FORTRAN with VMS Extensions, Modula-2 and Pascal. All four are based on the same technology as used in our previous Sun-2 and Sun-3 compilers, as described in [GhoM86]. Since that paper describes the basic technology in detail, we concentrate here on the new SPARC-oriented components and the additional optimizations which have been added recently.

The SPARC versions of the C, FORTRAN and Pascal compilers include global optimization and all four include a new code generator, assembler and peephole optimizer targeted to SPARC. The compilers are structured as shown in Figure 2.[4] The arrows describe the path followed when global optimization and inlining are both enabled. When either is disabled, certain components are skipped, in some cases depending on the source language being compiled.

In contrast to our Sun-2 and Sun-3 compilers, which ran *c2* as a separate pass before the assembler, the SPARC *c2* is integrated into the assembler and operates on an internal linked-list form of the assembly language. This results in nontrivial savings in compilation time, since we read and write the assembly code once each, rather than twice, as a result.

The compilers support several levels of optimization which require various amounts of compilation time and produce various qualities of code. For example, the C compiler has four levels of optimization (in addition to the "no optimization" level):

- O1 This invokes only the peephole optimizer.
- O2 This and the following levels invoke both the global and peephole optimizers. At the O2 level, expressions involving global variables and pointers are not candidates for optimization.
- O3 Expressions involving global variables are optimized, but worst case assumptions are made about pointers.
- O4 This level traces what pointers may point to as assiduously as possible.

In general, the amount of compilation time required and the speed of the resulting code increase as the optimization level increases. However, it is interesting to note that O3 and O4 almost always produce the same code, but that compilation with O4 tends to be faster since it typically uses less virtual memory. Some examples for which O4 does produce better code than O3 are C programs which take the addresses of local variables and dereference them and Pascal programs containing `with` statements.

7. The Global and Peephole Optimizers

The SPARC global optimizer *iropt* is shared with our Sun-2 and Sun-3 compilers. Tailoring it for one architecture or another involves describing the register model to the global register allocator and tuning a few other components in minor ways, such as to determine which types of common subexpressions are worth reevaluating rather than saving and the degree of loop unrolling appropriate to use. The global optimizer performs the following optimizations:

Loop-invariant code motion
Induction-variable strength reduction
Common subexpression elimination (local & global)
Copy propagation (local & global)
Register allocation (modified graph coloring)

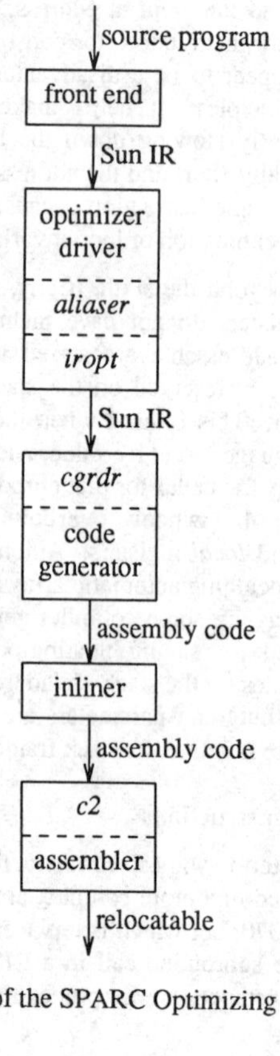

Figure 2. Structure of the SPARC Optimizing Compilers

[4] The component names which may not be familiar are as follows: *aliaser* determines which variables may at some time point to the same location; *iropt* is the global optimizer; *cgrdr* translates the Sun IR intermediate code used by the global optimizer into the PCC trees expected by the code generator; *c2* is the peephole optimizer.

Dead Code Elimination

Loop unrolling

Tail recursion elimination

and the peephole optimizer does

Elimination of unnecessary jumps

Elimination of redundant loads and stores

Deletion of unreachable code

Loop inversion

Utilization of machine idioms

Register coalescing

Instruction scheduling

Leaf routine optimization

Cross jumping

Constant propagation

In addition, inlining of language-defined (and user) routines is done by a separate pass after code generation. Most of these optimizations are discussed in [GhoM86], and so we shall discuss only the new ones in detail here, namely tail recursion elimination and loop unrolling, and make a few comments about instruction scheduling as it applies to SPARC.

7.1. Tail-Recursion Elimination

Given a self-recursive procedure whose only action upon being returned to is to itself return (and to always return the same value, if any), tail recursion elimination converts the body of the procedure into a loop.[5] On SPARC this typically saves many register window overflows and underflows and on all Sun architectures it saves stack allocation, manipulation and deallocation.

Call by reference (or the ability to pass the address of a local variable to another routine, as found in C) poses some tricky issues when combined with recursion. In this case, it may be essential that two invocations of the routine have different stack areas for their local variables. Our optimizer detects this situation and does not do the tail recursion elimination.

7.2. Loop Unrolling & Instruction Scheduling

Loop unrolling replaces the body of a loop with several copies of the body, adjusting the loop control code accordingly. While this optimization is generally valuable for loops with constant bounds, since it reduces the overhead of looping, it is particularly valuable for an architecture like SPARC because it typically increases the effectiveness of instruction scheduling.

We apply loop unrolling to loops which satisfy four conditions. Namely, the loop must 1) contain only a single basic block (i.e. straight-line code), 2)generate at most 40 triples of Sun IR code[6], 3) contain floating-point operations, and 4) have simple loop control. If the conditions are satisfied, the loop body is copied once. A special compiler flag makes it possible to unroll more copies in the relatively rare cases where that is appropriate.

SPARC has branches with a one-instruction delay and with an option to conditionally nullify (i.e. not execute) the delay slot instruction. SPARC's load instructions may overlap with the execution of the following instruction, if that instruction does not use the value loaded. Also, it allows integer instructions and one or more floating-point instructions (how many is implementation-dependent) to proceed in parallel. The implementation used in the Sun-4, in particular, allows one floating-point additive operation and one floating-point multiplicative operation at the same time. So the Sun-4 instruction scheduler must pay attention to scheduling as many as four operations at once: 1) a branch or load, 2) an integer unit instruction other than a branch or load, 3) a floating-point additive instruction, and 4) a floating-point multiplicative instruction. It uses the technique described in [GibM86].

8. Compiler Performance Analysis

In this section we briefly compare the effects of the various optimization levels on Sun-4 code and compare Sun-4 and Sun-3 code size.

8.1. Effect of Optimizations

We compare the effects of the various optimization levels of the SPARC C compiler on the Stanford benchmark. The numbers represent percentage improvements in execution time[7] over totally unoptimized code.

Effect of Optimization Levels Percentage improvements				
	O1	O2	O3	O4
Perm	28	62	62	62
Towers	26	54	57	57
Queens	16	58	58	58
Intmm	17	55	56	56
Mm	14	45	47	47
Puzzle	28	68	73	73
Quick	27	60	63	63
Bubble	25	64	73	73
Tree	13	77	81	81
FFT	16	28	28	28

For these benchmarks, O1 improves the code by an average of 21%, O2 by an average of 57%, and both O3 and O4 by an average of 59%, though there is considerable variation from one benchmark component to another.

8.2. Code and Program Size

In this section we compare code and total program size for several large programs. We would include the Stanford benchmark, but it is too small to show a significant difference, due to UNIX's predilection for rounding sizes up to the next full page. Instead, we show ratios of sizes for the C shell, the troff text formatter, the SPARC C front end, and the SPARC code generator, compiled on the Sun-3 (based on the Motorola MC68020) and Sun-4 with O2 optimization.

	Sun-4/Sun-3 Ratios	
	text	overall
C shell	1.50	1.45
troff	1.50	1.04
SPARC C front end	1.42	1.23
SPARC code generator	1.38	1.18

[5]Our optimizer currently does not deal with fully general tail recursions.

[6]This restriction is imposed in order to keep the blocks of code unrolled relatively short so as not to unduly expand the object code.

[7]For example, the number 54 at the intersection of row Towers and column O2 in the first table indicates that Towers compiled with O2 optimization runs in (100 - 54)% = 46% of the time a totally unoptimized version of Towers requires.

Thus with O2 optimization, SPARC code is, on average, about 45% larger than corresponding Sun-3 code and whole programs are about 25% larger.

9. Conclusion

The primary design considerations for SPARC were to provide an architecture which (1) is scalable through several technologies and performance levels, (2) is well-matched to available and near future compiler technology, (3) provides in its first implementation a significant performance improvement over previous Sun processors, and (4) could gain wide acceptance as an industry standard. This paper has concentrated on the second of these goals.

10. References

[Deut87] Deutsch, L. P., Personal communication, 22 Oct. 1987.

[GarA88] Garner, R., A. Agrawal, M. Namjoo & D. Jackson, The Scalable Processor Architecture (SPARC) and a CMOS Gate Array Implementation, this proceedings.

[GhoM86] Ghodssi, V., S. Muchnick & A. Wu, A Global Optimizer for Sun FORTRAN, C and Pascal, *Proceedings of the Summer 1986 USENIX Conference*, June 1986, pp. 318 - 334.

[GibM86] Gibbons, P. & S. Muchnick, Efficient Instruction Scheduling for a Pipelined Architecture, *Proc. of SIGPLAN Symp. on Compiler Constr.*, Palo Alto, CA, June 1986.

[Kaph87] Kaphan, S., Personal communication, 23 Oct. 1987.

[Kate83] Katevenis, M., **Reduced Instruction Set Computer Architectures for VLSI**, Ph.D. dissertation, Computer Science Div., Univ. of California, Berkeley, 1983. Also published by M.I.T. Press, Cambridge, MA.

[Klei88] Kleiman, S., UNIX on SPARC, this proceedings.

[MagP87] Magenheimer, D., L. Peters, K. Pettis & D. Zuras, Integer Multiplication and Division on the HP Precision Architecture, *Proc. 2nd Intl. Conf. on Arch. Support for Prog. Lang. and Oper. Sys.*, Palo Alto, CA, Oct. 1987.

[Smal87] Smalltalk 80 on the Sun-4—Call for Beta Testers, *Smalltalk-80 Newsletter*, No. 11, Sept. 1987, p. 5.

[UngB84] Ungar, D., R. Blau, P. Foley, A. D. Samples & D. Patterson, Architecture of SOAR: Smalltalk on a RISC, *Proc. of 11th Annual Intl. Symp. on Comp. Arch.*, Ann Arbor, MI, June 1984.

[Weic84] Weicker, R. P., Dhrystone: A Synthetic Systems Programming Benchmark, *CACM*, vol. 27, no. 10, Oct. 1984.

SunOS on SPARC

S.R. Kleiman and D. Williams

Sun Microsystems, Inc.
2550 Garcia Ave.
Mountain View, CA 94043

ABSTRACT

This paper describes the port of SunOS, a derivative of the UNIX operating system, to the SPARC™[1] RISC CPU. SPARC makes tradeoffs between hardware and software complexity. Operations implemented by microcode on CISC CPUs are supported by low-level operating system routines.

Hardware Architecture

SPARC specifies both integer and floating-point execution units. SPARC implementations also require a surrounding system architecture. The system architecture used in the port of SunOS to SPARC is called Sun-4™. The specific implementation of the Sun-4 architecture that was used is called the Sun-4/200 series. The core of the Sun-4 architecture contains a SPARC Integer Unit (IU), an optional SPARC Floating-Point Unit (FPU), a memory management unit (MMU), an optional virtually addressed cache, an optional VMEbus interface and several control registers.

Virtual Memory Management

The SPARC CPU has no built-in knowledge of the Sun-4 MMU. It merely emits addresses and processes memory exceptions. The MMU provides both protection and mapping.

Sun-4 Memory Mapping Hardware

The Sun-4 MMU consists of a two-level static-RAM based translation table (see Figure 1). The first-level translation table is called the segment map. Each entry in the segment map contains an index into the second-level table, which is called the page map. Entries in the page map contain the actual physical page address, protection information and statistics bits. Pages contain 8 kilobytes of memory. Page map entries are grouped into 32 entry units called *page map entry groups* (PMEG). Each PMEG maps 256 kilobytes of memory. Entries in the segment map are grouped into units called contexts. The context used to translate the current virtual address is provided by the context register. Each context represents a memory mapping of a virtual address space for a process. The Sun-4 architecture does not require that the entire 32-bit virtual address space for a process be mappable. An implementation may choose to mark a part of the middle of the virtual address space as permanently invalid. Thus, depending on the implementation, the "hole" in the middle of a process will grow or shrink. The Sun-4/200 has 16 contexts each having 1 gigabyte of mappable virtual address space; 512 megabytes at the top, and 512 megabytes at the bottom.

UNIX is a trademark of AT&T. SPARC and Sun-4 are trademarks of Sun Microsystems, Inc.

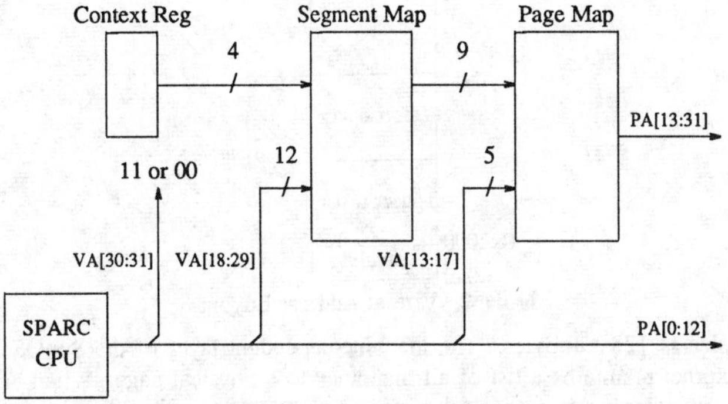

Figure 1. Sun-4/200 MMU

Virtual Address Layout

The typical layout of a SunOS process is shown in Figure 2. The kernel occupies the top 128 megabytes in all contexts to allow the kernel to switch freely among them. The kernel stack is contained in the per process global structure called the *u area.* The *u area* resides at the very top of the address space so it can be addressed absolutely. The upper 1 megabyte of the address space is also used by external I/O devices. Memory requests from these devices are translated through this portion of the MMU to provide fully mapped memory access. This technique is called Direct Virtual Memory Access (DVMA).

MMU Management

The operating system allows more runnable processes and more total virtual address space than can be accommodated by the MMU at any one time. Therefore the MMU is managed as a cache of entries. For example, when a process is started, it initially runs in a context which is reserved by the kernel for processes without contexts. The user portion of the address space of this context is completely invalid. When the process exits the kernel and attempts to run user code it gets a page fault. The kernel then tries to allocate a free context and a free PMEG to the process to provide the mapping capability to satisfy the fault. If an unused context and/or PMEG cannot be found, one is taken away from another process.

Virtual Address Cache

On the Sun-4/200 the SPARC CPU accesses main storage through a virtually addressed cache. On such caches there is a problem of cache consistency between *synonyms*; i.e. two or more virtual addresses which map to the same physical address[2] [3]. One solution is to turn off the cache for those pages which have synonyms. Sun-4 allows cached synonyms if the virtual addresses are the same modulo the cache size[4]. On the Sun-4/200 the cache

CH2539-5/88/0000/0289$01.00 © 1988 IEEE

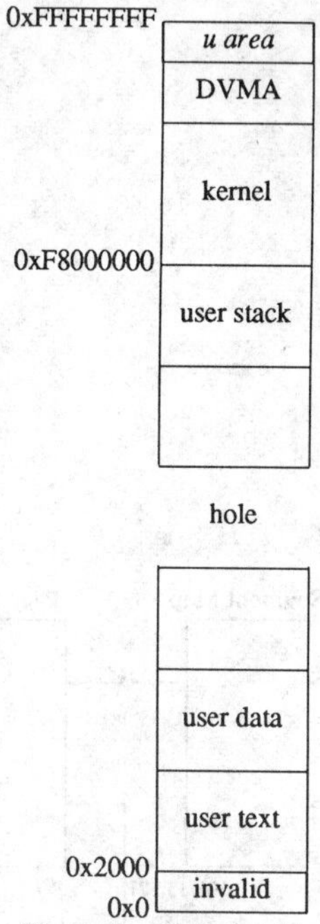

Figure 2. Virtual Address Layout

size is 128 kilobytes. The machine-dependent layer of the SunOS kernel maintains a list of all mappings to a physical page. When a new mapping to a physical page is requested by the virtual memory subsystem, the new virtual address is checked against the current mappings to see if it is the same modulo the cache size. If it is, all the mappings may be cached. Otherwise, the old mappings are flushed from the cache and the pages are marked non-cacheable. SunOS contains mechanisms[5] which allow the machine-dependent layer to pick appropriate cache-consistent virtual addresses for mappings where the user does not insist on a particular virtual address. The machine-independent layer of SunOS has no knowledge of the virtual cache.

Trap handling

Trap handlers on SPARC are the very lowest level of software. They do many things normally reserved for microcode in CISC architectures. Trap handlers can be split into three broad categories: 1) window overflow and underflow, 2) generic traps and interrupts, and 3) floating point.

Processor State

This paper assumes that the reader is familiar with the concept of register windows in general and SPARC[1] in particular. However, before going further, we review some of the SPARC processor state that is of particular interest to trap handlers:

- Current Window Pointer (CWP). A field in the Processor State Register (PSR) which contains an integer index which points to the current active register window. Decrementing the CWP moves to the "next" window. Incrementing it moves to the "previous" window.
- Window Invalid Mask (WIM) register. Any register window may be declared invalid by setting the corresponding bit in this register. Normal instructions that cause window motion cannot enter invalid windows.

When a trap is taken, further traps are disabled, the CWP is decremented (regardless of the value of the WIM), the program counters (there are 2) are saved in registers in the new window, and processing continues at the appropriate vector.

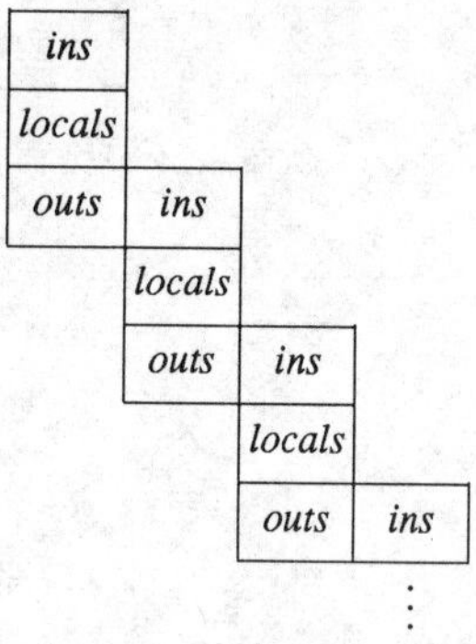

Figure 3. Register Window Model

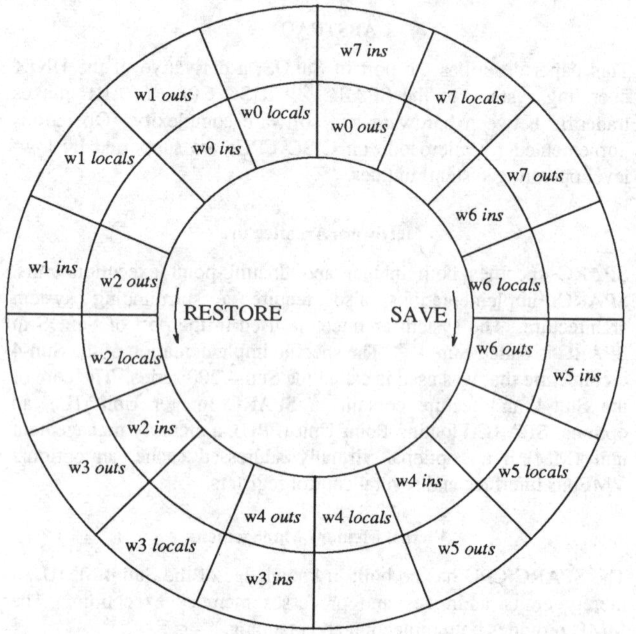

Figure 4. Register Window Implementation (8 windows)

Traps and Register Windows

The purpose of the window overflow and underflow trap handlers is to give user programs the illusion that they have an (effectively) infinite supply of overlapping register windows. Conceptually these register windows form a normal LIFO stack (see Figure 3). Normally a program uses the SAVE instruction to "push" a new window on the stack, or a RESTORE instruction to "pop" a window from the stack. In actuality the register windows are implemented as a ring (see Figure 4). Eventually, new register windows wrap around to overwrite previously used windows. This is called a window overflow. When the register window wraps around software must save the contents of the old window in memory. Similarly, the software must restore previously used register windows when the register file is emptied (window underflow). The software detects window overflow and underflow by marking at least one window between the least recently used window and the most recently used window as invalid in the WIM. If a SAVE or RESTORE instruction would move the current window to one that is marked invalid, the instruction traps instead.

If the software were to use all the implemented register windows, the *out* registers for the last window would overlap the *in* registers for the least recently used window. In addition, since the CWP is decremented in the trap sequence, the software must ensure that at least one window is available to handle a possible trap whenever traps are enabled. Thus, even though there are *n* implemented windows only *n*–1 are available for general use. The window which is marked invalid to detect overflow and underflow also serves to guarantee that there will be at least one window (the invalid window) which is free for use by the trap handler. However, it is likely that the *in* registers for the trap window are in use by the program that took the trap and the *out* registers for the trap window may be in use as the *in* registers of the least recently used window. Thus, the trap handler may always use the local registers in the trap window, but it may not use the *in*, *out*, or *global* registers without first checking whether they are in use and possibly saving and restoring them.

It is not required that one use register windows in this way. For example, one can provide one register window for users, one register window for the operating system, and several other windows for interrupt handlers. In this mode of operation, general software should not attempt to use SAVE or RESTORE instructions, but should instead use only the 32 registers in one window. The different window contexts can be protected from each other by marking register windows as invalid through the Window Invalid Mask register (WIM). Context switching would involve just setting the CWP to point to the appropriate register window and saving/restoring the global registers. This effectively removes the advantages[6] of register windows.

Window Overflow and Underflow Trap Handlers

The window overflow trap handler is responsible for saving one or more of the least recently used windows to memory. There are at least two alternative places to save overflowed register window data; On the normal program stack or on a special window save stack. In a virtual memory environment, saving window data on a separate window save stack has the advantage that it is relatively easy to make the top of the window stack be always resident in memory. This means that the window overflow and underflow trap handlers do not have to test for residency before doing the actual save or restore of the window data. However, a separate window save stack effectively doubles the stack maintenance effort since two independent growable regions must be maintained. Because of this we chose the former alternative. The trap handlers designate one of the *out* registers in each window as a pointer to a 16-word save area for window overflow or underflow. In general, this register is also used as the stack pointer. The stack pointer must be maintained whenever traps are enabled since traps may happen at any time.

Simulation data[7] has shown that saving and restoring one window at a time is the simplest and most effective algorithm for handling overflow and underflow.

Simple Window Trap Handlers A simple trap handler assumes that reading or writing words to the window save area pointed to by the stack pointer will not cause a trap. If it does, a reset trap occurs. This means that the stack pointer must be aligned to a word boundary and must point to a valid area of memory. The trap handler assumes that the WIM is initialized to a value with only one bit set, which invalidates the window before the initial CWP. The algorithm is as follows:

```
window_overflow:
    !
    ! Current window is marked invalid. Next
    ! window must be saved and marked invalid.
    !
    save;                   ! go to next window
    %wim = ror(%wim, 1); ! rotate WIM right by 1
    save window data (ins and locals) to stack
    restore;                ! back to trap window
    rett;                   ! return from trap

window_underflow:
    !
    ! Previous window is last active window.
    ! The window before that is marked invalid
    ! and must be restored. The window before
    ! that becomes the new invalid window.
    !
    %wim = rol(%wim, 1); ! rotate wim left by 1
    restore; restore;       ! back 2 windows
    restore window data (ins and locals) from stack
    save; save;             ! go to trap window
    rett;                   ! return from trap
```

In many SPARC implementations it is faster to load and store doublewords than to load and store words. The SunOS trap handlers assume that the stack pointer is doubleword-aligned so that they can use the load doubleword and store doubleword instructions to save and restore windows.

Full Window Overflow and Underflow When running in a multiprogramming environment, such as UNIX, the window trap handlers must do more checking before actually saving or restoring a window. The system must make sure that the save area is aligned and is resident in memory. If the save area is misaligned or is non-resident then the overflow trap handler must temporarily save the overflow window to an internal buffer so that the system can continue.

The operating system can run the register file in one of two ways: 1) save the entire register file on system entry and restore it on system exit, or 2) share the register file with the user. The first approach has the advantage of making the trap handler less complex. Sharing the register file with the user has that advantage of possibly not saving or restoring user windows that have not overflowed/underflowed. This can improve the performance of interrupts and simple system calls. The algorithm below assumes that the register file may contain both user and supervisor windows.

```
window_overflow:
    save;                   ! go to next window
    %wim = ror(%wim, 1); ! rotate wim right by 1
    if (window to be saved is a user window) {
        if (%sp & 7) {
            save window data to internal buffer
            goto user_alignment_trap;
        }
        if (stack is writable) {
            save window data to stack
        } else {
            save window data to internal buffer
            if (user_trap)
                goto user_page_fault;
        }
    } else {                ! system window
        save window data to stack
    }
    restore;                ! back to trap window
    rett;                   ! return from trap
```

```
window_underflow:
    %wim = rol(%wim, 1);  ! rotate wim left by 1
    restore; restore;     ! back 2 windows
    if (user_trap) {
        if (%sp & 7)
            goto user_alignment_trap;
        if (stack is not readable)
            goto user_page_fault;
    }
    restore window data from stack
    save; save;           ! back to trap window
    rett;                 ! return from trap
```

Generic Trap Handlers

A generic trap handler is a standard preamble and postamble for any non-window trap that requires register windows. Examples of this type of trap are page faults, interrupts and system calls. Certain other traps may not require the use of the generic trap handler, but they must work in the restricted environment left immediately after a trap.

The generic trap preamble first saves the global registers and the PSR. Then it checks for a window overflow condition. If there is an overflow condition it must save the next window. Next, if the trap is an interrupt it must set the appropriate processor interrupt level. Lastly, it re-enables traps and dispatches the trap to higher-level code.

The generic trap postamble first checks for a window underflow condition. If there is an underflow condition it restores the previous window. Then it restores the global registers and the PSR. When restoring the PSR it must make sure that the CWP field reflects the current CWP, not the CWP at the time of the trap, as these may be different (see Context Switching below). Lastly, it returns from the trap, which reexecutes the instruction which took the trap.

In a multi-programming environment it is also necessary to make sure that kernel data is not accessible to the user. Since, the user and the kernel share the register file the generic trap postamble must "clean" (zero) the register windows used by the kernel before returning to the user.

Page Faults Page faults use the generic trap handler. When a page fault on data is taken, the page fault handler must compute the address of the fault. It may do this by decoding the faulted instruction and computing the effective address. On the Sun-4, the effective address of a data fault is latched in an external register. The register is read by the page fault handler to determine the faulted address.

VMEbus Interrupts After the preamble, the VMEbus interrupt handler reads an external system register to get the VME interrupt vector and complete the interrupt acknowledge cycle. The vector is then used to find the correct interrupt handler to call.

Floating-Point Trap Handlers

A bit in the Processor State Register enables the SPARC floating-point unit. Processes are started with the FPU disabled. When a process executes its first floating-point instruction, a trap is generated. The floating-point trap handler enables the FPU, initializes the FPU registers to NaNs, and marks the process as using the FPU so that a context switch will save the FPU state.

SPARC defines a set of floating-point operations (FPops) that an implementation may provide. FPops which are not implemented are simulated by the kernel for compatibility. Configurations without an FPU generate traps on every execution of a floating-point instruction. The floating-point trap handler calls a simulator for floating-point operations in this case. The simulator runs at the lowest interrupt priority until it completes. Interrupts can be taken during simulation but the kernel will not context switch until the simulator finishes.

A SPARC FPU may execute several FPops in parallel while other non-floating-point IU operations are proceeding. The number of FPops that may execute in parallel is implementation-dependent. A queue in the FPU stores the necessary state for all the concurrently executing FPops when exceptions occur. The floating-point unit and trap handler together guarantee a user model (ANSI/IEEE 754 compatible) in which the floating-point instructions appear to finish in sequence, even though they are executing in parallel.

Exceptions are generated asynchronously, by the FPU yet are only taken by the IU synchronously when another floating-point instruction is encountered in the instruction stream. The trap handler for floating-point exceptions normally gets control at a point where the IU has advanced the program counter many instructions after the FPop that generated the exception. The floating-point queue contains sequence of address/instruction pairs which are the current set of instructions being executed by the FPU. The trap handler dumps the queue and takes action appropriate to the type of exception. The following exceptions may be generated (with the noted actions):

- IEEE exceptions - The kernel sends a signal to the user with a code and the address of the instruction generating the exception.
- Unfinished FPops - An implementation may not be able to fully implement correct handling of some instructions in all cases. The trap handler simulates the instruction in this case.
- Unimplemented FPops - An implementation may not implement all FPops. The trap handler simulates the instruction.

Context Switching

The general procedure for context switching is shown below:

```
cswitch:
    store stack pointer
    store PC (return address)
    save global registers (if required)
    save floating point registers (if required)
    flush active register windows to the stack
    save; save; ... NWINDOWS–2 times
    restore floating point registers (if required)
    restore global registers (if required)
    load new return address
    load new stack pointer
    restore;
    return;
```

The main action that is unique to register window architectures is flushing the register windows to the stack. One way to do this is to do NWINDOWS–2 SAVE instructions, where NWINDOWS is the number of implemented windows in the ring. The reason we can do two less than the number of windows is that one window is always invalid and we don't have to flush the window that the context switch is operating in. The restore at the end of the context switch (part of the normal return sequence) is guaranteed to cause an underflow which fetches the window data from the new stack.

This is the method the kernel uses to context switch. However, it is undesirable to have user programs know how many windows are implemented on a particular implementation of SPARC. Therefore, a process may use a special software trap instruction which causes the kernel to flush its register windows. Also note that a process which is context switched may return to a different window than the one it left. Therefore, users never know which register window (CWP) they are in currently.

Measurements of the Sun-4/200 kernel (which has seven implemented windows) suggest that on average three active register windows are flushed to the stack.

Kernel Context Switching

Switching processes in the kernel is more complicated than ordinary context switching. After the state of the old process has been saved, the context switch routine must switch kernel stacks by switching the MMU entries for the *u area*, which is at a fixed address. Before this can be done, the current stack must be flushed out of the virtual address cache. This is the most expensive operation in kernel context switching (about 75% of the context switch time). It is possible to avoid this by not requiring the UNIX *u area* to reside at a fixed address. After this, the context switch routine loads the context register with the context number of the new process, if it has one. If it doesn't, it uses the reserved kernel-only context.

Conclusions

The most difficult part of porting SunOS to SPARC was dealing with the register windows. Once the trap handler "microcode" was written the port proceeded much like for other microprocessors. The simplicity of RISC architecture allowed processor state saving to be tailored exactly to the needs at hand, without extra overhead. Simple instruction restarting provided easy exception handling.

REFERENCES

1. R. Garner, A. Agrawal, W. Brown, D. Hough. W.N. Joy, S.R. Kleiman, S. Muchnick, D. Patterson, J. Pendelton, R. Tuck, "The Scalable Processor Architecture", *Compcon Conference Proceedings*, March 1988.
2. A.J. Smith, "Cache Memories", *ACM Computing Surveys*, September 1982.
3. R. Cheng, "Virtual Address Cache in UNIX", *USENIX Conference Proceedings*, Summer 1987.
4. Sun Microsystems, Inc., "Sun-4 Architecture: A Sun Technical Report".
5. R.A. Gingell, J.P. Moran, W.A. Shannon, "Virtual Memory Architecture in SunOS", *USENIX Conference Proceedings*, Summer 1987.
6. D.A. Patterson, C.H. Sequin, "RISC I: A Reduced Instruction Set VLSI Computer", *Proceedings of the 8th Symposium on Computer Architecture*, May 1981.
7. Y. Tamir, C.H. Sequin, "Strategies for Managing the Register File in RISC", *IEEE Transactions on Computers*, vol. C-32, no. 11, November 1983.

The New Apollo Workstations

Chair: P. Levine

The Network Computing Architecture and System: An Environment for Developing Distributed Applications

Terence H. Dineen, Paul J. Leach, Nathaniel W. Mishkin, Joseph N. Pato, Geoffrey L. Wyant

Apollo Computer Inc.

1. Introduction

The Network Computing Architecture (NCA) is an object-oriented framework for developing distributed applications in a heterogeneous computing environment. The Network Computing System™ (NCS™) is a portable implementation of that architecture that runs on Unix® and other systems. By adopting an object-oriented approach, we encourage application designers to think in terms of what they want their applications to operate on, not what server they want the applications to make calls to or how those calls are implemented. This design increases robustness and flexibility in a changing environment.

NCS currently runs under Apollo's DOMAIN/IX™ [Leach 83], 4.x BSD and System V Unix (and their derivatives), the IBM PC®, and VAX/VMS®. Apollo Computer has placed NCA in the public domain.

NCA defines a network-transport independent Remote Procedure Call (RPC) protocol. (RPC is a mechanism that allows programs to make calls to subroutines where the caller and the subroutine run in different processes, most commonly on different machines [Birrell 84].) NCS implements this protocol using Berkeley Unix sockets as the interface to any datagram facility. The NCA/RPC protocol provides at-most-once procedure call semantics over the datagram layer, with optimizations if an operation is declared to be idempotent.

NCA defines the Network Interface Definition Language (NIDL), a high-level language used to specify the interfaces to procedures that are to be invoked through the RPC mechanism. NCS includes a portable NIDL compiler that takes NIDL interfaces as input and produces stub procedures that, among other things, handle data representation issues and connect program calls to the NCS RPC runtime environment that implements the NCA/RPC protocol. The relationships among the client (i.e. the caller of a remoted procedure), server, stubs, and NCS runtime is shown in figure (1).

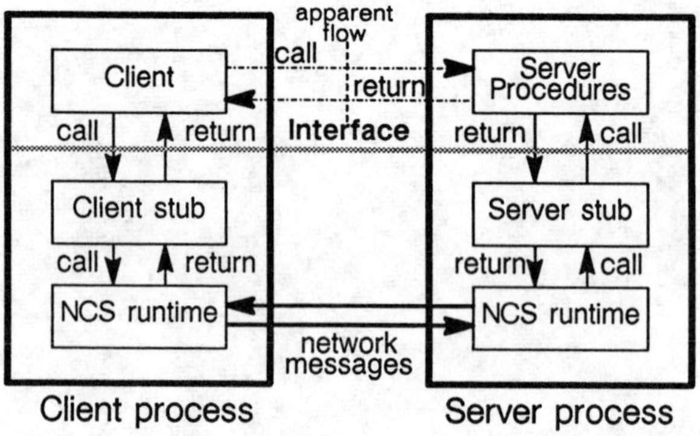

Figure 1. Relationships among client, server, stubs and NCS runtime

Network Data Representation (NDR), NCA's data representation protocol, supports multiple scalar data formats, so that similar machines do not have to convert data to a canonical form, but can instead use their common data formats.

NCA defines several interfaces (written in NIDL) to support a replicated global location database: Using it, the locations of an object can be determined given its object ID, its type, or one of its supported interfaces. NCS includes servers that implement the location interfaces.

2. The Object-Oriented Approach

NCA is object-oriented. By this we mean that it follows a paradigm established by systems such as Smalltalk [Goldberg 83], Eden [Almes 83, Lazowska 81], and Hydra [Wulf 75, Cohen 75]. The basic entity in an object-oriented system is the *object*. An object is a container of state (i.e. data) that can be accessed and modified only through a well-defined set of *operations* (what Smalltalk calls *messages*). The implementation of the operations is completely hidden from the client (i.e. caller) of the operations. Every object has some *type* (what Smalltalk calls a *class*). The implementation of a set of operations is called a *manager* (what Smalltalk calls a set of *methods*). Only the manager of a type knows the internal structure of objects of the type it manages. Sets of related operations are grouped into *interfaces*. Several types may support the same interface; a single type may support multiple interfaces.

For example, consider an interface called *directory* containing the operations *add_entry*, *drop_entry*, and *list_entries*. This interface might be supported by two types: *directory_of_files* and *print_queue*. There are potentially many objects of these two types. That there are many objects of the type *directory_of_files* should be obvious. By saying that there are many *print_queue* objects we mean that a system (or a network of connected systems) might have many print queues — say, one for each department in a large organization.

The reason for using the object-oriented approach in the context of a network architecture is that this approach lets you concentrate on *what* you want done, instead of *where* it's going to be done and *how* it's going to be done: objects are the units of *distribution, abstraction, extension, reconfiguration,* and *reliability*.

Distribution. Distribution addresses the question of where an operation is performed. The answer to this question is that the operation is performed where the object resides. For example, if the print queue lives on system A, then an attempt to add an entry to the queue from system B must be implemented by making a remote procedure call from system B to system A. (This implementation fact is hidden from the program attempting to add the entry.)

Abstraction. Abstraction addresses the question of how an operation is performed. In NCA, the object's type manager knows how the operation is performed. For example, a single program *list_directory* could be used to list both the contents of a file system directory and the contents of a print queue. The program simply calls the *list_entries* operation. The type managers for the two types of objects might represent their information in completely different ways (because, say, of the different performance characteristics required). However, the *list_directory* program uses only the abstract operation and is insulated from the details of a particular type's implementation.

Extension. The object-oriented approach allows extension; i.e. it specifies how the system is enhanced. In NCA, there are two kinds of extensions allowed. The first is extension by creation of new types. For example, users can create new types of objects that support the *directory* interface; programs like *list_directory* that are clients of this interface simply work on objects of the new type, without modification. The second kind of extension is extension by creation of new interfaces. A new interface is the expression of new functionality.

Reconfiguration. Because of partial failures, or for load balancing, networked systems sometimes need to be reconfigured. In object-oriented terms, this reconfiguration takes place by moving objects to new locations. For example, if the system that was the home for some print queue failed because of a hardware problem, the system would be reconfigured by moving the print queue object to a new system (and informing the network of the object's new location).

Reliability. The availability of many systems in a network should result in increased reliability. NCA's approach is to foster increased reliability by allowing objects to be replicated. Replication increases the probability that least one copy of the object will be available to users of the object. To make replication feasible, NCS provides tools to keep multiple replicas of an object in sync.

While NCA is object-oriented and we believe that applications that use the object-oriented capabilities of NCA will be more robust and general than those that don't, it is easy to use NCS as a conventional RPC system, ignoring its object-oriented features.

3. Network Interface Definition Language

The Network Interface Definition Language (NIDL) is the language used in the Network Computing Architecture to describe the remote interfaces called by clients and provided by servers. Interfaces described in NIDL are checked and translated by the NIDL compiler.

NIDL is strictly a *declarative* language — it has no executable constructs. NIDL contains only constructs for defining the constants, types, and operations of an interface. NIDL is more than an interface definition language however. It is also a *network* interface definition language and, therefore, it enforces the restrictions inherent in a distributed computing model (e.g. lack of shared memory).

A NIDL interface contains an constant and type definitions, and operation descriptions.

A standard set of programming language types is provided. Integers (signed and unsigned) come in one, two, four, and eight byte sizes. Single (four byte) and double (eight byte) precision floating point numbers are available. Other scalars include signed and unsigned characters, as well as booleans and enumerations.

In addition to scalar types, NIDL provides the usual type constructors: structures, unions, pointers, and arrays. Unions must be discriminated. (Non-discriminated unions are not permitted. The actual data values must be known at runtime so that it can be correctly transmitted to the remote server.) Pointers, in general, are restricted to being "top-level." That is, pointers to other pointers, or records containing pointers are not permitted. Arrays can be fixed in size or have their size determined at runtime.

Operation declarations are the heart of a remote interface definition. These define the procedures and functions that servers implement and to which clients make calls. All operations are strongly typed. This enables the NIDL compiler to generate the code to correctly copy parameters to and from the packet and to do any needed data conversions. Operation declarations can be optionally marked to have certain semantic properties, for example whether they are *idempotent*. (An idempotent procedure is one that can be executed many times with no ill-effect.)

All operations are required to have a *handle* as their first parameter. This parameter is similar to the implicit "self" argument of Smalltalk-80 or the "this" argument of C++ [Stroustrup 86]. The handle argument is used to determine what object and server is to receive the remote call. NIDL defines a primitive handle type named *handle_t*. An argument of this type can be used as an operation's handle parameter. Clients can obtain a *handle_t* by calling the NCS runtime, providing an object UUID and network location as input arguments.

More abstract types can also be used as handles. To do so the interface writer must supply a subroutine that converts the abstract type into a *handle_t*. This routine is automatically invoked by the client stub. Handle arguments can be implicit. An interface definition can declare that a single global variable should be treated as the handle argument for all operations in the interface.

Earlier we stated that pointers could not be nested. The reason is that such nesting would require the NIDL compiler to generate code to transmit general graph structures. However, permitting only top-level, non-nested pointers can be a severe limitation in the design of an interface. For example, it excludes passing tree data structures to remote procedures.

To provide an escape from this restriction, NIDL allows a type to have an associated "transmissible" type. The transmissible type is a type that the NIDL compiler *does* know how to marshall. Any type that has an associated transmissible type must have a set of procedures to convert that type to and from its transmissible type.

4. Network Data Representation

Communicating typed values in a heterogenous environment requires a data representation protocol. A data representation protocol defines a mapping between typed values and *byte streams*. A byte stream is a sequence of bytes indexed by nonnegative integers. Examples of data representation protocols are Courier [Xerox 81] and XDR [Sun 86]. A data representation protocol is needed because different machines represent data differently. For example, VAXes represent integers with the *least* significant byte at the low address and 68000s represent integers with the *most* significant byte at the low address. A data representation protocol defines the way data is represented so that machines with different local data representation can communicate typed values to each other.

NCA includes a data representation protocol called Network Data Representation (NDR). NDR defines a set of data types and type constructors which can be used to specify ordered sets of typed values. NDR also defines a mapping between ordered sets of values and their representations in messages.

Under NDR, the representation of a set of values consists of two items: a *format label* and a byte stream. The format label defines how scalar values are represented (e.g. VAX or IEEE floating point) in the byte stream; its representation is fixed by NDR as a data structure representable in four bytes.

NDR supports the scalar types *boolean, character, signed integer, unsigned integer*, and *floating point*. Booleans are represented in the byte stream with one byte; *false* is represented by a zero byte and *true* by a non-zero byte. Characters are represented in the byte stream with one byte; either ASCII or EBCDIC codes can be used. Four sizes of signed and unsigned integers are defined: *small, short, long*, and *hyper*. Small types are represented in the byte stream with one byte, short types with two bytes, long types with four bytes, and hyper types with eight bytes. Either big- or little-endian representation can be used for integers; two's complement is assumed for signed integers. The two sizes of floating point type are *single* and *double*. Single floating point types are represented with four bytes and double floating point types use eight bytes. The supported floating point representations are IEEE, VAX, Cray, and IBM.

In addition to scalar types, NDR has a set of type constructors for defining aggregate types. These include *fixed size arrays, open arrays, zero terminated strings, records*, and *variant records*.

NDR is abstract in that it does not define how the format label and the byte stream are represented in packets. The NIDL compiler and the NCA/RPC protocol are users of NDR: They work together to generate the format label and byte stream, encode the format label in packet headers, fragment the byte stream into packet-sized pieces, and put the fragments in packet bodies.

5. The NCS NIDL Compiler

NCS includes a compiler which mediates between NIDL on the one hand and NDR and the NCS runtime on the other. The functions of the compiler are: checking the syntax and "semantics" of interface definitions written in NIDL; translating NIDL definitions into declarations in implementation languages such as C; and generating client and server stubs for executing the remote operations of an interface.

NCS's NIDL compiler is implemented for portability in C using YACC and LEX. It is available in source form to encourage its use and extension in heterogeneous networked environments.

6. Location Broker

A highly available location service is a fundamental component of a distributed system architecture. Objects representing people, resources, or services are transient and mobile in a network environment. Consumers of these entities cannot rely on a priori knowledge of their existence or location, but must consult a dynamic registry. When consumers rely solely on a location service for accessing objects, it becomes essential that the location server remain available in the face of partial network failures.

The NCA *Location Broker* (NCA/LB) protocol is designed to provide a reliable network-wide location broker. This protocol is defined by a NIDL interface and is thereby easily used by any NCA/RPC based application.

The NCA/LB, unlike location services like Xerox SDD's Clearinghouse [Oppen 83] or Berkeley's Internet Name Domain service (BIND) [Terry 84], yields location information based on UUIDs rather than on human readable string names. The advantages of using UUIDs were described earlier.

An object's type manager must first advertise its location with the Location Broker in order for that object to locatable. A manager advertises itself by registering its location and its willingness to support some combination of specific objects, types of objects, or interfaces. A manager can choose to advertise itself as a global service available to the entire network, or limit its registration to the local system. Managers that choose the latter form of registration do not make themselves unavailable, but rather limit their visibility to clients that specifically probe their system for location information.

Clients find objects by querying the Location Broker for appropriate registrations. A client can choose to query for a specific object, type, interface, or any combination of these characteristics. When operations are externally constrained to occur at a specific location, a client can choose to query the location broker at the required system for managers supporting the appropriate object.

7. The NCA/RPC Protocol and NCS Implementation

The NCA/RPC protocol is designed to be low cost for the common cases and independent of the underlying network protocols on top of which it is layered. The NCS runtime implementation of the NCA/RPC protocol is designed to be portable.

The NCA/RPC protocol is designed so that a simple RPC call will result in as few network messages and have as little overhead as possible. It is well known that existing networking facilities designed to move long byte streams reliably (e.g. TCP/IP) are generally not well suited to being the underlying mechanism by which RPC runtimes exchanges messages. The primary reason for this is that the cost of setting up a connection using such facilities and the associated maintenance of that connection is quite high. Such a cost might be acceptable if, say, a client were to make 100 calls to one server. However, we don't want to preclude the possibility of one client making a call to 100 servers in turn. In general, we expect the number of calls made from a particular client to a particular server to be relatively small. The reliable connection solution is also unacceptable from the server's perspective: A popular server may need to handle calls from hundreds of clients over a relatively short period of time (say 1-2 minutes). The server does not want to bear the cost of maintaining network connections to all those clients.

Rather than depending on reliable connections, all the NCA/RPC protocol assumes is an underlying unreliable network service. The protocol is robust in the face of lost, duplicated, and long-delayed messages, messages arriving out of order, and server crashes. When necessary, the protocol ensures that no call is ever executed more than once. (Calls may execute zero or one times and, in the face of network partitions or server crashes, the client may not know which.)

The NCS RPC runtime is written in portable C and uses the BSD Unix *socket* abstraction. This abstraction is intended to mask the details of various *protocol families* so that one can write protocol-independent networking code. (A protocol family is a suite of related protocols; e.g. TCP and UDP are part of the DoD IP protocol family; PEP and SPP are part of the Xerox NS protocol family.) Bringing up the NCS runtime on a new protocol family should *not* require any changes to the NCS runtime proper. All that should be required is to add some relatively trivial routines to the socket abstraction extension library.

References

[Almes 83]
Guy T. Almes. Integration and distribution in the Eden system. Technical Report 83-01-02, Department of Computer Science, University of Washington, 1983.

[Birrell 84]
Andrew D. Birrell and Bruce Jay Nelson. Implementing remote procedure calls. *ACM Transactions on Computer Systems*, II(1):39-59, 1984.

[Cohen 75]
Ellis Cohen and David Jefferson. Protection in the Hydra operating system. In *Proceedings of the Fifth Symposium on Operating Systems Principles*, pages 141-160. ACM Special Interest Group on Operating Systems, 1975.

[Goldberg 83]
Adele Goldberg and David Robson. *Smalltalk-80: The Language and its Implementation*. Addison-Wesley, 1983.

[Lazowska 81]
Edward D. Lazowska, Henry M. Levy, Guy T. Almes, Michael J. Fischer, Robert J. Fowler, and Stephen C. Vestal. The architecture of the Eden system. In *Proceedings of the Eighth Symposium on Operating Systems Principles*, 148-159. ACM Special Interest Group on Operating Systems, 1981.

[Leach 82]
Paul J. Leach, Bernard L. Stumpf, James A. Hamilton and Paul H. Levine. UIDs as Internal Names in a Distributed File System. In *Proceedings of the Symposium on Principles of Distributed Computing*, 34-41. Association for Computing Machinery, 1982.

[Leach 83]
Paul J. Leach, Paul H. Levine, Bryan P. Douros, James A. Hamilton, David L. Nelson, and Bernard L. Stumpf. The architecture of an integrated local network. *IEEE Journal on Selected Areas in Communications*, SAL-I(5):842-857, 1983.

[Oppen 83]
D. C. Oppen and Y. K. Dalal. The Clearinghouse: A decentralized agent for locating named objects in a distributed environment. *ACM Transactions on Office Information Systems* I(3):230-253, 1983.

[Stroustrup 86]
Bjarne Stroustrup. *The C++ Programming Language*. Addison-Wesley, 1986.

[Sun 86]
Sun Microsystems. Networking on the Sun workstation. Part no. 800-1324-03. 1986.

[Terry 84]
D. B. Terry, M. Painter, D. Riggle and S. Zhou. The Berkeley Internet Name Domain Server. In *Proceedings of the Usenix Association Summer Conference*, 21-31. 1984.

[Wulf 75]
W. Wulf, R. Levin, C. Pierson. Overview of the Hydra operating system development. *Proceedings of the Fifth Symposium on Operating Systems Principles*, pages 122-131. ACM Special Interest Group on Operating Systems, 1975.

[Xerox 81]
Xerox Corporation. Xerox System Integration Bulletin, OPD B018112. 1981.

The Cache Architecture of the Apollo DN4000

Craig R. Frink, Paul J. Roy

Apollo Computer Inc.
Chelmsford, MA 01824

Abstract

The cache architecture of the Apollo DN4000 workstation utilizes a virtual cache to provide a cost-effective approach to high-performance computing. Of particular interest is how our use of a virtually tagged, write-through cache made it possible to use a low-cost, off-the-shelf MMU and resulted in inclusion of a virtual write buffer. This architecture enables the processor to execute zero wait-state memory reads and writes. We also show how the way that objects are accessed in Apollo's system led to a write-allocate cache update policy to solve the virtual address synonym problem.

1. Introduction

The Apollo DN4000 is a high-performance workstation that fits in the mid-range of Apollo's product family. It is based on Motorola's 25Mhz MC68020 microprocessor [Moto85], MC68881 floating-point coprocessor, and the MC68851 Paged Memory Management Unit (PMMU) [Moto86]. The system has a 1 Gigabyte per-process virtual address space, supports between 4 and 32 Megabytes of physical memory, and utilizes a PC/AT®-compatible bus to support a wide range of system and user peripheral devices [Apol87a].

Cache memories [Smit86] are used in many high-performance microprocessor designs to achieve the highest possible performance. A cache is a fast memory placed between the processor and the main memory subsystem. When the processor references a memory location that has data stored in the cache, the effect of a slower main memory subsystem is eliminated. It is then possible for the processor to operate at a much higher speed than a design which depends on the main memory store for each reference.

The DN4000 achieves its high performance using a virtual cache architecture in which both the cache indices and cache tags are derived from virtual addresses. This made it possible to use a low-cost, off-the-shelf MMU, which subsequently resulted in inclusion of a virtual write buffer†. This approach allowed us to implement a zero wait-state, write-through cache.

The virtual cache in the DN4000 does present some problems, however. First, because the cache is virtually tagged, many memory accesses will not result in MMU activity. As a result, some of the MMU housekeeping functions, such as ensuring the validity of virtual-to-physical mappings, are not always exercised and the operating system must play a significant role in maintaining cache coherency (discussed in detail in a previous work [Frin88]). Secondly, virtual address synonyms [Smit82] must be dealt with. Our solution is an outgrowth of the way that objects are accessed in Apollo's system, and is discussed in Section 3.

A final consideration was the creation of a virtual write buffer to achieve zero wait-state writes. Figure 1 shows the location of the virtual write buffer between the cache and MMU in the DN4000 processor/memory subsystem.

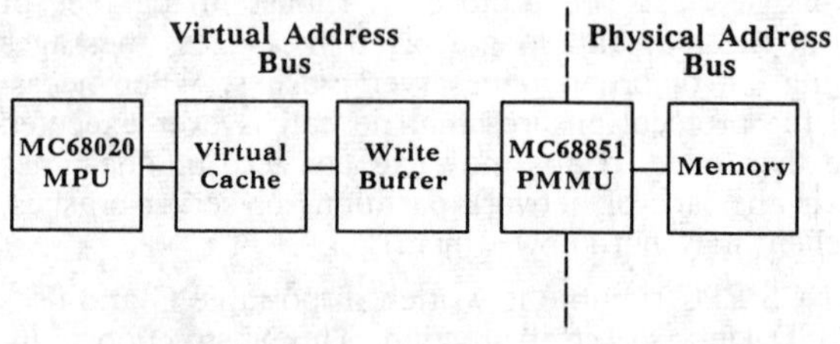

Figure 1. Processor/Memory Subsystem

The next section describes the cache architecture in detail and Section 3 discusses the solution to the virtual address synonym problem. Section 4 describes the functioning of the virtual write buffer and how it allows the processor to execute writes in zero memory wait-states.

† Certain aspects of this technology are subject to patents which are pending with the United States Patent and Trademark Office.

CH2539-5/88/0000/0300$01.00 © 1988 IEEE

2. Cache Architecture

The cache memory subsystem in the DN4000 has both its indices and tags derived from virtual addresses. On a read access, a cache hit does not require the MMU to translate and validate the virtual address because it was done previously when the data was entered in the cache. The MMU, therefore, need only be involved in processor read operations that generate cache misses. Similarly, write accesses that hit in the cache will be captured by the write buffer, thus effectively hiding the MMU translation time from the processor. This important aspect of the virtual cache architecture allowed a large amount of the entry-level Apollo DN3000 workstation architecture [Apol87a] to be reused, most importantly its use of the inexpensive PMMU, a lower-speed memory management unit.

The cache employs a write-through, with write-allocate write policy. On a memory write, both the cache and main memory are updated. If a cache miss occurs then the indexed cache line is allocated to contain the new data. Section 3 discusses why the write-allocate update policy of the cache is crucial to maintaining cache coherency in the face of virtual address synonyms.

The cache is 8 Kbytes in size and contains both instructions and data. It is direct mapped, organized as 2048 lines of 4 bytes each. Each line has a data and tag field associated with it. The data field stores the data values associated with each processor reference. The tag field, which is comprised of an address and condition code tag, is used in the validation of all cache references. Figure 2 shows the organization of the virtual cache.

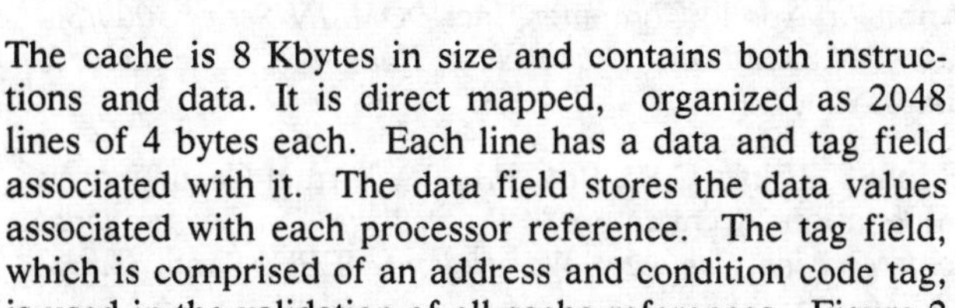

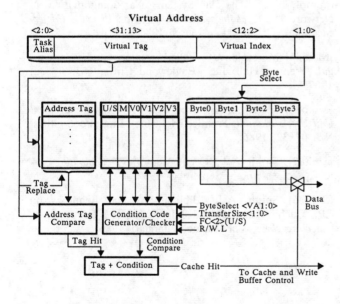

Figure 2. DN4000 Virtual Cache Organization

The address tag is derived from the upper 19 virtual address bits and a 3-bit task alias field. This 3-bit field is provided by the PMMU on context switch and reflects one of eight most-recently-used processes in the system. It effectively acts as an approximation to full address space identifiers, and serves to reduce cache flushing due to context switches. The address tag is the first indication that a processor reference will find valid data in the cache and is used to terminate the processor cycle.

The condition code tag contains information about the data values stored in each cache line. This information is generated and stored on each cache refill or write operation. The user/supervisor status, validity of each byte, and the modified status of each cache line are checked on each cache reference to determine if the reference should generate a cache hit.

The "user/supervisor" or "U/S" bit in each cache line provides protection to encached data. Since the MMU does not check the permissions of all cache references, this status must be reflected in each cache line. Thus, for instance, a user access to data inserted in the cache while the processor was in supervisor mode will result in a cache miss. This then allows the MMU to become an active participant in the transaction and reflect any possible access violation to the operating system. However, a supervisor reference to a cache entry that was created by a user process will succeed.

The cache supports the write-allocate policy by containing information about the validity of each byte in the cache line. Each byte has a "valid" or "V" bit associated with it. For example, if the write of a single byte allocates the byte to the indexed entry, only that byte is valid for future references. Referencing a byte which is not marked as valid, results in a cache miss and the entire line being refilled from physical memory. This way the cache accommodates all types of read and write operations including aligned, and misaligned byte, word, and longword references.

Status of the modification state of each cache line is also maintained. This is the "modified" or "M" bit. This bit is used to support the virtual write buffer in determining whether a write operation is a candidate for buffering (see Section 4).

3. Virtual Address Synonyms

Virtual address synonyms, or aliases, exist when two or more virtual addresses point to the same physical data. There are some inherent problems associated with synonyms. The first is the case where multiple synonyms do not index to the same cache line.

Consider the following situation in which two processes have access to shared data. Each process uses its own virtual address. Process One reads from address VA1 and the data is inserted in the cache at line L1. Process Two then writes to address VA2 (which is a synonym to VA1), but line L1 is not affected because VA1 and VA2 do not index to the same cache line. When Process One reads VA1, it accesses stale data from line L1 instead of the new data that's been written by Process Two.

The solution for the DN4000 was an outgrowth of the way that objects are accessed in Apollo's system [Leac85]. In this system, a program accesses an object by "mapping" 32 Kbyte segments into the program's virtual address space (and subsequently accessing the mapped addresses to result in demand-paging). Because all the mappings are chosen by the operating system on a modulo 32 Kbyte boundary — and because the cache size is less than the segment size — all virtual address synonyms are guaranteed to index to the same cache line.

Another problem with virtual address synonyms exists if only a write-through *without* write-allocate policy is used. In this situation, Process One reads from address VA1, and the data is inserted in the cache at line L1. Process Two then writes to address VA2 (which is a synonym to VA1 and indexes to line L1), but L1 is not affected because a write miss occurs as the result of a cache tag mismatch. When Process One reads VA1, it accesses stale data from line L1 instead of the new data that's been written by Process Two.

To solve this problem, a write miss must do one of two things: invalidate the indexed cache entry, or allocate the entry to the new data. So that subsequent accesses to the same data would result in cache hits, we used the latter approach in the DN4000.

4. Virtual Write Buffer

The DN4000's write buffer is a single longword deep and resides on the virtual side of the MMU (hence the name "Virtual Write Buffer"). A write that has been captured in the write buffer allows the processor to complete its cycle in zero wait-states and continue execution out of the cache. Concurrently, the write buffer writes the data through the MMU to physical memory.

The placement of the write buffer on the virtual bus provides a great degree of overlap by hiding the MMU virtual-to-physical address translation time from the processor on many write operations. This provides a substantial performance win for the DN4000 because of the write-through nature of its cache, and its use of a lower-cost, lower-speed MMU [Frin88].

All writes that have an address tag match and "modified" bit set in the indexed cache entry are buffered. If the tag mismatches or the "modified" bit is not set, the write cannot be buffered because the processor must wait while the write access is validated. Once the write has successfully completed, the "modified" bit is set to indicate that subsequent writes may be buffered.

The virtual write buffer produces another performance benefit related to the autonomous nature of the DN4000 bus architecture. Because multiple bus operations may occur concurrently on both the virtual and physical buses, the write buffer can arbitrate for the physical bus (e.g., with a DMA controller), while the processor continues to access the virtual cache. Of course, because the write buffer is a single longword deep, only one write may be pending.

5. Conclusion

The Apollo DN4000 workstation achieves its high performance using a virtual cache-based architecture. In this paper, we described the DN4000's virtually tagged, write-through cache and virtual write buffer. This architecture enables the processor to execute zero wait-state memory reads and writes, while using a low-cost, off-the-shelf MMU. Virtual caches, however, require solving the virtual address synonym problem. The DN4000 solution was an outgrowth of the way that objects are accessed in Apollo's system, and consisted of implementing a write-allocate cache update policy.

References

[Apol87a] Apollo Computer, Inc. *DOMAIN Series 3000/Series 4000 Hardware Architecture Handbook.* Chelmsford, MA 01824, 1987.

[Frin88] Frink, C.R., Roy, P.J. "A Virtual Cache-Based Workstation Architecture," *Proceedings 2nd International Conference on Computer Workstations*, IEEE, Santa Clara, CA, March 1988.

[Leac85] Leach, P.J., Levine, P.H., Hamilton, J.A., Stumpf, B.L. "The File System of an Integrated Local Network," *Proceedings of ACM Computer Science Conference*, New Orleans, LA, March 1985.

[Moto85] Motorola. *MC68020 Microprocessor User's Manual.* Prentice-Hall, Inc., Englewood Cliffs, N.J. 07632, 1987.

[Moto86] Motorola. *MC68851 Paged Memory Management Unit User's Manual.* Prentice-Hall, Inc., Englewood Cliffs, N.J. 07632, 1986.

[Smit82] Smith, A.J. "Cache Memories," *Computing Surverys*, Vol. 14, no.3, September 1982.

[Smit86] Smith, A.J. "Bibliography and Readings on CPU Cache Memories and Related Topics," *Computer Architecture News,* Vol. 14, no.1, January 1986.

A PORTABLE AND EXTENSIBLE ENVIRONMENT FOR DEVELOPING INTERACTIVE APPLICATIONS

Kee Hinckley and Andrew Schulert

Apollo Computer Inc.
330 Billerica Road
Chelmsford, MA 01824

Abstract

This paper describes work that is being done in the User Environment Group at Apollo Computer on an architecture for the construction of interactive applications. Originally, on Apollo workstations, almost all support for interactive applications was embedded in a single application, the Display Manager. While this has been a useful and long-lived tool, it has not been easy to extend it for new applications or to customize its components for reuse. The new architecture is modular, defining a set of cooperating tools that are both extensible and replaceable, while maintaining the advantages of the earlier, more integrated approach.

Introduction

When Apollo introduced its first workstation in 1981, an integral part of the product was the **Display Manager** (DM), a special application that ran in its own process and performed several functions. Because the DM included facilities for window management, text editing, and terminal emulation, it defined virtually the entire user interface. In addition, it had a procedural interface that gave applications some access to the underlying window system.

The DM is still a part of standard Apollo software, but it is undergoing a radical transformation. This is not due to unhappiness with the functions it provides. What it does, it does well. Furthermore, due to its integrated design, it provides a consistent interface to the entire system. However, its monolithic construction has made it difficult to customize and extend. For the last few years the User Environment Group at Apollo has been redesigning the DM architecture into a more modular system. This has resulted in a set of cooperating tools, each of which can be separately replaced by alternate tools filling the same role, and each of which is designed to be extensible.

This paper describes the DM as it was originally conceived, covering its advantages and disadvantages. It then describes the new user environment architecture and how it maintains the advantages and eliminates the disadvantages of the DM. Finally, the paper covers two relatively unplanned results of the redesign: the ability to merge the DM with the X Window System™ (trademark of the Massachussets Institute of Technology), and the ability to develop system-independent (portable) tools.

The Display Manager

The Display Manager is the first process that is started when an Apollo workstation is booted. It takes over, and mediates application access to the display and input devices. Each application accesses the DM through a global library that manages the interprocess communication between the two. This procedural interface provides primitives for window creation, deletion, resizing, etc., filling the role of a window server.

In the simplest case, the DM provides windows to the Graphics Primitives Routines (GPR), allowing the application to obtain raw input events and perform low-level graphical output. However, the DM also provides higher-level text-editing facilities. It provides three types of text-editing windows: **input**, **transcript**, (output), and **edit** (input/output). (To be precise, it keeps the text in **pads**, and allows any number of windows to view those pads.) Edit windows provide a view onto a text file, providing a standard system editor. Input windows allow the user to enter text to be read by an application via a streams interface (e.g., stdin). Transcript windows display text written by an application via a streams interface (e.g., stdout). An input/transcript pair form a terminal emulator. The combination of these text windows provides an almost universal editing facility. Text is entered the same way in all places, and can be cut and pasted between any text windows.

CH2539-5/88/0000/0303$01.00 © 1988 IEEE

In addition to mediating application access to the interaction devices, the DM also consumes input events and uses screen space to implement a user interface to the windowing system, allowing the end user to create, destroy, and position windows. As such, it fills the role of a window manager. This interface is heavily oriented towards keyboard input, providing a key definition facility that allows any key to perform any sequence of operations in the DM command language. Universal text editing means that key definitions can be applied in all text windows. Since the DM handles both window management and text editing, key definitions can combine both types of operations. So, for example, a key definition can copy text from a transcript window into an input window, or extract a file name from some text and open a window onto it.

There are several aspects of the DM that we thought were important to carry over into the new user environment. The new user environment had to provide a similarly consistent, well-tuned user interface. It had to provide a universal editing facility. And it had to be possible for users to customize it, using a common facility such as the DM command language.

The primary disadvantage of the DM is that it is monolithic. There is no way for users to take those aspects of it that they like and replace the rest. For instance, some users would like to replace the window management part of the DM with a more graphical, mouse-driven interface. Others would like to provide an alternative command language for specifying key bindings. There is no way of extricating these pieces from the rest of the DM. There is also no way of extending the existing pieces. Some users would like to take the text editor and simply add a few application-specific functions. Others would like to use the DM command language to let users define application-specific key bindings. Again, this is impossible.

A second disadvantage of the DM, related to its lack of extensibility, is that it provides no real support for the development of user interfaces to applications. While it has a few internal facilities that are used by the window manager, these are not accessible to the application, and there was no attempt to integrate any kind of dialogue manager or toolkit into the DM.

Because of these disadvantages, the User Environment Group at Apollo developed a new user environment architecture to address these problems while maintaining the advantages of the DM.

The New User Environment Architecture

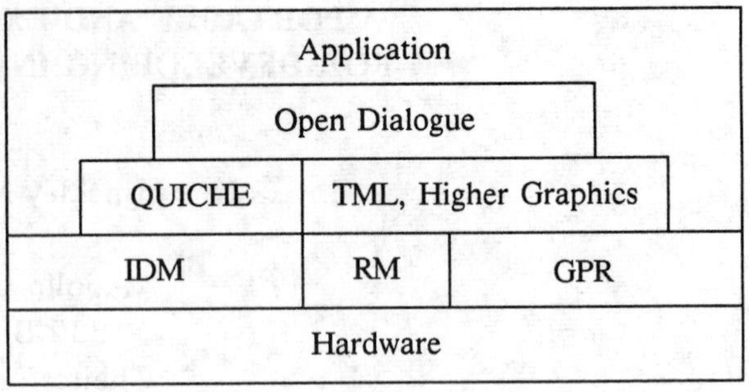

Figure 1. The New Architecture

Figure 1 shows a somewhat simplified view of the new architecture. It is layered, with each layer providing a more powerful set of functions to the one above it. However, the application is not constrained to use only the highest layer. Each component can be bypassed if necessary. The structure can be divided into two parts, with input flowing up one side and output down the other. Input and output are merged at the higher levels by the application and Open Dialogue™.

At the center of the lowest level is the **Rectangle Manager** (RM). The RM actually does no input or output. It simply maintains a database of rectangles that are used to coordinate access to the screen for both input and output. The rectangles form a hierarchy, where siblings may overlap.

The lowest component on the input side is the **Input Demultiplexor** (IDM). The IDM handles all input events received from the hardware devices, as well as events queued by other software. It uses the RM to determine which rectangle (and therefore which application) is interested in the event, translates the hardware event into a logical event of the type expected by the application and places it into the appropriate queue.

Immediately above the IDM is the **Quick User Interface and Command Handling Extension** (QUICHE) [HINC87]. QUICHE is an interpreter based on the Icon [GRIS83] programming language. The user or a program can bind any input event to a QUICHE function. When an application requests input, the IDM checks to see if the next event in the queue has a binding. If it does, the associated function is interpreted. This function can insert more events into the queue, make system calls, or call back directly to the application. When it has completed, control returns to the IDM, which checks the next event in the queue. This lets the user customize key bindings for a specific application.

QUICHE also allows the user to define key bindings that can be applied to multiple applications. This is made possible through a system-wide **trait** facility [REES86]. A trait is a collection of operations that define common behavior across applications. For instance, an editing trait might support operations for searching, inserting, and deleting text. A QUICHE function can call the application indirectly through these traits. So, for instance, a *delete word* key binding might be defined in terms of operations in the editor trait. This key binding will work with any application that supports this trait, regardless of the underlying implementation.

At the lowest level on the output side is GPR, the **Graphics Primitive Routines**. These actually do output to the display, either directly or (more often) clipped to a particular rectangle in the RM database.

GPR provides simple, two-dimensional, non-retained graphics. There are several components that are layered on it, providing higher-level primitives. These include implementations of graphics standards such as CORE and TEK4014.

The **Text Management Library** (TML) is a special kind of graphics library [WALD86]. TML manages the representation, display (rendering), and storage of hierarchical text. Leaf nodes in the hierachy contain strings of characters. Parent nodes impose order on the text. TML allows properties to be associated with nodes in the hierarchy. Some of these properties, such as font and character set, have meaning to TML and affect the rendering of the text; others are application specific. While not itself an editor, TML is intended to be the basis for any number of editors, from WYSIWYG document preparation systems to syntax-directed program editors.

Finally, **Open Dialogue** is a user interface management system (UIMS) that is intended to provide the level at which most applications interact with the user. It is based on a prior UIMS developed at Apollo [SCHU85]. Open Dialogue has the dual goals of providing high-level interaction primitives for constructing user interfaces (e.g., menus and sliders) and insulating the application from variations in users and interaction hardware. It allows the user interface to be defined separately from the application, and encourages programmers to write their applications as subroutine packages that are called by Open Dialogue.

Comparing Old and New

Some of the functions of the DM are broken into their own components in the new architecture. Window server functions are now performed by the Rectangle Manager and Input Demultiplexor. The DM command language has been replaced by QUICHE.

A number of the functions provided by the DM do not appear directly in the new architecture. Window management (the user interface to the window system), editing, and terminal emulation are now performed by standard applications. This makes it easy to replace them, or even to support multiple implementations.

This distribution of functions could lead to a less consistent user interface. While the new architecture does not prevent this, it discourages it by providing Open Dialogue and QUICHE. Open Dialogue provides a common set of interaction primitives. It also simplifies the task of interface development, allowing more effort to be spent on maintaining consistency. QUICHE provices a common key definition facility to all users. When used with traits, it also allows standard key definitions to be used across multiple applications, even third party applications, which could not use the DM's command language.

Universal editing has been retained, and even expanded, through QUICHE and the editor traits. Furthermore, applications that use TML will find it much easier to implement the editor traits.

Finally, while the DM allowed access to only the windowing and graphics layers, the new architecture lets the application access whatever layer of the system is appropriate for its particular task.

Additional Advantages

Subsequent to our initial design we were faced with two unplanned challenges. First, the popularity of the X Window System [SCHE86] required its integration into the architecture. However, compatibility requirements prohibited using it in place of RM, IDM, and GPR (its functional counterparts in the new architecture). We were faced with the problem of supporting two separate window system interfaces (X and the DM) simultaneously. Fortunately, RM and IDM turned out to provide an appropriate base for both systems. As a result of implementing both systems on them the new environment will support both existing Apollo windowing applications and X windowing applications at the same time on the same screen. Any window manager will be able to manipulate both kinds of windows.

A second challenge was the increasing importance of supporting heterogeneous environments. With people using multiple systems, and applications running on multiple platforms, providing a consistent interface requires portable tools. By taking a more modular approach, we have isolated the higher layers of the architecture from system dependencies. We expect this to simplify the problem of porting these tools to other systems, and have announced plans to support at least Open Dialogue on foreign machines.

Summary

The Display Manager has defined the primary interface to window management and text editing functions on Apollo workstations. To do this, it has made use of internal facilities for such functions as screen allocation, input demultiplexing, text management, and key binding.

The User Environment Group at Apollo has been redesigning the DM to give other applications access to these internal facilities, so they can be replaced, extended, or customized. We have developed a new user environment architecture that meets this goal while maintaining the advantages of the old, integrated DM. The new architecture contains individual components for screen management, input demultiplexing, user-defined key bindings, text management, and user interface management.

In addition to meeting its original goal of providing a more extensible environment, the new architecture has also proven useful in allowing simultaneous support of two different windowing systems, and in providing the basis for the development of portable tools.

Bibliography

[GRIS83] Ralph Griswold and Madge Griswold. *The Icon Programming Language*. Englewood Cliffs, NJ, 1983.

[HINC87] Kee Hinckley. An Object Oriented Extension Language for Integrating Disparate Applications. In *Human-Computer Interaction – INTERACT'87* (Stuttgart, Sept. 1-4, 1987), Elsevier Science Publishing Co., Inc., New York, pages 529–533.

[REES86] Jim Rees et al. An Extensible I/O System, in *USENIX Association Summer Conference Proceedings* (Atlanta, June 9–13, 1986), USENIX, El Cerito, CA., pages 114–125.

[SCHE86] Robert W. Scheifler and Jim Gettys. The X Window System. *ACM Transactions on Graphics* V(2):79–109, April 1986.

[SCHU85] Andrew J. Schulert, George T. Rogers, and James A. Hamilton. ADM – A Dialog Manager. In *Proc. CHI '85 Human Factors in Computing Systems* (San Francisco, April 14–18, 1985), ACM, New York, pages 177–183.

[WALD86] James Waldo. Modeling Text as a Hierarchical Object., in *USENIX Association Summer Conference Proceedings* (Atlanta, June 9–13, 1986), USENIX, El Cerito, CA., pages 270–283.

CAD Track

Update on New Standards for Hardware Design: VHDL and EDIF

Chair: Y. Huh

THE VHSIC HARDWARE DESCRIPTION LANGUAGE (IEEE STANDARD 1076) LANGUAGE FEATURES REVISITED

Ronald Waxman and James H. Aylor
Center for Semicustom Integrated Systems
School of Engineering and Applied Science
Thornton Hall
University of Virginia
Charlottesville, Virginia 22901

Erich Marschner
CAD Language Systems, Inc.
51 Monroe St.
Suite 606
Rockville, MD. 20850

ABSTRACT

The VHSIC Hardware Description Language (VHDL) is now an IEEE standard (VHDL 1076). The original language (VHDL 7.2) has been refined by the IEEE. The resulting language has broader capabilities than originally anticipated. In this paper, the features and capabilities of VHDL and the refinements made by the IEEE over the original language are discussed. Examples of some of the enriched function are given.

INTRODUCTION

In April, 1986, the Computer Society published a Special Issue of Design and Test magazine [1] on the subject of the VHSIC Hardware (Design and) Description Language (VHDL)[1]. An article in that issue [2] discussed the major features of VHDL and analyzed several other hardware description languages. The analyses discussed how each of the other languages related to the objectives to be met by VHDL Version 7.2 [3]. VHDL 7.2 was also compared to the objectives established for it during the requirements phase of the development effort. Since the completion of that work, the IEEE has improved on the base VHDL [4]. The VHSIC Hardware (Design and) Description Language (VHDL) has become IEEE Standard 1076.

This paper revisits the language features that were discussed in [2] (the reader should refer to [2] for a detailed discussion of the features). The new capabilities provided by Standard 1076, as well as areas to which VHDL is being applied, are discussed and related to the language features. Also addressed are language capabilities still desired by some.[2]

VHDL is a very important standard in the design automation community for two reasons. First, it will provide the ability for designers of electronic systems and subsystems to share design data much more easily and completely than they have been able to in the past. The purpose of a description language is to permit efficient communication among design communities, within and between companies. Because of the variety of languages and formats that currently exist, effective communication has been a problem. Also, the purpose of a design language is to permit efficient communication between the designer and the application design tools. A standard language for which design tools can be developed will greatly encourage the development of sophisticated new tools. The availability of application design tools to be used with a language are essential to the acceptance and effective use of the language by the design community.

A comprehensive set of measurable hardware description language requirements were developed as a part of the VHDL development activity. The language requirements have been abstracted to a set of generally useful language features. This set has not changed since the original language development effort. What has changed are some of the capabilities provided by the language to enable the designer to more easily utilize the features. The list of features to be examined are:

(1) Scope - Range of Hardware to be Described;

(2) Management of Design;

(3) Description of a Design's Timing;

(4) Description of a Design's Architecture;

(5) Description of a Design's Interface;

(6) Description of a Design's Environment; and

(7) Language Extensibility.

The features examined relate to utilization of the language for design as well as documentation. The reader is referred to [5] and [6] where the rationale for many of the features described here are developed.

VHDL RELATED ACTIVITY

VHDL was developed to be independent from the design tools it must drive. However, it was implemented with consideration for them. This statement is underscored by our understanding that several companies are presently developing commercial tools for use with VHDL. Many of these commercial tools have not yet been announced. Such tools will undoubtedly operate on various computers. Figure 1 shows some of the publicly acknowledged VHDL related work that is underway, much of which is at least partially funded by the Department of Defense. The semantics of VHDL are independent of any particular programming language implementation of the tools. Work is underway in the DASS to develop a standard intermediate format for VHDL. Such a standard will simplify the task of developing tools for use with VHDL.

Ease of data extraction and insertion, minimization of effort to describe a design, ease of readability to understand an existing design, are all key attributes required for a hardware design and description language. Based on our experience with the VHDL benchmark activity, VHDL is user oriented, understandable and usable by hardware designers. The parts of the language that are procedural in nature have a programming language orientation. VHDL also supports documentation of design data, which may be

[1] The Very High Speed Integrated Circuit (VHSIC) project is a Government program that has been underway since 1980. The objective of the VHSIC program is to advance the state-of-the-art of microelectronics. Development of VHDL has been an important part of that program. The VHDL effort started in 1983, with the award of the development contract to Intermetrics (prime contractor), IBM and TI (subcontractors). The work on VHDL Version 7.2 was completed during 1985. In 1986, the Design Automation Standards Subcommittee (DASS), in concert with the Automatic Test Program Generation (ATPG) Committee, started work on making VHDL a standard for industry (IEEE Standard 1076). The DASS is a subcommittee of the Technical Committee on Design Automation, which is a standing committee of the Computer Society of the IEEE. The ATPG is a subcommittee of the IEEE Standards Coordinating Committee #20 (the ATLAS Committee). VHDL met the IEEE requirements for standardization in December, 1987.

[2] The VHDL Analysis and Standardization Group (VASG), the working group within the DASS that developed the Standard 1076, is continuing its work in a maintenance mode sharing the responsibility with the ATPG.

• Intermetrics	Upgrade VHDL 7.2 tools to IEEE Standard VHDL tools. Expected completion in 1988.
• Bell Northern Research	Port VHDL Tools to IBM 370, VM/CMS environment (for IEEE Standard VHDL). Expected completion in 1989.
• Harris	Tester Independent Software Support System.
• Honeywell	VHDL version of Mimola (VHSIC Synthesizer).
• Unisys	VHDL version of MIXSIM (VHSIC Simulator).
• JRS Research	VHDL ---> Microcode. Ada algorithms ---> VHDL. Silicon compilation from a high level VHDL description of a chip.
• Research Triangle Inst.	VHDL interface to ADAS and Genesil.
• Silicon Compilers Inc.	VHDL cell library from National Semiconductor.
• VISTA	VHDL design capture.
• General Electric	Hardware/software rapid prototype environment (VHDL workstation).
• University of Virginia	VHDL benchmarks. VHDL system level modeling and synthesis. VHDL test philosophy. VHDL in mixed analog/digital systems. VHDL validation requirements.
• Virginia Tech.	Behavioral modeling and test philosophy.
• University of Cincinnati	VHDL in the manufacturing environment.
• Renssalaer	Object oriented design approach.
• U. of Southern Ca.	VHDL --> Silicon VHDL to USC's D. A. system (ADAM).
• Dartmouth	Analog extensions to VHDL.
• Stanford	Formal verification of VHDL design descriptions using an annotation language for specification.
• DoD plans	System design tools - R & D activity. Engineering Information System development. Computer-Aided Acquisition and Logistics Support System.
• Industry plans	Many companies developing VHDL tools for commercial application. Some companies developing VHDL tools for internal use.

Figure 1 -- VHDL in Government, Industry and Academia

organized for ease of data extraction and insertion, as well as for understanding. Many of the improvements in the language that resulted from the IEEE DASS activity addressed these areas.

LANGUAGE FEATURES

The reader is reminded that to benefit fully from the following discussion, he or she should refer to [2] for a detailed discussion of the features. The requirements stated in that paper have been largely met and, in general, exceed expectations.

Two concepts, hierarchical design and descriptive continuum, must be understood before features of a hardware description language can be fully appreciated. Figure 2 links these two concepts to the consequences of various language implementations possible when one considers hierarchy. This concept is fully discussed in [2].

Scope - the Range of Hardware to be Described

There exists a rich environment of design data description capability provided by languages and formats other than VHDL [7]. VHDL development focused on providing the ability to support the complete description and design process of digital systems, a subset of the total VLSI data environment. The original scope of VHDL included views ranging from an algorithmic mathematical description of desired hardware to a precise logic gate description of a desired function, for both combinational and sequential machine designs.

Work now going on at the University of Virginia, as well as elsewhere, indicates that the range of applicability is broader than was anticipated for the original language design. The creation of "uninterpreted" VHDL models that are simulatable in the same simulation environment as "interpreted" models appears to be possible [8] . Initial results indicate that a new "uninterpreted" model for abstract (high-level) descriptions of digital systems can be implemented using VHDL. The concept is based on petri-net

Language Supports:	Consequences:
Structural Hierarchy --------->	Real structures may be represented at any level of the hierarchy. Primitives at the lowest level give behavioral information.
Behavioral Hierarchy --------->	Pure behaviors may be represented at any level of the hierarchy. A purely behavioral description should have no implied structure.
Structural Hierarchy plus Behavioral Abstraction ------->	Behavior and structure may be described at any level of the hierarchy.
Disjoint------------->	Descriptions will be either purely behavioral or purely structural.
Continuum------------>	Behavior and structure, both within the description of a design unit.
No separation of control flow from data flow --->	No guarded statements. All statements may execute in parallel.
Separation of control flow from data flow---->	Guarded statements. Statements for which guards are true execute in parallel. Supports parallelism and concurrency. Provides hooks for synthesis.

Figure 2 -- Kinds of Design Descriptions

modeling where the value of system variables are neither defined or operated upon. The methodology and modeling concept permits a hierarchical single path design environment that will support the simultaneous simulation of system descriptions at different levels of interpretation and abstraction.

Analog functions may be modeled in VHDL at a high level of abstraction and work is progressing to lower the level of abstraction, or to show how to bridge from VHDL to existing analog simulation environments [9]. A bridge between VHDL and EDIF, at the NETLIST level of detail, is being created by a DASS working group. The concept is discussed in [10], [11] and [12]. The application of VHDL to the design and manufacturing environment is discussed in [13], [14] and [15].

Some of the extended capabilities of VHDL 1076 help to increase the scope of the language. One of the areas in which VHDL 1076 has been improved is that of support for high- level system design. In particular, the language now includes a general I/O facility, and it has been extended to support access (i.e., pointer) types for building dynamic data structures. I/O features allow a system designer to abstractly model the input/output characteristics of a system by reading and writing data files. This makes it possible to defer decisions regarding the low-level design of those parts of the system until the critical parts are worked out. Similarly, access types allow a system designer to defer the detailed implementation of structures such as stacks, queues, and other more complex memory structures by modeling them abstractly. Readers wishing to gain a basic understanding of VHDL and the IEEE technical issue resolution process should refer to [16] and [17].

Management of Design

Design methodology drives design management, and relates to a designer's organization of the design process. Design methodologies encompass the notions of hierarchical design, top-down design and bottom-up design (or a mixture of the two), separation of dataflow design from the control-logic design, and so forth. Depending on design objective, design methodologies differ within the design community and may vary for a particular designer from day to day.

A DASS working group is developing recommended practices to address all elements required to manage digital computer system design, manufacture and life-cycle support. The group plans to provide a draft document, within the next year, describing these practices.

Some of the extended capabilities of VHDL 1076 help to improve the design management process. The management of design data revolves around the conceptual structure of the library system used to organize such data. Earlier versions of VHDL had a fairly complex design library structure, one that was hierarchical and that supported multiple revisions of each design unit in the library. This was intended to help support version and revision management of designs within the library. However, two problems became evident with this structure. First, the name of a given sub- library within the design library system was dependent upon its placement within the hierarchy, and therefore designs that made reference to the design library structure were portable only if the same hierarchical library structure existed in many places. Second, the concept of a revision in the VHDL design library did not quite match that of a revision of a design: modifying something as trivial as the name of a constant used within a design, followed by reanalysis of the design, would create a new revision within the library. This proliferation of revisions with every iteration in the design process made it difficult to know whether a given revision was ready for use in other designs or whether it was still under development.

In VHDL 1076, a much simpler library model has been adopted. VHDL 1076 assumes that any number of libraries may exist, each containing only design units. A logical name facility allows each design unit to state the names by which it knows each library that it uses; the support environment is responsible for binding the logical names to actual libraries in a given installation. This avoids having library names dependent upon local naming conventions, be they hierarchical or otherwise, and therefore improves the portability of VHDL 1076 design descriptions. In addition, the concept of revisions has been removed from the language. This tends to enforce a design management methodology in which design iterations are performed in a local working library; only when the design is frozen is it "released" for use elsewhere by moving it to a global library where others can find it. This style of revision management is very similar to methodologies already in use in many places.

Description of Timing

The timing concept embodied within VHDL is oriented toward hardware simulation. However, this orientation does not prevent the use of the language with any hardware simulator. To ensure that designers can describe all digital systems, the language supports timing concepts that apply at all levels of design hierarchy and abstraction.

To satisfy a range of design styles, VHDL provides a general timing model that supports both event-driven designs and cycle-driven designs. The timing model allows designers to define timing granularity in terms of real-time values, in units related to real time values, or in clock cycles. All times are definable as multiples of the smallest granular time unit. Propagation delay specifications are supported, and inertial and transport delay models are allowed. Specification of timing characteristics and constraints are also supported.

With respect to timing, VHDL 1076 differs only minimally from previous versions of VHDL. The primary difference is the fact that type TIME is now defined to include negative values. This provides for a more natural expression of negative setup and hold times. The primary timing issue, that of back-annotation, generated much discussion in the course of the standardization of VHDL, but no language changes were introduced in this area. The consensus of those involved in the standardization effort was that existing language features were adequate, although not optimal, for back-annotating designs with timing derived from layout analysis. Even so, back-annotation remains an issue, because the multiple levels of hierarchy involved in a VHDL description complicate the process.

Description of Architecture

The discussion on a continuum of descriptive capability, given in [2], describes the importance of providing such a continuous spectrum for design description. Behavioral, structural and mixed behavioral/structural models are supported by VHDL. The high level of abstraction that may be modeled makes it possible to investigate hardware/software trade-offs early in the design process. As refinements are made in the design, detailed models may be evaluated in the total system modeling environment.

Although VHDL supports a continuum of design styles, its support for register- transfer styles of description has been somewhat limited in previous versions of the language, and the "flow-through" process model of VHDL 7.2 forced a somewhat unnatural representation of certain kinds of behavior. Both of these problems have been alleviated in VHDL 1076. The standard language now supports "guarded signals" whose semantics have been tailored to represent abstract memory elements (registers) and multiplexed communication channels (buses). The addition of registers and buses makes possible a standard register-transfer style description of hardware. In addition, the addition of the wait statement, in conjunction with a more general process model, provides greater flexibility in the modeling of behavior.

A guarded signal is one that exhibits special behavior when assigned to by a guarded signal assignment statement. A guarded signal assignment statement, in turn, is an assignment that only takes place when the guard expression of an enclosing block statement evaluates to TRUE. Block statements can be written in such a way that their guard expressions will evaluate to TRUE in a mutually exclusive fashion; this allows a designer to express the behavior of a device in the form of a state machine, where each guard expression defines a distinct state. The addition of guarded signals in VHDL 1076 provides the multiplexing semantics associated with such a state machine when a given signal is driven in more than one state.

For example, consider an RS latch modeled as a state machine. A description of the latch in VHDL 1076 appears in Figure 3.

In this example, guarded signal M represents the memory element embodied by the latch. Each assignment drives M only when the corresponding guard expression is TRUE, e.g., when R = '1' or S = '1', so provided that R and S are not both controlling at the same time, the assignments to M will be multiplexed. Note, however, that VHDL 1076 makes no assumption that states are mutually exclusive in the example, both assignments would attempt to control M if both R and S were "1" simultaneously. A resolution function can be used to model the behavior of M in such a case.

While guarded signals improve the concurrent behavioral modeling capabilities of the language, the generalized process model and wait statement of VHDL 1076 make easier the modeling of response to sequences of events. In VHDL 7.2, processes always began executing at the first statement of the process and terminated at the last statement of the process. In VHDL 1076, a process may suspend at any point in its execution and resume later on at that same point. This capability allows a process to represent its internal state in terms of its last suspension point rather than as a collection of explicit state variables. As a result, the algorithmic description of a state machine becomes easier to express.

For example, consider the following description of an I/O controller (Figure 4). This description models a device that services I/O requests for a board: it performs the handshaking necessary to communicate with another copy of itself that is servicing I/O requests for a different board, where all boards are attached to a common bus. The sequencing of actions involved in the handshaking process are a good example of the utility of the general process model and the wait statement. For simplicity, this example assumes the existence of only two communicating boards.

The description of the I/O Controller shown in Figure 4 is fairly natural; the correspondence between the states of the communicating devices are easy to see. In VHDL 7.2, the example could only be modeled as one giant case statement, with one entry for each distinct state, and the overall behavior of the controller would be much more difficult to understand.

Description of a Design's Interface

VHDL provides a mechanism to define interfaces to design descriptions. The VHDL defined interface can be equivalent to the hardware interface for the hardware being described. The interface definition includes the I/O ports and assertions about the design description that apply to all of the design alternatives described within a design entity. Interface description is supported at all design abstraction and hierarchy levels. The mechanism requires that all alternative models for a particular design description be functionally equivalent and consistent with the explicit interface. User-supplied data may be referenced from the interface description. Input and output ports described in the interface are strongly typed, providing the means to check for consistency in connecting various models.

In VHDL 1076, the interface of a design entity may contain statements as well as the declarations of the ports and generics of the

```
entity RS_Latch
        port(   R,S:     in Bit;
                Q,QB:    out Bit);
end;

architecture RTL_Style of RS_Latch is
        signal M: Bit register := '0';
begin
        Set:
                block (S = '1')
                begin
                        M <= guarded '1' after 15ns;
                end block;
        Reset:
                block (R = '1')
                begin
                        M <= guarded '0' after 12ns;
                end block;
        Q <= M;
        QB <= not M;
end;
```

Figure 3 -- RS Latch Modeled as a State Machine

```
entity IO_Controller
        port(   Sending:     inout   Bit;
                Receiving:   inout   Bit;
                DataRdy:     inout   Bit;
                DataBus:     inout   Byte;
                IOReq:       in      Bit;
                IOMode:      in      Bit;
                Data:        inout   Byte);
end;

architecture IO_Cycle of IO_Controller is
begin
        process
        begin
                wait until IOReq = '1';
                case IOMode is
                        when '0' =>                 -- send operation
                                Sending <= '1';
                                wait until Receiving = '1';
                                DataBus <= Data;
                                DataRdy <= '1' after 10ns;
                                wait until Receiving = '0';
                                Sending <= '0';
                        when '1' =>                 -- receive operation
                                wait until Sending = '1';
                                Receiving <= '1';
                                wait until DataRdy = '1';
                                Data <= DataBus;
                                Receiving <= '0';
                                wait until Sending = '0';
                end case;
        end process;
end;
```

Figure 4 -- Architectural Description of an I/O Controller

entity. These statements can be used to monitor the behavior of the device or the environment of the device and detect any anomalous conditions. For example, setup and hold times could be monitored in this way. This additional capability subsumes the VHDL 7.2 assert directive within a much more general and powerful monitoring capability. Detection of sequencing errors as well as single-point error conditions is now possible.

For example, the IO_Controller entity declared in Figure 4 could be extended to verify that the handshaking protocol is correctly observed (see Figure 5). This is accomplished by using a process statement that tracks the state transitions that occur as the handshaking progresses. If the appropriate combination of values for Sending and Receiving are not present at each state, the process will report a protocol error.

Description of a Design's Environment

Environmental data are necessary to fully define the environment where hardware being described must operate. These include the following categories: package data (for example, the number of ground planes), design process (for example, CMOS), design-audit data (for example, the release number), logic design rules (for example, fanout), circuit and technology data, physical-design data (for example, metal pitch), simulation-and-test data, cross-reference data(for example, physical to logical names), and operating environment data (for example, temperature). There is nothing new in VHDL 1076 that changes the language's ability to describe environmental factors associated with a design.

CONCLUSIONS - LANGUAGE EXTENSIBILITY

VHDL has reached a major milestone: standardization. However, work on the language will continue. New requirements will unfold as the application of VHDL grows within industry. The DASS, in concert with the ATPG, is responsible to maintain the language, investigate problems and suggested improvements, and at an appropriate future time, ballot on possible revisions. Other DASS working groups are evaluating how VHDL may relate to other standards and how to provide a suitable interface between VHDL and design tools. Work is proceeding to create VHDL "packages" of useful application functions and models. The use of VHDL to model very abstract design concepts (system design capability) and to model analog function is being studied. A standard hierarchical language with the power and scope of VHDL may allow us to take the next step in the process of design synthesis.

However, as satisfying as the present state of VHDL may be to some of us, there are still some issues known to us today. The ballot to standardize VHDL passed with 92% voting affirmatively. That means that 8% of of those who voted still have reservations. Despite the extensions incorporated into VHDL 1076, there remain areas in which the language could be improved. We have already mentioned the issue of back- annotation, which involves mapping timing data derived from a flattened representation of a circuit back onto a hierarchical representation of the same circuit. This is difficult, and appropriate language extensions to support it will probably have to wait for a better understanding of the mapping problem itself. Another area in which VHDL 1076 could be extended is that of abstract inter-process communication. The current version of the language requires that all communication occur via signals, and that processes must respond when an event occurs on a signal or else the message is lost. In system-level design, however, the ability to queue messages for later processing by the recipient is essential. These and other areas continue to generate active discussion.

```
entity IO_Controller
        port(   Sending:      inout   Bit;
                Receiving:    inout   Bit;
                DataRdy:      inout   Bit;
                DataBus:      inout   Byte;
                IOReq:        in      Bit;
                IOMode:       in      Bit;
                Data:         inout   Byte);
begin
        process
        begin
                wait on Sending, Receiving;
                assert Sending = '1' and Receiving = '0'
                              report "Protocol Error";
                wait on Sending, Receiving;
                assert Sending = '1' and Receiving = '1'
                              report "Protocol Error";
                wait on Sending, Receiving;
                assert Sending = '0' and Receiving = '1'
                              report "Protocol Error";
                wait on Sending, Receiving;
                assert Sending = '0' and Receiving = '0'
                              report "Protocol Error";
        end process;
end;
```

Figure 5 -- An Interface Description Containing Statements

REFERENCES

(1) IEEE Design and Test of Computers, Special VHDL Issue, Vol. 3, No. 2, April, 1986.

(2) J. Aylor, R. Waxman and C. Scarratt, "VHDL: Feature Description and Analysis," *IEEE Design and Test of Computers,* Vol. 3, No. 2, April, 1986.

(3) IBM, "Language Requirements for VHDL, Revision 5.0," July, 1984

(4) IEEE,"VHDL Language Reference Manual, Draft Standard 1076/B", May, 1987

(5) Intermetrics, "VHDL (7.2) Design Analysis and Justification," July 30, 1984.

(6) CAD Language Systems Inc., "VHDL (1076) Language Refinement Rationale," August, 1987.

(7) R. Waxman, "The Design Automation Standards Environment," *Proceedings of the 24th ACM/IEEE Design Automation Conference,* Miami Beach, Florida, June 29,-July 1, 1987

(8) J. H. Aylor and R. J. Auletta, "A Non-Interpreted Model for Digital Systems," *Proceedings of the 1986 IEEE Southeastcon,* March 24-25, 1986, Richmond, VA.

(9) R. Waxman, L. A. Belfore, J. H. Aylor, B. W. Johnson and R. D. Williams, "VHDL Representation of Analog/Digital Systems," *Center for Semicustom Integrated Systems, White Paper,* University of Virginia, 1987.

(10) R. Waxman, "Design Automation Standards Development," *Proceedings of the Reliability and Maintainability for Computer Aided Engineering workshop,* Leesburg, Virginia, August 25, 26, 1987.

(11) M. Shahdad, "An Interface Between VHDL and EDIF," *Proceedings of the 24th Design Automation Conference,* June 28 to July 1, 1987, Miami Beach, Florida.

(12) R. Waxman, K. Schulz and R. Alvarodiaz, "An Open Architecture - VHDL and EDIF Access to an Integrated Data Base," *Proceedings of the 1987 Government Microcircuit Applications Conference (GOMAC)*, Orlando, Florida, October 27-29, 1987.

(13) R. Waxman and R. Alvarodiaz, "Standards for Electronic Design and Their Effect on the Transition to Production," *Proceedings of the Symposium on Engineering for Electronics Production*, Indiana University, Bloomington, Indiana, June 24, 25, 1987.

(14) R. Waxman, "Hardware Design Languages for Computer design and Test," *IEEE Computer*, Vol. 19, No. 4, April, 1986.

(15) L. Saunders, "The IBM VHDL Design System," *Proceedings of the 24th Design Automation Conference*, June 28 to July 1, 1987, Miami Beach, Florida.

(16) CAD Language Systems, Inc., "VHDL Tutorial for IEEE Standard 1076 VHDL," June, 1987.

(17) CAD Language Systems, Inc., "Proceedings of the VHDL Analysis and Standardization Group," Volumes 1-4, August 19, 1987.

AN INTERFACE BETWEEN VHDL AND EDIF

Moe Shahdad

CAD Language Systems, Inc.
51 Monroe Street Suite 606, Rockville, MD 20850
301 424-9445

Abstract

The VHSIC Hardware Description Language (VHDL) [1] and the Electronic Design Interchange Format (EDIF) [2] are industry standards for describing design data. It is of interest to understand the application range of each standard and the way each standard relates to the other. This paper discusses the motivation for relating VHDL and EDIF, as well as scenarios in which VHDL and EDIF can contribute to different aspects of the design process. An earlier version of this paper which focused on VHDL Version 1076/A and EDIF Version 1 1 0 appeared in the Proceedings of the 24th Design Automation Conference [3].

Motivation

Traditionally, IC vendors have used data books to document and communicate characteristics of their components. However, this form of documentation is not machine processable. Recent increases in the complexity of the design of VLSI circuits has motivated widespread use of design automation tools, and thereby the need for machine processable descriptions. This in turn has led to development of formal notations that can serve both documentation and design of hardware. EDIF and VHDL are two such notations. Their relationship is of interest for two major reasons:

Standard Selection. The electronics industry spans aerospace companies, computer system manufacturers, electronic communication companies, and defense contractors. These companies design electronic systems made up of components that are internally manufactured, components that are purchased off-the-shelf, or components that are custom-made through external sources. Since components originating from different sources have to be integrated into the same system, there is a need for a standard notation for documentation of such components. When multiple standards can potentially serve the same purpose, the relationship between these standards is critical.

Standard Implementation. CAD tool vendors need to understand the relationship between VHDL and EDIF both from a market viewpoint and from an implementation viewpoint. The market viewpoint will determine the level of investment and the nature of the tools that have to be developed. The implementation viewpoint will determine if both VHDL and EDIF tools can be supported as part of the same design environment.

It would be of interest to know if a neutral intermediate form can be developed to support both VHDL and EDIF descriptions. Presence of such a form will allow CAD tool vendors to develop and market tools that are targeted to this neutral form, without regard to the notation in which the design was first described.

Design Paradigm

The relationship between VHDL and EDIF must be investigated in the context of a design paradigm. The design paradigm considered here involves three phases: specification, logical design, and physical design, as shown in Figure 1. The outcome of the specification phase is the top-level functional behavior of the design. During the logical design phases, the functional behavior of the design is decomposed in terms of its subcomponents. This decomposition process is repeated until a level is reached where the subcomponents are primitives that are already implemented and are available to the designer. The logical design phase is followed by a physical design phase, where routing and placement are performed. Timing data obtained from physical representation is then used to back-annotate the logical representation of the design. These three design phases are repeated as many times as necessary until the desired functional and physical characteristics are achieved. Finally, the mask layout representation of the design is submitted to a fabrication facility for implementation.

A design takes on three representations throughout the design life cycle: schematic representation, functional representation, and physical representation. The schematic representation graphically depicts the primitive; the functional representation defines the time-dependent input/output transformation performed by the primitive; and the physical representation is used to define the layout of the primitive.

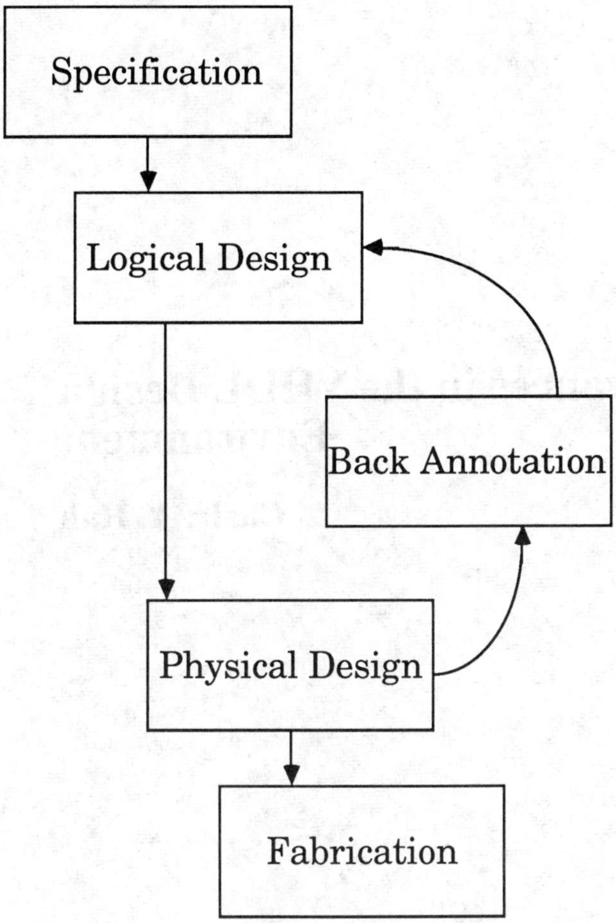

Figure 1. Design Life Cycle

VHDL / EDIF Design Interface

VHDL is more effective at the conceptual levels of the design hierarchy, while EDIF is more effective at the concrete levels of the hierarchy. Therefore, it is likely that system design houses would tend toward using VHDL, while fabrication facilities would tend toward using EDIF. To support this scenario, an interface between VHDL and EDIF is required. The EDIF model library used in the design process must contain schematic, layout, and functional representations of each primitive in the library in order to support the design process described in the previous section. The EDIF schematic and functional representations of primitives must be translated from EDIF into VHDL. Since EDIF behavioral constructs are somewhat restricted, functional representations of the corresponding primitives in the VHDL environment may have to be hand coded or developed independently. Such VHDL descriptions are then analyzed into a VHDL design library to establish a set of design primitives.

Designers would be able to use a VHDL design environment to perform a design task, as described in the previous section. All the leaf nodes of the design hierarchy created in the VHDL design environment must be primitives. This hierarchy is translated into EDIF for physical design. Timing data obtained from the EDIF environment must be used to back-annotate the VHDL design, and to repeat the design cycle as necessary. When such a design is completed, the VHDL structural hierarchy may be translated into an EDIF netlist hierarchy for physical design.

The above methodology requires translation of EDIF schematic and functional data into VHDL, and translation of VHDL structural data into EDIF. A strategy for performing this translation is discussed in [3]. This strategy demonstrates that VHDL has the necessary syntax to represent all the semantics of EDIF. For those cases where EDIF semantics is not supported in VHDL, a separate tool must be developed to elaborate and enforce these semantics in the VHDL design environment. Furthermore, this strategy shows that no feature of VHDL has semantics which conflicts with EDIF. The same strategy demonstrates that VHDL structural data can be easily translated into EDIF.

Concluding Remarks

VHDL and EDIF can contribute to different aspects of the design process. A likely design scenario will involve the use of VHDL by system design houses and the use of EDIF by fabrication facilities. Readability and richness of the operational semantics of VHDL supports its use for design communication, maintenance, second sourcing, and simulation. Richness of declarative semantics of EDIF supports its use for physical design.

EDIF model libraries can be translated into VHDL to provide schematic and functional representations of a set of design primitives. Since EDIF behavioral constructs are somewhat restricted, the functional representation of such primitives may have to be hand coded in VHDL. A VHDL design environment can then be used for designing systems in terms of such primitives. A design hierarchy defined in VHDL may then be translated back into an EDIF design environment for layout, timing analysis, and back-annotation.

References

[1] "VHDL Language Reference Manual", IEEE Standard 1076, in preparation by CAD Language Systems with permission from the IEEE, to be released in December 1987.

[2] "EDIF Version 2 0 0", Electronic Industries Association, May 1987.

[3] Shahdad, Moe, "An Interface between VHDL and EDIF", Proceedings of the 24th Design Automation Conference, IEEE, 1987.

Advances in the VHDL Design Environment

Chair: Y. Huh

A STATE OF THE ART VHDL SIMULATOR

David R Coelho Alec G Stanculescu

Vantage Analysis Systems, Inc.

Abstract

The VHDL language [7,8] promisses to be one of the most significant contributions to simulation technology in the last five years. By offering the hardware designer a tool independent language, which spans a wide range of design abstraction levels and methodologies, VHDL offers the potential to integrate a wide range of tools and organizations, and provide a standard basis for electronic design representation.

In order to be effective over such a wide range of uses, the VHDL language has considerably more features than most other hardware description languages. One of the concerns that emerges, is whether an efficient implementation of VHDL can be achieved, while still maintaining a full language implementation. This paper will address this question, and will summarize the results that have been achieved in the implementation of a state-of-the-art VHDL simulator.

1 Introduction

The problems facing hardware designers are becoming increasingly complex. There are numerous steps in the hardware design process including problem definition, analysis, specification, description at various levels, simulation of the various levels, layout and fabrication. The design community has become increasingly concerned with establishing standards which allow more effective integration of tools and data throughout the design process. The VHDL effort, initiated by the US Department of Defense is one of the more important contributions in this area. By establishing a single standard hardware description language which is tool and methodology independent, significant progress can be made towards the goal of integrating the design environment and allowing effective interchange of design information between organizations.

The VHDL language has an ambitious goal and must span a wide range of design abstraction levels as summarized here:

- Architecture
- Block/Functional
- Gate/Logic

Each of these design abstraction levels has a set of requirements which are unique. At the gate and logic level, VHDL has specific features which allow accurate handling of timing details including propagation delay, inertial delay, spike suppression, setup and hold constraints, and others. At the block and functional level, the ability to describe data-flow style behavior, and to effectively handle concurrency of processing is important. At the architecture level, algorithmic style software modelling is required. The net effect is a language which has considerably more flexibility and more power than most hardware description languages.

The difficulty from an implementation standpoint is that the simulation environment which supports VHDL must be inherently more complex to handle the wide range of features available in the language. Complexity of implementation does not necessarily imply inefficient execution, and the remainder of this paper will address some of the issues related to efficient implementation of the VHDL language and will draw some conclusions as to whether a VHDL-based simulation environment is competitive with state-of-the-art simulators that are based on other hardware description languages.

2 System Overview

The VHDL simulation environment which is discussed in this paper provides many of the capabilities typical of production quality simulators, and a few facilities which are specific to the VHDL language.

Heavy reliance on interactive graphics and the multi-windows graphics capabilities of engineering workstations provide a user friendly and easy to use tool. Industry standards provided a basis for the design of the user interface. Of particular interest are the following standards:

- Microsoft Windows
- X-Windows

- Unix

The following sections will summarize the key capabilities of the environment.

The simulation environment has an open architecture making it possible to derive structural information from commercially available schematic entry systems. In addition, back-annotation of delay information from physical layout packages is also supported.

2.1 VHDL Compiler and Design Library

A full IEEE 1076 VHDL compiler front-ends the simulation environment. The compiler performs complete syntax and semantic analysis of VHDL source files and produces an intermediate format suitable for use during simulation. VHDL features of particular interest which are supported include:

- External compilation
- Configurations
- Overloading of operators

Both netlist as well as behavioral information can be input using VHDL source code to the system. As an alternative, structural information can also be derived from a schematic entry system.

Because of the specific VHDL features which support description of project management related data, the VHDL simulation environment supports a design library in which each VHDL entity is stored after compilation. This design library facilitates separate compilation of VHDL descriptions, and makes it possible to avoid complete recompilation where possible.

2.2 Simulator

A high-performance behavioral simulator which supports VHDL is supported. The user specifies stimulus and control to the simulator using a powerful simulation control language. The following summarizes some of the features of this control language:

- Control constructs (if, while, etc)
- Stimulus vectors
- Variables

All results generated during simulation are displayed using the results display facility described in the next section.

2.3 Results Display

The results display facility provides an interactive graphics environment in which three primary forms of data are displayed:

- Waveforms
- Tabular text based output
- Superimposed values on schematic diagram

The user has control over what signals are displayed, and the form in which those values are shown. Waveforms allow a logic-analyzer style of result. The tabular output facilities provide for a user definable ascii style of display. Finally, it is possible to display values from simulation simultaneously with the schematic data.

3 Results

During the development of this system, substantial experience has been derived regarding the efficiency of implementing VHDL. As was discussed earlier, VHDL is a considerably more complex language from the implementation standpoint than many other hardware description languages. The author has direct experience with two previous behavioral simulation environments, ADLIB-SABLE [5] and the HELIX [3,5] simulation environment. Experience with VHDL indicate that the resources required to implement a VHDL based system are considerably greater than many other systems including these latter two.

Although, the implementation effort is greater, it is possible to build a very efficient simulator because of characteristics of VHDL. Specific features which are unique and important to VHDL in this regard include:

- Support for separate compilation of design units
- Well-defined semantics for the processing of time
- Tool independent language definition
- Excellent support for busses
- Strong typing of data
- Well-defined simulation semantics
- Very powerful syntactic features
- Well-defined and powerful handling of concurrency

Each of these features gives VHDL significant advantages in providing for very efficient simulation environment performance. The following sections will discuss specific experience in regards to VHDL performance.

3.1 VHDL Compilation

By utilizing modern compiler-compiler technology and an efficient programming language (C), excellent results have been obtained in the performance of the VHDL compiler. Previous experience by Intermetrics resulted in a VHDL compiler which operated at approximately 350 lines per CPU minute on a VAX 11/785 [6]. This Intermetrics version was implemented in ADA which in itself introduces significant performance penalties. Current indications are that VHDL can be compiled much more efficiently, with lexical analysis speeds exceeding 10,000 lines per minute on a two MIPS machine. Although semantic analysis will slow this throughput, preliminary benchmarks indicate that VHDL compilation speeds including external compilation units are competitive with modern programming languages including C and Pascal.

VHDL offers potential to far exceed the design turnaround performance of other hardware description languages by leveraging separate compilation capabilities. Very few HDLs offer the powerful separate compilation features in VHDL which allow incremental changes to large databases of VHDL source code to be made without a significant volume of recompilation being required. The implementation discussed in this paper fully utilizes this advantage.

The strongly typed nature of VHDL makes it possible for the VHDL compiler to perform a significantly greater number of checks on VHDL inputs making it possible to produce more efficient run-time support. Conceptually, VHDL allows some of the processing which typically occurs during run-time to be shifted to compile time. As a result, VHDL has some advantages over other HDLs.

VHDL has a number of very powerful syntactic features which make it possible to describe complex hardware behavior in a terse fashion. The generate statement supports the description of complex repetitive structure in a succinct fashion, potentially saving tens if not hundreds of lines of source code. Many of the shorter forms of concurrent statements are very effective in describing typical hardware function. Clearly, the built-in semantics in the handling of timing offer advantages over other HDLs. In sum, it is possible to describe hardware designs more effectively in VHDL than many other languages, and as a result the compile efficiency associated with these descriptions is increased.

3.2 Simulation Run-Time

The VHDL language offers more flexibility than many other HDLs in the wide range of abstraction levels which are supported. Of particular interest, are the many modelling styles which are supported:

- Data-flow
- Structural
- Algorithmic

Each of these modelling styles has specific VHDL constructs which must be supported at run-time during simulation. VHDL provides a number of key characteristics that make it possible to build a highly optimized simulation engine including:

- Well-defined semantics for the processing of time
- Tool independent language definition
- Excellent support for busses
- Well-defined simulation semantics
- Very powerful syntactic features
- Well-defined and powerful handling of concurrency

Because of the tool independence that VHDL supports, it is possible to isolate the language from the actual implementation. In this environment, transformations of the VHDL source input can be performed. Such transformations may lead to (1) enhanced functionality, as in the transformation supporting the VHDL Annotation Language (VAL) [1], (2) enhanced performance, or (3) multiple system-level design alternatives [2].

The well-defined semantics of VHDL in the areas of hierarchical description, conflict resolution, handling of time, and concurrency make it possible to validate the operation of the simulation algorithms and guarantee that every implementation will be compatible at a VHDL source level.

By leveraging the well-defined nature of VHDL and by performing significant optimizations during code-generation, experience with the implementation described in this paper indicates that VHDL can in fact be very efficient. Early benchmarks have resulted in performance of approximatively two thousend events per second per MIPS. This performance exceeds the currently available commercial behavioral simulator performance by a factor of two. Although more extensive benchmarking has yet to be performed, indications are that VHDL simulation can execute very efficiently.

4 Conclusion

VHDL is a very powerful and flexible hardware description language which offers a significant improvement from a design tool standpoint over other currently used languages. VHDL is a standard language that is independent from the tools that support it. VHDL is suitable for multi-level design ranging from the gate level to the architectureal level. VHDL also suports a wide range of description methodologies including data-flow, algorithmic and structural.

One of the primary concerns with VHDL is the difficulty of developing an efficient simulator. Experience as summarized in this paper indicates that in fact VHDL has specific features which make it possible to build a simulation environment with significantly better performance than many of the state-of-the-art tools which use proprietary languages.

Based on this experience, it is clear that VHDL will become a very important language for the design community. Production quality tools that are efficient and have sufficient functionality to support hardware design can be built, and these tools when combined with the advantages of the VHDL language offer a potent enhancement to current design environments and languages.

References

[1] L.M.Augustin, B.A.Gennart, Y.Huh, D.C.Luckham, and A.G.Stanculescu, *VAL: An Annotation Language for VHDL*, ICCAD 87, Digest of Technical Papers

[2] R.A.Walker, and D.E.Thomas, *Design Representation and Transformation in The System Architect's Workbench*, ICCAD 87, Digest of Technical Papers

[3] D.Coelho, *HELIX, A Tool for Multi-Level Simulation of VLSI Systems*, International Semi-Custom IC Conference, November 1983

[4] D.Coelho, *High-Level Design Using HELIX*, ACM Computer-Science Conference, March 1985

[5] D.Coelho, D.Hill, *Multi-Level Simulation for VLSI Design*, Kluwer Academic Publishers, 1987

[6] UTMC, *VHDL Software Evaluation Report, Release 3.0*, VHDL Independent Validation and Verification contract F33615-85-C-1760, April 1987.

[7] IEEE, *VHDL Language Reference Manual*, Draft Standard 1076/B, May 1987.

[8] CAD Language Systems, Inc., *VHDL Tutorial for IEEE Standard 1076 VHDL*, Draft, May 1987.

VHDL in an Object Oriented VLSI Design Environment

*Moon Jung Chung**, *Edwin Rogers*** *Yoohun Won*†

*Department of Computer Science
Michigan State University
East Lansing, MI 48824

**Department of Computer Science
RPI
Troy, NY 12180

† Department of Computer Science
Hong Ik University
Seoul, Korea

ABSTRACT

We describe the principal structures used in a new object-oriented CAD design environment (OOCADE) intended for use in connection with VHDL design. VHDL is a specification language for hardware systems, not a design environment. As such it defines a scope for VLSI design and provides a means of communicating designs of complex hardware systems. Those engaged in design need more. OOCADE establishes a hierarchical knowledge representation system for design entities (objects) using multiple inheritance (and inferential distance to resolve ambiguities) across a variety of user-definable relations. Behavior, state, structure and other attributes are incorporated in objects. Relationships among objects may include COMPONENT-OF, VERSION-OF and others that a designer may define. A designer interface will use icons, templates and knowledge-base searches in a multi-window environment. Designer freedom to deal with various parts of a design simultaneously and to explore design options in a largely independent way are important. However, design activities will be monitored to track consistency in aggregate design objects formed and integrity among versions or levels of specification of a design.

This paper gives further details concerning the design of this object oriented design system.

1. Introduction

Hardware design is a series of transformations from the behavioral to the logic level description, and finally to layout. Most hardware description languages are primarily for simulation [4,5,7,14]. Recently, there have been developments on object oriented VLSI CAD databases [1,2,3]. Wolf developed an object oriented VLSI design system based on flavors [8]. We have designed an object oriented computer aided design environment (OOCADE) which uses VHDL [7] as a specification language. OOCADE is a tool for carrying out such design transformations in a seamless way. It will be used for the design, specification, simulation and synthesis of VLSI systems. One output of OOCADE will be a VHDL description. To complement VHDL, OOCADE has extra supporting features such as abstraction mechanisms, class hierarchy, constraint checking, and dynamic binding.

OOCADE has three part: data base, design environment, and user interface. The former is a repository for design data and an object library, while the latter presents the design environment to the user. The design environment, called *VIOLET*, is the central part of OOCADE. *VIOLET* supports data abstraction, attribute inheritance, and dynamic binding. Hardware design entities, called objects, have attributes and messages. Design processes are modeled as messages carried out by methods applied to design objects icon actions in the designer interface. Constraint checking functions, defined by designers, check constraints during design stages. *VIOLET* supports the top-down design of VLSI structures wherein spatial and logical connections between hardware modules with prescribed behavior are specified. *VIOLET* can be also used in bottom up design by searching through the design library and combining components to form modules.

2. Basic Concepts

2.1. Objects and Messages

VLSI design entities inherently are objects with their own attributes (or properties). Each object has its own behavior and attributes. It also has a set of messages to which it can respond. In *VIOLET*, objects include not only the design entities of VHDL but also components or characteristics of the hardware at any level of abstraction, ranging from an entire system to a single transistor. An object can also be a port, a net or a signal, although they may not be hardware design entities. In this sense, *VIOLET* is different from [1,2,9].

Attributes describe how objects behave and how they are structured. An attribute of an object can be bound by supplying a constant value of the attribute or a corresponding method

† This work has been supported in part by the Air Force VHDL program.

CH2539-5/88/0000/0324$01.00 © 1988 IEEE

which describes the computation of an attribute. In this way, an attribute may be a message related to the design entity specification. For example, a specification "delay <- 5" for object A says the attribute delay for object A is 5, and whenever the object receives a message "delay'A", it must return the value 5. Also, functions such as computing the channel requirement, estimating area and computing power consumption may be regarded as methods for correponding attributes.

A special kind of attribute is called a state. A state changes its value upon receiving a message. The object behavior describes how an object changes its state. In *VIOLET*, the behavior and state of an object are described in the behavior part of the object.

Built-in messages are provided for simulation, layout, and timing analysis. Designers can override these methods by supplying their own methods. For example, the message "SIMULATE ADDER(x,y)" will invoke the design object ADDER to add two numbers and return the result. If ADDER consists of two half adders HA1 and HA2, then ADDER may send other messages such as SIMULATE HA1 and SIMULATE HA2 in order to execute the message SIMULATE ADDER.

2.2. Class Hierarchy

Similar objects are grouped together to form a class. If an object is in a class, we say that the object is an instance of the class. Instances in the same class will inherit the same set of messages from the parent class. Sometimes a class may have constraints to be satisfied by all objects which are instances of the class. This facility is convenient for checking the integrity of a design. A class may be divided into subclasses from which instances may be drawn. Thus, a design class is defined by its messages, attributes, behavior, constraints, and its super-class.

The object oriented approach gives us mechanisms for abstraction and inheritance. Inheritance means simply that the scope of the messages and attributes contained in a class B includes each sub-class A of class B. Thus, all instances of class A will inherit the attributes of class B.

Consider Figure 1 which shows the class hierarchy of ADDER. A class of circuits which performs addition can be modeled as a class ADDER. An instance of ADDER will inherit its I/O ports attributes and its functionality from the class ADDER. Suppose ADDER may be implemented in two ways, by means of half adders or by means of a PLA. A PLA implementation of ADDER may be classified according to its technology, such as CMOS, NMOS etc. In this hierarchy, CMOS adders will inherit I/O port and behavioral attributes from the class ADDER and from the PLA adder subclass, while they will inherit attributes such as power consumption and area estimates from the class CMOS_ADDER.

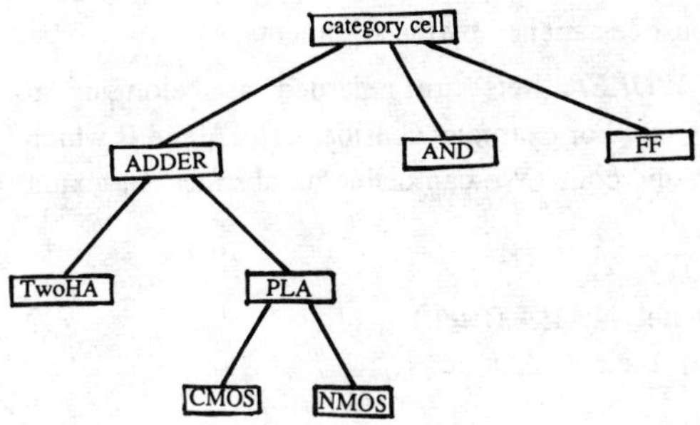

Figure 1. Hierarchy for Adders

3. Features of VIOLET

VIOLET has several built-in classes called categories. They are *cell, net, port* and *behavior*.

Objects in the *cell* category are very similar to VHDL design entities. They have ports, behavior, components, and other attributes. When we declare that A is a cell, we define a class of cells called A. When we use A to design other cells, we create an instance of the cell class A. Even though our system is primarily targeted for iconic design, users can also define a cell textually. For the textual description of a cell, the syntax is very similar to VHDL syntax. In this case the system will ask for the class hierarchy. The syntax of a cell declaration is as follows.

define cell cellname: superclass_name
generic parameters;
port specification;
attribute specification;
constraint specification;
component specification;
net specification;
behavior specification;

If the user does not specify a super class, the super class is the category cell. If the superclass of cell A is B, then cell A will inherit all of B's attributes and messages. Generic parameters can be used to describe parameterized circuits. Actual values can be bound during instantiation of the object. The syntax and semantics of port specification and behavior specification come from VHDL.

All attributes can be retrieved by **AttributeName'ObjectName.** For example, an attribute area of an object cell A can be denoted by **area'A.** Constraints impose restrictions on the attributes of a design entity. One way of specifying such constraints is by using VHDL assertion statements. Also, we can include predicate functions which must be satisfied by the arguments.

In *VIOLET*, nets are regarded as belonging to the category *net*. For example, consider cells A and B which have ports cin and cout. We can define an abstract net textually as follows.

```
define net Net1(A,B:cell)
  begin B.cin <- A.cout;
  end
```

After binding an icon to Net1, we can create a connection between object A and B by picking the Net1 icon and then picking objects A and B. Users can define a net which connects several ports with delay as follows.

```
define net Net2(A:cell, a,b,s : port)
  begin
     A.ain <- a  after 3;
     A.bin <- b  after 2;
     s <- A.sum  after 3;
  end
```

An abstract net such as Net2 can be used textually or graphically to define other cells. Nets Net1 and Net2 can be regarded either as classes of nets with given attributes or as templates which can be used to create connections. Thus, by regarding Net1 and Net2 as templates, we can still use Net1 and Net2 without creating classes under the net category. In this case, such objects will be stored in the design library of the design window where we define a cell.

In *VIOLET*, structural relationships are represented explicitly by **net** statements. In VHDL and ZEUS, they are represented implicitly by a signal assignment statement. One advantage of such explicit specification of **net** statement is that, with the graphics interface, **net** and **component** instantiation can be done easily by picking I/O ports for the net or by copying a cell icon. Note that from the structural description given by component instantiation and net, we can deduce the behavioral description. Simulation can be done at the behavioral description level or at the structural description level.

4. Dynamic Binding

Abstraction mechanisms and dynamic binding allow hiding of design details, which simplifies the design process and makes it more robust. Suppose that component X is used to design cell A. The statement

component X:Y;

declares that a component X is a cell of type Y. Later in the design, we may refine component X to be a subtype Z of cell type Y, by making the following assignment.

component X:Z;

For example, an instance of cell type ADDER may be used to design an ALU. We can later bind an instance X of the ADDER subclass ParaAdder within the design of ALU. This can be done simply by

X <- ParaAdder.

An object whose components are bound is called a version. Thus, a version is similar to a VHDL design entity which has a configuration body. But in *VIOLET*, the binding is restricted according to the class hierarchy. This restriction can prevent unnecessary error. That is, a user can specify the class (type) of cell which can be used, and the binding of a component can be done only if the new type to be bound is a subclass of the original type.

5. The Iconic User Interface

Icons will be used to represent various objects (such as circuits, interconnections and pins), messages and templates in *VIOLET*. OOCADE allows an icon which corresponds to several design steps. Thus, a user can design a circuit by manipulating icons. For example, in a pattern matching systolic array, certain connections appear repeatedly. In design systems, such as [1,8,9], representing such connection patterns is not easy. In this system, we can group several ports as a port cluster and define the cluster as a single object. A "connect" message can be defined with respect to this port cluster and used to implement the connection. Thus, a new design paradigm can be accommodated easily without modifying the language syntax. Thus this system can be regarded as both a design language and a design environment. In this sense, OOCADE is similar to the Smalltalk system [12]. However, in *VIOLET* the manipulation of object classes is tailored to VLSI design.

VIOLET uses four types of window: *class window, design window, text window,* and *buffer window.* A class window shows the class hierarchy of objects. Using class windows, a user can go up and down the design hierarchy. For example, Figure 2 denotes a sample window through which we can move down to the CMOS implementation of ADDER.

A design window is used to design a cell. We can create an object, place it in a window, instantiate an object from a class window or from the buffer window. A text window is necessary when a user wants to describe an object textually.

A buffer window stores icons, objects and other information which are used to design a cell. Using a buffer window,

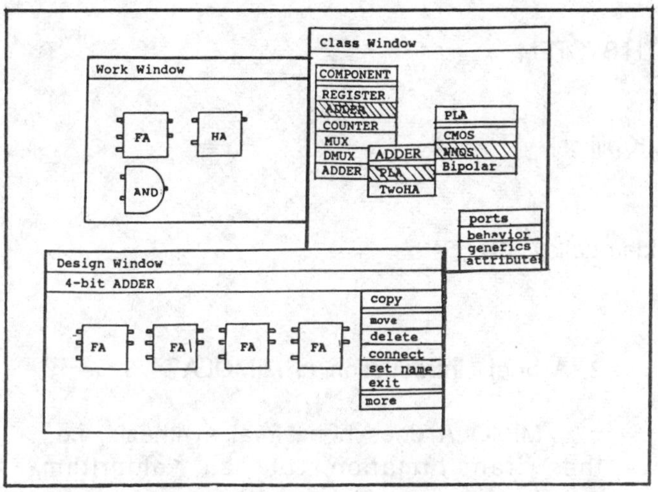

Figure 2. A sample window for the design of 4 bit ADDER

we need not scroll a whole class window or store intermediate results in a class hierarchy. Figure 2 shows examples of these windows for a four bit adder design.

6. Constraints and Integrity Checking

The attributes of an object may be regarded as constraints, as for example, the delay or area of a cell. In the top down design of a system, constraint checking is important. The attributes specified for an entity may not correspond to the values which are obtained after combining its components. Such constraints may be related to logical values, delays, or geometry, among other things. For example, suppose the maximum power of FullAdder is specified as 10μA but, after designing HA and combining it to construct FullAdder, the power consumption of FullAdder is larger than the original specification. In this case the lower level design violates the constraint of the FullAdder circuit.

In *VIOLET*, such constraints may be checked automatically. For each built-in attribute such as area, power, and delay, there is a built-in procedure which computes the actual attribute value of an entity from its structural and behavioral descriptions when these are avialable. If they wish, designers can override this constraint checking procedure. For example, if a user wants to use his own function Fun1 which computes power from its structural and behavioral description, he can set the attributes of the power as

attributes power <- Fun1;
constraints power < 10;

7. Conclusion and Current Status

The design of hardware in an object oriented design environment has been described. VHDL is used as a basis for the design entities and their behavioral description. To complement VHDL, we have a class hierarchy, dynamic binding and inheritance mechanism. Using icons representing objects and messages, designers can model design objects and design processes and thus be free from the idiosyncracies of the syntax of the VHDL. Currently, the iconic representation of objects and messages are being designed. The VIOLET system is being implemented on SUN workstations.

Acknowledgements We are grateful to D. Robinson and J. Zhou for their help during the preparation of the paper.

8. References

[1] Afsarmanesh, H., D. McLeod, D. Knapp, and A. Parker, "An Extensible Object-oriented Approach to Databases for VLSI/CAD", Proc. VLDB, Stockholm, 1985.

[2] Batory, D.S. and W. Kim, "Modeling Concepts for VLSI Objects", ACM TODS, 10, 3 (1985), 289-321.

[3] Copeland, G and D. Maier, "Making Smalltalk a Database System", Proc. ACM International SIGMOD Conference, Boston, June, 1984.

[4] IEEE Computer, Special Issue on Hardware Design Languages, February 1985.

[5] Lieberherr K. J., Knudsen S.E., "Zeus: A Language for Expressing Algorithms in Hardware," Unpublished manuscript.

[6] Veiga P., Lanca M., "Harpa: A Hierarchical Multi-level Hardware Description Language," Proceedings 21-st Design Automation Conference, June 1984.

[7] VHDL Language Reference Manual, 1987.

[8] Wolf W., "Fred, A Procedural Database for VLSI Chip Planning", Technical Report, AT&T.

[9] R.V. Zara and D. R. Henke, "Object Oriented Mixed-Mode Functional Simulation System," Proceedings 22-nd Design Automation Conference, 1985.

[10] A. Goldberg and D. Robson, Smalltalk-80, Addison Wesley, 1983.

[11] A. Borgida, "Features of Languages for the Development of Information Systems at the Conceptual Level," IEEE Software, Vol. 2 No. 1, Jan. 1985, pp. 63-72.

[12] Kowalski, T. J., The VLSI Design Automation Assistant: A Knowledge-Based System, Ph. D. Thesis, Dept. of EECS, CMU, 1984.

[13] W.H. Evans, J.C. Ballegeer and Nguyen H. Duyet, "ADL: An Algorithmic Design Language for Integrated Circuit Synthesis," 21-st Design Automation Conference, pp. 66-72, June 1984.

[14] Riloty, R. and D. Borrione, "The Conlan Project: Concepts, Implementation, and Application," Computer, Vol. 18, No. 2, February 1985, pp 81-92.

THE V-SYNTH SYSTEM

Stanley J. Krolikoski

Honeywell CSDD, Golden Valley, MN 55427

Abstract

The V-Synth system, a major updating of the MIMOLA Software System is described. A brief overview of MIMOLA is presented, followed by description of the changes made to it. These changes include integration of MIMOLA into the VHDL environment, development of a new tool called the "process graph analyzer", changes to the MIMOLA control structure and the addition of the capability to accept pipelined designs as input.

1. Introduction

The MIMOLA Software System (MSS) is a behavioral synthesis program originally developed by G. Zimmermann at the University of Kiel [Zimm]. It was brought to Honeywell in 1980, where it has been greatly enhanced. Currently a new expanded version of MIMOLA called "V-Synth" (for "VHDL Synthesis") is being developed at Honeywell's Corporate Systems Development Division and was delivered to the Air Force in November of 1987. In this paper we shall discuss V-Synth.

The work reported in this paper was sponsored by the Avionics Laboratory, Air Force Wright Aeronautical Laboratories, Aeronautical Systems Division (ASSC), United States Air Force, Wright-Patterson AFB, Ohio 45433-6543 under contract no. F33615-85-C-1861

2. A brief introduction to MIMOLA

MIMOLA does behavioral synthesis, i.e., the transformation of an algorithm specified in some high level language into an application-specific register transfer level architecture which will execute this algorithm. In MIMOLA, the designer can control the nature of the synthesized architecture through the mechanisms of hardware restrictions and hardware binding. Setting or loosening hardware restrictions, i.e., controlling the amount of hardware able to be used in a design, effectively controls the amount of behavior done in parallel in an architecture during a given machine cycle. For example, two additions can be done during the same clock cycle if at least two adders are available, but at least two cycles will be needed if there is only one one adder available.

The designer is given additional control over the results of synthesis through the mechanism of hardware binding. This allows specific hardware elements to be associated with individual behavioral statements in the algorithm. For example, instead of simply indicating that the synthesized architecture is to execute (among other things) the following piece of behavior:

(1) a := b + c ,

MIMOLA allows the designer to write something like:

(2) S_cache(a) := S_main(b)/
S_assoc(c) -> B_carry_lookahead(+) .

This latter line (which is written in the original MIMOLA language) describes the same behavior as (1), but also indicates where b and c are located (viz., in the main memory and an associative memory, respectively), what adder (a carry lookahead adder) is to do the addition, and in which memory (a cache in this case) the results are to be stored. The designer is also free to not bind some behavior to any specific piece of hardware. In this case MIMOLA will attempt to reuse already existing hardware or, subject to any hardware restrictions, will allocate new hardware as needed.

An important point here is that the designers can either use the default generic library of hardware components provided by MIMOLA, or may suppply their own libraries for MIMOLA to use during the synthesis process. In the former case, the design can stay "technology independent" as long as possible, while in the latter case, a design can be targeted toward a specific technology.

As shown in Figure 1, MIMOLA is typically used iteratively. Once an algorithm has been chosen, a designer will use MIMOLA to synthesize several functionally equivalent architectures. The differences between these designs, which will be reflected in the utilization and cost figures, result from changes made in hardware restrictions/bindings to alter performance. The GEMS software [Venkat] provides a graphical interface through which the user easily may change hardware restrictions and/or bindings.

3.0 V-Synth

V-Synth is an extended synthesis system which has MIMOLA as its core. In this section we shall discuss the key features of V-Synth

3.1 Integration into the VHDL environment and the process graph analyzer

VHDL (VHSIC Hardware Description Language) is the DoD and IEEE standard hardware description language. [Shahdad]. One of the most important changes changes in V-Synth is the ability of MIMOLA to input and output this important new HDL.

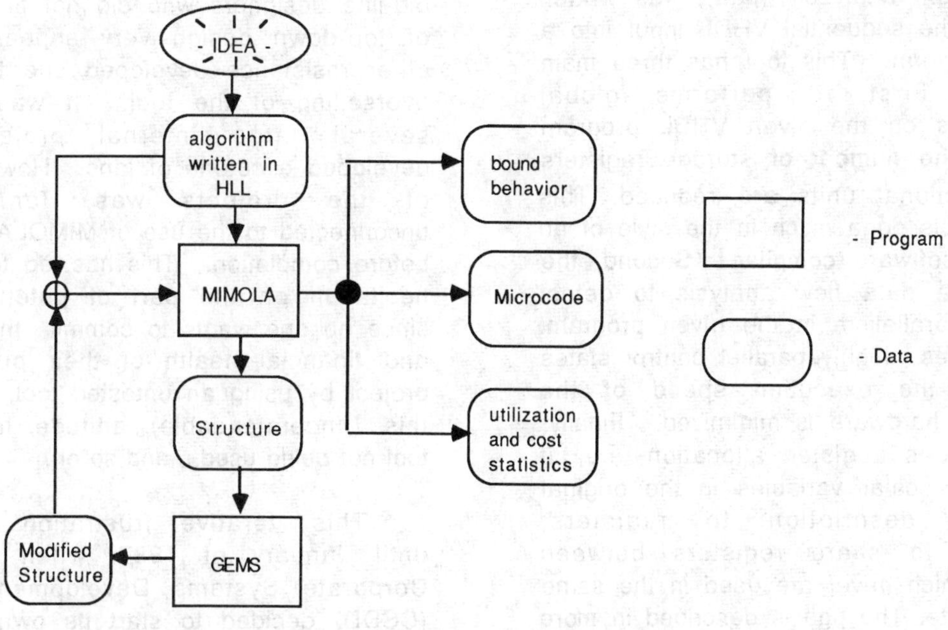

Figure 1. The Synthesis Process in MIMOLA

One of the limitation of the orginal MIMOLA tool was that it required the designer to consider the machine being synthesized as a state machine. That is to say, the behavior to be performed in parallel during each state of this machine and all state transitions must be detailed by the designer. This type of input is appropriate in many situations, particularly when the designer has a very good preconception of the machine to be synthesized. As such it will continue to be supported under V-Synth, except that such algorithms must be now written in VHDL.

On the other hand, the designer may wish, in many cases, to develop sequential algorithms which more closely resemble programs written in a higher-level language. V-Synth allows the user to do this, using the part of VHDL which is similar to Ada. This will free the user from having to decide which behavior needs to be done in parallel during a particular machine state, and will allow full concentration to be given to algorithm development.

However, the decision as to what behavior is to be done in parallel during the states of the synthesized machine must eventually be made. Thus, a tool, called the "process-graph analyzer" (pga), was written to convert the sequential VHDL input into a parallelized form. This tool has three main functions. First, it performs global optimizations on the given VHDL program such that the number of storage registers and/or functional units are reduced. This optimization is done much in the style of an optimizing software compiler. Second, the pga does a data flow analysis to detect maximum parallelism in the given program. This produces highly parallel control states such that the execution speed of the synthesized hardware is minimized. Finally, the pga does register allocation, i.e, it assigns the scalar variables in the original behavioral description to registers, attempting to share registers between variables which never are used in the same machine state. The pga is described in more depth elsewhere. [Bhask]

V-Synth outputs a register-transfer level architecture written in VHDL. It will also output in VHDL the fully bound behavior associated with this architecture. Finally, it will output the microcode for this architecture. This output may subsequently be used as the input to lower level design tools such as silicon compilers.

3.4 Elimination of current limitations

Until V-Synth, MIMOLA has existed as a laboratory, i.e., prototype, tool. We have worked to take it beyond this status into the realm of industrial-quality tools. This involves making the changes listed above, removing all known bugs, plus producing a new set of users manuals. These changes will, we believe, make MIMOLA a tool able to fit nicely into the design cycle of application specific integrated circuits.

4 Use of V-Synth

Since the original MIMOLA system has come into Honeywell it has only seen limited use within the corporation. Part of the resistance to the tool came from old-line designers who did not find the idea of top-down design very appealing, while other resistance developed due to a gross overselling of the tool. It was used on several large internal projects, and developed a coterie of fans. However, each of the projects was, for reasons unconnected to the use of MIMOLA, cancelled before completion. This has led to a certain hesitation on the part of potential users, since no one wants to commit the technical and financial health of their project their project by using an untested tool. Naturally, this (understandable) attitude led to the tool not being used... and so on.

This iterative frustration continued until January of 1987, when Honeywell Corporate Systems Development Division (CSDD) decided to start its own test chip design. The results of this project, it was felt, would at least provide information regarding V-Synth performance for designers in other Honeywell divisions to examine in considering the use of the tool. Shortly thereafter, Honeywell Solid State Electonics Division (SSED), Systems and Research Center (S&RC) and Marine Systems Divisions (MSD) became interested in participating in this project. This was a fortunate occurence, since now a bona fide product division (MSD), the main chip design and fabrication division (SSED) in Honeywell, and the Honeywell Aerospace and Defense Research Center (S&RC) were using the tool. This joint MSD/SSED/S&RC/ CSDD project is continuing on the design of a VHSIC chip. We are confident that this project will provide the catalyst to get V-Synth regularly used within our corporation.

5. Porting V-Synth To 1076 VHDL

As this paper is being written (October 1987), V-Synth has not yet been delivered to the Air Force. Delivery is scheduled for the end of November 1987. The immediate next phase in the development of the tool is to convert it to use the new IEEE VHDL.

6 Summary

In this paper we have briefly described MIMOLA and the changes made to it to produce the V-Synth system. These changes include the integration of MIMOLA into the VHDL environment, and the creation of a new tool, the process graph analyzer, which will take sequential VHDL code and break it into optimized control states. MIMOLA will also be able to do more sophisticated synthesis of the control path of a design, and will be able to accept pipelined algorithms as input. Finally, the tool will now be as bug-free as possible, making it suitable to use in an industrial design environment.

Bibliography

[Bhask] J. Bhasker, "Process Graph Analyzer," in Proceedings of the 1987 Hawaii International Conference on Circuits and Systems, 1987.

[Shahdad] M. Shahdad, "An Overview of VHDL Language and Technology," in Proceedings of the 23rd Design Automation Conference, Las Vegas, pp.320-326, 1986.

[Venkat] V. Venkataraman and C.Wilcox, "GEMS: An Automatic Layout Tool for MIMOLA Schematics," in Proceedings of the 23rd Design Automation Conference, Las Vegas, pp. 131-137, 1986.

[Zimm] Zimmermann, G.,"The MIMOLA Design System, a Computer Aided Processor Design Method," in Proceedings of the 16th Design Automation Conference, San Diego, pp.55-59, 1979.

Standards and Benchmark Circuits in Logic Testing

Chair: S. Mourad

BENCHMARKING OF TEST-GENERATION SYSTEMS

Prabhakar Goel and Harry Chen

Gateway Design Automation Corporation
Six Lyberty Way, Westford, MA

Abstract

Many factors come into play in the selection of an automatic test-generation system. The choice is complicated by the ever-growing number of system suppliers, as well as the in-house ATG capabilities of many manufacturers. Benchmarking can simplify the selection process. This paper discusses several aspects to consider in the benchmarking of automatic test-generation systems.

Introduction

A number of commercial and in-house ATG systems are in use in the electronics industry today. The need exists, therefore, to perform careful evaluations when making build-or-buy decisions. Even those manufacturers already using in-house ATG systems must make comparative evaluations of commercially available systems. The need for an evaluation process is even more pressing for those manufacturers that have not yet built or procured an ATG system.

The establishment of a well-defined benchmarking methodology reduces the risk of making wrong decisions. It is very important that the criteria used in ATG benchmarking be well understood. An analogous situation exists in benchmarking simulator products[1]; many issues associated with simulator benchmarking are applicable to ATG evaluation. The benchmarking tests for automatic test generation break down into three distinct categories:

(a) human interface/documentation
(b) functionality tests
(c) speed/capacity (or stress) tests

Because the human-interface/documentation aspect is easily analyzable and product-specific, this paper will not discuss category (a); the intent of the paper is, rather, to present generic issues in ATG benchmarking. Benchmarks for the functionality-test criterion are the easiest to devise. It's a relatively simple matter to build small, simple circuits that contain the different features, and that provide tangible proof of functionality. Therefore, this paper will concentrate on speed/capacity (stress) tests.

Historically, a substantial part of the efforts in the industry toward devising benchmarks for automatic test generation have been devoted to stress tests. The Brglez-Fujiwara circuits[2], for example, represent an early effort toward developing standardized benchmarks for testing combinational circuits. This paper will list the parameters that come to bear in speed/capacity tests, and will discuss the impact each of these parameters has on benchmarking ATG systems.

Before discussing in detail the benchmarks in category (c), it's useful to list the issues associated with automatic test generation. Table 1 gives the taxonomy of the key functionality features. This table is modelled after the performance-test table for simulators presented in Reference 1.

Speed/capacity tests

Benchmarks for stress testing of test-pattern generation tools require a keen awareness of the parameters that influence the speed and/or capacity of such tools. Some of the key parameters encountered in stress testing are:

(a) depth of circuitry
(b) local vs global feedback loops
(c) synchronous vs asynchronous logic
(d) number of primitives
(e) structural characteristics of subcircuits

Depth of circuitry

In the case of combinational logic, depth of circuitry is defined to be the maximum number of gates or primitives in any path from an input pin to an output pin. Depth is a key parameter in determining the complexity of test generation for combinational-logic circuits. It has been shown empirically[3] that the cost of test generation for an "unpartitionable" combinational circuit varies as G^2, where G is the number of gates. In this context, "unpartitionable" means the circuit can not be separated into unconnected sections--ie, most of the gates in the circuit feed each output of the circuit.

It is easy to see that the gate count of an unpartitionable circuit is closely related to the depth of the circuit. For example, a tree-structure circuit having two input gates has a gate

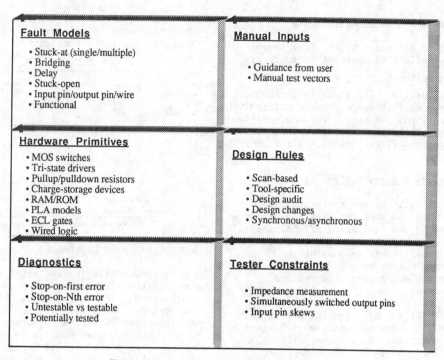

Fault Models • Stuck-at (single/multiple) • Bridging • Delay • Stuck-open • Input pin/output pin/wire • Functional	**Manual Inputs** • Guidance from user • Manual test vectors
Hardware Primitives • MOS switches • Tri-state drivers • Pullup/pulldown resistors • Charge-storage devices • RAM/ROM • PLA models • ECL gates • Wired logic	**Design Rules** • Scan-based • Tool-specific • Design audit • Design changes • Synchronous/asynchronous
Diagnostics • Stop-on-first error • Stop-on-Nth error • Untestable vs testable • Potentially tested	**Tester Constraints** • Impedance measurement • Simultaneously switched output pins • Input pin skews

Table 1. Automatic test-generation issues

count of 2^d-1, where d is the depth. Many unpartitionable circuits (but not necessarily all) exhibit a similar exponential growth in gate count as depth increases. Hence, test-generation costs can also be expected to grow exponentially with depth.

In the case of unstructured sequential-logic circuits, it is well known that counters present a real challenge for test generation. The depth of the circuitry is linked to the lengths of the sequences (initializing sequences) needed to reach different internal states, and to the lengths of the sequences (distinguishing sequences) needed to distinguish different states. Thus, shift registers entail short sequences, while counters require long sequences. Although no empirical relationship has been established, it appears that the cost of ATG for sequential-logic circuits can also be expected to increase exponentially with increasing lengths of the required initializing and distinguishing sequences.

<u>Local vs global feedback</u>

A simple extension of the combinational-logic circuit structure is the case of an acyclic interconnection of logic gates and D-type latches. In the absence of global feedback loops, and with direct exercisability of the clock signals to a latch, it is easy to see that the initializing and distinguishing sequences are relatively small[4]. Test generation is relatively easier to devise when global feedback loops are absent. Global feedback loops generally increase the difficulty of test generation, because they increase the difficulty of constructing initializing and distinguishing sequences.

<u>Synchronous vs asynchronous logic</u>

Most successful automatic test generation has been done with synchronous logic circuits, because the practically useful algorithms ignore the propagation delays of gates. A sequential-logic circuit is modelled as if it were synchronous for the purposes of test-pattern generation. Any "bad" (invalid) test introduced as a result of using asynchronous logic is subsequently screened out by the more accurate model used in the fault-simulation process.

It would be a safe assumption that general asynchronous-logic circuits having upwards of several hundred gates will cause most automatic test-pattern generation systems to do poorly. However, if there are smaller sections of easily characterizable asynchronous logic (eg, an asynchronous set/reset latch) scattered among other synchronous logic, then the synchronous-logic model used by test-pattern generators can be expected to work in most instances.

<u>Number of primitives</u>

As pointed out in Reference 3, the number of gates in a circuit is not a significant parameter in ATG costs unless it is also known that the circuit is unpartitionable. In the case of combinational logic, the gate count of an unpartitionable circuit is an important parameter in determining ATG costs. However, in an unpartitionable sequential-logic circuit, the presence of counters or of global feedback loops can override the gate-count issue and reduce the significance of the gate count in the determination of costs.

Structural characteristics of subcircuits

As explained in Reference 5, the ECAT (error correction and translation) class of circuits are difficult to test with the D-algorithm[6], but not with the PODEM algorithm. It is similarly possible to construct examples that would present difficulty to the PODEM algorithm, but not to the D-algorithm. It is thus obvious that benchmarks used to evaluate ATG must incorporate different circuit structures to be complete.

Approach to creating benchmark circuits

In creating circuits to use in benchmarking ATG, a choice exists: to seek out existing circuits in a facility, or to use available, off-the-shelf, circuit blocks. However, the already-realized circuits in the facility may be subject to proprietary issues, may be more difficult to characterize, or may not possess the desired benchmarking features.

Off-the-shelf SSI and MSI circuits are quite representative of the commonly used subcircuits found in larger circuits, as is borne out by the ASIC macrocells implemented to model the SSI/MSI cells. Further, gate-level models of the SSI/MSI cells are readily available. Because delays are impractical to consider in ATG, accurate delay modelling of the SSI/MSI circuits is of no concern.

Combinational-circuit benchmarks are easy to construct by configuring an acyclic interconnection of different combinational SSI/MSI subcircuits. It is thus possible to obtain circuits of almost any desired depth and combination of structural characteristics. An example is shown in Figure 1; this acyclic circuit uses two ALUs, parity trees with fanout and reconvergence, and a multiplexer.

The benchmarks can be assembled by using schematic-capture systems that have graphical symbols for the SSI/MSI parts, then generating a netlist. However, the benchmarks constructed in this manner can give rise to untestable circuitry, as the assembly process gives no clue as to the function of the circuitry. Unless large portions of untestable circuitry exist, however, these benchmarks are valuable because they help to determine the ability of an ATG system to identify untestable faults.

Figure 2 provides another example of using off-the-shelf SSI/MSI circuits to build ATG benchmarks. The basic cell is an Advanced Micro Devices Am2505 4x2-bit two's-complement multiplier. By iterating cells both vertically and horizontally, any MxN (assuming M and N are multiples of 4) multiplication array can be constructed[7]. The circuit in Figure 2 is an 8x8-bit multiplier.

The multiplication array is a good example of a circuit that is unpartitionable because of extensive cross-coupling among the cells. The gate-level description of the Am2505 is readily available. The ease of varying both the width and the depth of the multiplier makes the circuit an ideal benchmark to measure how ATG costs grow as a function of circuit complexity.

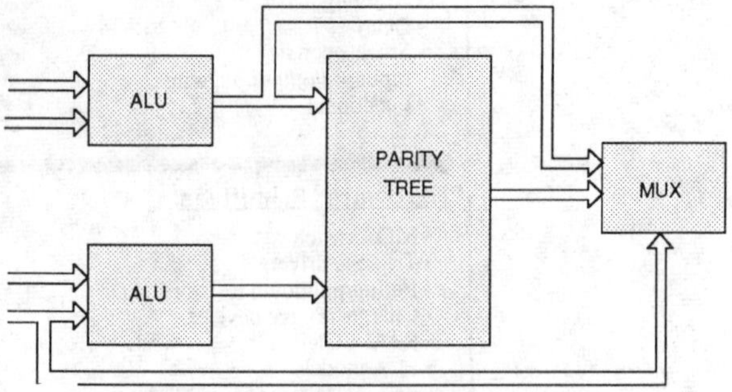

FIGURE 1. Acyclical combinational-logic circuit

Sequential-logic benchmarks

The sequential-logic circuit shown in Figure 3a contains two edge-triggered, D-type flip-flops and a set-reset latch. A single global feedback loop also exists. In Figure 3b, sections of the circuit are connected in series to construct a benchmark of greater depth. More complexity can be introduced by inserting global feedback logic between the iterated blocks. This circuit was iterated without regard to functionality. Note, however, that iterated sequential-logic circuits are more apt to produce untestable circuitry than are combinational-logic circuits.

Among sequential-logic circuits, further classification based on increasing order of test-generation difficulty can be made: scan logic, synchronous logic, and asynchronous logic.

Scan-logic benchmarks basically require combinational-logic circuitry bounded by SRLs (scan latches), in additional to some gated clock logic (gated from pins and SRLs). In many cases, an adequate benchmark is attainable without the use of the gated clock logic. The process for creating scan-logic benchmarks is generally similar to that used for combinational-logic circuitry.

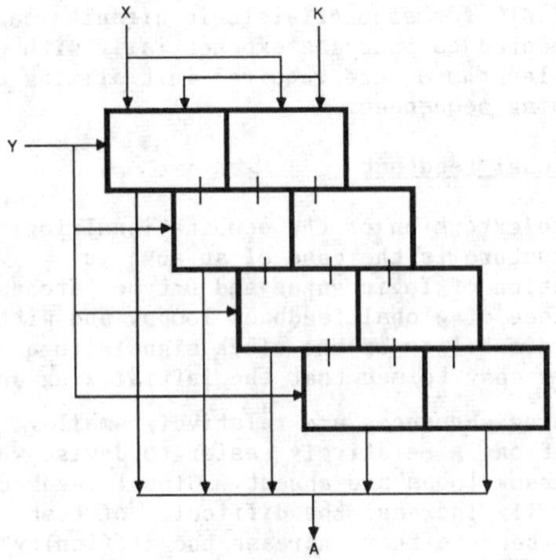

Figure 2. An 8 x 8-bit multiplier, A = X * Y + K using 8 Am 2505 cells

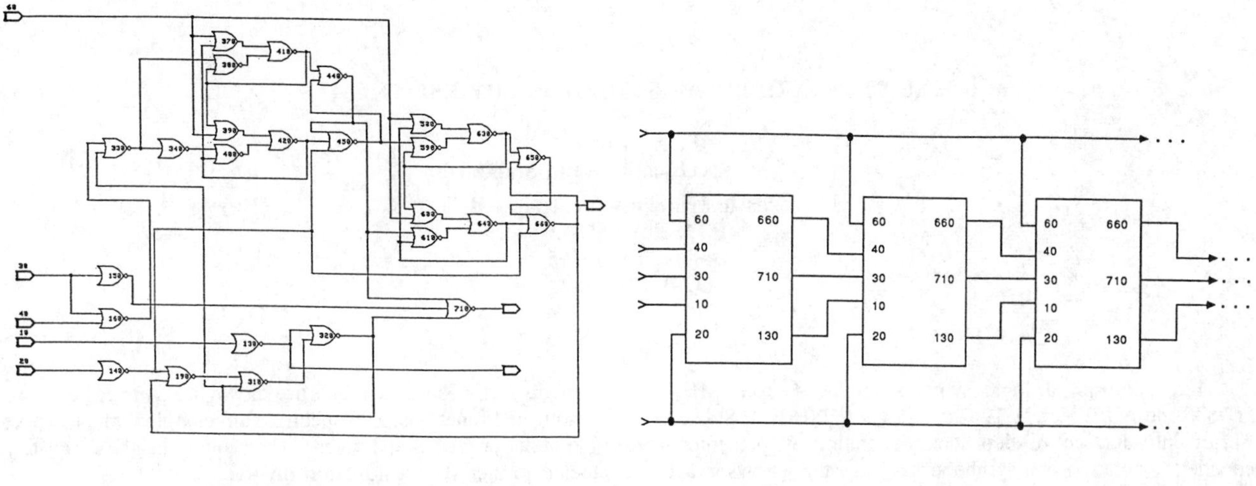

(a) Gate-level sequential circuit

(b) Sequential circuit

Figure 3. Building a sequential benchmark circuit

Benchmarks for synchronous sequential-logic circuitry can also be constructed similarly to those for combinational logic; however, it is necessary to ensure that no global feedback loops exist that are not interrupted by a clocked latch. In a synchronous circuit, the clocks must be directly controllable from the input pins. Finite state machines are good examples of synchronous benchmarking circuits.

In an asynchronous circuit, the control of clock signals and data is less clearly separable. By introducing a mix of counters of various sizes and types, shift registers, parallel registers, and other structures, it is possible to build benchmarks that have various depths, global loops, numbers of primitives, and circuit structures.

One can also vary complexity by mixing scannable, synchronous, and asynchronous logic in the benchmark. The essential element in these benchmarks is the control of the clock signals. Most practical ATG algorithms make assumptions about clock control. The limitations inherent in these assumptions need to be exposed by benchmarking. Different clocking schemes--eg, single-phase, multiphase, level-sensitive, and edge-sensitive--also have an effect on the performance of the ATG program.

Some of the benchmarking circuits discussed here may have no recognizable functionality. In most cases, however, functionality of a benchmark circuit is of no relevance to ATG systems that are seeking structural defects. Lack of functionality becomes an issue in ATG only when the nonfunctional circuits introduce massive redundancies. How to avoid these redundancies is an open question.

Conclusion

This paper has explored the important issues in creating benchmark circuits for automatic test-pattern generation, with the emphasis placed on speed/capacity (stress) testing. The paper has attempted to explain the ways in which depth of circuitry, local vs global feedback, synchronous vs asynchronous logic, number of primitives, and structural characteristics of subcircuits relate to the costs of automatic test generation.

Acknowledgment

The authors gratefully acknowledge the assistance of Ronna Alintuck, Karen Dapkus, and George Hwa in the preparation of this manuscript.

References

1. Greer, David L., "The Quick Simulator Benchmark", VLSI Systems Design, November 1987.

2. Brglez, F., and Fujiwara, H., "A Neutral Netlist of 10 Combinational Benchmark Circuits and a Target Translator in Fortran", Special Session on ATPG and Fault Simulation, Proceedings 1985 IEEE ISCAS, Kyoto, Japan, June 1985.

3. Goel, Prabhakar, "Test Generation Costs Analysis and Projections", 17th Design Automation Conference, 1980.

4. Goel, Prabhakar, "The Feedforward Logic Model in the Testing of LSI Logic Circuits", PhD Thesis, Carnegie-Mellon University, 1973.

5. Goel, Prabhakar, "An Implicit Enumeration Algorithm to Generate Tests for Combinational Logic Circuits", Volume C-30, IEEE Transactions on Computers, March 1981.

6. Roth, J.P., "Diagnosis of Automata Failures, a Calculus and a Method", Volume 10, IBM Journal of Research and Development, July 1966.

7. Levy, R., "How to Multiply and/or Divide in Two's Complement Hardware", Digital Signal Processing Handbook, Advanced Micro Devices, 1976.

IEEE STANDARD LOGIC SYMBOLS, WHY USE THEM?

F. A. Mann
Manager, Specifications and Standards
Texas Instruments Incorporated
P.O. Box 655012
Dallas, TX 75265
(214) 995-2659

ABSTRACT

The evolution of logic symbols is traced from MIL-STD-806 and AIEE No. 91-1962 to today's ANSI/IEEE Std 91. A brief introduction to dependency notation is presented. Dependency notation is a symbolic language that shows exact relationships between ports without necessarily showing how they are implemented. Some users refer to symbols in accordance with IEEE 91 as Functional Logic Symbols or FLS. The requirements for understanding FLS are outlined. The arguments against FLS are examined, and the alternatives are considered.

1. INTRODUCTION

As yet no one seems to be seriously questioning the fact that logic diagrams are still a necessary part of the required documentation for a system, be it for commercial or military use. And logic diagrams in some form are still used by designers as thought organizers and as a means of communication to others involved in the project from the conceptual stage onward. Unless one depends entirely on block diagrams with a good deal of supplementary text, symbols must be used that convey to others the essential facts in the mind of the originator.

One relevant definition of a symbol is "an arbitrary or conventional sign used in writing or printing relating to a particular field to represent operations, quantities, elements, relations, or qualities". This implies that there must be a standard or standards to define those symbols and their use, else they will not be understandable. See Figure 1.

SYMBOLS ARE ARBITRARY, THEY MUST BE DEFINED

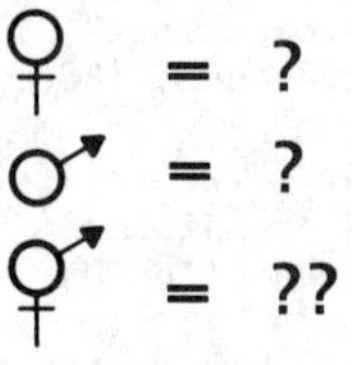

FIGURE 1

2. THE EVOLUTION OF PRESENT-DAY STANDARDS

In 1962, we had MIL-STD-806B and AIEE No. 91. These two standards were very similar in scope as the most complex device they had to deal with was the shift register. MIL-STD-806 recognized only positive logic, and it showed exactly how to handle a shift register with serial and parallel inputs and the capability to shift in both directions. The rectangle was used as the basic shape for all symbols except AND, OR, AMPLIFICATION, DELAY, and SINGLE-SHOT functions. These distinctive-shape symbols are shown in Figure 2. For more complicated functions, 806 specified a rectangle with an aspect ratio of 2:1 or greater and stated "The symbol shall be adequately labeled to identify the function involved".

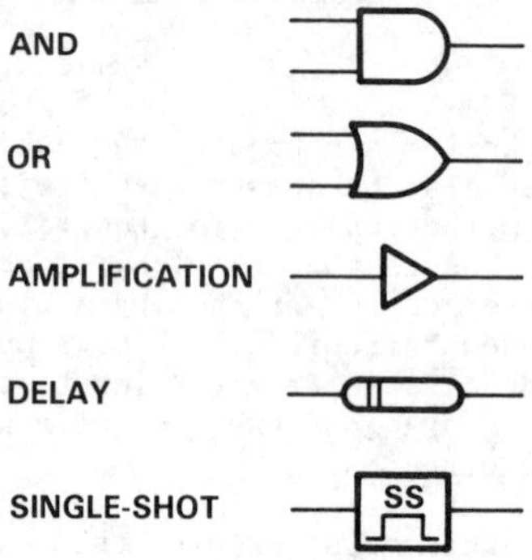

FIGURE 2

The standard produced by the American Institute of Electrical Engineers, AIEE No.91, tried to be more general. It covered positive logic, negative logic, and so-called "mixed logic". It recognized the distinctive shapes for AND and OR, but also permitted these to be represented by rectangles with the qualifying labels "A" or "OR" inside, as shown in Figure 3. A shift register was shown in some of their example diagrams, but the functions of several of its inputs are largely a matter of conjecture today. The rectangle was specified as the basic shape, but methods for representing more complex devices were not addressed.

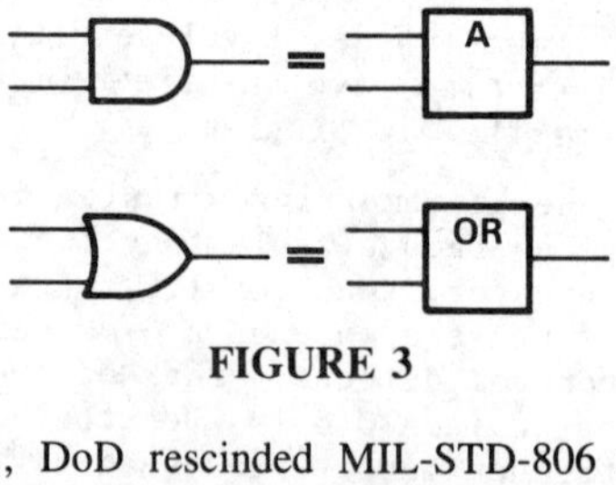

FIGURE 3

In 1973, DoD rescinded MIL-STD-806 and accepted ANSI/IEEE Std 91-1973. This standard included in rudimentary form a new concept, dependency notation. This allows one to show the exact effect of an input on one or more outputs, or on other inputs, by means of labels at the affecting input. The logic that implements the relationship is not shown. The form was rudimentary in that dependency notation could be used only when an AND-gating relationship existed, and several alternative means were shown for formulating the labels.

CH2539-5/88/0000/0338$01.00

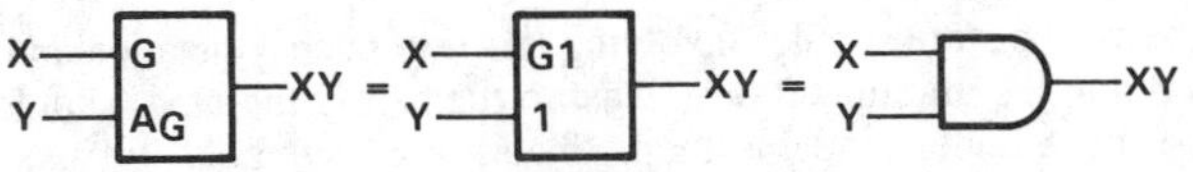

FIGURE 4

The symbols committees of the International Electrotechnical Commission (IEC), with IEEE participation, continued to evolve this revolutionary concept and to publish frequent supplements to the IEC standards in the 1970s. Unfortunately, the IEEE did not keep its own standard up to date. Some American companies, notably Allen-Bradley, AT&T, Control Data, Digital Equipment, General Electric, Hewlett-Packard, Honeywell, Sperry, Texas Instruments, and others, had seen the benefits in the system and helped in its evolution. The IEEE and the IEC worked together very closely to perfect the system and to harmonize their standards, and the results were published in 1983 [IEC 83] and 1984 [IEEE 84]. Many who use the IEEE symbols refer to them as Functional Logic Symbols or FLS.

3. AN INTRODUCTION TO DEPENDENCY NOTATION

How dependency notation works in the case of AND relationships can be seen from the example illustrated in Figure 5.

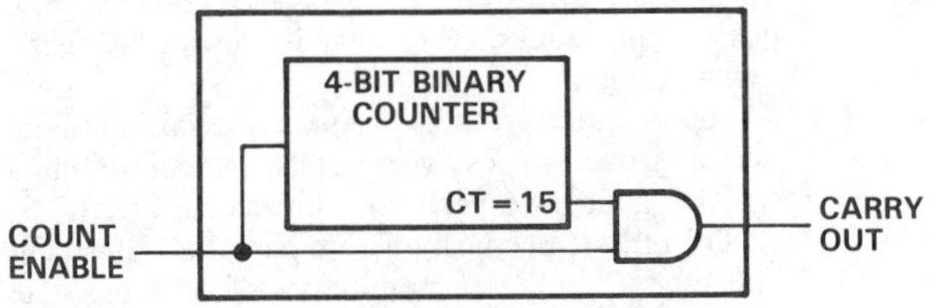

FUNCTION TABLE

COUNT	LOGIC STATES		
	CT = 15	COUNT ENABLE	CARRY OUT
0 thru 14	0	L = 0	0 = L
0 thru 14	0	H = 1	0 = L
15	1	L = 0	0 = L
15	1	H = 1	1 = H

FIGURE 5A

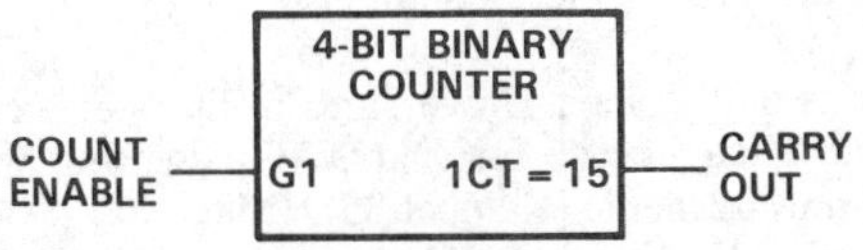

FIGURE 5B

Assume positive logic, meaning that a high level at an input or output pin will correspond to the internal 1-state at that input or output unless negation is shown. Suppose we have a 4-bit binary counter with a carry output that takes on the 1-state (becomes active) whenever the internal count reaches maximum, that is, 15. In the symbol, that output would be labeled "CT = 15". This is simple output labeling; it does not involve dependency notation. Now suppose this counter has an input called Count Enable, which must be in its 1-state to enable the Carry Output to take on its 1-state at the appropriate time. That is, if the Count Enable input is at its 0-state, it will impose the 0-state on the Carry Output. Thus, an AND relationship exists in this instance. Figure 5A shows the logic involved and Figure 5B shows a basic counter symbol with the relationship between the Count Enable input and the Carry Output shown by dependency notation. The letter G is prescribed by the standards to represent AND gating. The G inside the symbol indicates this input is ANDed with something. That something could be another input or an output. To specifically link it, the G is followed by an arbitrarily chosen number, e.g., "1". That same number is then placed at the affected input or output. In this case, it can be placed either before or after the other output label, CT = 15, since in ANDing, it doesn't matter which state is taken into account first: the internal state developed by the counter logic, or the state of the affecting G input. If either is a 0, the output result will be 0.

Figure 6 adds a little more complexity to the counter. How do we know it's a counter? By the general qualifying symbol "CTR" in the top center of the symbol. The "DIV16" part of the general qualifying symbol gives us the count modulo, 16. Inputs to parallel load the counter have been added at pins 1 through 4, a Load Enable has been added at pin 5, and parallel outputs have been added at pins 8 through 11. The letter "C" indicates Control Dependency. Thus the label "C2" tell us that this input has a "control" relationship to other inputs labeled "2". The standard would tell us that when a C input stands at its 1-state, the affected input has its normal effect on the circuit, that effect being determined by its defined nature. But while the C input stands at its 0-state, the affected input function no longer has any effect, that is, it is disabled. To find what inputs are affected, we look for inputs labeled with the number that follows the C, that is, 2. We see these are D inputs. D inputs are defined as data inputs to storage elements. The storage elements follow the D inputs while the latter are enabled; they hold their last state when the D inputs are disabled. So in this example, the four inputs labeled "2D" are controlled by the input labeled "C2". When the C2 input stands at its 1-state, the D inputs enter data. When the C2 input is at its 0-state, the storage elements retain their last-entered data until counting starts or C2 again takes on its 1-state.

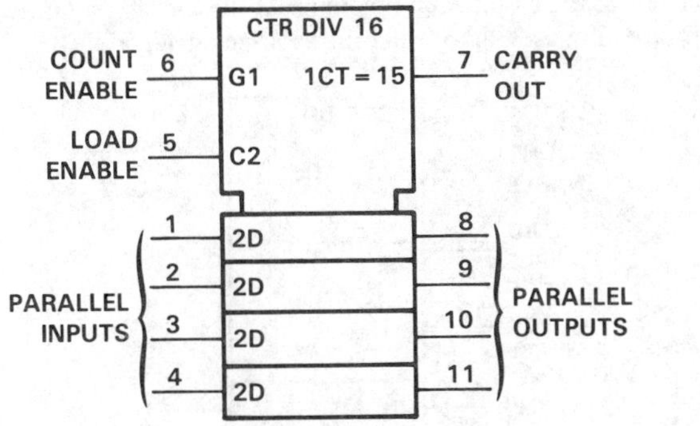

FIGURE 6

Note the upper rectangle separated from the array of four flip-flops by a narrowed "neck". This is a common control block, which may be used in conjunction with an array of related elements as a point of placement for inputs or outputs associated with more than one element of the array, or possibly the array as a whole but no single element in particular.

Figure 7A adds the input that causes counting, pin 12. The right-pointing skinny triangle indicates that this input is dynamic and that its momentary 1-state occurs on the external transition from low to high, having assumed positive logic. The plus sign means that each time this input takes on its 1-state, the count is incremented by one.

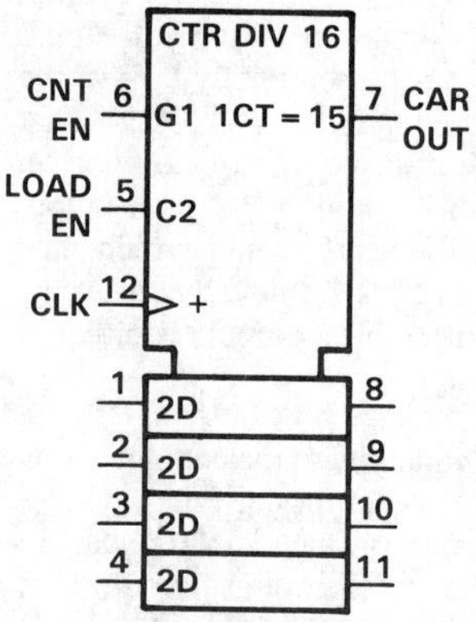

FIGURE 7A

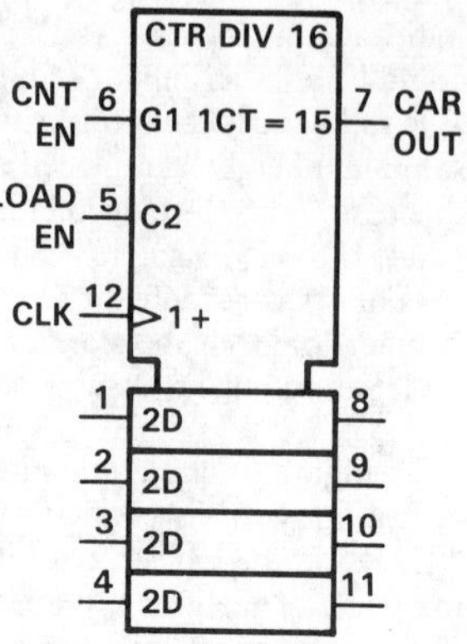

FIGURE 7B

Figure 7B adds refinement by showing that this dynamic input also is also affected by an AND relationship with the Count Enable input. This is done simply by putting that input's identifying number (1) in front of the plus sign. Thus, if pin 6 stands at the 0-state, that 0-state would be imposed on the incrementing function and transitions at pin 12 would have no effect.

If we need to show that the Count Enable is subordinate to the Load Enable input, this can be done as in Figure 8. In addition to acting in a control relationship with the D inputs, the Load Enable affects the Count Enable in an AND relationship. G dependency is used and this additional function of pin 5 is indicated by a "G3" label separated from the other function label, "C2", by a slash. Actually, pin 6 is ANDed with the complement of pin 5. Since it is the complement of G3 that affects pin 6, the numeral 3 at the affected input is shown with a bar over it. This means that when G3 stands at the 1-state, its complement stands at the 0-state and this imposes the 0-state on G1, which in turn imposes the 0-state on its affected functions.

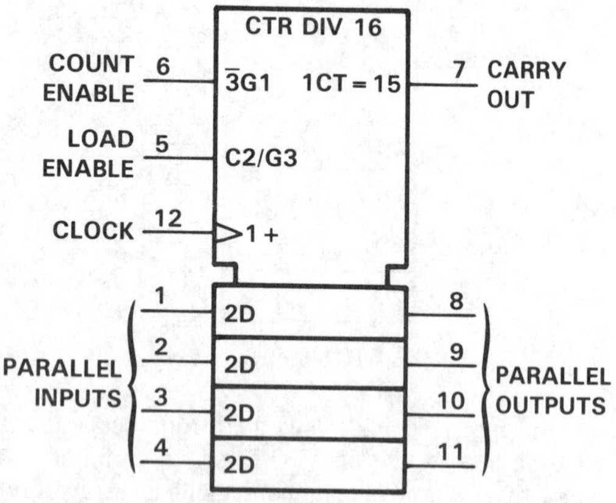

FIGURE 8

The symbol in Figure 8 is about average in complexity for the TTL and CMOS product lines up to the LSI level. Some symbols are more complex. For example, in a combination symbol, one element, such as this counter, might be shown driving a register made up of transparent latches. But many of the symbols are simpler involving less dependency notation and, even to the uninitiated or at least to the barely initiated, should be more understandable than "black-box" symbols.

4. WHAT IT TAKES TO UNDERSTAND FUNCTIONAL LOGIC SYMBOLS

It must be understood that IEEE Std 91-1984 is no mere catalog of symbols. Rather it spells out a symbolic language. This means you have to learn the "alphabet" and you have to learn the "grammar". Fortunately, it, like other languages, is much easier to read than it is to write. The writing can usually be left to experts who will put the results in data books, company drafting manuals, CAD libraries, and symbols in sticky-back form.

That all may sound more formidable than it really is. To be able to understand most IEEE functional logic symbols, you need to know the following:

(1) Some 28 to 33 general qualifying symbols. Most of these are quite obvious and easily remembered. Many are common acronyms, such as MUX, ALU, RAM, and FIFO. Others are mathematical symbols.

(2) Less than 20 symbols for inputs and outputs. Most of these are already in common use, such as those designating negation (○), active level (⊾), and dynamic inputs (▷).

(3) About 20 more symbols defining special input and output characteristics. Many of the symbols defining type of input have been used for decades (J, K, S, R, D); others, primarily the output labels for open-collector (<u>◇</u>), open-emitter (◇̄), three-state (▽), etc., are newer and less well known, but quite useful.

(4) The core of "what's new" is dependency notation. This paper has briefly covered two types, G and C. There is a total of 13 types, some of which are used infrequently. As previously explained, some of these impose logic states; others enable or disable inputs and outputs; and others set, reset, or address storage elements, transfer signals from point to point, cause negation, or determine modes of operation. The general rules for application of dependency notation are more or less common to all 13 types.

Help is on the way. Universities in Europe and a few in the USA have taught FLS for years. An increasing number of books are now available [Kampel 85], [Mann 84], [Mann 87], [Peatman 80], [McCluskey 86] in addition to the formal standards.

5. THE ARGUMENTS AGAINST FUNCTIONAL LOGIC SYMBOLS, AND COMMENTS THEREON

Since 1980 when Texas Instruments started using FLS in data books, I have received less than 10 letters objecting to their use. While the points were often made in colorful language, they boil down to three somewhat overlapping statements.

(1) We liked the old symbology; everyone understood it.

The real problem here is determining exactly what "the old symbology" was that "everyone understood". That is why I included the historical portion of this paper. Once we go beyond the relative handful of devices that were actually covered by the 1962 standards, the so-called symbols in use were not consistent from one source to another, although the techniques were fairly uniform. That is, a box was used but inputs and outputs often joined the box from four directions, often at random. You could not tell an input from an output, and the only clue to the function of the ports and the total device were pin names, often arbitrary and abbreviated to the point of total obscurity. Possibly not everyone understood these drawings as well as their preparers thought. The only recourse was to have at hand, and refer to, a data sheet for every symbol in the drawing.

(2) The new symbols are too complicated. They give more information than is required.

This is very much more dependent on the users of the diagram than the preparer. A designer may work with a system until he knows every part of it in detail, but that is of little comfort to those who are trying to follow the trail he blazed.

A device like a microprocessor can be represented fairly simply under rules given in the standards for so-called ''gray boxes'', which are more informative than a ''black box'' but less informative than a 'white box, which tells all. But in this day of custom circuitry, no catchall name, such as microprocessor, may yet exist for someone's latest creation. It is nice that a system exists that can be used to describe a device to whatever detail necessary. If the user is given more than he needs, that should be preferable to the alternative.

(3) It's 20 years too late.

It is a fact that logic symbology fell far behind hardware development. Assuming that hardware development is not about to stop, does the fact that we got behind mean we must abandon any attempt to catch up? Maybe we will never catch up. That does not mean that we should not do the best we can to continue the evolution in a logical and consistent manner.

6. WHAT ARE THE ALTERNATIVES?

No standard should ever be adopted without giving some consideration to all the reasonable alternatives. We considered additional use of distinctive shapes but no serious proposal was ever made to try to find shapes to represent counters, shift registers, multiplexers, adders, ALUs, memories, parity detectors, coders, and so on. In effect, that approach was ruled out in 1962 when the standards said ''use rectangles''. Even if enough different distinctive shapes could be found, they would get bulky and certainly would not lend themselves to be combined to form more complex symbols.

Another alternative would be for JEDEC or IEC to try to standardize pin names. The list would be endless, and certainly never up to date. No one has ever thought of really descriptive names for a majority of all the pins, and even common ones like ''clock'' affect different devices in different ways. Many pins have a multiplicity of functions, and these may be mode dependent. Use is made of manufacturers' pin names in the ''gray-box'' symbols mentioned earlier and suggested for symbolizing very complex devices. But these devices are still the exceptions — the devices that people may study for a semester in college. For these devices, the symbol cannot and need not tell all.

7. CONCLUSIONS

Functional logic symbols, as defined by ANSI/IEEE Std 91-1984 and its international counterpart [IEC 1983], provide a powerful and efficient means of representing logic devices more complex than basic gates in a way that can be completely understood without reference to supplementary documentation. A reasonable number of building blocks must be learned. The only alternative methods seen so far involve ''black box'' symbols, which tell almost nothing about the devices they represent and so depend heavily on previous device knowledge or expensive supplementary documentation.

BIBLIOGRAPHY

[IEC 83] *IEC Publication 617-12, Graphical Symbols for Diagrams*, ANSI, NY, 1984

[IEEE 84] *ANSI/IEEE Std 91-1984, IEEE Standard Graphic Symbols for Logic Functions*, IEEE, NY, 1984

[Kampel 85] Kample, Ian, *A Practical Introduction to the New Logic Symbols*, Butterworths, Boston, 1985

[Mann 84] Mann, F. A., *Overview of IEEE Std 91-1984*, Texas Instruments Incorporated, Dallas, TX, 1984

[Mann 87] Mann, F. A., *Using Functional Logic Symbols*, Texas Instruments Incorporated, Dallas, TX, 1987

[McCluskey 86] McCluskey, Edward J., *Logic Design Principles*, Prentice-Hall, Englewood Cliffs, NJ, 1986

[Peatman 80] Peatman, John B., *Digital Hardware Design*, McGraw-Hill, NY, 1980

EDIF: TEST GENERATION AND FAULT SIMULATION

John P. Eurich

Engineering DataXpress, Inc.
5 Town & Country Village, Suite 736
San Jose, CA, 95128-2026
(408) 243-8786

Abstract

Throughout this decade the availability of commercially developed digital simulation products has flourished. There seems to be a need in the industry to establish a standard set of tests or benchmarks against which these products can be evaluated and compared. But to be of any value, these benchmarks must be in a form that will allow them to be easily installed on the many different systems available. This paper analyzes the Electronic Design Interchange Format (EDIF) to determine if it is a viable form in which to distribute digital simulation benchmarks and tests.

Introduction

The Problem

The range of electronic design verification and test generation tools that are now commercially available is considerable when compared to those of the last decade. At the start of 1987 at least 33 commercial vendors were supplying at least one type of simulation product, with new entries coming into the CAE/CAD market at the rate of six per year [7]. In addition to the behavioral, logic, switch, analog, and fault simulators offered, there are automatic test pattern generation and timing verification products being released to the design verification and test generation markets.

This large availability of similar products could mean that the customer has a better chance of finding a set of tools which closely meets its engineering design needs. But how does one determine which product is the best match? Evaluating the literature, reviews and surveys can help somewhat, but normally the final decision is based on tests or benchmarks prepared by the customer and ported through one means or another to the environment of each product being considered. With so many products now available, this testing procedure can be a costly task for both customer and vendor.

The Solution

In the computer and system software industry, where there is a large number of different configurations of CPUs, buses, memories, disks, operating systems, compilers and languages, etc., standard benchmarks (whetstones, etc.) have been developed which give a good approximation of a particular system's performance and capabilities. Therefore, there is a need in the electronic design verification and test generation industry to establish a standard set of benchmarks against which these products can be evaluated and compared. The computer benchmarks are specified in standard programming languages such as FORTRAN, C, and Pascal so that they are easily ported to the different computer systems available. Likewise, so that the design verification and test generation benchmarks can be ported easily to different systems, they need to be specified in a neutral data format which is capable of representing the information required to test the products.

The Electronic Design Interchange Format (EDIF), which was released in May 1987 as the Electronic Industries Association (EIA) Interim Standard No. 44 [3], is proposed to be a good candidate for such a neutral data format. Examples will be presented to substantiate that EDIF is a viable form in which to distribute design verification and test generation benchmarks. In particular, the requirements of automatic test pattern generation and digital fault simulation will be considered.

The Electronic Design Interchange Format

The EDIF standard was developed as a neutral data format through which electronic design data can be exchanged between companies and CAE/CAD systems. Hundreds of companies from all over the world have participated in its development over the past four years. EDIF is capable of representing information for electrical netlists, schematics, schematic symbols, IC mask layout, symbolic layout, PCB layout, simulation stimulus and response, logic models, timing, physical design rules, and documentation [2,3,4,5,6]. The EDIF data file is a stream of ASCII characters and has a LISP like syntax. The syntax and semantics of EDIF are rigorously defined in the EDIF 2 0 0 reference manual [3].

The Simulation Information Environment

Simulation information requirements are very similar for the different tools on the market. They all require a design description or model to simulate, and a set of stimulus for all input and bidirectional pins and an optional expected response for the output pins. The design description can be specified at different levels (e.g. behavioral, block-functional, gate, electrical or switch, etc.) depending on the type of simulator. The gate level model with timing and delay information is most often used with fault simulators, but functional and circuit level can also be used. The stimulus can be automatically generated by an automatic test pattern generator (ATPG). The ATPG in most cases uses as input the same design description as the fault simulator. The fault simulator creates information which confirms the detection of faults for test patterns created by an ATPG, computes fault coverage, produces a fault dictionary used in fault diagnosis, and identifies circuit areas which have not been tested [1].

The EDIF standard was designed to represent all of this information except for that provided as fault simulation output, i.e. the fault coverage reports and fault dictionary [3,5,6].

Design Descriptions

Design descriptions can be either flat or hierarchical specifications of gate level connectivity. Benchmark designs can range from very simple, containing only a few gates, to very complex containing over one hundred thousand gates. The complex designs are used to stress the limits and comprehensiveness of the tool. Although the actual gate count is high, the benchmark test data can be kept relatively small by using hierarchy to construct the test design.

Descriptions of design hierarchy and electrical connectivity are easily represented in EDIF through the use of the *cell*, *view*, *instance*, and *net* constructs. The representation of the connectivity of a circuit is normally specified using EDIF's NETLIST view, although the SCHEMATIC view may be also be appropriate.

Primitive Design Objects

Connectivity at the lowest level of the hierarchy references gate level primitives, such as nand, nor, and latch gates. The actual logical behavior of these primitives is expressed in EDIF using the LOGICMODEL view [3,6]. The logic states, or values, used in the logic model description are declared in EDIF with the *simulationInfo* construct. Example 1 illustrates the declaration of the four states H, L, Z, and X.

In Example 2, an EDIF logic model specification for an XOR gate is illustrated using the four states defined above. EDIF's *follow* statement specifies that the output "O" has a relationship to the inputs, "I1" and "I2", as specified by the *table* construct. Timing information is included in the model by the *duration* and *delay* statement.

Simulators usually have a library of generic primitive design objects built into them and only require timing and delay information to complete their definition. EDIF also has the mechanism for specifying such timing and delay data. Example 3 is an EDIF description for a D type flip flop. The *timing* statement is used here to specify the pin to pin delays and set up and hold times for the DFF.

Hierarchical Connectivity

In Example 4, the primitive gates, XOR2 and DFF, are referenced in an EDIF hierarchical netlist description. This example represents a hierarchical benchmark circuit designed by Greer [7] in the EDIF format. The top cell of the instance hierarchy is "TopOfDesign". The *net* and *instance* statements are used to specify the hierarchical connectivity.

Test Patterns

Test patterns include the stimulus, expected response, and information which specifies when a value is to be driven on an input pin and when a value should be sampled off an output pin and compared to the expected response. The test pattern may be automatically or manually generated. In either case, the test pattern is required as part of a benchmark test for digital fault simulators. With EDIF's *simulate* construct, test patterns can be specified [3,5]. Example 5 illustrates a simple test pattern with 18 test vectors for the XOR gate defined earlier.

A test pattern for the hierarchical design called "TopOfDesign" is specified in Example 4 within the *simulate* construct. This pattern contains 1000 test vectors.

Summary

The design verification and test community needs tools with which to evaluate and compare the many simulation and automatic test generation products offered commercially. Development of a standard set of benchmarks is proposed while using the Electronic Design Interchange Format (EDIF) to specify them in a neutral and industry compatible form. Because EDIF contains the mechanisms with which to capture the benchmark information for digital simulation and test generation (e.g., logic models, timing and delay information, hierarchical connectivity, test patterns, etc.) and other electronic design features, it has been accorded an eager acceptance by industry leading companies who view it as a viable solution to the problems of the status quo.

References

[1] A. Miczo, Digital Logic Testing and Simulation, Harper and Row, 1986, pp118-171.

[2] J. P. Eurich, "A Tutorial Introduction To The Electronic Design Interchange Format," Proc. 23rd. ACM IEEE Design Automation Conference, June 1986, pp. 327-333.

[3] Electronic Industries Association, Electronic Design Interchange Format Version 2 0 0, EIA Interim Standard No. 44, May 1987.

[4] A. R. Newton, "Electronic Design Interchange Format, Introduction to (EDIF 2 0 0)," Proc. of the IEEE 1987 Custom Integrated Circuits Conference, May, 1987, pp 531-535.

[5] A. Etherington, "Interfacing Design To Test Using The Electronic Design Interchange Format (EDIF)", Proc. of the IEEE 1987 International Test Conference, 1987, pp 378-383.

[6] W. Angevine, "Transferring Simulation Models in EDIF", VLSI Systems Design, May 4, 1987, Vol. VIII No. 5, pp 32-40.

[7] D. L. Greer, "The Quick Simulator Benchmark", VLSI Systems Design, Nov. 1987, Vol. VIII No. 12, pp 40-57.

Example 1

```
(SimulationInfo
 (logicValue H
  (booleanMap (true))
  (voltageMap (mnm 2 (e 24 -1) 5))
  (currentMap (mnm (e 1 -5)(e 2 -5)(e 4 -5))))
 (logicValue L
  (booleanMap (false))
  (voltageMap (mnm 0 (e 4 -1)(e 8 -1)))
  (currentMap (mnm (e 4 -4)(e 8 -4)(e 16 -4))))
 (logicValue Z
  (isolated)
  (currentMap (mnm (e 5 -6)(e 1 -5)(e 2 -5))))
 (logicValue X
  (compound H L Z)
  (resolves H L)))
```

Example 2

```
(cell XOR2 (cellType GENERIC)
 (view logicmodel (viewType LOGICMODEL)
  (interface
   (port O (direction output))
   (port I1 (direction input))
   (port I2 (direction input)))
  (contents
   (follow O
    (table
     (entry
      (steady (portList I1 I2) (duration 3)
       (becomes (logicList L L)))
      (logicRef L))
     (entry
      (steady (portList I1 I2) (duration 3)
       (becomes (logicList L H)))
      (logicRef H))
     (entry
      (steady (portList I1 I2) (duration 3)
       (becomes (logicList H L)))
      (logicRef H))
     (entry
      (steady (portList I1 I2) (duration 3)
       (becomes (logicList H H)))
      (logicRef L))
     (tableDefault (logicRef X)))
    (delay 5)))))
```

Example 3

```
(cell DFF (cellType GENERIC)
 (view logicmodel (viewType LOGICMODEL)
  (interface
   (port Q (direction output))
   (port R (direction input))
   (port C (direction input))
   (port D (direction input))
   (timing (derivation MEASURED)
    (pathDelay
     (delay (mnm (e 18 -1)(e 37 -1)(e 84 -1)))
     (event (portRef C)(transition H L))
     (event (portRef Q)(transition H L)))
    (pathDelay
     (delay (mnm (e 13 -1)(e 27 -1)(e 59 -1)))
     (event (portRef C)(transition H L))
     (event (portRef Q)(transition L H)))
    (forbiddenEvent
     (timeInterval
      (offsetEvent
       (event (portRef C)(transition H L))(e -48 -1))
      (offsetEvent
       (event (portRef C)(transition H L))(e 24 -1)))
     (event (portRef D)))
    (forbiddenEvent
     (timeInterval
      (event (portRef C)(transition H L))
      (duration (e 87 -1)))
     (event (portRef C)(transition L H)))))))
```

Example 4

```
(cell LFSR (cellType GENERIC)
 (Comment "Linear Feedback Shift Register [7]")
 (view netlist (viewType NETLIST)
  (interface
   (port B1 (direction output))
   (port A1 (direction input))
   (port Reset (direction input))
   (port Clk (direction input)))
  (contents
   (instance Xor1 (viewRef logicmodel (cellRef XOR2)))
   (instance Dff1 (viewRef logicmodel (cellRef DFF)))
   (instance Dff2 (viewRef logicmodel (cellRef DFF)))
   (instance DffM (viewRef logicmodel (cellRef DFF)))
   (instance DffN (viewRef logicmodel (cellRef DFF)))
   (net A1
    (joined
     (portRef A1)(portRef I2 (instanceRef Xor1))))
   (net CLK
    (joined (portRef Clk)
     (portRef C (instanceRef Dff1))
     (portRef C (instanceRef Dff2))
     (portRef C (instanceRef DffM))
     (portRef C (instanceRef DffN))))
   (net RESET
    (joined (portRef Reset)
     (portRef R (instanceRef Dff1))
     (portRef R (instanceRef Dff2))
     (portRef R (instanceRef DffM))
     (portRef R (instanceRef DffN))))
   (net O
    (joined
     (portRef O (instanceRef Xor1))
     (portRef D (instanceRef Dff1))))
   (net Q1
    (joined
     (portRef Q (instanceRef Dff1))
     (portRef D (instanceRef Dff2))))
   (net Q2
    (joined
     (portRef Q (instanceRef Dff2))
     (portRef D (instanceRef DffM))))
   (net QM
    (joined
     (portRef Q (instanceRef DffM))
     (portRef I1 (instanceRef Xor1))
     (portRef D (instanceRef DffN))))
   (net B1
    (joined
     (portRef B1)(portRef Q (instanceRef DffN)))))))
(cell J2 (cellType GENERIC)
 (view netlist (viewType NETLIST)
  (interface
   (port Reset (direction input))
   (port Clk (direction input))
   (port A2 (direction input))
   (port B2 (direction output)))
  (contents
   (instance Lfsr1 (viewRef netlist (cellRef LFSR)))
   (instance Lfsr2 (viewRef netlist (cellRef LFSR)))
   (instance Lfsr3 (viewRef netlist (cellRef LFSR)))
   (instance Lfsr4 (viewRef netlist (cellRef LFSR)))
   (net CLK (joined (globalPortRef Clk)))
   (net RESET (joined (globalPortRef Reset)))
   (net A2
    (joined
     (portRef A2)(portRef A1 (instanceRef Lfsr1))))
   (net B1_1
    (joined
     (portRef B1 (instanceRef Lfsr1))
     (portRef A1 (instanceRef Lfsr2))))
   (net B1_2
    (joined
     (portRef B1 (instanceRef Lfsr2))
     (portRef A1 (instanceRef Lfsr3))))
   (net B1_3
    (joined
     (portRef B1 (instanceRef Lfsr3))
     (portRef A1 (instanceRef Lfsr4))))
   (net B2
    (joined
     (portRef B2)(portRef B1 (instanceRef Lfsr4)))))))
(cell TopOfDesign (cellType GENERIC)
 (view netlist (viewType NETLIST)
  (interface
   (port Reset (direction input))
   (port Clk (direction input))
   (simulate TopOfDesign_Test1
    (waveValue C 5 (logicWaveform L H H L))
    (apply (cycle 5 (duration 20))
     (logicInput Reset (logicWaveform L L L L L))
     (logicInput Clk (logicWaveform C)))
    (apply (cycle 995 (duration 20))
     (logicInput Reset (logicWaveform H))
     (logicInput Clk (logicWaveform C)))))
  (contents
   (instance Lfsr1 (viewRef netlist (cellRef J2 )))
   (net CLK (joined (globalPortRef Clk)))
   (net RESET (joined (globalPortRef Reset)))
   (net FEEDBACK
    (joined
     (portRef A2 (instanceRef Lfsr1))
     (portRef B2 (instanceRef Lfsr1)))))))
```

Example 5

```
(simulate XOR_test1
 (apply
  (cycle 18 (duration 20))
  (logicInput I1
   (logicWaveform L L L L H L H L L H L H H H H H L H))
  (logicInput I2
   (logicWaveform L L H L L L H H H L H H L L H H L H))
  (logicOutput O
   (logicWaveform L L H L H L L H H H H L H H L L L L))
))
```

LEGAL ISSUES Track

Software Compatibility and Copyright Law

Chair: R. Wedig

RECENT DEVELOPMENTS IN COPYRIGHT LAW

R. Ben-Yehuda, Esq.
R.L. Johnston, Esq.
Blanc Gilburne Williams & Johnston
1900 Avenue of the Stars, Suite 1200
Los Angeles, California 90067

Computer programs, whether written in source or object code, have been protectable as "literary works" under federal copyright law for several years. Apple Computer v. Franklin Computer, 714 F.2d 1240 (3d Cir. 1983). Recently, several courts have extended the scope of this protection in two important directions. First, Whelan Associates v. Jaslow Dental Laboratory, 797 F.2d 1222 (3d Cir. 1986), and succeeding cases held that, in addition to the literal code, copyright may protect the structure, sequence or organization of a program. Second, several cases have protected the general "concept and feel" of the user interface. In both types of cases, however, the extent of protection is unclear because the relevant cases are not particularly helpful guides for predicting how future cases will be decided, several courts have criticized and refused to follow the leading decisions in these areas, and the Supreme Court has, so far, declined to lay down the law.

I. COPYRIGHT GROUND RULES

There are three ground rules necessary to understand the scope of copyright protection for computer software. First, the item sought to be protected must be proper subject matter for protection under copyright law. Thus, for example, several recent cases have considered whether the structure and engineering of a computer program or the general "concept and feel" of a user interface is proper subject matter for copyright protection.

Second, unlike patent law, a plaintiff alleging copyright infringement must prove the defendant copied his program. Since infringers usually are secretive, direct evidence of copying is rarely available. Hence, the law will presume copying, absent contrary evidence, if plaintiff can show defendant had access to his program and defendant's program is substantially similar to plaintiff's program.

Third, copyright protection does not extend to ideas, but only to particular expressions of ideas. Further, if there is only one way to express a particular idea, that expression is denied copyright, because otherwise the copyright would effectively protect the idea as well. Whelan at 1234. Several recent cases have said that the purpose of the program or user interface is its idea, and that the particular implementation of that purpose is the expression. Therefore, if there are several ways to implement the purpose -- as will almost always be the case with such a general idea -- the expression in question will not be an unprotectable idea.

The Whelan case illustrates these concepts. Elaine Whelan had written a program for use with the IBM Series One Machine to help run the business operations of dental laboratories. Rand Jaslow, who had initially hired Whelan to write the program, decided that there would be a wider market for such a program if it could be used on the smaller computers in most dental laboratories. He then wrote such a program, and Whelan sued.

Whelan did not argue that Jaslow had copied her source or object code. Rather, she alleged -- and the court found -- that the overall structure of the programs was similar. Since Jaslow admitted access, therefore, the questions presented were whether this structure was proper subject matter and, if so, whether it was the expression rather than the "purpose" or "idea" of the program.

The court held, first, that the structure, sequence or organization of a computer program is copyrightable subject matter. Second, the purpose -- and thus idea -- of Whelan's program "was to aid in the business operations of a dental laboratory." Id. at 1238. Since the court chose such a general description of the "idea," any description of the program less general than that very general purpose, including the structure of the particular programs at issue, would presumably be "expression." In addition, since there were other programs on the market performing the same functions with different structures, the court concluded that several structures could implement the purpose of running a dental laboratory. Hence, since Whalen had shown access and substantial similarity to the copyrightable subject matter or expression -- rather than the "idea" -- the court found infringement.

II. SCOPE OF PROTECTION -- STRUCTURE AND ORGANIZATION OF PROGRAM?

The court in Whelan concluded that the overall structure and organization of the programs in question were similar by comparing their file structures, screen displays and subroutines. It stated that the file structures "require certain information and order that information in a particular fashion." Such structures may be copyrighted "if they are sufficiently innovative that their arrangement of information is itself informative." Aside from noting the complexity of these structures, however, the court did not describe them.

Regarding screen displays, the court held that similarity between user interfaces is not, by itself, sufficient to prove a violation of the copyright in the underlying code; however, such similarity could be considered as some evidence leading to that conclusion. The court's opinion did not describe the testimony regarding the screen displays.

Finally, the court held that the "marked" similarity between five of the programs' many subroutines was enough to establish substantial similarity. More specifically, the court relied on expert testimony that the invoicing, accounts receivable, order entry, day's end and month's end subroutines were clearly copied. For example, plaintiff's expert witness testified that, at the end of the month, both systems do

> 'accounts receivable aging, since a month has gone by they have to update all the 30 days, 60 days, et cetera, calculate service charges. Then they print the monthly AR reports that had to do with service charges, only those that involve service charges, they both do that. Then they both print the age file balance, balance report, and following that they print the month and accounts receivable report.'

There was similar testimony comparing the other subroutines.

In SAS Institute v. S&H Computer Systems, 605 F. Supp. 816 (M.D. Tenn. 1985), SAS Institute marketed "SAS," a statistical analysis program that operated exclusively on IBM and IBM-compatible computers. The court found that S&H extensively and systematically used SAS to create its own statistical analysis program for use on VAX machines. As a result, S&H had actually copied several lines of source code. Even absent such copying, however, the court held that S&H infringed on SAS's copyright because it had copied the organizational and structural details of SAS.

Unfortunately, the court did not describe the structures of the programs or explain how they were similar. Rather, the opinion concentrated on the fact that S&H personnel obtained copies of SAS under false pretenses, violated the terms of their licence, advertised that their program would work like SAS, attempted to hide their copying through artificial and meaningless changes, and destroyed evidence. As is often the case in difficult infringement cases, the court in SAS found against the defendants at least partially because it disapproved of their conduct.

In Williams v. Arndt, 626 F. Supp. 571 (Mass. 1985), the court protected the English language expression of a computer program's function. Williams had written a specific, step-by-step method for trading in various commodities. Arndt wrote a program that performed all the functions and calculations required by Williams' method and provided the user with the results much more quickly than was possible without a computer. The court did not describe the program or Williams' method in any detail. It simply held that the program was not a different or unique expression of Williams' ideas. It was a mere translation from English to source code, and, as such, was substantially similar to Williams' publication and an infringement of his copyright.

Prior to these cases, it was generally believed that protection for the engineering and coherence of a computer program was available only, where appropriate, under trade secret law. It remains to be seen whether Whelan and SAS will lead the protection available under copyright law into this domain.

Plains Cotton Cooperative v. Goodpasture Computer Service, 807 F.2d 1256 (5th Cir. 1987), for example, apparently refused to grant as much protection as Whalen had. In Plains Cotton, Plains had developed the Telcot program to provide members of its cooperative with information regarding cotton prices and availability. Later, Goodpasture developed GEMS, a program "very similar to Telcot on the functional specification, programming, and documentation levels," id. at 1256, by hiring several former Plains employees.

Plains Cotton stated that it refused to "embrace" Whelan. It is not clear if the court considered the structure of the program improper subject matter for copyright, however, because the court based its decision on the fact that "the externalities of the cotton market" play a "significant role in determining the sequence and organization of cotton marketing software." Without going into any detail, the court held that adapting to these "market factors" (one of which was the need to provide the same information as is contained on a "cotton recap sheet") constituted the type of "idea" that should protect Goodpasture from an infringement claim.

Note that this analysis could be consistent with Whelan, which denied protection to the structure of a program if that structure embodied the only possible expression of an idea. Since, in this case, the court held that the idea of providing useful information regrading cotton is closely constrained by the organization of the cotton market, the court in Whelan may not have found infringement either.

III. SCOPE OF PROTECTION -- LOOK AND FEEL

A. The Trend Toward Protection of User Interfaces

There is a strong trend to accord greater protection to user interfaces as courts realize that designing an interface may involve more creativity and effort than writing the code.

The user interface cases are difficult to comprehend because courts do not agree on what type of copyright is involved. Copyright law protects several categories of works, including literary works (which include computer programs), audiovisual works, and compilations. Some courts believe it is illogical to protect the user interface as part of the total literary work under the program's copyright because completely different code could produce the identical interface. Further, user interfaces seem to be better described as audiovisual works, which "consist of a series of related images which are intrinsically intended to be shown by the use of machines or devices . . . ," 17 U.S.C.A. Section 101 (1977), or as compilations, which are works "formed by the collection and assembling of . . . data that are selected, coordinated, or arranged in such a way that the resulting work as a whole constitutes an original work of authorship." Id.

Regardless of the copyright chosen, however, the emerging trend is to protect the structure and organization -- or "look and feel" -- of the interface. In Broderbund Software v. Unison World, 648 F. Supp. 1127 (N.D. Cal. 1986), Broderbund owned the copyright to a commercially successful graphics program for Apple computers. Unison developed a program with a strikingly similar user interface for use on IBM computers. The court held that the menu screens, input formats and sequencing of screens was proper subject matter for copyright. Further, it described very broadly the "idea" or "purpose" involved as a menu driven program that allows its users to print greeting cards, banners, etc. Since another program on the market accomplished this purpose with a very different interface, Broderbund's interface was protectable.

Other cases are coming to similar conclusions. In Digital Communications v. Stofklone Distributing, 659 F. Supp. 449 (N.D. Ga. 1987), plaintiff's program, Crosstalk, enabled the user's computer to communicate with other computers. The issue was whether defendant had copied Crosstalk's "status screen," and, if so, whether it was protectable. The court described the status screen as follows:

> [It] contains in its upper portion an arrangement and grouping of parameter/command terms under various descriptive headings. Next to each of the parameter/command terms are values, either numerical or verbal. The value of each parameter/command reflects the value at which the program is operating and is either selected by the user or by the computer program . . . . Two letters of each parameter/command are capitalized and highlighted.

The upper portion of defendant's status screen was nearly identical to Crosstalk's. The court found that the arrangement and collection of commands on the status screen was protectable as a compilation of data. It relied heavily on the fact that the layout of the screen was not arbitrary, but, rather, was designed for greater ease of use.

Nor has protection been limited to standard interfaces. In Worlds of Wonder v. Vector Intercontinental, 653 F. Supp. 135 (N.D. Ohio 1986), the user interface was Teddy Ruxpin, an animated toy bear. The programs in question were on two-track cassette tapes that the user inserted into Teddy. One track was audio and played through Teddy's speaker, and the other controlled motors making Teddy's eyes, nose and mouth move in a life-like fashion as it performed songs and stories.

Defendant Vector Intercontinental created tapes designed to tell stories through Teddy. These stories themselves were unprotected fairy tales, however, and the "idea" of telling stories through a toy bear was similarly unprotectable. Nevertheless, the court held that the tapes as used violated World of Wonder's copyright, because the particular pitch, gender and speed of the voice and the movements of the eyes, nose and mouth were protectable expression.

Finally, although the trend towards expanding copyright protection is unmistakable, not all courts consistently follow along. In Frybarger v. IBM, 812 F.2d 525 (9th Cir. 1987), the ninth circuit court of appeals defined the "idea" of a computer game's display to include much of the general structure of the user interface, which, therefore, was not subject to copyright protection. More specifically, the court found that copying the following specific features was not actionable, because the features constituted the basic ideas of the video games in question.

> 1) The display screen of each game is filled with straight rows of pivot points on a solid colored background.
>
> 2) Between some of the pivot points are solid lines, connecting two pivot points.
>
> 3) There is a single protagonist.
>
> 4) The single protagonist has legs and a face.
>
> 5) The single protagonist moves vertically and horizontally between rows of pivot points.
>
> 6) The single protagonist may cause one end of a line to come unattached from one pivot point and attach to a different pivot point by bumping into the line as the protagonist moves between rows of pivot points.
>
> 7) There is more than one antagonist.
>
> 8) Each antagonist moves toward the general location of the protagonist.
>
> 9) If an antagonist bumps into the protagonist, the progress of play stops.
>
> 10) An antagonist will be immobilized if it is surrounded on three sides by lines and the protagonist bumps a line across the

fourth side, closing off the only remaining avenue of exit.

11) The player may obtain points by causing the protagonist to elude and 'trap' antagonists.

12) The speed at which the protagonist and antagonists move increases as the game progresses.

B. THE LOTUS CASES

One of the most important cases in the user interface area is the current litigation by Lotus against Mosaic Software and Paperback Software International. Mosaic's and Paperback's programs intentionally and thoroughly imitate 1-2-3's user interface and, in addition, provide some new functions of their own.

What makes this case interesting is that 1-2-3 has become an industry standard. Users accustomed to 1-2-3 do not want to bother learning a different system. Mosaic and Paperback, therefore, can each argue that its "idea" or "purpose" was to create integrated software compatible with the industry standard, and, since true compatibility could be achieved only by fairly strict copying, its software does not infringe. Thus, the key issue may be whether conforming to a standard is the type of "idea" that allows copying.

C. Other Interface/Compatibility Cases

In Apple v. Franklin, 714 F.2d 1240 (3d Cir. 1283), Franklin claimed that it was permitted to copy Apple's operating system because to do so was the only way to implement its "idea" of making an Apple-compatible computer. In holding for Apple, the court stated that this was not an "idea" within the meaning of the copyright law since it was a "commercial and competitive objective." This may suggest that adapting to a standard similarly does not justify copying.

On the other hand, in Synercom Technology v. University Computing, 462 F. Supp. 1003 (N.D. Tex. 1978), the court appeared to hold that an effort to conform to a standard was the sort of "idea" that was not subject to copyright protection. That case involved a structural analysis engineering program. Defendant had copied plaintiff's input formats to make its program easier for persons trained on Plaintiff's program to use. The court held for defendant, finding that the sequence of data input was an "idea" unprotectable under copyright.

IV. CONCLUSION

All creative work is, to some extent, built upon the work of predecessors. Under current law, the computer programmer who wants to build (or simply capitalize) upon another's program must take care not to borrow protectible expression.

The problem is two-fold. First, the scope of copyrightable subject matter may have been greatly expanded by recent cases. Second, the distinction between "purpose" or "idea" and "expression" disappears under scrutiny, because a purpose or idea can be described on any level of abstraction; the term "idea" merely states that court's legal conclusion. Indeed, the better reasoned decisions admit that the distinction between idea and expression is decided on a case-by-case basis rather than by applying legal doctrine to specific facts. Peter Pan Fabrics v. Martin Weiner Corporation, 274 F.2d 487, 489 (2d Cir. 1960).

For example, the purpose of Whelan's program could have been anything from running the business operations of a dental laboratory more efficiently, as the court found, to running the laboratory more efficiently by automatically updating certain accounts at certain times through certain procedures on Jaslow's IBM System One machine. And this more specific characterization of purpose is not very far-fetched. The court found that Jaslow had initially tried to make his laboratory more efficient by developing a computer program to run its business operations. When he realized that he did not have the expertise to complete that task, he hired Whelan "to develop a program that would run on Jaslow Lab's new IBM Series One computer . . . ."

CLONING THE IBM PS/2 SERIES
Legal and Practical Problems

G. Gervaise Davis III, Esq.

Schroeder, Davis & Orliss Inc.

Cloning the IBM PS/2 is not a trivial task, and should under no circumstances be undertaken without an advance appreciation of the extremely complex legal issues involved. Aside from the expensive engineering aspects of doing so, illegal activities engaged in by the clone company or its suppliers could be the death of the whole company, should IBM select the company for its test case. This article discusses the legal and practical problems of cloning.

Cloning For Survival.

The market imperative of following the IBM PC standards in the personal computer business is well known, although some would argue that building microcomputers to duplicate the IBM Micro Channel Architecture (MCA) is unnecessary to compete. Without entering the latter argument, we assume for purposes of this discussion that a decision has been made to "clone" the upper end of the IBM PS/2 line -- the Model 50, 60 and/or the 32 bit Model 80 -- all of which utilize the MCA. The lower end PS/2 models are essentially repackaged PC-XT's and PC-AT's, which have already been cloned by many competitors.

Webster defines a clone as "one that appears to be a copy of the original." In the context of this discussion, cloning an IBM PS/2 is the act of designing and building a microcomputer which is so functionally compatible that software written for the IBM PS/2 runs on the clone as though it were a PS/2. Except for purposes of aesthetics, however, the external design of the clone does not need to duplicate the appearance of a PS/2.

While InfoWorld says IBM Senior Vice President Allen Krowe recently stated at the Seybold Executive Forum that the "PS/2 was never envisioned to be clone-proof," he also noted, however, that clone builders must "do it with the sweat of their brow."

This summarizes the clone builders dilemma. IBM has intentionally designed the PS/2 series hardware with the objective of making it expensive and time consuming to clone. It is a legal and practical strategy directed at giving IBM a 12 to 18 month technical and marketing lead time over competitors. In so doing, IBM has utilized a clever combination of legal and practical defenses against cloners.

These defenses are more likely to be successful against the low cost Far Eastern clone producers, rather than the Compaq's and other major American computer manufacturers, for reasons explained below. Our purpose, in this paper, is to identify these obstacles and to suggest means of overcoming the defenses against cloning built into the PS/2.

The IBM PS/2 Strategy and Defenses.

Contrasting the design of the original IBM PC series (referred to as the "PC") versus the PS/2 series, the most obvious physical differences lie in the use of PS/2 proprietary chips (ASIC's) and other components that are not available off the shelf, as hardware elements were with the PC series. At this point in the life of the PC (whether dealing with the original PC, the XT, or even the AT), it is possible for anyone with even a modicum of engineering knowledge to purchase motherboards, power supplies, controllers, cases, disk drives, and other required components and to assemble their own PC clone.

The PS/2 is an entirely different matter, both as to legal considerations and with regard to practical design and manufacturing problems. Unlike the PC, for example, there is no published BIOS code, no schematics, very little in the way of detailed specifications as to components used in the PS/2 machines, and sketchy documentation for many aspects of the design and implementation of the PS/2. The PC had, from the outset, published specifications, schematics, and source code for the BIOS.

CH2539-5/88/0000/0354$01.00 © 1988 IEEE

From a legal standpoint, IBM has set up a series of legal defense posts that cause the cloner to pause, to think through the means of overcoming the specific defense, to actually overcome it, and then to go on to the next defense post and start the process all over. It is almost like playing Monopoly, where you keep getting sent to GO, only to be put back on another property, and then having to start over again. You make some progress and manage to stay out of JAIL, but never seem to get to Boardwalk or Park Place.

IBM's PS/2 legal defenses are based on a combination of copyright, semiconductor chip mask protection, patent, and trade secret protection rarely seen in a consumer or over the counter business level product. These defenses, like the legs of a spider web, are such that if one is destroyed, the rest still hold up the structure. It is a strategy based on stalling for time, which is a key defensive tool when technology is not unique and can be reverse engineered.

<u>The Cloner's Dilemma -- Time To Market</u>.

For historical and engineering reasons, the initial problem for the cloner is duplicating the functionality of the software involved in the Basic Input/Output System (BIOS) -- a legacy from the venerable CP/M operating system. However, there is not one, but two BIOS in these machines -- the CBIOS for compatibility with earlier software, and the ABIOS that is intended to add the machine level features needed to support future software like the OS/2 operating system. Both BIOS are protected by copyright under U.S. and foreign laws. We will discuss the legal problems related to copyright in a moment.

IBM has reportedly filed worldwide patent applications on many of the features and functions of the PS/2, which patents provide a second line of defense for IBM. These patent applications, some of which have surfaced in European publications, cover both hardware and software aspects of the PS/2 and the earlier RT model. The principal difficulty this presents to the cloner, at this point, is determining which, if any, of the features and functions selected to be used by the cloner would potentially infringe the eventual IBM patents. The word "potentially" is used here, since until the IBM patents issue sometime in the next three years, it is almost impossible to determine what IBM's claims entail, because under U.S. patent law and practice the nature and extent of the claims are not disclosed until the patent is issued. This fact, alone, increases the risk factor for cloners who have to go to market under a cloud that in the future the IBM patents may be the basis for an infringement claim by IBM.

Finally, IBM has made very clear that while it may, on appropriate terms, license the IBM utility patents, it will license neither the copyrighted BIOS nor the technical know-how to design and build the PS/2 machines. Because this information is embedded in the machine, it is possible for the cloner to discern this only by extensive (and expensive) reverse engineering of both the BIOS and the various proprietary chips used in the PS/2.

In short, IBM has (as it may legally do) declined to license the IBM copyrights and trade secrets involved in the development and manufacture of the PS/2, the knowledge of which would substantially shorten development time for IBM's competitors. To our knowledge IBM has not yet signed any specific licenses for the PS/2 utility patents, although it is reportedly negotiating with many companies on a worldwide basis, and already has some cross licenses with existing mainline computer systems companies.

Beyond the IBM patents, the cloner must further contend with the possibility that other patents held by Computer Automation and perhaps others related to the MCA design and use. Even though IBM has licensed the CA patents this does no good for companies that license the IBM patents.

<u>Understanding Some Legal Concepts</u>.

Before examining the PS/2 cloning techniques that may be available, let's review briefly the legal significance of each of the several bodies of intellectual property law on which IBM apparently relies. The importance of IBM's use of these differing bodies of law, in combination, cannot be overemphasized, since it is this one factor that makes cloning the PS/2 all the more difficult, from both the legal and practical standpoint.

The current situation also demonstrates that the legal system, and the lawyers and their clients who must work within this system, is being sorely strained because the traditional intellectual property law is behind the power curve in its ability to deal with rapidly evolving high technologies. Whether the final outcome will be an accommodation of the existing law to this new technology, or a call for changes in the existing intellectual property laws, cannot be foreseen at this point.

What is clear, is that there will be some litigation over these conflicts, and that that litigation will be expensive and potentially disastrous for some of the potential defendants. As others have learned, wrestling with a giant 2000 pound blue bear can be very hazardous to your company's financial health.

The Different Bodies of Law.

Ideas, processes, inventions, and industrial know-how, in general, are potentially protectible under the copyright, patent, trade secret, and sometimes trademark laws. Semiconductor chip masks are protected in a manner similar to copyrights. Each of these subdivisions of the law have different purposes, different conditions under which they are available, different terms of protection, and, generally, afford a very different scope of protection to the technology.

Copyrights. For example, the purpose of copyright laws is to protect the written expression of ideas from copying by others, but not against use of the ideas or the functionality expressed in the writing. While protection was originally limited to the writings of authors, in the most traditional sense, this body of law has recently been extended to protect computer software in source, object, and even microcode form.

Procedurally, anything fixed in writing is protected from the day of creation, if the work is registered with the Copyright Office within three months of publication, and if the work carries a proper copyright notice. Registration is a simple process of filing out a two-sided form, signing it, and mailing it to the Copyright Office with a $10 filing fee. Registration is usually complete in three to four months.

The term of a copyright is for the life of the author plus 50 years, or 75 to 100 years if the copyright is held by a business. Assuming that the various legal conditions are met, protection becomes effective, retroactive to the date of publication, upon issuance of the registration certificate. It is very difficult to defend a copyright infringement action where the second work is substantially similar to the original and the second author had access to the original work while preparing the second work. Furthermore, the successful plaintiff almost always recovers damages and attorney fees for a copyright infringement.

Remember that a key element of copyright is that it does not prevent others from using the same ideas and processes, so long as the written materials on which the second party bases its right to use was "independently developed," i.e., not copied from the original work.

Semiconductor Mask Protection. Several years ago the computer industry and Congress finally agreed upon what is essentially a special form of copyright for semiconductor chip masks. In theory the law only protects the masks themselves, but due to some of the language in the legislative history of this law there is some reason to believe it may go beyond that.

Probably the most significant aspect of this law is that it expressly authorizes reverse engineering of semiconductors by examining the layers of metalization and insulation in order to create a functional duplicate of the original chip. The Act, however, does require that some original engineering be involved in the process. The Act gives this protection for a period of approximately ten years from the date of registration with the Copyright Office or commercial exploitation of the mask, whichever first occurs.

The law authorizes, but does not require, the marking of protected chips with either a circle M or the mark *M* to differentiate from copyright notices. The Act provides for remedies similar to those provided for proven infringement of copyrights, including damages and injunctions, attorney fees, and costs.

There are a number of IBM proprietary chips on the PS/2 circuit boards that carry an *M* mark, in addition to copyright notices. These chips are the technological heart of the PS/2 system, in that they contain disk controllers, video controllers, and other key components of the system.

Patents. The purpose of a patent is to prevent others from using, selling, or otherwise benefitting from a patented invention, if the claim is properly registered with the U.S. Patent Office and the patent has been issued. Different types of patents cover designs, versus machines or processes, the latter being referred to as "utility patents." IBM has offered only licenses on its utility patents on these machines. Utility patents may protect the way a machine or process works, the manner in which software works, and many other aspects of an invention.

Contrary to the ease of obtaining a copyright, registering and prosecuting a utility patent is an expensive, time consuming process that can take any where from three to six or more years, depending on the technology and the country of filing. The inventor must show, in a detailed application for the patent, the general background of the invention, the specific elements of the invention, and the specific claims made and to be covered by the issued patent. The inventor must demonstrate that the invention is new, novel, nonobvious, and useful. The Patent Office examiner conducts an exhaustive search of prior industry publications and prior patents to verify the claims of the inventor, and only after comparison of the prior art to the inventor's claims is the patent issued.

The term of the patent is generally 17 years from the date of filing, which means that some of the term is gone by the time the patent issues. Unlike copyright law, patent protection does not commence until the date the patent issues, so the inventor cannot assert infringement claims for use of his invention prior to that time. By U.S. law, the contents of the application are kept confidential until the patent issues, although under European patent practice, the application must be published for public information (and opposition) within approximately 18 months of the original filing date.

Once issued, however, a patent gives its owner a much more pervasive right to restrict others from using or selling the protected invention. Regardless of independent development, the ideas and concepts reduced to practice in the invention, if claimed and granted, are protected from use by others. The only way to deal with a patent is to license it, try to design around the claims, or litigate over the validity of the patent. Patent protection protects against use of an applied idea, unlike copyright law.

An infringer is liable for damages, costs and attorney fees in some cases, and may be enjoined from producing or selling the infringing device. Thus many IBM competitors may eventually be forced to license, for a stiff royalty payment, the IBM utility patents that may issue on the PS/2 technology. Even then, the patents do not themselves tell the reader in any detail how to implement or use the technology.

Trade Secrets. A trade secret is commercial information not generally known, developed or acquired by a company, and treated by its owner as secret or proprietary, which if obtained by a competitor would have value to the competitor. Unlike copyright and patent law, trade secret law is based on various state statutes and case law, although it has become fairly uniform in recent years.

The purpose of trade secret law is to prevent competitors from acquiring secret or proprietary commercial information through improper means -- such as hiring away employees or unauthorized removal or use of documentation, schematics, specifica-tions, and the like. It works only if the owner of the information takes reasonable steps to protect the information -- such as marking it as confidential, not releasing it except under license or contract, and requiring employees to keep the confidence imposed in them.

It is not illegal or improper to obtain the information a company would consider a trade secret by reverse engineering, so long as the product is on the market and unusual or extraordinary means are not used. The source code of computer software many simultaneously be a trade secret and be protected by copyright, if handled correctly. However, since dumping a ROM containing object code is not illegal, if the purpose is only to read it and to ascertain how it works, it may be possible to reverse engineer copyrighted code.

The one failing of trade secret law is that the information in question is only a trade secret until it is legally disclosed or discovered by reverse engineering. Once it is legally published or disclosed, it ceases to be a trade secret. Thus, its term is indefinite. The cost of obtaining a trade secret may be small or great, and the cost of protecting it may exceed the cost of creating the information in the first instance. Except as may be provided in statutes or in contracts protecting the trade secrets, attorneys fees and costs are not usually recoverable, although other damages and possible injunctive relief may be available.

Most computer companies consider the source code of important programs a trade secret, as well as the details of board and component design and manufacture. IBM quite clearly treats much of the PS/2 information as a trade secret, including the source code of the PS/2 BIOS. As evidenced by the fact that IBM has refused to disclose most of the information needed by someone else to build a compatible PS/2 clone. IBM has also clearly said it would not license such information, so that it can only be obtained by an extensive and expensive reverse engineering process by its competitors.

Trademarks. IBM has already asserted its trademark rights against AST and others who used the term PS/2 in product names without clearly identifying it as a trademark of IBM. In this sense, a trademark may also protect technology and make selling clone or related products harder.

A trademark is any mark, either words, letters, or images, that identifies for the public the customary source of a particular product. Thus, GM trucks are made by General Motors, and IBM computers by International Business Machines Corporation.

Trademarks may be registered in a particular state, but more usually are registered in the Trademark Office connected with the U.S. Patent Office. Marks claimed are examined by that office for conflicts with other similar ones, and if there is no apparent conflict a registration certificate is issued entitling the holder to the exclusive use of that mark. This is a perpetual right if the mark is continually used, and if certain filing requirements are met. The cost of obtaining a trademark is usually less than $500, unless other trademark holders object and claim a conflict exists.

So What Has All This Got To Do With Cloning? The relevance of this legal discussion is simply that IBM has managed to design and build a new series of computers that rely on the protection of all these complex bodies of law in such a way that anyone building a clone must spend an inordinate amount of legal and engineering time to duplicate the functional aspects of the PS/2 series, if the cloner expects to avoid litigation with IBM over infringement claims.

This carefully planned defense perimeter has bought IBM time in the marketplace, and time to engineer further improvements that will make it even more time consuming and expensive for competitors to clone future editions of the PS/2.

<u>What It Takes To Clone A PS/2</u>.

Specifically, to design and build an IBM PS/2 clone the cloner must first examine the various circuit boards, board and chip sockets, disk drives, controllers, power supplies, etc. in detail in order to derive the necessary specifications and components needed to build a compatible machine. As there are no schematics and very few specifications available for the machine, this information must be obtained solely by reverse engineering -- a tedious, error prone, time-consuming, and very expensive process.

As many of the chips and other components are non-standard parts, they cannot simply be purchased from industry suppliers, but must be spec'd out and custom built. Or the cloner can buy PS/2 clone parts now being offered by various chip suppliers, and hope against hope that the cloned parts were legally produced and not just copied from the IBM masks and ASIC's.

Then the lucky cloner has to build and test the machine, as a whole, testing for compatibility with the IBM PS/2 series by running complex software on the clone that runs correctly on the PS/2. If the clone machine creates errors, then an iterative process ensues while the developer tries to make the machine function as though it were a PS/2. The clone maker then has to pray that the testing procedures were inclusive enough to cover all probable incompatibilities.

Meanwhile, the clone builder must either reverse engineer or acquire from other software houses, a functional, noninfringing ABIOS and CBIOS in order for the hardware to run the MS-DOS or OS/2 operating systems. The cloner must then license these operating systems from the friendly folks at Microsoft, as they did for the earlier IBM PC and AT clones.

Finally, a year and a half later, the cloner is ready to market the machine, at a point in time when IBM announces its next step in PS/2 hardware --the model "XX", featuring a faster MCA or some other key element not in the cloned competitive machine.

And if this were not enough to discourage anyone, about this time the U.S. IBM PS/2 and RT patents will be issued, covering the MCA and numerous other features. This, of course, provokes a request for payment of license fees to IBM, or a patent infringement action by IBM, which permanently kills all sales of the clone.

<u>Can The Cloner Replicate The PS/2</u>?

Given the legal constraints outlined above, what alternatives does the cloner have if it makes the decision it must develop and market a functional clone to the PS/2?

Copyrights. First, it is clear under the U.S. copyright laws that source code "independently developed" is not an infringement of the copyright on the BIOS, for example. What this means is that the clone company should be able to set up a so-called "clean room" procedure for the purpose of extracting the functional specifications from a reading of the disassembled BIOS code, obtained by reverse engineering. These ideas in the form of specifications can then be used by another group of programmers who did not read the IBM code, but only the specifications, to create new source code. The details of the clean room procedure for doing so is beyond the scope of this paper, but will be covered by other participants in the panel.

Mask Works. Second, it is permissible under the Semiconductor Chip Protection Act ("SPCA") for the cloner to have the IBM ASIC and other chips taken apart and studied carefully, for the purpose of ascertaining the function and relationship of each component on the chip, and then building a duplicate of that functionality, but not of the original masks used by IBM.

Although there have been almost no test cases yet under the SCPA, it is believed that the intent of Congress was that the party examining the protected chip must do some independent work sufficient to understand what the components are actually doing. If this interpretation is correct, merely microscopically examining and obtaining a network ("net") list of connections and identifying the components on the chip, and then using a silicon compiler to create a functionally identical chip would not meet the requirements of the law.

It would appear that some companies in the market have done just this, and those companies may be at substantial risk, as would be board manufacturers who acquire such chips and use them on their boards. Note that relying on someone else not to have infringed IBM's rights in preparing the components you use is not a defense to copyright, SCPA, or patent infringement, although it would no doubt mitigate the damages that might otherwise be assessed.

Utility Patents. Protecting the clone company from patent infringement in the case of the PS/2 system may be a far more difficult situation. The cloner has only three alternatives, short of simply deciding to risk an eventual patent infringement action: (1) sign up for an IBM utility patent license and pay the required royalties to IBM, assuming that the cloner can figure out how to build the machine; (2) attempt to design around the various patent claims that IBM has made in those patents and patent applications that your attorney can find of record at this time, and hope that no more patents show up in the future and that your attorney and you did not miss any salient patents; and (3) decide to contest the validity of the IBM patents and applications presently thought to apply to the PS/2 and pay the cost in time and money of doing so.

The first alternative is clean and expensive; the second is exceedingly dangerous since most of those patent applications thought to apply to the PS/2 have not yet become public under U.S. and foreign patent procedures; and the third alternative is so costly and time consuming that no company acting alone could afford to do so, although a consortium might decide to do so.

In the final analysis, those American and foreign companies that have their own patent portfolios may be able to obtain, if they do not already hold, a cross license for the needed IBM utility patents, which may or may not bear royalties, depending on the strength of the patent portfolio. This is far more economical than litigating or risking infringement by attempting to design around the patents expected to be issued to IBM. The companies that are at real economic risk, in the case of potential IBM patents, are the smaller clone makers who do not have the cash to pay IBM large upfront royalties, and must instead pay high per unit or dollar volume royalties. They may have no alternative, unless they want to risk making and shipping PS/2 clones until the patents issue in a particular country, and then stop using and shipping those on hand when the patents issue. This may be a risky but practical alternative in those countries like Japan where it takes 5 to 7 years for a patent to issue, which time lapse could be the effective useful life of the PS/2 features. We would not recommend this approach, however.

Trade Secrets. Under U.S. law a cloner is not deemed to have misused an IBM trade secret so long as it is not obtained illegally. This means that unless the cloner hired away IBM personnel for the purpose of improperly obtaining the information, or purchased stolen or misappropriated schematics or the like, the use of information gathered solely by taking a PS/2 machine apart, component by component, and from reading published manuals and documentation, is not improper or illegal. This technique is in use all over the U.S. and the world today, although engineers should be aware that this process may not be legal in some foreign countries, where it is treated as unfair competition to do so.

Trademarks. Finally, avoiding problems related to trademark infringement are less difficult. Simply do not use marks confusingly similar to those owned by IBM, and when referring to IBM marks, such as "IBM PS/2 compatible," make certain that the manual or advertisement makes clear that these are marks registered or owned by IBM. It is legally permissible to refer to a competitor's trademarks, if they are identified as such.

Conclusion

Cloning the IBM PS/2 is not a trivial task, and should under no circumstances be undertaken without an advance appreciation of the extremely complex legal issues involved. Aside from the expensive engineering aspects of doing so, illegal activities engaged in by the clone company or its suppliers could be the death of the whole company, should IBM select the company for its test case.

It is a foregone conclusion that a company that spends the time and effort IBM did to clone proof its PS/2 line of computers will not pass up an opportunity to make an example of a clone thief.

FUNCTIONAL COMPATIBILITY AND THE LAW:

FROM THE NECESSITY OF CLEAN ROOM DEVELOPMENT OF COMPUTER SOFTWARE TO THE COPYRIGHTABILITY OF COMPUTER HARDWARE

Daniel R. Siegel

Skjerven, Morrill, MacPherson, Franklin & Friel
Santa Clara, California

SUMMARY OF OUTLINE

Copyright protection of computer software illustrates the conflict between the policies underlying patent and copyright law, as well as between the means by which patent and copyright law encourage progress in the computer industry. As a general rule, patent law encourages a "better mouse trap," and protects functional articles of industry; whereas copyright law encourages the "free exchange of ideas," and protects literary expression.

Patent law thus encourages functional compatibility achieved through reverse engineering, as a means of encouraging the incremental progress which eventually leads to true innovation. Copyright law, on the other hand, discourages this practice of copying and improving upon the works of others, at least to the extent that concrete expression, as opposed to more general underlying ideas or functions, is taken.

This conflict is not, in and of itself, very disturbing. It is currently being resolved by prohibiting reverse engineering to the extent that "computer programs" are duplicated. This limitation on otherwise legitimate reverse engineering is made necessary due to the ease with which mass-marketed computer software can be copied (relative to the much higher cost of independently developing that software). Traditional reverse engineering generally requires a significantly greater cost relative to the cost of independent development.

Unfortunately, however, copyright law is currently expanding in two major directions, both of which are having a significant negative impact on the development of functionally compatible devices.

The first area of expansion concerns the increasing scope of copyright protection afforded computer programs. Although copyright law protects not the general "ideas" or functions underlying computer programs, but only the more concrete "expression" of those general ideas, courts have interpreted a copyrighted program's ideas very narrowly, resulting in broad protection of functionality which, if unpatented, could otherwise legally be reverse engineered. Such broad protection of functionality goes well beyond that necessary to prevent software piracy, and prevents a practice more akin to traditional reverse engineering.

Even more significantly, functionally compatible devices may naturally or inevitably result in software similarities, particularly if hardware-dependent programs are involved. Due to the complexity of computer software, courts have had difficulty determining whether such natural or inevitable similarity is the result of impermissible copying, or merely the result of legitimately expressing the same idea.

This uncertainty has, as a practical matter, made it necessary for the developer of certain functionally compatible products to prove that copying could not possibly have occurred, by documenting the complete lack of access to the copyrighted software via "clean room" procedures (an expensive and time consuming measure).

The second area in which copyright law is expanding concerns the "copyrightability" of computer software — <u>i.e.</u>, what constitutes a "computer program?" The next likely area of expansion involves the copyrightability of computer hardware. In essence, the argument can be made (although it has never been raised in any reported case) that the sequence of functions performed by a hardwired logic device constitute a copyrightable computer program (the "instructions" of which correspond directly to that sequence of functions) embodied within that device.

This argument raises a number of unique issues which further underscore the conflicting policies of patent and copyright protection of computer software, and which, unfortunately, threaten the continued legal viability of reverse engineering and development of functionally compatible products.

CH2539-5/88/0000/0361$01.00 © 1988 IEEE

I. INTRODUCTION

A. Progress, Functional Compatibility and the Law

1. Progress in any field occurs in two distinct varieties: the few great leaps of **innovation**, in between which occur the frequent relatively minor **improvements**.

2. Both varieties of progress should be encouraged; for, without permitting the small improvements which ultimately lead to innovation, such innovation might never occur.

3. The computer industry is no exception; but **functional compatibility** with the industry standard may also be necessary to achieve commercial success.

4. Even the innovative leaders in the computer industry recognize that functional compatibility is, at the very least, a necessary evil.

5. BUT, the problem is that the **patent and copyright laws** (the primary means by which the United States government encourages progress) **ultimately conflict** as to whether functional compatibility should be encouraged.

   a. Copyright protection of computer software is at the root of the problem; and, although such protection will not (and should not) be eliminated, this conflict must be understood.

   b. This conflict is currently being resolved in a manner which is discouraging functional compatibility and threatening to overturn the deeply ingrained notion of reverse engineering as a legitimate development process.

B. Copyright Protection of Computer Programs: the Source of the Conflict Between the Patent and Copyright Laws

1. Patent law encourages **functional progress**
(a "better mouse trap").

   a. Patent law protects only sufficiently innovative ("novel and nonobvious") products and processes.

   b. Patent law permits unpatented products and processes to be reverse engineered (copied and improved upon).

2. Copyright law encourages **literary progress**
("the free exchange of ideas")

   a. Copyright law protects the sufficiently concrete **expression** in any original (non-copied) work.

   b. Copyright law permits the relatively general **ideas** expressed in a work to be copied (expressed by subsequent authors).

3. Both patent and copyright law protect (at least to some extent) **the functionality of computer programs.**

4. But, it is often argued that patent and copyright protection of computer programs do not conflict, because copyright law does not protect the **functions** performed by computer programs, but only the particular **literary expression of such functions** as a series of instructions to a computer.

   a. Yet, because computer programs, unlike other copyrightable works, are perceived directly by a computer (without human intervention), there is little, if any, practical distinction between performing the functions specified by computer programs and copying the literary expression in such programs. [**But see** the problems raised by this distinction below in the context of **copyright protection of computer hardware.**]

   b. There is, however, a distinction between protecting the **general** functions (ideas) specified in a computer program and protecting the **particular sequence of subfunctions** (or expression) of such general functions — copyright law protects only the latter.

   c. Thus, at least to some extent, both patent and copyright law protect the functionality of computer programs.

5. The current resolution of this conflict between patent and copyright law is to **prevent reverse engineering** of unpatented products and processes **to the extent** that **computer programs are duplicated**.

a. This balance of patent and copyright law policies is equitable, because it encourages the proper degree of investment in both software and hardware.

b. Without this limitation on reverse engineering, there would be an insufficient incentive to invest in the development of computer programs, due to the ease with which computer programs can be duplicated (relative to the cost of program development).

c. The disadvantages of legitimizing software piracy far outweigh the benefits of incremental progress achieved by permitting such "reverse engineering."

6. BUT, the problem is that the **courts are interpreting** both the **scope of copyright protection** and the issue of **copyrightability** (i.e., what constitutes a "computer program") **too broadly**, thereby discouraging functional compatibility.

II. THE EXPANDING SCOPE OF COPYRIGHT PROTECTION OF COMPUTER SOFTWARE

A. The Idea-Expression Dichotomy

1. Under a principle known as the "idea-expression dichotomy," copyright law protects not the general ideas expressed by an author, but only the particular expression of those ideas.

2. Where to draw the line between unprotected ideas and protected expression is a **difficult policy decision** which is based upon the breadth of the monopoly deemed necessary to encourage sufficient investment in a particular type of software.

   a. It is useful first to divide a work into various **levels of abstraction** (from the most abstract idea to the most concrete expression), so as to provide a framework in which individual similarities between two works can be analyzed in perspective — i.e., in relation to the work as a whole. Moreover, such a procedure facilitates the court's determination as to whether particular similarities lie on the idea or the expression side of the line.

   b. Computer programs, particularly those developed utilizing "top-down" programming techniques, are well-suited to the levels of abstraction analysis.

3. BUT, the problem is that the **complexity of computer programs has confused courts**, causing some to abdicate their responsibility for making this policy decision and, instead, simply declare that the most general function performed by a computer program is an unprotected idea, but that all other more concrete aspects or subfunctions of this general idea are protected expression (with one exception, discussed in the next section below).

4. Yet, as courts decide more of these types of cases, they will become more proficient at gauging the proper degree of protection afforded computer programs (**but functional compatibility raises a far more significant problem**, discussed in the next section).

B. The Merger Doctrine

1. Developing a computer program which is functionally compatible with an industry standard program often results in certain **natural or inevitable similarities** between the two programs — i.e., similarities which are the result not of copying but of expressing the same idea.

2. Traditionally, copyright law, under a corollary of the idea-expression dichotomy known as the "merger doctrine," permits the copying not only of a work's underlying ideas, but also of any expression which is the natural or inevitable result of expressing those unprotected ideas.

   a. Because copying can almost never be proven directly (absent a videotape of the defendant in the act of copying), **copyright infringement is proven circumstantially**, by evidence of **access** and **substantial similarity**.

   b. It usually is the case that, if the defendant's work was prepared with access to a copyrighted work and is substantially similar to that copyrighted work, then the defendant probably copied that copyrighted work.

   c. BUT, if the same types of similarities would have occurred whether or not the defendant copied, then such **natural or inevitable similarities do not support an inference of copying**.

   d. To protect natural or inevitable similarities of expression would, in essence, protect the underlying idea expressed, thus undermining the policy of encouraging the free exchange of ideas.

3. BUT, the problem is that the **complexity of computer programs has confused courts,** making it difficult to distinguish similarities which are the result of impermissible copying of another author's work from those which are the natural or inevitable result of legitimately expressing the same ideas.

   a. Eventually, courts may become familiar enough with these types of cases to know which expert opinion to believe, or at least which questions to ask.

   b. In the interim, however, given the significant risk that a court may fail to understand the complex argument that similarities were the result not of copying but of expressing the same idea (functional compatibility), it may be advisable to avoid legitimate access to copyrighted computer programs in order to provide the strongest and simplest possible defense to copyright infringement — "I couldn't have copied it because I never saw it."

   c. The lack of access to a copyrighted computer program can be established most effectively by utilizing clean room development procedures (discussed in the next section below).

C. Clean Room Development of Computer Software

1. Clean room procedures generally involve two groups, a **Functional Specification and Testing Group** and a **Coding Group**, and an **Intermediary** between the two groups.

   a. The Functional Specification and Testing Group prepares a written specification of the "idea" or task to be performed by the Coding Group — e.g., to write a microcode interpreter which will cause the specified microarchitecture hardware (of an industry standard microprocessor) to execute the specified macroinstruction set.

      i. It is permissible for the Functional Specification and Testing Group to reverse engineer the unpatented (or licensed) hardware, for example, of an industry standard microprocessor.

      ii. It is also permissible for the Functional Specification and Testing Group to have access to the copyrighted code in that industry standard product. Such access may well facilitate the reverse engineering of that product.

   b. The Coding Group writes code to perform the task specified in the written specification.

      i. It is critical that the Coding Group not have access to the copyrighted code.

      ii. It is preferable to avoid even the appearance of access by having the Intermediary review all substantive communications to the Coding Group as a "devil's advocate."

   c. The Intermediary insures that the two groups communicate only by written or electronic means, and that all such substantive communications are recorded.

      i. The Intermediary also reviews and edits all substantive communications to the Coding Group to insure that such communications do not contain even the appearance of access to the copyrighted code.

      ii. It is important that all substantive communications to the Coding Group be reviewed by one familiar with both the subtleties of copyright law and the relevant technology.

2. By insuring that no substantive communications to the Coding Group provide access to the copyrighted code, the clean room process provides documented proof that the functionally compatible code was prepared without access to the copyrighted code, and thus that no copying occurred.

3. Clean room development may be significantly more expensive and time consuming than traditional reverse engineering, or even development from scratch (without access).

   a. Nevertheless, such procedures may be the only feasible means of developing a device which is to be functionally compatible with a commercially significant industry standard product, while maintaining a sufficiently low risk of liability for copyright infringement (based, unjustifiably, on certain natural or inevitable similarities).

   b. Yet, even clean room procedures do not guarantee that a court will refrain from holding the defendant liable for copyright infringement. No cases have been decided directly on this issue; and there is nothing to prevent an expert from making the complex, technical argument (even if it is not true) that access to the specification constitutes access to the copyrighted code.

III. THE FUTURE: COPYRIGHT PROTECTION OF COMPUTER HARDWARE

A. Computer Hardware as a Copyrightable "Computer Program"

1. Copyright law protects **"computer programs:"** a set of statements or instructions to be used directly or indirectly in a computer in order to bring about a certain result."

2. Copyright law protects only **intangible** works embodied in **tangible** objects, but does not protect the tangible objects themselves.

3. Thus, the general issue is not really whether computer hardware is copyrightable, but whether a hardwired logic device embodies a copyrightable computer program (in particular, **whether the sequence of functions performed by a hardwired logic device constitutes a copyrightable computer program**).

4. The issue of computer hardware copyrightability is likely to arise in two contexts:

   a. Company B "hardwires" Company A's copyrighted computer program, by creating a logic device which performs the same functions in precisely the same order as those which Company A's program directs a computer to perform. **Does Company B's hardwired logic device embody Company A's computer program, thereby rendering Company B liable for copyright infringement?**

   b. Company B "functionally duplicates" Company A's unpatented hardwired logic device, by creating a logic device which performs the same functions in precisely the same order as does Company A's device. **Does Company A's hardwired logic device embody a copyrighted computer program (literally duplicated in Company B's device), consisting of the sequence of instructions corresponding to the sequence of functions performed by that device, thereby rendering Company B liable for copyright infringement?**

B. The Copyright Law Requirement of Fixation

1. Copyright law requires that the copyrighted work (as well as the infringing work copied from the copyrighted work) be **fixed** in a tangible object — i.e., that its embodiment in that tangible object be **"sufficiently permanent or stable to permit it to be perceived, reproduced or otherwise communicated, either directly or with the aid of a machine or device, for a period of more than transitory duration."**

   a. A computer program is fixed whether it is embodied on paper, on diskette or in a ROM or PLA; because it can repeatedly be reproduced from any of those tangible objects.

   b. Courts have held that the screen displays generated by a video game program are fixed in the ROM or diskette in which that program is embodied (even though it appears that only the code is stored in ROM, while the screen displays are merely generated by that code).

   c. **Fixation is thus a broader concept than mere memory or storage**; it also includes the ability to generate or reproduce repeatedly (i.e., for more than a period of transitory duration).

2. With a hardwired logic device, however, the distinction between the stored instructions of a computer program and the execution of those instructions disappears, indicating that, technically, **hardwired logic devices do not embody any instructions** (corresponding to the functions performed by that device).

C. Logic v. Memory: the Dual Role of Computer Hardware

1. All logic devices perform not only a logic function, but also a memory function.

   a. The **logic** function is the **mapping of a set of inputs to a set of outputs** (e.g., a two-input logical AND gate which maps the four permutations of "0" and "1" to the set of outputs, "0," "0," "0" and "1").

   b. The **memory** function is the **storing of a set of outputs, accessible by input addresses** (e.g., a two-input logical AND gate which stores the four numbers "0," "0," "0" and "1," each accessible by its input address, one of the four permutations of "0" and "1").

c. A ROM, for example, performs a particular combinational logic function, although it is generally utilized for its memory function.

2. This is true whether the logic device truly stores, or merely generates, its outputs (i.e., regardless of whether a unique set of transistors actually corresponds to each bit of output).

a. Sequential logic devices simply perform a different memory (as well as combinational logic) function for each of their possible "states."

b. Ordered array logic devices can be said to store their outputs (e.g., in a ROM in which a unique set of transistors may correspond to each bit of output), or merely generate their outputs (e.g., in a PLA in which there may not be a unique set of transistors which correspond to each bit of output).

c. Random logic devices generate their outputs; no unique set of transistors corresponds to each bit of output.

3. The converse, however, is not true; some tangible objects (e.g., paper or a diskette) perform only a memory function, but not a logic function.

D. Does a Hardwired Logic Device Embody a "Computer Program"?

1. **Company B Hardwires Company A's Copyrighted Computer Program**

a. The logic function performed by Company B's device is identical to that performed by the device embodying Company A's copyrighted computer program — i.e., the sequence of functions performed by Company B's device corresponds directly to the sequence of instructions in Company A's copyrighted computer program.

b. The memory function performed by Company B's device is the storing of the set of outputs generated by that device (identical to the outputs generated by the device embodying Company A's copyrighted computer program).

c. Thus, the information embodied in Company B's device (the set of outputs it generates) does not constitute, or correspond in any way to, the sequence of instructions in Company A's copyrighted computer program; rather, such information constitutes the results generated when that sequence of instructions is executed (or when Company B's device performs the sequence of functions corresponding to that sequence of instructions).

d. [Note that if Company B's device merely "hardwired" Company A's program (but not also the hardware which executes that program), then that device would generate output corresponding to the instructions of Company A's program, and might thus be deemed to embody an infringing copy of that program.]

2. **Company B Functionally Duplicates Company A's Hardwired Logic Device**

a. The logic function performed by Company B's device is identical to that performed by Company A's device — i.e., both devices perform the same sequence of functions.

b. The memory function performed by Company B's device is the storing of the set of outputs generated by that device (identical to the outputs generated by Company A's device).

c. It appears, however, that neither hardwired device embodies a computer program, because hardwired devices eliminate any distinction between the stored instructions of a computer program and the execution of those instructions. Thus, Company A's hardwired logic device does not embody a copyrightable sequence of instructions (computer program) corresponding to the sequence of functions performed by that device.

3. PROBLEM: Conflicting Policies Result in Either the **Elimination of Reverse Engineering** or the **Encouragement of a New Form of Software Piracy**

a. If Company B's hardwiring of Company A's copyrighted computer program constitutes copyright infringement, then Company B's device embodies a copy (albeit an infringing copy) of a computer program.

i. Such a result would seem to imply that Company B's functional duplication of Company A's hardwired device also constitutes copyright infringement (because the same hardwired device either does or does not embody a computer program).

ii. There is, however, some difficulty in identifying the instructions embodied within a hardwired device (because, without reference to another computer program, it is difficult to determine at which level of abstraction the sequence of functions performed by that hardwired device should be described).

iii. PROBLEM: the **functional duplication (or lesser form of reverse engineering) of virtually any logic device might be held to constitute copyright infringement**, on the theory that a copyrighted computer program embodied in the plaintiff's hardwired device was copied by the defendant.

b. If Company B's hardwiring of Company A's copyrighted computer program does not constitute copyright infringement, then Company B's hardwired device does not embody a computer program.

i. Such a result would seem to imply that Company B's functional duplication of Company A's hardwired device also does not constitute copyright infringement (because the same hardwired device either does or does not embody a computer program).

ii. PROBLEM: **a future "silicon compiler"** which could take as input a copyrighted computer program and generate as output a functional description of a hardwired logic device (that would perform the precise sequence of functions which the copyrighted computer program directs a computer to perform) **would, in essence, create a new form of software piracy**, because the essence of the computer program's expression — the sequence of functions corresponding to the program's sequence of instructions — could be copied freely on the theory that such sequence of functions does not constitute a computer program.

4. **Possible Solutions**

a. Enact legislation to enforce the seemingly contradictory rule (which a court is unlikely to devise) that hardwiring a copyrighted computer program constitutes copyright infringement, but functionally duplicating a hardwired logic device does not.

i. Such a rule would balance the conflicting policies of patent and copyright law, by permitting traditional reverse engineering of computer hardware while preventing the essence of a computer program (the sequence of functions corresponding to the program's sequence of instructions) from being pirated.

ii. It is unlikely, however, that such seemingly contradictory legislation will be enacted, absent a compelling lobbying effort against a frequent, significantly harmful practice, such as that envisioned by the future silicon compiler mentioned above.

b. Judicially eliminate (in essence) reverse engineering, by ruling, as cases arise, that both hardwiring a copyrighted computer program and functionally duplicating a hardwired logic device constitute copyright infringement.

i. Such a sweeping result is unlikely, given the deeply ingrained notion in the law that the reverse engineering of unpatented products and processes is permissible, indeed necessary to encourage progress (by permitting the small improvements which ultimately lead to innovation).

ii. The difficulty of identifying the computer program embodied in a hardwired logic device makes this result all the more unlikely.

c. It appears, however, that the better judicial rule would be one under which neither the hardwiring of a copyrighted computer program nor the functional duplication of a hardwired logic device constitutes copyright infringement.

i. This result continues to encourage progress by confirming the legitimacy of reverse engineering.

ii. The potential evil of a new form of software piracy could be handled by future legislation, if and when it arises.

iii. In any event, even the future silicon compiler contemplated above would require the building of the "pirated" hardwired logic device, and thus would be more similar to traditional reverse engineering than to software piracy (because the ratio of the cost of copying to the cost of development is nearer that found in traditional reverse engineering).

Patent Protection for the Computer Industry

Chair: R. Wedig

THE PATENT/COPYRIGHT INTERFACE FOR SOFTWARE PROTECTION: DETERMINING THE PROPER ROLE OF EACH

Ronald S. Laurie

Townsend and Townsend

ABSTRACT

A comparative overview of copyright and patent protection for computer software under U.S. law. The two forms of protection are compared in terms of a number of factors including subject matter, scope of protection, level of disclosure required and relative cost. In addition, a number of "second generation" software copyright issues are discussed such as protection of the "structure, sequence and organization" of programs, and the "look and feel" of user interfaces as well as the "clean room" approach to the design of compatible software.

I. COPYRIGHT PROTECTION FOR COMPUTER SOFTWARE

Historically the United States has been, and continues to be, the leader in the development and distribution of new computer software. As such the U.S. was in the forefront of establishing copyright protection for computer programs in order to encourage the continued growth of this industry. The Copyright Revision Act of 1976, effective January 1, 1978, made significant changes in U.S. copyright law. The 1976 Act, which replaced the Copyright Act of 1909, was designed specifically to adapt copyright law to the technological advances which had created new mediums and forms of expression and new methods of reproduction and dissemination.

A. Copyrightability of Computer Programs: The "First Generation" Cases

The legislative history of the 1976 Copyright Act made it clear that computer programs, to the extent they represent a programmer's original expression, are entitled to copyright protection as a "literary work". In the 1980 amendments to the Act, a computer program was defined as a "set of statements or instructions to be used directly or indirectly in a computer in order to bring about a certain result."

Not long after the passage of the 1976 Act the Courts were presented with a series of "first generation" software copyright cases. The cases involved virtually verbatim copying and the legal issue to be decided was the copyrightability of the particular *kind* of software involved. These cases ultimately led to the Third and Ninth Circuit Court of Appeals decisions in Apple v. Franklin and Apple v. Formula, which clearly upheld the copyrightability of computer programs irrespective of form (source or object code), function (applications or systems programs), and fixation medium (magnetic or electronic). The recent District Court decision in NEC v. Intel held that even microcode, the collection of elemental bit patterns which regulates the flow of data through the electronic circuits deep within a computer's central processing unit, is entitled to copyright protection.

B. The Scope of Software Copyrights: "Second Generation" Issues

Given the protectability of all types of computer programs under copyright law, the courts are now deciding "second generation" cases which seek to define the *scope* of that protection. That is, what kinds of "copying" (in the broadest sense of the word) will and will not constitute copyright infringement.

It is a fundamental principle of U.S. copyright law that a copyright does not protect the ideas embodied in a work of authorship but only the author's particular *expression* of those ideas. This so-called "idea-expression dichotomy" is found in Section 102(b) of the Copyright Act which provides that:

"In no case does copyright protection for an original work of authorship extend to any idea, procedure, process, system, method of operation, concept, principle, or discovery, regardless of the form in which it is described, explained, illustrated, or embodied in such work."

The legislative history of Section 102(b) discusses the application of the idea-expression dichotomy to computer programs in the following terms:

"Some concern has been expressed lest copyright in computer programs should extend protection to the methodology or processes adopted by the programmer, rather than merely to the ´writing´ expressing his ideas. Section 102(b) is intended, among other things, to make clear that the expression adopted by the programmer is the copyrightable element in a computer program, and that the actual processes or methods embodied in the program are not within the scope of the copyright law."

Thus, programmers are free to use the ideas (e.g. "methodology or processes") employed in existing programs but they may not copy the specific way in which those ideas have been expressed.

A corollary of the idea-expression dichotomy is the "merger doctrine" which states that when an idea can only be expressed in one way, or a limited number of ways -- i.e. when the idea and the expression merge -- copying the expression will *not* constitute copyright infringement. In 1978, a commission appointed by Congress to study and report on the effects of new technology, including computers, on copyright law discussed application of the merger doctrine to computer software as follows:

"The ´idea-expression identity´ exception provides that copyrighted language may be copied without infringing when there is but a limited number of ways to express a given idea. This rule is the logical extension of the fundamental principle that copyright cannot protect ideas. In the computer context this means that when specific instructions, even though previously copyrighted, are the only and essential means of accomplishing a given task, their later use by another will not amount to an infringement."

The Copyright Act does not use the verb "copy" to define a prohibited act. Rather, a copyright owner is given the exclusive rights to "reproduce" and to "prepare derivative works based upon", i.e. to adapt, the copyrighted work. Thus, unauthorized reproduction or adaptation constitutes copyright infringement.

In order to establish a case of copyright infringement in court, the plaintiff must prove: (a) that the defendant *used* (i.e. referred to or had in mind) the plaintiff´s copyrighted work during the creation of the alleged infringing work; *and* (b) that the nature and extent of the use amounted to the *unlawful appropriation of the protected expression* in the work, beyond the mere use of the underlying ideas.

Some unclarity in judicial decisions on copyright infringement results from the fact that courts sometimes use the terms "copying" and "copied" to refer to step (a) above, sometimes to refer to step (b) and sometimes without indicating which is meant. Thus, it is often said that copying may be proved from circumstantial evidence in the form of "access plus substantial similarity." Properly construed, this is legal shorthand for the principle that an inference of *use* (as that term is defined above) may be drawn from the facts that the defendant had access to the plaintiff´s work and that the two works are substantially similar *at the level of the ideas presented*. In order to be infringing, however, as stated above the two works must also be substantially similar *at the level of expression*.

A very controversial, and currently unsettled, issue is whether the expression in a computer program extends above the level of abstraction represented by the literal code and, if so, how far. In Whelan v. Jaslow, the Third Circuit Court of Appeals held that the *idea* in a program is its purpose or function and that everything else, including the "structure, sequence and organization" of the program, constitutes protectable expression. There is disagreement among copyright lawyers as to the validity of this principle and the Fifth Circuit Court of Appeals, in Plains Cotton v. Goodpasture, declined to embrace it. In any event, in a footnote the Whelan opinion specifically noted that in certain cases the purpose or function of a program may be to accomplish a particular result *in a particular way* and, in such a case, those aspects of the program which are necessary to accomplish the desired result are unprotectable ideas. It can be argued that functionally compatible software falls within this category. Under this view, those aspects of the internal structure, sequence and organization of a program which are *dictated* by external programming constraints such as hardware or software interface requirements *may* be copied without infringement. Similarly, it can be argued that under the merger doctrine even program code may be copied when there is no other practical or efficient way to achieve functional compatibility.

The "clean room" approach to the design of compatible software is intended to eliminate *access* to the copyrighted program by the programmers who create the compatible program. This approach requires that those responsible for writing the compatible program have no knowledge of the source code for the program to be emulated but rather work from functional specifications prepared by other programmers based on analysis of the copyrighted source code. In order to avoid a finding of access in subsequent litigation, the functional specification must extract from the copyrighted code the unprotectable ideas *without* taking the protected expression. In those instances where it is impossible or impractical to communicate the function in any other way and still achieve compatibility, even those program elements which would otherwise qualify as protected expression may be used. Thus, the purpose of the clean room approach is to insure (and to later demonstrate) that any similarities between the original code and the compatible code arise not from "copying" but from compatibility requirements.

The scope of copyright protection in computer programs and the viability of the clean room design approach will be further developed in the second phase of the NEC v. Intel case which involves the question of the circumstances under which the "reverse engineering" of copyrighted software to achieve a functionally compatible program do or do not constitute infringement.

Another second generation issue of great interest is whether the copyright in a computer program protects the "look and feel" of the program´s user interface (i.e. screen displays, keystroke sequences, command sets, etc.) or whether, in order to be protected these program attributes must *independently* qualify as a more traditional form of copyrightable subject matter such as an audio-visual or pictorial work, compilation, etc.

C. Registration and Deposit with the U.S. Copyright Office

In the U.S., copyright vests when an original work of authorship is first "fixed" in a tangible medium of expression. Neither publication nor registration is necessary in order for copyright protection to attach. However, registration is normally required before one is permitted to seek the aid of a Federal court in enforcing a copyright. In addition, there are a number of "incentives" for early registration of computer programs (and data bases) with the Copyright Office including the following:

- registration within three months of publication or prior to commencement of infringement of the work entitles the copyright owner to recovery of statutory damages and attorneys´ fees in appropriate cases;
- registration within five years of publication will establish *prima facie* evidence in court of the validity of the copyright and of the facts recited in the registration certificate;
- registration within five years after discovery that a work has been published without notice (coupled with reasonable efforts to add notice to copies still under the control of the copyright owner) will avoid loss of copyright; and
- where a work has been published by or under the authority of the copyright owner with the name of someone other than the owner in the copyright notice, an innocent transferee or licensee who

relied on the notice will not be liable for infringement *unless* the copyright was registered at the time of the purported transfer or license.

In order to register a copyright with the U.S. Copyright Office, an applicant must submit:

- a properly completed application on the appropriate form (TX for literary works; VA for visual arts; PA for performing arts, etc.);
- a filing fee of $10.00 for each application; and
- suitable deposit material for examination and archival purposes -- in the case of computer programs, the first and last twenty-five pages of source code printout.

While relatively easy to comply with, the deposit requirement has caused concern among software developers who are understandably reluctant to provide source code to the Copyright Office in view of the public accessibility of the deposit and the consequent potential for use by competitors. In response to these concerns, the Copyright Office will automatically grant "special relief" from the normal deposit requirements to anyone who files a paper claiming trade secrets in the software and submits a deposit in one of the following forms:

- first and last twenty-five pages of object code plus any ten consecutive pages of source code;
- first and last ten pages of source code; or
- first and last twenty-five pages of source code with up to fifty percent of the material masked out.

If an applicant chooses not to submit any source code, the Copyright Office will nevertheless issue a registration based on the deposit of the first and last twenty-five pages of object code, *but* the registration will indicate that it was issued under the "rule of doubt." This refers to the Copyright Office rule which gives an applicant the benefit of the doubt in cases where the Office is not able to determine whether the deposited material constitutes an "original work of authorship." The effect of registration under the rule of doubt is unclear, but it does provide a defendant in an infringement suit with an additional argument to use in opposing a temporary restraining order or preliminary injunction. The Copyright Office will not accept a deposit in any form other than visible printout, e.g., a ROM chip, diskette, tape, etc.; however, some types of machine-readable media may be accepted within the near future.

The normal term of copyright protection in the United States is the author´s lifetime plus 50 years. If a work is created by an employee within the scope of his or her employment, i.e. a "work for hire," the term is 75 years from publication or 100 years from creation, whichever expires first.

II. PATENT PROTECTION FOR COMPUTER SOFTWARE

While it has only recently become fashionable to consider patent protection for software products, the U.S. law in this area has not changed significantly over the past several years.

There are three major inquiries which are pertinent to a discussion of software patents. The first two are legal questions and relate to: (1) the patentability of the *kind* of software involved; and (2) the patentability of *the particular program* under consideration. The third involves practical business considerations and asks the question, even if the software *is* patentable should this form of protection be pursued?

A. Patentability Requirements in General

In order to be legally eligible for patent protection a software related invention must: (a) constitute "statutory subject matter"; and (b) satisfy the dual requirements of novelty and nonobviousness. On the practical side, the process of obtaining patent protection has the following characteristics relative to the other two primary forms of software protection, copyright and trade secret:

- it is more expensive;
- it requires more time to complete;

- it requires full public disclosure of the preferred implementation of the software.

These disadvantages are balanced by the fact that a patent provides, in effect, a seventeen year monopoly on the product or process defined by the patent claims. Thus, in a patent infringement suit independent derivation is not a defense as it is in a copyright or trade secret case. In addition, patents offer broader protection than copyrights because the former cover technological ideas while the latter only protect "expression."

B. The Statutory Subject Matter Requirement

Most of the reported software patent decisions over the last eighteen years have involved the question of statutory subject matter, i.e. whether software is the *kind* of thing which should be protected by the patent laws. Beginning in 1969, patent applications for software-based inventions were routinely rejected on the grounds that the claims recited "mental steps". This basis of rejection was replaced in the early 1970´s by the Examiner´s conclusion that the claims recited a "mathematical algorithm". The case law has now evolved into the rule that computer programs *are* statutory subject matter *unless* the claims "wholly preempt a mathematical algorithm". This means that the claims directly or indirectly recite a mathematical algorithm *and* that the use of the algorithm is not limited to a specific physical environment, i.e. structure or process. Under this standard it is apparent that most software created today *will* satisfy the statutory subject matter requirement.

C. The Novelty/Nonobviousness Requirement

The most frequent basis on which the U.S. Patent and Trademark Office denies patent protection to an applicant is that the claimed invention is either not novel, or if novel, would have been "obvious" at the time it was made to a "person having ordinary skill in the art to which the subject matter pertains." The nonobviousness requirement alone probably accounts for upwards of eighty percent of the patent applications that are rejected. In the case of software, some argue that, given the problem to be solved, the process of creating a computer program is nothing more than doing the obvious. The percentage of software written today that would satisfy the obviousness requirement is probably in the five to ten percent range. The question of obviousness is necessarily a case by case inquiry. Moreover, because the Patent Office has a limited collection of programming "prior art," many of the software patents which *are* granted will ultimately be held to be invalid in litigation based on prior publications, foreign patents or commercial uses which were not available to the Patent Office.

D. Practical Business Considerations: Cost

The cost of preparing and filing a patent application covering a complex software system can easily reach, and occasionally exceed, the ten to twenty thousand dollar range. About a year after the application is filed, the "prosecution" phase begins during which several written exchanges occur between the patent examiner and the applicant´s attorney. During this period, the applicant may narrow the patent claims in order to distinguish, to the examiner´s satisfaction, prior art which the examiner finds in his or her search. The attorney may have a number of telephone interviews with the examiner or may request a face-to-face interview at the Patent Office. The prosecution phase may generate another several thousand dollars in legal costs.

E. Practical Business Considerations: Time

Assuming the applicant´s patent attorney and the patent examiner can ultimately agree on claims which patentably distinguish the invention from the prior art, the average time between filing and issuance of a patent is in the range of two to four years. However, it may be another five to eight years before meaningful protection is obtained. This is because one of the most effective forms of protection provided by a patent is the right to obtain a preliminary injunction prohibiting further manufacture and sale of the infringing item by the defendant during the pendency of the litigation. Generally, a preliminary injunction is not available in a patent case in the absence of a prior adjudication of the patent´s validity (or long standing recognition of the patent in the industry, e.g. by licensing or conscious avoidance). Because of the extensive discovery required it may take five years to bring a patent case to trial with another three years for appeal. Thus, measured from the time of filing the application, it may be ten years or more before a preliminary injunction is available. This is to be contrasted with copyright and trade secret protection where temporary restraining orders and preliminary injunctions are routinely obtained upon the filing of litigation provided the plaintiff can demonstrate a likelihood of success on the merits and irreparable injury if the defendant's activity continues.

F. Practical Business Considerations: Disclosure

The level of technical disclosure which is necessary in order to obtain protection under the patent law is much higher than with copyright (and obviously with trade secret) protection. Specifically, the patent application must disclose a preferred implementation of the invention in sufficient detail to enable any person skilled in the art to which the invention pertains, e.g. a programmer, to practice, i.e. utilize, the invention (after the patent expires) without "undue experimentation." In addition, the applicant is required to disclose the "best mode" of practicing the invention known at the time of filing the application. In practical terms this *usually* means submission of a complete source code listing to the Patent Office. If and when the patent issues, the source code becomes publicly available for teaching purposes, though, if it is also copyrighted, not for use in a computer. This is to be contrasted with the Copyright Office deposit requirements of from ten to fifty pages of source code (see above). Where the source code listing is ten pages or less it is printed as an appendix to the patent; where longer, it must be submitted to the Patent Office in microform and copies are made available to the public upon request.

G. Conclusions

Based on the above considerations, in order to be a good candidate for patent protection a software product should possess the following attributes:

(1) long commercial life in the range of five to ten years;

(2) substantial commercial value in terms of potential sales or licensing revenue;

(3) an internal structure and logic which would not be obvious to a programmer of ordinary skill.

Finding the Trap Door Through Patent Protection of Busses

David M. Simon

Spensley Horn Jubas & Lubitz
Los Angeles, CA

Abstract

As the prices of CPU's decline, CPU manufacturers are likely to protect their revenues by increasing their manufacture of peripherals. Further, to block peripheral manufacturers from competing by building peripherals to be linked to the CPU's, CPU manufacturers will increasingly resort to patents to protect their busses. However, implied licenses may allow peripheral manufacturers to avoid the CPU manufacturer's patent protection. Implied licenses exist whenever a patent owner sells part of a patented combination where the part sold has no practical use except in the patented combination.

Background

Many of us spent countless hours in college breaking into computer systems. No matter how hard the system operators strived, no security system stopped the "computer hackers." Frequently, "calling cards" were left behind for the system operators. Hidden from the operators were trap doors into the computer systems to circumvent the frustrated system operators' security efforts.

Today, another battle goes on with stakes of billions, but not between college students and system operators. CPU manufacturers instead of system operators fight to maintain the "security" of their busses from peripheral manufacturers. Due to the high profitability of peripherals designed for new busses, peripheral manufacturers continually break the security of CPU manufacturer's new busses.

Faced with falling prices for CPU's, CPU manufacturers, and particularly minicomputer manufacturers, have tried to supplement their lagging CPU revenues by making more of their own peripherals. Although some, most notably IBM, have sought to protect their market by aggressive pricing, other CPU manufacturers have found this undesirable.

A common strategy, most notably tried by DEC with some success, is to patent the CPU's bus. Because a patent prevents others from making, using or selling what is patented, a patent on a CPU's bus furnishes a legal mechanism to exclude peripheral manufacturers from making products linked to the bus. After all, if peripheral manufacturers can be prevented from manufacturing products designed to link their peripherals to a CPU's bus, the CPU manufacturer has protected its product "world" from competitors.

Yet even in the face of aggressive bus patent owners protecting their CPU busses, peripheral manufacturers may have a trap door past the patent wall to the bus. This trap door is an implied license.

The Traditional Implied Licenses

Implied licenses arose from nineteenth century manufacturers suing purchasers of their machines that infringed the manufacturers' patents on methods performed by those machines. Although, the purchaser was literally a direct infringer by using the patented method, the courts refused to allow the patent owners/manufacturers to recover for patent infringement. Instead, the courts held that the patent owner/manufacturers had granted an implied license for their patents when they sold machines designed to perform the patented methods.

Over the years, implied licenses have been broadened. If a patent owner sells an unpatented article that has <u>no practical</u> use except in the patented combination, the purchaser of that article has an implied license -- a license that effectively allows the purchaser to buy additional components required to complete the patented combination.

That implied license also serves to protect the manufacturers of the additional components (the peripheral manufacturers). Ordinarily, the peripheral manufacturers would be liable to the patent owner for either contributory infringement or inducing infringement. (Contributory infringement involves the sale of a part that has no substantial use other than being used in a patented invention while inducing infringement involves aiding a third party to infringe a patent.) Because both contributory infringement and inducing infringement require someone to infringe -- and the peripheral manufacturer does not infringe by only making an unpatented component of the patented combination -- the purchaser's implied license means that no one is liable. Without the purchaser having infringed because of its license, the peripheral manufacturer cannot be a contributory infringer or be an inducer of infringement.

Busses and Implied Licenses

The nature of a bus is favorable for finding implied licenses on bus patents. A bus typically involves a group of wires, a bus interface that responds to signals on those wires according to a protocol and additional hardware and software in the host processor. Because a mere collection of wires is itself obvious, and therefore not patentable, the patent must cover at least the wires and the bus interface. Frequently, to avoid having the bus patent be obvious over prior designs -- i.e., to be patentable subject matter -- the patent must also include within the patented combination parts of the CPU.

By inclusion of any part of the CPU in the patented subject matter, an implied license to such bus patents is granted to anyone who purchases the CPU from the manufacturer. The CPU and the bus interface probably has no practical use other than being linked to the bus. Therefore, the sale of the CPU probably grants the purchaser of the CPU an implied license to complete the patented combination by attaching peripherals not provided by the patent owner to the bus. That license also protects peripheral manufacturers.

Limitations on Implied Licenses

Although implied licenses can be useful for peripheral manufacturers, they do have limits. Only in peculiar situations such as may arise with busses will implied licenses exist.

For an implied license to exist, the part sold by the patent owner must have no practical uses other than as part of the patented combination. For example, if DEC's CPU has practical uses other than being linked to the patented bus, no implied license to the bus patent is granted by the purchaser of the CPU. Because the purchaser has no implied license from DEC, the peripheral manufacturer has no implied license. In this example, the peripheral manufacturer who sells the other components of the patented bus to the purchaser of the CPU may be liable to DEC.

Also, the peripheral manufacturer's freedom from liability requires the customer to purchase the CPU from the patent owner. Returning to the DEC example, if third parties other than DEC make and sell the CPU -- a situation that exists with IBM CPU's -- and the customer purchases its CPU's from the third parties, no implied license is granted to the customer. Therefore, the peripheral manufacturer is probably liable to the patent owner.

The peripheral manufacturer's ability to avoid infringement depends on what is patented. If the patent merely covers one or more peripherals and the electronics linking the peripherals to the bus, the CPU is not part of the patented combination. Therefore, sale of the CPU does not carry with it any implied license to the CPU purchaser to practice the patented combination. Without the purchaser of the CPU having the right to practice the patented combination, the peripheral manufacturer may be liable.

Finally, the CPU manufacturer can avoid granting implied licenses to its customer by specific disclaimers. Overt steps taken before the sale to a customer by the patent owner can negate an implied license. For example, if DEC tells its customers <u>before</u> selling its CPU's that no license is granted, DEC avoids granting an implied license to that customers. If the customers then purchase the peripheral from a peripheral manufacturer, the peripheral manufacturer may be liable because the customer has received no implied license.

Extending Implied Licenses

Although implied licenses normally exist only when a patent owner sells a product that has no use except as part of its patented invention, implied licenses may arise in other situations.

Most such implied licenses result from the patent owner's conduct.

An implied license could arise from a patent owner advertisements. For example, assume IBM has patented the PS/2 micro-channel bus and a peripheral manufacturer's sells an accelerator board that couples to the bus and forms part of an infringing combination. To claim that the PS/2 may be as fast as competitors' products, IBM encourages purchase of that infringing accelerator board. By its conduct of affirmatively encouraging customers to purchase an infringing product, IBM has probably granted an implied license to its customers and to the peripheral manufacturer.

Further, implied licenses may arise whenever a court deems it unfair for a patent owner to recover. In one recent case, the patentee's licensee had sold expensive equipment that was part of a patented combination and encouraged its customers to add various components to make several different combinations -- one of which was the patented combination. Based on the expense and the patent licensee's encouragements, the Court found that an implied license existed.

Thus, close attention must be paid to the patent owner's actions. Given that CPU manufacturers frequently entice potential customers by promoting the number of products that may be linked to their busses, reviewing a CPU manufacturer's advertising can often support a basis for an implied license.

Conclusion

An implied license occurs whenever the patent owner sells one part of a patented combination that has no use except as part of the patented combination. Because bus patents frequently have to include part of the CPU as part of the bus, implied licenses may frequently be created by the sales of the CPU that includes part of the patented bus.

NEURAL NETWORKS Track

Introduction to Neural Networks

Chair: F. Coury

Neurobiology 101: A One Semester Course in the Neurosciences instead of a Coffee Break

Charles H. Clanton

Aratar
220 Downey Street
San Francisco, CA 94117

Abstract

The fundamentals of neurobiology and some of the more interesting details are discussed in the jargon of the computer sciences. This presentation is intended for computer professionals, technologists, and anyone else who would like to better appraise the neurobiology contained intalks and papers on artificial intelligence and "neuro-computing" or is just interested in how the brain works. No prerequisites.

INTRODUCTION

Energy economics promotes the evolution from single celled organisms to larger and larger multicellular organisms. With increased size comes increased specialization. Sensors must communicate via nerves with effectors like muscles and glands. The nervous "system" evolves. In its most primitive form, the neurons travel more or less directly where they need to go--a neural network architecture. As complexity of activity and responsiveness grows, some intermediary processing of information evolves and clumps of neurons emerge in a ganglionic architecture connected by a large neuronal "wiring harness". More sensors inthe front of the organism and more complex processing are accommodated by the enlargement of the frontmost ganglion, which becomes the brain of the brain/spinal cord nervous system architecture.

THE NEURONAL BUILDING BLOCKS

A nervous system isbuilt out of nerve cells called "neurons". Neurons come in many shapes and sizes but to explain how one works, we will consider only the fashionable neuron inhabiting beginning neuroanatomy textbooks. This neuron consists of a single bush of dendrites on one side of its cell body and a long axon coursing out from the other side. The axon ends extremely close to a muscle or gland cell or another another neuron that it helps control.

Lets start with the axon. It can be quite long, as for example the neurons whose cell bodies are in your lower back have axons stretching all the way to the muscles inyour foot. Axons provide frequency encoded digital transmission of information via all-or-none voltage "spikes" that travel down their length. The study of how this occurs is fascinating but involves words like neurochemistry and electrophysiology which are too long for this account.

Since the voltage change is stereotyped, only the frequency of the spikes are meaningful. Because the rate of firing can only vary over a very limited range, a single neuron can only tell about one to two orders of magnitude in variation of its inputs. This is much smaller than the range of most of our sensors, so neurons of different sensitivites must be "recruited" to measure the many orders of magnitude of stimulus energies we are exposed to.

When thespike reaches the end of the axon, its endplate, it causes chemical "transmitters" to be released into the synapse. The synapse is the very small space between the axonal endplate and the muscle or gland cell or neuron it terminates on. These transmitters bind to "receptors" on the other side and cause a voltage change that may result in contraction (muscle), secretion (gland), or transmission of information (neuron).

Again, lets consider the fashionable axon. It terminates on a dendrite. The transmitter it releases attaches to the receptors on the dendrite and causes a voltage change. This change is not a spike, but instead is a graded voltage change. It is graded over time and distance due to the "cable" properties of the dendrite. The actual time course depends on what transmitter is involved, how fast that transmitter is digested by circulating enzymes, or removed from the synaptic space by active uptake bythe endplate. Both these processes can be altered by circulating hormones and other aspects of body chemistry. Also, some transmitters raise the voltage and others lower it. All of these voltages spread across the dendrites and to the cell body where their effects are summed. When the voltage reaches a certain threshold on the cell body, the axon fires.

Of course, not all axons are fashionable. The cell body is covered with axon terminations and in fact so are the ends of the axons themselves. This vast multiplicity of inputs all interact to create the firing rate, and everything discussed here are important control variables in determining the outcome of the system.

THE BRAIN

The brain is composed of massive numbers of these neurons. When youcarefully study the cross-section of a brain, you can identify primitive areas that resemble those of lower animals. These primitive areas control so-called "vegetative" functions like the heart beat and breathing. Overlying these are areas thatprovide more abstract control, affect and drive state. Around this area are the cortical regions which perform complex information processing including, as the forehead squares off, personality.

The brain is not just a large random network of neurons however. As you look at it ever more closely, you discover ever finer structure. Each information pathway is massively parallel, and there are huge numbers of pathways. Information from one sensor may be processed by many different channels, each with differing structures related to the differing processing it performs. The human brain uses considerable brute force to implement its data processing. Much research has revealed neuronal wiring diagrams reflecting information processing activities, all of which are composed of enormous numbers of parallel units.

THE MIND

The brain implements both our conscious mind and our nonconscious mind. While not implying that these are singular entitites in themselves, lets look at the peculiar characteristics of each.

The conscious mind is experienced as a serial, linguistic, symbol processor. It has very limited short term memory and slow unreliable access to a huge information store. It is easy to study, because we can talk about it. The conscious mind does not do well with probability theory or analytic solution methods of any complexity so it uses very clever heuristics to make good decisions.

The nonconscious mind is not linguistic nor serial. It is highly parallel and vastly associative. It is experienced more indirectly, as when we solve a problem whle not thinking about it or find ourselves surprized at what we are saying. This mind is highly reliable in the face of failure of individual components because it depends on the vast parallel machinery that seems well suited for pattern matching. However, the nonconscious is difficult to characterize or study.

THE SILICON CARBON METAPHOR

Why study biological systems if youare interested in computer sciences? I can think of four ways these areas interact.

First, attempts to simulate or explore biological systems using computer models has proven very valuable for understanding human information processing. Information processing terminology has proven a valuable language for describing much of what humans do with their brains, though not everything. For example, I do not believe we have any language that is suitable for talking about personality. But careful modelling has been very useful in clarifying cerebellar neuronal mechanisms.

Second, biological systems provide insight into the solution space. The chess machines initially used quite simple analaysis, not at all like human players. Then, to try to improve, human strategies were studied and attempts made to incorporatethem. This did not result in the hoped for improvement. Then chess computers were built from more specialized hardwareusually highly parallel. These machines are often described as being less "human" than their predecessors, despite the consistent metaphor of the highly specialized and parallel processing of the human brain.

Third, the study of both brain and computers can generate provocative suggestions for the other. I suspect that the adfvent of highlyparallel multiprocessing computer systems will encourage the development of the concepts and language necessary to understand better the implementation of the nonconscious mind. In the other direction, better understanding of how the mind provides satisfactory solutions to problems that it cannot solve analytically aids us in finding tractable solutions and in designing reasoning assistance.

Finally, either system can help understanding of the other at many levels of abstraction--from primitive neurons to global concepts of the architecture of mind. However, poor biology adds no more to computer science than poor computer science adds to biology. In the face of the fascinating claims and speculations surrounding the current resurgence ofinterest in "neuro-computing", it can be useful to clarify where the real carbon-silicon metaphor lies.

NEURAL MODELS AND LEARNING RULES

Patrick Ransil

Lockheed Artificial Intelligence Center

Abstract

Models of neural networks which focus on information processing capabilities have demonstrated a number of valuable properties. The basic computing element is a "neural" unit whose output is a function of the sum of its inputs. Information is stored in "synapses" or connection strengths between units. Networks of these neurons are not programmed like standard computers, but trained by data input. Unsupervised learning algorithms allow networks to find correlations in the input. Supervised learning algorithms allow the pairing of arbitrary patterns.

Introduction

Detailed neural models can be used by neurophysiologists to study the behavior of neurons or networks of neurons and to help compare theoretical models with real data. Other models focus on the computational abilities of *neural-like* elements and their capability to perform specific information processing tasks. While these models do not attempt to behave like real neurons, they have been shown to have valuable computational abilities.

One of the earliest models of the neuron as an information processor was developed by McCulloch and Pitts[1] in 1943. This model used networks of simple neural elements connected together by synapses which passed information from one neuron to the next. The input from excitatory synapses was summed by the neuron which then turned on (1) if the sum exceeded a threshold, or off (0) if not. Active inhibitory synapses could turn a neuron off regardless of the amount of excitatory input.

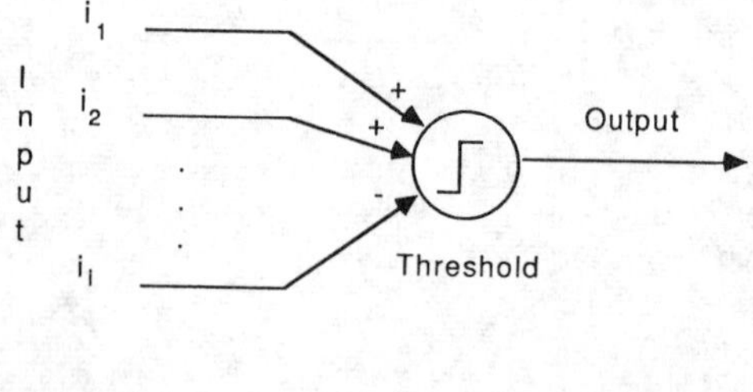

Figure 1. The threshold neural element of McCulloch and Pitts.

McCulloch and Pitts demonstrated an equivalence between this network model and propositional logic in which synapses represented logical relations, and a neuron turning on corresponded to the assertion of a proposition.

In 1949 Donald Hebb's book *Organization Of Behavior*[2] presented the first plausible theory for learning and memory in neural networks. Hebb hypothesized that information was stored throughout the network in the strengths of synaptic connections between neurons, and that learning occurred when synapses were strengthened due to simultaneous activity of pre- and post-synaptic neurons. This "Hebbian Learning" rule was shown to be able to learn input correlation patterns and formed the basis for a class of algorithms called "unsupervised learning rules".

Unsupervised Learning

Unsupervised learning rules train a system to classify inputs based on similarity of the training data set. The name comes from the fact that the system requires no supervisor or teacher to tell it how to classify each input. The system self-organizes by finding statistical regularities or correlations in the training data. In Hebbian unsupervised learning, the connection strength between neuron i and neuron j, w_{ji}, is increased if both neurons are simultaneously active:

$$\Delta w_{ji} = \eta o_i o_j \quad (1)$$

where o_i and o_j are the (binary) output values of the neurons, and η is a learning rate constant. This rule learns correlations of inputs, but is not very robust. Input patterns that are not orthogonal interfere with each other and cause errors. This severely limits the storage capacity of such a system.

Competitive Learning

The Competitive Learning Mechanism described in Chapter 5 of *Parallel Distributed Processing* [3] uses an unsupervised learning algorithm which classifies input patterns by similarity.

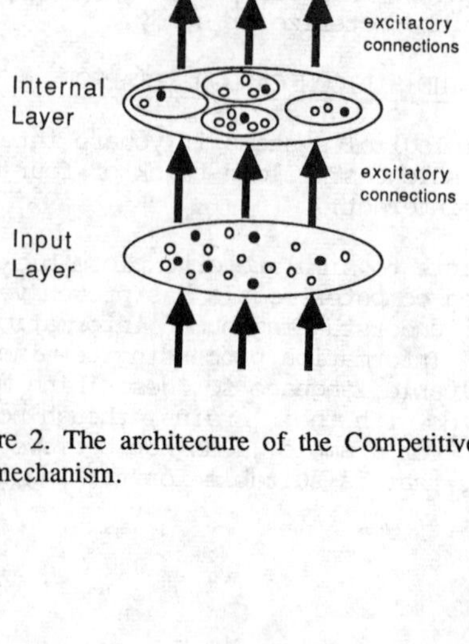

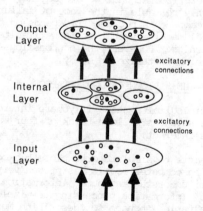

Figure 2. The architecture of the Competitive Learning mechanism.

The system is composed of layers of unit clusters (see Figure 2). Units in each layer receive excitatory inputs from every unit in the previous layer, and send excitatory outputs to each unit in the next layer. Within each cluster the units are connected to each other with negative or inhibitory weights providing "lateral inhibition". The total input to unit j for input pattern $\vec{I}_p$ is

$$i_{pj} = \sum_i w_{ji} o_{pi} + \sum_{j' \neq j} w_{jj'} o_{j'} \tag{2}$$

where the first term is the input from the previous layer and the second term is lateral inhibition from other units in j's cluster. This creates a "winner take all" (WTA) system in which the output of the unit with the largest total excitatory input from the previous layer goes to one, while the outputs of all other units in that cluster are forced to zero. The winner in each cluster is then trained by updating its weights so that it will respond even more strongly to this input next time. The weights of losing units do not change. The training rule is:

$$\Delta w_{pji} = \begin{cases} 0 & \text{if unit } j \text{ loses on pattern } \vec{I}_p \\ \eta \dfrac{c_{pji}}{n_{pj}} - \eta w_{ji} & \text{if unit } j \text{ wins on pattern } \vec{I}_p \end{cases} \tag{3}$$

where η is the learning rate constant, c_{pji} is the input (1 or 0) from unit i in the previous layer to unit j in this layer, for this input pattern $\vec{I}_p$, and n_{pj} is the number of active inputs to unit j in input pattern $\vec{I}_p$. The term $(-\eta w_{ji})$ keeps all weight vectors normalized, preventing one weight vector from growing large enough to win all input patterns.

The result of training is that the units in each cluster classify the input patterns on the basis of similarity. A cluster with N units divides the input patterns into N classes. Exactly how the input space is divided into these N classes is determined by the distribution of the training patterns, the order in which they are presented, and by the initial settings of the weights. Units can also be thought of as feature detectors, with units in higher layers detecting "higher order features" made up of conjunctions of features from the previous layer.

Competitive learning systems develop feature sets based on statistical regularities in the training data set, without the use of a "teacher". This can be a very useful function for large data sets where much of the information is redundant or the data is clustered so that it will naturally will fall into useful classes. On the other hand, often there may be several ways to split data clusters, and the categorization developed by the system may not be what was expected. Also, there are many classification schemes which this type of system can not learn such as putting all horizontal lines in one group and vertical lines in another, or classification based on small details while ignoring larger features.

Supervised Learning

Supervised learning algorithms can be used to train a system to perform an arbitrary mapping of inputs to outputs. The basic idea is to present an input pattern $\vec{I}_p$, allow the network to compute the output $\vec{O}_p$, and compare this to the desired output $\vec{T}_p$ which is provided by the "supervisor" or teacher. The error, $\vec{\delta}_p$ is then used to modify connection weights in the network to improve its performance.

The Widrow-Hoff Rule

The Widrow-Hoff rule[4] is a supervised training algorithm which implements an approximate gradient descent in mean-squared-error/weight space by iteratively changing weights to reduce the error and train single layer networks. For such a network (see Figure 3) and a linear output function the input/output mapping is

$$\overline{W}\vec{I}_p = \vec{O}_p \tag{4}$$

where $\overline{W}$ is the weight matrix of connections w_{ji} between input unit i and output unit j.

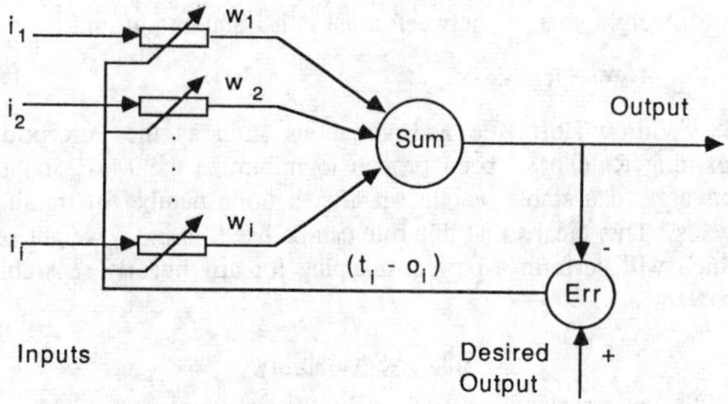

Figure 3. A supervised linear processing element. Weighted inputs are summed and compared with the desired output. The error is used to modify weights.

The mean squared error (MSE) over all training patterns $\vec{T}$ is

$$\xi = \sum_p (\vec{T}_p - \vec{O}_p)^2 = \sum_p \delta_p^2 \tag{5}$$

This will define a quadratic error surface such as the one shown in Figure 4.

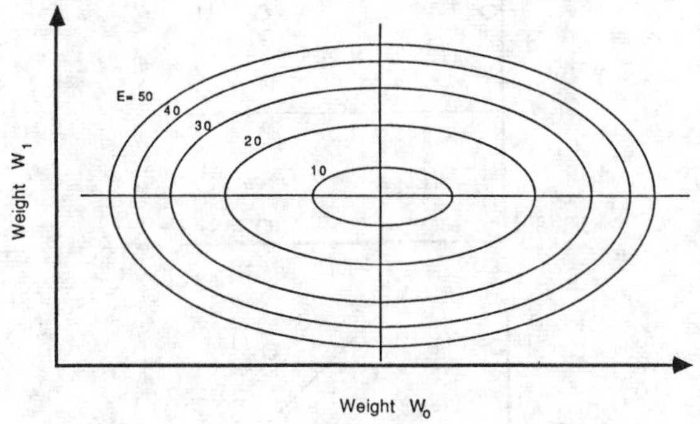

Figure 4. The quadric MSE surface for a network with two inputs, one output and two weights, w_0 and w_1.

The training procedure begins by presenting an input pattern $\vec{I}_p$, and calculating $\vec{\delta}_p$ an estimate of the error

$$\vec{\delta}_p = \vec{T}_p - \vec{O}_p \tag{6}$$

The derivative of $\vec{\xi}_p$, the estimated MSE with respect to the weights is then

$$\nabla\vec{\xi}_p = \begin{bmatrix} \frac{\partial\hat{\delta}_{p0}^2}{\partial w_0} \\ \vdots \\ \frac{\partial\hat{\delta}_{pL}^2}{\partial w_L} \end{bmatrix} = \begin{bmatrix} \frac{\partial\hat{\delta}_{p0}^2}{\partial o_{p0}}\frac{\partial o_{p0}}{\partial w_0} \\ \vdots \\ \frac{\partial\hat{\delta}_{pL}^2}{\partial o_{pL}}\frac{\partial o_{pL}}{\partial w_L} \end{bmatrix} = -2\vec{\hat{\delta}}_p\vec{I}_p \quad (7)$$

Weight changes are made by

$$\Delta\overline{W}_p = \eta\vec{\hat{\delta}}_p\vec{I}_p \quad (8)$$

or for weight changes between input unit i and output unit j,

$$\Delta w_{ji} = \eta\hat{\delta}_{pj}i_{pi} \quad (9)$$

The Widrow-Hoff rule and variations such as the Perceptron Learning Rule have been proven to minimize the MSE and to converge to a stable weight set after a finite number of training cycles. This means that this rule can be used to find a weight set which will perform a perfect mapping for any linearly separable problem.

Linear Separability

Single layer systems can only solve linearly separable problems. Figure 5a depicts a linearly separable problem in which the two-bit binary input is separated into two classes. Odd inputs are above the decision line while even inputs are below the line. Another linear separation of this space would be a vertical decision line for which all inputs less than two are on the left, while all inputs greater than or equal to two fall on the right. Figure 5b shows a simple non-linearly separable problem, the exclusive or, (XOR). No single line can divide the space putting (00) and (11) on one side while (10) and (01) are on the other side. A higher dimensional non-linearly separable problem is parity (XOR is parity with two bits).

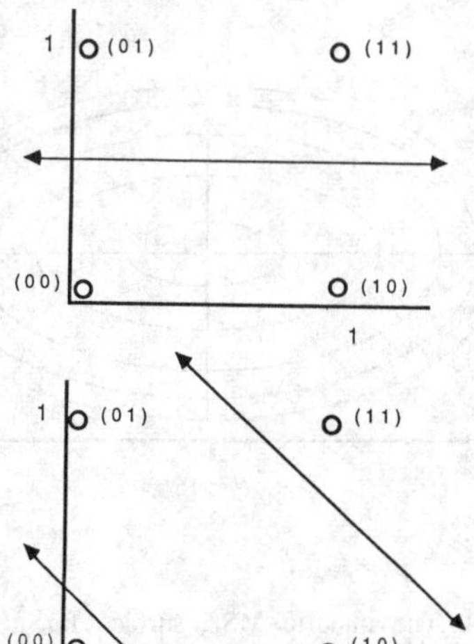

Figure 5(a) A linearly separable problem in 2-space. A single unit can form a decision line separating odd numbers from even numbers. (b) A non-linearly separable problem, XOR. No single line can divide this space with (00) and (11) on one side while putting (10) and (01) on the other.

Single layer networks can't solve these problems because each unit can only produce a linear decision surface in the space. This is a line in 2-space, a plane in 3-space, and a hyper-plane in higher dimensional space. Using a multiple layer system with linear output functions does nothing to improve the situation because this system can always be replaced by an equivalent single layer system.

Multilayer systems with non-linear output functions can solve non-linearly separable problems. For the XOR problem, one solution is to have the first layer composed of one unit which responds to (00) and another unit responding to (11). The second layer can have one unit which will respond if either of its inputs is on.

Until recently, one of the main problems with multilayer systems has been that they could not be trained. The output layer is trainable using the Widrow-Hoff rule if we have a teacher because we know what the output of all units in this layer should be for any input. For the internal or hidden layers we don't know what the outputs of the units should be, so an error term can't be calculated for training. This is known as the credit assignment problem, and has been a major problem holding back the development of neural networks for many years. Some solution to this problem are described later in this session by M. Jurik's paper.

Applications

The unique properties of neural networks make them useful for many applications in which conventional computers are not well suited. Neural architectures similar to those described above are being used as content addressable and associative memories where their tolerance for noisy, distorted, or incomplete data can be a great advantage. These systems are also inherently parallel and can be very fast when implemented in custom parallel hardware. Many signal processing applications using single layered nets with supervised learning are described in Widrow and Stearns[4]. These applications range from adaptive control systems to designs for interference canceling in electrocardiography and long distance telephone lines.

Conclusions

Studies of the information processing capabilities of neural networks has lead to the development of network architectures which are being applied to many problems that have been difficult to solve using conventional techniques. Although much further research and development is needed, neural network architectures have the potential to become a very useful complementary technology when used with standard signal processing and computing methods.

References

[1] McCulloch, W.S., Pitts, W.H., "A Logical Calculus Of The Ideas Immanent In Nervous Activity", Bull. Of Math. Biophy., Vol 5, pp. 115- 133, 1943

[2] Hebb, D., "The Organization of Behavior", Wiley, 1949

[3]Rumelhart, D.E., McClelland, J.L., "Parallel Distributed Processing," MIT Press, 1986

[4] Widrow, B., Stearns, S.D., "Adaptive Signal Processing", Prentice Hall, 1985

BACK ERROR PROPAGATION

A Critique

Mark Jurik

ESL Incorporated
Intelligent Systems Group
Sunnyvale, California 94088

ABSTRACT

This paper will describe and critique a neural-net algorithm known as Back Error Propagation (BEP). First a generic black box view is presented, followed by a description of several noteworthy experiments. A review of the learning algorithm is given with a critique. Next, some handy training tips are offerred along with a few variations on the basic design. Lastly, a possible trend in neural net evolution is discussed, suggesting the BEP could be heading toward a genetic dead end, despite early successes in small scale experiments.

INTRODUCTION

Life can be viewed as a complex mini-max game, where performance usually involves a sophisticated mixture of both long and short term plans. Such plans exploit the environment's predictability in space and time. For any cybernetic system, man or machine, predictive capability implies having some form of an internalized model of its external world. It is reasonable to require that such models 1) capture the spatio-temporal redundancy of its surroundings with a minimum of assumptions (maximum entropy approach), 2) be robust regarding future learning, forgetting and its own physical imperfections, and 3) emulate non-linear association (spatio-temporal logic). Obviously, the proper organization of such models is highly context dependent, governed largely by the system's physical constraints, performance goals and environmental interaction.

The artificial neural net (ANN) philosophy is loosely based on the assumption that internalized models can exist as non-linear dynamical systems possessing at least one stable system state. The hope is that when given any initial condition, the system should evolve within its state space by approaching at least one of these stable points. (Fig 1) In a sense, these points have a "gravitational-like" field about themselves and are thus referred to as ATTRACTORS. Simple pattern recognition could then be accomplished by labelling each attractor with a unique symbol, such as "cat" or "dog". When an input vector initializes the system's dynamical state, the system then proceeds to converge (sometimes immediately) to an attractor, thereby resulting in a classification such as "the input matches a dog".

Adaptive adjustment of internal models of the external environment involves the judicious placement of these attractors, as needed, within the system's model space. One cause for ANN's popularity with engineers is the belief that such placement of attractors can occur automatically via machine adaptation (learning). This hope envisions a new way toward achieving adaptive pattern recognition and signal processing within domains that typically lack analytical solutions, such as weather forecasting and speech recognition.

This essay contains the following parts :

A - A black box view of the BEP ANN
B - A review of some noteworthy experiments
C - A review of the dataflow and learning algorithms
D - A critique on BEP's mathematical philosophy
E - A list of handy heuristics for better training
F - A few alterations to the basic algorithm
G - A comparison between BEP and new ANN trends

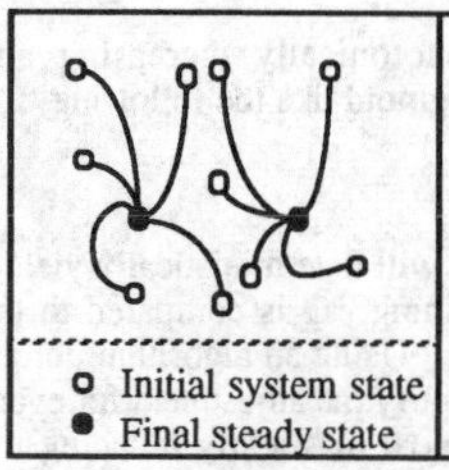

Fig 1 - Paths from initial state to a steady state

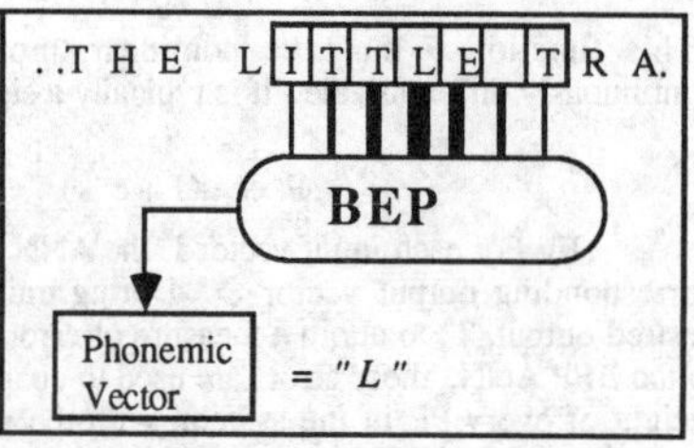

Fig 2 - NETtalk learns to pronounce the 4th (middle) letter in window

A. A BLACK BOX VIEW

An artificial neural network (ANN) consists of many primitive processing elements (PE's) connected together in one of many generic arrangements or architectures. Each arrangement has its own dataflow paths and algorithms for both information processing and self-organization (adaptation) Once a net of some specific architecture has been built (via hardware or software), the tabula rasa is simply shown examples of "stimulus-response" pairs. During repeated showings, the neural net is expected to self-adjust and display not only its having learned how to associate the various inputs (stimuli) and outputs (responses), but also that it can generalize the abstraction sufficiently for optimal performance on stimuli not presented during training.

Optimization, however, requires a performance metric, and each such metric can carry many subtle assumptions about the statistical nature of both the input and output data. In a later section, we'll see how this seemingly small issue is the basis for some of BEP's current disadvantages.

For this discussion, consider the BEP to be a black box with the following notation and properties :

A) The input is represented as a vector of parameters that describe the system's stimulus environment. For radar classification, such parameters might represent signal PRI, RF hop rate, scan rate, power spectral coefficients,..etc. If there are N parameters, then let any input vector's notation be

$$\mathbf{I} = (i_1, i_2, i_3, \ldots i_n)$$

B) The output is also represented as a vector of parameters, whose dimension is the number of different responses that is desired from the system. For radar classification, some responses might be "type A signal", "type B signal", ,"take response action 1", "run for the hills"....etc. If there are P such parameters, then let any output vector's notation be

$$\mathbf{O} = (o_1, o_2, o_3, \ldots o_p)$$

C) Training the system entails comparing the output vector with what we desire the system to produce. This desired output vector must obviously have the same dimensionality as vector **O**. Let its notation be

$$\mathbf{T} = (t_1, t_2, t_3, \ldots t_p)$$

D) Input data travels through the BEP ANN via one row of parallel PE's at a time. (See fig 7) The first row of PE's are forced to do no more than simply reflect the system's input vector **I**, one PE for each element of **I**. In a sense, their role resembles that of unity gain buffers. The last row of PE's in the ANN defines the system's output vector **O**, one PE for each element of **O**. The intermediate rows, if any, can have any number of PE's and can be connected to any number of PE's in either of its two adjacent rows.

E) Dataflow is strictly feedforward, from row to row. Every PE in the system determines its output using the same algorithm, that is, the output of each unit is some function of the weighted sum of its inputs. (See [10] in these proceedings.)

$$o_j = F\left(\Sigma_i w_{ij} o_i \right)$$

where o_i = output of cell i
o_j = output of cell j
w_{ij} = scaling weight on data from cell i to cell j

This function F must be nonlinear, monotonically increasing and continuously differentiable. It is typically a sigmoid like the following :

$$F(x) = (1 + e^{-x})^{-1}$$

F) For each input vector **I**, the ANN will deterministically yield a corresponding output vector **O**. During training, **O** is compared to the desired output, **T**, to attain a measure of error. Using an algorithm unique to the BEP ANN, these errors are used to quantify the adjustment for every weight of every PE in the system, with the goal of slightly reducing the system's error for the current stimulus-response (S-R) being presented. The hope is that after enough cycles through all the training S-R pairs, the BEP will yield a satisfactory response for these pairs as well as for other similar pairs the BEP has never seen.

The unique manner in which error "messages" are propagated through the system to all the PE's within a BEP ANN has been rediscovered several times. [9,11,14]

A highly parallel pipelined version of a BEP could translate input to output in less than a millisecond, the time for data to traverse all the rows of PE's. However, to date, most realizations of the BEP ANN are software simulated, (and consequently very slow), due to the immature state of ANN hardware.

B. SOME NOTEWORTHY EXPERIMENTS

There have been several noteable experiments with BEP. I have chosen a few examples related to acoustic analysis / synthesis because this field is rich with many difficult-to-analyze real world problems.

A still popular BEP experiment was the NETtalk system of Sejnowski & Rosenberg[12] which translated English text to speech phonemes. Its input was the successive presentation of 7-letter groups, where the middle letter of any group was the target for the desired phonemic output, and the surrounding six letters provided context for shaping the target's pronunciation. (See fig 2) During the evolution of NETtalk's training, the system first learned to be silent when the target character was a space between words. Eventually it began to sound like a young child talking,exhibiting proof of its ability to discover, keep and utilize generalized "rules" of speech synthesis.

Another acoustic application, Elman and Zipser [2], involved BEP speech analysis and recognition. Addressing the age-old problem of finding useful parameters for speech representation, they proved that a BEP model could spontaneously develop its own set of speech units which sometimes, but not always, correspond to currently popular linguistic representations. One elegant way to achieve this is to present vectored speech data (eg, vectored FFT coeficients) as both input **I** and target output **T**. Rather than evolving into an identity transform, where the input feeds straight into the output, (as one might expect from a linear system), the nonlinear BEP would learn to find salient features of the signal, and then "reverse" transform the features back into a speech vector at the output. (See fig 3)

In addition to discovering salient features within a signal, numerous experiments have proven that a BEP could, in some cases, figure out how to compress the reresentation of its input data as well This encoding process would convert input, represented by n PE's at the first row, into a representation needing less than n PE's at some other row downstream. [11] This encoding is somewhat analogous to compressing a Roman numeral, such as MDCCCLXXXVIII, into the compact 1888.

A third experiment , also acoustic, was a BEP that could classify sonar echoes as a reflection off either a rock or a metal mine. [3] In this case, the spectral analysis (FFT) of a returning sonar echo gave Fourier vectors which were utilized (after some preprocessing) as input vectors **I** for the ANN. The output had two PE's, one for "rock" and one for "metal mine". After training was over, the PE that produced the larger output determined the rock/mine class of the echo. Results revealed a system that performed as well as some trained people.

3 humans	88-93% correct
BEP ANN	92-99% correct

Other notable uses of BEP included political forecasting and consumer energy consumption modeling [14].

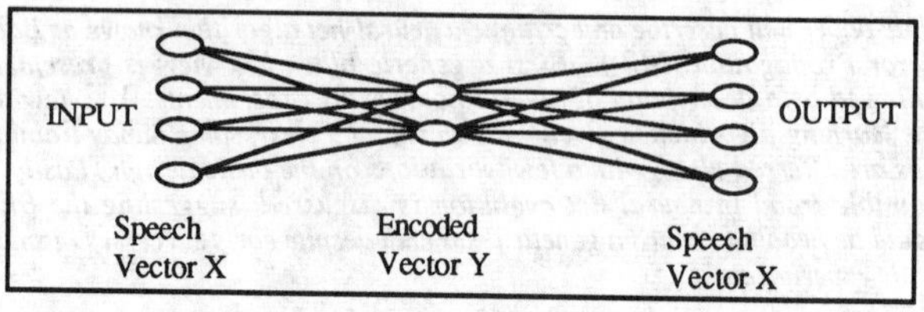

Fig 3 - Nonlinearity of BEP enables it to find and encode salient features of input as well as decode them back into original form

C. REVIEWING BEP'S ALGORITHMS

Assume the trainer has a collection of input **I** and output **O** vector pairs. The first row in the BEP ANN must contain the same number of PE's as there are elements in **I**, thus all the **I**'s must have the same dimensionality. For example, each **I** vector could contain data about a different person, where elements would represent sex (M/F), employed (Y/N), ...etc. Likewise, the **O** vector, associated with a particular **I**, might represent eventual cause of death for that person, one element for each of many possible causes. For example, **O** = (0,0,1,1) might represent high blood pressure and heart failure. All **O**'s must have the same dimensionality, although it is typically unequal to that of the **I**'s.

One training *exposure* constitutes inputing the values of one **I** into the BEP and, based on its output, feeding the error back into BEP for minor internal adjustments. One training *cycle* constitutes exposing the BEP to the complete set of **I-O** vector pairs.

During one exposure, the value of each element of **I** enters its corresponding PE in the first row. The internal value of any PE is represented by the variable u, and the subscript notates the PE within that row. Figure 7 nomenclature uses subscript ***i*** for cells in the first row (system input), ***j*** for the second row (middle layer), ***k*** for the third (another middle layer), and ***l*** for the last (system output) row. A generic BEP can have any number of middle rows, including no middle rows at all.

The output of any PE, or cell, is represented by variable o, again with the appropriate subscript. A Cell's output is not the same as its internal value, since the output o is a nonlinear transform of u, represented as

$$o = F\,(\,u + \text{bias}\,)$$

where F is the sigmoid already described in section A. The only exception is the first row where o is forced to reflect the input. The output o is then transmitted to every cell in the next layer that has a potential link between the two cells. The system designer determines what PE's can be physically connected, and usually each cell is "wired" to every PE within the next successive row.

At the receiving end, the o values are collected and weighted before getting summed. A bias is then added which, in effect, shifts the sigmoid along the u domain. This bias is automatically adjusted during training. The unique weight attached to every intercell link is of prime importance, since what a BEP learns from training is mostly reflected in these weight values.

Data flows unidirectionally, from row to row. At the last row, each PE's output is compared to its corresponding target (desired) value and the difference is an error. The degree to which any cell in the net can reduce these errors determines to what extent that cell's weights and bias will be modified. This "credit assignment" that's judged upon each PE is analytically feasible (thanks to the simplicity of mean square error techniques) and is given as explicit equations in fig 7.

For any cell, its evaluated relevance toward lowering system error is annotated as epsilon. This value can be negative, indicating the cell should seek to lower its output under current conditions, otherwise a positive value would dictate an increase in cell output. The epsilon of an arbitrary cell *l* in the last row is simply the difference (error) between output o and target t :

$$error_l = (o_l - t_l)$$

scaled by the value of the first derivative of the cell's sigmoidal output :

$$F' (u_l)$$

This epsilon travels *backwards* through the net in a manner similar to how the input data travelled forward. At the next row, traveling backwards, each PE cell takes the weighted sum of the epsilons and scales the sum by the first derivative of its sigmoidal output. This repeated process back-propagates the error through the entire net, hence its name "Back Error Propagation".

When all the PE's get their assigned epsilon, then each cell's bias and weights can be incrementally adjusted. The change in bias is proportional to the cell's epsilon, by a scaling factor that's typically small, such as 0.1. The change in each weight is proportional to both epsilon and the value of the feedforward data currently on that weight's link. Thus links transmitting large data values will have their weights experience large adjustments.

This sequence of events is repeated for each **I**,**O** exposure in a cycle, and for many cycles. There is no precise algorithm indicating when to stop training; indeed, that is just one of many difficulties with the BEP ANN.

D. CRITIQUING BEP'S PHILOSOPHY

Recall that each input vector **I** has a corresponding desired ouput vector **T**. In response to **I**, the system yields its own output vector **O**. The BEP philosophy considers performance error to be the vector difference between **T** and **O**, that is, error vector **E** is ....

$$\mathbf{E} = \mathbf{T} - \mathbf{O} = ([t_1 - o_1], [t_2 - o_2], \ldots [t_n - o_n]).$$

In many adaptive signal processing applications, finding the least mean square error works quite well with linear systems. Minimizing the squared length of error vector **E** amounts to minimizing the sum of the squares of each of its elements, ..

$$||\mathbf{E}||^2 = [t_1 - o_1]^2 + [t_2 - o_2]^2 + \ldots [t_n - o_n]^2$$

The main idea to follow is this : we'd like to minimize $||\mathbf{E}||$ by adjusting each weight in the ANN. The BEP technique is similar to the Widrow-Hoff algorithm[15] for linear systems, even though an ANN is typically nonlinear. The entire approach rests on the desire to modify each weight by an amount proportional to how it can decrease the output error. In other words, ...

$$\frac{d\mathbf{w}}{dt} = -k \frac{d\,||\mathbf{E}||^2}{d\,\mathbf{w}} . \qquad (1)$$

where **w** is the collection of input weights at any one cell and dw/dt is the amount of adjustment each weight would receive for one training exposure to an S-R pair. With this in hand, each weight would be updated in the following manner :

$$\mathbf{w}(t+1) = \mathbf{w}(t) + d\mathbf{w}/dt$$

The critical difference between the BEP and the Widrow-Hoff model, is that the former uses PE's with nonlinear output transfer functions, such as the sigmoid F(*) mentioned earlier, and the latter is linear. This poses a problem for BEP. In a linear system, any arrangement of rows of PE's with linear data processing could always be reduced to just two rows, (since any series of matrix multiplications could also be achieved using only one matrix). As a consequence, error minimization amounts to adjusting those weights which will maximize the descent down an n-dimensional parabolic basin, the least mean square error surface. (See fig 4.1) This makes implementation of equation (1) pretty straightforward in linear systems.[15]

An ANN with rows of nonlinear PE's cannot, in general, be reduced to fewer rows. This has two major consequences : 1) we must carry out the same algorithm for *all* rows when adjusting the weights and 2) the error surface is gutted with *many* basins, of which few should ever resemble the analytically appealing paraboloid. (See fig 4.2)The consequences of these two issues, as well as a few others will now be examined in detail.

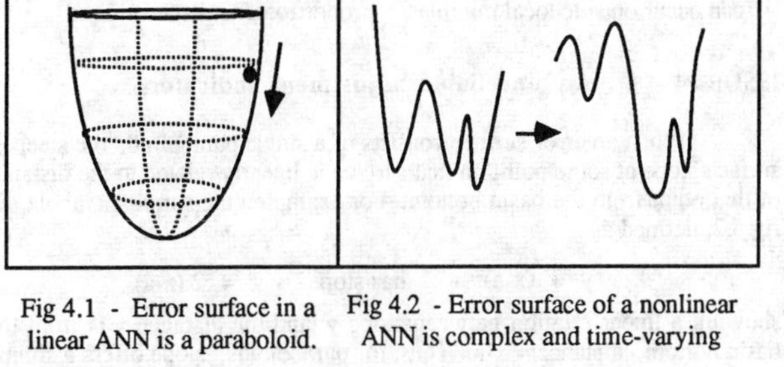

Fig 4.1 - Error surface in a linear ANN is a paraboloid.

Fig 4.2 - Error surface of a nonlinear ANN is complex and time-varying

ISSUE #1 Backpropagation through noise

Since system error is first derived at the output, the error signal must propagate back through the rows in order to reach every row. But initially, each row of PE's has weights that are random. Thus the error becomes increasingly meaningless as it back-propagates through the net of randomized weights. As a consequence, the front rows get "misled" into what adjustment was truly needed. After this almost random correction at the front rows, the back rows will now receive data corrupted by the updated front rows. This noisy communication appears to be very inefficient, since some simple training tasks can require thousands of training cycles.

ISSUE #2 Simultaneous change

The mathematical derivation of the formula for weights adjustment uses partial derivatives, which assumes nothing else is being changed except the weight in question. However, in practice, and for the sake of expediency, all the weights are changed per training exposure. Rumelhart[11] offers this comment :

> "... By changing [all] the weights after each pattern is presented we depart to some extent from a true gradient descent....nevertheless, provided the learning rate [β] is sufficiently small, this departure will be negligible ..... In particular, with a small enough learning rate, the delta rule will find a set of weights minimizing this [LMSE] error function. "

The problem is that small learning rates imply long training sessions, making the BEP unsuitable for real-time adaptive processing. This contrasts against linear adaptive nets which can adjust in real-time.[15]

ISSUE #3 Numerous basins and crests

One reason why the mean square error method works well for linear systems is that the error function yields only one n-dimensional parabolic error surface. In this error space, the surface has only one place where its value is minimal : at the paraboloid's bottom. It is therefore safe to use equation (1) since then the only time weight adjustments will stop, ie. when $d\,\mathbf{w}/d\,t = 0$, is when the system has reached the basin's bottom, the ultimate goal.

Nonlinear systems, on the other hand, will typically have an error surface indented with numerous basins. For BEP, the problem is enhanced since these basins are usually non-parabolic and time varying. One can attain zero slopes within regions *between* any two such basins as well as at the bottom of any basin (local minima). See fig 5.1 This implies the possibility that weight modification may be very slow within regions of relative *maximum* error, as well as at relative minimas. This is yet another cause for slow learning.

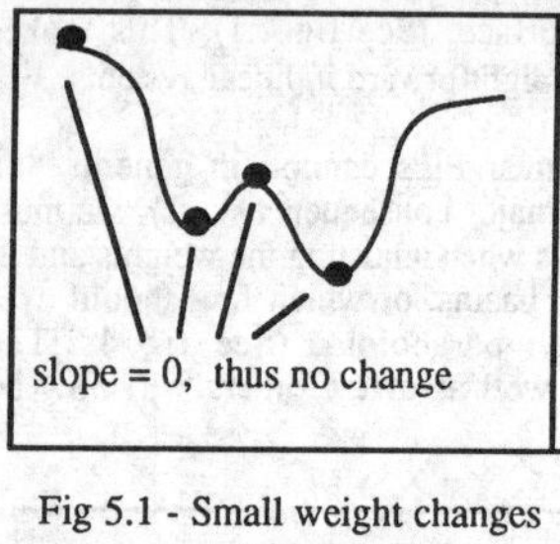

Fig 5.1 - Small weight changes can occur outside local minimas.

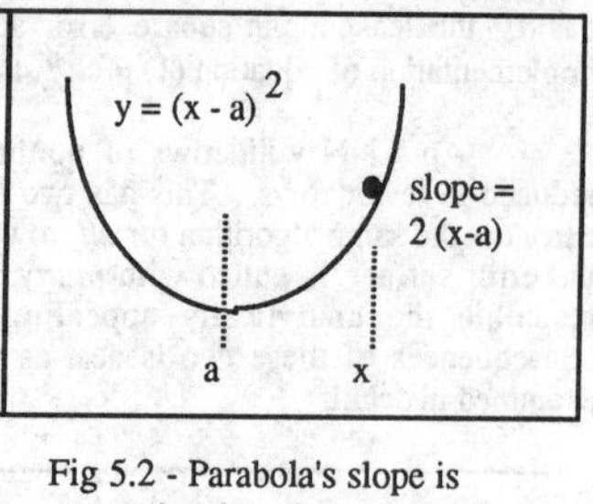

Fig 5.2 - Parabola's slope is proportional to distance x - a .

ISSUE #4 **An unreliable adjustment indicator**

When an error surface consists of a single paraboloid, the steepest surface slope at some point on that surface is linearly related to the distance of that point from the basin bottom. For example, the simple parabola, in fig 5.2, defined as ...

$$y = (x-a)^2 \qquad \text{has slope} \qquad y' = 2\,(x-a)$$

showing a linear relation between slope y' and the distance x is from the basin bottom, distance = x-a. Thus, for paraboloids, slope offers a simple indication of how far the system is from a local minima : a large slope implies a large distance and the need to make a large adjustment to the weights. We now see a reason why equation (1) works so well with single paraboloid surfaces.

The problem lies in extending this assumption for basins that can be of almost any complex curvature, including those attained in a BEP. In this case, there is no simple relation between slope and distance to a relative minima, despite the fact that BEP mathematics also uses (1) as its primary equation. As a consequence, large misguided adjustments can frequently occur, sending the system state straight down through the local minima and far up the other side, giving the system an error performance worse than prior to the adjustment.

ISSUE #5 **Lack of digital convergence proof**

It is mathematically provable that if one uses infinitesimally small weight adjustments (plus infinitely long patience), then convergence to an optimal behavior will occur in a BEP ANN. However, reality usually requires a finite training period, and therefore a fixed valued learning constant (unless an analog computer is used). The consequence is that digital applications may not necessarily converge. In fact, an experiment by Wasserman [13] showed how a BEP managed to achieve near perfect performance, and then upon further training with the same training set, the BEP proceeded to degrade, achieving an RMS error *increase* of two orders of magnitude. How does one know when to stop the training session? Just like wanting to know when to pull out of the stock market, there is no easy reliable answer.

ISSUE # 6 **Dependence upon initial conditions**

Another debatable issue about BEP learning centers around the significance of numerous minimas with unequal depths. This means that convergence toward one minima may yield a lower mean square error than convergence toward another. Although some basins may be as deep as the deepest one, there is no direct way to determine whether or not the BEP is at a near optimal minima, short of randomizing the weights and retraining again and again, hoping for better results.

The ultimate basin of convergence can have significant impact on performance. For example, when the weights of NETtalk were slightly altrered and retraining occurred, the system's performance rose from 84% to 93% correct [12]. One strong argument for this could be that the randomized weight adjustments placed NETtalk near a basin that was better than that of the first training session, and therefore converged to it instead. We see now that final performance is partially dependent upon the randomized initial conditions for training -- a sobering fact .

ISSUE #7 **Self - disabling tendancy**

One widely agreed upon problem with applying equation (1) to non-linear cells is that the adaptation algorithm requires using the first derivative of sigmoid F. Since F' can have large domains where its value is near zero, then a cell, once accidentally placed into one of these regions (by method discussed in issue #5), will have a very slow time trying to get back into proper operation. This is true because both a cell's weights and bias are varied according to equations that have F'(*) as a factor. (See fig 7)

ISSUE #8 **Non-real time adaptation**

Unfortunately, one cannot simply add a new pattern to the BEP's repertoire without also reinforcing the old patterns too. For each pattern a BEP must learn, it tends to fade its memory of prior learned patterns. This must occur since it is how BEP achieves long term noise immunity during training. The consequence of this is that in-the-field training will require cycling through all the old patterns as well as whatever new pattern(s) the BEP would need to learn in real-time.

Many heuristics are available for attaining some improvement in the BEP's adaptation convergence rate, and are discussed in section E. For some cases, training could be reduced from 4000 cycles to only 100. Yet even with a requirement of 100 training cycles for acceptable convergence, a large number of patterns per cycle would still render the system non-realtime.

An alternative use for BEP would be as a pattern decoder at the receiving end of a communications link. Assume a BEP has been trained to decode a fixed number of patterns that have been distorted in a manner similar to the way a communications channel might distort a signal (eg. via additive noise). Then the BEP could be used to pattern match against an incoming distorted signal, and deliver the encoded version.

A experiment similar to this has been demonstrated by Hecht-Nielsen [5]. A BEP was trained to translate a noisy EKG signal of a horse into a clean signal. During training, the system would learn the regular heartbeat pattern from the noisy cycloperiodic signal, so that it could extract, via pattern matching, the beating waveform pattern from a signal deeply embedded in noise.

E. SOME TRAINING HEURISTICS

Heuristics are rules that work most of the time, at least that's the idea. Here are some helpful ones :

1. **Generalization**

If you are using middle rows (highly recommended), start with a number of PE's in each of these rows at least as large as the total number of PE's in the first plus last rows. Then retrain with fewer middle row cells. Repeat this process until any further reductions seriously degrade the system's performance. By doing so, the BEP is being forced to generalize as much as is possible from the training session. This will *usually* yield better system performance on degraded patterns that the ANN has never seen, than if the ANN does not generalize at all.

2. **Training variability**

Train with as much variability as can be reasonably imposed upon the input data. This will encourage the ANN to find prototypes, rather than memorize each pattern as a special case (which it will do when given half a chance). The simplest method is to add noise to the input data and train with the largest set as is feasible.

Also, before each cycle, randomize the sequence of exposure of the training set. This will discourage the net from finding subpatterns based on fixed sequential exposures of specific input patterns.

3. **Error thresholding**

The practice of back propagating only those errors that exceed a minimum threshold may enhance the quality of convergence as well as its speed. This practice was applied during the training of NETtalk. [12]

4. **Error averaging**

For some cases, averaging the error over a few exposures before back propagation may also enhance convergence quality and speed. Although this technique has intuitive appeal, it is missing theoretical support. Specifically, weight adjustments are determined by a combined interaction of both back propagating epsilons and forward propagating data. The obvious question is "to what forward flowing data should the averaged error of many training patterns be combined to determined weight adjustments ? " Although averaging may make sense in linear systems, it remains unclear how they should work in nonlinear ANNs.

5. **Biased Training**

Just as a teacher would spend more time with a pupil on items poorly learned than on items well learned, so it makes sense to train a BEP in similar fashion. Remember to return to the "old" patterns once in a while to avoid their fading out of system memory.

6. **Simulated annealing of learning rate**

Try a few runs to estimate the average convergence time (if it converges at all). Now try again with the convergence rate constant, b, initially set to a "high" value, say 0.5. Then during the training session, successively lower b by 50%. This may help the ANN find a good sized basin before settling down inside it.

7. **Simulated annealing of weight changes**

With a philosophy similar to heuristic #6, add some noise to the amount by which each weight must change. During the course of a training session, slowly decrement the noise level until it reaches zero.

8. **Giving weight changes momentum**

The idea here is that convergence down the side of a large basin may be stopped cold by a small uphill climb that needed to be traversed before resuming downhill. Although annealing heuristic #8 could handle this difficulty, another technique is to add some momentum to the weight change. Then while cruising downhill, small uphills would be readily rolled over. This effect can be achieved by using the following equation for weight change :

$$\Delta w\ (t) \ = \ \beta_1 \varepsilon\ o \ + \ \beta_2\ \Delta w\ (t\text{-}1)$$

where $\beta_1 \varepsilon\ o$ is the original formula and $\beta_2 \Delta w\ (t\text{-}1)$ is the added momentum, a fraction of the weight adjustment used at the exposure prior to this one. β_1 and β_2 are fraction constants, such that $0<\beta_1<<1$ and $0<\beta_2<<1$.

The momentum heuristic serves as a stabilizer for a changing weight by bringing into each adjustment calculation a decaying history of that weight's earlier adjustments. Although this approach may aid the traversing across jagged error surfaces, its drawback is the potential for oscillation within steep, narrow basins.

F. ARCHITECTURAL VARIATIONS

Replace the standard series of rows with more localized modules, in such a manner that each output cell has its own collection of dedicated rows of PE's. (See fig 6.1)

If what the ANN needs to learn can be broken down into hierarchical stages, then try breaking the ANN into modules that would correspond to the different concepts that need to be trained. Training could then be accomplished one module at a time. (See fig 6.2)

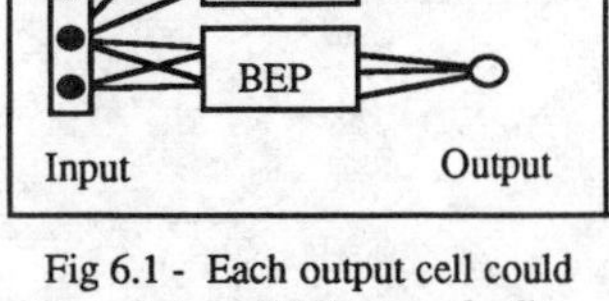

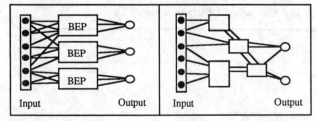

Fig 6.1 - Each output cell could have its own BEP array of cells

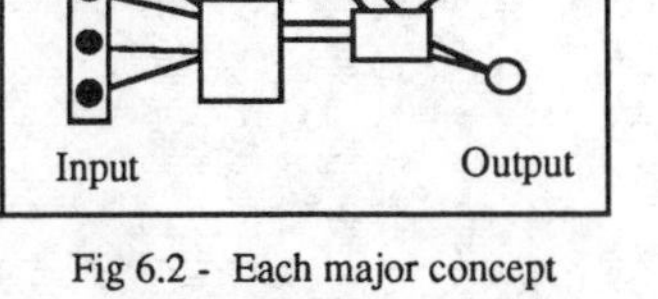

Fig 6.2 - Each major concept could be trained in a module

G. BEP VS. FUTURE ANN TRENDS

As mentioned in this paper's introduction, the interest in neural nets lie in their ability to emulate nonlinear system dynamics in such a way that it dissipates "energy" while settling into some steady state. If these states are labeled, then input data can be view as initial conditions for a system that would eventually rest at a labelled state and thus yield a labelled system output.

The BEP ANN, however, is slightly different in that convergence occurs during training for weight adjustments only, and not during its operational use as a pattern recognizer, when it is strictly a feedforward system. In a sense, after training, the BEP is "cast in stone" and remains static until retraining is again imposed by humans.

The future evolution of neural nets will probably not remain in this static mode for too long. Already, efforts towards more dynamic architectures have produced resonant models such as Kosko's BAM [7] and higher level system intra-action as found in Grossberg's ART. [4] But even these models may soon be overshadowed by newer concepts on the horizon[8]. These concepts integrate principles from many disciplines, including information theory, biophysics, game theory, non-linear dynamics, and neuropsychology.

For example, as a system converges, or simply moves about in its state space, the path of its sequential system states is called its TRAJECTORY. Although some trajectories spiral towards an attractor (the typical neural-net assumption), others may form a quasi-stable orbit about an attractor, or periodically hop around from one attractor to another (a limit cycle). Is there a relationship between the relative stability of limit cycles in complex nets and the apparent stability of simple circular reasoning, such as "A was angry because B occurred; B occurred because C didn't occur; and C didn't occur because A was angry." ?

Secondly, when a dynamic system's trajectory appears to unpredictably move from one orbit to another, it can be considered CHAOTIC. Such behavior can exhibit extreme sensitivity to initial conditions (input data) by quickly diverging into one orbit or the other. This effectively gives a system the ability to amplify a signal in order to discriminate and specialize [1], whereas absolute stability might help a system to associate and generalize (The popular application of neural nets) . A model which can alternate between these two modes on many hierarchical levels promises to possess the potential to build prototypes and allocate internal resources *as needed* in a supervised (directed error correcting) scenario. This would be quite useful for robust ANN pattern learning and recognition [6].

H. SUMMARY AND CONCLUSION

The Back Error Propagation model was reviewed and criticized. Although BEP can learn, there is no guarantee of performance since learning is dependent on initial conditions that should be random, as well as on the poor ability of least means square optimization to handle multiple minima with complex, time-varying, high order error surfaces. Nonetheless, BEP has had noteworthy experiments to attest to its pattern processing capability, and there exists a bag of heuristics to help it along. In the long term, BEP's static property may be its own undoing; but for the short term, its appeal leads me to conclude with the advice, *"caveat emptor."*

References

1. Crutchfield, Farmer, Packard & Shaw, "Chaos" , Scientific American, dec 86

2. Elman,J. & Zipser,D., "Learning the hidden structure of speech", ICS report 8701, Institute Cognitive Science, 1987, UC San Diego, La Jolla, CA 92093

3. Gorman,P. & Sejnowski,T., "Learned classification of sonar targets using a massively parallel network", Proc Workshop on Neural Network Devices and Applications, Feb 87, document JPL D4406, JPL, Pasadina, CA

4. Grossberg,S., "Competitive Learning : From Interactive Activation To Adaptive Resonance", Cognitive Science, v11, 1987

5. Hecht-Nielsen,R., "The Heartbeat Through An ANZA", HNC Networker, Nov 87, HNC Inc., San Diego, CA 92121

6. Jurik,M., This aspect of non-linear dynamics is currently under study at ESL, Sunnyvale, CA.

7. Kosko,B., "Competitive Adaptive Bidirectional Associative Memory", Proc. International Conference on Neural Networks, Jun 87, San Diego, CA

8. Nicolis,J., *Dynamics of Hierarchical Systems, an Evolutionary Approach*, Springer-Verlag, 1986

9. Parker,D., "Learning Logic", Invention report S81-64, File 1, Office of Technology Licensing, Stanford University, Oct 82. (copies available from the author)

10. Ransil,P., "Neural Models and Learning Rules", Proc. IEEE Compcon, Spring '88, San Francisco, (elsewhere in this proceedings)

11. Rumelhart,D.,Hinton,G.,&Williams,R., "Learning Internal Representation by Error Propagation", ICS report 8506, Institute Cognitive Science, 1985, UC San Diego, La Jolla, CA 92093

12. Sejnowski,T., & Rosenberg,C., "NETtalk, a Parallel Network that Learns to Read Aloud", EECS report 86-01, Biophysics Dept, Johns-Hopkins University, Baltimore MD, 21218

13. Wasserman,P., ANZA Research Corp., San Jose, CA , personal communication

14. Werbos,P., "Beyond Regression : New Tools for Prediction and Analysis in the Behavioral Sciences", thesis, Harvard University, Aug 74

15. Widrow,B. & Stearns,S., *Adaptive Signal Processing*, Prentice-Hall, 1985

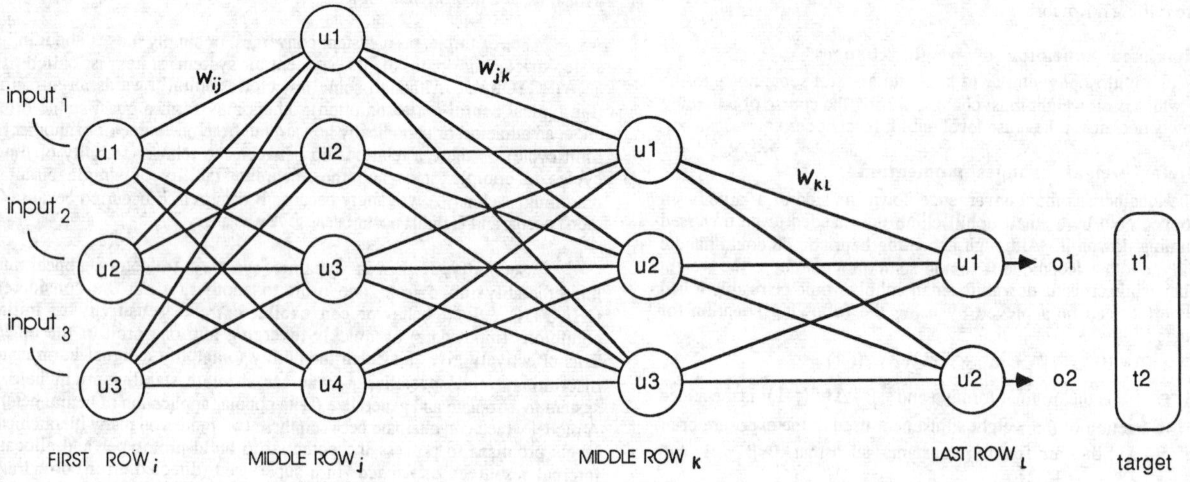

$o_i = \text{input}_i$

$u_j = (\Sigma_i w_{ij} o_i) + \text{bias}_j$ $o_j = F(u_j)$

$u_k = (\Sigma_j w_{jk} o_j) + \text{bias}_k$ $o_k = F(u_k)$

$u_l = (\Sigma_k w_{kl} o_k) + \text{bias}_l$ $o_l = F(u_l)$

$\varepsilon_j = F'(u_j)(\Sigma_k w_{jk} \varepsilon_k)$ $\varepsilon_k = F'(u_k)(\Sigma_l w_{kl} \varepsilon_l)$ $\varepsilon_l = F'(u_l)(t_l - o_l)$

$\Delta w_{ij} = \beta\, o_i\, \varepsilon_j$ $\Delta w_{jk} = \beta\, o_j\, \varepsilon_k$ $\Delta w_{kl} = \beta\, o_k\, \varepsilon_l$

$\Delta \text{bias}_j = \beta \varepsilon_j$ $\Delta \text{bias}_k = \beta \varepsilon_k$ $\Delta \text{bias}_l = \beta \varepsilon_l$

ε = proportional to $-\partial\text{Error} / \partial u$

β = a small constant, $0 < \beta << 1$

u = PE value before sigmoidal transformation

o = PE value after sigmoidal transformation

Δ = adjustment during training

F = sigmoidal transform

F' = first derivitive of F

w = link weight between two PE's

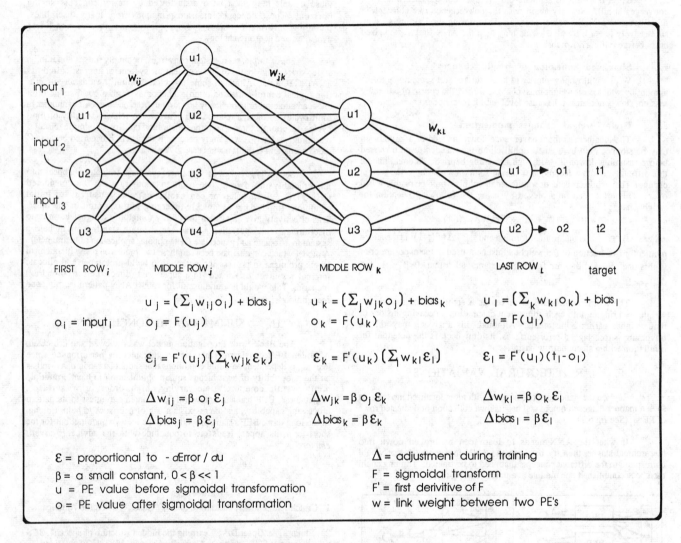

Fig - 7 A comprehensive view of PE linkage and the adjustment equations for cell weights and cell bias in a sample Back Error Propagation ANN.

Implementations of Neural Networks

Chair: F. Coury

A TEST VEHICLE FOR BRAITENBERG CONTROL STRUCTURES

Bruce R. Koball
Motion West
2210 Sixth Street
Berkeley, CA 94710

John H. Wharton
Applications Research
P.O. Box 2038
Sunnyvale, CA 94087

Abstract

This paper describes the implementation of model vehicles with neural network control systems based on Valentino Braitenberg's thought experiment. The vehicles provide a platform for experimentation with neural network functions in a novel format. Their operation is facilitated by the use of a commercially available neural network simulator to define the network for downloading to the vehicles.

Introduction

Several generations of researchers have been fascinated by the potential of networks of simple, interconnected processing units inspired by the model of biological nervous systems. While arguably imprecise, the term "neural network" has come to describe a wide variety of such computational models, some which strive for biological accuracy and others which are pursued as interesting alternatives to traditional computing paradigms.

Neuroanatomist Valentino Braitenberg[1] has proposed a series of thought experiments exploring the potential of these models and their implications regarding the evolution of real biological nervous systems. His experimental apparatus consists of hypothetical vehicles constructed of a number of simple components including sensors of various modalities (e.g. light, temperature, odor, etc.), a network of interconnected threshold units (i.e. units whose transfer function includes some threshold) and motors, controlled by the network, which propel the vehicles. Through a series of increasingly complex designs Braitenberg shows how these vehicles can exhibit behaviors which may be described in such high-level terms as "fear", "aggression" and "love," how they may be said to "evolve" new characteristics and capabilities, acquire "knowledge," have "ideas" and "foresight" and even display "egotism" and "optimism."

One advantage of the thought experiment as a tool is the ability to exceed the limitations imposed by current technology, and, in his more complex designs, that is indeed what Braitenberg has done. His simpler models, however, may be realized with existing technology and still offer interesting insights into the function and capabilities of neural networks.

We decided to attempt such an implementation. The motivations for this were several. The appeal of a small, mobile, autonomous entity scurrying about, behaving in perhaps unexpected ways, was obvious. The behavior of even simple networks can be surprisingly complex and difficult to analyze, so the ability to actually watch such a device function, interacting with its environment, can be instructive.

Sample Vehicles

Figure 1 illustrates some examples of simple Braitenberg vehicles. The vehicle in Figure 1a has two sensors at the front, each connected to the motor-driven wheel at the rear on the same side as the sensor. If the sensor-to-motor connections are excitatory, that is, if increasing sensor activation results in increasing motor activation, then it is easy to see that the vehicle will tend to turn away from a stimulus source to which the sensors respond. A vehicle close to a source will turn away rapidly, slowing down as sensor activation decreases with increasing distance from the source. Braitenberg says this vehicle appears to be "afraid" of the source.

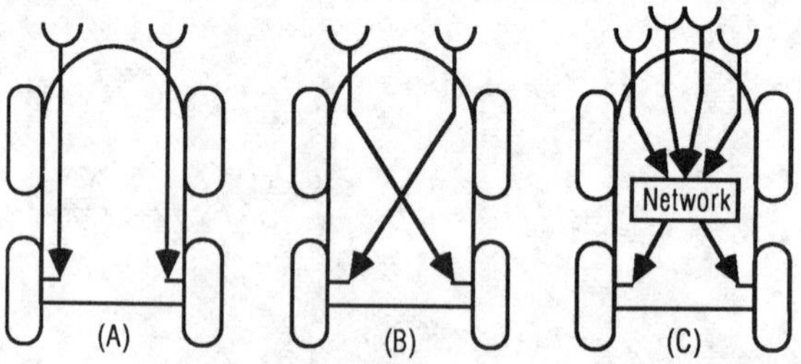

Figure 1. Simple vehicle examples

The vehicle in Figure 1b has each sensor connected to the motor on the opposite side. With excitatory connections this vehicle will tend to turn towards a source, its speed increasing the closer it gets. Braitenberg says this vehicle is showing "aggressive" behavior.

If we make the connections inhibitory, that is, increasing sensor activation results in decreasing motor activation, these two vehicles exhibit not quite opposite behaviors. For example, the vehicle in Figure 1a now turns towards a source but slows down as it approaches it. Braitenberg says this vehicle "loves" the source. Additional behavioral complexity may be added by making the transfer functions of the sensors and/or the motors nonlinear. Adding a threshold to the function is one simple way of doing this.

All these constructions, however, are familiar to designers of traditional control systems. It is with the vehicle in Figure 1c that we make a departure. This vehicle has a number of sensors, perhaps of different modalities, connected to a network of threshold units, which in turn are connected to

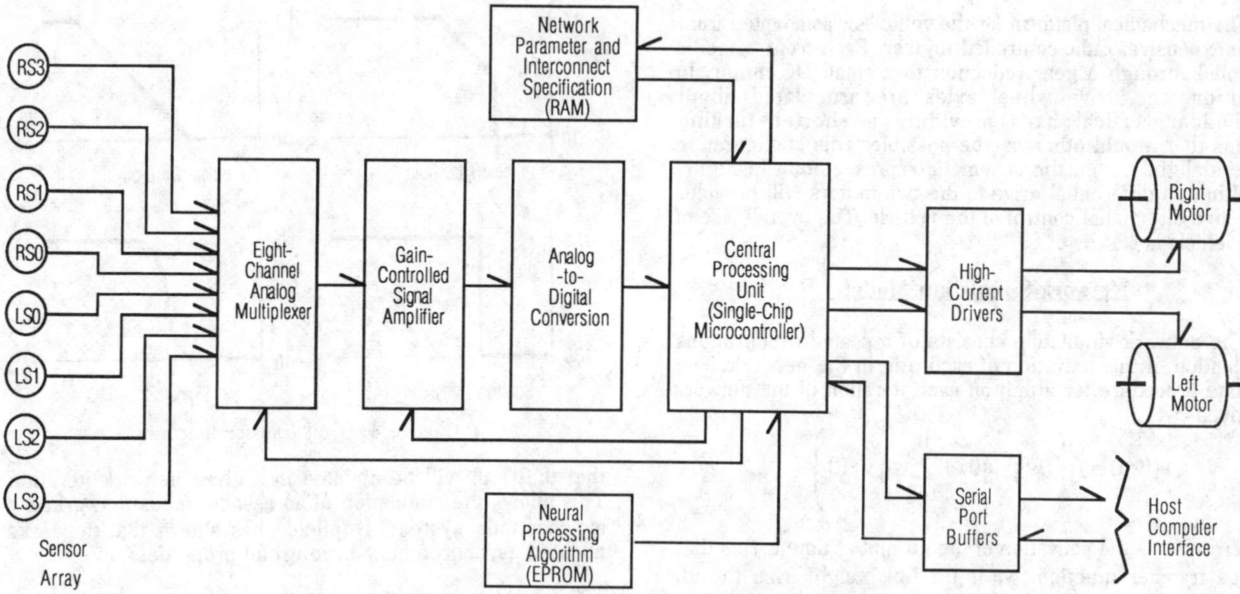

Figure 2. Braitenberg vehicle hardware block diagram

the motors. Within the network the threshold units are interconnected by excitatory and inhibitory links of differing weights. The topology of this network may be arbitrarily complex and it is from this complexity that interesting behaviors arise. Following the biological metaphor these units are analogous to neurons and the links to synapses. The operation of the individual units is simple. The activation of each unit is a function of the activation of the other units from which it has links and the weights of those links.

Hardware Implemention

The implementation of such a network may be approached in a number of ways. It would be possible, for example, to build individual units from op-amp integrators and comparators with discrete resistors determining the link weights. They might also be realized with digital logic as suggested by Dewdney[2]. In either case the interconnecting links would have to be hard-wired, perhaps using a sort of patchboard to provide some flexibility.

This approach has some obvious disadvantages. In general, the larger the network is, the more potential it has for exhibiting interesting behaviors. Unfortunately, adding units to such an implementation would increase its size and the interconnection patchboard would soon become unwieldly. Programming, revising and duplicating a large network patchboard would be tedious. Moreover, such a network would be necessarily static, unable to dynamically adjust its parameters during operation.

An alternate approach is to simulate the network using a microcomputer onboard the vehicle. Different network topologies may be easily defined and downloaded to the microcomputer. This method offers obvious advantages. The size is minimized and the patchboard is eliminated. The network could modify its own parameters in real time; it could "learn." In addition, since the network simulation model is defined in the microcomputer firmware it may be modified without changes to the hardware.

We decided to take the latter approach. The system block diagram is shown in Figure 2. The microcomputer used is a member of the Intel 8051 microcontroller family. The entire circuit is implemented on a 3" by 5" circuit board.

The sensor input consists of eight analog channels with provision for expansion to sixteen. Initially, all sensors were photodiodes, although sensors of other modalities may be used with the appropriate circuitry. One goal in the design of the front end was to accommodate sensory stimuli with a dynamic range of several orders of magnitude. A simple way to accomplish this would be to use sensors or amplifiers with logarithmic transfer functions. We opted, instead, to maintain an additional degree of flexibility and allow the microcomputer to control the gain of the sensor amplifier.

Each sensor is sampled by an analog multiplexer and its signal fed into the amplifier. The output of the amplifier is fed into an A/D converter. The microcomputer uses one of two selectable normalization algorithms, peak or averaging, to set the gain of the amplifier on each scan pass. The microcomputer reads the sensor activation values from the converter and uses them as inputs to the simulated network.

Those values, as well as other network parameters and interconnection specifications are stored in external RAM. The microcomputer's firmware is stored in an external EPROM. The network definition is down-loaded to the vehicle from a host computer via an RS-232c compatible serial port.

The activation output for each motor appears on the microcomputer's output pins in pulse frequency modulated form, and buffered by high current drivers for the motors. For a given motor, a pulse of constant width (approx. 8 ms) is output at intervals inversely proportional to that motor's activation. This drive scheme is effective in overcoming "stick-slip" friction in the mechanical system and provides good low-speed performance. The drive pulses are alternated between motors to minimize interaction and electrical noise..

Six 1.5 volt AA cells directly power the motors and a separate 9 volt unit supplies the analog and digital circuitry. Low power CMOS circuitry is used throughout to maximize battery life which exceeds eight hours of continuous use.

The mechanical platform for the vehicles was adapted from an inexpensive, radio-controlled toy car. Each front wheel is coupled through a gear reduction to a small DC motor. In addition, the drive wheel axles are articulated about individual vertical axes providing a shorter turning radius than would otherwise be possible. This configuration differs slightly from the schematic representation in Figure 1, although differential drive to the two motors still provides effective directional control of the vehicle. The overall size of the vehicle is 4.5" by 6".

Network Simulation Model

The network simulation consists of repeated synchronous evaluation of the activation of each unit in the network. The update procedure for a unit on each iteration of the network is given by:

$$\mu_j(t+1) = f_j\left((1-d_j)\,\mu_j(t) + \sum_{i=1}^{n} w_{ij}\,\mu_i(t)\right) \qquad (1)$$

where $\mu_j(t)$ is the activation of the jth unit at time t, f_j is that unit's transfer function, w_{ij} is the link weight from the ith unit to the jth unit (w = 0 for no link from i to j), d_j is the jth unit's decay parameter and n is the number of units in the network. The microcomputer firmware and onboard RAM can support up to 250 units with up to 3000 links. For the sake of execution speed fixed point math routines were used. Running at 12 MHz the system can perform approximately 30,000 link evaluations per second. For a fully connected network of 40 units (i.e. every unit connected to every other unit) a complete network update cycle would take approximately 50 ms.

```
BEGIN
I=10
L=LS0
T=+0.00000
D=+1.00000
A=+0.00000
C=0
R=+1.00000
F=1
NEXT
L=RS0
T=+0.00000
D=+1.00000
A=+0.00000
C=0
R=+1.00000
F=1
NEXT
L=LM
T=+0.00000
D=+1.00000
A=+0.00000
C=0
R=+1.00000
F=1
S=1
W=-0.500
S=2
W=+0.500
S=5
W=+0.100
NEXT
L=RM
T=+0.00000
D=+1.00000
A=+0.00000
C=0
R=+1.00000
F=1
S=1
W=+0.500
S=2
W=-0.500
S=5
W=+0.100
NEXT
T=+0.00000
D=+1.00000
A=+0.00000
C=1
R=+1.00000
F=1
END
```

Figure 3. Sample network definition file

Each unit in the vehicle's simulated network is characterized by a number of parameters which define its operation as well as the topology of the network. The simulation is initiated by downloading an ASCII network definition file containing this information to the vehicle via the serial interface. A sample network definition file is shown in Figure 3. The file consists of a list of tokens and values which define the following parameters:

Activation Value (A): Each unit has an activation value from 0.0 to 1.0 which is updated iteratively during the network simulation. The initial activation value for a unit in the down-loaded network definition is used by that unit in the first iteration of the network simulation.

Update Rate (R): There is an update rate parameter associated with each unit which determines the probability that that unit will be updated in a given network iteration. This allows the simulation of an asynchronous network in a synchronous system. Hopfield[3] has shown that networks updated asynchronously have useful properties.

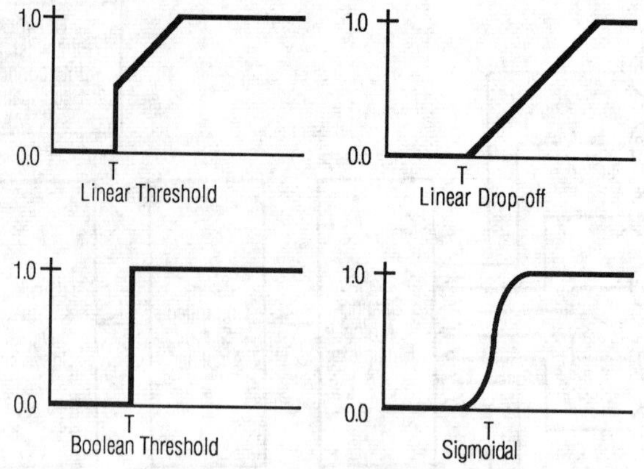

Figure 4. Unit transfer functions

Decay Value (D): Each unit has a decay value from 0.0 to 1.0. This value determines how much of a unit's previous activation is retained for the next iteration of the network. A decay value of 1.0 indicates that none of the previous activation is retained (i.e. activation in the next iteration is derived only from that unit's input links). A decay value of 0.0 indicates that all of a unit's previous activation is retained for the next iteration.

Transfer Function (F): Each unit may be assigned one of four transfer functions. For a given iteration, the sum of a unit's inputs and any previous activation is passed through this transfer function and the resulting value becomes that unit's output for the next iteration. The four available transfer functions are illustrated in Figure 4, where the horizontal axis is the sum of the inputs and the vertical axis is the activation output.

Threshold Value (T): A threshold value from 0.0 to 1.0 (T in Figure 4) is also associated with each unit's transfer function. Generally, on a given iteration, if the sum of the inputs to a unit plus any residual activation is less than this threshold, that unit's output will be zero for the next iteration (the sigmoid transfer function is an exception).

Unit Label (L): A label name may be assigned to each unit. The vehicle firmware recognizes certain label names for special handling. The labels LS0, LS1, LS2, LS3 and RS0, RS1, RS2, RS3 designate sensors in the left and right sensor arrays. Units with these labels take their activation from the sensor inputs and ignore any other input links. The labels LM and RM designate the left and right motors. The activation of a unit with one of these labels determine the speed of the respective motor.

Clamp Flag (C): Each unit also has an associated clamp flag. If this flag is true, it maintains the unit at its initial activation value regardless of any subsequent input changes. This is useful for providing "tonic" activation to specific units in the network.

Link Weight List: Each unit has a list of links from other units in the network and their associated weights. This list defines the network topology. The link parameter refers to the source unit (S) and is derived from the order in which that unit appears in the network definition file. The link weight

(W) may take values from -100.0 to +100.0 although -1.0 to +1.0 is the usual range.

Network Iteration Rate (I): A programmable delay from 0 to 500 ms allows the overall iteration rate for the network to be set.

The ASCII network definition file also contains tokens to mark the beginning and end of the file and the start of each unit in the network. The order in which a unit appears in the file is not significant to the operation of the network.

The network model implemented in the current firmware is similar to that used by MacBrain, a neural network simulator for Macintosh computers, created by Neuronics, Inc. of Cambridge, MA. MacBrain allows the user to create and edit networks on screen, load and save network definitions to disk, and run simulations of networks while observing the changing activation of the various network units.

These capabilities make MacBrain an ideal "development system" for the vehicles. A proposed network may be created, simulated, debugged, and saved to disk using MacBrain. The network definition file is then translated to the appropriate format and down-loaded to the vehicle using a special utility.

Sample Network Definitions

The network definition procedure and results can best be illustrated with some examples. In the following examples the interconnecting links are shown as arrows pointing in the direction of the flow of activation. The black arrows represent excitatory (positive weight) links and the grey arrows represent inhibitory (negative weight) links. For clarity, individual link weight values are not shown.

The network in Figure 5 is similar to the vehicle in Figure 1b. The eight units along the top of the figure are given labels (LS0, RS0, etc.) which define them as sensors, thus their activation is derived from the analog sensor inputs. At the bottom of the figure there are two units which have labels (LM, RM) defining them as motors. Their activation, therefore, determines motor speed.

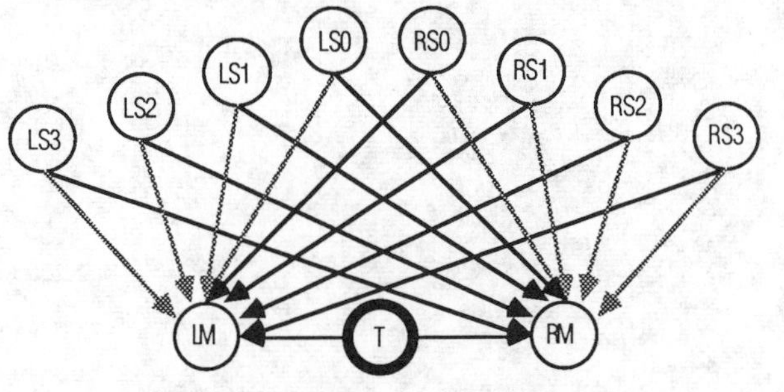

Figure 5. Moderated phototropic network

All the sensors make excitatory connections to the motor on the opposite side and inhibitory connections to the motor on the same side. In the case of photodiode sensors this results in light-seeking or "phototropic" behavior. This behavior is moderated, however, by the presence of both excitatory and inhibitory links so the vehicle will not tend to accelerate or decelerate as it approaches a light source.

The final unit, labeled T, is clamped to remain at some initial value as indicated by the bold outline. Its connections to the motor units provide a "tonic" activation level that assures that the vehicle will continue to move even in the absence of light.

The network represented in Figure 6 was designed to exhibit more complex behavior. Some simplifications have been made for clarity. Only two of the sensors, RS0 and LS0, are shown, although all eight could be used. They are connected to a "hidden layer" of units labeled H1 through H4 which are, in turn, connected to the motor units.

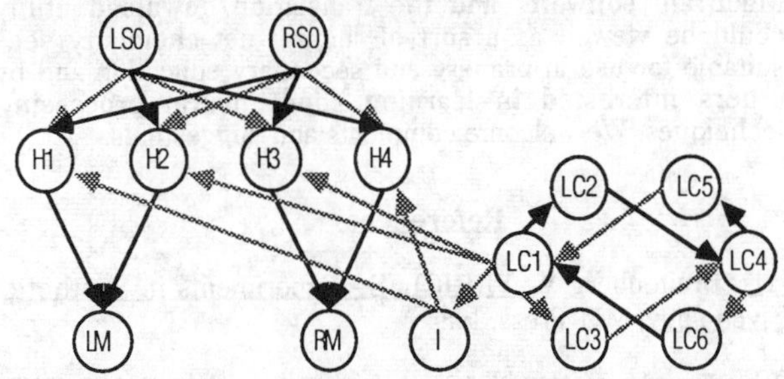

Figure 6. Alternating phototropic/photophobic network

The left sensor makes excitatory connections to units H2 and H4 and inhibitory connections to units H1 and H3. The right sensor is connected in a complementary fashion. It can be seen that the activation of units H1 and H4 would produce phototropic behavior if they were motor outputs while H2 and H3 would produce light-avoiding or "photophobic" behavior.

The array of six units at the right of the figure will produce a continuously repeating pattern of activation. This type of network behavior is called a "limit cycle" and is useful in developing behavioral "clocks." In this case, the activation of unit LC1 will rise to a maximum value, remain there for a period and then fall to a minimum, remaining there for a period until the cycle repeats. The period is set by the link weights in the limit cycle generator. Unit LC1 also makes an inhibitory connection to a unit, labeled I, whose activation is the inversion of LC1 (i.e. when LC1 is maximum, I is minimum).

Finally these two units make inhibitory links to pairs of hidden layer units, LC1 to H2,H3 and I to H1,H4. As the limit cycle progresses these links alternately inhibit the H1, H4 and H2, H3 pairs. The resulting action of a vehicle with this network is to alternate between phototropic and photophobic behaviors on a period determined by the limit cycle. Not shown in the figure are clamped units providing tonic activation to the motors, to the I unit, and to the limit cycle generator.

Further Work

One area of potential interest not addressed in initial version of the vehicle's network simulation model was the dynamic alteration of network parameters during operation based on sensory input and network activation. While any of the network's parameters could be changed in this manner, the most likely candidate would be the link weights. The alteration of link weights based on some criteria is a widely used model for "learning" in neural network experimentation and, indeed, is thought to be part of the mechanism of learning and memory in real biological nervous systems. MacBrain (Ver. 1.10)[4] has the capability of defining "modulation links", links between units and other links (instead of unit to unit) which can modulate the weight of the target link based on the activation of the source unit. Efforts towards adding this and other learning functions to the vehicle's network simulation model are underway.

Conclusion

We undertook this project out of interest in Braitenberg's models and neural networks in general. We found the vehicles to be reasonable platforms for experimentation with network functions. The combination of the vehicles, the MacBrain software, and the translation/download utility could be viewed as a sort of "neural net chemistry set," suitable for use in primary and secondary education and by others interested in learning about neural processing techniques. We welcome comments and suggestions.

References

[1] Braitenberg V., VEHICLES - Experiments in Synthetic Psychology, MIT Press, 1984.

[2] Dewdney A. K., "Computer Recreations," Scientific American, Vol.256, No.3, March 1987, pp. 16 - 24.

[3] Hopfield J. J., "Neural netwotks and physical systems with emergent collective computational abilities," Proc. Natl. Acad. Sci. USA, Vol. 79, pp. 2554 - 2558, April 1982.

[4] MacBrain Users Manual, Neuronics, Cambridge, MA, 1987.

[5] Lippmann R. P., "An Introduction to Computing with Neural Nets," IEEE ASSP Magazine, April 1987, pp. 4 - 22

[6] Hopfield J. J., Tank D. W., "Computing with Neural Circuits: A Model," Science, Vol. 233, 8 August 1987, pp. 625 - 633.

[7] Rumelhart D. E., McClelland J. L., Parallel Distributed Processing: Explorations in the Microstructures of Cognition, Vol. 1 and 2, MIT Press, 1986.

[8] Hoppensteadt F. C., An introduction to the mathematics of neurons, Cambridge University Press, 1986.

EXPERIMENTS IN TRANSLATING CHINESE CHARACTERS USING BACKPROPOGATION

Philip D. Wasserman

Anza Research Inc.
Cupertino, CA 95014

Abstract

An artificial neural network was trained to translate the Chinese characters representing numerals into their Arabic numeral equivalents. Pre-processing of the characters was minimized in an effort to test the network's ability to produce its own internal representations from a large input set. A modified backpropogation algorithm was used which incorporates several heuristics to reduce convergence time and avoid common training problems.

1. Introduction

Pattern recognition has proven difficult to implement on conventional computers. Tasks performed easily by a five-year-old child are often intractable for the most powerful hardware and sophisticated algorithms. Even relatively simple applications are expensive to implement using conventional computational methods, and frequently produce marginally acceptable results. Artificial neural networks have been shown to overcome many of these limitations. They are trained rather than programmed, learning much as a human does by repeated presentation of examples. Thus, there is no need for a programmer to understand the characteristics of the patterns and develop algorithms to detect them; the network develops its own internal representations during the training process. Also, they have the ability to generalize, a human-like capability which permits them to produce correct results despite distorted, incomplete, or noisy inputs.

Computer recognition of handwritten characters has long been an objective. Recently, impressive results have been reported by Burr[1,2,3]. The accuracy realized is adequate for certain applications, and could form the basis for commercial products.

In the design of systems to recognize handwritten characters, Burr has done considerable pre-processing to produce a compact representation. For example, he describes a system in which the character is represented by thirteen numbers obtained by projecting the segmented character onto an array of thirteen oriented bars. These thirteen numbers are then applied as inputs to the neural network. This compact representation reduces both training time and the computation needed for character recognition, compared with simply presenting the character as an image composed of hundreds of pixels.

Such pre-processing requires substantial computation and somewhat defeats the purpose of using an artificial neural network to do the classification. Thus, it seems desirable to use the network itself to construct the necessary compact internal representations. To overcome the massive computation associated with large input patterns, various heuristics were developed which significantly reduced training time. Those methods were then employed to train the network to recognize the Chinese characters representing the numerals 0 through 9, plus the characters for 10, 100, 1000, 10,000, 100,000,000, and 100,000,000,000. These characters are combined to form the full range of possible numbers in a manner reminiscent of Roman numerals.

These characters were chosen to explore the potential for Chinese-to-English character translation, an application of substantial practical interest. In order to start with a problem of reasonable size, the set was restricted to numerals. These are among the simpler characters, yet embody many of the properties of the full character set.

2. System Configuration

As shown in Figure 1, each character was written on a 13 by 17 array of "pixels." Each pixel with a line passing through it was weighted as a one, all others were weighted as zero. This simple representation was deliberately chosen to test the ability of the algorithm to operate without pre-processing.

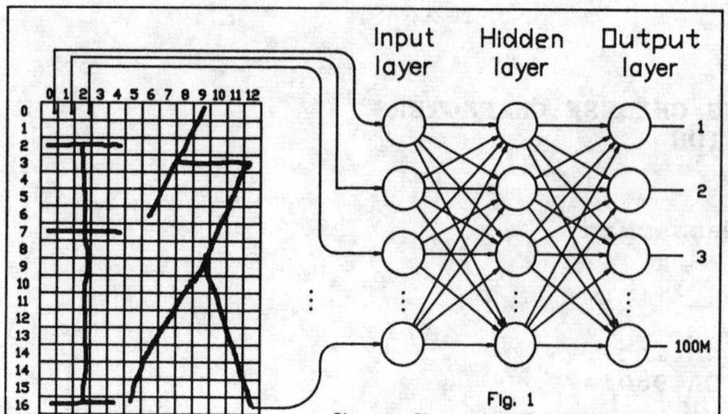

Fig. 1
Chinese Character Translation System

The 221 pixel inputs were applied to the first layer of the network where they fanned out through weighted connections in a fully connected pattern to 20 units in the hidden layer. These were then fully connected to 16 units in the output layer, each of which represents a single Arabic numeral. The number of units in the hidden layer was selected based on experience, and other choices may prove superior.

3. Training Set

Ten handwritten sets of the 16 Chinese numerals shown in Figure 2 were collected. Five sets were used for training; the others served as the naive set for evaluation of the trained network's ability to generalize, by producing correct answers despite minor variations in character formation. The patterns were adjusted to fill the array, both vertically and horizontally.

The outputs of the network were 16 real numbers, with one output trained to a level of +.8 for each input pattern, and all other outputs trained to -.8. The output having a level closest to +.8 was chosen as the "winner", indicating the corresponding Arabic numeral.

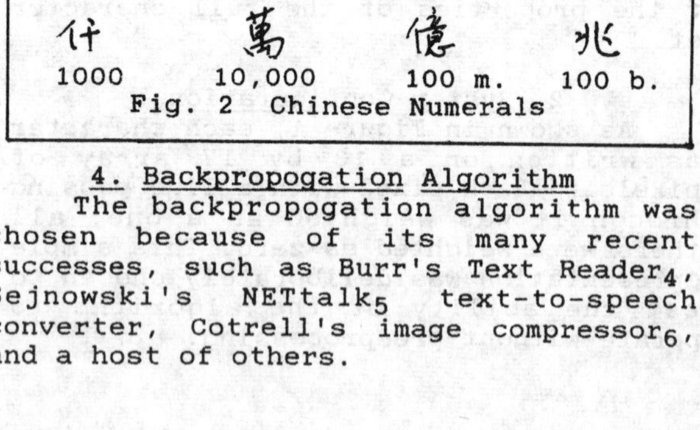

Fig. 2 Chinese Numerals

4. Backpropogation Algorithm

The backpropogation algorithm was chosen because of its many recent successes, such as Burr's Text Reader[4], Sejnowski's NETtalk[5] text-to-speech converter, Cotrell's image compressor[6], and a host of others.

Despite its demonstrated power and flexibility, the basic backpropogation training algorithm described by Werbos[7], Parker[8] and Rumelhart[9] exhibits a number of application dependent problems. To alleviate these, several heuristic modifications have been made which show promise in improving the predictability and speed of the training algorithm.

Training Time

The backpropogation algorithm is subject to long, unpredictable training times. Days and even weeks have been spent training networks without achieving convergence. In fact, there is no proof that a network will ever converge with a finite step size.

Parker[10] has proposed a second order backpropogation algorithm which speeds convergence in certain cases. Its benefits vary greatly from problem to problem, a characteristic typical of various attempts to improve the backpropogation algorithm.

The convergence proof presented by Rumelhart[11] assumes an infinitesimal step size. Since this implies an infinite convergence time, a finite step size must be employed. In general, a large step size will accelerate convergence, but if it is excessive, continuous oscillations, divergence, or paralysis (explained below) will result.

Unfortunately, there is no way to determine the optimal step size a priori. The maximum permissible step size is unpredictable and problem dependent. A step size which results in rapid convergence for one problem can cause a convergence failure for another which is superficially similar. Also, each time a training session is started, the weights are set to random values. A step size which is optimal for one set of initial values may not allow the network to converge with another set, even on the same problem.

Even more disconcerting, on some problems, the backpropogation algorithm has been observed to progress through a minimum of the objective function and then proceed to depart from that solution. This again appears to be a result of an excessive step size.

Adaptive Step Size Algorithm

From the preceding discussion it may be seen the step size selection is a critical factor in achieving convergence. What is less obvious is that the optimal step size changes during the course of the training process. To demonstrate this, an adaptive step size algorithm was developed. The program observes the progress of the adaptation process, and adjusts the step size in a direction which improves the convergence rate without causing instability.

To implement the algorithm, the mean

square error is calculated for the output neurons over the entire training set. If this error is equal to or less than that calculated for the previous pass through the training set, the step size is increased by a factor proportional to the improvement. If the error is worse, the step size is reduced, again by a factor proportional to the change in the error. In this way, a network which is training successfully is allowed to do so more rapidly; whereas, one which is not improving takes smaller steps.

The algorithm has been tested on a number of problems and generally achieves more rapid, consistent training times. The frequency of outright failures to converge was substantially reduced and less human judgment and monitoring is required during the training process.

Step Error Correction

The backpropagation algorithm propogates errors from the output layer to the lower layers. The weights associated with a layer are adjusted based upon these errors and the outputs of the previous layer. Because of the indirect nature of this process, these adjustments can be in error, slowing convergence or actually untraining a network in some cases.

To prevent this, an algorithm was tested which applies each training vector twice. On the first application the squared error is summed over the output neurons and the weights are adjusted. On the next application, the error is recomputed and compared with the previous error. If it is worse, the previous weight adjustment is removed. If it is better, an additional weight adjustment is made, assuming that further progress in the same direction is probably desirable.

This process is analogous to the way that a human would search a dark space for a low area when only the local slope is known. If a step in a direction which is downward where one stands produces an increase, one would step back to the original postition. If a decrease results, an additional step in the same direction would be taken.

If the step size is small, errors are infrequent but training becomes long. This algorithm allows larger steps to be taken, and hence, reduces training times on many problems.

Network Paralysis

The backpropogation algorithm is capable of entering a state where all of the output neurons are fixed near one extreme or another. A network in this condition may never recover despite the large values of error which result. Generally, this condition may be avoided if the step size is made small enough. Unfortunately, reducing the step size in a network which has entered the paralytic state may not permit it to converge. Under these conditions the only remedy is to start over with a smaller step size, an unfortunate alternative if days have been spent in a training session.

A solution has been studied which alleviates the problem by detecting the onset of paralysis and automatically reducing the step size. The numbers in parentheses represent typical values for the coefficients. In operation, the outputs of the neurons are examined after training on each input pattern. If more than k (1.0) percent of the neurons have outputs with magnitude greater than m (.9), the step size is reduced by multiplying it by a factor r (.8). Note that The algorithm operates on the results for each pattern, rather than over the composite of the set of input patterns. It has been found that rapid detection of the paralysis condition and subsequent step size reduction is essential if the problem is to be avoided. The anti-paralysis algorithm has been applied to a number of problems and the frequency of paralysis has been substantially reduced.

Local Minima

The backpropagation algorithm adjusts the network weights to minimize the error. There is, however, no guarantee that it will find the lowest minimum. It may become trapped in a shallow dip when there is a deep valley nearby.

In fact, this is seldom a practical problem, as in a complex network one minimum is about as low as another. Also, the finite step size seems to introduce a randomizing process which enhances the probability of finding a global minimum.

6. Results

Three separate networks were trained. The networks converged over the training set in an average of 105 iterations using a step size of .05. The program's momentum term was best set to zero in this case. Convergence was defined as a mean square error over the training set of less than .03. There were no errors in categorizing the characters in the training set.

On the naive set, accuracy averaged 84%. It is felt that a larger training set would improve the ability of the network to generalize, thereby reducing the errors over the naive set.

No major differences were noted among the results from the three training sessions. Starting from different random values of the weight variables, the worst session produced errors on the naive set only 5% more often than the best, a result which suggests that a global minimum may not help.

7. Conclusions

It has been demonstrated that artificial neural networks using the backpropogation training algorithm can learn a complex training set without extensive pre-processing. Learning time can be reduced and the probability of convergence increased through the use of heuristic methods. Accuracy of the result is encouraging and can probably be improved. Training times are acceptable without extensive pre-processing.

Acknowledgement

The author would like to thank Jiahn-Fei Lue, Jia-Wei Jang, and Juliet Lefevre for their contributions.

References

1. D. J. Burr, "Experiments with a Connectionist Text Reader," Proc. of the 1st Int'l Conf. on Neural Networks, San Diego, CA, June 1987.

2. D. J. Burr, "A Neural Network Digit Recognizer," Proc. of IEEE Conf. on Systems, Man and Cybernetics, pp. 1621-1625 Atlanta, GA, 1986.

3. D. J. Burr, "Designing a Handwriting Reader," IEEE Trans. on Pattern Analysis and Machine Intelligence, Vol. PAMI-5 No. 5, pp. 554-559, Sept. 1983.

4. Ibid 1.

5. T. J. Sejnowski, "Parallel Networks that Learn to Pronounce English Text," Complex Systems 1, pp.145-168, 1987

6. G. W. Cottrell, P. Munro, D. Zipser, Advances in Cognitive Science (Vol. 3), N. E. Sharkey (Ed.), Norwood NJ: Ablex.

7. Paul J. Werbos, "Beyond Regression: New Tools for Prediction and Analysis in the Behavioral Sciences," thesis in applied mathematics, Harvard University, Aug. 1974.

8. David B. Parker, "Learning-Logic," Invention Report, S81-64, File 1, Office of Technology Licensing, Stanford University, October, 1982.

9. D. E. Rumelhart, G. E. Hinton, and R. J. Williams, "Learning Internal Representations by Error Propagation," Parallel Distributed Processing, Vol. 1, p.330, Cambridge Mass: MIT Press, 1986.

10. David B. Parker, "Second Order Back Propagation: Implementing an Optimal O(n) Approximation to Newton's Method as an Artificial Neural Network," Computer, Sept.,1987.

11. Ibid 9, p.325.

12. N. Metropolis, A. W. Rosenbluth, M. N. Rosenbluth, and A. H. Teller, "Equation of State Calculations in Fast Computing Machines," Journal of Chemical Physics, Vol. 21, No. 6, 1953.

13. S. Kirkpatrick, C. D. Gelatt,Jr., M. P. Vecchi, "Optimization by Simulated Annealing," Science, Vol. 220, Number 4598, May 1983.

14. H. H. Szu, R. L. Hartley, "Nonconvex Optimization by Fast Simulated Annealing," Proc. IEEE, September 1987.

MACHINE EMOTION

Raymond Scanlon and Mark Johnson

US Army Armament Research, Development, and Engineering Center
Benet Laboratories
Watervliet, NY 12189-4050

ABSTRACT

A feeling-thinking machine has been designed using the mammalian brain as a model and current psychobiology concepts as a guide. The machine has been successfully run as a computer simulation. It mimics a primitive organism with eight functional brain centers. They are the reticular ascending substance (RAS), the amygdala, the cingulate gyrus, the medial forebrain bundle, the hippocampus, thalamus, hypothalamus, and the neocortex.

INTRODUCTION

Machine intelligence for autonomous systems must be capable of learning and especially thinking, if we are to go beyond the 'islands of autonomy' presently envisioned for teleoperated and remotely piloted vehicles. One approach is to use the mammalian brain as a model and investigate the possibility of duplicating its functions in electronic circuitry. This extension of neural network design is called non-living intelligence (NLI).

The brain consists of approximately 10**12 neurons intricately interconnected. Only a small part of this circuitry has been unravelled. The NLI effort at Benet Laboratories does not describe how the brain works, but involves electronic and computational experiments that provide insight into how the brain might work. We pursue NLI through the design and construction of feeling-thinking machines. Feeling is essential because without motivation, there is nothing. The machine must want to do things. In doing things, it will learn; and having learned, it will think. This report does not describe machines that "exhibit intelligent behavior"; but rather machines that feel, want, and think. The distant goal is to create a machine that thinks and acts like a man. This report discusses the first of a series of feeling-thinking machine designs.

THE MODEL

Our approach to designing this machine is to simulate a primitive organism which must survive within a contrived universe. We have given it the name "Pacrat". Pacrat's brain has eight brain centers. The electrical activity of these neural centers is not modeled, only the functional relationships. From these interactions arises a sophisticated structure which rests upon the anatomy of Pacrat's brain. The neural centers modeled are: the reticular ascending substance (RAS), the thalamus, the hypothalamus, the amygdala, the cingulate gyrus, the medial forebrain bundle, the hippocampus, and the isocortex.[1]

Individual neural response is not simulated, only the activity of assemblages of neurons called codons. A codon is the result or record of an experience. It exists as the altered synapses between the neurons which constitute the assemblage.[2,3]

Pacrat, in diagrammatic form, is shown in Figure 1. It shows that he has been provided with the ability to get about in his universe through four motor neurons. These are driven by the motor area of the isocortex as a final result of sensory input, channeled to the isocortex under the control of the thalamus, and filtered through the isocortex under the influence of the prevailing emotion.

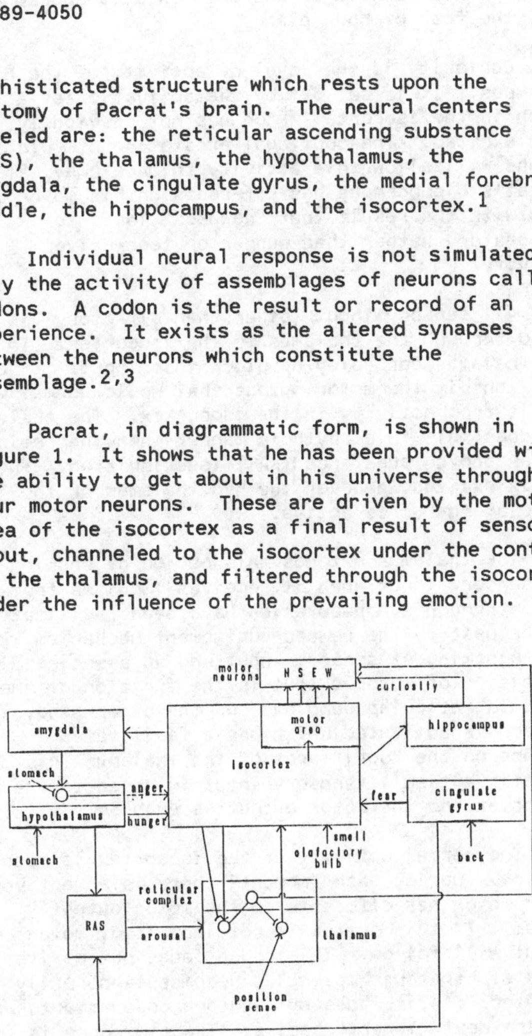

Figure 1. Anatomy of Pacrat.

Hunger is the level of neural activity in an area of the hypothalamus which we will call the hunger center.[4] The model assumes there are sensory neurons lining the stomach wall that respond to expansions and contractions of the stomach. These determine the level of activity of the hunger center. As the stomach empties, the hunger center becomes more active: as the stomach fills, it becomes less active.

Anger is also a level of neural activity in an area of the hypothalamus, but in this case the cause is the activation of certain codons in the isocortex as mediated through the amygdala. When this area is active, Pacrat experiences some level of anger or frustration. The activity in the amygdala is quickly inhibited by eating.[5,6]

Fear is the level of activity of the cingulate gyrus. This activity is, subjectively, unease escalating to terror. In Pacrat, it is assumed that sensory neurons excite the cingulate gyrus whenever his back is uncovered. This is agoraphobia, the fear of open places.

Curiosity is the level of activity of the hippocampus. It is set off by the activation of a codon in the isocortex which has not previously been excited. The continual excitation of "old" codons will allow this activity to fade away. Pacrat's hippocampus has efferents on his motor area with the result that "newness" leads to exploratory rather than hunger or fear-driven activity.

All sensory input (other than olfactory) is gated through the thalamus to the isocortex. Thus the thalamus can relay or block this input. It can also inhibit the motor output that would normally result from activity in the isocortex. The thalamus does this in a rhythmic manner when the reticular ascending substance (RAS) is stimulated. The RAS is excited whenever the hypothalamus or the cingulate gyrus is active.

The thalamus extends this period of choking off sensory input when it receives impulses from a codon through synapses which have been facilitated in the past by the reward-punishment mechanism. This blocking of sensory input and an associated inhibition of motor output is the function of the thalamic reticular complex. On the other hand, if a codon is activated which has a facilitated synapse on the "goal" area of the thalamus (cf. akinetic mutism[7]), sensory input is gated to the isocortex and the motor output is enabled.

The normal activity of the isocortex is association. During each "moment" there is an active codon which has efferents on the motor output system. If this system is not inhibited, motor output will follow. This codon fades out as its store of strategic molecules becomes temporarily depleted. As it fades out another codon starts up and the next "moment" begins. The new codon is determined by the sensory input (if not blocked), the previously excited codon, and the current dominant emotion.

A reward-punishment mechanism is started up by the medial forebrain bundle whenever activity in the hypothalamus or cingulate gyrus is reduced. The role of this mechanism is to facilitate all recently fired synapses.[6]

THE IMPLEMENTATION

Pacrat exists in a contrived universe: a very simple universe which is seen as partitioned by a rectangular grid (Figure 2). At each location in the grid one of Pacrat's sensory neurons, unique to that location, becomes active. This gives him a location sense. At genesis he does not know where one location is relative to another, but he does know that he is where he is. He has also been given the ability to sense his own trail, and has a general adversion to going where he has recently been. Again, the individual activity of the sensory neurons is not simulated, only the relationship with other active neurons. His burrow (or starting point) is always at row 11, column 1. This is indicated by shading that cell. Pacrat's current location is given by highlighting the cell he is in.[8,9]

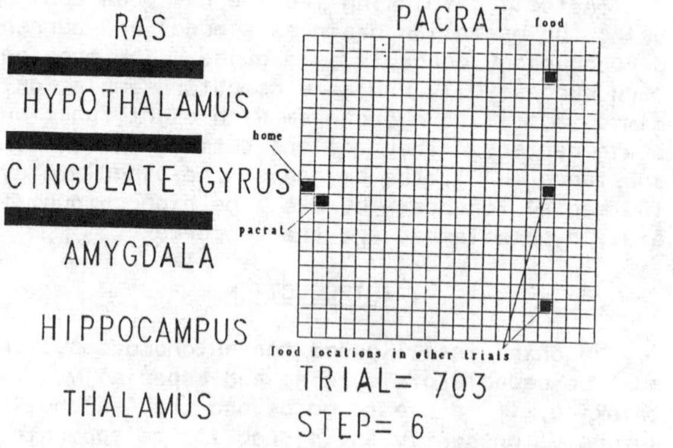

Figure 2. Pacrat.

One codon is active at any time and this represents a 'moment' in Pacrat's life. This codon is excited by current sensory input to the isocortex plus the previously excited codon and the prevailing emotion. The inputs are the location sense, which is gated through the thalamus (Figure 1), smell, and the axonal bundles from the hypothalamus, and cingulate gyrus. A codon in the simulation is simply a vector of scalars representing the current sensory input (if any), normalized synaptic weights to the four motor neurons, associative connections to other codons, dominant emotion, and synaptic weights to the amygdala, thalamus, and hippocampus.[10]

Pacrat's motivation is hunger and fear. When awake, Pacrat is forced to move by one or the other, or else he just goes to sleep as the RAS quiets down.[4] Initially this drive is hunger. In the simulation, the distension of the stomach is represented by a scalar. This number continually decreases unless Pacrat is at a food spot and is eating. When this number is low enough, the hypothalamus responds (again a scalar) and the RAS is excited. Pacrat wakes up. He is forced to explore his universe for food to satisfy hunger. Food is placed randomly in one of three locations. The three potential food spots are highlighted on the right side of the grid, with food located in one of the cells. When he reaches a food spot, he eats, his stomach fills up, and the activity in the hypothalamus is significantly reduced. This is simulated by simply increasing the number corresponding to distension of the stomach which is sensed by the neurons lining the stomach wall. These neurons have efferents to the hypothalamus.

Pacrat can move north, south, east, and west within the boundaries of his universe. Motor neurons drive Pacrat in one of these directions one cell at a time. Each active codon in the isocortex has efferents on each of these motor neurons and the relative effectiveness of these efferents determines the direction of travel. At the outset, i.e., trial 1, there is no preferred direction of movement. The synaptic weights from any given codon to the motor neurons are identical. Pacrat moves about his universe randomly until food is found. When it is, a reward mechanism is activated through the medial forebrain bundle which facilitates all recently fired synapses. This is learning and will generate a preferred direction of movement when similar codons are active in the future. The vectors representing codons are changed so that elements corresponding to synaptic connections between simultaneously active neurons are increased. Facilitation is proportionally lower for codons active earlier in time.

After hunger is satiated and the level of activity of the hypothalamus reduced, fear is no longer masked by hunger. Fear keeps the activity of the RAS high. An active cingulate gyrus drives Pacrat back to his burrow. Again, if this is the first trial, there is no preferred direction, but the codons which are activated are those associated with fear rather than hunger. The neurons in the cingulate gyrus, not the hypothalamus, excite neurons in the isocortex. When his burrow is reached, Pacrat's back is covered. The activity of the cingulate gyrus is abruptly decreased. The reward mechanism is again activated through the medial forebrain bundle and recently fired synapses are facilitated. This will generate biased movement in the future if these codons are active. Henceforth, at any cell in the grid, he will tend to go in a direction depending on which neurons are active in the brain centers. An active hypothalamus may move him east, an active cingulate gyrus with the same sensory input may drive him north.

During epigenisis, Pacrat learns to survive. Randomness forces Pacrat out of obsessive behavior patterns. Although a reward mechanism may increase synaptic strength between a codon and a given motor neuron, there is always a chance Pacrat will move in a different direction. A built-in random element raises the level of activity of motor neurons with a lower synaptic weight to the currently active codon. An active hippocampus increases the effect of this random element. If this were not present, Pacrat would not survive. Once food were found, he would follow the same path again and again. However, as the synaptic strength between a codon and motor neuron is increased, it becomes more and more difficult for Pacrat to alter his behavior. He will continue searching for food in locations where it does not exist. To resolve this we have given Pacrat an amygdala. An active amygdala mediates anger. Excited neurons in the amygdala generate unique active codons in the isocortex. Figure 1 shows the role of the amygdala in Pacrat. When the reward mechanism is active, all recently fired synapses are facilitated through the medial forebrain bundle. These include synapses from the active codon in the isortex to the amygdala. Therefore, if this same codon is excited in future trials, the amygdala also becomes highly active. This high level of activity excites a region in the hypothalamus associated with anger or frustration. Unless there is a concurrent good experience, such as eating, which will inhibit the amygdala; Pacrat will become angry. In other words, he gets mad when food is not where it is supposed to be. This anger quickly drives Pacrat out of the vicinity of a food spot by exciting different codons in the isocortex. These codons do not have synaptic weights to the motor area that favor any given direction. He is effectively 'bounced' randomly to neighboring locations in the grid. Without the amygdala, Pacrat would keep looking for food in the same spot almost indefinitely. The level of activity in the hypothalamus is far greater than that of the hippocampus. When he is starving, he doesn't get bored.

The effect of the rhythmic action of the thalamus is that a moment (active codon n) that generates motor output is followed by several moments (active codons n+1, n+2,...) with motor output inhibited. This is the first of three forms that thinking takes. The sensory input is temporarily blocked, motor output inhibited, and associated codons in the isocortex are turned on. This form of thinking is implemented in Pacrat as he effectively evaluates the consequences of his last move.

A second form of thinking comes about when an excited thalamus results in an extended period of blocking of sensory input. Again, the normal state in the isocortex is association so codons continue to fade in and out. If the chain of associating codons reaches a codon with inhibitory efferents on the thalamus, activity of neurons in the reticular complex is reduced. The blocking cycle of sensory input is reduced to a minimum and Pacrat proceeds to move with intent. This form of thinking is recognition. It is initiated when Pacrat moves to an area of particular interest to him on the grid. This is a location where synapses from the isocortex to the thalamus have been facilitated from previous rewards.

A third form of thinking comes about when the extended period of blocked sensory input and inhibited motor output results in slightly different associated codon chains. This can occur because of the inherent randomness of neural actions. If one of these chains results in activating a codon quicker than recent paths have done, the neurons of this codon are in a different state of molecular depletion. It has had less time to recover from the last activation. It comes on with a burble which is transmitted to the reward system, and recently fired synapses are facilitated. This is insight and is the basic mechanism of rational thought. Pacrat has demonstrated this by "thinking" of more efficient paths to food.

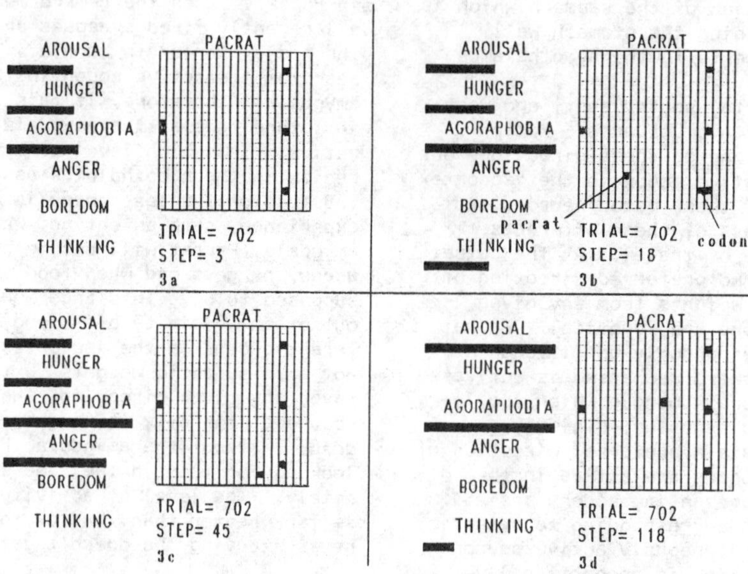

Figure 3. Snapshots of Dynamic Graphics Display.

TRIAL RUN

Figure 3 shows four static displays of a typical trial run of the simulation. Figures 3a through 3d are snapshots in trial 702. The activity of the brain centers is given by a bar chart on the left side of the display. The larger the bar, the more active that area of the brain. Even number trials (i.e., 702) display the effect of a particular neural center (i.e., hunger, anger), while odd number trials (i.e., 703) give the name of the center. The number of steps indicate the sequence of each snapshot in the trial.

In Figure 3a Pacrat has just left his burrow, the starting point. The activity of the hypothalamus was high enough to activate the RAS and wake him up. Figures 3a through 3c show Pacrat driven by hunger. Through epigenisis, which is his previous 701 trials, he has learned. Figure 3b shows Pacrat with his motor output inhibited by the thalamus. This is shown by freezing him at his current location and dynamically displaying his codon association chain. The reward cell for this trial is in the middle of the three possible food locations (row 11, column 18). From past experience, food has been known to be located in the last reward cell (row 19, column 18). Pacrat's codon chain eventually associates to this location and facilitated synapses from the isocortex stop the thalamus from blocking sensory input and inhibiting the motor area. His motor output is no longer inhibited. Figure 3c shows the active amygdala when food is not found where it was expected.

His frustration forces him out of the vicinity of the empty food cell and eventually he locates the food. Figure 3d shows Pacrat moving with intent back to his burrow, driven by fear. The activity in the thalamus (thinking) indicates it has been inhibited from blocking sensory input and from inhibiting motor output. This is a result of recognition resulting in strong inhibitory input from the isocortex.

IMPLEMENTING PACRAT AS A NEURAL NET

A simplified version of Pacrat has been implemented using only simulated neurons, formal definitions of neural activity, and synaptic facilitation. Neural activity is modeled using PID (proportional-integral-differential) control. The governing equations for cell activity and synaptic facilitation are given in Figure 4. Synaptic facilitation has both a Hebbian (associative) and a non-Hebbian (reward-punishment) component.

CELL ACTIVITY (PID)

i = postsynaptic , j = presynaptic

$$X_i = [AX_i + B\int_{-t}^{0}(K_i - X_i)dt + \dot{C}X + D*XI + E*R]^{+}$$

$$XI = XI + F*(\sum X_j W_{ij} - X_i)$$

X = cell activity
K_i = resting frequency
W_{ij} = synaptic weight
A,B,C,D,E,F = empirical constants
R = rectangular distribution on (0.0,1.0)

SYNAPTIC FACILITATION

$$W_{ij} = -AW_{ij} + B*H(X_i,X_j) + \Gamma(R,P)*\alpha*\int_{-t}^{0} H(X_i,X_j)dt$$

$$\alpha = C\alpha + D*H(X_i,X_j)$$

$$\Gamma(R,P) = E*R + F*P$$

$$H(X_i,X_j) = [X_i-K_i]^{+}[X_j-K_j]$$

A,B,C,D,E,F = empirical constants
K_i,K_j = resting frequencies
R = instantaneous reward level
P = instantaneous punishment level
R = P = 0 or E = F = 0 => Hebbian

Figure 4. Cell Activity and Synaptic Facilitation.

This simulation is called Mouse. Figure 5 gives a static display at one point in the simulation. The shaded circles on the left represent neurons. Mouse, like Pacrat, lives in a bounded universe. This universe is the ten by ten grid on the right. At each cell in the grid, a single sensory neuron becomes active. The color of the circles reflects the activity. The color changes gradually from blue to red to white as the activity increases. Since color is not reproduced in this report, the active neurons are circled. Each sensory neuron has excitatory efferents on each of four motor neurons. These motor neurons are labelled N (north), S (south), E (east), and W (west). When the activity of one of these motor neurons exceeds a preset threshhold, Mouse moves one cell in that direction (within the boundaries) and a different sensory neuron becomes excited. As in Pacrat, there are three potential reward cells. At the beginning of each trial, food is placed randomly in one of these cells. These cells are the three shaded cells in column 9 as shown in Figure 5. The dark cell gives the location of the reward cell for that trial. When Mouse reaches a cell where food is located, a reward mechanism is activated and recently fired synapses are facilitated. The normalized synaptic weights from the sensory neurons to the motor neurons are shown by the arrows in the grid. There is always an element of randomness associated with each move, but the larger the arrow the more likely Mouse will move in that direction. Initially, (i.e., trial one) Mouse has no preferred direction of movement and the arrows have zero length and direction. Figure 5 gives the normalized weights after 1000 trials. Mouse always starts at row 6, column 1 and his current location in the grid is highlighted. In order to avoid obsessive, compulsive behavior, Mouse has been given a sense of smell. He is designed to avoid his own trail. This is accomplished via four sensory neurons with inhibitory efferents on the motor neurons. These are labeled 1/N, 1/E, 1/S, and 1/W indicating their effect on that direction of travel. The necessity for these is evident if one imagines four arrows in the grid forming a loop.

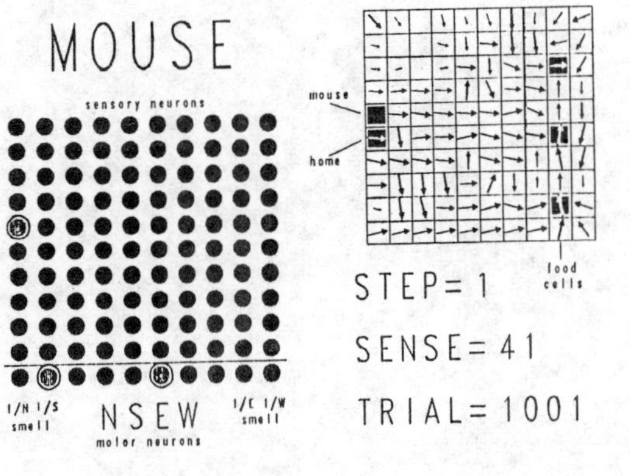

Figure 5. Snapshots of Mouse Display.

Figure 5 shows Mouse after a single move. He has just moved north so there is a high level of neural activity in the neuron inhibiting motor neuron S (south). Since this is the 1000th trial, Mouse has a preferred direction of movement. At this location, as shown by the arrow, it is east. The large synaptic weighting from the currently active sensory neuron to motor neuron E (east) is raising the activity of this motor neuron more than the others. It is therefore likely that Mouse will move east.

CONCLUSIONS

A brassboarded feeling-thinking machine is possible. We believe it is not practical at the moment to consider casting everything in silicon, therefore the neural network section of the machine will be emulated in a highly parallel computer ensemble.

ONGOING EFFORTS

The Pacrat simulation is being completely rewritten so that the neurons are explicitly modeled. This is preparatory to moving the simulation to a transputer network running under an Occam harness.

REFERENCES

1. Gregory RL (1975): Do we need cognitive concepts?, in Gazzaniga MS and Blakemore C (eds): Handbook of Psychobiology. New York, Academic Press pp. 607-628.
2. Palm G (1982): Neural Assemblies. Berlin, Springer-Verlag.
3. Palm G (1986): Associative networks and cell assemblies, in Palm G and Aertsen A (eds): Brain Theory. Berlin, Springer-Verlag.
4. Kissin B (1986): Conscious and Unconscious Programs in the Brain. New York, Plenum Publishing Corp.
5. Flynn JP, Vanegas H, Foote W, and Edwards S (1970): Neural mechanisms involved in a cat's attack on a rat, in Whalen RW, Thompson RF, Verzeano M, and Weinberger NM (eds): The Neural Control of Behavior. New York, Academic Press, pp. 135-173.
6. LeDoux JE (1986): The neurobiology of emotion, in LeDoux JE and Hirst W (eds): Mind and Brain. Cambridge, Cambridge University Press, pp. 301-358.
7. Girvin JP (1975): Clinical correlates of hypothalamic and limbic system function, in Mogenson GJ and Calaresu FR (eds): Neural Integration of Physiological Mechanisms and Behavior. Toronto, University of Toronto Press, pp. 412-434.
8. Walter WG (1950): An imitation of life. Scientific American 182:N5.
9. Walter WG (1951): A machine that learns. Scientific American 185:N2.
10. Mishkin M and Appenzeller T (1987): The anatomy of memory. Scientific American 256:N6.

Perspectives on Neural Networks: Panel

Chair: F. Coury

A POSITION PAPER ON NEURAL NETWORKS

Fred F. Coury

Fred Coury Associates, Inc.

There has been a great deal of discussion concerning the biological accuracy of the neural network models currently in use. Some believe that they are indeed accurate in the necessary details, and that they adequately represent the essential form and function of biological nervous systems. Others argue that they fall far short of a reasonable model of the real systems, and should be made to more faithfully represent the actual living systems before they can be at all useful.

My position on the subject can be summed up as follows:

(1) "Neural Networks" are good. They show great promise for the solution of many important problems which, to date, have been either difficult or impossible to solve.

(2) They really are not what they are claimed to be. They do not even come close to the way biological nervous systems are structured or function. We don't really know how real biological systems do what they do. And "neural networks" model only a small fraction of what we know about real nervous systems.

(3) However, I think that neural networks are valid in their own right. I do not recommend that they be made more biologically accurate. I think that is a losing proposition. Rather, I believe that the future of neural networks holds great promise if it is treated as a separate discipline.

Let me illustrate my third point by using the following analogy: Man has always wanted to fly. The first people who actually tried to fly did so by building bird-like contraptions, complete with flapping, feather-covered wings. None of them ever succeeded in getting off the ground.

Manned flight did not become a reality until three things occurred:

(1) The basic principles of flight (propulsion, lift, drag, etc.) were understood from observations of birds and from further experimentation. This research was inspired by birds, but independent of them.

(2) The specific practical problems to be solved were defined (e.g. carrying a person aloft, crossing the ocean, breaking the sound barrier).

(3) Contemporary technology (wood and cloth structures) was applied to the solution of those problems, or new technologies (jet propulsion) were developed where necessary.

There is a big difference between Aeronautical Engineering and Ornithology. Although originally inspired by birds in flight, aircraft designers no longer claim that their creations fly "the way birds do", because they don't. Modern aircraft are made of aluminum, not feathers, and they are powered by petroleum products, not birdseed. There is no need to claim biological accuracy by building feathered wings that flap.

However, by separating Aeronautical Engineering from Ornithology, people have been able to fly farther, faster, and higher than any bird ever could. And we have been able to carry cargo and passengers far beyond the capabilities of any living bird.

Another important result of separating aircraft design from bird observations is that we have realistic expectations for aircraft. We do not expect airplanes to eat worms or lay eggs. This may seem trite, but many equally unreasonable expectations about neural networks exist based on the assumption that they are accurate models of biological nervous systems.

Breaking the ties with biological systems will remove the source of most of the "hype" that we encounter today by removing tha claims that these systems work "like the human brain". At the same time, it will free neural networks from the constraints of biological accuracy and allow them to develop to their fullest potential.

CH2539-5/88/0000/0410$01.00 © 1988 IEEE

Hardware Intelligence

Peter Berke

UCLA Computer Science Department

Fifty years of machine-making and twenty years of psychology have endeavored to explain human behavior in computing terms. The future of machine-making will focus on perception. We will come to understand thinking, rational decision-making, as a special case of perceiving, of feeling our way through life. Artificial Intelligence has produed many innovative programming techniques, but it has failed to mechanize perception, and with it, knowledge.

Many times since being children, we have been told to "look both ways before crossing the street." Well, we can't look both ways before crossing the street, at least not at the same time. Since we cannot recognize it at a glance, "safe to cross" is not a primitive symbol in our human machines. It must be computed. The following procedure will suffice to compute the non-primitive condition "safe to cross:" (1) Look left; (2) remember "no cars on left;" (3) look right; (4) remember "no cars on right;" (5) infer "safe to cross."

Consider the overhead for the procedure. It requires order, object recognition, symbols (states of objects), memory, and explicit inference. Sensor flexiblity and a little rewiring could obviate this procedure by making it possible to directly sense the conditions one might otherwise compute. Imagine you could, upon approaching a street, swing your eyes out so you could see both ways at once.

If you had been born with such flexible eyes, the connections in your brain that implement vision would allow you to sense at a glance that it was safe to cross. What was, in the procedure, a fact arrived at by rational thought, is embodied in structure. In this way, knowledge may be viewed as connections in a network.

I may know something without being able to put it into words. As a result of Goedel's work we know that, even if I restrict myself to cases where I can put something I know into words, its being true may be independent of my or anyone being able to prove it. We simply perceive our beliefs: we feel, or sense something to be true. Linguistically inspired beliefs may be as much a matter of perception as vision-based beliefs. Both are subject to doubt, e.g., "I can't believe my eyes!" or, "I don't believe you!"

We expect applications for "neural networks" in pattern recognition, autonomic control, language translation, etc., the things that computers do poorly. In systems that react to their environment, recognition is a side-effect of reaction rather than a logical search-and-inference procedure.

A computer is a perfectly focused perceiver: it does one thing at a time. Computers are machines designed on a model of rational thought. We cannot program perception because perception is not a product of rational thought. There is just no way to say completely what perception is and how it works. So you can't tell an entirely rational being, a computer, how to perceive. Since knowledge is a perceptual process rather than a rational one, attempts to program knowledge have so far been futile.

In 1956 Shannon defined a universal Turing machine with only two states, and proved that there is no universal computer with only one state. This is the fundamental difference between sequential and combinational, programmable and non-programmable, computing and recognizing machines. Pattern recognition must be built in, or physically learned through experience. There may be no "universal perceiver" though there is a universal computer. Knowledge is domain-dependent. It depends on the perceiver and what has been previously perceived.

The re-emergence of connectionist thinking and the manufacture of modern "neural nets" impinges on major issues in many fields such as: distributed control of computer networks, associative memory, ambiguity, induction, DNA encoding, human memory, strategy, and discourse, to name a few. Significant results affecting all these fields will not come from handwaving, from writing a program and saying, "There, it thinks like a baby."

Bertrand Russell said, "The worse your logic, the more interesting the consequences to which it gives rise." Russell was speaking of Hegel's work, but for the field of Neural Nets in the late 1980's, we could add: The quicker your conclusions, the broader their scope. Many neural "network" models are computational models or computer simulations. Like flow-charts, neural nets may be a convenient way to partition problems, but to actually mechanize perception, they will have to learn physically, to grow.

There should be no backing out of the 'neural' in 'neural networks'. Software presumes recognition. That is, it uses objects and symbols are well-defined and well-recognized. Hardware produces recognition. This forms a basis for the belief that whatever neural nets have new to offer must be accomplished in hardware, e.g., VLSI.

Structural processing may be a larger form of processing than symbol processing. Computers perform numeric calculations by processing symbols rather than by "understanding" the numbers that the symbols represent. Similarly, it may be possible to create machines that perform symbolic operations by processing physical structures, rather than by "understanding," the symbols. It is toward that goal that neural networks strive.

Psychology, Philosophy, and Artificial Neural Nets

Stuart E. Dreyfus

University of California at Berkeley

Artificial neural nets have yet to demonstrate practical value, although they almost certainly will. They have, however, already impacted in important ways cognitive psychology and philosophers interested in cognition. New issues have arisen in these areas, and new distinctions have been made.

A few philosophers anticipated the sorts of problems that rule-based artificial intelligence eventually encountered, and had they been heeded, AI would have evolved quite differently. In particular, artificial neural net research would not have almost ceased between 1965 and 1980. Philosophically and psychologically oriented thought, if taken seriously, may now influence the evolution of connectionism.

I will discuss: (1) issues concerning the proper treatment of connectionism as it relates to understanding human cognition; (2) the ability of a net to generalize as a human would after a few concrete examples; and (3) why I believe that no artificial net will ever learn to exhibit fully human intelligence.

Neural Nets in Perspective

Tom J. Schwartz, Founder

TSA, Mtn. View, CA

A unique fallacy of Artificial Neural Systems is that they are intimately involved with how the brain functions. This is evidently not the case. While we have many useful models of neural nets which are inspired by neural research, none of them can be proven to perform in the identical way to the brain. Most neural models are based on the observed electrical activity of the brain and dismiss the chemical aspects of neural function.

The best model of a single electro-chemical neuron we have to date contains about a 150 parameters and requires a 32 node 80286, Hyper Cube to model a single neuron. At the same time we have software which runs on a PC which models 4,000 Processing Elements (sometimes mistakenly referred to as neurons) with 16,000 interconnects (sometimes mistakenly referred to as synapses). Without question there are meaningful differences between the level of detail used in each of the preceding models.

For purposes of this paper non-chemical models will be referred to as Phase 1 models and electro-chemical neural models will be referred to as Phase 2 models. We will discuss four stages of commercialization: Stage 1, 1-3 years (the first products appear), Stage 2, 3-6 years (the beginnings of real commercial benefit), Stage 3, 6-10 years (wide commercial benefit), Stage 4, 10 years and beyond (common practice).

In the Stage 1 (1-3 year) time frame the major action will be in Phase 1 neural architect kits. These will include single exclusive paradigm kits and fully flexible products. The flexible software will come with a number of canned paradigms and this number will continue to grow. In this time frame we will maybe overwhelmed with the flexibility offered by this software.

During this time frame there will also be a number of accelerator boards offered. Most of them will be for roll your own Phase 1 nets or as a migration path from one particular product to an accelerator board. We will also see a few stand alone neural applications.

From years 3-6 we will see the previous trends intensify. Basic modeling software will become easier to use and will begin to become integrated with existing software and expert systems. We will also see Phase 1 modeling software and chips which will allow for the delivery of imbedded neural applications. At the same time the first Phase 2 modeling software which accounts for electro-chemical neural action will hit the market. These chemical models will be inordinately complex.

In the 6-10 year time frame complete, off the shelf, Phase 1 chip sets will be offered. Neural capability will be available of most new hardware and software workstations. This capability will also be offered in the aftermarket and will fully integrate into existing software. Many existing applications will be updated to include the new adaptive functionality offered by neural nets. While this is going on for the Stage 1 models, Stage 2 models will be moving into the second period of commercialization.

In the period after this we will see the Phase 2 Models to continue to improve and perhaps we will eventually attain silicon consciences

Tom Schwartz is the founder of Tom Schwartz Associates. This Mtn. View, CA firm offers consulting to vendors and users of advanced computing technologies like expert systems and neural computing. The firms services include: on site training, problem and product selection, deployment strategies, technology partnering, venture capital sourcing and strategic marketing . Mr. Schwartz holds a BSEE, MSEE and MBA. He can be reached at 415/965-4561.

DATABASES Track

High Performance Relational Database Systems

Chair: J. Gray

NonStop SQL - A DISTRIBUTED RELATIONAL DBMS FOR OLTP

Robert Holbrook

Tandem Computers Incorporated

NonStop SQL is a relational DBMS explicitly designed for on-line transaction processing (OLTP). An audited benchmark has verified that NonStop SQL can execute more than 200 debit-credit transactions per second on a network of Tandem mainframes. Two design decisions contribute to this result: first, DBMS function was pushed as low as possible into the system operating code; second, the DBMS efficiently exploits the advantages of distributed processing.

NonStop SQL is at the leading edge of commercially available relational technology. It has two distinctions in this regard. It is the first relational product able to handle very large OLTP applications. It is also the first relational product to support transparent distribution of data. NonStop SQL was first sold in September, 1987. The product went 'live' in a production application later that month.

PERFORMANCE

The performance of NonStop SQL grows linearly as hardware is added to a processor network. To demonstrate this claim, an audited benchmark of NonStop SQL was executed in January, 1987. The workload was based on a standard measure of transaction processing power (Datamation, April 1, 1985). The transaction executed performs the database activity that results when a bank customer withdraws money from an account. The workload includes a test for distribution: while most of the withdrawals are made from the customer's home branch, 15% are not. For the largest hardware configuration, a network of 2,560 branch banks was simulated, each with 10 tellers, and a total of 25,600,000 accounts. A two-node network (16 processors) executed 106 transactions per second (TPS) with 90% of the transactions completing in two seconds or less. When the hardware was doubled to four nodes, the system processed 208 TPS, a 98% increase in throughput.

208 TPS is enough capacity for almost all on-line applications in the world today. To understand how such throughput was achieved, it is necessary to examine Tandem's architecture and how NonStop SQL exploits it.

TANDEM ARCHITECTURE

NonStop SQL is deployed on Tandem NonStop computers. Tandem has been the leader in the fault-tolerant computer marketplace since its first product was shipped in 1976. Tandem solved the problem of fault tolerance with special hardware and software. The hardware is designed so that no single point of failure inhibits the use of the system -- a backup path is always available. System software uses 'checkpoints' that transfer key information about the state of a process to a backup process running in another processor. In the event of a processor failure, the backup process has enough information to continue processing as of the last checkpoint.

Specifically, a Tandem system consists of 2 to 16 processors connected by two high-speed 20Mb/second buses. Multiple systems can be connected by a 1Mb/second fiber optic connection. In total, 224 processors can form a processing network. Communication and disk controllers can be attached to these processors as needed. They are dual-ported for fault tolerance. Special software complements this hardware. In particular, all communication between processes occurs through messages. Interprocess communication via messages helps protect other processors from fatal software errors resulting from corrupted memory. Another advantage of messages for interprocess communication (as opposed to a shared memory scheme) is that the processors can be geographically distributed with no effect on the code that uses the operating system.

Several processes participate in executing a user's application. These processes can be allocated to different processors. At the highest level, the user's application executes as a process, typically in a processor on the user's node. When the user's application issues a request for data, the DBMS is invoked as part of the user's process. The DBMS reduces the user's request to a set of operations to be performed on physical files. Each of these operations is sent to a 'disk process'. Disk processes run in every processor to which disks are attached, and control the data on those disks. Thus, the disk process can be distant from the user.

AN INTEGRATED DBMS

NonStop SQL performs well for two reasons. First, it is tightly integrated with the system software. Relational functions have been pushed into low levels of system code. Because of this, path lengths are shorter and less data needs to be moved between processors. Performance is improved as operating overhead is reduced.

The database software supports three levels of abstraction with regard to data. The <u>physical file</u> corresponds to a set of sectors on a disk. The disk process manifests the data in these sectors as a logical set of rows and columns. Many physical files can contain related data. The file system coordinates the I/O to related physical files and presents them as a <u>logical file</u>. Within the context of a logical file, a physical file can take the role of a horizontal fragment of the file, an index of the file, or a horizontal fragment of an index of the file. Many logical files can form a <u>relation</u> (or table). This work is performed by the SQL executor. The disk process resides in the processor where the data is located; the file system and SQL executor run in the processor where the user's program executes.

With NonStop SQL, the disk process executes with a knowledge of the data types of the columns in the files it controls. Through the cooperation of the SQL executor and the file system, predicate information from a user query can be passed to the disk process. The disk process can evaluate this predicate and return only the rows and columns of interest to the user. Because the disk process runs in the processor closest to the data, less data needs to move between processors. This is critically important to the performance of a distributed system.

When a file is processed sequentially, data is sent from the disk process to the file system in blocks. If the disk process combines the service of predicate evaluation with this sequential block buffering, the result is a stream of blocked data containing only the rows and columns of interest to the user. This is called virtual sequential block buffering.
The situation is even better for set-oriented UPDATE or DELETE operations. The disk process can execute the entire request without the intervention of higher-level code. Tandem compared the speed of an update using an SQL cursor, which requires data to be sent to the user's program, with that of a set-oriented UPDATE statement, which does not. Whereas 40 rows per second could be updated using a cursor, 400 rows per second were updated when the disk process did all the work itself.

The Transaction Monitoring Facility (TMF) is intricately linked with the disk process. As the disk process changes data, it logs these changes to an audit trail in a compressed format. The audit trail file is usually managed by a separate disk process, although this is not necessary. In addition, the disk process supports a group commit feature which can be used to improve throughput at a small cost to response time. A two-phase commit protocol is used between processors participating in a transaction. Low-level message system code was enhanced to speed the execution of this protocol. A hierarchical two-phase commit protocol is used when more than one node is involved in a transaction.

A DISTRIBUTED DBMS

The first reason NonStop SQL obtains high performance is that it is integrated with the system operating software. The second reason NonStop SQL performs well is that it efficiently exploits the power of distributed processing. Work can be done by all of the processors in a system at the same time. To fully exploit the hardware, a workload is required that lends itself to being divided among several processors. On-line transaction processing (OLTP) applications present such a workload. An OLTP application typically involves many concurrent requests for a predefined transaction.

Performance is one aspect of distribution. Another aspect provided by NonStop SQL is location independence. The user can mix read and write access to data at multiple sites as if the data were all stored locally, with no loss of transaction protection. As a network grows, data may move, but application code is not affected because programs are not even implicitly aware of the data's location. Thus, a program written for a two processor system can work equally well in a 2000 processor system.

Participating in a distributed network need not imply any loss of control. The system administrator has complete authority over the objects at the local node. Moreover, users can always access local data, even if the rest of the network is unavailable. This principle, called 'local autonomy', is supported by NonStop SQL.

Managing a large database, distributed or not, can be a complex task. NonStop SQL comes with an assortment of utilities to make this task easier. These include FILEINFO, DUP, COPY, LOAD, BACKUP and RESTORE. Maintenance of applications is also easier. The data administrator can assess the impact of a proposed change by generating a 'where-used' report listing all programs and views that depend on the object to be altered.

NonStop SQL EXTENSIONS

Although NonStop SQL adheres closely to the SQL language defined by ANSI, it also extends the language for use in production environments. Extensions include support for partitioned files, flexible locking options, entry-sequenced, relative and key-sequenced files, non-audited tables, COBOL-like data declarations, and a variable-length character data type. Primary keys and system-enforced constraints are supported. The ANSI naming and authorization models are not supported. Instead, NonStop SQL is consistent with the naming and authorization scheme used by the rest of Tandem's software products. NULL values are not supported.

Locking deserves special attention in the context of high performance databases. NonStop SQL provides three lock modes: BROWSE ACCESS, STABLE ACCESS and REPEATABLE ACCESS corresponding to degrees 1, 2 and 3 consistency (sometimes called read-through locks, cursor stability, and repeatable reads). REPEATABLE ACCESS does not lock the end of a file when an insert is made to the end of the file, as full degree 3 consistency would require. This improves the performance of inserting entry-sequenced data. In addition, NonStop SQL provides an adjustable timeout value after which the system will return control to the user if a record is locked. Timeouts are used to resolve deadlocks. Three granularities of locks can be held: record-level, set-level and table-level. Set-level locks can be used for records that share a leading portion of their primary keys. For example, a set-level lock would be appropriate for a single order that has many line items in an order detail file. Finally, both shared and exclusive locks can be acquired for all locks.

NonStop SQL is one of several Tandem application development tools. PATHMAKER provides an ability to generate screens for the part of the application that deals with the user (the requestor). COBOL85 can be used with SQL to write the application servers that deal with the database. These requestors and servers can be combined in a PATHWAY environment. PATHWAY starts and stops server programs as needed, depending on the volume of requests coming from the requestor programs. When NonStop SQL is used in a PATHWAY environment, the user gets a special benefit: a fault tolerant application, without special coding.

COST

NonStop SQL runs on all Tandem NonStop systems, from a small departmental machine to a large network of mainframes. The transaction processing power of the processors that are used in these systems, the initial license fees per processor and the monthly license fees per processor follow:

	TPS	ILF	MLF
VLX	6.5	$4000	$500
TXP	4.5	$4000	$375
CLX	2.5	$3000	$300

These TPS numbers will be 10% higher when all the processors reside in the same node.

The full five-year life cycle cost of the benchmarked system, including hardware, software, and support fees, is $55,000 per TPS capacity. Fully mirrored disk drives (standard on most Tandem systems) cost 10% more. If the requirement to keep history data for 90 days is removed, the price drops to $46,700 per TPS capacity.

CONCLUSION

The high performance obtained by NonStop SQL is due to two design decisions. First, database function was embedded as deeply as possible in system code. Second, the distributed function of Tandem's hardware architecture was exploited. Less fundamental, but equally necessary, the SQL language was extended to allow the database administrator to fully utilize the high degree of concurrency permitted by the Tandem architecture.

INFORMIX-TURBO

Richard B. Curtis

Informix Software, Inc.

ABSTRACT:

Informix Software, Inc., has introduced a new database engine that has been designed for high OLTP performance and for fault tolerance under power failure and loss of magnetic media on UNIX systems. Informix-Turbo makes use of System V shared memory and raw I/O to manage concurrency and transaction logging. Use of these features allows database tables to span multiple disks and programmers to specify several levels of isolation.

What is Informix-Turbo?

Informix SQL-based products have a two-process architecture. The user program of front-end process handles the interaction between the user and the computer through forms, reports, menus, windows, etc. These programs can be written in C, in 4GL, or make use of Informix-SQL, an integrated package of forms, reports, and on-line query facilities. These front-end products, when executed by the user, spawn a database server process or back end that is responsible for the actual communication with the database. The back end consists of three distinct levels: the SQL parser, the optimizer, and the indexed sequential access method (isam). The back end and the front end communicate over a named pipe in the UNIX environment. The front end sending coded SQL statements to the back end and receiving the results of the execution of the SQL statements from the back end.

The original database server for the Informix SQL-based products uses C-ISAM as the isam level library. Informix-Turbo is an alternative database server for the Informix SQL products and differs mainly from the original back end in using a newly developed isam. With minimal modifications to the parser and optimizer, Informix-Turbo can be used with any of the Informix front-end products like Informix-SQL, Informix-4GL, Informix-ESQL/C and other embedded languages, and Datasheet Add-in.

What are its Major Benefits?

Informix-Turbo adds a number of benefits to the already successful Informix line of products.

High Performance

Informix-Turbo is from 80% to 150% faster than the Informix C-ISAM-based back end running the Debit-Credit benchmarks without simulating terminals across X.25 lines. Turbo shows the same range of performance improvement when compared to two of our competitors. The actual number of transactions per second is highly machine dependent.

Fault Tolerance under Power and Disk Failure

Through use of both physical (before image) and logical (before/after record) logs, Turbo can recover from a system failure within minutes after the system is rebooted to the end of the last completed transactions. No committed data is lost. The option of software-controlled disk mirroring permits the same level of recovery even with loss of magnetic media. No special hardware is required.

Unlimited Table Size

A database table in Turbo can span two or more physical devices. The table can

CH2539-5/88/0000/0422$01.00 © 1988 IEEE

grow into a new disk without having to be reconfigured. It is only necessary to tell Turbo what disk partition is available for it to use. Actually, there is a limit. A table must occupy less than 137,438,953,472 bytes and have no more than 4,294,967,296 rows.

Advanced Concurrency Control

C.J. Date defines five different locking strategies for read-only queries that he calls "levels of isolation." The most restrictive of these is "repeatable read" and is the level required for serializable transactions. Informix-Turbo has adopted three of these levels, including repeatable read, and has added "dirty read" for rapid access to static tables. Informix-Turbo's implementation of repeatable read uses key or predicate locking to provide the highest possible level of concurrency consistent with the requirements of repeatable read.

Tunable System Parameters

Reliance on the UNIX operating system to handle reading and writing to files, managing locks, and buffering data means that the database management administrator has little or no ability to modify the limits the system imposes. Informix-Turbo bypasses these UNIX controls. It reads and writes to files outside of the UNIX file system; it manages locks in shared memory; it maintains its own shared data buffering system. As a result, the database administrator can easily tune the number of simultaneously open tables, the total number of locks available, as well as the number of accessible data buffers. Changing these and several other operating parameters does not require bringing the UNIX operating system down. It is necessary only to cease database activity for several seconds.

Integrated Management Environment

The Turbo system can be managed totally within a menu-driven environment. The administrator can initialize the system, modify system parameters, observe the system performance, back-up and restore the system and the incremental logical logs, add additional disk space, and change the operating state of the Turbo system.

What Were the Driving Forces in its Development?

Informix had two principle goals in the creation of Informix-Turbo: to increase the performance of on-line transaction processing in the UNIX environment and to provide software fault tolerance for the system. Increasingly, as the capacity and power of UNIX machines has grown, there has been a desire on the part of firms to carry out on these much less expensive machines the kind of transaction processing that previously required mini-computers and mainframes. The data integrity implied by transaction processing requires that the data entered into the system not be lost and that recovery time be kept to a minimum. To provide these features, database activity on UNIX machines had to be efficient.

Increasing Performance

Increasing performance in the UNIX environment implied avoiding those components of the system that take time. Disk I/O was to be avoided whenever possible, consistent with data integrity and safety. The shared memory feature of System V made this possible. When it was necessary to go to disk, the problem of indirection had to be overcome. Data must be organized physically on the disk in such a way that it could be located directly and with minimum disk I/O's. This called for Informix-Turbo's organizing its own disk space and its not using the UNIX file system. Reads and writes to disk would be direct (raw I/O). System calls are expensive. Informix-Turbo would reduce its dependence on system calls. This meant that it would handle its own locking in shared memory. At the same time, the number of locks was liberated from kernel restrictions and the types of locks (shared, update, and exclusive on rows, pages, and keys) were definable by Turbo.

Solving these performance problems in these ways made it possible to solve several other problems. Using raw I/O and organizing the placement of data and indexes on disk means that each disk partition used by Turbo required a single file descriptor. UNIX's limit on open file descriptors became for Turbo a limit on number of disk partitions. There was no limit on the number of open tables; UNIX had no knowledge of how many tables were on a disk partition. Tables could span disk partitions with ease, even when they were on different physical devices. Managing data buffers in shared memory reduces data redundancy. Two or more processes could have sequential access to and could make modifications to the same row without having to perform disk I/O's. Turbo would handle the access in shared memory.

Fault Tolerance

A major strength of the UNIX file system is also a major difficulty. In order to speed the writing of files, UNIX buffers the writes, returning to the calling program a "success," but not yet actually writing the data to disk. This is efficient when UNIX stays up, but is disasterous when there is a power failure. The calling program has no way of knowing what data has been written to disk. A database management system that relies on the UNIX file system has no way of recovering from a system failure on its own. A database admininistrator must manually check the date and indexes to determine whether a committed transaction actually made to disk without corrupting the indexes. Actually, some UNIX systems have implemented synchronous writes, flushing the buffer on each call to write. This call, however, is very slow.

Turbo was written with fast recovery as a design goal. Between each line of code, the programmers asked, "How can we recover if there is a power failure here?" Turbo keeps two logs: a logical log and a physical log. The logical log is a record by record account of all changes to the database system. This is the conventional transaction log that allows roll back and roll forward of all database activity. The physical log is a temporary log recording the "before images" of all pages in the database that have been changed since the last checkpoint.

In order to understand the physical log and the fast recovery procedure of Turbo, it is necessary to know that there are periodic checkpoints at which time all memory is flushed to disk, with the logs being written before the data. At this time, the physical log is emptied and activity causes the logical log to continue to fill up and the physical log to contain unique before-image pages of all pages incurring a change since the checkpoint.

Suppose there is a system failure before the next checkpoint. Upon recovery of the system, the Turbo daemon wakes up and begins the recovery procedure. It first writes all the pages in the physical log into the database, thus restoring the database to its state at the last checkpoint. The corresponding checkpoint record is located in the logical log and the database is rolled forward from that point to the end of the logical log. Turbo then asks, "Are there any open transactions?" If so, it rolls each of them back and brings the Turbo system on line. The databases are all restored to the end of the last completed transaction. The only data that was lost was that in the transactions in process.

In a recent upgrade to Turbo, users are now able to designate various regions of the database system and logs to be disk mirrored. Every write to a mirrored region is actually written twice to separate physical devices. Reads are only from one of the devices. Should one of the mirrored disks crash, the system will automatically switch to the healthy disk and continue running. When the injured disk is replaced and Turbo notified that it is back on line, Turbo will bring the new replaced disk up to date as a background task while database activity continues. When the replaced disk has been restored to being identical with its mirrored partner, Turbo continues to write to both and to read from one. There exist expensive computer systems that provide disk mirroring as part of the hardware. Turbo makes this feature available to all UNIX machines.

The effect of having disk mirroring is that databases under Informix-Turbo are fault tolerant even under disk failure. Users never need lose data that has been entered.

What Are its Principle Features?

Many of the Informix-Turbo features have been mentioned and described in earlier sections. Its use of direct or raw I/O not only contributes to its performance gains, but also to its ability to handle very large tables spanning several devices. Because of its writing directly to disk and its logical and physical logs, it guarantees fast recovery. Disk mirroring extends fault tolerance beyond power failures to disk crashes. On-line archiving allows a busy system to be backed up without shutting down. Predicate or key locking allows full serializable transactions without locking other users out of the affected tables. Non-affected portions of the tables can be updated and new data can be inserted.

The newest version of Turbo also has a sophisticated optimizer that calculates the costs of the various brances of a decision tree before choosing the strategy for executing a complex SELECT statement. Users can elect to print out the selected strategy. The new optimizer guarantees full use of all defined indexes.

Beyond these features, the current release of Turbo meets full ANSI Level I SQL Compatibility and virtually all of ANSI Level II. Compiler options permit the programmer to get warnings on all non-ANSI compliant syntax.

Turbo can be the remote backend on a network, allowing users on PC's and other UNIX machines to enjoy all of Turbo's features. It is the underlying engine for Informix's distributed database design.

High Performance Transaction Processing Systems: Case Studies

Chair: A. Reuter

Design Considerations in Replicated Database Systems for Disaster Protection

Jim Lyon

Tandem Computers, Inc.

Abstract: As computer systems process higher and higher volumes of economic transactions, the cost of a breach in service due to a disaster becomes financially intolerable. In situations like this, it becomes economically feasible to maintain a standby system with an up-to-date copy of the database. This paper discusses the design issues in building such a system.

Introduction

In recent years, a number of corporations have implemented online transaction processing systems that manage the data at the core of their business. In many cases, the business is totally dependent on the correct and continuous operation of these systems. Some businesses require these systems to remain up 24 hours per day, 365 days per year, even in the face of fires, floods, earthquakes, terrorists, and software upgrades.

In response to this need, Tandem Computers, Inc, is developing a product to allow an application and its database to be replicated on two geographically separated computer systems. This product, is called the *Remote Database Facility (RDF)*.

This paper discusses some of the requirements for RDF, and the way in which they influence the design.

Architecture

RDF is layered on top of Tandem's *Transaction Monitoring Facility (TMF)*. TMF provides transaction atomicity and transaction, system and media recovery. It is a standard part of Tandem's operating system. TMF is the transaction monitor for both the older, VSAM-like file system and the newer ANSI-standard SQL file system. TMF supports distributed transactions in a network of Tandem systems using a traditional two-phase commit protocol.

RDF allows any individual file to be replicated on two different nodes in a network. At any time, one of these files is *primary*; the application only reads and writes primary files. RDF automatically keeps the other copy (the *backup*) in synch with the primary file.

RDF does this by monitoring the transaction journal as it is created by TMF. All updates that pertain to protected files are extracted from the journal at the primary node and transmitted to the backup node. RDF enters these updates into the journal at the backup node and then replays them against the backup file.

Should a disaster strike the primary node, the backup node will contain a copy of the database which is up to date except for at most the last few seconds' worth of transactions. If the backup node is asked to assume the duties of the primary node, RDF will first roll back the effects of any transactions that were only partially received from the primary node.

Constraints and TradeOffs

Availability

Some customers require totally continuous availability. This implies that there must be no routine operations that require taking the system down. While the application is running, customers must be able to make backups, add and/or reconfigure CPUs and disk drives, and upgrade the system and application software.

TMF already provides the ability to make backups of the databases while the application is running, using standard "fuzzy dump" technology.

The strategy to achieve the other operations is as follows:

A customer may stop his backup node and perform whatever maintenance is necessary. During this time, the primary node continues processing. After the backup node is restarted (possibly with a new configuration), RDF will start transmitting the accumulated journal records to the backup node. After the backup node has caught up with the primary, the operator can ask the two nodes to switch roles, allowing the application processing to proceed on the erstwhile backup node. The customer can then take the original primary node down for maintenance and reconfiguration. After it is restarted, and has caught up with its partner, the operator can again ask the two nodes to switch roles, thus moving the application processing back to the original node.

This strategy has two major implications:

First, configurations of the two partner nodes must be allowed to differ in all of the important variables. They must be allowed to have different numbers and types of processors. They must be allowed to have different numbers and types of disk volumes. They must also be allowed to distribute the files across the volumes differently. Finally, they must be allowed to run different versions of the system and application software.

Achieving these constraints required changing some of TMF's journal strategies, which previously stored information related to transaction rollback on a volume basis instead of a file basis.

Second, RDF must provide a very fast means to allow a primary and backup node to exchange their roles. When an operator asks RDF to exchange the roles of two nodes, RDF causes the primary node to refuse to start any new transactions. After any transactions that are in progress have finished, RDF will ship their journal records to the backup node. After the updates described by these records have been applied to the database at the backup node, the backup node will start processing new transactions.

Thus, switching roles between the two systems involves a brief period during which new transactions cannot be started. We estimate that, for typical configurations, this period will be between 1 and 10 seconds. We expect this to be acceptable for almost all applications.

Transaction Loss vs. Response Time

Transaction Loss: A straightforward implementation of RDF's journal-shipping strategy would imply that, when a disaster strikes, the last few seconds' worth of transactions would be lost. However, some customers have applications in which a typical transaction may represent a transfer of several millions of dollars. For these applications, RDF must be able to promise that, when the system tells an application that a transaction has been committed, that transaction will not be lost, even in a disaster.

To achieve this, the primary and backup systems use a variant of a non-blocking two-phase commit protocol. Thus, a transaction will not commit until the backup system has received sufficient journal information to retain that transaction in the event that a disaster strikes the primary.

The guarantee that a transaction will not be lost only applies to single disasters. If one of the partner nodes is already down, the other will commit transactions even though there is no backup for the transaction. (Otherwise, adding a backup node would *decrease* availability, not *increase* it.)

Response Time: Guaranteeing that no transactions will be lost in a disaster has one drawback: it increases the response time for each transaction by the amount of time necessary for one round-trip communication between the primary and backup nodes. For geographically separated systems, this can exceed one second.

For many applications, this is unacceptable. These applications are characterized by a very high volume of transactions, with stringent response-time requirements. Typical applications include ATM networks and airline reservation systems. For these applications, it is economically acceptable to lose a few transactions if a disaster strikes.

Therefore, RDF must allow customers to configure their systems so that some transactions cannot be lost in a disaster (but suffer a response-time penalty), and other transactions have no response-time penalty (but can be lost in a disaster).

Flexibility vs. Cost

In its simplest form, an RDF configuration would consist of a single primary node and a single backup node. Obviously, this is a 100% increase in the hardware cost for the system.

As a customer's business grows, he will probably install a network of nodes. If there is a backup node for each of these nodes, then there continues to be a 100% increase in the hardware cost for the system.

At some point, however, it makes sense to use a single backup node for several primary nodes. This backup node need only have sufficient processing capacity to take over for the largest of the nodes that it backs up. This can cut the cost of the backup hardware substantially.

As an extreme, each node in a network could contain its own primary files, and a few backup files for each of the other nodes. For example, in a ten-node network, each node could contain one ninth of the backup files from each of the other nine nodes. In the event of a disaster striking any individual node, each of the other nine would only need an additional 11% processing capacity. Of course, this may entail substantial additional communication costs if the nodes are very distant from each other. It also creates a network in which *every* double disaster will destroy some data.

In order to allow the customer to retain control of the tradeoffs in the degree of disaster protection required and the amount he is willing to pay for it, RDF must allow very flexible configurations in how the primary and backup copies of files are distributed among nodes.

Operational Issues

Configuring and operating a network that includes disaster protection is complicated. Following are some of the issues:

Testing: In order to have confidence that a disaster configuration will actually work when needed, the configuration must be periodically tested. This implies actually moving the application workload to the backup system, and observing that it works. RDF's planned switch feature, discussed earlier, is intended to make this relatively painless.

When to Takeover: In all of Tandem's previous fault-tolerance products, the backup of a resource is "spring-loaded" to take over. That is, when it discovers that the primary is no longer functioning, it immediately assumes the role of the primary, and only notifies the operator after doing so. With RDF however, the primary and backup resources may be many miles apart. At each node, the failure of the other node appears to the computer system to be indistinguishable from the failure of the communication lines connecting the systems. Thus, we leave the decision to take over in the hands of the operators. Before performing an unplanned takeover at a backup node, the operator should verify that the primary node is really not functional.

Partial Failures: Partial failures of nodes present unusual technical challenges for RDF. For example, if a disk volume fails at a primary node, any transactions in progress that require files on that volume will be aborted. They will be rolled back with respect to files on the volumes that are still up, but cannot be rolled back with respect to files on the volume that failed. In some cases, the operator may decide that this volume failure is sufficient reason to move processing to the backup node. If he does this, then RDF on the backup node needs to roll back these transactions, but only with respect to those files on which they have not already been rolled back. Similarly, when the failed volume gets repaired, RDF must know that some of the files contained on that volume have become backups while the volume was down.

Conclusion

While a number of the issues presented above require careful design, none of them is insoluble. We believe that the time has come for achieving continuously available systems, even in the face of disasters.

Hardware costs are continuing to decrease. Businesses are becoming ever more dependent on their transaction systems. As both of these trends continue, we expect that data replication and disaster recovery abilities will become standard features of database management systems, just as transaction atomicity is today.

THE MEAD INFORMATION RETRIEVAL SYSTEM

Samuel DeFazio
Charles Greenwald

Mead Data Central, Inc.
9393 Springboro Pike, Miamisburg, Ohio 45342

Abstract

The LEXIS®/NEXIS® information retrieval system during peak loads processes nearly eight thousand full-text searches an hour. Most often these searches are directed at databases on the order of one hundred billion bytes in size. The I/O and CPU resource requirements to service the LEXIS/NEXIS workload is approaching the limits of existing computer technology. For the information retrieval industry to remain cost effective as database size increases continuously, fundamental advances in computer architectures and full-text search algorithms are required.

Background

The requirement to service a peak load of nearly eight thousand transactions per hour sounds rather mundane. When each of these transactions is a full-text LEXIS or NEXIS search requiring four hundred or more input/output operations and over fifteen million CPU instructions, the workload pushes current mainframe computer technology to its limits. The complexity of this task derives primarily from the size of the databases, now more than two hundred billion characters of raw text, about evenly split between LEXIS and NEXIS services. Given this enormous data collection and the current target response time of twelve seconds, connectivity and access to data are critical architectural issues. The approach adopted by the LEXIS/NEXIS search system to satisfy these requirements is based on a highly parallel and distributed architecture. However, even with large numbers of processors, channels, controllers, and disk drives, limitations in current mainframe computing technology and commercial operating systems impose substantial restrictions on the degree of "real" parallel operation. This presentation focuses primarily on these limitations, approaches to dealing with them, and architectures which could improve the efficiency of searching large full-text databases.

Presentation Outline

The topics addressed in the LEXIS/NEXIS case study presentation include:

1. **Introduction to MDC services.** The discussion here centers on the LEXIS/NEXIS search and retrieval services.

2. **Processing environment.** A High-level overview of the current software and hardware configuration will be given to characterize the CPU and I/O resource requirements associated with searching large full-text data bases.

3. **Limitations of existing technology.** The limitations of current hardware and operating system technology with respect to searching large full-text data bases will be addressed.

4. **Architectural alternatives.** A number of alternative architectures that improve access to databases and processor-peripheral connectivity, thereby improving the efficiency of large full-text searching will be suggested.

In addition to the topics discussed above, this presentation also focus on the most important and distinguishing properties of large full-text retrieval systems.

Concluding Remarks

The LEXIS/NEXIS information retrieval system by present standards is a highly specialized application. Consider if you will, however, the amount of valuable textual information that will exist in magnetic form twenty years from now. It seems clear that _if_ full-text information retrieval is to become a major industrial activity, the current computer resource requirements at MDC are a clear indication of the need for more cost effective solutions.

CH2539-5/88/0000/0431$01.00 © 1988 IEEE

Camelot: A Flexible, Distributed Transaction Processing System

Alfred Z. Spector, Randy F. Pausch, and Gregory Bruell
Computer Science Department
Carnegie Mellon University
Pittsburgh, PA 15213

Abstract

Distributed transaction processing techniques are useful in many application domains, including commercial on-line transaction processing systems, general and special purpose database management systems, high availability mail systems, and the like. The Camelot Project has constructed a distributed transaction facility intended to support wide-spread use of transaction processing techniques. Camelot executes on a variety of uni- and multi-processors on top of the Unix-compatible, Mach operating system. This paper describes the design decisions that make Camelot a flexible, easy-to-use system, and briefly describes Camelot's programming interfaces and algorithms. The paper also discusses two applications of Camelot: an implementation of distributed ET-1 and a graphical room reservation system that uses the X window manager.

1. Introduction

Transaction processing facilities are recognized as essential elements in reliable, commercial applications. By a *transaction facility*, we mean a collection of components that supports the execution of transactions and the implementation of shared abstract data objects. Examples of such objects include databases, files, and mail queues. Although there is room for diversity in the exact functions of a transaction facility, it must make it easy to begin and end transactions, to call operations on objects from within transactions, and to implement abstract objects that have correct synchronization and recovery properties. Also, a transaction facility should make it possible to manage protected subsystems, which are groupings of abstract objects that perform a coherent function.

The transactional properties of failure atomicity, permanence of effect, and serializability free application programmers from many of the problems caused by concurrency and failures. Application programmers also benefit from functions that simplify the development, use, and management of protected subsystems. Additionally, a common transaction facility can permit the combined use of separately implemented subsystems. For example, a computer aided design system might be built using a transactional database management system and a transactional file system.

New uses of transaction processing techniques will benefit from, and perhaps require, a collection of improvements to existing transaction facilities. First, distributed operation is crucial: there must be easy access to objects on other network nodes. Second, transaction facilities should be made easy to use by programmers with standard programming skills. Third, transaction facilities should operate in the standard computing environments that organizations use for their main computing needs: heterogeneous hardware and networks, and operating systems such as Unix™. This permits transactions to be more easily used in existing application areas. Fourth, transaction facilities should support nested transactions (to support intra-transaction parallelism and partial roll-back), and the definition of user-defined shared abstract objects. Fifth, transactions should execute with increased performance, particularly to support replication. Finally, the cost of hardware to support distributed transactions should be close to the cost of hardware to support ad hoc techniques.

Various subsets of these features have been demonstrated in a number of systems. IBM's CICS and Tandem's TMF are examples of commercial distributed transaction processing facilities [9, 7]. IBM's R*, Relational Technology's Ingres/Star, and Tandem's NonStop SQL are relational database systems that contain embedded transaction processing facilities [11, 13, 20]. MIT's Argus is a programming language that includes support for distributed transaction processing [12]. IBM T. J. Watson's CPR, UCLA's Locus, and IBM Almaden's Quicksilver are operating systems with support for transactions [2, 21, 6]. Other examples abound.

2. Design Goals

Camelot [17, 15, 18] is a distributed transaction facility that runs on the Mach [14] operating system. Presently, Release 1 of Camelot is nearing completion and is running on Digital uni-and multi-processor Vaxes, IBM RT PCs, Sun 3s, and an Encore MultiMax, all of which are on the DARPA Internet[1]. We anticipate that Camelot would run, if recompiled on Sequent and other computers that support Mach.

Broadly, Camelot supports the execution of distributed transactions, and the definition, management, and use of *data servers*, which encapsulate shared, recoverable objects. Camelot is based on the client-server model and uses RPC both locally and remotely to provide communication among applications and servers.

Designing Camelot entailed making a number of difficult deci-

This research was sponsored by the Defense Advanced Research Projects Agency (DOD), ARPA Order No. 4864 (Amendment 20), under contract F33615-87-C-1499 monitored by the Avionics Laboratory, Air Force Wright Aeronautical Laboratories, Wright-Patterson AFB. The views expressed are those of the authors.

[1]As of 2 December 1987, we are releasing Camelot Release 0.9(36), which supports all Camelot interfaces, but which does not support media recovery. The Camelot 1.0 Alpha release will be complete in the first quarter of 1988.

CH2539-5/88/0000/0432$01.00 © 1988 IEEE

sions regarding which functions Camelot should support. Often, there were trade-offs between performance and ease-of-use. In addition, we had to chose a design that could be implemented in the roughly ten programmer years we had available. The following list summarizes the major features that we chose to include in Camelot Release 1.0:

- **Easily constructed applications and servers.** An easy to use library of powerful primitives makes it easy for Unix/C programmers to develop clients and servers. Applications and servers are easy to write because programmers can declare and access recoverable data objects in ways very similar to normal C practice. They need only pay attention to issues of locking, which Camelot assumes is best done by the server designer. Easily used RPCs make accessing servers as easy as local procedure calls. An easy to use library is part-way between full linguistic support, as in Argus or Avalon [12, 8], and raw system calls.
- **Automatic management of threads.** Thread management, layered on Mach-supplied threads, simplifies the development of clients and servers and reduces machine dependencies.
- **Nested transactions.** Nested transactions simplify handling concurrency within transactions and partial failures.
- **Flexible synchronization.** Logical locks, implemented within servers, and support for hybrid atomicity provide the possibility of high concurrency.
- **Long and short transactions on a wide variety of data objects, which are instances of user-defined types.** Supporting user-defined objects provides flexible, high performance access to shared data. This is in contrast to the approach being developed by researchers who are developing extensible, database management systems.
- **Support for small and large data objects.** Access to small data objects is efficient, because they generally reside in main memory. Camelot also aims to make accessing large (multi-gigabyte) data objects as efficient as possible so as to support large databases.
- **Transactions with non-blocking commit protocols.** Non-blocking commit protocols reduce the likelihood that access to data will be delayed due to node or network failures.
- **Flexible logging support.** Distributed logging, as well as local logging, permits the use of Camelot in environments where ultra high data integrity is required and/or there is no local stable storage.
- **Simplified node configuration.** An easy to use node configuration application permits authorized users, whether local or across a network, to install servers on nodes, start, shutdown, and restart servers, set quotas, and the like.
- **Support for multiple servers per node.** Supporting multiple servers makes possible cleanly supporting separate data abstractions and partitioning data into multiple servers. Separate servers can be installed, can crash, and can be restarted independently during normal system operation.
- **Support for multiple disks per node.** Supporting multiple disks makes possible storing large amounts of data and higher disk bandwidth.
- **Machine independent execution.** Execution on all the hardware running the Mach operating system, including shared memory multiprocessors, permits developers to purchase hardware having the lowest cost/MIPS, and to allocate the right types and sizes of processors to servers.

In performance, it is Camelot's goal to have low cost per transaction and per lock, and to add little to the cost of disk I/O and calls on other servers. Additionally, Camelot is designed to make efficient use of shared memory multiprocessors.

3. Interface and Implementation

3.1. Camelot Release 1.0 Interface

The interfaces to Camelot comprise the *Camelot library* (for C programs) and an interactive program for configuring a node. The interfaces are described in much greater detail in the *Guide to the Camelot Distributed Transaction Facility* [16]

The Camelot library comprises routines and macros that allow a user to implement data servers and applications. For servers, it provides a common message handling framework and standard processing functions for system messages; e.g., for performing recovery and participating in two-phase commit. Thus, the task of writing a server is reduced to writing procedures for the particular operations supported by the server.

The library provides several categories of support routines to facilitate the task of writing these procedures. Transaction management routines provide the ability to initiate and abort nested and top level transactions. Data manipulation routines permit the creation and modification of static recoverable objects. These routines perform logging of modifications as a side effect. Locking routines maintain the serializability of transactions and automatically support lock inheritance within families of nested transactions. The library provides macros to simplify calling remote procedures.

Applications that execute transactions and perform operations on data servers use a subset of the library facilities. In particular, they use transaction management and server access (remote procedure call) macros.

In addition to the Camelot library, we are completing an abstract data type library that supports b-trees, extensible hash tables, and dynamic storage allocation. When the implementations of these shared, recoverable abstract data types are complete, this library will be contain another important set of programming abstractions for server writers.

The other interface to Camelot is provided by the *node configuration application.* The node configuration application permits authorized users to create, delete, start, shutdown, and restart servers. It permits users to specify disk quotas for servers, the maximum recovery time that Camelot should take to recovery from a node failure, and the preferable times of the day for taking archival dumps. Also, it provides commands for authorizing and deauthorizing users, and for showing a node's current configuration.

3.2. Camelot Functions

The primitive building blocks of Camelot are provided by Mach. They include processes, threads of control within processes, shared memory between processes, and message passing. In addition, some other programs that run on Mach, such as the MIG RPC stub generator and the C thread management library provide additional functions on which Camelot is based [3, 10].

To support the Camelot interface, Camelot must support disk, recovery and transaction management functions, as described below. Release 2 will support deadlock detection and reliability/performance evaluation. Lock-based synchronization primitives are primarily implemented in the Camelot library.

3.2.1. Disk Management

Camelot provides each data server with up to 2^{48} bytes of recoverable storage that can be mapped into the address space of data servers. With the cooperation of Mach, Camelot permits data servers to remap their storage spaces when their data exceeds the virtual addressing limitations of the hardware. To simplify the allocation of contiguous regions of disk space, Camelot allocates and deallocates disk storage in *chunks*, large blocks of data comprising many contiguous pages. Data servers are responsible for doing their own microscopic storage management. Also, they may use semantic knowledge of data access patterns to issue commands to influence the paging of their data. For example, data servers doing sequential data scans may initiate prefetching and preflushing of data.

To allow operations on data in recoverable storage to be undone or redone after failures, Camelot provides data servers with logging services for recording modifications to objects. Camelot automatically coordinates paging of recoverable storage to maintain the write-ahead log invariant [5].

3.2.2. Recovery Management

Camelot's recovery functions include transaction abort, and server, node, and media-failure recovery. To support these functions, Camelot Release 1 provides both new value and old value/new value forms of write-ahead value logging. Camelot writes log data to locally duplexed storage or to storage that is replicated on a collection of dedicated network log servers [4].

3.2.3. Transaction Management

Camelot provides facilities for beginning new top-level and nested transactions and for committing and aborting them. Two options exist for commit: *blocking* commit may result in data that remains locked until a coordinator is restarted or a network is repaired; *non-blocking* commit, though about twice as expensive in the normal case, reduces the likelihood that a node's data will remain locked until another node or network partition is repaired. In addition to these standard transaction management functions, Camelot provides an inquiry facility for determining the status of a transaction. This is used by the Camelot library to implement lock inheritance.

Camelot and Master Control Tasks
Node Server and Node Configuration Application
Camelot Library
Transaction Management
Recovery Management
Disk Management
Inter-node Communication

Figure 3-1: Logical Structure of Camelot

This figure describes the logical structure of Camelot. Camelot is logically hierarchical, except that the disk manager uses the node server for retrieving information about servers, and for storing long term disk allocation information.

3.3. Camelot Structure

The major functions of Camelot and their logical relationship are illustrated in Figure 3-1. All of these layers, except the library routines, are implemented by a collection of Mach processes, which run on every node in a distributed system. Each of these processes is responsible for supporting a particular collection of functions. Processes use Mach-provided threads of control to permit intra-process parallelism. Calls to Camelot are made to the Camelot library (e.g., to begin or commit a transaction), which in turn directs them to a particular Camelot process. Frequently called functions such as log writes are invoked by writing to memory queues that are shared between a data server and a Camelot process. Other functions are invoked using messages that are generated by MIG.

Figure 3-2 shows the seven processes in Release 1 of Camelot: camelot process, master control, disk manager, communication manager, recovery manager, transaction manager, node server, and node configuration application.[2]

- **Camelot.** This interactive process permits a user to set the Camelot configuration options, stores and retrieves these options from a Unix file, and restarts Camelot automatically after crashes. (User's are expected to store critical configuration data off-line as well as in the Unix file system for reliability reasons.)

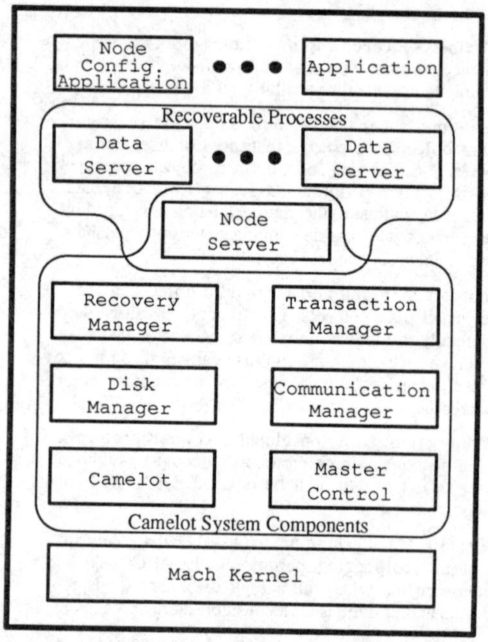

Figure 3-2: Processes in Camelot Release 1

This figure shows the Mach kernel and the processes that are needed to execute distributed transactions. The node server is both a part of Camelot and a Camelot data server because it is the repository of essential configuration data. Other data servers and applications use the facilities of Camelot and Mach. The node configuration application permits users to exercise control over a node's configuration.

[2]Camelot Release 2 will use additional processes to support reliability and performance evaluation, and deadlock detection.

- **Master Control.** This process restarts Camelot after a node failure, parses all switches, and redirects diagnostic output.
- **Disk Manager.** The disk manager allocates and deallocates recoverable storage, accepts and writes log records locally, and enforces the write-ahead log invariant. The disk manager works with dedicated network servers to support distributed logging. Additionally, the disk manager writes pages to/from the disk when Mach needs to service page faults on recoverable storage or to clean primary memory. Finally, it performs checkpoints to limit the amount of work during recovery and works closely with the recovery manager when failures are being processed. The disk manager is multithreaded to permit multiple I/O's in parallel.
- **Communication Manager.** The communication manager forwards inter-node Mach messages, and provides the logical and real clock services. In addition, it knows the format of messages and keeps a list of all the nodes that are involved in a particular transaction. This information is provided to the transaction manager for use during commit or abort processing. Finally, the communication manager provides a name service that creates communication channels to named servers. (The transaction manager and distributed logging service use IP datagrams, thereby bypassing the communication manager.)
- **Recovery Manager.** The recovery manager is responsible for transaction abort, server recovery, node recovery, and media-failure recovery. Server and node recovery respectively require one and two backward passes over the log.
- **Transaction Manager.** The transaction manager coordinates the initiation, commit, and abort of local and distributed transactions. It fully supports nested transactions.
- **Node Server.** The node server is the repository of configuration data necessary for restarting the node. It stores its data in recoverable storage and is recovered before other servers.
- **Node Configuration Application.** The node configuration application permits Camelot's human users to update data in the node server and to crash and restart servers.

4. Experience and Summary

The room reservation system (RR) [19] is an example of a special purpose office database application built using Camelot. As shown in Appendix 1, the RR application graphically displays (using X Windows) the reservations for departmental conference rooms and permits authorized users to make reservations. Almost all interaction is via mouse clicks.

The RR application can be run from any Mach workstation in the DARPA Internet, and it automatically finds a remotely located RR server, which stores one year's worth of reservations. Internally, the server represents the room reservation database as a hash table of rooms, where each room points to a large one-dimensional array. Each array contains 365 days x 24 (half-hour) room reservation slots. The server also uses a hash table for storing information about users. Not surprisingly, the overwhelming bulk of the code for RR is for the graphical interface, not the data server. The performance of the system on RT PC, Sun 3, and MicroVax II class workstations is fine, though some of the window management functions under X version 10 are a little sluggish.

A more traditional application of Camelot is distributed ET-1 [1]. In our experimental implementation, workstations send debit-credit requests to Camelot nodes, each of which has two servers: Bank and BankData. The Bank server receives input requests from simulated terminals, executes transactions on BankData, and then returns responses to the workstation. Fifteen percent of all ET-1 transactions are distributed and require access to two Camelot nodes. BankData stores its data in large arrays, but hash tables could be substituted with little performance impact.

The code for the main operation (`op_bankdata_et1`) in the BankData server is shown in Appendix 2. (This operation illustrates the use of the Camelot `LOCK`, `MODIFY` (assignment operator), `ABORT`, and `SERVER_CALL` primitives.) `Op_bankdata_et1` calls `op_acct_and_history`, either locally or remotely to update the account and history data. A *lazy* top-level transaction is used to update the history file's index so as to reduce contention. This permits the write lock on the index to be dropped immediately. A lack of space precludes us from listing the code for more of ET-1.

We executed 5 ET1 transactions/second/Camelot node, with 85% of the transactions executing in less than 1 second on an original Model IBM RT PC with non-DMA disks. We used two Camelot nodes running banking servers, and six workstations to drive the two nodes. While the zero second think time and number of workstations do not meet the specification of the ET1 benchmark, we essentially met the other requirements. Because we were not yet CPU or disk limited in the benchmark, we expect to find logical bottlenecks that will improve performance substantially.

Overall, we have been pleased with the programming interface to Camelot, and we have found it flexible enough. Debugging servers has not been easy, but we would expect that situation to improve as we get better multi-threaded debuggers and an Avalon/C++ language interface. The performance is good now, and it should improve further. (The *Camelot Interim Report* and Camelot User's Guide [18] provide detailed performance information.) We are looking forward to increasing the number of users of the system and more fully testing our distributed transaction processing support.

References

[1] Anonymous, et al.
A Measure of Transaction Processing Power.
Datamation 31(7), April, 1985.
Also available as Technical Report TR 85.2, Tandem Corporation, Cupertino, California, January 1985.

[2] A. Chang, M. Mergen.
801 Storage: Architecture and Programming.
ACM Transactions on Computer Systems 6(1Month=Febuary"), 1988.
Also appeared in SOSP-11 preprints. To appear.

[3] Eric C. Cooper.
C Threads.
June, 1986.
Carnegie Mellon Internal Memo.

[4] Dean S. Daniels, Alfred Z. Spector, Dean Thompson.
Distributed Logging for Transaction Processing.
In *Sigmod '87 Proceedings*. ACM, May, 1987.
Also available as Technical Report CMU-CS-86-106, Carnegie-Mellon University, June 1986.

[5] Jeffrey L. Eppinger, Alfred Z. Spector.
Virtual Memory Management for Recoverable Objects in the TABS Prototype.
Technical Report CMU-CS-85-163, Carnegie-Mellon University, December, 1985.

[6] R. Haskin, Y. Malachi, W. Sawdon, G. Chan.
Recovery Management in QuickSilver.
ACM Transactions on Computer Systems 6(??):??-??, ??, 1988.
Also appeared in SOSP-11 preprints. To appear.

[7] Pat Helland.
Transaction Monitoring Facility.
Database Engineering 8(2):9-18, June, 1985.

[8] M. P. Herlihy, J. M. Wing.
Avalon: Language Support for Reliable Distributed Systems.
In *Proceedings of the Seventeenth International Symposium on Fault-Tolerant Computing*. IEEE, July, 1987.

[9] *Customer Information Control System/Virtual Storage, Introduction to Program Logic*
SC33-0067-1 edition, IBM Corporation, 1978.

[10] Michael B. Jones, Richard F. Rashid, Mary R. Thompson.
Matchmaker: An Interface Specification Language for Distributed Processing.
In *Proceedings of the Twelfth Annual Symposium on Principles of Programming Languages*, pages 225-235. ACM, January, 1985.

[11] Bruce G. Lindsay, Laura M. Haas, C. Mohan, Paul F. Wilms, Robert A. Yost.
Computation and Communication in R*: A Distributed Database Manager.
ACM Transactions on Computer Systems 2(1):24-38, February, 1984.

[12] Barbara H. Liskov, Robert W. Scheifler.
Guardians and Actions: Linguistic Support for Robust, Distributed Programs.
ACM Transactions on Programming Languages and Systems 5(3):381-404, July, 1983.

[13] R. McCord.
INGRES/STAR: A Heterogeneous Distributed Relational DBMS.
In *Sigmod '86 Proceedings*, pages 1-1. ACM, May, 1987.

[14] Richard F. Rashid.
Threads of a New System.
Unix Review 4(8):37-49, August, 1986.

[15] Alfred Z. Spector.
Distributed Transaction Processing and the Camelot System.
In Yakup Paker et al. (editors), *Nato Advanced Study Institute Series - Computer and Systems Sciences: Distributed Operating Systems: Theory and Practice*, pages 331-353. Springer-Verlag, 1987.
Also available as Carnegie Mellon Report CMU-CS-87-100, January 1987.

[16] Alfred Z. Spector, Kathryn R. Swedlow, ed.
The Guide to the Camelot Distributed Transaction Facility: Release 1
0.7(33a) edition, Carnegie Mellon University, Pittsburgh, PA, 1987.

[17] Alfred Z. Spector, Joshua J. Bloch, Dean S. Daniels, Richard P. Draves, Dan Duchamp, Jeffrey L. Eppinger, Sherri G. Menees, Dean S. Thompson.
The Camelot Project.
Database Engineering 9(4), December, 1986.
Also available as Technical Report CMU-CS-86-166, Carnegie-Mellon University, November 1986.

[18] Alfred Z. Spector, Dean Thompson, Randy F. Pausch, Jeffrey L. Eppinger, Richard Draves, Dan Duchamp, Dean S. Daniels, Joshua J. Bloch.
Camelot: A Distributed Transaction Facility for Mach and the Internet - An Interim Report.
Carnegie-Mellon Report CMU-CS-87-129, Carnegie-Mellon University, June, 1987.

[19] Kathy Swedlow.
RR: The Camelot Room Reservation System.
December, 1987.
Camelot Working Memo 14.

[20] *NonStop SQL Benchmark Workbook*
84160 edition, Tandem, 1987.

[21] Matthew J. Weinstein, Thomas W. Page, Jr., Brian K. Livezey, Gerald J. Popek.
Transactions and Synchronization in a Distributed Operating System.
In *Proceedings of the Tenth Symposium on Operating System Principles*, pages 115-126. ACM, December, 1985.

Appendix 1

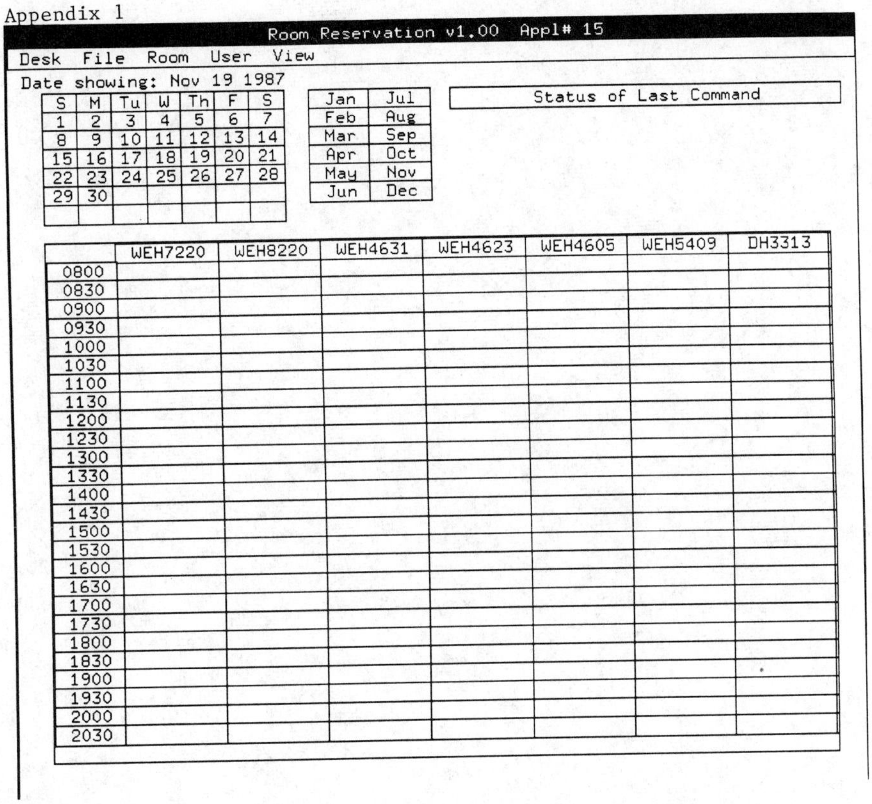

Appendix 2

```
/*
 * 'op_bankdata_et1' is the RPC entry point for et1 transactions. The branch and teller balances
 * are set, and then (either as an RPC, or as a local subroutine call), 'acct_and_history' is
 * invoked to set the account balance and add a history record at the appropriate node.
 */
EXPORT
void op_bankdata_et1(req, reply)
et1_request_t   req;
et1_reply_t     *reply;
{
        et1_reply_t             dummyAnswer;
        branch_balance_t        branch_temp;
        teller_balance_t        teller_temp;

        LOCK(LOCK_NAME(REC(branches[req.arrival.num].branch_balance)),
                LOCK_MODE_WRITE);

        branch_temp = REC(branches[req.arrival.num].branch_balance) + req.amount;
        if ( branch_temp < 0 )
                ABORT(AB_BANKDATA_BRANCH_FUNDS);
        MODIFY( REC(branches[req.arrival.num].branch_balance), branch_temp);

        LOCK(LOCK_NAME(REC(branches[req.arrival.num].tellers[req.teller])),
                LOCK_MODE_WRITE);

        teller_temp = REC(branches[req.arrival.num].tellers[req.teller]) + req.amount;
        if ( teller_temp < 0 )
                ABORT(AB_BANKDATA_TELLER_FUNDS);
        MODIFY( REC(branches[req.arrival.num].tellers[req.teller]), branch_temp);

        if ( STRMATCH(req.home.server.name, current_machine_name) )
                {
                op_acct_and_history(req);
                }
        else
                {
                camelot_string_t        server_name;
                (void) strcpy(server_name, "bankdata@");
                (void) strcat(server_name, req.home.server.name);
                SERVER_CALL(server_name, acct_and_history(ARGS req));
                }

        (void) strcpy(dummyAnswer.filler, "all done"); /* put something into answer */
        *reply = dummyAnswer; /* ensure 200 bytes are copied */
```

Distributed Databases

Chair: B. Mahbod

Site Autonomy in a Distributed Database Environment

by Bob Cornelis

Sybase, Inc.

Abstract

This paper discusses the issue of site autonomy in the model of a decentralized distributed database system. This issue is of paramount importance to database administrators in such an environment. The two major characteristics of site autonomy are identified and examined and examples are provided to demonstrate their significance. A system architecture is proposed which provides a flexible and powerful way of achieving the required degree of site autonomy.

Introduction

Distributed database management (DDBM) systems will be required to run in very diverse computing environments. Some of these environments will be composed of a central, controlling unit connected to, and directing the operation of, other peripheral units. Others may consist of several units participating equally in applications where performance is a key issue and the DDBM system is being used to manage load balancing. Still others will be made up of distinct functional units tied together in order to allow separate entities in an organization to become more functionally integrated while maintaining their independent integrity. In each of these models, the concerns of the database administrators in charge of the various sites will differ in relation to the rationale behind the use of a DDBM system in that environment.

In the centralized model, administrators will be interested in a system which allows them to easily set up and control the database schema all other sites will use and which allows them to restrict the activity of these sites. Their primary concern will be the ability to enforce policy.

In the performance model described, administrators will want to be able to set up a very dynamic environment. The location of both applications and the objects they run against should be easily changed to allow fine tuning of the environment while the system is running. The primary administrative concern in this environment is flexibility and the ability to monitor performance.

In the decentralized model, the administrators at each site will be primarily concerned with minimizing the degree to which the state of other sites in the system affects their own users. This local independence in a distributed database environment is the essence of site autonomy. The decentralized distributed environment is an important one to examine since many existing organizations will adopt that model when they choose a DDBM system rather than change the way they manage their various corporate entities. There is a general movement toward decentralization of computing in the business world as networks and workstations become widespread. This paper will discuss the specific requirements that are needed to insure site autonomy and will propose a model with which these requirements can be met.

Site Autonomy

There are two sides to the issue of site autonomy in a decentralized distributed environment. Administrators have the dual responsibility of protecting the integrity of the data at their sites from applications and users running elsewhere in the system and of insuring that their users can run applications with as little interference from other sites as possible. They must be concerned with the view of their data they present to the rest of the world and also with the view of the rest of the world that other sites provide them.

Protecting Data Integrity

The problem of protecting local data integrity is more difficult in a distributed environment than in a non-distributed one. An administrator has little knowledge of users that may be logging onto other sites in the system and has probably even less understanding of what their applications are going to try to do. We will present some scenarios to illustrate the potential consequences of providing insufficient control over local data.

Imagine a banking system in which there are branch offices in San Francisco and New York, each with databases containing account information about their respective customers. One of the New York customers visits San Francisco and tries to transfer funds from his New York account to the account of one of the San Francisco customers. There are numerous opportunities for disaster in this simple example, each of which will serve to illustrate a level of control that is required by distributed database administrators.

A teller having permission to access the San Francisco accounts should not necessarily have equivalent access to the New York accounts. While they may understand the details of their own business system, they may not necessarily understand those of the New York office. An ignorant user could inadvertently disrupt the accounts at another branch. The New York administrator will want to restrict access to its accounts to *authorized users* at other sites who have sufficient knowledge to use them properly.

Even if authorization for access to a particular table or database exists, there would be no way to insure that the correct operating procedures of the New York branch would be followed by a user running from the San Fran-

CH2539-5/88/0000/0440$01.00 © 1988 IEEE

cisco branch. Once given access to the accounts, the San Francisco teller could, for example, debit the New York account by a larger amount than the account holds. It would be up to the application running in San Francisco to perform this integrity check, a responsibility that the New York office could not afford to entrust to others. The New York office will want a means by which it can insure that certain *ineligible operations are not performed on its data.*

The San Francisco teller may not realize that the New York branch has a policy of recording every debit greater than a specified amount in a log file that is checked every day by a bank officer. There may be a requirement that once a specified threshold has been surpassed in the account table, another log file is updated. These important business steps could be inadvertently excluded when the New York account is debited. That branch will want a way to insure that when certain events happen to the database, *other events can be triggered automatically.*

In addition to triggering other events in the database, accesses to local data from remote sites may have other processing associated with them. For example, debiting the accounts in New York may involve a series of updates to various tables that have to be performed in a specific order. This logical sequence of steps may change as new requirements arise at the New York branch. It would be too much to expect of users at other branches to know what procedural steps are needed in New York to debit an account, and too much to ask of the New York administrator to rely on those people following the correct steps. They need a way to provide a *logical interface for complex operations* to users at other sites.

Finally, a failure to correctly manage a multi-site transaction could result in inconsistent accounts at the San Francisco and New York branches. If the San Francisco account is credited, we must insure that the New York account is debited. Each site must be able to decide whether its part of the transaction will commit or abort, with the understanding that the none of the parts of the transaction will commit unless all participating sites agree to do so. A transaction management system must be provided that will guarantee that *distributed transactions will be treated as atomic events* and that sites will be able to determine the state of such transactions when they are being rolled forward or aborted during a database recovery.

Meeting the above requirements will satisfy the major concerns database administrators have regarding the exposure of their data to remote users in a distributed environment. Different levels of control are provided, from high level user authorization to low level procedural logic. These capabilities should be provided in a manner that is easy to set up and maintain. Ideally they exist in the database itself, providing a single point of control that is easily accessible to the administrator and which allows a consistent enforcement of database integrity rules. An example of such an implementation is found in Sybase's proposed solution to the distributed database problem. This solution makes use of TRANSACT-SQL, an extension to the standard SQL database language, which provides tools to implement database enforced integrity and site autonomy. We will examine how each of the above site autonomy issues is dealt with in the Sybase model.

User authorization is controlled by the addition of a system catalog in the local data dictionary that provides a local identity to a user attempting to access data from a remote site. The name of the remote site, combined with the name the user has on that site, provide a unique mapping to a user identification on the local site. This local user identification can itself be unique or can be mapped to from various combinations, providing the ability to define "group" accounts to which users at remote sites belong. Database and object permissions can be granted to and revoked from these local users in the same manner they are assigned to "real" local users. The system catalog which does the mapping is solely under the control of the local database administrator, who decides which operations are permissible by users from other sites.

Ineligible operations are controlled by providing new database objects called *rules* and *defaults.* A rule is a database object which can be used to enforce the domain of acceptable values for any column in a table. No values outside of this domain are allowed in the specified column. A default is an object which assigns a value to a column in the absence of a user-supplied value. Both of these objects are defined in a single place, the database, and are central to the concept of database enforced integrity. Rules and defaults can prevent applications from introducing illegal values into local tables and can insure that legal values are assigned when the application fails to provide a value.

Necessary database events, defined by business rules, can be guaranteed to occur with the use of *triggers.* Triggers are database objects consisting of a sequence of TRANSACT-SQL statements that are executed every time a specified table is updated or queried. They can be used to provide referential integrity and to trigger events in the database when certain predefined conditions in that table are reached. Triggers are defined locally, *i.e.* at the site where the object they apply to is defined. They provide the administrator at that site a means of controlling the occurrence of events that are predicated on other states in their database being reached. The applications running on remote sites accessing local data do not even have to be aware of the execution of these events.

A logical interface between applications running remotely and local data is provided for in TRANSACT-SQL with *stored procedures.* A stored procedure is an object stored in the database which consists of (almost) any sequence of TRANSACT-SQL statements and is executed by simply calling the procedure, much like a subroutine call in high level programming languages. It can accept parameters and can contain complex logic based on control flow extensions (WHILE, IF-ELSE-THEN) to SQL. An application running at the San Francisco branch need only execute a procedure installed in New York to update the account table at that site. Any business (operational) logic involved can be included in the procedure and controlled by the administrator of the New York branch. This creates a very high level functional interface between applications and the data they operate on. More importantly in a distributed environment, it provides a high level interface between applications and distinct business operations that insures that the latter are under the control of the proper authority of the administrator rather than that of the application program.

The last requirement we have discussed is to insure consistent and predictable participation in distributed transactions. Sybase supports a two-phase commit protocol for committing transactions that mandates that all sites committing in a distributed transaction must agree to commit (PREPARE) before the transaction is committed. Once all sites have entered the PREPARE state, they will commit the transaction even in the event of a subsequent site failure. This protocol avoids partially committed distributed transactions since all sites must enter an intermediate state before committing their portion of the transaction. Site autonomy is enforced because the transaction a site participates in cannot commit unless the site agrees to it.

Independence from other Sites

The other side of site autonomy deals with the vulnerability of a site due to its dependence on other sites in the distributed system. This independence is the complement to the control we have been discussing in providing database administrators with the ability to maintain site autonomy. Two events will happen at sites that will impact other sites in the system—they can become unavailable or their schema can undergo structural changes. Sites trying to access sites where these events have occurred might experience failures of varying types. We will examine both of these events and demonstrate how the Sybase model of distributed computing can reduce the exposure other sites experience when these events occur.

Site Failures

When a site is unavailable there is obviously nothing that can be done to allow applications running elsewhere to continue if they are dependent on data that exists only at the failed site. There are two strategies that can be used to reduce the risk of site failure affecting applications. The first is to maintain replicated copies at other sites of tables on which the applications are running. The use of replication is up to administrators to decide upon since the robustness it provides is counterbalanced by the cost of maintaining the copies. Sybase provides the ability to replicate data with the use of triggers and stored procedures. Decisions can be made within the logic of these database objects regarding which copies should be updated and what should be done in the case of update failure. Managing data replication in an effective manner is complex, and while the Sybase architecture already provides tools that can be used to implement such a scheme, there will probably be further evolution of these requirements and the solutions to them.

The second strategy that can be used is to reduce any global reliance on a single site for information needed at other sites. The usual domain in which this dependence manifests itself is in the distributed data dictionary. In some systems, the dictionary information concerning objects which will be accessed in the distributed environment is located at a single site. All accesses to remote objects require information about those objects—where they are, the data types involved, the size of the objects for query optimization, etc. These accesses will fail if that information is located at a site which is not available, even if the site containing the object itself is available.

This dependence on the availability of the global data dictionary is an exposure that Sybase has eliminated in its distributed system architecture. Instead of a single source of distributed object information, this information is distributed throughout the system as it is needed. Data dictionary information about remote objects is retrieved from the site at which the object is located and cached locally for subsequent use by the current or other users. The distribution of object information in the system migrates to different sites as their applications reference remote objects. Only the sites participating in the query need be available for the query to be capable of running. The remote object data dictionary cache can be refreshed in a variety of ways based on timestamps in the dictionary itself or due to forced recompilations of queries when it is decided at the remote site that the cached data dictionary information was inaccurate. The result of this dictionary architecture is that the failure of any site only results in the unavailability of objects defined at that site.

Schema Changes

The second event which occurs at sites which impacts applications running against them is a schema change. Examples of this include an object changing location (to another database or site), an table being restructured into several table, or a data type change within the table. Ideally an application should not have to change every time one of the objects it references undergoes such a change.

We have already been introduced to the essential component of an environment in which application changes due to schema changes are minimized. It is the concept of providing a logical interface to the physical objects or events that are occurring. We have described how this logical interface can be achieved with the use of stored procedures. An application can be buffered from underlying physical changes to an object against which it is running by accessing it through stored procedures that are installed and controlled by the administrator of the objects database. By changing the procedure to conform to the new schema, the number of instances in which the application has to be changed can be reduced. It simply continues to call the stored procedure and provide it with the parameters required to perform the logical operation.

Stored procedures thus fill two roles in providing site autonomy in the distributed environment. First, they provide control to the administrator at the site they are installed at and, second, they provide independence to the applications executing them from other sites.

Another way in which schema changes can be hidden from applications is through the use of synonyms. In the Sybase architecture, synonyms are alternate names for database objects. A synonym can be defined in any database and can refer to a table in any database on any site. It can be used from any site, as if it were an ordinary table name in the database in which it is defined. If an object changes location, this fact can be hidden from an application by referring to that object through a synonym and then simply modifying the synonym to reflect the object's new location. It is transparent to the application or end user that the object referred to is, in reality, a synonym rather than the object itself. A synonym is another type of logical interface to objects that reduce an application's dependence on what configuration changes are occurring at other sites.

Summary

In a decentralized model of a distributed system, one of the primary requirements of database administrators is an architecture that can provide a high degree of site autonomy. Site autonomy is characterized by two aspects. The first is *local control* over data and the second is *site independence* from remote changes and failures. Sybase is proposing an architecture and a set of tools based on TRANSACT-SQL which can achieve a high level of autonomy, as defined by these requirements. Control is maintained by allowing database enforce integrity and a logical interface to objects and operations on those objects. Independence is attained in two ways. Data dictionary information about objects is distributed throughout the system, thus avoiding vulnerability to a single point of failure. Logical interfaces to objects create a loosely-coupled environment that is more robust when faced with schema changes. By using the tools supplied by the Sybase distributed architecture, database administrators can easily define and maintain the levels of local control and site independence that are appropriate to their business environment.

HIGH END SCIENTIFIC WORKSTATIONS Track

The Dana Personal Supercomputer

Chair: C. Maples

Single-User Supercomputers or How I Got Rid of the BLAS

Cleve Moler

Dana Computer, Inc.
Sunnyvale, California

Abstract

Dana's new Titan is a supercomputer with a price tag that makes it possible to devote the entire machine to a single user. Peak floating point performance is 64 megaflops. The Titan compilers automatically vectorize and parallelize standard code. Powerful, integrated graphics allow visualization of the results of computational experiments. The LINPACK Benchmark is one tool for analyzing how well computers approach their peak performance ratings.

The Titan Hardware

The Titan system from Dana Computer is a new class of machine: a single-user supercomputer with tightly integrated graphics. Titan closely couples the computation power of a supercomputer to dynamic, 3D, full-color, high-performance graphics in a single system. Titan is dedicated to individual scientists and engineers working on high-priority projects. Titan can also be accessed across a network and shared by other users, but without the graphics.

Titan is a symmetric multiprocessor with from 1 to 4 processors. Each processor incorporates a 64-bit, vector floating point arithmetic unit. The capabilities of the expandable system can be summarized by a few numbers:

- 16 - 64 MIPS
- 16 - 64 MFLOPS
- 50 "MIXELS"—Millions of pixels per second
- 8 - 128 MB of main memory
- 256 MB/second internal memory bandwidth
- 0.1 - 0.2 Megadollars per system.

The list price for a typical configuration is comparable with a "high-end" workstation whose arithmetic power is 1 to 2 orders of magnitude less. The list price is considerably below that of a "minisuper" with a comparable MFLOPS rating, but no graphics.

The Titan system is designed around multiple identical processing elements, running in parallel. Each processor has a general-purpose integer unit with high-speed caches coupled to a co-executing vector unit.

Each Titan integer unit acts as the control unit for the processor and performs all non-floating-point operations. It issues instructions to the vector unit for floating point operations, and it synchronizes with the vector unit. Its principle components are

- *RISC processor*. 16 megahertz clock and single cycle execution.
- *Large cache*. Two direct-mapped caches, one for instructions and one for non-floating-point data.
- *Bus watcher*. Ensures coherency among multiple data caches and main memory.

The combined effect of these features is a 16 MIPS peak performance level for each processor.

Each Titan vector unit has a peak floating point execution rate of 16 MFLOPS, with independent multiplier, adder, and divider. The unit supports 32- and 64-bit floating point formats that conform to IEEE standard 754. A key component of the unit is a vector register file containing a total of 8,192 64-bit elements that can be software configured into multiple vector registers of any length. The default configuration is 256 registers of length 32. This allows several concurrently executing processes to access distinct sets of vector registers, thereby significantly reducing the costs of context switches.

The memory subsystem supports Titan's high system throughput. A fully-configured Titan has a memory capacity of 128 MB with 16-way memory interleaving. Peak memory bandwidth is 256 MB per.second while supporting fully homogeneous addressing of system memory. The memory system provides error detection and correction.

The graphics output device is a 19-inch color, 1280× 1024, 60 Hz, non-interlaced display. Much of the processing associated with graphics is done by the general purpose integer and vector units. The only specialized graphics hardware is a rasterizing subsystem that, in a fully configured system, consists of 12 parallel pixel processors, 3 polygon processors, 48 image planes for double-buffered, 24-bit, full color images and a 16-bit Z-buffer with four overlay planes and three control planes. The system also has NTSC genlock circuitry to provide interfaces to monitors, tape recorders and other video devices. The speed of the graphics subsystem makes it possible, for example, to produce an animated sequence consisting of 10,000 Gouraud-shaded triangles per frame at 15 frames per second.

The Titan Software

As much effort has been devoted to the development of Titan's software as to its hardware. The major components are

- Supercomputing UNIX*.
- Titan Compilers.
- Doré**—Dana Object-Rendering Environment.

The Titan operating system provides full compatibility with standard AT&T UNIX System V.3 operating system and Berkeley 4.3 UNIX extensions. Dana's enhancements for supercomputing applications include

- Symmetric multiprocessing.
- Fast file system—1,000 KB/second with disk striping.
- Asynchronous I/O.
- Large, multi-volume files.
- X+ window system.

The basic design of the Dana-developed compilers for FORTRAN and C has focused on optimal performance in a vector and parallel environment. The key features include

- Automatic generation of vector and parallel operations from ordinary source programs in either FORTRAN or C.
- Inline expansion of selected functions and procedures.
- Powerful global optimizations.
- Compatibility with VAX† /VMS FORTRAN .
- Compatibility with Cray†† compiler directives.
- Features from ANSI C.

Language-dependent front ends for FORTRAN and C produce an intermediate parse tree which is then processed by common optimization and code generation phases. The vectorization, parallelization, and optimization algorithms are based on a rigorous, deep analysis of data interdependence, rather than on *ad hoc* pattern matching.

Doré, the Dana Object-Rendering Environment, is a powerful, interactive system for the generation of 3-dimensional, color graphics and for the visualization of the results of scientific computation. Its key features include

- Common scene database.
- Integral ray tracing and solid texture mapping.
- Interactive, real-time, dynamic imagery.
- Smooth balance of image realism against computation time.
- Simulation of a "virtual" photography studio.
- Easy extensibility.

LINPACK and the LINPACK Benchmark

The impression gained from recent articles in the electronics trade press, business journals, and computer ads is that LINPACK is a benchmark, something like the Whetstone benchmark or the Livermore Loops. That's only a small portion of the whole story.

LINPACK is primarily a FORTRAN subroutine library for matrix computation. It can be used to factor matrices, solve linear systems of equations, obtain determinants and inverses, analyze least-squares problems, estimate the accuracy of computed solutions, and so on. The package was developed between 1974 and 1979 at Argonne National Laboratory and at three universities—California at San Diego, New Mexico, and Maryland.

The LINPACK Users' Guide, by J. J. Dongarra, J. R. Bunch, C. B. Moler, and G. W. Stewart, is published by SIAM, the Society for Industrial and Applied Mathematics. The public-domain source code is available from several sources, including the National Energy Software Center at Argonne and through the software distribution services provided by NAG (Numerical Algorithms Group) and IMSL (International Mathematical and Statistical Libraries.)

The primary LINPACK library consists of 40 FORTRAN subroutines in each of four precisions—real, double, complex and double complex. For example, the two most commonly used subroutines are

- DGEFA, factor a double precision general matrix, and
- DGESL, use the factors to solve a linear system.

Replacing the leading D in the subroutine names with S, C, or Z leads to the same capabilities in other precisions.

Ten years ago, when LINPACK was being written, many FORTRAN compilers produced inefficient code for the "inner loop" operations on two dimensional arrays. Consequently, LINPACK makes use of a sublibrary known as the BLAS, for Basic Linear Algebra Subprograms, to perform fundamental vector operations. The three BLAS used by DGEFA and DGESL are

- IDAMAX, index of largest component of a vector,
- DSCAL, multiply a vector by a scalar,
- DAXPY, add a scalar multiple of one vector to another.

---

* UNIX is a trademark of AT&T.
** Doré is a trademark of Dana Computer, Inc.
† VAX is a trademark of Digital Equipment Corp.
†† Cray is a trademark of Cray Research, Inc.

Today, with powerful, optimizing FORTRAN compilers, the subroutine call overhead associated with the BLAS may be a source of inefficiency. The sophisticated memory architecture of the Titan allows the vector register load and store operations out of main memory to operate simultaneously with, and as fast as, vector arithmetic operations like DAXPY. Near peak performance can be obtained without concern for retaining intermediate results in vector registers or for keeping data caches full.

The Titan FORTRAN compiler is capable of "inlining"—effectively merging the source code for the BLAS into the source code for the primary LINPACK routines—and then producing optimally efficient vector and parallel object code. On the Titan, the operation represented by DAXPY, which is at the heart of many LINPACK routines, becomes a single vector multiply and accumulate instruction.

What is now called the LINPACK Benchmark began with the testing of the LINPACK library almost ten years ago. It consists of using DGEFA and DGESL to solve a random 100×100 system of simultaneous linear equations, timing the computation, and computing a megaflop rate. There is also a check on the residuals to verify that the computation was done correctly, but this is not counted in the timing. Jack Dongarra has collected the results for a wide range of machines and periodically issues a summary in an Argonne technical report, ANL-TM-23.

The popularity of the LINPACK Benchmark arises partly because the matrix algorithms it uses are prevalent in scientific and engineering computation and partly because it is well correlated with other performance measurements. Swanson Analysis Systems, Inc., has measured the performance of their ANSYS finite element analysis program on a wide range of machines and problems. One set of measurements, on four problems which they refer to as SP-1 through SP-4, has been made on 27 different machines from workstations to supercomputers with performance ranging over almost 3 orders of magnitude. The problems involve I/O and setup, as well as the floating point intensive solution phase. The following graph shows that the correlation with the LINPACK Benchmark is comparable with the correlation among the four different problems.

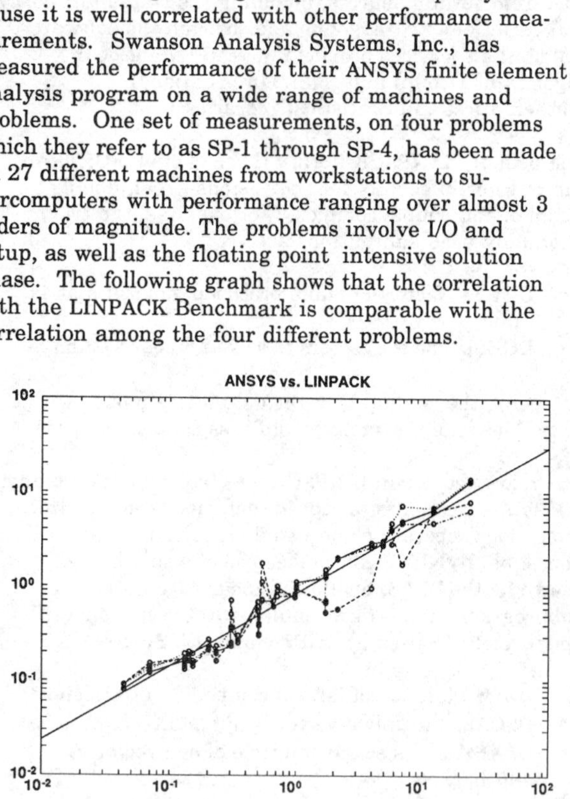

Appendices to Dongarra's report also give timing and megaflops results for two other programs. One involves solving a 300×300 linear system using an algorithm with reordered loops so that intermediate results may be retained in any faster memory that may be available. The other involves solving a 1000×1000 linear system with any algorithm that works correctly for general matrices. Technically, these appendices should not be called "LINPACK" benchmarks because they do not use the LINPACK library.

Useful information about performance can be also obtained by using DGEFA and DGESL to solve systems of varying order, including the Benchmark's 100×100, but not changing the algorithm or source code. As the order, n, of the matrix is increased, the MFLOPS rates of DGEFA and DGESL are eventually determined solely by the MFLOPS rate of the vector operation represented by DAXPY. Understanding how this peak rate is approached with varying n sheds some light on performance of realistic vectorized code. It is possible that such results may be better correlated with other, non-LINPACK, scientific computations than those in Dongarra's appendices.

We confine our analysis to the Gaussian factorization routine, DGEFA, because most of the time is spent there. In outline, the algorithm is:

FOR $k = n - 1$ DOWNTO 1
  IDAMAX of length $k + 1$
  DSCAL of length k
  k swaps of pairs of matrix elements
  k DAXPYs of length k

For machines like the Titan where performance of vector operations is not limited by memory references, we can model the performance of this algorithm by assuming the execution time for each vector operation is a linear function of the vector length.

time for IDAMAX(k+1) = $a_1 + b_1 k$
time for DSCAL(k) = $a_2 + b_2 k$
time for DAXPY(k) = $a_3 + b_3 k$
time to swap two elements = a_4

The total time is

$$t = \sum_{k=1}^{n-1} a_1 + b_1 k + a_2 + b_2 k + (a_4 + a_3 + b_3 k)k$$

which is approximately

$$t = \frac{1}{3} b_3 n^3 + \frac{1}{2} (b_1 + b_2 + a_3 + a_4) n^2$$

The algorithm requires about 1/3 n^3 multiplications and 1/3 n^3 additions, so the MFLOPS rate is

$$\text{MFLOPS} = \frac{\frac{2}{3} n^3}{t}$$

$$= \frac{2}{b_3} \frac{1}{1 + s/n}$$

where

$$s = \frac{3}{2} \frac{b_1 + b_2 + a_3 + a_4}{b_3}$$

The peak rate approached for large n is $2/b_3$, the asymptotic rate of DAXPY. For a single processor of the Titan, this is 16 MFLOPS.

In this model, the attenuation for finite values of n is determined by the quantity s. In particular, when $n = s$, the LINPACK megaflop rate is one-half of the peak rate of DAXPY. Note that s depends upon the peak rates for IDAMAX and DSCAL, the startup time for DAXPY, and the time to swap two matrix elements.

Roger Hockney introduced the notion of $n_{1/2}$, the vector length necessary to achieve one-half the peak performance. Our analysis here suggests regarding s as a matrix $N_{1/2}$, the matrix order necessary to achieve one-half the peak performance on the LINPACK Benchmark.

The following graph shows how this model of LINPACK Benchmark performance would behave on machines with peak rates of 16 MFLOPS and $N_{1/2}$ of 100 and 300. Both graphs are approaching 16 MFLOPS as n increases, but clearly the machine with a larger $N_{1/2}$ approaches the peak more slowly.

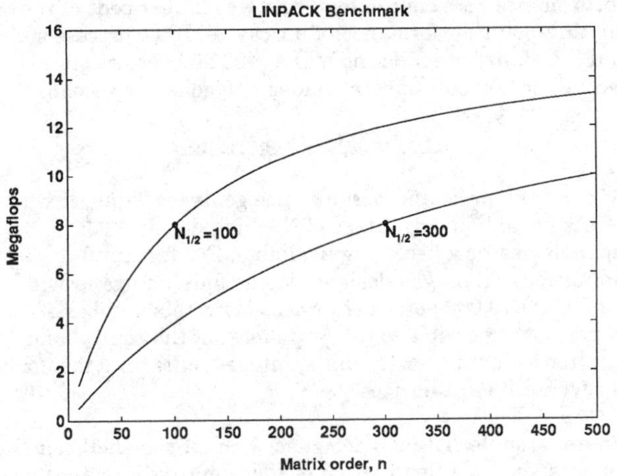

Conclusion

In summary, Dana's new Titan offers the computational scientist or engineer a new class of machine with

- A price tag that makes it possible to devote the entire machine to a single user.
- Peak floating point performance of 64 MFLOPS.
- Hardware and software features that allow a healthy percentage of peak performance to be obtained on realistic problems.
- Compilers that automatically vectorize and parallelize, eliminating the BLAS and other, similar programming constructs.
- Powerful, integrated graphics to visualize the results of computational experiments.

SQUEEZING A CRAY-CLASS SUPERCOMPUTER INTO A SINGLE-USER PACKAGE

Glen S. Miranker
Jon Rubinstein
John Sanguinetti

Dana Computer, Inc.
Sunnyvale, California

Abstract

The need for a low-cost machine to perform large-scale engineering and scientific computations is being addressed by a new class of computers—the single-user supercomputer. Advances in compiler technology and the speed and density of low-cost, high-speed semiconductors, combine to make these new machines possible. We describe how these technologies were used to construct Titan, a single-user supercomputer with integral high-performance graphics.

Goals of the Titan

Titan was conceived to be a *personal visualization tool.* It is a machine that allows an engineer or scientist to construct a model of a physical object or process and then visualize the results of some analysis of the model. Consequently, the machine must be able to do the computation required for physical modeling as well as be capable of rendering the resulting image in a reasonable amount of time.

Typical physical modeling tasks include fluid dynamics problems, solids modeling, and molecular modeling. For a 3D viscous fluid problem, a 500,000-point grid might take 1 billion floating point operations for a single iteration, and it might take up to 1,000 iterations for convergence. A Cray-class machine, averaging 25 MFLOPS, takes about 40 seconds per iteration.

Substantial computational power is also needed to view the results of such computations. Drawing a picture occupying one-half the screen area (655,360 pixels on a 1280×1024 screen) using a ray-tracing algorithm and Phong shading with 3 light sources, shadows, and environmental reflections typically takes 3.5 billion floating point operations.

These kinds of physical modeling problems are currently solved on a supercomputer, with images then drawn on a graphics workstation as a distinct back-end task. The main computer might be shared among many users, giving each user only a fraction of its computing resources. The "thin wire" connection between a computing resource and a display terminal limits the flexibility and rapidity with which the user can study, modify and re-analyze a problem. A machine dedicated to a single user providing a significant fraction of a supercomputer's performance provides more computation cycles to the user's problem than does a shared machine. Integrating the graphics processing as a part of the architecture of this machine allows rapid and immediate feedback of the results of an analysis.

These computational goals imply that Titan needs a fast processor and a very high bandwidth processor-to-memory interconnection. In order to do double-precision vector triad operations, the processor-to-memory connection must deliver 16 bytes to the processor and 8 bytes to memory for each operation, making a requirement of 24 MB per MFLOP. Such high computation rates imply large data sets that in turn require large main memories—32 MB and larger.

The goal of the Titan was to allow an individual to address visualization tasks on his own machine. The initial performance goal chosen for Titan was 25 per cent of the floating-point performance of a Cray X/MP (1 processor), and the ability to render images at 400,000 vectors per second, or 200,000 smooth shaded polygons per second.

Technology Constraints

To meet the price and performance goals for Titan, it was necessary to take advantage of the high density CMOS technologies now becoming available. For fast implementation, Titan was designed using gate arrays providing 30,000-40,000 gates per device. With this number of gates, it was possible to integrate most of the control and data paths for the vector units, integer units, and memory in seven different devices.

Where possible, Titan is designed with off-the-shelf components, such as floating-point adder/multipliers and dividers from Weitek Corporation, and a RISC integer processor from MIPS Computer Corporation. Use of these components allowed design efforts to be focused on portions of the system that were not readily available and on areas where Dana could make a significant contribution. In addition, commercially available components are typically less expensive, reducing overall system cost. The same CMOS technologies that made our gate arrays possible allowed the development of these custom devices.

CH2539-5/88/0000/0452$01.00 © 1988 IEEE

Providing a system that meets the memory requirements of supercomputer applications and high performance graphics requires the use of low cost, high density dynamic RAMS. The advent of the 1 MBit DRAM allows inexpensive memory subsystems as large as 128 MB, which is equivalent to the memory subsystem size in the Cray X/MP. Again, these RAMs are made possible by CMOS technologies.

For power and cost reasons, the portions of the system that are not integrated are designed with standard TTL and CMOS components.

These technology choices, necessitated by cost and size constraints, mean that the system clock frequency is limited to 16-20 MHz. To build a Cray class machine that operates at this comparatively low clock frequency requires innovations in architecture and implementation, primarily the exploitation of parallelism at many system levels. In order to see how this was done in Titan, a brief review of the machine architecture follows.

Titan Architecture

The major components of the Titan are shown in Figure 1. The Titan hardware was designed to support fully symmetric multiprocessing with one to four processors in the system. Except for processing of fatal hardware errors, all processors in the system are identical and consist of two distinct parts: an *integer processor* or IPU and a *vector processor* or FPU. Bus arbitration is "fair", allowing each processor an equal opportunity to access system resources. In order to support the peak execution rate of the IPU, each integer unit has its own 16 KB instruction cache and a 16 KB *write-through* data cache. Writes are buffered in a 4-deep queue. This minimizes the performance impact of the store stalls normally associated with a write-through cache. An additional benefit of the cache is that it significantly lowers the bus utilization and memory bandwidth requirements for the integer units, freeing these valuable resources for vector processing.

With multiple IPUs, as well as other devices such as I/O and graphics modifying memory, it is necessary to provide a mechanism to keep the caches in the system coherent. A bus watching mechanism was chosen since it requires no special bus protocols, allowing the vector units to operate at peak rates while still maintaining coherence. The data cache in each IPU contains its own bus watcher which maintains a duplicate set of tags. Duplicating the tag set minimizes degradation of IPU performance by allowing memory transactions to proceed at peak rate, interfering with IPU operation only if it accesses its data cache at the same time a bus watcher tag match occurs.

To provide for synchronization between processors, several mechanisms are provided. A load-and-clear instruction allows for simple semaphores and a load-and-increment instruction allows for counting semaphores. To assist with interprocessor communication, interrupt driven doorbells are available. Any processor may signal any other processor with this interrupt mechanism.

Titan Vector Unit

The Titan vector unit executes all floating-point instructions, both vector and scalar, as well as vector integer arithmetic. Its basic organization, shown in Figure 2, is basically Cray-like and consists of six major pieces:

- Interface to the IPU.
- Vector register file.
- Three independent arithmetic functional units: ALU, multiplier, and divider.
- Three independent memory pipes: two load pipes and one store pipe.
- Crossbar switch for routing of data among the system bus, the arithmetic functional units, and the vector register file.
- Translation look-aside buffers to translate the virtual memory pipe addresses to physical addresses.

The vector unit receives instructions from the IPU. Unless specifically directed to synchronize its operations with the IPU, once an instruction is received, FPU operation is completely independent of IPU operations. Concurrent operation of the IPU and FPU allows many scalar and integer operations, such as "bookkeeping" computations for strip-mining, to be overlapped with vector processing. The IPU interface supports this by allowing queuing of FPU instructions and providing the means for the two co-execution units to synchronize when explicitly required.

The vector unit contains four independent pipelines: the three memory pipes and the operation pipe. Each pipe can have a different instruction pending in each of its stages. Thus between concurrency within each pipe and among the four pipelines, greater than 50 instructions (in principle) can be in process in the vector unit at a given moment.

Even though there is such a large amount of concurrency, the programming model is simple. Hardware hazard and chain detection ensures that *all* operations complete in an order consistent with sequential execution, while achieving maximal overlap. The same hazard and chaining logic is used during scalar execution. As a result, sequences of data dependent scalar operations may be issued without regard to latency, and independent scalar operations complete at peak vector rates.

All operations of the vector unit (except synchronization instructions), loads, stores, and arithmetic operations use the vector register file as a source or sink of operands. The Titan vector register file is high bandwidth, supporting the simultaneous operation of all four vector unit pipes. It is also large, comprising 8 independent sets of 32 vector registers of length 32. Each vector register element can hold either 4 or 8 bytes. These 8 sets are assigned on a process by process basis to minimize context switching time.

The vector register file is unique in that operations may start at any point within a vector register. Thus convolutions and recurrences can be directly computed in the vector unit.

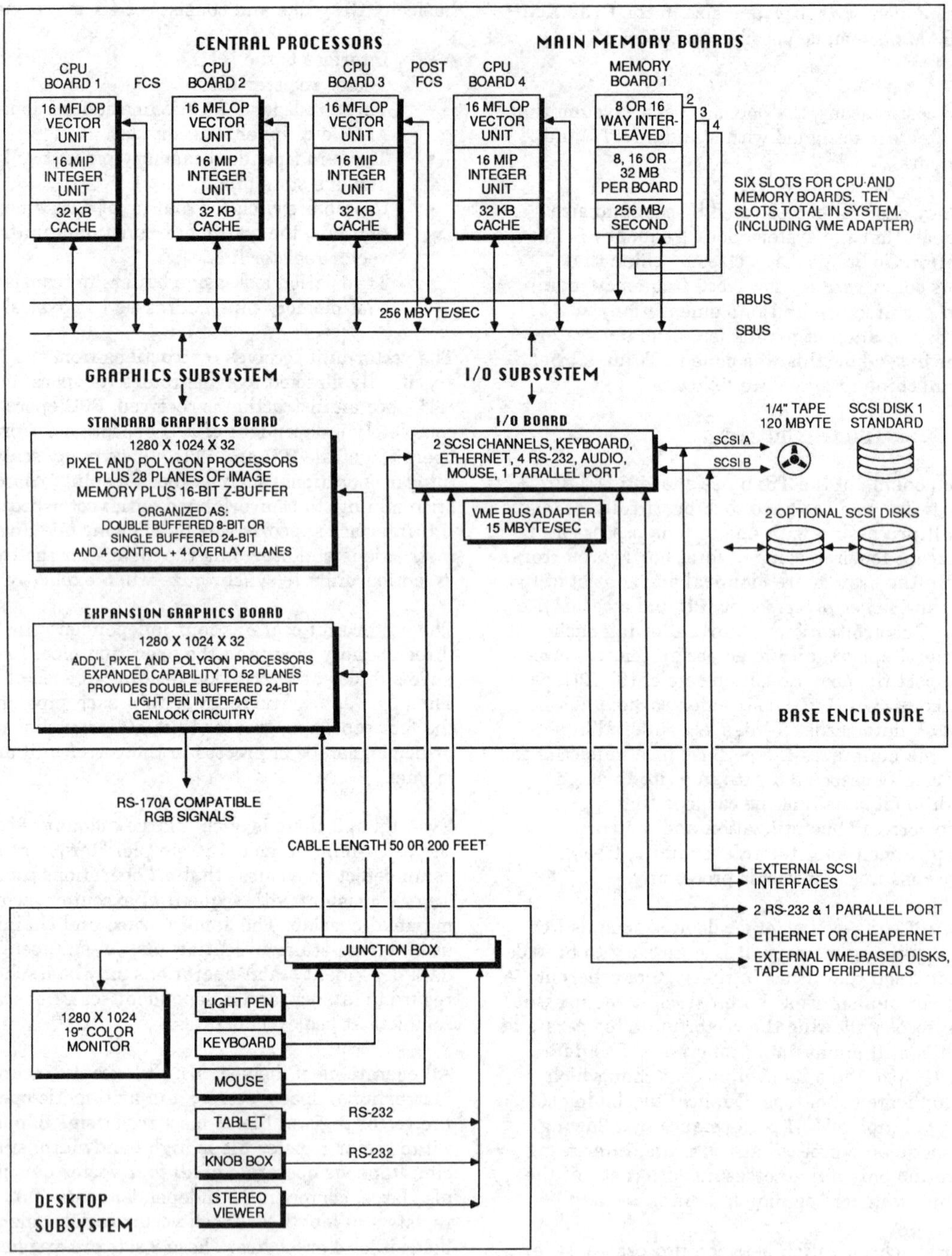
CENTRAL PROCESSORS
MAIN MEMORY BOARDS
CPU BOARD 1
FCS
CPU BOARD 2
CPU BOARD 3
POST FCS
CPU BOARD 4
MEMORY BOARD 1
16 MFLOP VECTOR UNIT
16 MIP INTEGER UNIT
32 KB CACHE
8 OR 16 WAY INTER-LEAVED
8, 16 OR 32 MB PER BOARD
256 MB/ SECOND
2
3
4
SIX SLOTS FOR CPU AND MEMORY BOARDS. TEN SLOTS TOTAL IN SYSTEM. (INCLUDING VME ADAPTER)
RBUS
256 MBYTE/SEC
SBUS
GRAPHICS SUBSYSTEM
I/O SUBSYSTEM
STANDARD GRAPHICS BOARD
1280 X 1024 X 32
PIXEL AND POLYGON PROCESSORS PLUS 28 PLANES OF IMAGE MEMORY PLUS 16-BIT Z-BUFFER
ORGANIZED AS: DOUBLE BUFFERED 8-BIT OR SINGLE BUFFERED 24-BIT AND 4 CONTROL + 4 OVERLAY PLANES
I/O BOARD
2 SCSI CHANNELS, KEYBOARD, ETHERNET, 4 RS-232, AUDIO, MOUSE, 1 PARALLEL PORT
SCSI A
SCSI B
1/4" TAPE 120 MBYTE
SCSI DISK 1 STANDARD
VME BUS ADAPTER 15 MBYTE/SEC
2 OPTIONAL SCSI DISKS
EXPANSION GRAPHICS BOARD
1280 X 1024 X 32
ADD'L PIXEL AND POLYGON PROCESSORS EXPANDED CAPABILITY TO 52 PLANES PROVIDES DOUBLE BUFFERED 24-BIT LIGHT PEN INTERFACE GENLOCK CIRCUITRY
BASE ENCLOSURE
RS-170A COMPATIBLE RGB SIGNALS
CABLE LENGTH 50 OR 200 FEET
EXTERNAL SCSI INTERFACES
2 RS-232 & 1 PARALLEL PORT
ETHERNET OR CHEAPERNET
EXTERNAL VME-BASED DISKS, TAPE AND PERIPHERALS
JUNCTION BOX
1280 X 1024 19" COLOR MONITOR
LIGHT PEN
KEYBOARD
MOUSE
TABLET
RS-232
KNOB BOX
RS-232
STEREO VIEWER
DESKTOP SUBSYSTEM

Figure 1.

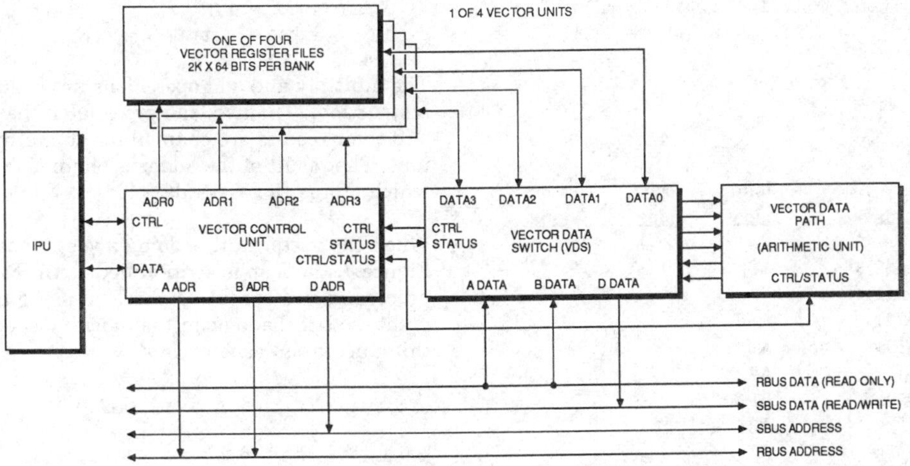

Figure 2.

To facilitate conditional computations, the memory pipelines support a rich set of operations: scatter/gather, and merge/compress/expand under mask. Similarly, the operation pipe supports merge and compress under mask of vector operations and nullification of scalar operations.

Titan Bus and Memory

Since the computational performance of any supercomputer cannot exceed the performance of its memory subsystem, a great deal of effort was focused on the implementation of the Titan bus and memory. The parity checked bus consists of two independent 8 byte data buses each with its own separate address and control lines. The buses are capable of simultaneous transfers at 16 MHz for an aggregate bus bandwidth of 256 MB/second. Synchronous, disconnect protocols ensure high bus utilization.

Titan's memory is provided on 1 to 4 memory boards. Each board holds 8-32 MB of SECMED protected memory organized as 8 independent interleaves. The 8 interleaves are connected by an 8x2 crossbar to the two system buses. Sixteen-way interleaving is achieved if 2 or 4 memory boards are installed.

Performance Through Parallelism

There are many levels in a machine design that allow parallel operation. In Titan, simultaneous operation is exploited in as many levels as we felt could be profitably used by the software.

Multiprocessing

By providing n complete copies of the processor, the basic processing rate is multiplied by n. Making effective use of multiple processors is currently a difficult problem for a compiler. However, compiler technology has advanced to the point where many instances of potential parallelism can be recognized and code can be generated for a shared memory model of computation. Many numerical applications that manipulate arrays of data are codes that have this kind of exploitable parallelism. In the Titan, there are up to 4 processors, each of which may work on a different task (standard multi-tasking), or any number of which may work on a single process (micro-tasking). Micro-tasking can be accomplished on very small code segments since inter-processor communication is achieved through shared memory, and inter-processor synchronization via the load-and-increment operation is fast, taking only a few instruction times.

Co-execution

Because the two major units of a processor, the IPU and FPU are independent, each can operate at the same time. The integer processor does basic instruction fetching and scalar integer and addressing operations, while the vector unit does all floating-point and vector operations.

Figure 3 gives an example of the effect of this overlapping execution. The example is a strip-mined loop, with a strip of length 8 (smaller than would normally be used). The code is shown in 3(a) and the run-time sequence of operations is shown in 3(b), along with the operation of the pipes in the vector unit. The load pipes are indicated by A and B. On any given cycle, one pipe is using the bus while the other pipe is generating its next address. The arithmetic pipe does an operation every other cycle, while the store pipe puts out results when they become available. Notice that the integer processor, by running independently, can stay ahead of the vector unit, allowing the computation rate to be limited solely by the speed of arithmetic operation.

Multiple functional units

A vector unit is made of several units, each of which can execute simultaneously. There are two load units, an arithmetic unit, and a store unit. This accommodates a triad of the form $x = y + z$. Since each unit can accommodate a vector operand, and results can be chained from one unit to another, all four units can be working at once on a given triadic operation.

```
      DO 12 I = 1,100
12       Z(I) = X(I+1) - X(I)
```

Figure 3a.

	integer processor	load pipe	op pipe	store pipe
$L1	<set up address(2)>			
	<set up address(1)>			
	<set up Load X(2)>			
	<start Load X(2)>	A1 *		
	<set up Load X(1)>	A2		
	<start Load X(1)>	B1 *		
	<start X(2)-X(1)>	A3		
	<set up Store Z(1)>	B2		
	<start Store Z(1)>	A4		
	<test for last strip>	B3		
	<loop back>	A5		
$L1	<set up address(10)>	B4	X2-X1 *	
	<set up address(9)>	A6		Z1 *
	<set up Load X(10)>	B5	X3-X2	
	<start Load X(10)>	A7		Z2
	<set up Load X(9)>	B6	X4-X3	
	<start Load X(9)>	A8		Z3
	<start X(10)-X(9)>	B7	X5-X4	
	<set up Store Z(9)>	A9 *		Z4
	<start Store Z(9)>	B8	X6-X5	
	<test for last strip>	A10		Z5
	<loop back>	B9 *	X7-X6	
$L1	<set up address(18)>	A11		Z6
	<set up address(17)>	B10	X8-X7	
	<set up Load X(18)>	A12		Z7
	<start Load X(18)>	B11	X9-X8	
	<wait for load pipe>	A13		Z8
	.	B12	X10-X9 *	
	.	A14		Z9 *
	.	B13	X11-X10	

* — beginning operation of a vector

Figure 3b.

Multiple arithmetic elements

There are an adder, a multiplier, and a divider in the arithmetic unit, all of which can be in operation simultaneously. Typically, the multiplier and adder will be chained together in a multiply-accumulate operation. The Titan uses a separate set of instructions to specify this chaining, putting the burden of chain-detection for such operations on the compiler.

Pipeline parallelism

Each of the functional units in the FPU is pipelined. Thus, each stage of each unit can be active at once on a different element. For a vector triadic operation, a high degree of parallelism can be achieved, as is shown in Figure 4. The operation being performed is Daxpy:

```
      DO 10 I = 1,N
10       Y(I) = Y(I) + A*Z(I)
```

The multiply and add operations are chained by the *mac* instruction. The two load pipes fetch the Y and Z operands, and their results are chained to the multiplier by the vector unit. The result of the adder is chained to the store pipe, which stores the Y result.

When the vector unit is doing a vector operation as in Figure 4, the loop is strip-mined as in Figure 3, and four processors are executing the loop using microtasking, a great deal of the logic in the machine can be doing something useful on each cycle.

```
i+1 2 3  4  5  6  7  8  9  10 11 12 13 14 15 16 17 18 19 20

Y(5)_____B  B  B  B  B  B
Z(6)________A  A  A  A  A  A
A*Z(3)______*  *  *  *  *  *
Y(6)___________B  B  B  B  B  B
Z(7)______________A  A  A  A  A  A
Y(1)+T1___________+  +  +  +  +  +
A*Z(4)____________*  *  *  *  *  *
Y(7)_________________B  B  B  B  B  B
Z(8)____________________A  A  A  A  A  A
Y(2)+T2_________________+  +  +  +  +  +
A*Z(5)__________________*  *  *  *  *  *
Y(8)_______________________B  B  B  B  B  B
Z(9)__________________________A  A  A  A  A  A
Y(3)+T3_______________________+  +  +  +  +  +
A*Z(6)________________________*  *  *  *  *  *
Y(9)_____________________________B  B  B  B  B  B
Z(10)_______________________________A  A  A  A  A  A
Y(4)+T4_____________________________+  +  +  +  +  +
A*Z(7)______________________________*  *  *  * *   *
Y(1)________________________________D  D  D  D  D  D
Y(10)_________________________________B  B  B  B  B  B
Z(11)____________________________________A  A  A  A  A  A
Y(5)+T5__________________________________+  + +   +  +  +
A*Z(8)___________________________________*  * *   *  *  *
Y(2)_____________________________________D  D  D  D  D  D
```

Figure 4.

Conclusion

By using new technology and making extensive use of parallelism at several levels, we were able to extend supercomputer performance to the single-user, graphics-oriented machine. Parallel operation at the pipeline, functional unit , and processor levels provides a very attractive price/performance ratio, while high levels of integration in CMOS gate arrays and off-the-shelf components provide a low absolute cost. A relatively fast processor-to-memory bus and a heavily interleaved main memory provide a sufficient data transfer rate to match the performance of the processors.

The result is a graphics supercomputer that has a peak processing rate of 64 MFLOPS and 64 MIPS, sustainable rates in excess of 10 MFLOPS and 20 MIPS, a double-precision 100x100 LINPACK rate of 10 MFLOPS (compiled), 200,000 shaded triangles/second, and 50 M pixels/second shading rate.

System Software for the Sciences: Taming the Single-User Supercomputer

Randy Allen
Bruce Borden
Steve Johnson
Michael Kaplan
Way Ting
Charles Wetherell

Dana Computer, Inc.
Sunnyvale, California

Abstract

The key measure of supercomputer performance is not peak speed, but rather the speed a programmer observes on an application and the effort expended to achieve satisfactory speed. In the past, supercomputers have tended to be unruly beasts, requiring much stroking and care to achieve significant fractions of peak speed. As supercomputer performance decreases in price, the ability of system software automatically to do that stroking increases in importance. This paper highlights the design aspects of the system software in the Titan (a single-user supercomputer) and describes how that software interacts with the hardware to provide supercomputer performance without superhuman effort.

Introduction

Realized computing speed advances come from two sources: increases in hardware performance and new developments in software. Recent advances in hardware performance have been dramatic and have received great attention. But software advances have been just as dramatic. For example, if one had the choice of solving a three dimensional partial differential equation for a particle in a box using present day software and 1960 hardware or using present day hardware and 1960 software, the solution would be obtained faster by using present day software and 1960 hardware [5].

Looking forward, current developments presage the nature of future computing systems. In hardware, RISC processors provide very fast, cost-efficient integer performance [6, 10]. Vector processors permit many codes to obtain fast floating point performance [7]. Parallelism is being extensively explored as a mechanism for achieving new speedups with existing hardware technology. In software, powerful restructuring and optimizing compilers have shown that user programs can utilize such hardware with little programmer intervention [3, 9, 2]. These developments all point to cheaper, more powerful computing. Dana Computer has followed this path to build a machine capable of supercomputing performance for a price that permits single-user usage. The resulting machine (codenamed Titan) is capable of 64 MFLOPS peak performance (16 MFLOPS per processor). A single processor Titan costs less than $100,000.

The availability of powerful, inexpensive computers such as the Titan will put a new slant on supercomputer software development:

1. *Graphics and visual applications will increase in importance.* Graphic interpretation of results is highly desirable in a number of areas, such as computational chemistry, computational fluid dynamics, and oil exploration. For example, one method for solving a partial differential equation (or any problem where a technique is iterated until a convergence criterion is reached) is to display the convergence graphically as the computation proceeds and allow the user to stop the computation when the results are satisfactory. At the moment, solutions like this are virtually impossible to explore. The underlying problems are computationally intensive, requiring supercomputer performance. Supercomputers are typically batch-oriented with few facilities for graphic display and their high cost must be amortized over a large number of users. Interactive graphics is not an option on these machines. The Titan will provide new opportunities to explore graphic and interactive solutions to computationally intensive problems.

2. *New software economics come into play* . Compared to the multi-million dollar hardware costs of a supercomputer, the cost of a programmer to rewrite codes to utilize that machine seems modest. Compared to the price of a $100,000 system, however, that cost is not so trivial. Accordingly, it is essential that compilers for a single user supercomputer be able to optimize user programs automatically. Adherence to industry standards also increases in importance.

Another way of saying all this is that a user buys not just a piece of hardware, but instead an entire computing system. The observed performance level depends upon the entire system—hardware, compilers, operating system, and graphics—and not just the hardware alone. In the past, the high cost of supercomputer hardware forced users to accept whatever software was presented because no other mechanism could deliver the desired performance. As supercomputer performance becomes more readily available, the effectiveness of the entire system will increase in importance.

The Titan single-user supercomputer has been designed from its very onset to have a close synergism of hardware, software, and graphics, to be a unified system that delivers supercomputer performance without requiring superhuman effort. To that end, Titan software development has been a careful amalgam of industry standards adapted for visualization and the supercomputer environment. This paper highlights the major aspects of the Titan software.

Operating System

Supercomputers traditionally run batch-oriented, proprietary operating systems (CTSS*, NOS**, SX†, and so on). However, proprietary operating systems require a substantial effort on the part of either the customer or some third party software vendor to convert existing applications. It is the goal of Dana Computer to provide an environment in which most existing applications can be ported readily. For this and other reasons stated previously (standardization and interactivity), Dana chose UNIX§ to be the operating system.

At the same time, it has to be recognized that applications that run on supercomputers are mostly "large" programs—that is, they are programs which

1. have a large instruction space;
2. have a large data space;
3. require a long execution time even on supercomputers;
4. read and write large amounts of data from disks; and,
5. potentially generate large files.

Any computer which is to be effective in supporting these applications must address each of the 5 points listed above. Traditional UNIX, unfortunately, does not meet these needs.

To properly support large applications, Dana's implementation of UNIX contains the following features:

1. *Total virtual address space (combined instruction, data, and stack) allowed is close to 2 Gbytes.* The paging system and the disk subsystem are capable of supporting such a large address space.

2. *Large files and high disk bandwith.* Dana's implementation of UNIX supports the idea of disk striping. Multiple physical disk drives can be configured to act as a single logical drive. Files are therefore no longer constrained to fit on a single physical drive. Furthermore, where the physical drives are connected to separate controllers, effective disk throughput can be doubled.

3. *Extent based file system.* The standard System V file system maintains a list of free disk blocks within a file system and allocates single blocks from this list. The net result , after a prolonged period of use, is that a file is likely to have its blocks scattered all over the disk drive. Accessing each block will typically incur the penalty of a seek and the average rotational latency. Dana has added a new, extent-based file system type which provides contiguity. Bandwidth in this file system is very high because the system issues large (typically more than a track's worth) reads and writes. Seek and rotational latency are kept to a minimum.

4. *Asynchronous file I/O.* The standard System V file system provides read-ahead. That is, when logical block *n* of a given file is read, a read for block *n+1* is also started asynchronously. This is often adequate in a time-sharing environment where there are multiple processes ready to run at any given moment, and each of the processes can make progress with small amounts of data from a disk file. A large application, however, often requires large amounts of data to start execution. Once execution has been started, it does not access the disk file for a relatively long time. Asynchronous file I/O exploits this program behavior very naturally. The process issues a read for a large block of data. When the read is completed, the process issues a read for the next block that it needs (not necessarily the next sequential block) asynchronously before it starts the execution on the first data block. Maximum overlap between I/O and computation may be achieved by this scheme.

5. *Multi-processing.* With multiple processors available to support one user, it is only natural to have different processors work on different tasks where possible. For instance, a user should be able to read mail in the foreground using one processor while other processors remain dedicated to a background computation-intensive task.

6. *Micro-tasking.* Effective use of parallelism within a single task requires efficient task spawning and low cost synchronization between processors. The Dana version of System V has incorporated the notion of a "lightweight" process (also known as a thread). The hardware, operating system, and compilers were designed together to make parallelism very efficient.

Compilers

The driving motivation behind the Titan compilers (both FORTRAN and C) is the philosophy that the user should not have to know the details of the Titan architecture. Instead, the compiler, as part of the optimization process, automatically utilizes the major features of the Titan hardware. In particular, standard code can obtain the benefits of

---

* CTSS is a trademark of Cray Research, Inc.
** NOS is a trademark of CDC, Inc.
† SX is a trademark of NEC, Inc.
§ UNIX is a registered trademark of AT&T.

1. *Multi-processors*. A Titan can have from one to four processors, each of which can be applied to a task.

2. *Vector hardware*. Each Titan processor contains a vector floating point unit.

3. *Low level parallelism*. Because each processor has independent integer and floating point units, these computations can be overlapped. Additionally, loads and stores can overlap computation.

The key to supercomputer performance is the capability to process many operands at once—either simultaneously, when vector hardware is invoked, or nondeterministically, when multiple processors are used. Because neither of these execution orders can be specified directly in standard C or FORTRAN programs, the compiler must determine when parallel or vector executions can produce the same results more quickly than sequential execution. To do so, the compiler captures all the execution constraints that *must* be observed for the correct results to be computed. For instance, in the following

S_1	R = 10
S_2	PI = 3.14
S_3	AREA = PI * R ** 2

S_3 must follow both S_1 and S_2 because it will use a wrong value of either PI or R if it does not. Nothing requires that S_2 follow S_1, however, and the correct results will be computed regardless of the relative execution of those two statements. The compiler records this fact by noting that S_3 *depends* on both S_1 and S_2. Once the compiler knows all the dependences in a program, it is free to optimize code for parallel and vector execution. So long as it does not violate any dependences, it will not change the results of the program.

The Dana compiler drives vectorization, parallelization, and scalar optimization from a dependence graph based on a significantly enhanced theory of data dependence. In this theory, sophisticated mathematical analysis is performed on array subscripts within loops to categorize dependences as being either *loop independent* or *loop carried* [1, 8]. Categorizing dependences in this manner provides a powerful but efficient basis for program transformations. The Dana compiler considers all loops within a nest to be viable candidates for vectorization and parallelization; after finding the best vector and parallel loops, it will interchange loops to move them into better positions. Because all optimizations were designed into the compiler from the beginning (and at the same time that the hardware was being designed), they cooperate to provide a very efficient, unified approach that creates highly optimized code.

The Dana compiler also exploits a dual side of dependence that has been largely unrecognized. A dependence arises when two statements access the same memory location. From a vectorization point of view, a dependence is a bad thing because it restricts some execution orders and may thereby inhibit vectorization. However, that same dependence means that two statements are referencing the same memory location, which can be useful information for allocating frequently used variables to registers. The Dana compiler is able to analyze dependences to uncover the most frequently accessed variables and to allocate them to vector and scalar registers. The result is that the Titan is more often able to operate at its processor speed, rather than at its memory speed. When this transformation has been hand-simulated on other machines, speedup factors of three have been obtained on key algorithms [4].

The Dana compiler contains a number of other technical features that help users automatically obtain efficient code.

1. *Automatic procedure inlining* . Procedure calls have always been a barrier to good optimization, primarily because they hide important information from the compiler. On vector machines, they provide a further hindrance: because procedure calls cannot be run in vector hardware, restructuring compilers cannot directly vectorize calls. Inlining procedures provides two major benefits: it opens the code for better vector/parallel analysis, and it tailors a call for a specific invocation, thereby eliminating unnecessary code at compile-time. Automatic procedure inlining allows users to write code in the most readable, maintainable fashion and still obtain very fast code.

2. *Sophisticated branch treatment*. Code containing conditionals and branches has always created problems for vector machines, primarily because vector hardware finds conditional execution difficult. Parallelism, however, provides a very natural, efficient mechanism for executing conditional code. Because the Dana compiler was designed from the beginning for the parallel-vector Titan hardware, it is able to parallelize many loops containing constructs such as assigned GOTOs and computed GOTOs which other compilers cannot handle.

3. *Postload optimization* . The limitations of addressing modes on many computers cause optimizing compilers severe problems. For instance, global data access can often be optimized, but only after the entire application has been loaded. The Dana compiling system contains a postload optimizer which is able to perform a number of optimizations that rely upon information from the entire program.

4. *Extensive vector reporting*. The Titan compiler contains an extensive vector reporting facility which not only shows the changes the compiler has made, but also gives suggestions to help improve performance in loops that it cannot vectorize.

5. *Compiler directives*. Most of the time, the Dana compiler should generate extremely efficient code from user programs. In certain cases, however, the compiler may lack key information necessary to generate the optimal code for an important loop. In those cases, the programmer can help the compiler by providing the information in the form of compiler directives, thereby overriding the compiler's natu-

ral caution. The compiler can also accept Cray compiler directives, easing the porting of many codes.

6. *Source level debugger*. Dana provides a source level debugger which allows a user to examine a running program to obtain the values of important variables at key points.

7. *Highly accurate profiling*. The Titan hardware contains a special clock dedicated to the task of providing highly accurate profiling information. The Dana compilers provide options for reporting this information back to users in very readable form.

Graphics

In support of visualization, Dana has created an abstract graphics environment called the Dana Object Rendering Environment, or Doré. Just as Dana's compilers simplify the task of writing high performance applications, Doré simplifies the task of writing high performance visual interfaces.

Existing graphics interfaces (including the various ANSI standards and vendor-specific graphics libraries) force each application to know a lot about graphics and to include a large amount of graphics specific code. This has several bad side effects:

1. As graphics hardware and software technologies change, applications must be modified to stay current. Because graphics is young and changing very fast, this leads to constant application changes.

2. Typically, standard graphics libraries have been very slow compared to vendor specific libraries, so many applications have their own intermediate graphics layer which provides interfaces to many different low level graphics drivers.

3. Applications programmers spend a disproportionate amount of their development and support time on graphics rather than on their own code.

Doré provides a graphics environment that simplifies the development of high performance visual interfaces. It supports dynamics for interactively viewing, rotating, panning, zooming, and modifying complex images, as well as high quality rendered images including shadows, reflections, and textures. Many graphics primitives and attributes are supported, providing all of the color, shading, and geometric primitives found in existing libraries. In addition, Doré supports advanced primitives and attributes such as solids, meshes, surfaces, transparency, texture, and more.

Doré is user extensible. That is, an application can add attributes, primitives, textures, shading, and rendering functions to Doré without requiring Doré source. These additions are portable across all Doré implementations. With these capabilities, an application can utilize graphics in terms which are most natural to the application.

Doré offloads the graphics visualization task from the application. A user of a Doré application can interactively select between different representations (points, wireframe, faceted, and smooth shaded), different shading models (ambient, diffuse, specular reflections and shadows), and different realism levels—interactively manipulating images with as much realism as the hardware allows or with high realism taking as long as the hardware requires.

Future Directions

The important measure of a computer is not the peak execution speed of the hardware, but rather the execution speed a user sees for a particular application and the amount of effort necessary to obtain that speed. The obtained speed measures not only the hardware, but also the cooperation between the hardware and the system software.

The Titan represents a new direction in the supercomputer arena; a system in which both the hardware and the software were designed with the intention of delivering supercomputer performance and interactive visualization without superhuman effort. Previously, supercomputer performance was not only expensive but also involved major investments in code conversion. With the onset of the Titan, those investments can be turned away from code conversion and into the development of highly interactive, graphical codes, providing a new wealth of supercomputer applications.

References

[1] J.R. Allen, "Dependence analysis for subscripted variables and its application to program transformations," Ph.D dissertation, Dept. of Mathematical Sciences, Rice University, April, 1983.

[2] J.R. Allen and K. Kennedy, "PFC: a program to convert FORTRAN to parallel form," *Supercomputers: Design and Applications*, K. Hwang (ed.), IEEE Press, 1984, pp. 186-205.

[3] F. Chow and J. Hennessy, "Register allocation by priority-based coloring," *Proc. SIGPLAN 84 Symposium on Compiler Construction, SIGPLAN Notices* 19, 6, June 1984, pp. 222-232.

[4] J.J. Dongarra and S.C. Eisenstat, "Squeezing the most out of an algorithm in Cray FORTRAN" Technical Report 9, Argonne National Laboratories MCS Division, Argonne, Illinois, May, 1983.

[5] D.R. Hamann, "Computers in physics: an overview," *Physics Today*, May, 1983, pp. 25-33.

[6] J.L. Hennessy, "VLSI processor architecture," *IEEE Transactions on Computers*, C-33(12) pp. 1221-1246 (Dec. 1984).

[7] T.L. Jordan, "A guide to parallel computation and some Cray 1 experiences," in *Parallel*

Computations, Garry Rodrigue (ed), Academic Press, 1982, pp. 1-50.

[8] K. Kennedy, "Automatic translation of FORTRAN programs to vector form," Rice Technical Report 476-029-4, Rice University, October 1980.

[9] D.J. Kuck, R.H. Kuhn, B. Leasure, and M. Wolfe, "The structure of an advanced vectorizer for pipelined processors," *Proc. IEEE Computer Society Fourth International Computer Software and Applications Conf.*, IEEE, October 1980.

[10] D.A. Patterson, "Reduced Instruction Set Computers," *Communications of the ACM* , 28(1) pp. 8-21 (Jan. 1985).

The Advent of the Personal Supercomputer Workstation

Chair: C. Maples

AN INTRODUCTION TO THE ARCHITECTURE OF THE STELLAR™ GRAPHICS SUPERCOMPUTER

Michael Sporer
Fellow, Hardware Engineering

Franklin H. Moss
VP, Software Development

Craig J. Mathias
Director, Marketing

Stellar Computer Inc.
85 Wells Avenue, Newton, MA 02159
(617) 964-1000

Abstract

The Stellar Graphics Supercomputer is a new class of system that tightly integrates the processing capabilities of mini-supercomputers with high performance three-dimensional graphics in a single user package. Scientific and engineering fields, such as finite element analysis, computational fluid dynamics and molecular modeling, will benefit greatly from the high levels of interactivity and real-time response provided by the Stellar system. This paper briefly introduces the novel architectural concepts used to meet Stellar's ambitious goals for performance, size and price.

Introduction

The way in which sophisticated technical professionals use computers is rapidly changing. It is moving to applications that blend realistic three-dimensional visualization with massive numerical calculations. Fields like finite element analysis, computational fluid dynamics and molecular modeling are all evolving in this direction . The Stellar Graphics Supercomputer architecture is tailored to meet the needs of these applications. The system delivers the highest levels of combined integer, floating point and graphics rendering performance available in a single user package at a single user price. It enables interactive visualization by providing extraordinarily high bandwidth between the compute and graphics components.

The Graphics Supercomputer design reflects a remarkable freedom of architectural choices. New tools and fabrication techniques are now available that enable rapid design of complex custom designed integrated circuits (ASICs). By designing our own ASICs throughout the system, we were able to balance the machine's resources to solve problems whose requirements range from intense computation to high performance 3-D graphics. Since many current and emerging applications have a mixture of these needs, they benefit greatly from our design.

Highly Integrated Architecture

A fundamental premise of the architecture is that high performance numerical processing and 3-D graphics rendering have a large number of common needs. This led to a highly integrated, uniform architecture where critical system resources can be efficiently accessed by both compute and graphics, as depicted in Figure 1. These resources are:

Vector Floating Point: A single vector floating point unit with a peak capacity of 40 MFLOPS services requests from both the CPU (Multi-Stream Processor, or MSP) and the Rendering Processor (RP). To exploit vectorization in compute programs, the Stellar FORTRAN and C compilers are capable of automatic vectorization across all data types. The VFP is capable of executing vector or scalar floating point operations and forms the front end of a pipeline with the powerful Rendering Processor.

Large, Fast Memory Hierarchy: The system has a 1 MB cache, a 16K entry TLB, and 16 to 128 MB of main memory. By employing a novel architecture called "virtual pixel maps" (the VPM™ architecture), graphical images can be rendered directly to main memory. This capability eliminates the need for expensive, dedicated frame buffers and z-buffers. Also, the cache is shared by multiple execution streams in the CPU (described below under SPMP™ CPU Architecture), obviating the need for explicit cache synchronization. This design overcomes a weakness of conventional multi-processor architectures in which each procesor has a private cache.

High Performance I/O: Up to four independent I/O processors are available to meet the data transfer requirements for compute and graphics. Each processor has a peak transfer rate of 16 MB/sec. Two I/O processors are used internally to connect industry standard VME and PC I/O busses to

CH2539-5/88/0000/0464$01.00 © 1988 IEEE

the system. Up to three gigabytes of disk storage can be supported internally in the system; more than twenty gigabytes can be added in expansion chassis. For very high file system throughput, the operating system supports striping across multiple disks.

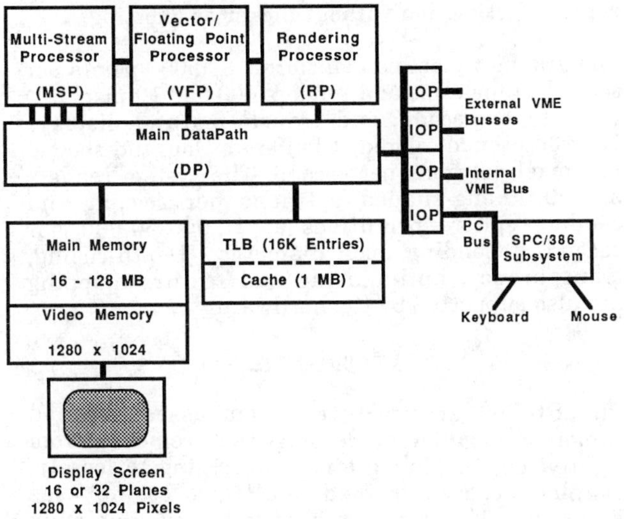

Figure 1 **Hardware Architecture**

The uniformity of the architecture is further exemplified by the instruction set architecture, which presents a single, consistent interface encompassing all machine operations: integer and floating point, scalar and vector, graphics, I/O and concurrency control. The hardware automatically handles all scheduling and synchronization requirements of the different subsystems, so the programmer does not need to be concerned with subsystem-level operations. The instruction set also incorporates many high performance features; notable is packetization, whereby two adjacent instructions are executed in a single cycle. The Stellar compilers exploit this capability by instruction re-ordering.

The SPMP CPU Architecture

The SPMP (Synchronous Pipelined Multi-Processor) is a novel CPU organization that simultaneously executes four instruction streams in a single, 12-stage, 50 ns pipeline. The SPMP selects a new instruction from the next sequential stream during each clock period. Thus, each stream has three instructions in the pipe at any point (see Figure 2). The SPMP provides two important benefits. First, each stream's instructions are separated sufficiently to minimize pipeline hazards like register conflicts, branches, and cache and TLB misses. Additionally, each functional unit is controlled by a different stage of the pipeline; this inherently eliminates resource contention. The system's resource management allows the use of a single cache and a single TLB and obviates cache coherency issues. These techniques combine to complete one instruction (two packetized instructions) every clock tick. Thus, the SPMP allows us to achieve the rated 20-25 MIPS in a compact, economical package.

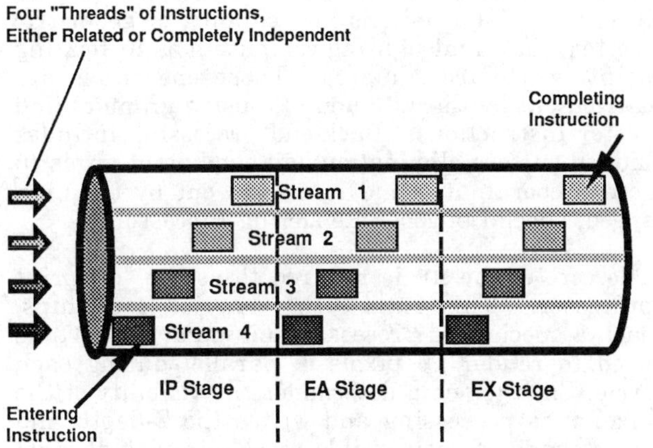

Figure 2 **SPMP Architecture**

DataPath™ Architecture

At the core of the processor is the DataPath, which provides the large bandwidth needed among all the functional units. This enables the high levels of integration for functional units and execution streams described above. The DataPath provides:

Functional Unit	Bandwidth (MB/sec) Between Functional Unit and DataPath
cache	1280
memory	320
integer (2 units)	480
vector	480
rendering	320
I/O processors (4 units)	160

By simultaneously providing these bandwidths, the DataPath permits each unit to operate independently and in parallel.

The DataPath exemplifies the architectural opportunities offered by ASICs. It is implemented in thirty-two 223-pin 1.5u CMOS gate arrays (LSI Logic Compacted Array ™), each with approximately 40000 used gates. These 1.2 million gates provide the interconnect and the register storage needed to implement the four stream processor.

The DataPath also includes a set of registers used for concurrency control among the four streams. This centralized location provides both efficient communication between the streams and various functional units and the high level of interactivity between computation and graphics.

Graphics

The Stellar graphics pipeline is divided into front-end processing, back-end processing, and image generation (see Figure 3). Front-end functions include transformations and clipping of geometric (vertex) data and lighting computations in floating point "world" coordinates. These operations are carried out by the MSP and VFP using graphics and vector instructions. Back-end processing includes hidden-surface elimination and shading of pixels in screen coordinates and is carried out by the high speed, special purpose Rendering Processor.

The core of the RP is referred to as the "footprint processor." This 4 x 4 SIMD array of "toe" chips, each a specialized processor running at 20 MIPS, is used to render 16 pixels in parallel during each cycle. Each toe chip determines the visibility of the pixel it is processing and writes the Z-depth and color shade of each visible pixel to a virtual pixel map (VPM™). The VPM holds the Z-buffer and image. In effect, the footprint processor "walks over" polygons whose edges have been defined by computations performed by the VFP.

Both 12-bit pseudo-color with 16-bit Z-values and 24 bit true color with 32-bit Z-values are supported using one or two VPMs per image. VPMs permit multiple, arbitrary-sized images to be processed and special purpose buffers (like Z-, alpha-, and shadow- buffers) to be created. These are all managed in a uniform way by the virtual memory management portion of the OS.

Image generation consists of window management and video display. Window management is accomplished by copying the visible portions of the VPMs to the video memory frame buffer using the 640 MB/sec Blt instruction.Video is generated directly from the 1280 x 1024 pixel frame buffer refreshed at 74 Hz. This unusually high rate coupled with short-persistence phosphor allows rapid object motion without flicker or ghosting.

The graphics pipeline transforms 800,000 points per second, transforms and renders 600,000 10-pixel 3-D vectors per second, and transforms and displays 150,000 pseudo-colored, Z-buffered, Gouraud-shaded 100-pixel polygons per second. The system renders 30,000 Phong-shaded polygons per second and renders sphere primitives at 12,000-50,000 per second, depending upon diameter. Depth-cueing, transparency, anti-aliasing and texture mapping are also supported by the hardware.

Concurrency

The Stellar architecture encompasses a broad range of parallel processing requirements from tightly-coupled, fine-grained processing to loosely-coupled, coarse-grained multi-processing (see Figure 4). The former is used to achieve minimum time-to-solution for a single application; the latter is used to achieve maximal throughput. Concurrency is supported by all aspects of the Stellar architecture. Medium-grained to coarse-grained concurrency is supported by shared cache and memory, lightweight processes (threads) and compiler directives. The special needs of fine grain concurrency are met by the concurrency registers and parallel region instructions; compiled code exploits these resources without operating system intervention.

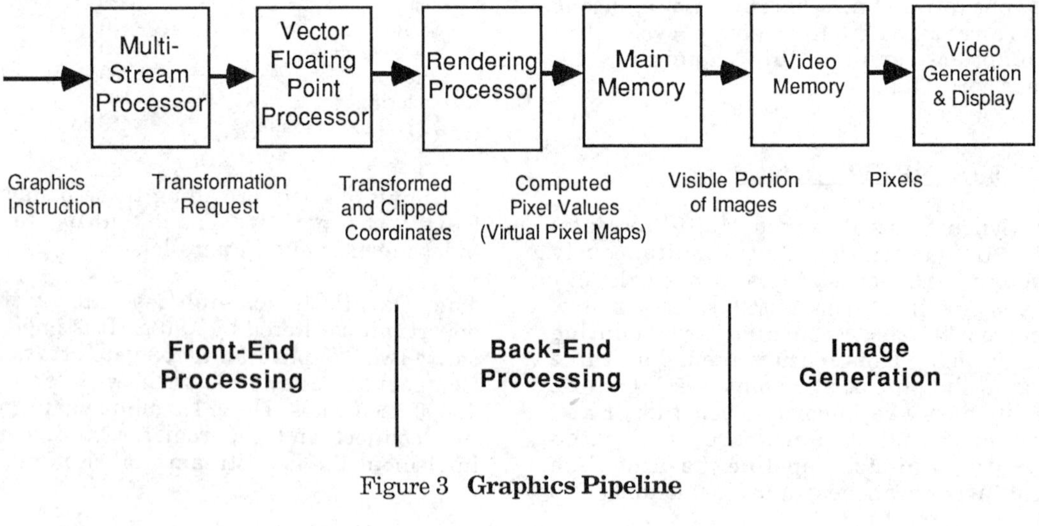

Figure 3 **Graphics Pipeline**

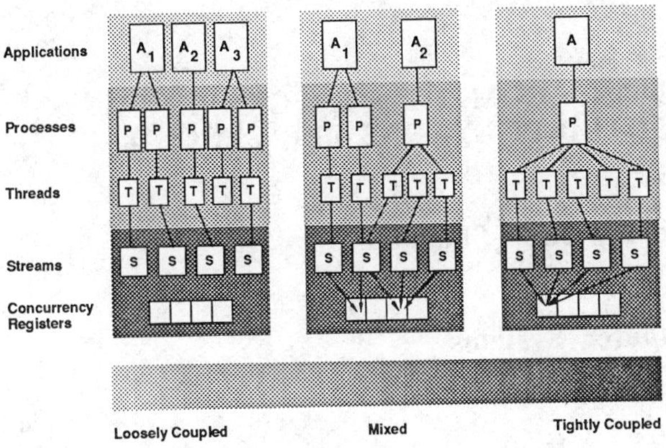

Figure 4 **Parallelism Spectrum**

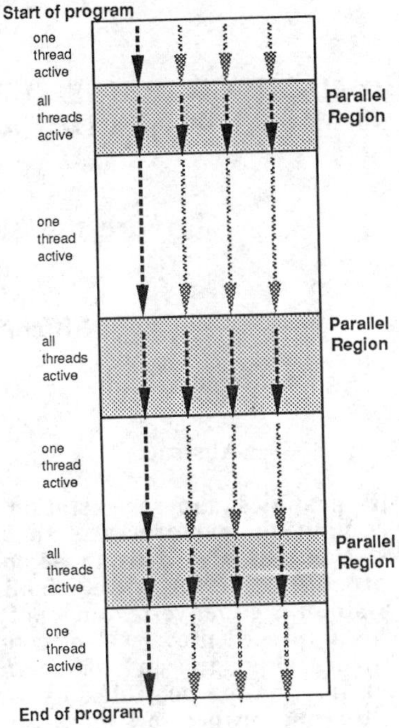

Figure 5 **Parallel Regions**

Stellar provides FORTRAN-77 and C compilers that automatically detect opportunities for vectorization and concurrency. The compilers produce concurrent code for loop constructs, such as outer loops around vectorized inner loops. In addition, the compiler parallelizes linear independent code sequences and can, if advised by programmer directives, parallelize code with conditionals or loops that contain such linear sequences. Compiler-generated concurrent code cooperates seamlessly with programmer-specified concurrent code. Concurrent code executes correctly regardless of the number of streams actually available at run-time, permitting maximum speed-up if all streams are available and less speed-up if other programs are contending for the processors.

A typical concurrent program is decomposed into multiple threads by the compiler. Each thread can be scheduled independently by the operating system, though generally all the threads for a program are run at the same time. The primary thread of a program computes the sequential sections until it encounters a parallel region, that is, a region of code that can be productively executed by multiple threads, each running on its own stream. All available threads then execute the code in the parallel region by using the concurrency registers to communicate and disperse the work among themselves. See Figure 5.

For example, consider the IDAMAX function from the LINPACK library: the goal of the function is to find the first index of the largest magnitude in a linear array. All threads execute the same code; they select elements to examine by incrementing, in one instruction cycle, the shared concurrency register that contains the index of the last examined element. Each thread remembers the index of the maximal element from the subset of the array that it examined. Finally, the threads compare their maxima and compute the final index value. Even though the threads are communicating approximately every six instructions, each thread executes as quickly as strictly sequential code that does not have the communication requirement. As a result, the computation can achieve a speed-up of nearly four.

Library support for programmer-specified concurrency extends the applications that can be parallelized. A multi-stream debugger and execution profiler are also included as part of programming language support.

Conclusion

The Stellar Graphics Supercomputer architecture is implemented in a one meter high single user package using 61 CMOS ASICs with over two million designed gates. Not discussed at great length in this paper is the machine's complete, standard software environment that allows the performance capabilities of the hardware to be exploited transparently. The system is scheduled for formal announcement during the first quarter of 1988.

Acknowledgements

The Graphics Supercomputer architecture was the joint effort of the entire engineering development team at Stellar Computer Inc., executed under the leadership of Paul Jones. Guiding light was provided by Bill Poduska and a guiding hand by Art Carr. Special thanks to our Technical Advisory Board, lead by Andy vanDam, for many important discussions and contributions. Thanks to Clare Campbell for expert manuscript preparation.

THE 4D-MP GRAPHICS SUPERWORKSTATION: COMPUTING + GRAPHICS = 40 MIPS + 40 MFLOPS AND 100,000 LIGHTED POLYGONS PER SECOND

Forest Baskett, Tom Jermoluk, Doug Solomon

Silicon Graphics Computer Systems

Abstract

The 4D-MP graphics superworkstation brings 40 mips of computing performance to a graphics superworkstation. It also delivers 40 megaflops of geometry processing performance enabling 100,000 lighted, 4-sided, concave-tested polygons per second. This unprecedented level of computing and graphics processing in an office-environment workstation is made possible by the fastest available Risc microprocessors in a single shared memory multiprocessor design driving a tightly coupled, highly parallel graphics system. Aggregate sustained data rates of over one gigabyte per second are achieved by a hierarchy of buses in a balanced system designed to avoid bottlenecks.

Introduction

Graphics workstations from Silicon Graphics have always provided state of the art workstation computing performance tightly coupled with custom-silicon graphics subsystems that provided sufficient floating point performance to enable the real time display and movement of three dimensional objects. Progress in the underlying technology has contributed to not only faster and more powerful computing subsystems but also faster and more powerful graphics subsystems.

The computing subsystems have moved from one-half mips to two mips to ten mips to today's forty mips. These speed improvements have been accompanied by improvements in memory size, both primary and secondary, improvements in file system speed and capability, and improvements in compiling and operating system sophistication.

The graphics subsystems have progressed from 50,000 3-D vectors per second to 150,000 to today's 400,000 vectors per second. The functionality has also improved from less than 1000 flat shaded polygons per second to today's 100,000 Phong lighted, Gouraud shaded, four sided, concave tested polygons per second. Thus early systems could provide real time motion of moderately complex 3-D wire frames. Today's systems can provide real time motion of even more complex, remarkably realistic, lighted and shaded solid objects.

These advances have been made possible not only by advances in the speed and density of the underlying technology but also by our ability to design increasingly complex hardware and software systems in balanced configurations. Today's 4D-MP system has a hardware logic complexity of over two million gates, about the logic complexity of the last generation of commercial mainframe computers.

Computing System Architecture

The key new element of the 4D-MP workstation design is its use of a tightly coupled multiprocessor. The particular configuration we describe in this paper is a 4 processor system, although the architecture will support from one to sixteen processors. The key design philosophy of the system is a hierarchy of buses, each tailored to the functional needs for which it is intended.

Figure 1 is a block diagram of the major components of the multiprocessor computing section of the system. Several of the important buses of the system are shown in this diagram. The sync bus is the bus that provides high speed synchronization between the main processors of the system in support of fine grained parallelism. The processor buses allow full speed access to instructions and data from the individual first level caches of each main processor. The read and write buffers allow for the efficient flow of information between the processors and the main memory of the system. The second level data cache provides the additional bandwidth needed to support an automatically consistent shared memory computing model with such high speed processors. The MP bus then supports the protocols for consistent data sharing and the high speed block transfers for fast data sharing among the processors, the main memory, the I/O subsystem, and the graphics subsystem.

The Sync Bus. The sync bus is designed for the synchronization needs of a multiprocessor supporting efficient fine grained parallelism. The goal is for a single application to be able to make efficient use of parallel processors even at the individual loop level, in addition to the kinds of larger grained parallelism found in many system simulation applications and the even larger grained parallelism found in the process structure of most Unix systems.

The sync bus provides 65,000 individual test-and-set variables. These variables are in a special part of the physical address space. They are addressed as memory and can be allocated to individual applications by the operating system. They are arranged 64 to a page and can be mapped into the virual address space of an application. The operating system itself makes use of them to provide very fine grained locks for the control variables of the operating system. The operating system is thus a very parallel, fully symmetric multiprocessing operating system. In other words, the Silicon Graphics verion of Unix V.3 is a well developed parallel processing application on the 4D-MP and its speed demonstrates some of the power of this approach to high speed computing.

Because the sync bus can provide synchronization operations to applications with an overhead of only tens of cycles, many programming and compiler techniques developed for vector processors are also suitable for this kind of parallel processor. For example, strip mining, the technique of taking a long vector and breaking it into a number of strips for use by a vector register, can be used by taking a long vector and breaking it into 4 strips, one for each processor. This technique, when properly applied, can result in super-linear speedups of applications because of the potential for taking advantage of the private cache organization of the multiprocessor.

The sync bus also provides for the distribution of interrupts from one processor to another, or from the I/O system to appropriate processors. The flexibility of the interrupt distribution system means that the operating system can provide scheduling algorithms that support the power of private caches rather than disrupt it.

The processor bus. Each processor provides both an address bus and a data bus that can support sustained data transfers at 8 bytes every clock cycle. Thus this four processor system has a total processor-to-cache sustainable bandwidth of 512 megabytes per second. In addition, the organization of this bandwidth on a modular basis means that smallar and larger configurations are possible in such a fashion that the bandwidth shrinks or grows with the processing power. This kind of bandwidth modularity is not only sensible, it is economical.

The modular processor bandwidth and private caches are also what make super-linear speedups possible. A super-linear speedup is defined as running an application more than N times faster on an N processor system than on a 1 processor system. Since large problems are often constrained by data bandwidth needs as much as by compute cycle needs, the addition of more data bandwidth in conjunction with more processor cycles can result in super-linear speedups. This phenomenon may not be common but its existence helps demonstrate the value and power of this type of system organization.

The first level caches, separate for instructions and data, are all 64 kilobytes. The total cache size is 512 kilobytes in a 4 processor system. The instruction caches are fed by a read

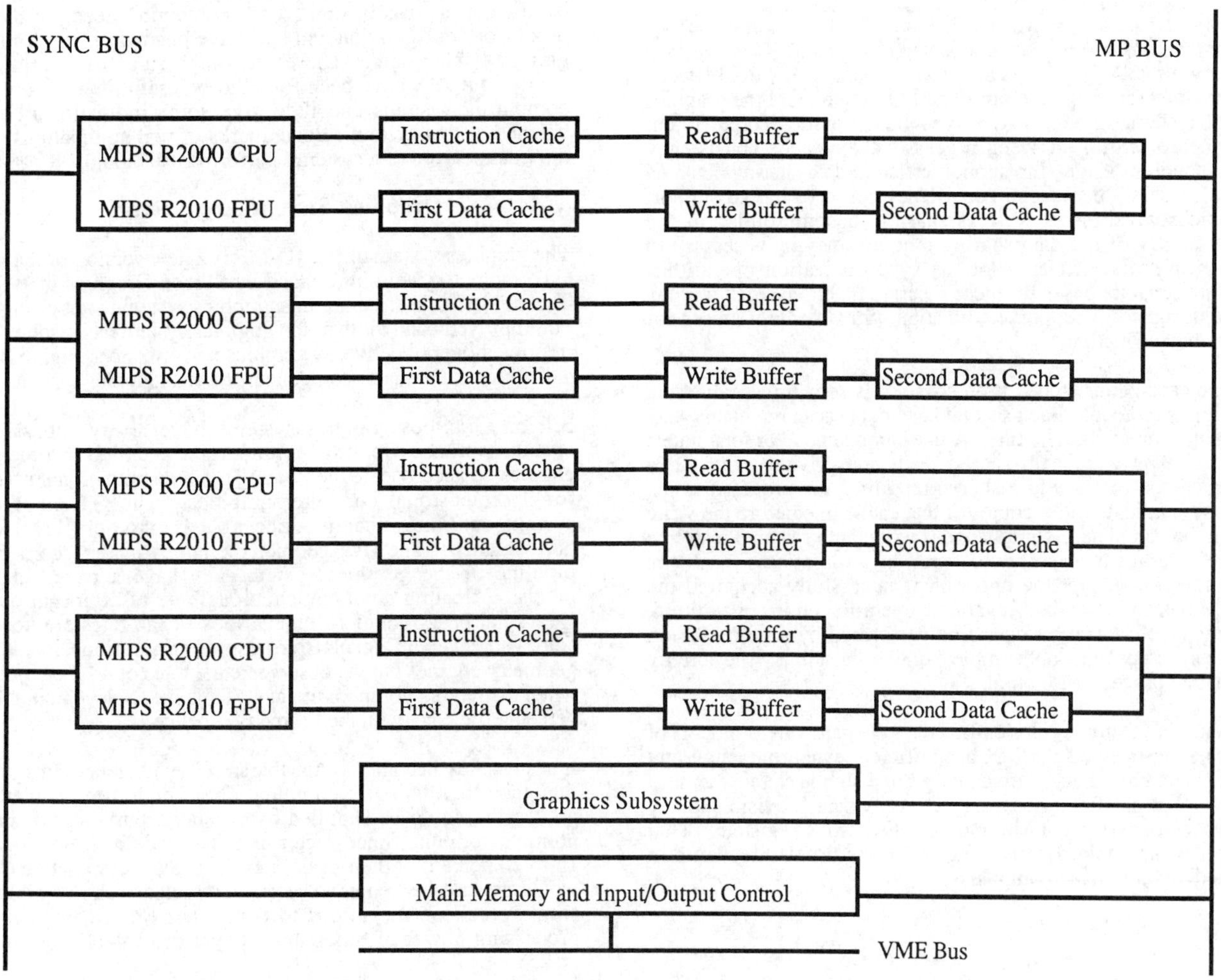

Figure 1. Computing System Architecture

buffer and the data caches drive a write buffer. These buffers also provide a convenient point for an asynchronous interface between the processors and the MP Bus. This asynchronous interface provides an added degree of modularity in the overall system. The clock speed of all the processors and the MP Bus is 16 megahertz but we anticipate faster processors in the future. The asynchronous interface makes it possible to upgrade to faster processors without having to replace the entire system.

Each second level data cache is 64 kilobytes in size, organized as 4 thousand lines of 16 bytes each. This cache provides the block transfer capability that the MP bus supports and it also provides the additional bandwidth for the cache line tag storage necessary to keep all the individual caches in a consistent state. The second level data cache watches every transaction on the MP bus and checks for transactions involving data in its data storage. This checking is performed by matching every address on the MP bus with the addresses in the tag storage section of the second level data cache. The first level data cache is always a subset of the second level data cache so consistent data is guaranteed. In addition, since all the caches are physical address caches rather than virtual address caches, there are no synonym problems caused by mapping different virtual addresses to the same physical address. The difficult system level issues that arrise when dealing with multiple virtual address caches are not present in this system.

The MP Bus. The MP bus is a pipelined, block transfer bus that supports the cache consistency protocol as well as providing 64 megabytes of sustained data bandwidth between the processors, the memory and I/O system, and the graphics subsystem. Because the sync bus provides for efficient synchronization between processors, the cache consistency protocol is designed to support efficient data sharing between processors. If a cache consistency protocol has to support synchronization as well as sharing, a compromise in the efficiency of the data sharing protocol may be necessary to improve the efficiency of the synchronization operations. With separate buses for these separate functions, each bus can be designed to support its function without compromises for the other function.

The cache consistency protocol used is sometimes called the Illinois protocol. Each second level data cache maintains state values for each cache line. A line can be in one of four states: invalid, private read, shared read, and private write. If a processor writes into a shared read line, the processor must first invalidate other copies of that cache line before the write can be completed. Simultaneous writes into a shared read line by several processors will result in write misses in all the processors except the one which successfully accquired the MP bus and issued an invalidate operation on it. In addition, any synchronization operation performed by a processor on the sync bus must not complete until all pending write activity by that processor is complete.

With these simple rules enforced by the hardware protocols of the sync bus and the MP bus, efficient synchronization and efficient data sharing are achieved in a simple shared memory model of parallel processing. The only data not visible to any processor is the data in another processor's registers. That sort of invisible data is handled by the usual safeguards in modern optimizing compilers.

The physical structure of the MP bus is 32 address lines and 64 data lines. An MP bus transaction is six cycles in length although the last two data transfer cycles can overlap with the first two cycles of the next transaction, resulting in a sustainable data transfer rate of 64 megabytes per second in a very economical configuration. New data arrives in the last two cycles. Old data from a swapped cache line is carried in the middle two cycles. Addresses are transferred in the first two cycles. Bus arbitration is pipelined and doesn't add to the cycle cost of transactions.

How does 64 megabytes of MP bus bandwidth balance with the computing requirements of this 4 processor configuration? Each individual MIPS R2000 processor and R2010 coprocessorat 16 megahertz would be a 12 mips processor in the absence of the cost of coordination overhead in a multiprocessor configuration. A conservative rating of the individual processors is thus about 10 mips. If we use the rule of thumb that we need about one megabyte per second of memory bandwidth for each mip, we need 40 megabytes per second for a 4 processor configuration. Each coprocessor has a peak floating point rate of 8 megaflops, double precision, and we can deliver 1.6 megaflops on applications like Linpack. If we use the rule of thumb that we need about 8 megabytes per second per delivered megaflop, we need about 50 megabytes per second to deliver over 6 megaflops of double precision floating point performance. Thus the MP bus bandwidth can easily support the computing needs of the 4 processor configuration and still have bandwidth left for the graphics subsystem. These are rough rules of thumb, of course, but they have been found to be useful in a variety of computing systems and they give some indication of the balance of this system. Benchmarks of real applications are the true measure of a system's performance, though.

Graphics System Architecture

The graphics system of the 4D-MP is a new version of the 4D GT graphics system introduced by Silicon Graphics in 1987. The architectural structure this graphics system is not changed but improved bandwidth to the graphics system has resulted in improved overall delivered graphics performance. Figure 2 is a diagram of the major components of this graphics system.

Silicon Graphics graphics systems have always provided special purpose floating point engines, called geometry engines, to accomodate the floating point computational needs for 3 dimensional computer graphics. The GT graphics system continues that practice at a remarkable level of performance. The five geometry engines in the geometry pipeline of the graphics system each have a peak single precision floating point computational rate of 20 megaflops, for a total peak rate of 100 megaflops. Peak rates are never achieved, even in special purpose configurations like the geometry engines but we observe actual rates of 40 megaflops when displaying complex images. Thus we achieve about 40 percent efficiency with the geometry pipeline.

It has recently become fashionable in some quarters to imagine that the floating point computational needs for geometry processing could be supplied by a general purpose floating point vector unit. Since vector units rarely deliver more than 15 to 20 percent of their peak rates for actual computations, it would presumably require a vector unit with a peak rate of 200 single precision megaflops to equal the realized geometry processing power of this graphics system. In addition, bus bandwidth requirements would go up substantially if our delivered megaflops versus bus bandwidth rule of thumb has any merit. Again, only actual application benchmarks will tell for sure.

The geometry pipeline feeds a polygon processor designed to handle arbitrarily shaped polygons. This generality usually simplifies applications and also makes it possible to handle the most common case of four sided polygons at a rate almost equal to our rate for three sided polygons. The more common situation is for the four sided polygon rate to be less than half the rate for triangles in those systems designed around triangle primitives. Thus we can render 100,000 independent four sided polygons that are Phong lighted, Gouraud shaded, concave tested, clip tested, and Z-buffered. For triangles, we can render 120,000.

The polygon processor then feeds a set of edge processors that iterate down the edges of a polygon to determine a sequence of vertical spans that must be rendered. These spans are broadcast to a set of 5 span processors over the pixel bus. Each of the span processors is responsible for one fifth of the spans and picks up every fifth span to render.

Each span processor broadcasts the pixel addresses of each pixel in the span to a set of four image engines. Each image engine is responsible for one twentieth of the pixels and picks up every fourth pixel from its span processor. This two dimensional interleaving of pixel processing means that even small polygons can be rendered with twenty way parallelism.

The resulting fill rates for pixels are 80 million pixels per second without Z buffering and 40 million pixels per second with Z buffering.

Of course, vector drawing is a special case and takes place at the rate of 400,000 vectors per second for plain vectors or 200,000 vectors per second for anti-aliased vectors. All these numbers are for polygons and vectors that are 10 pixels on a side.

Summary

The 4D-MP graphics superworkstation uses both general purpose and special purpose multiprocessing to provide minisupercomputer performance in a workstation package with the highest performance real time 3-D graphics available. The use of a hierarchy of buses, each designed to economically provide efficient performance for their particular functions is the organizing principle of this system. The resulting package illustrates the deliverable power of parallel processing.

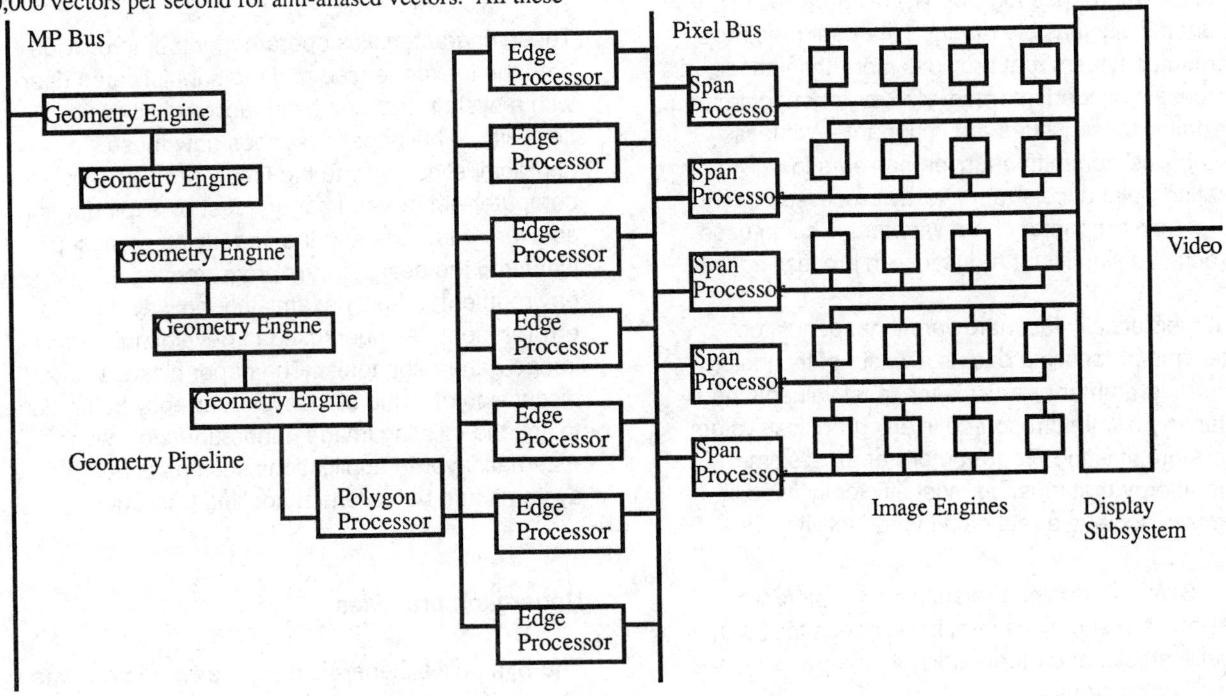

Figure 2. Graphics System Architecture

Increasing Users' Productivity in a High-Performance Graphics Environment

John L. Kulp

Symbolics Graphics Division

ABSTRACT: The production of 3D graphics requires a high-performance system that combines the right hardware architecture with the right software, including not only application programs with an easy-to-learn user interface, but also accessibility and extensibility so that advanced users can supply their own unique features. The Symbolics Genera™ software environment and the animation and paint system from the Symbolics Graphics Division provides such an open architecture and easily learned user interface.

In order to produce high-quality 3D graphics in an economically feasible manner, the user requires a computer system that provides more than sheer processing speed, memory size, or disk paging area. Certainly these issues are important -- witness Symbolics' commitment over the years to floating-point accelerators, array processors, and other new proprietary hardware that is being used to achieve significant reductions in processing time.

But theoretically fast hardware that spends too little time processing data is a waste of technology. The programmer or artist is the most valuable and often most limited resource in any graphics system; therefore, it is the programmer's or artist's time and energy that must be most efficiently used in order to achieve a real gain in productivity.

The Symbolics paint and animation system was designed to supply several basic needs for CAD users, artists, and other users of high-performance graphics systems:

- An underlying software substrate, embodying symbolic processing concepts, that lends itself to manipulation at any of several levels of abstraction.

- A set of applications that let the user start being productive quickly, with the ability to make incremental refinements as the artist's skill grows.

- An open software environment so that the more experienced user can extend the system's capabilities either by recombining existing features into new combinations, by developing new applications for the production of unique visual effects, or by linking with external software packages for special applications.

These characteristics operate together to provide both the inexperienced and the sophisticated user with a system that combines accessibility with flexibility. This paper describes how these characteristics apply to the timely production of computer-generated imagery, first by exploring the software substrate and the underlying premises that went into the design of the programming environment, then by examining the way this environment has been used to develop interactive image generation tools. The paper closes with a discussion of some of the work currently being done to link the existing image generation tools with external, layered applications such as expert systems and behavioral modelling packages.

Underlying premises

The Symbolics Genera software environment was designed originally with the software developer in mind, based on the premise that the developer's time

CH2539-5/88/0000/0472$01.00 © 1988 IEEE

is a valuable and limited resource. Although the initial assumptions that directed the choices made during the genesis of Genera were oriented towards software developers, the effects of these decisions have benefitted the graphics user.

One such assumption that guided the design of the environment was the need to provide support for complexity. Where a program developer needs tools for managing the relationship of the many parts of complex programs, graphics users need tools for managing the relationship between different parts of an image -- for example, the hierarchical relationship between components of a robot assembly cell, or between members of a simulated flock of birds. A system designed to simplify the association of many disparate programming modules in a complex program, as Genera was designed, is ideal for the support of a hundred or more autonomously directed animation characters.

One of the reasons behind Genera's aptness for the task of managing complicated graphics systems is its many links with the Lisp programming language. Since Genera not only supports Symbolics Common Lisp, one of the most sophisticated implementations of Lisp currently available, but was also designed, coded, and developed using Lisp, Genera can take full advantage of the useful features of the Lisp programming language.

Perhaps the most important aspect of Lisp as it applies to a graphics user's productivity is Lisp's facility for managing abstraction at many different levels. This gives the user tools with which he or she can find the level of abstraction most applicable to the task at hand.

For example, a programmer designing a graphical simulation of a robot assembly cell needs to be able to think abstractly on several levels of detail. At the lowest level of detail, the programmer must consider the transformations required to move the robot's arm to the correct location on the screen with respect to the parts bin that contained the desired part, also modelled on the screen at a certain location. Then the programmer must consider the transformations required so that the arm can reach into the bin and remove a semiconductor device for installation on the PCB assembly modelled at yet another location. Finally, another set of transformations must be calculated to show the arm dropping into the correct position and installing the device (pin side down and correctly aligned with respect to power and ground lines, one hopes).

However, devising the simulation would be greatly simplified if the programmer could think in more abstract terms. One way to manage this kind of abstraction is to contain the low-level details in the programmed representations of the various objects being simulated. In such a scheme, the programmed representation of the parts bin has an inventory listing of which devices it contained, the PCB has a map that indicated where the device in question belonged, and the robot arm maintains state information and information about how quickly it moves from point A to point B. This scheme much more closely approximates the way the user or programmer approaches the problem, since it links objects in the graphic simulation with attributes that would be inherent to them in the real world.

With such a programming scheme, the programmer can devise a simulation system that merely asks the user to think in terms of moving the robot arm over the parts bin that had the device of interest, moving the arm over the PCB, and installing the device at the correct location. The simulator polls the programmed representation of the parts bin, the robot arm, and the PCB assembly to obtain the appropriate data from each, and can also calculate the duration of the animation for virtually any combination of parts bins and PCB target locations.

The key to managing abstraction in this way is a technique called object-oriented programming. Object-oriented programming gives the graphics user two advantages over conventional data processing techniques. First, the state information for each object can be (and in the case of most high-level objects, is) a collection of other objects rather than a collection of raw data.

For example, consider a geometric model of a compound polyhedron, such as the robot assembly cell used in the previous example. At one level, it would simplify programming to think of the robot assembly cell as a single object -- for instance, to load the object from disk storage into memory. However, simulating the assembly process requires the independent manipulation of sub-objects, in this case the robot arm, the parts bin, and the platform that holds the PCB. The facility to address these different levels of abstraction -- whether to think of the robot assembly cell as one object or as many objects, depending on the situation -- means that the system can adapt to the user's mental framework, rather than the reverse.

The second advantage that object-oriented programming presents to graphics users is that objects can contain instructions as well as data. That is, in the Symbolics Flavors implementation of object-oriented programming, the programmer can perform a generic function on a specific object. The interaction of the procedural information in the function with the state information from the object, modified by any discrete behavioral information that might be unique to that object, determines the net effect of executing this generic function. Because the object contains enough specific information about its behavior, the generic operation causes the object to react in its own characteristic manner.

But how does this affect the graphics user? To begin with, different programs can share objects. Because each object's specific behavioral information is maintained by the object, not by the program, the behavioral information does not need to be coded into every program that might use these objects. This also means that the person using the program does not need to manipulate the objects to make the data used by one program available to another.

There is, however, a certain amount of irony in all this discussion of levels of abstraction, objects containing state and procedural information, and application-specific behavioral characteristics. The irony is that the system handles all this manipulation of objects in such a manner that the user never needs to know any of this in order to create images. The user sees a seamless transition from 3D wireframe image to rendered, shaded, full-color image, using nothing but the tools provided by the paint and animation system.

Paint and animation

The Symbolics paint and animation system comprises several tools for the creation and manipulation of graphical images:

- S-Paint, for 2D painting with complex special brush effects, simple 2D animation such as shape and color interpolation, and for the creation of visual textures for use as texture maps when rendering the final image.

- S-Geometry, the 3D database and editor, for creating and manipulating 3D models of real world objects.

- S-Dynamics, the animation scripting system, for controlling the behavior (rotation, translation, scale, color, transparency, and other arbitrary user-defined or compound characteristics) of objects over a specified period of time.

- S-Render, for generating shaded 3D images of objects, taking into account different shading models, reflectance, texture, and specular highlights.

Not only do these tools share the benefits of object-oriented programming as discussed above, but they also share a common design theme: the use of graphical feedback and flexible menu interfaces to help users more quickly to understand the effects and intents of different graphical editing operations.

One key to improving the user's productivity is to provide a flexible means of entering geometrical data. Flexibility, however, takes on new meanings in the context of Symbolics equipment. The flexibility of data input ranges from giving the user a choice between numeric or graphical input of position parameters, through a new automated geometry data capture system developed by ICAD (Cambridge, MA) for use on Symbolics workstations. Exploring both ends of this continuum will help point out some of the productivity gains that can be realized with object-oriented program based graphics systems.

The Symbolics paint and animation system offers many ways in which the user can specify data. For example, a color can be specified in any of several different ways. One way is to select the desired color model -- that is, selecting whether the color is specified by the intensity, hue, and saturation (IHS) component model, by the red, green, and blue (RGB) component model, or by the video standard (YIQ) component model. Each model has advantages for different circumstances.

However, the flexibility does not end here. To pick a color to use as the color of an object being rendered, the user can, if desired, type in the numeric specifications for each component. This makes color matching between systems (and system users) consistent: if the user needs to specify a value of 50% blue and 50% red using an RGB model, the numeric values for that object's color components and color model matches other objects built to the same specification, regardless of the user's color sense or the monitor's gamma correction curve.

However, many times the user is more interested in approximating a color from the natural world. The color editor provides an interactive way for the user to manipulate the individual color components in the selected color model. The color editor automatically redisplays the composite color each time the user alters one or more of the components.

This flexibility gives visually oriented users a way to interactively manipulate a color until it "looks right," as well as giving numerically oriented users a way to specify the exact numeric values from the outset. And since colors are stored as programming objects with the color components maintained as state variables, both numerically-specified and interactively-specified colors can be transferred between different workstations without a loss of accuracy.

But more important for overall productivity is the advent of automatic data capture systems for geometric and procedural data. The ICAD system previously mentioned offers a knowledge-based system that lets CAD designers build a database of rules that define a particular class of product. Then, when the user manipulates variables to specify individual variations, the system generates 3D models of the specific item. In addition, the ICAD system lets designers generate a bill of materials from the knowledge base.

Another user-definable knowledge base that can be used to create 3D graphics is the Concept Modeller from Wisdom Systems (Chagrin Falls, OH). The Concept Modeller lets the user interactively modify the object on the screen, rather than rewriting the rules for the knowledge base. But both these products reduce the repetitive aspects of drawing an object, and provide noticeable productivity enhancements by automating the process of object design. The underlying feature that simplifies the process of implementing these design automation tools is the open system architecture that characterizes the Symbolics Genera programming environment.

Open system architecture

The user who is familiar with the Genera programming environment can take advantage of Genera's open system architecture in many significant ways. In this type of architecture, the objects, the flavor system, and in fact the whole Lisp world is available at the click of a mouse button. The more experienced user can, if necessary, extend the system's capabilities either by recombining existing features into new structures, by developing new applications for the production of unique visual or behavioral effects, or by linking with external software packages for special applications.

A key point to the productive development of new features in the Genera environment is the fact that Genera has no core or kernel that cannot be modified; instead, everything -- functions and data both -- is in the same virtual memory. User functions and system functions are written in the same language, use the same development tools, call the same facilities, and are invoked the same way.

Furthermore, because object-specific information need not be coded into every program that might use the object, new utilities can be created much more quickly and in a much more modular fashion than if the complicated, object-specific data needed to be coded into every program. As a side benefit, this system tends to promote consistent, modular design of these object manipulation tools.

The ability to layer intelligent front-end systems on top of the paint and animation substrate is already demonstrating a significant productivity advantage for the Genera software environment. In addition to the graphical design systems from ICAD and Wisdom Systems mentioned previously, Symbolics has progressed with research into the simulation of the behavioral interaction within flocks, schools, and herds.

This behavioral animation system, demonstrated at SIGGRAPH 1987, relied heavily on the Flavors object-oriented programming system. As noted previously, objects can (and often do) contain other sub-objects. In the case of the flocking system, a new class of object was created, for which one of the sub-objects was a graphical representation of the kind of animal whose flocking was being represented (for instance, a bird or a fish).

Once the behavioral characteristics were encoded into the object, for example one of the birds from the film, a generic function could be executed by the animation system, with the bird as the object of the function's operation. However, the specific effect of the generic operation would be determined by the bird's state and behavioral information. For instance, a generic operation such as "fly south" is executed by the individual bird only after taking into consideration not only its current state (such as distance from other flockmates, distance from other obstacles, orientation, and altitude), but also its behavioral characteristics (such as "flocking instinct," a tendency to remain near the centroid of the flock which requires some awareness of the position of a number of flock members).

Such a behavioral animation system suggests several applications, in the fields of entertainment, CAD/CAM, and pure scientific research. For example, it would be possible to apply the flocking simulation system, coupled with classic solutions to the "travelling salesman" problem, to the problem of air traffic control.

By encoding the behavioral characteristics of various aircraft into individual objects, then encoding the rule base for simulating their most efficient operation, it would be possible to determine the most efficient algorithms for takeoff, landing, circling, and other aspects of air traffic control. (This does not suggest the immediate possibility of a real-time computer-controlled airport, but it does point out that there already exist research tools -- a flocking-oriented behavioral simulation system geared toward object-directed motion in three dimensions, coupled with a rule base for determining the most efficient operation of the members of the flock -- that could be put to work on this application almost immediately.)

Conclusions

This paper has pointed out the advantages of the Symbolics Genera system as a highly productive software environment for the generation and manipulation of images by computer. On the one hand, the system has tools that speed the process of image generation, including Symbolics-designed products as well as third-party products. In addition, the basic system design concepts lend themselves to the development of productivity-enhancing applications such as distributed behavioral simulation, rule-based object design and encoding, and graphically interactive shape, color, and even procedural editing systems.

Most important, all the tools described in this paper for these applications are available (in released or experimental form) today. This observation reinforces the assertion made at the beginning of this paper: fast hardware is useless unless it can be used immediately and continually. The most significant gains in productivity come, not from adding megaflops and gigabytes, but rather from software that offers the user a steeper learning curve, from an environment that gives the user the tools required to build even more specific tools quickly and simply, and from a system that lets the user spend his energy solving the problem rather than defining it.

References

Janet H. Walker, David A. Moon, Daniel L. Weinreb, and Mike McMahon, "The Symbolics Genera Programming Environment," *IEEE Software,* November 1987.

Craig W. Reynolds, "Flocks, Herds, and Schools: A Distributed Behavioral Model," in *Computer Graphics*, Volume 21, Number 4, July 1987.

Craig W. Reynolds and Scott Fisher, "Soft Tools for Hard Problems," internal publication, February 1986.

Scott Fisher, "The Symbolics Computer for Advanced Graphics," *Computer Graphics World*, January 1988.

Scott Fisher, "Automated Reasoning for Intelligent SImulation," *S-News*, December 1987.

"Automated Knowldge," Stephen Porter, *Computer Graphics World*, November 1987

Integration of Symbolic, Numerical, and Graphical Techniques in Scientific Computing Environments

Chair: S.A. Abdali

MATLAB—A Mathematical Visualization Laboratory

Cleve Moler

Dana Computer
Sunnyvale, California
and
The MathWorks
Sherborn, Massachusetts

MATLAB began its life ten years ago as a "matrix laboratory," an interactive matrix calculator built on top of the LINPACK and EISPACK subroutine libraries[1-3]. It has now evolved into a general, high-level, mathematical computing environment, integrated with 2- and 3-dimensional graphics. MATLAB's implementation on Dana Computer's new single user supercomputer, the Titan, takes advantage of both high performance, vector floating point arithmetic and high performance graphics facilities to provide an especially powerful integrated environment for visualizing mathematical objects.

MATLAB's only data structure is a matrix—a rectangular array of real or complex numbers. The fundamental operations are taken from linear algebra and include addition, multiplication, transposition, inversion, factorizations, eigenvalues, singular values, submatrices, partioned matrices, compositions, and so on. The basic mode of interaction is through a one-line-at-a-time interpreter with a natural, easy to read and learn, mathematical notation. Simple programming constructions like if-statements, for-statements and while-statements are also available. Frequently used or more elaborate commands can be encapsulated in "M-files"—text files that extend the capabilities of the system well beyond its core operations. Two-dimensional, x-y plotting commands can automatically scale data, label axes, vary line types, and so on.

At this level, MATLAB is similar to APL, except that it works with matrices rather than arrays, it has a more natural syntax, and it "knows" more numerical analysis.

One example of the use of MATLAB involves understanding computer performance data. Execution times are measured as a function of, say, problem size and number of parallel processors, and then plotted, smoothed and fit by models. A glimpse at some results of this kind can be seen in another paper at this conference, "Single User Supercomputers, or How I Got Rid of the BLAS." The graphs in both that paper and this one were produced by running MATLAB on a Titan, translated into PostScript* by the MATLAB graphics post processor, sent across a network to an Apple Macintosh**, then merged with the text in a Microsoft† Word document and finally output to an Apple LaserWriter†† Plus.

Three-dimensional graphics arise when the matrices are regarded as functions of their two indices and the resulting surface is plotted. An example is provided by a partial differential equation problem involving the wave equation. The basic mathematical model occurs in the study of structures, semiconductors and wave guides, but the simplest application involves the vibration of a membrane. We are particularly interested in an L-shaped membrane formed from three unit squares. The nonconvex corner in the domain generates singularities in the solutions, thereby providing challenges for the underlying mathematical theory and the computational algorithms.

The solution of the wave equation can be expressed as a linear combination, with coefficients which vary sinusoidally with the time variable, of static eigenfunctions which depend upon the shape of the membrane. Each eigenfunction is, in turn, expressed as a linear combination of fundamental solutions comprised from Bessel functions in polar coordinates. The two figures show the contour plot and the wire-frame surface plot of the twelfth eigenfunction.

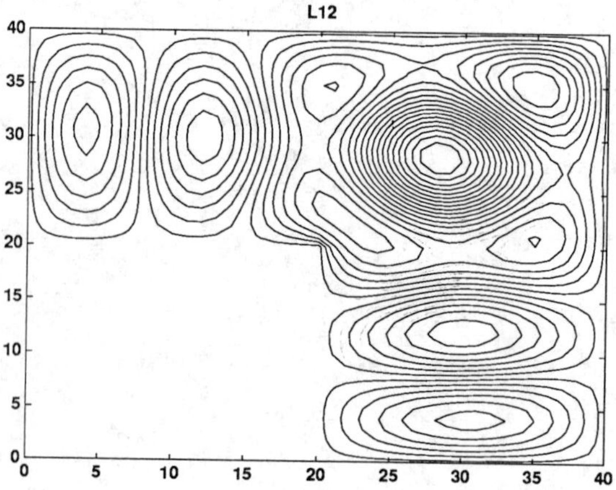

* PostScript is a trademark of Adobe Systems Inc.
** Macintosh is a trademark licensed to Apple Computer, Inc.

† Microsoft is a registered trademark of Microsoft Corp.
†† LaserWriter is a trademark of Apple Computer, Inc.

CH2539-5/88/0000/0480$01.00 © 1988 IEEE

L12

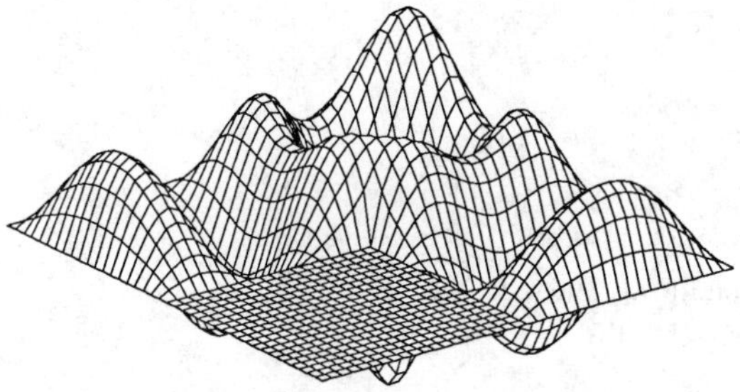

The M-file which initially computes the eigenfunctions and then produces an animated display of their time-varying linear combination is probably the most complicated MATLAB program we've written, but it is less than 2 pages of text. We don't consider short programs a virtue if they are difficult to understand. We do feel that MATLAB allows a powerful, concise, clear way of expressing such computations.

The Dana Titan allows us to go two steps beyond what we have shown here. The Dana Object Rendering Environment, Doré*, produces smoothly shaded representations of the surface. The Titan processor is fast enough to generate several frames of the time dependent solution per second. The combination of the shading and the animation leads to a much deeper understanding of the mathematical model and its solution.

References

[1] Cleve Moler, MATLAB—An interactive matrix laboratory, University of New Mexico Mathematics Department, Report 369, 1979.

[2] Cleve Moler, MATLAB Users' Guide, University of New Mexico Computer Science Department, Report CS81-1, 1981.

[3] Cleve Moler, John Little, Steve Bangert, and Steve Kleiman, MATLAB Users' Guide, The MathWorks, Inc., 1985, 1986, 1987.

* Doré is a trademark of Dana Computer, Inc.

Integration of Symbolic and Numerical Processing in Control Engineering Design

O. Akhrif† G.L. Blankenship†
P. Chancelier†† C. Gomez†† J.P. Quadrat†† A. Sulem††

Summary

In this talk we shall describe a prototype Computer–Aided–Design system integrating symbolic and numerical processing for the analysis and design of control engineering and signal processing systems. The system has five major components:

(i) a modular system of programs written in Macsyma which "solve" certain stochastic, nonlinear control and filtering problems in symbolic form;

(ii) an "intelligent" command language interface using Oblogis, a Prolog system written in Lisp [1];

(iii) a "theorem proving module," also using Oblogis, capable of checking the well-posedness (existence and uniqueness of solutions on a Sobolev space determined by the module) of certain classes of linear and nonlinear PDE's in symbolic form;

(iv) a general purpose collection of macros written in Macsyma for generating Fortran programs from the symbolic manipulation modules of the system; and

(v) a general collection of macros for the production of a report summarizing the results of the systems operation for a particular design problem.

The function of the system is to accept specifications of design problems from the user with model equations expressed in symbolic form, to "expertly" (automatically) select a solution technique for the design (control or filtering) problem, to reduce the model equations by symbolic manipulations to a form appropriate for the technique, checking well-posedness of the model along the way; to automatically generate a numerical language (Fortran) program realizing the solution algorithm, to execute the program and generate a report (LaTeXfile) summarizing the design, including a summary of the methods used and some background material supporting the choice of the design methods.

In this way the system serves as a kind of **symbolic compiler** for control systems engineering. This is its intended purpose. See Figure 1.

The system which now exists is capable of treating, among other problems,[1] stochastic optimal control problems by symbolically evaluating a Hamilton-Jacobi dynamic programming nonlinear partial differential equation for the evolution of the optimal return function, selecting from four methods for the analysis, and then producing a Fortran code for the numerical solution of this equation [3]. The system can also produce a report summarizing the design results. This is written using the MacroTex system developed to pass from Macsyma expressions and a Prolog database of facts about the design problem to a LaTeXfile in the form of a technical paper [4].

To execute the system, one inputs the system model equations in symbolic terms, identifying state and control variables, and specifies in general terms the type of optimization problem involved. The cost function, the initial conditions, and any other boundary conditions are also entered. Functions written in Macsyma carry out the calculations involved in implementing dynamic programming for the optimization problem. That is, they carry out, in symbolic form, the differentiations, function minimizations, and routine algebra necessary to compute the Hamilton-Jacobi equation which describes the evolution of the optimal cost and the functional form of the optimal control law. This portion of the code is realized in terms of a grammar based on Macsyma expressions describing this class of control problems. See Figure 2.

†Electrical Engineering Department and Systems Research Center, University of Maryland, College Park, Maryland 20742. This research supported in part by NSF Grant CDR-85-00108 and in part by Grant INT-84-13793 from the NSF International Programs Office.

††INRIA, Domaine de Voluceau, Roquencourt, B.P. 105, Le Chesnay Cedex, France.

[1] It can also handle stochastic approximation, decentralized stochastic control, optimal control by the Maximum Principle, system identification, and certain nonlinear control and filtering problems [2].

A subsequent portion of the code which is written in Macsyma and Lisp evaluates Fortran expressions for the appropriate Macsyma expressions and produces "dimension", "write", "format", "goto", "logical if", "numerical if", and other standard Fortran lines for the construction of a Fortran program. The Fortran (subroutine) is written using a Macrofort language [5]. For typical stochastic control problems execution of the Macsyma program and generation of the Fortran code takes about 30 seconds. The programmer can at this point enter numerical values for the system functions and data and then execute the Fortran code. (These could be also entered automatically from preassigned files, and the Fortran code executed automatically.)

The advantages of this system are clear. Given a new design problem, the time involved in analyzing the dynamic programming equation and then writing the Fortran code to execute it is eliminated. The mistakes and the time required to test and debug the Fortran code are also eliminated. This is a major advantage of the system in its present form. Most importantly, the system allows the engineer to interact with the computer for design in terms of symbolic expressions. In this way he can modify his analysis or design problem by modifying the symbolic functional form of the model. The Fortran subroutines that he might have to modify by hand to accomplish this in conventional design procedures are written automatically for him. The advantages of working at the higher level are clear.

The stochastic control portion of the system also has *production rules* written in Oblogis which take advantage of the special structures associated with such problems to select or guide the selection of analytical or numerical procedures to treat specific applications.

Several systems for computer-aided-design of control systems have been developed recently:

- ORACLS by NASA [6];
- DELIGHT.MIMO by the University of California, Berkeley and Imperial College, London [7];
- DELIGHT.Maryland by the University of Maryland [8];
- CACE-III by the General Electric Company and RPI [9];
- The Federated System by the General Electric Company [10];
- and various commerical packages like Matrix_X, Program CC, and Cntl-C.

In addition, there has been some excellent work on general and specific algorithms for numerical problems associated with control system design [11]. The cumulative product of these efforts is a strong library of *numerical* systems and packages for the analysis and design of numerically defined control systems.

The system in [9] is closest to ours in spirit. It has an interface written in Lisp which provides an "intelligent" interaction with pre-existing design packages.

The system described here has a different function. It is designed to automatically generate numerical programs (and reports) for the solution of problems posed in symbolic form. By using symbolic manipulation programs, the system permits design efforts to take place at the "next level up" from Fortran code. It interfaces more naturally with AI constructs since it is based in Lisp and Prolog and uses symbolic expressions in its database to represent problems, as opposed to the numerical structures of Fortran. In this way it facilitates the incorporation of an intelligent interface for assistance in the development of problems and selection of algorithms for their solution. It would be difficult to design such an interface in a language like Fortran; and it would be equally awkward to write theorem proving modules in Fortran.

In this talk we shall discuss the current status of this system, plans for its future development, and the role systems of this type

References

[1] P. Gloess and J. Marcovitch, "Oblogis: A flexible implementation of Prolog logic and applications to DBMS interfacing and expert systems design," *Proc. First Int. Conf. Appl. Artificial Intelligence to Engineering Problems, Southampton University,* April 1986.

[2] O. Ahkrif, and G.L. Blankenship, "Computer algebra algorithms for nonlinear control systems," *Proc. NATO Advanced Study Institute on CAD of Control Systems,* M. Denham and A. Laub, eds., Springer-Verlag, New York, to appear.

[3] C. Gomez, J.P. Quadrat, and A. Sulem, "Towards an expert system in stochastic control: the Hamilton-Jacobi part," in *Lecture Notes in Control and Information Sciences,* A. Bensoussan and J.L. Lions, eds., Springer-Verlag, June 1984.

[4] J.P. Chancelier and A. Sulem, "MACROTEX: A LATEX code generator in MACSYMA," preprint, INRIA, 1987.

[5] J.P. Chancelier and J.P Quadrat, "Un Interface Macsyma - Fortran : Macrofort," preprint, INRIA, 1987.

[6] E.S. Armstrong, *ORACLS. A Design System for Linear Multivariable Control,* Marcel Dekker, Inc., New York, 1980.

[7] D. G. Mayne, W. T. Nye, E. Polak, P. Siegel, and T. Wuu, "DELIGHT-MIMO: An interactive, optimization-based multivariable control system design package," *Control System Magazine,* vol. 2, 1982.

[8] M.K.H. Fan, W.T. Nye, and A.L. Tits, *DELIGHT.MaryLin User's Guide,* Electrical Engineering Department, University of Maryland, College Park, Feb. 1985.

[9] J.R. James, P.P. Bonissone, D.K. Frederick, and J.H. Taylor, "A retrospective view of CACE-III: Considerations in coordinating sysmbolic and numeric computation in a rule-based expert system," *Proc. Second Conf. Artificial Intelligence Applications,* Miami, FL 1985.

[10] H.A. Spang III, "The Federated Computer-Aided control design system," *Proc. IEEE,* vol. 72, 1984, pp. 1724-1731.

[11] A. J. Laub, "Numerical linear algebra aspects of control design computations," *IEEE Trans. Automatic Control,* vol. AC-30, 1985, pp. 97-108.

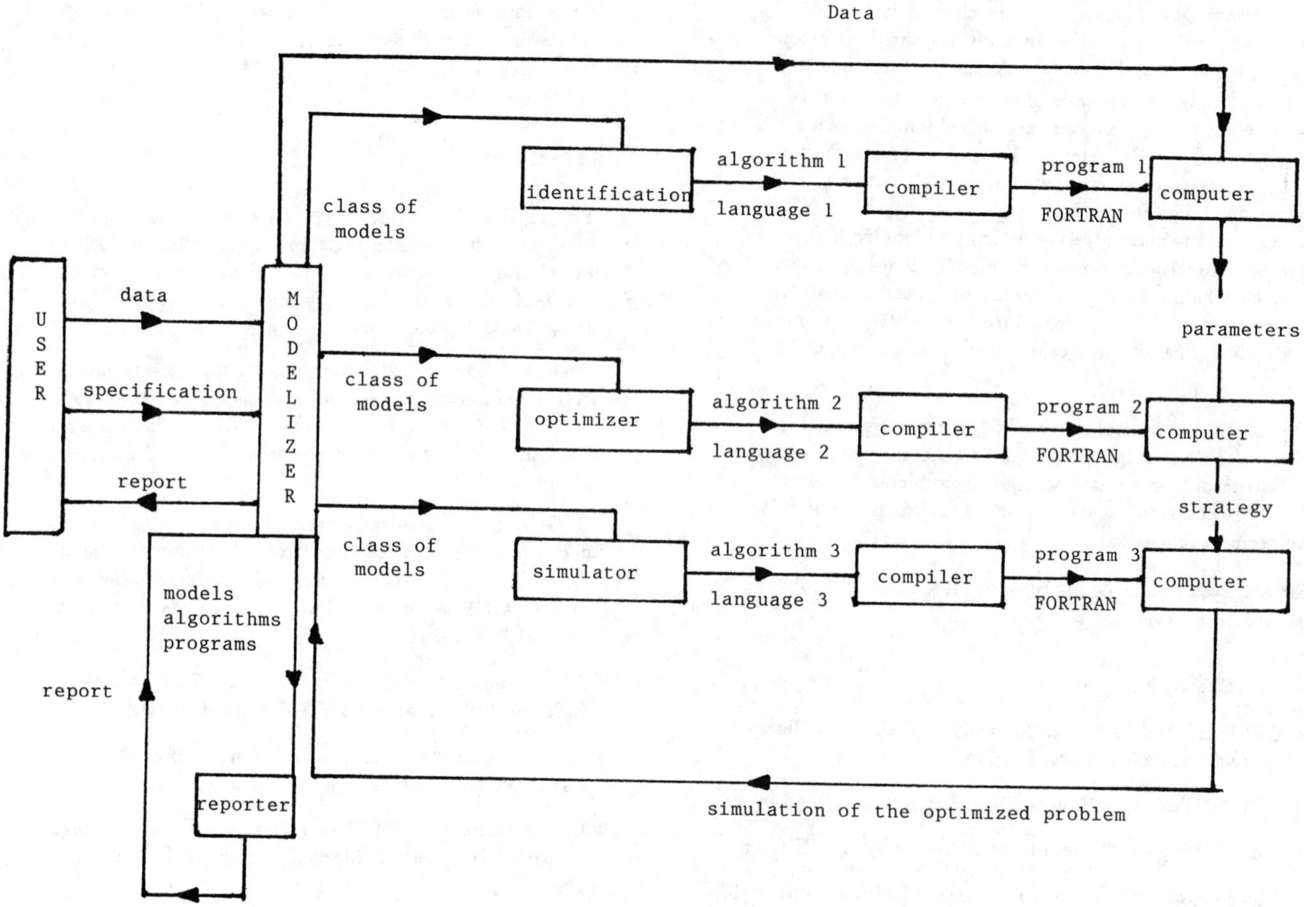

Figure 1: Structure of the expert system.

$$< \textit{stochastic-control-problem} >::=< \textit{domain} >, < \textit{inside-condition} >, < \textit{boundary-condition} >$$

$$< \textit{domain} >::= [0,1]^n | [0,1]^n \times [0,T].$$

$$< \textit{boundary-conditions} >::= \sum_{<\textit{boundary-element}>} < \textit{boundary-conditions} >, < \textit{boundary-element} >$$

$$< \textit{boundary} - \textit{element} >::= \{< y >:< y >\in< \textit{domain} >, < x_i >= 1\}|$$

$$\{< y >, < y >\in< \textit{domain} >, < x_i >= 0| \{(x,1), x \in [0,1]^n\}$$

$$< x_i >::= x_1 | x_2 | \ldots | x_n$$

$$< y >::= x | (x,t)$$

$$< \textit{boundary} - \textit{condition} >::= V = f | \frac{\partial V}{\partial n} = f$$

$$< \textit{operator} >::=< \textit{evolution} - \textit{operator} > + < \textit{space} - \textit{operator} >$$

$$< \textit{evolution} - \textit{operator} >::= \ldots | \frac{\partial V}{\partial t}$$

$$< \textit{operators} >::=< \textit{operator} > | < \textit{operator} > + < \textit{operators} > | \min\{< \textit{operator} >, < \textit{operators} >\}$$

$$< \textit{inside} - \textit{condition} >::=< \textit{operators} >= 0$$

$$< \textit{space} - \textit{operator} >::= -\lambda(< y >)^V + \sum_{i=1}^{n} b_i(< y >)\frac{\partial V}{\partial x_i} + \sum_i a_i(< y >)\frac{\partial^2 V}{\partial x_i^2} + C(< y >)|$$

$$\min\{u \in \Re^m : -\lambda(< y >), u)V + \sum_{i=1}^{n} [b_i(< y >, u)\frac{\partial V}{\partial x_i}$$

$$+ a_i(< y >, u)\frac{\partial^2 V}{\partial x_i^2}] + C(< y >, u)\}$$

Figure 2: Prototype grammar for stochastic control.

GRAPHICAL USER INTERFACES AND AUTOMATIC GENERATION OF SEQUENTIAL AND PARALLEL CODE FOR SCIENTIFIC COMPUTING

Paul S. Wang*

Kent State University
Kent, Ohio 44242

ABSTRACT

A workstation-based integrated scientific computing system should be a powerful tool for contemporary scientists and engineers. When symbolic, numeric and graphics computing techniques are combined in an integrated environment, these techniques should reinforce one another so that the whole is bigger than the sum of the parts. We present some recent developments in this direction: (1) symbolic derivation of numerical code for finite element analysis; (2) automatic numeric code generation based on derived formulas; (3) generation of parallel code; and (4) graphical user interfaces for mathematical systems. We also describe several software packages in these directions.

1. Introduction

Symbolic computation systems specialize in the exact computation with numbers, symbols, formulas, vectors, matrices and the like. When a problem is solved symbolically, the answers are exact mathematical expressions and there is no loss of precision. In some cases, the expressions obtained can provide a great deal of insight. However, many practical problems do not have neat exact solutions. Numerical packages, on the other hand, use floating-point numbers, and iterated approximate computations to solve problems. Many efficient numeric algorithms have been developed and programmed to solve a wide variety of scientific and engineering problems. A principal difficulty with numeric computation is loss of precision. Sometimes estimating the error in the final numerical solution is still a problem. It is usually the case that a problem has some parts that are suitable for symbolic processing and other parts that are better solved numerically. Thus, the two computational approaches are complementary and should be made available in an integrated scientific computing environment. In addition such an environment must also have adequate graphics facilities. Graphics can be used to convey information visually and in many situations is much more effective than formulas or tables of numbers. Obvious applications include the display and manipulation of points, curves and surfaces. Graphics is also important for advanced user interface design which is an important factor of whether a powerful, multi-functional system is easy to learn and use. The combination of symbolic, numeric and graphics computing techniques in a single scientific computing environment can bring not only convenience but also new approaches for problem solving.

*Work reported herein has been supported in part by the National Science Foundation under Grant DCR-8504824

Powerful workstations make it feasible to investigate such integrated computing environments. A workstation-based integrated scientific system should be the tool of choice for contemporary scientists and engineers. It is relatively simple to bring numeric, symbolic and graphics computing capabilities to a single computing system. What is more difficult is to have a truly integrated system where these techniques work together with very little barrier between them. More importantly, these three techniques should reinforce one another so that the whole is bigger than the sum of the parts. We present some recent developments in this direction:

1. symbolic derivation of numerical code for finite element analysis;
2. automatic numeric code generation based on derived formulas;
3. generating code for advanced parallel computers;
4. graphical user interfaces for mathematical systems.

We shall also describe some software packages being developed in these areas.

2. Symbolic Derivation of Finite Element Code

Finite element analysis, has many applications in structural mechanics, heat transfer, fluid flow, electric fields and other engineering areas. It plays a vital role in modern Computer Aided Design. Large numerical packages such as NFAP [3] and NASTRAN [16] exist for finite element analysis. They provide facilities for frequently used models and cases. Only slight modifications of the "canned" computational approaches are allowed via parameter setting. Without extensive reprogramming of the formulas involved, these "canned" packages can not be used in situations where new formulations, new materials or new solution procedures are required. At Kent State University, we have implemented a prototype software system to automate the derivation of formulas in finite element analysis and the generation of programs for the numerical calculation of these formulas. Some previous work in this area can be found in [6] and [8]. The promise and potential benefit of such an approach are clearly indicated. However, it is not enough for the approach to work well on simple problems that are limited in size and complexity. Practical problems in finite-element analysis involve large expressions. Without more refined techniques,

CH2539-5/88/0000/0486$01.00

the formula derivation can become time consuming and the generated code can be very long and inefficient. Thus, several problems must be solved before this approach can become widely accepted and practiced:

(i) the derivation of symbolic formulas must be made efficient and resourceful to handle the large expressions associated with practical problems,

(ii) methods must be employed to reduce the inefficiencies that are usually associated with automatically generated code, and

(iii) the system and its user interface must be designed for ease of use by engineers and scientists who have no extensive computer experience.

The system we have constructed is called FINGER (FINite element code GEneratoR) [13]. FINGER is a self-contained package written in franz LISP running under MACSYMA [9] at Kent State University. The computer used is a VAX-11/780 under Berkeley UNIX (4.2 bsd). The techniques developed are applicable not only to finite element analysis but in the general context of automatic symbolic mathematical derivation interfaced to numerical code generation.

2.1. FINGER Functionalities

From input provided by the user, either interactively or in a file, FINGER will derive finite element characteristic arrays and generate FORTRAN code based on the derived formulas. The initial system handles the isoparametric element family. Element types include 2-D, 3-D, and shell elements in linear and nonlinear cases. The system allows easy extension to other finite element formulations. From a functional point of view, FINGER will

1. assist the user in the symbolic derivation of mathematical expressions used in finite elements, in particular the various characteristic arrays;
2. provide high-level commands for a variety of frequent and well-defined computations in finite element analysis, including linear and non-linear applications, especially for shell elements;
3. allow the mode of operation to range from interactive manual control to fully automatic;
4. generate, based on symbolic computations, FORTRAN code in a form specified by the user;
5. automatically arrange for generated FORTRAN code to compile, link and run with FORTRAN-based finite element analysis packages such as the NFAP package [3];

2.2. Formula Derivation

In finite element analysis, the mathematical derivation leading to the material properties matrix is quite tedious and error prone. Although the manipulations involved are straightforward. By automating this process, many weeks of hard computation by hand can be avoided.

The computation involves vectors, matrices, partial differentiation, matrix multiplication etc. Expressions involved can be quite large. Thus, care must be taken to label intermediate expressions and to use symmetry relations in symbolic derivation and in generating code. The first applications of FINGER have been on elasto-plastic materials. It is interesting to note that, using the package, we have found an error (a term missing) in the plastic matrix generally accepted in the literature In reference [4], for example, equation 12.100 in page 580 shows:

$$\frac{1}{\omega} = (1-2v)(2J_2+3^2_\rho)+9v\rho^2+ \tag{1}$$

$$\frac{H(1+v)(1-2v)}{E}\left[2J_2+3\rho^2\right]^{\frac{1}{2}} \quad 1-\frac{1}{3}Bp$$

Our material matrix module derived the following:

$$\frac{1}{\omega} = (1-2v)(2J_2+3\rho^2)+9v\rho^2+ \tag{2}$$

$$\frac{H(1+v)(1-2v)}{E}\left[2J_2+3\rho^2+2\left(r^2_{xy}+r^2_{yz}+r^2_{zx}\right)\right]^{\frac{1}{2}}\left(1-\frac{1}{3}Bp\right)$$

After we found the discrepancy between the equations (1) and (2), painstaking hand computation was undertaken which verified equation (2). It is conceivable that there exist numerical finite element packages that use the incorrect material matrix formula (1).

In addition to material property matrices, FINGER also derives the element strain-displacement matrix and the element stiffness matrix in the isoparametric and hybrid-mixed formulations.

3. FORTRAN Code Generation

Actual generation of FORTRAN code from symbolic expressions or constructs is performed by the GENTRAN package [11] that we developed. It is a general purpose FORTRAN code generator/translator. It has the capability of generating control-flow constructs and complete subroutines and functions. Large expressions can be segmented into subexpressions of manageable size. Code formating routines enable reasonable output formating of the generated code. Routines are provided to facilitate the interleaving of code generation and other computations. Therefore, bits and pieces of code can be generated at different times and combined to form larger pieces. For example, consider the following sequence of steps.

1. A FORTRAN function header line is generated for the function XYZ.

2. Declarations of formal parameters of XYZ are generated.

3. Computation proceeds for the derivation and generation of the function body.

  3.1 Some assignment statements are generated.

  3.2 Another FORTRAN function ABC now needs to be generated (into a different output file).

  3.3 The function ABC is generated.

  3.4 More statements are generated for the function XYZ. Some such statements may call the function ABC.

4. The generation of XYZ completes.

The flexibility afforded by GENTRAN is evident from this example. To allow the user to control details of code generation and to specify the exact form of certain parts of the final code, GENTRAN allows a user-supplied "template" file to guide code generation. The template file contains literal parts and variable parts. The literal parts follow regular FORTRAN syntax. The variable parts contain code derivation and generation statements. When the template file is use to guide code generation, its literal parts stay and its variable parts are replaced by generated codes. Thus, after being processed, the template file is transformed into the desired FORTRAN code. With properly specified templates, the generated code can be directly combined with existing FORTRAN code whether it's the NFAP package or something else. GENTRAN can also generate RATFOR or C code. GENTRAN has been ported to run under REDUCE [17]. The REDUCE-version of GENTRAN is available for distribution [5]. User's manuals for GENTRAN exist for both the REDUCE and MACSYMA versions.

At the present time, work is going on to add to GENTRAN an independent module to handle the generation of parallel/vectorized code.

4. Techniques for Generating Efficient Code

Our experiences in automatic code generation indicate that code generated naively will be voluminous and inefficient. We have used several techniques to generate better FORTRAN code.

(a) Automatic expression labeling: In the symbolic derivation of expressions certain intermediate results should be generated with machine created labels. These results can be remembered to prevent the re-computation and re-generation of the same expressions in subsequent computations.

(b) Using symmetry by generating functions and calls: Symmetries arise in practical problems and these symmetries are reflected in the mathematical formulation for solving the problem. Therefore techniques for taking advantage of symmetry are of great interest. For example, the expression $x+y-z$ is related to $x-y+z$ by symmetry, although the two can not be regarded as identical computations. If we have a function $F(x, y, z) = x + y - z$ then the latter expression is $F(x, z, y)$. If $F(x, y, z)$ is a large expression then we can simplify the resulting code generated by first generating the function definition for $F(x, y, z)$ then generate calls to F with the appropriate arguments wherever F or its symmetric equivalent occurs. We are not proposing an exhaustive search for symmetric patterns in large expressions. The symbolic derivation phase should preserve and use the symmetry in the given problem [12].

This technique greatly reduces the volume of the generated code in the finite element applications. The generated code is also more structured for reading. The price to pay is the additional function calls at run time which is insignificant if the functions contain nontrivial computations.

FIGURE 1. Functions and calls in generated RATFOR code

```
t0=g11(y,y)
t1=g11(x,y)
t2=g11(x,x)
sk(1,1)=(m1*t0+2*m3*t1+m6*t2)/detk
sk(1,2)=(m3*t0+m2*t1+m6*t1+m5*t2)/detk

function p1p1(aa,bb)
implicit real *8(a-h,0-z)
dimension aa(4),bb(4)
v0=vi(12,aa); v1-vi(12,bb); v2=vi(10,bb); v3=vi(10,aa)
return (16.0/3.0*v0*v1+16.0/9.0*v2*v3
end

function q1p1(aa,bb)
implicit real*8(a-h,0-z)
dimension aa(4),bb(4)
v0=vi(9,aa); v1=vi(12,bb0; v2=vi(10,aa); v3=vi(10,bb)
return (-4*v0*v1-4.0/3.0*v1*v2-4.0/3.0*v0*v3-4.0/9.0*v2*v3)
end

function q1q1(aa,bb)
implicit real*8(a-h,o-z)
dimension aa(4),bb(4)
v0=vi(9,aa); v1=vi(9,bb); v2=vi(10,aa); v3=vi(10,bb)
return (16.0/3.0*v0*v1+16.0/9.0*v2*v3)
end

function g11(aa,bb)
dimension aa(4),bb(4)
return (p1p1(aa,bb)+q1p1(aa,bb)+q1q1(aa,bb)+q1p1(bb,aa))
end
```

Figure 1 shows generated code (in RATFOR) where functions g11, p1p1, q1q1 and q1p1 are automatically generated with appropriate declarations. Then calls to these functions are generated to compute t0, t1 and t2 (generated labels). The function names are program generated. These functions are generated by interleaving calls to code generation routines with the formula derivation steps, resulting in great flexibility and control of the code generated.

(c) Optimizing the final expressions before code generation: Using the Horner's rule for polynomials and a search for common subexpressions for limited size expressions can help improve the efficiency of the generated code as well.

(d) Generate subroutines: Instead of generating repeated assignments or array store operations in straight-line code, subroutines with flow control structures can be generated to reduce the code size.

5. Generating Code for Parallel Processors

Carrying the automatic code derivation and generation idea one step further, current research at Kent State University addresses the derivation and generation of code for advanced parallel computers. Automatic generation of parallel code not only reduces manual mathematical manipulations but also helps engineers and scientists who are not computer experts take advantage of advanced parallel computers. At Kent State, we have access to two very different parallel computers: the STARAN-E and the WARP. Our department maintains the STARAN-E which is a SIMD (Single Instruction Multiple Data) computer with 256 simple processing elements. The STARAN-E is a precursor of the massively parallel MPP [2] and the ASPRO computers of the former Goodyear Aero Space Corporation. We also have access to the Carnegie Mellon University WARP computer [7] through dialin lines. The WARP we use has a linear array of 10 identical powerful processors (cells) connected in a systolic fashion.

For finite element analysis, our approach is to identify key portions of the finite element computation process for parallelization and to map such computations to available parallel architectures. The necessary parallel routines are automatically derivated and generated. By building the expertise needed to take advantage of parallelism into a software system, it is hoped that the powers of advanced parallel computers can be brought to a larger number of engineers and scientists. FINGER is being extended to map finite element computations to these parallel computers.

The architecture and the programming language for the two parallel computers mentioned are very different. Generating code for each of these computers will give us much experience and insight into the various techniques necessary for the successful generation of different parallel programs. The parallel counterpart of GENTRAN is GENPAL, a software system being constructed at Kent State. GENPAL is written in Franz lisp to run under MACSYMA. From well-defined lisp-level representations of parallel computations, GENPAL can generate either W2 code, a high-level language for WARP or ASPROL code, an associative programming language for the ASPRO and the STARAN-E. The design of GENPAL allows it to be easily extended to generate code in other parallel languages.

6. Graphical User Interfaces for Scientific Computing

The user interface for a scientific computing system which combines numeric, symbolic and graphical capabilities should also be of advanced design which not only provides functionalities to control computations but is easy to learn and use. Recent studies in this direction include the MathScribe [10] system of Tektronix, and the GI/S [15] at Kent State University. They are user interface systems for REDUCE and MACSYMA respectively. MathScribe features incremental two-dimensional display of mathematical expressions as the user types the input, command skeleton forms to be filled by the user and distilling the structure of long expressions under user control. Another recent system is CaminoReal [1] of Xerox Palo Alto Research Center which ties scientific computing environments also with document processing and electronic mail. These represent the initial steps in an investigation into suitable user interface designs for complicated scientific computing systems.

The trend is to take full advantage of the capabilities of a modern workstation. Multiple windows are provided to allow concurrent control of multiple activities. A mouse is used as a pointing device to select windows and expressions, to pop up menus and to issue commands. High resolution graphics is used for mathematical symbols, fonts and interactive plotting of points, curves and surfaces. An emacs style editor is active whenever and wherever user input is typed. Mouse-assisted "cut and paste" allows the user to rearrange text and graphics between windows. Mathematical expressions are displayed in a textbook-like two dimensional format. Using the mouse, subexpressions of mathematical formulas can be selected interactively. User specified operations can be applied to selected subexpressions. The GI/S system will be discussed in more detail.

6.1. GI/S Windows

In the GI/S user interface system, two standard windows (Figure 2) are displayed on the screen when the system begins. These are the input and display windows. The input window provides a command-line editor and a history mechanism to recall past commands. Results of computations are displayed in two dimensional form in the display window. Other windows may be opened by the user as needed. There are several different types of windows:

1. Display window
2. Scratch window
3. Graphics window, and
4. Help window.

Windows are named. Each can be relocated and re-sized interactively by the user. A corner of each output window contains status information on how the computation controlled by the window is progressing. The mouse buttons are used for selection and for appropriate pop-up menus.

6.2. Mouse Apply

One way to exploit the capability of the mouse in a scientific system is to use it to enhance mathematical operations. One such operation is singling out a part of a large expression and apply a user specified function to it with the result of the function replacing the original part *in place*. Let us call this operation "mouse apply". Figure 3 and figure 4 show the "before and after" of *mouse applying* the function **factor**.

Studies of user interface design of complicated scientific systems have just begun. Standards, protocols and conventions are still largely lacking. However, one can be sure that advances will be made and users will benefit much from the next generation interface systems.

6.3. Graphics for Scientific Computing

Graphics display plays an important role in an integrated scientific computing environment. In such an environment graphics display is an integral part of the user interface. A graphics package [14] for this purpose has been implemented for GI/S. This package features a highly interactive environment in a multiple window format with extensive help facilities. The capabilities include full color graphics, efficient hidden line removal, solid shading and cubic spline and least square curve fitting.

The package can display curves and surfaces given in either implicit or parametric form. The equations can be results of prior symbolic derivations. For plots involving many points, Fortran code is automatically generated to compute the function values more efficiently. The user has control over color, viewpoint, rotation, hidden line treatment etc. of plots. The control is provided alternatively through interactive menus or commands typed on the keyboard. Plots can be superimposed using different colors.

The curve fitting capability allows the user to enter data points which are plotted as discreet points on the graphics display. A least square interpolation functions can then be calculated and the curve defined overlays the points. The equation for the fitted curve can be returned for further manipulation.

7. Conclusions

Modern workstations offer a practical way to integrate numeric, symbolic and graphics computing systems into one comprehensive scientific computing environment. Operations such as symbolic formula derivation, automatic numerical program generation, graphics display of data points and mathematical equations, and advanced user interfaces can work together and offer many desirable features and capabilities that are otherwise unavailable. Using such an integrated environment with attached parallel processors that can provide near-supercomputer performance at a fraction of the cost may develop into a major trend. Automatic generation of parallel code can help scientists and engineers take advantage of the computational power of parallel processors. Evolution of such integrated environments will bring increasing computing power and convenience to scientists and engineers for substantially improved productivity.

8. References

[1] Arnon, D., Beach, R., McIsaac, K., and Waldspurger, C., "CaminoReal: An Interactive Mathematical Notebook," (to appear) Proceedings of the International Conference on Electronic Publishing, Document Manipulation, and Typography, Nice, France, April 20-22, 1988, Cambridge University Press.

[2] Batcher, K. E., "The Massively Parallel Processor System Overview," in THE MASSIVELY PARALLEL PRO CESSOR, MIT Press, To be published Spring 1985.

[3] Chang, T. Y., NFAP - A Nonlinear Finite Element Analysis Program, Vol. 2 - User's Manual. Technical Report, College of Engineering, University of Akron, Akron Ohio, USA 1980.

[4] Chen, W. F., *Limit Analysis and Soil Plasticity*, Elsevier Scientific Publishing Co., New York, 1975.

[5] Gates, B. L., "GENTRAN : An Automatic Code Generation Facility for REDUCE," ACM SIGSAM Bulletin, Vol. 19 No. 3, Aug. 1985, pp. 24-42.

[6] Korncoff, A. R., Fenves, S. J., "Symbolic generation of finite element stiffness matrices," Comput. Structures, 10, 1979, pp. 119-124.

[7] Kung, H. T., "The Warp Computer: A Cost-Effective Solution to Supercomputing", DARPA Workshop on Parallel Architectures for Mathematical and Scientific Computing, June 29 - July 1, 1987, Syracuse, New York.

[8] Noor, A. K., Andersen C. M., "Computerized Symbolic Manipulation in Nonlinear Finite Element Analysis", Comput. Structures 13, 1981, pp. 379-403.

[9] Pavelle, R. and Wang, P. S., "MACSYMA from F to G", Journal of Symbolic Computation, vol. 1, 1985, pp. 69-100, Academic Press.

[10] Smith, C. J., Soiffer, N., "MathScribe: A User Interface for Computer Algebra Systems," Proceedings, the 1986 Symposium on Symbolic and Algebraic Computation, 1986, pp. 7-12.

[11] Wang, P. S. and Gates B., "A LISP-based RATFOR Code Generator," Proceedings, the Third MACSYMA Users Conference, August, 1984, pp. 319-329.

[12] Wang, Paul S., "Taking Advantage of Symmetry in the Automatic Generation of Numerical Programs for Finite Element Analysis," Proceedings, ACM EUROCAL'85 Conference, April 1-3 1985, Lecture Notes in Computer Science No. 204 (1985), Springer-Verlag, pp. 572-582.

[13] Wang, P. S., "FINGER: A Symbolic System for Automatic Generation of Numerical Programs in Finite Element Analysis," Journal of Symbolic Computation, vol. 2, 1986, pp. 305-316, Academic Press.

[14] Young D. A. and Wang, P. S., "An Improved Plotting Package for VAXIMA," abstract, presented at ACM EUROCAL'85 Conference, April 1-3 1985, Linz Austria, Lecture Notes in Computer Science No. 204 (1985), Springer-Verlag, pp. 431-432.

[15] Young D. A. and Wang, P. S., "GI/S: A Graphical User Interface For Symbolic Computation Systems," Journal of Symbolic Computation, Academic Press. (to appear in 1987).

[16] *COSMIC NASTRAN USER's Manual*, Computer Services, University of Georgia, USA.

[17] *REDUCE User's Manual*, Version 3.0, Edited by Anthony C. Hearn, The Rand Corporation, Santa Monica, California. April 1983.

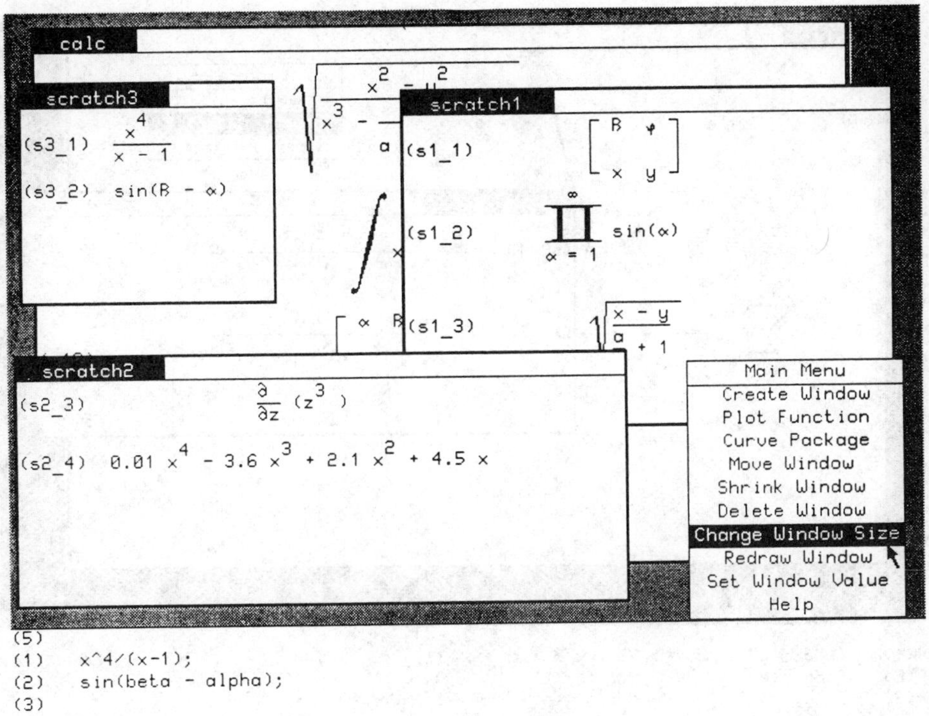

FIGURE 2. Multiple-window user interface

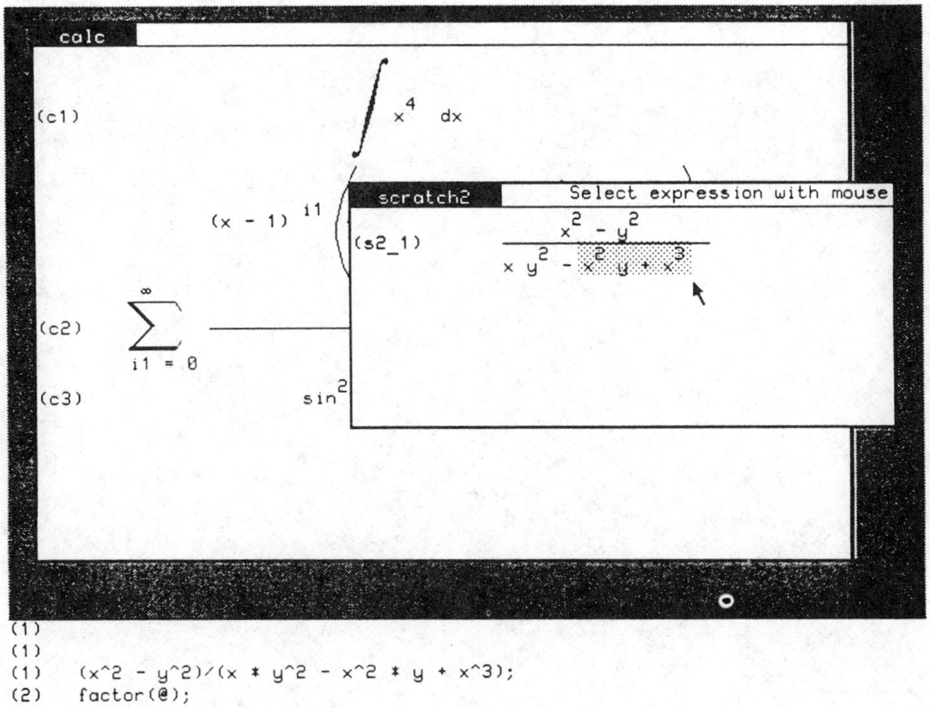

FIGURE 3. Before *mouse-apply* factor

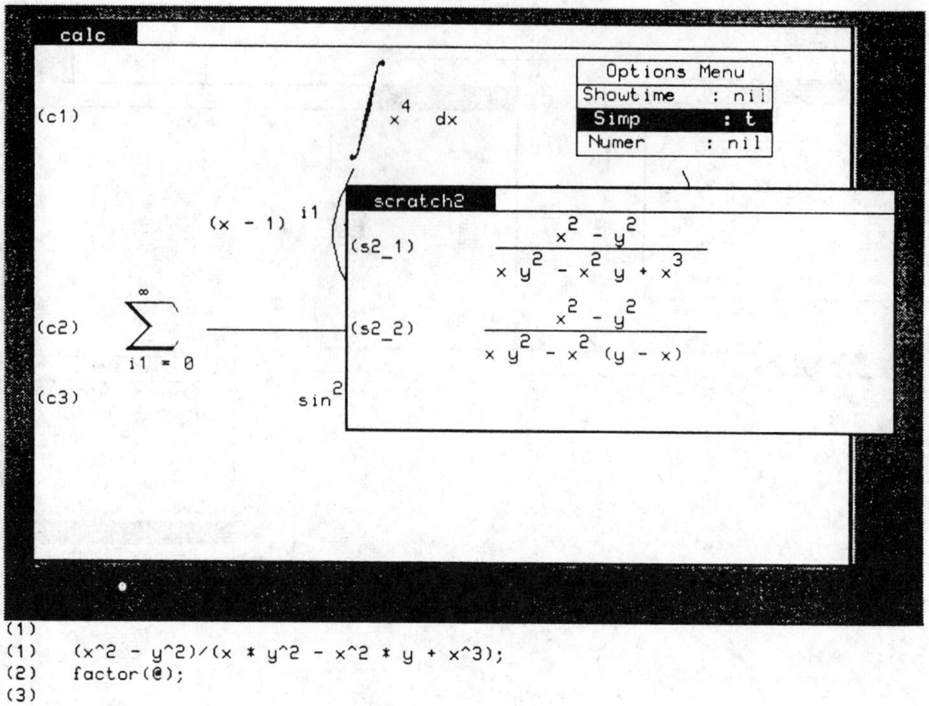

FIGURE 4. After *mouse-apply* **factor**

POTPOURRI Track

Next Generation Buses

Chair: A. Koganivich

NEW ADVANCES IN ECL BUS DESIGNS

Jeffrey A. West

Signetics Corporation

Abstract

Integrated circuits have been developed that provide 3-State high performance output structures in the 100K ECL product line. These outputs combine 25 ohm line drive capabilities when on with high impedance/low capacitance outputs when in the off state.

Introduction

3-State ECL is a new line of 100K circuits that adds a third high impedance state to the normal 2 levels of standard 100K ECL logic. The objectives of the 3-state family are to make a true bus structure available to the ECL designer and increase the level of circuit integration. Because there is no true bus structure in existing ECL board designs, designers have had to use substitute techniques like multiplexing signals and wire-ORing. And because ECL drivers are always on, the output impedance of the standard ECL driver is low which causes discontinuities in the transmission line impedance. With the addition of the high impedance mode, a true bus structure can be created with a high state, a low state and a high impedance state. A device is taken off the bus (placed in the high impedance mode) by disabling the outputs. Because this is both a low capacitance and a high impedance output state, the bus loading is minimal. A 50 ohm environment is maintained over the full length of the bus. Any driver or transceiver along the bus sees the same 50 ohm environment as any other driver or transceiver.

There are four basic groups of products in development. All are interface parts built around an eight or nine bit transceiver. The first group interfaces ECL to ECL. A typical application would be interfacing an ECL board to an ECL backplane. The second and third groups translate between ECL and TTL. The second group translates between ECL and TTL where they share a common single power supply. The third group translates between ECL and TTL where they use two power supplies, a positive 5 volt TTL supply and a negative ECL supply. The fourth, to be done later, will be buffers and transceivers with parity generation and checking.

3-state ECL - Objectives

The goal of 3-state ECL is to give the ECL designer the flexibility and product depth that is available with standard TTL, but in the higher performing ECL 50 ohm environment. The first objective is to create a true bus with buffers, receivers and transceivers placed anywhere along the bus without changing the characteristics of the 50 ohm transmission line (see Fig. A).

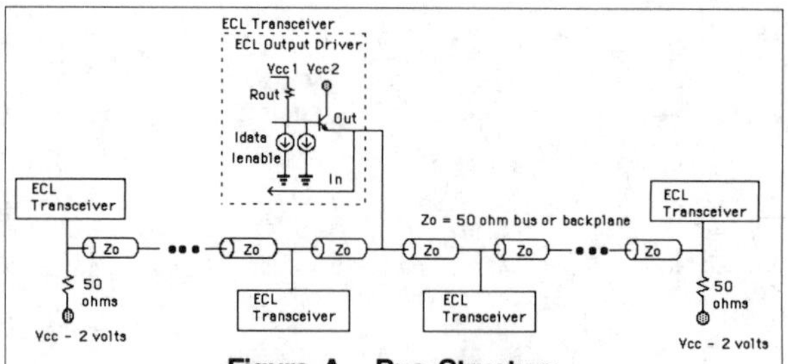

Figure A - Bus Structure

The second objective is to add flexibility through increased bit width, translating function between ECL and TTL and adding more functionality to the part by including registers or latches in the data path (see Fig. B).

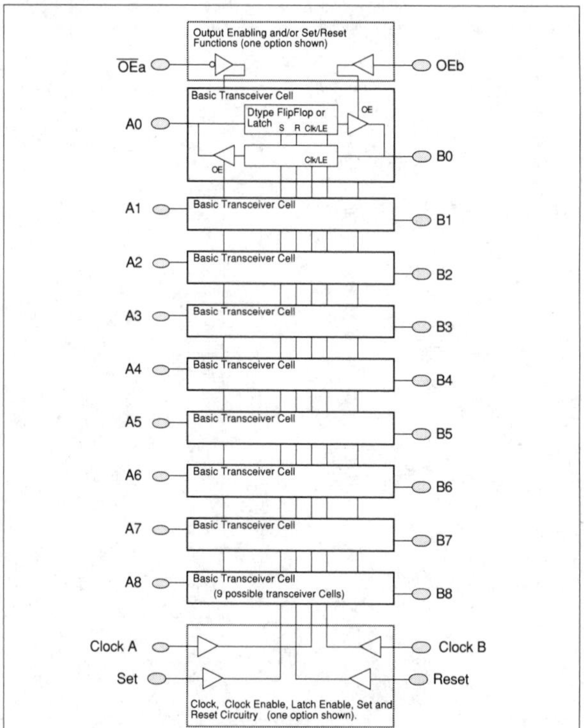

Figure B - General Logic Structure

The electrical performance of the TTL outputs is targeted to match that of standard FAST structures with 24mA 3-state performance. The ECL outputs are 100K ECL outputs capable of driving 25 ohms to the standard V_{CC}-2volts termination. This means the ability to drive a 50 ohm ECL transmission line from anywhere along the line. The three ECL output states are standard 100K V_{OH}, 100K V_{OL} and the new output level of V_{OZ}, where the output is high impedance with respect to the terminating voltage, V_{CC}-2volts.

Targets for propagation delays are 1ns for any ECL path and 3ns for any TTL path. The 25 ohm ECL outputs have controlled output rise and fall times, T_{rise} and T_{fall}, of 1ns measured from 20% to 80% of the range between initial and final values of Vout.

One of the major attributes of this product line is the wide range of its system applications. The primary application is a 25 ohm 3-state transceiver which allows the creation of a true ECL bus. With the addition of translation from ECL to TTL, many more types of functions can be generated. An ECL board can interface easily to a TTL backplane. A TTL system can interface with an ECL backplane or system. One major area of interest is memory interface. Most of the memory today is TTL, MOS or CMOS. Creating a large memory for a high speed ECL system would require interfacing between ECL and TTL levels. Having eight and nine bit translating transceivers with built-in registers or latches greatly reduces the number of integrated circuits required to implement a function. Typically these new parts are each designed to accomplish the function of five to seven standard ECL integrated circuits. This greatly reduces system cost and board space (see Fig. C).

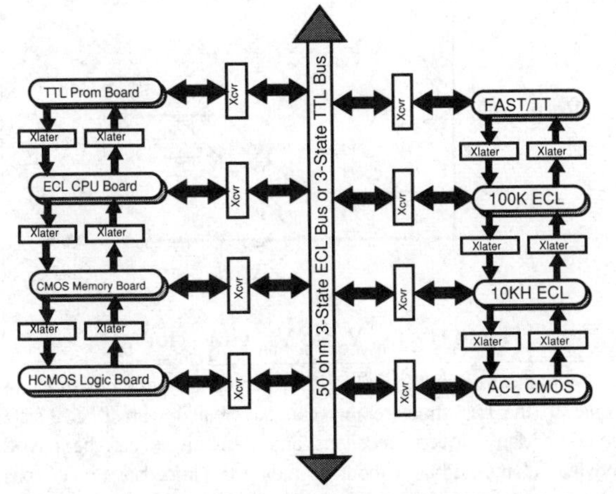

The structure of the Signetics 3-State Interface Family adds flexibility to system design

Figure C - Flexibility

A common complaint with the existing ECL product line is its lack of depth. There is just not the variety of functions in ECL to design with that there is in the FAST or other TTL lines. One of the most popular functions in the FAST product line is the octal transceivers and octal transceivers with registers or latches. It is popular because it is a very versatile product that can be used in many applications. Because it is a byte wide, it is a convenient size. The existing ECL line is weak in such eight and nine bit functions.

Another common complaint about the ECL product line is its lack of a 3-state output that functions in a manner similar to TTL 3-state parts. Without the ability to disable the outputs with a high impedance, low capacitance mode, ECL designers have had to use substitute techniques that have drawbacks in design and performance.

Drawbacks in Designing with Standard ECL

Since ECL is a bare emitter logic, like open collector logic, it is possible to wire-OR the outputs together. Logically this can be done, but electrically there is a penalty to pay in performance because of the wired-OR glitch phenomenon. The wired-OR glitch occurs when two or more signals on a bus are high at the same time and one of the drivers makes a transition from high to low. The terminating currents

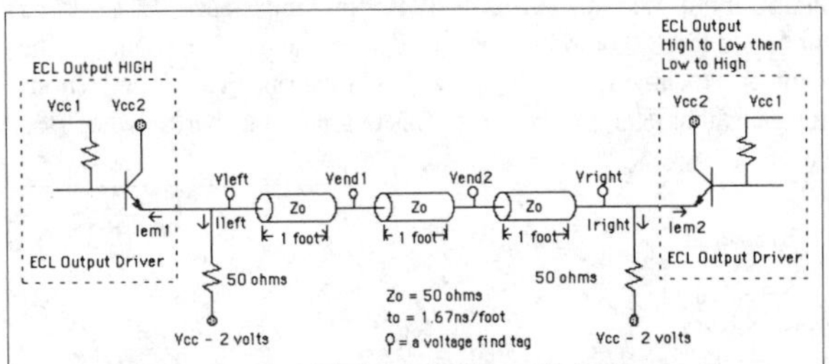

Figure D - Wired-Or Glitch Schematic

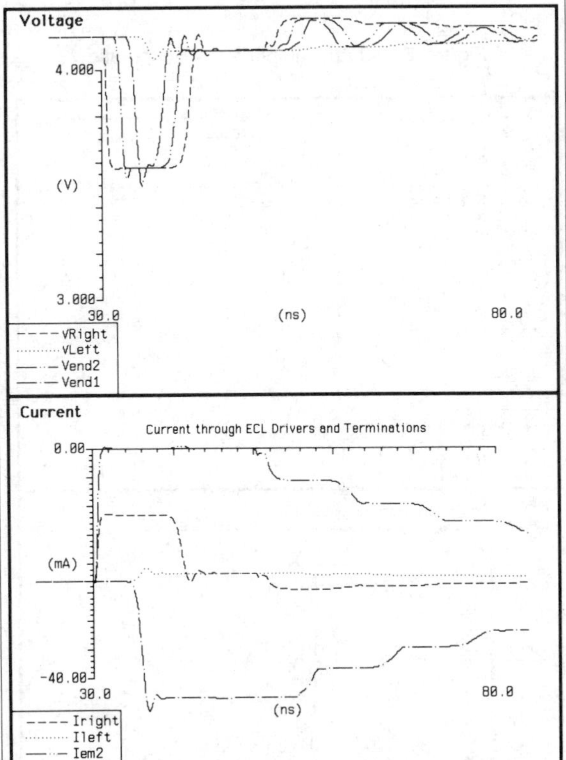

Figure E - Wired-Or Glitch Simulation

are shared by both drivers; each driver sees 50 ohms. Even though the logic is an OR function where one logical high should make a logical one, a glitch can occur when one driver goes low. If one of the drivers at one end of the line makes a transition from high to low, the termination at the end of the line near the driver that went low pulls the line low. This high to low transition propagates down the line until it reaches the other driver that is high, which holds the line high. The high reflection travels back down the line ending the wired-OR glitch. The single driver that is high now sees both terminating resistors, equivalent to 25 ohms (see Fig. D, E).

Another drawback in standard ECL logic is the output impedance of the ECL driver. Since the terminating voltage is V_{CC}-2volts and the output voltages V_{OH} and V_{OL} are about V_{CC}-0.95volts and V_{CC}-1.7volts respectively, the output transistor is always on. In the on-region, the transistor shows low resistance – usually a lot lower than the 50 ohm line or termination. A low impedance ECL driver connected to a 50 ohm bus shows a discontinuity in impedance at the point of attachment. A change in bus impedance causes reflections in signals that take time to settle. This degrades bus performance (see Fig. F, G).

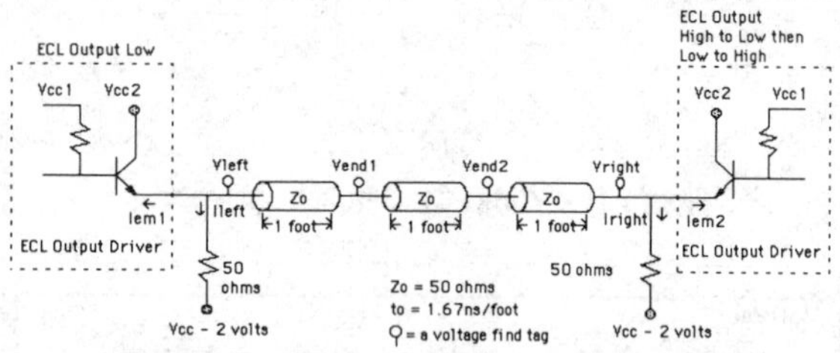

Figure F - Output Impedance Schematic

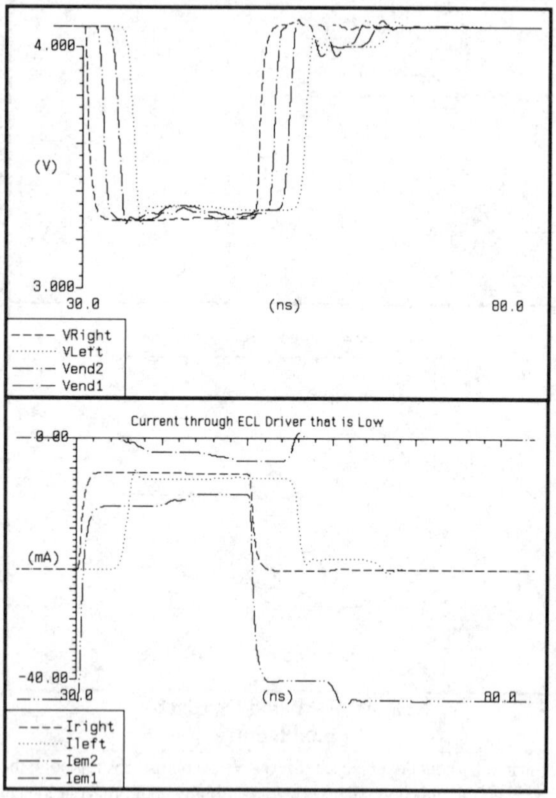

Figure G - Output Impedance Simulation

A third drawback to standard ECL is point to point wiring. Since there is no true busing in ECL, and since 50 ohm drivers dominate, a single wire must be routed from the output of one gate to the input of the next. If, as a substitute for a bus, incoming lines were multiplexed together so as to select between data bits, wires would have to be routed from different outputs to a common multiplexer where a selection would be made. If the data is very wide or if very many signals must be selected, this scheme could become cumbersome in design and layout.

Each of these drawbacks to the standard ECL design can be eliminated by implementation of a true 3-state bus structure.

3-State ECL Solution

The typical way to implement ECL busing is to use something like the 100123, where there are two levels only – a high state and a high impedance state. The low for the data signal is the same as the high impedance or disabled state. 3-State ECL has 3 true logic levels: the 100K V_{OH} at about V_{CC}-0.95 volts, the 100K V_{OL} at about V_{CC}-1.7 volts, and the high impedance V_{OZ} – which equals the terminating voltage, V_{CC}-2volts, where the emitter-base junction of the output driver is reverse biased to an OFF state. This not only allows the parts to function in a way logical similar to their TTL counterparts, but it also provides maximum performance for data transfer rates. Because the output edge rates are slowed down to minimize noise, having to change the output to a V_{OZ} instead of just a V_{OL} or from a V_{OZ} to a V_{OH} instead of a transition from V_{OL} to V_{OH}, would add delay to the signal path (see Fig. H).

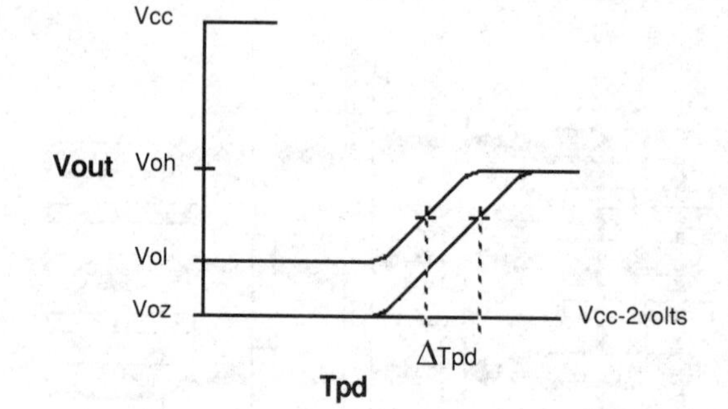

Figure H - T_{PD}, V_{OL} to V_{OH} vs V_{OZ} to V_{OH}

With the 3 distinct logic levels we can create a true bus structure similar to the bus structure that can be created with TTL 3-state circuits. Many drivers, receivers and transceivers can be placed anywhere along the bus without degrading the impedance of the bus and bus performance. The bus itself would perform in a manner similar to the TTL bus; one device would talk at a time and many devices could listen. When that device finishes, it would be disabled and another device would be enabled and then it would use the bus.

The second need that these devices will address is increased functional integration, thereby getting a reasonable amount of function into a package. An eight or nine bit data width with registers or latches seems to be a reasonable function for the buffers and transceivers. With the added function of the high impedance output, the problem of low output impedance is solved by disabling outputs that are not driving the bus (see Fig. I, J, K).

The 3-state bus structure replaces the wired-OR configuration and point to point wiring that have been used. This not only lends structure to the design, but also lends structure to layout, allowing

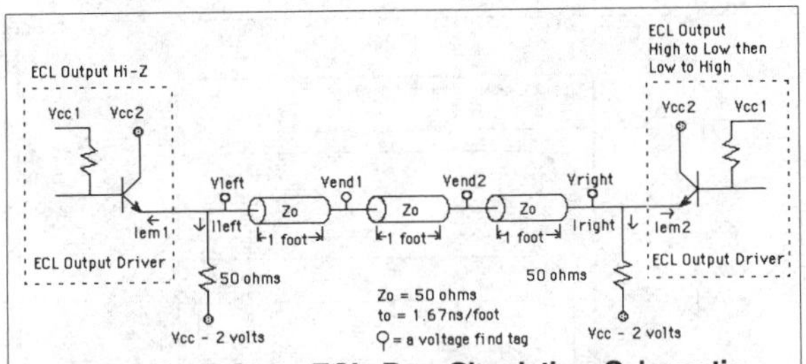

Figure I - 3-State ECL Bus Simulation Schematic

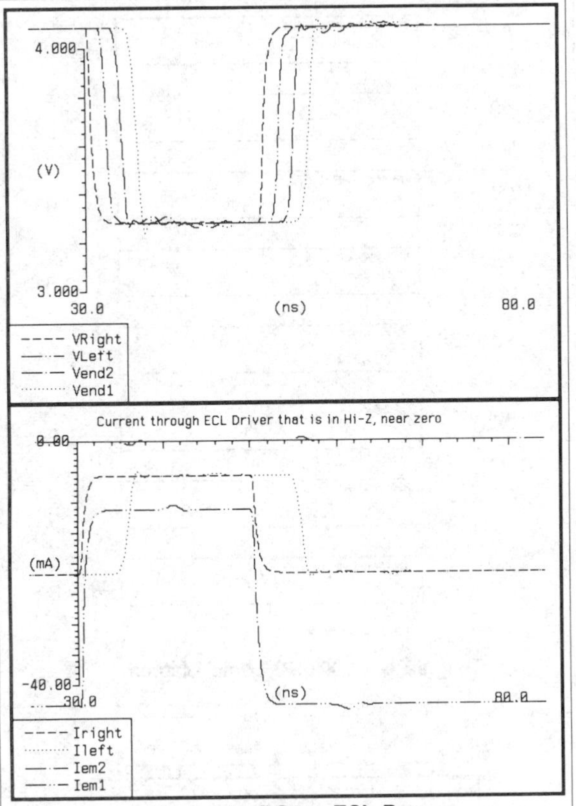

Figure J - 3-State ECL Bus Simulation

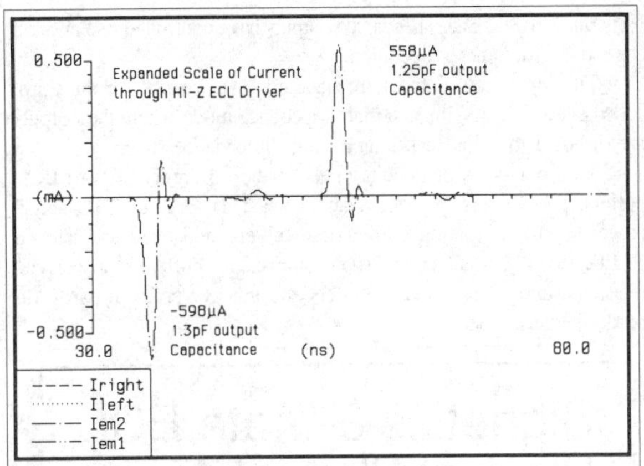

Figure K - 3-State ECL Bus Simulation

different functions to be laid out and grouped around a common bus for communication.

Electrical Description

The possibility of creating a 3-state output for ECL and increasing the functional density is due primarily to improvements in integrated circuit technology. Although the technology used for producing these 3-state ECL circuits is improved over the existing ECL technology, these parts are designed to have standard 100K input and output characteristics. The V_{CS} and V_{BB} are voltage and temperature compensated 100K bandgap references, with the V_{CS} reference about 1.32 volts and the V_{BB} reference about V_{CC}-1.32 volts. The inputs are NPN base inputs with ESD protection of over 2000 volts; typically 4000 volts. The outputs are 25 ohm emitter- follower outputs with controlled edge rates, having the three logic levels of 1) standard 100K V_{OH}, 2) standard 100K V_{OL} and 3) the added level of V_{OZ}. The high impedance state, V_{OZ}, is generated by pulling the base of the emitter-follower low enough to reverse bias the emitter-base junction of the output driver with respect to the termination voltage; V_{CC}-2 volts. The outputs also have ESD protection similar to the inputs (see Fig. L).

Output characteristics in the high impedance state will be less than 20 micro- amps output leakage current in the active ECL region down to about V_{CC}-2.1 volts and pin capacitance of about 5pF or less including pin, package and part.

Propagation delays on an ECL path is typically 1ns, and 3ns on any TTL path.

Voh = 100k Voh Level

Vol = 100k Vol Level

V hz < Vcc -2 volt termination

Figure L - V_{OUT} Chart

100K123 Type Output Option

A 123 type output structure is a wiring option for these parts. The output levels are V_{OH} and V_{OZ}. The V_{OL} level is the same as the disabled V_{OZ} level. Advantages to the 123 type output are familiarity of the output structure. It performs logically the same as the 3-state output but the V_{OL} level is at the lower V_{OZ} level like the 100K123. The disadvantage of the 123 type output is in the data transfer rate. Since the V_{OZ} level is lower than the V_{OL} level, it takes longer to make a transition between V_{OH} and V_{OZ} and between V_{OZ} and V_{OH} than between the standard V_{OH} and V_{OL} levels.

Summary

The 3-state ECL parts are designed to fill a void in the existing 100K line of logic parts. These parts are interface parts, transceivers and translating transceivers with 3-state ECL outputs capable of driving transmission lines with 25 ohm characteristics. Although the parts run at 100K ECL speeds, the outputs have controlled rise and fall edge rates for quieter operation.

The inputs and outputs are standard 100K except for the third, added state of V_{OZ}. This is a high impedance mode where the outputs are disabled to a low capacitance, high impedance state.

The four types of circuits to be developed are 1) ECL to ECL buffers, transceivers, registered and latched 2) ECL to TTL single power supply translating buffers, transceivers, registered and latched 3) ECL to TTL dual power supply translating buffers, transceivers, registered and latched and 4) buffers and transceivers with parity (to be done later). (See Fig. M.)

Signetics 3-State ECL Product Plan

1. ECLtoECL Transceivers
   - Buffers
   - Latched
   - Registered
   - With Various Enable Schemes
2. Single Power Supply
   - ECL to TTL Transceivers
   - Buffers
   - Latched
   - Registered
   - With Various Enable Schemes
3. Dual Power Supply
   - ECL to TTL Transceivers
   - Buffers
   - Latched
   - Registered
   - Wtih Various Enable Schemes
4. Buffers and Transceivers with Parity

Figure M - Product Plan

Product Example 100K990

The first product manufactured using the 3-state output is a nine bit ECL to ECL transceiver (see Fig. N, O).

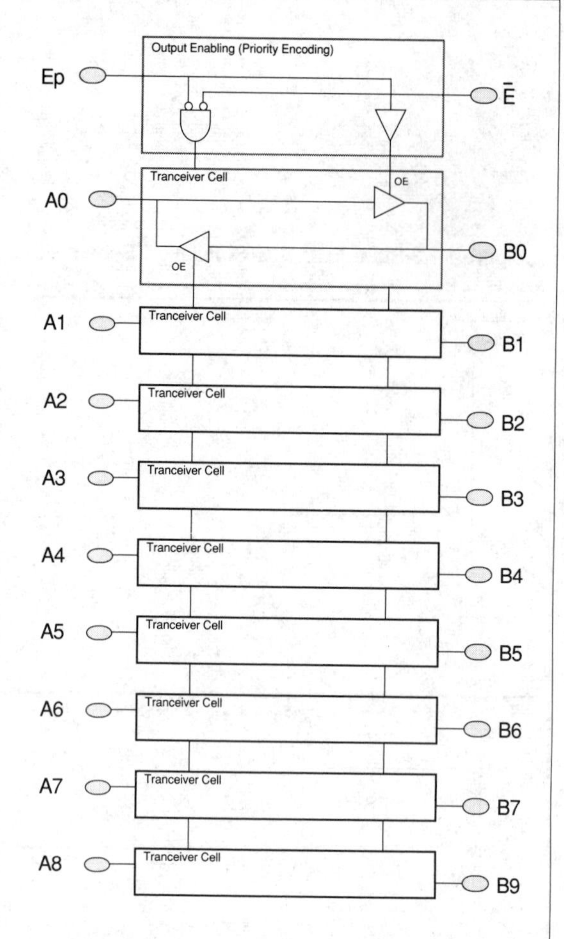

Figure N - 100k990 Logic Diagram

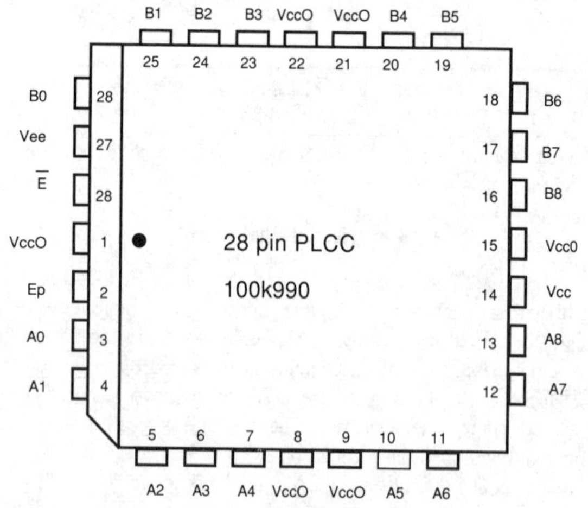

Figure O - 100k990 Pinout

The Futurebus Protocol

Paul L. Borrill

National Semiconductor Corporation,
Santa Clara, California

Abstract

This paper examines the innovative protocols used in the IEEE P896.1 Futurebus specification. The principles of technology independence, explicit connection and disconnection and orthogonality of protocol features will be seen to have remarkable ramifications on the the design longevity of the standard.

1. Introduction.

Futurebus is a very high-performance, forward-looking 32-bit, asynchronous, multiplexed address/data backplane bus standard, utilizing standard IEC mechanical specifications and with a requirement for a single +5V power supply.

The name ***Futurebus*** stems from the concept of *technology independence* embodied in the specification. By providing a protocol and electrical specification which solves all the fundamental barriers to backplane and system performance, whilst guaranteeing the compatibility of boards built over several generations of systems, the Futurebus will outlast, by a large factor, the design lifetime of all existing bus systems. In conjunction with the built-in hooks to extend the protocol to future system requirements, and the 2nd-layer work now being carried out in the P896.2 Working Group, the Futurebus is likely to become one of the most well- and completely-specified systems available in the public domain.

2. Principal Features.

The basic philosophies of technology, manufacturer and architecture independence pervade the entire Futurebus specification. Specifically, this was intended to give users the true benefits of a standard: freedom from obsolescence, freedom from the the technical and economic whims of any one manufacturer, and freedom to choose the particular architecture which suits their application -- and to change or evolve that architecture as the understanding of how multiprocessor systems should be built and programmed improves over the lifetime of the product family.

The principal objective of the Working Group was "to create a specification for a backplane bus standard which provided a *significant* step forward in the performance and facilities available to designers of future multiprocessor systems". The Working Group believe this objective has been met admirably by the final draft now adopted as an IEEE Standard[1].

Some of the features of the P896.1 specification are:

- **Asynchronous (compelled) handshake protocol.**
  Provides a "cause and effect" relationship between the events which take place during the arbitration for mastership of the bus and transfer of data over the bus. This allows the protocol to be specified in such a way that no arbitrary "technology dependent" timing information ,such as "set-up", "hold", or "bus settling" delays, were necessary with other buses.

- **Highest Attainable Throughput.**
  The block-transfer protocol provides a level of performance ultimately limited only by the speed of light of the signals traveling in the backplane. Coupled with the cache coherence model, this provides a realizable system performance many times that achievable with other buses.

- **High Integrity Electrical Specification.**
  A unified BTL (Backplane Tranceiver Logic) interface on all signal lines, along with well specified backplane parameters, affords a level of electrical performance (Speed and Integrity) unsurpassed in modern backplane bus systems driven from a 5V tranceiver technology, and rapidly approaching that attainable with the best ECL systems.

- **Large (Triple Eurocard) Format.**
  The "preferred" size of Futurebus boards affords a significant improvement in the ratio of bus interface (real-estate and cost) overheads to board functionality. This allows high performance systems to be implemented in fewer boards, or for fundamentally more powerful systems to be accommodated within a single 19" sub-rack.

- **Provision for Live Insertion.**
  A fundamental requirement for high availability systems is the ability to insert and withdraw cards without having to power down the system. The Futurebus provides both the electrical and the protocol "hooks" to enable the user to implement a full live-insertion and witdrawal functionality in his boards and systems.

- **Provision for Explicit Future Expansion.**
  Several hooks are provided in the protocol to allow additional functionality to be incorporated into the specification as industry knowledge and experience of the bus grows. Although perceived as antithetical to the theoretical notion of a "standard", the evolution of the design to meet practical future needs is a very necessary and often overlooked requirement in other buses.

3. Fundamental Protocol.

Prior to transferring data on the parallel bus, the modules must compete in a control acquisition procedure; explained in detail elsewhere[2].

Fundamentally, the Futurebus protocol is entirely different to that of conventional buses. There is an explicit "connection" and "disconnection" bounding the transactions between boards, with a guaranteed "broadcast" of the address enabling all boards to participate at least to the point of knowing if they need to respond in the subsequent data transfer phase or not, as shown in figure 1 below. It took some time for the design team to realize the true need for all boards to participate in the address (connection) phase of the transfer. Nowhere is this need more apparent than in the cache coherence protocols which fundamentally require "snooping" on all addresses as they appear on the backplane, in order that stale data in the caches can be "invalidated" by writes from other boards.

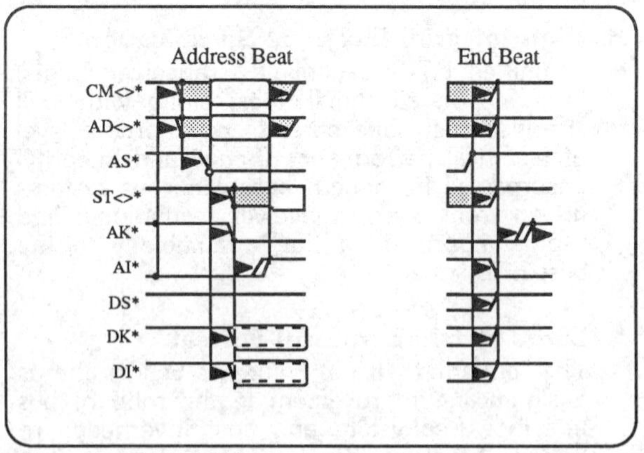

Figure 1: Futurebus Connection Protocol.

The connection phase of the protocol is implemented with an *address beat*. The first event line indicates an idle bus, the condition necessary before the current master can initiate a transaction. The second event line shows the master presenting its command and address information on the bus. The third event line is where the master "synchronizes" (or indicates the validity) of the address and command data with the assertion of the *address sync* signal **AS***. The fourth event line is where the first, or fastest, slave detects **AS*** asserted, after which all slaves present their status on the *status* lines **ST<>***, and handshake control information on **DK*** and **DI*** (named for their principal function of *Data Acknowledge* and *Data acknowledge Inverse* in the data transfer phase respectively). When all slaves have presented this information, (i.e. have completed their address decoding) they then release Address acknowledge Inverse **AI*** to synchronize this data. The slowest slave to respond allows **AI*** to be detected in the released state by the master on the fifth event line. This indicates the master may now begin the *data transfer* phase. All slaves not selected in the connection phase no longer participate in the handshake until the disconnection phase, implemented with the *end beat*, unless the master indicated in its initial command field that the entire transaction was to be a *broadcast*.

The end beat is initiated by the master releasing **AS***, and is terminated by all the slaves asserting **AI***, followed by the release of **AK***.

This explanation of the connection protocol serves as an example on how all the parallel bus protocols are implemented. Between the Address beat, and the End beat, comes the data transfer phase, which may comprise any number (including zero) Odd beats, followed by even, or nul beats. Each of these beats has orthogonal forms for single transfer or block transfer, and single slave or broadcast. The reader is referred to the specification for complete details of these protocols.

4. Unique Electrical Specifications.

For a considerable period prior to the development of the current specification, the designers floundered, as all other bus designers have in the past, with a backplane physics problem known as the "bus-driving" problem. Briefly, this is the phenomenon of a TTL device being unable to drive the very low characteristic impedances presented by a backplane loaded in each slot position, by the capacitance of other TTL devices of the same type. Previously, all TTL buses have avoided this problem by *delaying* the synchronization signal for some period of time to allow the information signals to propagate to, and to reflect from, the backplane terminators. The resulting staircase waveform, after one or more reflections, builds up to a point where it can be reliably received off the backplane with receivers which require standard TTL thresholds. These delays were a fundamental barrier to improving the performance capability of backplane buses, until the Futurebus team discovered the solution.

The Electrical Specifications Task-Group discovered that the principal problem was the fundamental construction of the tranceiver devices themselves. Tri-state TTL simply presented too much capacitance to the lines (with a backplane slot spacing ≤ 1") for these same devices to drive the resultant depressed characteristic impedance.

It was realized that TTL is an inappropriate technology to cope with the physics of modern high-speed backplanes. Figure 2 below shows the basic principle of isolating the capacitance of an *open collector* driver by a reverse-biassed schottky diode. So successful was this technique that National Semiconductor, Texas Instruments, and now Ferranti are to manufacture and sell devices which incorporate this feature, along with a high accuracy receiver threshold, to meet the Futurebus specifications.

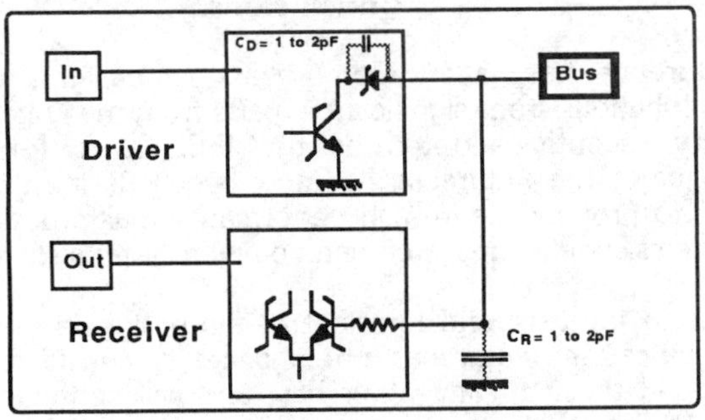

Figure 2. Backplane Tranceiver Logic.

5. Architecture Independence.

A particularly attractive feature of the Futurebus is its freedom from the constraints of system architecture as seen in the eyes of the designers of the initial specification (at least at the time they conceived the bus!). It is now widely recognized that a high performance bus alone is insufficient to guarantee a high performance system; and that architecture is the key to being able to extract the best performance from multiprocessor systems. The Futurebus is capable of supporting almost any kind of multiprocessor architecture, from the *functionally distributed*, which requires a message passing protocol, to the immensely versatile *shared memory architecture*, which requires a cache coherence protocol.

The hardware specification, 896.1, provides the basic protocol mechanisms. The P896.2 document, currently in definition, provides the higher level protocols needed for message passing, cache coherence, and *bus repeaters*. P896.2 is the next "layer" of Futurebus Family of standards.

6. Cache Consistency Protocol.

As processors are added to a system, soner or later the bus will become a bottleneck. With modern high-performance 32-bit microprocessors, this bottleneck becomes apparent often with only two or three processors sharing the same bus. This is due to the relative inefficiency of accessing memory "randomly" (as opposed to sequentially -- as in page mode, nibble mode, or static column mode). By somehow organising the system or the software, so that the available bandwidth is used more economically (and when it *is* used, more efficiently -- such as with block transfers of several words at a time), the system can be made to scale in performance much more linearly as processors are made available to the system.

Traditional methods to solve this problem are to persuade the programmers to keep all their code for execution locally, and only access the bus when the need for communicating data to other boards arises. In addition, by communicating only "results" of computations in messages between processors directly, rather than randomly and indirectly through pointers to data objects in main memory, the ratio of computational work to bus traffic can be lowered, albeit with a somewhat increased computational overhead to manage the messages. The problem with this traditional method, is the very need for the programmers to be aware of, and to work with, the constraints of this kind of architecture. Whilst this may be a natural organization in some systems (such as where tasks are assigned statically to processors in PROMs etc.), it is most often a burdensome and unwelcome constraint to the system programmers, who desire the freedom to manipulate the system code and data in ways which most naturally fit less specialized applications.

What is truly needed is some method which allows the programmers completely unrestricted access, by any of the processors in the system, to shared data objects, or code. This kind of system is often referred to as a shared memory system. The first step in understanding how to build a shared memory system without the consequent bottleneck imposed by the inefficient access of common memory through the bus, is to interpose a cache memory between each of the processors and its bus interface. Until recently, caches were used primarily for speed-up purposes, to make a large (and cheaper) memory behave much faster by imposing a much smaller and faster smart memory buffer (the cache) between the processor and its main memory. Due to the temporal and spatial locality characteristics of program behaviour, once a cache has obtained a copy of a data item after the first request by the processor (the miss), subsequent accesses are serviced by the cache directly rather than have to go to main memory for a copy.

In multiprocessor systems, however, an additional benefit is provided by the reduction in the need for bus traffic due to the hit-rate of the local cache. Thus, if a cache has a hit rate of say 90%, then typically, only 10% of the original (uncached) traffic will now appear on the bus. It is not difficult to see that this increases the number of processors which can now coexist on the same bus, by an order of magnitude--or more with higher hit-rates.

Unfortunately, a cache cannot guarantee to always have the *latest* data available to its client processor, since any processor on the bus could modify the original data in main memory. This is one aspect of what is known as the *cache-coherence* problem.

This problem could be solved by having a requirement, that all caches must *write-through* any data which modifies a cache data item. This would then ensure that at least all data modifications could be "seen" on the bus, and that if the caches were able to "snoop" on at least the address transactions (and the read/write command) . The caches would then have at least a sporting chance of invalidating the data if it saw it being modified by another processor, causing only fresh (as opposed to stale) data to be supplied to the client processors. Since, as described above, the Futurebus guarantees that the transaction header (address beats) can be monitored, in a technology independent way, by all other boards, this "write-through" method is rather easy to implement in Futurebus systems.

However by requiring all *write* transfers to create cache "misses", the effective hit-rate is now severely degraded, limiting the usefulness of the caches in reducing bus traffic. This is regrettable since, depending upon the application, the vast majority of writes from processors may not be to data objects which other processors (and caches) are interested in anyway (i.e. private or non-shared data). Of course, if *none* of the data were shared, we would have no need to write-through at all.

Ideally, what is needed is some method which can dynamically keep track of which data items are shared (used by more than one processor) and those which are not shared. We can then dynamically decide whether to write-through the cache, or to only write-back to the cache, on an access by access basis. The Futurebus provides the mechanisms necessary to maintain state information in each cache to do exactly that. A complete explanation of these mechanisms is beyond the scope of this paper and the reader is referred to a more specialized discussion[3].

7. Support for Fault-Tolerant Systems.

Many of the initial members of the Working Group were significantly interested in building systems which could be used in fault-tolerant or high-integrity applications. Support of these kind of systems therefore exists not only explicitly in the specification, such as mechanisms to support live-insertion, parity protection for the arbitration, and data transfer protocols, etc., but also in aspects which pervade the entire philosophy of the specification, such as: the lack of *centralized* boards or services; care in the design of the transaction protocol to ensure the *locking* mechanisms would work reliably in dual or triple bus systems; mechanisms to identify the current master, and to re-initialize only the bus interfaces of all the boards should the current master lock up for some reason.

8. Conclusions.

Futurebus has taken many years to design, with contributions from significant experts from many fields. Very recently adopted by the IEEE as a formal standard, the Futurebus has now begun its inevitable rise to prominence in high performance multiprocessor systems, both in research and commercial projects.

Due to the care and foresight of the designers of the specification, Futurebus offers benefits, considerably beyond those of any other bus, and will continue to do so for considerably longer than any other standard, or proprietary, backplane bus.

9. References.

1. IEEE 896.1, Draft 7.5b available from IEEE Standards Office, 345 East 47th Street, New York, N.Y. 10017–2394.

2. Taub, Matthew. Improved Control Acquisition Scheme for the IEEE 896 Futurebus. IEEE Micro, Vol 7 No 3, June 1987, pp 52..62.

3. Sweazey, Paul and Smith, Alan Jay, PROC ACM/IEEE Conference on Computer Architecture, Tokyo 1986, pp 414..423.

Shared Memory Systems on the Futurebus

Paul Sweazey

National Semiconductor Corporation
P. O. Box 58090
Santa Clara, CA 95052

Introduction

Shared Memory Architecture (SMA) is perhaps the most elegant and conceptually simple multiprocessor architecture. An SMA machine consists of multiple processing elements that all share the same system resources. Those system resources, including memory, appear in the same global address space and are equally accessible by all processing elements.

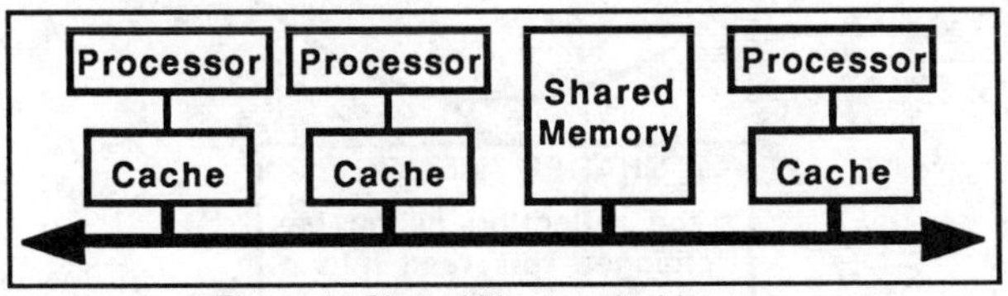

Figure 1: Shared Memory Architecture

SMA allows for the intuitively straightforward sharing of data between processing elements. Contrast this with a Distributed Resource Architecture (DRA)—a message passing scheme. With message passing, data that is to be shared between processors must be explicitly transmitted to the sharers, and if one processor modifies its copy of a data structure, then the copies no longer match. With shared memory, one processor needs only pass a pointer to another processor. They may then share the same copy.

An SMA machine based on a single shared backplane bus has an obvious bottleneck—the bus. A single microprocessor is already fully capable of completely utilizing the memory access bandwidth of a traditional backplane bus. That is one reason why VMEbus, Multibus II, and NuBus systems either use on-board memory or they access program memory on a private memory bus.

There is a way of making the system communications bus into a global memory bus also. Place a *cache memory* between each processing element and the system bus. As will be explained later, the addition of a cache has two beneficial results: (1) the bus traffic per processor is significantly reduced and (2) the bus traffic that is generated can be converted to highly efficient burst-mode packet transfers.

There is only one industry standard bus that supports sophisticated cache-based shared memory architectures. The *IEEE 896 Futurebus* has the richest set of multicache coherence mechanisms ever developed for a backplane bus. The Futurebus makes it possible to build cache-based architectures that have previously only been the realm of proprietary systems.

How Caches Work

A cache is a specialized memory system that keeps quasi-private copies of public, system memory data. The client processor cannot tell the difference between a memory access that reads data in the cache or that reads data in the system memory, except that the cache memory is much faster. From the client side of the cache, the processor performs random accesses. The cache acts like a memory access accelerator for the cached data. From the system side, the cache memory is a block transfer master that occasionally bursts contiguous words to or from the shared memory. The cache acts as a "packetizing filter", converting the client's random accesses into less frequent block transfers.

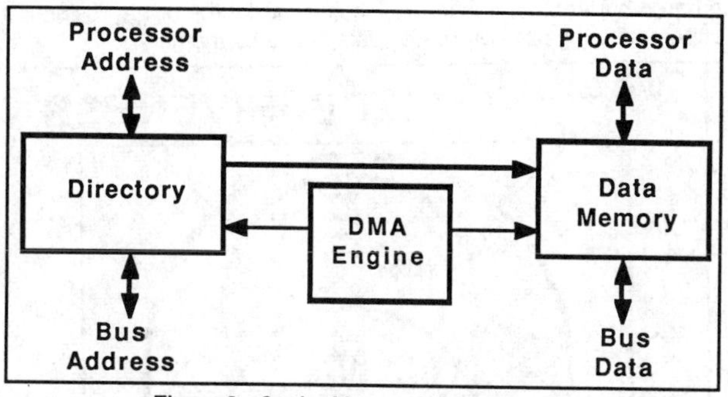

Figure 2: Cache Memory Block Diagram

The most complex cache memories can be described conceptually according to the diagram of figure 2. A data memory block provides local storage for the cached data. A directory block associates the data memory with client processor and system bus addresses. A direct memory access (DMA) engine or "data mover" moves data between the external memory and the cache's data memory. Note that there are times when the data memory block may pass data to or from the external bus as well as to and from the processor, so it is logically a dual-port storage block. The same is true of the directory. It deals with addresses from both the processor and the system. The goal is for the cache to transparently move data blocks between itself and main memory so that the average apparent speed of memory to the client processor is maximized.

Figure 3 illustrates what is meant by a cache "hit" or "miss". A hit occurs when a memory access corresponds to data held in a cache. Otherwise the access corresponds to a miss. A *client hit* or *client miss* refers to a memory access by the client, while a *bus hit* or *bus miss* refers to transactions appearing on the system bus.

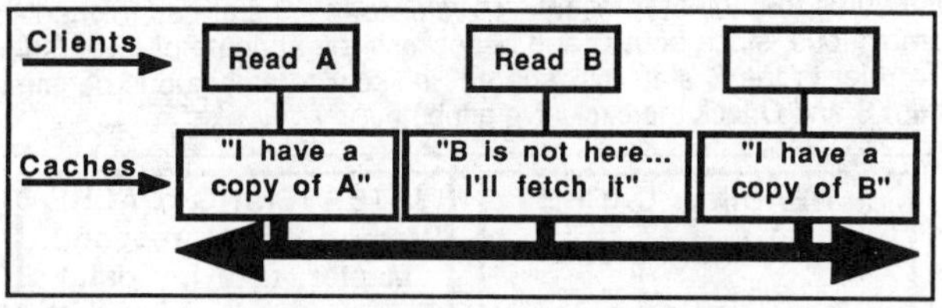

Figure 3: Client and Bus Hits and Misses

The term *cache line* or *cache block* are references to the way data is organized within the cache hardware, or transferred to and from main memory. Usually the granularity of storage of a cache memory is multiple processor words per entry. This may be the size of the block transfer of data to and from main memory. Perhaps most importantly, an invalidation message between caches must be applied to a block of data, called an *address line* or an *invalidation line*

Cache Coherence

Cache *coherence* or cache *consistency* is the property that all cache clients perceive the same *shared memory image* at any instant in time. (The shared memory image is different than the data in shared memory, since the data in the shared memory itself may be out-of-date.) Whenever there are multiple copies of the same information, the problem of keeping all of the copies consistent must be addressed. A system of coherent caches manages this problem.

Cache Attributes and the MOESI Model

A cache client is interested in two characteristics of data in its cache: *private read permission* and *private write permission*. In their absence a client must bypass the cache and (slowly) access the external memory directly. The Futurebus cache coherence mechanism allows a cache to establish private access permission by associating system cache *attributes* with each line in a cache. In the terminology of Futurebus, there are three attributes associated with each 64-byte data line—*validity*, *exclusiveness*, and *ownership*, for which the following informal definitions will suffice: A line is valid if it matches the shared memory image. A line is exclusive if it is not valid in (shared by) another cache. A line is owned if the owner cache data supercedes the possibly "stale" data in shared memory.

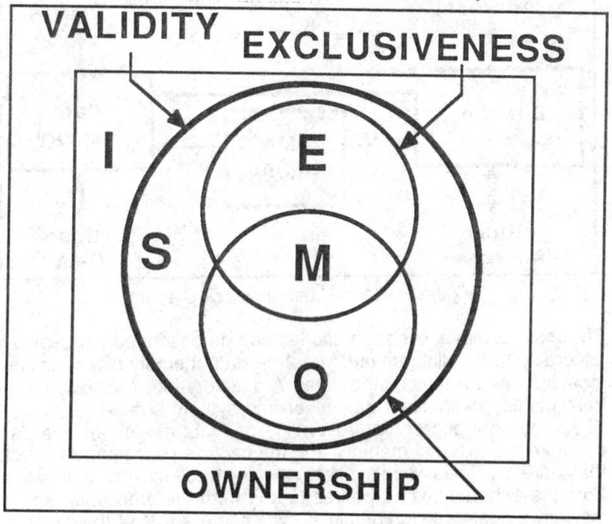

Figure 4: Three Attributes of Futurebus Cache Data

Any data that is exclusive or owned is also valid. Thus, as shown in figure 4, the three attributes correspond to five states of cached data, denoted by the letters **M**, **O**, **E**, **S**, and **I**. The **M** state is exclusive and owned, the **O** state is shared and owned, the **E** state is exclusive and unowned, the **S** state is shared and unowned, and the **I** state is invalid. These states are the source of the name for the so called "MOESI Model" of cache coherence. To avoid confusion, the states should be referred to by their letter names or by the combinations of attributes that they represent. To refer to the **O** state as "owned" is ambiguous, since both **O** and **M** possess the attribute of ownership. To refer to the **S** state as "shared" is likewise ambiguous because both **S** and **O** lack the exclusive attribute.

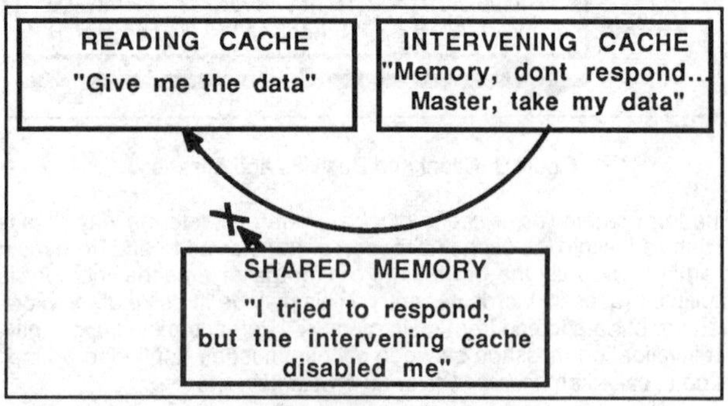

Figure 5: Access Intervention

Three-Party Transactions

Let's suppose that a cache client has modified data in its cache privately, without also writing to shared memory. To do so, it must first have an exclusive copy and become the owner (**M**). Now suppose that another cache wishes to read the same cache line. How does the owner cache keep the reader from getting an out-of-date copy from shared memory?

A Futurebus three-party transaction involves exactly three modules: a bus master, the shared memory, and an owner (**M** or **O**) cache. The owner cache responds in place of the shared memory module, because shared memory holds "stale" data, and the third party holds the most up-to-date copy. There are two types of three-party transactions: access *intervention* and access *reflection*. In intervention the shared memory is disabled, and the data transfer passes between the intervening owner and the master. In reflection the shared memory is not disabled but "diverted" into a store-only mode, so that it receives the updated line from the owner cache as it passes by. Either way, it is obvious that three-party transactions are an important thing for a caching bus to support, and the Futurebus is the only industry-standard bus that does so.

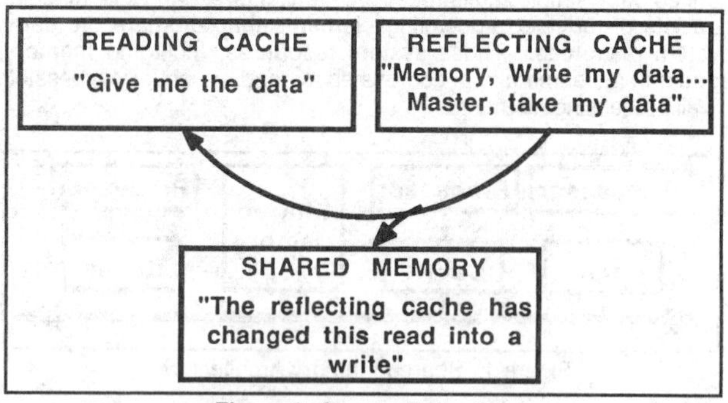

Figure 6: Access Reflection

Futurebus Technology Independence

Futurebus information transfer is constrained by the Futurebus parallel bus handshake to run as slow as the slowest participating module, but no slower!

The Futurebus is a so-called "asynchronous" bus, because its timing is not dependent on a single system clock. In fact, the Futurebus is *dynamically synchronizing* because the source of the "clock" is also the source of the information, so that they propagate together down the bus and eliminate clock skew problems. In Futurebus terminology there are synchronizers and there are information fields, and the synchronizers mark the beginning and ending of the validity of the information fields.

Skews

A module that emits information must guarantee that the synchronizer that marks its validity arrives at the backplane AFTER the information. A module that receives information is guaranteed only that the information will arrive at its backplane connector BEFORE the synchronizer arrives. A backplane must be manufactured so that the electrical length of the information traces is LONGER than that of the synchronizer traces. This is the Futurebus method for guaranteeing setup times. In all cases the setup time is guaranteed only to be greater than or equal to zero.

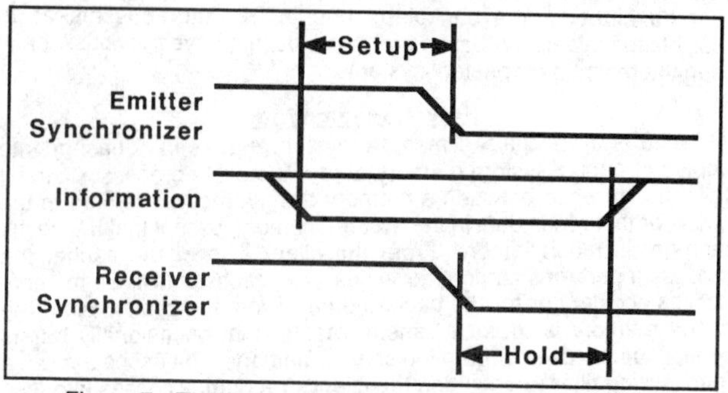

Figure 7: Technology-independent information transfer

Fully Compelled Protocol

An emitter of information must continue to emit the information until all receivers of the information permit it to be removed. This is the Futurebus method for guaranteeing hold times, assured to be greater than or equal to zero. In addition, every transition of a synchronizer signal is both a RESPONSE to a previous transition and a STIMULUS for the following transition. A simple set of synchronizer signals control the flow of information such as address, data, command, and status between multiple caching masters and the shared memory.

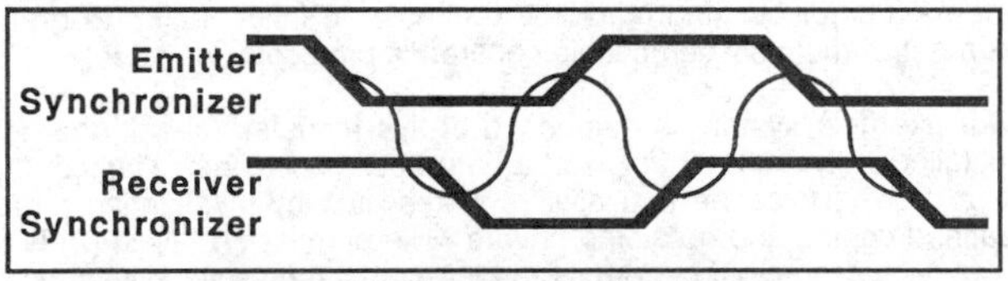

Figure 8: Fully-compelled handshake

Futurebus Information Transfer

Information that flows from a Futurebus master to be received by a Futurebus slave is called *command*. Information that flows from a slave to a master is called *status*. The period of time during which a command or status information field is valid on the bus is called a *beat*. Every command beat is followed by a status beat, and every status beat is followed by a command beat. An ordered pair of beats consisting of a command beat and a status beat is called a *transfer*. A *transaction* is the sequence of command and status beats associated with one transfer of address on the Futurebus. A single Futurebus *tenure* or *mastership* by any one master contains zero or more transactions.

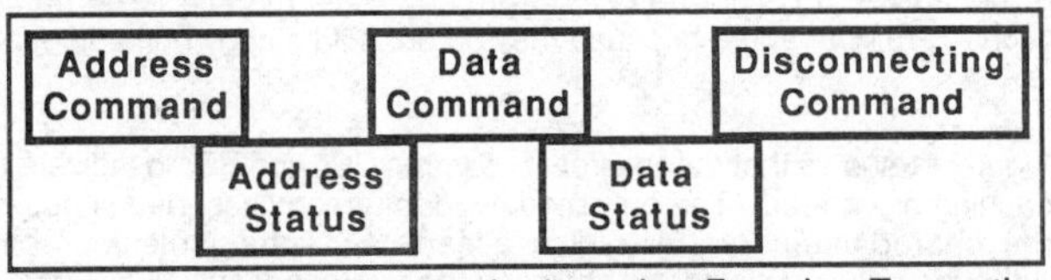

Figure 9: Five information-carrying beats in a Futurebus Transaction

There are five types of command and status beats: (1) an *address command beat*, during which the master transmits an address to all slaves, (2) an *address status beat*, during which the slaves respond to the master's address by connecting, remaining unselected, signalling an error response, etc., (3) a *data command beat*, during which the master either emits write data or requests read data, (4) a *data status beat*, during which the slave or slaves either indicate the acceptance or rejection of write data or emit requested read data, and (5) a *disconnecting command beat*, during which the master transmits to all slaves a final word about the outcome of the entire transaction. The minimum transaction is composed of an address command beat, an address status beat, and a disconnecting command beat. (There is actually also a disconnecting status beat in the handshake protocol, but no information is transmitted within it.) The fullest transaction consists of an address command beat, an address status beat, and any number of pairs of data command beats and data status beats (a single transfer, block transfer, or read-modify-write), plus a final disconnecting command beat.

There are bit fields associated with each beat of a transaction. The individual bits have clear and orthogonal meanings that indicate the sequence of succeeding beats in the transaction, the handshake mechanisms to use, the interpretation of the address and data fields, etc.

Address Command Bits

There are six control bits transmitted from the master to the slaves during the address command beat.

CC* Cache Command
The master may keep a copy of the addressed data in its cache memory.

IM* Intent to Modify
The value of the addressed data may change. Thus, even though no write data transfer appears on the Futurebus datapath, a cache invalidation may be required. Alternatively, if this bit is false, then even though write transfers appear on the parallel bus, cache invalidation is unnecessary.

LK* Lock
The atomicity of sequential data transfers with respect to the addressed slave and the current master must be preserved.

BT* Block Transfer
Each succeeding data transfer accesses the next word in the cache line.

BC* Broadcast
Use multislave handshakes for data transfers. Three-party transactions and multislave transactions are mutually exclusive.

EC* Extended Command
Reserved for future use; Ignore this transaction.

Address Status Bits

There are six control bits transmitted from the slaves to the master during the address status beat.

CS* Cache Status
This non-third-party cache will retain a copy of the accessed data at the end of this transaction.

SL* Selected
This module recognizes the address and wishes to transfer data with the master. Caches only assert SL* for multislave transfers.

ER* Error
An error has occurred.

BS* Busy
End the transaction without data transfer and try again later.

DK* (Data Acknowledge Synchronizer)
A third party wishes to intervene in this non-multislave transaction. During data transfers this is a slave synchronizer signal, but during the address status beat of a non-multislave transaction this signal is used as a slave status information bit.

DI* (Data Acknowledge Inverse Synchronizer)
A third party cache wishes to intervene or reflect in this non-multislave transaction. During data transfers this is a slave synchronizer signal, but during the address status beat of a non-multislave transaction this signal is used as a slave status information bit.

Data Command Bits

There are six control bits transmitted from the master to the slave or slaves during the data command beat. For our purposes there are two bits of interest.

TH* Three-party
This is a three-party transaction. The master detects the presence of a third party by the assertion of DI* during the address status beat. The master passes this information on to all slaves via TH*. This bit is defined for the first data command beat of a transaction.

WR* Write
This data command beat will transfer data from the master to the connected slaves. If WR* is false, then data will be transferred from the slave or slaves to the master during the immediately following data status beat.

Data Status Bits

There are four control bits transmitted from the slave or slaves to the master during the data status beat.

PM* Privately Modified
This cache is an owner of the cache line that may contain privately modified data. The implication is that shared memory will eventually need to be updated by the final owner of the line. This bit is defined for the first data status beat of a transaction.

SL* Selected
This module recognizes the address and wishes to transfer data with the master. Caches only assert SL* for multislave data transfers. Release of SL* during the first data status beat of a transaction is the acknowledgement that a module is disabled due to access intervention by a third party.

ER* Error
An error has occurred.

ED* End of Data
This data transfer moves the last data word for which the address is assumed to increment from the previous data transfer. The required response of the master is a disconnecting command beat. The continuation of, for instance, a block transfer, must be initiated with another address transfer in a new transaction.

Disconnecting Command Bits

There are three control bits transmitted from the master to the slaves during the disconnecting command beat.

DE* Disconnecting Error
During the previous beats the master detected ER* asserted by a slave, or some other indication of anomalous operation. Caches involved in the transaction should ignore any effects a successful completion of the transaction would have had on the state of cached data.

DB* Disconnecting Busy
During the address status beat the master detected BS* asserted by a slave. Caches involved in the transaction should ignore any effects a successful completion of the transaction would have had on the state of cached data, and should expect the transaction to be repeated shortly with a high probability of success.

DO* Disconnecting Owner
At the end of this transaction the slave that is the current owner of the addressed cache line shall cease to be the owner, and the master shall assume ownership.

Control Bits and Cache Coherence

Many of the control bits defined and described in the previous sections are required for normal slave addressing and data transfers that would be expected in any robust system bus. Some bits are more specialized with respect to caching modules and cache coherence. These bits support the kinds of information transfer that allow multiple caches to maintain a consistent and common copy of the same data.

A Unified, Multiple-Protocol, Coherent System

Let us investigate a system of Futurebus modules, and follow them as they interact in the sharing of a single cache line. Through this example it will become apparent that the Futurebus is not constrained by a particular cache coherence protocol, but provides the means for caching modules to choose to follow any of a great number of mutually compatible coherence protocols.

Our example system is composed of five modules (circuit boards) installed in five different slots of a Futurebus backplane. The first (1) is a copyback cache that always writes data by invalidating other cached copies and obtaining private write permission. Next (2) is a copyback cache that performs broadcast write transactions whenever it needs to write cache data that is shared by other caches. A write-through cache module (3) never seeks or obtains private write permission, but performs all data writes publicly across the Futurebus. The last master module is (4) a non-caching master that performs all reads and all writes publicly. The last module (5) is the shared memory slave, which is the final repository of all of the shared data.

Caching Master Reads Unshared Data

As shown in figure 10, the initial state of the addressed cache line is correct in the shared memory (5) and invalid **I** in all of the caching modules. The invalidating copyback cache (1) performs a block transfer and reads the entire line, identifying itself as a caching master via CC*, and marking the line internally as being exclusively cached, **E**, because CS* is not detected from any slave module. The other caches are unaffected because they do not hold a copy of the line.

Figure 11 shows that the master (1) asserts CC* and BT* to indicate a caching block read. The only module to return any asserted status is the shared memory (5), which asserts SL*, the "selected" bit. Although only two fields are shown in the figure, because it is a block transfer the two data beats are repeated for every 32-bit word in the cache line.

The remaining figures use the same format as figure 11, plus the inclusion of state and state transition information as in figure 10.

Caching Master Reads Shared Data

Figure 12 shows that a new master (2) now reads the same line, also indicating that it will keep a copy by asserting CC*. This causes the invalidating cache (1) to respond with CS*, and to change its cache line state to "shared", **S**. Because the master (2) detects CS* asserted, it also labels its cache line **S**. In this case, the data transfer flows from the memory (5) to the master (2). Note that threre are two responding modules in the address status beat: the memory (5) with SL*, and a sharing cache (1) with CS*.

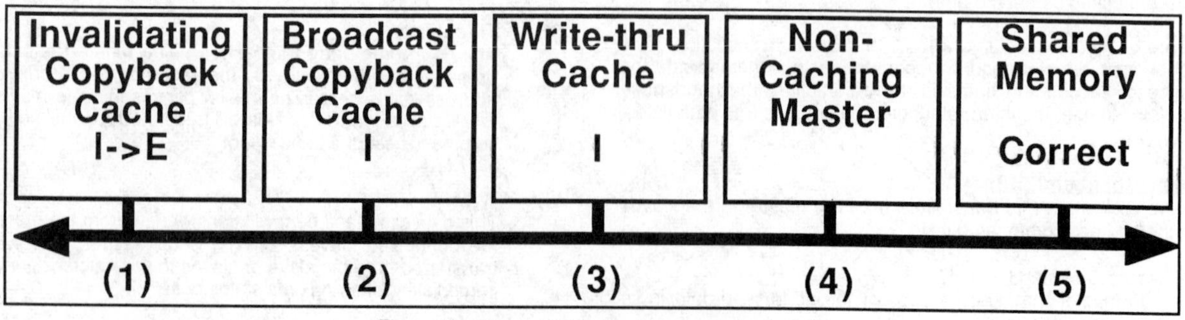

Figure 10: Five modules in a Futurebus backplane

	Address Command	Address Status	Data Cmd	Data Status	Disconnect Command
	CC,IM,LK,BT,BC,EC	CS,SL,ER,BS,DI,DK	TH,WR	PM,SL,ED,ER	DO,DE,DB
Invalidating Copyback Cache (1)	100100	------	00	----	000
Broadcast Copyback Cache (2)	------	000000	--	----	---
Write-through Cache (3)	------	000000	--	----	---
Non-caching Bus Master (4)	------	000000	--	----	---
Shared Memory (5)	------	010000	--	0100	---

Figure 11: Detailed information emission for each module

E->S (1)	------	100000	--	----	---
I->S (2)	100100	------	00	----	000
I (3)	------	000000	--	----	---
(4)	------	000000	--	----	---
Correct (5)	------	010000	--	0100	---

Figure 12: Broadcast copyback cache reads data

Invalidating Copyback Write

The invalidating copyback module (1) now wishes to obtain private write permission so that it can modify its copy of the line within its cache only. Figure 13 shows that (1) obtains private write permission, labeling its line **M**, for "modified", and the sharing cache (2) looses its copy, which enters the **I** state. The shared memory (5) copy is shown for the first time as being "stale" or "out-of-date". The master (1) issues both CC* and IM*, the "intent to modify" bit, and does not assert BC*, the multislave bit or WR*, the data write bit. The shared memory (5) responds with SL*, but the invalidated sharing cache (2) does not respond at all.

S->M (1)	110000	------	--	----	000
S->I (2)	------	000000	--	----	---
I (3)	------	000000	--	----	---
(4)	------	000000	--	----	---
->Stale (5)	------	010000	--	----	---

Figure 13: First private write creates stale memory

Cache-To-Cache Transfer of Dirty Data

The invalidated cache (2) is not, however, finished with the cache line, so it becomes the bus master and reads the line again. As can be seen in figure 14, the data cannot be read from shared memory (5) because that data is "stale". The only correct copy is now held by (1). Module (2) performs a full line read, and receives the data from the owner cache (1). The reading cache (2) assumes the **S** state because it did not try to invalidate the copy in (1), and the third party (1) enters the "owned" state, **O**, because it knows that another cache copy exists, but it must retain ownership since the shared memory (5) copy is "stale".

M->O (1)	------	100011	--	1000	---
I->S (2)	100100	------	10	----	000
I (3)	------	000000	--	----	---
(4)	------	000000	--	----	---
Stale (5)	------	010000	--	0000	---

Figure 14: Owner cache responds as third party

The owner cache (1) responds to the external access with DK* and DI* to indicate intervention. The shared memory also responds with the selected bit, SL*. During the data transfer phase the master (2) informs the shared memory (5) of a three-party transaction via TH*, and the shared memory (5) acknowledges this fact and the fact that DK* (its data synchronizer signal) is already asserted by releasing SL* in the first data status beat. The memory (5) does not participate in the actual transfer of data between the two cache modules. Incidentally, the owner (1) indicates to the master (2) that it holds a dirty copy of the line by emitting PM* during the first data status beat.

Broadcast Write for Ownership

What if the broadcast copyback cache (2) decides to modify the line? Figure 15 shows that it may broadcast the particular word of the cache line that has changed, and change that word in every other cached copy as well as the shared memory (5). In addition, it may acquire ownership of the line by asserting DO*. The previous owner (1) changes its line state to **S**, and the new owner (2) goes to **O**. The shared memory (5) remains stale because the writer (2) cannot know if the one word that it has written is the only stale word in the memory line.

O->S (1)	------	110000	--	1100	---
S->O (2)	110010	------	01	----	100
I (3)	------	000000	--	----	---
(4)	------	000000	--	----	---
Stale (5)	------	010000	--	0100	---

Figure 15: Ownership passes from one cache to another cache

The master (2) asserts CC*, IM*, and BC* during the address command beat, informing the sharer (1) of an attempt to write into it and any other sharers. Two modules respond. The shared memory (5) becomes selected, and the owner cache (1) indicates selection and sharing with CS* and SL*. The writer (2) indicates a write transfer with WR*. The shared memory (5) remains selected, and the owner cache (1) indicates that it holds a privately modified line by asserting PM* as well as SL*. The writer (2) causes the owner cache (1) to relinquish ownership by asserting DO*, to end the transaction.

Write-Through Cache Reads Data

Now the write-through cache (3) begins to read the cache line as shown in figure 16. It receives the data from the owner cache (2) via intervention, leaving cache (1) in the **S** state and cache (2) in the **O** state. The shared memory is still stale because the read did not involve access reflection. The sharing cache (2) indicates sharing with CS*, the shared memory (5) indicates its recognition of the address via SL*, and the owner cache (2) indicates its intention to become a third party via DK* and DI* during the address status beat. In the data command beat the master (3) echos the presence of a third-party cache with TH*. The broadcast copyback cache indicates that it owns dirty data by asserting PM*. A write-through cache typically is incapable of acquiring ownership, and therefore does not assert DO* in the disconnecting command beat.

S (1)	------	100000	--	----	---
O (2)	------	000011	--	1000	---
I->S (3)	100100	------	10	----	000
(4)	------	000000	--	----	---
Stale (5)	------	010000	--	0000	---

Figure 16: Data flows from copyback to write-through cache

Broadcast Write Without Ownership

Figure 17 illustrates a broadcast write emitted from the write-through cache (3). A single word is transmitted from the master (3) to both other sharing cache slaves (1 and 2) and the shared memory (5). No state change occurs and no loss or acquisition of ownership occurs, for DO* is not asserted by the write-through cache (3). Three slaves (1, 2, and 5) assert SL*, and two slaves (1 and 2) assert CS* to indicate slave cache sharing. During the data status beat the same modules assert SL*, and one module (2) asserts PM*. Note that the shared memory is still considered to be "stale".

S (1)	------	110000	--	0100	---
O (2)	------	110000	--	1100	---
S (3)	110010	------	01	----	000
(4)	------	000000	--	----	---
Stale (5)	------	010000	--	0100	---

Figure 17: Write-through cache updates all copies

Non-Caching Master Writes Data

If a non-caching master (or any master) performs a non-multislave write as shown in figure 18, then all unowned cache copies are invalidated, and the owned copy is updated. Since the non-caching master (4) does not indicate that it will retain a copy with CC* (of course), the owner cache may assume exclusive caching of the line and upgrade from the **O** state to the **M** state. If by some means beyond the scope of the Futurebus specification (such as a technology dependency!) another module might be able to absorb the write also, then it would have to account for this by asserting CS*, indicating the possibility of cache data sharing, and inhibiting the transition of the owner to the **M** state. Note that the master (4) does not assert CC* or BC*, that the owner (2) responds as a third party by asserting DK* and DI* while the shared memory (5) asserts selected, SL*, during the address status beat, that the owner (2) alone asserts status information, PM*, in the data status beat, and that the master (4) keeps DO* released in the disconnecting command beat.

S->I (1)	------	000000	--	----	---
O->M (2)	------	100011	--	1000	---
S->I (3)	------	000000	--	----	---
(4)	010000	------	11	----	000
Stale (5)	------	010000	--	0000	---

Figure 18: A non-caching master reads without breaking coherence

Owner Flushes Line To Shared Memory

Eventually, if a dirty line in a copyback cache is selected for replacement, the dirty line must be "flushed" back to shared memory. In figure 19 cache (1) and cache (3) retain copies of the line while the owner cache (2) flushes the line to shared memory (5). This finally restores the shared memory (5) so that it holds a "fresh" copy of the line. Even though the line was written across the Futurebus, the copies in (1) and (3) are not invalidated. This is because the master (2) does not emit IM*, in effect promising to the sharing caches that, even though they do not connect on the write transfer, the "shared memory image" is not actually changing, but is simply being copied across the bus. The shared memory (5) is the only slave module that participates in the data status beats during the transfer.

S (1)	------	100000	--	----	---
O->I (2)	000100	------	00	----	000
S (3)	------	100000	--	----	---
(4)	------	000000	--	----	---
->Correct (5)	------	010000	--	0100	---

Figure 19: A copyback cache restores memory by "flushing"

Reflection Updates Stale Memory

Now let us see how access reflection can eliminate the need to perform "flushes" to memory. Figure 20 shows invalidating cache (1) to be the master, reading the data line for the first time and updating its state from invalid, **I**, to shared, **S**. It receives the line from the owner (2), who responds via reflection rather than intervention. The difference is that the memory (5) is not disabled, but rather treats the read like a write and stores all of the data that appears on the bus, thus becoming "freshened" with the latest copy from the owner. The shared memory copy is therefore correct.

I->S (1)	100100	------	10	----	000
O->S (2)	------	100001	--	1000	---
S (3)	------	100000	--	----	---
(4)	------	000000	--	----	---
->Correct (5)	------	010000	--	0100	---

Figure 20: Reflection and full-line transfers eliminate flushes

We see that reflection is indicated rather then intervention because, in the address status beat, DK* does not accompany DI*. The master (1) still responds in the data command beat with TH* to indicate a three-party transaction, but the shared memory (5) does not remove SL* in the data status beat. Rather, it (5) uses DK* (not shown) to participate in the data transfer handshake with the master (1) and the owner (2) to obtain the privately modified data. During the data transfer, the owner (2) identifies itself with PM*. By virtue of the fact that a full line transfer was performed via reflection, the master (1) may remove ownership status from the broadcast cache (2), or the owner slave (2) may relinquish ownership of its own volition (having recognized that the memory has been updated), although either action is optional. If a master module expects the slave to check for full line reflection and the owner expects the master to check for full line reflection to enforce the loss of ownership, then efficiency may be lost, but coherence is not compromised.

Summary

The Futurebus is already the fastest non-ECL industry standard bus. Invariably though, users will find ways to consume all of its bandwidth. Nevertheless, the Futurebus provides yet another mechanism to increase the effective system bandwidth—its cache coherence support. Depending on the size of the caches and the level of actual data sharing, each processor in a multiprocessor system may perceive an order or magnitude more apparent bus bandwidth to shared memory than is actually available.

Not only are the mechanisms available to implement virtually every distributed-directory, shared-bus coherence protocol published in recent years, but the Futurebus makes it possible to allow them to coexist in the same system and share the same data. Thus, for instance, it is possible to treat semaphores using a broadcast write protocol, while dealing with less intensely shared data using an invalidating protocol. Straightforward extensions using module-internal state information (e.g., invalidate on multiple external broadcast writes without a client reference) can result in progressively higher performance for finely-tuned systems, for which the basic interface is an unchanging industry standard.

References

IEEE-896.1-1987, "A Backplane Bus for Multiprocessor Architectures".

James Archibald, "The Cache Coherence Problem in Shared-Memory Multiprocessors", Doctoral Dissertation and Technical Report 87-02-06, February, 1987, Computer Science Dept., University of Wachington, Seattle, Washington.

James Archibald and Jean-Loup Baer, "An Evaluation of Cache Coherence Solutions in Shared-Bus Multiprocessors", Technical Report 85-10-05, October, 1985, Computer Science Dept., University of Washington, Seattle, Washington.

J.M. Goodman, "Using Cache Memory to Reduce Processor-Memory Traffic", *Proceedings of the 10th International Symposium on Computer Architecture*, pages 124-131, June, 1983.

R.H. Katz, S.J. Eggers, D.A. Wood, C.L. Perkins, R.G. Sheldon, "Implementing a Cache Consistency Protocol", *Proceedings of the 12th Annual Symposium on Computer Architecture*, pages 276-283, June, 1985.

Mark S. Papamarcos and Janak H. Patel, "A Low-Overhead Coherence Solution for Multiprocessors with Private Cache Memories", *Proceedings of the 11th Annual International Symposium on Computer Architecture*, pages 348-354, June, 1984.

P. Sweazey, A.J. Smith, "A Class of Compatible Cache Consistency Protocols and their Support by the IEEE Futurebus", *Proceedings of the 13th International Symposium on Computer Architecture*, June, 1986.

Tandem CLX Design Methodology

Chair: T. Fredricks

A HIGHLY INTEGRATED, FAULT-TOLERANT MINICOMPUTER: THE NONSTOP CLX

Daniel E. Lenoski

Tandem Computers Incorporated
19333 Vallco Parkway
Cupertino, CA 95014

Abstract

The NonStop CLX, a highly integrated version of Tandem Computers' fault-tolerant NonStop architecture, is described. An overview of the system block diagram and a detailed description of the CLX processor is given. The processor is based on a custom CMOS chip-set developed using silicon compilation techniques. The CPU micro architecture is a hybrid of traditional minicomputer and high performance micro-processor architectures. This merging leads to a number of novel structures including a single static RAM array that is used as writeable control store, data cache and page table cache. The processor includes a high degree of fault checking in order to assure data integrity and fault-tolerant operation.

System Organization

The block diagram for the CLX™ is shown in Figure 1. The structure is that of a private memory multiprocessor and is similar to that of earlier Tandem NonStop™ systems (TNS) [1].

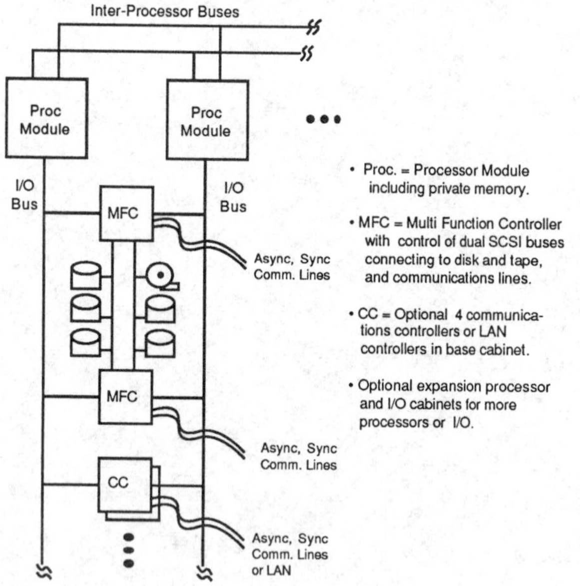

Figure 1. System Block Diagram

Each CPU communicates to other CPU's over two high speed Interprocessor buses (IPB's). Each bus operates synchronously on 16 bit wide data providing a peak bandwidth of 20 Mbytes / sec. The two buses transfer independently providing a total of 40 Mbyte / sec of bandwidth to the maximum of six processors in a CLX system.

CPU's communicate with I/O devices either through a local I/O bus or through the IPB to another CPU and its I/O bus. Each CPU contains a single asynchronous, burst multiplexed I/O bus which transfers data at a maximum rate of 3.7 Mbyte / sec. to a maximum of 16 controllers. I/O controllers are dual-ported and can be driven by either of the CPU's to which they are attached.

The CLX utilizes a Multi-Function Controller (MFC) based on a Motorola 68010 to control dual Small-Computer-System-Interfaces (SCSI) containing up to five disk drives and one tape drive. The MFC also contains 2 asynchronous and 1 synchronous communication lines together with a dedicated maintenance communication line. The MFC runs it's own real-time operating system kernel that coordinates the independent disk, tape, comm. and maintenance tasks.

Not shown in Figure 1 are the system maintenance buses. These buses allow maintenance and diagnostic information to travel between the system control panel, the processors, the multifunction controllers and the power and environmental monitors.

A fully populated single cabinet system contains two CPU boards with optional expansion memory, six I/O controllers, five 145 Mbyte disk drives and one cartridge tape drive. Fault-Tolerant (dual) power supplies and cooling fans are also provided within the cabinet. The entire system is designed to operate within the power, noise and size requirements of an office environment. Expansion beyond a single cabinet is handled with additional I/O or CPU cabinets.

The message based Guardian 90™ operating system [2] provides all processes with a seamless interface to all CPU's and peripherals. All resources are viewed in a uniform way regardless of their physical position within the system. Networking software extends this transparency between systems. Enhanced diagnostic software together with careful mechanical and electrical design of each customer replaceable unit allows 98% of all component failures to be serviced by the user.

The system is optimized for On-Line Transaction Processing.

The best measure of performance of such an OLTP system is Transactions Per Second (TPS) [3]. For a specific benchmark environment, the TPS rating gives a true measure of system performance that is independent of processor type and includes the performance of the I/O subsystem, the operating system and application code. The most widely used transaction benchmark is *debit-credit* (ET1). Each transaction in the ET1 benchmark represents a typical bank teller account update. The CLX system has demonstrated a performance of 2.5 TPS per processor on this benchmark (with less than 2 second response time for 90% of all transactions). This rating includes the use of a full SQL relational database and transaction logging. For OLTP applications it has also been demonstrated that the NonStop architecture shows linear performance growth in excess of 32 processors[4]. For the CLX this implies a 1-6 processor system can deliver between 2.5 to 15 TPS.

Fault-Tolerance is provided through module redundancy and fail-fast module operation. Module redundancy implies that each unit must be replicated so that the system can continue operation in the face of a failure of one module. The system as a whole will only fail if there is a second failure within the window of time it takes to repair an initial failure. This increases the mean time to failure of the system orders of magnitude greater than any individual module. Note that redundancy does not imply replicated units need to be idle. In the case of NonStop CPU's, checkpointing [5] allows CPU's to work independently, but still have all the necessary state to recover in the event of a failure of a primary CPU. Likewise, under normal conditions IPB's transfer data simultaneously and mirrored disks perform independent reads.

Fail-fast or fail-safe operation is required of each module so that the integrity of data is not compromised by an undetected faulty module. This implies that replicated components must fail in such a way as to stop operating. This assures that faulty outputs do not corrupt the module's back-up or both sections of a redundant system interface.

Processor Organization

The TNS processor architecture is optimized to support OLTP and a message based OS environment. In this environment operations such as interprocessor bus transfers and block moves are more important than in typical processors. Conversely, operations such as floating point arithmetic are not as critical to overall performance.

The CLX supports the entire instruction set of the TNS architecture[6]. The architecture defines a stack based CISC processor together with its interprocessor and I/O buses. The definition includes an explicit register stack used to accelerate stack computations and to hold array indices. Sixteen and thirty-two bit operations with thirty-two bit addressing are defined by the instruction set. The machine includes complex instructions that support OS operations, block operations, and decimal and floating point data types.

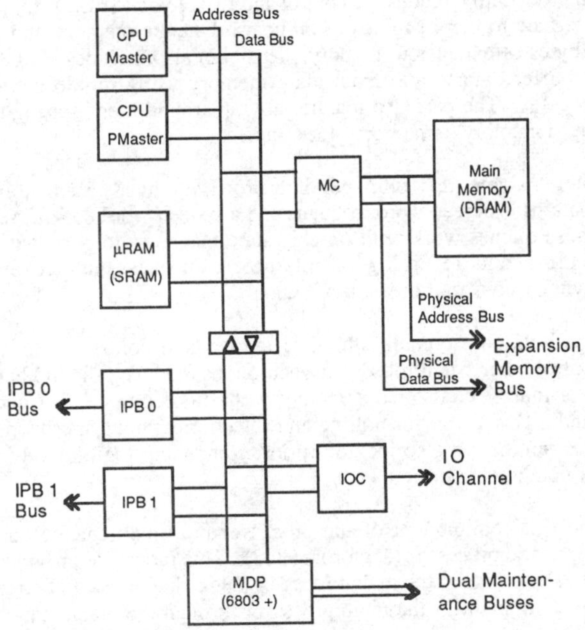

Figure 2. Processor Block Diagram

The processor block diagram is shown in Figure 2. The processor logic is implemented primarily within six custom CMOS chips. The chip set is fabricated in a 2µ drawn gate, n-well CMOS process and was designed using a silicon compiler supplied by Silicon Compiler Systems Corporation [7]. Some of the relevant statistics of chip set are shown in Table 1. The four chip types were implemented, inclusive of definition through to functionally correct silicon in the laboratory, by 6 engineers in 15 months.

Table 1. CPU Chip-Set Statistics

	CPU	MC	IOC	IPB
Vertical (mils)	495	352	309	300
Horizontal (mils)	496	367	311	300
Transistor Sites	78,301	29,408	14,785	19,565
Transistors	60,469	25,653	12,177	18,872
Power Dissipation	2.0 W	1.3 W	0.9 W	0.9 W
I/O pins	110	95	71	95
Power pins	15	13	11	10
Ground pins	15	12	11	10

The two CPU chips are identical and run in lock-step to form a totally self-checked module. These chips include the complete CPU function, and work together with a single bank of static RAM (µRAM) that functions as the microcode control store, page table cache and data/instruction cache. The µRAM is realized with thirty 16k x 4, 35ns SRAM parts organized as two banks of 16k by 60 bit words. This provides for 14k words of microcode and scratch pad memory, 2k words of page table cache with two entries per word, and 16k words of instruction / data cache with four bytes per word.

The MC chip includes the control and ECC logic (SEC/DED) to interface to the 4 Mbytes of on-board dynamic memory and 8 Mbytes of expansion memory. This chip also includes FIFO's to buffer data to and from main memory using nibble mode accesses. The part also features a wrap around mode for high-speed memory to memory block transfers.

There is one IPB chip per interprocessor bus. Each chip contains a sixteen word in-queue and a sixteen word out-queue. These queues work with on-chip state machines to permit the sending and receiving of interprocessor message packets asynchronous to processor execution.

The IOC chip contains the data latches and control logic to control a burst-multiplexed, asynchronous I/O bus. The I/O bus is primarily controlled directly by the microengine, but can handle DMA transfer polling and selection without microcode intervention. It also includes priority encoding logic to aid in servicing I/O interrupts.

The final component of the processor is a maintenance and diagnostic processor (Motorola 6803). This processor provides overall control of the main processor, and a diagnostic and error reporting path for the main processor through the maintenance buses.

CPU Architecture

The CLX CPU architecture is a hybrid of minicomputer and microcomputer architectures. The CPU chip's external interface is similar to a microprocessor. It contains one address bus, one data bus and one status bus along with miscellaneous signals such as an interrupt request, memory wait controls and tri-state input controls. A closer look, however, reveals that the address bus is only 18 bits wide, and the data bus is 60 bits wide. This structure is actually more akin to that found in minicomputer architectures. The CLX CPU external interface is the merging of many buses that would normally be separate in a minicomputer architecture. In particular, an external cycle on the CLX can have the following meanings:

- Microcode control store access.
- Instruction or Data cache access.
- Page Table cache (TLB) access.
- Main Memory access.
- Microcode Scratch Pad Memory access.
- Special Module (IPB, IOC, MDP) access.

This merging of buses reduces the cost of the processor in terms of the number of static RAM parts and their associated support logic, and the pins and packaging of the CPU chip itself. If implemented blindly however, this merging would lead to a significant degradation in performance. In order to reduce the bandwidth required on these buses and thus the performance impact, a variety of techniques were used. These include:

- Utilization of a small on-chip microcode ROM.
- Use of a virtually addressed cache.
- Use of nibble mode DRAM with block operations to the main memory controller.
- Higher-level control operations for special modules.

The on-chip ROM (μROM) has the biggest effect on reducing the performance impact of the merged buses. The μROM contains 160, 54 bit words of microcode with an identical encoding as external microcode. This ROM is addressed by either the microcode PC (μPC) or through an explicit index specified in the previous line of microcode. The μPC addressing is used to implement the inner loops of IPB and IOC transfers, cache filling routines and block memory moves.

The index addressing is used throughout the microcode to implement short common sequences such as instruction prefetch, interrupt testing, and cache loads and stores to the top of the register stack. The explicit indexing acts like a microcode call, but does not modify the μPC. It simply overlays the microcode that would have been fetched from external control store with a line from the μROM. The index specifier of the overlaying line does not conflict with other microfields (unlike a call to the μROM). Index addressing is also used in critical instructions where such a micro branch would be costly. The explicit addressing provides for maximal sharing of small amount of μROM code without the overhead of a μCode call and return.

The virtually addressed cache reduces the number of page table accesses, and thus the required band-width to the shared μRAM. Likewise the use of block-mode commands to the memory controller reduces the number of memory commands needed during cache filling and block moves. Finally, the use of higher-level commands to the IPB and IOC reduce the control transfers needed to receive and transmit data to these devices. The on-chip μROM together with these other features reduces the penalty of using a single bus approach from over 50% to less than 12%.

The primary alternative to the μROM used on the CLX is an emulation scheme where a set of emulation instructions and a subset of the CISC instructions are implemented entirely by an internal ROM. The μROM scheme has two primary benefits when compared with the numerous emulation schemes that have been reported in the literature[8][9]. First, it provides much higher performance when the amount of ROM space is limited relative to the number of instructions that must be implemented. Second, the dispatch of each instruction is to external writeable control store enabling any ROM code errors to be corrected externally (albeit with some performance penalty).

CPU Chip Internal Architecture

The block diagram of the CPU chip is shown in Figure 3. This structure supports concurrent ALU execution, address formation, external access and microcode branching in a pipelined fashion.

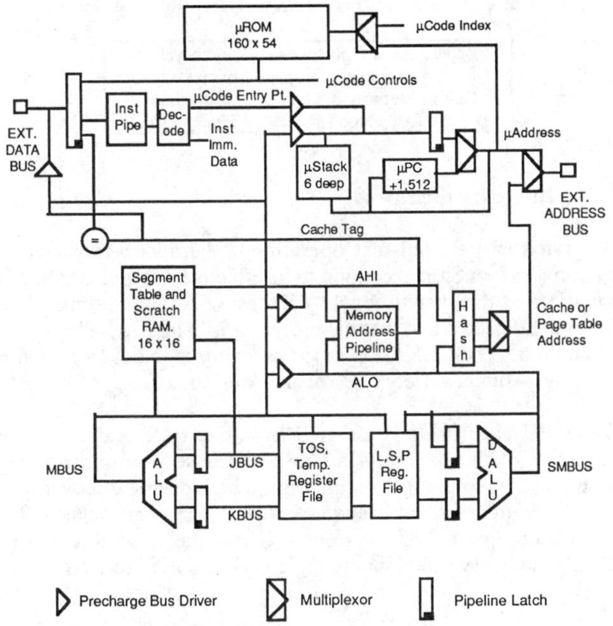

Figure 3. CPU Chip Block Diagram

The lower section of Figure 3 shows the main execution datapath with its two 16 bit ALU's. The primary ALU operates on the architecturally defined register stack along with other miscellaneous registers external to the datapath. This primary ALU supports arithmetic and logical operations along with multiply and divide step operations. The other ALU (DALU) is used in memory address formation. This includes the formation of instruction specified stack or frame pointer relative addresses, PC incrementing, and limit checking of TNS extended addresses. The main datapath also includes two 3-port register files, one which is 10 locations deep and the other which is 3 deep.

Above the main ALU in Figure 3 is an additional three port register file that is used to hold microcode temporary values and memory segment addresses. One read port and one write port of this RAM is accessed by the main ALU. The other read port is used to access segment addresses. Memory addresses are pipelined by the address datapath shown to the right of the register file in Figure 3 for subsequent cache hit and breakpoint detection. This datapath also contains the first level of multiplexing logic used in choosing between cache and page table cache addresses for use in external accesses.

The μROM discussed in the previous section is shown at the top of Figure 3 with the micro sequencer and instruction pipeline just below it.

The micro sequencer supports a variety of microcode addressing functions. These include a sequential address, a microcode explicit address (call or goto), a return address, a main datapath computed address (case) or a macro instruction dispatch address. All branch decisions are conditional on the true or complement state of 32 test conditions and are delayed by one micro instruction that can be conditionally NOP'd. Microcode call and return is provided through the use of a six deep micro-address stack.

The Instruction Pipeline holds two fixed length, TNS macro-instructions. Together with microcode pipelining this implies that up to four macro-instructions can be executing concurrently. The pipeline timing will be described in the next section, but the structure includes the two instruction registers and a number of PLA's that decode the next instruction register.

Along with the interface to the μROM, another unique feature of the micro sequencer is it's use of two sequential addressing mechanisms. Unlike most minicomputers that use an entry point RAM to determine the starting microcode address for each macro-instruction, the CLX implements this dispatch with a hard coded PLA within the CPU chip. This presents a problem because it is undesirable to force a microcode branch to occur on the first microcode line of an instruction simply to get to the rest of the microcode for that instruction. Likewise, if the dispatch address is shifted left and padded with zeros this will reserve more than 1 microcode line per instruction, but would either still have the branch problem or would be wasteful of control store space because most instructions would not fit in the 2^n words reserved by this mechanism. The solution used on CLX is to have a second sequential increment equal to the number of entry points (512 in the CLX). The use of a second increment allows there to be any number of microcode lines reserved per entry point and for the total number of words reserved for dispatching to be any multiple of the 512. An instruction will execute one line in each block of 512 and continue to execute one line per block until it has reached the end of the "Skipping" region (which is 3k deep on CLX, i.e. six microcode lines per instruction). In addition to the freedom of the number of reserved microcode lines per instruction, the "Skipping" scheme allows more freedom of branching when the end of the "Skipping" region is reached. In the 2^n scheme, an instruction with more than 2^n lines of microcode must branch after the initial 2^n lines. In the "Skipping" scheme an instruction that has not branched after six increments of 512 will simply sequence into the location one after its seventh line. This location is normally reserved for seventh line of another instruction, but by separating critical entry points this line and subsequent lines of microcode can be arranged to be empty. The multi-mode incrementing requires only a small amount of logic since it amounts to a simple decode of the current microcode address and an assertion of one of two carries into the μPC incrementer.

CPU Chip Internal Timing

Internal to the CPU chip both microcode and macrocode execution are pipelined. The microcode pipeline is 3.5 stages. The pipelined execution of the main ALU and the micro sequencer are shown in Figure 4 (the a and b refer to individual clock phases of the non-overlapping clock):

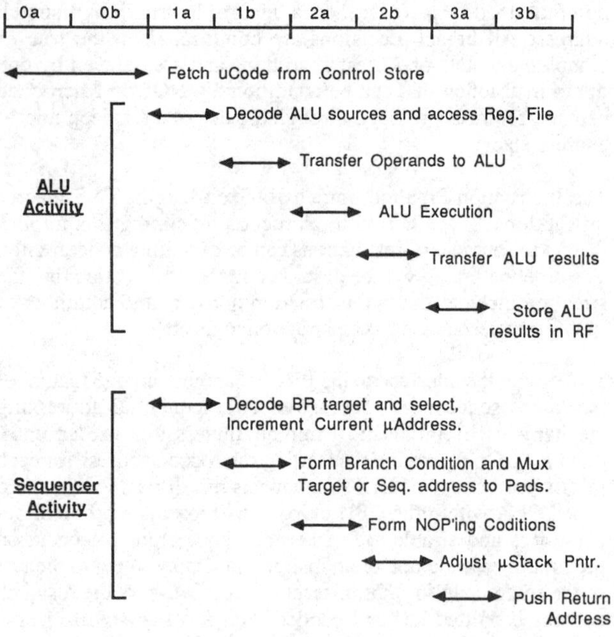

Figure 4. Microcode Pipeline

The macrocode pipeline is controlled by microcode and executes at a maximum rate of one macro instruction per two micro cycles. The general flow of macro instructions is illustrated in Figure 5.

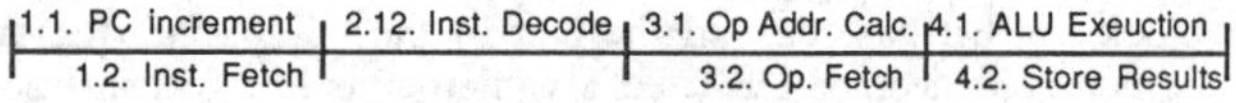

Figure 5. Macroinstruction Pipeline

This macro pipeline is not fully realizable, however, because there is not enough resources to perform the operand calculation and fetch of the instruction in parallel with the instruction address calculation and fetch for the instruction two downstream. One solution to this problem would be to increase the number of microcycles per macropipeline stage, but this would result in a penalty for simple instructions that do not use memory operands. Another solution would be to allow short instructions to omit the operand fetch, but this would require that the microcode for short instructions control the operand fetch part of the macropipeline. This, in turn, would require a deeper microcode pipeline with the undesirable increase in the penalty for pipeline breaks and interlocks. The final solution used in the CLX is to have the contents of the next macro instruction register modify the semantics of certain microcode operations. In particular, when the microcode sequence of the instruction preceding a short instruction specifies the operand calculation and fetch for the short instruction this operation is modified to actually do an instruction calculation and fetch of the instruction two downstream from the short instruction. Since these two operations are similar (both have an address calculation using the DALU and a memory fetch from cache) the only additional logic is a decode of the next instruction register to single out all short instructions.

The overall result is a fast pipelined micro engine which controls the macro pipeline, but whose operations can be altered by the contents of the macro pipeline. This configuration gives high speed execution of complex instructions without penalizing simple instructions. Some sample timing for simple instructions is given in Table 2.

Table 2. Simple Instruction Execution Times.

Register Stack Operations	2 microcycles
Memory to Stack	3 microcycles
Stack to Memory	5 microcycles
Branch Taken/Not Taken	3/3 microcycles

Data Integrity Features

As stated earlier, fail-fast operation of hardware modules is essential to NonStop execution to be effective in providing fault-tolerance at the system level. Fail-fast operation requires that faults are detected and that the processor is halted upon detection of an fault. The CLX CPU supports a very high degree of fault coverage using a variety of error checking strategies.

The CPU chip itself is covered by a duplicate and compare scheme. This scheme was chosen because it minimizes the amount of internal logic required for a high degree of coverage, and it maximizes the utilization of existing library elements in the silicon compiler CAD system. The implementation of the CPU's duplicate and compare logic is shown in Figure 6.

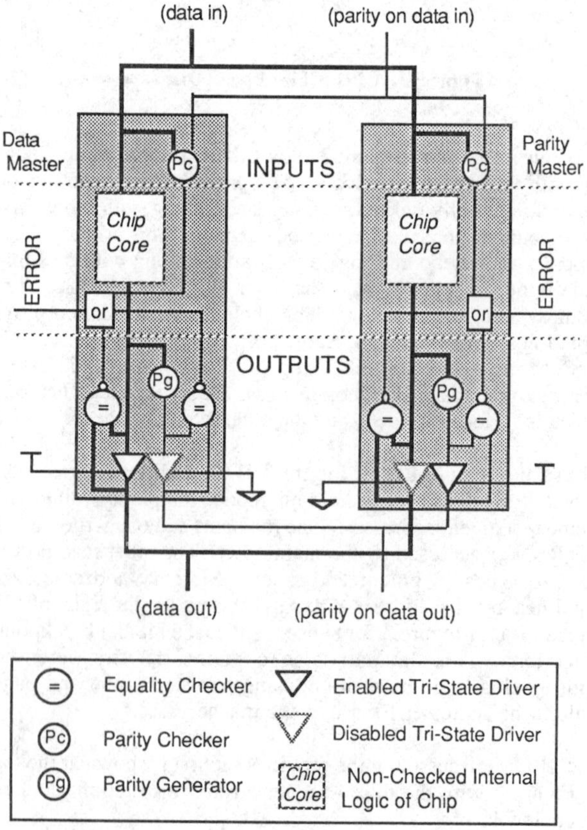

Figure 6. CPU Cross-Coupled Checking.

This scheme improves the fault coverage of other duplicate and compare schemes reported in the literature[10][11] by providing for a cross-coupling of data and parity outputs. One chip is designated the data master and drives all data outputs while the other is designated the parity master and drives all parity outputs. This insures that both chips' outputs and checking logic are active, and that latent errors in the checking logic can not lead to an undetected double failure. The parity out of the CPU also functions to cover the address and data lines connecting the CPU to other parts of the processor and the µRAM.

Within the memory system ECC with encoded address parity is used to provide checking of all memory system data paths. In addition, redundant state machines are used within the MC chip and in the external RAS/CAS generation logic. The state transitions of these machines are encoded into CRC registers whose outputs are compared. The resulting structure contains a high degree of fault coverage for both the data and control sections of main memory.

The IOC and IPB provide for parity protection of the data and control lines that they are interfaced to. In addition, they are protected by end-to-end checksums supported in software that guarantee the integrity of their respective buses, I/O controllers and devices.

Conclusion

The NonStop CLX is a prime example of the benefits of using high density ASIC technologies in the design of high performance minicomputers. The architecture of such machines must blend the structures used on previous board level minicomputers as well as the structures used in VLSI microprocessors in order to be effective. This includes the matching of the pin limits of VLSI to the wide buses utilized on minicomputers, and the use of a high degree of pipelining throughout the design. The machines resulting from this merger can provide low-cost through integration while maintaining or increasing the performance, data-integrity and fault-tolerance of previous machines.

Acknowledgement

The CLX system is the result of the hard work of over 35 hardware and software engineers together with an even greater number of support personnel. This work was greatly aided by the leadership and environment provided by Tandem management.

References

[1] Tandem Computers Inc., *Introduction to Tandem Computer Systems*, Tandem Part No. 82503, March 1985.

[2] Tandem Computers Inc., *Guardian Operating System Programmer's Guide*, Tandem Part No. 82357, March 1985.

[3] Anon et al., "A Measure of Transaction Processing Power," *Datamation*, April 1, 1985, pp. 112-118.

[4] R. Horst, T. Chou, "The Hardware Architecture and Linear Expansion of Tandem NonStop Systems", *Proceedings of the 12th International Symposium on Computer Architecture*, June 1985.

[5] J. Bartlett, J. Gray, R. Horst, "Fault Tolerance in Tandem Computer Systems", *The Evolution of Fault-Tolerant Computing, Vol 1*, ed. A. Avizienis et al., May 1987, pp. 55-76.

[6] Tandem Computers Inc., *System Description Manual*, Tandem Part No. 84017, October 1986.

[7] S. C. Johnson, "Silicon Compiler Lets System Makers Design Their Own VLSI Chips", *Electronic Design*, Oct. 4, 1984, pp. 168-181.

[8] R. M. Supnik, "MicroVAX 32, A 32 Bit Microprocessor", *IEEE Journal of Solid-State Circuits*, October 1984, pp. 675-681.

[9] H.H. Chao et al, "Micro/370: A 32-bit Single-Chip Microprocessor", *IEEE Journal of Solid-State Circuits*, October 1986, pp. 733-740.

[10] D. Johnson, "The Intel 432: A VLSI Architecture for Fault-Tolerant Computer Systems," *Computer*, August 1984, pp. 40-48.

[11] D. Ajmera et al, "Bipolar Building Blocks Deliver Supermini Speed to Microcoded Systems", *Electronic Design*, Nov. 15, 1987, pp 230-246.

[12] J. Bartlett, "A NonStop Kernal", *Proceedings of the Eighth Symposium on Operating System Principles*, Dec. 1981, pp. 22-29.

[13] R. Horst and S. Metz, "A New System Manages Hundreds of Transactions / Second", *Electronics*, April 19, 1984, pp. 147-151.

[14] Anon, "Tandem Makes a Good Thing Better", *Electronics*, April 14, 1986, pp. 34-38.

™ Tandem, NonStop, Guardian 90 and CLX are trademarks of Tandem Computers Inc.

BUILT-IN-SELF-TEST FOR THE TANDEM NONSTOP CLX PROCESSOR

David J. Garcia

Tandem Computers Inc.
19333 Vallco Parkway
Cupertino, CA 95014

Abstract

A built-in self-test (BIST) method is presented that uses pseudo-random test vectors and scan path design. The BIST method followed on the Tandem NonStop CLX™ processor is shown as an example. The pseudo-random test covers several custom ICs, commercial MSI logic, a static RAM array and their interconnects. Also, the BIST does a functional test of the dynamic RAM main memory and its control logic. Requirements for the BIST were that it be low cost and require minimal overhead to support the test function. Control of the test is handled by maintenance processor software, simplifying the hardware dedicated to BIST.

CLX Introduction

The Tandem NonStop CLX is a low-cost multiprocessor computer for online transaction processing. A CLX system can have from 2 to 6 single-board processors. The processor design is based on 4 custom CMOS chips, a 32K x 60 cache/control store static RAM array, and a 4 MB main memory array [1]. An optional expansion memory board of 2, 4, or 8 MB may be added to each processor.

Apart from the traditional Tandem design requirements of fault tolerance, data integrity and reliability, the CLX is required to be inexpensive and user serviceable. Furthermore, its use in an office environment requires such operations as diagnostics to be speedy and require no user intervention. A BIST function to test the CPU and memory met these requirements.

CLX Built In Self Test

The BIST on the NonStop CLX processor is based on scan, in which the majority of state elements within the processor are made of shiftable latches and registers. The BIST repetitively shifts pseudo-random patterns into the registers and latches, single steps the machine, and then shifts the results out, incorporating the results into a signature [2]. This is repeated until 2^{16} test vectors have been shifted in. The signature is then compared against that of a known good board, giving a pass/fail result. The system responds deterministically to the pseudo-random stimulus, responding with the same signature for good boards but a different signature for boards containing a detectable failure.

The test is completely self contained; it does not require control or data from other boards. The processor board and its external memory board are covered by BIST. The total test time is less than one minute. The test is run at power-on and on request by a maintenance process running in a separate CPU.

The BIST covers failures throughout the processor and memory boards, as well as within the core of the custom chips. The control logic for large RAM arrays is well tested, but the arrays themselves (cache static RAMs and main memory dynamic RAMs) are tested to a lesser extent.

The test does not cover the Tandem IO Bus interface, nor does it cover the Tandem Inter-Processor Bus interface. Testing these areas would involve different processors, and BIST is only intended to verify the one processor. Running in a single processor, BIST has no way to control and observe these external interfaces without affecting the shared bus.

The BIST test of memory changes the memory contents. Because of this the BIST can be done in two ways -- either cold BIST or warm BIST. The two techniques differ in the way they affect memory. In cold BIST the contents of the main memory are written to and tested. This type of test is suitable for use before a cold start of the processor when the contents of main memory are not important. In a warm BIST the contents of main memory are not disturbed. Of course this version of the test is not as thorough. A warm BIST is suitable for testing the processor after a power fail when battery backup preserved the contents of main memory, allowing a resumption of existing jobs. Unless specified, for the rest of this paper BIST refers to cold BIST.

While the scan-based design necessary for BIST is expensive, it allows for many other attractive features. The NonStop CLX uses the scan feature within development engineering, manufacturing, and in the field. For test and debug, scan gives excellent observability and controllability of registers and latches [3]. A stand-alone tester to screen custom chips uses a pseudo-random scan/step/collect signature method. Another tester does board-level repair using scan techniques. The board level tester does pseudo-random pattern testing, and when a failure is found, it masks off scan strings until the problem is isolated. Finally, scan is used in the field to determine the state of failing boards. This information allows diagnostic software to determine the cause of failure and prescribe an appropriate fix [4].

Scan Implementation

Most of the state elements on the CPU board are scannable. That is, they operate in one of three modes: normal, frozen, or scanning. When frozen, registers or latches hold their state. When scanning, the registers and latches are configured into a large shift register, allowing their entire contents to be shifted in and out.

Among the numerous scan methods [5] a single-clock multiplexed-data scheme was chosen. That is, a free-running clock is distributed to all registers, and the normal, frozen, or scan modes are determined by control lines (fig. 1).

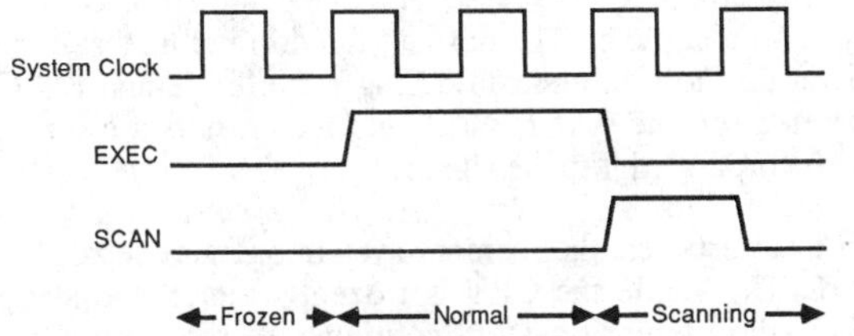

Figure 1, Scan Control Signals

This scan method allows state elements from different technologies and clocking regimes to coexist in one scan string and use the same control signals. The custom CMOS chips have shifting latches which use two-phase non-overlapping clocks [6], while the scannable MSI FAST parts and PALs use a single, edge-triggered clock. The same free-running system clock is distributed to all state elements (the two-phase clocks for the custom chips are generated internally).

Pattern Generator/Signature Register

The BIST uses strings of pseudo-random bits generated by a 16 bit linear feedback shift register (LFSR) [7] called the PPG (pseudo-random pattern generator). The BIST signature is collected by another 16 bit LFSR called the SR (signature register). The characteristic polynomial of the two LFSRs is $x^{16} + x^{12} + x^9 + x^7 + 1$. Figure 2 shows the PPG and SR designs.

The PPG and SR must be writeable for initialization and the SR must be readable to determine the results of the test. Both registers reside in a custom chip, occupying less than 5% of the chip's logic area. To minimize IO connections to the chip, the PPG and SR are connected to a scan string. When not doing BIST the registers may be examined and set using scan. During the BIST, the two registers are removed from the scan string and operate as LFSRs.

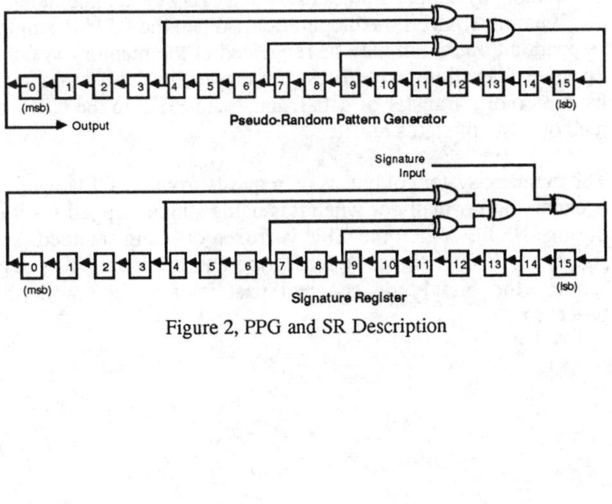

Figure 2, PPG and SR Description

MDP Software Control of BIST

The decision to include a BIST feature on CLX was made after the decision to include scan in the processor design. To achieve the CLX design requirement of low-cost, control of the BIST function had to added with minimum hardware overhead. The requirement was met by maximizing the use of MDP software to control the BIST function.

The main function of the MDP, the Maintenance and Diagnostic Processor, is to manage microcode loading, fault analysis, and scan functions. The MDP, based on the 6803 8-bit microprocessor, is central to the control of the BIST function. The MDP executes the proper sequence of steps for initialization and directs the scanning and stepping of the processor. During the BIST function, the MDP software is completely deterministic. There are no real-time interrupts or data-dependent steps allowed.

The MDP can control the scan strings to shift one bit at a time into or out of scannable registers. To transfer a bit between the MDP and a scan string (one of 13), the MDP writes a certain address, causing the corresponding scan string to shift in the high order bit of the microprocessor data bus. A read to the same address gives the current scan-data-out of the string on the low order data bus bit. This allows direct observability and controllability of all scannable registers. This mode of scanning could theoretically be used for BIST, i.e. one bit could be read from the PPG and then shifted into a scan string. This method would be slow, since at microprocessor speeds, several microseconds per bit would be needed.

The BIST on the CLX uses a faster way to load the scan strings with pseudo-random data (fig. 3). When in BIST mode, the decoders that assert the individual scan control signals operate differently. Normally, the SCAN<nn> control line is asserted for one system clock when the appropriate MDP address is written to. In BIST mode, a write to this address causes the SCAN<nn> signal to assert continuously, and all other SCAN signals to deassert. The input to the scan strings, SCAN_IN, is driven by the PPG output. With this method, the scan strings can be loaded at a rate of one bit per system clock.

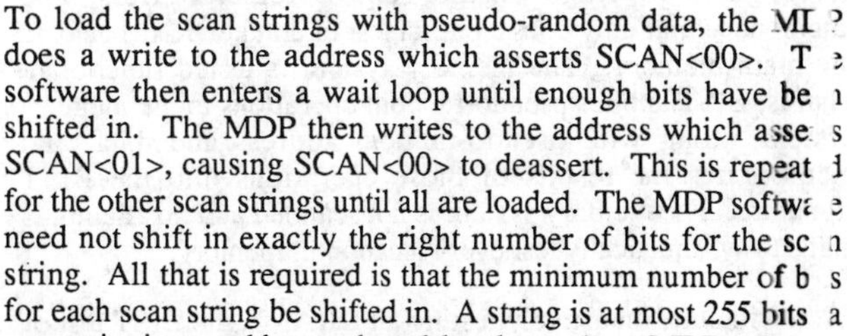

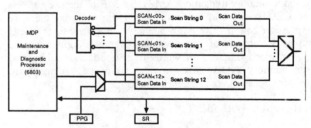

Figure 3, Block Diagram of BIST Structure

To load the scan strings with pseudo-random data, the MDP does a write to the address which asserts SCAN<00>. The software then enters a wait loop until enough bits have been shifted in. The MDP then writes to the address which asserts SCAN<01>, causing SCAN<00> to deassert. This is repeated for the other scan strings until all are loaded. The MDP software need not shift in exactly the right number of bits for the scan string. All that is required is that the minimum number of bits for each scan string be shifted in. A string is at most 255 bits (a constraint imposed by our board-level tester), so MDP software shifts a fixed number of bits into each string.

The BIST loads a test vector into all scannable registers/latches before single stepping the machine. The length of the test vector generated by the PPG is determined by the total number of bits shifted into the scan strings, not simply the number of bits in the scan string (since MDP software shifts in a number greater than 255). Since the pseudo-random pattern is generated by an LFSR, the test vector length determines the number of unique test vectors generated.

Initialization for BIST

For the BIST to return a stable signature, all data incorporated into the signature must be deterministic. This requires that all state bits affecting the signature be initialized. Scannable registers/latches are initialized through scan, non-scannable state elements through different processes.

Small RAM arrays and register files (non-scannable) are initialized by repeating the BIST, and only using the signature from the second pass. That is, the 2^{16} iterations of scanning in test vectors and single stepping the machine are repeated twice. The PPG and SR are reinitialized between the two passes. Since the RAMs are small, the first BIST pass will write all those locations that the second BIST pass will read.

A different method is required for large RAM arrays, as there is a distinct probability that BIST will read a location that it never writes to. For these RAMs, initialization is also done in a two pass approach. During the first pass, a control signal is asserted which forces all read operations to writes. Then, during the second pass, the control signal is deasserted, and the same pseudo-random test vectors are applied. Thus, all the locations that the BIST second pass reads contain initialized, pseudo-random data.

Further initialization issues are covered in the section on initializing a memory system.

Memory System Operation

The CLX memory system includes an instruction/data cache and page table cache in static RAM and between 4 and 12 megabytes of main memory dynamic RAM [1]. 4 MB of memory are on the CPU board and the rest are on the optional memory expansion board. The main memory interface to the CPU supports transfers of single words at random addresses, and higher speed transfers of words from contiguous addresses. The memory system also provides support for memory to memory block moves and data alignment.

Integration With BIST

The main memory system is functionally tested by BIST. BIST gives good coverage of the control logic, buffers, and interconnect but only does a partial test of actual DRAM cells in the main memory. The memory system is tested functional. That is, BIST applies pseudo-random operations to the memory system, along with pseudo-random address and data, and incorporates the results of those operations into the BIST signature. The memory system is not scanned and no attempt is made to systematically test every location in memory.

Even without exhaustively testing all DRAMs, the BIST test of main memory is quite adequate for our needs. First, it tests at least a few memory locations in each dynamic RAM along with all the memory support circuitry external to the DRAMs. Total failure of a dynamic RAM, such as a missing component or a floating pin, is detected. Failures undetected by BIST would be confined to a single DRAM and would be easily detected by a microcode diagnostic.

The BIST must test the memory system differently from the rest of the processor. The processor is tested by scanning in pseudo-random data, single stepping the machine, and scanning out the data. The memory system cannot be tested in this fashion because of the DRAMs. The dynamic RAMs' periodic refresh would be interrupted if pseudo-random data were to be scanned into the control logic. Also, DRAM operations take longer than one CPU system clock, e.g. a memory read takes 4 cycles to complete. The normal pseudo-random test expects all operations to complete in a single cycle. Thus, the CPU is operated for one system clock and then results are scanned out and incorporated into the signature.

For test purposes, the memory system operates separately from the CPU. While the CPU is frozen, scanned and stepped by BIST, the memory system continues to run normally, doing periodic refreshes of the dynamic RAMs. The BIST test of the memory system occurs when the CPU interacts with the memory system. During BIST the CPU pseudo-randomly does reads and writes of pseudo-random addresses with pseudo-random data. Results of these memory operations are loaded by the CPU and then incorporated into the BIST signature. In effect, the BIST does a functional test of the memory system.

This type of testing places several requirements on the memory system. Special memory system features to support BIST are listed below:

- The memory system must be able to accept single stepped operations from the CPU.
- The memory system interface to the CPU must ignore pseudo-random bits scanning past the interface.
- The memory system must respond deterministically to any command from the CPU presented in any sequence.
- The memory system must give a deterministic response to the CPU in the presence of events such as refresh.
- There must be a mechanism for initializing all state elements observable by BIST.
- The memory refresh must occur deterministically relative to the start of BIST.

During the BIST, the CPU is scanned and single-stepped while the memory system continues executing every cycle, maintaining the dynamic RAM refresh operation. When the CPU is single-stepped, an operation may be requested of the memory system. Possible operations are writes to memory, initiation of a read from memory, transfer of data from a read FIFO to the CPU, or read or write of status registers.

The memory system only acts on requests from the CPU when it is executing normally or when it is being single stepped (as it is during BIST). When the CPU is frozen or being scanned (see fig. 1) the EXEC signal is deasserted and the memory system ignores the bits being scanned past its interface with the processor.

When the BIST single steps the CPU, the memory system takes the pseudo-random bits at its interface with the CPU and executes the command. The command is executed in successive clocks. That is, the memory system is not single stepped like the CPU.

In the case of a read or write to a memory system status register the operation is completed in one cycle and the results are loaded by the CPU and are incorporated into the scan string.

In the case of a multi-word read , the operation is completed in 7 cycles (for a 4 word read) and the read data is buffered in a memory system FIFO. The data waits in the FIFO until a single stepped pseudo-random FIFO-to-CPU transfer operation occurs. Once transferred to the CPU, the data is incorporated into the scan string and hence influences the BIST signature. The read data cannot bypass the FIFO and go directly to the CPU because data is being read from the DRAM in a stream of back-to-back clocks. The CPU is unable to accept data on back-to-back clocks while it is being scanned for the next BIST iteration.

In normal operation, a CPU microinstruction advances down a multistage pipeline. For example, Figure 4 diagrams a line of microcode to do a memory write. The interface signals between the CPU and memory system are derived from both R1 and R2 pipeline stages.

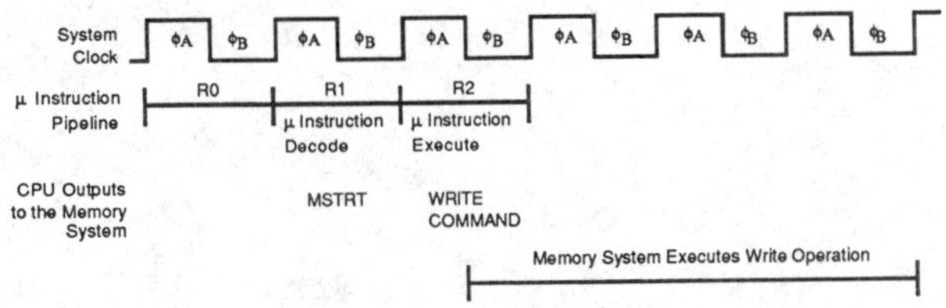

Figure 4, Microinstruction Pipeline for Memory Operation

In the case of memory reads and writes, the R1 signal MSTRT always precedes the R2 encoded signal to do a read or write. When a line of microcode is single-stepped, the pipeline advances one stage for each single step. There may be many cycles between R0 and R1 or between R1 and R2 where the processor is frozen. When a memory operation is single-stepped in R2 (i.e. EXEC is asserted by the falling edge of ϕ_A) the operation is said to be committed. The committed operation will complete in the next 4 system clocks, even if EXEC is freezing the processor.

During BIST, pseudo-random data is scanned into all pipeline stages of the processor (but not into the memory system pipeline stages). For example, in order for the memory system to do a read operation, the memory system expects to see an MSTRT in the R1 stage and in the following single-step see the appropriately encoded read command in R2. For this sequence to happen, pseudo random data has to, by chance, load the pipeline correctly on successive BIST iterations. If the BIST does not load the pipeline correctly, the memory operation will not complete. Instead of accessing the memory, there is some other deterministic response (such as not doing anything).

Deterministic Pseudo-Random Memory Operations

The memory system's response to any request during BIST must be deterministic. This is also true of invalid requests such as would occur if the previously described pipeline stages were set to an invalid state. Not only should the response of the memory system be deterministic, the control logic should remain in a state where it can service further memory requests and service the DRAM refresh. That is, it is not acceptable for a normally illegal sequence of requests to cause the memory control state machines to halt or go to undefined states. While this would most likely be deterministic, it would prevent the memory system from participating in any further functional tests.

The memory system must respond to any sequence of operations without producing nondeterministic results. For example, a series of read FIFO-to-CPU transfers could empty the FIFO. The data value transferred from the empty FIFO must be some deterministic constant, and not be dependent on a random power-on state for example.

Initialization of the Memory System

Unlike most of the processor, the memory system is not initialized by scan, as the memory system control logic must preserve the dynamic RAM refresh function. The refresh interval is initialized by synchronizing its count to the start of BIST. During a refresh, the memory system asserts a control signal to the CPU indicating that it is busy and cannot respond to any requests. Failure to synchronize BIST with refresh would result in nondeterministic results being sent back to the CPU and cause an unstable BIST signature.

The refresh counter and other control logic is synchronized by the MDP software asserting a signal at the start of the BIST. This ensures that refresh interactions will always be consistent across every run of the BIST. Note that the refresh interval may change during the course of BIST due to the CPU pseudo-randomly writing to the memory system's refresh interval register.

Test Coverage

The exact test coverage of the BIST on CLX is unknown as we were unable to run a complete fault simulation. The large number of test vectors with over 350 chips, including commercial and custom VLSI and large static and dynamic RAM arrays, are an obstacle to simulation.

The BIST does not cover the IO channel interface or interprocessor bus interface. Both of these connect to external sources which cannot be controlled or observed by the BIST. Of the remaining logic, very high fan in circuits, such as the comparators for the cross-coupled chips, are known not to be covered. The logic known not to be covered by BIST is 5-10% of all the logic on the board.

Even though the DRAMs are not exhaustively tested, the BIST coverage of the memory system is quite good for control logic, board wiring, and address/data paths.

In the first 160 processor boards built, there were no cases of failures (outside of the areas known not to be covered by BIST) that were undetectable by BIST. In some cases BIST indicated a board to be bad even though the board passed all other tests and seemed to function normally. In these cases it is assumed that BIST detected a failure in a path not sensitized by normal operation.

BIST Signature Management

After the BIST is completed, MDP software determines if the test passed or failed. The generated signature is compared against known good signatures kept in EEPROM. There is more than one valid signature possible. The signature is dependent on the type of BIST, either warm or cold, and the size of the external memory board installed.

A simple solution would be to require that the correct warm and cold BIST signatures be updated any time a processor or memory board is installed. This is undesirable for a system intended to be user serviceable, as it would add a manual step to the installation process.

Keeping a list of known good signatures only on the processor or memory board presents a version control problem. A new size or version of memory board unknown to the processor would cause a signature miscompare and erroneously indicate a failing board.

The solution is a list of signatures in non-volatile memory kept on both the processor and memory boards. On the processor board, a list is kept of all good signatures possible when that processor board is paired with any memory board. On the memory board, a list is kept of all good signatures possible when that memory board is paired with any processor board.

After completing the BIST, the maintenance processor scans the list on both the processor board and the memory board. Failure to find a match on either list indicates that the board does not pass the BIST. This approach allows engineering changes or new versions of either board to change the correct BIST signature without updating the signature list previously stored on the other board.

Conclusion

The BIST design presented here does a good test of the board without high hardware overhead. Keeping control of the test in maintenance processor software minimized hardware overhead. The test of the processor board covers much of the dynamic RAM memory system as well as the scannable logic.

References

[1] Lenoski, D.E., "A Highly Integrated, Fault Tolerant Minicomputer: The NonStop CLX", *Digest of Papers, Compcon Spring 1988*, San Francisco, CA 1988.

[2] McCluskey, E.J., *Logic Design Principles: With Emphasis on Testable Semicustom Circuits*, Prentice-Hall, Englewood Cliffs, NJ 1986.

[3] Staas, G., "TDL: A Hardware/Microcode Test Language Interpreter", *17th Annual Microprogramming Workshop*, New Orleans, LA 1984.

[4] Tandem Computers Inc., *Tandem Maintenance and Diagnostics Manual*", Tandem Part No. 82387, 1986.

[5] McCluskey, E.J., "A Survey of Design for Testability Scan Techniques", *VLSI Semicustom Design Guide*, Summer 1986.

[6] Mead, C.A. and Conway, L.A., *Introduction to VLSI Systems*, Addison-Wesley, Reading, MA 1980.

[7] Peterson, W.W. and Weldon E.J., *Error Correcting Codes*, MIT Press, Cambridge, MA 1972.

DESIGN METHODOLOGY FOR SYSTEM CORRECTNESS: LESSONS FROM THE TANDEM NONSTOP CLX

Peter L. Fu

Tandem Computers Incorporated
19333 Vallco Parkway
Cupertino, CA 95014

Abstract

This paper presents a methodology which allows a small design group to quickly produce a highly integrated processor. The methodology presented here is based on the design experience of the CPU for the Tandem NonStop CLX. The first section focuses on system design correctness, who shares the correctness responsibilities and some of the likely design errors. The second section gives an account of the design and verification process of the NonStop CLX CPU. The last section draws lessons from this process and introduces parallels between the techniques for implementing highly reliable or fault-tolerant system and the design methodology for system correctness.

Introduction

Most of today's system projects, though modest in size and scope, use aggressive circuit technology for performance and competitiveness. To be successful, these projects must seek an optimal investment in time, people and design tool resources. There is a need for system design environments which enable a small number of system designers to define, implement, verify and deliver such a product on time. Most of today's silicon compilation, standard cell and gate-array vendors are striving to provide such an environment.

The methodology presented here is based on the design experience of the Tandem NonStop CLX™ CPU [1]. It grew out of planning, on-the-job decisions and lessons learned in retrospect. Examples, taken from the design and verification process of the CLX CPU, are used for illustration. Although the processor was designed using silicon compilation, the methodology applies equally well to other forms of ASIC designs.

System Design Correctness

This section of the paper focuses first on the particulars of what design correctness encompasses. This is followed by a discussion on whom design correctness responsibilities fall, in the context of a layered technology partnership between vendors or groups within a company. Finally, a discussion on common design errors concludes this section.

Areas of Correctness

The designer should be aware of the following areas of correctness:

- **Feature correctness and completeness.** It is obvious that in a fully functional design, each feature must be implemented and perform as specified.
- Correctness should also be viewed in context. **External interface correctness** is as important as internal design correctness.
- **Cost, Performance and Flexibility.** A design is not correct if it costs too much to manufacture or does not meet performance or capacity requirements. Beyond mere meeting specifications to the letter, a good design should also consider some flexibilities in its implementation. Such flexibility might be needed later on in the project to make up for some lost performance in other areas.
- A design is not correct if it exceeds specified **physical constraints** such as size, weight and power consumption.
- A design is also not correct if the intended **testability coverage** is not implemented. This is important for manufacturability and system maintenance.
- **Data Integrity Coverage.** System designer must consider the appropriate amount of protection from component failures as a correctness issue, since error detection and recovery techniques are difficult to be retrofitted into systems.

Correctness Responsibilities

Any state-of-the-art system project requires expertise from multiple disciplines. From project management and efficiency points of view, it is desirable to partition project responsibilities according to these disciplines, where there can be well-defined interfaces and accountable shares of design correctness responsibilities. A multi-vendor partnership may involve a system manufacturer doing the system design, a tools vendor providing silicon compilation or other ASIC tools and a semiconductor foundry providing fabrication and testing services. An inter-group partnership may consist of a design group, a CAD group and the fab-line of the same company.

System designers must have a full understanding of the system requirements and the technology base. The full flexibility and limitations of the tools and technology capabilities must be taken into account in assessing design implementation

CH2539-5/88/0000/0525$01.00 © 1988 IEEE

and design process options. Appropriate aggressiveness and conservativeness need to be weighed against system correctness in the final product.

Technology/CAD tools suppliers must fully understand and be able to exploit the capabilities of the underlying circuit technology. The overall responsibility to the system designer is to present a level of abstraction, which facilitates the system design process. To maintain design correctness, all tools must be carefully verified. To *enhance* design correctness, all tools should be made extensible where appropriate, especially simulation tools. Tool development must stay ahead of intended usage. Size and other limits in the tools should be aggressively tested in advance of usage.

Semiconductor foundries or fab-line services form the third partner in creating correct systems. Besides maintaining correctness internally in their manufacturing process, they must ensure correctness in their interfaces with the CAD tools. Further responsibilities include correlating the performance of their process with the tools supplier so that the latter can calibrate their performance prediction tools for the system designers.

Common Design Errors

Given the capabilities of the current CAD tools and fab-line automation, many of the more obvious design errors such as inconsistent netlists, electrical and physical design rule violations are automatically screened out. Aside from errors within CAD tools or the fabrication process itself, imperfect designs tend to be due to errors such as:

- mis-communicated specifications
- interface/protocol mismatch
- incomplete or erroneous error/exception handling
- mishandling of boundary conditions for some operations or algorithms
- missing feature
- incorrect initialization or unresettable state
- no source on bus under certain conditions
- unintended and undesirable side effects of some functions
- missed testability coverage

Design Methodology for the CLX CPU

System design methodologies to ensure correctly designed products are evolving. Not long ago, the standard procedure was to first produce a careful paper design, reducing concepts to good practical implementations. Prototypes were then built, debugged, revised and debugged again. The advent of VLSI made this obsolete. With its inherent complexities and high cost of making revisions to a design, it is paramount that the confidence in design correctness be high before commitment to silicon.

The current approaches span a spectrum ranging from full system modeling and simulation [2][3], to hierarchically structured design validation and correct-by-construction techniques [4], to proof of hardware design correctness [5]. But for most projects with few designers, using highly leveraged tools to manage complexity, the former two approaches may be too costly, in terms of time and resources. On the other hand, the proof of design correctness tools are not yet available commercially. The methodology used at Tandem for the design of the NonStop CLX CPU is an example of utilizing available tools to the fullest, under the constraints of time, human and machine resources. This methodology is based on the GENESIL® design system from Silicon Compilers Systems Corporation. In addition, complementary tools for design verification, firmware development, lab debug and chip test support were developed by Tandem.

Conceptual Design

The design goal of the NonStop CLX was to build a fault-tolerant, high performance and low-cost minicomputer compatible with the existing line of Tandem NonStop computers. The investigation of the micro-architecture and the target technology was an interactive process, started in early 1985. Various ASIC alternatives were evaluated, with key sections of logic serving as test design vehicles. It was decided that silicon compilation based on GENESIL provided the best leverage for integration, performance and design efficiency from a rich set of high-level functional blocks. Much effort was applied to understand the capabilities and limitations of the tools before logic design was begun. The result was an architecture that matches well with the technology, thus enhancing the probability of a correct implementation.

Logic Design

A careful top-down paper design was made, resulting in a detailed block diagram of the functions of a chip-set, the major blocks within, and all the major buses. Since there were few designers — three for the most complex of the four chips — communication problems on design interfaces were minimal. Actual logic implementation and data entry proceeded bottom-up.

Micro-code Design

When the micro-architecture crystallized, the micro-word field definitions were documented. Key micro-instruction sequences were written to verify the capabilities of the micro-engine to support the functionality and performance of the macro-architecture. Firmware designers then customized a universal macro-assembler to generate CLX micro-code. In order to manage the inter-field dependencies, parameterized templates were used to ensure consistency. The multi-stage pipeline also involved many multi-line interactions, and a post-processing constraint checker was built to monitor possible conflicts between sequentially executed lines of micro-code. This was possible with the help of a network builder program, which finds all paths of execution the micro-code could take.

Special hardware features deserved special attention. The micro-ROM within the CPU chip cannot be changed once the design was committed to fab. Besides having a need to be correct (and complete), it needed to avoid hard-coded references to relocatable sections of code or data. Also, as an optimizing feature, the first lines of each macro-instruction were to reside in a skipping region (see [1]) and do not sequence like normal micro-instructions. Instead of fragmenting the code, source reorganization was chosen as a postprocessing step, relieving firmware designers from this complexity. Overall, automation was used wherever possible to enhance code correctness.

Integration

The integration of sub-blocks into chips happened rather rapidly, partly due to many of the high-level functional blocks available from the GENESIL. A tradeoff was made in the areas of control and decoding logic, which would take more time to optimize. Many of these design details such as logic partitioning and state assignment problems (for size and timing), are still best handled by human designers. Rather than waiting for time consuming optimizations, preliminary functional designs were made such that the whole system could be modeled to obtain global functionality, timing analysis and chip sizing feedback as soon as possible.

In retrospect, this was instrumental for functional simulation, but these early estimates for size and timing were too optimistic.

Two Levels of Modeling

There were two simulation efforts, one for hardware and the other for firmware development. The hardware simulation modeled as much of the processor as possible at the functional level with logic strengths and don't-cares. This included full functional models of all custom chips, full control store, address and data caches, full-sized main memory and interface logic, which were all done on the GENESIL functional simulator. Models for the chips were automatically generated when the designs were entered into the system. Off-chip TTL interface logic was also constructed within GENESIL, as if they were other chips.

This modeling effort was notably streamlined by the full programming language and underlying operating system interface support in the very extensible GENESIL simulator. For example, the full 16 MBytes address space of main memory with ECC and nibble-wide don't-cares was modeled without too much effort (see Appendix A).

The firmware simulation model was extracted from the hardware structure and was kept up-to-date as the design changed. The firmware simulator used behavioral models of hardware blocks, optimized for speed. Its primary purpose was for low-level diagnostic program development and verification. The firmware simulator ran on a Tandem system and was more than 100 times faster than the GENESIL simulator. Given that the firmware model tracked that of the hardware, a translation tool was built such that the extraction and updating could be automated and errors minimized. This was possible because the GENESIL design information was accessible and presented in a well-defined and parsable table format. This eliminated the problem of the two groups verifying their design to an inconsistent model.

Verification

Extensive simulation is key to design verification. Limited **interactive simulation** of individual functional areas was done to flush out local design errors. **Exhaustive testing** was used for some critical areas. For example, all 64K possible macro-instructions were simulated to check the address formation logic against a behavioral model. The most thorough verification were achieved when the whole or at least a major part of the system was simulated using the hardware model. The logic was then simulated in context, revealing a number of interface problems. **Micro-coded diagnostics** were written to test the low-level functionality of specific portions of the chips. These tests were first checked out using the firmware simulator. Since these were self-contained micro-programs, they were loaded directly into the full control store model, and were executed by the simulated processor.

Once instruction-set micro-code was loaded into the simulated control store, macro-code could be directly simulated. Simple programs or segments of compiled object code were used as **macro-instruction based tests**. The program and data segments were loaded into either the cache or main memory models. At this point, the ability to generate meaningful tests that simultaneously stressed many area of the design was greatly improved. For example, the many cache operations and memory interactions, such as cache fill, write-through, address translation and cache conflicts, were exercised. Throughout each stage of the verification process, and especially when many memory elements were involved, the use of **the don't-care or indeterminate state** proved to be extremely helpful. Many errors, from reset or initialization problems, to unintentional operations, to subtle non-deterministic behavior showed up as indeterminate outputs. Still more design errors were caught early because they accessed uninitialized locations in control store, cache or memory.

Design Commitment

Aside from functional verification, other aspects of design correctness needed attention before committing chips to silicon. Much time was spent on optimizing the speed performance of the CPU chip. GENESIL provided a static timing analyzer, as opposed to timing simulation. Indeed, worst-case timing under all logic conditions, not just the timing under normal operations, was required due to pseudo-random testing.

The NonStop CLX includes many fault-detection mechanisms such as parity, ECC, cross-coupled checking, and testability mechanisms such as non-destructive freeze and scan, single-stepping, built-in pseudo-random self-test support [6]. All of these were tested before design commitment. Freeze and scan were especially critical for hardware debugging (see below). Hence, in addition to free-running mode, most tests were executed in freeze-step mode and some were executed in freeze-scan-step mode. Routines written in the GENESIL simulation environment simulated this debugging environment.

The length of the regression test suite totaled over 250,000 clocks. Before the design commitment of the second revision of the CPU chip, this regression test was done in one and a half weeks.

Hardware Debugging

The CLX CPU contains a maintenance microprocessor which can interrogate and set all register and memory elements through the freeze, scan and single-step mechanisms. When all the components were realized in hardware, the exact same tests created earlier were loaded and used for initial system bring-up.

Without exception, all tests ran exactly as simulated. All four chips were functional on first pass, but there were indeed minor design errors that escaped simulation, forcing small changes in micro-code. Only the CPU chip was revised, primarily for speed improvements.

Production Tests

The system simulation model was leveraged to generate test vectors for production chip tests. Micro-coded diagnostics and segments of macro-instruction tests were executed on the simulator and signals at the chip boundaries were captured to use as test vectors. Even hand-generated and specialized scan-related test vectors were simulated and recaptured, giving them full chip pin coverage on every vector.

Finally, the GENESIL simulator's list-processing capability (a la LISP) even allowed partial fault-coverage analysis. A toggle analysis of most simulator visible nodes ran only a few times slower than normal (see Appendix B). After the chips were released, idle time on the GENESIL CAD system was used to run stuck-at-fault simulation on the same nodes. It took a few months, but the results provided the first basis for improving fault coverage of the test vectors (see Appendix C).

A "Fault-Tolerant" Design Methodology

It is every designer's ideal to achieve perfection, to do it right the first time and on time. But given the time pressure of the commercial competitive environment, it is practically impossible to be 100% thorough in the design verification process. The task of building "perfect" systems is likened to the reliability of computer systems. Each single Tandem processor is designed to be no less failure-prone than other vendors' processors, being built with similar components. But because of two key features of Tandem NonStop systems — data integrity and fault-tolerance — the probability of a Tandem NonStop system being unavailable or delivering an erroneous result is substantially reduced. Likewise, providing some degree of "fault-tolerance" in the design process points to solutions to deal with real-life design for correctness problems, just as a fault-tolerant computer deals with real life component failures.

It is perhaps wiser to address the system design correctness problem in terms of a cost measure of design errors in each feature. A priority for verification can be established based on this cost. This error cost is often not binary — complete success versus catastrophic failure. In many cases, especially for computer systems, there are alternate means or workarounds to do a certain function, possibly causing some performance or cost penalty, but without requiring the complete removal of the error.

Following are known techniques used in building highly reliable systems, and their parallels applied to a "fault-tolerant" design for correctness methodology. [7][8]

Graceful Degradation

The ability to isolate a failure, while operating the system at reduced performance, is called graceful degradation.

In the context of design correctness, wherever possible and especially for complex areas of the design, some fall-back strategy could make the difference between a non-functional system or a reduced performance system. Examples include patchable ROMs or optimized sequences that could be run non-optimized. In the NonStop CLX, most of the micro-code lines in ROM within the CPU chip can be run in the external control store, with reduced performance.

Design for Testability

Just as a physical system that is highly testable enhances manufacturing efficiency, if a designer considers how the unfinished design is to be verified, overall design time is reduced. There is often some flexibility in partitioning and structuring a design. Choosing the more intuitive alternatives could help the design debug effort, thus enhancing correctness.

High Fault Coverage Self-Tests

Periodic self-tests improve system reliability and availability, by spotting failures before they actually cause the system to shut down or run at reduced performance or reduced fault-tolerance. Similarly, in system design verification, it helps to have a set of high fault coverage regression tests, such that as the design moves closer to full implementation, the validity of earlier designed modules can be assured. In general, the sooner lower level models can be integrated into a more complete model, the sooner more leveraged tests can be written for the subsystem, in terms of fault coverage and future conversion into production system tests. For this reason, integration happened early in the design cycle of the CLX CPU.

Modularity

Modularity encourages localization of complexity, simplification of inter-module interfaces and reduction of error detection latency. The same applies to the design process.

Fault Avoidance

Fault avoidance seeks to increase system reliability by reducing the possibility of failures. If a particular fault can cause a total system failure, it deserves critical analysis. In the design for correctness realm, selective exhaustive testing should be applied in critical areas intolerant of design errors. In the CLX, macro-instructions are dispatched to starting micro-addresses with a hard-coded PLA in the CPU chip. A serious performance penalty would be incurred if certain high frequency instructions were involved in any incorrect mapping. Consequently, this PLA was exhaustively tested with all possible opcodes.

Fault Masking

Fault masking as used constructively in a fault-tolerant system is employed to prevent erroneous outputs. Conversely, fault masking is to be avoided in system verification. Care must be taken not to certify correctness of a design prematurely just because a program or diagnostic has run successfully. Consider a fault which causes a whole section of the test to be skipped. The test may not be designed with such a fault in mind, and indicates no errors found at the end. At least for the first time such a test is run, the entire execution should be followed in detail. In many cases, it is true that such tests have coverage of faults beyond its intended fault set. Careful tracing may reveal such design flaws in logic unrelated to a particular test.

Another potentially more serious type of fault masking is unintended side-effects. If possible, as much state information in the system as practical should be checked after each diagnostic test.

Fault Secureness

Fault secure techniques used in reliable systems ensure that the outputs are correct unless an error is indicated. Error-detecting and correcting codes are typically used to implement a fault-secure system. In the context of design verification, system tests and diagnostics are most often included in a regression test suite for future retesting as the design progresses. When these are rerun, there will not be an opportunity to trace the execution in detail again, as suggested above. It would be highly desirable to strengthen these tests with error detection or watchdog mechanisms separate from the actual tests. One effective yet simple mechanism is to associate with each test a measure of reasonableness. For example, the number of simulated clock cycles as well as the final system state for each test can be captured. These can then be compared against the carefully monitored first run.

Self-checking Design

A self-checking circuit produces an error indication when there is an internal fault or inconsistency. In data or transaction processing, data integrity is just as important as availability. Many systems today try to provide both features, particularly in memory systems or communication subsystems where parity, error-detecting and correcting codes are used. Including these built-in fault detection mechanism in the modeling during system verification will improve design error sensitivity. For example, enabling the checksum mechanism in a receiver may reveal errors in a data packet early, before further error propagation, saving the time necessary to backtrack. In the CLX lab debug phase, the totally self-checked duplicate and compare cross-coupled checking scheme was very sensitive to uninitialized state in the CPU chips. Some otherwise difficult to trace operating system support micro-code problems were uncovered early.

Conclusions

As computer-aided design technology progresses, a greater portion of the task of mapping design concepts to appropriate implementations is being automated. The focus of design correctness issues are moving away from the mechanical aspects of the design process into more global and complex aspects. This paper presented the strategy taken by the Tandem NonStop CLX design team to manage these issues, resulting in the successful introduction of the system. Further analysis of this process revealed many parallels with the techniques used in fault-tolerant computing. It is hoped that lessons learned here will result in further improvements of future design methodologies for system design correctness.

References

[1] Lenoski, D. E., "A Highly Integrated, Fault-Tolerant Minicomputer: The NonStop CLX," *Digest of Papers, Compcon Spring 1988.*

[2] Bak, D. T. and C. Wiecek, "VAX 8800 Design Tools and Methodology," *Digest of Papers, Compcon Spring 1987*, pp. 329-332.

[3] Ohno, Y., et al., "Principles of Design Automation System for Very Large Scale Computer Design," *The 23rd Design Automation Conference Proceedings*, 1986, pp. 354-359.

[4] Ryan, R. J., "The CLIPPER™ CAD System Integrated Hierarchical VLSI Design," *Digest of Papers, Compcon Spring 1986*, pp. 186-190.

[5] Barrow, H. G., "Proving the Correctness of Digital Hardware Design," *VLSI Design*, July 1984, pp. 64-77.

[6] Garcia, D. J., "Built-In-Self-Test for the Tandem NonStop CLX Processor," *Digest of Papers, Compcon Spring 1988.*

[7] McCluskey, E. J., "Hardware Fault Tolerance", *Digest of Papers, Compcon Spring 1985*, pp. 260-263.

[8] Siewiorek, D. P., et al., *The Theory and Practice of Reliable System Design*, 1982.

Appendices

The following GENIE™ code segments were developed at Tandem and used for design verification of the CLX. GENIE is the programatic interface of the GENESIL functional simulator for advanced simulation. It has C-like statements and LISP-like prefix operators or commands and list-processing support. Binary numeric values have 3 states: 0, 1 and indeterminate.

Appendix A

```
/*
** Functions to Model Arbitrary Sized RAM
** Written by: Peter Fu, Charles Spirakis.
**             Tandem Computers, Inc.
**
** These functions use a UNIX™ file to model
** a 22 bit wide RAM, each RAM location takes up
** exactly 10 bytes, as modeled by the C string:
** " 0xhhhhhh\n", where h is a hex digit or 'X'
** for a nibble-wide indeterminate value.
** The file seek function allows random access.
** In most UNIX systems, locations that have not
** yet been written to are "holes" in the file
** and do not occupy unnecessary disk space.
** If read, these unwritten locations return
** ASCII NULs.  Remember to remove apparently
** huge files when done!
**
** Ram_Init: initialize the details of the RAM
*/
func Ram_Init {
   set ram_width 22
   set ram_hexwidth 6
   set ram_offset 10

   /* Now open RAM file for reading and writing. */
   open ram_file "RAM_model" r+
```

```
   /* Define a 22-bit indeterminate value to */
   /*    present on errors.                    */
   set ram_indeterminates 0biiiiiiiiiiiiiiiiiiiii
   set ram_status 1      /* 1 == status ok */
   return @ram_status
}
/*
** Ram_Write: writes to the ram file. Accepts an
**    address and a value, and deposits the value
**    in the location defined by the address.
**    If the address has any indeterminate bits,
**    no write is performed, and RAM status is set
**    to corrupted.
*/
func Ram_Write { args addr value
   /* make sure the address does not contain */
   /*     any indeterminate bits             */
   /* an XOR between 2 indeterminate bits    */
   /*     does not result in a 0             */
   if (== 0 (bitxor @addr @addr)) {
      seek ram_file (* @ram_offset @addr)
      writeto @ram_file " 0x%s\n" (hex @value
@ram_hexwidth)
   } /* else */ {
      println "diskram zapped!!"
      set ram_status 0
      return @ram_indeterminates
   }
   return @value
}
/*
** Ram_Read: reads from the RAM file. Accepts an
**    address.  If it has no indeterminate bits,
**    and the status of the RAM is good,
**    and there is a value for that address, that
**    value is returned.  Otherwise, indeterminates
**    are returned.
*/
func Ram_Read { args addr
vars tstchr retval
  if (== 1 @ram_status) /* see if corrupted */ {

   /* if all address bits are determinate */
   if (== 0 (bitxor @addr @addr)) {

      seek ram_file (* @ram_offset @addr)

      /* Look for an ASCII space to indicate if */
      /*    there is real data here             */
      if (== 1 (readfrom @ram_file "%c" tstchr)) {

         if (== (ord " ") (ord @tstchr)) {
            /* Yes, there is data */
            if (== 1 (readfrom @ram_file "%x" \
                        retval)) {
               return @retval
            }
         }
      }
   }
  }
  return @ram_indeterminate
}
```

Appendix B

```
/*
** Simplified version of Activity Simulation
** Written by: Peter Fu, Tandem Computers, Inc.
**
** This core routine samples the nets in the
** node_list and updates in actv_list the
** corresponding list of triplets for each net.
** Each net has as many triplets as its bit width.
** Called once each clock, Actv_Update will
** increment one of three counters, depending on
** the value of the bit being 0, 1 or indeterminate
** The following is an associative list, mapping
** each logic strength to the three values.
*/
set actv_ref '( ("0" 0) ("1" 1) ("i" 2) ("p" 2) \
                ("L" 0) ("H" 1) ("I" 2) \
                ("l" 0) ("h" 1) ("x" 2) ("z" 2) )

func Actv_Update {
vars n nw bn bv lp la bc nc
   setptr la actv_list 0
   foreach n @node_list {
      picknet @n
      set nw (netwidth)
      set nv (bin (shownetvalue) @nw)
      for bn 0 (- @nw 1){
         set bv (getref @actv_ref (substr @nv @bn 1))
         setptr lp la 0 @bn @bv
         set nc (+ 1 (first @lp))
         deleteat lp
         insertat lp @nc
      }
      ++ la
   }
   return
}
```

Appendix C

```
/*
** Poor Man's Fault Simulation (simplified)
** Written by:  Peter Fu, Tandem Computers, Inc.
*/
func FaultSim {
   /* Process ALL simulator visible nets */
   foreach n net {
      if (StuckVec @n "L") { /* found errors */
         println "Net" @n "stuck-at-0 covered."
      } /* else */ {
         println "Net" @n "stuck-at-0 NOT covered!"
      }
      if (StuckVec @n "H") { /* found errors */
         println "Net" @n "stuck-at-1 covered."
      } /* else */ {
         println "Net" @n "stuck-at-1 NOT covered!"
      }
   }
func StuckVec { args  node val
   /* Force a particular net hi or lo, then run   */
   /* the available tests. If there is no error   */
   /* the net is not covered for stuck at faults */
   bindnet @net @val
   /* Insert code here to run test vectors */
   /*    until error or done               */
   return (geterrcnt)    /* return # of errors */
}
```

™ Tandem, NonStop and CLX are trademarks of Tandem Computers Incorporated. UNIX is a trademark of AT&T Bell Laboratories. GENIE is a trademark of Silicon Compiler Systems Corporation.

® GENESIL is a registered trademark of Silicon Compiler Systems Corporation.

Computer-Aided Perception: Enhancement for Tele-Operation

Chair: S. Ellis

Enhancement of Man-machine Communication: the Human Use of Inhuman Beings:

Stephen R. Ellis, Arthur Grunwald[*]*, Stephen Smith, and Mitchell Tyler*[**]

NASA Ames Research Center
Moffett Field, CA 94035

Abstract

A conference session on enhancement of man-machine communication is introduced by reviewing some aspects of the social impact of computer technology. Worries that computers will be a dehumanizing influence on everyday life may be partially alleviated by better design of the human interface to the technology. Examples of human perceptual and motor limitation are cited to show how specific understanding of these limitations can determine ways that computers can be used to enhance man-machine communication.

Introduction

In 1950 Norbert Wiener, the father of the modern theory of cybernetics, wrote the first edition of a short book titled *The Human Use of Human Beings* (1). In this book he explored the social and moral consequences of the intellectual revolution arising from the widespread application of automatic control technology, most of which was computer based. At this time, the computer was seen mainly as an arcane tool of big government or big business; many nontechnical people were seriously worried, in the words of the book's jacket, about the "formidable and potentially dangerous power" of these vaguely "manlike machines." In short, the machines were seen as potential tools of the ultimate social control of an overt or covert totalitarian state.

Times have changed. The widespread use of microcomputers in scientific and engineering laboratories as well as in newsrooms, stock brokers offices, airline counters and in many other nontechnical settings, especially in video game arcades, has resulted in a generally far less fearful popular approach to computer technology. The technology is seen now not as a implement of governmental control but as a tool that can provide a kind of personal intellectual amplifier, not a master but a servant.

New computer architectures based on homeomorphic models of neural nets, such as described by Task and Hopfield (2), promise quantum leaps in computing capabilities which will allow mass access to computationally intensive processing such as automatic image recognition. Such access will be the basis for currently unimagined applications for currently unanticipated mass markets.

But no matter how powerful the computer or sophisticated the application, the final constraint on the availability of the machine's power to a user is the user interface. The user quite literally *sees* the intellectual amplification afforded by the machine through the interface. It is the interface that constrains the human use of inhuman beings.

The papers presented in this session will focus on questions related to the design of this interface, questions that must be answered so that the promised intellectual amplification is achieved.

Design questions of the type to be discussed are not new and have had to be answered for the intellectual tools of the past. Paper, pens, books, movable type, erasers, megaphones, microphones, tape recorders, telescopes, and televisions all are technologies that amplify human abilities, albeit sometimes in simple ways. Nevertheless, the human interface to these mechanical, electrical, or optical, technologies had to be effectively designed. Since these older technological enhancements were generally focused on the physical aspects of speech, hearing, writing, or drawing, the parameters of their designs were primarily physical. In many cases, the design was simply a generalized kind of *impedance matching*. For example, the size of a pencil would be adjusted so it could fit comfortably in a average person's hand.

Though they do still have important physical and physiological implications, the newer technological

[*] Department of Aeronautical Engineering, TECHNION, Haifa, ISRAEL
[**] Department of Physical Education, University of Wisconsin, Madison, WI.

enhancements are more of an intellectual type. The development of appropriate intellectual enhancements for computer based systems dealing with pictorial information can provide a case study of how these enhancements may be selected.

Spatial Displays and Spatial Instruments

In order to understand how the spatial information presented in pictures may be communicated, it is helpful to distinguish between images which may be described as *spatial displays* and those that were designed to be *spatial instruments*. One may think of a *spatial display* as any dynamic, synthetic, systematic mapping of one space onto another. A picture or a photograph is a spatial display at an instant of time. A silhouette cast by the sun is not, because it is a natural phenomena and not synthesized by man.

A *spatial instrument*, in contrast, is a *spatial display* that has been enhanced either by geometric, symbolic, or computational techniques to insure that the communicative intent of instrument is realized. A simple example of a *spatial instrument* is an analogue clock. In a clock the angular positions of the arms are made proportional to time, and the viewer's angle estimation task is assisted by radial tic marks designating the hours and minutes.

A second aspect of the definition of a *spatial instrument*, which the clock example also illustrates, is that the communicated variable, time, is made proportional to a spatial property of the display, such as an angle, area, or length and is not simply encoded as a character string.

The *spatial instruments* that we wish to focus attention on are generally interactive. That is to say that the communicated information flows both to and fro between the viewer and the instrument. Some of this bidirectional flow exists for practically all *spatial instruments* since movement of the viewer can have a major impact on the appearance of the display. However, the displays in which we wish to focus attention are those incorporating at least one controlled element, such as a cursor, which is used to extract information from and input information to the instrument.

Maps when combined with mechanical aids for their use certainly meet the definition of a spatial instrument. The map projection may be chosen depending upon the spatial property of importance. For example, straight line mapping of compass courses could be preserved as in Mercator projections or area could be conserved as in Lambert-type, equal-area projections. The projection choice illustrates a geometric enhancement of the map. The overlaying of latitude and longitude illustrate symbolic enhancement.

Specific Examples of Enhancements.

The following two descriptions provide concrete examples of how the computational power of a computer can be used to improve the human interface to a tool.

The first shows evidence of natural perceptual biases in open-loop direction judgements made with 3-dimensional maps such as might be used to provide air traffic information to commercial aircraft pilots (3). Compensation for these biases can be achieved by predistorting the projection with an inverse based on the measured bias.

The subjects task in this example is to judge the azimuth of a target presented on a 3D map with respect to a reference position and a reference straight-ahead direction. The subject made this judgement by adjusting the position of a dial next to the image as shown in Figure 1.

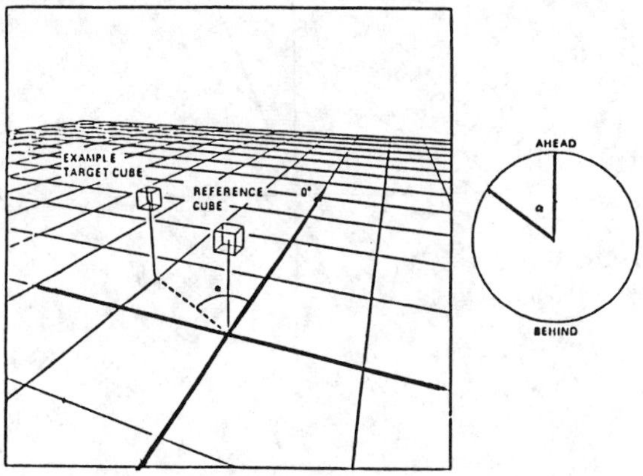

Figure 1. Sketch illustrating the direction judgement task from a right viewing station with viewing rotation of 22 degrees azimuth and -22 of elevation. The subject adjusted the dial at the right to match the depicted azimuth of the target.

We examined the angular errors subjects make when making these judgements in a variety of viewing situation ranging from actual scenes to computer-generated images with varying amount of geometric detail on the ground reference symbols. In general, we find a tendency for our subjects to make errors towards the axis crossing the reference direction when judgements are made with the computer generated pictures (4,5,6,7). These errors occur even when the subjects viewpoint is adjusted to be at the geometric center of projection. The pattern of the error allows the computation of an inverse distortion. Wide angle distortion approximates the kind of correction that is necessary.

The second example shows how the computations necessary to maintain alignment between display and control axes in closed-loop 3 dimensional tracking task can improve tracking performance. In this task the sub-

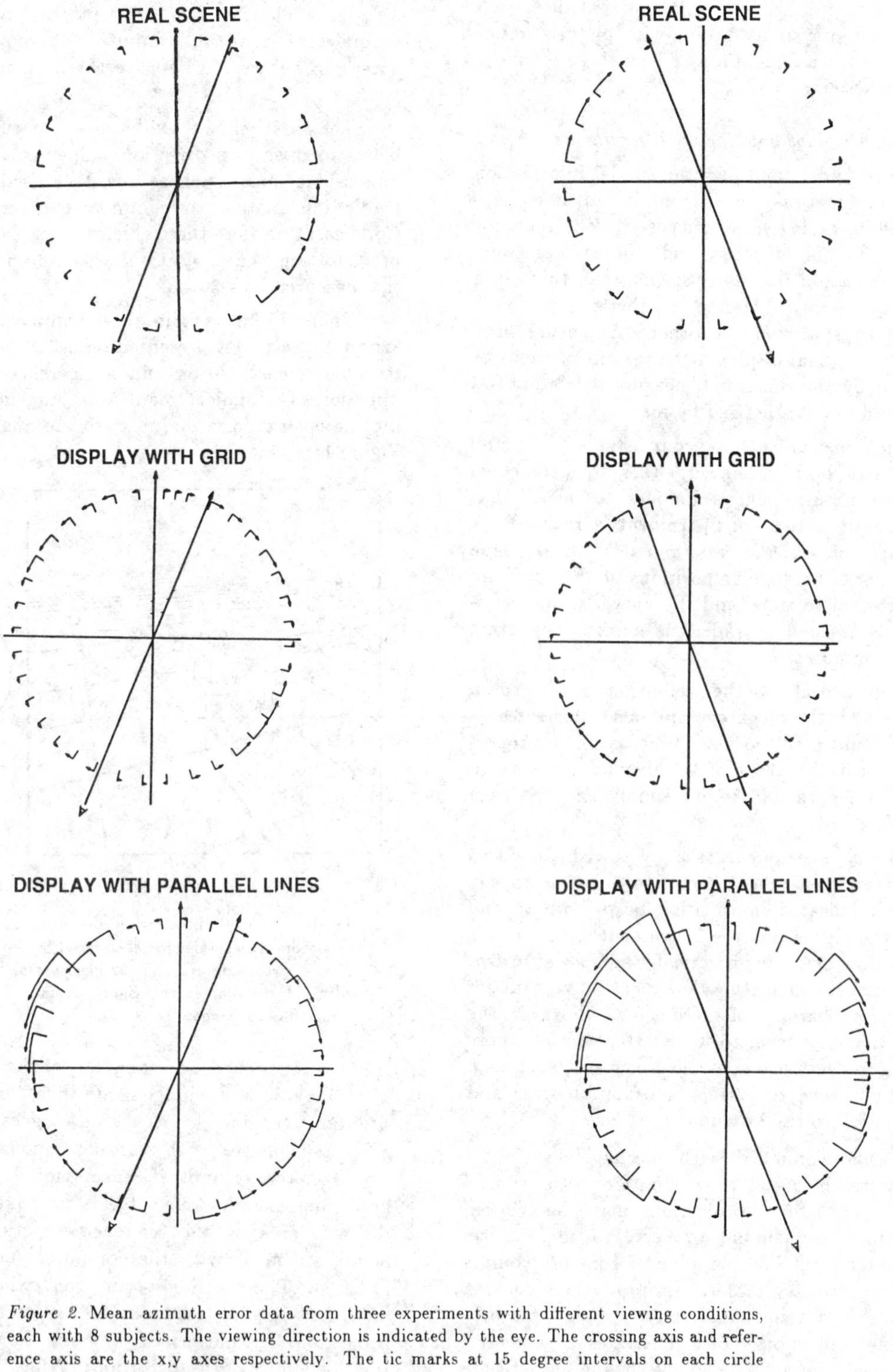

Figure 2. Mean azimuth error data from three experiments with different viewing conditions, each with 8 subjects. The viewing direction is indicated by the eye. The crossing axis and reference axis are the x,y axes respectively. The tic marks at 15 degree intervals on each circle represent the depicted positions of the targets for each experiment. The arrows at each tic show the direction and amount of mean estimation error for each target. All results were statistically significant beyond the 0.01 level.

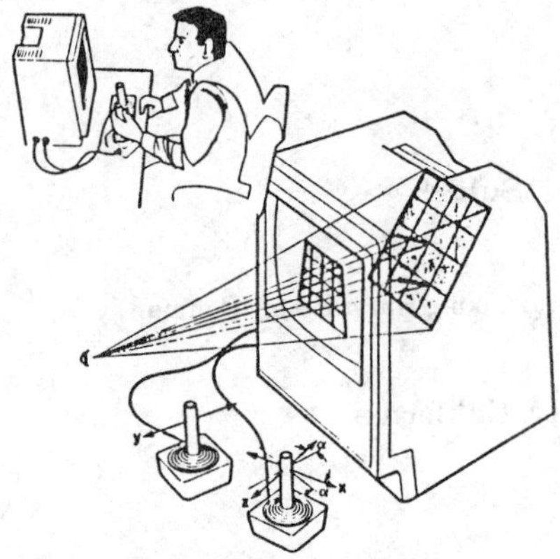

Figure 3. Illustration of the viewing conditions of the 3 dimensional tracking task. The control axes of the right joystick could be rotated into or out of alignment with the display axes of the controlled element.

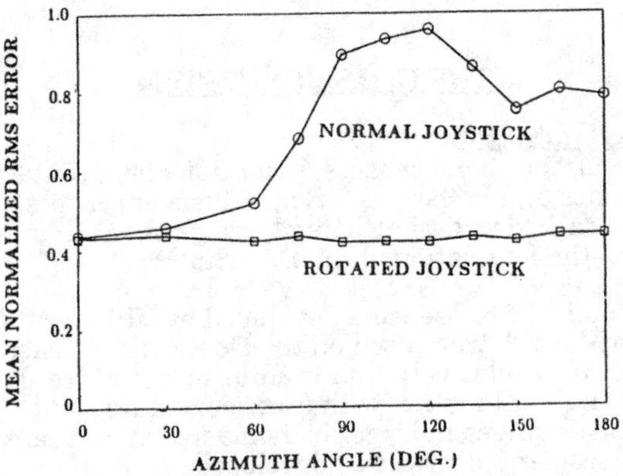

Figure 5. Mean slant-range RMS tracking error from 6 subjects who were in a repeated measures experiment in which they used each of the 11 azimuth rotation conditions with and without rotation of their control axes. Presentation order was separately randomized for each subject. The statistical interaction ploted here was highly significant ($F=6.54$ $df=10,40$ $p < .0009$).

ject is required to use two 2-axis joysticks to superimpose the position of a 3D cursor on a target that moves irregularly in 3 dimensions (8,9,10,11). The experimental variable was the alignment between the lateral and longitudinal control axes with the axes of the display. As may happen in a telerobotic control task, the misalignment of these axes can degrade control performance. As shown by Figure 5, rotation of the control axes into alignment with the display axes totally eliminates the additional tracking error due to misalignment. Interestingly, however, human trackers seem to be able to tolerate about +/- 50 degrees of misalignment before their tracking performance seriously deteriorates.

These two above examples show how understanding the biases and limits of human perceptual and motor capacities can be used to direct computation resources to improve man-machine communication.

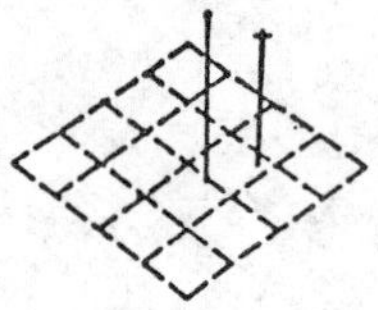

Figure 4. Sample display from the 3 dimensional tracking task illustrating a view of the target, the dot on the end of the reference line, and the cursor, the cross at the end of the other reference line. Viewing azimuth and elevation are here both 45 degrees. Elevation was kept constant while azimuth was changed during the experiment.

References

(1) Wiener, Norbert (1954) *The human use of human beings* Anchor Books, New York.

(2) Task, David W. and Hopfield, John J. (December, 1987) Collective computation in neuronlike circuits. *Scientific American, 257,* 104-114.

(3) Ellis, Stephen, McGreevy, Michael W., Hitchcock, Robert (1987) Perspective traffic display format and airline pilot traffic avoidance. *Human Factors, 29,* 371-382.

(4) McGreevy, Michael W. and Ellis, Stephen R. (1986) The effect of perspective geometry on judged direction in spatial information instruments. *Human Factors, 28,* 439-456.

(5) Grunwald, Arthur, & Ellis, Stephen R. & Smith, Stephen. (1988) Spatial orientation in pictorial displays. *IEEE Trans. on Systems Man and Cybernetics*, (accepted for publication).

(6) Grunwald, Arthur, Ellis, Stephen R. & Smith, Stephen (1986) Spatial orientation in pictorial displays. *Proceedings of the 22nd Annual Conference on Manual Control,* July, 1986, Wright Patterson AFB, Ohio.

(7) Grunwald, Arthur, & Ellis, Stephen R. (1986) Spatial orientation by familiarity cues. *Proceedings of the 6th European Annual Conference on Decision Making and Manual Control,* June, 1986, University of Keele, Great Britain.

(8) Kim, W. S., Ellis,S.R., Tyler, M., Hannaford,B., & Stark, L. (1987) A quantitative evaluation of perspective and stereoscopic displays in three-axis manual tracking tasks, *IEEE Trans. on Systems Man and Cybernetics, SMC-1,*, 61-72.

(10) Ellis, S.R., Kim, Won Soo, Tyler, Mitchell, McGreevy, M. W. ,Stark, L. (1985). Visual enhancements for perspective displays: perspective parameters. Proceedings of the International Conference on Systems Man and Cybernetics. IEEE Catalog # 85CH2253-3, 815-818.

(11) Kim, Won Soo, Ellis, S.R. Tyler, M., Stark, L. (1985). Visual enhancements for telerobotics: perspective parameters. Proceedings of the International Conference on Systems Man and Cybernetics. IEEE Catalog # 85CH2253-3, 807-812.

FROM DataGlove™ TO DataSuit™

Ann Lasko-Harvill, Chuck Blanchard, William Smithers, Young Harvill, Amy Coffman

VPL Research, Inc. Redwood City, California

ABSTRACT

This paper reports on the development of an interface system which captures, records, and renders the movement of the human body. Sensors on the DataSuit™, a garment covering the body from neck to ankles, register the position and orientation of the joints of the body. An absolute positioning system tracks the movement of the individual in six degrees of freedom within the room.

Application of the DataSuit™ include use as a user input device for teleoperation, telepresense, human performance modeling and animation.

KEY WORDS: User Interface Device, Man-Machine System, Control Design, Teleoperator, Virtual Environment

INTRODUCTION

VPL Research Inc has developed the DataSuit™, a whole-body input device which captures the motion, the bends, gestures and spacial orientation of the human being who wears it. The DataSuit™ offers the capacity for telepresence with a vastly increased sphere of performance: full body participation in virtual realities, simulations and teleoperations. Coupled with the DataGlove™, complex remote effectors can be manipulated simply and naturally.

BACKGROUND

The DataGlove™

Developed by Tom Zimmerman, the DataGlove™ and ZGlove™ were introduced by VPL Research at SigCHI in 1987. [6] Formative research with the DataGlove was performedby Scott Fisher at NASA. [2] and Joe Rosen at the VA.[5] A Polhemus 3Space sensor supplimented with lower-cost optical guides for sensing finger motions was found to be a promising tool as a telepresence effector and for evaluation of range of joint movement in rehabilitation. An improvment in the bend sensor technology by Young Harvill for the DataGloveII allows the glove to measure hyperextension an abduction while improving the accuracy and linearity of the sensor. [3]

THE DataSuit™ SYSTEM

The DataSuit™

Optical fiber bend sensors, potentiometers, contact switches and Polhemus 3-Space Tracker sensors are attached to a tightfitting lycra garment that forms the foundation of the DataSuit™.

The optical fiber sensors developed by VPL for the DataGlove™ were used on the DataSuit to measure joints with relatively small radius of curvature. To measure joint motion with large curvatures and surface changes in larger body masses an optical displacement sensor was developed.

Data Acquisition

The system acquires data at 60 Hz. when polling the DataSuit™ alone and at 20 hz. when two DataGloves are polled simulanteously with the suit sensors.

Absolute Positioning

The current version of the system relies on the Polhemus 3Space Tracker for absolute positioning. This imposes limits
on the range of operation in a DataSuit to be within a 15 foot diameter hemishere. Systems with greatly increased areas are under development.

The DataSuit™ Application

Charles Blanchard has authored a new system for acquiring, massaging, recording, rendering and replaying data on the MacIntosh.

The Tree

A editable linked tree model represents the human figure in 16 nodes: *Head, neck, thorax, pelvis, and right and left upper and lower arms, upper and lower legs, feet, and right and left hands.* When DataGloves are added to the system, the hands represent 16 degrees of freedom each.

Tree editing capabilities include building entirely new trees, modifying trees by adding, subtracting, or altering specific nodes, and constraining the links between nodes.

Constraints can limit yaw, pitch and roll (or x, y, z) individually, and specify allowable ranges of rotation.

The Record

The record produced from the massaged data consists of an enumeration of the number and nature of nodes in the tree, their initial orientation, and the series of delta changes.

DataFlow

Data Massage and Data Acquisition modules (DMm's and DAm's) are chainable units of code that operate to direct data flow and massage operations within the sysem.

As the tree is edited or a new tree is created, DAm's and DMm's can be chained and associated to the nodes as needed.

Scripts

An interpreted language for user interface embedded in the DataSuit™ application, Scripts, takes the user through calibration routines, directs file handling operations, and allows the user interface to be custom configured for specific environments and users.

Real Time Rendering

The DataSuit™ application renders a line-drawn tree in 3 Space on a real time basis. This rendering can be used as visual feedback to the teleoperator, as well as a check on system performance.

The tree data structure wholly defines the rendering. Tree editing can be accomplished interactively with the mouse operating on the rendered tree.

Multiple trees can be driven by the same DataSuit™ inputs. Trees representing the operator and the teleoperated device could be rendered simultaneously.

Figure 1. A WireFrame Rendering Dubbed "Jake" used in the DataSuit™ Development System

Extended Rendering Capabilitilies:

LinkModel II, a linked solid modeling system developed by Young Harvill, for the interaction with the DataGlove, can accept DataSuit™ files and display them in a variety of rendering styles including wire frame, tonal shading, and color.

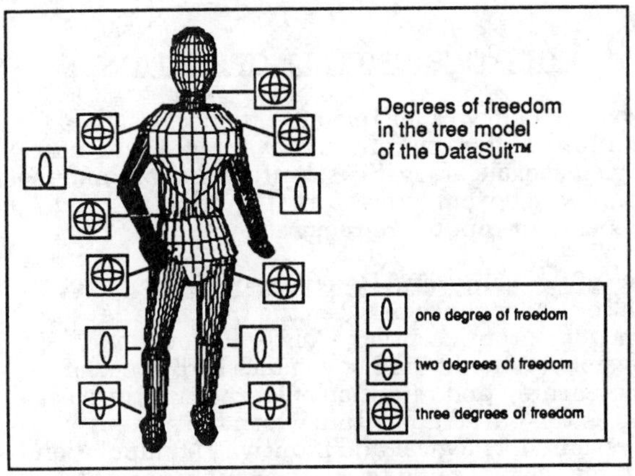

Figure 2. A LinkModel II rendering of a DataSuit™ File showing degrees of freedom measured.

SIMULATIONS AND VIRTUAL ENVIRONMENTS

Simulation for Training

Simulations are commonly used for training personnel when the danger of the environment is significant due to radiation, biological or chemical toxicity, or the stakes on human performance ride too high to allow learning in the actual system (aircraft, supertankers).

Use of the DataSuit™ in such simulations will allow monitoring and feedback of many more aspects of the human performance than is presently the case: habitual postures, gestures, angles of attack can be analyzed.

Education

The DataSuit™ adds the capability for kinesthetic learning within a virtual learning environment.

Teleconferencing

"Body English", the non-verbal human language, will become part of remote communications when DataSuited individuals are linked in a shared virtual reality. The telepresence of the participant becomes fully articulated.

Projection of self - the psychological perception of personal involvement in the virtual reality may be enhanced by full body representation.

Entertainment

The DataSuit™ is a natural user input device for interactive video and its descendants. The projected self in the game enviroment participates in a three dimensional world, in which he or she moves freely.

When used in a Virtual Reality environment, the rendering representation of the figure can correspond interactively with the contextual system of the reality (ie the rendered figure could lieterally reassemble himself).

ROBOTICS AND TELE-OPERATION

As a control device for remote end-effectors, the DataSuit™ offers significant advantages over a the tangled console of joysticks, buttons, knobs, and foot pedals which would necessary if multiple independant inputs are required.

Ease of Learning and Retention of Skill

The correspondance between the tree and the operator's proprioception of his or her own movement should tend to enhance both speed of task learning and retention of learned routines as long as the paradigm within which the system is represented is logical and intuitive. Manipulation of a robotic arm could become smoothly natural when operated by the rotation, and flexion of a human arm capable of corresponding motions. Simple deviations in the paradigm, (elbows that bend backwards, for instance) could be learned by the experienced operator through visual feedback , or massaged by software for a novice user.

Optimizing Path and Sequence of Operations

Teleoperation sequences could be modeled on actual human performance, allow much preprocessing of path optimization. Programing of systems operations can become an iterative process choreographed by the computer and human operator in a virtual environment before the system is placed on line.

The human operator is bound by similar limitations placed on the remote operator. Both are bound by inertia, often by gravity; human motions are already "optimized" to some extent for less joint wear and effacacy of movement. These factors augmented by training operators with visual feedback could improve control sequences by reducing wear and finding more optimum paths .

Interesting Future Applications

Teleoperation of legged vehicles, and joint motion clusters in servomanipulator operations are two areas that present problems in display and control that would be interesting to approach using a DataSuit™ or analogous system for input and display.(1. and 4.)

CONCLUSIONS

The DataGlove™ has stretched the range of operation of the the human being's most used end-effector, the hand from the proximal physical world, to both virtual environments and remote physical ones. The DataSuit™ offers an extended range of control. It also offers significant psychological advantages in simulation off whole person presence or projection of self.

The potential applications of the system that have been presented in this paper are only a small glimpse of the possibilities the DataSuit™ system opens up for the future.

ACKNOWLEDGEMENTS

The authors wish to to thank Jean-Jacques Grimaud, Jaron Lanier, Thomas G. Zimmerman, Tony Fabiani, Bea Holster and Daniel Christomo for their many contributions to the DataSuit™.

REFERENCES

1. Draper, J.V., Sundstrom, E., and Herndon, J.N., " Joint Motion Clusters in Servomanipulator Operation" (1986) In: A Cradel for Human Factors. Proceedings of the Human Factors Society 30th Annual Meeting, Dayton, Ohio Vol 1 1986 pp 552-555

2. Fisher, S."Telepresence Master glove controller for dexterous robotic end-effectors", (1986) SPIE Cambridge Symposium on Optical and Optoelectronic Engineering Oct. 86, Cambridge, Mass.

3. Foley, J.D., "Interfaces for advanced computing" Scientific American October 1987 pp 126-135

4. Gerth, R.J., Beringer, D.B., and Mundt, J.C. "Teleoperation of Legged Vehicles: Unique Problems in Walking and Foot Placement" (1985) In: Progress for People. Proceedings of the Human Factors Society 29th Annual Meeting, Balitimore, Maryland, Vol 2, pp 834-838

5. Wise, S. A, *et al* "Initial Experiences with the DataGlove™, a System for quantification of Hand Function" Proceedings of the 10th Annual RESNA Conference, June 1987, San Jose, California

6. Zimmerman, T.G. *et al*, "A Hand Gesture Interface Device", (1986) Proceedings of the SIGCHI conference ACM

AUTHOR'S ADDRESS

Ann Lasko-Harvill
VPL Research, Inc.
656 Bair Island Rd. Suite 304
Redwood City, CA 94063

IMAGE MODEL CONTROL OF IMAGE PROCESSING

An H. Nguyen, Huy X. Ngo, and Lawrence W. Stark

Department of Electrical Engineering and Computer Sciences
University of California at Berkeley, 94720

INTRODUCTION

Telerobotics studies remote control of distant robots by a human operator using supervisory or direct control. Even if the robotic manipulator and/or mobility device has vision or other senses, problems arise involving control, communications, and display (Stark et al., 87). The communication delays that may be expected with telerobots working in a space station and being controlled from an Earth laboratory have led to a number of experiments attempting to circumvent this problem. It is a main motivating factor in moving from well-understood instantaneous hands-on manual control to supervisory control; a further step would be the realization of a fully autonomous robot --- just like the movies!

Similarly, these communication restrictions and especially severe bandwidth limitations have suggested that transmitting large numbers of video camera pictures frame-by-frame may not be the most expeditious means of providing display feedback to the human operator. Our design, suggested by the top-down "scanpath" theory of human vision, provides for model control of image processing at the distant space station site (Stark and Ellis, 81; Lettvin et al., 59). Then only essential paramenters representing updating and correcting the model of the robot and its RWE, robotic work environment, need be communicated to the Earth Laboratory.

We present some early studies of our image processing algorithms operating under model control.

METHODS

Several types of standard TV cameras are used, all with standard RS-170 type formats, and a frame grabber, with usual performance characteristics.

As an initial test bed of our visual processing concepts, we selected the Radio Shack Armatron Mobile Manipulator, model 60-2396. This inexpensive device has important advantages over standard industrial manipulators. It is mobile and has a variety of control modes, in addition to its usual control pad. We have developed a multiple relay-switch board so that we can use a keyboard, joysticks, or mouse via parallel ports to the device. Also, we have programs to store and replay control sequences in what is called a teaching mode by the industry.

Image processing is carried out using a combined system with a PC/AT PGA graphics monitor and an IRIS workstation (Silicon Graphics). Display of results is accomplished in part with a driver for a pen-plotter using primitives to control the pen to create various forms (NGA).

Various algorithms for generating 2D profections of the 3D model have been considered; these are similar to those our group has previously used in simulating stereo views for our HMD (Kim et al., 87).

RESULTS

1.- Overview of the Telerobotic System

The RWE includes the robotic manipulators; work pieces; on-the-scene enhancements such as fiducial markers and bar coded identifications; and, of course, the locations and orientations of the multiple TV cameras (see figure 1.- Control Pathways for TR).

The control panel enables the operator to move the armatron and its manipulator and as well to update the 3D model. Not shown on figure 1 is a control path from the operator to his display that enables him to alter his point of view. Also possible is direct control from the model to the armatron. Control of the cameras is especially important during calibration and reviewing procedures (Sobel, 74) . Various control schemes have been proposed for control of telerobots --- our 3D model might naturally lend itself to model reference control, etc. However, for the purposes of this paper we wish to emphasize the use of the 3D model to control the many parallel lower-level image processing procedures.

The frame-grabbers are the direct pathway for visual information flow for the image processing scheme as a whole. While we are aware of important possible roles to be played by other sensory modalities, such as force feedback for

CH2539-5/88/0000/0539$01.00 © 1988 IEEE

bilateral control and vibrational drivers to provide non-visual clues to the operator, our present scheme relies on vision. (personal communication, Drs. A. Bejczy and B. Hannaford, JPL; and Cecilia Nguyen, UCB; also Schmid and Bekey, 78).

2.- Image Processing Scheme

Our 2D image processing includes, in the present bread-board system, a variety of thresholding and centroid operators as well as edge detectors and differential (Sobel) and integrating (low-pass smoothing) algorithms. Local feedback from one line-scan to the next enables adjustments to local image characteristics (see figure 2. Image Model Control of Image Processing).

More important is our use of global feedback. Here we use our knowledge of where an edge is expected to simplify and control the lower-level 2D image processing. The region in the video image where a particular edge is expected to be is isolated and transfered to another image buffer. Thus the pixel intensity histograms can be very simple and predictable since they deal with only one isolated feature, rather than an entire complex image.

The 3D model together with previous knowledge of the camera position and direction, is of course used as a guide to project the appropriate 2D slice of the 3D model onto the video image being abstracted, processed and ready

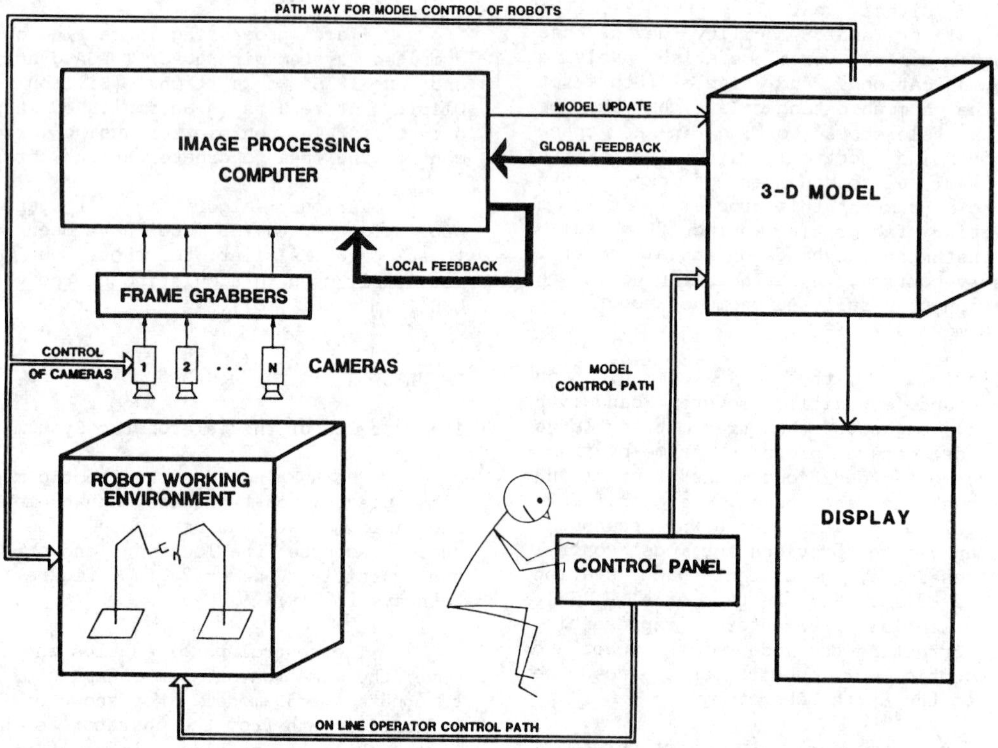

Figure 1: Overall Telerobotic System.

Control paths are shown as double lines; information paths as thin lines; while thick, solid lines are feedback paths.
In normal situations, operator controls the remote robots to perform a particular task and also the 3D model. Cameras are also directed so that essential visual information can be obtained. This is achieved by using the 3D model in 2D projections appropriate to the various video frames in order to simplify the image processing tasks. The image processing computers process information received from the frame grabbers. Local feedback provides local information to speed up image processing algorithms. Global feedback from the 3D model guides the image processing to collect essential information as to locations of joint angles, links and other features of the robot. The resultant visually obtained parameters are then used to update the 3D model so that it represents actual chieved positions.

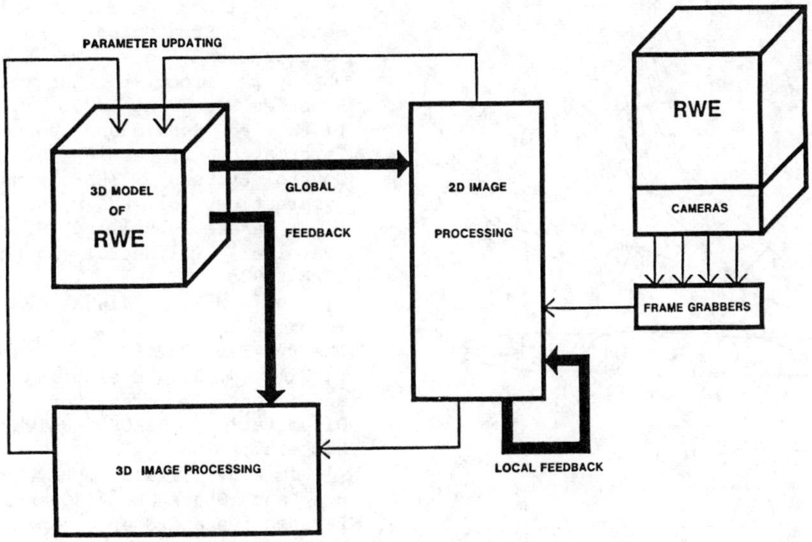

IMAGE PROCESSING SCHEME

Figure 2: Image Processing Scheme

The image processing scheme consists of three main tasks, the 3D model of the RWE, 3D image processing and 2D image processing. The robots activities are monitored by several video cameras which send video signals to the frame grabbers for digitizing. The raw information is first low-level-processed by 2D image processing where appropriated threshold levels, edges, sizes, object orientations are determined. Local feedback provides quick corrections and adjustments in local regions to improve efficiency in decision makings. The 3D image processing system receives information from the 2D image processing stages and thencomputes distances and depths of objects; it also estimates dynamical information of moving objects, as well as determining space constancy.Results from the 2D and 3D image processing stages are used to update the 3D model of the RWE. The 3D model, utilizing prior information, provides global feedback to the image processing computer so that the visual information is processed in a robust, rapid, and effective way.

to guide LLV image processing of video frame. (See figure 3.- 2D projection of the 3D model). Figure 3 shows a sequence of such 2D projections of the armatron as it is being controlled to lift its arm and bend its wrist.

From these many regions we obtain important parameters that are used to updated the model. Least-squares algorithms, now being tested by Dr. Won Soo Kim, of our laboratory, can of course be employed if an overabundance of parameters estimates result.

The Model, or 3D model, is central to our scheme of image processing. Through its "Global feedback" it controls both the LLV, lower level vision, 2D image processing algorithms, and the MLV, middle level vision, 3D image processing.

DISCUSSION

Our schema is based upon the "Scanpath Theory" proposed as an explanation of several aspects of HLV, higher level vision, in human vision. Here, a cognitive model drives successive fixations of the eye movements, so that individual features or subfeatures of a scene can be successively processed to check and confirm the expected visual information. Thus human vision is supposed to be not a passive, bottom-up, receiving of retinal images but an active looking, top-down, perceptual process.

However, our approach can utilize the important bottom-up work that has developed in computer vision in the last decades, including 2D image processing algorithms (Hu, 62; Castleman, 79; Canny, 86) and 3D object contruction (Roberts, 65; Brooks, 81; Besl & Jain, 85; Tanaka, 85; Grimson & Loranzo-Perez, 85; Silberberg et al., 86; Thompson & Mundy, 87).

ACKNOWLEDGMENTS: --- We are pleased to acknowledge support from the NASA-Ames Research Center (Technical Monitor, Dr. Stephen Ellis), and from the Jet Propulsion Laboratory, Calif. Inst.

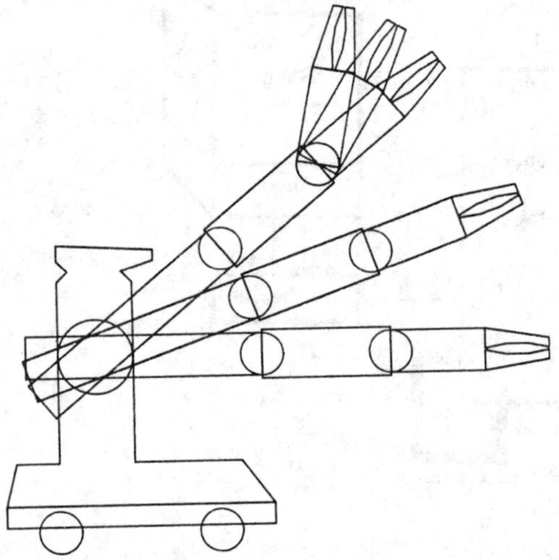

Figure 3: 2D Projection of Amartron Robot

From the initial position at 0 degrees, the model of a armatron is being controlled to lift its arm upward to 40 degrees with display increments of 20 degrees. The wrist is then moved up another 40 degrees, also with 20 degree increment display steps. These are then the global feedback bases for locations of regions to control 2D image processing of the video pictures.

of Tech., (Technical Monitor, Dr. Antal Bejczy). The Thoratec Corp., Berkeley provided graphics and other support to A.H.N. We also thank the students in ME210 (Biological Control Systems: Telerobotics) and especially the ICM, image compression by modeling, group(Anthony Maurer, Naresh Vermani, Magaret Wong, Srinivas Devadas, William Baringer, Wayne Chang); also Dr. Irwin Sobel, HP Corp., and Ms. Barbara Mills, Sandia Corp. provided helpful discussion and suggestions.

REFERENCES

[] Bazakos, Michael and Vu, Ngoc-chi, "Methodogies for Understanding and Evaluating and Evaluation of Image Processing Algorithms", Proceedings of SPIE: Intelligent Robots and Computer Vision, 1984, Vol. 521, pp. 134-141.

[] Brooks, R.A., "Symbolic Reasoning Amomg 3D Models and 2D images" Artificial Intelligence 17, 1981, p.285.

[] Canny, John, "A Computational Approach to Edge Detection", IEEE transactions on Pattern Analysis and Machine Intelligence, vol. PAMi-8, No. 6, Nov. 1986.

[] Castleman, K. R., "Digital Image Processing", Prentice-Hall Inc, 1979.

[] E. Grimson and T. Loranzo-Perez, "Search and Sensing Strategies for Recognition and Localization of Two- and Three-Dimesional Objects," Proc 3rd International Symposium on Robotics Research, 1985.

[] H. P. Schmid and George A. Bekey, "Tactile Information Processing By Human Operators in Control Systems", IEEE Trans. on System, Man, and Cybernetics, Vol. SMC-8, No. 12 Dec 1978

[] H. Tanaka, D.Ballard, S. Tsuji, and M. Curtiss, "Parallel Polyhedral Shape Recognition," Proc CVPR, 1985.

[] Hu, M-K, "Visual Pattern Recognition by Movement Invariants", IRE Trans. on Information Theory, Feb 1962.

[] Kim, W. S., "Evaluating Visual Display Designs and Control Modes for Telerobotics", Ph.D. Dissertation, EECS, University of California, Berkeley, 1986.

[] Kim W.S., Ellis S. R., Tyler M. E., Hanaford B., and Stark L., "Quantitative Evaluation of Perspective and Stereoscopic Display in Three-Axis Manual Tracking Task", IEEE Trans. System ,Man and Cybernetics, Vol. SMC-17, No. 1. pp 61-72, 1987.

[] L. Stark, W.S. Kim, F. Tendick, B. Hanaford, S. Ellis et al., "Telerobotics: Display, Control, and Communication Problems", IEEE J. of Robotics and Automation, RA-3 (1): 67-75 (1987)

[] Lettvin, J. Y., H. R. Maturana, W. S. McCulloch, and Pitts, W. H., "What the Frog's Eye Tells the Frog's Brain", Proc. IRE, vol. 47, no. 11, Nov. 1959.

[] L.G. Roberts, "Machine Perception of Three-Dimensional Solids, Optical and Electro-Optical Information Processing," J.T Tippett et al., Eds., MIT Press, Cambridge Mass, 1965.

[] P. Besl and R. Jain, "Three-Dimensional Object Recognition," Computing Surveys, Vol. 17, No. 1, March 1985.

[] Sobel, Irwin, "On Calibrating Computer Controlled Cameras for Preceding 3-D Scenes", Artificial Intelligent 5 (1974) 185-198.

[] Stark, L. W., Ellis S. R., "Scanpaths Revisited: Cognitive Models Direct Active Looking", Eye Movements: Cognition and Visual Perception, Dennis F. Fisher, Richard A. Monty, and John W. Senders, eds., Lawrence Erlbaum Assoc., New Jersey, 1981.

[] Stark L., Kim W. S., et. al., "Telerobotics: Display, Control, and Communication Problems", IEEE J. Robotics and Automation, Vol. RA-3, No. 1, pp. 67-75, 1987.

[] Ruetz Peter, "Architectures and Design Techniques for Real-Time Image Processing ICs" Memorandum No. UCB/ERL M86/37, May 1986.

[] Teresa M. Silberberg, David A. Harwood, and Larry S. Davis, "Object Recognition Using Oriented Model Points", Computer Vision, Graphics and Image Processing Vol. 35, pp. 47, 1986.

[] Thompson, D. W. and Mundy, J. L., "Three-Dimensional Model Matching From an Unconstrained Viewpoint", Proc. IEEE International Conference Robotics and Automation, pp. 208-220 (1987).

December 1, 1987

A HELMET MOUNTED DISPLAY FOR TELEROBOTICS

Won S. Kim, Andrew Liu, Katsuya Matsunaga* and Lawrence Stark

Telerobotics Unit, University of California, Berkeley

Abstract - An experimental helmet mounted display (HMD) system was constructed to provide the human operator with an enhanced visual interface during the performance of telemanipulation tasks. The HMD system tracks the human operator's head orientation and displays the corresponding simulated task environment. Results of pick-and-place experiments indicate improved performance for stereoscopic displays with appropriate interocular distances over monoscopic displays. To evaluate the HMD system, large work-space three-axis pick-and-place tasks were employed, in which the telemanipulation work space was assumed to be very large and only a partial view was displayed on the screen at a time. Experimental results show that performance with the HMD system is superior to that with the fixed display system. The results also show that appropriate adjustment of the joystick control reference frame improves the performance.

INTRODUCTION

Since 1960, head-coupled monocular display techniques have been investigated as a possible means of enhancing the visual interfaces of the aircrew to various aircraft systems (Hall and Miller, 1960, 1963; Fedderson, 1962; Furness, 1981). The head-mounted stereoscopic display system that provides the viewer with a synthetic computer-generated three-dimensional environment was constructed first by Sutherland (Sutherland, 1968, 1970; Vickers, 1973). Ordinarily, the image source and optical components of the head-coupled display system are affixed to the helmet worn by the operator, and thus the system is usually called the helmet-mounted display (HMD) system. Recently, an experimental HMD system has been constructed at the NASA Ames Research Center for a possible use in the space station (Fisher, McGreevy, Humphries and Robinett, 1986; Foley, 1987; Ellis, Grunwald and Velger, 1987).

The motivation of using the HMD for telemanipulations is to provide the human operator with telepresence, the feeling of being physically present at the remote site during the performance of telemanipulation tasks (Stark, Kim et. al., 1987). The HMD system detects the human operator's head motion, and controls the remote camera accordingly. Therefore, the camera control is made naturally by the human operator's head movement. The HMD can provide the human operator with panoramic views covering a very wide viewing angle for the telemanipulation scene, which is hard to achieve with conventional fixed (desk-top or panel-mounted) displays.

Little literature has been found regarding the performance of the HMD for use in telerobotic manipulation tasks. The purpose of this paper is to present a preliminary evaluation of the HMD system. The human operator's task performance with HMD and the performance with conventional fixed display are compared. In our experiments, a three-axis pick-and-place task was employed as a typical telemanipulation task. The remote telemanipulation environment for the pick-and-place task was simulated and the stereoscopic pictures for the HMD were generated by the computer. First, small work-space three-axis pick-and-place experiments were performed to investigate the performance of the stereoscopic display of the HMD system. Then, effects of misorientation between joystick control and display reference frames were investigated. Finally, large work-space three-axis pick-and-place experiments were performed to compare HMD with fixed display.

HELMET MOUNTED DISPLAY DESIGN

A two-axis magnetic Helmholtz coil arrangement was used as a head orientation sensing device to detect horizontal and vertical head rotations. It is composed of a search (sensing) coil mounted on or beneath the helmet (Figure 1a) and two pairs of field coils fixed with respect to human operator's control station. The right-left pair and the top-bottom pair generates the magnetic fluxes of 50 and 75 KHz square waves, respectively. The search coil detects the induced magnetic flux, which is

This work was supported in part by the Jet Propulsion Laboratory, under Contract 956873 and in part by the NASA Ames Research Center, NCC 2-86 Cooperative Agreement.

*on leave from Kyushu University, Japan

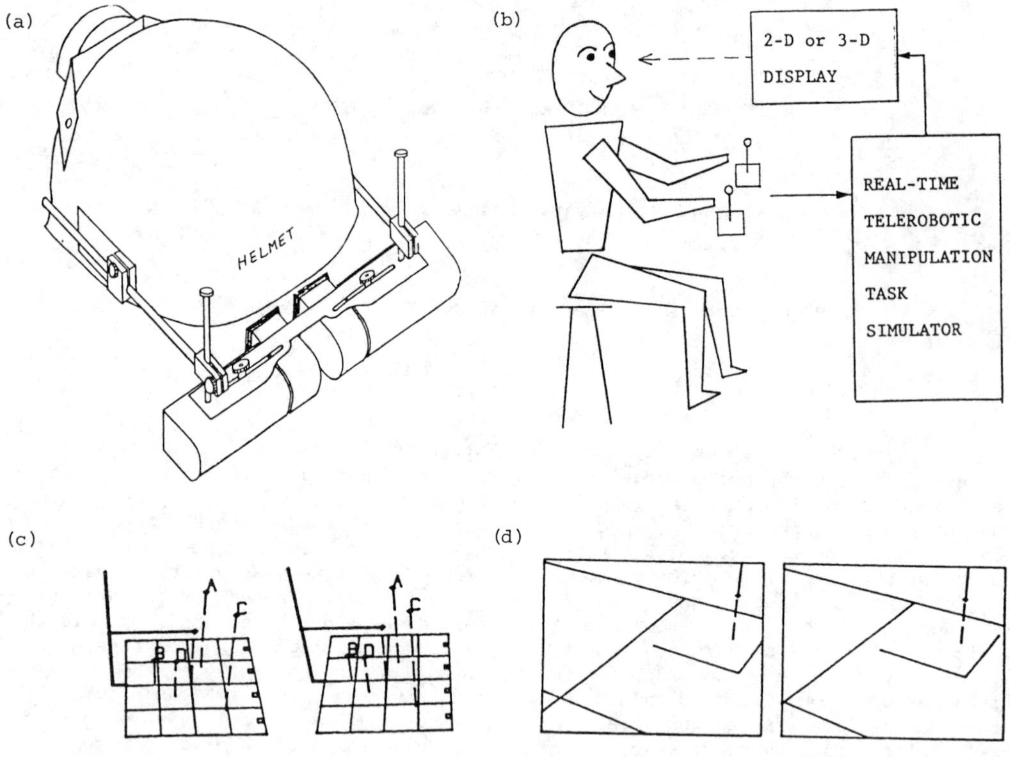

Figure 1. (a) A fully assembled helmet with CRT displays. (b) Simulated telerobotic control arrangement. (c) An example of the stereoscopic presentation for small work-space three-axis pick-and-place tasks. (d) An example of the stereoscopic display presentation for large work-space three-axis pick-and-place tasks.

amplified and separated into horizontal (50 kHz) and vertical (75 KHz) components. The magnitude of each frequency component depends upon the orientation of the search coil with respect to the corresponding field coil.

In our current model of the HMD system, two Sony viewfinders (Model VF-208) are mounted on the helmet (Figure 1a). Each viewfinder has a 1-inch cathode ray tube (CRT) screen and a converging lens through which the human operator views the CRT screen. The computer-generated stereo picture pair (stereogram) is displayed on the CRT screens; one for the left eye and the other for the right. The converging lens forms the virtual image of the stereogram behind the actual display screen with an image magnification of 6. The stereoscopic display formulas used to generate the stereogram for the helmet mounted display are described elsewhere (Kim, 1986; Kim, Ellis, Tyler, Hannaford, and Stark, 1987; Kim, Tendick, and Stark, 1987).

Five degrees of freedom were provided for the mechanical adjustment of the position and orientation of each viewfinder; three orthogonal slidings and two rotations (Figure 1a). A 1 lb. counterweight was attached to the back of the helmet for counterbalancing.

TESTING STEREOSCOPIC DISPLAY DESIGN

In order to test whether the stereoscopic display works properly for the helmet mounted display system, three-axis pick-and-place tasks (Kim, 1986; Kim, Tendick, and Stark, 1987) were performed with different values of the apparent interocular distance. In our simulated three-axis pick-and-place task, as depicted in Figure 1b, the human operator controlled the manipulator (3-degree-of-freedom cylindrical arm) on the display using two joysticks to pick up each object (point targets A, B, C, and D) with the manipulator hand and place it in the corresponding box. The apparent interocular distance is directly related to the inter-camera separation, the distance between the right and left cameras of the remote stereo camera. The apparent interocular distance is obtained by scaling up or down the inter-camera separation according to the magnification or reduction ratio of the display picture size to the true size.

A typical stereoscopic presentation for the pick-and-place task is shown in Figure 1c. When the apparent interocular distance is zero (Figure 2, lower left), the right and left pictures are identical. Namely, the stereoscopic view with zero apparent interocular distance is equivalent to the monoscopic view; the human viewer cannot perceive depth directly, although the human brain may interpret the flat view as a 3-D space scene. When the apparent interocular distance is other than zero, a disparity between the right and left pictures exists (Figure 2, lower right). Stereo disparity allows the human viewer to perceive relative depth between the objects in the view. As the apparent interocular distance increases, the depth perception becomes profound. When the apparent interocular distance is about the actual interocular distance of the human eyes (6 centimeters), the stereoscopic view appears to be excellent, neither flattened nor stretched along the depth direction. As the apparent interocular distance increases further above 6 centimeters, the stereoscopic view appears to be distorted or stretched out along the depth direction.

The experimental results of the three-axis pick-and-place tasks with apparent interocular distances between 0 and 10 centimeters are shown in Figure 2 for one subject with one repetition (other subjects produced very similar results). The results indicate that the stereoscopic display with an appropriate value of the apparent interocular distance is superior to the stereoscopic display with a zero apparent interocular distance. When the apparent interocular distance is zero or close to zero, the mean completion time of the pick-and-place operation is very long. This is because depth information is lacking and the human operator must sweep the manipulator along the depth direction in order to reach the correct object position. Note that in this experiment, the reference line indicating the vertical separation of the object from the grid plane was not presented on the display.

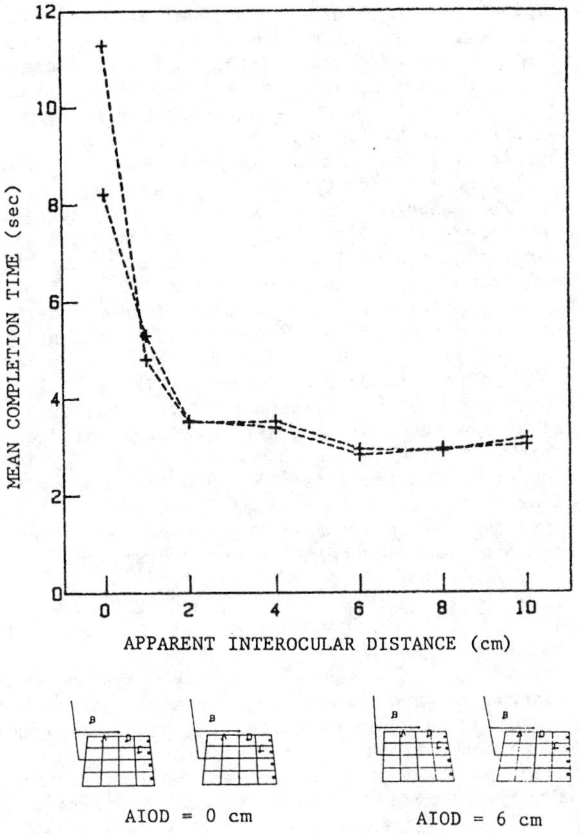

Figure 2. Mean completion time as a function of the apparent interocular distance of the stereoscopic display.

When the apparent interocular distance is above 2 centimeters, the mean completion time is shortened. This performance improvement is because the stereoscopic view now provides relative depth information, assisting the human operator in locating the object in 3-D space unambiguously with some precision. When the apparent interocular distance is 6 centimeters, subjects in our experiment felt that the stereoscopic view provided a nice 3-D view, neither flattened nor stretched. Further increase in the apparent interocular distance to 8 or 10 centimeters did not appear to improve the performance in our pick-and-place task. Note that the working volume of our pick-and-place task was a cube. An exaggerated interocular distance may, however, improve the performance, if the working volume of the telemanipulation task is very shallow in depth.

LARGE WORK SPACE TELEMANIPULATION TASKS

In the previous small work-space pick-and-place experiment, the entire work space was displayed on the screen. It was implicitly assumed that the manipulator work space was small or at least not very large as compared to the joystick control space. However, if the size of the manipulator is very large like the 50-foot-long space shuttle remote manipulator system, most pick-and-place operations of practical interest would require an enlarged, partial display for successful operations. Thus, in the large work-space pick-and-place experiment, only a small portion of the work space is displayed on the screen. Figure 1d shows an example of the stereoscopic presentation for the large work-space pick-and-place task when the stereo camera is directed towards the right side of the grid plane. In order to perform telemanipulation tasks successfully with such a wide work-space telemanipulator, an appropriate means of controlling the orientation of the remote stereo camera must be provided. The conventional method is to control the camera orientation manually. In this method, the human operator controls the telemanipulator and the camera alternately. An alterative method is to use the HMD. In the HMD system, the camera control is made naturally by the human operator's head movement. Thus, the helmet mounted display system allows simultaneous control of the manipulator and the camera.

Computer generation of the display picture for the large work-space pick-and-place task required computations for line clipping and perspective projection. In order to increase the sampling rate above 20 Hz, camera pan and tilt angles were discretized into 15 degrees increments, and the pictures of the objects in the work-space except for the manipulator were precomputed for each of the possible discrete pan and tilt angles. Only the picture of the manipulator was computed at every sampling interval to display the motion of the manipulator in real time.

CONTROL REFERENCE FRAME ADJUSTMENT

When the joystick control reference frame is excessively rotated relative to the display reference frame, the human operator has difficulty in control due to the misorientation. Figure 3 shows the effect of the azimuth angle on the three-axis pick-and-place performance (Kim, 1986; Kim, Frank, and Stark, 1987). As the azimuth angle exceeds the range of -45 to + 45 degrees, the mean completion time increases markedly. Pick-and-place performance is especially poor when the azimuth angle is about -90 or +90 degrees, even worse than the case when the azimuth angle is 180 degrees.

The above result suggests that the adjustment of the joystick reference frame according to the camera pan (azimuth) angle should improve the human operator's tele-manipulation performance, especially when the camera is directed towards the left or right corner with -90 or +90 degrees pan angle. In Figure 1d, when the joystick control reference frame is fixed, right/left and forward/backward joystick controls are oriented to the grid lines on the display, indicating a rotation of the control reference frame relative to the display reference frame. The joystick control reference frame can be rotated by a coordinate frame transformation according to the camera pan angle so that right/left and forward/backward joystick controls are oriented to the horizontal and vertical display axes. This joystick control reference frame adjustment maintains concordance (alignment, matching) between the display reference frame and the joystick reference frame for different camera orientations.

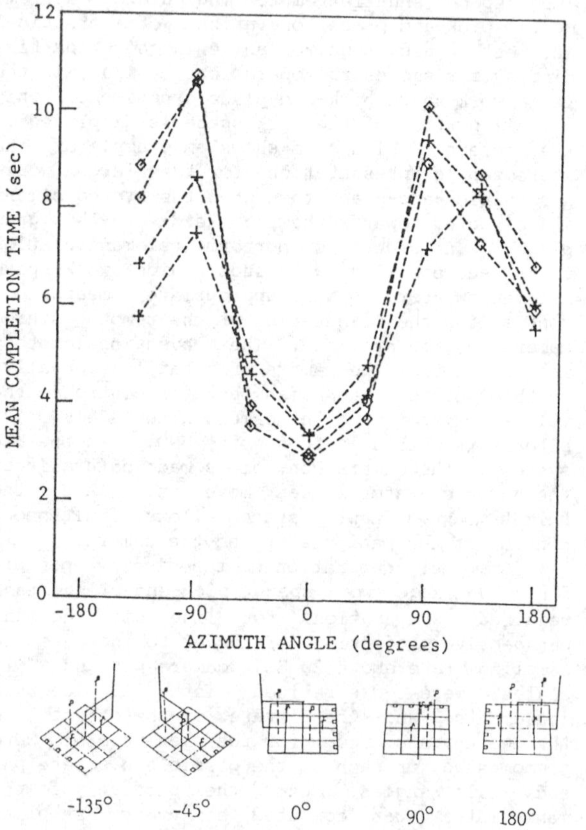

Figure 3. Mean completion time plots as a function of azimuth. Subjects: WK (diamond), FT (cross). Two runs for each subject.

EVALUATING HELMET MOUNTED DISPLAY DESIGN

In order to evaluate the performance of our helmet mounted display design, three-axis pick-and-place tasks were performed at four experimental conditions; (i) using the HMD with control reference frame adjusted, (ii) using HMD with control reference frame fixed, (iii) using conventional fixed display with control reference frame adjusted, and (iv) using fixed display with control reference frame fixed. Two subjects participated in this experiment. Each subject performed 40 pick-and-place operations (4 sessions of 10 pick-and-place operations in forward-reverse experimental order) for each of the four conditions.

In this experiment, the work space of the telemanipulator was assumed to be very large, and only a small portion of the work space was displayed on the screen. In the HMD system, the human operator could obtain different views by simply rotating his/her head while controlling the joysticks. In the conventional fixed display, its was necessary for the human operator to control the manipulator and the remote stereo camera alternately. The operator was allowed to switch modes by flipping a toggle switch on the joysticks. For a fixed display, the monoscopic display on a 9-inch CRT screen is used.

The experimental results for two subjects are shown in Figure 4. The vertical bar represents the 90 % confidence interval for the mean completion time based on the 40 pick-and-place operations. The 90 % confidence interval for the estimated mean based on 40 observations is given by $m \pm 1.68\, s / \sqrt{40}$, where m is the mean and s is the standard deviation. The results in Figure 4 (a) and (b) show that the use of the helmet mounted display improved the pick-and-place performance as compared to the fixed display. The results also show that concordant adjustment of the control reference frame improves the human operator's task performance for both fixed and helmet mounted displays.

CONCLUSION

A helmet mounted display system was constructed and tested as a possible means of providing an enhanced visual display interface for teleoperations. Our preliminary experiments indicated that the use of the helmet mounted display improved the human operator's three-axis pick-and-place performance for the large work-space telemanipulation tasks, as compared to the fixed display method with manual camera control. Adjustment of the joystick control reference frame in accordance with the display reference

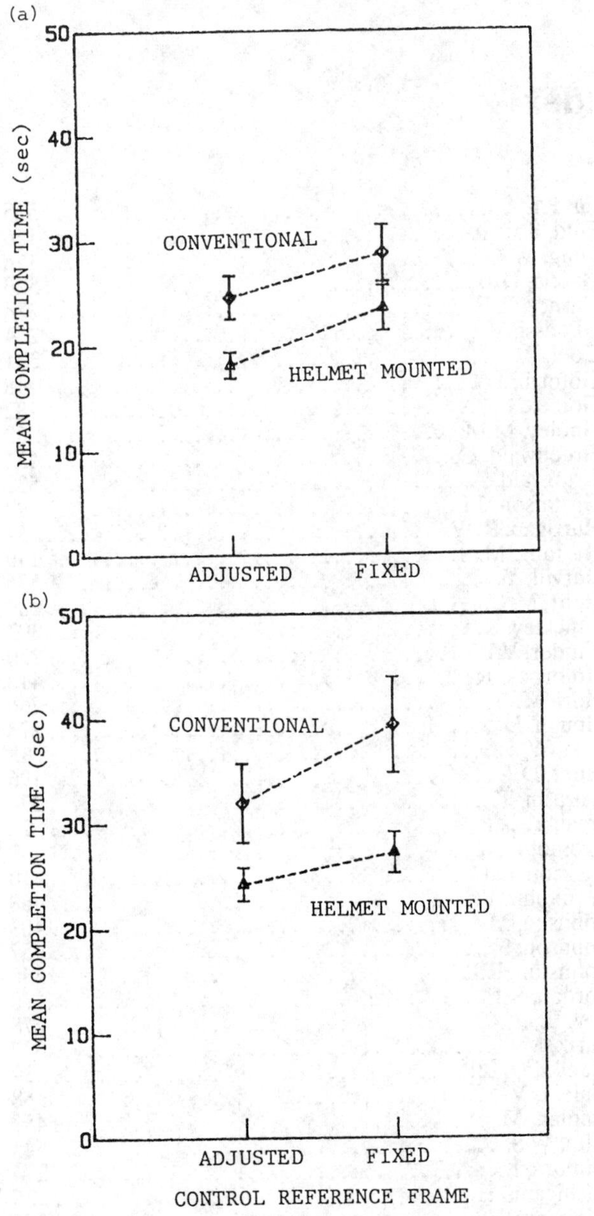

Figure 4. Performance comparison of fixed display and helmet mounted display. Subjects: (a) WK (b) KM.

frame appeared to assist the performance improvement. Further experiments with more sophisticated tasks using a 6-degree-of-freedom manipulator and an improved graphics display are on-going.

REFERENCES

[1] Ellis S. R., Grunwald A. and Velger M., "Head-Mounted Spatial Instruments: Synthetic Reality or Impossible Dream", Proc. 1987 AGARD Meeting, Belgium, 1987.

[2] Feddersen W. E., "Simulation Evaluation of a Head Mounted Orientation Display", Bell Helicopter Company, Technical Report No. D228-421-012, 1962.

[3] Fisher S. S., McGreevy M. W., Humphries J and Robinett W, "Virtual Environment Display System", ACM 1986 Workshop on 3D Interactive Graphics, North Carolina, 1986.

[4] Foley D. F., "Interfaces for Advanced Computing", Scientific American, pp. 127-135, October, 1987.

[5] Furness, T. A., The Effects of Whole-Body Vibration on the Perception of the Helmet-Mounted Display, Ph.D. Dissertation, University of Southampton, 1981.

[6] Hall R. J. and Miller J. W., "Feasibility Study for a Monocular Head-Mounted Display", Hughes Aircraft Company, Special Technical Document 5060-70, 1960.

[7] Hall R. J. and Miller J. W., "Head-Mounted Electrocular Display: A New Display concept for Specialized Environments", Aerospace Medicine, Vol. 34, No. 4, 1963.

[8] Kim W. S., Evaluating Visual Display Designs and Control Modes for Telerobotics", Ph.D. Dissertation, EECS, University of California, Berkeley, 1986.

[9] Kim W. S., Ellis S. R., Tyler M. E., Hannaford B., and Stark L., "Quantitative Evaluation of Perspective and Stereoscopic Displays in Three-Axis Manual Tracking Tasks", IEEE Trans. System, Man and Cybernetics, Vol. SMC-17, No. 1, pp. 61-72, 1987.

[10] Kim W. S., Tendick F., and Stark L., "Visual Enhancements in Pick-and-Place Tasks: Human Operators Controlling a Simulated Cylindrical Manipulator", IEEE J. Robotics and Automation,

[11] Stark L., Kim W. S., et. al., "Telerobotics: Display, Control, and Communication Problems", IEEE J. Robotics and Automation, Vol. RA-3, No. 1, pp. 67-75, 1987.

[12] Sutherland, I. E., "A Head-Mounted Three-Dimensional Display, Proceedings of the Fall Joint Computer Conference, Vol. 33, pp. 757-764, 1968.

[13] Sutherland I. E., "Computer Displays", Scientific American, 222, pp. 57-81, 1970.

[14] Vickers, D.L., "Sorcerer's Apprentice: Head-Mounted Display and Wand", pp. 193-304, in Remotely Manned Systems: Exploration and Operation in Space, ed. by E. Heer, California Institute of Technology, 1973.

Author Index

NOTES

NOTES

NOTES

NOTES

NOTES

NOTES

NOTES

NOTES

NOTES

NOTES